Linux®

FOURTH EDITION

Bill Ball, David Pitts, et al.

SAMS

A Division of Macmillan USA
201 West 103rd Street, Indianapolis, Indiana 46290

Unleashed

Linux® Unleashed, Fourth Edition

International Standard Book Number: 0-672-31688-9

Library of Congress Catalog Card Number: 99-62402

Printed in the United States of America

First Printing: **October 1999**

01 00 99 4 3 2 1

Trademarks

Warning and Disclaimer

Associate Publisher
Michael Stephens

Acquisitions Editor
Don Roche

Development Editor
Rosemarie Graham

Managing Editor
Charlotte Clapp

Project Editor
Carol L. Bowers

Copy Editors
Tonya Maddox
Sean Medlock

Indexer
Sandra Henselmeier

Proofreaders
Andrew Beaster
Cynthia Fields
Christina Smith
Maryann Steinhart
Mary Ellen Stephenson

Technical Editors
Jason Byers
Rory Bray
Paul Love
Ken Murray
Doug Eckhart

Team Coordinator
Carol Ackerman

Interior Design
Gary Adair

Cover Design
Aren Howell

Production
Brandon Allen
Darin Crone
Steve Geiselman
Susan Geiselman
Ayanna Lacey
Eric Miller
Heather Miller
Mike Poor
Louis Porter, Jr.
Staci Somers

Contents at a Glance

Table of Contents

About the Lead Authors

Bill Ball is the author of *Sams Teach Yourself Linux in 24 Hours*, Que's *Using Linux*, *Sams Red Hat Linux Unleashed*, and Sams' *How to Use Linux*. A reformed Macophile, Bill broke down and bought a PC after using Apple computers for nearly 10 years. Instead of joining the Dark Side, he started using Linux! He is a technical writer, editor, and magazine journalist, and has been using computers for the past 25 years. He first started working with Linux after moving from Tenon's Machten (BSD4.3) for the Apple Macintosh. He has published articles in magazines such as *Computer Shopper* and *MacTech Magazine*, and first started editing books for Que in 1986. An avid fly fisherman, Bill builds bamboo fly rods and fishes on the nearby Potomac River. He lives in the Shirlington area of Arlington County, Virginia.

David Pitts has co-written more than a half-dozen books covering Linux, UNIX, and CGI programming in Perl. He is an author, consultant, systems administrator, programmer, instructor, Web developer, and Christian. David can be reached at `dpitts@mk.net`. His Web page, `www.dpitts.com`, contains more information about him. Currently, David lives in Sacramento, California with his first wife, Dana, her beautiful teen-aged cousin, Ashley, and their invisible cat, Spot. David's favorite quote comes from Saint Francis of Assisi: "Preach the Gospel, and, if necessary, use words."

About the Contributing Authors

Bruce Balden is a seasoned user and programmer, with more than 10 years of experience with UNIX and Linux and more than 20 years of industry experience. He lives in the Vancouver area and has been active in the Vancouver Linux Users Group (VanLUG) and the Canadian Linux Users Exchange (CLUE). He maintains VanLUG's online directory of Linux professionals and was on the steering committee for the CLUE presence at COMDEX Canada West 1999 in Vancouver. His consulting activities frequently have taken him to Hong Kong and China. He is now a senior associate with the Fireplug Consulting Group (`http://www.fireplug.net`) in Vancouver, a firm specializing in ISP software and administration. His principal hobbies are classical piano, MIDI-assisted orchestration, and chess variants, particularly Xiangqi (Chinese chess) and Raumschach (an old form of three-dimensional chess).

Rich Bowen is president of RCBowen.com, a consulting company that has configured servers for MindStep Corporation, General Motors' Desert Proving Ground, and Textron. Rich has been administering Apache Web sites since 1994. Before that, he was managing Web sites running on NCSA HTTPd, on which Apache was built. Rich is currently running Apache on Linux, FreeBSD, Solaris, Windows NT, and Windows 95 machines. He manages the intranet site for DataBeam Corporation, as well as several of his own Web sites, all on Apache. He has been working with Perl for about five years, and now does much of his NT system administration with Perl. He has also written numerous Perl CGI applications for the DataBeam intranet.

Mario Camou has been working with Linux for more than six years, since the days of the 0.99 kernels. He has worked with almost all Linux distributions on hardware ranging from a 386 SX to Pentium IIIs, doing everything from software development to systems and network management. He is currently the director of technology at Umbral, one of the fastest-growing international Internet portals. Mario lives in Mexico City, and in his free time he likes to read science fiction and watch movies with his lovely wife, Angie.

Matthew Gillard has been working in the information technology field for the past five years as a UNIX and Windows NT consultant for Cybersource Pty, Ltd. Cybersource (`www.cyber.com.au`), based in Melbourne, Australia, specializes in UNIX and Windows systems integration. He has experience with implementing and supporting large Windows NT- and UNIX-based environments, and has also worked on Internet security- and firewall-related projects.

John Goerzen has been a developer for the Debian GNU/Linux operating system project since 1996 and currently works with package integration and porting to the 64-bit Alpha platform. He currently works as a system administrator and developer for an Internet firm. As the founder of the Air Capital Linux Users Group of Wichita, Kansas, John has been active in getting people involved with Linux for some time.

David B. Horvath, CCP, is a senior consultant in the Philadelphia area. He has been a consultant for over 14 years and is also a part-time adjunct professor at local colleges, teaching topics that include C programming, UNIX, and database techniques. He completed his M.S. degree in Organizational Dynamics at the University of Pennsylvania on December 22, 1998 (and is taking more classes as this book is being published). He has provided seminars and workshops to professional societies and corporations on an international basis. David is the author of *UNIX for the Mainframer* (Prentice-Hall/PTR) and a contributing author to *UNIX Unleashed*, 2E (with cover credit); *Red Hat Linux*, 2E; *Using UNIX*, 2E (Que); *UNIX Unleashed*, 3E; and *Learn Shell Programming in 24 Hours*. He has written numerous magazine articles. When not at the keyboard, he can be found working in the garden or soaking in the hot tub. He has been married for 12 years and has several dogs and cats (the number of which seems to keep going up). David can be reached at `rhu4@cobs.com` for questions related to this book. No spam, please!

Frank Hum, Jr. has 17 years of experience in the computer industry doing system engineering, development, and project management. He is currently Vice President of Engineering for Glebe Electronics, Inc. He has worked with numerous government agencies, Fortune 500 firms, and small firms on IT systems. Mr. Hum received his undergraduate degree in Computer Science from Duke University and his Masters Degree in Information Management from George Washington University. He resides in Oak Hill, VA, is married, and has three children.

Robert E. Lee currently works as a network engineer for Access Graphics in Boulder, Colorado. His first computer was a Vax 11/780 running bsd 4.3, which played a mean game of Worm. With a passion for learning, he has found himself holding Sun Workgroup and Enterprise Certifications in addition to several others. In his current position he has been a vocal advocate (aka, the yowling cat of sanity) for the GNU project, and will continue to help translate the technical merits of Linux in ways even PHBs can appreciate. He has also enjoyed various consulting opportunities, primarily designing Linux-based solutions. When he's not working with computers, Robert and his beautiful wife, Katie, enjoy plotting world domination. They currently own a home in Broomfield, CO, but will always have a spot in their hearts for their native state of California. He can be reached at `rel@gulbransen.com`.

Steve Litt is a central Florida-based software consultant specializing in legal and medical industry software creation and Linux software and services. He is the maintainer of the Universal Menu System software project. As Webmaster and lead content provider for the Troubleshooters.Com Web site, Steve has described and delivered the 10-step Universal Troubleshooting Process, as well as related material on bottleneck analysis, intermittent analysis, and software debugging. He has created numerous tutorials for Linux, Perl, Python, CGI, C++, Windows 9x installation, and accelerated learning techniques. Steve can be reached at the Troubleshooters.Com Web site.

Jeff Licquia has had an interesting and diverse career in the 10 years he has worked professionally in the information industry, from process control driver programming on Windows to network administration of one of the largest NT-based networks in the world. He first discovered Linux in 1991 (before it could boot multiuser) and became an avid proponent in 1993, successfully deploying it in varied environments for many purposes. Currently, he is network administrator for Springfield Clinic, a regional health clinic in his home town of Springfield, Illinois. Outside of the wired world, Mr. Licquia is active in his church and enjoys his time with his wife and two children.

Richard R. Morgan is an intranet systems engineer with Winstar Communications in Herndon, VA and has a range of experience that includes system integration, Web design, and software development. He began his computing odyssey many, many years ago by teaching himself Basic on the Timex-Sinclair 1000. Riding the crest of the Linux revolution, Richard uses Linux exclusively on his desktop machines at work and at home. He is also the Webmaster for the Northern Virginia Linux User's Group (`http://novalug.tux.org`). He might even be considered a Linux zealot. Richard lives in Haymarket, VA with wife, Laura, and their pets. He is soon to be a father. He can be reached via email at `rmorgan@tux.org` or visited online at `http://www.tux.org/~rmorgan`.

Gary Lawrence Murphy is President of TeleDynamics Communications, Inc., the ISP and telecommunications consultancy he founded in 1983. Gary currently lives in the idyllic Lake Huron shoreline forests of Sauble Beach, Ontario, in a converted cabin home he shares with the beautiful and ever-supportive May, young Nolan Man-hon, #5 due in November '99, and 90 pounds of Doberman. Gary has been a vocal Linux advocate since the 0.99-based Yggrasil distributions. He has been listed in the Linux Consultants HOWTO since 1993, has contributed to several open source projects, including VoGL, Argo/UML, and Apache/JServ's GSP, and has brought Linux and open source systems into production use at many regional ISPs and to Fortune 500s, such as Mitel, Bell Canada, Sympatico, and CBC Radio News.

Jeffrey Pajor (`pajor@ipass.net`, `http://www.ipass.net/~pajor`) has been working with IBM Global Services for two years as an e-business consultant. Jeff graduated from Purdue University in 1997, where he earned a Bachelor of Science degree in computer science. Jeff first started working with Linux and Java while attending Purdue University. Jeff is always interested in your comments and feedback.

Dedication

This book is dedicated to TM3 and Associates. Thanks, guys (non-gender)!!—David

To Paul Powers and Dan Dewell, comrades-in-arms and good friends—Billy

Acknowledgments

Thanks are due to the following people at Macmillan: Theresa Ball, Lynette Quinn, Don Roche, Rosemarie Graham, Carol Bowers, Tonya Maddox, and Trina Wilson. Kudos to all the tech editors on this project for their expertise and a job well done. Thanks are also due to Richard Stallman, the Free Software Foundation, and Linus Torvalds. And once again, thanks to Bill Gates and the Microsoft Corporation for making Linux more popular than ever!—Billy Ball

Many thanks need to go to the many people at Macmillan Publishing who do what they do to get a book of this size published! In addition, I would like to say a special thanks to the people at SMS who put up with me while I worked on my book: Perry Brandiezs, Beverly Chandler, Michael Cho, Rodd Cosby, David Hemsley, Marcie Herman, Frank McClean, Bonnie Phan, Reuben Pierce, George Xiromamos, Michael Bessey, Scott Fraser, Dan Grigsby, Yasin Mohammed, Alpesh Patel, and Maya Patel. To my wife and best friend, Dana: I cannot adequately express in words the depths of my love for you!—David Pitts

Tell Us What You Think!

As the reader of this book, *you* are our most important critic and commentator. We value your opinion and want to know what we're doing right, what we could do better, what areas you'd like to see us publish in, and any other words of wisdom you're willing to pass our way.

As a publisher for Sams, I welcome your comments. You can fax, email, or write me directly to let me know what you did or didn't like about this book—as well as what we can do to make our books stronger.

Please note that I cannot help you with technical problems related to the topic of this book, and that due to the high volume of mail I receive, I might not be able to reply to every message.

When you write, please be sure to include this book's title and authors as well as your name and phone or fax number. I will carefully review your comments and share them with the author and editors who worked on the book.

Fax: 317.581.4770

Email: `mstephens@mcp.com`

Mail: Michael Stephens
Associate Publisher
Sams
201 West 103rd Street
Indianapolis, IN 46290 US

Introduction

Welcome to Linux! This book has brought together a team of authors to teach you about installing, administering, and using the latest version of the best alternative computer operating system for today's PCs. Linux is the core of the operating system, the *kernel*, while the Linux operating system and its collection of software are formally known as the *distribution*. Many of the programs in the Linux distribution come from Berkeley Software Distribution, or BSD UNIX, and the Free Software Foundation's GNU software suite. Linux melds SysV UNIX and BSD features with POSIX compliance and has inherited many of the best features from more than 25 years of UNIX experience. Linux has also helped provide the recent impetus for the open source software movement.

First released on October 5, 1991, by its author and trademark holder, Linus Torvalds, and then at the University of Helsinki (now at Transmeta in California), Linux has spawned an increasingly vocal legion of advocates, users, and contributors from around the world. Originally written as a hobby, Linux now supports nearly all the features of a modern, multitasking, multiuser operating system.

Red Hat, Inc. is a computer software development company that has sold products and provided services related to Linux since 1993, and whose revenues have gone from a little over $400,000 to more than $10 million in the last several years. Red Hat's mission is to "provide professional tools to computing professionals." Red Hat provides these tools by doing the following:

- Building tools and releasing them as freely redistributable software available for unrestricted download from thousands of sites on the Internet.
- Publishing books and software applications.
- Manufacturing shrink-wrapped software versions of the Linux OS, making Linux accessible to the broadest possible range of computer users.
- Providing technical support.

Red Hat's customer-oriented business focus has forced it to recognize that the primary benefit of the Linux OS is not the advanced and reliable features for which it is famous. The primary benefit is the availability of complete source code and the freely distributable GNU General Public License (also known as the *GPL*). This allows any home, corporate, academic, or government user to modify Linux to his or her needs and to contribute to the ongoing development of the technology, which benefits all users. Working with Linux provides benefits, such as security and reliability, that commercially restricted, binary-only operating systems simply cannot match. Some of these benefits include the following:

There are no royalty or licensing fees. Linus Torvalds has control over the Linux trademark, but the Linux kernel and much of the accompanying software is distributed under the GNU GPL.

Linux runs on nearly any CPU. Linux runs on more CPUs and platforms than any other computer operating system. One of the reasons for this, besides the programming talents of its rabid followers, is that Linux comes with source code to the kernel and is quite portable.

Linux extends the life of legacy hardware. Recent trends in the software and hardware industries have pushed consumers to purchase faster computers with ever-increasing amounts of system memory and hard drive storage. Linux doesn't suffer the prevalent bloat of "creeping featurism," and it works quite well even on aging x486-based computers with limited amounts of RAM.

Linux controls the software, and you control Linux. This means that in the rare event that a program crashes, Linux won't collapse like a house of cards. You can kill that program and continue working with confidence. Linux uses sophisticated, state-of-the-art memory management to control all system processes. You won't lose control, and you won't have to suffer the indignity of rebooting the system.

Linux works very well as a personal computer UNIX for the desktop. You'll find that many popular applications are available for Linux, such as Netscape Navigator and Corel's WordPerfect. Red Hat Linux includes 2,000 or more programs (such as word processors, spreadsheets, and graphics applications) and a graphical interface—the X Window System. Red Hat Linux 6.0 is one of the newest Linux distributions, uses version 2.2.5 of the Linux kernel, and provides the X11 Enlightenment window manager with the latest GNOME software libraries. Red Hat includes a customized version of the `linuxconf` utility, which makes system administration a snap!

Linux works well for server operations. If you need a support platform for server operations, Linux has real advantages when compared to the cost of other operating systems, such as Windows 2000 (also known as Windows NT 5.0). Linux just makes sense for many home budgets and business financial models.

Red Hat Linux is easier to install and maintain because of advanced package management, graphical (point-and-click) system installation and control, and system administration tools.

The terms of the GNU GPL have allowed research institutions, universities, commercial enterprises, and hackers to develop and use Red Hat Linux and related technologies cooperatively without fear that someday their work may be controlled and restricted by a commercial vendor.

The huge development effort and wide distribution of the Linux OS have ensured its place as a real, viable, and significant alternative to commercially restricted operating systems. The open development model, availability of source, and lack of license restrictions are features that commercial OS developers simply cannot offer. Examples of software development groups that need this model range from government-affiliated research organizations to academic teaching projects to commercial software application developers.

The recent, rapid increase in new applications for Linux and the fast-growing user base for these technologies are causing even the largest computer industry organizations to take Linux seriously. Red Hat, Inc. is a serious contender, with corporate customers such as Boeing, Burlington Coat Factory, Cisco Systems, Deutsche Bank, GTE, Hewlett-Packard, Hughes, IKEA, Intel, New York Life, Nationwide Insurance, Southwestern Bell, and Suzuki. Red Hat, Inc. is also involved with academic institutions such as Carnegie Mellon University, CERN Laboratories, the University of North Carolina, and the University of Rochester. Red Hat Linux is even used by government entities such as NASA and the Internal Revenue Service!

By purchasing this book, you are taking the first step in regaining control of your computer from a closed-source operating system. There's an exciting future for Red Hat Linux, and we're glad that you're a part of it!

Who Is This Book's Intended Audience?

This book is aimed at the intermediate-to-advanced computer user. You should be familiar with Linux or another version of the UNIX operating system. If you're a new user, this book will help you install Red Hat Linux and configure the X Window System for your Intel-based computer.

What Can This Book Offer?

Linux, like UNIX, is a very modular operating system. The skills required to select, compile, link, and install the various components needed for a complete Linux OS may be beyond most people who might want to use Linux. Although the Red Hat Linux distribution goes a long way toward solving administrative and management tasks for the average Linux user, this book provides technical advice on advanced topics, such as setting up the Domain Name Service, configuring Apache, or understanding how to control system services.

How This Book Is Organized

This book is divided into the following parts:

- **Part I: Introduction and Installation of Linux**—Here you'll find detailed instructions and technical tips on installing and configuring Linux for your computer. You'll learn how to configure and get the most out of the X Window System, and you'll discover ways to choose the best X window manager or graphical interface for Linux.
- **Part II: Configuring Services**—This part will help you set up local and network services for your system—essential information that's required for Internet operations.
- **Part III: System Administration and Management**—All Linux systems require administration and management. Whether you have one user or 1,000 users, these chapters contain critical advice and analysis of software tools and administrative procedures that are used every day with Linux.
- **Part IV: Programming in Linux**—Linux comes with a wealth of programming languages. This section gives an overview of several popular computer languages and shows you how to put them to work right away.
- **Part V: Advanced Topics**—After you've mastered the basics, you'll find a host of more sophisticated applications you can add to your bag of Linux tricks. In this section, we provide the information you'll need to tackle some of the special tasks you may encounter as you expand your knowledge of Linux.
- **Appendixes**—Here you can learn more about Linux, read about the most popular software tools, or use advanced software such as emulators and virtual network systems.

Conventions Used in This Book

The following typographic conventions are used in this book:

- Code lines, commands, statements, variables, and any text you type or see onscreen appears in a `mono` typeface. **`Bold mono`** typeface is often used to represent the user's input.
- Placeholders in syntax descriptions appear in an *`italic mono`* typeface. Replace the placeholder with the actual filename, parameter, or whatever element it represents.
- *Italics* highlight technical terms when they're being defined.
- The ➥ icon is used before a line of code that is really a continuation of the preceding line. Sometimes a line of code is too long to fit as a single line on the page. If you see ➥ before a line of code, remember that it's part of the line immediately above it.

Introduction and Installation of Linux

PART I

IN THIS PART

CHAPTER 1

Introduction to Linux and UNIX

IN THIS CHAPTER

UNIX (not to be confused, as Dilbert's boss once did, with a eunuch) is one of the most popular operating systems in the world. UNIX is a trademark of The Open Group, but was originally developed by Ken Thompson, Dennis Ritchie, and others at AT&T. UNIX is a real operating system. A real operating system has, as a minimum, two qualifications: More than one person can access the computer at the same time and, while doing so, each person can run multiple applications, making it a *multiuser* and *multitasking* operating system. UNIX was originally designed to be such a multitasking system back in the 1970s, running on mainframes and minicomputers.

With UNIX, each user logs in using a login name. Optionally (and highly recommended), the user must also supply a password. The password ensures that the person logging on with the user login name is really who she claims to be. Users don't just log in to any no-name computer, either. Each computer has a "personality," if you will, which, at a minimum, is a hostname (mine is Lolly). If the computer is attached to a network, it has several other identifying items, including, but not limited to, a domain name and an IP address.

UNIX will run on just about every platform made. Many vendors purchased the source code and have developed their own versions. The various vendors (IBM, Hewlett-Packard, Sun, and so on) have added special touches over the years, but they are not the only ones to further modify UNIX. When UNIX was first developed, the source code was given out freely to colleges and universities. Two schools, the University of California at Berkeley and the Massachusetts Institute of Technology, have been on the front edge of development since the beginning.

As you can imagine, with this wide-ranging distribution, UNIX development went haywire. People all over the globe began to develop tools for UNIX. Unfortunately, there was no coordination to guide all the development, resulting in a lot of differentiation between the various versions of UNIX. Finally, standards started to appear. For UNIX, many of the standards fall under the IEEE POSIX.1 standard.

The downside of UNIX is that it is big. It is also expensive, especially for a PC version. This is where Linux comes in. Linux, as explained in a little more detail later in this chapter, was designed to be small, fast, and inexpensive. So far, the designers have succeeded. Albeit, as the Kernel has become more robust, it has gotten larger and larger.

Linux was originally created by Linus Torvalds of the University of Helsinki in Finland. Linus based Linux on a small PC-based implementation of UNIX called *minix*. Near the end of 1991, Linux was first made public. In November of that same year, version 0.10 was released. A month later, version 0.11 was released. Linus made the source code freely available and encouraged others to develop it further. They did. Linux continues to be developed today by a world-wide team, led by Linus, over the Internet.

The current stable version of Linux is version 2.2. Linux uses no code from AT&T or any other proprietary source. Much of the software developed for Linux is developed by the Free Software Foundation's GNU project. Linux, therefore, is very inexpensive; as a matter of fact, it is free (but not cheap).

Advantages of Linux

So, why would you choose Linux over UNIX? As already mentioned, Linux is free. Like UNIX, it is very powerful and is a real operating system. Also, it can be fairly small compared to other UNIX operating systems. Many UNIX operating systems require 500MB or more, whereas Linux can run on as little as 150MB of space and 2MB of RAM. There are even instances of recovery CDs for Linux that only use 16MB! Realistically, though, you will want to have room for development tools, data, and so on, which can take up 1000MB or more, and your RAM should be 12–16MB (although the more, the merrier!). See Chapter 2, "Installing Linux," for more specifics on space requirements and later in this chapter for more information on system hardware requirements. Here's what you get in exchange for that valuable space:

- Full multitasking—Multiple tasks can be accomplished, and multiple devices can be accessed at the same time.
- Virtual memory—Linux can use a portion of your hard drive as virtual memory, which increases the efficiency of your system by keeping active processes in RAM and placing less frequently used or inactive portions of memory on disk. Virtual memory also utilizes all your system's memory and doesn't allow memory segmentation to occur.
- The X Window System—The X Window System is a graphics system for UNIX machines. This powerful interface supports many applications and is the standard interface for the industry.
- Built-in networking support—Linux uses standard TCP/IP protocols, including Network File System (NFS) and Network Information Service (NIS, formerly known as YP). By connecting your system with an Ethernet card or over a modem to another system, you can access the Internet.
- Shared libraries—Instead of keeping its own copy of software, each application shares a common library of subroutines it can call at runtime. This saves a lot of hard drive space on your system.
- Compatibility with the IEEE POSIX.1 standard—Because of this compatibility, Linux supports many of the standards set forth for all UNIX systems.

- Nonproprietary source code—The Linux kernel uses no code from AT&T or any other proprietary source. Other organizations, such as commercial companies, the GNU project, hackers, and programmers from all over the world have developed software for Linux.
- Lower cost than most other UNIX systems and UNIX clones—If you have the patience and the time, you can freely download Linux off the Internet. Many books also come with a free copy (this book includes three distributions on CD-ROM).
- GNU software support—Linux can run a wide range of free software available through the GNU project. This software includes everything from application development (GNU C and GNU C++) to system administration (`gawk`, `groff`, and so on) and even games (for example, GNU Chess, GnuGo, NetHack).

At this point, the question is usually asked, "Okay, if Linux is so great, which version should I get and why should I get it?" I am glad you asked.

There are good reasons to use each version of Linux. Here are some of the highlights for each of the three version discussed in this book—Red Hat, Caldera, and Debian.

Red Hat

Here is a reason or two to use Red Hat:

- Red Hat Package Manager is included—For the same low cost (free), you get Red Hat Package Manager (RPM). This means that after you load Red Hat, you'll never have to load it again. The RPM is a sophisticated tool that includes intelligent file-handling across package upgrades, shared file-handling, documentation searching support, and package installation via FTP. You can install, uninstall, query, verify, and upgrade individual RPM packages.
- `Disk Druid`—`Disk Druid` is Red Hat's disk management utility. In particular, Disk Druid enables you to add and delete partitions through a GUI interface.

Here are a couple reasons to use Caldera's OpenLinux:

- `glibc` Compatibility —OpenLinux is the first Linux for Business solution to offer the 2.1 `glibc` libraries in a *self-hosted* (matching source and binaries) environment. Self-hosting allows corporate developers to optimize binaries for secure, high-performance turnkey solutions. With the inclusion of the new 2.1 `glibc` libraries, OpenLinux 2.2 offers 100% forward and backward compatibility with `glibc` 5 applications. This compatibility enables VARs, systems integrators, corporate customers, and users to run and upgrade those libraries when convenient for them.
- COAS—The Caldera Open Administration System builds upon the current Linux administration system by providing full graphical administration of the existing Linux administration architecture. Users and system administrators can utilize both

the old way of using Linux/UNIX and the new graphical environment of COAS without requiring redundant entry. Unlike other Linux graphical administration environments, COAS keeps track of both sides.

Finally, for Debian, there is one really good reason to use it:

- Maintenance—It is maintained by its users. Currently there are more than 500 registered Debian developers.

Copyright and Warranty

Linux is copyrighted under the GNU General Public License. This section doesn't include the entire license, but it does highlight a few items. Basically, the license provides three things:

1. The original author retains the copyright.
2. Others can do with the software what they wish, including modifying it, basing other programs on it, and redistributing or reselling it. The software can even be sold for a profit. The source code must accompany the program as well.
3. The copyright cannot be restricted down the line. This means that if you sell a product for one dollar, the person you sold it to can change it in any way (or not even change it at all) and sell it to a second person for $10—or give it away at no charge to a thousand people.

Why have such unique licensing? The original authors of Linux software didn't intend to make money from the software. It was intended to be freely available to everyone, without warranty. That is correct; there is no warranty. Does this mean you are left out in the cold when you have problems? Of course it doesn't. Numerous resources, including this book, newsgroups, and the Web, are available to assist you. What the no-warranty provision does do, though, is provide the programmers the ability to release software at no cost without the fear of liability. Granted, this lack of liability is a two-edged sword, but it is the simplest method for providing freely available software.

Where to Get Linux

You can get the latest patches, upgrades, and versions for each distribution by pointing your browser to each respective Web site:

Caldera's Web site is `http://www.calderasystems.com`.

Debian's Web site is `http://www.debian.org`.

Red Hat's Web site is `http://www.redhat.com/`.

Many of these sites include other distribution information for each platform that a particular distribution supports (Intel, Alpha, and SPARC), as well as upgrades, updates, answers to frequently asked questions, mailing lists, and much, much more.

System Requirements

Each of the distributions keeps a listing of the system requirements and supported hardware for the various platforms on which each distribution will run. As with anything, these lists change. If the particular hardware you have is not listed, check its Web pages to see if it has been listed there.

System Requirements—Linux

According to Red Hat, these are the system requirements for running Red Hat Linux on an Intel platform. Since it is pretty much the same basic list for each distribution, only one distribution is listed. Again, check out the distribution's Web site for additional information and updates!

- Intel Pentium and compatible processors (Pentium I/MMS/Pro/II/Celeron/III, AMD K6/K6-2, Cyrix 6x86/M-II)
- 500MB of hard drive space in character mode, or 1GB+ is recommended
- 16MB of memory required (although 64 or more is recommended)
- Most video cards supported
- CD-ROM drive
- 3.5-inch disk drive

Plug and Play hardware is not, at the time of this writing, wholly supported. (There is some level of PnP support with the `isapnp` software.) Most Plug and Play hardware has jumpers or BIOS settings that turn off the Plug and Play support. If you turn off this support, the equipment should work with Red Hat Linux. Some Plug and Play support equipment (such as the SoundBlaster 16 PnP) doesn't have a way of physically turning off the Plug and Play option. For these pieces of hardware to work with Linux, some sort of workaround must be performed.

The requirements listed here would be for one version of Linux. If you load multiple versions at the same time (multiple boot machine), you need to double the hard drive space, but not the memory.

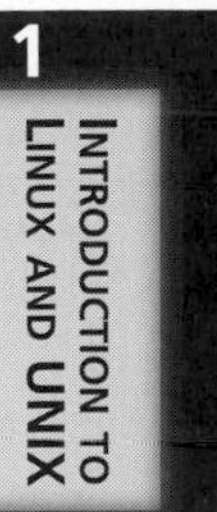

The list of supported hardware is not a list set in stone—new device drivers are constantly being revised. To find the most up-to-date listing of supported hardware, check Web sites listed earlier.

Summary

UNIX, as a real operating system, is a viable solution to many of the business needs today. It has been estimated that more than half of the Web servers currently on the Internet are actually Linux systems running Apache. Although I cannot confirm or deny that number, I do know that Linux, with its support infrastructure, its multiplatform usability, and its reliability, is the choice of many system administrators trying to work on real-world problems and come up with real-world solutions. To quote Mike Kropinack of MK Computer Associates (`http://www.mk.net`), "Linux is an awesome system, be it Red Hat, Slackware, or whatever. I'd choose it over Microsoft or Novell any day because in over five years of using it, I've never seen it crash in any of our production servers."

CHAPTER 2

Installing Linux

IN THIS CHAPTER

This chapter will guide you through the installation process for Red Hat, Debian, and Caldera. Before looking at the methods used to install an operating system, you should understand the hardware on which the operating system will be installed. After examining the hardware, the rest of this chapter guides you through the installation process step by step, breaking it down to show some of the differences between the four basic methods of installation. This chapter briefly presents the installation of LILO (Linux Loader), but it leaves many of those details to Chapter 3, "Boot Management."

Be Prepared... Be *Very* Prepared...

As Linux has matured over the years, its installation and configuration have gotten simpler and simpler. My colleague Mike Essinger asks why Linux doesn't make a program that probes the hardware, instead of having the installer figure it out. The Linux community is doing just that! Unfortunately, things can still go wrong during an installation. Just as unfortunately, not every piece of equipment ever produced is supported.

Because of this, it is important that you take a few minutes and fill out the following sheet to the best of your ability. Not only will it help you in configuring the system, but it will help you in case something goes wrong.

Most of the following information can be found in the manuals for the particular piece of equipment you're using. Other pieces of information can be gathered by talking to your system administrator. The boldface items have been problem areas, historically speaking. Obtaining the correct information on these areas may be critical if you are to have a successful installation.

Type and Number of hard drives:
Size of each hard drive (MB):
Primary hard drive:
Amount of RAM (MB):
Type and number of CD-ROMs: IDE
SCSI
Make and model of each CD-ROM:
Make and model of SCSI adapter(s):
Type of mouse:
Number of buttons on mouse:
If mouse is serial, COM port it is attached to:
Video card make, model, and amount of RAM:
Monitor's make and model:

Allowable horizontal refresh range:

Allowable vertical refresh range:

Networking:

IP:

Netmask:

Gateway address:

Domain name server's IP address:

Domain name:

Host name:

Network card make and model:

Additional OS's either installed or to be installed on system:

LILO, if used, will be installed here:

Installed on master boot record:

Installed on Linux partition:

Sound card make and model:

Sound card IRQ:

Sound card I/O address:

Note

If you are running OS/2, you must create your disk partitions with the OS/2 partitioning software; otherwise, OS/2 might not recognize the disk partitions. Do not create any new partitions during the installation, but do use the Linux `fdisk` to set the proper partition types for your Linux partitions.

After you have answered these questions, the rest of the installation is fairly easy. The entire process is menu-driven, which means you don't have to remember all the configuration information that you'd have to remember for other Linux versions you might want to install.

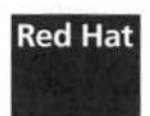

Installing Red Hat Linux

One of the obvious differences between Red Hat Linux and other Linux versions is the ease with which Red Hat can be installed. The process is quite straightforward and is automated by the Red Hat installation program. This installation program can handle many different system configurations and problems nicely, so most of these things are taken care of for you.

The installation or upgrading of Red Hat Linux can be done via several methods. Depending on which method you use, you need either one or two formatted, high-density (1.44MB), 3.5" disks. For most installations, you'll only need the setup disk.

Creating the Startup and Supplemental Disks

Before you make the startup and supplemental disks, label the disks. The process for making the two disks differs in only one way: When the program asks for the filename, you enter `boot.img` for the startup disk and `supp.img` for the supplemental disk. To create the floppy disks under MS-DOS, you need to use the following commands (assuming your CD-ROM is drive D):

```
d:
cd \images
\dosutils\rawrite.exe
```

`rawrite` asks for the filename of the disk image. Enter **`boot.img`**. Insert a floppy disk into drive A. You are asked for a disk to write to. Enter **`a:<return>`** and label the disk "Red Hat boot disk." Run `rawrite` again, enter **`supp.img`**, insert another disk, and type **`a:`**. Label this disk "Red Hat supplemental disk."

You can use the `dd` utility to create the disks under Linux. Mount the Red Hat Linux CD-ROM, insert a floppy disk into the drive (do not mount it), and change directories (`cd`) to the `images` directory on the CD-ROM. Use this command to create the startup disk:

```
dd if=boot.img of=/dev/fd0 bs=1440k
```

To make the supplemental disk, use the following command:

```
dd if=supp.img of=/dev/fd0 bs=1440k
```

Installing Without Using a Startup Disk

If you have MS-DOS on your computer, you can install without using a startup disk. The Red Hat installation program can be started by using these commands:

```
d:
cd \dosutils
autoboot.bat
```

Virtual Consoles

Red Hat's installation process goes beyond a simple sequence of dialog boxes. In fact, while you're installing, you can look at different diagnostic messages. You can actually switch between five virtual consoles, which can be helpful if you encounter problems during installation. Table 2.1 shows the five consoles, the key sequence to switch to each console, and the purpose of each console.

TABLE 2.1 Virtual Console Information

Console	*Keystroke*	*Purpose*
1	Alt+F1	Installation dialog box
2	Alt+F2	Shell prompt
3	Alt+F3	Install log (messages from the install program)
4	Alt+F4	System log (messages from the kernel and other system programs)
5	Alt+F5	Other messages

Most of the installation time will be spent in console 1, working through the dialog boxes.

Dialog Boxes

Each dialog box consists of a simple question or statement. You choose one or more responses. To choose these responses, it is necessary to navigate the boxes. Most dialog boxes have a cursor you can move via the arrow keys. You can also use the Tab key to to the next section and the Alt+Tab key combination to back up to the previous section. The bottom of each dialog box indicates which movement keys are valid for that particular box.

In addition to moving the cursor, you need to make selections. You select two things: a button (OK, for instance) and an item from a list. If you're selecting a button, use the spacebar to push the button. A second push of the button returns it to its original setting. To select a single item, press the Enter key. Use the spacebar to select one or more items from a list. Again, a second push of the spacebar deselects a selected item.

Press the F12 button to accept the current values and proceed to the next dialog box. In most cases, this is the same as pressing the OK button.

Caution

Do not press random keys during installation. Unpredictable results might occur if you do.

Step-by-Step Installation for Red Hat

This next section takes a step-by-step look at the installation process.

Starting the Installation

If you do not choose to use the autoboot program and start the installation directly from the CD-ROM, you have to start with the startup disk.

Insert the startup disk you created into the A: drive and restart the computer. At the `boot:` prompt, press Enter to continue.

You can load the Red Hat Linux installation program and begin the installation process from the `boot:` prompt. In most cases, the best way to get started is to simply press the Enter key.

You can pass a number of parameters to the Linux kernel at startup. These do not include parameters for devices such as CD-ROM drives or Ethernet cards.

Certain hardware configurations sometimes have trouble with the automatic hardware detection during the installation. This is unusual, but it does happen. If you experience problems during the installation, restart the installation using the Expert mode.

Expert Mode

The default method of installing Red Hat Linux uses autoprobing to detect the hardware in your system automatically. Although most systems can be autoprobed without difficulty, there can be problems in certain cases. You can overcome these problems by using Expert mode.

To start the installation using Expert mode, type **`expert`** and press Enter at the `boot:` prompt.

While you're in Expert mode, you have complete control over the installation process. You can also enter optional module parameters while in Expert mode.

Note

This chapter does not cover Expert mode installation.

Rescue Mode

The Red Hat installation program has undergone changes that enable you to create a custom startup disk for your specific system. This new startup disk is customized according to your system's hardware configuration, ensuring that you will be able to start your system even if LILO has been overwritten by another operating system.

You may also create a startup disk after the installation process has been completed. To do this, consult the `mkbootdisk` man page. Note that the `mkbootdisk` package must be installed to create a startup disk after the installation.

Your startup disk is the first disk in a two-part rescue disk set. The second disk required for Rescue mode must be created from the `rescue.img` image file, which is located in the Red Hat Linux CD-ROM's `images` directory. To create the second disk, insert a blank floppy in your system's floppy drive and type the following:

```
dd if=rescue.img of=/dev/fd0 bs=72k
```

You can then start in Rescue mode by booting from your startup disk and typing **`rescue`** at the `boot:` prompt. Insert the disk created from `rescue.img` when you're prompted to do so.

Kickstart Mode

Red Hat provides a method for unattended installation of a system, using a text configuration file. To enter Kickstart mode, type **`linux ks`** at the `boot:` prompt and press Enter.

Kickstart mode works with both NFS and CD-ROM installations. New options for the kickstart file include the capability to use a wider variety of networking options, including `bootp`, DHCP, and static IPs.

The installation program looks in the following places for the config files:

- On the broadcast server from `bootp`
- On the `bootp` server if no other server name is broadcast
- On the startup floppy disk if you type **`linux ks`** and press Enter

The `bootp` server gives the file it looks for. If a directory is given, `kickstart` looks for a file in that directory with the IP of the client as the filename, followed by `-kickstart` (for example, `172.13.128.44-kickstart`). If the floppy drive argument is given, it looks for a file named `ks` on that floppy disk.

Kernel Parameter Options

Some kernel parameters can be specified on the command line and thus passed to the running kernel. This does not include options to modules such as Ethernet cards or devices such as CD-ROM drives.

Use the following format to pass an option to the kernel:

```
linux <options>
```

If you want a different installation mode, enter it after the option(s). For example, to install on a system with 128MB of RAM, using Expert mode, type the following:

```
linux mem=128M expert
```

To pass options to modules, you need to use the Expert mode to disable PCI autoprobing. When the installation asks for the device type to which you need to pass an option or parameter, it gives you a place to type it.

Watch the startup information to ensure that the kernel detects your hardware. If it doesn't properly detect your hardware, you might need to restart and add some options at the `boot:` prompt. The following is an example:

```
boot: linux hdc=cdrom
```

If you need to enter any extra parameters here, write them down—you will need them later in the installation.

The Installation Program

The installation program greets you with "Welcome to Red Hat Linux!" Press Enter to go to the next screen. It asks you what language you prefer to use during the installation process. The default is English, but other options include Czech, Danish, Finnish, French, German, Italian, Norwegian, Romanian, Serbian, Slovak, Swedish, and Turkish. Use the arrow keys to highlight your choice and press the Tab key to move to the OK button. Press Enter to continue.

The next dialog box asks which keyboard configuration you have (see Figure 2.1). Use the Tab key to select the correct one and then press Enter.

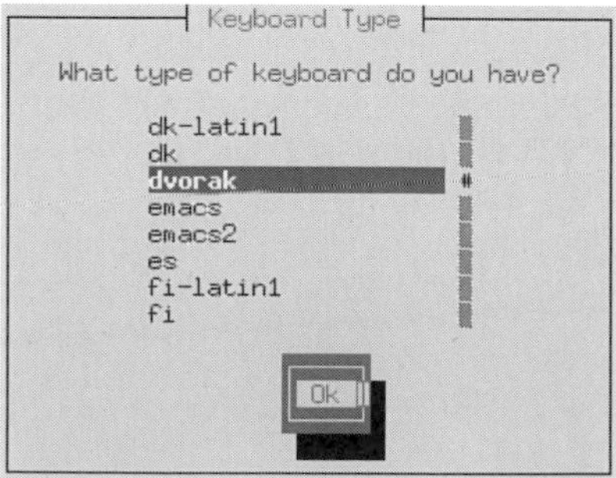

FIGURE 2.1
The Keyboard Type dialog box.

The next dialog box asks which type of installation you want to use (see Figure 2.2).

FIGURE 2.2
The Installation Method dialog box.

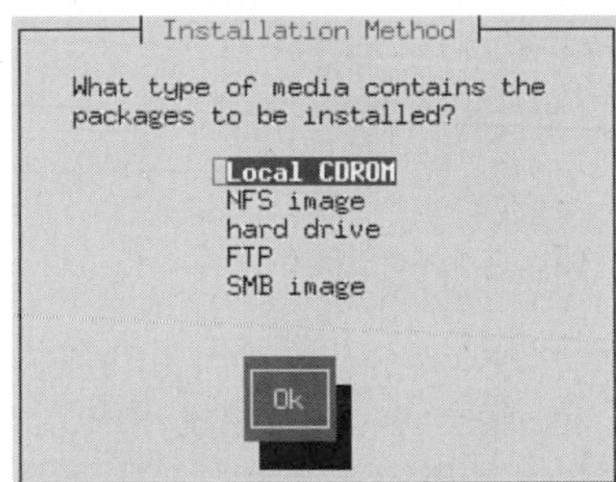

Before looking at the installation process for a CD-ROM, let's look at the other ways of installing Red Hat.

Selecting an Installation Method

There are five basic methods of installing Red Hat Linux:

- Local CD-ROM—If you have a supported CD-ROM drive, a Red Hat Linux CD-ROM, and a startup disk, you can install Red Hat Linux with your CD-ROM.
- FTP—You must have a startup disk and a supplemental disk to perform an FTP install. You need to have a valid nameserver configured, or the IP address of the FTP server you will be using. You also need the root path of the Red Hat Linux directory on the FTP site.
- Hard drive—To install Red Hat Linux from a hard drive, you need the same startup and supplemental disks used in the FTP install. You must first create a Red Hat directory called `RedHat` at the top level of your directory tree. Everything you install should be placed in that directory. Copy the base subdirectory, and then copy the packages you want to install to another subdirectory, called RPMS. You can use available space on an existing DOS partition or a Linux partition that is not required in the install procedure (for example, a partition that would be used for data storage on the installed system).

  If you are using a DOS filesystem, you might not be able to use the full Linux filenames for the RPM (Red Hat Package Manager) packages. The installation process does not care what the filesystem looks like, but it is a good idea to keep track of it so you will know what you are installing.
- NFS Image—If you want to install over a network, you need to mount the Red Hat Linux CD-ROM on a machine that supports ISO-9660 filesystems with Rock Ridge extensions. The machine must also support NFS. Export the CD-ROM filesystem via NFS. You should either have nameservices configured or know the NFS server's IP address and the path to the exported CD-ROM.

- SMB Image—Select this option if you want to install over a network from a disk shared by a Windows system (or a Linux system running the Samba SMB connectivity suite). This is similar to installing from a hard drive, except that in this case the hard drive is on another system.

The rest of the installation procedures presented here are for a CD-ROM installation. As you can tell from the previous descriptions, using other methods is not much different. As a matter of fact, the installation is the same; the difference is just a matter of the installation's origin. For example, if you are installing from a shared volume on a Windows 95 or Windows NT server, you have to supply the name of the server, the name of the shared volume, and the account name and password for the volume.

CD-ROM Installation

When you select Local CDROM, you are told to insert your Red Hat CD-ROM into your drive. Do this if you have not already done so. Tab to the OK button and press Enter.

The installation continues to the second stage.

Note

The installation process uses autoprobing to determine the type of CD-ROM you have. If you have problems with the CD-ROM at this point, refer to the `boot:` prompt information earlier in the chapter.

New or Upgrade?

The installation program now asks whether you are installing a new system or upgrading a system that already contains Red Hat Linux 2.0 or greater. You are installing a new system, so highlight Install and press Enter.

There are three classes of installation: Workstation, Server, and Custom. You are installing the Workstation class. As you go along, I'll point out the differences between the Workstation and Server classes.

SCSI Adapters?

The system scans for any (SCSI) adapters. On most systems, the autoprobe will detect if you have any adapters.

Because this is a new installation, the installation program assumes you do not have your Linux partitions set up. It does, however, give the following warning:

All of the Linux partitions on your hard drive(s) will be erased. This means that all of your previous Linux installations will be destroyed. If you do not want to lose all of your Linux partitions, select Cancel now and perform a Custom install.

This warning should be heeded because the installation will indeed write over any previously installed Linux partitions. You should get this warning only if the system sees Linux partitions already present on your system.

Caution

If you install it as a Server class, all of your partitions will be overwritten. This means you'll lose everything else on the disks—including other operating systems.

If you do have a Linux partition and you did not choose Custom, the system assumes you want to use the same partitions for the new system and begins to overwrite what is already there. It loads 336MB of data into your Linux partition.

Note

This means you can install more than one version of Linux on your system, but you must do a Custom install after the first one.

Depending on the speed of your CD-ROM (and the system as a whole), this package install could take anywhere from 10 to 30 minutes. (It takes approximately 16 minutes on a Pentium Pro 200 with a 12x CD-ROM.)

If you are performing a new install and you did not previously have a Linux partition, or if you chose Custom, you are next asked which tool you want to use for setting up your disk(s).

Two tools that come with Red Hat Linux can be used to set up Linux partitions. First is the old standby, `fdisk`. Second is the new tool, Disk Druid. Both are acceptable methods for configuring your partitions, but Disk Druid is easier. That is what is used here.

Disk Druid

Disk Druid is a tool that first shipped with Red Hat version 5.0. It is a graphical interface that enables you to configure your hard disk partitions.

There are three sections associated with Disk Druid. Each is explained in detail here.

The Current Disk Partitions Section

Each line in the Current Disk Partitions section represents a disk partition. Note the scrollbar to the right.

> **Note**
>
> In Europe they call these *elevators*, not scrollbars.

The scrollbar indicates additional items that cannot all be displayed at one time. Use the up and down arrow keys to look for any additional partitions. Each line (partition) has five fields:

Mount Point	Indicates where the partitions will be mounted after the Red Hat Linux system is up and running. (At least one partition must have a mount point of \ before you can move past the Disk Druid screen in the installation process.) Swap space does not get a mount point.
Device	The partition's device name.
Requested	The minimum size requested when the partition was defined.
Actual	The actual amount of space allocated to that partition.
Type	Shows the partition's type.

Drive Summaries

This section shows the hard disk(s) on the system. Just like the Current Disk Partitions section, this section has a scrollbar in case more than a couple of drives are attached to this computer. Each line contains six fields:

Drive	Shows the hard drive's device name.
Geom [C/H/S]	Shows the hard drive's geometry, which consists of three numbers representing the number of cylinders, heads, and sectors as reported by the hard drive.
Total	Shows how much space is on the entire hard drive.
Used	Shows how much space is currently defined to a partition.
Free	Shows how much space is currently available on the hard drive. Indicates how much is unallocated.
[######]	A bar graph visually represents the space currently used on the hard disk. The more pound signs there are between the brackets, the less free space is available.

Disk Druid's Buttons

The third section of Disk Druid contains the buttons. This section has five buttons across the bottom of the screen and six references to F keys:

Add	Used to request a new partition. When this button is selected, a dialog box appears with fields that must be filled in.
Edit	Used to modify the attributes of the partition currently highlighted in the Current Disk Partitions section. Selecting the Edit button opens a dialog box with fields that can be edited.
Delete	Use this button to delete the partition currently highlighted in the Current Disk Partitions section. Selecting Delete brings up a confirmation box.
OK	When this button is selected, any changes made are written to disk. At this time, you can confirm that you want the changes written to disk. This information is also passed to the installation program for later filesystem creation.
Back	This is the abort button. If you select the Back button, Disk Druid exits without making any changes and you are returned to the previous window, where you can select `fdisk` or Disk Druid to start over.
Function keys	As mentioned earlier, Disk Druid also has six handy function keys. Four of them map directly to the buttons just described (Add, Edit, Delete, and OK). Two are different:

F2—Add NFS	The F2 function key opens a dialog box in which you can define a read-only NFS served filesystem.
F5—Reset	This function does just what you think it does. (Unless you think it resets your computer—that's Ctrl+Alt+Del.) F5 resets the partitions to the way they were before you started editing them in this section.

Adding a Partition

To add a new partition, select the Add button and press Enter. A dialog box opens that contains the following fields:

Mount Point	Highlight this field and enter the partition's mount point.
Size	Enter the size (in megabytes) of the partition. The default of 1 can be removed with the Backspace key so you can enter a new number.

Growable?	This check box indicates whether the size you entered in the previous field is to be considered the partition's exact size or its minimum size. Press the spacebar to check and uncheck this box. When it's checked, the partition will grow to fill all available space on the hard disk.
Type	This field contains a list of partition types. Select the appropriate type by using the up and down arrow keys.
Allowable Drives	This field contains a list of the hard disks installed on your system, with a check box for each disk. If a box is checked, this partition can be created on that hard disk. If a box is not checked, the partition will never be created on that hard disk.
OK	Click this button and press the spacebar when you finish the settings for this particular partition. Then you're ready to create it.
Cancel	If you click this button, the partition you just defined will not be created.

Note

You must define at least two filesystems, one for Linux native and one for Linux swap space. However, the recommendation is six filesystems. One is swap space, and the other five are `/`, `/usr`,`/var`, `/home`, and `/usr/local`.

`fdisk`

For you old-timers out there, here are some pointers for `fdisk`. Again, Disk Druid is the recommended (and safer) way of partitioning the disks.

Caution

This is the most volatile step of the entire procedure. If you mess up here, you could delete your entire hard drive. I highly recommend that you make a backup of your current system before proceeding with the disk partitioning.

Here are some commands and a walkthrough of `fdisk`:

`m`	Provides a listing of the available commands.
`p`	Provides a listing of the current partition information.
`n`	Adds a new partition.
`t`	Sets or changes the partition type.
`l`	Provides a listing of the different partition types and their ID numbers.
`w`	Saves your information and quits `fdisk`.

Use `p` to check the current partition information, but add your root partition beforehand. Use `n` to create a new partition, and then select either `e` or `p` for extended or primary partition. Most likely you want to create a primary partition. You are asked what partition number should be assigned to it, at which cylinder the partition should start (you will be given a range—choose the lowest number), and the size of the partition. For example, for a 500MB partition, enter **`+500M`** for the size.

Formatting Swap Space

The installation program continues after you have defined the partitions. The next thing it asks you is the device to be used for swap space. There's a check box you can click to have the computer check for bad blocks during formatting. This is a wise thing to do.

To create your swap partition, you need to use `n` for a new partition. Choose either primary or extended; you probably need primary. Give the partition a number and tell it where the first cylinder should be. Lastly, tell `fdisk` how big you want your swap partition to be. Now you need to change the partition type to Linux swap. Enter `t` to change the type and enter the partition number of your swap partition. Enter `82` for the hex code for the Linux swap partition.

Now that you have created your Linux and Linux swap partitions, it is time to add any partitions you might need (for example, Windows 95). Use `n` again to create a new partition and enter all the information just as before. However, after you enter the size of the partition, you need to change the partition type. Enter `l` to get a listing of the hex codes for the different partition types. Find the type of partition you need and use `t` to change the partition type. Repeat this procedure until all your partitions are created. You can create up to four primary partitions. Then you must start putting extended partitions into each primary partition.

After your partitions are created, the installation program looks for Linux swap partitions and asks to initialize them. Choose the swap partitions you want to initialize, click the Check for Bad Blocks During Format box, and click OK. This formats the partition and makes it active so Linux can use it.

Formatting Partitions

After the swap space has been formatted, you are asked which partitions you would like to format. I strongly suggest that you format all system partitions (`/`, `/usr`, and `/var`, if they exist). You do not need to format `/home` or `/usr/local` if they have been configured during a previous install. Again, checking for bad blocks is a good thing.

The question that generally arises at this point is how big the partitions need to be. The following table gives a breakdown of the sizes of a typical installation. Of course, you can just have one great big partition called slash (`/`)if you decide not to have individual partitions for each major section.

Partition Type	*Minimal Size*	*Suggested Size*
`/`	80MB	100–200MB
`/usr`	850MB	850+ applications and other documentation
`/var`	22MB	50MB
Paging space	0MB	Up to 2,047MB

Although minimal and suggested sizes are given, your system's particular needs may require that you go above or below these numbers. For example, `/usr` at 850MB assumes that you have both text- and Web-based documentation loaded for at least one language. In addition, you see nothing here about a `/home` directory. Depending upon the needs of your system and your users, you can elect to leave them in the `/` partition or put them in a separate partition. The recommendation is that they be put into a separate partition. This is so you will not lose your home data during a system upgrade.

A Comment on Swap Space

When you create your swap partition, give some extra thought to the size of this partition (versus blindly picking a number or taking another person's recommendation). The swap partition is used for swapping the unused information in your RAM to disk to make room for more information. You should have at least 16MB total between your RAM and swap space. If you are running X Windows, you should have at least 32MB between them.

The problem with using the generic formula is that it doesn't take into consideration what the user might be doing. A formula for determining the amount of swapping you need is given here. Note that if you run out of swap space, your system will thrash about, trying to move memory pages into and out of the swap space. This will bring your system to its knees.

A better way to estimate how much RAM you need is to figure out the sizes of all the programs you would run at one time. To this number, add 8MB to cover the OS. If the total is less than 32MB, use a 32MB swap space; otherwise, use the actual value.

You should always configure some swap space, regardless of how much RAM you have. Even a small amount of swap space will produce good results on a system with a lot of RAM. For example, I have 64MB of RAM on my system, which is more than enough for all of the programs I run. I have 32MB of swap space for programs I have running but that I'm not actively using.

Components to Install

The next dialog box asks which components you want to install.

Note

If you want to install everything, just go to the bottom of the list and click Everything. Everything takes up about 942MB of total disk space. Keep in mind, though, that this includes almost 200MB of documentation. (Remember how many languages you can install in?)

When you have told the program which packages you want to install and have worked out all the dependencies, a window tells you that a complete log of your installation will be in `/tmp/install.log` after you restart your system.

Click OK, and then the system formats your partitions and loads the packages you selected. Depending on your CD-ROM speed and how many packages you requested (and, to a limited extent, your hard drive speed), this could take 25 minutes or longer.

Configuring Your Hardware

This section covers the final part of the installation: hardware configuration.

Choosing a Mouse

Note

Push down both buttons to emulate the third mouse button.

Configuring the X Window System

The next window that comes up asks you about the X Window server you want to run. Autoprobe identifies your graphics card and loads the card driver. It then asks about your monitor.

Be sure to select a monitor that exactly matches your model. If your model isn't listed, choose Custom and fill in the values listed in your monitor's manual.

> **Caution**
>
> Choosing the wrong monitor frequencies can—to use the vernacular—fry your monitor. Make sure you have the correct settings.

Xconfigurator is the program that configures your monitor. These settings can be changed at any time by rerunning Xconfigurator.

If you chose the generic VGA card, you are asked whether you want to probe for settings using `X - probeonly`. Choose not to probe; after a moment, you should move on to the next section of the installation.

> **Caution**
>
> The probe locks up some systems. This means you'll have to restart the system and begin again.

If you do probe and there are errors, you are asked for some specifics about your video card, amount of memory, and clockchip. You are then asked to select video modes.

Configuring the Network

The next question is whether you want to configure LAN (not dial-up) networking for your system.

If you will be installing this machine on a LAN and want to set up networking now, click the Yes button. If not, click No. You can always configure the networking later.

If you chose Yes, you are asked which network card driver to try. Scroll down the selection bar until you see one that matches your card.

Setting the Time Zone

Next you are asked to set up your system's time zone. The first selection area asks whether your computer's BIOS clock is set to GMT. The next area asks which time zone you are in. Scroll to the zone that best matches your time zone and select OK to continue.

Selecting Services to Start Automatically

The next section of the installation goes through the services or daemons to start when the system restarts. The dialog box contains a long scrollable list of check boxes. Pressing F1 will provide help on the item that's currently selected. You can change these services later with the `ntsysv` command.

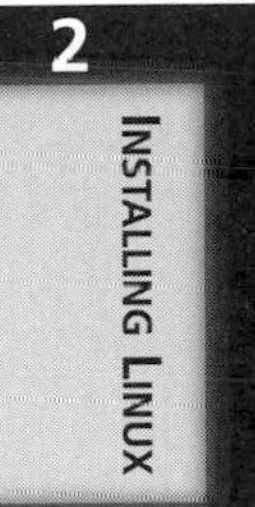

Configuring Your Printer

You are next asked if you want to configure a printer. Clicking Yes brings up a dialog box that asks where the printer is, with three selections available:

Local	A printer connected directly to the computer.
Remote `lpd`	A printer connected to your LAN, with which you can communicate via `lpd`.
LAN Manager	Use this if you print to the network printer via a LAN manager or SMB print server.

Root's Password

Root is the all-powerful administrative account. This account has no limitations; therefore, the password for this account must be kept secure. You are asked to enter a password twice. The password must be six to eight characters long. As you type in this new password, notice that nothing is shown on the screen. This is a security feature. Enter the password into the system twice to make sure you typed it correctly.

Authentication Configuration

Additional authentication configuration settings follow the setting of root's password. In this section you are asked if you want to have NIS enabled. If you do, you also need to supply the NIS domain and server. (See Chapter 14, "NIS: Network Information Service," for more information on NIS.) You can also choose to have the system request services via a broadcast instead of providing a server name.

The next two choices have to do with added password security. It is recommended that you at least turn on shadow passwords, if not both shadow passwords and MD5 password.

Creating a Startup Disk

A custom startup disk provides a way of starting your Linux system without depending on the normal bootloader. This is useful if you don't want to install LILO on your system, another operating system removes LILO, or LILO doesn't work with your hardware configuration. A custom startup disk can also be used with the Red Hat Rescue image, making recovery from severe system failures much easier.

> **Note**
>
> Creating a startup disk is highly recommended at this stage in the game.

If you select Yes, you are asked to insert a blank floppy disk into the first drive (`/dev/fd0`). The system creates a startup disk after you have inserted the blank disk.

Selecting Startup Options

The next screen (and one of the last) presents you with possible startup loader locations. A comment ensures that you do not overwrite the correct one. The choices are the Master Boot Record and the First Sector of Boot Partitions.

The Master Boot Record is the entire system's boot record. Replacing this causes LILO to start every time the system starts.

The First Sector of Boot Partitions can be used if you have another bootloader on your system. If these loaders are already in the primary drive's Master Boot Record, you probably do not want to replace them.

Bootloader

A few systems need to pass special options to the kernel at startup time in order for the system to function properly. If you need to pass startup options to the kernel, enter them at the next screen. The second part of bootloader states that it can start other operating systems that are on your system. If you have Windows 95 or 98, bootloader recognizes this and gives it a DOS startup label.

Done

Installation is complete. You need to remove the disk and press Enter to restart. You are now ready to log in to your Red Hat Linux system.

The Red Hat Package Manager

Installing and Removing Packages with RPM

The basic use of the `rpm` command to install a package is as follows:

```
rpm -I packagename.rpm
```

Use the following to uninstall a package:

```
rpm -u packagename.rpm
```

Many other options are available for RPM, but these two are the most common.

Packages for use with RPM are available at `ftp://ftp.redhat.com/pub/redhat/current/i386/RedHat/RPMS/` or any of its mirror sites.

Debian Installation Overview

Between Red Hat, Debian, and Caldera, Debian is probably the most complicated to install. The base system setup is painless. Things get muddy when you're using the package installer, but once users are accustomed to the Debian package installer, they do not want to use anything else. Given the huge number of packages available to Debian, the package installer must pay far more attention to dependencies. However, problems should be rare for the install in this chapter.

The first step in installing Debian is to boot the Debian installation system with the Rescue Floppy or from the CD-ROM. Once you've booted into the installation system, it will guide you through the initial system configuration. After you've gone through some basic configuration steps, the base system will be installed.

The Debian base system is a core set of packages that are required to run Debian in a minimal, standalone fashion and set up network access. Once you have configured and installed the base system, your machine can stand on its own.

> **Note**
>
> Debian is extremely network-oriented for its install. If you have a fast Internet connection, the base system can be installed and the rest of the packages can be fetched and installed from a Debian ftp mirror. The `dselect` package maintainer is highly automated. Once the network connection is configured, you can select the ftp mirror and the packages you want and go for a pizza. It will take care of the download and install. Usually the only time `dselect` stops is when a package needs to know your preferences before completing its install.

The final step is installing the remainder of the Debian system. This includes the applications and documents that you actually use on your system. The rest of the Debian system can be installed from CD-ROM. At this point, you'll be using the standard Debian package management tools, such as `dselect`.

Choosing Your Installation Media

First, choose the boot media for the installation system. Next, choose the method you will use to install the base system.

To boot the installation system, you have the following choices: bootable CD-ROM, floppies, or a non-Linux boot loader.

CD-ROM booting is one of the easiest ways to install. Not all machines can boot directly from the CD-ROM, so you may still need to use floppies. Booting from floppies is supported for most platforms. Floppy booting is described later in this section.

Installing from a CD-ROM

You don't need any floppy disks if your system supports booting from a CD-ROM. Put the CD-ROM into the drive, turn your computer off, and then turn it back on. You should see a Welcome screen with a `boot` prompt at the bottom. You can now skip the "Booting from Floppies" section of this chapter and continue the installation as described in the "Booting the Installation System" section.

> **Note**
>
> Note that you may need to go into your bios to take advantage of the CD-ROM boot option. To do this, go into bios and look for the boot sequence option. It is usually under Bios Setup Features. You want the CD-ROM to be listed before the primary hard drive.

If your computer can't boot from the Debian CD-ROM, make boot floppies as described in the next section.

Booting from Floppies

Your Debian CD-ROM contains all the information necessary to create boot disks for you. For these instructions, you will need two disks. Label the first one "Debian 2.1 Install/Rescue Disk" and the second one "Debian 2.1 Modules/Drivers Disk."

Creating Floppies from Disk Images

The steps outlined in the Red Hat installation section earlier in this chapter for writing raw disk images to a floppy can easily be adapted for Debian floppy creation. However, this section only discusses installation from Windows 95 and assumes you will be using the Debian CD-ROM during the installation.

Disk images, such as the rescue disk image `resc1440.bin`, should not simply be copied to a floppy disk. Instead, a program called `rawrite2` should be used to write the image files to floppy disk in *raw* mode.

First, you need to get to a DOS prompt. In Windows 95 and later, do this by double-clicking on an MS-DOS icon or by selecting the MS-DOS prompt menu selection in the Start, Programs menu. Insert your Debian GNU/Linux CD-ROM and change to your CD-ROM drive. In most cases, this is D:

```
C:\WINDOWS> D:
```

Now change to the directory containing the disk images:

```
D:\> CD \DISTS\SLINK\MAIN\DISKS-I386\2.1.8-1999-02-22
```

If that directory does not exist, issue `CD \DISTS\SLINK\MAIN\DISKS-I386`, and then run `DIR` to find out the actual name of the current directory. Debian makes periodic updates to its distributions, so the directory name may change between releases.

Now you will create the first of two disks. Start `rawrite2` as follows:

```
D:\DISTS\SLINK\MAIN\DISKS-I386\2.1.8-1999-02-22> rawrite2
RaWrite 2.0 - Write disk file to raw floppy diskette
```

`rawrite2` starts and displays its welcome message. Enter the boldface text shown in the following examples for each of these questions:

```
Enter disk image source file name: resc1440.bin
```

```
Enter target diskette drive: a:
```

`rawrite2` now asks you to insert a disk into the floppy drive. Do so and press Enter.

At this point, `rawrite2` will have created the first of the two necessary boot disks. Repeat the process for the driver disk image, `drv1440.bin`. By now, your boot disks have been created and you can now use the first one to boot.

Note

If the boot disks are not present or you want the latest disks, you can always download them from a Debian site, along with `rawrite`, if you encounter problems during an install. It is a good idea to make sure you have the latest disks.

Booting the Installation System

Shut down your computer and insert your newly created Rescue Disk floppy into the floppy drive. Turn on your computer. Soon you should have the `boot` prompt. Simply press Enter at this point.

Once you press Enter, you should see several boot messages. Ignore these messages for now. Just wait until you see the Color Selection screen. Be patient because this can take a couple of minutes from a floppy.

Step-by-Step Installation for Debian

`dbootstrap` is the program that is responsible for initial system configuration and the installation of the base system. The main job of `dbootstrap`, and the main purpose of your initial system configuration, is to configure core elements of your system. `dbootstrap` is very easy to use. It will guide you through each step of the installation process in a sequential manner. You can also go back and repeat steps if you make a mistake. Navigation within `dbootstrap` is accomplished with the arrow keys, Enter, and Tab.

Select Color or Monochrome Display

The first thing that `dbootstrap` asks about is your display. You should see the Select Color or Monochrome display dialog box. If your monitor is capable of displaying color, press Enter. The display should change from black and white to color. Next, use the arrow keys to move the cursor to the Next menu item, and then press Enter to continue with the installation.

Debian GNU/Linux Installation Main Menu

You will be able to see the main Debian installation menu throughout the installation process. The choices at the top of the menu will change to indicate your progress in installing the system. The first choice on the installation menu is the next action that should be taken. Continue the installation by selecting the Next menu item.

Configure the Keyboard

Make sure the Next item is highlighted, and then press Enter to go to the keyboard configuration menu.

Use the arrow keys to move the highlight to the keyboard selection you desire, and then press Enter. In most cases, you can just use the default U.S. layout.

Partition a Hard Disk

If the Next menu item isn't the Partition a Hard Disk menu selection, simply use the down-arrow key to select Partition a Hard Disk and then press Enter.

The Partition a Hard Disk menu item presents you with a list of disk drives you can partition and runs a partitioning application called `cfdisk`. You must create at least one Linux native (type 83) disk partition, and you probably want at least one Linux swap (type 82) partition, as explained later in this section.

You will now create the partitions that you need to install Debian, assuming that you are partitioning an empty hard disk.

> **Caution**
>
> Any partition resizing should have been done before this point. If you have to resize your partitions, first reboot into your other operating system and make the appropriate changes.

The `cfdisk` program should now be running. The boot partition *must* reside within the first 1,024 cylinders of your hard disk. Keeping that in mind, use the right-arrow key to highlight the New menu selection, and then press Enter. You will be presented with the choice of creating a *primary* partition or a *logical* partition. To help ensure that the partition containing the boot information is within the first 1,024 cylinders, create a primary partition first. This primary partition will be your Linux native partition.

Highlight the Primary menu selection and press Enter. Next, you will need to enter how large you want that partition to be. Refer to the partitioning suggestions in the Red Hat installation section earlier in this chapter to help you decide how large you want your Debian GNU/Linux partitions to be. Debian will require a similar amount of space. Enter the partition size you want and then press Enter. Next you will be asked if you want to place the partition at the beginning of the free space or at the end. Place it at the beginning to ensure that it lies within the first 1,024 cylinders. Highlight Beginning and press Enter. At this point you will be brought back to the main screen. Notice that the partition you created is listed. By default, a Linux native partition was created. This partition must now be made bootable. Make sure that the Bootable menu selection is highlighted and press Enter. The partition should now have Boot listed under the Flags column.

With the remaining space, create another primary partition. Using the down-arrow key, highlight the free space entry in the partition list. Now highlight the New menu selection and proceed just as you did when you created the first primary partition. Notice that the partition is listed as a Linux native partition. Because this partition will be your swap partition, it must be denoted as such. Make sure the partition you just created (your swap partition) is highlighted, press the left-arrow key until the Type menu selection is highlighted, and then press Enter. You will be presented with a list of supported partition types. The Linux swap partition type should already be selected. If it is not, enter the number from the list that corresponds to the Linux swap partition (82), and then press Enter. Your swap partition should now be listed as a Linux swap partition under the FS Type column on the main screen.

Until now, nothing on your disk has been altered. If you are satisfied that the partition scheme you've created is what you want, press the left-arrow key until Write is highlighted and press Enter. Your hard disk has now been partitioned. Quit the `cfdisk` application by selecting the Quit menu selection. Once you have left `cfdisk`, you should be back in Debian's `dbootstrap` installation application.

Caution

This is where many people run into mistakes. Make sure you press the left-arrow key until Write is highlighted and press Enter.

Initialize and Activate a Swap Partition

There is no problem in reinitializing a swap partition, so select Initialize and Activate a Swap Partition. This menu choice will first present you with a dialog box reading "Please select the partition to activate as a swap device." The default device presented should be the swap partition you've already set up; if so, just press Enter.

Next, you have the option to scan the entire partition for unreadable disk blocks caused by defects on the surface of the hard disk platters. This is especially useful if you have very old disk drives, but it can be useful nonetheless. Finally, there is a confirmation message because initialization will destroy any data currently on the partition. If all is well, click Yes. The screen will flash as the initialization program runs.

Initialize a Linux Partition

At this point, the next menu item presented should be Initialize a Linux Partition. If it isn't, either you haven't completed the disk partitioning process or you haven't used any of the swap partition-related menu choices.

You can initialize a Linux partition, or you can mount a previously initialized one. Note that `dbootstrap` will *not* upgrade an old system without destroying it. If you're upgrading, Debian can usually upgrade itself and you won't need to use `dbootstrap`. The Debian 2.1 release notes contain upgrade instructions.

If you are using old disk partitions that are not empty—that is, if you want to just throw away what is on them—you should initialize them. You must initialize any partitions that you created in the disk partitioning step. The first partition that you mount or initialize will be the one mounted as the root partition. Select the Next menu item to initialize and mount the root `/` disk partition. You will be offered the choice to scan the disk partition for bad blocks, just as when you initialized the swap partition. If you don't mind waiting, scanning for bad blocks is suggested. Depending on the size and speed of the drive, this can take from a few seconds to several minutes.

Install Operating System Kernel and Modules

Once you've mounted the `/` partition, the Next menu item will be Install Operating System Kernel and Modules unless you've already performed some of the installation steps. Use the arrow keys to select the menu items to initialize or mount disk partitions if you have any more partitions to set up. If you have created separate partitions for `/var`, `/usr`, or other filesystems, you should initialize or mount them now.

During this step, you will be asked to confirm that the device you have mounted on root is the proper one. Next, you will be offered a menu of devices from which you can install the kernel. Choose the appropriate device from which to install the kernel and modules; this will either be a CD-ROM device or the first floppy device.

If you are installing from floppies, make sure that the Rescue Floppy is in the floppy drive. Soon you will be asked to insert the Drivers Floppy and the remaining install floppies, depending on the install method.

Configure Device Driver Modules

Select the Configure Device Driver Modules menu item and choose devices that are installed in your system. Modules for the devices you select will be loaded every time your system boots. You can reconfigure your modules with the `modconf` program at any point after the system is installed.

Configure the Network

Now it is time to configure your network. Even if you don't have a network, you still need to specify a hostname and whether or not your system is connected to a network. If you are connected to a network, you'll need the information described in the Red Hat network installation section earlier in this chapter. However, if your primary connection to the network is through a telephone line, choose the Do Not Configure Network option.

You will be asked a number of questions about your network. Fill in the answers as requested. The installation system will ask you for confirmation. Next, specify the network device that your primary network connection uses.

Install the Base System

If you will be installing from a CD-ROM or hard drive, you will be prompted to specify the path to the `base2_1.tgz` file. If you have an official Debian CD-ROM, the default value should be correct. Otherwise, enter the path where the base system can be found, relative to where the CD-ROM was mounted.

If you are installing the base system from floppies, you will be prompted to insert each base disk floppy. Once all of the floppies have been read, the base system will be extracted and installed.

Configure the Base System

Now that the base system has been installed, you need to configure it. You'll be asked to select your time zone. The suggested way of specifying your time zone is to go to the Directories: pane and select your country (or continent). Now select the appropriate time zone in the Timezones: pane.

You must now specify if your system time is set relative to Greenwich Mean Time (GMT) or local time. If you will only be running Linux on your computer, select GMT by clicking Yes. Otherwise, select No to specify that your system will be using local time. Linux generally keeps GMT time on the system clock and converts visible time to the local time zone, whereas other non-UNIX-like operating systems usually do not.

Make Debian Bootable Directly from the Hard Disk

Now it is time to specify how Debian will be booted. You will be asked if you want to install a master boot record. If you aren't using a boot manager and you have no other operating system installed on the same machine, answer Yes to this question. You will then be asked whether you want to boot Debian from the hard disk when you turn on your system. This sets the Linux partition you created to be the *bootable partition*.

Make a Boot Floppy

Make a boot floppy if you intend to boot your Debian system from the hard disk. In case your hard drive doesn't boot correctly, you'll always be able to boot from a floppy disk to correct any problems. Select Make a Boot Floppy from the menu and insert a blank floppy as directed. Write-protect the newly created boot floppy and label it "Custom Boot."

The First Standalone Boot

At this point, your base system should be installed and configured. Your system will now be rebooted into a completely functional, yet minimal, installation of Debian GNU/Linux. Make sure there's no floppy disk in your floppy drive, and then select the Reboot the System menu item.

Debian should boot and you should see the same messages as when you first booted the installation system, followed by a long series of messages. Do not worry about these messages. You will not have to answer any prompts at this point.

Set the Root Password

At some point the whirl of messages will end and you will be asked for the root password. The *superuser* account or *root* account is an account that bypasses all security mechanisms on your system. You should use it only to perform system administration tasks. Remember to pick a non-obvious root password, but one that you will remember. You should *not* use the root account for daily use or as your personal login.

Create an Ordinary User

Next, the system will ask you to create an ordinary user account. Use this account as your primary, day-to-day account.

Shadow Password Support

Next, the system will ask whether you want to enable shadow passwords. This is an authentication system that makes your Linux system a bit more secure. It is generally a good idea to enable shadow password support. If you need to reconfigure shadow password support, use the `shadowconfig` program.

Remove PCMCIA

If you installed PCMCIA support and you have no use for it, you can choose to remove it at this point. In general, you will only need PCMCIA support when installing Debian on laptop systems.

Select and Install Profiles

You now have the option of installing predetermined software configurations offered by Debian. Select the profile that best suits your needs.

Once you are done selecting the installation profile, if any, Debian's primary package management tool, `dselect`, will be started. If you selected tasks or profiles, remember to skip the Select step in `dselect`, since the selections have already been made for you.

Package Installation with `dselect`

Software package installation on your Debian system is done using Debian's package management tool, `dselect`. `dselect` will be started for you during the installation, and it will step you through the package installation process.

As each step is completed successfully, `dselect` will lead you on to the next. In general, you should go through the steps in order without skipping any. However, skip the Select step if you selected an installation profile. Descriptions of each of the steps follow.

Access

Here, `dselect` is told where packages are located. The available access methods will be listed. Only the `multi_cd` and `apt` methods will be described in this section.

`multi_cd`

This access method is the recommended way of installing recent versions of Debian from a set of multiple binary CDs. When you first select this method, be sure the CD-ROM you will be using is not mounted. Place the last *binary* disk of the set in the drive and answer the questions you are asked.

After you've updated the available package list and selccted which packages to install, you will need to run an Install step for each of the CDs you have, in turn. Here's the procedure:

1. Insert the CD into your CD-ROM drive.
2. Select Install from the main `dselect` menu.
3. Once it's installed, press Enter to go back to the main `dselect` menu.
4. Repeat this procedure for the remaining CDs.

You may have to run the installation step more than once because some packages may be installed prior to the ones they depend on. This is very common, so it is a good idea to run it at least twice during the install.

Finally, the Configure menu selection aids in fixing any package installations that were not properly configured (if they were not installed in the proper order, for example).

Upgrading with `apt` and `dselect`

There are two major upgrading methods, `apt` and `dselect`.

`apt`

This is the recommended method for installation from a mirror of the Debian archive. It performs complete dependency analysis and ordering to ensure that packages are installed in the proper order.

Configuration of this method involves selecting any number of different locations that contain the package list. Locations are specified using a URL format. Available URL formats include the following:

`file:`	For obtaining packages found on local or NFS mounted disks.
`http:`	For obtaining packages from a site that uses the HTTP protocol.
`ftp:`	For obtaining packages from a site that uses the FTP protocol.

This information should be specified in `/etc/apt/sources.list`. You are specifying only the location of the package lists. From this, `apt` can figure out what is available and where to get it. There should be a couple of examples in the files that you can use, and you can add your own favorite ftp mirrors. `apt` is a very powerful package maintenance tool. It should take only a few minutes to configure, and later on it will be well worth the effort.

`apt` is a young package and the documentation is pretty good, so I would highly recommend reading the man pages on `apt` and `apt-get` and the `apt` user guide. They are brief and informative. After you have updated your `source.list` file and verified that you indeed have a network connection, you can use `apt`. When you're using `apt`, I recommend updating your lists before fetching anything. This can be done with the following commands:

```
# apt-get update

# apt-get check
```

The update command updates the package lists and the check command examines the packages that are currently installed. With the thousands of packages available for

Debian, it is a good idea to keep your package list as current as possible. In this book we will be installing individual packages, but `apt` can do full distribution upgrades.

To install individual packages, simply enter the package name as follows:

```
# apt-get install (package names)
```

It is possible to specify multiple packages. Keep in mind that it wants the package name, not the fully qualified name. A package name could be something like `xquake`, while the fully qualified name would be something like `xquake_1.2.3-1.deb`.

Even though `apt` is very powerful, problems still can occur. Be patient and read all the messages `apt` returns. When `apt` encounters an error, it will usually return all the information needed to resolve it. If you read through the man pages, you will notice an `-f` option. It looks like a quick and easy fix, but make sure you check your error message before using it. Remember, when you use the `-f` option, you are telling `apt` to go fix it. It will just try to fix the dependency problem, and may do so in a way you do not want.

dselect

`dselect` will read the file containing a list of all available packages using the access method you selected, and will create a database on your system of all available packages. Debian currently has over 2,000 packages, so this step may take some time on slow machines or network connections.

Select

This menu selection will allow you to select which packages are installed, updated, and removed. When you enter the Select step (this can take a few seconds), you will get a help screen. Once you are done reading the displayed help, press the spacebar to enter the package selection screen. Some useful keys are listed in Table 2.2.

TABLE 2.2 Useful `dselect` Keys

Key	*Description*
+	Selects a package for installation.
=	Places a package on hold.
-	Removes a package.
_	Removes a package and its configuration files.
i, I	Cycles through highlighted package information.
o, O	Cycles through the sort options.
v, V	Terse/verbose toggle.

The four leftmost columns describe the status of each package listed in the `dselect` package selection screen. Table 2.3 lists what each column denotes.

TABLE 2.3 `dselect` Package States

Flag	*Meaning*	*Possible Values*
E	Error	Space, R, I
I	Installed state	Space, *, -, U, C, I
O	Old mark	*, -, =, _, n
M	Mark	*, -, =, _, n

For example:

```
** Opt graphics gimp <none> 0.77-1 The GNU Image Manipulation Program
```

This means that the `gimp` package was selected when you last ran `dselect`, but it is not installed because the package is not available from the locations specified in your access method of choice.

There are times when `dselect` cannot get around a package dependency problem. Generally, such a situation occurs when a package depends on another package that isn't available, perhaps due to problem with the archive where the missing package is supposed to be stored. Pressing the Q (notice the capitalization) key will force `dselect` to ignore broken package dependencies and continue. The X key will revert to the selections you made and cause `dselect` to exit. For now, stick with the packages already selected and don't add any more. You can always add, update, and remove packages later. Press Enter to accept your package selections and return to the main screen.

Install

During this step, `dselect` will install the selected packages. Some packages may expect interaction from you, so be prepared to make some decisions. If a package is not installed because of dependency problems, try running the Install step again. More than likely, the package that was causing the dependency problems will have been installed, which will allow the package that had problems to be installed. If your access method was `apt`, you probably won't have this problem.

Configure

Package configuration generally occurs during the Install step. However, configuration errors may occur during package installation. In those situations, the Configure step can be used to correct packages that haven't been completely configured.

Remove

If you select packages for removal, this step will cause them to be removed. If you use `apt` as your access method, packages will be removed automatically during the Install step.

Quit

This step is self-explanatory. It simply causes `dselect` to be exited. After selecting this option, you should be back at the root prompt with a loaded Debian system ready to be configured.

Caldera OpenLinux Installation

The installation procedure for Caldera OpenLinux is fairly straightforward and relatively painless, but it usually pays to be prepared. Between Red Hat, Debian, and Caldera, the Caldera installation is the easiest.

Before you start the installation process, it is important to know what your current system looks like and what kind of hardware you are using. You should know what video card you have, the brand and model of your monitor, what type of ethernet card you are using (if any), and the modem that's connected. To that effect, you should probably fill in the little questionnaire earlier in this chapter.

The way you begin the installation process will depend on the platform you are currently using before installing Caldera. The first part of this section is divided by platform:

- Windows
- CD autoboot
- DOS
- UNIX or another version of Linux

After you've worked through the preinstallation and have partitioned Caldera with your specific platform, go to the section later in this chapter titled "Package Installation." This section will take you through the rest of the installation process.

Preinstalling and Partitioning Caldera Using Windows

If you already have a running computer with, say, Microsoft Windows 9x on it, you can simply insert the Caldera CD-ROM and it will autostart the installation procedure. From the first screen, you can do the following:

- Install products
- Browse CD contents
- View Caldera's Web site
- View multimedia presentations
- Register now
- Contact Caldera
- Find support and training

(If you contain yourself long enough, we recommend you try out the multimedia presentation. It's quite funny.)

When you are ready, go to the main menu (use the main menu button if you got yourself lost) and select Install Products. The first item there is the Full Install Preparation in English, German, French, and Italian. This will install some handy programs on your existing operating system to help you with the installation process. It's not a requisite to install these because you can just walk through the other items on the menu and then run and install programs from the CD as they are needed. If you do select this menu item and go with the default settings, you will be presented with an open window and a new entry in Start Menu, Programs, OpenLinux. If you have inadvertently closed this window, you should be able to use the Start Menu to get to the programs.

Creating the Install Floppies

The first thing to do is create the necessary install floppies. This is always a good idea, even if you have a computer that can boot from a CD-ROM. Go to Install Products, Create Floppy Install Diskettes. The Lizard install diskette is the latest and greatest in install disks and the follow-up to the LISA install diskette. When you click here, a DOS window will open where you type the drive letter of your floppy (normally A for your A: drive). This process lasts a couple of minutes because it has to write a whole floppy with information. You should also create the Lizard Modules diskette. The process is identical after you've selected the menu item on your screen. Make sure you label the disks so you know which is which. It might not be a bad idea to insert the Lizard install disk and reboot your computer, just to make sure that the floppy is without errors. If this works, you can remove the install disk from the floppy drive and safely press the reset button on your computer to get back into Windows.

Partitioning Linux Using Windows

The next thing you want to select is Partition & Install Linux. This is the Partition Magic program, Caldera edition, and it will install itself on your hard disk. When Partition Magic has been installed, you need to remove the CD-ROM from the tray before you can continue. Windows will shut down and give control to the Partition Magic program after your computer reboots. Partition Magic allows you to easily shrink the size of your current operating system on your first hard disk to make room for Linux. As explained elsewhere, Linux needs its own partition on the disk to set things up. If you already have a Linux partition defined, Partition Magic will alert you about this.

Caution

Partition Magic may be a commercial utility, but if not used properly it can still do a great deal of damage. This utility alters the partitions on your hard drive. A mistake can easily lose all of the data on the drive. So please back up your data, follow all directs, and read ever bit of information Partition Magic displays before making any selections.

Delete a Linux Partition

We encountered a problem with a program called Delete a Linux Partition. After invoking it twice in a row and rebooting the computer, Windows did not boot any more. After some investigation, it turned out that Delete a Linux Partition had removed all traces of the Windows partition as well! If this happens to you, it *might* be possible to retrieve the information without going back to your backups. (You *do* have backups, right?)

Here's a possible remedy: Boot the computer with the LISA install disk and answer the first couple of questions about keyboard settings and some other configuration issues (just hitting Enter will work most of the time) until you get to a screen titled "Hardware found (IDE/ATAPI)". There you can use the Alt+F2 keyboard combination and log in as root at the login prompt. After the ominous (and true) warning—"If you are root, you should know what you are doing"—type **`fdisk`** and press **`p`** at the command prompt. This shows you the known partitions on your hard disk. It helps if you know where your Windows partition used to be, but for most people this will be the whole disk. Enter **`n`** for new partition, **`p`** for primary partition, and **`1`** for the partition to fill in (provided it's available; otherwise, choose another digit).

When you get First cylinder (..-...), enter the number you wrote down before or choose the lowest number it allows you to pick. At Last cylinder, choose the highest number available. You're almost there! First you need to change the type of the partition you just created, since Linux's `fdisk` assumes you want to create Linux partitions. Type **`t`** (for type), check the partition number (1), and when it asks for a hex code, enter **6**. Set the boot flag with **a** and **1**, and then use the **w** command to write the information to your hard disk. You're then taken back to the number sign prompt.

Remove the floppy from the disk drive, make sure the CD-ROM drive is empty, press the reset button on your computer, and anxiously watch your computer reboot.

If all has gone according to plan, your computer will reboot with your old operating system.

If all else fails, you can always go back to your backups.

Depending on the size of your hard disk and the amount of free space you have available, you can select one of the default sizes. The package selection process happens later on, but at this point you need to decide what you are going to use.

Preinstalling and Partitioning Caldera Using CD-Autoboot

If your machine can boot from CD-ROM, you are in for the easiest install possible. The only thing you have to do is create a Linux native and a Linux swap partition. Just decide if you want to use a Windows, DOS, or Linux utility to do so, based on your current system configuration. If you want to use a Windows utility, please refer to the "Partitioning Linux Using Windows" section earlier in the chapter. If you choose a DOS-based utility, please follow the instructions provided with the utility. If you already have a Linux install, just use your favorite partitioning tool. After you have created the desired partitions, proceed to the "Package Installation" section later in the chapter and use the CD-ROM boot method.

Preinstalling and Partitioning Caldera Using DOS

If you are using DOS and you have a good partition utility, go ahead and use it, creating the Linux native and swap partitions as specified in the "Formatting Partitions" section under the Red Hat install earlier in this chapter. Remember, these are only suggestions. You only need a single Linux native partition and a single swap partition for the install to work. If you do not have any partitioning utilities, don't worry. You can just create some Lizard boot disks and do it the old-fashioned way. If you have already created the partitions, you can switch to your CD-ROM and run the following install, assuming the CD-ROM is the D: drive:

```
D:\col\launch\dos\install
```

Occasionally this method doesn't work. If you encounter any problems and have CD-ROM boot capability, just skip down to the "Package Installation" section later in this chapter and follow the procedures there.

Creating Boot Disks in DOS

To create boot disks in DOS, switch to the following directory on your CD-ROM:

```
D:\col\launch\floppy
```

In this directory you will find the `rawrite` utility, a couple of scripts, and a couple of disk images. You need two blank floppies to start with. Insert one and type `install`. It will prompt you for a drive letter. Enter the letter of the floppy. It will take a couple of minutes to create the install disk. Switch disks and run the `modules` script. It is the same procedure. Make sure you label the disks.

Now you just have to create those partitions. If you have already created them, skip to the "Package Installation" section.

Creating Linux Partitions Using the Boot Disks

Just insert the install disk and reboot the computer. This is assuming you have free space for partitions. If you need to shrink any partitions, do so first and refer to the "Partitioning Linux Using Windows" section earlier in this chapter if you only wish to shrink the primary Windows partition. Once you get to the language selection screen, enter Ctrl+Alt+F2. This will take you to another virtual terminal. Log in as root. It will give you a warning, but do not worry about it.

Next, you have to figure out what drive you need to partition. If it is the primary master IDE drive, it is `/dev/hda`. The primary slave is `/dev/hdb`, and so on. For SCSI drives, the first drive is `/dev/sda`, the next is `/dev/sdb`, and so on. So to get things started, enter the following:

```
# fdisk (your drive here)
```

This will start the Linux `fdisk` utility. Enter **`m`** to see the menu. First, I highly recommend you print your existing partition table with the **`p`** option. If you need to create a new partition, do so and create primary partitions if possible. Then change the type of one partition to Linux native (83) and one to Linux swap (82). Now all you need to do is select Write to Disk and exit. Your partitions have been created and you are ready to reboot and start the "Package Installation" section of this chapter.

Preinstalling and Partitioning Caldera Using Another Version of UNIX or Linux

Installing Caldera on a system with another version of Linux is probably the easiest method possible. To begin with, you need to create the partitions for Caldera. Just pop up your favorite partition tool—say, `fdisk` or Disk Druid—and create root, swap, and any other desired partitions. Of course, this is assuming that there are partitions or empty spaces available. If any partitions have to be compacted, please do so first using an appropriate Partition Magic-style tool. Remember to set the root partition to type 83 and swap to type 82. The Caldera install is very, very simple, but it can be touchy about the partitions. Do as much as you can beforehand.

If your machine is bootable by CD-ROM you can move on to the "Package Installation" section. Otherwise you will have to make a set of boot disks. You can do this with any disk writing utility in Linux like dd. The disk images are located in `/col/launch/floppy` on the CD-ROM. Otherwise you can follow the methods in "Creating the Install Floppies" for systems with Windows or the "Creating Boot Disks in DOS" section, if you prefer those methods. Once you have the install and modules disks created, you are ready to proceed to the next section.

Package Installation

Regardless of the platform you are using, eventually you will come to this part of the process. Now that you have the preinstallation and partitioning completed, you need to install packages. Here are the four default package installation options that you can choose from:

- Minimal install—This uses about 160MB of disk space. You can probably make do with 200MB, but 300MB is better. This installation should be used only if you don't have enough space, or if you intend to set up a Linux server as opposed to a Linux desktop. This doesn't mean that you cannot use your computer as a desktop, but you won't have as many nice tools available to you.
- Recommended packages—This uses about 600MB of disk space, so you should probably reserve at least 750MB. This will give you a nice and fairly complete desktop environment.
- Recommended packages plus commercial—This will take up about 850MB, so you should count on using about 1GB of disk space at a minimum. Here you get the value for your money, with a multitude of tools and gadgets that turn your computer into a real power machine.

- Everything—This will take up about 1.2GB of space, and it contains so many programs that you won't get bored. You should reserve at least 1.5GB, but 2GB is probably a better bet.

Try to make as much room as you can, and determine which option you will choose later on when the install procedure asks for it.

Note

Remember, even if you are booting from floppy, the CD-ROM still needs to be in the drive. While it's booting up, the floppy is searching for the source of the install files. If the CD-ROM is not in the drive at boot time, it cannot find them.

Insert the Lizard install disk in your floppy drive and reboot your computer. If you've seen Linux systems boot before, prepare to be impressed by the work that the Caldera folks have put into the interface. Wait until it asks you for your preferred language (we're going to assume it's English). The next step is detection of the mouse. Make sure you move the mouse slowly, or else the auto-detection might fail. If it does fail, you can always choose your own settings with the keyboard (hint: use the Tab key and the cursor keys).

The installation target menu allows you to select the location of your new operating system. If you're setting up a Linux machine with nothing else, the Entire hard disk would be a good selection. If you've played around with Linux and its partitions before, you might choose Custom, but the Prepared partition will work just fine if you've used Partition Magic. You also have to select a root partition, which will contain your complete set of installed programs. If you have only one option, go with that. Depending of the size of the partition, you can now select the install of your choice.

Video and Monitor Settings

Next is the keyboard setting and selection of your video card. Try out the probe if you are not sure about your hardware. Unless you have a very new video card, this should auto-detect just fine. If the detection fails or you just want to put in the details directly from your owner's manual, you can do that as well. When you are happy with the settings for the video card, move on to the monitor section. It is very important to choose the right monitor settings. When in doubt, check your manual. It is possible to damage your monitor if you choose settings beyond what your monitor can support. Luckily, there is a large database with monitor models (1,700 entries), so you should be able to find your specific monitor brand and model in there.

Video Mode

The video mode (next menu) helps you define what resolution you would like to have. The rule of thumb "More is better" is largely true, but pay attention to the second column: Refresh. The higher the refresh rate, the less flicker there will be. If you are sensitive to flicker, opt for a lower resolution with a higher refresh rate to keep headaches from flickering monitors at bay.

Adding Your Password

When you are asked to type in the root password, you know you're almost done. Make sure to choose a password that will not be easy for someone else to guess. (Very bad passwords include the make and model of your car, your home phone number, your work phone number, your boss's name, and your boss's name backwards.) You can create an account for yourself, and it is probably a good idea to do so because you do not want to log in as the root user as a matter of course. Don't forget to click the Add user button before you continue to the next menu!

We'll leave the next menu as a surprise. But be careful! You might get hooked on installing new Linux systems because of it!

Click Finish and log in to your newly installed Caldera OpenLinux operating system. You are almost done with the whole installation process.

Installing Boot Magic

You need to shut down and reboot the system. When you get back into Windows, select Install Products, Install Boot Magic from the OpenLinux CD. This last piece is needed to make sure you can boot Windows as well as Linux. The program will come up with some suggestions of what it thinks are installed operating systems on your machine. It's a good bet to go with the defaults. Save your configuration and quit the program.

Now for the moment of truth…

Reboot your computer and select the operating system of your choice. Enjoy!

Summary

After going through this chapter and following the step-by-step installation, you should now have a running Linux system. Keeping your system updated with the latest versions of utilities and libraries will ensure compatibility with most new applications being developed for Linux and keep your system operating efficiently.

If you do have problems, the Red Hat Web site (`http://www.redhat.com`) contains installation documentation and errata sheets for Red Hat Linux. This is also available at the Debian site at `http://www.debian.org` and the Caldera site at `http://www.calderasystems.com`.

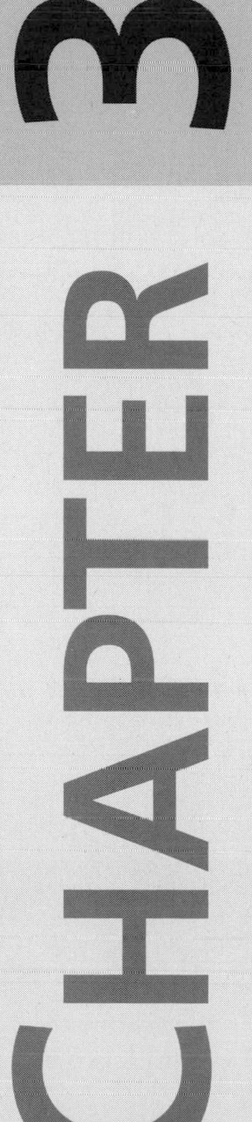

Boot Management

In This Chapter

Booting Linux requires you to install a program to load the kernel into your computer. Which program you use depends on the computer you're using: You'll use LILO for Intel-compatible PCs, MILO for Digital Equipment Corporation Alpha PCs, and SILO for SPARC-compatible workstations. This chapter focuses on LILO, which—according to its author, Werner Almesberger—stands for *Linux Loader*.

This chapter will help if you chose not to install LILO when you first installed Red Hat Linux or if you need help properly starting Linux with certain kernel options. You've probably already decided how you want to start Linux on your computer, but you should know there are other ways to fire up your system.

Instead of using LILO, you can start Linux from DOS with `LOADLIN.EXE`, which is included on your CD-ROM under the `Dosutils` directory. I'll discuss `LOADLIN.EXE` later in this chapter in the section "Using `LOADLIN.EXE` to Boot Linux."

You can also use your computer as a diskless workstation by booting Linux over a network. A discussion on this subject is beyond the scope of this chapter, but you'll find the details on how to do this in Robert Nemkin's Diskless-HOWTO, under the `/usr/doc/HOWTO/mini` directory after you install Linux.

Yet another approach is to use a commercial boot loader, such as V Communications, Incorporated's System Commander, which can come in handy if you need to run other operating systems such as OS/2, Solaris, or Windows NT on your computer.

Before installing LILO, you should know where your Linux partition is; if you have other operating systems, you must know where they are located. For example, your Linux partition might be at `/dev/hdb1`, and your Windows 95 partition might be at `/dev/hda1`.

If Linux is the only operating system on your computer or if you have Windows 95 or Windows NT, you will want to install LILO as the MBR of the boot drive. If you have OS/2 also, you will want to install LILO on the `root` partition of your hard drive and use OS/2's boot loader on the MBR.

Note

Some operating systems, such as Windows 98, write over the MBR. This means that if you are going to use your machine as a dual boot system, you need to either install the Microsoft type product first and then overwrite the MBR with LILO, or use another type of software that performs the same type task, such as Partition Magic.

NOTE

Most distributions of GNU/Linux install LILO at the end of an initial Linux installation or upgrade. You'll have the chance to create a bootdisk right before the LILO installation process—do it! Even if you don't use the disk, you'll benefit from having a little insurance in case things ever go awry. If you don't install LILO, you'll definitely need the disk.

You will usually want to install LILO after you have partitioned your hard drives and after you have installed either Linux or other operating systems.

LILO has capabilities similar to commercial solutions, but it's free. For now, I'll assume that you're going to use LILO to boot one of three traditional ways:

- From your hard drive's master boot record (MBR)
- From the superblock of your `root` Linux partition on your hard drive
- From a floppy disk

The following section shows you a list of LILO's configuration parameters and its command-line arguments, as well as points out some special features.

Installing and Configuring LILO

Although LILO is easy to install by using the `lilo` command (located under the `/sbin` directory), you should first take the time to read its documentation, which you'll find under `/usr/doc`. Along with the documentation, you'll find a shell script called `QuickInst` which can be used for a first-time install (under Red Hat the file is `QuickInst`, under Debian it is `QuickInst.gz`, and it does not come with Caldera). LILO's documentation contains details of its features and provides important tips and workarounds for special problems, such as installing boot loaders on very large-capacity hard drives or booting from other operating systems.

Caution

Before trying anything with LILO, you should have an emergency boot disk (see `/usr/doc/HOWTO/Bootdisk-HOWTO` for more info). Having a system that won't boot is not much fun, and if you don't have a boot disk, you might think there is no way to get back in and change things. Spending a few minutes making yourself a boot disk can save you a big headache down the road. Whatever happens, don't panic!

Installing or Reconfiguring LILO

If you don't install LILO during your Linux install or decide not to use the `QuickInst` script, you can install LILO in two basic steps:

1. Configure `/etc/lilo.conf`.
2. Run `/sbin/lilo` to install LILO and make it active.

This discussion describes modifying an existing `lilo.conf` file. Before making any changes, do yourself a favor and create a backup of the file either in the same directory or on a separate disk. Several files are important to LILO and are created during an initial install:

- `/sbin/lilo`—A map installer; see `man lilo` for more information.
- `/boot/boot.b`—A boot loader.
- `/boot/map`—A boot map that contains the location of the kernel.
- `/etc/lilo.conf`—LILO's configuration file.

Configuring LILO

Under Linux, your hard drives are abstracted to (referenced to or referenced as, for example) device files under the `/dev` directory. If you have one or more IDE drives, your first hard drive is referred to as `/dev/hda` and your second hard drive is `/dev/hdb` (hard drive a and hard drive b). SCSI drives are referred to as `/dev/sda` and `/dev/sdb` (SCSI drive a and SCSI drive b). When you installed Linux, you most likely partitioned your hard drive. The first partition on your first drive would be `/dev/hda1` or `/dev/sda1`, your second partition would be `/dev/hda2` or `/dev/sda2`, and so on.

Before configuring LILO, you should know which partitions have what operating system on them. You should also know where you want to install LILO. In almost all cases, you will want to put LILO on the MBR. You shouldn't do this, however, if you run OS/2, Partition Magic, or other similar products. OS/2, Partition Magic, and other similar software use the MBR. If you are using these types of software packages, LILO should be installed on the superblock of the `root` partition.

You can look to see what partitions you are currently using (from within Linux) by running the `df` command (`/bin/df`):

```
$df
Filesystem  1k-blocks      Used Available Use% Mounted on
/dev/hda1     1973472   1161391    710070  62% /
/dev/hda3     4036649      2443   3825361   0% /home
/dev/hdc       592892    592892         0 100% /mnt/cdrom
/dev/fd0         1423        57      1366   4% /mnt/floppy
```

Armed with your information, you are now ready to edit LILO's configuration file, `/etc/lilo.conf`.

Editing `lilo.conf`

Editing `lilo.conf` is easy. Make sure you're logged in as `root` and load the file into your favorite editor, making sure to save your changes and to save the file as ASCII text. You'll edit `lilo.conf` for a number of reasons:

- You are testing a new kernel and want to be able to boot the same Linux partition with more than one kernel. This is done by using multiple entries of the `image =` section of `lilo.conf`. You may have multiple kernels installed on your Linux partition and can boot to a different kernel by typing its name (specified in the `label =` section).
- You want to add password protection to a partition.
- You have a hardware setup that requires you to specify special options, such as booting a remote file system.
- Your kernel is called something other than `/vmlinuz` or is in a nonstandard place, such as `/etc`.

Listing 3.1 shows a sample `lilo.conf` file.

> **Note**
>
> Need more information about configuring LILO? Although you'll find a lot of detailed technical information under the `/usr/doc/lilo*` directory, don't overlook Cameron Spitzer's LILO mini-HOWTO under the `/usr/doc/HOWTO` directory. You'll find additional troubleshooting tips on how to configure your `lilo.conf` file.

LISTING 3.1 A Sample *`lilo.conf`*

```
boot=/dev/hdb2
map=/boot/map
install=/boot/boot.b
prompt
timeout=50
images=/boot/vmlinuz-2.2.2-1
label=linux
root=/dev/hdb2
initrd=/boot/initrd-2.2.2-1.img
read-only
```

```
other = /dev/hda1
  label = dos
  table = /dev/hda
```

You can add the parameters listed in Table 3.1 to your /etc/lilo.conf file. They could also be given at the boot prompt, but it is much simpler for them to reside in your /etc/lilo.conf file. Note that only 13 of LILO's 23 options are listed here. See LILO's documentation for details.

TABLE 3.1 /etc/lilo.conf Configuration Parameters

Parameter	*Description*
boot=*<boot_device>*	Tells the kernel the name of the device that contains the boot sector. If boot is omitted, the boot sector is read from the device currently mounted as root.
linear	Generates linear sector addresses instead of sector/head/cylinder addresses, which can be troublesome, especially when used with the compact option. See LILO's documentation for details.
install=*<boot_sector>*	Installs the specified file as the new boot sector. If install is omitted, /etc/lilo/boot.b is used as the default.
message=*<message_file>*	You can use this to display the file's text and customize the boot prompt, with a maximum message of up to 65,535 bytes. Rerun /sbin/lilo if you change this file.
verbose=*<level>*	Turns on progress reporting. Higher numbers give more verbose output, and the numbers can range from 1 to 5. This also has -v and -q options; see LILO's documentation for details.
backup=*<backup_file>*	Copies the original boot sector to *<backup_file>* (which can also be a device, such as /dev/null) instead of to /etc/lilo/boot.*<number>*.
force-backup*<backup_file>*	Similar to backup, this option overwrites the current backup copy, but backup is ignored if force-backup is used.
prompt	Requires you to type a boot prompt entry.
timeout=*<tsecs>*	Sets a timeout (in tenths of a second) for keyboard input, which is handy if you want to boot right away or wait for longer than the default five seconds. To make LILO wait indefinitely for your keystrokes, use a value of -1.

Parameter	Description
serial=<*parameters*>	Allows input from the designated serial line and the PC's keyboard to LILO. A break on the serial line mimics a Shift-key press from the console. For security, password-protect all your boot images when using this option. The parameter string has the syntax `<port>,<bps><parity><bits>`, as in `/dev/ttyS1,8N1`. The components `<bps>`, `<parity>`, and `<bits>` can be omitted. If one of these components is omitted, all of the following components have to be omitted as well. Additionally, the comma has to be omitted if only the port number is specified. See LILO's documentation for details.
ignore-table	Ignore corrupt partition tables.
password=<*password*>	Use this to password-protect your boot images. If you use this option but do not have `lilo.conf` set to root read-only permission (`-rw-------`), LILO issues a warning—the password is not encrypted!
unsafe	This keyword is placed after a definition for a partition. The keyword tells LILO not to attempt to read the MBR or that disk's partition table entry. You can declare all of the partitions in your system as a log of all existing partitions and then place the `unsafe` keyword entry to prevent LILO from reading it.

After making your changes to `lilo.conf`, make sure to run `/sbin/lilo`. You should also always run `/sbin/lilo` after installing a new kernel otherwise, the changes will not take affect.

LILO Boot Prompt Options

The following sample list of options can be passed to LILO at the boot prompt to enable special features of your system or to pass options to the Linux kernel to enable a proper boot. Knowing any needed options for your system is especially handy during the Linux installation process because you'll be asked for any special options if you choose to install LILO at that time.

Although you'll normally type **`linux`** or **`dos`** at the `LILO:` prompt, you can also try one or two of the following options. For a more up-to-date list of kernel messages or options, read Paul Gortmaker's BootPrompt-HOWTO under the `/usr/doc/HOWTO` directory.

Note

If you can't remember the exact labels you've specified in `lilo.conf` for the `LILO` prompt, press the Tab key to have LILO print a list of available kernels. If this doesn't work, you can also try pressing the Alt or Shift keys before the `LILO` prompt appears.

- `rescue` —Boots Linux into single-user mode to allow system fixes. (Note: Several distributions, such as Red Hat and Mandrake, have this as an option while other distributions, such as Caldera, do not.)
- `single` —Similar to `rescue`, but attempts to boot from your hard drive.
- root=<*device*> —Similar to the `/etc/lilo.conf` entry, this option allows you to boot from a CD-ROM or other storage device.
- vga=<*mode*> —Enables you to change the resolution of your console; try the `ask` mode.

Using `LOADLIN.EXE` to Boot Linux

`LOADLIN.EXE` is a program that uses the DOS MBR to boot Linux. This handy program by Hans Lermen also passes along kernel options. `LOADLIN.EXE` is very helpful when you must boot from DOS to properly initialize modems or sound cards to make them work under Linux.

You need to do two things before using `LOADLIN.EXE`:

1. Copy `LOADLIN.EXE` to a DOS partition (for example, `C:\LOADLIN`).
2. Put a copy of your kernel image (`/vmlinuz`) on your DOS partition.

For example, type the following from the DOS command line to boot Linux:

```
loadlin c:\vmlinuz root=/dev/hda3 ro
```

Make sure you insert your `root` partition in the command line. The `ro` stands for read-only. When you are first booting a Linux partition, it should be mounted as read-only to prevent data loss.

If you have a UMSDOS file system, you can type this:

```
loadlin c:\vmlinuz root=/dev/hda1 rw
```

The rw stands for read/write. Starting a UMSDOS file system this way is safe. Again, make sure you substitute your own partition. LOADLIN.EXE accepts a number of options; see its documentation in the LOADLIN.TGZ file under the Dosutils directory on the book's CD-ROM.

How to Uninstall LILO

You can uninstall LILO by using the `lilo -u` command; if LILO is not installed on the MBR, you can disable it by using `fdisk` under either Linux or MS-DOS to make another partition active. If LILO has been installed as the MBR, you can restore the original MBR by booting under MS-DOS and using the command `fdisk /mbr`.

Troubleshooting LILO

You shouldn't have any problems with LILO, but if you do, you'll get one of 70 warnings or error messages. They're not all listed here, but Table 3.2 lists six of the most probable LILO: prompt or initial errors.

TABLE 3.2 *LILO:* Prompt Errors

Prompt	*Description*
L<*nn*>	*nn* represents one of 16 disk-error codes.
LI	The second-stage boot loader loaded, but could not run.
LIL	The descriptor table could not be read.
LIL?	The second-stage boot loader loaded at an incorrect address.
LIL-	LILO found a corrupt descriptor table.
LILO	LILO ran successfully.

Disk error codes can indicate problems such as an open floppy door, a drive timeout, a controller error, a media problem, a BIOS error, or even transient read problems (which can be overcome by rebooting). Overall, some common problems with LILO include the following:

- Not rerunning `/sbin/lilo` following a kernel change
- Incorrect use of `/sbin/lilo` in creating a new boot map
- Installing and booting Linux from a very large (2GB+) partition
- Installing another operating system (such as Windows 95, which overwrites the MBR) after installing Linux and LILO

- Errors in `/etc/lilo.conf` after manual edits
- A corrupted MBR
- Installation of LILO in a Linux swap partition (which should be impossible)
- A missing Linux kernel image (error in `/etc/lilo.conf`)
- Installing Linux on and booting from a DOS partition and then defragmenting the DOS partition
- Passing incorrect kernel messages at the `LILO:` prompt

If you run into trouble, definitely peruse Almesberger's readme file, which is found under the `/usr/doc/lilo` directory. Take his advice: Don't panic! With a little forethought, detection, and perseverance, you should be able to avoid or overcome problems.

Summary

This chapter covered the basics of configuring, installing, and using LILO and introduced you to the `LOADLIN.EXE` boot utility. Hopefully, you've seen that using LILO can give you additional flexibility in the number of operating systems installed on your PC and that Linux can be used along with these other systems. Don't forget to read LILO's documentation, because you'll not only learn about how operating systems boot from your hard drive, but also how you can customize the Linux boot prompt.

CHAPTER 4

The X Window System

IN THIS CHAPTER

The X Window System

The X Window system is a networking windowing system that provides a base set of communications protocols and functions for building graphical interfaces for computers with bitmapped displays. You should never refer to the X Window system as X Windows; the proper terms of reference are X, X11, X Version 11, or the X Window system, version 11.

X was first developed at the Massachusetts Institute of Technology in the early 1980s. The first commercial release of the X was X10 in the mid-80s, with the first X11R1 release in 1987. Though the original MIT consortium has since disbanded and X now falls under ownership of The Open Group (a large consortium of computer companies), X11's general client/server model of operation has remained unchanged.

X was designed from the ground up to support networking graphics. Programs or applications under X are known as *clients*. X clients do not directly draw or manipulate graphics on your display but instead communicate with your X server, which in turn controls your display. Although many home users will run clients and an X server on a single computer, it is also possible to run multiple X servers (and X sessions) on a single computer and to launch clients from remote computers—and to then have them displayed locally by a local server. This also means that it is possible to run X over various types of networks or even through a serial dial-up line!

The X Window system used with most Linux distributions is a collection of programs from The XFree86 Project, Incorporated (see the sidebar in this chapter on "The Future of X").

The version of X11 included with Red Hat Linux 6.0 is XFree86 3.3.3.1 and is based on X11R6.3.

The latest version of X is X11R6.4, and according to the XFree86 folks, "XFree86-4.0 will be X11R6.4 based."

Note

You can verify the version of XFree86 in use, even during an X session, by using `-showconfig` with the `X` command like this:

```
# X -showconfig
XFree86 Version 3.3.3.1 / X Window System
(protocol Version 11, revision 0, vendor release 6300)
Release Date: January 4 1999
...
```

Not all the output is shown here.

You can also buy a commercial version of the X Window system from vendors such as XiGraphics (`http://www.xig.com`) or Metro Link, Incorporated (`http://www.metrolink.com`). These distributions range in price from $39 to $299. However, the XFree86 distribution is free. This chapter focuses on configuring and using XFree86's version of X.

Setting Up Your XFree86 System

The X Window System is the foundation of the graphical interface for Linux. Although you can use Linux without using X, you'll be less productive and will miss out on a lot of useful programs.

If you installed and configured X11 when you installed Linux, you'll find that most of the X Window system resides under the `/usr/X11R6` directory. If you have an older version of X11 installed, you can use Red Hat's `rpm` command to upgrade X.

Red Hat

First, insert your Red Hat CD-ROM and mount it (as `root`) like this:

```
# mount /mnt/cdrom
```

Since Red Hat Linux 6.0 provides an entry in the filesystem table `/etc/fstab`, you could also mount the CD-ROM under the `/mnt/cdrom` directory by specifying your system's CD-ROM device, `/dev/cdrom` (a symbolic link to your CD-ROM's device):

```
# mount /dev/cdrom
```

Start X11. Use `rpm` from the command line of a terminal window:

```
# su -c "rpm -Uvh /mnt/cdrom/RedHat/RPMS/XFree86*rpm
```

If you did not install X, you can use Red Hat's `rpm` command to install the software. However, you should know that the official *Red Hat Getting Started Guide* advises that "While it is possible to manually install the required packages, you'll probably find it easier to re-do the installation...."

To install the software manually, mount your Red Hat CD-ROM and navigate to the `RedHat/RPMS/i386` directory. Use the `rpm` command at the command line of your console:

```
# su -c "rpm -i /mnt/cdrom/RedHat/RPMS/XFree86*rpm
```

This command installs the XFree86 software.

Note

Red Hat Linux users can also try using the `gnorpm` command to install the software. Select Preferences and then set the interface preference RPM path to the RPMS directory on your mounted Red Hat CD-ROM.

For Debian users, the install procedure is a bit different. You can get a basic X setup by simply running this:

```
# apt-get install xbase xserver-vga16 xserver-svga wmaker
```

If necessary, you may also elect to install other X servers as appropriate for your hardware; for instance, if you have a Mach64-based graphics card, you can select the `xserver-mach64` package. `dselect` contains a nice list of available servers, and if in doubt, you can install all of the `xserver-*` packages. The `XF86Setup` or `xf86config` program can also tell you which files you need.

X11 is configured when you install OpenLinux, even if you request a minimal installation using a 300MB partition. If you incorrectly configure X11 using Caldera's `Lizard` utility, your display may not work correctly or use a resolution too low to be of use (such as 320×200). You can bypass the default `kdm` graphical login by pressing Ctrl+Alt+F4 and then logging in through the OpenLinux console. After logging in as `root`, you can rerun the `xf86config` or `XF86Setup` client to reconfigure X.

After the software is installed, you'll find a series of directories under the `/usr/X11R6` tree, including

`/usr/X11R6/bin`	Where most (but not all) X11 clients are stored
`/usr/X11R6/include`	Programming header files and directories of bitmaps and pixmaps
`/usr/X11R6/lib`	X11 software libraries needed by X clients and programmers
`/usr/X11R6/man`	X manual pages

Depending on the software installed, these directories can take up 40–400MB of hard drive space, and even more if you install a lot of X window managers, programming libraries, or other software. (A typical full installation of XFree86 is about 75MB.)

The major components of XFree86 consist of a series of 10 X servers, configuration files, clients, programming header files and libraries, fonts, resource (client configuration) files, and manual pages. For details about XFree86, your X server's configuration file `XF86Config`, and various X servers, read the `README.Config` document found in the /usr/X11R6/lib/X11/doc directory. Debian users can find this file in /usr/doc/xserver-common.

The Future of X

At the time of this writing, the latest version of X11—X11R6.4—is no longer under fee-based licensing restrictions. This is good news. The Open Group (TOG), a consortium of nearly 200 companies (whose membership includes Apple and Microsoft), had decided on January 30, 1998, that X11R6.4 would no longer be available to anyone for profit without payment of an annual licensing fee. The fee schedule started at $7,500 for "non-Project" members distributing up to 50,000 units and reached upward to $65,500 for unlimited distribution rights. To be eligible for slightly lower distribution fees, a person or company could become an X Project Team member at a cost of $30,000 and had to sign a contract with a nondisclosure agreement, or NDA clause.

For many members of the Open Source community and programmers dedicated to distributing software under the GNU General Public License, this was a great fear (ever since the MIT consortium disbanded) quickly realized. However, response was rapid, and the XFree86 Project returned fire 90 days later in a news release on April 7, 1998:

"The XFree86 Project will continue its development based on the freely available X11R6.3 SI [sample implementation] and, where appropriate, attempt to implement future developments to the X11 standards independently of TOG."

Fortunately, TOG changed its mind in early September 1998 and reverted X11R6.4's license to the same as X11R6.3. What would have happened otherwise?

Basically, the development of X would have split. Although many companies, programmers, and users felt it was a bad time for a rift to occur—especially in light of the massive growth of the Linux user base—the effect may not have been noticed for some time. Many TOG members, such as Hewlett Packard and Digital Equipment Corporation (now Compaq), still only distribute X11R5, a much older version of X. Although you may have had to pay a licensing fee to distribute X11 library or server binaries, no restrictions were placed on distributing patches to the source; people could build their own X distribution, and without the fees associated with distributing source to X clients that might use X11R6.4 libraries.

The good news is that the XFree86 Project stepped up to the plate and, with the blessing of Linus Torvalds, committed to providing future free distributions of X. The XFree86 Project rightfully deserves the support of the worldwide Linux community. For details about TOG's X11 licensing and fees for other software, such as Motif, see http://www.opengroup.org. For the latest version of free X11 and to pledge support for The XFree86 Project, see http://www.xfree86.org.

Configuring Your XFree86 System

The largest hurdle most new X users face after installing XFree86 is coming up with a working `XF86Config` file. This file is initially generated during your install if you configure X11 using the Red Hat installer or the OpenLinux `lizard` installer.

As you know, if you choose to install X11 during your Red Hat Linux 6.0 installation, you're almost forced to come up with a working GUI for a successful install, even if at a lower resolution. Fortunately, you can always reconfigure `XF86Config` later if you upgrade your computer's video memory or install a new graphics card.

If you already have a working setup, chances are your old `XF86Config` will work. If you're starting from scratch, one of the first things you should do after installing X is read as much of the documentation as possible. Although the daring and brave will launch right into configuring X11, even experienced users will benefit from reading about the latest XFree86 developments and checking the XFree86 documentation for tips about their specific hardware.

You'll find just about everything you need under the `/usr/X11R6/lib/X11/doc` directory. Table 4.1 contains the details of this directory for XFree86 3.3.3.1 (included with Red Hat Linux 6.0 and Caldera OpenLinux 2.2). You'll find detailed information regarding protocols, libraries, clients, and other services under the `/usr/doc/XFree86-doc-3.3.3.1` directory or `/usr/doc/xserver-common` in Debian. Also check the XFree86 HOWTO under the `/usr/doc/HOWTO` directory—it contains valuable tips on configuring your X software.

TABLE 4.1 XFree86 Documentation

File	*Description*
`AccelCards`	A list of tested accelerated graphics cards
`BUILD`	How to compile the XFree86 X distribution from source
`COPYRIGHT`	Copyright statement
`Devices`	An old file of contributed `XF86Config` Device sections
`Monitors`	An old file of contributed `XF86Config` Monitor sections
`QuickStart.doc`	A quick-start guide to setting up XFree86
`README`	General information about the current XFree86 release
`README.3DLabs`	Info for 3DLabs chipset users
`README.Config`	Detailed, step-by-step guide to configuring XFree86
`README.DECtga`	Information for DEC 21030 users

File	*Description*
`README.DGA`	How to program for the XFree86 DGA interface
`README.I128`	Information about Number Nine I 128 cards
`README.LinkKit`	Specific information on how to build XFree86 from scratch
`README.Linux`	Good information for Linux users about installing and using XFree86
`README.MGA`	Information about the Matrox Millennium and Mystique video cards
`README.Mach32`	Information about the Mach32 XFree86 X server
`README.Mach64`	Release notes about the Mach64 XFree86 X server
`README.NVIDIA`	Notes for NVidia NV1, SGS-Thomson STG2000, and Rival128 video cards
`README.Oak`	Notes for Oak Technologies, Inc., chipset users
`README.P9000`	Release notes for the P9000 XFree86 X server
`README.S3`	Notes for S3 chipset users
`README.S3V`	Notes for S3 ViRGE, ViRGE/DX, ViRGE/GX, ViRGE/MX, and ViRGE/VX users
`README.Sis`	Notes for Sis chipset users
`README.Video7`	A readme file about the Video7 drivers
`README.W32`	Notes for W32 and ET6000 chipset users
`README.WstDig`	Notes for Western Digital chipset users
`README.agx`	Information about the AGX XFree86 X server
`README.apm`	Notes about the Alliance Promotion chipset
`README.ark`	Notes for ARK Logic chipset users
`README.ati`	Information about XFree86's ATI Adapters video drivers
`README.chips`	Notes about Chips and Technologies chipsets
`README.cirrus`	Information about XFree86 support for Cirrus Logic chipset
`README.clkprog`	Programming information about external video clock setting programs
`README.cyrix`	Info for Cyrix MeidaGX users
`README.epson`	Info for EPSON SPC8110 users
`README.mouse`	Details about XFree86's X11 mouse support
`README.neo`	Info for NeoMagic chipset users
`README.rendition`	Details about Rendition chipset users

continues

TABLE 4.1 continued

File	*Description*
`README.trident`	Notes for Trident chipset users
`README.tseng`	Notes for Tseng chipset users
`RELNOTES`	The definitive release notes for XFree86
`ServersOnly`	How your directories should look when building XFree86 X servers
`VGADriver.Doc`	A HOWTO on adding an SVGA or VGA drive to XFree86
`VideoModes.doc`	Eric S. Raymond's comprehensive treatise on building `XF86Config` modelines
`xinput`	General information on input device (such as joystick) support in XFree86

If you're new to X11, first read the man pages for X and XFree86 for an overview of X. Before you begin configuring X, you should also read the `QuickStart.doc` text. You need to know some technical details about your computer and your computer's video card and monitor. Here is some of the information that will help:

- The type, make, name, or model of video card installed in your computer
- How much video RAM (not system RAM) is installed for your card
- The type of clockchip used by your video card chipset
- The type of mouse you use (PS/2 or serial, for example)
- The type, make, name, or model of monitor attached to your computer
- The vertical and horizontal refresh rates for your monitor (such as 55–100 vertical, 30–60 horizontal)
- The type of keyboard you use

Armed with this information, you then have to choose the method or tool for configuring XFree86 and generate a correct `XF86Config` file for your system.

Red Hat Linux provides a graphical X11 setup tool, called `Xconfigurator`, in addition to XFree86's `XF86Setup`, XFree86's text-mode tool, `xf86config`.

You can also manually build your own `XF86Config` file. Both the `Xconfigurator` and `xf86config` programs will run from your console's command line or from a terminal window's command line.

Red Hat's `Xconfigurator` and XFree86's `XF86Setup` have the advantage of providing a graphical interface; `xf86config` asks a series of questions in a text-mode screen. If you're lucky, your computer's hardware will exactly match the configuration generated by these programs. Problems can arise if the settings don't work, if you've entered incorrect information, or if your video chipset is not fully supported by the XFree86 servers.

In general, video hardware several years old will fare much better than "bleeding-edge" video cards because software contributors have had a chance to work with the video chipsets. Laptop users can also run into special problems, and it can be disheartening to buy the latest laptop, only to find that the embedded video system will not work with X—it pays to research!

Desktop users have the option of installing a new, supported video card. Laptop users should definitely check the Linux laptop user site at `http://www.cs.utexas.edu/users/kharker/linux-laptop`.

If you find you cannot get correct settings, or if your chipset is not supported, you can also buy a commercial X distribution from one of the vendors mentioned in the introduction. Finally, your last resort is to whine at, plead with, cajole, or bribe a knowledgeable programmer to build a server for you from the XFree86 sources (but this rarely works).

The `XF86Config` File

Without a doubt, the most important configuration file for XFree86 is the `XF86Config` file. This file is used to properly feed font, keyboard, mouse, video chipset, monitor capabilities, and color-depth setting information to your selected X11 display server. When you start an X session, your X server will search for this file.

`XF86Config`, although normally located under the `/etc/X11` directory, may also be located under the `/usr/X11R6/lib/X11` directory; if you launch X as the root operator, it can reside under the `/root` directory.

OpenLinux users will find `XF86Config` under the `/etc` directory following initial installation and configuration.

`XF86Config` is a single text file, consisting of several sections:

- `Files`—Tells the X server where colors, fonts, or specific software modules are located
- `Module`—Tells the X server what special modules should be loaded
- `ServerFlags`—On/off flags that allow or deny special actions, such as core dumps, keyboard server shutdown, video-mode switching, video tuning, and mouse and keyboard configuration
- `Keyboard`—Tells the X server what keyboard to expect and what settings to use

- `Pointer`—Tells the X server what pointer to use and how buttons are handled
- `Input`—A special section for input devices such as graphics pads or styluses
- `Monitor`—Specific details and settings for your monitor, such as name, horizontal sync, vertical sync ranges, and modelines (one for each video resolution, such as 640×480, 800×600, 1,024×768)
- `Device`—Details about your video chipset, such as RAM or clockchips
- `Screen`—Tells what X server to use, the color depth (such as 8, 16, 24 or 32 bits per pixel), screen size (such as 640×480, 800×600, or 1,024×768), the size of the virtual screen

Caution

Do not use an `XF86Config` from someone who does not have the same graphics card and monitor that you have. Incorrect settings can harm your monitor. Do not use monitor settings outside your monitor's specifications. You have been warned! On the other hand, if you do come up with a good `XF86Config`, document it and share it with others. Read postings on `comp.os.linux.x` or `comp.os.linux.portable` and check the Linux laptop users Web pages for hints, tips, tricks, and places to share your information.

Before you begin, make sure you read `README.Config`.

Using Red Hat's Xconfigurator

Although you can manually administer Linux and manually create a configuration file for the X Window system, Red Hat Linux comes with a graphical configuration utility named Xconfigurator (a similar utility, named `XF86Setup`, is included with XFree86).

Debian users should use `XF86Setup`; in fact, the installation configuration system will offer to do this as X is being installed. This is generally a good idea; skip down to the `XF86Setup` section.

Red Hat's Xconfigurator generates an `XF86Config` file after it probes your system and asks several questions. This program may be used from the console (without X11) when you need to generate a new configuration file, such as after you change your computer's graphics card. You must run this program as the root operator. Start Xconfigurator from the command line of your console or from an X11 terminal window, like this:

```
# su -c Xconfigurator
```

The screen clears and a dialog box appears, as shown in Figure 4.1.

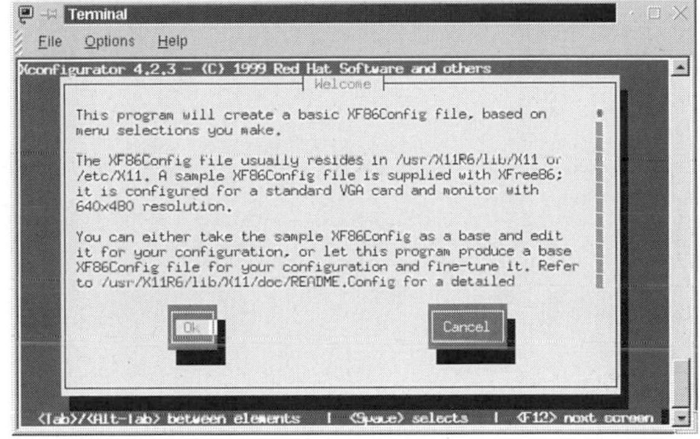

FIGURE 4.1
Red Hat's Xconfigurator generates the required `XF86Config` *file for XFree86.*

Use the Tab key to navigate to different buttons on the screen, and then press the Enter key when the OK button is highlighted. Xconfigurator first checks to see if a symbolic link from `/usr/X11R6/lib/X11/XF86Config` exists to the `/etc/X11/XF86Config`. If the link exists, Xconfigurator probes your video card and reports with a dialog box, as shown in Figure 4.2.

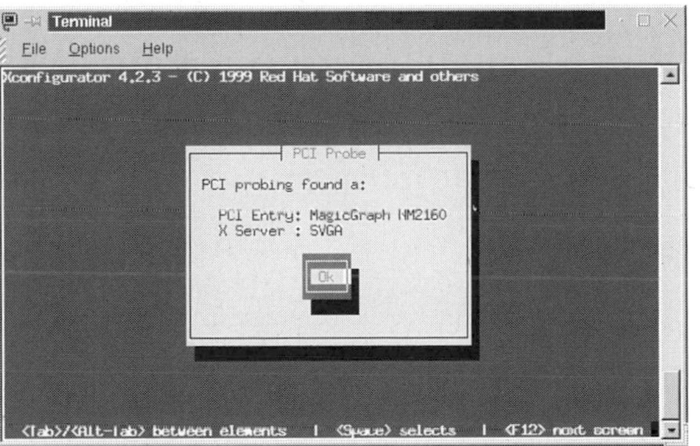

FIGURE 4.2
Xconfigurator reports on your video card with a small dialog box.

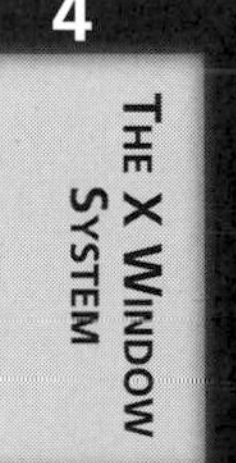

After you click the OK button, you are presented with a dialog box that asks for the type of monitor attached to your computer (see Figure 4.3). Nearly 200 monitors are listed in the Xconfigurator's database; desktop users will probably find their model listed. Scroll down the list until your model is highlighted and then click OK. Unfortunately, laptop users have to select the Custom monitor at the top of the list. If you have a desktop computer and your monitor is not listed, check the `Monitors` file under the `/usr/X11R6/lib/X11/doc` directory—you might find yours there, along with the supported horizontal and vertical frequencies.

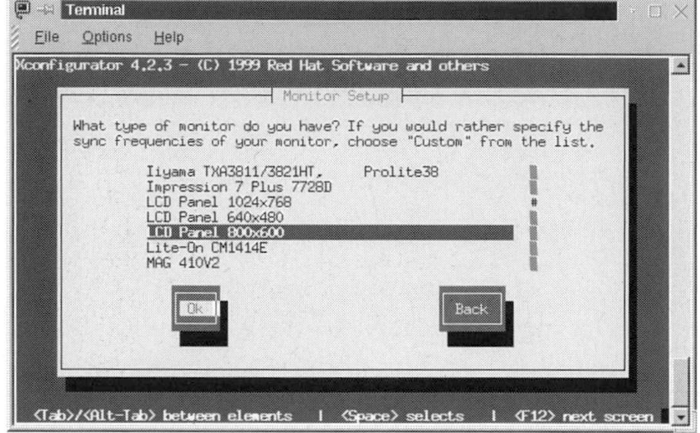

FIGURE 4.3
Xconfigurator has nearly 200 monitors in its model database.

Don't panic if you don't find your monitor listed or are using a laptop. Select the Custom monitor and click the OK button. Xconfigurator presents an introductory dialog box. When you click the OK button, you're presented a list of monitor resolutions and frequencies, as shown in Figure 4.4.

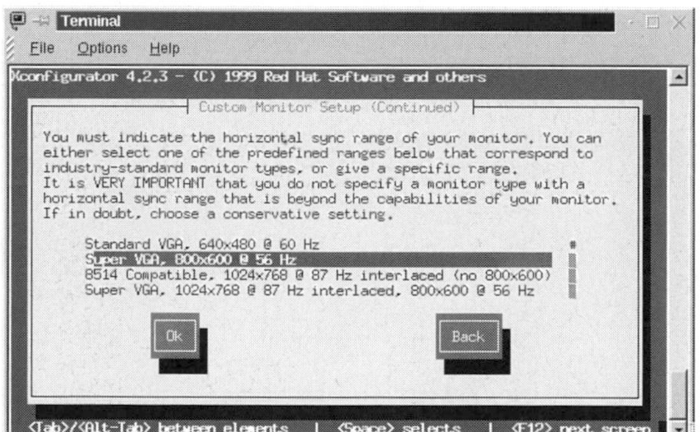

FIGURE 4.4
Xconfigurator allows custom monitor settings.

At this point, using Xconfigurator might be somewhat confusing. Although the program says a horizontal frequency is being selected, you are asked to select a video resolution and monitor frequency. The best bet is to pick a resolution you know is supported by your monitor and click the OK button. If you're not sure the correct information for your monitor will be inserted into your `XF86Config` file (which Xconfigurator will create after you've finished entering all the information), make sure to edit and change the inserted horizontal frequency settings before starting your first X session.

The next dialog box, shown in Figure 4.5, asks for the vertical frequency range of your monitor. Although the dialog box says you can enter a custom range, you have to pick the range closest to your monitor's and then edit your `XF86Config` file after Xconfigurator is done.

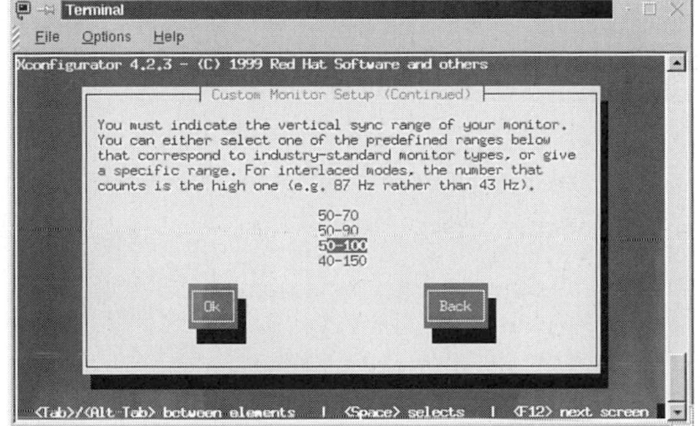

FIGURE 4.5
Xconfigurator offers four vertical frequency monitor settings.

Select your frequency range and click the OK button. The next dialog box asks if you want Xconfigurator to probe your video card for resolution (such as 640×480, 800×600, or 1,024×768) and color depth (such as 8-, 16-, or 24-bit color). Although the safest approach is not to probe, especially if you have a laptop or unsupported monitor, some users with supported video cards and monitors will benefit by this automatic configuration. Select either the Don't Probe or Probe button (as shown in Figure 4.6).

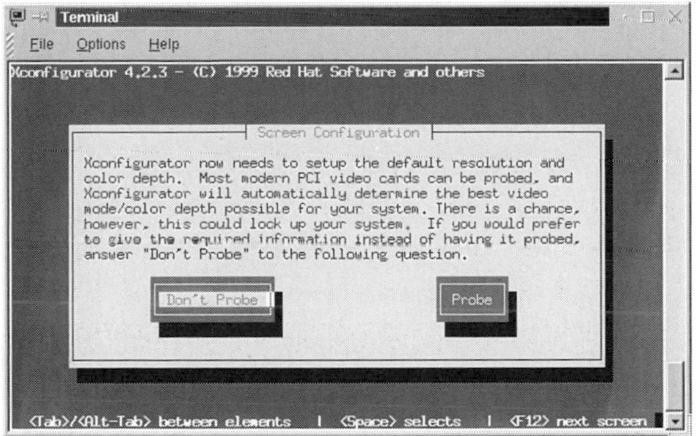

FIGURE 4.6
If you choose, Xconfigurator automatically probes your video for the best resolution and color-depth settings.

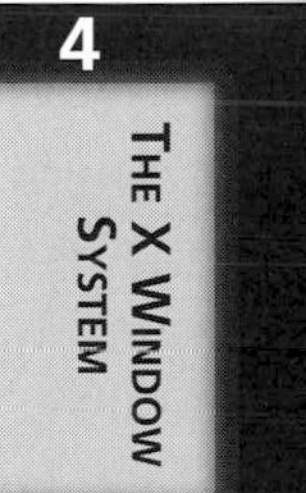

The next dialog box, shown in Figure 4.7, asks for the amount of video memory installed in your computer's motherboard or video card. In general, the more video memory you have, the higher the resolution or color depth supported by your computer. If you have upgradable video memory, you may benefit by adding memory (depending on your monitor and support by the XFree86 server for your video chipset).

Interestingly, no matter what memory value you select, Xconfigurator inserts the value but leaves it commented out in the final `XF86Config` file. In some cases—especially where the correct video RAM values are not correctly probed at startup by the server—this means you'll have to edit `XF86Config` manually to use your selected memory setting.

If you have more than 8MB of memory, you need to edit your final `XF86Config` file to correct the setting (and you have one heck of a video system installed). Select the currently installed amount of memory and click the OK button.

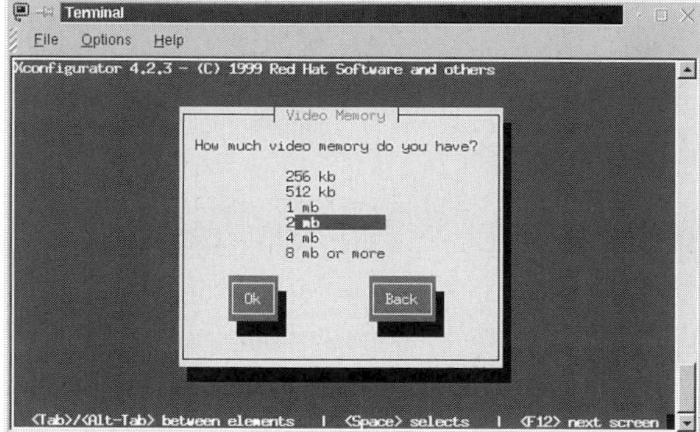

FIGURE 4.7
Xconfigurator offers six video memory configurations.

Xconfigurator next asks for the type of clockchip in your video subsystem (see Figure 4.8). If you're not sure whether your video card uses clockchip settings, select No Clockchip Setting. If you're sure about the type of clockchip used (by checking your video card or computer documentation), select one of the 12 clockchips listed and click the OK button.

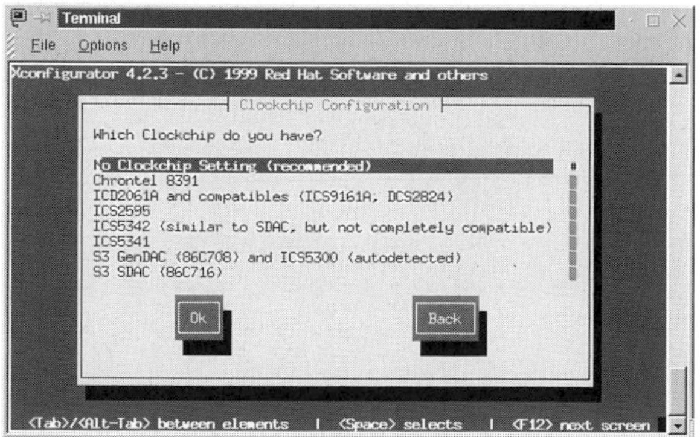

FIGURE 4.8
Xconfigurator lists 12 clockchips.

The next dialog box (shown in Figure 4.9) asks if you want to run hardware detection routines. This can help determine settings used later in your `XF86Config` file. This step could lock up your system, so you have the opportunity to skip it.

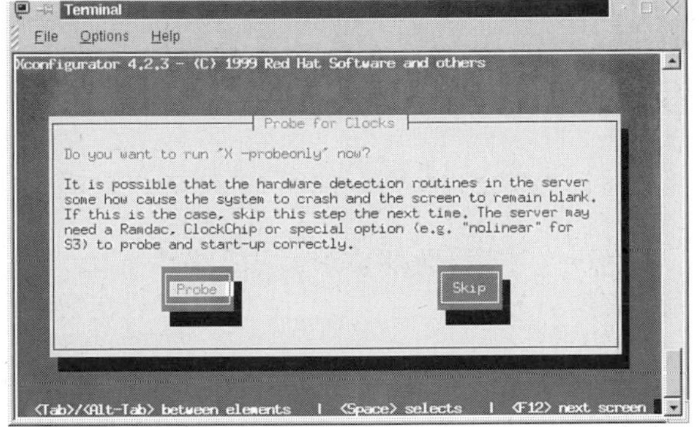

FIGURE 4.9
Probing your computer's video hardware has the potential to lock up your system.

After either probing your video or skipping the probe, Xconfigurator will ask (as shown in Figure 4.10) for the desired video resolutions (such as 800×600) and color depths (such as 8-bit, or 256 colors, or 16-bit for thousands of colors). Select different settings by navigating with your Tab and cursor keys and pressing the Spacebar. Do not select video resolutions greater than allowed by your monitor unless you want to use *virtual resolutions* (in which your display becomes a movable window on a large display).

When you're finished, click the OK button.

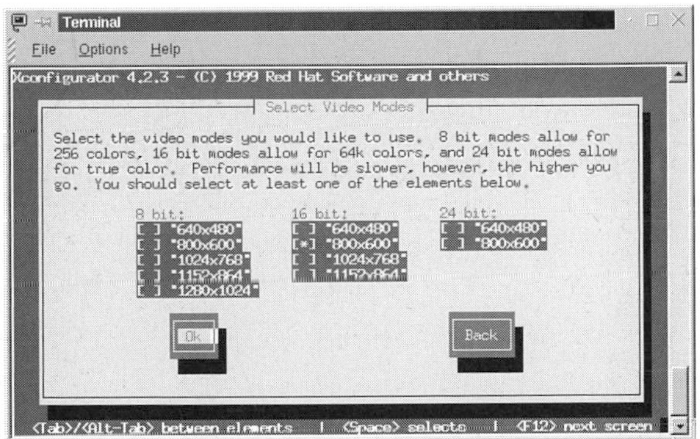

FIGURE 4.10
Xconfigurator configures a combination of video resolutions and color depths.

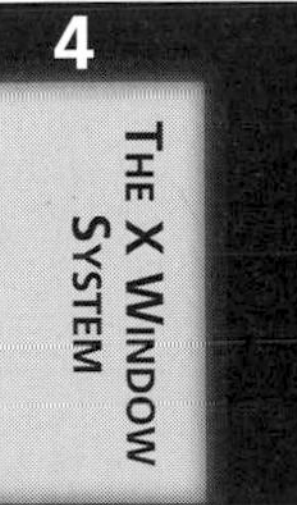

In the next step, Xconfigurator attempts to start X in order to test your settings (as shown in Figure 4.11). You can skip the test or press the OK button to start the X server. If you skip the test, Xconfigurator then creates and saves your `XF86Config` file, saving it under the `/etc/X11` directory.

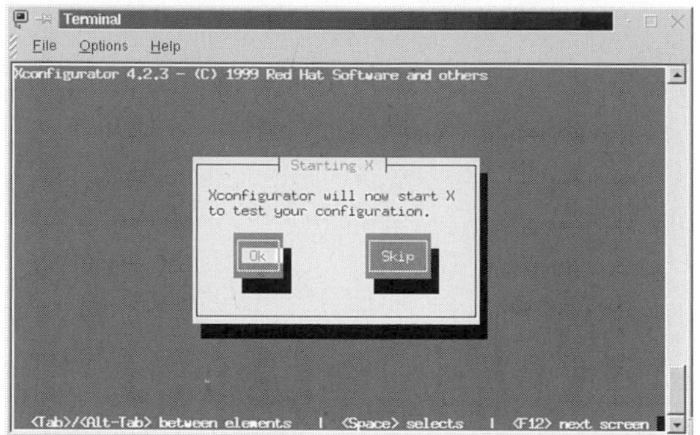

FIGURE 4.11
Xconfigurator offers to test your graphics card and monitor settings.

After you start the test (which uses the Xtest client found under the `/usr/X11R6/bin` directory), the screen clears and you may see a small dialog box. The dialog box asks if you can see this message. If you click the Yes button, you are then asked if you want to automatically start X upon booting. If you choose Yes, your Red Hat Linux system initialization table (the file `inittab` under the `/etc` directory) is modified to boot the Linux directory to runlevel 5. You then need to log in through the `gdm` or GNOME display manager (discussed in Chapter 5, "Window Managers"). If you click No, you have to use the `startx` command to begin your X sessions.

After clicking Yes or No, Xconfiguration then creates and saves your `XF86Config` file under the `/etc/X11` directory before quitting.

Examining the `XF86Config` File

Before you try to start an X11 session using your new `XF86Config` settings, open the file in your favorite text editor, making sure to disable line wrapping, and check the settings. Doing this is essential, especially for laptop users, in order to check the created settings, enable or disable some X server options, enter the correct amount of video memory, and fine-tune monitor settings.

Red Hat Linux users can open the file (as the *root* operator) with the `pico` text editor:

```
# su -c "pico -w /etc/X11/XF86Config"
```

OpenLinux users can also use the `pico` text editor, but must first install the `pine-4.10-1.i386.rpm` archive from the `col/contrib/RPMS` directory on the OpenLinux CD-ROM.

The next sections describe several of the more important parts of the `XF86Config` file you've generated. For an overview of the `XF86Config` file, see the `XF86Config` man page.

XF86Config Files Section

The `Files` section in Listing 4.1 (for Red Hat Linux) tells the X server the location of the color name database and system fonts.

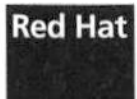

Note that as of Red Hat Linux 6.0, XFree86 is preconfigured to use the `xfs` font server, which supplies fonts to your designated X server.

When you installed Red Hat Linux 6.0, you may remember having the opportunity to automatically start the `xfs` server during bootup. If you've just installed and configured X from scratch, you need to use the `ntsysv` command (as `root`) to enable the font server, which runs in the background. Type this command from your console's command line:

```
# ntsysv
```

You'll see a dialog box like that shown in Figure 4.12. Scroll through the list of servers and select the `xfs` server with your Spacebar. When finished, click the OK button. Startup and shutdown of the server will be controlled by the `xfs` script under the `/etc/rc.d/init.d` directory.

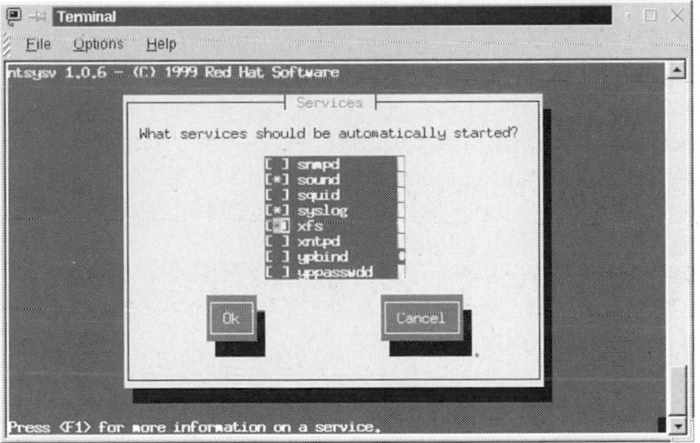

FIGURE 4.12
You must ensure that the `xfs` font server is running in order to easily use XFree86 with Red Hat Linux 6.0.

LISTING 4.1 The Red Hat Linux *XF86Config*'s *Files* Section

```
Section "Files"

# The location of the RGB database.  Note, this is the name of the
# file minus the extension (like ".txt" or ".db").  There is normally
# no need to change the default.

    RgbPath      "/usr/X11R6/lib/X11/rgb"

# Multiple FontPath entries are allowed (they are concatenated together)
# By default, Red Hat 6.0 and later now use a font server independent of
# the X server to render fonts.
```

continues

LISTING 4.1 continued

```
    FontPath    "unix/:-1"

EndSection
```

OpenLinux does not use the X font server and instead defines the paths (directories) where X11 will find fonts:

```
# Multiple FontPath entries are allowed (which are concatenated together),
# as well as specifying multiple comma-separated entries in one FontPath
# command (or a combination of both methods)

FontPath        "/usr/X11R6/lib/X11/fonts/75dpi/:unscaled"
FontPath        "/usr/X11R6/lib/X11/fonts/Type1/"
FontPath        "/usr/X11R6/lib/X11/fonts/misc/"
```

The `xfs` configuration file is found under the `/etc/X11/fs` directory and is named `config` for Red Hat users. Debian users should look under the `/etc/X11/xfs` directory.

The `xfs` configuration file includes a list of font directories under a `catalogue` entry, like this:

```
catalogue = /usr/X11R6/lib/X11/fonts/misc:unscaled,
        /usr/X11R6/lib/X11/fonts/75dpi:unscaled,
        /usr/X11R6/lib/X11/fonts/100dpi:unscaled,
        /usr/X11R6/lib/X11/fonts/misc,
        /usr/X11R6/lib/X11/fonts/Type1,
        /usr/X11R6/lib/X11/fonts/Speedo,
        /usr/share/fonts/default/Type1,
        /usr/X11R6/lib/X11/fonts/100dpi,
        /usr/X11R6/lib/X11/fonts/75dpi,
        /usr/X11R6/lib/X11/fonts/cyrillic,
        /usr/share/fonts/ISO8859-2/misc,
        /usr/share/fonts/ISO8859-2/100dpi,
        /usr/share/fonts/ISO8859-2/75dpi,
        /usr/share/fonts/ISO8859-2/Type1,
        /usr/share/fonts/ISO8859-9/misc,
        /usr/share/fonts/ISO8859-9/100dpi,
        /usr/share/fonts/ISO8859-9/75dpi
```

As you can see, you may find additional fonts for X11 installed under the `/usr/share/fonts` directory. The ISO8859-2 fonts are part of a collection of nearly 400 central European (or Latin 2) fonts and provide support for encoding characters in nearly a dozen Slavic and Central European languages.

Debian users should note that this list varies, depending on which packages are installed; in particular, note the list in `/etc/X11/XF86Config`; packages will automatically add or remove lines there as appropriate when being installed or removed.

You can verify the inclusion and availability of these fonts with the `xfontsel` client. Use `xfontsel` like this at the command line of a terminal window:

```
# xfontsel
```

You'll see a window (as shown in Figure 4.13) from which you can select different foundry and families of fonts.

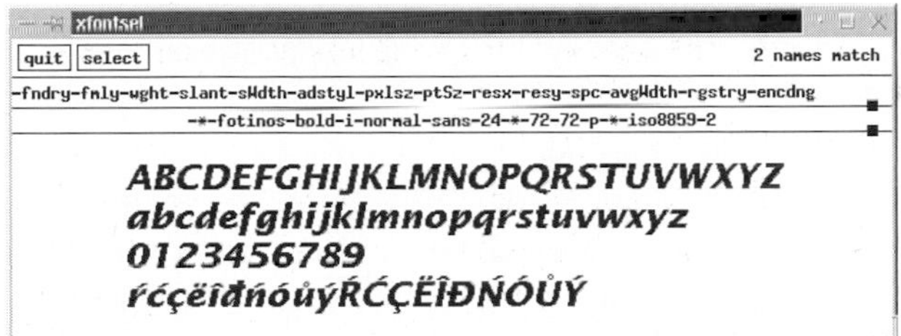

FIGURE 4.13
Use the `xfontsel` client to view the variety of X11 fonts included with Red Hat Linux 6.0.

XF86Config ServerFlags Section

Several parts of the `ServerFlags` section, shown in Listing 4.2, can be used to configure special actions allowed by your XFree86 X server. Enable a particular action by removing the pound sign (#) in front of the specific flag. Most users will not disable the DontZap feature because it provides a quick way to exit an X session. The DontZoom feature may be disabled if you use X in only one video resolution, such as 800×600 pixels.

LISTING 4.2 *XF86Config's ServerFlags* Section

```
# **********************************************************************
# Server flags section.
# **********************************************************************

Section "ServerFlags"

    # Uncomment this to cause a core dump at the spot where a signal is
    # received. This may leave the console in an unusable state, but may
    # provide a better stack trace in the core dump to aid in debugging
    #NoTrapSignals

    # Uncomment this to disable the <Crtl><Alt><BS> server abort sequence
    # This allows clients to receive this key event.
```

continues

LISTING 4.2 continued

```
    #DontZap

    # Uncomment this to disable the <Crtl><Alt><KP_+>/<KP_-> mode switching
    # sequences. This allows clients to receive these key events.
    #DontZoom

EndSection
```

XF86Config Keyboard Section

The Keyboard section in Listing 4.3 tells the X server what type of keyboard to expect and what settings to use, such as language type, key character layout, and manufacturer.

LISTING 4.3 *XF86Config's Keyboard* Section

```
# **********************************************************************
# Keyboard section
# **********************************************************************

Section "Keyboard"

    Protocol    "Standard"

    # when using XQUEUE, comment out the above line, and uncomment the
    # following line
    #Protocol   "Xqueue"

    AutoRepeat  500 5

    # Let the server do the NumLock processing. This should only be
    # required when using pre-R6 clients
    #ServerNumLock

    # Specify which keyboard LEDs can be user-controlled (eg, with xset(1))
    #Xleds      1 2 3

    #To set the LeftAlt to Meta, RightAlt key to ModeShift,
    #RightCtl key to Compose, and ScrollLock key to ModeLock:

    LeftAlt        Meta
    RightAlt        Meta
   ScrollLock      Compose
   RightCtl        Control

# To disable the XKEYBOARD extension, uncomment XkbDisable.

#    XkbDisable
```

```
# To customise the XKB settings to suit your keyboard, modify the
# lines below (which are the defaults). For example, for a non-U.S.
# keyboard, you will probably want to use:
#    XkbModel    "pc102"
# If you have a US Microsoft Natural keyboard, you can use:
#    XkbModel    "microsoft"
#
# Then to change the language, change the Layout setting.
# For example, a german layout can be obtained with:
#    XkbLayout   "de"
# or:
#    XkbLayout   "de"
#    XkbVariant  "nodeadkeys"
#
# If you'd like to switch the positions of your capslock and
# control keys, use:
#    XkbOptions  "ctrl:swapcaps"

# These are the default XKB settings for XFree86
#    XkbRules    "xfree86"
#    XkbModel    "pc101"
#    XkbLayout   "us"
#    XkbVariant  ""
#    XkbOptions  ""

   XkbKeycodes     "xfree86"
   XkbTypes        "default"
   XkbCompat       "default"
   XkbSymbols      "us(pc101)"
   XkbGeometry     "pc"
   XkbRules        "xfree86"
   XkbModel        "pc101"
    XkbLayout       "us"
EndSection
```

XF86Config Pointer Section

The `Pointer` section in Listing 4.4 tells the X server what pointer, or mouse, to use and how the buttons are handled. Note that Listing 4.4 shows a configuration for a PS/2 mouse. Other Protocol settings are Auto for a serial mouse and BusMouse for a bus mouse. The Device entry, `/dev/mouse`, is a symbolic link to the actual device (such as `/dev/psaux` for a PS/2 mouse or `/dev/ttyS0` for a serial mouse).

Two-button mouse users will definitely want to enable a three-button emulator, in which a simultaneous depressing of both buttons simulates the middle (or Button 2) press. One common use of Button 2 is to paste text or graphics. For more information about configuring a mouse, see the file `README.mouse` under the `/usr/X11R6/lib/X11/doc` directory.

LISTING 4.4 *XF86Config's Pointer* Section

```
# **********************************************************************
# Pointer section
# **********************************************************************

Section "Pointer"
    Protocol    "PS/2"
    Device      "/dev/mouse"

# When using XQUEUE, comment out the above two lines, and uncomment
# the following line.

#    Protocol   "Xqueue"

# Baudrate and SampleRate are only for some Logitech mice

#    BaudRate   9600
#    SampleRate 150

# Emulate3Buttons is an option for 2-button Microsoft mice
# Emulate3Timeout is the timeout in milliseconds (default is 50ms)

    Emulate3Buttons
    Emulate3Timeout    50

# ChordMiddle is an option for some 3-button Logitech mice

#    ChordMiddle

EndSection
```

XF86Config Monitor Section

The first several parts of the `XF86Config` file are easy to understand, but many XFree86 users whose initial `XF86Config` file does not work will want to pay specific attention to the `Monitor` section (a sample for a high-resolution laptop is shown in Listing 4.5), the `Device` section (Listing 4.6), and the `Screen` section (Listing 4.7). The `Monitor` section contains specific details and settings for your monitor, such as your monitor's name, its horizontal and vertical sync ranges, and critical modelines (one for each video resolution—for example, 640×480, 800×600, 1,024×768). Understanding the modeline is key to fine-tuning your X11 display.

For the best details, Red Hat and Caldera users should see the files `VideoModes.doc` and `README.Config` under the `/usr/X11R6/lib/X11/doc` (or `/usr/doc/xserver-common` for Debian) directory before fine-tuning modelines in your `XF86Config` file. Note that Debian 2.1 does not ship with a `VideoModes.doc` file. Another good tutorial is the XFree86-Video-Timings HOWTO under the `/usr/doc/HOWTO` directory.

The basic parts of a modeline are 10 different values representing (from left to right):

- A label of the screen resolution, such as 800×600
- A video frequency in MHz
- The number of visible dots per line on your display
- The Start Horizontal Retrace value (number of pulses before video sync pulse starts)
- The End Horizontal Retrace value (end of sync pulse)
- The total number of visible and invisible dots on your display
- The Vertical Display End value (number of visible lines of dots on your display)
- The Start Vertical Retrace value (number of lines before the sync pulse starts)
- The End Vertical Retrace value (number of lines at the end of the sync pulse)
- The Vertical Total value (total number of visible and invisible lines on your display)

LISTING 4.5 The *XF86Config Monitor* Section

```
# **********************************************************************
# Monitor section
# **********************************************************************

# Any number of monitor sections may be present

Section "Monitor"

    Identifier  "LCD Panel 1024x768"
    VendorName  "Unknown"
    ModelName   "Unknown"

# HorizSync is in kHz unless units are specified.
# HorizSync may be a comma separated list of discrete values, or a
# comma separated list of ranges of values.
# NOTE: THE VALUES HERE ARE EXAMPLES ONLY.  REFER TO YOUR MONITOR'S
# USER MANUAL FOR THE CORRECT NUMBERS.

    HorizSync   31.5-48.5

# VertRefresh is in Hz unless units are specified.
# VertRefresh may be a comma separated list of discrete values, or a
# comma separated list of ranges of values.
# NOTE: THE VALUES HERE ARE EXAMPLES ONLY.  REFER TO YOUR MONITOR'S
# USER MANUAL FOR THE CORRECT NUMBERS.

    VertRefresh 60
```

continues

LISTING 4.5 continued

```
# Modes can be specified in two formats. A compact one-line format, or
# a multi-line format.

# These two are equivalent

#    ModeLine "1024x768i" 45 1024 1048 1208 1264 768 776 784 817 Interlace

#    Mode "1024x768i"
#        DotClock 45
#        Htimings     1024 1048 1208 1264
#        Vtimings     768 776 784 817
#        Flags        "Interlace"
#    EndMode


# This is a set of standard mode timings. Modes that are out of monitor spec
# are automatically deleted by the server (provided the HorizSync and
# VertRefresh lines are correct), so there's no immediate need to
# delete mode timings (unless particular mode timings don't work on your
# monitor). With these modes, the best standard mode that your monitor
# and video card can support for a given resolution is automatically
# used.

# 640x400 @ 70 Hz, 31.5 kHz hsync
Modeline "640x400"     25.175 640  664  760  800   400  409  411  450
# 640x480 @ 60 Hz, 31.5 kHz hsync
Modeline "640x480"     25.175 640  664  760  800   480  491  493  525
# 800x600 @ 56 Hz, 35.15 kHz hsync
ModeLine "800x600"     36     800  824  896 1024   600  601  603  625
# 1024x768 @ 87 Hz interlaced, 35.5 kHz hsync
#Modeline "1024x768"    44.9   1024 1048 1208 1264   768  776  784  817 Interlace

# 640x480 @ 72 Hz, 36.5 kHz hsync
Modeline "640x480"     31.5   640  680  720  864   480  488  491  521
# 800x600 @ 60 Hz, 37.8 kHz hsync
Modeline "800x600"     40     800  840  968 1056   600  601  605  628 +hsync
+vsync

# 800x600 @ 72 Hz, 48.0 kHz hsync
Modeline "800x600"     50     800  856  976 1040   600  637  643  666 +hsync
+vsync
# 1024x768 @ 60 Hz, 48.4 kHz hsync
Modeline "1024x768"    65     1024 1032 1176 1344   768  771  777  806 -hsync
-vsync

# 1024x768 @ 70 Hz, 56.5 kHz hsync
Modeline "1024x768"    75     1024 1048 1184 1328   768  771  777  806 -hsync
-vsync
```

```
# 1280x1024 @ 87 Hz interlaced, 51 kHz hsync
#Modeline "1280x1024"   80     1280 1296 1512 1568  1024 1025 1037 1165 Interlace

# 1024x768 @ 76 Hz, 62.5 kHz hsync
Modeline "1024x768"    85     1024 1032 1152 1360   768  784  787  823
# 1280x1024 @ 61 Hz, 64.2 kHz hsync
Modeline "1280x1024"  110     1280 1328 1512 1712  1024 1025 1028 1054

# 1280x1024 @ 74 Hz, 78.85 kHz hsync
Modeline "1280x1024"  135     1280 1312 1456 1712  1024 1027 1030 1064

# 1280x1024 @ 76 Hz, 81.13 kHz hsync
Modeline "1280x1024"  135     1280 1312 1416 1664  1024 1027 1030 1064

# Low-res Doublescan modes
# If your chipset does not support doublescan, you get a 'squashed'
# resolution like 320x400.

# 320x200 @ 70 Hz, 31.5 kHz hsync, 8:5 aspect ratio
Modeline "320x200"     12.588 320  336  384  400   200  204  205  225 Doublescan
# 320x240 @ 60 Hz, 31.5 kHz hsync, 4:3 aspect ratio
Modeline "320x240"     12.588 320  336  384  400   240  245  246  262 Doublescan
# 320x240 @ 72 Hz, 36.5 kHz hsync
Modeline "320x240"     15.750 320  336  384  400   240  244  246  262 Doublescan
# 400x300 @ 56 Hz, 35.2 kHz hsync, 4:3 aspect ratio
ModeLine "400x300"     18     400  416  448  512   300  301  602  312 Doublescan
# 400x300 @ 60 Hz, 37.8 kHz hsync
Modeline "400x300"     20     400  416  480  528   300  301  303  314 Doublescan
# 400x300 @ 72 Hz, 48.0 kHz hsync
Modeline "400x300"     25     400  424  488  520   300  319  322  333 Doublescan
# 480x300 @ 56 Hz, 35.2 kHz hsync, 8:5 aspect ratio
ModeLine "480x300"     21.656 480  496  536  616   300  301  302  312 Doublescan
# 480x300 @ 60 Hz, 37.8 kHz hsync
Modeline "480x300"     23.890 480  496  576  632   300  301  303  314 Doublescan
# 480x300 @ 63 Hz, 39.6 kHz hsync
Modeline "480x300"     25     480  496  576  632   300  301  303  314 Doublescan
# 480x300 @ 72 Hz, 48.0 kHz hsync
Modeline "480x300"     29.952 480  504  584  624   300  319  322  333 Doublescan

EndSection
```


XF86Config Graphics Device Section

The Graphics Device section in Listing 4.6 contains details about your video chipset, such as RAM or clockchips. Note that even though you told Xconfigurator (or `xf86config`) you have 2MB of video RAM, the program commented out your choice with a pound sign (#). To properly configure for X, you need to remove the pound sign in front of the VideoRam setting in this part of the `XF86Config` file.

This section of your `XF86Config` file is critical—the device definition is used to tell the X server exactly what type of video chipset and options to support. (Your `XF86Config` will definitely look different from this one, which is for an IBM i1451 laptop with a NeoMagic NM2160 chipset.) For a list of device Identifiers and options, see the readme file under the `/usr/X11R6/lib/X11/doc` directory corresponding with your chipset.

LISTING 4.6 The *XF86Config Device* Section

```
# **********************************************************************
# Graphics device section
# **********************************************************************

# Any number of graphics device sections may be present

Section "Device"
    Identifier        "Generic VGA"
    VendorName        "Unknown"
    BoardName "Unknown"
    Chipset   "generic"

#    VideoRam 256

#    Clocks   25.2 28.3

EndSection

# Device configured by Xconfigurator:

Section "Device"
    Identifier  "My Video Card"
    VendorName  "Unknown"
    BoardName   "Unknown"
    #VideoRam    2048
#    Chipset    "NM2160"
#    IOBase     0xfea00000
#    MemBase    0xfd000000
#    VideoRam   2048
#    DacSpeed   90
#    Option     "linear"
#    Option     "nolinear"
#    Option     "swcursor"
#    Option     "hw_cursor"
#    Option     "no_accel"
#    Option     "intern_disp"
#    Option     "extern_disp"
#    Option     "mmio"
#    Option     "no_mmio"
#    Option     "lcd_center"
#    Option     "no_stretch"
    # Insert Clocks lines here if appropriate
EndSection
```

XF86Config Screen Section

The XF86Config Screen section in Listing 4.7 tells what X server to use, the color depth (such as 8, 16, 24 or 32 bits per pixel), the screen size (such as 640×480, 800×600, or 1,024×768), and (possibly) the size of a virtual screen. This particular listing shows that you have the option to use the startx command's -bpp option to have 8- or 16-bit planes of color (256 or thousands) for X sessions.

The startx command is an easy way to start an X session if you're working on a single computer. There are other ways to start X (see the section "Using xdm," later in this chapter). If your video card and monitor support these features, you can start a 16-bit X session like this:

```
# startx -- -bpp 16
```

The Screen section contains directions for your chosen X server (the XF86_SVGA or other color server, the 4-bit or 16-color XF86_VGA16 server, or the monochrome server, XF86_Mono) on what resolutions and virtual screen size to support.

For example, according to the configuration in Listing 4.7, if you're using the 8-bit or 256-color mode of the XF86_SVGA server, you have the choice of a 1,024×768, 800×600, or 640×480 display (not all modes may work). If you choose to start an X session with millions of colors, you'll find a lower resolution available. You can toggle resolutions during your X session by holding down the Ctrl+Alt keys and depressing the plus (+) or minus (–) key on your keypad. Laptop users need to use the NumLock key before switching resolutions.

Remember that Listing 4.7 was generated for a computer different than yours, so your XF86Config file will be different.

LISTING 4.7 The *XF86Config Screen* Section

```
# **********************************************************************
# Screen sections
# **********************************************************************

# The Colour SVGA server

Section "Screen"
    Driver      "svga"
    # Use Device "Generic VGA" for Standard VGA 320x200x256
    #Device      "Generic VGA"
    Device      "NeoMagic (laptop/notebook)"
    Monitor     "My Monitor"
    Subsection "Display"
        Depth       8
```

continues

LISTING 4.7 continued

```
        # Omit the Modes line for the "Generic VGA" device
        Modes       "1024x768" "800x600" "640x480"
        ViewPort    0 0
        # Use Virtual 320 200 for Generic VGA
    EndSubsection
    Subsection "Display"
        Depth       16
        Modes       "1024x768" "800x600" "640x480"
        ViewPort    0 0
    EndSubsection
    Subsection "Display"
        Depth       24
        Modes       "800x600" "640x480"
        ViewPort    0 0
    EndSubsection
EndSection


# The 16-color VGA server

# The 16-color VGA server

Section "Screen"
    Driver      "vga16"
    Device      "Generic VGA"
    Monitor     "My Monitor"
    Subsection "Display"
        Modes       "640x480" "800x600"
        ViewPort    0 0
        Virtual     800 600
    EndSubsection
EndSection

# The Mono server

Section "Screen"
    Driver      "vga2"
    Device      "Generic VGA"
    Monitor     "My Monitor"
    Subsection "Display"
        Modes       "640x480" "800x600"
        ViewPort    0 0
        Virtual     800 600
    EndSubsection
EndSection

# The accelerated servers (S3, Mach32, Mach8, 8514, P9000, AGX, W32, Mach64
# I128, and S3V)
Section "Screen"
```

```
    Driver      "accel"
    Device      "NeoMagic (laptop/notebook)"
    Monitor     "My Monitor"
    Subsection "Display"
        Depth       8
        Modes       "1024x768" "800x600" "640x480"
        ViewPort    0 0
    EndSubsection
    Subsection "Display"
        Depth       16
        Modes       "1024x768" "800x600" "640x480"
        ViewPort    0 0
    EndSubsection
    Subsection "Display"
        Depth       24
        Modes       "800x600" "640x480"
        ViewPort    0 0
    EndSubsection
EndSection
```

Using xf86config

An alternative way to create an `XF86Config` for your X session is to use the `xf86config` command, found under the `/usr/X11R6/bin` directory. This command is part of the XFree86 distribution and works from the command line of your console or an X11 terminal window. Start the command like this:

```
# xf86config
```

Press the Return key twice (after reading two introductory screens) to get to the mouse configuration screen, which contains this text:

```
First specify a mouse protocol type. Choose one from the following list:

 1.  Microsoft compatible (2-button protocol)
 2.  Mouse Systems (3-button protocol)
 3.  Bus Mouse
 4.  PS/2 Mouse
 5.  Logitech Mouse (serial, old type, Logitech protocol)
 6.  Logitech MouseMan (Microsoft compatible)
 7.  MM Series
 8.  MM HitTablet
 9.  Microsoft IntelliMouse
10.  Acecad tablet

If you have a two-button mouse, it is most likely of type 1, and if you have
a three-button mouse, it can probably support both protocol 1 and 2. There are
two main varieties of the latter type: mice with a switch to select the
```

```
protocol, and mice that default to 1 and require a button to be held at
boot-time to select protocol 2. Some mice can be convinced to do 2 by sending
a special sequence to the serial port (see the ClearDTR/ClearRTS options).

Enter a protocol number: 4
```

As you can see, you have a choice of nine different pointers. Enter a number corresponding with your pointer and press Enter. You're asked whether you want three-button emulation:

```
If your mouse has only two buttons, it is recommended that you enable
Emulate3Buttons.

Please answer the following question with either 'y' or 'n'.
Do you want to enable Emulate3Buttons? y
```

Press the Y key if desired, followed by the Enter key. Next you're asked for the Linux device corresponding with your pointer. For Red Hat users, this is `/dev/mouse`.

```
Now give the full device name that the mouse is connected to, for example
/dev/tty00. Just pressing enter will use the default, /dev/mouse.

Mouse device:
```

If you have a different pointer, enter its device name from the `/dev` directory and press Enter. The next screen asks if you want to use XFree86's XKeyboard extension:

```
Beginning with XFree86 3.1.2D, you can use the new X11R6.1 XKEYBOARD
extension to manage the keyboard layout. If you answer 'n' to the following
question, the server will use the old method, and you have to adjust
your keyboard layout with xmodmap.

Please answer the following question with either 'y' or 'n'.
Do you want to use XKB? y
```

This is a good idea for most users; unless you have a specialized keyboard or want to customize your keyboard's characters by using the `xmodmap` client, answer with a **y** and press the Enter key. The `xf86config` command follows up with a series of dialog boxes, asking about your choice of keyboards:

```
List of preconfigured keymaps:

  1  Standard 101-key, US encoding
  2  Microsoft Natural, US encoding
  3  KeyTronic FlexPro, US encoding
  4  Standard 101-key, US encoding with ISO9995-3 extensions
  5  Standard 101-key, German encoding
  6  Standard 101-key, French encoding
  7  Standard 101-key, Thai encoding
  8  Standard 101-key, Swiss/German encoding
```

```
  9  Standard 101-key, Swiss/French encoding
 10  None of the above

Enter a number to choose the keymap. 10

 You did not select one of the preconfigured keymaps. We will now try to
compose a suitable XKB setting. This setting is untested.
Please select one of the following standard keyboards. Use DEFAULT if
nothing really fits (101-key, tune manually)

  1  Standard 101-key keyboard
  2  Standard 102-key keyboard
  3  101-key with ALT_R = Multi_key
  4  102-key with ALT_R = Multi_key
  5  Microsoft Natural keyboard
  6  KeyTronic FlexPro keyboard
  7  DEFAULT

Enter a number to choose the keyboard.  2
Please choose one of the following countries. Use DEFAULT if nothing
really fits (US encoding, tune manually)
Press enter to continue, or ctrl-c to abort.

  1  Belgium
  2  Bulgaria
  3  Canada
  4  Czechoslovakia
  5  Denmark
  6  Finland
  7  France
  8  Germany
  9  Italy
 10  Norway
 11  Poland
 12  Portugal
 13  Russia
 14  Spain
 15  Sweden
 16  Thailand
 17  Switzerland/French layout
 18  Switzerland/German layout

Enter a number to choose the country.
Press enter for the next page

 19  United Kingdom
 20  USA
 21  DEFAULT

Enter a number to choose the country.
Press enter for the next page 20
```

After you choose a keyboard, `xf86config` presents a short introductory screen before asking for your monitor's specifics. Press the Enter key, and you'll see the following text:

```
You must indicate the horizontal sync range of your monitor. You can
either
select one of the predefined ranges below that correspond to industry-
standard monitor types, or give a specific range.

It is VERY IMPORTANT that you do not specify a monitor type with a
horizontalsync range that is beyond the capabilities of your monitor.
If in doubt, choose a conservative setting.

    hsync in kHz; monitor type with characteristic modes
 1  31.5; Standard VGA, 640x480 @ 60 Hz
 2  31.5 - 35.1; Super VGA, 800x600 @ 56 Hz
 3  31.5, 35.5; 8514 Compatible, 1024x768 @ 87 Hz interlaced (no 800x600)
 4  31.5, 35.15, 35.5; Super VGA, 1024x768 @ 87 Hz interlaced, 800x600 @ 56 Hz
 5  31.5 - 37.9; Extended Super VGA, 800x600 @ 60 Hz, 640x480 @ 72 Hz
 6  31.5 - 48.5; Non-Interlaced SVGA, 1024x768 @ 60 Hz, 800x600 @ 72 Hz
 7  31.5 - 57.0; High Frequency SVGA, 1024x768 @ 70 Hz
 8  31.5 - 64.3; Monitor that can do 1280x1024 @ 60 Hz
 9  31.5 - 79.0; Monitor that can do 1280x1024 @ 74 Hz
10  31.5 - 82.0; Monitor that can do 1280x1024 @ 76 Hz
11  Enter your own horizontal sync range

Enter your choice (1-11): 11
```

Enter a number corresponding to your monitor's characteristics. If you prefer, enter the number **11** to give a specific horizontal sync range. You then see this text:

```
Please enter the horizontal sync range of your monitor, in the format used
in the table of monitor types above. You can either specify one or more
continuous ranges (e.g. 15-25, 30-50), or one or more fixed sync frequencies.

Horizontal sync range: 31.5-37.9
```

Press the Enter key. You are then asked to enter the vertical range.

```
You must indicate the vertical sync range of your monitor. You can either
select one of the predefined ranges below that correspond to industry-
standard monitor types, or give a specific range. For interlaced modes,
the number that counts is the high one (e.g. 87 Hz rather than 43 Hz).

 1  50-70
 2  50-90
 3  50-100
 4  40-150
 5  Enter your own vertical sync range

Enter your choice: 5
```

If you prefer to enter your own range, choose **5** and press the Enter key. Now you'll see this text:

```
Vertical sync range: 50-70
```

Enter your monitor's vertical range, such as **50-70**, and press the Enter key. You are asked to enter three lines of description for your monitor. Enter a description, as well as your monitor's manufacturer and model. You can also just press the Enter key, as this information is not critical.

```
You must now enter a few identification/description strings, namely an
identifier, a vendor name, and a model name. Just pressing enter will fill
in default names.

The strings are free-form, spaces are allowed.
Enter an identifier for your monitor definition:
Enter the vendor name of your monitor:
Enter the model name of your monitor:
```

After you enter the model name and press the Enter key, `xf86config` presents an introduction dialog box to video card selection and asks if you want to look at the card database:

```
Now we must configure video card specific settings. At this point you can
choose to make a selection out of a database of video card definitions.
Because there can be variation in Ramdacs and clock generators even
between cards of the same model, it is not sensible to blindly copy
the settings (e.g. a Device section). For this reason, after you make a
selection, you will still be asked about the components of the card, with
the settings from the chosen database entry presented as a strong hint.

The database entries include information about the chipset, what server to
run, the Ramdac and ClockChip, and comments that will be included in the
Device section. However, a lot of definitions only hint about what server
to run (based on the chipset the card uses) and are untested.

If you can't find your card in the database, there's nothing to worry about.
You should only choose a database entry that is exactly the same model as
your card; choosing one that looks similar is just a bad idea (e.g. a
GemStone Snail 64 may be as different from a GemStone Snail 64+ in terms of
hardware as can be).

Do you want to look at the card database? y
```

You'll see the following list of the first 18 video cards in XFree86's card database of more than 600 cards (located in the file `Cards`, under the `/usr/X11R6/lib/X11` directory):

```
 0  2 the Max MAXColor S3 Trio64V+                      S3 Trio64V+
 1  3DLabs Oxygen GMX                                   PERMEDIA 2
```

```
  2  928Movie                                       S3 928
  3  AGX (generic)                                  AGX-014/15/16
  4  ALG-5434(E)                                    CL-GD5434
  5  ASUS 3Dexplorer                                RIVA128
  6  ASUS PCI-AV264CT                               ATI-Mach64
  7  ASUS PCI-V264CT                                ATI-Mach64
  8  ASUS Video Magic PCI V864                      S3 864
  9  ASUS Video Magic PCI VT64                      S3 Trio64
 10  AT25                                           Alliance AT3D
 11  AT3D                                           Alliance AT3D
 12  ATI 3D Pro Turbo                               ATI-Mach64
 13  ATI 3D Pro Turbo PC2TV                         ATI-Mach64
 14  ATI 3D Xpression                               ATI-Mach64
 15  ATI 3D Xpression+                              ATI-Mach64
 16  ATI 3D Xpression+ PC2TV                        ATI-Mach64
 17  ATI 8514 Ultra (no VGA)                        ATI-Mach8

Enter a number to choose the corresponding card definition.
Press enter for the next page, q to continue configuration.
```

Your choices are to enter a number corresponding to your card (or a card recommended as a close choice by the readme file for your card under the `/usr/X11R6/lib/X11/doc` directory), to press the Enter key to page to the next screen, or to press Q to continue the configuration. Note that if you press Q, `xf86config` uses Unknown for your graphics device. On the other hand, if you pick a specific card, `xf86config` reports with an identifier, chipset, and selected server appropriate for your chipset (after choosing entry 97 in the database).

```
Your selected card definition:

Identifier: NeoMagic (laptop/notebook)
Chipset:    MagicGraph 128 series
Server:     XF86_SVGA

Press enter to continue, or ctrl-c to abort.
```

You're asked to select the type of server after pressing the Enter key:

```
Now you must determine which server to run. Refer to the manpages and other
documentation. The following servers are available (they may not all be
installed on your system):

 1  The XF86_Mono server. This a monochrome server that should work on any
    VGA-compatible card, in 640x480 (more on some SVGA chipsets).
 2  The XF86_VGA16 server. This is a 16-color VGA server that should work on
    any VGA-compatible card.
 3  The XF86_SVGA server. This is a 256 color SVGA server that supports
    a number of SVGA chipsets. On some chipsets it is accelerated or
    supports higher color depths.
 4  The accelerated servers. These include XF86_S3, XF86_Mach32, XF86_Mach8,
```

```
   XF86_8514, XF86_P9000, XF86_AGX, XF86_W32, XF86_Mach64, XF86_I128 and
   XF86_S3V.

These four server types correspond to the four different "Screen" sections in
XF86Config (vga2, vga16, svga, accel).

 5  Choose the server from the card definition, XF86_SVGA.

Which one of these screen types do you intend to run by default (1-5)? 5
```

Unless you specifically want your X sessions to use black and white or the 16-color server (`XF86_VGA16`), choose the default server preselected by `xf86config` by entering **5** and pressing the Enter key. You're asked whether you want `xf86config` to create a symbolic link called X under the `/usr/X11R6/bin` directory. Don't create the link!

```
The server to run is selected by changing the symbolic link 'X'. For example,
'rm /usr/X11R6/bin/X; ln -s /usr/X11R6/bin/XF86_SVGA /usr/X11R6/bin/X' selects
the SVGA server.

Please answer the following question with either 'y' or 'n'.
Do you want me to set the symbolic link?
```

Note

Because of a recent security update to XFree86, the symbolic link X should point to the `Xwrapper` client, found in the `/usr/X11R6/bin` directory. These files should look like this:

```
# ls -l /usr/X11R6/bin/X
lrwxrwxrwx   1 root  root       8 May  8 07:29 /usr/X11R6/bin/
➥X -> Xwrapper
# ls -l /usr/X11R6/bin/Xwrapper
-rws--x--x   1 root  root    6116 Apr 18 19:33 /usr/X11R6/bin/
➥Xwrapper
```

If you don't find X as this link, log in as the root operator and use the `ln` command to create the link like this:

```
# ln -s /usr/X11R6/bin/Xwrapper /usr/X11R6/bin/X
```


Type **n** and press the Enter key. You're asked to enter the amount of video memory installed in your graphics card:

```
Now you must give information about your video card. This will be used for
the "Device" section of your video card in XF86Config.

You must indicate how much video memory you have. It is probably a good
idea to use the same approximate amount as that detected by the server you
intend to use. If you encounter problems that are due to the used server
```

```
not supporting the amount memory you have (e.g. ATI Mach64 is limited to
1024K with the SVGA server), specify the maximum amount supported by the
server.

How much video memory do you have on your video card:

 1  256K
 2  512K
 3  1024K
 4  2048K
 5  4096K
 6  Other

Enter your choice:
```

Either enter a number corresponding to the amount of memory or enter **6**, press Enter, and then enter the amount of memory, in kilobytes, supported by your card. Note that, like Xconfigurator, the `xf86config` command generates an `XF86Config` file with the video RAM setting commented out. You'll have to edit the file after you're done to ensure your video RAM setting is used (unless this value is probed correctly by your X server).

You're asked to enter information as you did for your monitor, but now about your video card:

```
You must now enter a few identification/description strings, namely an
identifier, a vendor name, and a model name. Just pressing enter will fill
in default names (possibly from a card definition).

Your card definition is NeoMagic (laptop/notebook).

The strings are free-form, spaces are allowed.
Enter an identifier for your video card definition:
You can simply press enter here if you have a generic card, or want to
describe your card with one string.
Enter the vendor name of your video card:
Enter the model (board) name of your video card:
```

Again, it's not necessary to fill out this information. After pressing the Enter key, you may be asked about your video's clockchip settings:

```
A Clockchip line in the Device section forces the detection of a
programmable clock device. With a clockchip enabled, any required
clock can be programmed without requiring probing of clocks or a
Clocks line. Most cards don't have a programmable clock chip.
Choose from the following list:

 1  Chrontel 8391                                          ch8391
 2  ICD2061A and compatibles (ICS9161A, DCS2824)           icd2061a
 3  ICS2595                                                ics2595
```

```
 4  ICS5342 (similar to SDAC, but not completely compatible)    ics5342
 5  ICS5341                                                     ics5341
 6  S3 GenDAC (86C708) and ICS5300 (autodetected)               s3gendac
 7  S3 SDAC (86C716)                                            s3_sdac
 8  STG 1703 (autodetected)                                     stg1703
 9  Sierra SC11412                                              sc11412
10  TI 3025 (autodetected)                                      ti3025
11  TI 3026 (autodetected)                                      ti3026
12  IBM RGB 51x/52x (autodetected)                              ibm_rgb5xx

Just press enter if you don't want a Clockchip setting.
What Clockchip setting do you want (1-12)?
```

If your video card uses a clockchip (see your card's readme file under the `/usr/X11R6/lib/X11/doc` directory), select the appropriate setting, followed by the Enter key. Press Enter only if you don't need or want a clockchip setting in your `XF86Config`'s `Device` section. The `xf86config` command then asks if you'd like to probe your video card for clockchip settings. Note that your earlier choice of the Cirrus Logic chipset said to avoid probing the clocks (because a clockchip is not used).

Handy Command-Line Diagnostics

Probing your video card for clockchip settings is one way to fine-tune your `XF86Config` file. Another handy way to diagnose your `XF86Config` settings before you start your first X session is to use a tip detailed by Eric S. Raymond in his XFree86 HOWTO (found under the `/usr/doc/HOWTO` directory). This method saves the output of the chosen X server, such as `XF86_SVGA`, while it reads your `XF86Config`. You can save the output to a file such as `myX11.txt` with a command line like this: **`X > myX11.txt 2>&1`**. If you jump into your X session, kill the session by holding down the Alt+Ctrl keys and pressing the Backspace key. You can then read the X server's output with the more-or-less command `less myX11.txt` to ensure that everything is okay. This command is handy because the output normally scrolls too fast to be read.


```
For most configurations, a Clocks line is useful since it prevents the
slow and nasty sounding clock probing at server start-up. Probed clocks
are displayed at server startup, along with other server and hardware
configuration info. You can save this information in a file by running
'X -probeonly 2>output_file'. Be warned that clock probing is inherently
imprecise; some clocks may be slightly too high (varies per run).

At this point I can run X -probeonly, and try to extract the clock
information from the output. It is recommended that you do this yourself
and add a clocks line (note that the list of clocks may be split over
```

```
multiple Clocks lines) to your Device section afterwards. Be aware that
a clocks line is not appropriate for drivers that have a fixed set of
clocks and don't probe by default (e.g. Cirrus). Also, for the P9000
server you must simply specify clocks line that matches the modes you
want to use.  For the S3 server with a programmable clock chip you need
a 'ClockChip' line and no Clocks line.

You must be root to be able to run X -probeonly now.

Do you want me to run 'X -probeonly' now?
```

Enter either a **y** or an **n** and press the Enter key. (You may be again asked to confirm a probe if you type a y.)

The `xf86config` command now asks about your desired screen resolution and color depths. It is unnecessary to make any changes, as the X server will not accept a display size or color depth out of range for your video card, but you should generate a cleaner `XF86Config` file by changing the modes or settings to match the capabilities for your video and monitor. For example, settings of 1,024×768 or greater at 16, 24, or 32 bits per pixel don't make sense if your display and video cannot support the settings.

```
For each depth, a list of modes (resolutions) is defined. The default
resolution that the server will start-up with will be the first listed
mode that can be supported by the monitor and card.
Currently it is set to:

"640x480" "800x600" "1024x768" "1280x1024" for 8bpp
"640x480" "800x600" "1024x768" for 16bpp
"640x480" "800x600" for 24bpp
"640x480" "800x600" for 32bpp

Note that 16, 24 and 32bpp are only supported on a few configurations.
Modes that cannot be supported due to monitor or clock constraints will
be automatically skipped by the server.

 1  Change the modes for 8pp (256 colors)
 2  Change the modes for 16bpp (32K/64K colors)
 3  Change the modes for 24bpp (24-bit color, packed pixel)
 4  Change the modes for 32bpp (24-bit color)
 5  The modes are OK, continue.

Enter your choice:
```

If you choose to change some of the settings, you're asked to choose specific resolutions for each color depth and whether you'd like a virtual screen size larger than your display (such as an 800×600 virtual screen when using a 640×480 display). Change the settings for each mode by pressing a key (1 through 4; press 5 to accept the defaults) and then press Enter to continue. The `xf86config` command asks if you want to save the generated `XF86Config` file in the current directory. Enter a **y** and press the Enter key—you're done.

```
I am going to write the XF86Config file now. Make sure you don't accidentally
overwrite a previously configured one.

Do you want it written to the current directory as 'XF86Config'? y

File has been written. Take a look at it before running 'startx'. Note that
the XF86Config file must be in one of the directories searched by the server
(e.g. /usr/X11R6/lib/X11) in order to be used. Within the server press
ctrl, alt and '+' simultaneously to cycle video resolutions. Pressing ctrl,
alt and backspace simultaneously immediately exits the server (use if
the monitor doesn't sync for a particular mode).

For further configuration, refer to /usr/X11R6/lib/X11/doc/README.Config.
```

The `XF86Config` file may be located in several different places in your system:

`/etc/XF86Config`

`/etc/X11/XF86Config`

`/usr/X11R6/lib/X11/XF86Config`

`/root/XF86Config` (only if you use X as `root`)

Finally, if you don't want to use Xconfigurator or `xf86config` to generate an `XF86Config` file, you can create your own. Red Hat and Caldera users will find a template file, `XF86Config.eg`, under the `/usr/X11R6/lib/X11` directory. Debian users can find the same file in `/usr/doc/xserver-common/examples/XF86Config.eg`. Copy this file to your directory and edit it in your favorite text editor, inserting specifications for your system and X server.

Configuring with XF86Setup

You can also try the `XF86Setup` command, a graphical interface client included with XFree86 that you can use to set up X11. From the command line of a console or an X11 terminal window, start `XF86Setup` like this:

```
# XF86Setup
```

After you press Enter, you may see a dialog box similar to that in Figure 4.14, especially if you are running an X11 session.

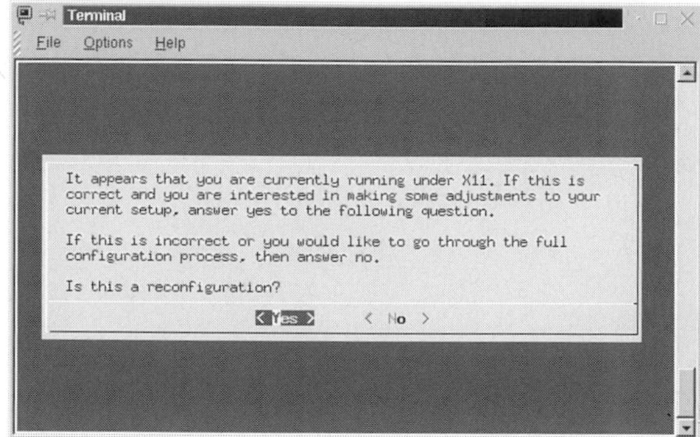

FIGURE 4.14
The `XF86Setup` client will detect whether you have an X11 session in progress before starting.

If you're running X, you can use `XF86Setup` to reconfigure or fine-tune different settings, such as your mouse, keyboard, and mode selections for color depths. Select Yes if you're running X11; you then see the main `XF86Setup` dialog box, as shown in Figure 4.15.

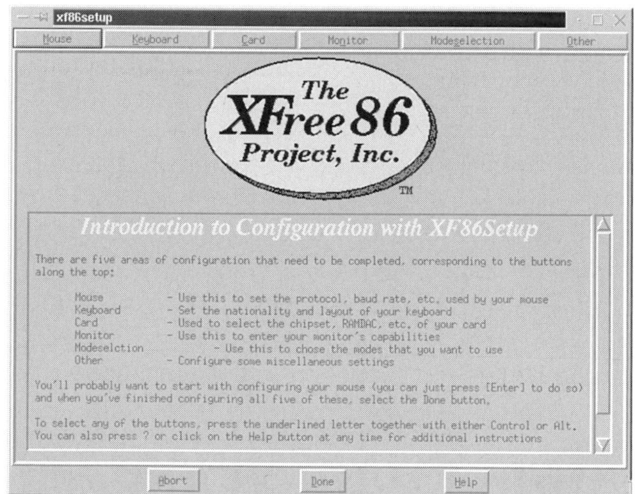

FIGURE 4.15
The `XF86Setup` client can be used to reconfigure `XF86Config` settings while running an X11 session.

For example, if you click the Mouse tab at the top of the dialog box (shown in Figure 4.15), you'll see the Mouse protocol dialog box, as shown in Figure 4.16. You can use this dialog box to change a mouse on-the-fly, add three-button emulation, or test your current mouse.

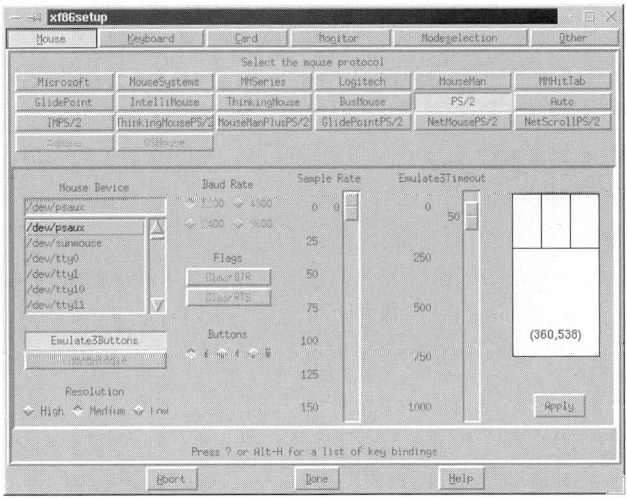

FIGURE 4.16
XF86Setup's Mouse dialog box can reconfigure a pointer while running an X11 session.

If you click the Keyboard tab, you'll see a dialog box like that in Figure 4.17. Here you can reconfigure or install a new keyboard, use different language settings through the Layout drop-down menu, or modify the behavior of various keystrokes (similar to using the `xmodmap` client).

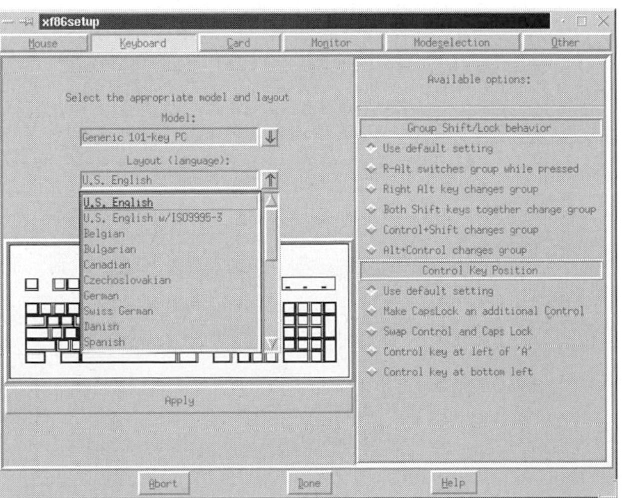

FIGURE 4.17
XF86Setup's Keyboard dialog box can be used to reconfigure a keyboard for your X11 session.

You can also use `XF86Setup` to configure a new `XF86Config` file from scratch. In this case, use the Card dialog box to select a new video card. Figure 4.18 shows the Card dialog box.

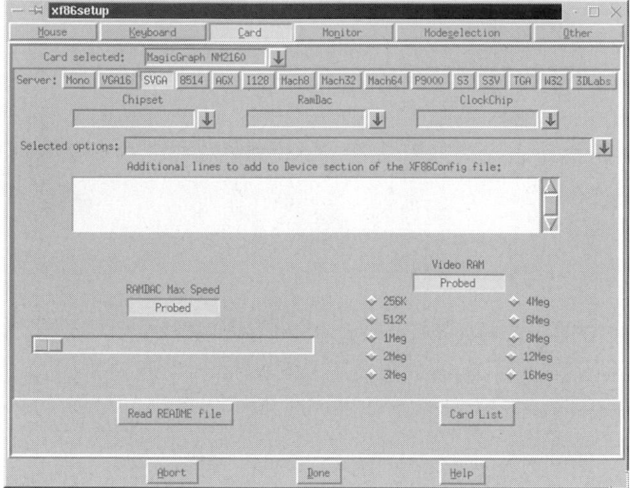

FIGURE 4.18
Use `XF86Setup`'s Card dialog box to configure a new video card for X.

Click the drop-down Card Selected menu to scroll through the list of current cards. Additional cards are selected through the Card List button in the lower-right portion of the dialog box. Select a server by clicking the appropriate server button at the top of the dialog box. When finished, click the Monitor tab.

The Monitor dialog box, shown in Figure 4.19, is used to enter new synch rates for a new monitor and to change current settings.

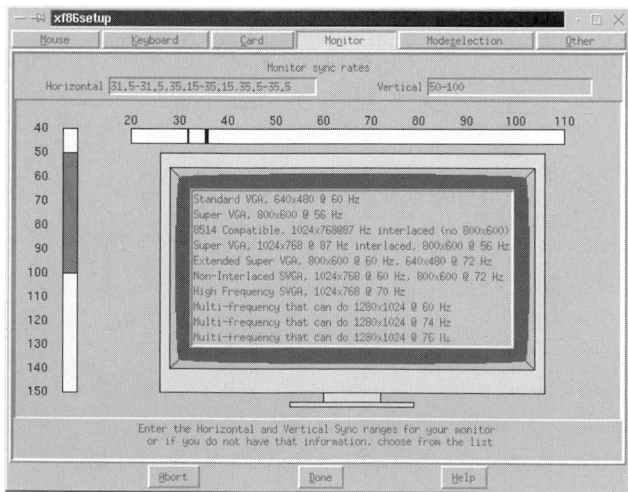

FIGURE 4.19
The `XF86Setup` client's Monitor dialog box can be used to install a new monitor for X11.

If you'd like to change the default color depths or resolutions for your X session, use the Modeselection dialog box, shown in Figure 4.20, to change your `XF86Config` file's settings.

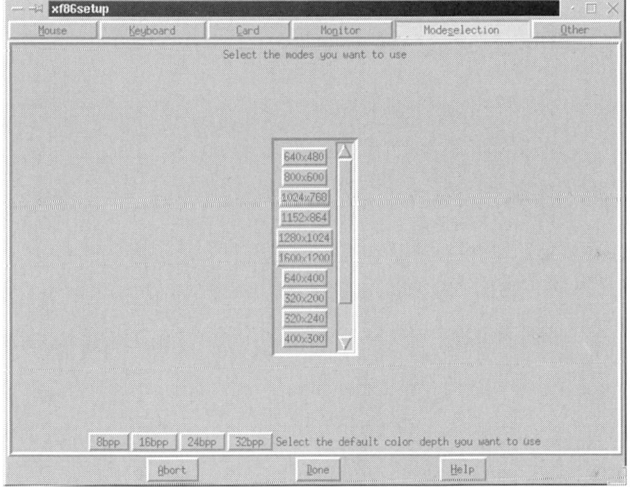

FIGURE 4.20
The `XF86Setup` client's Modeselection dialog box changes the resolution and color-depth settings of your `XF86Config` file.

The Other tab is used to change settings found in the `Server` section of the `XF86Config` file, along with allowing or disallowing video mode, keyboard, or mouse setting changes across a network. If you are satisfied with your changes using `XF86Setup`, click the Done button. The Abort button cancels all your changes.

The `.xinitrc` File

When you use the `startx` command to initiate an X session on your computer, details about which window manager to use or other X clients to start can be found in a file called `.xinitrc` in your home directory. A sample or template file called `xinitrc` is installed in the `/etc/X11/xinit` directory. You can copy this file to your home directory with the filename `.xinitrc` and modify it.

OpenLinux provides a modified version of the `startx` command named `kde` (and found under the `/opt/kde/bin` directory) that will launch an X session using KDE.

Although the default `.xinitrc` file contains shell script logic to load system resources or set different environment variables, you can define a simpler version from scratch, such as the one in Listing 4.8, which can be used to start 12 different X window managers. (For more information about various X window managers, see Chapter 5.)

LISTING 4.8 Sample *.xinitrc* File

```
# Sample .xinitrc file
#
# This .xinitrc file has configuration support for the following X11
# window managers: AnotherLevel, fvwm, fvmw2, KDE, twm, mlvwm, AfterStep
#                  WindowMaker, wm2, wmx, mwm, GNOME
#
# Use AnotherLevel's configuration of the fvwm2 window manager
# fvwm2 -cmd 'FvwmM4 -debug /etc/X11/AnotherLevel/fvwm2rc.m4'
#
# Use fvwm2
# fvwm2
#
# Use fvwm
# fvwm
#
# Use the K Desktop Environment
startkde
#
# Use twm - note: needs an X terminal started
# twm
#
# Use the mlvwm (Macintosh-like) window manager
# mlvwm
#
# Use AfterStep
# afterstep
# or
# RunWM.AfterStep
#
# Use WindowMaker
# exec wmaker
# or
# RunWM.WindowMaker
#
# Use the wm2 window manager
# wm2
#
# Use the wmx window manager
# wmx
#
# Use Motif's or LessTif's mwm
# mwm
# or
# RunWM.MWM
#
# Use GNOME
# exec gnome-session
```

Note that the sample .xinitrc file in Listing 4.8 is for Red Hat Linux and is currently set to use the K Desktop Environment.

To use a different window manager (if installed on your system), add or remove the appropriate pound sign in the file; then use the startx command to start a new session:

```
# startx
```

Using Red Hat's wmconfig Command

Each X window manager in Listing 4.8 has its own set of configuration files. Some use a single, default systemwide file, and others require numerous files and a complex series of support files for different code modules. To make the job of configuring your window manager easier, Red Hat Linux includes the wmconfig, or window-manager configuration command.

The wmconfig command, found under the /usr/X11R6/bin directory, creates resource files for use in your home directory for (at the time of this writing) seven X window managers. The resource files are built according to entries in different program files under the /etc/X11/wmconfig directory. This directory contains 106 entries for different commands and X clients. For example, here's the entry for emacs:

```
emacs name "emacs"
emacs description "emacs Editor"
emacs exec "emacs &"
emacs group Utilities
```

The entry shows the program's name, its description, the command line to start the client, and under what menu the program will be found. Unfortunately, it's hard to determine how the different programs are grouped just by looking at the contents of the wmconfig directory; however, if you use wmconfig's --output= with the debug option, you get a tree-like list of how the programs are grouped, along with the names of the main menus that will be built. Here is an example:

```
# wmconfig --output=debug
+-Red Hat Linux:
|  +-Administration:
|  |  +-package   : apachecfg
|  |  |  group     : Administration
|  |  |  name      : Apache Configuration
|  |  |  icon      : comanche.xpm
|  |  |  mini_icon: mini-comanche.xpm
|  |  |  exec      : comanche &
|  |  |  desc      : A graphical configuration tool for the Apache web server
```

```
|   |   |   Xresource:
|   |   |   copy      :
...
```

Not all the output is included, but you can see that the wmconfig command shows the first entry in the Red Hat Linux menu's Administration submenu is the apachecfg tool. To build a configuration file for other window managers, such as the fvwm2 window manager, use wmconfig, along with its --output= option:

```
# wmconfig --output=fvwm > .fvwm2rc
```

This command line creates a new .fvwm2rc file, so make a copy of your original files before using wmconfig. If you'd like to create your own set of configurations, create a .wmconfig directory in your home directory and copy the configuration files from the /etc/X11/wmconfig directory like this:

```
# mkdir .wmconfig ; cp /etc/X11/wmconfig/* .wmconfig
```

You can then edit and create window manager resource files from your .wmconfig directory instead of using the systemwide defaults.

The Debian Menu System

Debian GNU/Linux has a similar system, but it operates in a different and somewhat more transparent way. Whenever a user-level application is installed on a Debian system, it registers itself with the Debian menus. You can take advantage of these by installing the menu package, like so:

```
# apt-get install menu
```

Now, every window manager on the system that is capable of displaying menus (as well as a few related programs that display menus but are not window managers) will automatically have menus populated with programs you can run. These menus are automatically maintained by the system and are the same in any window manager. They are enabled by default for each person if you install the menu package; there is no additional configuration necessary.

The Personal X Resource File

Most default settings for the various X clients are found in individual files under the /usr/X11R6/lib/X11/app-defaults directory. Here is an example:

```
# ls /usr/X11R6/lib/X11/app-defaults
Beforelight     XCalc          XMailbox        XTerm-color
Bitmap          XCalc-color    XMdb            Xditview
```

```
Bitmap-color    XClipboard   XMixer           Xditview-chrtr
Chooser         XClock       XOsview          Xedit
Clock-color     XConsole     XPaint           Xfd
Editres         XDaliClock   XPat             Xfm
Editres-color   XDbx         XPlaycd          Xgc
Fig             XFontSel     XPlaymidi        Xloadimage
Fig-color       XGammon      XRn              Xmag
GV              XGetfile     XScreenSaver     Xman
GXditview       XLoad        XSm              Xmessage
KTerm           XLock        XSysinfo         Xmh
Viewres         XLogo        XSysinfo-color   Xvidtune
X3270           XLogo-color  XTerm
```

These are text files each client uses for default window size, color, or other options. As a trivial example, edit the `xplaycd` client's resource file, `XPlaycd`, and change the line containing `!*reverseVideo: off` to have the client use a reverse-video window. Do this by removing the exclamation point (`!`) and changing the word `off` to `on`:

```
*reverseVideo:  on
```

Save the file and run the program from the command line of an X terminal window like this:

```
# xplaycd &
```

The before and after `xplaycd` windows are shown in Figure 4.21.

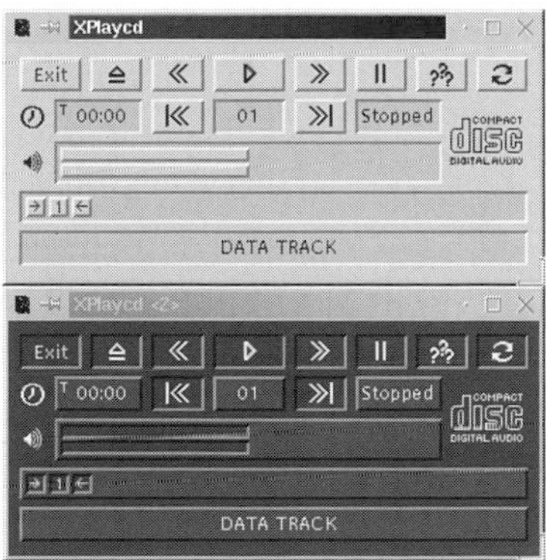

FIGURE 4.21
The `xplaycd` client's display (such as reverse video) and other features can be customized through its resource file.

Changes like these affect all users on your system if you make the change to a client's file in the `app-defaults` directory. To avoid systemwide changes, create a file called `.Xresources` in your home directory with an entry for your application and specific settings. This file's format is detailed in the X man page, but you can easily change defaults by specifying the client name, followed by the client's resource and a value. For example, to change how `xplaycd` displays (using our previous example), create this entry in your `.Xresources` file:

```
xplaycd*reverseVideo: on
```

Save the file and then use the `xrdb`, or X resource database, utility, to merge the values into your current X session:

```
# xrdb -merge .Xresources
```

If you create numerous settings and customized resources for clients during your X sessions and use the sample Listing 4.8, insert the `xrdb` line into the beginning of your `.xinitrc` file. (The systemwide `.xinitrc` file merges in these settings by default.)

Using xdm

The `xdm`, X display manager, is an X client and one of several display managers available for Linux that you can use to provide a small level of security when booting Linux. You can use `xdm` to log into Linux and directly to an X session, either locally or using a remote computer. However, if you choose to not use a display manager or boot directly to X, you can try `xdm` from the command line as the root operator by using the `-nodaemon` option:

```
# xdm -nodaemon
```

The display clears, and you see an `xdm` login display similar to the one in Figure 4.22. You can then log into X or use the Ctrl+Alt+F1 keys to go back to your console display and kill the daemon with a Ctrl+C.

Red Hat

Previous versions of Red Hat's Linux distributions used the `xbanner` command to customize the `xdm` login screen (see Figure 4.22). If you'd like to use `xbanner` to customize the `xdm` login screen, see the documentation under the `/usr/doc/xbanner` directory. If you don't want to use the default screen used with Red Hat Linux 6.0, you have to edit the file `Xsetup_0` under the `/usr/X11R6/lib/X11/xdm` directory and remove these lines:

```
/usr/bin/xsri -geometry +5+5 -avoid 300x250 -keep-aspect \
        /usr/share/pixmaps/redhat/redhat-transparent.png
```

Red Hat Linux now uses the `xsri` client to display the Red Hat logo in the `gdm`, `kdm`, and `xdm` login screens.

Note

To learn more about the GNOME display manager, `gdm`, and the K display manager, `kdm`, see Chapter 5. You'll find out how to set up Red Hat Linux to use different display managers and login screens.

After you have a working XF86Config, you may want to start Linux directly to X. To do this, change the default init entry in your system's initialization table file (/etc/inittab). Look for this line:

```
id:3:initdefault
```

Change it to this line:

```
id:5:initdefault
```

This is applicable only for Red Hat systems. For Debian users, you can simply install the xdm package and thus have xdm ready to go.

Caution

Be careful—editing inittab is dangerous, and any errors could render your system unbootable. Make sure you have an emergency boot disk on hand, and make a backup copy of the inittab file first. Also note that other distributions of Linux (such as SuSE) may use different runlevel designations. You have been warned!

Tip

You can also boot directly to runlevel 5 through the LILO boot prompt. Turn on your computer, and type the following at the LILO boot prompt:

```
linux 5
```


After you make this change, restart your system by using this shutdown command:

```
# shutdown -r now
```

Although this will work quite handily, a much better alternative (and less disruptive for a system with active users) is to use the telinit command, followed by the desired runlevel number, like this:

```
# telinit 5
```

FIGURE 4.22
You can customize the Red Hat Linux `xdm` login screen for X11 by editing simple command lines in an `xdm` configuration file.

Starting X Sessions

If you don't use a display manager, you'll most likely use the `startx` command, a handy shell script that will pass on command-line options to your X server for your X sessions. The `startx` command is typically used to pass starting color-depth information to the X server, as well as to find client commands or options to run for the session (usually your `.xinitrc` file in your home directory).

The preferred method to log into OpenLinux is with the `kdm` client, which will then start an X session using the K Desktop Environment. In order to use a different window manager, such as `twm`, OpenLinux system administrators must first create a `twm` session using the login manager available through the K Control Center. For security reasons, session types are controlled through the `Xsession` file under the `/etc/X11/kdm` directory. To then allow users to log in and use the `twm` command, the `root` operator should open the `Xsession` file and insert a `twm` section (shown here in boldface):

```
case $# in
1)
        case $1 in
        kde)    KDEDIR=/opt/kde; export KDEDIR
                PATH=$KDEDIR/bin:$PATH
                exec /etc/X11/xinit/kdeinitrc
                ;;

        twm)    PATH=$PATH
                exec /etc/X11/xinit/xinitrc
                ;;

        failsafe)
                exec xterm -geometry 80x24-0-0
                ;;
        esac
esac
```

After making the changes, save the file and then either restart X or log out of KDE.

Unless you've used the `DefaultColordepth` option in your system's `XF86Config` file to set a specific color depth, using `startx` by itself will usually start an X session using 8-color bitplanes or 256 colors. However, you can pass color-depth options to your server by using the `--` and `-bpp` options:

```
# startx -- -bpp 16
```

This command line will start an X session (if supported by your computer's graphics card and monitor) using thousands of colors. Color values typically passed with the `-bpp` option also include 24 and 32 for millions of colors.

You can also use `startx` to start multiple X11 sessions on the same computer, possibly using different window managers, and then navigate between the sessions using virtual consoles. Red Hat Linux supports up to six different login screens or consoles, accessed by pressing Alt+F*X*, where *X* is F1 through F6. For example, if you log in to Linux without using a display manager, you'll be at the first virtual console. After you log in, press Alt+F2; you'll then see another login prompt at the second console. To get back to your first login, press Alt+F1.

When you log into Linux and start an X11 session with `startx`, X uses a seventh virtual screen. Since you've started X from the first virtual console, this console will be unavailable for use. However, you can get to another virtual console, such as the second, by pressing Ctrl+Alt+F2. You'll then see the Linux login prompt. To go back to your X session, press Alt+F7. Using this approach, you can jump back and forth between your X session and different text consoles.

To use multiple X11 sessions at different color depths on different virtual consoles, first start a session with the `startx` command. After the X desktop appears, press Ctrl+Alt+F2 and log in to Linux again. If your graphics card supports thousands of colors again, use the `startx` command to start an X session. This time, however, include the `:1`, `-bpp 16`, and `vt8` command-line options:

```
# startx -- :1 -bpp 16 vt8
```

The screen clears and you'll be running an X session with a different color depth! To jump to your other session, press Ctrl+Alt+F7. To jump to another virtual console, press Ctrl+Alt+F3 (since the first and second consoles are in use). To jump back to your original X session, press Ctrl+Alt+F8.

Troubleshooting XFree86

One of the best sources for troubleshooting installation or other problems when using XFree86's X11 is the XFree86 FAQ, which is found at `http://www.xfree86.org`. The FAQ contains seven sections and covers difficulties such as

- Configuration problems
- Keyboard and mouse problems
- Display problems
- Problems using fonts
- Problems using configurations with symbolic links to X (Xwrapper)
- Chipset support fixes
- Other known problems

Note

If you cannot find the answer you need in the X manual pages, the FAQ, or other documentation, try lurking for a while on the `comp.os.linux.x` Usenet newsgroup. You can post a question, clearly stating your distribution and version of Linux, along with the version of XFree86 you've installed.

Note

If your ISP doesn't have `comp.os.linux.x`, or if you don't feel like using a Usenet newsreader to look for answers about Linux and X11, point your favorite Web browser to `http://www.dejanews.com`.

Summary

This chapter covered the basic installation and configuration of the XFree86 X11 distribution for Linux. If you're a new user, you found out how to correctly configure and install X with fewer problems; if you're an experienced user, you hopefully discovered some new features (such as Xwrapper, Red Hat's `wmconfig`, or multiple X sessions) that will make your X sessions more productive and enjoyable.

CHAPTER

Window Managers

IN THIS CHAPTER

This chapter covers a variety of window managers for the X Window System. As you learned in Chapter 4, "The X Window System, Version 11," X11 provides the basic networking protocols and drawing primitives used to build the platform for various graphical interfaces, or window managers, you can use with Linux. A number of *clients*, such as `twm`, are from the XFree86 distribution, while others, such as Carsten Haitzler's GNOME-enabled Enlightenment window manager, use additional clients developed with support by various developers to provide a complete desktop environment. Some distributions include the K Desktop Environment (KDE), a similar desktop distribution with features and a following that rivals the commercial Common Desktop Environment (CDE).

What Is a Window Manager?

Using Linux and the XFree86 distribution of X11 means freedom of choice—the choice of an operating system and the choice of how you'd like your computer's desktop or `root` window in X to look. Although a window manager is nothing more than an X11 client, you'll find that using a window manager is virtually necessary if you want to run different programs, drag windows around the display, use icons, create virtual desktops, resize windows, or customize how your X sessions work. Of course, you can run X without a window manager, but you'll lose a lot of functionality.

Note

Want to try X without a window manager? If you've configured Linux to use a *display manager*, such as the GNOME display manager, gdm, select the Failsafe session. If you don't use an X display manager (such as `gdm`, `kdm`, or `xdm`), create an `.xinitrc` file in your home directory with your favorite text editor and then enter just one line:

```
exec xterm
```

When X starts (or you use `startx`), you'll get an `xterm` window, as shown in Figure 5.1—but you won't be able to move or resize it. To quit your X session, either type the word **`exit`** at the command line of the `xterm` terminal window or use the Ctrl+Alt+Backspace key combination to kill your X session. Without a window manager to provide support for movable windows, you're pretty much stuck with a static `xterm` screen. Now do you see why window managers are so much fun (and necessary)?

[bball@localhost bball]$ xwd -out nowinmgr.xwd -display 0:0

FIGURE 5.1
You can run X11 without a window manager, but is it worth it?

Most Linux distributions come with several window managers for X.

Several window managers are part of the XFree86 X11 distribution, while others are supported by Red Hat for your use. This chapter starts by discussing the GNOME software libraries for X11, and then concentrates on Red Hat's default X11 window manager, Enlightenment.

Debian comes with more than a dozen different window managers for the X Window System. You can choose which ones you want to install; among those available are Enlightenment, Afterstep, and various GNOME software. Debian has no particular default window manager; the default is set in /etc/X11/window-managers.

This chapter also introduces you to the default X11 desktop for OpenLinux: the K Desktop Environment, or KDE.

After covering several of the more popular or distribution-specific window managers, this chapter wraps up with the XFree86 window managers.

The GNOME X Environment

This section covers GNOME, the GNU Network Object Model Environment, which is supported by and is being developed by programmers from around the world. GNOME has received increasing interest because it is distributed under the GNU GPL, unlike the underlying graphics software libraries, Qt, for KDE. Arguments about licensing constraints aside, GNOME is an important part of the future of the graphical X desktop for Linux for a number of reasons:

- The software is fully Open Source and vendor neutral; commercial software may be built upon the software without purchasing a software license.
- Contributions, changes, and modifications may be made without control by a central source, and there are no licensing restrictions on making and distributing changes.

- The software supports multiple operating systems and external programming languages.
- The software works with any GNOME-aware X11 window manager, such as Enlightenment.

What Is GNOME?

GNOME is a set of software libraries and X11 clients built to support an X11 desktop environment. GNOME can be used with any GNOME-aware window manager or any window manager that will support its panel component and client features, such as drag-and-drop desktop actions. GNOME is initialized and runs before you start your window manager. Like KDE, GNOME provides a rich user environment with application frameworks, a file manager, a panel, a suite of applications with consistent look and feel, and session management, so that a working desktop is restored between X11 sessions.

GNOME Installation Components

GNOME consists of a number of software components and, for Red Hat Linux, is distributed in a series of RPM files. You can install GNOME using the `glint` control-panel X11 client or through the `rpm` command. Debian GNU/Linux also includes GNOME files; of course, in Debian, they're `deb` files. You can install GNOME using `dselect`, `dpkg`, or `apt-get`. The current distribution of GNOME at the time of this writing consists of the following files, as shown in Table 5.1. The names may vary slightly between distributions.

TABLE 5.1 GNOME Components

RPM File	*Description*
`control-center-1.0.5`	GNOME desktop control utility
`control-center-devel-1.0.5`	Development libraries to build GNOME capplets
`ee-0.3.8`	Electric Eyes image viewer
`gdm-1.0.0`	The GNOME display managers (similar to the `kdm` and `xdm` clients)
`gedit-0.5.1`	A GNOME-enabled text editor
`gedit-devel-0.5.1`	Libraries to support building plug-ins for the `gedit` client
`gmc-4.5.30`	The GNOME Midnight Commander
`gnome-audio-1.0.0-6`	Sounds for GNOME events
`gnome-audio-extra-1.0.0-6`	GNOME sounds
`gnome-core-1.0.4-34`	Thirty basic GNOME applets (programs)

RPM File	Description
gnome-core-devel-1.0.4-34	Software libraries for GNOME panel development
gnome-games-1.0.2-10	More than a dozen GNOME games
gnome-games-devel-1.0.1-1	Minimal game development libraries
gnome-libs-1.0.8-8	Required software libraries
gnome-libs-devel-1.0.8-8	GNOME software development libraries
gnome-linuxconf-0.22-1	GNOME interface for linuxconf
gnome-media-1.0.1-3	GNOME-aware multimedia clients, such as a music CD player, mixer
gnome-objc-1.0.2-4	Support libraries for GNOME Objective C clients
gnome-objc devel-1.0.2-4	Programming libraries for GNOME Objective C clients
gnome-pim-1.0.7-2	Personal information manager clients, such as `gnomecal` and `gnomecard`
gnome-pim-devel-1.0.7-2	Development support for the GNOME PIM clients
gnome-users-guide-1.0.5-4rh	Contains the GNOME users' guide
gnome-utils-1.0.1-6	At least 20 different GNOME clients, such as an editor, calculator, and other clients
gnorpm-0.8	A GNOME-enabled front-end client to version 3.0 of the `rpm` command
gnumeric-0.23	A GNOME-enabled simple spreadsheet client
gtop-1.0.1	A GNOME-enabled system monitor
pygnome-1.0.1	Python extension modules that provide GNOME support

The majority of the GNOME-specific clients for X11 are installed under the `/usr/bin` directory when you install Red Hat Linux. Systemwide configuration and support files will be installed under the `/usr/share/gnome` directory, but you may also find other GNOME client directories (such as those for `gedit`, `gnibbles`, or `gnotepad+`) under `/usr/share`.

If you'd like to get the latest software libraries, GNOME distribution, and the GNOME FAQ or download the newest GNOME applications, you can find them at `http://www.gnome.org`.

Just because Caldera does not include the GNOME software, development libraries, and the `Enlightenment` window manager, does not mean that you cannot install and run GNOME with OpenLinux. Check the `contrib` directory at `ftp://ftp.caldera.com` or download and build the GNOME libraries and Enlightment window manager from scratch.

Configuring X11 to Use the GNOME or Other Display Managers

The GNOME distribution of X11 clients and software libraries does not include a window manager. GNOME libraries and clients, such as the panel application, are designed to work with your favorite X11 window manager.

If you install Red Hat Linux, configure an XFree86 X11 server to work with your computer's graphics card, and choose to boot directly to X, you'll end up using the Enlightenment window manager with the GNOME libraries by default. Your login will be through the GNOME display manager, `gdm` (as shown in Figure 5.2). However, Red Hat Linux comes with other display managers, such as the K display manager (`kdm`), and the X display manager (`xdm`).

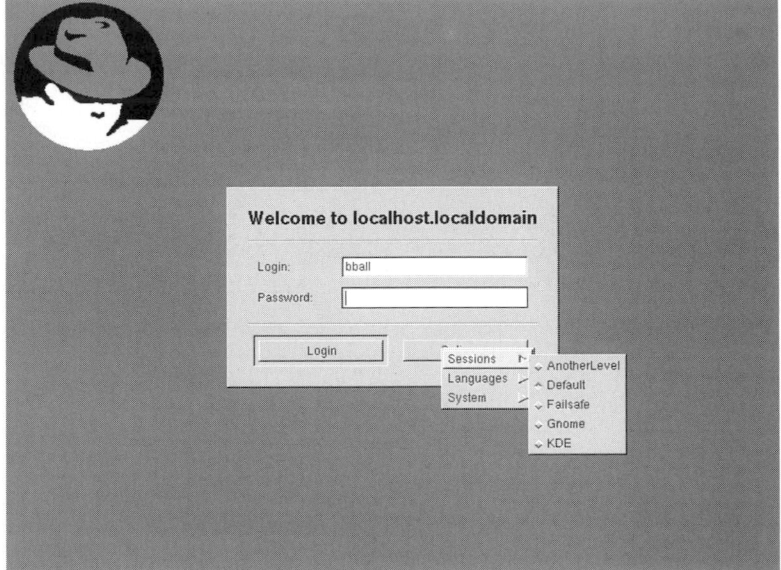

FIGURE 5.2
The GNOME gdm display manager is the default graphical login for Red Hat Linux 6.0 when booting directly to X11.

Initially you may think that the default display manager launched at startup would be according to a symbolic link named `prefdm` under the `/etc/X11` directory. If you look at the runlevel entry for runlevel 5 in your Red Hat 6.0 system initialization table, the file `/etc/inittab` shows this:

```
x:5:respawn:/etc/X11/prefdm -nodaemon
```

When you examine the `prefdm` file under the `/etc/X11` directory, you'll see this:

```
lrwxrwxrwx   1 root  root    17 May  8 11:57 /etc/X11/prefdm -> ../../
```

```
➥usr/bin/gdm
```

You may think, according to this example, that the default display manager is `gdm`. You may think all you have to do to change the default display manager is delete the `prefdm` file and then use the `ln` command to create a new symbolic link named `prefdm`, which points to `xdm` or `kdm`. This is not the case!

The `prefdm` symbolic link is created during boot up by the `rc.sysinit` script, found under `/etc/rc.d`. This script contains logic to determine the default display manager when booting. The pertinent portion of the `rc.sysinit` script looks like this:

```
# Set preferred X display manager link
preferred=
if [ -f /etc/sysconfig/desktop ]; then
        if [ -n "`grep GNOME /etc/sysconfig/desktop`" ]; then
                preferred=gdm
        elif [ -n "`grep KDE /etc/sysconfig/desktop`" ]; then
                preferred=kdm
        elif [ -n "`grep AnotherLevel /etc/sysconfig/desktop`" ]; then
                preferred=xdm
        fi
fi
```

As you can see, `rc.sysinit` first looks for a filename desktop under the `/etc/sysconfig` directory. To set the default display manager, create the desktop file under `/etc/sysconfig`, then enter a keyword such as `GNOME`, `KDE`, or `AnotherLevel`. If you further examine the `rc.sysinit` script, you'll see it then creates the `prefdm` link like this:

```
if [ -n "$preferred" ] && which $preferred >/dev/null 2>&1; then
        ln -snf ../..`which $preferred` /etc/X11/prefdm
else
        if [ ! -L /etc/X11/prefdm ]; then
                if which gdm >/dev/null 2>&1; then
                        ln -snf ../..`which gdm` /etc/X11/prefdm
                elif which kdm >/dev/null 2>&1; then
                        ln -snf ../..`which kdm` /etc/X11/prefdm
                elif which xdm >/dev/null 2>&1; then
                        ln -snf ../ ..`which xdm` /etc/X11/prefdm
                fi
        fi
fi
```

In Debian, the default window manager is stored in the file `/etc/X11/window-managers`. Simply edit that file and place the full pathname for your preferred window manager at the top and save; your preferences will take effect the next time you start X.

If you want to use `gdm`, simply run the following:

```
apt-get install gdm
```

The default *Session*, or type of window manager launched by the gdm display manager, is defined in the /etc/X11/gdm directory. If you examine the Sessions directory under /etc/X11/gdm, you'll see this:

```
AnotherLevel  Default  Failsafe  Gnome  KDE  default
This list can vary between distributions.
```

Most of these files are short shell scripts and show up under the Sessions drop-down menu in the gdm dialog box. The scripts use the Xsession command, found under the /etc/X11/xdm directory, to start a particular X session.

For example, the AnotherLevel session script contains:

```
#!/bin/bash -login
/etc/X11/xdm/Xsession anotherlevel
```

If you examine the Xsession script, you'll find this section:

```
case $# in
1)
    case $1 in
    failsafe)
        exec xterm -geometry 80x24-0-0
        ;;
    gnome)
        exec gnome-session
        ;;
    kde)
        exec startkde
        ;;
    anotherlevel)
        # we assume that switchdesk is installed.
        exec /usr/share/apps/switchdesk/Xclients.anotherlevel
        ;;
    esac
esac
```

This shows the different commands used to start your X session after selection through a display manager. Note that the Failsafe session only launches the xterm client.

Note

For more information about shell scripts and shell programming, see Chapter 25, "Shell Programming."

If you do not use a display manager to log in to Linux and you want to use GNOME for your X session, your .xinitrc should contain the following entry:

```
exec gnome-session
```

You would then use the `startx` command to start your X session:

```
# startx
```

The session will start the major GNOME components—such as the panel (a taskbar client from which to access root menus, configure your desktop, or launch X11 clients)—along with desktop, keyboard, and mouse control software. Finally, the Enlightenment window manager is launched. Figure 5.3 shows what your X11 desktop might look like with several clients running.

FIGURE 5.3
The X11 desktop using the GNOME environment uses a panel, and nearly all clients provide common features, such as menus and toolbars.

Using GNOME Clients and Tools

The most obvious and first GNOME client you'll see is the panel client, which offers a taskbar at the bottom of your X desktop. From the `root` menu of the taskbar (displayed by pressing the left mouse button, or mouse button 1 on the GNOME button), you can launch a variety of other GNOME clients:

Applications	Editors, browsers, and productivity clients, such as `gnomecard` or the Gnumeric spreadsheet
Games	Such as Mahjongg, Yahtzee, Mines
Graphics	Editors such as Electric Eyes or the GIMP
Internet	FTP, electronic mail, and other clients, such as Netscape

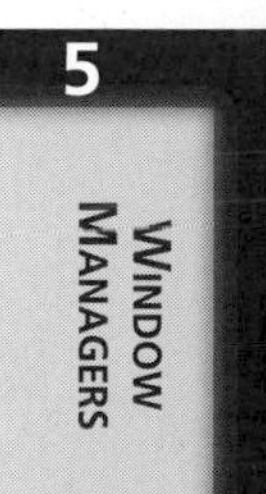

Multimedia	Audio CD players, mixers and sound utilities
System	Change password, finger information, and manage software
Settings	Wallpaper or screensaver settings, mouse handling, keyboard configuration, session management, menu editing, and general desktop controls
Utilities	Various terminal clients and system utilities
File Manager	The GNU Midnight Commander, a graphic desktop file manager
Help	To get help on GNOME
Run program	A command-line dialog box
AnotherLevel Menus	A submenu system from other window managers that includes traditional X11 clients
KDE Menus	A submenu system providing access to KDE clients
Panel	The panel's configuration and control menu
Lock screen	To lock (password protect) the desktop
About	About the GNOME Panel dialog box
About GNOME	About GNOME dialog box
Log out	To end your X11 session

Note

The desktop panel menu described here applies to Red Hat Linux 6.0's GNOME environment. If you install GNOME and use it with another window manager, your menus will certainly be different.

Because many of the GNOME clients are installed in the Linux file system in the normal places (such as the `/bin`, `/usr/bin`, or `/usr/X11R6/bin` directories), you can also start them from the command line of an X11 terminal window. You'll quickly recognize a GNOME client because most clients follow the GNOME style guide. This guide stipulates that each program should have supporting documentation and each client should have a File and Help menu, with an Exit menu item on the File menu and an About menu item on the Help menu (see Figure 5.4).

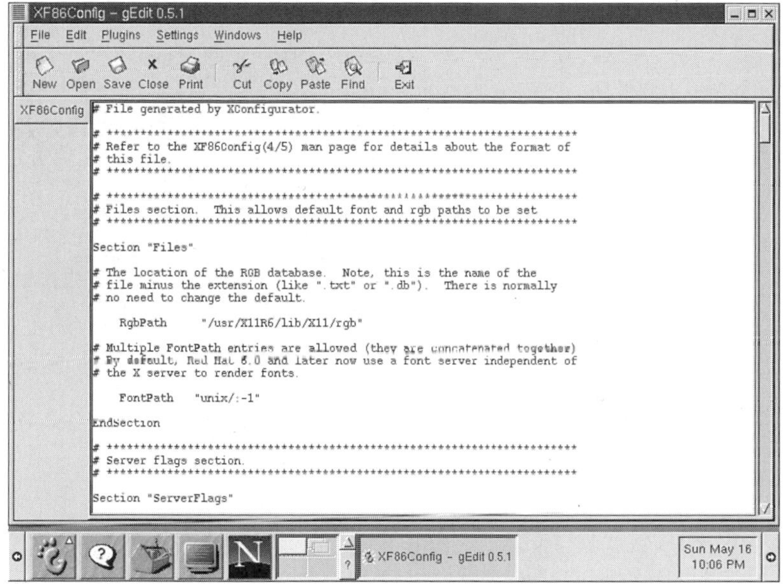

FIGURE 5.4
GNOME clients, such as the gEdit editor, generally have a consistent interface with a standard menu and toolbar.

Other features in common among many GNOME clients include tear-off menus and toolbars. To tear off a menu bar, click and drag the mottled, vertical rectangle on the left end of the menu bar. The bar will drag with your mouse pointer. You can use this approach to rearrange the order of the controls of a GNOME client (such as placing the menubar of a terminal at the bottom of the terminal window), or placing controls as floating tool windows beside a client's window. Each client will remember the toolbar or menu bar settings between launches.

Configuring Your Desktop with the GNOME Control Center

The GNOME Control Center, shown in Figure 5.5, configures your system and desktop. The Control Center can be started by clicking the GNOME Configuration tool button on the desktop panel, or by clicking the panel menu, selecting Settings, and then clicking the GNOME Control Center menu item.

For example, to configure your desktop's background, launch the Control Center and then click the Background item, or *capplet*, under the Desktop group in the left side of the Control Center's window. The right side of the Control Center will clear, and you'll have access to a dialog box (as shown in Figure 5.5) to configure your desktop's background color or wallpaper.

FIGURE 5.5
Use the GNOME Control Center to configure your system and session's desktop.

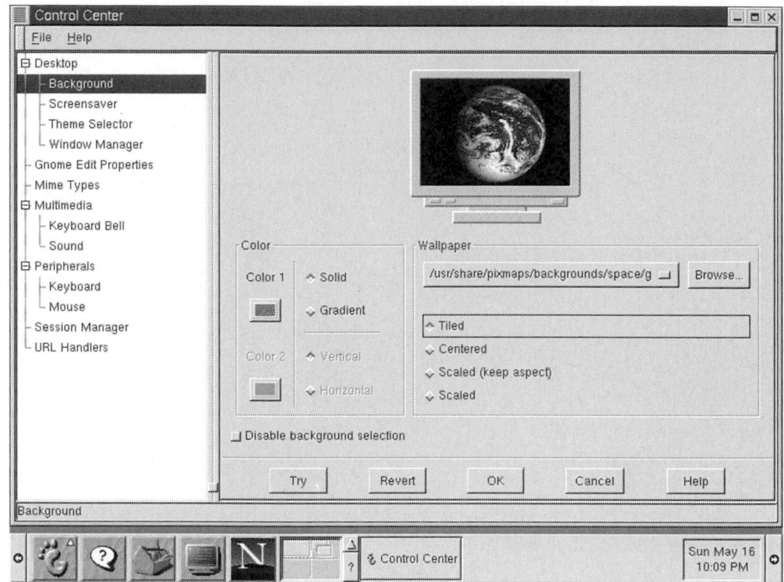

You can radically change your desktop's appearance by selecting other controls, such as the Theme Selector. The GNOME libraries included with Red Hat Linux 6.0 include 11 different *themes*, or color and decoration schemes you can use with the currently running window manager. Another way to alter your desktop is to change the current window manager on-the-fly through the Window Manager capplet.

By default, only Enlightenment and Window Maker are included as alternative window managers. However, you can add others, such as the AnotherLevel configuration of `fvwm2`, `AfterStep`, `fvwm`, or `twm`. Start the Control Center, then click the Window Manager capplet. In the Window Manager dialog box (as shown in Figure 5.6), click the Add button and then type in the name of the window manager in the Name field. Next, type in the complete pathname and command line used to run the window manager in the Command field. If the window manager has a configuration tool, enter the complete pathname and necessary command-line options to the Configuration Command field. Do not click the Window Manager Is Session Managed button unless you are absolutely sure that the window manager is GNOME-aware. When finished, click the OK button.

You can then try your new choice by highlighting the name of the new window manager and clicking the Try button in the Window Manager dialog box.

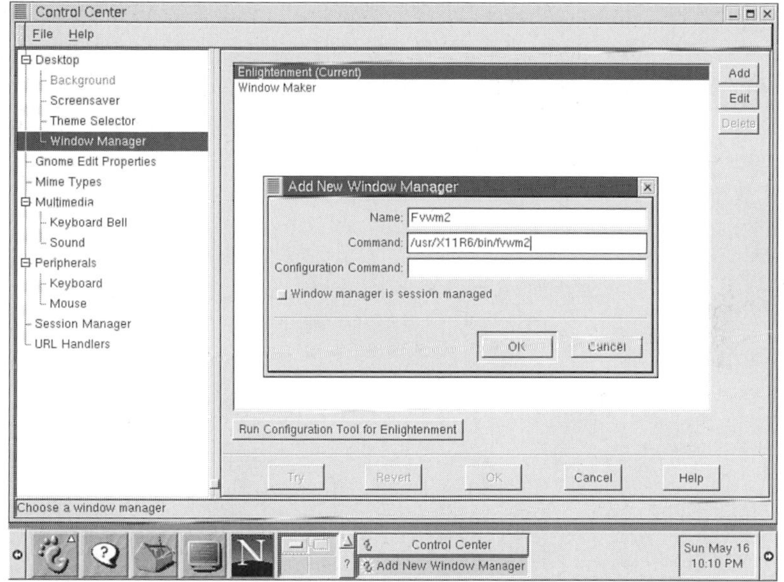

FIGURE 5.6
The Window Manager capplet in the GNOME Control Center may be used to switch window managers on-the-fly, or even add new window manager choices.

> **Note**
>
> The GNOME Control Center houses many types of desktop settings in one convenient dialog box, but you should know that you can also launch the individual settings capplets from the Settings menu on the GNOME desktop. These capplets (and other clients) cover desktop, sound, keyboard, and mouse settings, along with menu editing of the GNOME panel.

GNOME Panel Configuration

The GNOME Panel is an application and menu launcher for the GNOME desktop. By default, the panel is home for a number of important desktop elements, such as

- System menus for a dozen categories of clients and including menus for the AnotherLevel window manager and KDE desktop
- GNOME help
- GNOME configuration
- Virtual desktop navigation through the GNOME pager
- A taskbar container for currently running applications
- The date and time

The panel is configured by clicking the Panel menu item on the panel's pop-up menu, or by right-clicking a blank area of the panel. The pop-up Panel menu, shown in Figure 5.7, offers a choice of 10 different configuration settings. You can create new panels on the top, bottom, left, or right edges of the display, and add or remove menus, drawers (to contain launcher applets), icons, or other applications. If you need a bit more screen real estate, click the Hide Panel button on either end of the panel to minimize or maximize the panel.

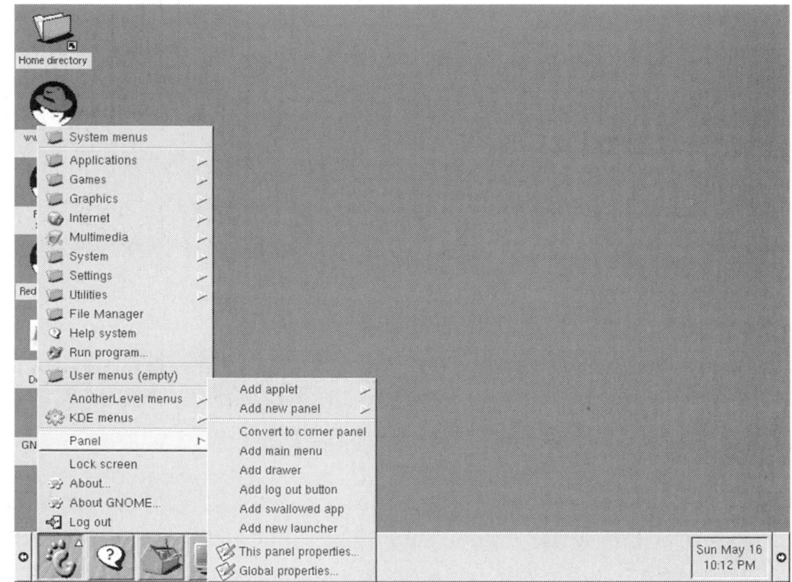

FIGURE 5.7
The Panel menu configures the appearance, contents, and location of your GNOME desktop's panel.

Launcher applets may be added to the panel in at least two ways. One way is to use GNOME's drag-and-drop. Use the GNU Midnight Commander to navigate to a directory containing various commands, such as `/usr/bin`. Next, drag an icon of a command, such as e-conf from the icon view window and drop the command directly on your desktop's panel. The Create Launcher applet appears, as shown in Figure 5.8.

Type in a name for the command as well as a short comment. If the command usually runs inside a terminal window or from the console, click the Run in Terminal button. You can also assign an icon if you click the Icon button; a visual directory of the `/usr/share/pixmap` directory will appear. When finished, click the OK button. A new icon will appear on your panel.

Panel elements such as icons can be changed, moved, or removed directly on the panel. Right-click an element and a small pop-up menu appears with several selections.

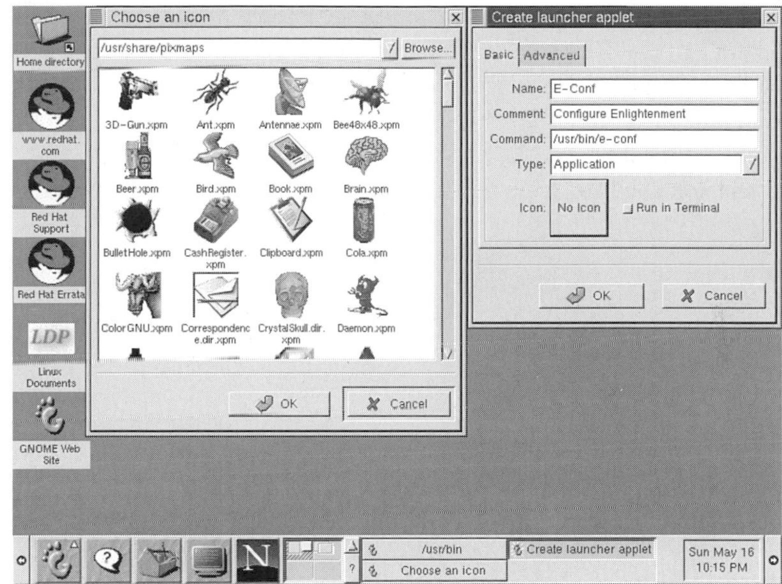

FIGURE 5.8
The Create Launcher applet dialog box is a handy way to create customized applications (with icons) for your GNOME desktop's panel.

Features of the Enlightenment Window Manager

The Enlightenment window manager, also known as E, is the default GNOME-aware window manager used by Red Hat Linux for X11 sessions and is also an option for Debianusers. This is one of the newest window managers available for X11, and has been specifically configured to work well with the GNOME libraries.

The systemwide E configuration file are stored under the `/usr/share/enlightenment` directory. However, you'll find an `.enlightenment` directory installed in your home directory the first time you use this window manager. This directory is used to store the currently used E *theme*, or window-management and decoration settings. Theme settings are only one of eight different settings categories used by E. Others include

- Basic options, such as window movement, resizing, and focus
- Virtual screen settings, such as the number and separation
- Window, pointer, and ToolTip behavior
- Sound effects for window operations
- Special effects for window, desktop, and menu animation
- Distinct background settings for desktops
- Keyboard shortcuts for nearly 80 actions, such as window handling, desktop navigation, or cursor movement

There are at least three ways to launch the Enlightenment configuration editor. One way is through the Configuration Tool button in the GNOME Control Center's Window Manager capplet. Another way is to press the middle mouse button (a simultaneous left and right button press for two-button mouse users) in a blank area of the desktop, and then to click the Enlightenment Configuration menu item from the pop-up GNOME menu. Yet another way is to start the editor, e-conf, from the command line of a terminal window like this:

```
# e-conf &
```

After you press the Enter key, you'll see the Enlightenment Configuration Editor, as shown in Figure 5.9.

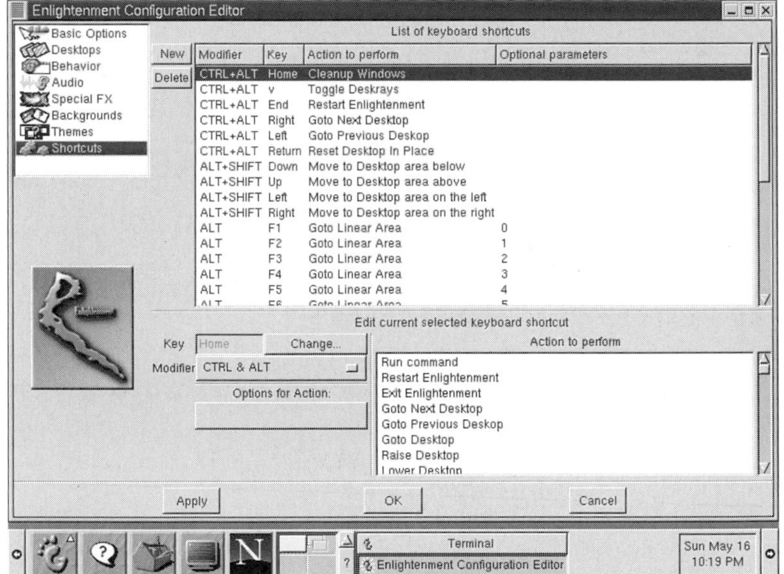

FIGURE 5.9
The Enlightenment Configuration Editor is a complex tool, offering more than 130 different settings and configurations of the E window manager.

Features of the K Desktop Environment

One of the newest X11 window managers for Linux is the K Desktop Environment. However, KDE is much more than an X11 window manager—it is a complete desktop environment with more than 150 clients with a consistent interface, much like those included with GNOME.

KDE is the default X11 window manager and desktop environment for OpenLinux. This section also highlights the differences between the Red Hat and OpenLinux KDE installations.

KDE supports many of the features you'd expect in a modern desktop environment, including those commonly found in commercial software libraries such as Motif, and the Common Desktop Environment, or CDE (which is now only offered by one vendor, Xi-Graphics, for Linux). These features include

- A suite of personal productivity tools, such as disk and network utilities, designed to use the desktop interface; these tools have the capability to import and export data to other tools
- Session management, so open applications and window positions are remembered between sessions
- "Sticky Buttons" to put an application or window on every desktop
- Network Transparent Access, or NTA, so you can click or drag and drop a graphic document's icon in an FTP window to display or transfer the graphic
- Pop-up menus and built-in help for nearly any desktop action and KDE client
- A desktop trash can for safer file deletions
- Graphic configuration of your system's desktop, keyboard, mouse, and sound
- Programs and other data represented as icons on the desktop or in windows with folder icons
- Drag-and-drop actions (such as copy, link, move, and delete) for files and devices

KDE Installation Components

Although KDE can be downloaded in source form from `http://www.kde.org`, you'll usually find one of the latest distributions included with your Linux distribution. KDE and other KDE clients are usually installed from precompiled binaries in RPM files.

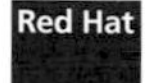

Red Hat includes KDE 1.1.1, consisting of the following RPM files:

`kdeadmin-1.1.1pre2-1`	KDE system administration tools
`kdebase-1.1.1pre2-2`	KDE's window manager and other base clients, such as `kdehelp`
`kdegames-1.1.1pre2-2`	More than a dozen KDE games, such as ksame
`kdegraphics-1.1.1pre2-2`	KDE graphics clients, such as `kghostview`
`kdelibs-1.1.1pre2-2`	Shared software libraries
`kdemultimedia-1.1.1pre2-2`	KDE media and sound clients, such as the `kscd` audio CD player

`kdenetwork-1.1.1pre2-2`	KDE network clients and utilities
`kdesupport-1.1.1pre2-2`	Software support libraries
`korganizer-1.1.1pre2-1`	A KDE calendar and scheduling productivity client
`kpilot-3.1b8_pgb-1`	KDE communications and synchronization client for Palm PDAs
`kppload-1.04-4`	PPP load monitor client
`kdeutils-1.1.1pre2-1`	Various KDE utilities, such as the `kvt` or `konsole` emulators

Unlike other distributions, such as OpenLinux, KDE 1.1.1 clients under Red Hat Linux 6.0 are installed in the `/usr/bin` directory, with support and configuration files stored under the `/usr/share` directory. KDE may be installed during your initial Red Hat Linux installation, or afterward using the `gnorpm` or `rpm` commands. Most disappointing for Red Hat Linux KDE developers is the fact that Red Hat Linux 6.0 does not include the required files to build new KDE clients or to upgrade the existing KDE distribution from scratch.

OpenLinux 2.2 includes a mix of KDE 1.1 and KDE 1.1.1 components, consisting of the following RPM files:

`kdeapps-1.1-6`	Various KDE clients
`kdebase-1.1-13`	KDE's window manager and other base clients, such as `kdehelp`
`kdebase-opengl-1.1-13`	OpenGL support for KDE
`kdedoc-990211-1`	KDE documentation (`.html`)
`kdegames-1.1-1`	More than a dozen KDE games, such as ksame
`kdegraphics-1.1-1`	KDE graphics clients, such as `kghostview`
`kdelibs-1.1-2`	Shared software libraries
`kdelibs-devel-1.1-2`	Shared software libraries development support
`kdelibs-doc-1.1-2`	KDE software libraries documentation
`kdemultimedia-1.1-2`	KDE media and sound clients, such as the `kscd` audio CD player
`kdenetwork-1.1-2`	KDE network clients and utilities
`kdestart-1.1-14`	KDE replacement for `startx` script
`kdesupport-1.1-1`	Software support libraries
`kdesupport-devel-1.1.1`	Development support clients
`kdesupport-devel-static-1.1.1`	Development support for building static KDE clients
`kdethemes-2.0.0-1`	Themes for the KDE desktop

`kdetoys-1.1-1`	Fun, but non-essential KDE clients
`klyx-0.9.9-1`	WYSIWYG LaTeX KDE word processor
`korganizer-1.1.1-1`	A KDE calendar and scheduling productivity client
`kpackage-1.1.2-2`	Graphic RPM file-management client
`kpilot-3.0.2-2`	KDE communications and synchronization client for Palm PDAs
`kquery-0.9-2`	CGI script support for KDE searches
`ktop-0.9.9-1`	Graphic KDE system monitor client
`kdeutils-1.1-2`	Various KDE utilities, such as the `kvt` or `konsole` emulators

Caldera OpenLinux supports a much richer KDE experience out of the box compared to other Linux distributions. Support is included for local development of new KDE clients or to easily upgrade an existing desktop distribution. Under OpenLinux, the suite of KDE clients is installed in the `/opt/kde` directory, with systemwide support and configuration files stored under the `/opt/kde/share` directory.

Logging In with `kdm`

The `kdm`, or K display manager (shown in Figure 5.10), is KDE's replacement of `xdm` or `gdm`. Using `kdm` is one way to boot directly to X and KDE after you start your computer.

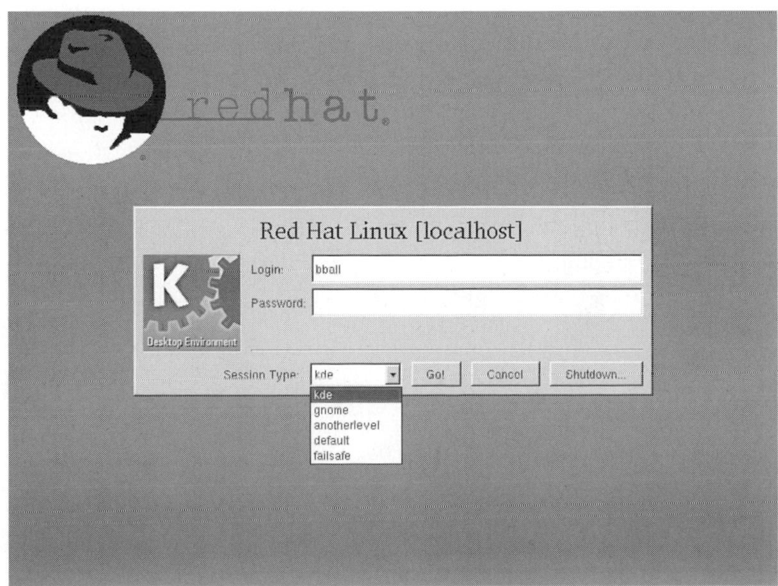

FIGURE 5.10
The K display manager manages logins and desktop sessions when you boot directly to X11.

The K display manager, `kdm`, is the default graphical login when you install and then boot OpenLinux. The OpenLinux system initialization table, `/etc/inittab`, is preconfigured to use `kdm` and to boot OpenLinux to runlevel 5 with this entry:

```
# Default runlevel
id:5:initdefault
```

The pertinent runlevel entry in the OpenLinux `/etc/inittab` file follows:

```
kdm:5:respawn:/opt/kde/bin/kdm -nodaemon > /var/log/kdm 2>&1
```

To log in, click your username's icon and type in your password. Like `gdm`, `kdm` offers a choice of session type. Click the drop-down menu by the `kdm` Session Type field and then click the Go! button to log in to your favorite desktop environment.

The default OpenLinux sessions are defined in the file `Xsession` under the `/etc/X11/kdm` directory.

To shut down, reboot your computer, or restart your X server, click the Shutdown button on the `kdm` dialog box and select the desired action.

Features of the KDE Desktop

The KDE desktop is an alternative X11 session offered through the `gdm` client's Options, Sessions menu or `kdm` client's Session Type menu. If you do not use a display manager to boot directly to X after starting Red Hat Linux, you can start KDE manually from the command line of your console. Insert the command `startkde` in the `.xinitrc` file in your home directory, and then start X11 with the `startx` command:

```
# startx
```

The screen will clear and you'll see a desktop similar to that shown in Figure 5.11. When KDE first starts, a `Desktop` and `.kde` directory will be created in your home directory (according to the skeleton file system configuration under the `/etc/skel` directory). Changes, configurations, or modifications to your desktop or KDE clients will be saved under your `.kde` directory. The `Desktop` is a directory representing your home folder under the KDE desktop (as shown in Figure 5.11).

Performing Basic Desktop Actions

When you first start KDE, you see the `kfm`, or K file manager window, and a `root` display, or desktop, as shown in Figure 5.11.

FIGURE 5.11
The KDE is one of the most popular of the newer desktop environments for the X Window System and Linux.

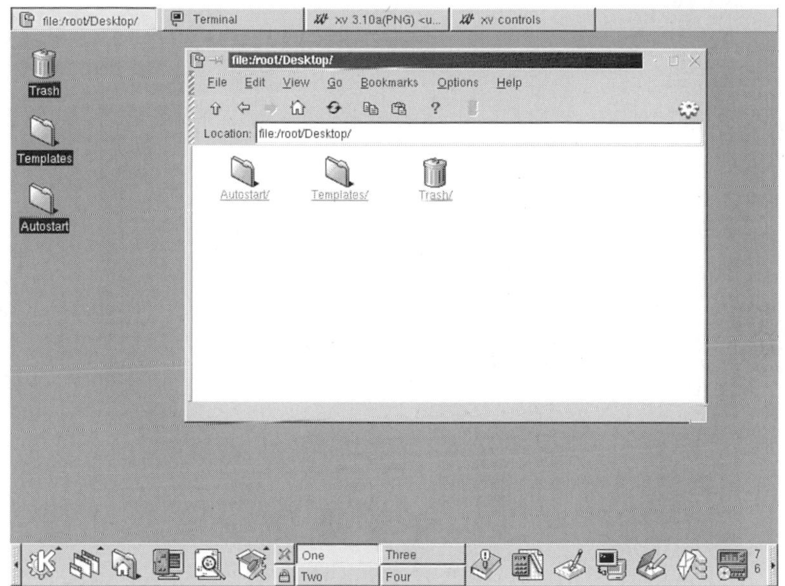

The KDE desktop consists of several elements: a *taskbar* across the top of display, the `root` background (or *root display*), and the *desktop panel* along the bottom of your screen. In the panel, starting from the left, is the *Application Starter* button (the large K), followed by several icons representing different applications, folders, and directories. There are four buttons representing the default four *virtual desktops*, or displays, followed by more application icons.

Using Desktop Panel

The KDE panel, like the GNOME panel, is used to hold the Application Starter menu (accessed when you click the Application Starter menu), other application icons, the screen lock or logout button, virtual desktop buttons, and other program icons. KDE uses a separate taskbar, unlike the GNOME panel, to store buttons of currently running clients.

To change the panel's size or orientation, click the Application Starter button, select Panel, and then click Configure. You can also right-click a blank area of the panel to access the Configuration dialog box, as shown in Figure 5.12. You can select different settings. When you're finished, click Apply and OK.

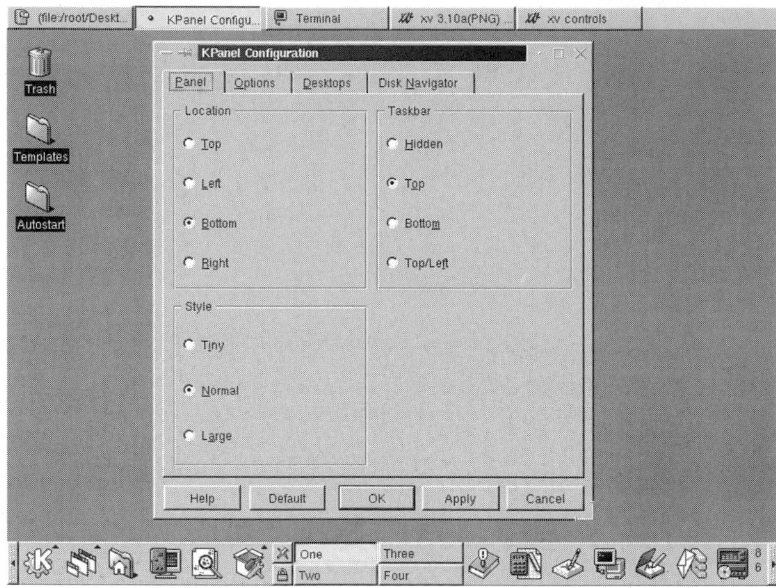

FIGURE 5.12
The Panel Configuration dialog box is used to change the panel and taskbar appearance and location.

If you want to change how icons are placed or arranged on the panel, right-click a desired icon, and then select Remove (to delete the item) or Move from the small pop-up menu. If you click Move, you can drag the icon across the panel to a different place. If the panel is getting in the way during your KDE session, click the small button to the far left or right of the panel to temporarily hide the panel from your screen. To restore the panel, click the small button again.

Editing the KDE Panel Menu

To edit the desktop's panel menus, click the Application Starter button, select Panel, and then click Edit Menus. The KDE Menu Editor dialog box appears as shown in Figure 5.13. If you're logged in as the `root` operator, you can change and edit menu items on the panel menus by using drag-and-drop to shift items in the menu list or create items using the Empty menu item.

Tip

If you're logged in as a regular user, you can only change menu items for which you have permission. If you right-click a KDE panel item, you see the message `! PROTECTED Button !`. You can, however, edit a single applink menu item in your desktop's panel. To this menu, you can add nearly any other command or client.

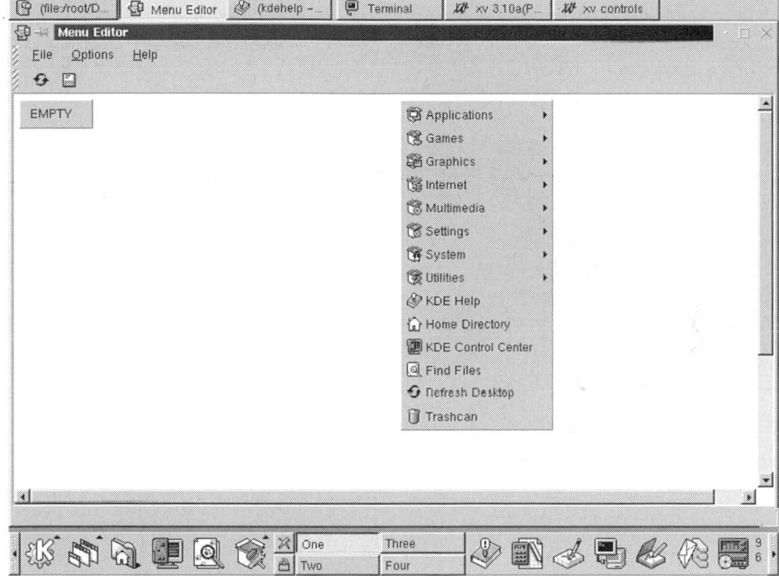

FIGURE 5.13
The panel Menu Editor enables you to add or remove menu items from the panel's menus.

Using the `kfm` File Manager

The K file manager, or `kfm`, is at the center of KDE's magic. This file manager provides a usable desktop where you can drag, drop, multiple-select, copy, move, or delete icons of data files or programs. Many of the desktop actions supported by `kfm` become apparent when you drag or right-click a file's icon.

The `kfm` root display, which includes your home directory and your `root` display (as shown in Figure 5.11), is represented by the directory named `Desktop` in your home directory. If you drag files to this folder, the files' icons appear on your `root` display. Similarly, if you drag a file from another folder or directory to the desktop, it appears in your `Desktop` directory.

Configuring KDE with the KDE Control Center

The KDE Control Center is the main dialog box through which you can change numerous settings of your desktop, get system information (such as the currently mounted devices and capacities), or (if logged in as the `root` operator) configure and control KDE's appearance, background, fonts, and sessions for all users.

Click the Application Starter button on your desktop's panel, and then click KDE Control Center to display the Control Center dialog box. The main dialog box appears, as shown in Figure 5.14.

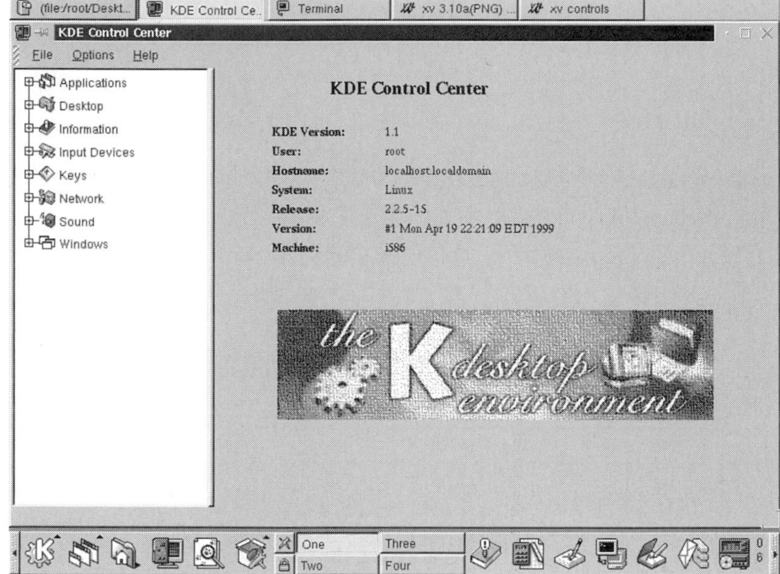

FIGURE 5.14
The KDE Control Center dialog box provides access to many different controls of your system's KDE sessions.

Using Display Manager Options

Use the Login Manager item under the Applications group in the Control Center to change the appearance or contents of the `kdm` login dialog box. You must be logged in as the `root` operator to access this portion of the Control Center, but you can get around this limitation without logging out of the current KDE session. Open a terminal window and type the **`su`** command, followed by the **`kcontrol`** client, on the command line:

```
# su -c kcontrol &
```

The Login Manager dialog box, shown in Figure 5.15, enables you to change how the `kdm` login dialog box appears when you set Linux to boot directly to X. You can change the greeting strings, the type of logo used (by dragging and dropping an icon onto the logo), and even the language used for your KDE sessions. By clicking different tabs at the top of the dialog box, you can change the fonts, background, icons for users (perhaps using a scanned image of a person's face?), and sessions using other window managers. After you make your changes, click the Apply button.

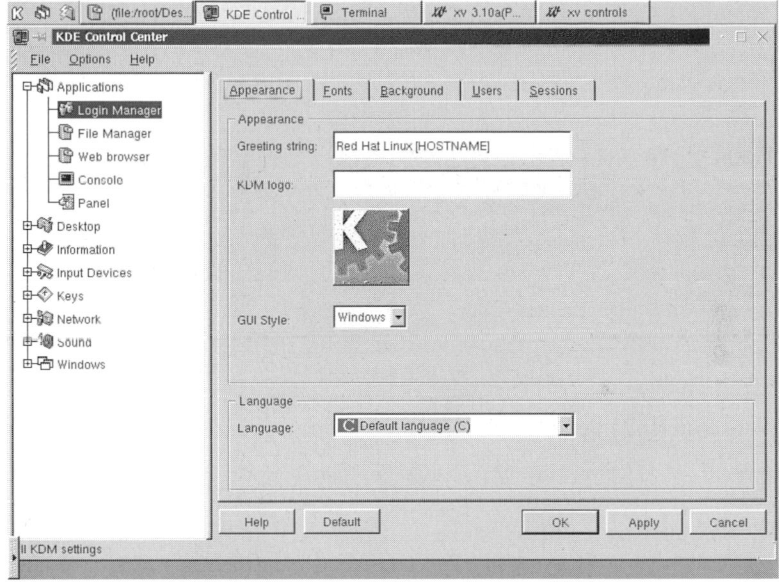

FIGURE 5.15
Use the Login Manager dialog box to change `kdm`*'s login screen and session settings.*

You can also control which users are permitted to log in. Click the Users tab in the Login Manager dialog box. The Users dialog box appears, as shown in Figure 5.16. To selectively control user logins, click the Show Only Selected Users button and then click and add users to the Selected Users section of the dialog box using the >> button.

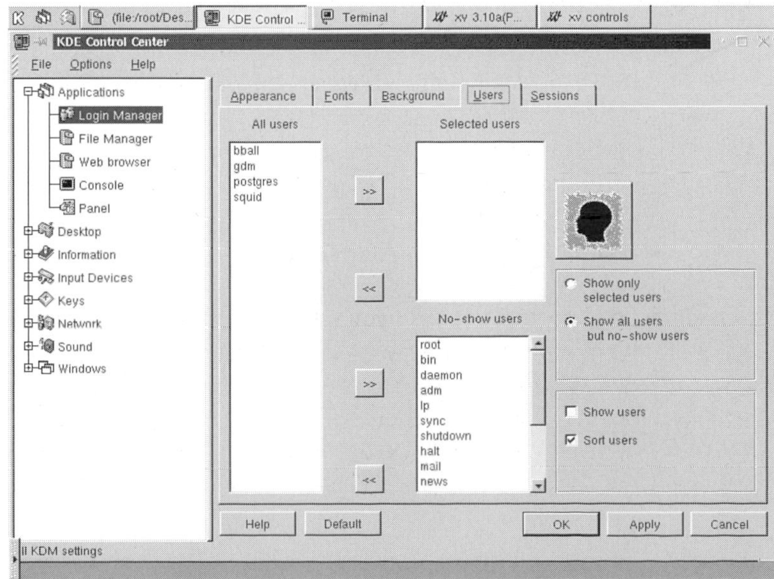

FIGURE 5.16
The Users dialog box can control who is permitted to log in to Linux through `kdm`*.*

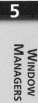

To control reboot or shutdown through the `kdm` login screen, click the Sessions tab of the Login Manager dialog box and then click the Allow to Shutdown drop-down menu. Select None, All, Root Only, or Console Only. When finished, click the Apply button.

Changing Your Desktop's Wallpaper

KDE comes with nearly 150 different wallpapers to fill the `root` display or to background of your desktop. To configure the current desktop's wallpaper, right-click a blank area of the desktop and select Display properties. You can also click the drop-down Desktop menu in the Control Center and then click Background. Additionally, you can click the Application Starter button on the desktop panel, and select Settings, Desktop, Background.

All default KDE wallpapers are in JPEG format. Under Red Hat Linux 6.0, they are stored under the `/usr/share/wallpapers` directory. Many of these wallpapers look best when used with a display using thousands of colors. Although the default KDE wallpapers are in JPEG format, other graphics formats may be used. Look under the `/usr/share/pixmaps/backgrounds/tiles` directory for nearly two dozen images suitable in tiled format as a background. You'll find 6 directories of 230 swirling, colorful images under the `/usr/share/pixmaps/backgrounds/Propaganda` directory. You'll also find an excellent selection of stunning NASA photos under the `/usr/share/pixmaps/backgrounds/space` directory.

OpenLinux users should browse to the `/opt/kde/share/wallpapers` directory to change the KDE desktop wallpaper.

The Background dialog box, shown in Figure 5.17, enables you to set the name of each desktop, each desktop's colors, and whether the desktop uses a wallpaper. To set a different wallpaper, click the Wallpaper pop-up menu in the Wallpaper section of the dialog box and then click Apply. A random setting may be used to show wallpapers on the desktop from different directories in different order and at specified intervals.

Changing Your Screensaver

KDE comes with 20 different screensavers. To configure a screensaver for your KDE desktop, click Screensaver from the Desktop drop-down menu in the KDE Control Center. You can also click the Application Starter button on the desktop panel, and then select Settings, Desktop, Screensaver. As another alternative method, you can right-click a blank area of your desktop and then click the Screensaver tab in the Display settings dialog box.

FIGURE 5.17
Use the Background dialog box to set your desktop's name, colors, and wallpaper.

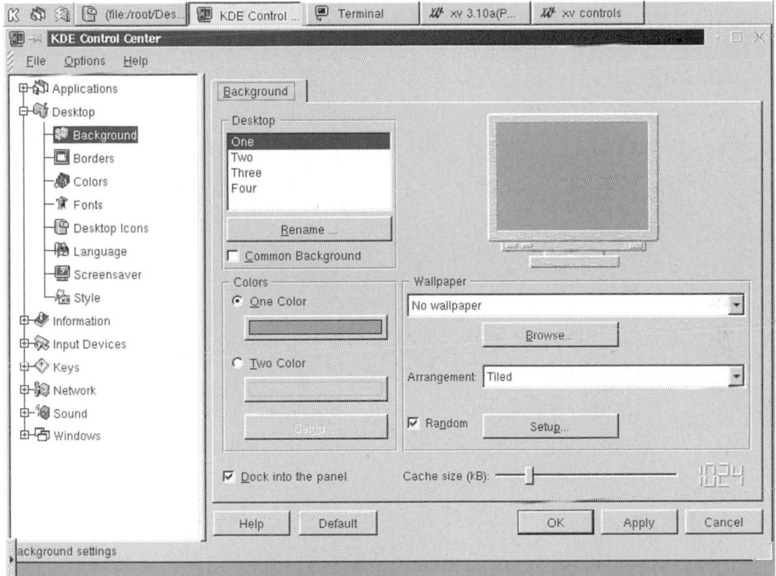

The Screensaver dialog box, shown in Figure 5.18, has a number of settings, such as the type of screensaver, the time delay before activating the screensaver, a random setting to cycle through installed screensavers, and whether you want to require a password to go back to work. After you make your changes, click the Apply button; click OK to close the dialog box.

FIGURE 5.18
The Screensaver dialog box has different settings you can use to test a screensaver, set a time delay, or require a password.

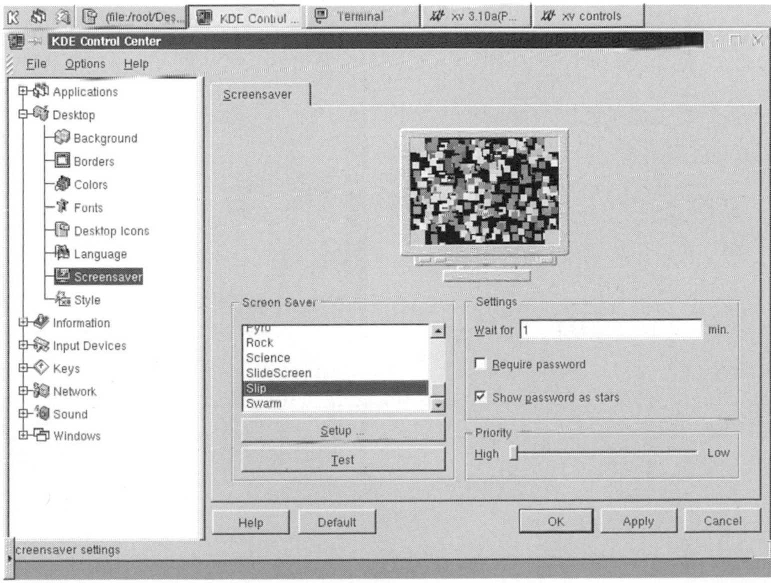

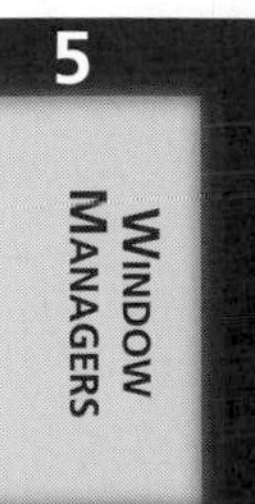

> **Note**
>
> Right-click different corners of the sample display in the Screensaver dialog box to set automatic screen-saving or screen-locking! A small pop-up menu appears, and you can select Ignore, Save Screen, or Lock Screen for each corner. For example, if you set the lower-left corner of the sample display to start screen saving, the next time you move your mouse pointer into the left corner of the display (and leave it there for a second), screen saving starts.

Installing System Sounds

Click the Sound drop-down menu in the KDE Control Center, and then click System Sounds to configure KDE to use sound during your X sessions. KDE recognizes 27 separate system events to which you can assign a sound. For example, to have KDE play a sound when it first starts, click Enable Systems Sounds in the Sound dialog box (shown in Figure 5.19), and then click the Startup system event.

Under OpenLinux, KDE sounds are located in the `/opt/kde/share/sounds` directory.

You can then either drag the icon of a sound file into the Sounds area of the dialog box or click an existing sound from the list of sounds. When finished, click the Apply button. You hear the sound file play the next time you start KDE.

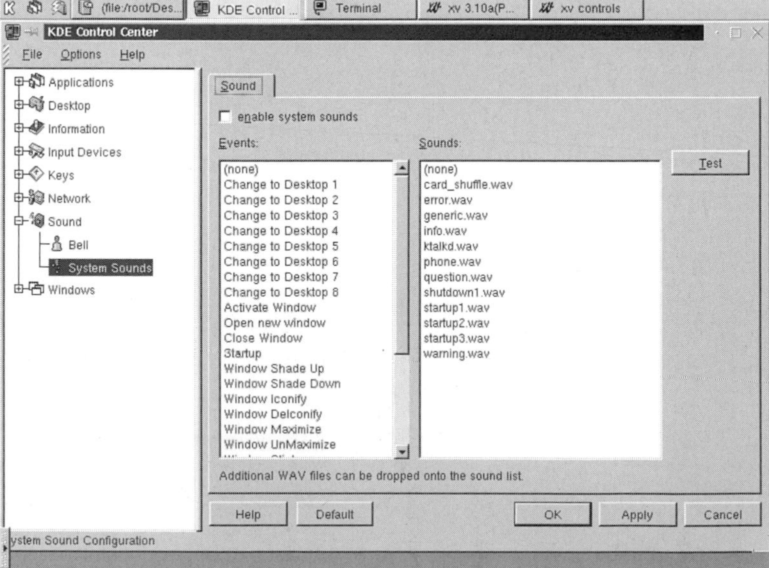

FIGURE 5.19
The Sound dialog box is used to assign sounds to different session events, such as window changes.

Note

At the time of this writing, KDE sounds must be in .wav format. If you've installed StarOffice 5.0, a full directory of various sounds is located under the `Office50/gallery/sounds` directory. Navigate to the `Sounds` directory through your home directory, then drag the file `Applause.wav` into the Sound dialog box, click the Startup event, and then click Apply. The next time you start KDE, you'll hear applause!

Changing Keyboard and Mouse Settings

Click Keyboard from the Input Devices drop-down menu in the KDE Control Center to toggle keyboard character repeat (repeated printing of a character when a key is held down), and whether each key-press generates a key-click sound. Click the Apply button (shown in Figure 5.20) when you finish with your selection.

FIGURE 5.20
The Keyboard dialog box toggles Keyboard repeat and key-click sounds.

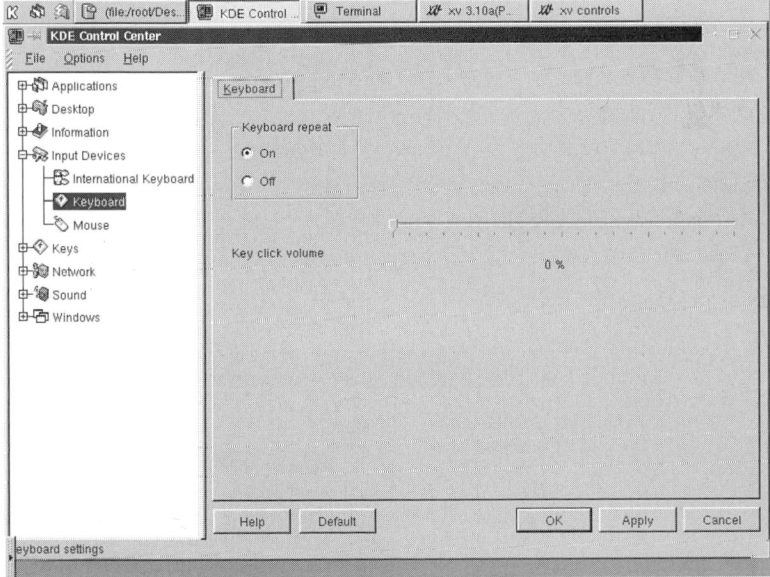

You can also access keyboard and mouse settings through the Input Devices submenu off the Settings panel menu. The Mouse dialog box lets you change how fast your mouse cursor moves across the screen and the sequence of mouse buttons for right- or left-handed users. This dialog box (shown in Figure 5.21) offers functions similar to using the `xset` and `xmodmap` commands from the command line.

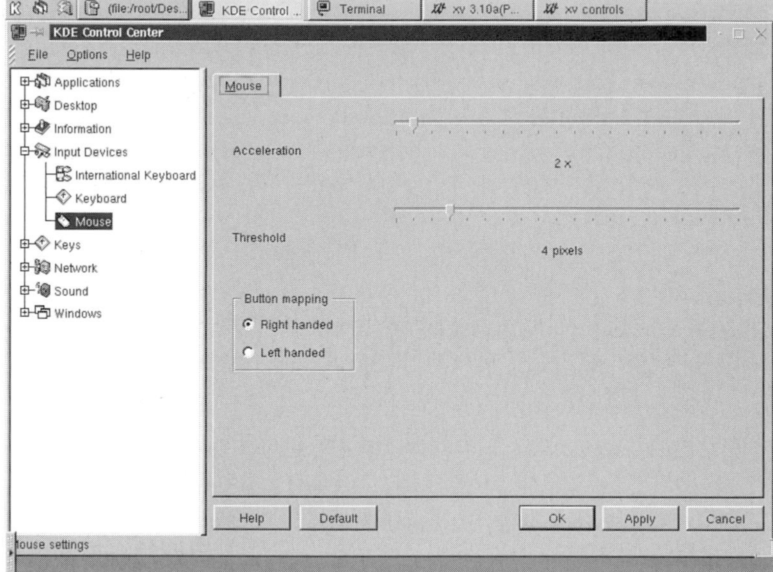

FIGURE 5.21
Left-handed mouse users can benefit from KDE's flexible mouse configuration!

Changing Window Buttons

Click the Windows drop-down menu to access the Buttons, Mouse, Properties, and Titlebar dialog boxes. You can also click the Application Starter button on the desktop panel and then select Settings and Windows to get to these settings. Toggle respective buttons under Left, Right, or Off in the Button dialog box, shown in Figure 5.22, to add, remove, or place different window controls. The sample window's buttons will change according to your selection!

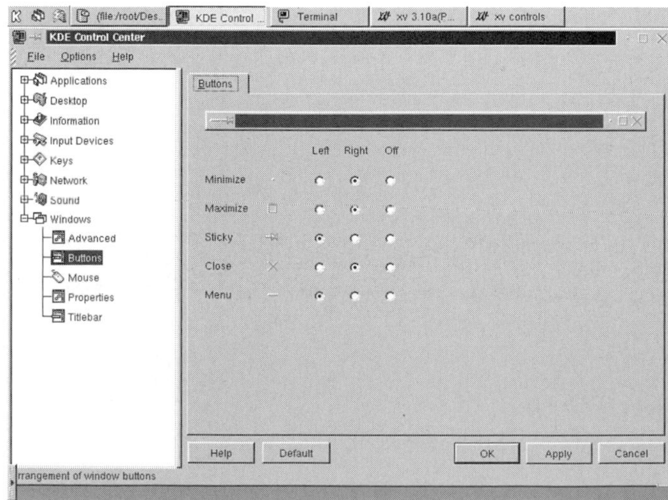

FIGURE 5.22
Use the Buttons dialog box to change the appearance of all windows during your KDE sessions.

In the Titlebar dialog box shown in Figure 5.23, click different buttons to change how KDE windows' title bars appear (controlling elements such as shading or whether a picture is used). Drag the Title Animation slider to change how fast a window's title moves back and forth for a KDE client (when the title is wider than the window's title bar). The Mouse action pop-up menu is used to set how windows react when you double-click in the title bar. (The default setting might use a "window shade" effect, but normally under X11, a window enlarges or shrinks.)

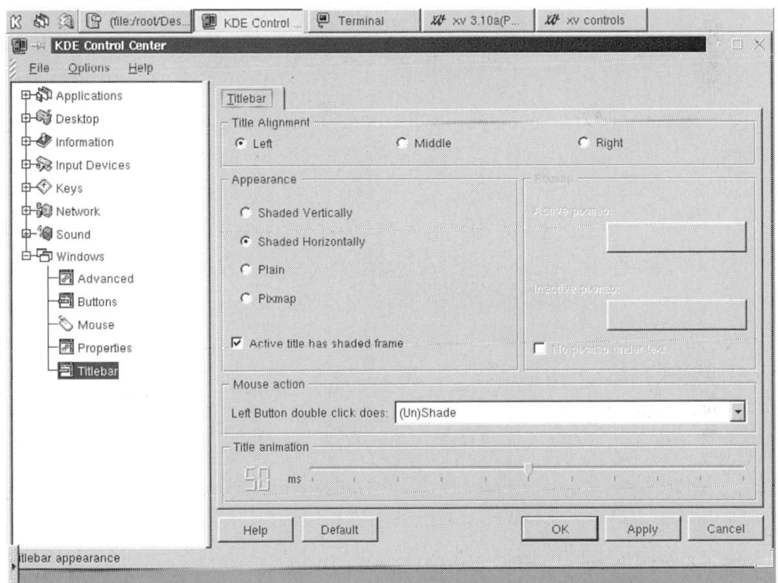

FIGURE 5.23
The Titlebar dialog box sets how KDE windows act and look during your KDE sessions.

For more complex window control, click Properties to use the Windows dialog box, shown in Figure 5.24, to tell KDE how to move, place, resize, or activate windows on your desktop. For example, the Focus Policy section tells KDE how to make a window active. The default action is that you must click a window to activate it, or enable it to receive keyboard input; other policies make a window active when your mouse pointer is over the window.

> **Note**
>
> The Mouse dialog box under the Windows drop-down menu is used to set how you want KDE windows to react to your mouse clicks. You can find a dozen different mouse actions (such as left-, middle-, or right-clicks on active windows) you can customize.

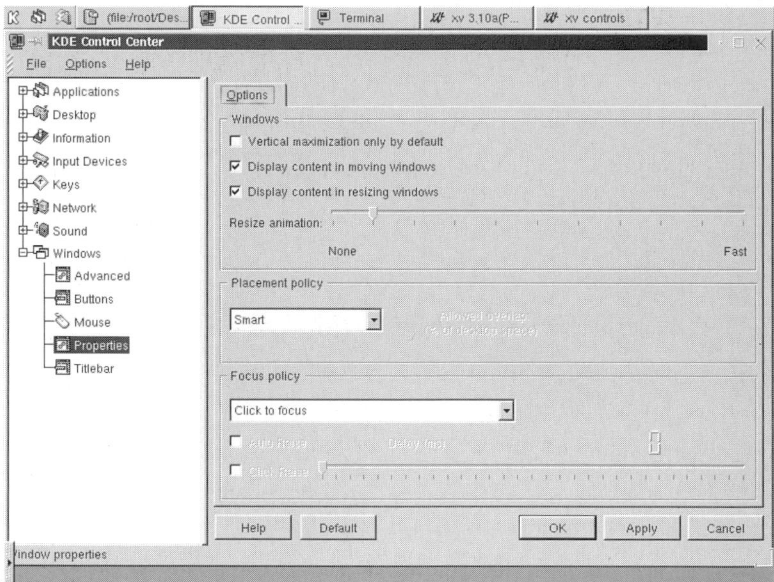

FIGURE 5.24
You can fine-tune how KDE handles windows on your desktop with the Windows dialog box.

Controlling Cursor Movement Through Desktops

The Borders dialog box, accessed through the Settings and Desktop menu items from the Application Starter menu of your panel, is used to control cursor movement between virtual desktops. By default, you'll have to click a virtual desktop button on your desktop's panel to move between desktops. If you click the Enable Active Desktop Borders check box in the Borders dialog box (shown in Figure 5.25) and then click the Apply button, you can move to a different desktop by moving your mouse cursor to the edge of the current desktop.

Note

Don't want to click the panel's desktop buttons or drag your mouse to move between desktops? Use the keyboard instead! Press Ctrl+Tab to walk through the desktops. Press Alt+Tab to walk through (activate) windows in the current desktop.

You can also drag the different sliders to set the time delay for desktop switching and the width of the sensitive edge of each desktop.

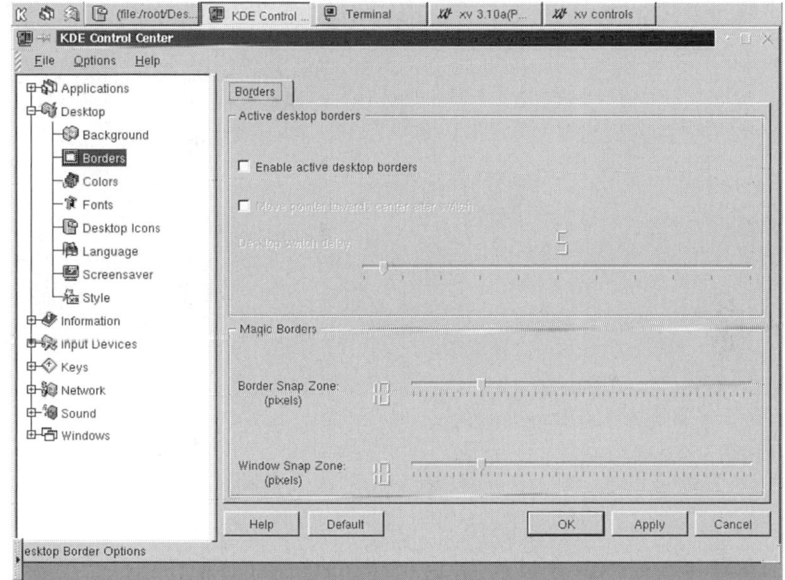

FIGURE 5.25
The Borders dialog box is used to tell KDE whether to use the mouse to move between desktops, how fast to make the switch, and when to make the change.

Features of the `fvwm2` `AnotherLevel` Configuration

Red Hat Linux 6.0 also includes the now-familiar `AnotherLevel` configuration of the `fvwm2` window manager (see Figure 5.26). `AnotherLevel`, which is built with X11 resource files to enhance `fvwm2`, provides many window decorations, such as close, zoom, and minimize buttons; 3D scrollbars; support modules for virtual desktops; a taskbar with Start menu; and even an AfterStep wharf.

The `fvwm2` window manager is not included with OpenLinux 2.2, but may be built from scratch or installed from contributor's RPM files; try `ftp://ftp.caldera.com`.

Important Files

`AnotherLevel`'s default configuration files are found under the `/etc/X11/AnotherLevel` directory. Unlike other window managers, which may use a single configuration file, `AnotherLevel` uses `fvwm2`'s `-cmd` configuration option to load in a series of configuration files (although you can just use a single `system.fvwm2rc` or `.fvwm2rc` file). Most of `AnotherLevel`'s fancy window decorations, menus, and specialized features (such as audio) are built and processed through this mechanism.

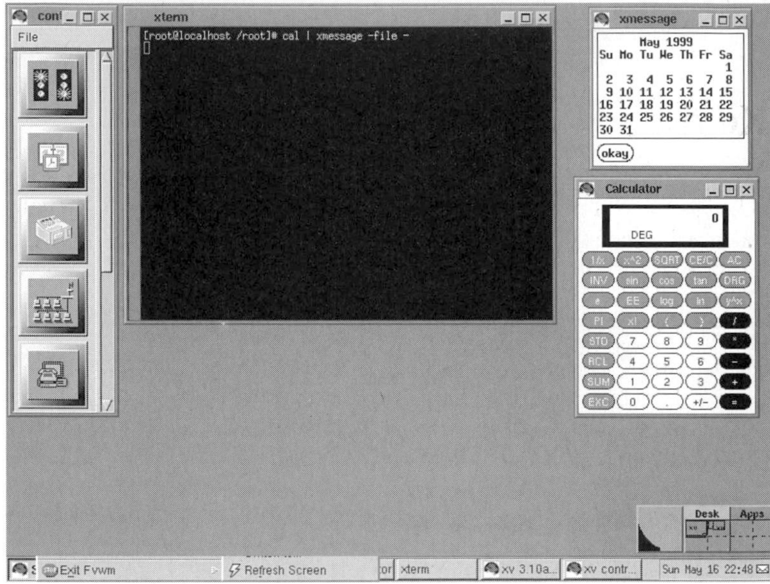

FIGURE 5.26
The `AnotherLevel` configuration of the `fvwm2` window manager provides a simple start menu and windowing scheme.

You can choose an `AnotherLevel` session through the `gdm` or `kdm` login dialog boxes. However, if you choose not to use a display manager, and instead start your X sessions with the `startx` command, your `.xinitrc` file should have an entry like this:

```
fvwm2 -cmd 'FvwmM4 -debug /etc/X11/AnotherLevel/fvwm2rc.m4'
```

Configuring `AnotherLevel`

Although one way to configure `AnotherLevel` is to edit its startup scripts under the `/etc/X11/AnotherLevel` directory, you can also build and configure your interface and then choose Preferences, Save Desktop to `new.xinitrc`. `AnotherLevel` creates a file called `new.xinitrc` in your home directory. That file contains the names of all running applications, along with window settings such as size, color, and placement. Here is a sample listing of this file:

```
rclock -bg red -fg yellow -update 1 -geometry 80x80-3+3 &
xmessage -title Calendar -file - -geometry 163x142+627+86 &
rvplayer /tmp/M035F9413D0150E3E.rmm -geometry 348x309+520+199 &
rxvt -fg black -bg white -geometry 80x24+5+5 &
applix -wp -geometry 581x416+6+6 &
rxvt -fg black -bg white -geometry 80x11+5+373 &
```

In this example, the `rclock`, `xmessage`, `rvplayer`, `applix`, and two `rxvt` terminals were in use when the settings were saved. Each of these lines is a command line that can be modified and used either in your `.xinitrc` file or in `AnotherLevel`'s `fvwm2rc.init` file under the `/etc/X11/AnotherLevel` directory.

By using the Exit `fvwm` menu's Switch To item, you can quit `AnotherLevel` and launch a different window manager, such as AfterStep or WindowMaker.

Keyboard Controls

Many window managers support keyboard control of the display, the windows, or the X11 pointer. Table 5.1 details the default keyboard controls for `AnotherLevel`. In some instances, such as moving or resizing a window, the window must be active or highlighted (do this by clicking the window's title bar).

TABLE 5.2 Common *AnotherLevel* Keyboard Commands

Command	*Keyboard Command*
Display Window list (menu)	Alt+Esc
Display desktop preferences menu	Ctrl+Shift+Alt+p
Display window operations menu	Ctrl+Shift+Alt+w
Lower window to bottom	Ctrl+Alt+Return
Make next window active	Alt+Tab
Make previous window active	Shift+Alt+Tab
Maximize window horizontally	Ctrl+Shift+right_cursor
Maximize window vertically	Ctrl+Shift+up_cursor
Minimize (iconify) window	Ctrl+Shift+down_cursor
Move to first virtual desktop	Ctrl+Shift+Alt+Home
Move to last virtual desktop	Ctrl+Shift+Alt+End
Move window	Ctrl+Shift+F7
Next desktop down	Ctrl+Shift+Alt+down_cursor
Next desktop to left	Ctrl+Shift+Alt+left_cursor
Next desktop to right	Ctrl+Shift+Alt+right_cursor
Next desktop up	Ctrl+Shift+Alt+up_cursor
Pointer down 100 pixels	Ctrl+Alt+F10
Pointer down 5 pixels	Ctrl+Shift+F10
Pointer left 100 pixels	Ctrl+Alt+F9
Pointer left 5 pixels	Ctrl+Shift+F9
Pointer right 100 pixels	Ctrl+Alt+F12
Pointer right 5 pixels	Ctrl+Shift+F12
Pointer up 100 pixels	Ctrl+Alt+F11
Pointer up 5 pixels	Ctrl+Shift+F11
Raise window to top	Ctrl+Alt+Return
Resize window	Ctrl+Shift+F8

Note

To be able to use your keyboard properly during your X11 sessions, make sure you've configured X with the correct keyboard setting for your computer. See Chapter 4, "The X Window System," for details about the `XF86Config` file.

Features of the AfterStep Window Manager

The AfterStep window manager (see Figure 5.27) is yet another descendant of the `fvwm` window manager. This X window manager's interface is somewhat similar to the NEXTSTEP interface and incorporates a *wharf* (floating window) for application buttons, a `root` menu, and distinctive icons. You might also like its default window-handling animation (displayed after you press the Minimize or Zoom buttons on windows).

The `AfterStep` window manager is not included with OpenLinux 2.2, but may be obtained from `http://www.afterstep.org`.

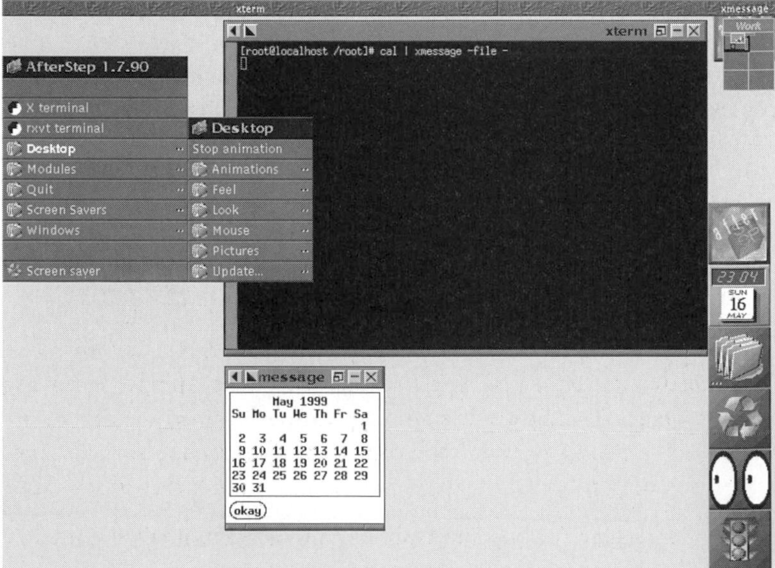

FIGURE 5.27
The AfterStep window manager for X offers sophisticated X client windows and extensive menus.

Important Files

Unlike other window managers included with Linux, AfterStep's default, systemwide configuration files are found under the `/usr/share/afterstep` (or `/etc/X11/afterstep` in Debian) directory. This directory of configuration files also contains AfterStep's documentation in Red Hat. In Debian, the documentation is in `/usr/doc/afterstep`. You can read this documentation (which is Andrew Sullivan's *AfterStep FAQ*) with your favorite Web browser, such as lynx, like this:

```
# lynx afterstep.html
```

To use AfterStep for your X11 sessions, specify its name, **`afterstep`**, in the `.xinitrc` file in your home directory. In Debian, you can instead edit `/etc/X11/window-managers`. Start X (or switch to an AfterStep session from another window manager).

When you run AfterStep for the first time, it creates local configuration files under the `GNUstep` directory in your home directory. The default wharf contains buttons for (starting at the top) getting help, displaying the time and date, virtual desktop control, display of the current system load, launching clients, logging out, and restarting.

Configuring AfterStep

You can control many AfterStep features, including background pictures, color schemes, or handling of windows, through menu items on AfterStep's `root` menu. You can change the look of your desktop, its color scheme, or its handling of windows. For details about other ways to configure AfterStep, read its FAQ or browse to `http://www.afterstep.org`.

Features of the GNU Window Maker Window Manager

The Window Maker window manager (see Figure 5.28) is another window manager that attempts to emulate the NEXTSTEP interface. Like AfterStep, Window Maker incorporates a wharf (floating window) for application buttons, a `root` menu, and distinctive icons. To use Window Maker for your X session, use the `wmaker` command in the your `.xinitrc` file. In Debian, you can instead edit `/etc/X11/window-managers`.

The `WindowMaker` window manager is not included with OpenLinux 2.2, but may be found at `http://www.windowmaker.org`.

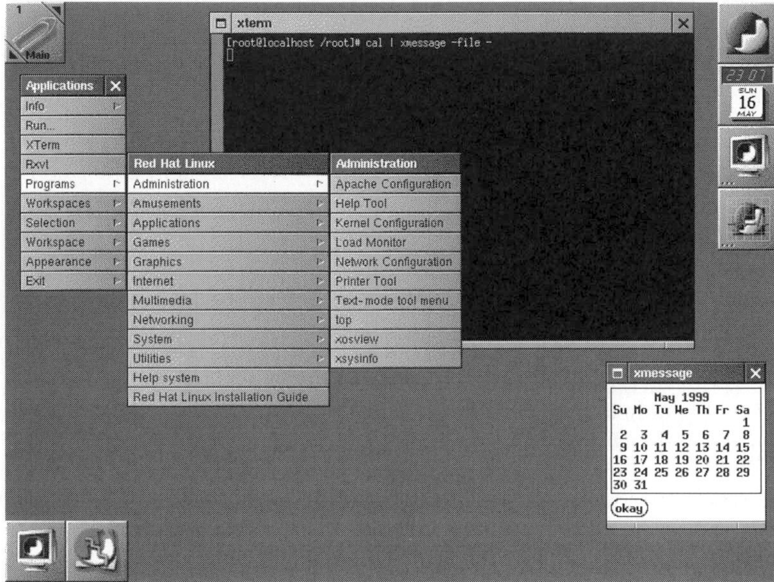

FIGURE 5.28
The GNU Window Maker window manager, like AfterStep, offers sophisticated X client windows and extensive menus.

Important Files

Window Maker's default, systemwide configuration files are found under the `/usr/share/WindowMaker` directory. This directory contains backgrounds, icons, graphics files, and style and theme directories, along with configuration and startup scripts.

You won't find much documentation for Window Maker included with Red Hat Linux 6.0. However, you can read some documentation (such as a readme file and an FAQ) under the `/usr/doc/WindowMaker` directory, or you can browse to `http://people.delphi.com/crc3419/WMUserGuide/index.htm`.

Configuring Window Maker

You'll find some configuration files under the `/etc/X11/WindowMaker` directory. By editing the WMRootMenu file, you can change systemwide settings for the desktop's `root` menu. You can also save changes to the look of your desktop, its color scheme, or its handling of windows, by using the Save Session menu item from the Workspace menu on the desktop's `root` menu (accessed by pressing the right mouse button when the cursor is in a blank area of the desktop).

Like other window managers, Window Maker also supports cursor and mouse operations from the keyboard. Keyboard mouse control support is provided by the `XKB` extension of the `XFree86` server distribution. In general, the Ctrl+NumLock key is used in conjunction with your keyboard's numeric keypad, which provides cursor movement and mouse button events to the window manager, like this:

Numeric Key	*Pointer/Button Action*
*	Select middle mouse button
+	Double-click current button
.	Release current button
/	Select left mousc button
0	Click and hold current button
1	End
2	Mouse pointer down
3	PageDown
4	Mouse pointer left
5	Click current button
6	Mouse pointer right
7	Homc
9	PageUp

Note that these keys will not work with all window managers. Other window managers, such as Enlightenment, KDE, or `fvwm2`, may use other settings and key combinations.

The `fvwm2` Window Manager

The `fvwm2` window manager (see Figure 5.29) has a configurable taskbar, 3D window frames, buttons, scrollbars, and the capability for extensive customization. Customized configurations of this window manager have been the basis of several complex and popular X desktops provided with Red Hat Linux in the last several Red Hat distributions (such as `TheNextStep` and `AnotherLevel`).

The `fvwm2` window manager is not included with OpenLinux 2.2; however, you may be able to build this window manager from scratch using the `fvwm2` source code.

This window manager's default startup file is found under the `/etc/X11/fvwm2` directory as `system.fvwm2rc`. Copy this file to your home directory as **`.fvwm2rc`** and make changes to customize your X sessions. To use **`fvwm2`**, insert its name in your `.xinitrc` file and use the **`startx`** command to start your X session.

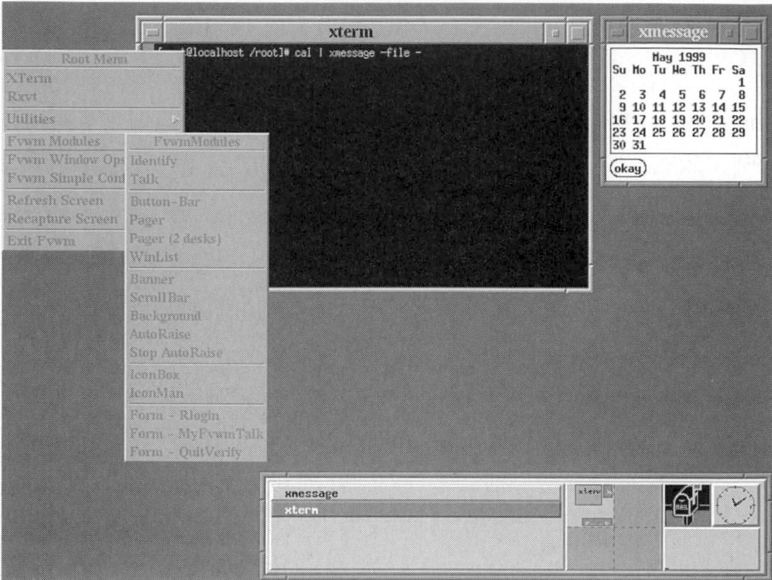

FIGURE 5.29
The `fvwm2` *window manager provides many sophisticated window controls.*

The `fvwm` Window Manager

The `fvwm` window manager (shown in Figure 5.30) is a descendant of the `twm` window manager but has several advantages, such as using less memory, supporting fancier window decorations, and providing virtual desktops or offscreen displays. Virtual desktops are especially handy if you don't want to litter your display with icons or overlapping windows. You can also group your windows by function, such as using one desktop for Web browsing, another for word processing, and perhaps a third for drawing graphics.

The `fvwm` window manager is not included with OpenLinux 2.2.

You'll find `fvwm`'s default file under the `/etc/X11/fvwm` directory with the name `system.fvwmrc`. Copy this file to your home directory with `.fvwmrc`, and make changes to customize it for your use. `fvwm`'s startup file contains sections for customizing window colors and style, menus, and the number of virtual desktops. Look for the desktop section, which looks like this:

```
# Set up the virtual desktop and pager
#set the desk top size in units of physical screen size
DeskTopSize 2x2

# and the reduction scale used for the panner/pager
DeskTopScale 32
```

fvwm's default startup file defines four different virtual desktops. You can move to a different desktop by pressing your left mouse button on the appropriate square in the desktop pager's window. By changing the DeskTopSize value, you can either reduce or increase the number of virtual desktops. For example, use a setting like this to add another two desktops:

```
DeskTopSize 2x3
```

FIGURE 5.30
The fvwm window manager is an improvement over the X11's twm window manager.

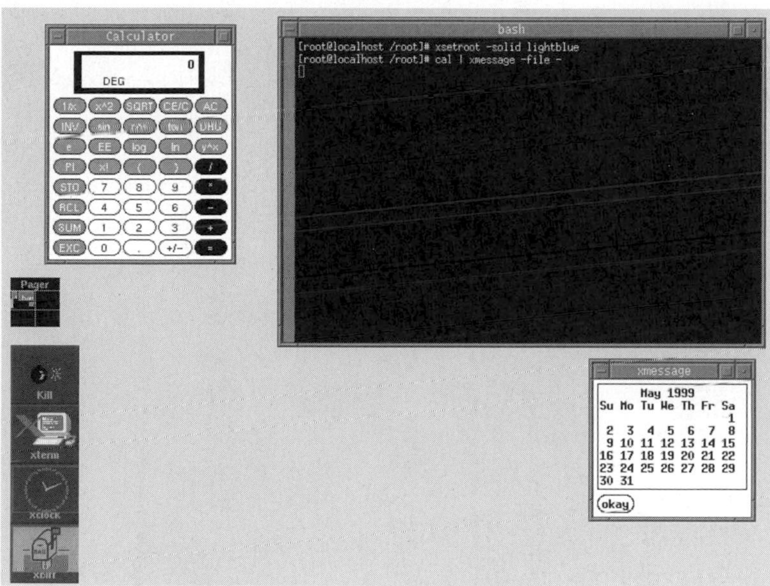

When you restart fvwm, you'll see that an additional two desktops have been added to the fvwm pager window. Use fvwm by inserting the word **fvwm** in your .xinitrc file and use the startx command to start your X session.

The twm Window Manager

The twm, or Tab window manager (shown in Figure 5.31), comes with the XFree86 X Window distribution, and is included with most Linux distributions. You'll find this window manager installed if you install XFree86. Installed under the /usr/X11R6/bin directory, the twm window manager provides the basics of window management for X:

- Custom keyboard commands
- Custom mouse commands
- Icon dock

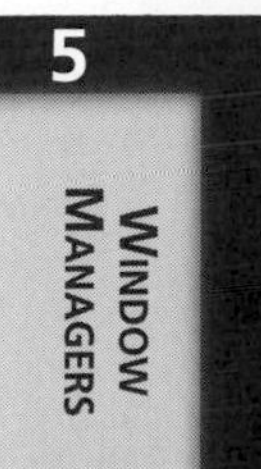

- Icons
- Resizable windows
- Window titles

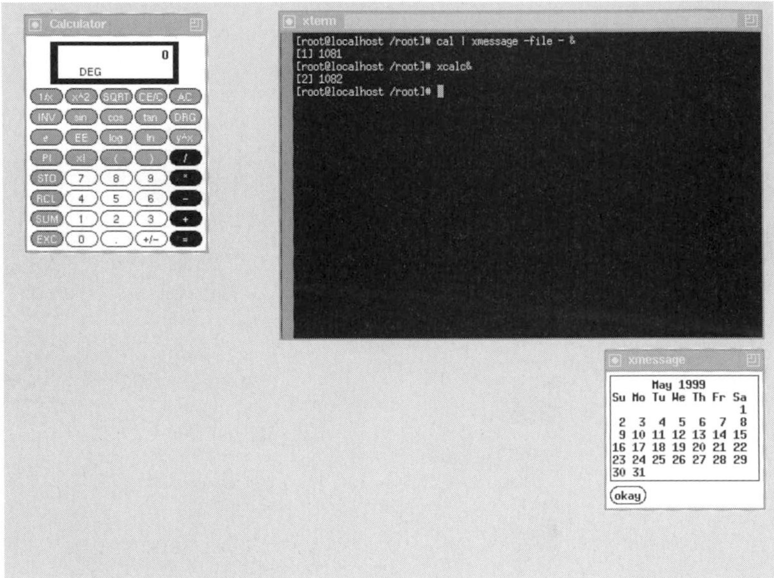

FIGURE 5.31
The `twm` provides basic window operations for your X sessions.

You'll find `twm`'s systemwide configuration file, `system.twmrc`, under the `/etc/X11/twm` directory. This file contains default definitions you can change and use for yourself. Copy `system.twmrc` to your home directory as **`.twmrc`** to make your changes. If you use the `startx` script to start your X sessions, you can use `twm` by inserting the `twm` command in your `.xinitrc` file.

`twm`'s default startup file, which defines `twm`'s `root` menu (accessed by pressing the left mouse button in a blank area of the desktop) does not include a menu item definition for a terminal. Before using `twm`, open your copy of `.twmrc` in your favorite text editor, such as `pico`, and insert a menu definition to start a terminal:

```
# pico -w .twmrc
```

The `pico` editor is part of the `pine` email package. OpenLinux users won't find `pine` available for installation through the default file locations for `lisa`. Instead, you must browse to the `col/contrib/RPMS` directory on your OpenLinux CD-ROM and then install the `pine-4.10-1.i386.rpm` archive.

Debian does not ship `pico` due to licensing issues. You might want to try `emacs`, `vi`, or `ae` instead.

Look for the section defining the `root` menu:

```
menu "defops"
{
"Twm"   f.title
"Iconify"       f.iconify
"Resize"        f.resize
"Move"          f.move
"Raise"         f.raise
"Lower"         f.lower
""              f.nop
"Focus"         f.focus
"Unfocus"       f.unfocus
"Show Iconmgr"  f.showiconmgr
"Hide Iconmgr"  f.hideiconmgr
""              f.nop
"Kill"          f.destroy
"Delete"        f.delete
""              f.nop
"Restart"       f.restart
"Exit"          f.quit
}
```

Insert a menu item for `xterm` (or your favorite X11 terminal client):

```
{
"Twm"   f.title
"Iconify"       f.iconify
"Resize"        f.resize
"Move"          f.move
"Raise"         f.raise
"Lower"         f.lower
"------------"  f.nop
"Focus"         f.focus
"Unfocus"       f.unfocus
"Show Iconmgr"  f.showiconmgr
"Hide Iconmgr"  f.hideiconmgr
"------------"  f.nop
"xterm Window"  !"/usr/X11R6/bin/xterm &"
"------------"  f.nop
"Kill"          f.destroy
"Delete"        f.delete
"------------"  f.nop
"Restart"       f.restart
"Exit"          f.quit
}
```

This section of `.twmrc` contains `root` menu labels, followed by an appropriate command for the `twm` window manager. For example, to "kill" a window, you press your left mouse button on the desktop, drag down to select the Kill menu item, and then press your mouse button over the top of a desired window—`twm` then removes the selected window.

Notice that the blank areas in the new menu definition have been spiffed up with hyphens for a bit more readability. After making your changes, save the new `.twmrc` file. If you're running `twm`, press your left mouse button and drag down to select the Restart menu item (which restarts `twm`) using the newly defined menu. This is how you can customize not only `twm`, but also other window managers discussed in this chapter.

Features of the Common Desktop Environment

In 1993, several major software and hardware vendors joined in an effort to eliminate many of the arbitrary and confusing discrepancies among the various versions of UNIX. These ranged from the monumental, such as key programming interfaces that made support of several UNIX versions difficult for software developers, to less complicated but no less bothersome or expensive issues, such as unnecessary variations in file locations, formats, and naming conventions. Regardless of how "big" these differences were, the vendors recognized that some standardization would have to take place if UNIX were to withstand the tough competition provided by Microsoft's Windows NT, which was finally becoming a serious competitor to UNIX in the server arena.

As a solution to the problem of inconsistent user interfaces, the Common Desktop Environment (CDE) was presented in 1995 by Hewlett-Packard, Novell, IBM, and SunSoft (the software division of Sun Microsystems). The CDE not only addresses the problem of inconsistencies among versions of UNIX and among OEM versions of the X Window System, but also greatly increases the accessibility of UNIX to nontechnical users accustomed to environments such as Windows and Macintosh. The CDE presents the same look and feel on all supported platforms and also provides base applications—such as a networked workgroup calendar, a printer manager, context-sensitive help, and file and application managers—that enable users to completely avoid the often intimidating shell prompt and occasionally confusing manual pages. However, a power user can choose to turn off some of these features and interface directly with the shell and command-line tools while still enjoying a consistent interface when using more than one UNIX variant. The CDE is so consistent in UNIX versions that many vendors even distribute much of the same documentation.

Installing Red Hat's CDE and Library Fixes Using RPM

For a short time (from 1997 until 1998), Red Hat Software marketed and sold a version of CDE prepared by the TriTeal Corp. This version of CDE was designed to install cleanly with Red Hat Linux 4.2. However, changes were made to the standard shared software libraries included with Red Hat's Linux distribution after the CDE 1.2 release. Incompatibilities arose with the very next version of Red Hat Linux, 5.0. If you have Red Hat Linux 5.0 or later and still want to use CDE 1.2, you need to go to Red Hat's Web site and download two RPM files that must be installed after you install CDE on a 5.0 or later system.

> **Note**
>
> There is no guarantee that Red Hat's CDE 1.2 will work with Red Hat Linux 6.0, OpenLinux 2.2, or the current Debian Linux distribution. If you must use CDE, you can try one of at least four versions from the sole CDE vendor for Linux: Xi-graphics. Browse to `www.xig.com` for more information about maXimum cde.

These files are located at `ftp://ftp.redhat.com/pub/redhat/updates/cde/1.2/rpms`.

These files are `TEDlibc5fix-4.2-00.i386.rpm` and `ld.so-1.9.5-5.i386.rpm`.

Download and install them after installing but before running CDE. Use the `rpm` command, along with its `-i` (install) command-line option like this:

```
# rpm -i *.rpm
```

Details about this fix are on Red Hat's site at `http://www.redhat.com/support/docs/cde`.

Summary

This chapter presented an overview of various window managers for X11, including AfterStep and Window Maker, along with a discussion of the current method of configuring different Linux systems for different display managers. You also read about how other window managers, such as `fvwm2`, `fvwm`, and `twm` are configured for use. Don't be intimidated just because an interesting X11 window manager is not included with your favorite Linux distribution: You can download the source code for more than 100 different window managers, and then build and install from scratch.

For links to the source for many other window managers, or for pointers to the latest version of your favorite window manager, see `http://www.PLiG.org/xwinman`. You'll find lots of links to additional window themes, icons, and graphics you can use with your X11 desktop.

Configuring Services

Part II

In This Part

CHAPTER 6

System Service Tools

In This Chapter

One of the great things about Linux and Open Systems is the enormous variety of third-party tools, especially networking tools, that are available as add-ons, frequently with source code available.

While the availability of the source code is wonderful to the hacker, it has also meant that many hands have contributed to that writhing mass of software known as Linux, just as many hands have contributed to Microsoft Windows NT. In the latter case, however, Microsoft has contributed very significant resources to creating a uniform Windows-based administrative interface.

However, a central precept of the UNIX and Linux communities is to make every system configuration file configurable with a text editor, provided you know how. When an Ethernet interface is added to a Linux boot configuration, it documents exactly which text files are affected. A sufficiently knowledgeable system administrator can use a text editor even when more complex tools cannot be used, for whatever reason.

This application of the "Keep It Simple, Stupid" (KISS) principle is good for system robustness, but something of a problem for the novice.

Therefore, from the beginning of commercial versions of Linux, major vendors such as Red Hat and Caldera have put major resources into developing various types of high-level administration tools which manipulate the underlying text-based configuration files.

In the spirit of the Open Software movement, these tools are generally available in source form, and may even be available across vendor lines. `COAS`, for instance, although funded by Caldera, is developed by a separate organization with its own Web site.

The nature of the Open Software movement is that at first everybody boldly dashes off in all directions, giving rise to many tools of overlapping purpose. The high-level administration tools area is no different. Gradually, however, certain tools have risen above the others. It is too much to expect that only one would be so blessed; there are a variety of older Red Hat tools, and one older Caldera tool. Then there is the modern entry in each camp.

The `COAS` tool is written partly in the Python programming language, described in Chapter 31, "Programming with Python." This is probably the easiest method for average programmers to write programs with graphical interfaces.

Finally, we take a peek under the hood, at what really happens when Linux starts up. The *booting*, or loading the Linux kernel, was described earlier in Chapter 3, "Boot Management," but that is only the beginning. Look at what happens after that. For ordinary purposes, the high-level tools correctly control the behavior of assorted services, from low-level networking to the Apache Web server. Even experts mostly trust that this is done properly. But when something breaks, it's time to go back to basics. This doesn't mean that you're editing configuration files, but at least you may be able to tell what the high-level tool you're using is really up to.

Given the variety of such tools, it is inevitable that some of them are more complete than others, or better at a particular task, or have better help screens.

Classification of System Service Tools

System service tools can be classified either according to what they do, or by the interface they present to the user. Accordingly, the following two sections are named "Configuration, Analysis, and Control," and "User Interface," respectively.

Configuration, Analysis, and Control

One useful classification of system service tools is by whether the tool performs *configuration*, *analysis*, or *control*:

- *Configuration* tools alter the permanent state of the system, normally by changing the way the system is set up or shut down. Configuration changes usually do not take effect until the next system boot.
- *Analysis* tools have no effect at all, but look around to see what is there.
- *Control* tools have an immediate but temporary effect, sometimes with an option to make it permanent.

To illustrate the difference between control and configuration, consider the sample administration tasks in Table 6.1.

Table 6.1 Examples of Related System Control and Configuration Tasks

Topic	*Control*	*Configuration*
Disk partitions	Mount a disk partition immediately but temporarily	Add an entry to the list of disk partitions automatically mounted at boot time

continues

Table 6.1 continued

Topic	*Control*	*Configuration*
Network interfaces	Bring up a network interface now with ad hoc (command-line) parameters	Change control files that control the initialization of network interfaces at boot time
Modules	Load a module now	Arrange for a certain module to be loaded at boot time
Apache Web server	Start the Apache Web server	Change the startup options of the Apache server (`httpd`)

The difference is immediacy and permanence. A good administrative principle to follow is this: It is better to try things before relying on them. Therefore, even when you ultimately want a change to be permanent, you should first use a control tool to see if the change is useful.

User Interface

System service tools may also be classified according to the type of user interface:

- *Command line, noninteractive, with immediate effect.* For instance, referring to the first entry in Table 6.1 above, the `mount` command mounts an additional filesystem (partition), immediately (if possible), but does not cause the partition to be mounted in the next boot sequence. Thus, it causes an immediate change in the system's running configuration, which persists only until system shutdown. The `mount` command can mount any mountable resource whether it is listed in `/etc/fstab` or not (see next bullet).
- *Text editors.* Traditionally, every aspect of the boot sequence of a Linux or UNIX system can be controlled by human-readable text files. Continuing the example of the previous bullet, the file `/etc/fstab` controls which filesystems are mounted during the boot sequence, Therefore, the traditional way of adding a filesystem to a system's permanent running configuration is to use a text editor to modify `/etc/fstab`. Naturally, UNIX lore is replete with horror stories of minor typographical errors in this file which caused incredible grief, as well as compensating stories of clever administrators fixing problems which a buggy high-level editor

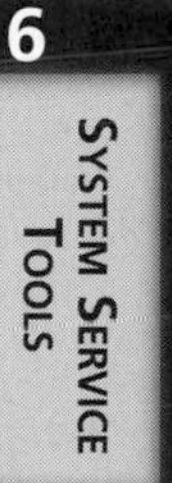

caused. Similarly, the startup sequence of the Apache Web server is controlled by a complex series of control files. Early Apache administration required editing these files directly, and using the very latest features sometimes still does.

- *Curses-based semi-graphical tools, such as `lisa` (OpenLinux).* These tools offer menus, wizards, and overlapping windows within a context of 80×25 text mode. These programs have the advantage that they can be run much more readily across a network connection than a fully graphical tool and run a lot faster, especially on slower machines. However, they are a lot less visually appealing, and overlapping windows cause screen clutter in a hurry.
- *True (X Windows-based) graphical tools, such as Red Hat's `linuxconf` and OpenLinux's `COAS`.* These tools offer the maximum degree of convenience. In fact, the two tools just mentioned can function both in curses and graphical modes. Although current vendor trends are to let curses-based tools languish in favor of the graphical tools, it should be noted that curses tools (or multi-modal tools in curses mode) may be only tools available, either because of limited network bandwidth, firewalls (the X protocol is generally blocked at firewalls), or simply because the X environment is not working (because you installed a new graphics card, or made a mistake in setting up Xfree86). So for administering your own workstation, X-windows tools may be extremely convenient, but for office machines you are administering from home or elsewhere, you may prefer to use curses tools.

The integration of the latter two administration tool types is one of the major contributions of Red Hat and Caldera to the Linux community. Debian does not have equivalent tools of its own, but some, if not most, administration tools are open-source, so that they could be adapted to Debian without excessive effort.

Introduction to Red Hat Tools

Earlier versions of Red Hat Linux offered a `control-panel`, which appeared during a `root fvwm2` session. This tool is still available in Red Hat 6, but is being rapidly eclipsed by `linuxconf`.

`linuxconf`

One of the great things about Red Hat Linux is the number of system-management tools included in the distribution. One important tool is Jacques Gelinas's `linuxconf`, which can be called from a command line in a terminal window while running X, from the command line of your console screen, or through your favorite Web browser. You should use `linuxconf` for a number of reasons:

- `linuxconf` provides a comprehensive graphic interface for administering your Red Hat system.
- You can save different system configurations, allowing you, for example, to set up your computer as a desktop machine or Internet server at different times with a single command line.
- `linuxconf` replaces and maintains a number of user, file, and network utilities (such as the old `usercfg`, `fstool`, and `cabaret`); the program is used as a configuration tool and service activation tool.
- `linuxconf` has the capability to use modules to add features or capabilities.
- The program features built-in help for many services or actions.
- `linuxconf` allows system maintenance over a network, enabling more efficient management of in-house or remote computers and networks.
- In X mode, `linuxconf` has the concept of overlapping administrative tasks. When you select one leaf of its tree, begin making changes, and then select another without committing the changes, `linuxconf` starts another configuration panel which runs in parallel with the other one. This allows several related configuration tasks to be coordinated. For instance, adding a virtual Web site to Apache may also involve adding an ethernet alias and making DNS changes. Although this should be counted as a feature, it can also come as a bit of a surprise to the unwary, because starting another panel does not commit the changes from the current panel.

The `linuxconf` main executable is found under the `/bin` directory and is about 715K in size, which used to be considered large—not any more. The program, written with more than 80,000 lines of C++ code, also comes with a support directory `/usr/lib/linuxconf` contains more than 6MB of data, help files in several languages, and code modules.

After you log in as the `root` operator, start the `linuxconf` program from the command line with the following and press the Enter key:

```
# linuxconf &
```

If you're running X and have installed the GNOME software libraries, the program's main window will appear as shown in Figure 6.1.

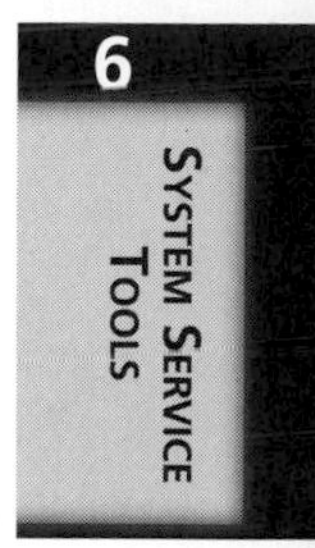

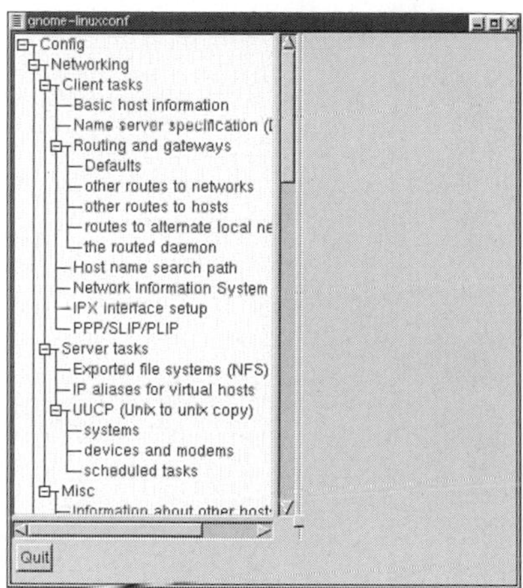

FIGURE 6.1
The `linuxconf` client represents a new generation of graphical Linux administration tools.

When used without GNOME libraries or from the console, the program (which started life as a configuration tool for the XFree86 X11 distribution) responds to keyboard commands just like Red Hat's Linux installation tool. Navigate around the program's dialog box by pressing the Tab key and then use the Enter key when the cursor is on a desired button or list item.

`linuxconf` can be used not only interactively, but also from the command line. The following related commands (and perhaps others by the time you read this) can be found in your filesystem after you install `linuxconf` (part of Red Hat Linux since version 5.1):

- `fixperm`—A utility that checks system file permissions.
- `fsconf`—A utility that manipulates the filesystem table, `/etc/fstab`, as shown in Figure 6.2.

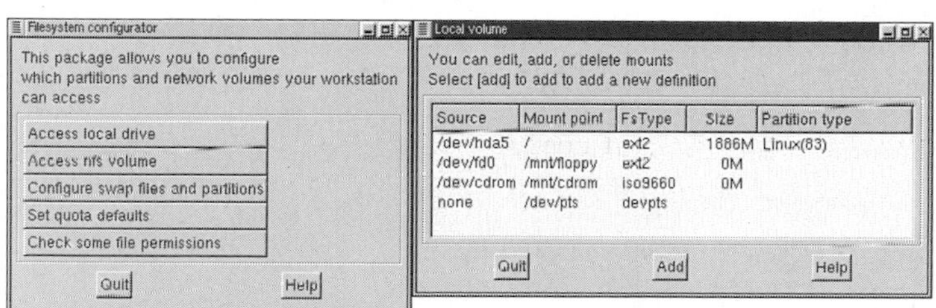

FIGURE 6.2
The `fsconf` command manipulates your system's filesystem table and can be used to configure mounting options.

- `lpdconfig`—A print-spooling configuration utility.
- `netconf`—A TCP/IP services configuration utility, as shown in Figure 6.3.

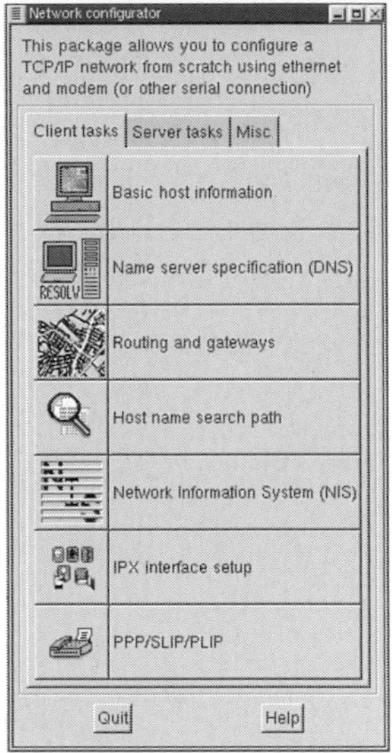

FIGURE 6.3
The `netconf` *command is a graphical network configuration tool.*

- `linuxconf --shutdown`—This brings up a graphical display similar to that shown in Figure 6.4, and allows the system to be gracefully shut down. This means that first a warning message is sent to all users every minute for a specified grace period, after which the actual shutdown sequence begins. There is also a `Shutdown/Reboot` item in the main `linuxconf` menu tree which brings up the same dialog box.

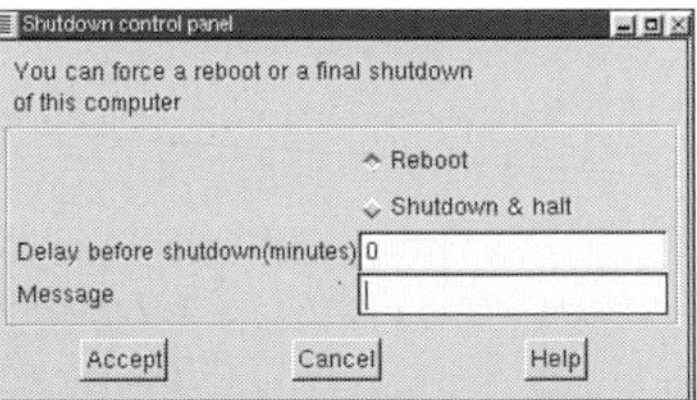

FIGURE 6.4
`linuxconf`'s graphical shutdown control utility, as invoked directly from the command line.

- `userconf`—User and group configuration (to add or delete users and groups).
- `xconf`—X11 configuration utility (see Chapter 4, "Configuring the X Window System," for details).

Most of these programs are invoked by a symbolic link to `linuxconf`. For example, to delete the user `cloobie` from the command line, use `linuxconf`'s symbolic link `userconf`:

```
# userconf --deluser cloobie
```

You can get help for each utility by using the `--help` command-line option, or if using X11, by clicking the Help button in the utility's main dialog box.

The `linuxconf` command will also help you properly start and stop services under Linux while the system is running. Although you can selectively "kill" processes with the following code (where `pid` is the number of the running process), this is a crude, ineffective, and potentially harmful way to stop processes and system services.

```
# kill -9 pid
```

As you learn later in this chapter, the approved method of stopping a service is to call the appropriate script in the `/etc/rc.d/init.d` directory, illustrated here for the Apache Web server (`httpd` daemon):

```
# /etc/rc.d/init.d/httpd.init stop
```

This method has the virtue of shutting down the service gracefully, but is still a manual process. The Red Hat folks have taken great pains to make system administration easier; why not take advantage of menu convenience? When you use the Service/Control facility of `linuxconf`, you can enable or disable multiple services, either temporarily or permanently in a single operation.

Note

Other tools included with Red Hat Linux include `ntsysv` and `tksysv`. `ntsysv` is a curses tool, used to decide which services are started at boot time. `tksysv` is a *runlevel editor* which performs a somewhat similar service as `linuxconf`'s Service/Control facility described above. Runlevels and the boot sequence are described in great detail later in this chapter.

If you manually configure your system's services by hand-editing configuration files, be careful—making changes to default runlevels in `/etc/inittab` or indiscriminately using administration tools to change services or runlevels can put your system into an unusable state. If you run into trouble, reset your computer and enter the following at the `LILO` prompt:

```
LILO boot: linux single
```

> **Note**
>
> If you don't feel like typing the entire word *single*, use this:
>
> `LILO boot: linux 1`
>
> It works just as well. The value `1` (or its alias `single`) overrides the *default runlevel* for the system, as explained in the section "The `init` Process," later in this chapter.

Booting into single-user mode might allow you to fix any problems (a similar approach to another operating system's "safe mode"). When you boot into single-user mode, you go directly into a `root` operator command line, which is handy for enabling a quick fix or performing other system administration tasks.

You should also know that `linuxconf` is a work in progress; not every item in the program is documented or has an associated Help menu or complete help text. For some additional details about `linuxconf`, tips on using modules, or other errata, see `linuxconf`'s home page at `http://www.solucorp.qc.ca/linuxconf/`.

You can also subscribe to the `linuxconf` mailing list, `linuxconf@hub.xc.org`, or read archives of discussions about `linuxconf` through this site.

`control-panel` Tools

Although `linuxconf` is getting better all the time, there are still tasks for which you need Red Hat's older `control-panel`. This is accessible through the same System menu from a `root` shell window:

```
#control-panel &
```

The `control-panel` items are as follows:

- A runlevel editor (see the section on runlevels later in this chapter). Allows you to change the default runlevel. Useful values are `3` (text mode login) and `5` (start the GNOME Display Manager graphical login screen)
- Time and date manager (Time Machine).
- Printer setup tool (`printtool`).
- Network Configurator.
- Modem setup tool.
- System setup (`linuxconf`): See above. This has grown from a part of `control-panel` to Red Hat's major high-level tool.

Figure 6.5 shows a screenshot with several of the control-panel tools active simultaneously.

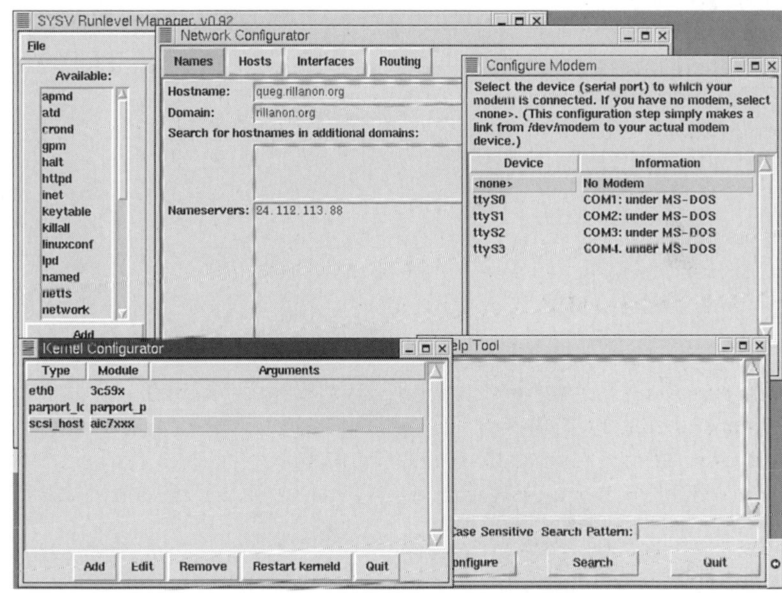

FIGURE 6.5
Several different `control-panel` *tools in simultaneous use.*

Introduction to Caldera OpenLinux Tools

Caldera OpenLinux offers two independent tools: Linux Installation and System Administration (`lisa`) and Caldera Open Administration System (`COAS`). The former is curses-based, and predates `COAS`. The latter, `COAS`, can operate in both curses and graphical modes. The following sections describe `lisa` and `COAS` in turn.

lisa

`lisa`, or Linux Installation and System Administration, is a curses-based administration tool developed by Caldera. It works best on one of the text virtual consoles (accessed by pressing Ctrl+Alt+F1 through Ctrl+Alt+F5; the graphical screen is restored by Ctrl+Alt+F8 or sometimes Ctrl+Alt+F7) or a classic `xterm`. An `xterm` can be launched from inside a `kvt` console window with this command:

```
/usr/X11R6/bin/xterm &
```

If you launch `lisa` from a KDE term (`kvt`), most of `lisa` will work as expected. The F1 key, however, will not work as expected.

Once you have a `root` command prompt, `lisa` can be launched with the following command:

```
lisa
```

At this point, the following messages are sent to the screen but you will not see them until the `lisa` session is finished:

```
Kill is control-U (^U).
Interrupt is control-C (^C).
```

What you will see is the `lisa` main screen, approximately as shown in Figure 6.6.

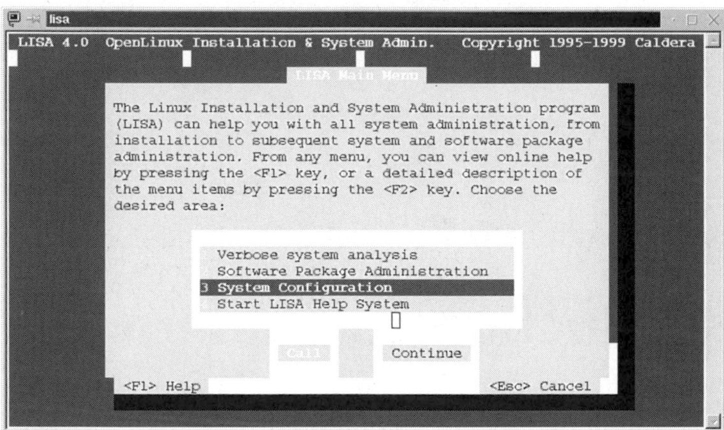

FIGURE 6.6
The opening screen from `lisa`.

As of this writing, items 1 and 3 on the screen are the most useful. Software package administration (item 2) is handled better by use of other tools (see Chapter 19, "Software Management") and the `lisa` help system (item 4) seems to be quite spare.

Navigation is quite simple: Use the arrow keys or the numerals to highlight a menu option and then use the Tab key to select either Call or Continue. Select Call and press Enter to call the highlighted `lisa` subsystem. Select Continue and press Enter, or simple press Esc, to exit the menu and return to the previous menu (or the command prompt if you're already at the top level).

The following subsections take a look at some of the deeper layers of the tree.

Verbose System Analysis

Selecting Verbose System Analysis (item 1) reveals the following submenu:

```
1 Automatic System Analysis
2 Automatic Kernel Analysis
3 Automatic Hardware Analysis
4 Automatic Partition Analysis
5 Automatic Network Analysis
6 Display Boot Process Messages
7 Display Script Configuration File
8 Display System Configuration File
```

> **Note**
>
> `lisa` is updated from time to time. The menu shown here corresponds to the latest update at the time of writing, which is dated July 1, 1999. If you install an update, use `rpm` from the command line instead of one of the graphical tools (such as `COAS` or `kpackage`) so that you can see the `rpm` messages. See Chapter 19 for more information on software installation and updating.

All eight menu items produce various types of report about the system. The first five are particularly useful, but may take a noticeable length of time to complete, even on a fast system. Figure 6.7 shows a screenshot of Automatic System Analysis, and Figure 6.8 shows a screenshot of Automatic Kernel Analysis.

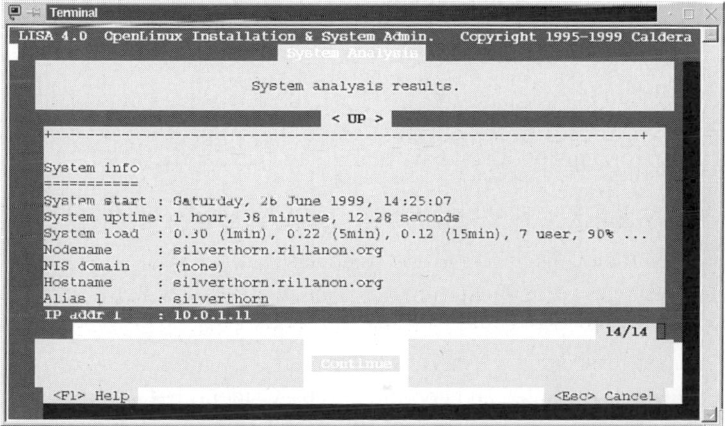

FIGURE 6.7
Output of my system's Automatic System Analysis.

These are just analyses; we can't use this subsystem to change anything. For longer reports, the up and down arrows and the PgUp and PgDn keys can be used.

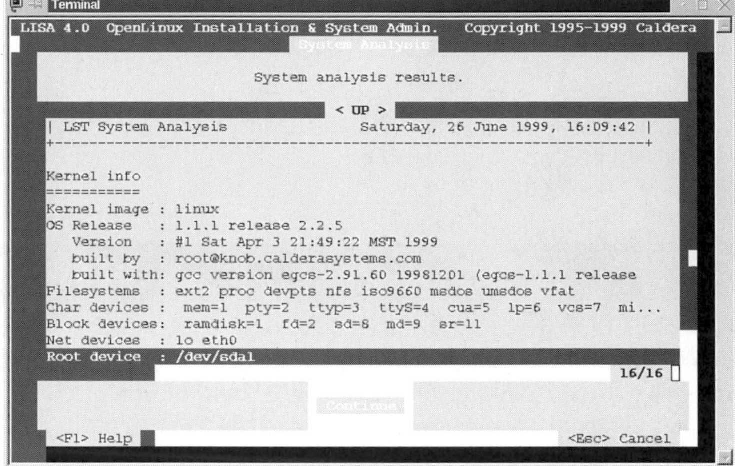

FIGURE 6.8
Output of my system's Automatic Kernel Analysis.

System Configuration

Selecting System Configuration from the main menu calls up the next layer of menus. You are again confronted with a menu with the same System Configuration item highlighted. You could be forgiven if you thought nothing had happened, but if you look more closely you'll see that it's now item 2 instead of item 3, and that the menu title at the top is also System Configuration.

This time, however, you see several very useful menu items such as User Administration, Configure Mount Table, Configure Swap Space, Set Hostname, and Configure Timezone. Note that if you use the Set Hostname item, then you will not be able to launch any more graphical programs until you have started a new X session.

The first item, User Administration, leads to yet another menu of user administration activities, such as Display System Users, Add New Users, and Delete users.

COAS

COAS stands for Caldera Open Administration System. It is developed by the COAS Project, which is funded and coordinated by Caldera, but incorporates the work of others. In keeping with the general trend in the Linux community, it is placing the entire results of the project under the GNU Public License.

The COAS Project aims to create a comprehensive, unified, administration environment for Linux which is *multimodal*, meaning that it can be used from the command line in text interactive mode (curses), X (KDE), or (ultimately) Java. This is a very ambitious set of goals, and it is remarkable how much has been achieved so far—and there is more yet to come.

The COAS Project maintains an independent Web site at `http://www.coas.org`, where you can find out how to complain about `COAS` bugs and contribute yourself to the `COAS` effort.

In addition, Caldera provides periodic updates of `COAS` in RPM format on its own Web site (as of the time of writing, `COAS` 1.0-8 is available) There is also a `COAS` mailing list where you can keep with the latest happenings in the `COAS` world. To sign up, send a text-only message to `majordomo@lists.calderasystems.com` containing the following two lines:

```
subscribe COAS
quit
```

Note

As noted on the Caldera Web site, `COAS` 1.0-8 fixes a security breach involving permissions on the file `/etc/shadow`. Although the fix prevents the permissions from being weakened by future `COAS` sessions, you can use the following command to make sure they have not already been weakened:

```
# chmod 600 /etc/shadow
```

COAS Architecture

`COAS`, like `linuxconf`, is primarily an administration framework, into which various particular modules (and submodules) are fitted. The `COAS` jargon for an individual module is *CLAM* (for *Caldera Loadable Administration Module*.)

The current set of CLAMs (administrative modules) shipping with `COAS` follows:

- Network administration
- System administration
- Peripherals administration
- Kernel modules
- Install/remove software packages

The first four CLAMs are discussed here; software installation using COAS is discussed in Chapter 19.

Launching COAS

COAS can be launched from the COAS icon on the KDE panel, as shown in Figure 6.9.

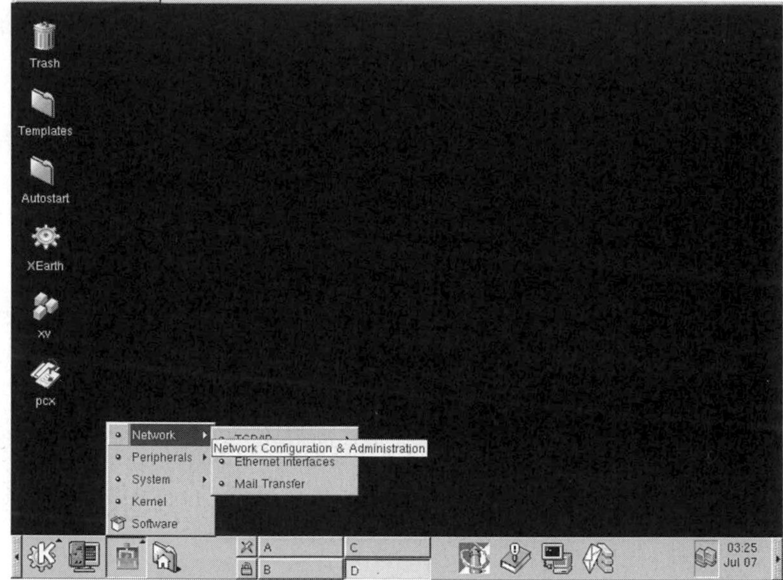

FIGURE 6.9
The COAS menu, which is produced by clicking Tool at the foot of the KDE screen.

Alternatively, if you are sitting at the command prompt as `root` (either you originally logged in as `root` or you previously used the `su` command to launch a `root` shell), the simplest way to launch COAS is with the following command:

```
# coastool
```

Tip

When you execute the `su` command, it starts a new shell belonging to a different Linux user, for example, `root`. This user may not have the right to connect to your X display. If you get messages like "Xlib: connection to :0.0 refused by server", execute the following command from a diffferent terminal window

```
$ xhost +
```

> This command disables access control to your screen. Access control will be reenabled the next time X is restarted. Other variations on this command relax access control less severely. In particular the following may suffice
>
> ```
> $ xhost +localhost
> ```

If you are not currently logged in as `root` and you are using X (KDE), then you can launch `COAS` as follows:

```
kdesu root coastool
```

This method will produce a somewhat different display, but with the same capabilities, as shown in Figure 6.10.

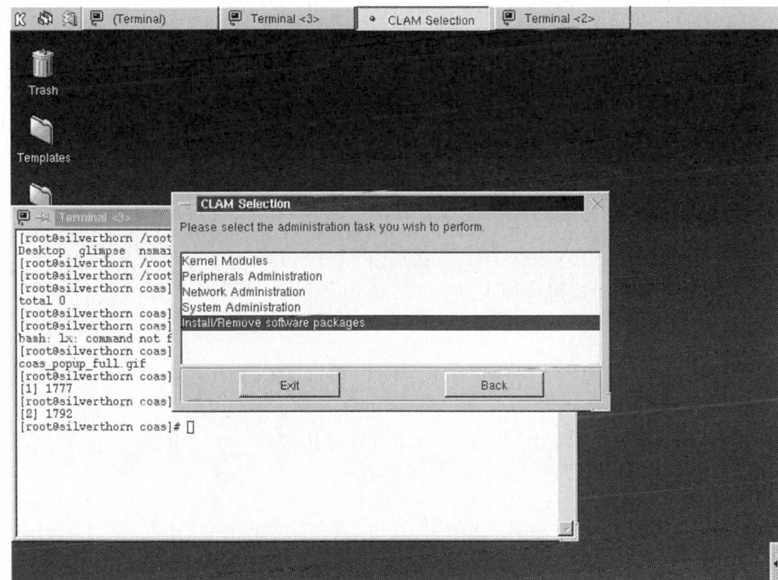

FIGURE 6.10
The COAS main menu, which is shown only when launched from a command line.

You can also launch particular CLAMs as with the following command to start the network administration module:

```
$ kdesu root 'coastool network'
```

It is also possible to reach deeper into the COAS menu tree from the command line with a command like the following:

```
$ kdesu root 'coastool network.tcpip.nis'
```

When not running as root, the items on the KDE menu wrap all the COAS calls in kdesu as shown earlier, so that you can successfully use them just by entering the root password into the COAS su wrapper dialog box, as shown in Figure 6.11.

FIGURE 6.11
COAS su *wrapper dialog box requesting the* root *password.*

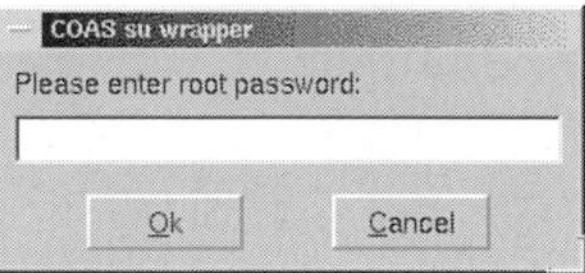

You will get a notice if you mistype the root password, but no second chance to enter it correctly.

Tip

root privilege is only needed to change things. Therefore, if you want to play with COAS without any danger of making unintentional system changes, simply launch it as an ordinary user from the command line without the kdesu wrapper. Some of the COAS screens will no longer be available, and others will not function properly, but you will be automatically prevented from making any system changes.

Note

COAS normally senses the availability of X using the DISPLAY environment variable, but you can force it to use text mode using the curses keyword:

```
coastool curses
```

See Chapter 25, "Shell Programming," for a full discussion of environment variables.

COAS Network Administration

The COAS network administration module provides the following options, with the primary COAS name shown first, followed by the KDE menu path; alternate names are shown in parentheses. The primary name is the name shown in Figure 6.12.

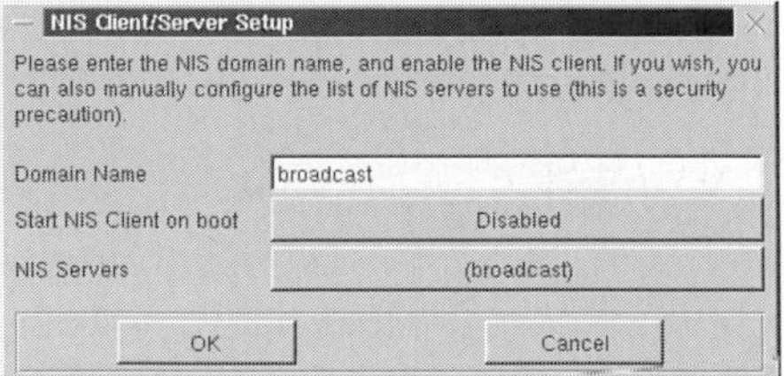

FIGURE 6.12
COAS dialog box for setting up NIS (Network Information Service).

- Network Information Service—`COAS`->Network->TCP/IP->NIS—Also known as `yp`. NIS is discussed in detail in Chapter 14, "NIS: Network Information Service." Briefly, however, you will need this item if you are part of a cluster of Linux and UNIX machines. This item can be used to enable starting the NIS client at boot time, which sets the NIS domain name (not necessarily the same as the DNS domain name) it will listen to. NIS can discover nearby servers automatically without putting them in this file, but this is insecure. This item may mysteriously fail to operate on newly installed systems, mainly because as shipped, NIS's main configuration file `/etc/nis.conf` contains an invalid line. If this is the case for you, save the file `/etc/nis.conf` (just in case it contains something useful) and then delete `/etc/nis.conf`. If `COAS` is running, exit `COAS` and relaunch it; select the NIS item again. This time it should work. Type in the word **`broadcast`** (or whatever your NIS domain name is) into the Domain Name field and click OK. The dialog box closes and another one asks for confirmation to save the changes.
- Hostname resolution—`COAS`->Network->TCP/IP->Resolver—Linux has three sources of information about the network: the local file `/etc/hosts`, NIS, and DNS (domain name service). The Resolver menu item opens the Name Resolver Setup dialog box similar to that shown in Figure 6.13. When a name is looked up, the services are consulted in a particular order, initially set to `hosts, nis, dns`. If you are not running NIS, you may want to remove NIS from the list; it is similar with DNS. Also, you may want to give NIS or DNS priority over `/etc/hosts`. If you have fixed DNS servers, you may want to set them here. A typical situation with variable DNS servers is an ADSL or cable modem Internet connection. In such cases, the DNS servers are set by the script that connects the user to the Net.
- TCP/IP Network Options—no KDE menu item—Sets two flags, one of which can turn off all networking! The other controls IP forwarding, which indicates whether your kernel will route packets from one interface to another. This is a general policy. The actual instruction to route-particular addresses is done by means of separate commands. If IP forwarding is turned off, IP packets may only originate or terminate at your machine, not transit, despite any kernel routing commands in effect.

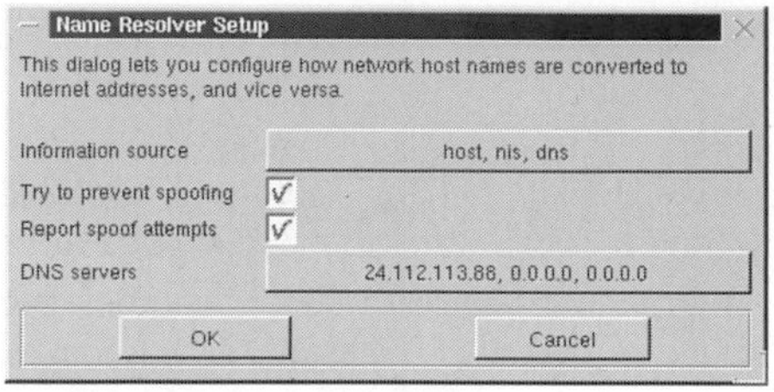

FIGURE 6.13
COAS Name Resolver (host-name resolution) dialog box.

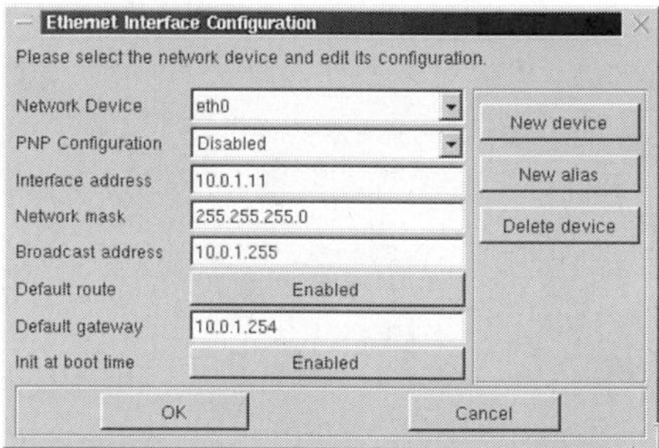

FIGURE 6.14
Main dialog box of COAS Network Interface module.

- Common Networking Functions—COAS->Network->Ethernet Interface—This module can be used to add new networking interfaces (Ethernet cards) or to create new *aliases* (virtual interfaces) for existing Ethernet cards. When the module loads, a dialog box similar to that shown in Figure 6.14 is displayed. Using the drop-down selection in the first field, you can get configuration information for all real interfaces and their aliases. Aliases are the way to give the same machine multiple IP addresses using a single Ethernet card. You can also enable/disable Plug and Play (PNP), as well as set the IP address of the interface, the broadcast address, the default route, and whether the interface is activated at boot time. If you use DHCP (ADSL or cable modem) to get your Ethernet information, setting PNP to DHCP is necessary, but perhaps insufficient, depending on your particular network provider's policy.
- Mail Transport Configuration—COAS->Mail Transfer—Allows setting of simple options for `sendmail`. See Chapter 9, "SMTP and Protocols," for more information about sendmail and other mail software.

COAS Peripherals Administration

This module allows you to set the keyboard layout, set up the printers and text mouse mode (which is not the same as the mouse used under X Windows).

The `lisa` printer administration tool is more flexible than the COAS tool. For instance, my own older HP laser printer is listed under the `lisa` menus, but not under COAS.

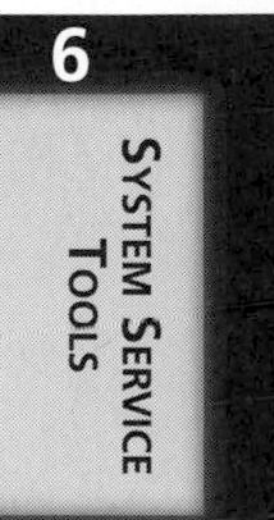

Otherwise, the COAS tool is considerably snazzier if that's what impresses you or your superiors.

OpenLinux uses a commercial print spooler called LPRng, which is compatible with lpd, the sprint spooler shipped with other versions of Linux, including Red Hat. LPRng is very similar to lpd and interoperates with it. While Red Hat's printtool provides a way to submit a Linux print job to Windows using Windows-native protocols (smbprint), LPRng takes the opposite approach. It provides a Windows 95/98 tool that can accept native Linux lpd jobs. Microsoft itself supplies a similar tool for Windows NT. Printing under Linux is discussed further in Chapter 24, while the SMB networking tools (for interworking with Microsoft operating systems) are discussed in Chapter 16.

Under COAS, adding printers is mostly a matter of selecting the printer type and its connection location (a parallel or serial port). Figure 6.15 shows a typical dialog box displayed when a printer definition is edited. It's a big dialog box and so the rest of the KDE screen is not shown.

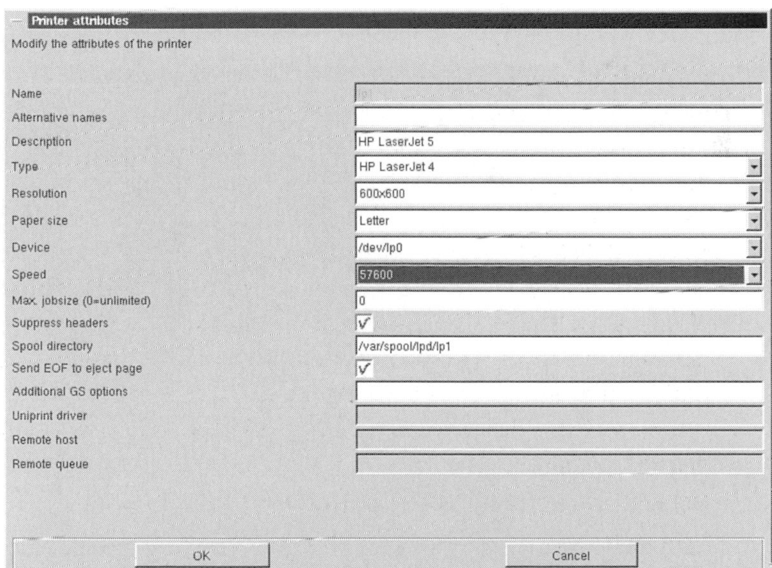

FIGURE 6.15
Printer Attributes dialog box under COAS.

Finally, note that nearly all the printer support is actually provided by Peter Deutsch's Ghostscript. Linux programs (such as Netscape Communicator) produce all printer output in PostScript format and Ghostscript is used to convert the result to another format, such as HP PCL5. Some Linux applications, however (such as WordPerfect), do have their own printer driver support. When you select the WordPerfect HP Laserjet 5 driver,

WordPerfect is already producing a PCL5 stream and `Ghostscript` needs to be bypassed altogether.

COAS System Administration

This module contains the most frequently used tools, under the following headings:

- Account Administration—Allows you to examine the list of user accounts and to add, modify, or remove entries. This dialog box benefits from a lot of screen real estate, and so this dialog box alone is shown in Figure 6.16 for a typical newly installed system. For the existing entries, the dialog box is organized like a spreadsheet. Highlight a particular row and then pull down the Actions menu; pull down Action and select Edit User or Delete User, as appropriate. For new users, just pull down Actions and select Create User. Two points about this item: first, the security advisory about `/etc/shadow` mentioned at the beginning of the `COAS` section above; second, at the time of writing this tool does not successfully modify the Name field of the `/etc/passwd` file, which contains the human readable name of the user (for example, Fred Jones).

User Accounts

File Actions View Options

Login	UID	Name	Home Directory
root	0	root	/root
bin	1	bin	/bin
daemon	2	daemon	/sbin
adm	3	adm	/var/adm
lp	4	lp	/var/spool/lpd
sync	5	sync	/sbin
shutdown	6	shutdown	/sbin
halt	7	halt	/sbin
mail	8	mail	/var/spool/mail
news	9	news	/var/spool/news
uucp	10	uucp	/var/spool/uucp
operator	11	operator	/root
games	12	games	/usr/games
gopher	13	gopher	/usr/lib/gopher-data

FIGURE 6.16
COAS User Accounts dialog box.

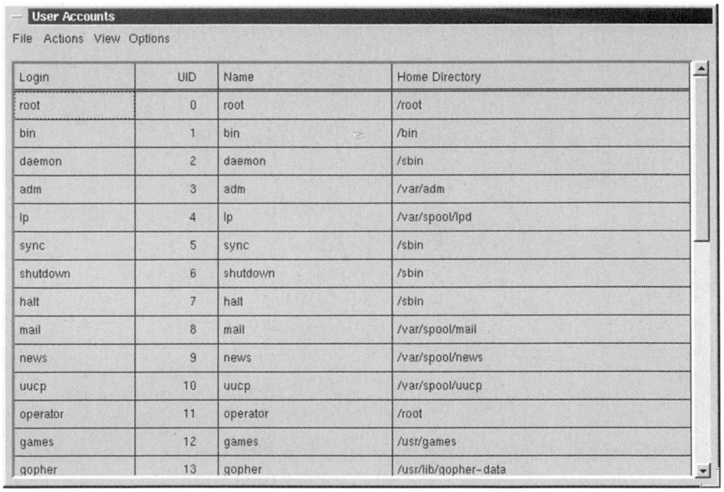

- Enable/Disable System Services—Enables/disables services via check boxes next to their names; takes effect at next system boot, as shown in Figure 6.17.
- Filesystem Administration—Controls mount points of existing partitions and removable devices.

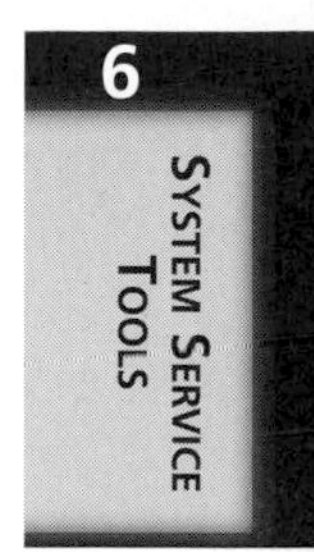

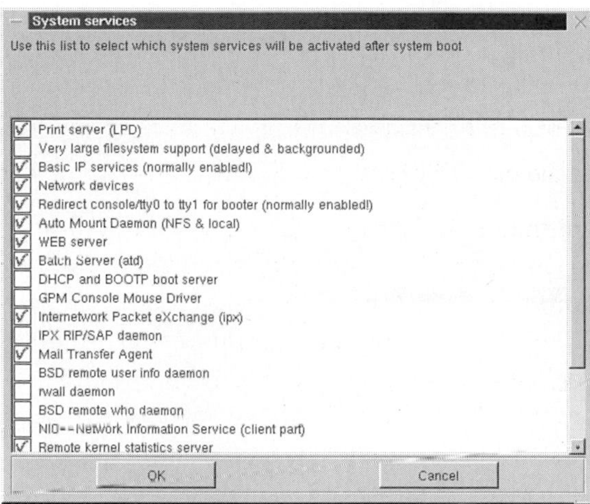

FIGURE 6.17
Typical list of services to disable or enable.

- System Hostname—This should have been set when OpenLinux was installed. If you want to change it, log out of KDE immediately afterwards; you will no longer be able to launch new X clients!
- System Resource Information—This is a list of information about the CPU's in your system, such as whether it has several bugs, and the bogomips (the Linux kernel's bogus estimated MIPS) value.
- System Time—This item allows you to view the current system time, change it, and to view and set the kernel timezone (now the kernel interprets the hardware clock).

COAS Kernel Modules Administration

`COAS` is capable of loading kernel modules on the spot and arranging for them to be loaded at boot time. It also has built-in intelligence on what parameters they need at boot time and what their purposes are (multimedia, networking, and so on).

When a Kernel Modules Administration Module (CLAM) loads, you are initially presented with two long lists, one of kernel modules that can be loaded and another of modules already loaded, as shown in Figure 6.18.

For instance, if you decide to load the `smc-ultra` module (supporting the SMC Ultra Ethernet cards), `COAS` first presents a dialog box similar to that shown in Figure 6.19.

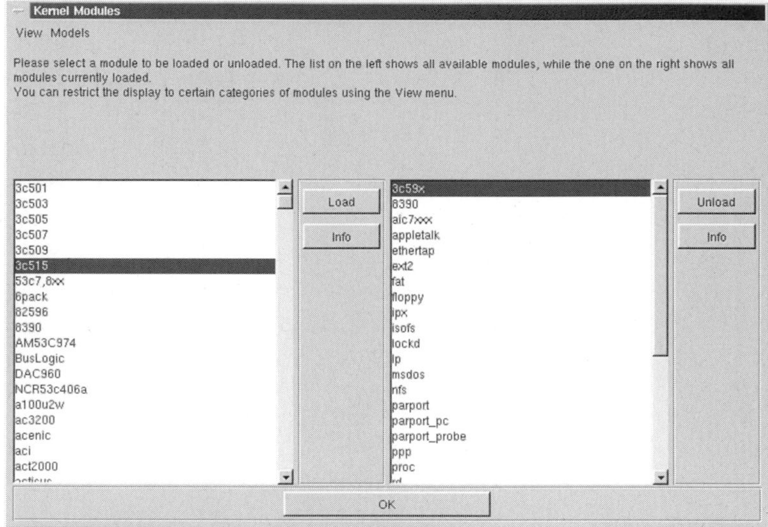

FIGURE 6.18
COAS lists of kernel modules: available and already loaded.

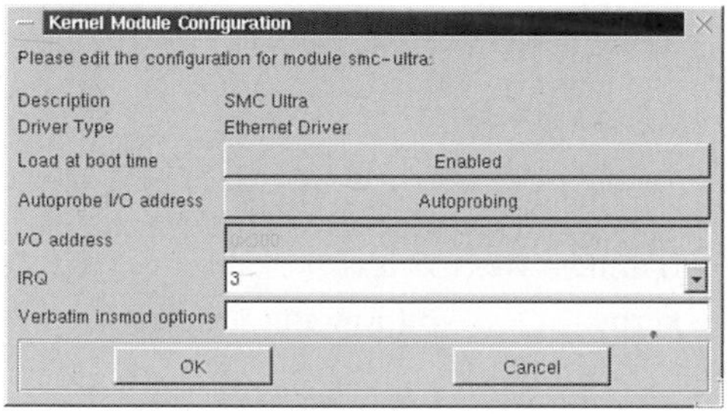

Kernel Module Configuration
Please edit the configuration for module smc-ultra:
Description SMC Ultra
Driver Type Ethernet Driver
Load at boot time Enabled
Autoprobe I/O address Autoprobing
I/O address
IRQ 3
Verbatim insmod options
OK Cancel

FIGURE 6.19
Loading the SMC Ultra module under COAS.

The module is set to Autoprobe in the displayed configuration. The Linux kernel does this by default when it loads. However, if you have more than one Ethernet card of the same type, you may want to control the order that the driver tries different addresses so that the right card turns out to be `eth0` (so you don't have to switch the cables).

Using the box Load at Boot Time, you control whether the module is loaded only temporarily or on all future boots as well.

The Boot Process

The high-level tools presented earlier in this chapter are designed to insulate you from what is going on under the hood. Just as the first thing you should do after buying a new car is get its repair manual, you should have some awareness of what is really happening when Linux boots—even if you do not tamper with it yourself.

In Chapter 2, "Installing Linux," you learned how to install Linux, and in Chapter 3 you found out how to install and use different loaders for different computers. There are a number of ways to start Linux with different computers, and there are different ways to load the Linux kernel. Intel Linux users will most likely use LILO, LOADLIN, SYSLINUX, BOOTLIN, or commercial alternatives, such as System Commander or BootMagic. BootMagic and a limited version of PartitionMagic are supplied as part of the OpenLinux 2.2 distribution. SPARC users will use SILO, and Alpha users will probably use MILO. For Red Hat Linux, the basic steps are outlined in the *Red Hat Linux User's Guide* (from the official distribution) or on the Red Hat Web site at `http://www.redhat.com/linux-info`. It is also described in Chapter 12 of the *OpenLinux 2.2 Getting Started Guide*, part of the official Caldera OpenLinux 2.2 distribution package.

Debian GNU/Linux 2.1 users may find this information on the Debian Web site at `http://www.debian.org/releases/slink/`.

From now on, this chapter assumes that readers will install one of the Intel distributions, particularly Red Hat Linux 6.0 or Caldera OpenLinux 2.2. These remarks also apply to most up-to-date distributions of Linux, including Debian.

PCs start by looking at the first sector of the first cylinder of the boot drive and then trying to load and execute code found there (which is one way LILO can work). This is also the case with other (but not all) hardware systems and versions of UNIX. You should be able to set the order in which your PC looks for the boot drive, usually through a BIOS change in a setup menu you can invoke when you first turn on your machine (usually accomplished by pressing Del, F1, F2, or even F10). Setting the order can be handy if you never use a boot floppy disk; for example, laptop users with an external floppy drive can speed the boot process by directing the computer to look first at the internal hard drive or CD-ROM.

You can also start Linux over a network and run a diskless Linux box. For more information on how to do this, see Robert Nemkin's Diskless Linux Mini HOWTO, under `/usr/doc/HOWTO/mini`. Although Linux shares many traits with both System V and BSD UNIX, Linux is closer to the former in the case of booting and starting the system. This means Linux uses the `init` command and a similar directory structure of associated scripts to start running the system and loading processes (see "Using `bootpc` for Remote Booting" in this chapter).

The System V approach is flexible and powerful, and therefore is the way of the future in Linux. However, it is a nuisance to administer via traditional command-line tools. Fortunately, the advent of such tools as Red Hat's `linuxconf` and Caldera's `COAS` (described earlier in this chapter) have almost put an end to this.

The init Process

Once the kernel has loaded, it builds process 0 "by hand" and then loads a special process: init. init is the ancestor of all other processes in the system's uptime. This process always has process ID 1. Here, for instance, is part of the output of the pstree (process tree) command for a running Red Hat system:

```
init-+-atd
     |-cardmgr
     |-crond
     |-2*[enlightenment]
     |-gdm-+-X
     |     `-gdm---gnome-session
     |-gen_util_applet
     |-gmc
     |-gnome-name-serv
     |-gnome-smproxy
     |-gnome-terminal
...
```

Although the entire output of pstree is not shown here, you can see that init has spawned the start of the system as the first process, and the parent of all subsequent processes.

The operation of the init process is controlled throughout the uptime of the system by the control file /etc/inittab. One of the various activities that is controlled by this file is the mounting of additional (non-root) filesystems. Therefore, this file is needed before that, and therefore the /etc directory must be located in the root (primary) filesystem. Otherwise /etc/inittab will not be accessible when it is first needed.

Here is part of /etc/inittab for my Red Hat 6.0 system:

```
# System initialization.
si::sysinit:/etc/rc.d/rc.sysinit

l0:0:wait:/etc/rc.d/rc 0
l1:1:wait:/etc/rc.d/rc 1
l2:2:wait:/etc/rc.d/rc 2
l3:3:wait:/etc/rc.d/rc 3
l4:4:wait:/etc/rc.d/rc 4
l5:5:wait:/etc/rc.d/rc 5
l6:6:wait:/etc/rc.d/rc 6

# Things to run in every runlevel.
ud::once:/sbin/update
```

```
# Trap CTRL-ALT-DELETE
ca::ctrlaltdel:/sbin/shutdown -t3 -r now

# When our UPS tells us power has failed, assume we have a few minutes
# of power left.  Schedule a shutdown for 2 minutes from now.
# This does, of course, assume you have powerd installed and your
# UPS connected and working correctly.
pf::powerfail:/sbin/shutdown -f -h +2 "Power Failure; System Shutting Down"
```

The beginning of each line is a label with no particular meaning, except to the human reader.

The second field, surrounded by colons, may be empty, or may contain one or more digits. In the latter case, the digits form a list of *runlevels* (see the next section) to which the line applies. When empty, the line applies to all runlevels.

The third field controls when and how often to perform the action. For instance, `respawn` means to keep doing something (run it, and then restart it again after it exits), and `sysinit` means to perform the action once at system init time.

The fourth and last field, the rest of the line, which may be empty in certain cases, contains the system command to perform.

Lines beginning with an octothorpe (hash mark) are comments.

Runlevels

At any given time, the Linux system has a global system state known as the runlevel. This is simply a one-digit parameter used by `init` to selectively execute entries in `/etc/inittab`. A special entry in `/etc/inittab` specifies the *default* runlevel, which is normally used as the *initial* runlevel at boot time.

The default runlevel for the system can be overridden from the prompt of most boot loaders, including LILO. The current runlevel of a fully booted system can also be changed by interactive use of the `init` system command.

Runlevels are small single-digit decimal integers, from 0 to 9, with 0, 1, 2, 3, 5, 6 and sometimes 4 being the only values commonly used.

Runlevels, also known as system states, grew from the need to separate how the system ran according to the forms of maintenance being performed on a system. Linux is a multiuser, networked operating system with both character and graphical interfaces available. Under certain conditions, it is convenient to start selected parts of the system, and in particular to disallow multiple users, or not automatically start the X Windows

System. For instance, if you buy a new monitor or video card, your current X Windows parameters may not work. Therefore, you will want to start your system without X, run `XF86Setup`, and then go back to graphics mode. This can be done without a full reboot.

In the past, configuring new hardware—except for external modems—necessitated rebooting the system in single user mode (runlevel 1). This is similar to performing a software or hardware upgrade on older PCs, which generally requires a reboot or shutdown and restart of the computer. These days, however, this practice is partially obviated through new software and hardware technologies. *Hot-swappable* hardware and software indicates that you can change hard drives, PC cards, or associated software on-the-fly—while the system is running (such as loading or unloading Linux kernel modules with the `insmod` and `rmmod` commands).

Although runlevel values are purely arbitrary, consistency with the behavior of AT&T's System V Release 4 (SVR4) (of which Solaris 2 is a derivative) has fixed the meaning of levels 0, 1, 2, 3, and 6, and has created the impression there are already too many runlevels. There is no need to go above 6! Therefore, as a practical matter, only 4 and 5 were available for Red Hat and Caldera. Essentially, 4 is left unused, although Caldera makes it the same as 3, and 5 is used for graphics mode. Debian defines level 2 as the default and it brings up everything; you are free to modify this if desired. Here is the consolidated list for all three systems:

> 0—Halt; the system runlevel is normally changed to 0 to effect an orderly shutdown.
>
> 1—Single-user mode, comparable to MS Windows safe mode.
>
> 2—Multiuser mode without NFS. In Debian, this is full-blown multiuser mode with NFS and X.
>
> 3—Multiuser mode with NFS.
>
> 4—Under Red Hat, not used; Caldera also has no purpose for it, but makes it identical to 3.
>
> 5—Multiuser mode with X11 started automatically.
>
> 6—Reboot; this is the same as runlevel 0, except that the machine is rebooted at the last step instead of being halted.

As mentioned, the various runlevels are defined in the file `/etc/inittab`. Although it's not immediately evident from examining this file, a series of scripts in `/etc/rc.d/rcX.d` is run whenever a runlevel is entered or exited. `X` stands for the level number. For example, the scripts in `/etc/rc.d/rc5.d` are used for runlevel 5, the runlevel reserved under Red Hat and Caldera for graphical mode (GNOME or KDE login screen, respectively, instead of a text-mode prompt).

sysinit

Before anything else happens, `init` runs lines in `/etc/inittab` with `sysinit` in the third field. As shipped, a Red Hat system has exactly one such line that reads as follows:

```
si::sysinit:/etc/rc.d/rc.sysinit
```

Caldera has three such lines, as shown next:

```
s0::sysinit:/bin/bash -c 'C=/sbin/booterd; [ -x $C ] && $C'
si::sysinit:/bin/bash -c 'C=/etc/rc.d/rc.modules; [ -x $C ] && $C default'
s2::sysinit:/bin/bash -c 'C=/etc/rc.d/rc.serial; [ -x $C ] && $C'
```

Debian has one corresponding line that reads as follows:

```
si::sysinit:/etc/init.d/rcS
```

Red Hat and Debian put all the parts of system initialization common to all runlevels in a single script (`rc.sysinit` or `rcS`), whereas Caldera divides it into three parts.

The Red Hat Linux `sysinit` script, the Debian `rcS` script, and the three parallel Caldera scripts perform some or all of the following functions:

- Sets some initial `$PATH` variables
- Configures networking
- Starts swapping for virtual memory
- Sets the system hostname
- Checks `root` filesystems for possible repairs
- Checks `root` filesystem quotas
- Turns on user and group quotas for `root` filesystems
- Remounts the `root` filesystem read/write
- Clears the mounted filesystems table `/etc/mtab`
- Enters the `root` filesystem into `mtab`
- Readies the system for loading modules
- Finds module dependencies
- Checks filesystems for possible repairs
- Mounts all other filesystems
- Cleans out several `/etc` files: `/etc/mtab`, `/etc/fastboot`, and `/etc/nologin`
- Deletes UUCP lock files
- Deletes stale subsystem files

- Deletes stale pid files
- Sets the system clock
- Turns on swapping
- Initializes the serial ports
- Loads modules

That's a lot of work for the first startup script, but it's only the first step in a number needed to start your system. You've seen that the init command is run after the Linux kernel is loaded. After the rc.sysinit is run by init, init runs rc.local. If you look at the Red Hat Linux rc.local script, you'll see that it gets the operating system name and architecture of your computer and puts it into a file called /etc/issue, which is later used for display at the login prompt. Red Hat manufactures /etc/issue inside the /etc/rc.d/rc.local script, while Caldera will read it from /etc/.issue if this file exists. In Debian, the appropriate script is /etc/init.d/bootmisc.sh, which replaces rc.local.

Note

The purpose of rc.local is not to provide a place to put system-specific initializations, although some people do. In BSD UNIX, rc.local is generally used for controlling network services. Linux has not always used the same initialization scripts or approach to starting. You might find differences between distributions, such as Red Hat Linux, Caldera, Debian, Slackware, SuSE, or others. For Red Hat Linux, use one of the graphical interface tools (such as tksysv, ntsysv, or linuxconf) to control your system's services. Although you can do it manually by copying a skeleton script from the init.d directory and setting up the proper symbolic links, you'll find most of your needs met by the proper Red Hat tool.

When the Runlevel Changes

When the system boots, it is deemed to enter its default runlevel, or the value that overrode that value from the LILO prompt. Similarly, the following interactive command requests that the runlevel be changed to that new runlevel:

```
#init N
```

N is a runlevel.

In particular, this command initiates a shutdown of the system:

```
# init 0
```

When a change of runlevel is requested, the scripts beginning with `K` (for *kill*) in the old runlevel's `rcX.d` directory are run in alphabetical order. Scripts beginning with `S` (for *start*) in the new `rcX.d` directory are run, also in alphabetical order. However, if you do a listing from one of these directories (such as the following one from `/etc/rc.d/rc5.d`) on an OpenLinux 2.2 box, you will see that these directories only contain symbolic links to various files in `/etc/rc.d/init.d`. To investigate this further, I used the following command on both a Red Hat 6.0 and an OpenLinux 2.2 system:

```
# find /etc/rc.d -type d -print | xargs symlinks -v | sort
```

The command indicates that all `/etc/rc.d` subdirectories should be found and their names piped to the program `xargs`. This program in turn translates the list of names into a long line that it uses to complete the list of arguments to `symlinks`, and to sort the result alphabetically. The `symlinks` command (which is not distributed with OpenLinux, but is freely available from various places on the internet) looks for symbolic links in a directory and finds out where, if anywhere, they point. After some editing to conserve printing space, I got the following result under OpenLinux:

```
/etc/rc.d/init.d/local -> ../rc.local
/etc/rc.d/init.d/reboot -> halt
/etc/rc.d/rc0.d/K09samba -> ../init.d/samba
/etc/rc.d/rc0.d/K25gpm -> ../init.d/gpm
/etc/rc.d/rc0.d/K25httpd -> ../init.d/httpd
/etc/rc.d/rc0.d/K30logoutd -> ../init.d/logoutd
/etc/rc.d/rc0.d/K39rwalld -> ../init.d/rwalld
/etc/rc.d/rc0.d/K40rstatd -> ../init.d/rstatd
/etc/rc.d/rc0.d/K44dhcpd -> ../init.d/dhcpd
/etc/rc.d/rc0.d/K47rusersd -> ../init.d/rusersd
/etc/rc.d/rc0.d/K48rwhod -> ../init.d/rwhod
/etc/rc.d/rc0.d/K50mta -> ../init.d/mta
/etc/rc.d/rc0.d/K59atd -> ../init.d/atd
/etc/rc.d/rc0.d/K60cron -> ../init.d/cron
/etc/rc.d/rc0.d/K65lpd -> ../init.d/lpd
/etc/rc.d/rc0.d/K70amd -> ../init.d/amd
/etc/rc.d/rc0.d/K70ntp -> ../init.d/ntp
/etc/rc.d/rc0.d/K73ipxripd -> ../init.d/ipxripd
/etc/rc.d/rc0.d/K74ipx -> ../init.d/ipx
/etc/rc.d/rc0.d/K79nis-client -> ../init.d/nis-client
/etc/rc.d/rc0.d/K85inet -> ../init.d/inet
/etc/rc.d/rc0.d/K95syslog -> ../init.d/syslog
/etc/rc.d/rc0.d/K95urandom -> ../init.d/urandom
/etc/rc.d/rc0.d/K99network -> ../init.d/network
/etc/rc.d/rc0.d/K99zap -> ../init.d/zap
/etc/rc.d/rc0.d/S99halt -> ../init.d/halt
/etc/rc.d/rc1.d/K09samba -> ../init.d/samba
/etc/rc.d/rc1.d/K25gpm -> ../init.d/gpm
/etc/rc.d/rc1.d/K25httpd -> ../init.d/httpd
/etc/rc.d/rc1.d/K30logoutd -> ../init.d/logoutd
```

```
/etc/rc.d/rc1.d/K39rwalld -> ../init.d/rwalld
/etc/rc.d/rc1.d/K40rstatd -> ../init.d/rstatd
/etc/rc.d/rc1.d/K44dhcpd -> ../init.d/dhcpd
/etc/rc.d/rc1.d/K47rusersd -> ../init.d/rusersd
/etc/rc.d/rc1.d/K48rwhod -> ../init.d/rwhod
/etc/rc.d/rc1.d/K50mta -> ../init.d/mta
/etc/rc.d/rc1.d/K59atd -> ../init.d/atd
/etc/rc.d/rc1.d/K60cron -> ../init.d/cron
/etc/rc.d/rc1.d/K65lpd -> ../init.d/lpd
/etc/rc.d/rc1.d/K70amd -> ../init.d/amd
/etc/rc.d/rc1.d/K70ntp -> ../init.d/ntp
/etc/rc.d/rc1.d/K73ipxripd -> ../init.d/ipxripd
/etc/rc.d/rc1.d/K74ipx -> ../init.d/ipx
/etc/rc.d/rc1.d/K79nis-client -> ../init.d/nis-client
/etc/rc.d/rc1.d/K85inet -> ../init.d/inet
/etc/rc.d/rc1.d/K95syslog -> ../init.d/syslog
/etc/rc.d/rc1.d/K95urandom -> ../init.d/urandom
/etc/rc.d/rc1.d/K99zap -> ../init.d/zap
/etc/rc.d/rc1.d/S99single -> ../init.d/single
/etc/rc.d/rc2.d/K09samba -> ../init.d/samba
/etc/rc.d/rc2.d/K25gpm -> ../init.d/gpm
/etc/rc.d/rc2.d/K25httpd -> ../init.d/httpd
/etc/rc.d/rc2.d/K30logoutd -> ../init.d/logoutd
/etc/rc.d/rc2.d/K39rwalld -> ../init.d/rwalld
/etc/rc.d/rc2.d/K40rstatd -> ../init.d/rstatd
[SNIP]
/etc/rc.d/rc2.d/K44dhcpd -> ../init.d/dhcpd
/etc/rc.d/rc2.d/K47rusersd -> ../init.d/rusersd
/etc/rc.d/rc2.d/K48rwhod -> ../init.d/rwhod
[SNIP]
/etc/rc.d/rc2.d/S99zap -> ../init.d/zap
/etc/rc.d/rc3.d/S01network -> ../init.d/network
/etc/rc.d/rc3.d/S05syslog -> ../init.d/syslog
/etc/rc.d/rc3.d/S05urandom -> ../init.d/urandom
/etc/rc.d/rc3.d/S15inet -> ../init.d/inet
/etc/rc.d/rc3.d/S21nis-client -> ../init.d/nis-client
/etc/rc.d/rc3.d/S26ipx -> ../init.d/ipx
/etc/rc.d/rc3.d/S27ipxripd -> ../init.d/ipxripd
/etc/rc.d/rc3.d/S30amd -> ../init.d/amd
/etc/rc.d/rc3.d/S30ntp -> ../init.d/ntp
/etc/rc.d/rc3.d/S35lpd -> ../init.d/lpd
/etc/rc.d/rc3.d/S40cron -> ../init.d/cron
/etc/rc.d/rc3.d/S41atd -> ../init.d/atd
/etc/rc.d/rc3.d/S50mta -> ../init.d/mta
/etc/rc.d/rc3.d/S56dhcpd -> ../init.d/dhcpd
/etc/rc.d/rc3.d/S60rstatd -> ../init.d/rstatd
/etc/rc.d/rc3.d/S61rwalld -> ../init.d/rwalld
/etc/rc.d/rc3.d/S62rwhod -> ../init.d/rwhod
/etc/rc.d/rc3.d/S63rusersd -> ../init.d/rusersd
/etc/rc.d/rc3.d/S70logoutd -> ../init.d/logoutd
/etc/rc.d/rc3.d/S75gpm -> ../init.d/gpm
```

```
/etc/rc.d/rc3.d/S75keytable -> ../init.d/keytable
/etc/rc.d/rc3.d/S85httpd -> ../init.d/httpd
/etc/rc.d/rc3.d/S91samba -> ../init.d/samba
/etc/rc.d/rc3.d/S98local -> ../init.d/local
/etc/rc.d/rc3.d/S99bigfs -> ../init.d/bigfs
/etc/rc.d/rc3.d/S99rmnologin -> ../init.d/rmnologin
/etc/rc.d/rc3.d/S99skipped -> ../init.d/skipped
/etc/rc.d/rc3.d/S99zap -> ../init.d/zap
[SNIP]
/etc/rc.d/rc5.d/S01network -> ../init.d/network
/etc/rc.d/rc5.d/S05syslog -> ../init.d/syslog
/etc/rc.d/rc5.d/S05urandom -> ../init.d/urandom
/etc/rc.d/rc5.d/S15inet -> ../init.d/inet
/etc/rc.d/rc5.d/S21nis-client -> ../init.d/nis-client
/etc/rc.d/rc5.d/S26ipx -> ../init.d/ipx
/etc/rc.d/rc5.d/S27ipxripd -> ../init.d/ipxripd
/etc/rc.d/rc5.d/S30amd -> ../init.d/amd
/etc/rc.d/rc5.d/S30ntp -> ../init.d/ntp
/etc/rc.d/rc5.d/S35lpd -> ../init.d/lpd
/etc/rc.d/rc5.d/S40cron -> ../init.d/cron
/etc/rc.d/rc5.d/S41atd -> ../init.d/atd
/etc/rc.d/rc5.d/S50mta -> ../init.d/mta
/etc/rc.d/rc5.d/S56dhcpd -> ../init.d/dhcpd
/etc/rc.d/rc5.d/S60rstatd -> ../init.d/rstatd
/etc/rc.d/rc5.d/S61rwalld -> ../init.d/rwalld
/etc/rc.d/rc5.d/S62rwhod -> ../init.d/rwhod
/etc/rc.d/rc5.d/S63rusersd -> ../init.d/rusersd
/etc/rc.d/rc5.d/S70logoutd -> ../init.d/logoutd
/etc/rc.d/rc5.d/S75gpm -> ../init.d/gpm
/etc/rc.d/rc5.d/S75keytable -> . ./init.d/keytable
/etc/rc.d/rc5.d/S85httpd -> ../init.d/httpd
/etc/rc.d/rc5.d/S91samba -> ../init.d/samba
/etc/rc.d/rc5.d/S98local -> ../init.d/local
/etc/rc.d/rc5.d/S99bigfs -> ../init.d/bigfs
/etc/rc.d/rc5.d/S99rmnologin -> ../init.d/rmnologin
/etc/rc.d/rc5.d/S99skipped -> ../init.d/skipped
/etc/rc.d/rc5.d/S99zap -> ../init.d/zap
/etc/rc.d/rc6.d/K09samba -> ../init.d/samba
/etc/rc.d/rc6.d/K25gpm -> ../init.d/gpm
/etc/rc.d/rc6.d/K25httpd -> ../init.d/httpd
/etc/rc.d/rc6.d/K30logoutd -> ../init.d/logoutd
/etc/rc.d/rc6.d/K39rwalld -> ../init.d/rwalld
/etc/rc.d/rc6.d/K40rstatd -> ../init.d/rstatd
/etc/rc.d/rc6.d/K44dhcpd -> ../init.d/dhcpd
/etc/rc.d/rc6.d/K47rusersd -> ../init.d/rusersd
/etc/rc.d/rc6.d/K48rwhod -> ../init.d/rwhod
/etc/rc.d/rc6.d/K50mta -> ../init.d/mta
/etc/rc.d/rc6.d/K59atd -> ../init.d/atd
/etc/rc.d/rc6.d/K60cron -> ../init.d/cron
/etc/rc.d/rc6.d/K65lpd -> ../init.d/lpd
/etc/rc.d/rc6.d/K70amd -> ../init.d/amd
```

```
/etc/rc.d/rc6.d/K70ntp -> ../init.d/ntp
/etc/rc.d/rc6.d/K73ipxripd -> ../init.d/ipxripd
/etc/rc.d/rc6.d/K74ipx -> ../init.d/ipx
/etc/rc.d/rc6.d/K79nis-client -> ../init.d/nis-client
/etc/rc.d/rc6.d/K85inet -> ../init.d/inet
/etc/rc.d/rc6.d/K95syslog -> ../init.d/syslog
/etc/rc.d/rc6.d/K95urandom -> ../init.d/urandom
/etc/rc.d/rc6.d/K99network -> ../init.d/network
/etc/rc.d/rc6.d/K99zap -> ../init.d/zap
/etc/rc.d/rc6.d/S99reboot -> ../init.d/reboot
```

The lines marked `[SNIP]` are where material has been left out in the name of brevity. However, the contents of `/etc/rc.d/rc0.d`, `/etc/rc.d/rc1.d`, `etc/rc.d/rc3.d`, `/etc/rc.d/rc5.d`, and `/etc/rc.d/rc6.d` are given in full.

Basically, the `rcX.d` directories contain only symbolic links to real files in the `/etc/rc.d/init.d` directory.

In Debian machines, these directories contain links to files in `/etc/init.d`.

At first, the naming pattern in the `rcX.d` directories seems strange, but it is done to make sure the associated services are started and stopped in a specific order, and there is no particular connection between a service's readable name and its correct position in an alphabetical startup sequence unless the strange `S` and `K` prefixes are added.

Runlevel 0, as shown earlier, is special and reserved for orderly system shutdown. Certain system commands (such as `halt`, `poweroff`, and `reboot`) only perform their obvious function by changing to runlevel 0. For instance, the `shutdown` system command actually only warns the users of the impending shutdown and then, if it hasn't been aborted because of somebody's protest, executes the following system command to perform the actual shutdown.

```
# init 0
```

The Default Runlevel

In the absence of boot-time directive from the user (via the LILO boot prompt for instance), `init` uses `initdefault` line in `/etc/inittab` to select the default runlevel. This level can be manipulated directly by editing the `/etc/inittab` file (not recommended) or indirectly via so-called runlevel editors, such as the one built into Red Hat's `linuxconf`. The normal default runlevel for the latest Linux distributions is 5, meaning that it will automatically start the designated X Display Manager (such as kdm for KDE or gdm for GNOME). The value `3` generally means to start everything else. The user logs in using a traditional text login, and types `startx` or a similar command to start up the X system. Absolutely never set the default runlevel to 0 or 6. The runlevel 1 is also known as single, which explains why single can be used in place of 1 at the LILO prompt to request single-user mode.

The init.d directory

By convention, startup, shutdown, and restart of each service is done by the same script, called in a different way. By further convention, the directory /etc/rc.d/init.d contains the primary copies of the scripts, and the various rcX.d directories contain symbolic links to the appropriate script in the init.d directory.

When a service is started, the script is called with the single argument start. When it is stopped, it is called with the single argument stop. Lastly, the argument restart may or may not do what the word suggests; it is only invoked with that argument interactively, and not through the regular boot or shutdown sequences.

Using Red Hat as the basis for analysis, here is a survey of what the various scripts in init.d can do. Whether they actually have any effect depends on whether appropriate symbolic links exist in the current runlevel's script directory.

The details about each are not given here, but you should be able to guess at the function of some by their names and short description, as shown in Table 6.2. Many of them are described elsewhere in this book.

TABLE 6.2 Red Hat Linux System Initialization Scripts

Name	*Description*
amd	Controls the automount daemon
apmd ging	Directory contains apmd.init for control of power management and log-
arpwatch	Tracks Ethernet and Internet protocol address pairings
atd	Controls the at (personal scheduling) daemon
autofs	Controls the automount filesystem daemon
bootparamd	May be used to network boot older Sun workstations
crond	Controls the cron system scheduling daemon
dhcpd	Controls the Dynamic Host Control Protocol daemon
functions	Shell script functions used by init scripts
gated	Controls the routing gateway daemon
gpm	Controls the console mouse server (console cut-and-paste utility)
halt	Controls how shutdowns and reboots are handled
httpd	Controls the Apache Web server and HTTP services

continues

TABLE 6.2 continued

Name	*Description*
`inet`	Controls TCP/IP and other services
`kerneld`	Controls autoloading/unloading of kernel modules
`keytable`	Controls keyboard map loading
`killall`	Utility script used by `amd`, `crond`, `inet`, `kerneld`, `mars-nwe` and the `nfs init` scripts to kill processes
`linuxconf`	Utility script for Red Hat's `linuxconf` tool
`lpd`	Controls print spooling services
`mars-nwe`	Controls Netware-compatible system services
`mcserv`	Controls Midnight Commander remote services
`named`	Controls starting and stopping of DNS
`network`	Controls starting and stopping system networking
`nfs`	Controls NFS services
`nfsfs`	Controls mounting of NFS filesystems
`nscd`	Controls the `Name Switch Cache` daemon
`pcmcia`	Controls Card services for laptops
`portmap`	Controls RPC services
`postgresql`	Controls `PostgreSQL` database daemon
`random`	Controls random number generation
`routed`	Controls `network routing table` daemon
`rstatd`	Controls the `rpc.statd network kernel statistics` daemon
`rusersd`	Controls the `rpc.rusersd` Network services
`rwalld`	Controls the `rpc.rwalld` Network Wall services
`rwhod`	Controls the `rwhod` daemon network `rwho` services
`sendmail`	Controls mail transport services
`single`	Used by `init` when Linux is booted to runlevel 1 or single-user administrative mode
`smb`	Controls the Samba `smbd` and `nmbd` daemons
`snmpd`	Controls the `Simple Network Management Protocol` daemon
`sound`	Saves and restores mixer information and levels
`squid`	Controls `httpd` object caching service
`syslog`	Starts and stops System Logging services

`xdm`	Controls whether to start or stop the X display manager, K display manager, or GNOME display manager for runlevel 5
`xfs`	Starts and stops the X11 `font` server
`xntpd`	Starts and stops the `Network Time Protocol` (`NTPv3`) daemon for time synchronization
`ypbind`	Controls NIS binding services
`yppasswdd`	Controls the `YP password` server
`ypserv`	Controls Network Information services

In general, each script listed in Table 6.1 is designed to respond to commands of the following form:

```
script {start¦stop¦status¦restart}
```

This means that a particular service may be controlled from other programs, depending on the syntax used.

Debian defines the options as start, stop, reload, and restart. The reload option is used to tell a running daemon to reset itself (generally, to reload its configuration file).

Note

Not all scripts will respond to a restart or a status call.

Kernel Modules

Kernel modules have revolutionized software and hardware installation.

Originally, there was a sharp line between the kernel and user realms that was deliberately unbreachable. The user realm was flexible: New programs could be loaded at will and it had virtual memory, it (eventually) had multithreading (multiple processes sharing the same memory and I/O resources). The kernel realm was much different. It had a fixed linear memory space, with no dynamic allocation at all, and the only code in it was the kernel loaded at boot time.

The advent of universal interfaces such as SCSI started to change that. It didn't matter exactly what kind of SCSI disk you had as long as you knew its parameters: The hardware and kernel interfaces were not very different.

UNIX kernels always had provision for *device drivers*, which were jump tables with standardized entry points and some kernel glue to get data between parts of the driver run at interrupt time (when many kernel services don't work) and task time (when regular kernel services are available). New device drivers were provided in object form, with link symbols still attached, and the module was simply linked into the device driver table.

Kernel modules work the same way except that the symbols are resolved when needed, not when the kernel is first loaded. This, of course, may fail if the requested module is not around.

For this reason, there are user-level tools for loading modules, unloading modules, and for testing for the presence of modules in the kernel.

In addition to simply loading a module, it is possible to reach into the module and adjust it slightly before loading. Why would you want to do that? For instance, most device driver kernel modules have a small array called `io`, which is a list of the I/O interface addresses to search. If I'm not on a PCI system and want to tell the NE2000 module to look for my NE2000 card at address 0x340, I can issue this command:

```
#insmod ne2k.o io=0x340
```

Naturally, this isn't the sort of command I like to issue all the time, and so I prefer to use autodetect of ethernet cards at boot time if I can. If the automatic card search at boot time fails to find or properly configure a new card, I use Red Hat's `Kernel Configurator` (in the `control-panel`) or Caldera's `COAS`. Those tools ask for the I/O address (and other parameters) in a dialog box.

Just as `insmod` installs a module, `rmmod` removes one (if possible). `modprobe` loads a group of modules, or just the first one to actually work (such as the first ethernet module to work), and `depmod` determines which other modules a given group of modules might depend on.

Summary

This chapter provided an introduction to the high-level tools available for administering Red Hat and Caldera Linux. It also provided some insight into what happens during the startup and shutdown process of Linux and some insight into the world of loadable kernel modules.

TCP/IP and Network Management

In This Chapter

TCP/IP (Transmission Control Protocol/Internet Protocol) is the most widespread networking protocol in use today and forms the base of many networks, including the Internet. Like all UNIX systems, Linux has extensive support for TCP/IP built in to itself. This chapter discusses the essentials needed to understand and configure network services under Linux.

The Internet Engineering Task Force (IETF) is the body charged with standardizing TCP/IP. IETF standards documents are called *Requests For Comments*, or *RFCs*. There are currently a couple thousand RFCs, although many RFCs have become obsolete. To keep track of RFCs, each one is assigned a number that never changes. For example, RFC 796, written in 1981, is still the RFC dealing with classful IP network address mappings. RFCs are the last word on Internet standards, and can be found at the IETF's Web site (`http://www.ietf.org`).

TCP/IP Basics

Before diving head first into the TCP/IP network stack, you may want to read up on some TCP/IP basics. If you're familiar with how TCP/IP works and would like to go straight to the nitty-gritty of configuring your Linux system, you can skip this part and go straight to the "Configuring the Network" section of this chapter.

IP Addresses

Every network interface in a TCP/IP network is assigned a unique *IP address*. The IP address is used to identify and differentiate an interface from other interfaces on the network. In the current IPv4 specifications, an IP address is a 32-bit number. We often think of this 32-bit number as a sequence of four 8-bit octets. Computers understand base 2 numbers (1s and 0s), while humans tend to think in base 10 (0–9). We then convert each octet to decimal and separate the decimal values with periods. This 32-bit, 4-octet sequence of base 2 can be represented as `192.168.1.1`:

```
11000000 10101000 00000001 00000001
```

It is important to carefully select and keep track of IPs that are assigned to network interfaces. If the network is directly connected to the Internet, you may only assign IPs that have been set aside for your network by the Internet Assigned Numbers Authority (IANA). If the network isn't connected to the Internet or is separated from the Internet by a firewall, addresses should be selected from the block of private network addresses discussed in the next section. The *network administrator* is the person responsible for assigning IP addresses within an organization. You should contact him before assigning an IP address to any device.

Dividing the Network

As its name implies, *IP* (Internet Protocol) was designed from the ground up for *internetworking*. This means it was designed for interconnecting networks. Thus, an IP address is divided into two parts: a *network part* and a *host part*. The network part distinguishes one network from another, while the host part identifies a particular host within that network.

Netmasks and Network Classes

The *network mask* (or *netmask*) identifies what part of the IP address represents the network number, and what part represents the host address. The netmask is another 32-bit number that is converted into four 8-bit octets, translated into decimal, and separated by periods as in Figure 7.1. The 1 bits in the netmask designate the network portion of an IP address. The 0 bits in the netmask correlate with the host portion of an IP address. For example, if a network interface were assigned the IP address `172.17.24.83` (`10101100 00010001 00011000 01010011`) with a netmask of `255.255.0.0` (`11111111 11111111 00000000 00000000`), then the network part of the IP address would be `172.17`, while the unique host address within that network would be `24.83`.

FIGURE 7.1
Netmasks divide hosts from networks.

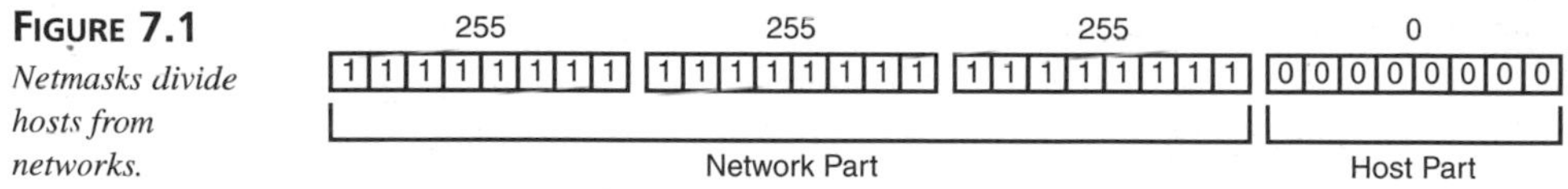

Each logical IP network has a network address and a broadcast address. The *network address* is used to identify the network itself and is the lowest number (all 0 bits in the host part) in its respective IP network. The *broadcast address* is a special address that all of the devices in the IP network listen for. It is the highest number (has all 1s in the host part) in its respective IP network. This means that number of assignable addresses is always two less than the actual range of numbers being used. If you had a network number of `192.168.1.0` and a netmask of `255.255.255.0`, your broadcast address would be `192.168.1.255`. You would have a maximum of 254 assignable host addresses, even though your actual range of numbers is `0–255`.

Historically (due to RFC 796), depending on the first few bits of an IP address, networks were assumed to have default netmasks based on their network *class*. Class A networks have an 8-bit network part and a 24-bit host part. Class B networks have 16 bits each in the network and host parts. Class C networks have a 24-bit network part and an 8-bit host part. Class D networks are considered multicast addresses. See Table 7.1 for the octet-to-network class definition chart.

TABLE 7.1 Network Classes According to RFC-796

First Byte of Address	*Default Network Class*
1–127 (starts with `0`)	A
128–191 (starts with `10`)	B
192–223 (starts with `110`)	C
224–239 (starts with `1110`)	D
240–254 (starts with `1111`)	Reserved

CIDR (Classless Interdomain Routing)

Although IP classifications are still used in the networking world, this way of thinking has been made obsolete since the release of RFCs 1517, 1518, 1519, and 1520. Those RFCs define CIDR (Classless Interdomain Routing). One of the main reasons CIDR came to be was a lack of an appropriate network class size for a mid-sized company. The class C network—with a maximum of 254 host addresses—is too small, while class B—which allows up to 65,534 addresses—is too large for an ethernet's limit of 12,000 attachments. The result is inefficient utilization of class B network numbers.

To begin thinking in terms of CIDR notation, here is a visual exercise that shows you how the netmask for a given range of IPs is calculated.

Say you wanted to have communication starting with `10.168.0.0` all the way through `10.168.255.255`. Understand that the netmask you use lets the computer know which IP networks to listen to, and which ones to mask out. To see this masking in action you would first need to visualize which bits are common between the two ranges. Wherever the bits match, the corresponding bit in the netmask becomes a `1`.

Tip

To simplify the exchange of routing information and to lower the odds of human error in defining a netmask, it is illegal to have discontiguous 1 bits in the netmask. Once you calculate the first 0 bit in the netmask, all of the remaining bits must be 0.

```
00001010 10101000 00000000 00000000 (10.168.0.0) Start of Range
00001010 10101000 11111111 11111111 (10.168.255.255) End of Range
=================================================================
11111111 11111111 00000000 00000000 (255.255.0.0) Netmask
```

Tip

Since this example network starts with a `0` `(00001010)` as its first bit, it would have traditionally been called a *class A network*. By using the new rules defined by CIDR, it's now effectively in a *class B size*.

Instead of representing this network by its *network number* (the lowest IP address of an IP network) and its netmask, in CIDR notation you simply count all of the *one* bits (1s) in the netmask and represent this network as `10.168.0.0/24`. This network is now said to be a *24-bit network*. The traditional class C network is another example of a 24-bit network.

Subnetting

The act of dividing an IP network into smaller networks is called *subnetting*. It is usually done when an organization has a block of addresses that it needs to share between two or more physically separate sites. For example, an organization may request a 24-bit block of address for use on the Internet and then need to share those addresses between two offices. Instead of wasting two full 24-bit networks, you can cut the 24-bit network into two different networks by extending your netmask one more bit. This changes your netmask from `255.255.255.0` (24 1s, aka `/24`) to `255.255.255.128` (25 1s, aka `/25`). This netmask is applied to both of the newly created networks. Where you once had a network of `192.168.1.0/24`, there are now two networks of `192.168.1.0/25` and `192.168.1.128/25`. The `192.168.1.0/25` network has a host range of `0–127`, where `192.168.1.0` is the network number and `192.168.1.127` is the broadcast. The second network has a host range of `128–255`, where `192.168.1.128` is the network number and `192.168.1.255` is the broadcast.

To see why this works, try the visualization test shown before on the second created network:

```
11000000 10101000 00000001 10000000 (192.168.1.128)
11000000 10101000 00000001 11111111 (192.168.1.255)
=====================================================
11111111 11111111 11111111 10000000 (255.255.255.128 or 25-bit)
```

Supernetting

As you saw in the subnetting section, adding one bit to the network mask splits the network in half. To double a network's size, you simply take away one bit from the network mask. To continue with the visualization tests, assume you were working with the `192.168.126.0/24` and `192.168.127.0/24` networks. Now say you wanted to be able to have all of the IPs from both 24-bit networks communicate in their own expanded, or *super logical*, IP network. This would define the range of `192.168.126.0–192.168.127.255`, which looks like the following written out:

```
11000000 10101000 01111110 00000000 (192.168.126.0)
11000000 10101000 01111111 11111111 (192.168.127.255)
=======================================================
11111111 11111111 11111110 00000000 (255.255.254.0 or 23-bit)
```

The resulting netmask has 23 one bits, so the new supernet is represented as `192.168.126.0/23`. It has a network number of `192.168.126.0` and a broadcast of `192.168.127.255`. There are now 510 assignable IPs in this logical IP network.

This prefix/bit-count notation does not work when joining just any ranges of numbers. For example, look at the range of `192.168.10.0–192.168.13.255`:

```
11000000 10101000 00001010 00000000 (192.168.10.0)
11000000 10101000 00001011 00000000 (192.168.11.0)
11000000 10101000 00001100 00000000 (192.168.12.0)
11000000 10101000 00001101 11111111 (192.168.13.255)
=====================================================
11111111 11111111 11111110 00000000
```

It is illegal to represent this range as `192.168.10.0/22` because it points to a different address range than expected. This can be very confusing to humans and is bound to lead to error. If you apply the bit count to the address, you're referencing the same network as `192.168.8.0/22`. To correctly write out this particular range, you must specify two networks: `192.168.10.0/23` and `192.168.12.0/23`. Here's the general rule that lets you know whether the continuous base addresses may be grouped together: For the number *X* of continuous base addresses to have a common prefix (network number), *X* must be a power of two and the last octet containing the network number must be evenly divisible by *X*.

With that rule in mind, revisit the 192.168.8.0/22 network. To apply the bit-count (netmask) against the network prefix (network number), you can write out their binary values and visualize which ranges fall into the mask.

```
11000000 10101000 00001000 00000000 (192.168.8.0)
11111111 11111111 11111100 00000000 (255.255.252.0 or 22-bits)
=============================================================
11000000 10101000 00000111 00000000 (192.168.7.0 is masked out)
10000000 10101000 00001000 00000000 (192.168.8.0 obviously is in)
11000000 10101000 00001001 00000000 (192.168.9.0 is in)
11000000 10101000 00001010 00000000 (192.168.10.0 is in)
11000000 10101000 00001011 00000000 (192.168.11.0 is in)
11000000 10101000 00001100 00000000 (192.168.12.0 is masked out)
```

In this example, *X* equals 4 because you're combining four continuous base addresses. 4 is a power of two and 8 (the last octet of the base address) is evenly divisible by 4.

Reserved Network Numbers

There is also a standard reserved block of addresses, defined in RFC 1918, for use in *private networks*. These are networks that will never be connected directly to any public network (specifically the Internet). The private-network addressing standard is shown on Table 7.3.

TABLE 7.3 Private Network Addresses According to RFC 1618

Address Range	*Network Class*
10.0.0.0–10.255.255.255	A (1 class A network)
172.16.0.0–172.31.255.255	B (16 class B networks)
192.168.0.0–192.168.255.255	C (256 class C networks)

There is another reserved class A network, with addresses in the range of 127.0.0.0–127.255.255.255. This is known as the *loopback* network. It is a virtual network that points to the same host where the packet originates. The usual loopback address in any system is 127.0.0.1. If you want a program to connect to the localhost (the same system) it's running on, you can open a connection to 127.0.0.1. This is useful, for example, when running networking software in a system that isn't connected to a network, or for testing daemons on the local system.

Routing

Networks are connected by means of routers. A *router* is a device that has connections to two or more networks and takes care of moving packets between them. When a host sends out a packet whose destination lies in the same network, it sends it directly to the destination host. However, if the packet's destination lies in a different network, it sends the packet to a router so that the router will send it to the correct network. This is why it's so important to set a host's netmask correctly—it's the parameter that tells the host whether to send the packet either directly to the destination host or to the router (see Figure 7.2).

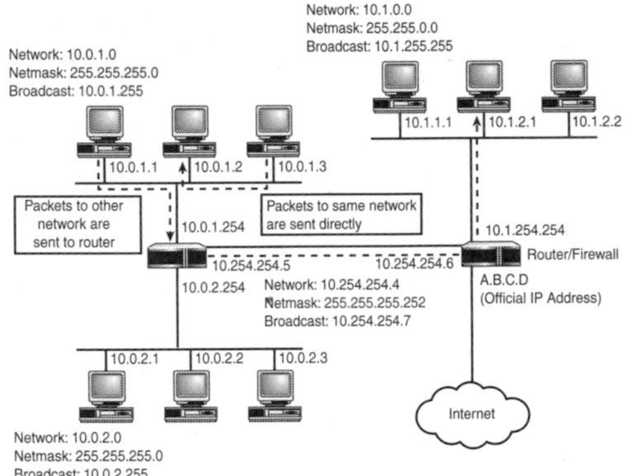

FIGURE 7.2
Routers connect networks.

A network usually has a *default router*, which connects it to other networks. In such a setup, all traffic whose destination is outside the local network gets sent to the default router. There may be several routers in a network; one to the Internet and another one to other internal networks is an example. In this case, it may be necessary to use a *static route* to tell the host to send packets destined for specific subnets to a specific router, or use *dynamic routing* by means of a routing daemon (such as `routed`). These daemons are discussed in the "Network Daemons" section in this chapter.

The TCP/IP Protocol Suite

TCP/IP is actually not just one protocol, but a protocol suite. At the low level, it's composed of the following protocols:

- IP
- TCP
- UDP

IP is the lowest common denominator of TCP/IP. Every protocol at a higher level must eventually be translated into IP packets. An IP packet is self-contained in the sense that it contains within itself its source and destination addresses. However, it may be part of a larger conversation.

TCP is a *connection-based*, or *stream-oriented*, protocol on top of IP. This means that an application that communicates with another using TCP sends and receives data as a stream of bytes, and the TCP/IP stack takes care of splitting the data into packets and putting the packets back together again at the receiving end. It also ensures that the packets arrive in order and requests retransmission of missing and corrupt packets.

On the other hand, the UDP protocol is a *datagram-based*, or *packet-oriented*, protocol. It is a connectionless protocol. This protocol does not have built-in checking to ensure that the packets arrive in order, or check for missing packets. However, due to this missing protocol overhead, UDP can be quite efficient for use with applications that send small amounts of information, or on a network that is fast and reliable, such as Ethernet on a private LAN.

Application-specific protocols work on top of TCP and UDP. Some of these follow:

- SMTP (Simple Mail Transfer Protocol)
- HTTP (HyperText Transfer Protocol)
- FTP (File Transfer Protocol)
- SNMP (Simple Network Management Protocol)
- NFS (Network File System)

Each has different characteristics, depending on its intended use. Figure 7.3 shows the layers of the TCP/IP suite and the corresponding layers in the OSI reference model.

Ports

A single computer may provide several services. To distinguish one service from the next, something more is needed than just the host's IP address. We use different ports on the computer to respond to specified services, as in Figure 7.4. *Ports* are analogous to the jacks in an old-fashioned manual switchboard.

FIGURE 7.3
TCP/IP is a protocol suite composed of several layers.

Application	Telnet, FTP, HTTP, etc...
Transport	TCP, UDP, etc...
Network	IP and others
Link	Network interface and device driver

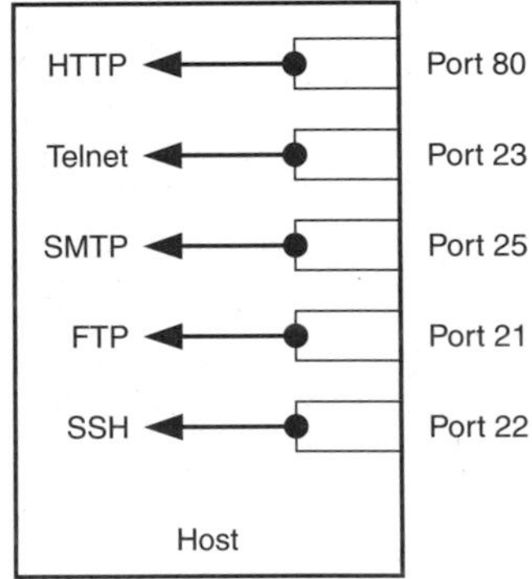

FIGURE 7.4
A single computer may host different services in different ports.

A server daemon can be configured to listen on any port. However, things would be very complicated if this decision were entirely arbitrary, because there would be no easy way of finding out what port a given service was listening on. To help, some well-known ports have been defined in RFC 1700. Some of these well-known ports are listed in Table 7.4.

TABLE 7.4 Some Well-Known Port Numbers

Port/Protocol	*Name*	*Use*
7/tcp	echo	Echoes everything it receives
13/tcp	daytime	Sends back the current date and time
23/tcp	Telnet	Remote terminal emulation
25/tcp	smtp	Email transfer
53/udp	domain	Domain Name System
80/tcp	www	World Wide Web traffic
110/tcp	pop3	Post Office Protocol, version 3
443/tcp	https	Secure Web traffic

Sockets

In network parlance, a *socket* is a network connection between two processes, which may be running on the same or different computers. Technically, an open socket has four parts (source host, source port, destination host, destination port). A closed socket has only the source port and source host.

Note that a socket has ports on both sides of the connection. When a client tries to connect to a server, it first asks the system for a *free* port (one that isn't being used by any other program). It then asks the system to connect to a destination host and port using that source port. That is why there can be several programs connected between the same two hosts; for example, a browser can have two or more windows open to the same host. The system keeps track of both the source and the destination port, and has different sockets for each connection.

Configuring the Network

In every modern Linux distribution, basic network configuration is done at installation time, when configuring the base system. As with other UNIX systems, all configuration data is stored in text files in the `/etc` tree.

An important thing to consider is that Linux, like other UNIX systems, can be reconfigured on-the-fly. In other words, almost any parameter can be changed while the system is operating, without rebooting. This makes it easy to experiment and correct configuration problems. However, if you are new to making permanent configuration changes, it is recommended that you reboot after making any important configuration changes, to ensure the correct configuration will be used when the system reboots.

This section deals with configuring the network statically, by editing the files stored in `/etc`. NIS is covered in Chapter 14, "NIS: Network Information Service."

Configuration Files

The most important network configuration files in a Linux system follow:

- `/etc/sysconfig/network`
- `/etc/HOSTNAME`
- `/etc/hosts`
- `/etc/services`
- `/etc/host.conf`
- `/etc/nsswitch.conf`
- `/etc/resolv.conf`

Each is covered in turn. All of these files can be modified while a system is running. Modifications (except for /etc/sysconfig/network or /etc/init.d/network) take place immediately, without having to start or stop any daemons. Note that most of these files accept comments beginning with a hash (#) symbol. Each of these files has an entry in section 5 of the UNIX manual, so you can access them with the man command.

Red Hat

Network Setup: /etc/sysconfig/network

The network file contains information that will control how other network related files and daemons get populated. Here is a sample network file:

```
NETWORKING=yes
FORWARD_IPV4=false
HOSTNAME=ltorvalds.tech.access.com
DOMAINNAME=tech.access.com
GATEWAY=205.185.225.1
GATEWAYDEV=eth0
NISDOMAIN=looneytunes
```

This file is best edited through the GUI tool netcfg. This tool requires you to have display access to an X server.

Debian

Debian also has an /etc/init.d/network file, but it's very different from Red Hat. Unlike Red Hat's network file, which defines environment variables that are interpreted to set up the network, Debian's network file is a shell script containing the literal commands to set up the network properly. Here's a sample Debian /etc/init.d/network file:

```
#! /bin/sh ifconfig lo 127.0.0.1
route add -net 127.0.0.0
IPADDR=192.168.1.1
NETMASK=255.255.255.0
NETWORK=192.168.1.0
BROADCAST=192.168.1.255
GATEWAY= ifconfig eth0 ${IPADDR} netmask ${NETMASK} broadcast ${BROADCAST}
route add -net ${NETWORK} [ "${GATEWAY}" ] && route add default gw ${GATEWAY}
metric 1
```

This particular sample file sets up the lo interface as well as the eth0 interface. The eth0 interface is configured with a default gateway.

Caldera

Caldera uses an `/etc/sysconfig/network` file, but it is in a different format than Red Hat. Here is a sample `/etc/sysconfig/network` file from Caldera:

```
NETWORKING=yes
HOSTNAME=caldy.foobski.net
IF_LIST='lo eth tr sl ppp'
```

As you can see, this file is quite minimalistic. Caldera stores additional information in the `/etc/sysconfig/network-scripts` directory, which contains a number of files beginning with the name "ifcfg-<interface>". Let's take a look at a sample `/etc/sysconfig/network-scripts/ifcfg-eth0` file:

```
#! /bin/sh
#>>>Device type: ethernet
#>>>Variable declarations:
DEVICE=eth0
IPADDR=192.168.1.1
NETMASK=255.255.255.0
NETWORK=192.168.1.0
BROADCAST=192.168.1.255
GATEWAY=none
ONBOOT=yes
DYNAMIC=
#>>>End variable declarations
REMIP=0.0.0.0
MTU=1500
```

As you can see, this is where most of the network configuration specifics reside. If you use COAS to change the configuration of your network interfaces, these are the files that get modified.

Hostname: /etc/HOSTNAME or /etc/hostname

The `/etc/HOSTNAME` (`/etc/hostname` in Debian) file contains just one line with the primary name of the host. In Red Hat, this file gets its content at boot time from the `HOSTNAME` line in the `/etc/sysconfig/network` file. This file is used when booting to set the primary hostname of the system. Here'san example of the `/etc/HOSTNAME` file:

```
mycomputer
```

Map Between IP Addresses and Host Names: /etc/hosts

The /etc/hosts file contains the mapping between IP addresses to hostnames, and aliases for hostnames. IP addresses were designed to be easily readable by computers, but it's hard for people to remember them. That's why the /etc/hosts file was created. Here's an example:

```
127.0.0.1     localhost
192.168.1.1    mycomputer
192.168.1.2    server
192.168.1.3    router
192.168.3.45    othercomputer   otheralias
199.183.24.133    www.redhat.com
```

In this case, othercomputer also has an alias. It can be also referred to as otheralias.

In practice, /etc/hosts usually contains the host's name, the localhost entry, and system aliases that the systems administrator commonly uses. Other hostnames are usually resolved using the Internet's Domain Name System (DNS). The client portion of DNS is configured in the /etc/resolv.conf file.

Map Between Port Numbers and Service Names: /etc/services

The /etc/services file contains the mapping between port numbers and service names. This is used by several system programs. This is the beginning of the default /etc/services file installed by Red Hat:

```
tcpmux      1/tcp              # TCP port service multiplexer
echo        7/tcp
echo        7/udp
discard     9/tcp    sink null
discard     9/udp    sink null
systat      11/tcp   users
```

Note that /etc/services also allows for aliases, which are placed after the port number. In this case, sink and null are aliases for the discard service.

Configure the Name Resolver: /etc/host.conf and /etc/nsswitch.conf

These two files configure the UNIX name resolver library by specifying where the system will find its name information. /etc/host.conf is the file used by version 5 of the libc library, while /etc/nsswitch.conf is used by version 6 (also known as glibc. The important thing here is that some programs will use one and some will use the other, so it's best to have both files configured correctly.

/etc/host.conf

The /etc/host.conf file specifies the order in which the different name systems (/etc/hosts file, DNS, NIS) will be searched when resolving hostnames. Each line of the /etc/host.conf file should consist of one of the following directives, followed by a parameter:

Directive	*Function*
order	Indicates the order in which services will be queried. Its parameter may be any combination of lookup methods separated by commas. The lookup methods supported are bind, hosts, and nis; respectively, DNS, /etc/hosts, and NIS.
trim	Indicates a domain that will be trimmed of the hostname when doing an IP address-to-hostname translation via DNS. trim may be included several times for several domains. trim doesn't affect /etc/hosts nor NIS lookups. You should take care that hosts are listed appropriately (with or without full domain names) in the /etc/hosts file and in the NIS tables.
multi	Controls whether a query to the name system will always return only one result, or whether it may return several results. Its parameter may be either on, meaning that several results may be returned when appropriate, or off, meaning that just one result will be returned. Default value is off.
nospoof	Controls a security feature to prevent hostname spoofing. If nospoof is on after every name-to-IP lookup, a reverse IP-to-name lookup will be made. If the names don't match, the operation will fail. Valid parameters are on or off. Default value is off.

Directive	*Function*
`alert`	If the `nospoof` directive is on, `alert` controls whether spoofing attempts will be logged through the `syslog` facility Default value is `off`.
`reorder`	If set to `on`, all lookups will be reordered so that hosts on the same subnet will be returned first. Default value is `off`.

Here is a sample `/etc/host.conf` file. The `/etc/host.conf` file on your system will be similar, if not identical:

```
order hosts,bind
multi on
```

This indicates that lookups will be done first to the `/etc/hosts` file and then to DNS. If several hosts match, all will be returned. This file is appropriate for most installations, although installations using NIS or where the `nospoof` behavior is desired will have to modify it.

/etc/nsswitch.conf

The `/etc/nsswitch.conf` file was originally created by Sun Microsystems to manage the order in which several configuration files are looked for in the system. As such, it includes more functionality than the `/etc/host.conf` file.

Each line of `/etc/nsswitch.conf` is either a comment (which starts with a hash (#) sign, or a keyword followed by a colon and a list of methods listed in the order they will be tried. Each keyword is the name of an `/etc` file that can be controlled by `/etc/nsswitch.conf`. The keywords that can be included follow:

Keyword	*Function*
`aliases`	Mail aliases
`passwd`	System users
`group`	User groups
`shadow`	Shadow passwords
`hosts`	Hostnames and IP addresses
`networks`	Network names and numbers
`protocols`	Network protocols
`services`	Port numbers and service names

Keyword	*Function*
ethers	Ethernet numbers
rpc	Remote Procedure Call names and numbers
netgroup	Networkwide groups

The methods that can be included follow:

Keyword	*Meaning*
files	Valid for all keywords except netgroup. Look up record in the corresponding /etc file.
db	Valid for all keywords except netgroup. Look up record in the corresponding database in the /var/db directory. This is useful for extremely long files, such as passwd files with more than 500 entries. Under Red Hat and Debian, you can create these files from the standard /etc files, cd into /var/db, and run the make command. Other distributions, such as Caldera and SuSE, appear to have forgotten to fully support the use of the /var/db directory. If you're technically inclined, you may want to add this directory to your system and either copy /var/db/Makefile from Red Hat or Debian, or track it down in the glibc sources (a much more difficult and time-consuming undertaking.)
compat	Compatibility mode, valid for passwd, group, and shadow files. In this mode, lookups are made first to the corresponding /etc file. If you want to do NIS lookup of the corresponding NIS database, you need to include a line where the first field (username or groupname) is a plus character, followed by an appropriate number of colons (six for /etc/passwd, three for /etc/group, eight for /etc/shadow). For example, in /etc/password, the following line would have to be included at the end: +:*:::::
dns	Valid only for the hosts entry. Lookups are made to the DNS as configured in /etc/resolv.conf

Keyword	*Meaning*
`nis`	Valid for all files. Lookups are made to the NIS server if NIS is active.
`[STATUS=action]`	Controls the actions of the Name Service. `STATUS` is one of `SUCCESS` (operation was successful), `NOTFOUND` (record was not found), `UNAVAIL` (selected service was unavailable), or `TRYAGAIN` (service temporarily unavailable, try again). `action` is one of `return` (stop lookup and return current status) or `continue` (continue with next item in this line). For example, a line such as `hosts: dns nis [NOTFOUND=return] files` would result in looking up the host first in DNS and then in NIS. Only if neither of these were available would the `/etc/hosts` file be used.

This is a typical `/etc/nsswitch.conf` configured to use the local files for everything, and adds the ability to do DNS-based hostname queries:

```
passwd:         compat
group:          compat
shadow:         compat

hosts:          files dns
networks:       files

protocols:      db files
services:       db files
ethers:         db files
rpc:            db files

netgroup:       db files
```

With this configuration, all names except network names will be looked up first in `/var/db` (for efficiency). If not found there, it will be looked up in the corresponding `/etc` files. There are quite a few databases that could be looked up via NIS if an appropriate entry exists in the corresponding database.

Configure the DNS Client: `/etc/resolv.conf`

The `/etc/resolv.conf` file configures the DNS client. It contains the host's domain name search order and the addresses of the DNS servers. Each line should contain a keyword and one or more parameters separated by spaces. The following keywords are valid:

Keyword	*Meaning*
`nameserver`	Its single parameter indicates the IP address of the DNS server. There may be up to three `nameserver` lines, each with a single IP address. `nameservers` will be queried in the order they appear in the file. `nameservers` after the first one will only be queried if the first `nameserver` doesn't respond.
`domain`	Its single parameter indicates the host's domain name. This is used by several programs, such as the email system, and is also used when doing a DNS query for a host with no domain name (with no periods, for example). If there's no domain name, the hostname will be used, removing everything before the first dot.
`search`	Its multiple parameters indicate the domain name search order. If a query is made for a host with no domain name, the host will be looked up consecutively in each of the domains indicated by the `search` keyword. Note that `domain` and `search` are mutually exclusive; if both appear, the last one that appears is used.
`sortlist`	Allows sorting the returned domain names in a specific order. Its parameters are specified in network/netmask pairs, allowing for arbitrary sorting orders.

There is no generic default `/etc/resolv.conf` file provided with Linux. Its contents are built dynamically depending on options given at installation time. This is an example `/etc/resolv.conf` file:

```
search my.domain.com other.domain.com
nameserver 10.1.1.1
nameserver 10.10.10.1
sortlist 10.1.1.0/255.255.255.0 10.0.0.0/255.0.0.0
```

This file indicates that unqualified hosts will be searched first as `host.my.domain.com` and then as `host.other.domain.com`. The `nameserver` at IP address `10.1.1.1` will be contacted first. If that server doesn't answer after a timeout, the server at `10.10.10.1` will be contacted. If several hosts are returned, the hosts in the class C network `10.1.1.0` will be returned first, followed by any other hosts in the class A network `10.0.0.0`, followed by any other hosts.

Configuration Programs

The files detailed in the previous section serve to configure many general network parameters. Most of these networking options can be modified dynamically just by editing the proper file. Configuring the host's IP address and routing table dynamically however requires special commands.

Configure the Host's Network Interfaces: `ifconfig`

The `ifconfig` program is used to configure a host's network interfaces. This includes basic configuration such as IP address, netmask and broadcast address, and advanced options such as setting the remote address for a point-to-point link (such as a PPP link).

Under Linux, all network interfaces have names composed of the driver name followed by a number. These are some of the network driver names supported by Linux:

Driver Name	*Device Type*
`eth`	Ethernet
`tr`	Token Ring
`ppp`	Point-to-Point Protocol
`slip`	Serial Line IP
`plip`	Parallel Line IP

Interfaces are numbered starting from `0` in the order the kernel finds them. By default, the Linux kernel will only find one network interface. If you have several network cards with drivers compiled into the kernel, you need to add a line like the following to the `/etc/lilo.conf` file and then re-run the `/sbin/lilo` command:

```
append="ether=IRQ,I/O,eth1 ether=IRQ,I/O,eth2"
```

This tells the kernel to add two more Ethernet devices—`eth1` and `eth2`—whose cards are at the IRQ and I/O address specified, and is required because the kernel normally autoprobes for only one card by default, unless told otherwise. If you want the kernel to autoprobe the cards' I/O addresses and IRQs, you can use `0` for IRQ and I/O.

If you are using the stock kernel that came with your distribution, your Ethernet card driver is most likely in a kernel module which can be loaded at runtime. In this case, you should configure your `/etc/modules.conf` so that it contains the appropriate information to configure your cards. Here is a sample excerpt, which you can see simply uses the identical parameters as the `lilo.conf` line above:

```
alias eth0 wd
alias eth1 3c503
options wd io=0x280
options 3c503 io=0x350
```

In the above example, "wd" and "3c503" are names of kernel modules that provide support for a particular kind of Ethernet card.

Basic Interface Configuration

This is the basic form of the `ifconfig` command:

```
ifconfig interface IP-address [netmask <netmask>] \
[broadcast broadcast-address]
```

This form of the `ifconfig` command can only be used by `root`. The netmask and broadcast parameters are optional. If they are omitted, `ifconfig` gets their values from the default class for the IP address. (See "Netmasks and Network Classes" in this chapter for more details.) They should be included if subnetting is being used.

This command will load the proper network driver and configure the interface.

Caution

The command will do exactly as it's told: It won't check whether the broadcast address corresponds to the IP address and netmask supplied, so be careful!

Tip

It's not enough to configure the interface. You need to tell the kernel how to get to the hosts on the network connected to that interface using the `route add` command. (See the "Manipulating the Routing Table: `route`" section in this chapter.)

Enabling and Disabling an Interface

An interface can also be temporarily brought down (*deactivated*) and brought back up without having to be reconfigured. This is useful for temporarily disabling a server's network connection (such as when reconfiguring a critical service). This is done with the following commands:

```
ifconfig interface down
ifconfig interface up
```

These forms of the `ifconfig` command can be used only by `root`.

Checking Interface Status

If you want to know the status of a network interface, just issue the command `ifconfig` *`interface`*. If you want to know the status of all active interface, use `ifconfig -a`. These versions of the `ifconfig` command can be used by any user. They show all of the configuration information for an interface, including its IP address, subnet mask, broadcast address, and physical (hardware) address. (The hardware address is set by the network card's manufacturer.) They also display the interface status, such as whether it is up or down and whether it's a loopback interface, and other information: the Maximum Transfer Unit (the size of the largest packet that can be sent through that interface), the network card's I/O address and IRQ number, and the number of packets received, packets sent, and collisions.

You can also check the status of an interface with the `ifconfig -a` command. This prints out all of the interfaces that are currently active with their parameters. Here's an example of the output of `ifconfig -a`:

```
$ /sbin/ifconfig -a
lo        Link encap:Local Loopback
          inet addr:127.0.0.1  Bcast:127.255.255.255  Mask:255.0.0.0
          UP BROADCAST LOOPBACK RUNNING  MTU:3584  Metric:1
          RX packets:1600 errors:0 dropped:0 overruns:0 frame:0
          TX packets:1600 errors:0 dropped:0 overruns:0 carrier:0
          Collisions:0

eth0      Link encap:Ethernet  HWaddr 00:20:87:3E:F0:61
          inet addr:10.0.1.10  Bcast:10.0.1.255  Mask:255.255.255.0
          UP BROADCAST RUNNING MULTICAST  MTU:1500  Metric:1
          RX packets:90506 errors:0 dropped:0 overruns:0 frame:0
          TX packets:92691 errors:0 dropped:0 overruns:0 carrier:1
          Collisions:667
          Interrupt:3 Base address:0x310
```

Network Aliasing—One Interface, Several Addresses

It is sometimes useful for a single network interface to have multiple IP addresses. For example, a server may be running several services, but you may want clients to access different IP addresses for each service to make reconfiguration easier in the future (if you need to split some services off to another server, for example).

Linux, like most other UNIX flavors, provides a feature called *network aliasing*, which does just that. To be able to use network aliasing, you must have reconfigured and recompiled your kernel, and enabled the Network Aliasing and IP: Aliasing Support options in the Networking Options configuration section. The options can be either compiled into the kernel or compiled as modules.

Once you are running a kernel with aliasing enabled, creating an alias is as easy as issuing a standard `ifconfig` command. All you need to do is append a colon and an alias number to the interface name. Here is an example:

```
ifconfig eth0:0 10.1.1.1 netmask 255.255.255.0 broadcast 10.1.1.255
```

This creates an alias `eth0:0` for Ethernet interface `eth0`, with the provided parameters.

To automate the creation of an alias each time the host boots, you can add the command to create it to `/etc/init.d/network`.

Other `ifconfig` Options

There are other options to `ifconfig` for some special circumstances:

`ifconfig` *`interface local-address`* `pointopoint` *`remote-address`* will enable a Point-to-Point interface—one that connects only to a single other host, not to a network. The interface must also be enabled in the remote host, switching the *`local-address`* and *`remote-address`* parameters.

`ifconfig` *`interface local-address`* `tunnel` *`remote-address`* will create an IPv4 tunnel between two IPv6 networks. IPv4 is the current TCP/IP standard on the Internet. IPv6 is the next-generation IP standard. If there are two IPv6 networks that need to be connected via the Internet, a tunnel that uses the IPv4 protocol must be made.

Manipulating the Routing Table: `route`

The `/sbin/route` command manipulates the kernel's routing table. This table is used by the kernel to see what needs to be done to each packet that leaves the host—whether to send it directly to the destination host or to a gateway, and on which network interface to send it.

The general form of the route command follows:

```
route [options] [command [parameters]]
```

Viewing the Routing Table

The simplest form of the command (with no options and no command) simply outputs the routing table. This form of the command can be utilized by any user:

```
$ /sbin/route
Kernel IP routing table
Destination     Gateway         Genmask         Flags Metric Ref    Use Iface
localnet        *               255.255.255.0   U     0      0       16 eth0
127.0.0.0       *               255.0.0.0       U     0      0        2 lo
default         router.company. 0.0.0.0         UG    0      0       71 eth0
```

The output has eight columns:

1. The first column (`Destination`) indicates the route destination. The name is substituted if a corresponding entry exists in either `/etc/hosts` or `/etc/networks`. The special name `default` indicates the default gateway.
2. The second column (`Gateway`) indicates the gateway through which packets to this destination are sent. An asterisk (`*`) means that packets will be sent directly to the destination host.
3. The third column (`Genmask`) indicates the netmask that applies to this route. The netmask is applied to the value in the `Destination` column.
4. The fourth column (`Flags`) can have several values. The most common flags are

   `U` Route is up. This route is enabled.

   `H` Target is a host. This is a static route to a specific host (see "Host-Based Static Routes" in this chapter).

   `G` Use a gateway. That packet will not be sent directly to destination host. The gateway will be used instead.
5. The fifth column (`Metric`) indicates the distance to the target. This is used by some routing daemons to dynamically calculate the best route to get to a target host.
6. The sixth column (`Ref`) isn't used in the Linux kernel. In other UNIX systems, it indicates the number of references to this route.
7. The seventh column (`Use`) is the number of times the kernel has performed a lookup for the route.
8. The eighth column (`Iface`) shows the name of the interface through which packets directed to this route will be sent.

There will always be at least one active route—the `localhost` route, which is set up in the `/etc/init.d/network` script. There should also be at least one route per network interface, pointing to the network the interface is connected to.

The `-n` option modifies the display slightly. It doesn't do host or network name lookups, displaying instead numerical addresses:

```
$ /sbin/route -n
Kernel IP routing table
Destination     Gateway         Genmask         Flags Metric Ref    Use Iface
10.0.1.0        0.0.0.0         255.255.255.0   U     0      0       16 eth0
127.0.0.0       0.0.0.0         255.0.0.0       U     0      0        2 lo
0.0.0.0         10.0.1.254      0.0.0.0         UG    0      0       71 eth0
```

In this case, the `default` destination and the `*` gateway are replaced by the address `0.0.0.0`. This output format is often more useful than the standard output format because there is no ambiguity as to where things are going.

Tip

If you issue a `route` command and it hangs, press Ctrl+C to interrupt it and issue `route -n`. Issuing `route` without the `-n` parameter means `route` tries to do a reverse lookup of every IP in the routing table. If DNS is configured and the host is currently not connected to the network, issuing route by itself can take a long time.

Manipulating the Routing Table

The `route` command also adds and removes routes from the routing table. This is done via the following commands:

```
route add¦del [-net¦-host] <target> [gw <gateway>] \
[netmask <netmask>] [[dev] <interface>]
```

The `add` and `del` commands indicate, respectively, whether you want to add or delete a route.

The optional `-net` and `-host` options indicate whether you want to operate on a net or a host route. (See "Host-Based Static Routes" in this chapter for more information on net or host routes.) Providing `route` information to eliminate any ambiguity is usually best. (For example, the address `10.0.1.0` can be either the network address of a class C network, or the address of a host in a class A or B network.)

The *`target`* parameter is the host address or network number of the destination. You would use the keyword `default` as the target for setting or deleting the default route.

The optional *`gateway`* parameter indicates which gateway to use for this route. If omitted, the `route` command assumes that the host or network is connected directly to this host. It's important to add a route to the local network after configuring an interface with `ifconfig`:

```
# /sbin/ifconfig eth0 10.1.1.1 netmask 255.255.255.0 broadcast 10.0.1.255
# /sbin/route add -net 10.1.1.0
```

As its name implies, the optional *`netmask`* parameter sets the netmask for the route, which will be applied to the *`target`* address. If omitted, the netmask will be taken either from the default netmask for the IP address or (in the case of routes to local networks) from the interface's netmask. (See "Netmasks and Network Classes" in this chapter for more information on the default netmask.)

The optional *dev* parameter sets the interface on which the packets to this destination will be sent. If omitted, the `route` command checks the current routing table to find which interface has a route to the *gateway*. If no *gateway* is provided, it determines which interface can be used to get directly to the *target*.

Host-Based Static Routes

While the `route` command is most often used to manipulate *network* routes (those that point to a remote network), sometimes it is necessary to add routes to specific hosts. This can be necessary, for example, if a host is connected through a point-to-point link (for example, through a modem or serial cable). See Figure 7.5 for an example.

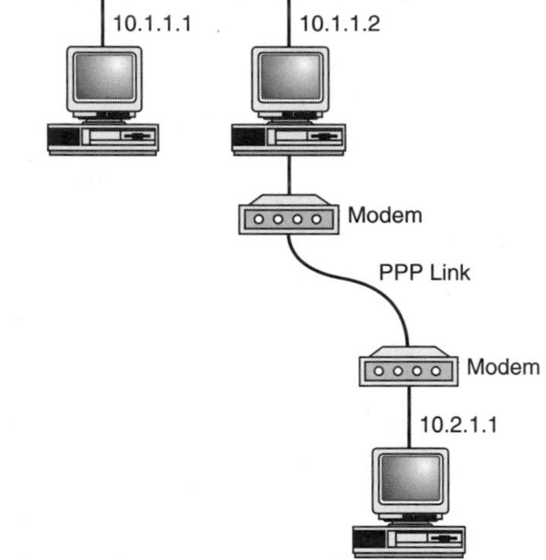

FIGURE 7.5
Host-based static routes are needed when a host is connected via a point-to-point link.

In this example, host `10.1.1.1` won't know how to get to host `10.2.1.1` without the following `route` command:

```
# /sbin/route add -host 10.2.1.1 gw 10.1.1.2
```

Checking Network Status: netstat

The `/bin/netstat` command displays the status of all TCP/IP network services. It has several options, depending on the information you want to display.

`netstat` by itself lists all connected sockets. The `-a` (all) option lists all open or listening sockets, not just those that have connections. The information listed for each socket includes

- The protocol (`tcp` or `udp`).
- Number of bytes currently in the send and receive queues (bytes that the local process hasn't read or that the remote process hasn't acknowledged).

- Addresses of the local and remote hosts. The remote host address is displayed as `*:*` for sockets that are in `LISTEN` state.
- Socket state. This can be `ESTABLISHED`, `SYN_SENT`, `SYN_RECV`, `FIN_WAIT1`, `FIN_WAIT2`, `TIME_WAIT`, `CLOSED`, `CLOSE_WAIT`, `LAST_ACK`, `LISTEN`, `CLOSING`, or `UNKNOWN`. In general, the `SYN_` states indicate that a connection is in the process of being opened, the `_WAIT` states indicate the socket is in the process of being closed, `ESTABLISHED` means the socket is connected, `LISTEN` means a daemon is waiting for clients to connect, and `CLOSED` means the socket is unused.

The `netstat -e` (extended) option lists, in addition to this information, the user currently using the socket.

`netstat -r` (routes) lists the routing table. It lists the same information as the `route` command with no parameters.

`netstat -i` (interfaces) lists the network interfaces and statistics on each interface. It displays the same statistics as the `ifconfig` argument, but is in table form for easy parsing.

As with the `route` command, you can also add the `-n` option to view numeric IP addresses instead of hostnames.

Network Daemons

A *daemon* is a program that waits for another program to ask it to do something. Network daemons in particular are similar to the jacks in an operator's switchboard. They create one or more sockets and listen to it, waiting for another process to connect. In Linux, as with most variants of UNIX, network services can be provided in one of two ways: as standalone daemons that handle each session themselves or as daemons incorporated into another configuration such as `inetd`, which handles the connections and disconnections for them.

Standalone TCP/IP Daemons

Originally, all UNIX network servers were standalone daemons. When you wanted to start a server, you ran a program that created the socket and listened to it. Many UNIX server programs still run in this manner. Examples are squid, the Web cache/proxy server; Samba, the SMB file/print server; Apache, the Web server, and many others (see Chapters 11, "Apache Server," and 16, "Samba").

Even though they have many functions, most network daemons usually share a few characteristics:

- Their names end with a *d* (for *daemon*).
- They respond to the HUP (HANG UP signal, `man 7 signal` for more information) signal (sent by the `kill -HUP` command) by rereading their configuration files.
- They are usually started at boot time by scripts in the `/etc/init.d` directory. These scripts minimally accept the `start` and `stop` parameters to start and end the daemons. Most of them accept the `restart` parameter to tell the daemon to reread its configuration files.
- When they receive a p request, they create another copy of themselves to service it. Thus, there may be several copies of each daemon running simultaneously at any given time.

The Internet Super-Server: `inetd`

In the standalone daemon model, each service you run on a server has a corresponding daemon. This poses several problems:

- If you have many services on a server, you need to have many daemons running, even if they are idle. Although inactive daemons will probably be swapped out to disk, they still take up valuable resources, such as virtual memory and process table entries.
- There is no centralized way of modifying the daemons to provide services such as encryption or access control. Each daemon program must be modified to provide these services.
- If a daemon dies because of user or programmer error, the service will be unavailable until it is restarted. The restart procedure can be automated, but then the program that restarts the daemon can also die.
- Programming a network daemon isn't easy, especially because most daemons must be multithreaded. Being multithreaded makes them able to manage several requests at once.

Eventually someone came up with a solution. How about a single daemon that could be configured to listen to any number of sockets and transfer control to different programs when it was needed? This daemon would also take care of multithreading and of managing the sockets. Thus was born `inetd`, the so-called "Internet super-server."

`inetd` is a daemon that is started when the host boots. It reads a configuration file, `/etc/inetd.conf`, that tells it what sockets to listen to and what program to start when a connection is received in each. It handles the creation of the socket by listening on specified ports until a connection is made. Then it creates a new process to handle that connection, and hands data off to the new process, as standard input p and standard output, connections to the socket.

There is, however, one disadvantage to starting servers via `inetd`: The start-up time for the server is longer. This is because the server process with a standalone daemon is always up and running. However, `inetd` has to load the server process each time it runs. Some servers, notably the Apache Web server, can be started either as standalone daemons or via `inetd`. For sites that have a low load or on which the Web server is accessed only sporadically, starting the server through `inetd` is an excellent choice. However, the best option in high-traffic sites is a standalone daemon.

`inetd` Configuration

As stated, `inetd` is configured by means of the `/etc/inetd.conf` file. Each line of this file has the following format:

```
service socket-type protocol wait/nowait[.max] user[.group] \
server-program program-arguments
```

`service` is the name of the service, taken from the `/etc/services` file. `inetd` gets the port number from this. It must be the official service name; no aliases are allowed.

`socket-type` is usually `stream` or `dgram`, depending on whether stream-oriented or datagram-oriented (basically TCP or UDP) service is desired.

`protocol` is a valid protocol taken from `/etc/protocols`. It is usually `tcp` or `udp`.

The *`wait/nowait[.max]`* entry applies only to datagram services. All other services should have `nowait` in this entry. There are two types of datagram servers. One of them, the *multithreaded* server, receives the connection and then connects to its peer, freeing the socket so that `inetd` can continue receiving messages on it. The other kind, the *single-threaded* server, starts only one thread that receives all packets sequentially and eventually times out. You should use `nowait` for multithreaded servers, and `wait` for single-threaded servers. The optional *`max`* field, separated from *`wait/nowait`* by a period, specifies the maximum number of processes that may be created (in the case of a `nowait` server) in 60 seconds.

`user[.group]` specifies the username and, optionally, the group name that the server should run as.

`server-program` is the full pathname of the program executable. Some services (notably `echo`, `chargen`, `discard`, `daytime`, and `time`) can be handled directly by `inetd`. In that case, the `server-program` should be the keyword `internal`.

`program-arguments` is the list of p arguments to the server program, if any. In most cases it should include as first argument the program name (without the path).

Take as an example the following line from /etc/inetd.conf:

```
telnet stream tcp nowait root /usr/sbin/in.telnetd telnetd
```

This line means that inetd should listen on port 23/tcp, the port assigned to the telnet service in /etc/services. It is a connection-oriented service. When a connection is made to that port, it should run the /usr/sbin/in.telnetd program with the single parameter telnetd.

Aside from ease of programming and a lower memory and process-table use on the host, the biggest advantage of using inetd is security. Because all connections can go through one centralized point (the inetd program), and because there is now a standardized way in which daemons are started, programs that enhance security may be built using the "building blocks" approach: Don't modify the whole program—just build a small block that plugs into the program and gives it additional security. One such program included with Red Hat is tcpd. Part of the tcp wrappers package Briefly, tcpd is a program that is run from inetd instead of the standard server and provides host-based access control to any inetd-based server by means of rules coded into the /etc/hosts.allow and /etc/hosts-deny files.

Configuring a PPP Server

The Point-to-Point Protocol (PPP) is p the most popular way of connecting to the Internet. It is most often used to connect two hosts or networks by means of a modem. This section covers how to make your Linux host accept calls from other hosts and connect them to the Internet.

First of all, you must configure your Linux box so it will accept calls coming from a modem. Once a user can log on to your host through a modem using a terminal emulator, it is time to set up the PPP server. This allows other hosts to dial into your host to connect to the Internet (see Figure 7.6).

There are two ways of allowing users to use a PPP connection. The first way involves allowing them to log in with a standard shell. This is useful if you want to allow your users both kinds of access: shell and PPP. If a user wants a PPP connection, he logs on and then executes a program that starts the PPP process.

The second option has the user's shell be the PPP process itself. If you don't want users to have shell access (for many resource management reasons, many want to be able to restrict who has shell access), you will want to use the second way discussed.

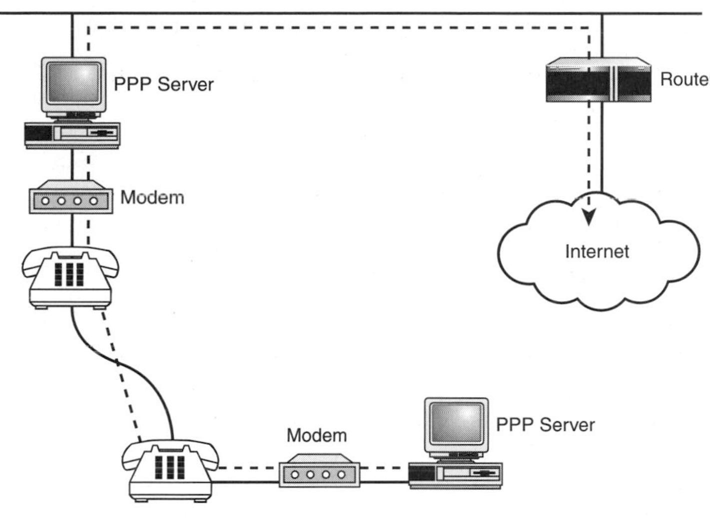

FIGURE 7.6
A PPP server allows other computers to connect to the Internet through it.

Basic Configuration

There are some configuration steps that need to be performed regardless of which way your users connect. First of all, you need to compile your kernel with the following options set (either as modules or as built-in drivers):

PPP (from Network Device Support)

IP: forwarding (from Networking Options)

You must have installed the `ppp` and one of the `getty` packages. If you don't want your users to have shell access, it's best to install one of the `mgetty` packages instead of the standard `getty`.

The `ppp` daemon is called, appropriately enough, `pppd`. It is configured by editing the `/etc/ppp/options` file. Note that `/etc/ppp/options` should contain options that apply to all PPP connections, incoming and outgoing. Here's a useful `/etc/ppp/options` file that should work for any connection:

```
asyncmap 0
netmask 255.255.255.0
proxyarp
lock
crtscts
modem
```

`asyncmap` sets which control characters should be escaped. Some modems have problems with some characters (notably Ctrl+S and Ctrl+Q), so those characters should be escaped. The parameter to `asyncmap` is a 31-bit number in which each bit represents one of the 31 control characters (from ASCII 0 to ASCII 31).

`netmask` sets the netmask for the PPP interface.

`proxyarp` tells the host to answer any ARP (Address Resolution Protocol) queries on behalf of the remote system. An ARP query is sent by a host on a local network, effectively asking all other hosts which one can handle a particular IP address. A *proxy ARP* means that this host tells all hosts on its LAN that it "owns" the remote host's IP address, thereby allowing other hosts on the LAN to see the remote host.

`lock` tells `pppd` to create a lockfile so that no other process will try to use the same serial port.

`crtscts` tells `pppd` to use hardware handshaking through the serial port. All modern modems and modem cables support hardware handshaking.

`modem` tells `pppd` to use all other modem control signals, such as carrier detect, in its operation.

Once the default `/etc/ppp/options` file has been set up, you should set up a file called `/etc/ppp/options.ttyXX` for each serial port you want to have a PPP server on. The most important configuration option in this file are the local and remote IP address. This is done so you have *dynamic IP addressing*, where IP addresses are not assigned to a particular remote host, but to a particular modem. The `/etc/ppp/options.ttyXX` file should minimally contain a line of this form:

```
localaddress:remoteaddress
```

`localaddress` is the address of the local side of the PPP interface, and *`remoteaddress`* is the address you want to assign the remote host. You must assign different local and remote addresses to each remote host. In this case, a netmask of `255.255.255.252` is useful, since it contains only two hosts per subnet. If different netmasks are desired for each connection type (incoming and outgoing), you can set the netmask using the `netmask` option in each of the `options.ttyXX` files instead of the general `options` file.

Once the general setup is finished, it is time to decide which kind of setup you want: shell or PPP-only.

Setting Up PPP Access via the Shell

If you want your users to log in with a shell and from there start the PPP program, you must follow a series of steps:

1. Starting a PPP link involves several operations, including configuring a kernel device. This requires `root` privileges. Since the user will be starting `pppd` from her own account, the `/usr/sbin/pppd` executable has to be `setuid-root`, using the following command:

   ```
   chmod u+s /usr/sbin/pppd
   ```

   For more information regarding `chmod` and the `setuid` bit, type **`man chmod`**.

2. To make it easier for users to start PPP, there should be either a global alias (set in the `/etc/bashrc` and `/etc/csh.cshrc` files) or a shell script in one of the directories accessible by all users through their `PATH` (`/usr/local/bin`, for example). The alias or script should point to or contain the following command:

   ```
   exec /usr/sbin/pppd -detach
   ```

   The `exec` command tells the shell to replace itself with the `pppd` program, thus saving memory. The `-detach` option tells `pppd` to remain in the foreground. This will ensure that no processes remain when `pppd` exits.

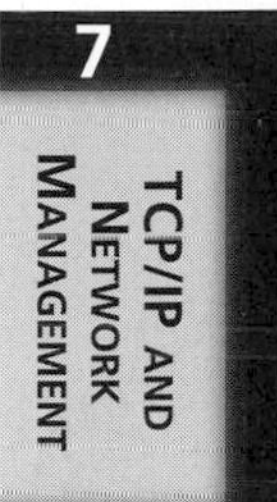

If you have this alias/script setup, when your users log in with their standard shell accounts, all they need to do is execute the alias you created for them (I like to call it `ppp`) to start the PPP connection. This can be automated through a dial-in connection script, which will vary depending on which software you use to dial in.

Setting Up Direct PPP Access Without Shell Access

If you want the PPP program to start automatically when a user connects, you can use a type of authentication called *PAP* (Password Authentication Protocol) or *CHAP* (Challenge Handshake Authentication Protocol). Both are supported by many `gettys` used by Linux; however, some PPP clients—notably old Windows 3.1 TCP/IP stacks and others—don't support PAP or CHAP. For this kind of client to work, you have to configure the `ppp` script already described as the user's shell (configured in the `/etc/passwd` file). This is discussed in detail here.

To add automatic PAP/CHAP authentication, you need to make sure you're running one of the mgetty variants, not just standard getty or agetty. This means making sure the mgetty package is installed (rpm -qa ¦ grep mgetty) and then making sure your /etc/inittab entries for the modem ports point to mgetty. Once this is done, PAP/CHAP authentication should automatically work. If it doesn't, edit the file /etc/mgetty/login.config. It should have a line like the following:

```
/Autoppp/ -     A_Ppp     /Usr/Sbin/Pppd Auth -Chap     Pap Login Debug
```

If the line isn't there, add it; if it's commented, uncomment it. If the line is there and PAP/CHAP still doesn't work, you might need some extra PPP options. Check the pppd(8) man page for more information.

If some or all of your users' PPP programs don't support PAP or CHAP, you need to perform a trick: Create the ppp script outlined in the previous section (it has to be a script, not an alias). Set your users' login shell to /usr/local/bin/ppp in /etc/passwd (just as an example). This makes the getty login process start the PPP daemon instead of the standard shell.

Caution

This method isn't as secure as it should be. A knowledgeable user could use Ctrl+C to stop the script's execution, and in some cases would end up in a shell. Because of that, the best way is to write a C program to start the pppd daemon. The following simple C program does just that:

```
#include <stdio.h>
#include <stdlib.h>

int main(void) {
    system("exec /usr/sbin/pppd auth -Chap +Pap Login");
    exit(0);
}
```

Save this file as "mypppd.c", and at the shell prompt, type

```
gcc mypppd.c -o mypppd
```

You will now have an executable program called "mypppd" in your current directory, which can be copied to /usr/local/sbin and set to the user's default shell.

TCP/IP Troubleshooting Tools

Problems rarely appear once a TCP/IP network is configured. However, networking equipment fails, lines go down, and cables get disconnected. Also, problems can arise during the initial configuration of a networked host.

Linux has three basic network troubleshooting tools. Two of them, `ping` and `traceroute`, are concerned with the capability of a host to reach another, while the third one, `tcpdump`, is useful for analyzing the flow of traffic in a network.

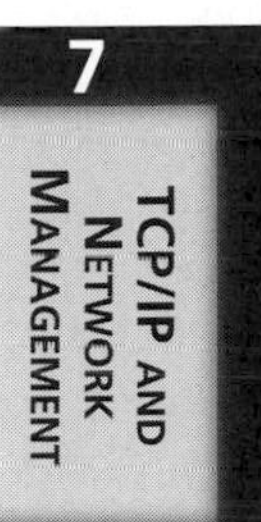

ping

The most basic network troubleshooting tool is the `ping` program. Named after the pinging sound made by submarine sonars, `ping` sends out packets to another host and waits for that host to reply. `ping` uses ICMP (Internet Control Message Protocol), which runs over IP and is designed for control messages used for things such as routing and reachability information.

The most common way of using `ping` is to pass it a hostname or address:

```
% ping server.company.com
PING server.company.com (10.0.1.10): 56 data bytes
64 bytes from 10.0.1.10: icmp_seq=0 ttl=245 time=83.239 ms
64 bytes from 10.0.1.10: icmp_seq=1 ttl=245 time=80.808 ms
64 bytes from 10.0.1.10: icmp_seq=2 ttl=245 time=82.994 ms
64 bytes from 10.0.1.10: icmp_seq=3 ttl=245 time=81.635 ms
^C
--- server.company.com ping statistics ---
4 packets transmitted, 4 packets received, 0% packet loss
round-trip min/avg/max = 80.808/82.169/83.239 ms
```

In this case, `ping` pings the target host one time per second, until you hit Ctrl+C. At that moment, it prints out the statistics for the run. In the statistics, aside from the number of packets transmitted and received, you can see the minimum, average, and maximum round-trip times, which will help you find out how congested the path to the destination host is at the moment.

`ping` has many options. Here are the most commonly used options:

Option	*Function*
`-c count`	Only sends *count* number of packets instead of pinging forever.
`-n`	`ping` displays numeric addresses instead of hostnames. Useful when you can't get to the DNS server or when DNS queries take too long.
`-r`	Record route. Sends an option in every packet that instructs every host between the source and the target to store its IP address in the packet. This way you can see which hosts a packet is going through. However, the packet size is limited to nine hosts. Besides, some systems disregard this option. Because of this, it is better to use `traceroute`.
`-q`	Quiet output. Outputs just the final statistics.
`-v`	Verbose. Displays all packets received, not just `ping` responses.

When troubleshooting network problems, you should first ping the IP address of the source host itself. This verifies that the originating network interface is set up correctly. After that, you should try pinging your default gateway, your default gateway's gateway (the next hop out), and so on, until you reach the destination host. That way you can easily isolate where a problem lies. However, once you've verified that you can get to the default gateway, it is better to use the `traceroute` program (which is described in "`traceroute`," next) to automate the process.

Note

All TCP/IP packets have a field called `Time-To-Live`, or `TTL`. This field is decremented once by each router on the network. The packet is discarded the moment it reaches `0`. While `ping` uses a default TTL of `255` (the maximum value), many programs such as `telnet` and `ftp` use a smaller `TTL` (usually `30` or `60`). That means that you might be able to ping a host, but not telnet or FTP into it. You may use the `-t ttl` option to `ping` to set the `TTL` of the packets it outputs.

traceroute

The traceroute program is the workhorse of TCP/IP troubleshooting. It sends out UDP packets with progressively larger TTLs and detects the ICMP responses sent by gateways when they drop the packets. In the end, this maps out the route a packet takes when going from the source host to the target host.

This is how it works: traceroute starts by sending out a packet with a TTL of 1. The packet gets to a gateway, which can be the target host or not. If it is the target host, the gateway sends a response packet. If it isn't the target host, the gateway decrements the TTL. Since the TTL is now 0, the gateway drops the packet and sends back a packet indicating this. Whatever happens, traceroute detects the reply packet. If it has reached the target host, its job is finished. If not (it received notification that the packet was dropped, for instance), it increments the TTL by 1 (its new value is 2) and sends out another packet. This time the first gateway decrements the TTL (to 1) and passes it through to the next gateway. This gateway does the same thing: determine whether it's the destination host and decrement the TTL. This goes on until either you reach the target host or you reach the maximum TTL value (which is 30 by default, but can be changed with the -m *max_ttl* option).

traceroute sends three packets with each TTL and reports the round-trip time taken by each packet. This is useful for detecting network bottlenecks.

traceroute is usually used the same way as ping—by giving it a destination address. Listing 7.1 shows an example of the output from traceroute:

LISTING 7.1 Sample Output from *traceroute*

```
mario@chaos:~ 511 $ /usr/sbin/traceroute www.umbral.com
traceroute to xmaya.umbral.com (207.87.18.30), 30 hops max, 40 byte packets
 1:  master.spin.com.mx (200.13.80.123)  120.75 ms  126.727 ms  109.533 ms
 2:  octopus.spin.com.mx (200.13.81.32)  110.042 ms  104.654 ms  99.599 ms
 3:  200.33.218.161 (200.33.218.161)  119.539 ms  105.697 ms  109.603 ms
 4:  rr1.mexmdf.avantel.net.mx (200.33.209.1)  131.556 ms  112.767 ms  109.6 ms
 5:  bordercore1-hssi0-0.Dallas.cw.net (166.48.77.249)  159.54 ms  155.378 ms
169.598 ms
 6:  core9.Dallas.cw.net (204.70.9.89)  159.483 ms  156.364 ms  159.628 ms
 7:  dfw2-core2-s1-0-0.atlas.digex.net (165.117.59.13)  169.505 ms  156.024 ms
149.628 ms
 8:  lax1-core1-s8-0-0.atlas.digex.net (165.117.50.25)  199.497 ms  194.006 ms
189.621 ms
 9:  sjc4-core2-s5-0-0.atlas.digex.net (165.117.53.74)  199.489 ms sjc4-core2-
s5-1-0.atlas.digex.net
```

continues

LISTING 7.1 continued

```
(165.117.56.110)  191.025 ms sjc4-core2-s5-0-0.atlas.digex.net (165.117.53.74)
210.25 ms
10:  sjc4-core6-pos1-1.atlas.digex.net (165.117.59.69)  201.031 ms  196.195 ms
199.584 ms
11:  sjc4-wscore2-p1-0.wsmg.digex.net (199.125.178.37)  360.468 ms  366.267 ms
199.481 ms
12:  sjc4-wscore4-fa1-0.wsmg.digex.net (199.125.178.20)  582.272 ms  207.536 ms
198.275 ms
13:  xmaya.umbral.com (207.87.18.30)  209.457 ms  3076.14 ms *
```

`traceroute` can give you quite a bit of information if you know how to look for it. For example, you can see a few things in Listing 7.1:

- `www.umbral.com` is actually an alias for `xmaya.umbral.com`. `traceroute` always does a reverse DNS lookup and reports the official hostname of the host it's tracing.
- `xmaya.umbral.com` is connected to the Internet through a service provider whose domain is `digex.net` (probably an ISP called Digex). (Lines 7–12 are all in the IP networks belonging to the domain of the last gateway.)
- You are connected to the Internet through an ISP called Spin, which is in Mexico. (Lines 1 and 2 are the first gateway. The domain ends with `.mx`.)
- The Digex hosts that appear on line 9 are actually several hosts with the same IP address. This is done for redundancy.
- There seems to be some kind of bottleneck between hosts in lines 10, 11, and 12. Notice how the response time, after slowly growing steadily until line 9, suddenly jumps from about 200 milliseconds to more than 300, and then to more than 500? This might be a temporary bottleneck (caused simply by the traffic load at the moment) or it may be a continuous problem, caused perhaps by a physical media problem or not enough capacity in the link.

As you can see, `traceroute` can be an invaluable tool. Much more information can be gleaned from `traceroute` output; it is best to read the `traceroute(8)` man page for a complete discussion.

tcpdump

`tcpdump` is another invaluable tool for debugging some types of network problems. It basically works as a *packet sniffer*—it listens to the network, looks at any packets that come by (whether destined for the host on which it is running or not), and operates on it. It can store all or just some interesting parts of the traffic it sees, or perform a rudimentary analysis of the information it contains.

`tcpdump` works by setting the network card into what is known as *promiscuous mode*. Normally, a network card will only see packets that are meant for it. However, in promiscuous mode, it will see all packets that pass through the network and pass them to the operating system above. The OS then passes the packets to `tcpdump`, which can then filter and display or store them. Since it modifies the configuration of the network card, `tcpdump` must be run by `root`.

Caution

`tcpdump` is a potential security hole. It falls into the category of programs known as *sniffers*, which listen to the network and can listen to all packets in the network and store them. If users use programs such as `telnet`, which send passwords in the clear, a cracker might use a sniffer to sniff out their passwords. Because of this, `tcpdump` should never be installed `setuid-root`.

To detect whether a network interface is in promiscuous mode (and thus might have a sniffer running on it), use the `ifconfig` command to display the interface's configuration. The `PROMISC` flag will appear if the interface is in promiscuous mode:

```
# /sbin/ifconfig eth0
eth0      Link encap:Ethernet  HWaddr 00:60:97:3E:F0:61
          inet addr:10.0.1.50  Bcast:10.0.1.255  Mask:255.255.255.0
          UP BROADCAST RUNNING PROMISC MULTICAST  MTU:1500  Metric:1
          RX packets:0 errors:0 dropped:0 overruns:0 frame:0
          TX packets:5 errors:0 dropped:0 overruns:0 carrier:5
          Collisions:0
          Interrupt:3 Base address:0x310
```

If you run `tcpdump` without any arguments, you get a listing of all the packets that pass through the network:

```
# /usr/sbin/tcpdump
tcpdump: listening on eth0
22:46:12.730048 renato.1445323871 > vishnu.nfs: 100 readlink [|nfs]
22:46:12.734224 tumbolia.1012 > vishnu.808: udp 92
22:46:12.746763 tumbolia.22 > atman.1023: P 142299991:142300035(44)
➥ ack 3799214339 win 32120 (DF) [tos 0x10]
22:46:12.763684 atman.1023 > tumbolia.22: . ack 44 win 32120 (DF) [tos 0x10]
22:46:12.778100 vishnu.808 > tumbolia.1015: udp 56
22:46:12.780084 gerardo.1448370113 > vishnu.nfs: 124 lookup [|nfs]
22:46:12.780153 tumbolia.22 > atman.1023: P 44:596(552) ack 1 win 32120 (DF)
➥ [tos 0x10]
```

The dump will stop when you press Ctrl+C.

As you can see, `tcpdump` by default converts IP addresses to hostnames and port numbers to service names. It also attempts to interpret some packets (such as those where the line ends with `lookup [|nfs]`, which are NFS lookups). In some cases, the number of bytes that `tcpdump` looks at (68) might not be enough to fully decode the packet. In this case, you may use the `-s` option to increase the number (see the `-s` option in Table 7.6).

You don't often want to see all the packets, especially in medium to large networks. Sometimes you want to see all the packets going between two specific hosts, or even those that use a specific service. `tcpdump` takes as a parameter an optional filter expression that will select only certain packets.

`tcpdump`'s filter expressions consist of one or more primitives joined by the keywords `and`, `or`, and `not`. Each primitive consists of a qualifier followed by an ID. A *qualifier* consists of one or more keywords, the most common of which are shown in Table 7.5. The ID specifies the value the corresponding field must have to match the filter.

TABLE 7.5 Most Common *tcpdump* Qualifiers

Qualifier	*Matches*
`src host`	The IP address of the host from where the packet comes.
`dst host`	The IP address of the host to which the packet is going.
`host`	The IP address of the source or the destination host.
`src port`	The port the packet is coming from.
`dst port`	The port the packet is going to.
`port`	The source or the destination port.
`tcp`, `udp`, or `icmp`	The packet's protocol is the specified one.

Tip

One common mistake is to run `tcpdump` through a remote connection, such as when connected through `telnet` or `ssh`, with a filter that includes all the `telnet` or `ssh` packets. An example is including just `host thishost`, where `thishost` is the host on which `tcpdump` is running. In that case you end up with an incredible amount of output. This is because the first packet that comes through generates output, which is transmitted through the network and captured by `tcpdump`, which generates more output, which is also transmitted through the network, and so on.

To prevent that, be more specific in your filter expressions. For example, you might include the primitive `not port 22` to filter out `ssh` packets.

`tcpdump` also takes several switches, the most common of which are shown in Table 7.6.

TABLE 7.6 Most Common *tcpdump* Switches

Qualifier	*Matches*
`-c` *`count`*	Exit after receiving *`count`* packets.
`-i` *`interface`*	Listen on *`interface`*. By default, `tcpdump` listens on the first interface found after the loopback interface. You can see the order the interfaces are searched using the `ifconfig -a` command.
`-n`	Don't convert numeric addresses and port numbers to host and service names (print numeric output).
`-N`	Print out only the hostname, not its fully qualified domain name.
`-r` *`file`*	Read packets from *`file`*, which must have been created with the `-w` option.
`-s` *`snaplen`*	Grab *`snaplen`* bytes from each packet. The default is `68`, which is enough for IP, ICMP, TCP, and UDP packets. However, for certain protocols (such as DNS and NFS), a *`snaplen`* of `68` will truncate some protocol information. This is marked by `[¦`*`protocol`*`]`, where *`protocol`* indicates the protocol part where truncation occurred.
`-v`	Verbose mode. Print some more information about each packet.
`-vv`	Very verbose mode. Print much more information about each packet.
`-w` *`file`*	Capture the packets into *`file`*.
`-x`	Print out each packet in hex. Will print out either the whole packet or *`snaplen`* bytes, whichever is less.

Network Security Tools

There are several tools that help you secure your networks. First of all, you must have a firewall to separate your internal network from the Internet and to prevent hackers from getting in. Then there is the problem of getting into your network from the outside, and from your network to the outside world, without leaving a wide-open door for hackers.

You must remember that the most important factor in security is usually the human one. You might have the best firewall in the world, perfectly configured, and an employee might simply copy confidential information to a floppy disk and hand it to a competitor. Security starts with people and with a good security policy. This particular subject cannot be discussed in depth here, however. If you want to learn more (and you should!), an excellent reference is *Maximum Internet Security: A Hackers Guide* (ISBN 1-5752-1268-4, Sams Publishing). To buy this book online, head over to `http://www.price-hunter.net` and type in the ISBN. This site scans the various Web sites that sell books online, and provides you with a list that shows the least expensive place, up to the most expensive place to buy your book.

Firewalls

A *firewall* is a computer that stands between a trusted network (such as your internal network) and an untrusted network (such as the Internet), and controls what traffic passes between them. It is an essential piece of the information security puzzle.

There are two general types of firewalls (which may be combined): application-level firewalls (known as *proxies*), and packet-filtering firewalls. A *packet-filtering firewall l*simply allows or disallows packets, depending on their content. Most packet-filtering firewalls determine what packets to allow or disallow based on the source or destination addresses, source or destination port, and whether the packet is part of an ongoing conversation.

An application-level firewall or proxy acts as an intermediary between client and server programs. Instead of connecting directly to the server, a client application connects to the proxy and asks it for the information. The proxy opens a connection to the server, sends the request, and continues to pass information back and forth between server and client (see Figure 7.7).

FIGURE 7.7
Packet-filtering and application-level firewalls are compared.

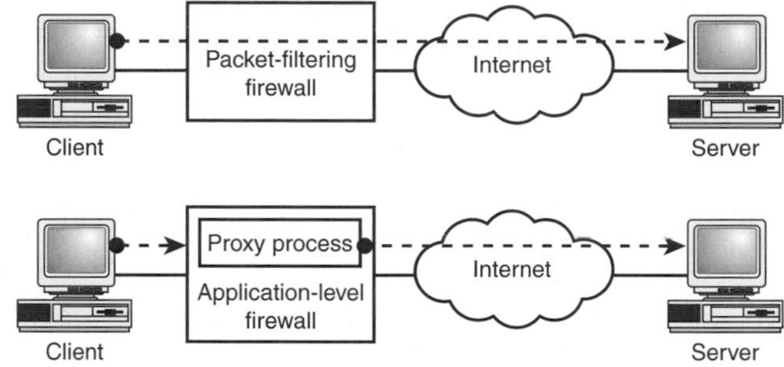

Both types of firewalls have advantages and disadvantages, and many sites implement both. A packet-filtering firewall is regarded as less secure than a proxy-based firewall, since the a proxy-based firewall will actually make a network connection on your behalf, and pass back all of the data it receives. In other words, when a proxy-based firewall is set up well, the only way to access systems outside your network is to use your firewall as a proxy to retrieve data for you. The design of proxy-based firewalls can thus completely shield your internal network from outside influences.

Another advantage of proxies is that sometimes they may be used to reduce bandwidth usage. For example, an organization may implement a proxy on its firewall that stores the Web pages requested by users. If another user requests the same page again, the proxy can grab it from its local storage and send the page to the user, without having to connect to the origin server again. If you multiply this by tens or hundreds of users, you can appreciate the bandwidth savings.

On the other hand, an application-level firewall must be built for each protocol. Thus, there are HTTP proxies, FTP proxies, Telnet proxies, SMTP proxies, and so on. This brings up the problem of *unsupported applications*—applications whose protocols don't have a proxy yet. There are *generic proxies* available, but applications must be modified and recompiled to use them. Since they work on single packets, packet filters are transparent to applications.

A packet-filtering firewall may also do what is known as *network-address translation* or *masquerading*. This means that the firewall converts the source addresses on outgoing packets so the other host thinks it's connecting to the firewall itself, and to the destination addresses on incoming packets so they go to the host that requested the connection initially. This has several advantages. For example, a whole network may connect to the Internet using a single IP address. Also, because internal addresses aren't visible to the outside, hosts on the internal network are more secure against attacks from the outside. The downside to this is that any hosts that provide services to the outside must be outside the firewall; otherwise, the firewall must be specifically configured to pass some packets straight to a particular host.

Linux Firewalling Concepts

The Linux kernel itself contains support for packet filtering and masquerading. There are also several packages available for proxy-based firewalls, such as the Squid HTTP/FTP proxy cache and the SOCKS proxy. To determine whether your kernel supports IP chains, look for the file `/proc/net/ip_fwchains`. If the file exists, your current kernel has support for IP chains.

If the file doesn't exist, you need to enable the kernel firewall. To do this, you must configure the kernel and enable Network Firewalls and IP: Firewalling. You might also want to enable IP: Always Defragment, IP: Masquerading, and ICMP: Masquerading if you're doing masquerading. After that, recompile and install the kernel and reboot.

Starting with version 2.2 of the Linux kernel, the packet filter is based on the concept of chains, which are configured using the `/usr/sbin/ipchains` utility. If your system doesn't contain this utility, simply install the ipchains package included with your distribution.

The ipchains tool inserts and deletes rules from the kernel's packet filtering section. Every rule in the kernel's packet filter belongs to a group of rules known as *chains*. Initially, the kernel contains three default chains:

- The *input chain*, which is applied to arriving packets, before passing them to the rest of the kernel or to applications
- The *output chain*, which is applied to packets just before they leave the host
- The *forwarding chain*, which is applied to packets that have passed the input chain but whose target host is a different host; when the host is being used as a firewall or router, for example

When a packet enters a chain, it is tested to determine if it matches each of the rules on the chain. If it does, it is passed to the target of that rule. If it reaches the end of a chain, it is passed to the chain's default target.

A target specifies what to do with a packet that matches a particular rule or, in the case of the default targets, that reaches the end of a chain. There are six system targets; they are presented in Table 7.7.

TABLE 7.7 *ipchains* System Targets

Name	*Function*
ACCEPT	Lets the package through.
DENY	Drops the package silently.
REJECT	Drops the package, notifying the sender.
MASQ	Valid only in the `forward` chain or chains called from it. Masquerades the package.
REDIRECT	Valid only in the `input` chain or chains called from it. Sends the package to a port on the firewall host itself, regardless of its real destination. May be followed by a port specification to redirect the package to a different port regardless of its destination port.
RETURN	Transfers immediately to the end of the current chain; the package will be handled according to the chain's default target.

A target may also be another chain, including a user-defined chain. You may create your own chains at any time, and attach them to any of the predefined chains. The default target of a user-defined chain is always the rule following the one in which the chain is called, so a user-defined chain can be used as a sort of subroutine; you may reuse its rules in several chains. This is useful in reducing the total number of rules and to better document what is happening, since you may name chains after what they do. For example, if a firewall has different rules for two departments (call them the *bosses* and the *masses*), you might define different chains called *bosses* and *masses*, and then simply apply each chain depending on where the packet is coming from.

Building a Firewall with `ipchains`

Consider the network shown in Figure 7.7. There is an internal network using private addresses connected to the public Internet. You want to allow all hosts in the internal network to access the Internet, while providing protection from external hackers. No one needs to access the internal hosts from the outside (thus, this kind of firewall is known as a one-way firewall).

Listing 7.2 shows a shell script that sets up a basic one-way packet-filtering and masquerading firewall using `ipchains`.

LISTING 7.2 A Basic Firewall Using *ipchains*

```
#!/bin/sh -x
# To enable logging if necessary
#LOG=-l

# Constants
ANYWHERE=0.0.0.0/0
EXT_IF=eth0
INT_IF=eth1

# Networks
INTERNAL_NET=10.0.1.0/24
EXTERNAL_ADDR=205.142.24.1/32

# Disable packet forwarding while we set up the firewall
echo 0 > /proc/sys/net/ipv4/ip_forward

# Flush all rules
/sbin/ipchains -F input
/sbin/ipchains -F output
/sbin/ipchains -F forward

# Deny all packets by default - this is a mostly-closed firewall
/sbin/ipchains -P input DENY
/sbin/ipchains -P output DENY
/sbin/ipchains -P forward DENY

# Accept anything to/from localhost
/sbin/ipchains -A input -j ACCEPT -p all -s localhost -d localhost -i lo \
$LOG
/sbin/ipchains -A output -j ACCEPT -p all -s localhost -d localhost -i lo\
 $LOG

# Spoofing protection - deny anything coming from the outside with an \
internal
# address
/sbin/ipchains -A input -j RETURN -p all -s $INTERNAL_NET -d $ANYWHERE –I\
 $EXT_IF $LOG

# Accept TCP packets belonging to already-established connections
/sbin/ipchains -A input -j ACCEPT -p tcp -s $ANYWHERE -d $ME -i $EXT_IF \! -y
$LOG

# Accept and masquerade all packets from the inside going anywhere
/sbin/ipchains -A input -j ACCEPT -p all -s $INTERNAL_NET -d $ANYWHERE –I\
 $INT_IF $LOG
```

```
/sbin/ipchains -A forward -j MASQ -p all -s $INTERNAL_NET -d $ANYWHERE –I\
 $INT_IF $LOG

# Accept all TCP packets going to the outside net
/sbin/ipchains -A output -j ACCEPT -p all -s $ME -d $ANYWHERE -i $EXT_IF \
$LOG

# Accept type 3 ICMP queries (Destination Unreachable)
/sbin/ipchains -A input -j ACCEPT -p icmp -s $ANYWHERE -d $ME -i $EXT_IF \
--icmp-type destination-unreachable $LOG
/sbin/ipchains -A output -j ACCEPT -p icmp -s $ME -d $ANYWHERE -i $EXT_IF\
 --icmp-type destination-unreachable $LOG

# Catch-all rules to provide logging
/sbin/ipchains -A input -j DENY -l
/sbin/ipchains -A output -j DENY -l
/sbin/ipchains -A forward -j DENY -l

# Enable packet forwarding
echo 1 > /proc/sys/net/ipv4/ip_forward
```


First, you should define a few shell variables to help keep your script readable and manageable. Next, for safety, disable packet forwarding in the kernel now while building the firewall rules. This is important, since the first step in actually building the firewall is flushing the system chains, so the system might be left in an insecure state.

There are two broad ways of thinking about firewall policies: mostly-open and mostly-closed. In a *mostly-open firewall*, your system lets everything through except the packets you specify. A *mostly-closed firewall* does the reverse, denying or rejecting everything except that which you specifically allow. This second kind of firewall is usually regarded as more secure, since you know exactly what is going through and won't be subject to future attacks based on now-unused protocols. As you can see in Listing 7.1, to build a mostly-closed firewall you first set the default target of all chains to `DENY` or `REJECT` and then add rules to `ACCEPT` those packets you want to let through. A mostly-open firewall, obviously, is just the opposite: You set the default target to `ACCEPT` and then add rules to `DENY` or `REJECT` those packets you don't want to let through.

You should now add rules for each of the packets you want to let through. Rules are added by executing the `ipchains` program with parameters that specify the packet characteristics and the action to take. Tables 7.8 and 7.9, respectively, show the commands `ipchains` will take and its most common options.

TABLE 7.8 *ipchains* Commands

Command	*Action*
`-A` *chain*	Adds rule to *chain*.
`-D` *chain* `[`*rulenum*`]`	Deletes rule number *rulenum* from *chain*. If *rulenum* is omitted, the default is the first rule (number `1`).
`-I` *chain* `[`*rulenum*`]`	Inserts rule into *chain* before rule number *rulenum*.
`-R` *chain rulenum*	Replaces rule number *rulenum* in *chain*.
`-F` *chain*	Flushes *chain*. Equivalent to using `-D` on all rules one by one.
`-L` *chain*	Lists the rules in *chain*.
`-N` *chain*	Creates new user-defined chain.
`-X` *chain*	Deletes user-defined chain.
`-P` *chain target*	Sets defaulttarget for *chain* to *target*.

TABLE 7.9 Most Common *ipchains* Options

Option	*Specifies*
`-s [!]` *address*`[/`*mask*`] [!] [`*port*`[:`*port*`]]`	Source address and port of the packet.
`-d [!]` *address*`[/`*mask*`] [!] [`*port*`[:`*port*`]]`	Destination address and port of the packet.
`-i [!]` *interface*	Interface the packet is arriving on (in the `input` chain) or leaving on (in the `output` and `forward` chains).
`-p [!]` *protocol*	Packet protocol. It may be any protocol specified in the `/etc/protocols` file.
`-j` *target* `[`*port*`]`	Target to send the packet to.
`[!] -y`	Packet is a `SYN` packet; only for rules that specify `-p tcp`.
`--icmp-type` *type*	ICMP type is *type*; only for rules that specify `-p icmp`.
`-l`	That packet is logged to `syslog`.`-n` or `--numeric`. Used with the `-L` option. Displays numeric host and port addresses instead of names.

Some of these options allow the use of the `!` (short for `not`) sign. The `not` sign can be used to negate or reverse the condition. For example, specifying `-p ! icmp` in a rule will match packets whose protocol is not ICMP to the conditions of this rule.

The source and destination addresses can be specified in several ways. To specify a particular host, you may use its IP address or its hostname. To specify a network, you can either use the CIDR notation or its normal expanded dotted-quad format. Thus, `1.1.1.0/24` is equivalent to `1.1.1.0/255.255.255.0`. Source and destination port numbers can be specified numerically or by service name (mapped from `/etc/services`). You may also specify a range of ports by using a colon (`:`) to separate the beginning and ending ports.

The `-y` option is used when you want to allow TCP connections in one direction only. When building a firewall, for example, you may want to allow your internal hosts to connect to the outside without letting outside agents connect to the internal hosts. Because a connection needs packets going both ways, blocking packets coming from the outside is a naive approach.

The solution is to block just those packets used to initiate a connection. These packets are called `SYN` packets because they have the `SYN` flag set in their headers and the `FIN` and `ACK` flags cleared. (The *flags* are specific bits set in the packet's header.) If you block any packets with the `SYN` bit set, your hosts can talk to hosts on the outside without allowing the outside hosts to initiate the connections to your hosts.

The Internet Control Message Protocol (ICMP) is used for control messages, such as `host not found` or `ping` responses. It is usually the most secure means to disable most ICMP messages. However, some message types are needed by various utilities or other parts of the system. The `--icmp-type` option matches those packets with a specific ICMP message type. For example, ICMP messages such as `destination unreachable` are used extensively by TCP and UDP. You might also want to allow your internal users to use other utilities such as `ping` or `traceroute`. Table 7.10 shows the most common ICMP message types.

TABLE 7.10 The Most Common ICMP Message Types

Number	*Name*	*Required By*
0	`echo-reply`	`ping`
3	`destination-unreachable`	Any TCP/UDP traffic
5	`redirect`	Routing, if not running routing daemon
8	`echo-request`	`ping`
11	`time-exceeded`	`traceroute`

You can find more detailed information on `ipchains` and its options in the `/usr/doc/ipchains-1.3.8/HOWTO.txt` file.

Proxies

As mentioned, there are two kinds of firewalls: packet-filtering and proxy-based. A basic packet-filtering firewall may be complemented with a proxy to enhance its security and, in some cases, cache data to reduce network bandwidth usage.

The most common kind of proxy on the Internet today is the Web caching proxy. Linux includes a Web caching proxy called Squid. Under Red Hat, run the `rpm -q squid` command to see whether it is installed. If the package isn't installed, you must install the `squid-2.2.STABLE1-1.i386.rpm` file included in the RedHat/RPMS directory of the CD. Caldera does not include a Squid RPM. It is recommended that you visit `http://freshmeat.net` and search for "squid" to track down either the Squid source archive or the RPM.

To configure Squid, go to the `/etc/squid` directory and copy the `squid.conf.default` file to `squid.conf`. Edit `squid.conf` to suit your site. The file is extensively commented, so most of its options are self-documenting. They also typically have sensible defaults that you can leave unmodified unless you want to tune the cache. Table 7.11 shows the options you should modify before starting Squid.

TABLE 7.11 Options You Should Modify in `/etc/squid/squid.conf`

Option	*Meaning*
`cache_dir` *`dirname mbytes level1 level2`*	The cache is stored in *`dirname`*. It occupies at most *`mbytes`* megabytes of disk space. *`dirname`* contains *`level1`* first-level directories, each of which contain *`level2`* second-level directories. The default values are `100`, `16`, and `256`, respectively. You should change only the first value to reflect the amount of disk space you want to use for the cache; the second and third values are used for tuning.
`pid_filename` *`filename`*	Create *`filename`* to store the Squid process ID, which is used by the `/etc/rc.d/init.d/squid` script to kill the process when called with the `stop` parameter. You should uncomment this line and leave the value unchanged.
`logfile_rotate` *`nfiles`*	When rotating logs, keep *`nfiles`* archived copies. Although the Squid installation will create a `/etc/logrotate.d/squid` file to handle log rotations, the number of archived copies is modified here.
`ftp_user` *`user@domain.name`*	Some FTP sites require that you pass a valid email address as a password. You should modify this parameter so that it contains a valid user ID (usually the site administrator).
`cache_mgr` *`user@domain.name`*	Email address of the site administrator. This person is emailed if a problem arises with the cache.

continues

TABLE 7.11 continued

Option	*Meaning*
`cache_effective_user` *`username`*	Squid is usually started from `/etc/rc.d/init.d/squid`, which is run as `root` at startup. It is unsafe to run Squid as `root`, so you must create a new user in `/etc/passwd` and add its username and group name to the `squid.conf` file. Squid will set its effective user and group IDs to the ones configured here.
`cache_effective_group` *`groupname`*	See `cache_effective_user`.
`err_html_text` *`html_text`*	This should be modified to contain HTML code including the cache administrator's email address. It is added to the end of all error pages presented by Squid to the users.

Once you have configured Squid, you may start it by running `/etc/rc.d/init.d/squid start`. The first time Squid starts, it will take a long time to create its cache directory hierarchy. Be patient. Squid will log its errors to the `/var/log/squid/squid.out`, so you can do a `tail -f` on this file to check whether there are any startup errors.

Secure Remote Access—SSH, the Secure SHell

You have just completely secured your site. You have an airtight firewall in place and have set up your proxy. You have a good security policy and your users have been educated on it. You can sit at your console basking in the feeling of a job well done and use `telnet` to log in to one of your servers to start a backup.

But what of a few days later? You discover your server has been compromised. Someone logged in as `root` and played amateur sysadmin on it. What could have happened?

This scenario is more common than you might think, and it has bitten many a sysadmin. What happened here was that someone on the internal network was using a *sniffer*, a program that captures all traffic on the LAN. It saw your complete `telnet` session, including the server's `root` password, and reported it to whoever was running the sniffer. That user, armed with the password, went into your server.

The problem with most Internet protocols is that the Internet was initially created without security being a main goal. Most companies today use these same Internet protocols on their internal networks. Even if your network isn't visible from the Internet, don't undervalue the importance of good network-wide security. It has been reported that over 70 percent of system compromises originate within the firewall, either by disgruntled employees, curious employees who want to see how systems work, or by competitors' spies.

What is a sysadmin to do? Use only the console? What about remote sites that are only connected via the Internet?

Enter the Secure SHell, also known as SSH. SSH is a suite of programs that allow you to log on to remote servers and transfer files in a secure manner. It is meant to be a replacement for `rlogin`, `rsh`, `telnet`, and `rcp`, which are insecure because they don't encrypt the data they transfer as it moves from one host to another. SSH on the other hand scrambles the data that goes through the network so it is indecipherable to someone using a sniffer. A full discussion of security and encryption technologies is beyond the scope of this book; however, an excellent reference is *Internet Security Professional Reference*, Second Edition (New Riders Publishing, ISBN 1-5620-5760-X).

With SSH, each host and user has a *private key* and a *public key*. The public key is stored on the server, while the private key is kept on the client. Data encrypted with one key can only be decrypted with the other, and vice versa. This means that SSH can be used both for secure communications and for strong authentication, where you need to be sure that the host on the other side of the connection is actually who it claims to be.

Since SSH contains encryption technology, it is illegal to export it from the United States. That is why it isn't included in the stock Red Hat Linux 6.0 distribution. To get SSH, you must download it from the Internet. The master site for the SSH RPM is `http://www.replay.com/redhat/ssh.html`. There are four RPMs: `ssh`, `ssh-server`, `ssh-clients`, and `ssh-extras`. (Version numbers aren't mentioned here because they might change over time; get the latest versions available.) `ssh-server` must be installed on the servers (the hosts you are logging on to), `ssh-clients` on the clients (the hosts you are logging on from), and `ssh` on both; `ssh-extras` can be optionally installed on either or both. It is often best to install all packages on all hosts.

The `ssh-server` package contains default `/etc/ssh/sshd_config` and `/etc/ssh/ssh_config` that work well for most purposes. It also contains an `/etc/rc.d/init.d/sshd` script for starting the `sshd` daemon when you boot the host. To start the `sshd` daemon manually, run `/etc/rc.d/init.d/sshd start`. If you want to start it automatically when the server boots, create an appropriate softlink in the `/etc/rc.d/rc?.d` directory that corresponds to your server's `initdefault` runlevel.

The ssh and ssh-clients packages contain several programs. The most useful are ssh and scp. ssh allows you to log on to a remote host, execute remote programs, and redirect ports from the local host to the remote host, and vice versa. scp, which allows you to copy files securely from one host to another, is a replacement for the rcp program.

The ssh Command

The ssh command is used to log on to a remote server and execute a command. It has the following syntax:

```
ssh [options] host [options] [command]
```

ssh also handles X connection forwarding. Whenever you log on to a remote host using ssh from a host that is running X windows, sshd creates a dummy X server and sets the DISPLAY variable to point to it. All X traffic going to this dummy server is actually forwarded to the X server on your local host. X authentication is automatically taken care of via xauth. That way, the X traffic is also encrypted and secure. You don't have to do anything to make this happen, just log on to the remote server from an X session.

There are many options to the ssh command that can be included either before or after the hostname. The most common options to ssh are listed in Table 7.12.

TABLE 7.12 Most Common *ssh* Options

Option	*Meaning*
-f	Send process to background after authentication. Useful when you need to enter a password.
-l *user*	Log in as *user* to the remote server.
-o '*option*'	Set option in the same format as the configuration file. Useful for some options that don't have command-line switch equivalents.
-v	Activate verbose mode. Useful for debugging connections.
-C	Compress. All data in the connection will be compressed. Useful especially over modem lines. The compression algorithm used is the same one used by gzip.
-L *port*:*host*:*hostport*	Forward TCP port *port* to *hostport* on remote host *host*. What this does is open a local server socket on *port* and a socket on the remote host that connects to port *hostport* on *host*. All connections to *port* on the local host will be forwarded to port *hostport* on *host*.
-R *port*:*host*:*hostport*	The reverse of -L. Forward TCP port *port* on the remote host to port *hostport* on *host*.

Port Forwarding

The -R and -L options deserve special mention. They are useful especially in cases where you need to make a secure "tunnel" through an insecure network (such as the Internet). Consider a case where you have a Web server in California and a database server in Florida. You want the Web server to access the database, but for security purposes you want the communication to be encrypted. Suppose the database listens by default to port 3306. You might run the following shell script on the Web server:

```
#!/bin/sh
while /bin/true
do
  ssh dbserver -L 3306:localhost:3306 sleep 87600
done
```


The `while` loop is needed because the `ssh` command (and thus the port forwarding) will run only as long as the command given on the `ssh` command line specifies. In this case, the `sleep 87600` command simply waits for 87,600 seconds (24 hours) before exiting. This command forwards port 3306 of the Web server (where you're running the command) to port 3306 on the `localhost` of the database server.

If you want to run this script on the database server, you would use the -R option and invert the two port numbers. Since they are the same, the command would be identical except for the option name.

Authentication

This scheme poses a problem, though. The `ssh` command will ask for the password of the remote user. There are only two ways to automate the password login process:

- Using `.rhosts` authentication
- Using private/public key authentication

To use `.rhosts` authentication, you create a `.rhosts` file in the home directory of the remote user, just as if you were using the `rsh` command. The difference here is that the remote host will be authenticated by its public key, instead of just by its IP address. Assuming the command was run by the `admin` user and that the Web server host is called `webserver`, the `.rhosts` file should contain the following line:

```
webserver  admin
```

If you don't like the idea of using a `.rhosts` file or you are sitting behind a firewall, the only option left is to use private/public keys. What you need to do follows:

1. Log on to the local server.
2. Run the `/usr/bin/ssh-keygen` program to generate the private and the public

keys. They are saved under the user's home directory as `.ssh/identity` and `.ssh/identity.pub`, respectively. `ssh-keygen` asks you for a passphrase, which is used to encrypt the keys and has to be keyed in every time you want to log on remotely. Since the purpose of this is precisely to avoid having to use a password, leave the passphrase blank.

3. Copy the `.ssh/identity.pub` file to the `/tmp` directory of the remote server:

   `scp $HOME/.ssh/identity.pub remoteserver:/tmp.`

4. Log on to the remote server:

   `ssh remoteserver.`

5. Append the `/tmp/identity.pub` file to the `.ssh/authorized_keys` file under the remote user's home directory:

   `cat /tmp/identity.pub >> .ssh/authorized_keys.`

6. Log off the remote server and log back on using `ssh`. This time `ssh` shouldn't ask for a password.

Caution

You should never use this procedure with the `root` user. If you want to use strong authentication when logging in as `root`, be sure to use a passphrase! The passphrase should be 10–30 characters, and is preferably not a phrase based on words. If you forget the passphrase, you'll have to regenerate the keys.

For this kind of batch process, it is usually best to have a special user whose only function is to perform these processes. If a host is compromised, the attacker will get access only to an unprivileged account.

The `ssh_config` and `.ssh/config` Files

The SSH client programs read their configuration from the `/etc/ssh/ssh_config` and the `$HOME/.ssh/config` files. There are many options that can be placed in these files. The most common are shown in Table 7.13.

TABLE 7.13 *ssh_config* Options

Option	*Meaning*
`Host` *hostname*	Introduces a new section. The *hostname* is matched against the hostname given on the command line. The options that follow apply to this host until the next `Host` directive. The `?` and `*` characters may be used as wildcards. You may use `Host *` to set defaults that apply to all hosts.
`HostName` *hostname*	The connection is made to *hostname*. This is useful to create aliases for particular connections (such as with different usernames or for port forwarding).
`BatchMode {yes¦no}`	When set to `yes`, `ssh` never asks for a password. It fails if it can't log in without a password.
`Compression {yes¦no}`	When set to `yes`, `ssh` compresses all data transferred to this host. The compression algorithm is the same one used by `gzip`. Equivalent to the `-C` command-line option.
`CompressionLevel {1-9}`	Specifies how much to compress the data. A `CompressionLevel` of `1` provides the least and fastest compression, while a level of `9` provides the most and slowest compression. The default value is `6` and is appropriate for most applications.
`User` *username*	Log in as *username*. Equivalent to the `-l` command-line option.
`LocalForward` *port host:hostport*	Forward local *port* to remote *hostport* on *host*. Equivalent to the `-L` command-line option.
`RemoteForward` *port host:hostport*	Forward remote *port* to local *hostport* on *host*. Equivalent to the `-R` command-line option.

Summary

The TCP/IP protocol suite forms the basis of the Internet.

An IP address has a host part and a network part. The decision of which bits are in which part is based on the netmask.

Routing is the process by which packets travel from one network to another. Most networks have a single default router that connects them to another, upstream network.

The main tools for troubleshooting TCP/IP problems are `ping`, `traceroute`, and `tcpdump`.

Linux provides several security tools. In the first place, the Linux kernel itself provides a firewall, which is configured with ipchains.

The networking rules are ever changing and fast paced. Becoming a network engineer can be a lot of fun and provide a very profitable source of income. This chapter should be all you need to take your first steps in this exciting world of networking.

CHAPTER 8

The Domain Name Service

In This Chapter

Referring to hosts by their IP addresses is convenient for computers, but humans have an easier time working with names. Obviously, we need some sort of translation table to convert IP addresses to hostnames. With millions of machines on the Internet and new ones popping up every day, it would be impossible for everyone to keep this sort of table up-to-date. This is where DNS comes in.

The *Domain Name Service* (DNS) is the system by which each site maintains only its own mapping of IP addresses to machine names. Each site puts this mapping into a publicly accessible database, so anyone can find the IP address corresponding to a hostname in the site simply by querying the site's database.

To access this database, you need to run a DNS server for your site. A DNS server is also known as a *nameserver* (NS). These servers come in three varieties:

- Master (also called *primary*)
- Slave (also called *secondary*)
- Caching

If you are connecting to an existing network (through your school or company network, for example), you only need to run a caching server. On the other hand, if you are setting up a new site to be accessed through the Internet, you need to set up a primary server. Secondary servers eliminate the single point of failure represented by a lone master server, and also share the query load.

This chapter shows how to configure each of these nameservers and gives you an overview of the tasks involved in maintaining a DNS database.

A Brief History of the Internet

To understand the Domain Name System, it is important to know a little about the history of the Internet and its precursor, ARPAnet.

The Internet began in the late 1960s as an experimental wide area computer network funded by the Department of Defense's Advanced Research Projects Agency (ARPA) . This network, called ARPAnet, was intended to allow government scientists and engineers to share expensive computing resources. During this period, only government users and a handful of computers were ever connected to ARPAnet. It remained that way until the early 1980s.

In the early 1980s, two main developments led to the popularity of ARPAnet. The first was the development of the Transmission Control Protocol and the Internet Protocol

(TCP/IP). TCP/IP standardized connectivity to ARPAnet for all computers. The second was U.C. Berkeley's version of UNIX, known as BSD, which was the first UNIX distribution to include TCP/IP as a networking layer. Because BSD was available to other universities at minimal cost, the number of computers connecting to ARPAnet soared.

All of a sudden, thousands of computers were connected to a network that had been designed to handle just a few computers. In many cases, these new computers were simultaneously connected to a university network and to ARPAnet. At this point, it was decided that the original ARPAnet would become the backbone of the entire network, which was called the Internet.

In 1988, the Defense Department decided the ARPAnet project had continued long enough and stopped funding it. The National Science Foundation (NSF) then supported the Internet until 1995, when private companies such as BBNPlanet, MCI, and Sprint took over the backbone.

Now millions of computers and millions of users are on the Internet, and the numbers keep rising.

The `hosts.txt` File

In the early days, when there were only a few hundred computers connected to ARPAnet, every computer had a file called `hosts.txt`. UNIX modified the name to `/etc/hosts`. This file contained all the information about every host on the network, including the name-to-address mapping. With so few computers, the file was small and could be maintained easily.

The maintenance of the `hosts.txt` file was the responsibility of SRI-NIC, located at the Stanford Research Institute in Menlo Park, California. When administrators wanted a change to the `hosts.txt` file, they emailed the request to SRI-NIC, which incorporated the requests once or twice a week. This meant that the administrators also had to periodically compare their `hosts.txt` file against the SRI-NIC `hosts.txt` file, and if the files were different, the administrators had to FTP a new copy of the file.

As the Internet started to grow, the idea of centrally administering hostnames and deploying the `hosts.txt` file became a major issue. Every time a new host was added, a change had to be made to the central version and every other host on ARPAnet had to get the new version of the file.

In the early 1980s, SRI-NIC called for the design of a distributed database to replace the `hosts.txt` file. The new system was known as the Domain Name System (DNS). ARPAnet switched to DNS in September 1984, and it has been the standard method for publishing and retrieving hostname information on the Internet ever since.

DNS is a distributed database built on a hierarchical domain structure that solves the inefficiencies inherent in a large monolithic file such as `hosts.txt`. Under DNS, every computer that connects to the Internet does so from an Internet domain. Each Internet domain has a nameserver that maintains a database of the hosts in its domain and handles requests for hostnames. When a domain becomes too large for a single point of management, subdomains can be delegated to reduce the administrative burden.

The `/etc/hosts` File

Although DNS is the primary means of name resolution, the `/etc/hosts` file is still found on most machines. It can help to speed up the IP address lookup of frequently requested addresses, such as the IP address of the local machine. Also, during boot time, machines need to know the mapping of some hostnames to IP addresses (for example, your NIS servers) before DNS can be referenced. The IP address-to-hostname mapping for these hosts is kept in the `/etc/hosts` file.

The following is a sample `/etc/hosts` file:

```
IP Address    Hostname    Alias
127.0.0.1       localhost
192.168.42.7    vestax        www
192.168.42.8    mailhub       mailhub.domain.cxm
192.168.42.6    technics
```

The leftmost column is the IP address to be resolved. The next column is the hostname corresponding to that IP address. Any subsequent columns are aliases for that host. In the second line, for example, the address `192.168.42.7` is for the host `vestax`. Another name for `vestax` is `www`. The domain name is automatically appended to the hostname by the system. However, many people append it themselves for clarity (for example, `www.domain.cxm`).

Note

Use of the .cxm domain name prevents conflict with any existing .com domain.

At the very least, you need to have the entries for

- Localhost
- Your NIS server (if you use NIS or NIS+)
- Any systems from which you NFS mount disks
- The host itself

In this example, `localhost` is the first line, followed by `vestax`, which is a WWW server. The machine `mailhub` is used by `sendmail` for mail transfers. Finally, there is `technics`, the name of the machine from which the `/etc/hosts` file came.

BIND 8

Most DNS implementations, including those shipping with Red Hat, Caldera, and Debian, use BIND, which stands for Berkeley Internet Name Domain. BIND has recently undergone a major version change, from version 4.x.x to version 8.x.x. Red Hat Linux 6.0 ships with BIND version 8.2.6, Caldera OpenLinux 2.2 with BIND version 8.1.1, and Debian GNU/Linux 2.1 with 8.1.2.

BIND version 8 represents a substantial improvement over its version 4 predecessors. There are several security improvements, including restriction of queries or zone transfers to and from specific IP addresses/subnets. Note that some of these security improvements existed in the latest of the version 4 series BIND implementations. Version 8 uses a new, easier boot file (`named.conf`) syntax. Version 4 and before used semicolons to comment out lines in the boot file. Version 8 no longer tolerates semicolons as comments in the boot file, but it gives the administrator three excellent new choices:

```
/* C type comments for multi line comments */

// C++ comments are great for single line or partial line

# Shell type comments are familiar to Unix admins
```


Note

The preceding comments are used in the boot file. The zone data files still use semicolons as comments.

The comment change brings up the fact that BIND 8 config files are absolutely incompatible with their BIND 4 predecessors. Although there are scripts to convert the configuration files, the quickest option is likely to be rewriting the files. Because BIND 8 configuration files are more straightforward than BIND 4, this rewrite should be a fairly simple task for all but the most complex setups.

By default, BIND 8 has the DNS boot file `/etc/named.conf`. Version 4 implementations default to the boot file `/etc/named.boot`. Both Red Hat 6.0 and Debian 2.1 come with an `/etc/named.boot` file, but that file has no effect on any system set up with the DNS that ships with Red Hat 6.0 or Debian 2.1.

BIND 8 has hostname checking, which may break with naming conventions accepted by older BIND versions. Rather than letting this deter you from using the superior BIND 8, you can temporarily turn hostname checking off with the following three lines in the `options` section of `named.conf`:

```
check -names master ignore;
check -names slave ignore;
check -names response ignore;
```

Because BIND 8 comes with Red Hat Linux 6.0, Caldera OpenLinux 2.2 and Debian 2.1—and because it's easier and more secure—BIND 8 is covered exclusively in this chapter.

A Word About This Chapter's Examples

The examples in this chapter were created to illustrate specific points and to allow the reader to safely run them on a two computer network. To accomplish this with minimal risk to the worldwide DNS system or your company's DNS system, all examples use the imaginary top level domain name .cxm.

In addition, all examples use private IP subnet 192.168.42. This is one of the subnets set aside for local, non-Internet use. You can see the complete list of private IP subnets in document `RFC 1918`, mirrored at `http://www.isi.edu/in-notes/rfc1918.txt`. If, by chance, your company already uses the 192.168.42 numbers for in-house IP addresses, you must pick another private subnet for this chapter's examples.

If running this chapter's examples happens to release any information to a higher level or to the worldwide DNS, the bogus top-level domain and the private IP numbers would instantly brand it as garbage to be ignored.

DNS is complex, and one of the few systems on your network that depends intimately on the correct working of machines elsewhere. Likewise, machines elsewhere depend intimately on the correct working of your DNS system. In the world of real top-level domains and public IP addressees, an unnoticed error in your DNS setup can cause serious problems for other people thousands of miles away, which in turn may cause serious problems for you.

When doing real-world DNS, please keep these rules in mind:

- Do not set up DNS for a zone until you have received delegation of authority over that zone.
- Always make sure your reverse and forward zones agree with each other.

- Always maintain at least one secondary DNS server over a zone to avoid having a single point of failure.
- Check and recheck your setup for errors.

In order to best illustrate specific points, this chapter's examples do not consistently follow all these rules. It's suggested that if you want to run this chapter's examples, you do so on a pair of machines not presently serving DNS for your organization, and make sure to use the bogus .cxm top-level domain and the private 192.168.42 subnet.

Bringing Up a Trivial Caching DNS

A trivial caching DNS is a proof of concept and a solid foundation for the remainder of the chapter. This section details steps needed to accomplish this.

The Red Hat installation creates a slightly flawed DNS, the repair of which is discussed in the remainder of this section. Caldera creates no DNS, so we'll start with a brief discussion of bringing Caldera to the Red Hat level.

Upon installation, Debian's bind package queries you regarding the type of installation you prefer. A caching setup is one option, and it does work. The files it creates are different than the examples in this book. You can choose to either use the examples here or use the existing structure with Debian; either way will work.

Special Steps for Caldera

Unlike Red Hat, Caldera installs no DNS files other than `/etc/resolv.conf`. To bring your Caldera installation up to the level of a Red Hat–installed DNS, a few steps are necessary. Here's a summary of the steps:

1. Check for prior `named` install, and install if necessary.
2. Create a trivial **`/etc/named.conf`**.
3. Create **`/var/named/named.local`**.
4. Procure and write **`/var/named/named.ca`**.
5. Test the configuration.
6. Make sure `named` starts on reboot.

Establish whether `named` itself has been installed; if not, install it. If the following command yields `No Such File or Directory`, it's not installed:

```
$ /usr/sbin/ndc
```

On the other hand, if the code brings back a syntax prompt, it is installed. If it is not installed, navigate to the Caldera installation CD-ROM's `Packages/RPMS` directory, `ls -l bind*.rpm`, and install each `bind*.rpm` file with the `rpm -ivh whatever.rpm` command. Note that some may say `Already installed`; that's okay. Once they're all installed, the `/usr/sbin/ndc` command should yield a syntax prompt.

Now create the following trivial **`/etc/named.conf`**:

```
options {
        directory "/var/named";
};

// a caching only nameserver config
zone "." {
        type hint;
        file "named.ca";
};

zone "0.0.127.in-addr.arpa" {
        type master;
        file "named.local";
};
Next, create the following /var/named/named.local:
@       IN      SOA     localhost. root.localhost.  (
                                      1997022700 ; Serial
                                      28800      ; Refresh
                                      14400      ; Retry
                                      3600000    ; Expire
                                      86400 )    ; Minimum
              IN      NS      localhost.

1       IN      PTR     localhost.
```

Procure an up-to-date copy of the DNS cache file. You can get one from a different Linux distribution. To get the latest and greatest, issue this command on an Internet-connected Linux box:

```
$ dig @b.root-servers.net . ns >named.ca.new
```

Once you've obtained your DNS cache file, copy it to `/var/named/named.ca`.

Test with these commands:

```
$ /usr/sbin/ndc stop
```

The preceding command should print either `Name Server Stopped` or `Stop: Named Not Running`, either of which is okay. Start it again with this command:

```
$ /usr/sbin/ndc start
```

This command should print `Name Server Started`. If it does not, troubleshoot.

Finally, make sure that named will start on reboot. The easiest way is to use LISA. Select System Configuration, System Configuration, Configure Daemon/Server Autostart and check Internet Domain Name Services. If appropriate, reboot to make sure your change was effective.

Note that this is not a functional DNS setup, merely an installed one roughly equivalent to that installed by the Red Hat distribution.

If `named` Was Not Previously Installed on Your Red Hat Machine

If you didn't install the `named` daemon with the Red Hat 6.0 operating system, you need to install it from the BIND distribution, available from `http://www.redhat.com`. The filename is `bind-8.1.2-6.i386.rpm`.

Note that the filename may be different on your distribution. If `/etc/named.conf`, `/var/named/named.local`, or `/var/named/named.ca` are not installed by the RPM file, create them using the instructions in the "Special Steps for Caldera" section in this chapter.

Special Steps for Debian

You can use this command in order to install (or upgrade) the name server and related tools:

```
apt-get install bind bind-doc dnsutils
```

If those packages are not installed, they will be; otherwise, they will be left alone.

As you install Debian's bind package, its configure script will ask you a few questions. If you would like to use Debian's default layout, you may answer the questions as warranted by your site. However, if you would like to follow along with the examples in this book, your answers will be irrelevant.

At this point, you have a BIND installation that will automatically start on reboot. If you want to use the examples in this book, you may skip to the preceding Caldera section that starts with creating a `named.conf` file.

After you follow the examples here, you can return to the Debian default system (which can make maintenance easier) by removing and reinstalling the name server. These commands will do that for you:

```
dpkg --purge bindrm -r /var/named
apt-get install bind
```

Caution

These commands remove any existing DNS configuration or zone files from your system. Use them only if you want to start from scratch!

Completing the Reverse DNS

Previously in the "Bringing Up a Trivial Caching DNS" section you've seen that a normal Red Hat 6.0 installation includes an almost-working caching DNS implementation, and you've learned how to mimic that default Red Hat installation default setup within the Caldera and Debian distributions.

This almost-working caching DNS implementation has a flaw, making it excessively slow on any reverse DNS lookup (more on reverse DNS later in this chapter). This problem can be verified by telnetting into the newly installed machine. Because of this flaw, Telnet will typically take 30 seconds or more to ask for the username, and may time out entirely.

This section explains how to cure the problem of slow reverse DNS lookup, discusses the fundamentals of a caching DNS, and introduces some terminology and concepts.

If you haven't yet, back up the installation-configured `/etc/resolv.conf` to `/etc/resolv.conf.org`. Once the backup file is verified, delete `/etc/resolv.conf`. Try telnet again, and notice how it takes only a second to prompt for username. What has happened is that you've just disabled the machine's DNS client (not server) by renaming `/etc/resolv.conf`, thereby eliminating the symptom. The root cause is in the DNS server configuration, so that must be addressed.

At this point, prepare to fix the root cause by restoring `/etc/resolv.conf`. Copy `/etc/resolv.conf.org` back to `/etc/resolv.conf`.

The Real Solution

For the purposes of this exercise, assume brand new machine `numark`, domain `domain.cxm`, assigned IP address 192.168.42.1 with primary DNS set to that same IP.

Caution

Before editing any configuration file, back it up. Original distribution or installation-default files should be backed up to files with `.org` appended to the end (such as `resolv.conf.org`). Other revisions can be backed up with the naming convention of your choice, as long as they don't overwrite the `.org` files. Take care never to change or overwrite an `.org` file.

Note

This chapter will use hypothetical top-level domain `.cxm` (note the `x`) to prevent any chance of causing confusion on the Internet. For the same reason, we use IP addresses in the Private Address Space defined in RFC 1918, mirrored at `http://www.isi.edu/in-notes/rfc1918.txt`. These names and addresses will work for the examples in this book.

Of course, if you're doing a genuine Internet-connected DNS, put in the domain name and IP address assigned to your organization by the proper authorities.

Listing 8.1 contains the installation default `/etc/resolv.conf` file for new host.

LISTING 8.1 The */etc/resolv.conf* File

```
search domain.cxm
nameserver 192.168.42.1
```

The `resolv.conf` file configures the DNS client, not the DNS server, even though in many cases they coexist on the same computer. The first line of `resolv.conf` defines `domain.cxm` as the client's default domain. That's the domain that's appended to machine names. The second line defines the IP address of the DNS server used by the client.

Listing 8.2 contains the installation default `/etc/named.conf` file for new host.

LISTING 8.2 The */etc/named.conf* File

```
// generated by named-bootconf.pl

options {
        directory "/var/named";
        /*
```

continues

LISTING 8.2 continued

```
         * If there is a firewall between you and nameservers you want
         * to talk to, you might need to uncomment the query-source
         * directive below.  Previous versions of BIND always asked
         * questions using port 53, but BIND 8.1 uses an unprivileged
         * port by default.
         */
        // query-source address * port 53;
};

//
// a caching only nameserver config
//
zone "." {
        type hint;
        file "named.ca";
};

zone "0.0.127.in-addr.arpa" {
        type master;
        file "named.local";
};
```

> **Note**
>
> The preceding file listing was generated by the Red Hat installation. If your `named.conf` was created manually or by a different distribution, it might have different comments.

In this file, anything preceded by `//` or enclosed in `/* */` is a comment. In English, the preceding file says the following:

- All zone data files mentioned in `named.conf` shall be relative to directory `/var/named`.
- Zone `"."` is the root of the DNS tree, hints to which are given in file `named.ca`, which is a list of the `root` servers.
- Any IP address in subnet 127.0.0 shall be resolved according to zone data file `named.local`, which is used, but not created, by the DNS server. Had it been `type slave` instead of `type master`, the file would have been created by the DNS server out of data from a zone transfer from a master zone on another computer.

When you're working with named.conf, remember that syntax is important. Make sure all quotation marks, braces, and semicolons are in place. If you prefer, everything between braces may be placed on a single line.

This /etc/named.conf configuration has a problem: It does not provide for reverse DNS lookup for its 192.168.42 subnet. However, it does provide reverse DNS lookup for the loopback subnet at 127.0.0 with zone "0.0.127.in-addr.arpa", which points to the file named.local in the directory /var/named specified in the options section. The solution to the reverse DNS problem is to provide a similar reverse DNS lookup for the 192.168.42 subnet. Here's a summary of how it's done:

1. Add code in /etc/named.conf to point to /var/named/named.192.168.42.
2. Copy /var/named/named.local to /var/named/named.192.168.42.
3. Modify /var/named/named.192.168.42 appropriately.
4. Restart named.

Adding Code to /etc/named.conf

A zone must be created to handle reverse DNS queries for the domain's subnet. In this case, that subnet is 192.168.42. The zone data file will be named.192.168.42. This file must be pointed to by the added zone in /etc/named.conf.

If you haven't already, back up the /etc/named.conf that is created by the Linux Installation (such files are sometimes called *distribution originals*) to /etc/named.conf.org. Add the following lines to the bottom of /etc/named.conf:

```
zone "42.168.192.in-addr.arpa" {
        type master;
        file "named.192.168.42";
};
```

This allows subnet 192.168.42/255.255.255.0 addresses to be resolved to names as instructed by the contents of zone data file /var/named/named.192.168.42.

Creating and Modifying /var/named/named.192.168.42

First, copy /var/named/named.local to /var/named/named.192.168.42.

> **Note**
>
> Anytime you modify a zone data file, you must be sure to increment that file's serial number. The serial number is the first number after the first opening
>
> *continues*

parenthesis and is usually expressed as yyyymmdd## to give you 100 chances per day to increase it.

Never use a serial number greater than 2147483647, as it will overflow the 32-bit internal representation of the serial number. This would produce a very hard-to-find bug, as your secondaries get bogus serials and won't update as needed. Fortunately, this will no longer be an issue by the year 2147, as compilers and operating systems will then accommodate much bigger numbers than 32 bits.

Obviously, serial numbers must never be more than 10 digits, and must never include non-numerics.

Failure to increment will result in various slave and cache DNS servers failing to pick up your modifications. It must be incremented—not changed to a lesser value.

When you're creating a brand new zone data file, the best practice is to set its serial number to the present date, revision 0. For instance, if you create it on February 21, 2000, the serial number for the new file should be 2000022100.

Listing 8.3 contains the `/var/named/named.local` file for new host, which you copied to `/var/named/named.192.168.42` for modification.

LISTING 8.3 The */var/named/named.192.168.42* File Before Modification

```
@       IN      SOA     localhost. root.localhost.  (
                                  1997022700 ; Serial
                                  28800      ; Refresh
                                  14400      ; Retry
                                  3600000    ; Expire
                                  86400 )    ; Minimum
                IN      NS      localhost.

1       IN      PTR     localhost.
```

This is a typical reverse DNS zone data file. The details will be discussed later in this chapter. What you need to do now is change this file to resolve `domain.cxm` names instead of `localhost` names.

Listing 8.4 shows the needed modification to the `/var/named/named.192.168.42` file you created with a copy from `/var/named/named.local`.

LISTING 8.4 The */var/named/named.192.168.42* File After Modification

```
@       IN      SOA     numark.domain.cxm. hostmaster.domain.cxm. (
                                    1997022700 ; Serial
                                    28800      ; Refresh
                                    14400      ; Retry
                                    3600000    ; Expire
                                    86400 )    ; Minimum
                IN      NS      numark.domain.cxm.

1       IN      PTR     numark.domain.cxm.
```

Basically, email address `root.localhost.` is changed to `hostmaster.domain.cxm.`, and every other instance of `localhost` is changed to the hostname, `numark`.

Host `numark.domain.cxm.` has authority over subnet `@`, which represents `42.168.192.in-addr.arpa.` due to the fact that this zone data file was called by zone `"42.168.192.in-addr.arpa"` in `named.conf`. This subnet uses `numark.domain.cxm` for a nameserver, and `1.42.168.192.in-addr.arpa.` resolves to `numark.domain.cxm`. (Remember that the `1` is relative to `@`.).

Caution

Punctuation is essential in all DNS configuration files. For instance, a domain ending in a period (.) is absolute, while a domain not ending in a period is relative to the called domain, which is represented by the `@` symbol. The same thing is true of IP addresses.

Completing the Job

Make sure the original `/etc/resolv.conf` is once again intact. (Earlier in this chapter, you were instructed to rename it and then copy it back.) Next, restart the DNS daemon `named` with this command:

```
# /usr/sbin/ndc restart
```

At this point, a trivial caching DNS should be running.

Testing Your Caching DNS

Verify that Telnet logs in properly. Run this command on another machine:

```
# telnet 192.168.42.1
```

If it takes about a second for the username prompt to appear, everything is good so far. If it takes 20 seconds or more, there's still a reverse DNS problem.

Note

The Telnet program is the *miner's canary* of reverse DNS. If there's a reverse DNS problem, Telnet will hang or be extremely slow. Other programs can hang, with much worse consequences, because of bad reverse DNS. Sendmail is one such program.

In the case of Sendmail, it's possible the hang will prevent successful boot, requiring a repair expedition with boot and rescue disks. Other programs that are sometimes run on bootup can also hang on bad reverse DNS. This is why it's vital to have Telnet working properly before you shut down or reboot the system.

If for some reason you can't repair reverse DNS before rebooting, temporarily rename `/etc/resolv.conf` before booting, and then return it to its original name after.

If everything seems okay, bring in `nslookup`:

```
$ nslookup 192.168.42.1 192.168.42.1
```

The first argument is the address to correlate to a name, while the second is the address of DNS server to query. In this example, they're the same. (Obviously, you should substitute IP addresses for the DNS server you're testing.) The preceding command should very quickly yield the following output:

```
Server:   numark.domain.cxm
Address:  192.168.42.1

Name:     numark.domain.cxm
Address:  192.168.42.1
```

Obviously, the name will be your server's hostname. If the output is delivered within a second, your reverse DNS is working. Note that at this point there's no forward DNS other than caching, so a lookup by `name` of the server `numark.domain.cxm` will still hang. This is addressed in "Configuring DNS Server Master Zones" later in the chapter.

Testing Non-Local Lookup

The time has come to test the lookup capability of your caching DNS. Although a caching-only DNS server cannot provide lookup for the local network, it can refer any queries for the Internet at large to the proper Internet DNS servers. /var/named/named.ca was simply a list of the world's root DNS servers. These servers are consulted unless your cache remembers a lower-level server that's authoritative over the domain.

Start by verifying a good Internet connection with the ping command. Remember that DNS cannot work without a good network connection. ping the IP addresses of several Web sites that are known to be up most of the time. If you cannot ping these addresses, look for network, PPP, or routing problems.

If you're using PPP, sometimes you'll need to make a new default route corresponding to your PPP.

Routing is often the cause with PPP connections. While pppd is running, start with the ifconfig ppp0 command:

```
# /sbin/ifconfig ppp0
ppp0      Link encap:Point-to-Point Protocol
          inet addr:10.37.60.188  P-t-P:10.1.1.1  Mask:255.255.255.255
          UP POINTOPOINT RUNNING NOARP MULTICAST  MTU:1500  Metric:1
          RX packets:7 errors:0 dropped:0 overruns:0 frame:0
          TX packets:7 errors:0 dropped:0 overruns:0 carrier:0
          collisions:0 txqueuelen:10
```

If you can ping the ppp0 inet address and P-t-P but cannot ping other Internet addresses, suspect routing. With pppd running, issue this command:

```
# /sbin/route add default gw 10.1.1.1 ppp0
```

Obviously, substitute the P-t-P address given by the ifconfig command. Try your ping again.

Once you can ping using IP addresses, you're ready to test your caching DNS itself by pinging an URL. Try this command:

```
# ping www.mcp.com
```

If all is well, the preceding ping command will display replies from www.mcp.com. If all is not well, carefully review the files and commands discussed up to this point. Once you can ping the URL, you know your caching DNS works.

If you have lynx installed, you can actually use it to browse the Web:

```
# lynx http://www.mcp.com
```

After a suitable delay, the Macmillan Publishing Web site should appear in your lynx browser.

Special PPP Considerations

The preceding was an example. To reduce bandwidth in real life you'd let your ISP do all your DNS by telling your DNS client that the nameserver is the ISP's nameserver. Simply put the following line in your `/etc/resolv.conf` file above all other nameserver lines:

```
nameserver ###.###.###.###
```

The `###.###.###.###` represents your ISP's primary DNS. You can also place the secondary DNS there. However, your DNS client will honor only three nameserver lines.

If you find that the additional nameserver(s) slows your normal network activities, you can have two different files you copy to `/etc/resolv.conf`: one for when you're online and one for when you're not.

Caching Server Summary

An almost-working caching server can be implemented with these three files: `/etc/named.conf`, `/var/named/named.ca`, and `/var/named/named.local`. The simple addition of reverse DNS resolution for the network subnet gives you a completely functioning caching-only server capable of resolving all Internet domain names, but not any that are declared locally.

Caching-only servers are the simplest and least authoritative of the three server types. The other two, master and slave, are discussed in the "Configuring DNS Server Master Zones" and "Adding a Slave DNS Server" sections later in this chapter. It is first necessary to discuss some important DNS facts and concepts.

Important DNS Facts and Concepts

There are several vital DNS facts and concepts. The most important are discussed in these sections.

The DNS Client and Server Are Distinct

Every network-enabled Linux computer has DNS client software, commonly called the *resolver*. The DNS client software simply queries its assigned DNS servers in the order they appear in file `/etc/resolv.conf`. A computer's DNS client can be assigned a server on the same computer, on another computer, or sometimes on one of each.

DNS servers are machines configured to return query data. The DNS server software relies on the `/etc/named.conf` file and the files pointed to by the zone references in that file. Clients ask, and servers answer (sometimes after asking other servers).

Confusion can arise, however, when a single computer has both a DNS client and server, with the client pointing to the server. The client and server can appear as one entity, with the resulting confusion. Always remember that `/etc/resolv.conf` pertains to the DNS client or resolver. All the other files, such as `/etc/named.conf` and the files it references, pertain to the DNS server.

DNS Terminology

Table 8.1 is a limited glossary of DNS terminology.

TABLE 8.1 Glossary of Essential DNS Terminology

Term	*Definition*
DNS client	The software component on all networked computers that finds the IP address for a name (or vice versa) by asking its assigned DNS server(s). The client gets its configuration information from `/etc/resolv.conf`. Sometimes the term *DNS client* is used to refer to the computer itself.
Resolver	For practical purposes, a synonym for *DNS client.*
DNS server	The software component that returns the name-to-IP translation (or vice versa) to the inquiring client. The DNS server may ask other DNS servers for help in doing this. The server gets its configuration from `/etc/named.conf` and the zone data files referenced in `named.conf`. On Linux machines used as DNS servers, DNS services are provided by a daemon called `named`.
Nameserver	A synonym for "DNS server".
Resolve	To convert a name to an IP address, or vice versa. Resolving is done by DNS, and sometimes by other software.
Zone	A subdomain or subnet over which a DNS server has authority.
Master	A nameserver with authority over a zone that derives its data from local zone data files. Note that a nameserver can be master for some zones, and slave for others.
Primary	A synonym for *master.*
Slave	A nameserver with authority for a zone that derives its data from another nameserver in a zone transfer. The other nameserver can be a master or another slave. Once the information is derived, it is stored locally so it can function even if its source goes down. Note that a nameserver can be master for some zones, and slave for others.
Secondary	A synonym for *slave.*

continues

TABLE 8.1 continued

Term	*Definition*
Zone transfer	A transfer of zone data from a master or slave DNS server to a slave DNS server. The receiving slave initiates the zone transfer after exceeding the refresh time or upon notification from the sending server that the data has changed.

DNS Maps Names to IP Numbers, and Vice Versa

DNS maps names to IP numbers, and vice versa—that's all it does. This is a vital concept to understand.

Almost everything you can do with a fully qualified domain name, URL, or any other name resolvable to an IP address, you can do with that IP address. If you use IP addresses, you needn't use DNS (except for a few reverse DNS situations). For the most part, if a command doesn't work with the IP address, the fault is not with DNS but with a lower-level network function. Trying commands with IP addresses instead of domain names and URLs is a great troubleshooting test.

The Forward and Reverse Zones Must Be Kept In Sync

The Forward and Reverse Zones Must Be Kept In Sync. If a host changes IP addresses, that fact must be recorded in both the forward and the reverse zone data files and the serial number for each incremented. Failure to keep forward and reverse zones in sync could cause a variety of hard to solve problems, possibly worldwide.

The HUP Signal Versus Restart

According to most literature, including the `named` man page, `named` can be forced to reload its zone data files by the following command:

```
# kill -HUP `cat /var/run/named.pid`
```

Unfortunately, this doesn't always work. A test that doesn't do what the troubleshooter thinks it does can waste hours. Therefore, the recommended way to get the zone data files to reload is with a restart:

```
# /usr/sbin/ndc restart
```

Restarting loses accumulated cache and eliminates DNS service during the restart process (20 seconds to four minutes). If that is unacceptable, you can try the HUP signal, but be very careful to verify that it does what you think it will. You can view the current `named` database and cache by sending `named` an INT signal. This is explained in "Troubleshooting and Debugging DNS" later in this chapter.

The `IN-ADDR.ARPA` Domain

All reverse mappings exist in the IN-ADDR.ARPA domain, thereby eliminating any possible confusion regarding the number's purpose. The network and subnetwork parts of the IP address are placed in reverse order to follow the standard way domain names are written. Domain names describe the hostname, the subnetwork, and then the network, whereas IP addresses describe the network, the subnetwork, and then the hostname. Placing the IP address in reverse order follows the convention established by the actual host and network names.

Host Naming Schemes

It is common for sites to pick a naming scheme for all of their hosts. This tends to make it easier to remember names, especially as the site grows in size. For example, the east wing of the office might use famous music bands to name their machines, and the west wing might use the names of *Star Trek* characters. This also makes it easier to locate a machine by its name.

Configuring the DNS Client: `/etc/resolv.conf`

This is a more detailed explanation of material covered earlier. Every machine in your network is a DNS client. Each DNS client runs resolver code to query DNS servers. The resolver gets its configuration from file `/etc/resolv.conf`. To find out which DNS server to use, you need to configure the file `/etc/resolv.conf`. The file should look something like this:

```
search domain.cxm
nameserver 192.168.42.1
```

`domain.cxm` is the domain name of the site, and the IP address listed after `nameserver` is the address of the DNS server that should be contacted. You can have up to three nameserver entries, each of which will be tried sequentially until one of them returns an answer. In PPP-connected machines, one or more of the nameservers can be at the ISP, relieving the local DNS server of work and decreasing traffic on the phone line.

Note

The search directive in the preceding resolv.conf is used to resolve incomplete domain names. The search command can take up to 6 space delimited domains. The following line has three:

```
search domain.cxm subdomain.domain.cxm domain2.cxm
```

If the user types the command ping brett, domain.cxm will be searched for a brett.domain.cxm, then subdomain.domain.cxm will be searched for a brett.subdomain.domain.cxm, then domain2.cxm will be searched for a brett.domain2.cxm. The first success terminates the search.

Note

You must supply the nameserver's IP address, not its hostname. After all, how is the resolver going to know what the nameserver's IP address is until it finds the nameserver?

The /etc/host.conf Order Statement

A client computer can choose its method of name resolution or specify a hierarchy of methods to use. This is done with the order statement in /etc/host.conf. One very efficient and reliable hierarchy is to try the /etc/hosts file first, and then try DNS. This has two advantages:

- A /etc/hosts lookup is very fast.
- The computer can look itself up when DNS is down.

To accomplish this, make sure the following line is in /etc/host.conf:

```
order hosts,bind
```

The Software of DNS

To configure a DNS for your site, you need to be familiar with the following tools:

- named
- The resolver library
- nslookup
- traceroute

named

The named daemon needs to run on DNS servers to handle queries. If named cannot answer a query, it forwards the request to a server that can. Along with queries, named is responsible for performing zone transfers. Zone transferring is the method by which changed DNS information is propagated across the Internet.

The named daemon is normally started at bootup. Here are the commands to manually start, stop, and restart named, respectively:

```
$ /usr/sbin/ndc start
$ /usr/sbin/ndc stop
$ /usr/sbin/ndc restart
```

After you make any change to /etc/named.conf or any of the files referenced by named.conf, you must restart named before the changes will take effect.

The Resolver Library

The *resolver library* enables client programs to perform DNS queries. This library is built into the standard library under Linux. The resolver library takes its configuration information from /etc/resolv.conf.

nslookup

The nslookup utility is one of your best troubleshooting tools. Correct use of nslookup saves considerable time and trouble.

> **Note**
>
> nslookup delivers many powerful features when used interactively. It can also lead to frustrating hangs. For enhanced troubleshooting, learn about nslookup from its man page.

The nslookup command is a utility invoked from the command line to ensure that both the resolver and the DNS server being queried are configured correctly. It does this by resolving either a hostname into an IP address or an IP address into a domain name. To use nslookup, simply provide the address you want to resolve as a command line argument. For example, here is the one argument version:

```
# nslookup mtx.domain.cxm
```

On a properly configured DNS, the result should look something like this:

```
# nslookup mtx.domain.cxm
Server:  numark.domain.cxm
Address:  192.168.42.1

Name:    mtx.domain.cxm
Address:  192.168.42.2
```

The two-argument version specifies the IP address of the DNS server as the second argument. In the absence of the second argument, the first server line in `/etc/resolv.conf` is used. Here's a two-argument example:

```
# nslookup mtx.domain.cxm 192.168.42.1
```

This command returns the exact same output as the one-argument version. The two-argument version is used when reverse DNS isn't functioning correctly, or if `/etc/resolv.conf` has been temporarily renamed or deleted.

traceroute

The `traceroute` utility enables you to determine the path a packet is taking across your network and into other networks. This is very useful for debugging network connection problems, especially when you suspect the trouble is located in someone else's network.

Using the ICMP protocol (same as `ping`), `traceroute` looks up each machine along the path to a destination host and displays the corresponding name and IP address for that site. Along with each name is the number of milliseconds each of the three tiers takes to get to the destination.

Preceding each name is a number that indicates the distance to that host in terms of hops. The number of *hops* to a host indicates the number of intermediate machines that had to process the packet. As you can guess, a machine that is one or two hops away is usually much closer than a machine that is 30 hops away.

To use `traceroute`, give the destination hostname or IP address as a command-line argument. Here is an example:

```
traceroute www.hyperreal.org
```

This should return something similar to the following:

```
traceroute to hyperreal.org (204.62.130.147), 30 hops max, 40 byte
➥packets
```

```
1  fe0-0.cr1.NUQ.globalcenter.net (205.216.146.77)  0.829 ms  0.764
➥ms  0.519 ms
2  pos6-0.cr2.SNV.globalcenter.net (206.251.0.30)  1.930 ms  1.839 ms
➥1.887 ms
3  fe1-0.br2.SNV.globalcenter.net (206.251.5.2)  2.760 ms  2.779 ms
➥2.517 ms
4  sl-stk-17-H10/0-T3.sprintlink.net (144.228.147.9)  5.117 ms  6.160
➥ms  6.109 ms
5  sl-stk-14-F0/0.sprintlink.net (144.228.40.14)  5.453 ms  5.985 ms
➥6.157 ms
6  sl-wired-2-S0-T1.sprintlink.net (144.228.144.138)  10.987 ms
➥25.130 ms  11.831 ms
7  sf2-s0.wired.net (205.227.206.22)  30.453 ms  15.800 ms  21.220 ms
8  taz.hyperreal.org (204.62.130.147)  16.745 ms  14.914 ms  13.018 ms
```

Note

Using a hostname for `traceroute` or `ping` might appear to hang if the name can't be resolved. It's best to learn a few strategic IP addresses (like your ISP's DNS, WWW, default gateway, and the like) and check those if hostnames appear to fail.

If you see any start characters (such as `*`) instead of a hostname, that machine is probably unavailable. This could be due to a variety of reasons, with network failure and firewall protection being the most common. Also, be sure to note the time it takes to get from one site to another. If you feel that your connection is excessively slow, it might be just one connection in the middle that is slowing you down and not the site itself.

By using `traceroute` you can also get a good measure of the connectivity of a site. If you are in the process of evaluating an ISP, try doing a `traceroute` from its site to a number of other sites, especially to large communications companies such as Sprint and MCI. Count how many hops, and how much time per hop, it takes to reach its network.

DNS Server Configuration Files

The DNS server is a potentially complex system configured by a surprisingly straightforward set of files. These files consist of a single boot file and several zone data files, each of which is pointed to by a zone record in the boot file. This section discusses these files and their features, syntax, and conventions.

The DNS Boot File: /etc/named.conf

The /etc/named.conf file is read in when named is started. Boot file comments can be done in three different ways:

```
/* C style comments can comment out multiple lines */
```

```
// C++ style comments comment one or fractional lines
```

```
# Shellscript style comments function like C++ style
```

Other statements take this form:

```
keyword {statement; statement; ...; statement;};
```

Because everything in this file is brace-, space-, and semicolon-delimited, multiple spacing and line breaks do not affect its functionality.

Caution

Bugs caused by syntax errors in the named files are hard to detect. Often there are no symptoms, and even when symptoms are observable, the messages are often cryptic and hard to trace to the bug. It is imperative to check the files carefully.

The two most common section-starting keywords in named.conf are options and zone. Listing 8.5 is a named.conf that does reverse DNS on its loopback and its eth0, and does forward DNS on domain.cxm:

LISTING 8.5 The Example *named.conf* File

```
options {
  directory "/var/named";       #referred files in /var/named
};

zone "." {
  type hint;                    #hints for caching
  file "named.ca";              #root servers file in
};                              #  /var/named/named.ca

zone "0.0.127.in-addr.arpa" {   #reverse on loopback
  type master;
  file "named.local";
```

```
};

zone "42.168.192.in-addr.arpa" { #reverse on eth0 subnet
  type master;                   #file is on this host
  file "named.192.168.42";       #rev dns file
};

zone "domain.cxm" {              #DNS for all hosts this domain
  type master;                   #file is on this host
  file "named.domain.cxm";       #dns file for domain
};
```

The `options` section holds information that's global to the DNS server. This one contains a single piece of information, the `directory` statement, which tells `named` the location of any filenames mentioned in the configuration.

Zone `"."` is the caching zone. A *caching zone* isn't a master or slave, but rather a set of hints for the server software to use. Hence the `type hint;` statement. The file for zone `"."` is `named.ca`, which contains a list of all the `root` DNS servers on the Internet. These `root` servers are needed to prime `named`'s cache. You can get the latest list of `root` servers from the InterNIC at `ftp://rs.internic.net/domain/named.cache`.

Each zone has a `type` statement indicating `master`, `slave`, or `hint`, and a `file` statement pointing to the file containing data for the zone. Files of type `slave` have a `nested` masters section. This is demonstrated in "Adding a Slave DNS Server" later in this chapter.

Each zone section defines a zone of authority, which is usually a domain, a subdomain, or, in the case of reverse DNS, a subnet. Almost every zone defines a file from which it derives its information. Every zone has a `type`.

notify

Another statement appearing frequently in zones and the `options` section is the `notify` statement, which can be `notify yes;` or `notify no;`. The default is `yes`, so there's no reason to put in a `notify yes;` except for documentation. If `notify` is `yes`, the zone's slaves are informed of zone data changes so they can initiate a zone transfer. If it's `no`, no notification is given. `notify no;` is often inserted to prevent bogus domains (like `domain.cxm`) from hitting real Internet nameservers. Note that if a `notify` statement appears in the `options` section, it serves as the default for all zones but is specified to be overridden by any zone-specific `notify` statement. The current version of `named` will not turn off `notify` if it's been turned on in the `options` section.

forwarders

With a `forwarders` statement in the `options` section, you can specify one or more nameservers to send queries that can't be resolved locally:

```
options {
  forwarders { 192.168.42.10; 192.168.42.20; };
...
```

This sends unresolved queries to the two servers mentioned instead of sending them to the local caching DNS. This can be advantageous when there's a premium on outside traffic. If all internal servers resolve outside names via one or two servers, those servers build up huge caches, meaning that more queries are resolved inside the building walls. Otherwise, all the servers might be making identical queries to the outside world.

If for some reason the forwarder cannot answer the query, the query is tried via the normal server caching DNS. To absolutely forbid any non-local query from a DNS server, place a `forward-only;` statement directly below the `forwarders` statement. Doing this makes the forwarder server(s) a single point of failure, so it's not recommended.

DNS Zone Data Files

Zone data files are pointed to by the file statements in the boot file's zone sections and contain all data about the zone. The first thing to understand is that the syntax of a zone data file is totally different from the syntax of the boot file `named.conf`.

Zone Data File Syntax Is Totally Different from Boot File Syntax

It's important to remember that the syntax of the zone data files is not the same as that of the DNS boot file (`named.conf`). The zone data file comment character is the semicolon. For each line, DNS will fail if the `name` data item has spaces before it.

Note

The `name` data item is normally the first on the line and must not be preceded with spaces. However, occasionally the `name` data item can be absent from the line, giving the appearance of space before the first data item. What's really happening is that the `name` data item was left off the line, allowing it to default to the `name` data item in the nearest previous line containing a `name` data item. For all practical purposes, the next data item after the `name` is either the word `IN` or a number representing a `Time To Live` (followed by `IN`). Knowing this can help you avoid much confusion.

Zone Data File Naming Conventions

A zone data file can be given any name. For maintainability, however, a naming convention should be used. This chapter uses the conventions described here.

This chapter has named the cache (`root` server) data file `named.ca` because the Red Hat installation creates it with that name. For the same reason, the reverse DNS file for the loopback at 127.0.0.1 is called `named.local`.

Master forward DNS data files are the word `named`, followed by a period, followed by the entire domain name. For instance, the master forward DNS data file for domain `domain.cxm` is called `named.domain.cxm`.

Master reverse DNS zone data files are the word `named`, followed by a period, followed by the IP number of the subnet. For instance, the reverse DNS zone data file for subnet 192.168.42 is `named.192.168.42`. Many people reverse the IP address to match the `42.168.192.in-addr.arpa` statement. The naming convention is entirely up to you.

Zone Data Substitutions

As mentioned, the file statement in the `named.conf` zone record points to the zone data file describing the domain named in the zone. Since the domain is specified by the `named.conf` zone record, that domain is substituted for the `@` symbol anywhere that symbol appears in the zone data file. The same is true for reverse DNS subnets. Furthermore, in the zone data file, any name not ending in a period is assumed to be relative to the domain specified in `named.conf`. For instance, if the domain specified in `named.conf` is `domain.cxm`, and the name `numark` appears unterminated by a period inside the zone data file, that word `numark` means the same as the absolute version, `numark.domain.cxm.` (note the terminating period).

Zone Data File Components

The zone's file line in the `/etc/named.conf` file points to a file containing the information that `named` needs in order to answer queries on the zone's domain. Unfortunately, the file format for these configuration files is a bit tricky and requires care when setting up. Be especially careful with periods —a misplaced period can quickly become difficult to track down.

The format of each line in the configuration file is as follows:

```
name     IN     record_type     data
```

`name` is the hostname you are dealing with. Any hostnames that do not end in a period have the domain name appended to them automatically.

The second column, IN, is actually a parameter telling named to use the Internet class of records. There are two other classes, CH and HS, but they're almost never used.

The third and fourth columns, record_type and data, indicate what kind of record you're dealing with and the parameters associated with it, respectively. There are seven possible records:

SOA	Start of authority
NS	Nameserver
A	Address record
PTR	Pointer record
MX	Mail exchanger
CNAME	Canonical name
RP and TXT	Documentation entries

SOA: Start of Authority

The SOA record starts the description of a site's DNS entries. The format of this entry is as follows:

```
domain.cxm. IN SOA ns1.domain.cxm. hostmaster.domain.cxm. (
    1997082401     ; serial number, YYYYMMDDxx
    10800          ; refresh rate in seconds (3 hours)
    1800           ; retry in seconds (30 minutes)
    1209600        ; expire in seconds (2 weeks)
    604800 )       ; minimum in seconds (1 week)
```

The first line begins with the domain for which this SOA record is authoritative. In most real zone data files, the hard-coded domain.cxm. in the first column would be replaced by the @ symbol. This first data item is followed by IN, to indicate that the Internet standard is being used, and SOA, to indicate start of authority. The column after SOA is the primary nameserver for this domain. Finally, the last column specifies the email address for the person in charge. Note that the email address is not in the standard *user@domain.cxm* form, but has a period versus the @ symbol. A good practice is to create the mail alias hostmaster at your site and have all mail sent to it and forwarded to the appropriate people.

At the end of the first line is an open parenthesis. This tells named that the line continues onto the next line, thereby making the file easier to read.

The five values presented in subsequent lines detail the characteristics of this record. The first line is the record's serial number. Whenever you make a change to any entry in this file, you need to increment this value so secondary servers know to perform zone transfers. Typically, the current date in the form YYYYMMDDxx is used, where YYYY is the year, MM is the month, DD is the day, and xx is the revision done that day. This allows for multiple revisions in one day.

The second value is the refresh rate in seconds. This value tells the slave DNS servers how often they should query the master server to see if the records have been updated.

The third value is the retry rate in seconds. If the secondary server tries to contact the primary DNS server to check for updates but cannot contact it, the secondary server tries again after retry seconds.

When secondary servers have cached the entry, the fourth value indicates to them that if they cannot contact the primary server for an update, they should discard the value after the specified number of seconds. One to two weeks is a good value for this.

The final value, the minimum entry, tells caching servers how long they should wait before expiring the entry if they cannot contact the primary DNS server. Five to seven days is a good guideline for this entry.

Don't forget to place a closing parenthesis after the fifth value.

NS: Nameserver

The NS record specifies the authoritative nameservers for a given domain. Here is an example:

```
IN NS    ns1.domain.cxm.
IN NS    ns2.domain.cxm.
```

If the NS records directly follow the SOA record, you do not need to specify the name field in the DNS record. In that case, the NS records will assume the same name field as the SOA record.

In this example, the domain.cxm domain has two nameservers—ns1.domain.cxm. and ns2.domain.cxm.. These are fully qualified hostnames, so they need to have the period as the suffix. Without the period, named would evaluate their value to ns1.domain.cxm.domain.cxm, which is not what you're looking for.

A: Address Record

The address record is used for providing translations from hostnames to IP addresses. There should be an A record for each machine that needs a publicly resolvable hostname. A sample entry using the A record follows:

```
mtx     IN A        192.168.42.2
```

In this example, the address is specified for the host mtx. Because this hostname is not suffixed by a period, named assumes it is in the same domain as the current SOA record. Thus, the hostname is mtx.domain.cxm.

MX: Mail Exchanger

The mail exchanger record enables you to specify which host on your network is in charge of receiving mail from the outside. sendmail uses this record to determine the correct machine to which mail needs to be sent. The format of an MX record looks like this:

```
domain.cxm.     IN MX 10    mailhub
                IN MX 50    mailhub2
```

The first column indicates the hostname for which mail is received. In this case, it's domain.cxm. Based on the previous examples, you might have noticed that you have yet to specify a machine that answers to domain.cxm., but the sample MX record shows that you can accept mail for it. This is an important feature of DNS; you can specify a hostname for which you accept mail even if that hostname doesn't have an A record.

As expected, the IN class is the second column. The third column specifies that this line is an MX record. The number after the MX indicates a priority level for that entry. Lower numbers mean higher priority. In this example, sendmail will try to communicate with mailhub first. If it cannot successfully communicate with mailhub, it will try mailhub2.

CNAME: Canonical Name

The CNAME record makes it possible to alias hostnames via DNS. This is useful for giving common names to servers. For example, we are used to Web servers having the hostname www, as in www.domain.cxm. However, you might not want to name the Web server using this convention at all. On many sites, the machines have a theme to the naming of hosts, and placing www in the middle of that might appear awkward.

To use a CNAME, you must have another record for that host —such as an A or MX record— that specifies its real name. For example:

```
mtx        IN A        192.168.42.2
www        IN CNAME    mtx
```

In this example, mtx is the real name of the server and www is its alias.

RP and TXT: The Documentation Entries

Providing contact information as part of your database is often useful—not just as comments, but as actual records that can be queried by others. You can accomplish this by using the RP and TXT records.

TXT records are freeform text entries in which you can place any information you see fit. Most often, you will only want to give contact information. Each TXT record must be tied to a particular hostname. Here is an example:

```
domain.cxm.     IN TXT "Contact: Heidi S."
                IN TXT "Systems Administrator/Ring Master"
                IN TXT "Voice: (800) 555-1212"
```

Because TXT records are freeform, you're not forced to place contact information there. As a result, the RP record was created, which explicitly states who is responsible for the specified host. For example:

```
domain.cxm.         IN RP heidis.domain.cxm. domain.cxm.
```

The first column states the domain for which the responsible party is set. The second column, IN, defines this record to use the Internet class. RP designates this to be a responsible party record. The fourth column specifies the email address of the person who is actually responsible. Notice that the @ symbol has been replaced by a period in this address, much as in the SOA record. The last column specifies a TXT record that gives additional information. In this example, it points back to the TXT record for domain.cxm.

PTR: Pointer Record

The pointer record, also known as the *reverse resolution record*, tells named how to turn an IP address into a hostname. PTR records are a little odd in that they should not be in the same SOA as your A records. Instead, they appear in an in-addr.arpa subdomain SOA.

A PTR record looks like this:

```
2.42.168.192.  IN PTR  mtx.domain.cxm.
```

Notice that the IP address to be reverse-resolved is in reverse order and is suffixed with a period.

Configuring DNS Server Master Zones

As mentioned earlier, DNS comes in three flavors:

- Master (also called primary)
- Slave (also called secondary)
- Caching only

We discussed creating a caching-only server earlier in the chapter. Caching-only servers cannot answer queries, but can only pass those queries on to other servers with master or slave zones that are authoritative over the domain in question. However, all DNS servers should be configured to perform caching functions.

Now turn your attention to adding DNS server master zones. A DNS server master zone can answer queries about its domain without querying other servers because its data resides on the local hard disk. A DNS server master zone is considered to have the most up-to-date records for all the hosts in that domain.

Adding Local Domain Resolution

Earlier in the chapter you created a caching-only DNS residing on the hypothetical host `numark` at address 192.168.42.1 in domain `domain.cxm`. Assume that this same subnet has host `mtx` at 192.168.42.2. It's an easy task to add local domain resolution, using master zones. Here is the basic procedure:

1. Add master zone `"domain.cxm"` to `named.conf`, pointing to zone data file `named.domain.cxm`.
2. Create zone data file `named.domain.cxm`, resolving both hosts, `sendmail`, and `www`.
3. Add resolution from 192.168.42.2 to `mtx` in the previously created `named.192.168.42`.
4. Restart `named`.
5. Test and troubleshoot.

Add Zone `"domain.cxm"` to `named.conf`

Add the following code to `/etc/named.conf`:

```
zone "domain.cxm" {               #DNS for all host this domain
  type master;                    #file on this host
  file "named.domain.cxm";        #dns file for domain
};
```

This says to refer any name or FQDN in domain `domain.cxm` to the data in `named.domain.cxm`. The `type master;` designation indicates that file `named.domain.cxm` is an input file to the DNS server rather than an output file from the DNS server or an intermediate file. Note that the text to the right of the pound signs (#) are comments. Next, create file `named.domain.cxm`.

Create Zone Data File `named.domain.cxm`

Create the following `/var/named/named.domain.cxm`:

```
@       IN      SOA     numark.domain.cxm. hostmaster.domain.cxm.  (
                                       1997022703 ; Serial
                                       28800      ; Refresh
                                       14400      ; Retry
```

```
                                  3600000     ; Expire
                                  86400 )     ; Minimum

                    IN    NS          numark
                    IN    MX 10       numark

numark              IN    A           192.168.42.1
mtx                 IN    A           192.168.42.2
www                 IN    CNAME       numark
```

Nameserver `numark.domain.cxm` has authority over zone `@`, which is set to `domain.cxm` via the zone call in `named.conf`. The information between the parentheses contains timing details explained earlier in this chapter. A single nameserver (`NS`) for `@` (`domain.cxm`) is at `numark`. `numark` handles the mail (`MX`) for `domain.cxm`. The `numark` and `mtx` hosts in `domain.cxm` have addresses 192.168.42.1 and 192.168.42.2, respectively. Alias `www` refers to `numark`, which by a previous line is set to 192.168.42.1.

The `IN NS` and `IN MX` statements have no name identifier in column 1. An `IN` item lacking a name identifier defaults to the name identifier of the last statement possessing an identifier, which in this case is the top line.

The preceding zone data file is built for simplicity. Real-life servers have an `ns IN A 192.168.42.1` type line so they can call the nameserver `ns` in all files. That way, if the nameserver is changed from `numark` to `mtx`, the only required change in any file is the `ns IN A` line. Real-life zones also have at least two `IN NS` lines, so if one nameserver goes down, the other one picks up the slack.

Note that syntax is important, especially because zone data file syntax is different from boot file syntax. All name identifiers must be in column 1. All periods are vital because a name ending in a period is considered absolute, while a name not ending in a period is considered relative to the `@` symbol, which is substituted by the domain from the `named.conf` zone record.

Add 192.168.42.2 to `named.192.168.42.`

You must be able to resolve 192.168.42.2 back to `mtx`, so add the following to reverse zone data file `named.192.168.42`:

```
2       IN      PTR     mtx.domain.cxm.
```

Restart `named` and then Test and Troubleshoot

Restart with this command:

```
# /usr/sbin/ndc restart
```

It could take a few minutes for this command to finish.

Once it finishes, test it. Try first telnetting in and making sure you get the `login:` prompt within a second or two. If Telnet hangs, investigate your reverse DNS zones and reverse DNS zone data files.

Next, try running the following commands:

```
ping 192.168.42.1
ping 192.168.42.2
```

Do each `ping` from each server. If any IP `ping` fails, there's a network connectivity problem that must be solved before you attempt to activate DNS. Once connectivity is proven, do the following:

```
ping numark
ping mtx
ping numark.domain.cxm.
ping mtx.domain.cxm.
ping www.domain.cxm.
```

Each of the preceding `ping` commands should succeed and deliver the right IP. If each of these commands succeeds, try the following:

```
nslookup numark
nslookup mtx
nslookup numark.domain.cxm.
nslookup mtx.domain.cxm.
nslookup www.domain.cxm.
nslookup 192.168.42.1
nslookup 192.168.42.2
```

Each command should quickly deliver the expected results. If you have `sendmail` up and running, test the `IN MX` statements with email operations.

Troubleshooting is essentially the process of elimination. Try to determine whether it's the forward or reverse lookups that are giving you problems. Try to narrow it to a single domain, server, or IP. Use `ping` to make sure you have network connectivity.

Adding Virtual Domain Resolution

Not all IP addresses denote actual hardware. Some are alias addresses intended to represent Web sites. Generally speaking, these Web sites are granted IP addresses. Here are the steps to add a virtual domain in the existing subnet:

1. Create the zone in **`named.conf`**.
2. Create a new zone data file.
3. Add an **`IN PTR`** line to the existing reverse DNS file for the subnet.
4. Restart `named`.

In the following example, add domain vdomain.cxm at IP address 192.168.42.101, which can be added by the following command:

```
# /sbin/ifconfig eth0:0 192.168.42.101 netmask 255.255.255.0
```

This IP is made into a virtual host Web site in /etc/httpd/conf/httpd.conf, so it only needs a domain name. Assuming you want to give 192.168.42.101 the name vdomain.cxm, add the following zone to named.conf:

```
zone "vdomain.cxm" {               #DNS for virtual domain
  type master;                     #file is on this host
  file "named.vdomain.cxm";        #dns file for domain
};
```

As you can see, the zone data file is named.vdomain.cxm. Create that file as follows:

```
@       IN      SOA     numark.domain.cxm. hostmaster.domain.cxm.  (
                                       1997022700 ; Serial
                                       28800      ; Refresh
                                       14400      ; Retry
                                       3600000    ; Expire
                                       86400 )    ; Minimum

                     IN    NS            numark.domain.cxm.

@                    IN    A             192.168.42.101
www                  IN    CNAME         @
```

Read the preceding as follows: numark.domain.cxm has authority over @ (vdomain.cxm). The nameserver for @ is numark.domain.cxm, and vdomain.cxm (@) has the address 192.168.42.101, as does www.vdomain.cxm.

Both vdomain.cxm and www.vdomain.cxm are resolved so they can be accessed as http://vdomain.cxm or http://www.vdomain.cxm.

Now add the reverse DNS for the virtual domain with this line in named.192.168.42:

```
101     IN    PTR        vdomain.cxm.
```

Note

The preceding example places the virtual domain in the host's subnet. It can be in a different subnet (and often is). In that case, a new reverse DNS zone data file must be set up for the additional subnet, and several routing and forwarding steps must be taken so the different subnet is visible to browsers around the world.

Delegating Authority

With millions of domain names and URLs on the Internet, the only way to keep track is with a distributed system. DNS implements this distribution through delegation to subdomains.

This section implements a trivial delegation whose purpose is illustrative only—no MX, no CNAME, no secondary server, not even reverse DNS; just the same subnet as the rest of the examples in this chapter.

Imagine that a new department, `subdomain`, wants to administer its own DNS. That makes less work for the `domain.cxm` administrators. Table 8.2 shows that the department has four hosts.

TABLE 8.2 The Subdomain Department's Servers

Host	*IP*
`sylvia`	`192.168.42.40`
`brett`	`192.168.42.41`
`rena`	`192.168.42.42`
`valerie`	`192.168.42.43`

From a DNS point of view, the four hosts are `sylvia.subdomain.domain.cxm`, `brett.subdomain.domain.cxm`, `rena.subdomain.domain.cxm`, and `valerie.subdomain.domain.cxm`. The nameserver for `subdomain.domain.cxm` is on host `sylvia`. Here is a synopsis of the steps to take to accomplish this:

1. Add authority for `subdomain.domain.cxm` on `sylvia`.
2. Test the `subdomain.domain.cxm` local resolution.
3. Delegate from `numark` to `sylvia` for the subdomain.
4. Test the `subdomain.domain.cxm` delegation.

Add Authority for `subdomain.domain.cxm` on `sylvia`

Start by adding a zone for the subdomain. Simply add this code to `sylvia`'s `/etc/named.conf`:

```
zone "subdomain.domain.cxm" {
  type master;
```

```
  file "named.subdomain.domain.cxm";
};
```

Create the zone data file `named.subdomain.domain.cxm` in the `/var/named` directory. Here's the file:

```
@ IN SOA sylvia.subdomain.domain.cxm. hostmaster.subdomain.domain.cxm. (
                                      1997022700 ; Serial
                                      28800      ; Refresh
                                      14400      ; Retry
                                      3600000    ; Expire
                                      86400 )    ; Minimum

                     IN    NS          sylvia.subdomain.domain.cxm.

sylvia               IN    A           192.168.42.40
brett                IN    A           192.168.42.41
rena                 IN    A           192.168.42.42
valerie              IN    A           192.168.42.43
```

Make sure there's reverse DNS resolution for `sylvia` and that you can quickly telnet into `sylvia`. (Review the "Bringing Up a Trivial Caching DNS" section earlier in this chapter, if necessary.) Remember that the same reverse resolution problems that can delay or time-out Telnet can prevent booting in certain situations.

When you can quickly telnet into `sylvia`, restart `named` on `sylvia` with this command:

```
# /usr/sbin/ndc restart
```

Test the `subdomain.domain.cxm` Local Resolution

This implementation has no reverse DNS for `brett`, `rena`, and `valerie`, so `nslookup` might fail. Use `ping` on all four hosts to test instead. The results should resolve to the correct IP addresses, similar to the following example:

```
# ping sylvia.subdomain.domain.cxm
PING sylvia.subdomain.domain.cxm (192.168.42.40): 56 data bytes
64 bytes from 192.168.42.40: icmp_seq=0 ttl=255 time=0.398 ms
--- sylvia.subdomain.domain.cxm ping statistics ---
2 packets transmitted, 2 packets received, 0% packet loss
round-trip min/avg/max = 0.235/0.316/0.398 ms

# ping brett.subdomain.domain.cxm
PING brett.subdomain.domain.cxm (192.168.42.41): 56 data bytes
64 bytes from 192.168.42.41: icmp_seq=0 ttl=255 time=0.479 ms
--- brett.subdomain.domain.cxm ping statistics ---
2 packets transmitted, 2 packets received, 0% packet loss
round-trip min/avg/max = 0.242/0.360/0.479 ms
```

```
# ping rena.subdomain.domain.cxm
PING rena.subdomain.domain.cxm (192.168.42.42): 56 data bytes
64 bytes from 192.168.42.42: icmp_seq=0 ttl=255 time=0.482 ms
--- rena.subdomain.domain.cxm ping statistics ---
2 packets transmitted, 2 packets received, 0% packet loss
round-trip min/avg/max = 0.244/0.363/0.482 ms

# ping valerie.subdomain.domain.cxm
PING valerie.subdomain.domain.cxm (192.168.42.43): 56 data bytes
64 bytes from 192.168.42.43: icmp_seq=0 ttl=255 time=0.471 ms
--- valerie.subdomain.domain.cxm ping statistics ---
2 packets transmitted, 2 packets received, 0% packet loss
round-trip min/avg/max = 0.234/0.352/0.471 ms
```

Once the DNS server on sylvia can resolve its hostnames to IP addresses, it's time to delegate from numark.

Delegate from numark to sylvia for the Subdomain

Add the following two lines to numark's /var/named/named.domain.cxm under all other NS statements to prevent breaking default names:

```
subdomain           IN     NS          sylvia.subdomain.domain.cxm.
sylvia.subdomain    IN     A           192.168.42.40
```

These lines say that sylvia.subdomain.domain.cxm is the nameserver for domain subdomain.domain.cxm.. (Remember that subdomain without a period is the same as subdomain.domain.cxm..) Since sylvia.subdomain.domain.cxm. has been mentioned, it must be locally resolved to an IP address; hence, the second line.

However, notice that there is no reference to brett, rena, or valerie anywhere on the numark server. That work is done on sylvia. This is the beauty of delegation. The subdomain subdomain could have 200 hosts and 1,000 subdomains below it, and you could pass on queries with just these two lines.

To finish the job, increment the serial number, save the file, and restart named.

Test the subdomain.domain.cxm Delegation

ping sylvia.subdomain.domain.cxm for starters. (Be sure to fully resolve it.) If that doesn't work, there's a problem with the local DNS; examine named.domain.cxm.

Once you can ping sylvia.subdomain.domain.cxm, try to ping brett.subdomain.domain.cxm. If that doesn't work, make sure it works on sylvia itself; troubleshoot accordingly.

Once you can `ping` all `subdomain.domain.cxm` hosts from `numark`, you know you've performed DNS delegation.

Note

To make the point as simply as possible, the preceding example did not implement reverse DNS or subnet splitting. In real life, the subdomain would probably be on a different subnet. In that case, reverse DNS could be implemented and delegated in much the same way as forward DNS, but using subdomains of the `IN-ADDR.ARPA` domain in reverse DNS zone definition files on the domain and subdomain hosts.

Adding a Slave DNS Server

The Internet would be an unpleasant place without slave servers. Slaves receive their data directly from a master DNS server, or from a slave receiving data directly from a master, and from something even more removed than that. Thus, you can control a large number of slaves by administering a single master.

The process of receiving that data is called a *zone transfer*. Zone transfers happen automatically when either of the following events occur:

- The zone's refresh time is exceeded. (The *refresh time* is the second number in the zone data file's `SOA` list.)
- The slave is listed as an `NS` server in the referring master or slave's zone data record, and neither the zone in `named.conf` nor the `options` section contains a `notify no;` statement. The administrator changes the master's zone record, increments its serial number (the first number in the zone data file's `SOA` list), and restarts `named`. This is called `NOTIFY`.

Note

`NOTIFY`—the second event—works only with BIND 8 servers and slaves.

With only one master to maintain, you can control a large number of slave DNS servers, making it practical to spread the work among numerous servers in different parts of the world.

The second advantage of slave DNS servers is that they present an easy way to create a second DNS server for each zone, enhancing reliability through redundancy while keeping only one point of administration. Note that although slave servers get their data from the master, they write it to disk so that the slave servers continue to provide DNS services even if the master goes down.

In this section you create a slave DNS server for the `domain.cxm` and 42.168.192 (reverse DNS) zones on host `mtx`. Here's a synopsis of how it's done:

1. On `mtx` `named.conf`, add slave zones `domain.cxm` and `42.168.192.in-addr.arpa`.
2. Restart `named` on `mtx`.
3. On `numark` `named.domain.cxm`, add `mtx` as a second nameserver.
4. On `numark` `named.192.168.42`, add `mtx` as a second nameserver.
5. Restart `named` on `numark`.
6. Test the configuration.

Note

If `domain.cxm` were a legitimate domain in the worldwide DNS system, both the master and any slaves would need to be delegated authority from above before they would work as DNS servers. However, since `domain.cxm` is a bogus domain constructed for this example, it is unnecessary in this case.

Changes to `mtx`

Add the following zones to `/etc/named.conf` on server `mtx`:

```
zone "42.168.192.in-addr.arpa" {
  type slave;
  file "slave.192.168.42";
  masters {192.168.42.1;};
};

zone "domain.cxm" {
  type slave;
  file "slave.domain.cxm";
  masters {192.168.42.1;};
};
```

On each one, the `file` statement names the file in which to write data obtained from the master, and from which to answer queries. The `masters {192.168.42.1;};` statement—and be sure to punctuate it exactly that way—tells `named` to acquire data from

192.168.42.1 whenever the refresh time is exceeded or whenever it's hit with a NOTIFY from 192.168.42.1, whichever comes first. The type slave statement tells named that this zone is allowed to do zone transfers to obtain the data from 192.168.42.1.

Notice that the files start with the word slave instead of named. This convention allows the administrator to refresh all slave zones with a rm slave.* command and a named restart command. Unlike the master zone data files, these slave zone data files are not maintained by humans and can be regenerated by the server. Contrast this with deleting a master's zone data file, which would be disastrous. Of course, if the master is down, deleting the slave files would be equally disastrous. Take care before you delete any slave zone data file.

Once the slave zones have been added, simply restart named with this command:

```
$ /usr/sbin/ndc restart
```

The named daemon creates the slave zone data files, and will in fact act as a slave DNS server in every respect except for receiving NOTIFY statements. (The master doesn't yet know about this slave server.)

It's perfectly possible to set up a slave to a master without the master knowing it. Due to the extra traffic burden placed on the master, however, this is not proper DNS etiquette. The administrator of the master should be informed of all slaves.

The master can defend itself against unauthorized slaves by limiting the servers that can receive zone transfers. Just put one of the following statements in named.conf's zone section(s), or in the global section:

```
allow-transfer {192.168.42.2; };    #only mtx can be slave

allow-transfer {192.168.42.2; 192.168.42.10};    #both

allow-transfer {192.168.42/24; };    #only hosts on subnet
```

Verify the existence of files /var/named/slave.domain.cxm and /var/named/slave.192.168.42. If they exist, verify that this list of commands quickly gives the expected output:

```
nslookup numark 192.168.42.2
nslookup mtx 192.168.42.2
nslookup numark.domain.cxm 192.168.42.2
nslookup mtx.domain.cxm 192.168.42.2
nslookup 192.168.42.1 192.168.42.2
nslookup 192.168.42.2 192.168.42.2
```

In the next section you make the master aware of the slaves so it can send the NOTIFY statements upon modification and restart.

Changes to numark

Add the following line below the `IN NS` statement in `named.domain.cxm`:

```
            IN     NS            mtx
```

Before you save your work and exit, be sure to increment the serial number (the first number in the parenthesized `SOA` list).

Now add this line below the `IN NS` statement in `named.192.168.42`:

```
            IN       NS       192.168.42.2.
```

Remember that the `mtx.domain.cxm` address is 192.168.42.2. Once again, be sure to increment the serial number. The incremented serial number is what tells the slave it needs to do the zone transfer.

Finally, restart the `numark` DNS server with this command:

```
$ /usr/sbin/ndc restart
```

The addition of the `NS` record enables `NOTIFY` statements to be sent to the DNS server on `mtx`, causing that server to initiate a zone transfer. The new `NS` record also enables `mtx` to be used as a backup nameserver.

To verify that the slave zones are working, perform the following shell commands and make sure you get the expected output:

```
nslookup numark 192.168.42.2
nslookup mtx 192.168.42.2
nslookup numark.domain.cxm 192.168.42.2
nslookup mtx.domain.cxm 192.168.42.2
nslookup 192.168.42.1 192.168.42.2
nslookup 192.168.42.2 192.168.42.2
```

Together with delegation, DNS slaves and their zone transfers give DNS the power to serve millions of URLs.

Troubleshooting and Debugging DNS

Many DNS troubleshooting techniques were discussed previously in this chapter, such as using the Telnet program to detect reverse-DNS problems. Other troubleshooting options include script programs and named logging options.

Using Scripting to Stress-Test Your DNS Setup

You can make two handy scripts to stress-test your DNS setup. They can be named anything, but this example calls them called `check1` and `check`. The `check1` script simply records the results of a `nslookup` in file `junk.jnk`, while `check` calls `check1` for each domain and IP under consideration. Here's the code for `check1`:

```
echo "nslookup $1 $2" >> junk.jnk
nslookup $1 $2 >> junk.jnk
echo " " >> junk.jnk
echo " " >> junk.jnk
```

`check1` simply writes the `nslookup` of its arguments to a file. `check` takes a single argument, which, if present, it passes as `arg2` to various `check1` calls. Here's the code for `check`:

```
rm junk.jnk
./check1 numark $1
./check1 mtx $1
./check1 numark.domain.cxm $1
./check1 mtx.domain.cxm $1
./check1 www.domain.cxm $1
./check1 192.168.42.1 $1
./check1 192.168.42.2 $1
less junk.jnk
```

The preceding script should run quickly and produce the right output. If not, there is a problem. By selectively commenting out lines of the `check` script, you can narrow the scope of the problem.

The `nslookup` program delivers many powerful features when used interactively. It can also lead to frustrating hangs. For enhanced troubleshooting, learn about `nslookup` from its man page.

Debugging with Dumps and Logs

One of the main debugging tools you have with `named` is having the daemon dump its cached database to a text file. To have `named` dump its cache, you must send the daemon an `INT` signal. The file `/etc/named.pid` contains the `named` process ID. The following command sends the `INT` signal to `named`:

```
# kill -INT  `cat /var/run/named.pid`
```

The file `/var/named/named_dump.db` contains the cache information that was dumped. The cache file will look similar to a zone database file.

The named daemon also supports debug logging. To start the daemon logging, send the daemon a USR1 signal like this:

```
# kill -USR1  `cat /var/run/named.pid`
```

The logging information is logged in the /var/named/named.run file. If the USR1 signal is sent to the daemon, the verbosity of the logging information increases. In fact, it's so verbose that you'll need to search for strings like error and not found. Send the daemon a USR2 signal to reset the debug level to 0.

The HUP signal can be sent to the named daemon each time a zone database is changed, and theoretically the HUP signal rereads the databases without having to kill and restart the named daemon. In fact, the HUP signal doesn't always work as advertised. The following example sends the HUP signal to named:

```
# kill -HUP  `/var/run/named.pid`
```

Caution

If alterations are made to the /etc/named.conf file, the named daemon must be stopped and restarted before you can see the changes.

Use this command in any situation when you want to make sure that all files are read and loaded:

```
# /usr/sbin/ndc restart
```

Another great debugging technique, especially after you've restarted named, is to look at the system log. You can find what file contains the appropriate log by looking in /etc/syslog.conf. Default for Red Hat 6.0 and Caldera OpenLinux 2.2 is /var/log/messages. By default, Debian stores information from named in /var/log/daemon.log. Since you're interested only in recent messages, grab the tail end of the file with this command:

```
# tail -n 400 /var/log/messages ¦ less -N
```

You would use this in Debian:

```
# tail -n 400 /var/log/daemon.log ¦ less -N
```

All log entries have date and time, so if need be you can read back more than 400 lines. Look especially for error, not found, no such, fail, and the like. Carefully evaluate any error messages and try to determine what they mean and what caused them.

Other DNS Documentation

Although this chapter covers the most needed DNS information, a complete discussion of DNS could easily fill a large book. Some further sources of DNS documentation follow.

The DNS HOWTO

The DNS HOWTO presents a slightly deeper view of DNS than does this chapter.

On Red Hat installations the DNS HOWTO is text file /usr/doc/HOWTO/DNS-HOWTO.

On Caldera the DNS HOWTO is available as HTML at /usr/doc/HOWTO/other-formats/html/DNS-HOWTO.html.

Debian users can find the DNS HOWTO as a compressed text file at /usr/doc/HOWTO/DNS-HOWTO.gz. It can also be found on the Internet at http://metalab.unc.edu/LDP/HOWTO/DNS-HOWTO.html.

The Network Administrator's Guide

The Network Administrator's Guide is found at /usr/doc/LDP/nag/index.html on Red Hat installations.

The DNS HOWTO is at /usr/doc/LDP/network-guide/nag/index.html on Caldera installations.

The NAG is in Debian's non-free section, and as such, is not included on Debian CD-ROMs. However, it is available on the Debian FTP site. If your apt is so configured, you may install it with this:

```
apt-get install ldp-nag
```

Then you can use /usr/doc/ldp-nag/network-guide-1.0.html/index.html.

The *Network Administrator's Guide* contains a simple overview of DNS. It can be found on the Internet at http://metalab.unc.edu/LDP/LDP/nag/nag.html.

/usr/doc/bind-8.2.6/

Note that the directory name might have a version number other than 8.2.6, depending on your distribution. This directory contains information on the installed version of bind.

Detailed documentation in Debian comes in the `bind-doc` package, which you installed earlier in this chapter. The documentation itself resides in `/usr/doc/bind/`.

`http://www.math.uio.no/~janl/DNS/`

This URL contains documentation for the old BIND 4.

`http://www.dns.net/dnsrd/`

This URL is the online DNS Resources Directory.

`http://www.isc.org/bind.html`

This URL is the Internet Software Consortium's BIND page, with BIND downloads and links to other valuable information. This page includes links to the Bind Operations Guide, in (BIND 4) HTML, Postscript, and Lineprinter.

Summary

This chapter covered the historical motivations for the creation of DNS. You see the different types of nameservers and a demonstration of a sample DNS query. You create and maintain DNS database files. You build a caching-only server, build master and slave zones, create zones for virtual domains, and delegate authority; you review essential DNS troubleshooting tools. With the material in this chapter, you should have a good idea of how to implement DNS throughout your local network.

CHAPTER 9

SMTP and Protocols

In This Chapter

This chapter begins with some brief background on Internet email and Sendmail; its underlying protocol, SMTP; the Washington University imapIMAP/popPOP package, which implements POP3 and IMAP4 support for Linux; and methods that retrieve your mail messages using the POP3 and IMAP protocols. By the Chapters end you should be able to install and setup a powerful email system with the Linux operating system.

A Brief History of Internet Email Standards

Electronic mail (email) is arguably the most useful application of any data network such as the Internet. (Yes, even more so than the relatively young World Wide Web.) Since the Internet's inception, there have been many public open standards published, which are referred to as *Requests for Comments* (RFCs). Many of these RFCs were (and still are) related to email standards. The SMTP specification originally started with the Mail Transfer Protocol in 1980, evolved into Simple Mail Transfer Protocol (SMTP) in 1981, and since has been enhanced into the protocol we know today (see `http://www.ietf.org/rfc.html`).

Introduction to `sendmail`

During this time of rapid change in email protocols, one package emerged as a standard for mail transfer—`sendmail`. `sendmail`, written by Eric Allman at University of California, Berkeley, was an unusual program for its time because it saw the email problem in a different light. Instead of rejecting email from different networks using so-called incorrect protocols, `sendmail` massaged the message and fixed it so the message could be passed on to its destination. Complexity is the tradeoff for this level of configurability flexibility. Several books have been written on the subject (the authoritative texts have reached more than 1,000 pages). However, for most administrators, this is overkill. `sendmail` was and still is written using the *open source* method of development—all the source code is freely available and can be freely distributed. Allman's established company, Sendmail, Inc. (`http://www.sendmail.com`), provides commercial products and add-ons for `sendmail`. However, the core `sendmail` product will always remain a free and open source.

One of the key `sendmail` features that differentiated it from other mail transfer agents (MTAs) during the 1980s was the separation of mail routing, mail delivery, and mail readers. `sendmail` performed mail routing functions only, leaving delivery to local agents that the administrator could select. This also meant that users could select their preferred email client as long as they could read the format of the messages written by the delivery software.

The Post Office Protocol (POP)

With the advent of larger, heterogeneous networks, the need for mail readers that worked on network clients and connected to designated mail servers to send and receive mail gave way to the Post Office Protocol (POP). The POP RFC has undergone many revisions since its inception. The latest revision of the protocol is POP3, which has been updated a number of times since 1988. Client software that is POP3 friendly is available for every imaginable platform; there is also POP3 server software for not only various implementations of UNIX (including Linux), but for other operating systems as well.

POP3 does have its fair share of limitations; the main one is that it's limited to accessing messages in only one mailbox (generally the user's incoming mailbox on the server). When you're reading email with a client program on Linux (`pine` or `elm`, for instance), you can create folders to manage your messages. When you're using a POP3 client, you can also create folders to organize your messages, but those folders will only exist on the machine that the POP3 client is running on. For example, if you run the Eudora email client on a Windows machine and access your mail via POP3 on a Linux server, you can save messages to Eudora folders, but these folders generally are located on the Windows hard diskdrive. If you use another PC to access your email with a POP3-compatible client, you will be unable to access those folders you created on the first Windows machine.

The Internet Mail Access Protocol (IMAP)

A protocol called Internet Message Access Protocol (IMAP) was developed to improve POP3. Its first RFC was based on version 4, so it is generally referred to as IMAP4. IMAP4 overcomes some of the limitations of POP3. The major feature is that a user can have multiple folders located on the server to save his read mail. Wherever you access your email using IMAP, you have full access to all your previously read and saved messages.

Another limitation of the POP3 protocol is that it does not keep the state of messages in your mailboxes—different messages can have different states, such as read, unread, or marked for deletion. Most POP3 clients download all the messages in the user's mailbox. IMAP4 overcomes this problem by only downloading the headers of all mail items, and depending on which message is selected, downloading only that particular message. Again, there are implementations of IMAP4 servers for most major network operating systems in use today.

SMTP and sendmail

The SMTP is the established standard for transferring mail over the Internet. The `sendmail` program provides the services needed to support SMTP connections for Linux.

This section covers the details you need to understand, install, and configure the `sendmail` package. Before getting into the details, however, read about the SMTP protocol in better detail and how the Domain Name Service (DNS) interacts with email across the Internet. (See Chapter 7, "TCP/IP and Network Management," for more details on DNS configuration.)

Armed with a better understanding of the protocols, you can understand `sendmail` itself, beginning with its various tasks (such as mail routing and header rewriting) and its corresponding configuration files.

Caution

As with any large software package, `sendmail` has its share of bugs. Although the bugs that cause `sendmail` to fail or crash have been almost completely eliminated, security holes that provide `root` access are still found from time to time.

When you're using any software that provides network connectivity, you must keep track of security announcements from the Computer Emergency Response Team (CERT) by either visiting its Web page at `http://www.cert.org`, joining its mailing list, or reading its moderated comp.security.announce newsgroup.

Internet Mail Protocols

To understand the jobs that `sendmail` performs, you need to know a little about Internet protocols. Protocols are simply agreed-upon standards that software and hardware use to communicate.

Protocols are usually layered, with higher levels using the lower ones as building blocks. For example, the Internet Protocol (IP) sends packets of data back and forth without building an end-to-end connection such as that used by SMTP and other higher-level protocols. The Transmission Control Protocol (TCP), which is built on top of IP, provides for connection-oriented services such as those used by Telnet and the SMTP. The TCP/IP protocols provide the basic network services for the Internet. Higher-level protocols such as the File Transfer Protocol (FTP) and SMTP are built on top of TCP/IP. The advantage of such layering is that programs that implement the SMTP or FTP protocols don't have to know anything about transporting packets on the network and making connections to other hosts. They can use the services provided by TCP/IP for that job.

SMTP defines how programs exchange email on the Internet. It doesn't matter whether the program exchanging the email is `sendmail` running on a Sun workstation or an SMTP client written for an Apple Macintosh. As long as both programs implement the SMTP protocol correctly, they can exchange mail.

The following example of the SMTP protocol in action might help demystify it a little. The user `betty` at `gonzo.gov` is sending mail to `joe` at `whizzer.com`:

```
$ /usr/sbin/sendmail -v joe@whizzer.com < letter
$ /etc/mta/sendmail -v joe@whizzer.com < letter
joe@whizzer.com... Connecting to whizzer.com via tcp...
Trying 123.45.67.1...  connected.
220-whizzer.com SMTP ready at Mon, 6 Jun 1997 18:56:22 -0500
220 ESMTP spoken here
>>> HELO gonzo.gov
250 whizzer.com Hello gonzo.gov [123.45.67.2], pleased to meet you
>>> MAIL From:<betty@gonzo.gov>
250 <betty@gonzo.gov>... Sender ok
>>> RCPT To:<joe@whizzer.com>
250 <joe@whizzer.com>... Recipient ok
>>> DATA
354 Enter mail, end with "." on a line by itself
>>> .
250 SAA08680 Message accepted for delivery
>>> QUIT
221 whizzer.com closing connection
joe@whizzer.com.. . Sent
$
```

The first line shows one way to invoke `sendmail` directly rather than letting your favorite Mail User Agent (MUA), such as `elm`, `pine`, or `mutt`, do it for you. The `-v` option tells `sendmail` to be verbose and shows you the SMTP dialog. The other lines show an SMTP client and server carrying on a conversation. Lines prefaced with >>> indicate the client (or sender) on `gonzo.gov`, and the lines that immediately follow are the replies of the server (or receiver) on `whizzer.com`. The first line beginning with `220` is the SMTP server announcing itself after the initial connection, giving its hostname and the date and time, and the second line informs the client that this server understands the Extended SMTP protocol (ESMTP), in case the client wants to use it. Numbers such as `220` are reply codes that the SMTP client uses to communicate with the SMTP server. The text following the reply codes is only for human consumption.

Although this dialog might still look a little mysterious, it will soon be very familiar if you take the time to read RFC 821. Running `sendmail` with its `-v` option also helps you understand how an SMTP dialog works. Here is an example of a verbose sendmail session so you can see what the SMTP dialog may look like:

```
[matt@gonzo init.d]$ /usr/lib/sendmail -v matt@gonzo.gov
This is a test email to me.
<Control-D>
matt@gonzo.gov... Connecting to mail.gonzo.gov. via esmtp...
220 mail.gonzo.gov ESMTP
>>> EHLO diamond.gonzo.gov
250-mail.gonzo.gov
250-PIPELINING
250 8BITMIME
>>> MAIL From:<matt@gonzo.gov>
250 ok
>>> RCPT To:<matt@gonzo.gov>
250 ok
>>> DATA
354 go ahead
>>> .
250 ok 933344259 qp 10635
matt@gonzo.gov... Sent (ok 933344259 qp 10635)
Closing connection to mail.gonzo.gov.
>>> QUIT
221 mail.gonzo.gov
```

Doing diagnosis using the sendmail verbose option is quite useful, especially when trying to diagnose why email is not working quite the way you expect it to!

The Domain Name System and Email

Names like `whizzer.com` are convenient for humans, but computers insist on using numerical IP addresses like `123.45.67.1`. The Domain Name Service (DNS) provides this hostname-to-IP-address translation and other important information.

In the old days (when most of us walked several miles to school through deep snow), only a few thousand hosts were on the Internet. All hosts were registered with the Network Information Center (NIC), which distributed a host table listing the hostnames and IP addresses of all the hosts on the Internet. Those simple times are gone forever. No one really knows how many hosts are connected to the Internet now, but they number in the millions, and it is physically impossible for an administrative entity such as the NIC to keep track of every Internet address. Thus was born the DNS.

The DNS distributes the authority for naming and numbering hosts to autonomous administrative domains. For example, a company called whizzer.com can maintain all the information about the hosts in its own domain. When the host `a.whizzer.com` wants to send mail or Telnet to the host `b.whizzer.com`, it sends an inquiry over the network to the whizzer.com nameserver, which might run on a host named ns.whizzer.com. The ns.whizzer.com nameserver replies to a.whizzer.com with the IP address of b.whizzer.com (and possibly other information), and the mail is sent or the Telnet connection made. Because ns.whizzer.com is authoritative for the whizzer.com domain, it can answer any inquiries about whizzer.com hosts regardless of where they originate. The authority for naming hosts in this domain has been delegated.

What if someone on a.whizzer.com wants to send mail to joe@gonzo.gov? ns.whizzer.com has no information about hosts in the gonzo.gov domain, but it knows how to find this information. When a nameserver receives a request for a host in a domain for which it has no information, it asks the root nameservers for the names and IP addresses of servers that are authoritative for that domain—in this case, gonzo.gov. The root nameserver gives the ns.whizzer.com nameserver the names and IP addresses of hosts running nameservers with authority for gonzo.gov. The ns.whizzer.com nameserver inquires of them and forwards the reply to a.whizzer.com.

From the preceding description, you can see that the DNS is a large, distributed database containing mappings between hostnames and IP addresses, but it contains other information as well. When a program such as sendmail delivers mail, it must translate the recipient's hostname into an IP address. This bit of DNS data is known as an A (address) record, and it is the most fundamental host data. A second piece of host data is the MX (mail exchanger) record. An MX record for a host such as a.whizzer.com lists one or more hosts willing to receive mail for it.

What's the point? Why shouldn't a.whizzer.com simply receive its own mail and be done with the process? Isn't a postmaster's life complicated enough without having to worry about mail exchangers? Although it's true that the postmaster's life is often complicated, MX records serve some useful purposes:

- Hosts not on the Internet (for example, UUCP-only hosts) can designate an Internet host to receive their mail and so appear to have Internet addresses. This use of MX records allows non-Internet hosts to appear to be on the Internet (but only to receive email).
- Hosts can be off the Internet for extended times for unpredictable reasons. Thanks to MX records, even if your host is off the Internet, its mail can queue on other hosts until your host returns. The other hosts can be onsite (in your domain), offsite, or both.
- MX records hide information and allow you more flexibility to reconfigure your local network. If all your correspondents know that your email address is joe@whizzer.com, it doesn't matter whether the host that receives mail for

whizzer.com is named `zippy.whizzer.com` or `pinhead.whizzer.com`. It also doesn't matter if you decide to change the name to `white-whale.whizzer.com`; your correspondents will never know the difference.

For the full details on configuring DNS for Linux, see Chapter 8, "The Domain Name Service."

Mail Delivery and MX Records

When an SMTP client delivers mail to a host, it must do more than translate the hostname into an IP address. First, the client asks for MX records. If any exist, it sorts them according to the priority given in the record. For example, `whizzer.com` might have MX records listing the hosts `mailhub.whizzer.com`, `walrus.whizzer.com`, and `mailer.gonzo.gov` as the hosts willing to receive mail for it (and the "host" whizzer.com might not exist except as an MX record, meaning that there might be no IP address available for it). Although any of these hosts will accept mail for whizzer.com, the MX priorities specify which host the SMTP client should try first, and properly behaved SMTP clients will do so. In this case, the system administrator has set up a primary mail relay `mailhub.whizzer.com` and an onsite backup `walrus.whizzer.com`, and has arranged with the system administrator at `mailer.gonzo.gov` for an offsite backup. The administrators have set the MX priorities so SMTP clients will try the primary mail relay first, the onsite backup second, and the offsite backup third. This setup takes care of problems with the vendor who doesn't ship your parts on time and the wayward backhoe operator who severs the fiber-optic cable that provides your site's Internet connection.

After collecting and sorting the MX records, the SMTP client gathers the IP addresses for the MX hosts and attempts delivery to them in order of MX preference. You should keep this fact in mind when you're debugging mail problems. Just because a letter is addressed to `joe@whizzer.com` doesn't necessarily mean a host named `whizzer.com` exists. Even if such a host does exist, it might not be the host that is supposed to receive the mail. You can easily check this using the `nslookup` command to determine whether any MX records are being used for a given domain name. Here is an example:

```
# nslookup -querytype=mx linux.org
Server:  dns1.whizzer.com
Address:  192.168.1.2

Non-authoritative answer:
linux.org       preference = 30, mail exchanger = border-ai.invlogic.com
linux.org       preference = 10, mail exchanger = mail.linux.org
linux.org       preference = 20, mail exchanger = router.invlogic.com

Authoritative answers can be found from:
linux.org       nameserver = NS.invlogic.com
linux.org       nameserver = NS0.AITCOM.NET
```

```
border-ai.invlogic.com  internet address = 205.134.175.254
mail.linux.org  internet address = 198.182.196.60
router.invlogic.com     internet address = 198.182.196.1
NS.invlogic.com internet address = 205.134.175.254
NS0.AITCOM.NET  internet address = 208.234.1.34
```

The *non-authoritative answer* means that you didn't get the answer from one of the DNS servers authoritative for the domain `linux.org`. A list of these authoritative servers is the last part of the response. The `MX` records that you requested are listed with their preference value. A lower preference means that these servers are tried first, followed by higher preferences, until the mail is delivered successfully. For the full details on configuring DNS for Linux, see Chapter 8.

Header and Envelope Addresses

The distinction between header and envelope addresses is important, because mail routers can process them differently. An example will help explain the difference between the two.

Suppose you have a paper memo you want to send to your colleagues Mary and Bill at the Gonzo Corporation and Ted and Ben at the Whizzer company. You give a copy of the memo to your trusty mail clerk Alphonse, who notes the multiple recipients. Because he's a clever fellow who wants to save your company 66 cents, Alphonse makes two copies of the memo and puts each in an envelope addressed to the respective companies (instead of sending a copy to each recipient). He writes "Mary and Bill" on the cover of the Gonzo envelope and "Ted and Ben" on the cover of the Whizzer envelope. When Alphonse's counterparts at Gonzo and Whizzer receive the envelopes, they make copies of the memo and send them to Mary, Bill, Ted, and Ben, without inspecting the addresses in the memo itself. As far as the Gonzo and Whizzer mail clerks are concerned, the memo itself might be addressed to the pope; they care only about the envelope addresses.

SMTP clients and servers work in much the same way. Suppose `joe@gonzo.gov` sends mail to his colleagues `betty@zippy.gov` and `fred@whizzer.com`. The recipient list in the letter's headers might look like this:

```
To: betty@zippy.gov, fred@whizzer.com
```

The SMTP client at `gonzo.gov` connects to the `whizzer.com` mailer to deliver Fred's copy. When it's ready to list the recipients (the envelope address), what should it say? If it gives both recipients as they are listed in the preceding To: line (the header address), Betty will get two copies of the letter because the `whizzer.com` mailer will forward a copy to `zippy.gov`. The same problem occurs if the `gonzo.gov` SMTP client connects to `zippy.gov` and lists both Betty and Fred as recipients. The `zippy.gov` mailer will forward a second copy of Fred's letter.

The solution is the same one that Alphonse and the other mail clerks used. The gonzo.gov SMTP client puts the letter in an envelope containing only the names of the recipients on each host. The complete recipient list is still in the letter's headers, but they are inside the envelope, and the SMTP servers at gonzo.gov and whizzer.com don't look at them. In this example, the envelope for the whizzer.com mailer lists only fred, and the envelope for zippy.gov lists only betty.

Aliases illustrate another reason header and envelope addresses differ. Suppose you send mail to the alias homeboys, which includes the names alphonse, joe, betty, and george. In your letter, you write "To: homeboys." However, sendmail expands the alias and constructs an envelope that includes all the recipients. Depending on whether the names are also aliases, perhaps on other hosts, the original message might be put into as many as four different envelopes and delivered to four different hosts. In each case, the envelope contains only the names of the recipients, but the original message contains the alias homeboys (expanded to homeboys@*your.host.domain* so replies will work).

A final example shows another way in which envelope addresses might differ from header addresses. With sendmail, you can specify recipients on the command line. Suppose you have a file named letter that looks like this:

```
$ cat letter
To: null recipient <>
Subject: header and envelope addresses
testing
```

You send this letter with the following command, substituting your own login name for *yourlogin*:

```
$ /usr/sbin/sendmail yourlogin < letter
$ /etc/mta/sendmail yourlogin < letter
```

Because your address was on the envelope, you receive the letter even though your login name doesn't appear in the letter's headers. Unless it's told otherwise (with the -t flag), sendmail constructs envelope addresses from the recipients you specify on the command line, and a correspondence doesn't necessarily exist between the header addresses and the envelope addresses.

sendmail's Jobs

To better understand how to set up sendmail, you need to know what jobs it does and how these jobs fit into the scheme of MUAs, MTAs, mail routers, final delivery agents, and SMTP clients and servers. sendmail can act as a mail router, an SMTP client, and an SMTP server. However, it does not do final mail delivery.

`sendmail` as Mail Router

`sendmail` is primarily a mail router, meaning that it takes a letter, inspects the recipient addresses, and decides the best way to send it. How does `sendmail` perform this task?

`sendmail` determines some of the information it needs on its own, such as the current time and the name of the host on which it's running, but most of its brains are supplied by you, the postmaster, in the form of a `sendmail.cf` configuration file. This somewhat cryptic file tells `sendmail` exactly how you want various kinds of mail handled. `sendmail.cf` is extremely flexible and powerful, and seemingly inscrutable at first glance. However, one of the strengths of `sendmail` version 8 is its set of modular configuration file building blocks. Most sites can easily construct their configuration files from these modules, and many examples are included. Writing a configuration file from scratch is a daunting task, so you should avoid it if at all possible!

`sendmail` as MTA: Client (Sender) and Server (Receiver) SMTP

As mentioned, `sendmail` can function as an MTA because it understands the SMTP protocol. (Version 8 `sendmail` also understands ESMTP.) SMTP is a connection-oriented protocol, so a client and a server (also known as a *sender* and a *receiver*) always exist. The SMTP client delivers a letter to an SMTP server, which listens continuously on its computer's SMTP port. `sendmail` can be an SMTP client or an SMTP server. When run by an MUA, it becomes an SMTP client and speaks client-side SMTP to an SMTP server (not necessarily another `sendmail` program). When your `sendmail` starts in daemon mode, it runs as a server. When in this server mode it performs two main tasks. The first is continuously listening on the SMTP port for incoming mail. The second is managing the queue of mail that has not yet been delivered and periodically retrying delivery until the message is successfully delivered or the retry limit is exceeded.

`sendmail` Is Not a Final Delivery Agent

One thing that `sendmail` doesn't do is final delivery. `sendmail`'s author wisely chose to leave this task to other programs. `sendmail` is a big, complicated program that runs with `superuser` privileges—that's an almost guaranteed recipe for security problems, and quite a few have occurred in `sendmail`'s past. The additional complexity of final mail delivery is the last thing `sendmail` needs.

`sendmail`'s Auxiliary Files

`sendmail` depends on a number of auxiliary files to do its job. Most important are the aliases file, /etc/aliases and the configuration file, `sendmail.cf`. The statistics file, sendmail.st, can be created or not, depending on whether you want statistics on how many messages are sent to and received from your host. This includes total amount of email traffic in kilobytes. sendmail.hf, which is the SMTP help file, should be installed if you intend to run sendmail as an SMTP server (most sites do).

The other file that might be required on your host is sendmail.cw, which contains all of the alternate hostnames for your email server. For example, if your main email server is mail.whizzer.com, which is specified as an MX record for whizzer.com, then you need to put whizzer.com in this file to tell sendmail to deliver mail addressed to *user*@whizzer.com email on the host mail.whizzer.com.

That's all that needs to be said about sendmail.st, sendmail.hf, and sendmail.cw. (Other auxiliary files are covered in the *Sendmail Installation and Operating Guide*, or *SIOG* for short.) The SIOG is usually found in /usr/doc/sendmail/doc/op/op.ps, /usr/doc/sendmail/op.ps.gz, or in sendmail's source distribution. The aliases and sendmail.cf files, on the other hand, are important enough to be covered in their own sections.

The Aliases File

sendmail always checks recipient addresses for *aliases*, which are alternative names for recipients. For example, each Internet site is required to have a valid address postmaster to whom mail problems can be reported. Most sites don't have an actual account of that name but divert the postmaster's mail to the person or persons responsible for email administration. For example, at the mythical fictional site gonzo.gov, the users joe and betty are jointly responsible for email administration, and the aliases file has the following entry:

```
postmaster: joe, betty
```

This line tells sendmail that mail to postmaster should instead be delivered to the login names joe and betty. In fact, these names could also be aliases:

```
postmaster: firstshiftops, secondshiftops, thirdshiftops
firstshiftops: joe, betty
secondshiftops: lou, emma
thirdshiftops: ben, mark, clara
```

In all these examples, the alias names are on the left side of the colon, and the aliases for those names are on the right side. sendmail repeatedly evaluates aliases until they resolve to a real user or to a remote address. To resolve the alias postmaster in the preceding example, sendmail first expands it into the list of recipients—firstshiftops, secondshiftops, and thirdshiftops—and then expands each of these aliases into the final list—joe, betty, lou, emma, ben, mark, and clara.

Although the right side of an alias can refer to a remote host, the left side cannot. The alias `joe: joe@whizzer.com` is legal, but `joe@gonzo.gov: joe@whizzer.com` is not.

Whenever you modify the alias file, you must run the command `newaliases`. Otherwise, `sendmail` will not know about the changes.

Reading Aliases from a File—The `:include:` Directive

Aliases can be used to create mailing lists. (The alias `postmaster` in the preceding section's example is, in effect, a mailing list for the local postmasters.) For big or frequently changing lists, you can use the `:include:` alias form to direct `sendmail` to read the list members from a file. Assume the aliases file contains this line:

```
homeboys: :include:/home/alphonse/homeboys.aliases
```

Assume also that the file `/home/alphonse/homeboys.aliases` contains this code:

```
alphonse
joe
betty
george
```

If these two assumptions hold true, the effect is the same as the alias:

```
homeboys: alphonse, joe, betty, george
```

This directive is handy for mailing lists that are automatically generated, change frequently, or are managed by users other than the postmaster. If you find that a user is asking for frequent changes to a mail alias, you might want to put it under her control. You must be careful: The latest versions of `sendmail` are very picky with permissions of files that it references. If any of these files or parent directories have group or world writable permissions, the files will most likely be ignored. That may cause `sendmail` to cease working or not even start at all. These sorts of problems are usually logged to your system messages file (`/var/log/messages` or `/var/log/maillog` depending on how your syslog is configured).

Mail to Programs

The aliases file also can be used to send the contents of email to a program. For example, many mailing lists are set up so you can get information about the list or subscribe to it by sending a letter to a special address, *`list`*`-request`. The letter usually contains a single word in its body, such as `help` or `subscribe`, which causes a program to mail an information file to the sender. Suppose the `gonzo` mailing list has such an address, called `gonzo-request`:

```
gonzo-request: |/usr/local/lib/auto-gonzo-reply
```

In this form of alias, the pipe symbol (¦) tells `sendmail` to use the program mailer, which is usually defined as `/bin/sh`. `sendmail` feeds the message to the standard input of `/usr/local/lib/auto-gonzo-reply`, and if it exits normally, `sendmail` considers the letter to be delivered.

Mail to Files

You can also create an alias that causes `sendmail` to send mail to files. This sort of alias begins with a forward slash (`/`), which will be a full pathname to the file you want to append to. An example is the alias `nobody`, which is common on systems running the Network File System (NFS):

```
nobody: /dev/null
```

Aliases that specify files cause `sendmail` to append its message to the named file. Because the special `/dev/null` file is the UNIX bit-bucket, this alias simply throws mail away.

Setting Up `sendmail`

The easiest way to show you how to set up `sendmail` is to use a concrete example.

First, you must install the `sendmail` package. For RPM-based distributions, you'll also need the `sendmail-cf` package, which installs all the files required to build your own configuration file. At this point, you may be done if you're using Debian.

If you're not using Debian, choose a `sendmail.mc` file that closely models your site's requirements and tinker with it as necessary. Make a `sendmail.cf` using the `make` utility. Test `sendmail` and its configuration file. Finally, install `sendmail.cf` and other auxiliary files.

Red Hat

The preceding are the basic steps, but you might also have to make sure that `sendmail` is configured to start correctly when your system reboots. The easiest way to do this is run the `control-panel` program as `root`. Select the first icon, which looks like two traffic-light symbols—this is the runlevel editor and it is shown in Figure 9.1.

After you click the runlevel editor, you will see a number of runlevels as displayed in Figure 9.2. Make sure `sendmail` is located in all runlevels in which you require it. By default, it should be in all of those displayed. If it isn't, put it in runlevel 3 for now by clicking in the leftmost window, scrolling down to and selecting `sendmail`, clicking Add, and selecting runlevel 3.

FIGURE 9.1
The Red Hat Control Panel.

FIGURE 9.2
The runlevel editor.

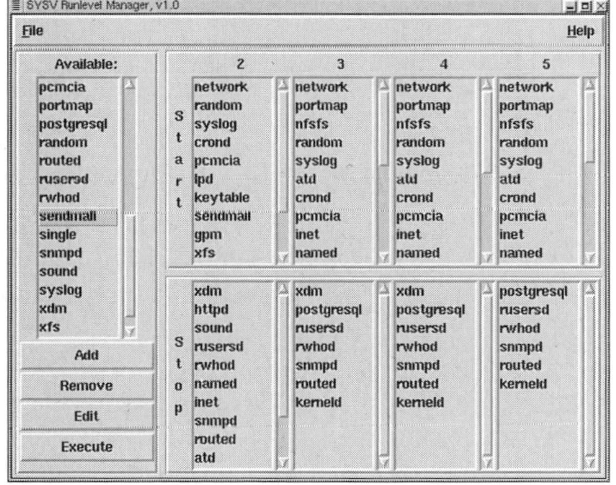

Those are the basic steps, but you might also have to make sure that `sendmail` is configured to start correctly when your system reboots. When you install Caldera OpenLinux, it creates a file called `/etc/rc.d/init.d/mta`. Links to this file are provided in the different runlevel subdirectories. In Caldera this startup file is called `mta` (rather than a more explicit name like `sendmail`) because these days other mail systems (such as `qmail`) are becoming more popular. Making the distribution as generic as possible is a good idea. This `mta` startup file looks for the directory `/etc/mta/options`. This directory will contain a file with the `mta` you want to use. In this case, there should be a file called `sendmail`, which contains the daemon name and command-line parameters with which to start it.

To install sendmail in Debian, simply type this code:

```
apt-get install sendmail
```

This fetches and installs the sendmail program. There is a short sendmail configuration system that runs as you install it. As you answer the questions, the Debian package generates a sendmail.mc and sendmail.cf package containing the appropriate defaults for your system.

If your system doesn't already have one, you must create an aliases file. If it is a Caldera system, it will be /etc/aliases; some systems might locate it in /usr/lib/aliases, depending on your version of UNIX. The location of the aliases file is given in sendmail.cf, so you can put it wherever you want. You might also have to make changes to your system's DNS database, but that information is not covered here (see Chapter 8). Future versions of sendmail will place all ancilliary sendmail files into the /etc/mail directory.

Obtaining the Source

Red Hat Linux and Debian GNU/Linux both ship with sendmail 8.9.3. Fortunately, this is the latest version at the time of writing. Caldera OpenLinux ships with sendmail 8.9.1. Unfortunately, this is not the latest version. If you are concerned with security (and you should be), you will want to keep track of any new versions by checking the comp.security.announce newsgroup regularly. The latest version of sendmail is always found at http://www.sendmail.org.

Debian users can find security updates on the Debian FTP site, ftp.debian.org, or at security.debian.org.

If there is a more recent version at this site than what is included in your Red Hat distribution, check for a newer RPM at ftp://contrib.redhat.com in the contrib directory. New versions or patches are quickly brought out when a security flaw is found, and you should upgrade your own system as soon as possible after a new version is released. It would be wise to wait for a Caldera RPM to be released with the new patches already applied. You otherwise need to get the patches and apply them to the source yourself, as well as the other Caldera configuration changes. This process is not trivial.

Check ftp://updates.redhat.com/6.0/i386 or the various Red Hat mirror sites around the world for any Red Hat RPM updates.

Check ftp://ftp.calderasystems.com/pub/openlinux/updates/2.2/current or the various Caldera mirror sites around the world for any Caldera RPM updates.

Note that the exact names of the files to download differ depending on the most current version of sendmail. In the case of the sendmail included in Caldera OpenLinux 2.2, the sendmail RPM is called sendmail-8.9.1-4.i386.rpm and for Red Hat 6.0 it is called sendmail-8.9.3-10.i386.rpm. Because the files are compressed, you must give FTP the binary command before transferring them. Note too that you should include your complete email address as the FTP password—for example, mylogin@gonzo.gov.

Unpacking the Source and Compiling sendmail

You only need to read this section if there is a new version of sendmail that is not yet released as an RPM and you need new features or bug fixes in place without delay. This step is generally unnecessary on Debian systems. I assume you have downloaded the source from ftp://ftp.sendmail.org.

Now that you have the source, you need to unpack it. Because it's a compressed tar image, you must first decompress it and then extract the individual files from the tar archive. Here is an example command:

```
[root@gonzo src]# gunzip -c sendmail-8.9.3.tar.gz | tar -xvf -
```

Now you're almost ready to compile sendmail. First read the following files, which contain the latest news pertinent to the specific release of sendmail you've downloaded:

- FAQ
- RELEASE_NOTES
- KNOWNBUGS
- READ_ME

You might also want to check the sendmail Frequently Asked Questions (FAQ) located at http://www.sendmail.org/faq. This is a useful source of information on common configuration mistakes or questions regarding how to set up a particular configuration.

Also take note that the *Sendmail Installation and Operation Guide* (*SIOG*) is in the doc/op subdirectory.

Now run cd and ls to see what files are in the source directory:

```
[root@gonzo src]# cd sendmail-8.9.3/src
[root@gonzo src]# ls
Makefile     collect.c    macro.c       parseaddr.c  srvrsmtp.c
Makefiles    conf.c       mailq.0       pathnames.h  stab.c
READ_ME      conf.h       mailq.1       queue.c      stats.c
TRACEFLAGS   convtime.c   mailstats.h   readcf.c     sysexits.c
alias.c      daemon.c     main.c        recipient.c  sysexits.h
aliases      deliver.c    makesendmail  safefile.c   trace.c
aliases.0    domain.c     map.c         savemail.c   udb.c
aliases.5    envelope.c   mci.c         sendmail.0   useful.h
arpadate.c   err.c        mime.c        sendmail.8   usersmtp.c
```

```
cdefs.h        headers.c      newaliases.0  sendmail.h    util.c
clock.c        ldap_map.h     newaliases.1  sendmail.hf   version.c
```

Thankfully, Eric Allman and the `sendmail` crew have done a fantastic job of making the installation process very straightforward. To compile your new version of `sendmail`, simply run the following (from the `sendmail src` directory):

```
[root@gonzo src]# ./Build
```

Watch it build.

> **Caution**
>
> Before installing the new `sendmail` configuration, be sure to make a backup of any files you are going to replace, especially the old `sendmail` daemon you have. In the event that the new `sendmail` doesn't work for you, you will need to restore the old versions while you troubleshoot the new version.

To install the new version of the `sendmail` executable, first stop the currently running daemon with the following command:

```
[root@gonzo src]# /etc/rc.d/init.d/sendmail stop
[root@gonzo src]# /etc/rc.d/init.d/mta stop
```

Type this code:

```
[root@gonzo src]# make install
[root@gonzo src]# ./Build install
```

With everything in place, you can restart the new daemon with the following:

```
[root@gonzo src]# /etc/rc.d/init.d/sendmail restart
[root@gonzo src]# /etc/rc.d/init.d/mta start
```

In Debian, this is the command:

```
/etc/init.d/sendmail restart
```

> **Note**
>
> Refer to Appendix E for information on sendmail.cf.

Automatically Generating the `sendmail.cf` File

Luckily, no one these days has to manually edit a `sendmail.cf` file.

With Debian, your m4 and sendmail cf systems will be automatically set up when sendmail is installed. No further action is needed.

Enter the following command:

```
[root@gonzo / ]# rpm -q sendmail-cf
sendmail-cf-8.9.3-2
```

If you get similar output, your configuration and macro files are already installed under the directory /usr/lib/sendmail-cf for Red Hat or /usr/share/sendmail for Caldera.

Otherwise, you will have to install the relevant RPM from your distribution CD-ROM.

A master makefile exists in /usr/lib/sendmail-cf/cf /usr/share/sendmail/cf/cf, which makes a sendmail.cf file from a sendmail.mc file using the m4 macro processor. The mc file is what is edited to create your site-specific sendmail.cf file. You need to check that you have the m4 package installed:

```
[root@gonzo /]# rpm -q m4
m4-1.4-10
```

m4 is available on your system if you get output similar to this (you might have different version numbers, but that's okay). Otherwise, the m4 RPM will be on your Caldera CD-ROM.

If you do a directory listing of /usr/lib/sendmail-cf on Red Hat it should look something like this:

```
[root@gonzo /usr/lib]# ls sendmail-cf/
README          cf              feature        m4             ostype
siteconfigREADME.check   domain         hack           mailer         sh
```

If you do a directory listing of /usr/share/sendmail/cf on Caldera it should look something like this:

```
[root@gonzo /usr/share/sendmail]# ls cf/
README          cf              feature        m4             ostype
siteconfigREADME.check   domain         hack           mailer         sh
```

The readme file is worth reading. It contains information on the different features that you can add to your mc file, as well as other important information, including a description of the anti-spam features that have made it into the later versions of sendmail.

Creating a sendmail.cf for your site is a matter of changing into the cf directory and selecting an appropriate template. The ls should produce a listing similar to this for Red Hat distributions:

```
[root@gonzo /usr/lib/sendmail-cf]# cd cf
[root@gonzo /usr/lib/sendmail-cf/cf]#  ls
Makefile                 generic-hpux10.mc        obj
```

```
Makefile.dist           generic-hpux9.mc          python.cs.mc
chez.cs.mc              generic-nextstep3.3.mc    redhat.cf
clientproto.mc          generic-osf1.mc           redhat.mc
cs-hpux10.mc            generic-solaris2.mc       s2k-osf1.mc
cs-hpux9.mc             generic-sunos4.1.mc       s2k-ultrix4.mc
cs-osf1.mc              generic-ultrix4.mc        tcpproto.mc
cs-solaris2.mc          huginn.cs.mc              ucbarpa.mc
cs-sunos4.1.mc          knecht.mc                 ucbvax.mc
cs-ultrix4.mc           mail.cs.mc                uucpproto.mc
cyrusproto.mc           mail.eecs.mc              vangogh.cs.mc
generic-bsd4.4.mc       mailspool.cs.mc
```

For Caldera it looks like this:

```
[root@gonzo /usr/share/sendmail/cf]# cd cf
[root@gonzo /usr/share/sendmail/cf/cf]#  ls
Makefile                generic-hpux10.mc         obj
Makefile.dist           generic-hpux9.mc          python.cs.mc
chez.cs.mc              generic-nextstep3.3.mc    generic-col2.2.cf
clientproto.mc          generic-osf1.mc           generic-col2.2.mc
cs-hpux10.mc            generic-solaris2.mc       s2k-osf1.mc
cs-hpux9.mc             generic-sunos4.1.mc       s2k-ultrix4.mc
cs-osf1.mc              generic-ultrix4.mc        tcpproto.mc
cs-solaris2.mc          huginn.cs.mc              ucbarpa.mc
cs-sunos4.1.mc          knecht.mc                 ucbvax.mc
cs-ultrix4.mc           mail.cs.mc                uucpproto.mc
cyrusproto.mc           mail.eecs.mc              vangogh.cs.mc
generic-bsd4.4.mc       mailspool.cs.mc
```

These are all the `mc` files you can choose from to create your `cf` file. For Red Hat you will use the `redhat.mc` file as a template or for Caldera you will use the `generic-col2.2.mc` file. I suggest copying it to another name. Here is an example:

```
[root@gonzo /usr/lib/sendmail-cf/cf]# cp redhat.mc gonzo.mc
```

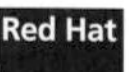

Here is a brief explanation of the various parts of this sample `mc` file:

```
divert(-1)
include(`../m4/cf.m4')
```

These are directives that the `m4` processor needs to process the file. You will find similar entries in some of the other `mc` files.

```
define(`confDEF_USER_ID',``8:12'')
OSTYPE(`linux')
undefine(`UUCP_RELAY')
undefine(`BITNET_RELAY')
```

The `define` indicates that you want to change a setting in `sendmail`, such as maximum hops allowed for a message or the maximum message size. In this case you're defining

which UID and group to run the sendmail program while it is not in privileged mode (running as root). All possible parameters you can define are listed in the readme file.

Different UNIX operating systems have different conventions for where to place files and which flags to give mailers. This is what the OSTYPE macro is for. In the example, sendmail should use the Linux conventions for file locations.

The two undefines remove the capability for this sendmail host to accept UUCP and BITNET addressed mail:

```
FEATURE(redirect)
FEATURE(always_add_domain)
FEATURE(use_cw_file)
FEATURE(local_procmail)
```

The FEATURE macros allow you to add the various sendmail features that your site requires.

The redirect feature rejects all mail addressed to address.REDIRECT with a 551 User not local; please try <address> message. That way, if Joe leaves the Gonzo company to go to Whizzer Inc., the email administrator at Gonzo can alias Joe to joe@whizzer.com.REDIRECT as a courtesy so Joe's friends and work contacts can reach him at his new job.

The second feature, always_add_domain, appends the fully qualified domain name of the local host, even on locally delivered mail to mail whose To: address is unqualified. For example, if I address mail to joe instead of joe@gonzo.gov, sendmail automatically appends @gonzo.gov to the To: header before delivery.

The use_cw_file feature indicates to sendmail to look in the file /etc/sendmail.cw for alternate names for the localhost. For example, if gonzo.gov also is a primary MX for the hiking club, hikers.org, then both gonzo.gov and hikers.org will have entries in the sendmail.cw file.

The next feature indicates that procmail is to be used as the local mailer:.

```
MAILER(procmail)
MAILER(smtp)
```

The two MAILER lines define only two mailers, procmail and SMTP. Remember that procmail was defined to be used as the local mailer. It must be defined here also, and SMTP is undefined as the mailer for remote mail deliveries:

```
HACK(check_mail3,'hash -a@JUNK /etc/mail/deny')
HACK(use_ip,'/etc/mail/ip_allow')
HACK(use_names,'/etc/mail/name_allow')
```

```
HACK(use_relayto,'/etc/mail/relay_allow')
HACK(check_rcpt4)
HACK(check_relay3)
```

In the V8.9 series of `sendmail`, relaying by external hosts is denied by default. This prevents other hosts from using your mailhost as a relay point for distributing junk mail (*spam*) or for other purposes. The preceding `HACK`s allow you to specify which hosts are allowed to use your mail server as a relay point and which machines on the Internet to never accept email from. This is especially handy for times when you and your users continually get spam from the same hosts. It is an exercise to read the `/usr/lib/sendmail-cf/README.check` file, which describes all the available `HACK`s and how to use them.

Here is a brief explanation of the various parts of this sample `mc` file:

```
divert(0)
divert(-1)
divert(0)dnl
VERSIONID(`$Id: generic-col2.2.mc,v 1.4 1999/02/23 15:36:07 okir Exp $')
divert(-1)
```

These are directives that the `m4` processor needs to process the file. You will find similar entries in some of the other `mc` files.

```
OSTYPE(`linux')
undefine(`UUCP_RELAY')
undefine(`BITNET_RELAY')
undefine(`LOCAL_MAILER_PATH')
```

Different UNIX operating systems have different conventions for where to place files and which flags to give mailers. This is what the `OSTYPE` macro is for. In the example, `sendmail` should use the Linux conventions for file locations.

The three `undefines` remove the capability for this `sendmail` host to relay UUCP and BITNET addressed mail and remove any previous macro definitions for `LOCAL_MAILER_PATH`:

```
define(`STATUS_FILE', `/var/log/sendmail.st')
define(`HELP_FILE', `/usr/share/sendmail/sendmail.hf')
define(`confUNSAFE_GROUP_WRITES', `True')
```

The define identifiers set certain macros that usually indicate where a file is located, or set a variable of some description. The first specifies where the `sendmail` statistics file should be located. This file is read using the `/usr/bin/mailstats` command. The second specifies where the `sendmail` help file is located and the last says that any `:include:` (included in an alias in `/etc/aliases`, for example) or `.forward` files in user home directories are to be considered unsafe if they have the group-writable bit set.

```
FEATURE(redirect)
FEATURE(always_add_domain)
FEATURE(use_cw_file)
FEATURE(mailertable, `hash /etc/sendmail/mailertable')
```

The FEATURE macros allow you to add the various sendmail features that your site requires.

The redirect feature rejects all mail addressed to address.REDIRECT with a 551 User not local; please try <address> message. That way, if Joe leaves the Gonzo company to go to Whizzer Inc., the email administrator at Gonzo can alias Joe to joe@whizzer.com.REDIRECT as a courtesy so Joe's friends and work contacts can reach him at his new job.

The second feature, always_add_domain, always appends the fully qualified domain name of the local host, even on locally delivered mail whose To: address is unqualified. For example, if I address mail to joe instead of joe@gonzo.gov, sendmail will automatically append @gonzo.gov to the To: header before delivery.

The use_cw_file feature tells sendmail to look in the file /etc/sendmail.cw for alternate names for the localhost. For example, if gonzo.gov also is a primary MX for the hiking club, hikers.org, both gonzo.gov and hikers.org will have entries in the sendmail.cw file.

The next feature indicates that a mailertable is to be defined and the location for it is /etc/sendmail:

```
ifdef(`COL_FEATURES',,`define(`COL_FEATURES',`/dev/null')')
include(COL_FEATURES)
MAILER(local)
MAILER(smtp)
MAILER(uucp)
```

The COL_FEATURES macro is predefined to include various Caldera-specific sendmail default information. Finally, the three MAILER lines define the different mailers for sendmail to use in order to be local (for local delivery), SMTP (for remote delivery), and UUCP (for UUCP addressed mail).

Tip

Suppose your users receive a lot of advertisements via email (or spam) and they complain about it to you. Suppose all the spam comes from the same host. You can prevent this host from sending any email to your site. If you are running

continues

Caldera OpenLinux you first need to add the following line to your `sendmail.mc` file:

```
HACK(check_mail3,'hash -a@JUNK /etc/mail/deny')
```

Then, it is a simple matter of editing the file:

```
/etc/mail/deny
```

and adding an entry such as this:

```
192.168.1.2"We do not accept mail from spammers"
```

Create the database for `sendmail` to use by typing in this command:

```
# makemap hash /etc/mail/deny.db < /etc/mail/deny
```

You need to use `nslookup` to look up the IP address of the spamming host to insert the `deny` file. When the host corresponding to the IP address `192.168.1.2` tries to talk to your `sendmail` process, it gets an error code as well as a configurable textual reason for the connection denial.

As you can see, the supplied `template` files provide a fairly good template for your own `mc` file. Debian systems build an `.mc` file for you based on your answers to the installation questions, so there is no need to make your own from scratch. You have already copied it to `gonzo.mc`. All you need to do now is add two more items; you can then create the `cf` file `sendmail` can use. Add the following after the list of `FEATURE`s:

```
FEATURE(masquerade_envelope)
MASQUERADE_AS(gonzo.gov)
```

Assume that your Gonzo mail host is called `mail.gonzo.gov`. Without these lines, all email you send out from your mail host will have a From: address in the envelope and message body that looks something like `joe@mail.gonzo.gov`. It would be nice to hide which host you sent the mail from and have the recipient From: address read something like `joe@gonzo.gov`. That is what the `MASQUERADE_AS` line does. The `masquerade_envelope` feature causes the message envelope From: header to be similarly masqueraded.

All you need to do now is build the `sendmail` configuration file:

```
[root@gondor cf]# make gonzo.cf
rm -f gondor.cf
m4 ../m4/cf.m4 gondor.mc > gonzo.cf
chmod 444 gonzo.cf
```

You can generate your `sendmail.cf` with the following in Debian after editing your `/etc/mail/sendmail.mc`:

```
/usr/sbin/sendmailconfig
```

If you are using GNU Make, which is almost certainly the case if you are running Caldera, you get an error after typing in the `make` command. Try `make -f Makefile.dist gonzo.cf` instead. If the `make` is successful, a `gondor.cf` file will appear in your `cf` directory. Congratulations—you have created your very first `sendmail.cf` file!

Testing sendmail and sendmail.cf

Before installing a new or modified `sendmail.cf`, you must test it thoroughly. Even small, seemingly innocuous changes can lead to disaster, and people often become irate when you mess up the mail system.

The first step in testing is to create a list of addresses that you know should work at your site. For example, at `gonzo.gov`, an Internet site without UUCP connections, the following addresses must work:

```
joe
joe@pc1.gonzo.gov
joe@gonzo.gov
```

If `gonzo.gov` has a UUCP link, those addresses must also be tested. Other addresses to consider include the various kinds of aliases (for example, `postmaster`, an `:include:` list, an alias that mails to a file, and one that mails to a program), remote addresses, source-routed addresses, and so on. If you want to be thorough, you can create a test address for each legal address format in RFC 822.

Now that you have your list of test addresses, you can use the `-C` and `-bt` options to see what happens. At a minimum, you should run the addresses through rulesets 3 and 0 to make sure they are routed to the correct mailer. An easy way to do so is to create a file containing the ruleset invocations and test addresses and then run `sendmail` on it. For example, assume the file `addr.test` contains these lines:

```
3,0 joe
3,0 joe@pc1.gonzo.gov
3,0 joe@gonzo.gov
```

You can test your configuration file `test.cf` by typing this code:

```
$ /usr/sbin/sendmail -Ctest.cf -bt < addr.test

rewrite: ruleset  3   input: joe
rewrite: ruleset  3 returns: joe
[etc.]
```

You also might want to follow one or more addresses through the complete rewriting process. For example, if an address resolves to the `smtp` mailer and that mailer specifies `R=21`, you can test recipient address rewriting by using `3,2,21,4` *`test_address`*.

If the `sendmail.cf` appears to work correctly so far, you're ready to send some real letters. You can do so by using a command like the following:

```
$ /usr/sbin/sendmail -v -oQ/tmp -Ctest.cf recipient < /dev/null
```

The `-v` option tells `sendmail` to be verbose so you can see what's happening. Depending on whether the delivery is local or remote, you can see something as simple as `joe... Sent` or an entire SMTP dialog. `-o` sets an option that overrides what is in the `sendmail.cf` file. You can also use `-O` (uppercase O) for long options.

The `-oQ/tmp` tells `sendmail` to use `/tmp` as its queue directory. Using this option is necessary because `sendmail` drops its `superuser` permissions when run with the `-C` option and can't write queue files into the normal mail queue directory. Because you are using the `-C` and `-oQ` options, `sendmail` also includes the following warning headers in the letter to help alert the recipient of possible mail forgery:

```
X-Authentication-Warning: gonzo.gov: Processed from queue /tmp
X-Authentication-Warning: gonzo.gov: Processed by joe with -C srvr.cf
```

`sendmail` also inserts the header `Apparently-to: joe` because, although you specified a recipient on the command line, none was listed in the body of the letter. In this case, the letter's body was taken from the empty file `/dev/null`, so that no To: header was available. If you do your testing as the `superuser`, you can skip the `-oQ` argument and `sendmail` won't insert the warning headers. You can avoid the `Apparently-to:` header by creating a file like the following and using it as input instead of `/dev/null`:

```
To: recipient

testing
```

You should be the recipient, so you can inspect the headers of the letter for correctness. In particular, return address lines must include an FQDN for SMTP mail. That is, a header such as `From: joe@gonzo` is incorrect because it doesn't include the domain part of the name, but a header such as `From: joe@gonzo.gov` is fine.

You should repeat this testing for the same variety of addresses you used in the first tests. You might have to create special aliases that point to you for some of the testing.

The amount of testing you do depends on the complexity of your site and the amount of experience you have, but a beginning system administrator should test very thoroughly, even for apparently simple installations.

When you are absolutely sure that the `sendmail.cf` file is correct, you can copy it into place in the `/etc` directory:

```
[root@gonzo cf]# cp /etc/sendmail.cf /etc/sendmail.cf.bak
[root@gonzo cf]# cp gonzo.cf /etc/sendmail.cf
```

The first copy backs up your current `sendmail` configuration in case you need to retrieve it for any reason. You can then stop and start `sendmail`; this causes `sendmail` to re-read its configuration file. For Red Hat you will use:

```
[root@gonzo]# /etc/rc.d/init.d/sendmail restart
```

And for Caldera you use:

```
[root@gonzo cf]# /etc/rc.d/init.d/mta reload
```

In Debian use:

```
/etc/init.d/sendmail restart
```

However, the `sendmail` config script offers to do this automatically for you.

Common `sendmail` Configuration Mistakes

There are three main common configuration errors when you are setting up a `sendmail`-based mail server.

The first is not having an alias for the postmaster user. All bounced messages get sent to this alias, which should point to a user that regularly reads their mail. When you get bounced messages for your site, you should read them! A lot of the time it helps you diagnose a problem before the users notice it and start complaining. It is also a widely known alias that Internet users commonly mail to if they need to contact an email administrator for a particular domain name.

The second is having an incorrectly configured `sendmail.cw` file. This file should list all the domain names for which the server is responsible for receiving mail.

The last is due to incorrectly configured DNS entries. Sites often have incorrect secondary `MX` records, which is of no use if your main email server goes down for a period of time. Your ISP will usually be happy to act as a secondary `MX` for your site.

POP

As much as you might love Linux, the reality is that you must contend with other operating systems out there. Even worse, many of them aren't even UNIX-based. Although the Linux community has forgiven the users of other operating systems, there is still a long way to go before complete assimilation occurs. In the meantime, the best thing that can happen is use of tools that tie the two worlds together.

The following sections cover the integration of the most often used application of any network: electronic mail. The Post Office Protocol (POP) was created because UNIX and other operating systems have very different views of how email should be handled. This protocol abstracts the details of email to a system-independent level so anyone who writes a POP client can communicate with a POP server.

Configuring a POP Server

The POP server you will configure on the sample systems is packaged as part of the freely available IMAP package. (Setting up IMAP is discussed in the next section.) This package was developed at the University of Washington (`ftp://ftp.cac.washington.edu/imap`). If you also need client software for non-UNIX systems, check out the Eudora Light email package available from Qualcomm (`ftp://ftp.qualcomm.com/eudora/eudoralight/`). Like the University of Washington (UW) POP package, Eudora Light is available for free. (The Professional version does cost money, however.) This chapter later shows you how to configure your Netscape browser for both POP and IMAP email retrieval.

Use the following to install both the POP and IMAP servers for Debian:

```
apt-get install ipopd imap
```

Caldera and RedHat have prepared an RPM of the UW IMAP package, which is available on the CD-ROM (`imap-4.5.BETA-1.i386.rpm` for Caldera and `imap-4.5.1.i386.rpm` for Red Hat). To install it from the CD-ROM, simply type a command similar to

```
rpm -i imap-4.5.1.i386.rpm
```

The `rpm` command installs three programs, all found in `/usr/sbin/`—`imapd`, `ipop2d`, and `ipop3d`—as well as the manual pages. You will not need to worry about using `ipop2d` because it implements the earlier POP2 specification. Almost every POP client available these days knows how to talk POP3.

Configuring `ipop3d`

Most of the `ipop3d` options are configured at compile time. Therefore, you don't have much say in how things are done unless you want to compile the package yourself. If you are interested in pursuing that route, you can fetch the complete package (which is version 4.5 at the time of this writing) from UW's FTP site at `ftp://ftp.cac.washington.edu/imap/imap-4.5.tar.Z`. However, it is highly recommended that you stick with the source RPM distributed on your Caldera CD-ROM, since it contains all the patches and other modifications that Caldera applied to the original codebase.

Using `ipop3d` gives you the following capabilities:

- Refusal to retrieve mail for anyone whose UID is `root`.
- Verbose logging to `syslog`.
- Supports for CRAM-MD5 and APOP for user authentication. For these to be enabled, the file `/etc/cram-md5.pwd` must exist. (See the section titled "How APOP Works" on setting up APOP support for details.)

To allow `ipop3d` to start from `inetd`, edit the `/etc/inetd.conf` file and make sure the following line is uncommented:

```
pop-3    stream    tcp    nowait    root    /usr/sbin/tcpd ipop3d
```

Don't forget to send the `HUP` signal to `inetd`. You can do so by issuing the following commands.

For Red Hat, restarting `inetd` is as simple as typing:

```
# /etc/rc.d/init.d/inet restart
```

For Caldera, type

```
# /etc/rc.d/init.d/inet stop
# /etc/rc.d/init.d/inet start
```

In Debian, you can use

```
/etc/init.d/inetd reload
```

to restart `inetd`. If this doesn't work, you might try the following, which works on other versions:

```
/etc/init.d/netbase reload
```

Now you're ready to test the connection. Enter the following at a command prompt:

```
$ telnet popserver pop-3110
```

`popserver` is the name of the machine running the `ipop3d` program. The `pop-3` at the end is what Telnet will reference in your `/etc/services` file for port 110.

You should get a response similar to the following:

```
+OK POP3 popserver.gonzo.gov v6.50 server ready
```

This result means that the POP server has responded and is awaiting an instruction. (Typically, this job is transparently done by the client mail reader.) If you want to test the authentication service, try to log in as yourself and see whether the service registers your current email box. For example, you enter the following to log in as `sshah` with the password `mars1031`:

```
user sshah
+OK User name accepted, password please
pass mars1031
+OK Mailbox open, 90 messages
quit
+OK Sayonara
```

The first line, `user sshah`, tells the POP server that the user for whom it will be checking mail is `sshah`. The response from the server is an acknowledgment that the username `sshah` is accepted, (however it may not necessarily exist on the system; see Note), and that a password is required to access the mailbox.

Note

The POP daemon will always accept a username as long as it complies to the UNIX username conventions. This is to stop a hacker from checking to see if an account exists on a machine or not. If a hacker knows that an account exists, then he has a starting point to try and break into the machine.

You can then type **`pass mars1031`**, where `mars1031` is the password for the `sshah` user. The server acknowledges the correct password and username pair by responding with a statement indicating that 90 messages are currently in user `sshah`'s mail queue. Because you don't want to actually read the mail this way, enter **`quit`** to terminate the session. The server sends a sign-off message and drops the connection.

How APOP Works

By default, the POP server sends all passwords in *cleartext* (not encrypted). If you are security- conscious, using cleartext passwords over your network is obviously a bad idea, and tighter control is needed on authentication. This is where APOP support comes in. APOP is a more security-minded way of authenticating users because the passwords are encrypted before they're sent over the network.

It works like this: The server issues a *challenge* to a connecting client. The client appends the user's password to the challenge and then encrypts it using `MD5` (this is called a *hash*) and sends the hash back to the server. The server then compares the client's response with its own calculated value of the checksum (challenge + user password). If there is a match, the client is then authenticated and logged on to the POP3 server.

As you can see, the advantage of this method is that rather than the plaintext password being transmitted in the clear, all that is transferred is a hash of text that means absolutely nothing to a cracker sniffing the network. If implemented correctly, the probability of the same challenge being issued twice by the server is very small! This stops cold the possibility of a replay attack, whereby the attacker grabs a MD5 hash that has come across the wire and tries to use it to log in to someone else's POP3 account.

Setting Up APOP Authentication

Luckily, `ipop3d` supports APOP. The APOP username and password information is in the `/etc/cram-md5.pwd` file. Because this database is kept in a cleartext format, you need to make absolutely sure that it has the permissions 0400 (`chmod 0400 /etc/cram-md5.pwd`).

When you installed `ipop3d`, the `/etc/cram-md5.pwd` database was not created. You need to create the file with your favorite editor and put some entries in, similar to this:

```
# CRAM-MD5 authentication database
# Entries are in form <user><tab><password>
# Lines starting with "#" are comments

fred    rubble
wilma    flintstone
barny    beret
betty    wired
```

Obviously, putting any plaintext passwords in any file is bad practice—one of the downfalls of the `ipop3d` software. At some point in the future, encryption will hopefully be added to the APOP database. In the meantime, you must continue to make sure that the file has the correct permissions. Additionally, it is not recommended that your users use the same password for APOP email access as that they use to log in to the server (the password that is specified in `/etc/passwd`).

The POP3 Protocol

The latest version of POP is POP3. POP2 was originally published as RFC 918 in October 1984 and was superceded by RFC 937 in February 1985.

POP3 was originally published as RFCs 1081 and 1082 in November 1988. RFC 1081 was superceded by RFC 1225 in May 1991. In June 1993, RFC 1460 superceded RFC 1225, and in November 1994, RFC 1725 made the standards track and rendered RFC 1460 obsolete.

IMAP

As noted at the beginning of the chapter, POP was a good first step toward enabling people to run on other non-UNIX operating systems to read their UNIX-based email. As time went on and distributed computing really took off, the deficiencies stood out. The POP server would not keep the read or unread state of messages. Messages would be downloaded to the user's PC and deleted from the server, so when the user moved to another PC, he had to move his mailbox between the two different machines. In this day of remote communication, people found that accessing email from home over a modem connection could be painfully slow if there were many messages to download, and they could not access the email folders they created on their work PC from home.

The IMAP protocol now allows people to store all their folders *online*. This makes it possible to access your email on your laptop while travelling, at home, or at work—without having to transfer the physical messages back and forth. It works by transferring all the message headers of the folder you are reading. Then, using your IMAP client software, you can select a message; it will display on your local screen. The main advantage, of course, is that the messages are left on the server so you can access them wherever you happen to be.

Similarly to the POP3 protocol, IMAP (also commonly referred to as IMAP4) is also an RFC standard, so it's a transparent protocol that can be added onto any messaging system. There exists IMAP implementations for not just UNIX systems, but Microsoft Exchange, Novell Groupwise, and countless others.

Configuring an IMAP Server

Installing IMAP on Debian is quite simple:

```
apt-get install imap
```

Configuring an IMAP server on your Caldera OpenLinux or Red Hat system is relatively straightforward. You need to make sure that the `imapd` RPM is installed:

```
 [root@gonzo /] # rpm -q imap
imap-4.5.BETA-1
```

If you get similar output, you are in business. Otherwise, you need to install `imapd`, which is on your Linux distribution CD-ROM.

You also need to check that `imapd` is mentioned in your `/etc/inetd.conf` file. There should be a line similar to this:

```
imap    stream  tcp     nowait  root    /usr/sbin/tcpd  imapd
```

If the line begins with a hash sign (#), it is commented out. You need to remove the hash sign and restart inetd. If you are unsure how to restart inetd, see the previous section on configuring ipop3d for examples.

By now, imapd is running and you should be able to connect to it. This is similar to the way you tested the connection to your POP server in the previous section.

Type in the following, where imapserver is the name of the machine running the imapd program:

```
telnet imapserver imap143
```

You should get a response similar to the following:

```
* OK imapserver IMAP4rev1 v11.241 server ready
```

This result means the IMAP server has responded and is awaiting an instruction (again, this is normally done by the client mail reader). If you want to test the authentication service, try to log in as yourself and see whether the service registers your current email box. For example, you enter the following to log in as sshah with the password mars1031:

```
A001 login sshah mars1031
A001 OK LOGIN completed
```

You are now logged into your IMAP server. Since you were just testing, you can log out now by entering this:

```
A002 logout
* BYE imapserver IMAP4rev1 server terminating connection
```

Your IMAP server is now set up and ready to use!

Mail Retrieval

With imapd set up on your server, you can access your mail using numerous methods. You can use a command-line program such as pine on the Linux console, an IMAP-compliant Windows or Macintosh-based email client (a list of which can be found at http://www.imap.org/products.html), or Netscape Communicator, which is available as part of the Caldera OpenLinux distribution.

Configuring Netscape for POP3 or IMAP Retrieval

It's fairly simple to set up Netscape to talk to your mail server. You just need to tell it your IMAP or POP server name, your login name, and if you want to use IMAP, the home subdirectory on the server where your folders are kept.

Start off by logging in to your account and creating a directory called `Mail`:

```
[fred@gonzo] $ mkdir Mail
```

You will use this directory to store your mail folders so they can be accessed by both your local email client and remote IMAP client.

Now start Netscape. You should be able to type in **`netscape`**. If you get a `command not found` error, you need to install it from your CD-ROM or FTP.

Click the Communicator menu and select Messenger Mailbox. This brings up the Netscape messaging system. Click Edit, Preferences, and then click Identity in the left half of the screen. You are faced with a dialog box like that shown in Figure 9.3.

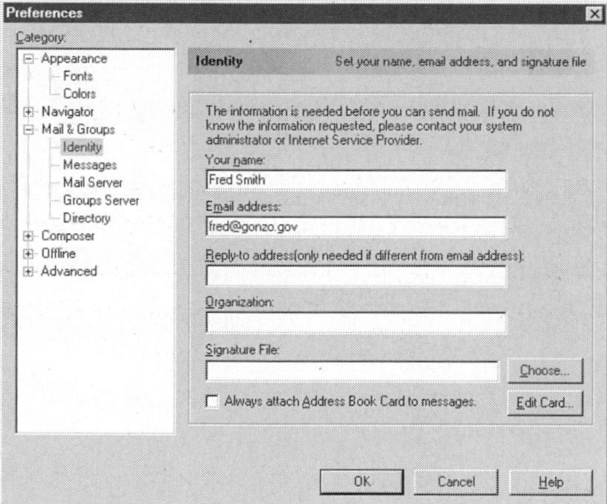

FIGURE 9.3
Setting your identity with Netscape Messenger.

Put your real name in. This name is what will be placed in the From: header for email messages you send out. Fill in your correct email address as well. This is the address that people will see in the From: header.

Click Mail Server and you will see a window similar to that shown in Figure 9.4.

In the first text box, enter the username that you use on your mail server in the first text box. Now enter your outgoing (SMTP) server name as well as the incoming server name (these are usually the same). Directly below the information you just entered, you can choose the incoming mail server type. We will choose IMAP for demonstration purposes, but you can just as easily choose POP3 if you don't want or need all the neat IMAP features. You can also choose to move your deleted messages into your Messenger trashcan, select SSL encryption if your IMAP server supports it, or you can select Set New Folders for Offline Download. This allows you to download messages you read so they physically reside on your local PC as well as the server for offline reading.

FIGURE 9.4
Setting your mail server details with Netscape Messenger.

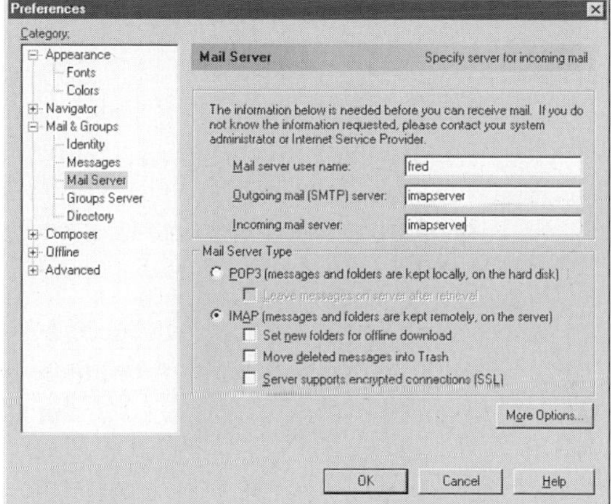

One final option needs to be set before you can begin reading your email with Messenger. Click More Options; in the IMAP server directory, enter the directory you created at the start of this section (`Mail`). This is the directory that Messenger uses for your online mail folders. Click twice (but do not double-click it) and then click the Get Msg button. Messenger asks for your password and then begins downloading all your email message headers. It displays them for easy browsing. You can easily switch to different folders using the drop-down box just under the toolbar.

fetchmail

`fetchmail` is best described with an example. Say your email is stored at your ISP. To access your mail using conventional means, using Netscape Messenger for instance, you set it up for POP3 access. That way, when you dial in it downloads all your messages to your personal Linux account, where you can read, reply, and sort through your messages as you please.

The `fetchmail` paradigm is slightly different. Instead of downloading your mail using your mail reader, `fetchmail` is executed as a separate program whose sole purpose is to log in to your POP3 or IMAP server and download all your messages. But that's not all it does! As it downloads your mail, each message is passed on to your regular Mail Delivery Agent (MDA). If you use `sendmail`, `qmail`, `smail`, or some other SMTP-compatible mail server, all the messages are passed to port 25 on your local Linux machine, just as if you were permanently connected on the Internet and email were arriving directly to your machine. Once the mail is delivered to your mail spool file (`/var/spool/mail/<username>`), you can read it using conventional methods, such as command-line mail, `elm`, `pine`, or even with Netscape Messenger on a Windows or

Macintosh machine elsewhere on your local LAN—long after you have disconnected from your ISP!

This method of mail pickup provides numerous benefits. If you use `procmail` scripts to filter incoming messages as they arrive and your `sendmail` is configured to use `procmail` as the local delivery mailer, your messages will be filtered correctly. Again, if you are using `sendmail` and you have a `.forward` file in your home directory, the `.forward` file will still be processed.

`fetchmail` is a very powerful program, and it has many advanced features that are not discussed here. If you want more information on what it offers, there is a reasonable amount of documentation in `/usr/doc/fetchmail-x.y.z`. (`x`, `y`, and `z` are the version numbers of the version you have installed.) In Debian, the path is `/usr/doc/fetchmail`.

To install `fetchmail`, run this code:

```
apt-get install fetchmail
```

To determine whether `fetchmail` is installed on your system, enter the following command:

```
[root@gonzo /] # rpm -qa ¦ grep fetchmail
fetchmail-4.5.8-2
```

If similar output appears, you are in business. Otherwise, install it from your Linux distribution CD-ROM using a command similar to this one (the version maybe different depending on which distribution of Linux you are running):

```
[root@gonzo /] # rpm -i fetchmail-4.5.8-2.i386.rpm
```

Configuring `fetchmail` for POP3 or IMAP Retrieval

When `fetchmail` executes, searches for a `.fetchmailrc` file in your home directory. This file usually contains all the options that are needed to log in to your ISP's POP or IMAP server. Anything that can be specified in this `rc` file can also be specified on the command line. It is usually easier, however, to put all the options you regularly use in a `.fetchmailrc` file. To start, create a configuration file to collect your mail from your ISP's POP3 server. It is fairly simple and shown in this line:

```
poll pop.isp.net protocol pop3 username joe password secret123
```

This is fairly self-explanatory: `poll` signifies the hostname to contact, `protocol` gives the protocol that you want to use to connect, `username` specifies your POP3 username, and `password` indicates that your password follows. If you want, you can leave your password out. If you choose to do it this way, you are asked for a password when `fetchmail` connects to your POP3 server.

Similarly, it is not hard to guess how to configure `fetchmail` to retrieve your mail from an IMAP server:

```
poll imap.isp.net protocol imap username joe password secret123
```

For security, you should also make sure you have the correct permissions on your `.fetchmailrc` file:

```
$ chmod 0400 .fetchmailrc
```

You can also start `fetchmail` as a daemon and have it automatically check your mail once every *n* seconds with the option `-d`. For example, use the following command to check your mail automatically every minute and put `fetchmail` in the background:

```
$ fetchmail -d 60 &
```

The `-v` option comes in handy when diagnosing mistakes. It outputs diagnostic information to the screen as it works to help you narrow a problem.

`fetchmail` has an excellent manual page that contains more details on how to configure some of the more advanced options. There are also numerous resources on the Internet, such as `http://www.tuxedo.org/~esr/fetchmail`.

Summary

In this chapter you learned how to install, set up, configure, and test `sendmail`, `ipop3d`, and `imapd`, as well as retrieve your mail using Netscape and `fetchmail`. The key things to remember about this process follow:

- An MTA is a Mail Transfer Agent, which actually routes and delivers mail. An MUA is a Mail User Agent, which is what the user uses to access mail after it has been delivered. `sendmail` is an MTA only.
- The Simple Mail Transfer Protocol (SMTP) is the actual protocol used to transfer mail. `sendmail` is a program that uses this protocol to communicate with other mail servers. Other mail servers don't need to run `sendmail`, but they do need to communicate via SMTP.
- `sendmail` does not deliver mail once it has reached the destination system. A special program that's local to the system, such as `/bin/mail` or `/usr/bin/procmail`, is used to perform the delivery functions.
- The aliases file can either remap email addresses to other usernames, redirect mail to files, or pass on email messages to another program for processing. Remember to run the `newaliases` program every time you change the alias file.

- sendmail is a large program with a history of security problems. Hence, be sure to keep up with the security bulletins. The security section at http://www.lwn.net (*Linux Weekly News*) is worth checking regularly, as well as ftp://updates.redhat.com (or mirrors) for security updates to your particular distribution. The security section at *Linux Weekly News* is worth checking regularly, as well as the updates directory at Caldera's FTP site (or mirrors) for security updates to your particular distribution.
- Whenever a new version of sendmail is released, download it from ftp.sendmail.org and install it.
- The Post Office Protocol (POP) is a protocol for allowing client machines to connect to a mail server and transfer mail. POP is not responsible for delivering mail to other users or systems.
- Although POP isn't nearly as large or complex as sendmail, it does have the potential to contain security problems (as does any Internet-accessible service). Watch for security announcements and upgrade accordingly.
- APOP is the means by which the POP protocol accepts passwords in an encrypted format.
- The Internet Message Access Protocol (IMAP) is a protocol for allowing client machines to connect to a mail server and access your email without having to download all your waiting messages at once. It also allows easy remote access to email when you are constantly moving around, by allowing you to manipulate mail folders on your mail server.
- Netscape Messenger can be configured to talk to either a POP or IMAP server quite easily.
- fetchmail is an alternative method to processing your mail from either a POP or an IMAP server.
- fetchmail passes mail to your local Mail Delivery Transfer Agent (MDTA) for processing. sendmail is an example.

Telling you all you must know about SMTP, POP, and IMAP in a single chapter is impossible, but as Yogi Bear (or maybe Casey Stengel) once said, "You could look it up," and you should. However, this chapter gives you a good basis for understanding the theory behind SMTP and related protocols.

CHAPTER 10

FTP

In This Chapter

Using the File Transfer Protocol (FTP) is a popular way to transfer files from machine to machine across a network. Clients and servers have been written for all the popular platforms, thereby often making FTP the most convenient way of performing file transfers.

You can configure FTP servers one of two ways. The first is as a private, user-only site, which is the default configuration for the FTP server. I cover this configuration here. A *private FTP server* allows only system users to connect via FTP and access their files. You can place access controls to either deny or grant access to specific users.

The other kind of FTP server is anonymous. An *anonymous FTP server* allows anyone on the network to connect to it and transfer files without having an account. Due to the potential security risks involved with this setup, you should allow access only to certain directories on the system.

Caution

Configuring an anonymous FTP server can pose a security risk. Because server software is inherently complex, it can contain bugs that allow unauthorized users to access your system. The authors of the FTP server you configure in this chapter have gone to great lengths to avoid this possibility; however, no one can ever be 100 percent sure.

If you decide to establish an anonymous FTP server, be sure to keep a careful eye on security announcements from the Computer Emergency Response Team (`http://www.cert.org`) and update the server software whenever security issues arise.

Depending on which packages you chose to install, you might already have the FTP server software installed. To determine whether you have the server software installed, check for the `/usr/sbin/in.ftpd`, `/usr/sbin/wu-ftpd`, or `/usr/sbin/wu-ftpd-academ` files. If at least one is present, the next section explains how to locate and install it.

Getting and Installing the FTP Server

One option with many Linux distributions is to use the freely availablefreely available `wu-ftpd` server `wu-ftpd` server. Debian users may find this as a `.deb` named either `wu-ftpd` or `wu-ftpd-academ`, depending on the distribution version. It can be installed with standard tools such as `apt-get`, `dselect`, or `dpkg`.

If you have apt configured for your system, you may simply use either one of these:

```
apt-get install wu-ftpd
```

```
apt-get install wu-ftpd-academ
```

This installs the wu-ftpd server. Furthermore, the postinst script automatically offers to configure anonymous FTP for you. If you will be using anonymous FTP, select Yes when asked. Other options in Debian diverge somewhat from the standard methods of configuration described here. These include such programs as proftpd.

wu-ftpd also comes as an RPM (Red Hat Package Manager) for users of Red Hat and is offered as an installation option during initial setup. If you decide you want to run an FTP server but did not install the RPM, fetch wu-ftpd-2.4.2b18-5.i386.rpm from the CD-ROM or check http://www.redhat.com for the latest edition. To install the RPM, mount your Red Hat CD-ROM and run the following as root:

```
# rpm -i /mnt/cdrom/RedHat/RPMS/wu-ftpd-2.4.2vr17-3.i386.rpm
```

If you plan to offer an anonymously accessible site, be sure to install the anonftp-2.8-1.i386.rpm from the CD-ROM as well. As always, you can check for the latest version at http://www.redhat.com.

To install the anonymous FTP file, log in as root and run the following:

```
# rpm -i anonftp-2.8-1.i386.rpm rpm
```

Now you have a working anonymous FTP server. Of course, you should also have an active Internet network connection and a valid host and domain name for a truly public server. See Chapter 8, "The Domain Name Service," for details about Domain Name Service (DNS).

To install the Caldera OpenLinux RPM, mount the Caldera CD-ROM, and as root run the following:

```
# rpm -i /mnt/cdrom/Packages/RPMS/wu-ftpd-2.4.2b17-9.i386.rpm
```

If you plan to offer an anonymously accessible site, be sure to install Red Hat's anon-ftp-2.8-1.i386.rpm or Caldera's anonftp-3.0-1.i386.rpm from CD-ROM as well, as these packages provide the directories and files that will reside under your system's /home/ftp directory.

To install the anonymous FTP file for Red Hat or Caldera, log in as root, navigate to the package's directory on CD-ROM, and run the following:

```
# rpm -i anonftp*.rpm
```

Now you have a working anonymous FTP server. Of course, you should also have an active Internet network connection and a valid host and domain name for a truly public server. See Chapter 11, "The Domain Name Service," for details about Domain Name Service (DNS).

Note

Although the `anonftp` package contains the files necessary to set up anonymous FTP service, and the `wu-ftpd rpm` file contains the FTP daemon, you'll find the `ftp` client program in the `ftp rpm` package. Install all three RPMs for complete service. With Debian, only the server package is needed; the `ftp client` is installed by default as part of the standard networking packages.

You should periodically check your distribution's Web site for updates to Linux FTP software, especially if you allow public access to your computer over the Internet. Many newer versions of Linux networking or communications software contain security fixes or other enhancements that are designed to protect your computers from intruders.

Although you can find the latest version of `wuftpd` at `ftp://ftp.academ.com/pub/wu-ftpd`, you should periodically check the Caldera and Red Hat Web sites for RPM updates to Linux FTP software, especially if you allow public access to your computer over the Internet. Many newer versions of the Linux networking or communications software contain security fixes or other enhancements that are designed to protect your computers from intruders.

To test whether the installation worked, simply use the FTP client and connect to your machine. For the sample FTP server, `aptiva`, you would respond to the following:

```
# ftp aptiva
Connected to aptiva.home.org.
220 aptiva.home.org FTP server (Version wu-2.4.2-academ[BETA-18](1)
Mon Aug 3 19:17:20 EDT 1998) ready.
Name (aptiva:): anonymous
331 Guest login ok, send your complete e-mail address as password.
Password: willie@thinkpad.home.org
230 Guest login ok, access restrictions apply.
Remote system type is UNIX.
Using binary mode to transfer files.
ftp> ls
200 PORT command successful.
150 Opening ASCII mode data connection for /bin/ls.
total 6
drwxr-xr-x   6 root     root          1024 Feb 17 13:21 .
drwxr-xr-x   6 root     root          1024 Feb 17 13:21 ..
```

```
d--x--x--x   2 root     root         1024 Feb 17 13:21 bin
d--x--x--x   2 root     root         1024 Feb 17 13:21 etc
drwxr-xr-x   2 root     root         1024 Feb 17 13:21 lib
dr-xr-sr-x   2 root     ftp          1024 Sep 11  1998 pub
226 Transfer complete.
ftp>
```

As you can see, you'll be in the `/home/ftp` directory after you log in. To quit the FTP clientsoftware, simply type **`bye`** or **`quit`** at the `ftp>` prompt. If you want to test the private FTP server, rerun the FTP client but use your login instead of the anonymous login. Here's an example:

```
# ftp aptiva
Connected to aptiva.home.org.
220 aptiva.home.org FTP server (Version wu-2.4.2-academ[BETA-18](1)
Mon Aug 3 19:17:20 EDT 1998) ready.
Name (aptiva:): bball
331 Password required for bball.
Password: mypassword
230 User bball logged in.
Remote system type is UNIX.
Using binary mode to transfer files.
ftp> ls
drwxr-xr-x   5 bball    bball        1024 Mar 24  1998 aim
drwxrwxr-x   5 bball    bball        1024 Apr  7 13:38 axhome
drwxrwxr-x   2 bball    bball        1024 Mar 10 11:50 current_work
drwxrwxr-x   2 bball    bball        1024 Apr 14 09:31 documents
drwxrwxr-x   2 bball    bball        1024 Apr 14 13:38 graphics
drwxrwxr-x   2 bball    bball        1024 Apr 14 14:17 mail
drwxrwxr-x  18 bball    bball        1024 Mar 23 15:11 pilot
drwxrwxr-x   2 bball    bball        1024 Apr 14 08:49 research
drwxrwxr-x   2 bball    bball        2048 Apr 14 16:15 rhunew
drwxr-xr-x   2 bball    bball        1024 Apr  2 14:48 screenshots
drwxrwxr-x   2 bball    bball        1024 Mar 18 16:59 tyl
226 Transfer complete.
ftp>
```

As you can see, when you log in with a registered username and password, you'll be placed in your home directory on the remote computer. The output of the Red Hat and Caldera versions of the FTP server is similar.

Tip

If you don't have access to a network, you can test your FTP server by using the hostname *`localhost`*. You must have an active loopback interface (usually configured by default when you install Linux).

How the FTP Server Works

FTP service is controlled from the /etc/inetd.conf file and is automatically invoked whenever someone connects to the FTP port. (Ports are logical associations from a network connection to a specific service. For example, port 21 associates to FTP, port 23 associates to Telnet, and so on.) When a connection is detected, the FTP daemon (/usr/sbin/in.ftpd, wu-ftpd, or wu-ftp-academ) is invoked and the session begins. In the /etc/inetd.conf file, the default distribution file usually contains the necessary line for this step to occur.

After the server is invoked, the client needs to provide a username and corresponding password. Two special usernames—anonymous and ftp—have been set aside for the purpose of allowing access to the public files. Any other access requires the user to have an account on the server.

If a user accesses the server server using her account, an additional check is performed to ensure that she has a valid shell. If she doesn't, she is denied access to the system. This check is useful if you want to limit user access to a server (for example, POP mail) and do not want them logging in via Telnet or FTP. A shell must be listed in the /etc/shells file to be valid. If you install a new shell, be sure to add it to your /etc/shells listing so that people using that shell can connect to the system via FTP.

Users accessing the FTP server are placed in their home directories when they first log in. At that point, they can change to any directories on the system to which they have permission. Anonymous users, on the other hand, have several restrictions.

Anonymous users are placed in the home directory for the FTP users. By default, this directory is set to /home/ftp. After the users get there, the FTP server executes a chroot system call, effectively changing the program's root directory to the FTP users' directories. Access is denied to any other directories in the system, including /bin, /etc, and /lib. This change in the root directory prevents the server from seeing /etc/passwd, /etc/group, and other necessary binaries (such as /bin/ls). To make up for this change, the server package creates bin, etc, and lib directories under /home/ftp. This is where necessary libraries and programs (such as ls) are placed; it's also where the server software can access them even after the chroot system call has been made.

For security reasons, files placed under the /home/ftp directory have their permissions set such that only the server can see them. (This is done automatically during anonftp's install.) Any other directories created under /home/ftp should be set up so they are world-readable. Most anonymous FTP sites place such files under the pub subdirectory.

Configuring Your FTP Server

Although the default configuration of the FTP server is reasonably secure, you can fine-tune access rights by editing the following files:

- `ftpaccess`
- `ftpconversions`
- `ftphosts`
- `xferlog`

Red Hat users may find the first three files in `/etc` and the fourth in `/var/log`.

Debian users can find the first three files under `/etc/wu-ftpd-academ` (or in `/etc/wu-ftpd` with older distributions). The fourth file is found in `/var/log/wu-ftpd-academ`.

- `/etc/ftpaccess`
- `/etc/ftpconversions`
- `/etc/ftphosts`
- `/var/log/xferlog`

With all these files, you can control who connects to your server, when they can connect, and where they can connect from. Also, you can create an audit trail of what they do after connecting. The `ftpaccess` file is the most significant of these because it contains the most configuration options; however, misconfiguring any of the others can lead to denied service.

Tip

When editing any of the files in the `/etc` directory (FTP-related or not), comment the file liberally and keep backups of original or previously working configuration files. Keeping an edit history at the end of the file—listing who last edited the file, when it was edited, and what was changed—is a good way to track down problems as well as the source of those problems.

Controlling Access—The `ftpaccess` File

The `ftpaccess` file is the primary means of controlling who can access your server. Each line in the file controls either defines an attribute or sets its value.

The following commands control access:

- `class`
- `autogroup`
- `deny`
- `guestgroup`
- `limit`
- `loginfails`
- `private`

The following commands control the information the server shares with clients:

- `banner`
- `email`
- `message`
- `readme`

These commands control logging capabilities:

- `log commands`
- `log security`
- `log syslog`
- `log transfers`

The following are miscellaneous commands:

- `alias`
- `cdpath`
- `compress`
- `tar`
- `shutdown`

Permissions controls are set by the following commands:

- `chmod`
- `delete`
- `overwrite`
- `rename`
- `umask`

- `passwd-check`
- `path-filter`
- `upload`

Controlling User Access

The ability to control user access to your site is a critical component in fine-tuning your anonymous FTP server. The commands described in the following sections define the criteria used to determine in which group each user should be placed.

class

The `class` command defines a class of users who can access your FTP server. You can define as many classes as you want. Each `class` line comes in this form:

```
class <classname> <typelist> <addrglob> [<addrglob> ...]
```

<classname> is the name of the class you are defining, *<typelist>* is the type of user you are allowing into the class, and *<addrglob>* is the range of IP addresses allowed access to that class.

<typelist> is a comma-delimited list in which each entry has one of three values: `anonymous`, `guest`, or `real`. Anonymous users are, of course, any who connect to the server as user `anonymous` or `ftp` and want to access only publicly available files. Guest users are special because they do not have accounts on the system per se, but they do have special access to key parts of the guest group. (See the description of the `guestgroup` command later in this chapter for additional details.) Real users must have accounts on the FTP server and are authenticated accordingly.

<addrglob> takes the form of a regular expression where `*` implies all sites. Several *<addrglob>*s can be associated with a particular class.

The following line defines the class `anonclass`, which contains only anonymous users:

```
class anonclass anonymous *
```

These users can originate their connections from anywhere on the network.

On the other hand, this line

```
class localclass real 192.168.42.*
```

allows only real users who have accounts on the FTP server to access their accounts via FTP if they are coming from the Local Area Network (LAN). By default, both Debian and Red Hat enable use of `ftpaccess`. This means you'll need, at a minimum, the `all` `class` definition (for real, `guest` and `anonymous`) found in `ftpaccess`.

autogroup

The autogroup command provides tighter controls of anonymous users by automatically assigning them a certain group permission when they log in. The format of the autogroup line follows:

```
autogroup <groupname> <class> [<class> ...]
```

<groupname> is the name of the group to which you want the anonymous users set and <class> is the name of a class that is defined by using the class command. You can have multiple <class> entries for an autogroup. Only the anonymous users referenced in <class> will be affected by autogroup.

Remember, the group to which you are providing user permission must be in the /etc/group file.

deny

The deny command enables you to explicitly deny service to certain hosts based on their names, their IP addresses, or whether their hostnames can be reverse-resolved via DNS. The format of the deny command follows:

```
deny <addrglob> <message_file>
```

<addrglob> is a regular expression containing the addresses that are to be denied and <message_file> is the filename containing a message that should be displayed to the hosts when they connect.

The following is a sample deny line:

```
deny evilhacker.domain.com /home/ftp/.message.no.evil.hackers
```

This line displays the contents of the file /home/ftp/.message.no.evil.hackers to anyone trying to connect via FTP from evilhacker.domain.com. To deny users access based on whether their IP addresses can be reverse-resolved to their hostnames, use the string !nameserved for the <addrglob> entry.

guestgroup

The guestgroup command is useful when you want to provide your real users with restrictive FTP privileges. The format of the command follows:

```
guestgroup <groupname> [<groupname> ...]
```

<groupname> is the name of the restricted group (as taken from /etc/group).

When a user's group is restricted, the user is treated much like an anonymous visitor; thus, the user's account requires the same setups used for anonymous visitors. Also, the user's password entry is a little different in the directory field.

The field for the user's home directory is broken up by the /./ characters. The effective root directory is listed before the split characters, and the user's relative home directory is listed after the split characters. For example, consider the following password entry:

```
user1:encrypted password:500:128:User 1:/home/ftp/./user1:/bin/false
```

Here, /home/ftp is the user's new relative root directory (the bin, etc, pub, and lib directories are under the /home/ftp directory by default, and /home/ftp/user1 is the user's home directory. Note that the false command is used when user1 logs in; although the ftpaccess man page documents the use of ftponly, this command will not be found with Linux—use of the false command is considered an acceptable substitute. (Don't forget to put /bin/false in your system's /etc/shells file.)

Note

There are also differences between Linux distributions in the type and number of binary commands available under the /home/ftp/bin directory. For example, Red Hat Linux 6.0 provides the compress cpio, gzip, ls, sh, tar, and zcat commands, while OpenLinux offers only the gzip, ls, tar, and zcat commands. In both instances, the zcat command is a symbolic link to gzip.

limit

The limit command enables you to control the number of users according to class and time of day. This is especially useful if you have a popular archive but the system needs to be available to your users during business hours. The format of the limit command follows:

```
limit <class> <n> <times> <message_file>
```

<class> is the class to limit, <n> is the maximum number of people allowed in that class, <times> is the time during which the limit is in effect, and <message_file> is the file that will be displayed to the client when the maximum limit is reached.

The format of the <times> parameter is somewhat complex. The parameter is in the form of a comma-delimited string, where each option is for a separate day. The days Sunday through Saturday take the form Su, Mo, Tu, We, Th, Fr, and Sa, respectively, and all the weekdays can be referenced as Wk. Time should be kept in military format without a colon separating the hours and minutes. A range is specified by the dash character.

For example, you would use the following `limit` line to limit the class `anonfolks` to 10 users from Monday through Thursday, all day, and Friday from midnight to 5 p.m.:

```
limit anonfolks 10 MoTuWeTh,Fr0000-1700 /home/ftp/.message.too_many
```

If the limit is reached in this case, the contents of the file `/home/ftp/.message.too_many` are displayed to the connecting user.

loginfails

The `loginfails` command enables you to disconnect clients after they've reached your predetermined number of failed login attempts. By default, this number is five; however, you can set it by using this command:

```
loginfails <n>
```

<n> is the number of attempts. For example, the following line disconnects a user from the FTP server after three failed attempts:

```
loginfails 3
```

private

You might find it convenient to share files with other users via FTP without placing the file in a 100 percent public place or giving these users a real account on the server. The clients use the `SITE GROUP` and `SITE GPASS` commands so they can change to privileged groups that require passwords.

To provide your FTP server with this capability, set the `private` flag by using this command:

```
private <switch>
```

<switch> is either `YES` (to turn it on) or `NO` (to turn it off).

Because passwords are required for these special groups, you must use the `ftpgroups` file. The format of an access group in `ftpgroups` follows:

```
access_group_name:encrypted_password:real_group
```

access_group_name is the name the client uses to reference the special group, *encrypted_password* is the password users need to supply (via `SITE GPASS`) access to the group, and *real_group* is the actual group referenced in the `/etc/group` file.

Tip

Use the UNIX `crypt` function to create the*encrypted_password* entry. To simplify generating of the encrypted password, use the following Perl script:

```
#!/usr/bin/perl
srand( time() ^ ($$ + ($$ << 15)));
@salts= ('46' .. '57','65' .. '90','97' .. '122');
print "Enter password to encrypt: ";
chop ($password=<STDIN>);
print "The encrypted password is: ",crypt ( $password,
 ( chr ($salts[int(rand $#salts+1)] ) .
   chr ( $salts[int(rand $#salts+1) ] ))), "\n";
```

Controlling Banner Messages

The commands in this section enable you to provide messages to FTP users when they connect to your site, or when they specify a special action. These commands are a great way to make your site self-documenting.

banner

The `banner` command displays a sign onscreen before the client provides a login and password combination. This is an important opportunity to display your server's security policies, information on where to upload software, and instructions for anonymous users regarding login procedures and software location. The format of this command follows:

```
banner <path>
```

<path> is the full pathname of the file you want to display. Consider this example:

```
banner /home/ftp/.banner
```

email

The `email` command specifies the site maintainer's email address. Some error messages or information requests provide this email address on demand. The default value in the `ftpaccess` file is `root@localhost`.

The format of the `email` command follows:

```
email <address>
```

<address> is the full email address of the site maintainer.

It is recommended that you create an email alias named *FTP* that forwards to the system administrators. Also, it's a good idea to provide this kind of information in the sign-on banner, so users know who to contact if they cannot log in to the system.

message

The `message` command sets up special messages that are sent to the clients when they log in and when they change to a certain directory. You can specify multiple messages. Here is this command's format:

```
message <path> <when> {<class> ...}
```

<path> is the full pathname to the file that will be displayed, *<when>* is the condition under which to display the message, and *<class>* is a list of classes to which this message command applies.

The *<when>* parameter should take one of two forms: either `LOGIN` or `CWD=`*<dir>*. If it is `LOGIN`, the message is displayed upon a successful login. If the parameter is set to `CWD=`*<dir>*, the message is displayed when clients enter the *<dir>* directory.

The *<class>* parameter is optional. You can list multiple classes for a specific message. This capability is useful, for example, if you want specific messages sent only to anonymous users.

The message file itself (specified by *<path>*) can contain special flags that the FTP server substitutes with the appropriate information at runtime. These options are as follows:

Option	*Description*
`%T`	Local time
`%F`	Free space in the partition where *<dir>* is located
`%C`	Current working directory
`%E`	Site maintainer's email address (specified by the `email` command)
`%R`	Client hostname
`%L`	Server hostname
`%U`	Username provided at login time
`%M`	Maximum number of users allowed in the specified class
`%N`	Current number of users in specified class

Remember, when messages are triggered by an anonymous user, the message path needs to be relative to the anonymous FTP directory.

This is the Linux default message command defined in `ftpaccess` in Linux:

```
message /welcome.msg    login
```

No message file is defined. Use your favorite text editor to create your own welcome.msg and type in the following:

```
Welcome to %L, %U,
you are %N out of %M users.
It is %T.
```

This message will print the hostname and login name and tell the user the user's number, along with the local time. Save the file under the /home/ftp directory. When an anonymous user logs in, he will see this:

```
230-Welcome to presario.home.org, anonymous
230-you are 1 out of unlimited users.
230-It is Tue May 25 21:13:32 1999.
230-
230-
```

readme

The readme command specifies the conditions under which clients are notified that a certain file in their current directory was last modified. This command can take this form:

```
readme <path> <when> <class>
```

<path> is the name of the file about which you want to alert the clients (for example, README), *<when>* is similar to the *<when>* in the message command, and *<class>* is the classes for which this command applies. The *<when>* and *<class>* parameters are optional.

Remember, when you're specifying a path for anonymous users, the file must be relative to the anonymous FTP directory.

Controlling Logging

As with any complex network service, security quickly becomes an issue. To contend with possible threats, you must track connections and their corresponding commands. Use the commands that follow to determine how much, if any, logging should be done by the server software.

log commands

For security purposes, you probably want to log the actions of your FTP users. The log commands option enables you to do this. Each command invoked by the clients is sent to your log file. The format of the command follows:

```
log commands <typelist>
```

<*typelist*> is a comma-separated list specifying which kinds of users should be logged. The three kinds of users recognized are `anonymous`, `guest`, and `real`. (See the description of the `class` command earlier in this chapter for each user type's description.) For example, specify the following to log all the actions of `anonymous` and `guest` users:

```
log commands anonymous,guest
```

`log transfers`

If you want to log only clients' file transfers (rather than logging their entire sessions with the `log commands` statement), use `log transfers`. The format follows:

```
log transfers <typelist> <directions>
```

<*typelist*> is a comma-separated list specifying which kinds of users should be logged (`anonymous`, `guest`, or `real`); <*directions*> is a comma-separated list specifying which direction the transfer must take in order to be logged. The two directions you can choose to log are `inbound` and `outbound`.

For example, you would use the following to log all anonymous transfers that are both `inbound` and `outbound`:

```
log transfers anonymous inbound,outbound
```

The resulting logs are stored in `xferlog`. See the section in this chapter on this file for additional information.

Miscellaneous Server Commands

The following set of commands provides some miscellaneous configuration items. Each command adds a good deal of flexibility to the server, making it that much more useful to you as its administrator.

`alias`

The `alias` command defines directory aliases for your FTP clients. These aliases are activated when the clients use the `cd` command and specify an alias. This capability is useful for providing shortcuts to often-requested files. The command's format follows:

```
alias <string> <dir>
```

<*string*> is the alias and <*dir*> is the actual directory to which the users should be transferred. The following is an example of this command:

```
alias orb_discography /pub/music/ambient/orb_discography
```

Hence, if clients connect and use the command `cd orb_discography`, they are automatically moved to the `/pub/music/ambient/orb_discography` directory, regardless of their current locations.

cdpath

Similarly to the UNIX PATH environment variable, the cdpath command establishes a list of paths to check whenever clients invoke the cd command. The format of the cdpath command follows:

```
cdpath <dir>
```

<dir> is the server directory that is checked whenever clients use the cd command. Remember, for security reasons, specify directories relative to the FTP home directory for your anonymous users. An example of the cdpath command follows:

```
cdpath /pub/music
cdpath /pub/coffee
```

If clients type the command cd instant, the server examines the directories in the following order:

1. ./instant
2. Aliases called instant (For more information, see the description of alias earlier in this chapter.)
3. /pub/music/instant
4. /pub/coffee/instant

compress

The wu-ftpd server (the FTP server I have currently installed) offers a special compress feature that enables the server to compress or decompress a file before transmission. With this capability, a client who might not have the necessary software to decompress a file can still fetch it in a usable form. (For example, a file on your server is compressed using gzip, and a Windows client machine needs to get it but does not have the DOS version of gzip available.)

The compress command's format follows:

```
compress <switch> <classglob>
```

<switch> is either YES (to turn on this feature) or NO (to turn it off). <classglob> is a comma-separated list of classes to which this compress option applies.

There is, of course, a catch to using this command. You need to configure the ftpconversions file so the server knows which programs to use for certain file extensions. The default configuration supports compression by either /bin/compress or /bin/gzip.

For more information, see the section titled "Converting Files On-the-Fly—The ftpconversions File" later in this chapter.

tar

Almost identical to the `compress` option, `tar` specifies whether the server will tar and untar files for a client on demand. The format of this command follows:

```
tar <switch> <classglob>
```

<switch> is either `YES` (to turn it on) or `NO` (to turn it off). The *<classglob>* option is a comma-separated list of classes that is specified by the `tar` command.

Like the `compress` command, this feature is controlled by the `ftpconversions` file. For more information, see the section on `ftpconversions` later in this chapter.

shutdown

The `shutdown` command tells the server to periodically check for a particular file to see whether the server will be shut down. By default, the RPMs you installed invoke the FTP server whenever there is a request for a connection; therefore, you don't really need `shutdown`. On the other hand, if you intend to change the system so the server software is constantly running in the background, you might want to use `shutdown` to perform clean shutdowns and to notify users accessing the site.

The format of the `shutdown` command follows:

```
shutdown <path>
```

<path> is the full path of the file that contains shutdown information. When that file does become available, it is parsed out and the information gained from it dictates the behavior of the shutdown process, as well as the behavior of the `ftpshut` program (discussed later in this chapter). While there isn't any standard place for storing this file, you might find it logical to keep it in `ftpshutdown` with the other FTP configuration files. Make sure the file is readable by `root`.

Here is the format of the file:

```
<year> <month> <day> <hour> <minute> <deny_offset> <disconnect_offset> <text>
```

<year> is any year after 1970; *<month>* is from `0` to `11` to represent January to December, respectively; *<day>* is from `0` to `30`; *<hour>* is from `0` to `23`; and *<minute>* is from `0` to `59`. The `<deny_offset>` parameter specifies the time at which the server should stop accepting new connections in the form `HHMM`, where `HH` is the hour in military format and `MM` is the minute. *<disconnect_offset>* is the time at which existing connections are dropped; it is also in the form `HHMM`.

The *<text>* parameter is a free-form text block displayed to users to alert them of the impending shutdown. The text can follow the format of the `message` command (see the description of this command earlier in the chapter) and can have the following special character sequences available:

Option	*Description*
`%s`	The time the system will shut down
`%r`	The time new connections will be denied
`%d`	The time current connections will be dropped

Controlling Permissions

Along with controlling logins and maintaininglogs, you will need to tightly control the permissions of the files placed in the archive. The following commands specify what permissions should be set under certain conditions.

chmod

The `chmod` command determines whether a client has authorization to change permissions on the server's files by using the client's `chmod` command. The format of this command follows:

```
chmod <switch> <typelist>
```

`<switch>` is either `YES` (to turn it on) or `NO` (to turn it off). `<typelist>` is the comma-separated list of user types affected by this command. The user types available are `anonymous`, `guest`, and `real`.

delete

The `delete` command tells the server whether FTP clients are authorized to delete files that reside on the server. The command's format follows:

```
delete <switch> <typelist>
```

`<switch>` is either `YES` (to turn it on) or `NO` (to turn it off). `<typelist>` is the comma-separated list of user types affected by this command. The user types available are `anonymous`, `guest`, and `real`.

overwrite

Use the `overwrite` command to control whether FTP clients can upload files and replace existing files on the server. Here is the format:

```
overwrite <switch> <typelist>
```

`<switch>` is either `YES` (to turn it on) or `NO` (to turn it off). `<typelist>` is the comma-separated list of user types affected by this command. The user types available are `anonymous`, `guest`, and `real`.

rename

Client FTP software can send a `rename` request to the server to rename files. The `rename` command determines whether this request is acceptable. The format of this command follows:

```
rename <switch> <typelist>
```

<switch> is either `YES` (to turn it on) or `NO` (to turn it off). *<typelist>* is the comma-separated list of user types affected by this command. The user types available are `anonymous`, `guest`, and `real`.

umask

The `umask` command determines whether clients can change their default permissions in a fashion similar to the `umask` shell command. The format of the `umask` command follows:

```
umask <switch> <typelist>
```

<switch> is either `YES` (to turn it on) or `NO` (to turn it off). *<typelist>* is the comma-separated list of user types affected by this command. The user types available are `anonymous`, `guest`, and `real`.

passwd-check

Providing a valid email address as a password is considered good manners when connecting to an anonymous FTP site. The `passwd-check` command lets you determine how strictly you regulate the string submitted as an anonymous user's email address. The format of the command follows:

```
passwd-check <strictness> <enforcement>
```

<strictness> is one of three possible strings: `none`, `trivial`, or `rfc822`. *<enforcement>* is one of two possible strings: `warn` or `enforce`.

If you select `none` for *<strictness>*, the password isn't checked. `trivial` is slightly more demanding, requiring that at least `@` appears in the password. `rfc822` is most strict, requiring the email address to comply with the RFC-822 "Message Header Standard" (for example, `sshah@domain.com`).

By using `warn` as the *<enforcement>*, users are warned if they fail to comply with the strictness requirement, but they can still connect. `enforce`, on the other hand, denies connection until users submit acceptable passwords.

path-filter

If you allow users to upload files to your server via FTP, you might want to set acceptable filenames (for example, control characters in filenames are not acceptable). You can enforce this restriction by using the `path-filter` command. This is the command's format:

```
path-filter <typelist> <mesg> <allowed-regexp> <denied-regexp>
```

<typelist> is a comma-separated list of users that are affected by this command; the user types available are `anonymous`, `guest`, and `real`. *<mesg>* is the filename of the message that is displayed if the file does not meet this criteria. *<allowed-regexp>* is the regular expression the filename must meet in order to be approved for uploading. *<denied-regexp>* is the regular expression that, if met, causes the file to be explicitly denied; *<denied-regexp>* is an optional parameter.

For example, the following line displays the file `/ftp/.badfilename` to `anonymous` or `guest` users if they upload a file that doesn't begin with the string `UL` or that ends with the string `gif`:

```
path-filter anonymous,guest /ftp/.badfilename UL* gif$
```

upload

You can use the `upload` command, along with `path-filter`, to control the files that are placed on your server. The `upload` command determines the client's permissions for placing a file in a specific directory. This command also determines the file's permissions once it is placed in that directory. The format for `upload` follows:

```
upload <directory> <dirglob> <switch> <owner> <group> <mode> <mkdir>
```

<directory> is the directory that is affected by this command, *<dirglob>* is the regular expression used to determine whether a subdirectory under *<directory>* is a valid place to make an upload, and *<switch>* is either `YES` or `NO`, thereby establishing that an upload either can or cannot occur there. The *<owner>*, *<group>*, and *<mode>* parameters establish the file's owner, group, and permissions after the file is placed on the server. Finally, you can specify the *<mkdir>* option as either `dirs`—which is able to create subdirectories under the specified directory—or `nodirs`—which is unable to do this.

Here is a sample entry:

```
upload /home/ftp * no
upload /home/ftp /incoming yes ftp ftp 0775 nodirs
```

This example specifies that the `/home/ftp/incoming` directory (`/incoming` to the `anonymous` client) is the only location in which a file can be placed. After the file is placed in this directory, its owner becomes `ftp`, `group ftp`, and the permission is `775`.

The `nodirs` option at the end of the second line prevents the anonymous client from creating subdirectories under `/incoming`.

Tip

It is recommended that you set uploads to group ownership by `ftp` with a 775 file permission. This allows read-only access, so the `/incoming` directory doesn't become a trading ground for questionable material—for example, illegal software.

Converting Files On-the-Fly—The `ftpconversions` File

The format of the `ftpconversions` file follows:

```
<1>:<2>:<3>:<4>:<5>:<6>:<7>:<8>
```

`<1>` is the strip prefix; `<2>` is the strip postfix; `<3>` is an add-on prefix; `<4>` is an add-on postfix; `<5>` is the external command that invokes to perform the conversion; `<6>` is the type of file; `<7>` is the option information used for logging; and `<8>` is a description of the action.

Confused? Don't be. Each optionis actually quite simple. The following sections describe them one at a time.

The Strip Prefix

The *strip prefix* is the string at the beginning of a filename that should be removed when the file is fetched. For example, if you want a special action taken on files beginning with `discography.`, where that prefix is removed after the action, you would specify `.discography` for this option. When clients specify filenames, they should not include the strip prefix. That is, if a file is called `discography.orb` and a client issues the command `get orb`, the server performs the optional command on the file and then transfers the results to the client. Although documented, this feature is not currently supported.

The Strip Postfix

The *strip postfix* is the string at the end of the filename that should be removed when the file is fetched. The strip postfix is typically used to remove the trailing `.gz` from a gzipped file that is being decompressed before being transferred back to the client.

The Add-On Prefix

An *add-on prefix* is the string inserted before the filename when a file is transferred either to or from the server. For example, you might want to insert the string `uppercase.` to all files being pulled from the server that are being converted to uppercase. Although documented, this feature is not currently supported.

The Add-On Postfix

An *add-on postfix* is the string appended to a filename after an operation performed on the file is complete. This type of postfix is commonly used when the client issues the command `get` *`largefile`*`.gz`, where the actual filename is only `largefile`; in this case, the server compresses the file using `gzip` and then performs the transfer.

The External Command

The key component of each line is the *external command*. This entry specifies the program to be run when a file is transferred to or from the server. As the file is transferred, it is filtered through the program where *downloads* (files sent to the client) need to be sent to the standard out, and *uploads* (files sent to the server) will be coming from the standard in. For example, if you want to provide decompression with `gzip` for files being downloaded, the entry would look like this:

```
gzip -dc %s
```

The `%s` in the line tells the server to substitute the filename that is being requested by the user.

The `Type of File` Field

The `type of file` field for `ftpconversions` is a list of possible filetypes that can be acted on, with type names separated by the pipe symbol (¦). The three file types recognized are `T_REG`, `T_ASCII`, and `T_DIR`, which represent regular files, ASCII files, and directories, respectively. An example of this entry is `T_REG¦T_ASCII`.

The `Options` Field

The `options` field of `ftpconversions` is similar to the type of file field in that it is composed of a list of names separated by the pipe symbol (¦). The three types of options supported are `O_COMPRESS`, `O_UNCOMPRESS`, and `O_TAR`, which specify whether the command compresses files, decompresses files, and uses the `tar` command, respectively. A sample entry is `O_COMPRESS¦O_TAR`, which says the file is both compressed and tarred.

The Description of the Conversion

The last parameter of `ftpconversions`, the description of the conversion, is a free-form entry in which you can describe the type of conversion.

Example of an `ftpconversions` Entry

The following is a sample entry that compresses files using `gzip` on demand. This allows someone who wants to get the file `orb_discography.tar` to instead request the file `orb_discrography.tar.gz` and have the server compress the file by using `gzip` before sending it to him. The configuration line that does this follows:

```
: : :.gz:/bin/gzip -9 -c %s:T_REG:O_COMPRESS:GZIP
```

The first two parameters are not necessary because you don't want to remove anything from the filename before sending it to the requester. The third parameter is empty because you don't want to add any strings to the beginning of the filename before sending it. The fourth parameter, though, does have the string `.gz`, which add the `.gz` suffix to the file before sending it. The fifth parameter is the actual command used to compress the file, where the `-9` option tells `gzip` to compress the file as much as it can, `-c` sends the compressed file to the standard output, and `%s` is replaced by the server from which the filename is requested (for example, `orb_discography.tar`). `T_REG` in the sixth parameter tells the server to treat the file as a normal file rather than an ASCII file or directory. The second-to-last parameter, `O_COMPRESS`, tells the server that the action being taken is file compression. The last parameter is simply a comment for the administrator so she can quickly determine the action being taken.

A bit daunting, isn't it? Don't worry, the sample `ftpconversions` file that came with the server package provides additional examples of using `tar` and `gzip`. In fact, most sites never need to add to this file because it covers the most popular conversion requests made.

Configuring Host Access—The `ftphosts` File

The `ftphosts` file rules on a per-user basis, determining whether users are allowed to log in from specific hosts.

Each line in the file can be one of two commands:

```
allow <username> <addrglob>
```

```
deny <username> <addrglob>
```

The `allow` command lets the user specified in `<username>` to connect via FTP from the explicitly listed addresses in `<addrglob>`. You can list multiple addresses.

The deny command explicitly denies the specified user <*username*> (or to deny anonymous access where *username* is *ftp*) access from the sites listed in <*addrglob*>. You can list multiple sites.

The FTP Log File—xferlog

Although xferlog isn't a configuration file, it plays an important role because all the logs generated by the FTP server are stored in this file. Each line of the log is described in Table 10.1.

TABLE 10.1 *xferlog* Fields

Log Field	*Definition*
current-time	The current time in DDD MMM dd hh:mm:ss YYYY format, where DDD is the day of the week, MMM is the month, dd is the day of the month, hh:mm:ss is the time in military format, and YYYY is the year.
transfer-time	The total time, in seconds, spent transferring the file.
remote-host	The hostname of the client that initiated the transfer.
file-size	The size of the file that was transferred.
filename	The name of the file that was transferred.
transfer-type	The type of transfer done, where a is an ASCII transfer and b is a binary transfer.
special-action-flag	A list of actions taken on the file by the server, where C means the file was compressed, U means the file was uncompressed, T means the file was tarred, and - means no action was taken.
direction	A flag indicating whether the file was outgoing or incoming, represented by o or i, respectively.
access-mode	The type of user who performed the action, where a is anonymous, g is a guest, and r is a real user.
username	The local username if the user was of type real.
service-name	The name of the service being invoked (most often FTP).
authentication-method	The type of authentication used: 0 means no authentication was done (anonymous user) and 1 means the user was validated with RFC-931 Authentication Server Protocol.
authenticated-user-id	The username by which this transfer was authenticated.
completion-status	(c)omplete or (i)ncomplete file transfer status.

FTP Administrative Tools

Several tools are available to help you administer your FTP server. These tools were automatically installed as part of the package when the server was installed. These utilities help you see the current status of the server and control its shutdown procedure:

- `ftpshut`
- `ftpwho`
- `ftpcount`

ftpshut

The `ftpshut` command eases the FTP server's shutdown procedures. This capability, of course, applies only if you are running the server all the time—instead of leaving it to be invoked from `inetd` as needed. The format of `ftpshut` follows:

```
ftpshut -l <login-minutes> -d <drop-minutes> <time> <warning message>
```

<login-minutes> is the number of minutes before server shutdown that the server will begin refusing new FTP transactions. *<drop-minutes>* is the number of minutes before server shutdown that the server will begin dropping existing connections. The default value for *<login-minutes>* is `10`, and the default for *<drop-minutes>* is `5`.

<time> is the time the server will be shut down. You can specify this time one of three ways. The first is to specify the time in military format without the colon (for example, `0312` to indicate 3:12 a.m.). The second is to specify the number of minutes to wait before shutting down. The format of this method is `+`*<min>*, where *<min>* is the number of minutes to wait (for example, `+60` shuts the server down in 60 minutes). The last option is the most drastic; if you specify the string `now`, the server shuts down immediately.

<warning message> is the message displayed to all FTP clients, instructing them that the server will be shut down. See the description of the `shutdown` command for the `ftpaccess` file earlier in this chapter for details on the formatting available for the warning message.

ftpwho

`ftpwho` displays all the active FTP users on the system. The output of the command is in the format of the `/bin/ps` command. The format of this command follows:

```
<pid> <tty> <stat> <time> <connection details>
```

<pid> is the process ID of the FTP daemon handling the transfer; *<tty>* is always a question mark (?) because the connection is coming from FTP, not Telnet. *<stat>* is the status of that particular instance of the daemon, where S means it's sleeping, Z means it has crashed (*gone zombie*), and R means it's the currently running process. *<time>* indicates how much actual CPU time that instance of the FTP has taken. Finally, *<connection details>* tells where the connection is coming from, who the user is, and that user's current function.

The following is an example of output from ftpwho:

```
Service class all:
10448  ?  S   0:00 ftpd: vestax.domain.com: anonymous/sshah@domain.com: IDLE
10501  ?  S   0:00 ftpd: toybox.domain.com: heidi: RETR mklinux-ALL.sit.bin
   -    2 users ( -1 maximum)
```

Here you can see that two users are logged in. (An unlimited number of users are allowed to connect.) The first user is an anonymous user who claims to be sshah@domain.com and is currently not performing any functions. The second user, who has the username heidi, is currently retrieving the file mklinux-ALL.sit.bin.

ftpcount

ftpcount, which is a simplified version of ftpwho, shows the current total of users in each class defined in ftpaccess. A sample output from ftpcount shows the following:

```
Service class all                         -    2 users ( -1 maximum)
```

Using FTP Clients

This section introduces you to several of the FTP clients included with various Linux distributions. Although the venerable ftp command has remained the standard network file transfer utility and tool of choice for millions of users worldwide, there's always room for improvement. However, the ftp command has a number of features, many of which users might not be aware.

Most new and experienced Linux users know how to access remote FTP servers by using ftp on the command line along with the name of a remote computer (as described at the beginning of this chapter). You can also speed up anonymous log-ins by using FTP's -a command-line option.

Debian users may be interested in the `wget` package. `wget` can download software using FTP or HTTP with a single command line, such as this:

```
wget ftp://aptiva.home.org/home/bball/happy2.jpg
```

Red Hat users may use the Red Hat `ftp` client to achieve the same effect for FTP servers:

```
ftp ftp://aptiva.home.org/home/bball/happy.jpg
```

Note that, although some of these utilities permit specifying passwords on the command line, doing so can pose a security risk and is therefore not recommended.

Another `ftp` command feature is `.netrc`. You can use it to accomplish the same task as the preceding command-line example. First, use your favorite text editor to create the file `.netrc` in your home directory; then enter a series of auto-login lines similar to this:

```
machine aptiva.home.org
login bball
password mypassword
macdef init
get happy2.jpg
bye
```

The first line in the file uses the `machine` keyword to specify a remote computer. The next two lines specify your remote `login` and `password`. The `macdef` and `init` keywords specify the start of an auto-executing macro. Any FTP commands placed following these keywords and two blank lines are executed. In this example, the `get` command is used to retrieve the file `happy2.jpg`, and the `bye` command is used to quit the connection.

Save the `.netrc` file and exit your editor. Next, use the `chmod` command to give the file read and write permissions of `600`, like this:

```
# chmod 600 .netrc
```

Finally, to test your `.netrc` file, use **`ftp`** with the hostname of the remote computer on the command line:

```
# ftp aptiva
Connected to aptiva.home.org.
220 aptiva.home.org FTP server (Version wu-2.4.2-academ[BETA-18](1)
 Mon Aug 3 19:17:20 EDT 1998) ready.
331 Password required for bball.
230 User bball logged in.
get happy2.jpg
local: happy2.jpg remote: happy2.jpg
227 Entering Passive Mode (192,168,2,36,5,0)
150 Opening ASCII mode data connection for happy2.jpg (34636 bytes).
100% |*******************************************| 34718      00:00 ETA
226 Transfer complete.
34718 bytes received in 0.05 seconds (696.50 KB/s)
bye
221 Goodbye.
```

As you can see, the .netrc file connected, logged in, retrieved the file, and quit the connection. You can use this approach to regularly retrieve files from remote computers (such as weather maps), to regularly upload files to remote sites (such as Web page directories), or to automate other file transfer tasks (such as regular, remote transfers of system logs through crontab entries).

autoexpect

The tool-rich Linux environment features many different software tools (such as expect) that you can use to accomplish difficult tasks. Yet another way to automate file transfers (and other tasks) is with the autoexpect command. The autoexpect command (packaged and installed with the expect rpm) will create an expect script to accomplish tasks performed during an autoexpect session.

To automate an FTP transfer, use the autoexpect command's -f command-line option, followed by the name of the desired command, and an initial command line:

```
# autoexpect -f eftp ftp aptiva.home.org
autoexpect started, file is eftp
Connected to aptiva.home.org.
220 aptiva.home.org FTP server (Version wu-2.4.2-academ[BETA-18](1)
Mon Aug 3 19:17:20 EDT 1998) ready.
Name (aptiva:): bball
bball
331 Password required for bball.
Password:mypassword

230 User bball logged in.
Remote system type is UNIX.
Using binary mode to transfer files.
ftp> get happy2.jpg
get happy2.jpg
local: happy2.jpg remote: happy2.jpg
227 Entering Passive Mode (192,168,2,36,5,64)
150 Opening BINARY mode data connection for happy2.jpg (34636 bytes).
100% |*************************************************
③| 34636       00:00 ETA
226 Transfer complete.
34636 bytes received in 0.03 seconds (1.10 MB/s)
ftp> bye
bye
221 Goodbye.
autoexpect done, file is eftp
```

This session creates an executable file named eftp, which connects to the remote computer, logs in, retrieves the file happy2.jpg, and then disconnects. To perform the automatic FTP session, type **eftp** on the command line:

```
# ./eftp
```

Tip

If the generated program works too fast, open the file (it is an `expect` command script) and look for this line:

```
set force_conservative 0  ;# set to 1 to force conservative mode even if
                          ;# script wasn't run conservatively originally
```

Change the `force_conservative` setting to `1` and then save the file. This slows the script to allow for slower connections.

ncftp

The `ncftp` command is another attempt at improving the `ftp` command. This program features utilities that help when building shell scripts to automate file retrieval, and offers a pseudo-graphical interface for FTP transfer from the shell command line. According to NcFTP's author, Mike Gleason, this command has a number of unique features:

- Auto-resume downloads
- Background processing
- Bookmarks
- Cached directory listings
- Command-line editing
- Downloading entire directory trees
- Filename completion
- Host redialing
- Progress meters
- Working with firewalls, proxies, and more

In its simplest form, `ncftp` may be used just like the `ftp` command, with the name of a remote computer:

```
# ncftp aptiva.home.org
```

For more details about `ncftp`, see its man page or the documentation under the `/usr/doc/ncftp` directory.

xtp

Like `ftp` and may `ncftp`, John Cristy's `xtp` command (not included with Caldera OpenLinux) may be used to log in and automatically retrieve one or more files from remote computers. For example, use the xtp command with a complete FTP command-line address like this:

```
# xtp ftp://bball@aptiva.home.org//home/bball/happy2.jpg
```

This logs in to the remote FTP server with your username (you'll be prompted for your password), then retrieves the file happy2.jpg and quits the connection. The xtp command has a number of command-line options. For details, see the xtp man page, or use the text-only lynx Web browser to read xtp's online documentation, like this:

```
# lynx /usr/doc/Image*/www/xtp.html
```

gFTP

Brian Masney's gFTP client is anan easy-to-use interface to FTP file transfers. You can start this client during an Enlightenment X11 session by clicking the Main Menu button in the GNOME Panel, selecting Internet, and then clicking the gftp menu item. You can also start gftp from the command line and specify a remote computer:

```
# gftp aptiva.home.org
```

The gFTP client will start, as shown in Figure 10.1.

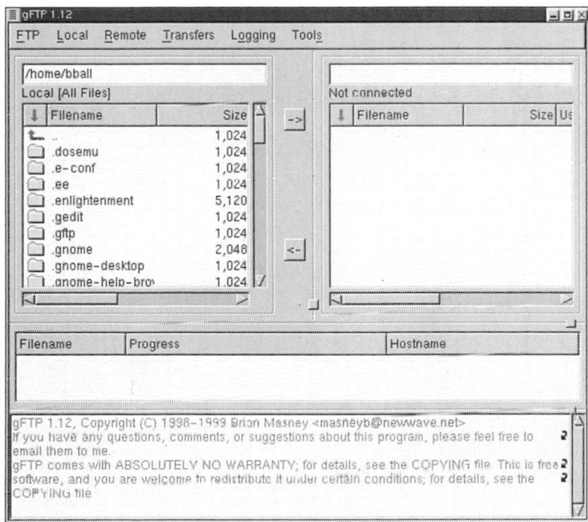

FIGURE 10.1
The gFTP client supports FTP file transfers with the click of a mouse, and it even supports drag-and-drop file transfers.

Like other FTP clients, the gftp command supports direct logins. The general syntax for the gftp command line follows:

```
# gftp [[ftp://][user:pass@]ftp-site[:port][/directory]]
```

This shows that you can use optional keywords, such as `ftp://`, along with a username, password, particular port number for the remote FTP server, and a destination directory for file transfers. Using this syntax, you can start an FTP session in your directory on a remote computer:

```
# gftp ftp://bball@aptiva.home.org/home/bball
```

This logs you in to your remote computer and uses a home directory for file transfers.

The `gFTP` main window (refer to Figure 10.1) features a menu bar with six drop-down menus, two directory windows for the local computer (on the left) and the remote computer (on the right), a progress window (showing the computer's filename, progress, and hostname), and a scrolling session window showing current activity.

The FTP menu is used to specify the type of file transfers and other options. The Local menu manipulates files and directories, while the Remote menu connects, disconnects, changes servers, and manipulates remote files and directories. Choosing to connect under the Remote menu produces the Connection Manager (see Figure 10.2). Use this dialog box to set up and save favorite FTP sites or logins.

FIGURE 10.2
The `gFTP` Connection Manager is used to initiate connections to remote computers for FTP transfers.

The Transfers menu controls the transfer session and uploads (or downloads) files. The Logging menu can be used to keep track of your FTP session. The Tools menu compares the local and remote directories and highlights files that aren't found in both windows. This can make synchronizing file directories between computers a snap!

After you connect, files are transferred between the local and remote computers by clicking a file and then clicking the appropriate direction arrow in the `gFTP` dialog box. This sends (or receives) files between computers. Another `gFTP` feature, when used during GNOME-enabled X11 sessions, is drag-and-drop. This means that you can transfer files to a remote computer by clicking and dragging a file from the desktop of the GNU Midnight Commander, then releasing the file onto the remote computer's file listing window.

Aside from a README file under the /usr/doc/gftp directory, you won't find any documentation for the gFTP client on your system. For the latest developments concerning gFTP, go to http://www.newwave.net/~masneyb.

Note

Both Caldera OpenLinux and Red Hat Linux offer other graphical clients you can use for FTP file transfers. For example, Netscape Communicator and the lynx Web browser accept FTP-type Uniform Resource Locator addresses, such as this:

```
ftp://ftp.caldera.com
```

KDE users with an active Internet connection, or who are connected to a LAN can also use the URL area of a number of KDE clients, such as the kfm file manager, to connect to a remote computer.

Summary

You might think the proliferation of the World Wide Web would make FTP servers extinct, but that is not the case. People are still deploying FTP sites in full force because of the ease with which they can be established and maintained. No cute HTML, no extra work—just put the file in the right place for downloading and let people get it.

The wealth of FTP clients and transfer tools available for Linux will make the job of transferring a large number of files between computers on a network a lot easier.

This chapter covered, in great detail, configuring the wu-ftpd server. The key points to remember when working with the FTP server are as follows:

- Keep a good watch on security announcements related to FTP servers, especially the wu-ftpd server.
- Monitor your logs for suspicious activity.
- Test your configuration carefully. With a large number of options available, make sure your server behaves the way you intended.
- When setting up file owners and permissions, be sure the permissions are correct.
- Use plenty of messages to help make your server self-documenting to outside users.

CHAPTER 11

Apache Server

IN THIS CHAPTER

This chapter covers the installation, configuration, and administration of the Apache Web server.

Apache is the most widely used Web server on the Internet today, according to the NetCraft survey of Web sites. The name Apache appeared during the early development of the software because it was "a patchy" server, made out of patches for the freely available source code of the NCSA HTTPd Web server. For a while after the NCSA HTTPd project was discontinued, a number of people wrote a variety of patches for the code, either to fix bugs or to add features that they wanted. There was a lot of this code floating around and people were freely sharing it, but it was completely unmanaged. After a while, Bob Behlendorf set up a centralized repository of these patches, and the Apache project was born. The project is still composed of a rather small core group of programmers, but anyone is welcome to submit patches to the group for possible inclusion in the code.

In the last year, there has been a surge of interest in the Apache project, partially buoyed by the new interest in Open Source. It's also due, in part, to IBM's announcement that it was going to devote substantial resources to the project because it made more sense to use an established, proven Web server than to try to write its own. The consequences of this interest have been a stable version for the Windows NT operating system and an accelerated release schedule.

The best places to find out about Apache are the Apache Group's Web site, `http://www.apache.org/`, and the Apache Week Web site, `http://www.apacheweek.com/`, where you can subscribe to receive Apache Week by email to keep up on the latest developments in the project.

Tip

In addition to the extensive online documentation, you will also find the complete documentation for Apache in the HTML directory of your Apache server. You can access this documentation by looking at `http://localhost/manual/`, on your new Red Hat system, `file:/home/httpd/apache/doc` on your new Caldera system, or `http://localhost/doc/apache` on your new Debian system. You can open these URLs with Netscape or Lynx, which can also be installed on your system.

Red Hat, Caldera, and the Debian distributions all ship with a version of Apache, but their version is typically several versions old due to Apache's rapid release schedule. You can obtain Apache as an RPM (Red Hat Package Manager) installation file from `http://rufus.w3.org/linux/RPM/`, as a `.deb` from `ftp://ftp.debian.org/debian`, or you can get the source code from the Apache Web site and, in true Linux tradition, build it for yourself.

This chapter covers Apache version 1.3.4+. Red Hat 6.0 ships with 1.3.6, Debian 2.1 with 1.3.3 (an update to 1.3.6 can be found online at `http://netgod.net/x/`) and Caldera 2.2 ships with 1.3.4.

Server Installation

You can install Apache with RPM/DEB or by building the source code yourself. The Apache source builds on just about any *nix operating system, and also on Win32.

Installing from the RPM

You can find the Apache RPM either on your distributions CD-ROM or from `http://rufus.w3.org/linux/RPM/`. You can install it with the command-line `rpm` tool, as you do any other RPM by typing the following:

```
rpm -Uvh latest_apache.rpm
```

where *`latest_apache.rpm`* is the name of the Apache RPM file.

The Apache RPM installs files in the following directories:

- `/etc/httpd/conf` (on Red Hat)

  `/etc/httpd/apache/conf` (on Caldera)

  This directory contains all the Apache configuration files, which include `access.conf`, `httpd.conf`, and `srm.conf`. See the section on configuration files later in this chapter.

- `/etc/rc.d/`

  The tree under this directory contains the system startup scripts. The Apache RPM installs a complete set for the Web server. These scripts, which you can use to start and stop the server from the command line, will also automatically start and stop the server when the workstation is halted, started, or rebooted.

- `/home/httpd/` (from the RPM)

  The RPM installs the default server icons, CGI programs, and HTML files in this location. If you want to keep Web content elsewhere, you can do so by making the appropriate changes in the server configuration files.

- `/usr/doc` and `/usr/man`

  The RPM contains manual pages and `readme` files, which are placed in these directories. As is the case for most RPM packages, the `readme` file and other related documentation is placed in a directory under `/usr/doc` that is named for the Apache server version.

- /usr/sbin

  The executable programs are placed in this directory. This includes the server executable itself.

- /var/log/http

  The server log files are placed in this directory. By default, there are two log files—access_log and error_log—but you can define any number of custom logs containing a variety of information. See the section on logging later in this chapter.

Note

If you are upgrading to a newer version of Apache, RPM will not write over your current configuration files. RPM moves your current files and appends the extension .rpmnew to them. For example, srm.conf becomes srm.conf.rpmnew. Don't underestimate the importance of a good backup. Before upgrading anything on a server you care about, always make a backup.

Installing from the .deb

To install the full Apache system on your Debian machine, run the following:

```
apt-get install apache apache-doc
```

Debian installs the files into the following locations:

/etc/apache for the configuration files

/etc/init.d contains the startup script.

/var/www is the document root for the Web server.

/usr/sbin holds the server binaries.

/var/log/apache contains the Apache log files.

Building the Source Yourself

There are two ways to install from the source—the old, familiar way and the new, easy way.

Both start the same way—you download the source from http://www.apache.org/ and unroll the tar file in a temporary directory somewhere nice, like /tmp. This will create a directory called apache_*version_number*, where *version_number* is the version that you have downloaded. For example, apache_1.3.6.

The Easy Way

To install Apache the easy way, just run the `./configure` in the directory just created. You can provide it with a `--prefix` argument to install in a directory other than the default `/usr/local/apache/`.

```
./configure --prefix=/preferred/directory/
```

This will create a file called `Configuration` in the `src/` subdirectory. It also generates the makefile that will be used to compile the server code.

Once this step is done, type **`make`** and then **`make install`** to compile the server code. Finally, type **`/usr/local/apache/bin/apachectl start`** to start the Web server process. If you used the `--prefix` parameter, change `/usr/local/apache/` to whatever path you provided.

> **Note**
>
> The Apache Autoconf-style interface (APACI), described here, is only available in version 1.3 and later.

The Old Way

If you want to do things the old-fashioned way, or you just want more control over the way that your server is built, follow these steps.

In the source directory, copy the file `Configuration.tmpl` to `Configuration` and open up `Configuration` with your favorite editor. Modify the compiler flags if, and only if, you know what you're doing. Uncomment those modules that you would like included, comment out modules that you don't want, or add lines for custom modules that you have written or acquired elsewhere.

Now, run the `Configure` script to create the makefile.

Finally, compile and install the server with `make` and `make install`.

> **Tip**
>
> You may want to symlink the existing file locations, listed in the RPM or Debian installation section earlier in this chapter, to the new locations of the files because the default install locations are not the same as when the RPM or Debian package installs the files. Failure to do this could result in your Web server process not being started at system startup.
>
> *continues*

I would recommend that you stick with the RPM or Debian package until you really know your way around what happens at system startup. Of course, you've already read about this, so you already know all about that.

File Locations After Manual Installation

As of version 1.3.4, all of the files are placed in various subdirectories of `/usr/local/apache` (or whatever directory you specified with the `--prefix` parameter). Before version 1.3.4, files were placed in `/usr/local/etc/httpd`.

- `/usr/local/apache/conf`—This directory contains all the Apache configuration files, which include `access.conf`, `httpd.conf`, and `srm.conf`. See the section on configuration files later in this chapter.
- `/usr/local/apache`—The `cgi-bin`, `icons`, and `htdocs` subdirectories contain the CGI programs, standard icons, and default HTML documents, respectively.
- `/usr/local/apache/bin`—The executable programs are placed in this directory.
- `/usr/local/apache/logs`—The server log files are placed in this directory. By default, there are two log files—`access_log` and `error_log`—but you can define any number of custom logs containing a variety of information. See the section on logging later in this chapter.

At this point, you have successfully installed the Apache server one way or another. It will run, but perhaps not quite the way that you want it to. The next section will talk about configuring the server so that it works exactly how you want it to work.

Runtime Server Configuration Settings

Traditionally, Apache had the runtime configurations in three files: `httpd.conf`, `access.conf`, and `srm.conf`. This was mainly because that's how the config files were written for NCSA, and Apache grew out of NCSA. And while there was some logic behind the original decision to split configuration options into three files, this made less and less sense over time—especially since you could put any configuration option in any file and it would work.

Starting with Apache 1.3.4, the runtime configurations are stored in just one file—`httpd.conf`. The other files are still there, but they contain only a comment telling you that the files are there for purely historical reasons and that you should really put all of your configuration in `httpd.conf`.

You should note, however, that while the RPM and Debian versions typically have the configuration still split into three files, this chapter assumes that you will combine your configuration files into one.

> **Note**
>
> You can still use the three-configuration-file approach if you really want to. It makes sense to some people. However, the distinction between what should go in one file or another has become increasingly blurred over the years.

Apache reads the data from the configuration file(s) when the process is started (or restarted). You can cause the Apache process to reload configuration information with the command `httpd reload`. We'll discuss this later in this chapter in the section on starting and stopping your server.

You perform runtime configuration of your server with *configuration directives*, which are commands that set some option. You use them to tell the server about various options that you want to enable, such as the location of files important to the server configuration and operation. Configuration directives follow this syntax:

```
directive option option...
```

You specify one directive per line. Some directives only set a value such as a filename, while others let you specify various options. Some special directives, called *sections*, look like HTML tags. Section directives are surrounded by angle brackets, such as `<directive>`. Sections usually enclose a group of directives that apply only to the directory specified in the section:

```
<Directive somedir/in/your/tree>
  directive option option
  directive option option
</directive>
```

All sections are closed with a matching section tag that looks like `</directive>`. Note that section tags, like any other directives, are specified one per line.

Editing `httpd.conf`

Most of the default settings in the config files are okay to keep, particularly if you have installed the server in a default location and are not doing anything unusual on your server. In general, if you don't understand what a particular directive is for, you should leave it set to the default value.

Tip

If you would like to use the single-file configuration but are using version 1.3.3 or earlier, you can still do this by simply concatenating the three files:

```
cat srm.conf >> httpd.conf
cat access.conf >> httpd.conf
```

Then make sure that `srm.conf` and `access.conf` are empty.

For those that want to keep using the three-file system, we've noted in the following list when these files appeared in `srm.conf` or `access.conf` prior to version 1.3.4.

The following are some of the settings that you might want to change.

`ServerType` This is mentioned more as a curiosity than anything else. The two server types are `standalone` and `inetd`. You will want this to be `standalone` in almost every imaginable case. Setting the `ServerType` to `inetd` will cause a new server to be spawned to handle every incoming HTTP request. That server will then die off immediately when the request has been served. This is presumably useful for testing configuration changes because the configuration files will be reloaded each time a new server process is spawned. Of course, this is extremely slow, since you have the overhead of server startup with every request.

`ServerRoot` This directive sets the absolute path to your server directory. It tells the server where to find all the resources and configuration files. Many of these resources are specified in the configuration files relative to the `ServerRoot` directory.

Your `ServerRoot` directive should be set to `/etc/httpd` for Red Hat or to `/etc/httpd/apache` for Caldera. If you installed the RPM, set it to `/etc/apache` for Debian. Set it to `/usr/local/apache` if you installed from the source.

`Port` The `Port` directive indicates which port you want your server to run on. By default, this is set to 80, which is the standard HTTP port number. You may want to run your server on another port, such as for running a test server that you don't want people to find by accident. (Don't confuse this with real security!)

`User` and `Group` The `User` and `Group` directives should be set to the user ID (UID) and group ID (GID) that the server will use to process requests. Generally, you will want to leave these settings as the defaults: `nobody` and `nobody`. Verify that the user `nobody` and the group `nobody` exist in your `/etc/passwd` and `/etc/group` files, respectively. (They are usually provided by your distribution, so they should already be defined.) If a `nobody` group does not exist, use the `nogroup` group instead. If you want to use a different UID or GID, you need to be aware that the server will run with the permissions of the user and group defined here. This means that in the event of a security breach, whether on the server or (more likely) on your own CGI programs, those programs will run with the assigned UID. If the server runs as `root` or some other privileged user, someone can exploit the security holes and do nasty things to your site. Always think in terms of the specified user running a command like `rm -rf /`, and that should convince you that leaving this as `nobody` and `nobody` is probably a good thing.

Instead of specifying the `User` and `Group` directives using names, you can specify them using the UID and GID numbers. If you use numbers, be sure that the numbers you specify correspond to the user and group you want and that they are preceded by the pound (#) symbol.

Here's how these directives look if specified by name:

```
User nobody
Group nobody
```

Here's the same specification by UID and GID:

```
User #-1
Group #-1
```

If you plan on specifying UID and GID directly, please check your `/etc/passwd` and `/etc/group` files and use UID and GID listed there. The UID and GID for these groups varies by distribution, and the UID and GID listed above may not be correct for your particular installation.

`ServerAdmin` The `ServerAdmin` directive should be set to the address of the Webmaster managing the server. It should be a valid email address or alias, such as *`webmaster@yourdomain.com`*. Setting this value to a valid address is important because this address will be returned to a visitor when a problem occurs on the server.

`ServerName` The `ServerName` directive sets the hostname the server will return. Set it to a fully qualified domain name. For example, set it to `www.your_domain.com` rather than simply `www`. This is particularly important if this machine will be accessible from the Internet rather than just on your local network. You really do not need to set this unless you want a different name returned than the machine's canonical name. If this value is not set, the server will figure out the name by itself and set it to its canonical name. However, you might want the server to return a friendlier address, such as `intranet.website.for.`*`your.domain`*. Whatever you do, `ServerName` should be a real Domain Name System (DNS) name for your network. If you are administering your own DNS server, remember to add an alias for your host. If someone else manages the DNS for you, ask that person to set this name for you.

`DocumentRoot` Set this directive to the absolute path of your document tree, which is the top directory from which Apache will serve files. By default, it is set to `/home/httpd/html` (for Red Hat), `/home/httpd/htdocs` (for Caldera), `/var/www` (for Debian) or, if you built the source code yourself, `/usr/local/apache/htdocs`. Prior to version 1.3.4, this directive appears in `srm.conf`.

`UserDir` This directive defines the directory relative to a local user's home directory where that user can put public HTML documents. It's relative because each user will have his own HTML directory. The default setting for this directive is `public_html`. Each user will be able to create a directory called `public_html` under his home directory, and HTML documents placed in that directory will be available as `http://servername/~username`, where *`username`* is the username of the particular user. Prior to version 1.3.4, this directive appears in `srm.conf`.

`DirectoryIndex` The `DirectoryIndex` directive indicates which file should be served as the index for a directory, such as which file should be served if the URL `http://www.server.com/Directory/` is requested. It is often useful to put a list of files here so that, in the event that `index.html` (the default values) is not found, another file can be served instead. The most useful application of this is to have a CGI program run as the default action in a directory. In this case, the directive would look like `DirectoryIndex index.html index.cgi`. Prior to version 1.3.4, this directive appears in `srm.conf`.

Caution

Allowing individual users to put Web content on your server poses several important security considerations. If you are operating a Web server on the Internet rather than on a private network, you should read the WWW Security FAQ by Lincoln Stein. You can find a copy at `http://www.genome.wi.mit.edu/WWW/faqs/www-security-faq.html`.

`.htaccess` Files and Access Restrictions

Almost any directive that appears in the configuration files can appear in an `.htaccess` file. This file, specified in the `AccessFileName` directive in `httpd.conf` (or `srm.conf` prior to version 1.3.4), sets configurations on a per-directory basis. As the system administrator, you can specify both the name of this file and which of the server configurations may be overridden by the contents of this file. This is especially useful for sites where there are multiple content providers and you want to control what these people can do with their space.

To limit what `.htaccess` files can override, use the `AllowOverride` directive. This can be set globally or per directory. To configure which options are available by default, use the `Options` directive.

Note

Prior to version 1.3.4, these directives appear in the access.conf file.

For example, you will see the following in your httpd.conf file:

```
# Each directory to which Apache has access can be configured with respect
# to which services and features are allowed and/or disabled in that
# directory (and its subdirectories).
#
# First, we configure the "default" to be a very restrictive set of
# permissions.
#
<Directory />
    Options FollowSymLinks
    AllowOverride None
</Directory>
```

Options Directives

Options can be None, All, or any combination of Indexes, Includes, FollowSymLinks, ExecCGI, or MultiViews. MultiViews is not included in All and must be specified explicitly. These options are explained in the following table.

None	None of the available options is enabled for this directory.
All	All of the available options, except for MultiViews, are enabled for this directory.
Indexes	In the absence of an index.html file or another DirectoryIndex file, a listing of the files in the directory will be generated as an HTML page for display to the user.
Includes	Server Side Includes (SSI) are permitted in this directory. This can also be written as IncludesNoExec if you want to allow includes, but don't want to allow the exec option in these includes. For security reasons, this is usually a good idea in directories over which you do not have complete control, such as UserDir directories.
FollowSymLinks	Allow access to directories that are symbolically linked to a document directory. This is usually a bad idea, and you should not set this globally for the whole server. You might want to set this for individual directories, but only if you have a really good reason to do so. This option is a potential security risk because it allows a Web user to escape from the document directory, and it could potentially allow the user access to portions of your file system where you really don't want people poking around.
ExecCGI	CGI programs are permitted in this directory, even if it is not a ScriptAliased directory.
MultiViews	This is part of the mod_negotiation module. When the document that the client requests is not found, the server tries to figure out which document best suits the client's requirements. See http://www.apache.org/docs/mod/mod_negotiation.html or the same document on your local copy of the Apache documentation.

Note

These directives also affect all subdirectories of the specified directory.

`AllowOverrides` Directives

The `AllowOverrides` directives specify which options `.htaccess` files can override. You can set this per directory. For example, you can have different standards about what can be overridden in the main document root and in `UserDir` directories.

This capability is particularly useful for user directories, where the user does not have access to the main server configuration files.

`AllowOverrides` can be set to be `All` or any combination of `Options`, `FileInfo`, `AuthConfig`, and `Limit`. These options are explained in the following table.

`Options`	The `.htaccess` file can add options not listed in the `Options` directive for this directory.
`FileInfo`	The `.htaccess` file can include directives for modifying document type information.
`AuthConfig`	The `.htaccess` file may contain authorization directives.
`Limit`	The `.htaccess` file may contain `allow`, `deny`, and `order` directives.

Virtual Hosting

One of the more popular services to provide with a Web server is to host a virtual domain, also known as a virtual host. This is a complete Web site with its own domain name, as if it were a standalone machine, but it's hosted on the same machine as other Web sites. Apache implements this capability in a simple way with directives in the `http.conf` configuration file.

There are two ways to host virtual hosts on an Apache server. You can either have one IP address with multiple CNAMEs, or you can have multiple IP addresses with one name per address. Apache has different sets of directives to handle each of these options.

Note

For information on setting up your Linux machine with multiple IP addresses or giving your Linux machine multiple CNAMEs, see Chapter 8, "The Domain Name Service," which covers DNS.

Address-Based Virtual Hosts

Once you have configured your Linux machine with multiple IP addresses, setting up Apache to serve them as different Web sites is quite simple. You need only put a `VirtualHost` directive in your `httpd.conf` file for each of the addresses that you want to make an independent Web site:

```
<VirtualHost www.virtual.com>
ServerName www.virtual.com
DocumentRoot /home/virtual/public_html
TransferLog /home/virtual/logs/access_log
ErrorLog /home/virtual/logs/error_log
</VirtualHost>
```

It is recommended that you use the IP address, rather than the hostname, in the `VirtualHost` tag.

You may specify any configuration directives within the `<VirtualHost>` tags. For example, you may want to set `AllowOverrides` directives differently for virtual hosts than you do for your main server. Any directives that are not specified default to the settings for the main server.

The directives that cannot be set in `VirtualHost` sections are `ServerType`, `StartServers`, `MaxSpareServers`, `MinSpareServers`, `MaxRequestsPerChild`, `BindAddress`, `Listen`, `PidFile`, `TypesConfig`, `ServerRoot`, and `NameVirtualHost`.

Name-Based Virtual Hosts

Name-based virtual hosts allow you to run more than one host on the same IP address. You need to add the additional names to your DNS as CNAMEs of the machine in question. When an HTTP client (browser) requests a document from your server, it sends with the request a variable indicating the server name from which it is requesting the document. Based on this variable, the server determines from which of the virtual hosts it should serve content.

> **Note**
>
> Some older browsers are unable to see name-based virtual hosts because this is a feature of HTTP 1.1, and those older browsers are strictly HTTP 1.0-compliant. However, many other older browsers are partially HTTP 1.1-compliant, and this is one of the parts of HTTP 1.1 that most browsers have supported for a while.

Name-based virtual hosts require just one additional step more than IP-address-based virtual hosts. You first need to indicate which IP address has the multiple DNS names on it. This is done with the `NameVirtualHost` directive.

```
NameVirtualHost 192.168.204.24
```

You then need to have a section for each name on that address, setting the configuration for that name. As with IP-based virtual hosts, you only need to set those configurations that need to be different for the host. You must set the `ServerName` directive because that is the only thing that distinguishes one host from another:

```
<VirtualHost 192.168.204.24>
ServerName bugserver.databeam.com
ServerAlias bugserver
DocumentRoot /home/bugserver/htdocs
ScriptAlias /home/bugserver/cgi-bin
TransferLog /home/bugserver/logs/access_log
</VirtualHost>

<VirtualHost 192.168.204.24>
ServerName pts.databeam.com
ServerAlias pts
DocumentRoot /home/pts/htdocs
ScriptAlias /home/pts/cgi-bin
TransferLot /home/pts/logs/access_log
ErrorLog /home/pts/logs/error_log
</VirtualHost>
```

Tip

If you are hosting Web sites on an intranet or internal network, there is often a chance that users will use the shortened name of the machine rather than the fully qualified domain name. For example, they might type `http://bugserver/index.html` in their browser location field, rather than `http://bugserver.databeam.com/index.html`. In that case, Apache will not recognize that those two addresses should go to the same virtual host. You could get around this by setting up `VirtualHost` directives for both `bugserver` and `bugserver.databeam.com`, but the easy way around this is to use the `ServerAlias` directive, which lists all valid aliases for the machine:

```
ServerAlias bugserver
```

Caution

If you plan to run a large number of virtual hosts on your system, you should consider sending all logged information to the standard Apache log files instead of to individual files. The reason is that you may reach your system's file descriptor limit (typically 64 per process) because you would be consuming one file descriptor per log file. Symptoms of this problem include error messages such as `unable to fork()`, no information being written to the log files, or poor response to `http` requests.

Logging

Apache provides for logging just about any information you might be interested in from Web accesses. There are two standard log files that are generated when you run your Apache server—`access_log` and `error_log`. All logs except for the `error_log` (by default, this is just the `access_log`) are generated in a format specified by the `CustomLog` and `LogFormat` directives. These directives appear in your `httpd.conf` file.

A new log format can be defined with the `LogFormat` directive:

```
LogFormat "%h %l %u %t \"%r\" %>s %b" common
```

The `common` log format is a good starting place for creating your own custom log formats. Note that most of the log analysis tools available will assume that you are using the `common` log format or the `combined` log format, both of which are defined in the default configuration files.

The following variables are available for `LogFormat` statements:

`%b`	Bytes sent, excluding HTTP headers.
`%f`	Filename.
`%{VARIABLE}e`	The contents of the environment variable `VARIABLE`.
`%h`	Remote host.
`%a`	Remote IP address.
`%{HEADER}i`	The contents of `HEADER`: header line(s) in the request sent to the server.
`%l`	Remote logname (from `identd`, if supplied).
`%{NOTE}n`	The contents of note `NOTE` from another module.
`%{HEADER}o`	The contents of `HEADER`: header line(s) in the reply.
`%p`	The canonical port of the server serving the request.

`%P`	The process ID of the child that serviced the request.
`%r`	First line of request.
`%s`	tatus. For requests that got internally redirected, this is status of the *original* request—`%>s` for the last.
`%t`	Time, in common log format time format.
`%{format}t`	The time, in the form given by `format`, which should be in `strftime(3)` format.
`%T`	The time taken to serve the request, in seconds.
`%u`	Remote user from `auth`; may be bogus if return status (`%s`) is 401.
`%U`	The URL path requested.
`%v`	The canonical `ServerName` of the server serving the request.

In each variable, you can put a conditional in front of the variable that will determine whether the variable is displayed. If it is not displayed, `-` will be displayed instead. These conditionals are in the form of a list of numerical return values. For example, `%!401u` will display the value of `REMOTE_USER` unless the return code is `401`.

You can then specify the location and format of a log file using the `CustomLog` directive:

```
CustomLog logs/access_log common
```

If it is not specified as an absolute path, the location of the log file is assumed to be relative to the `ServerRoot`.

CGI and SSI

The most common way to provide dynamic content on Web sites is with CGI (Common Gateway Interface) programs. The CGI is a specification of communication between server processes (such as programs that generate dynamic documents) and the server itself. SSI allow output from CGI programs, or other programs, to be inserted into existing HTML pages.

CGI

By default, you may put any CGI program in the `ScriptAlias` directory on your server. These programs must be executable by the user when the server is running. This usually means that you will need to change the mode of the files to `755` so that the user `nobody` can execute them.

```
chmod 755 program.cgi
```

In order to execute CGI programs outside of the ScriptAlias directory, you will need to enable the ExecCGI option for that directory. This is done either in your httpd.conf file (access.conf prior to version 1.3.4) or in an .htaccess file in the directory.

CGI programs can be written in any language. The most popular languages for CGI programming are Perl and C. You may want to pick up a good book on CGI programming, such as *CGI Programming With Perl*, Second Edition, since this is not intended to be a CGI book.

To test whether you have CGI configured correctly, try the following CGI program, written in Perl, which displays the values of the HTTP environment variables:

```
#!/usr/bin/perl
print "Content-type: text/html\n\n";
print "<html><head><title>Simple CGI program</title></head><body>\n";
for (keys %ENV)    {
    print "$_ = $ENV{$_}<br>\n";
}
print "</body></html>\n";
```

If you are going to be writing CGI programs in Perl, you may want to look at the CGI modules that come bundled with Perl.

SSI

Server Side Includes (SSI) are directives written directly into an HTML page, which the server parses when the page is served to the Web client. They can be used to include other files, the output from programs, or environment variables.

The most common way to enable SSI is to indicate that files with a certain filename extension (typically .shtml) are to be parsed by the server when they are served. This is accomplished with the following lines in your httpd.conf file (srm.conf prior to version 1.3.4):

```
# To use server-parsed HTML files
#
#AddType text/html .shtml
#AddHandler server-parsed .shtml
```

By uncommenting the AddType and AddHandler lines, you could tell the server to parse all .shtml files for SSI directives.

The less commonly used, and in my opinion much better, way of enabling SSI is with the XBitHack directive. XbitHack can be set to a value of on or off, and can be set in either your configuration file or in .htaccess files. If the XBitHack directive is on, it indicates that all files with the user execute bit set should be parsed for SSI directives.

This has two main advantages. One is that you do not need to rename a file, and change all links to that file, simply because you want to add a little dynamic content to it. The other reason is more cosmetic—users looking at your Web content cannot tell by looking at the filename that you are generating a page dynamically, and so your wizardry is just that tiny bit more impressive.

In addition to these directives, the following directive must be specified for directories where you want to permit SSI:

```
Options Includes
```

Or, alternatively, you can specify:

```
Options IncludesNOEXEC
```

This option enables SSI, but turns off a few of the most powerful and/or dangerous SSI directives, `exec` and `include`.

This may be set in the server configuration file or in an `.htaccess` file.

Basic SSI Directives

SSI directives look rather like HTML comment tags. The syntax is the following:

```
<!--#element attribute=value attribute=value ... -->
```

The `element` can be one of the following:

`config` This lets you set various configuration options regarding how the document parsing is handled. Since the page is parsed from top to bottom, `config` directives should appear at the top of the HTML document. There are three configurations that can be set with this command:

- `errmsg` Sets the error message that is returned to the client if something goes wrong while parsing the document. This is usually `[an error occurred while processing this directive]`, but it can be set to anything with this directive.

  Example: `<!--#config errmsg="[It's broken, dude]" -->`
- `sizefmt` Sets the format used to display file sizes. You can set the value to bytes to display the exact file size in bytes, or abbrev to display the size in KB or MB.

  Example: `<!--#config sizefmt="bytes" -->`
- `timefmt` Sets the format used to display times. The format of the value is the same as is used in the `strftime` function used by C (and Perl) to display dates, shown in the following list.

%%	PERCENT
`%a`	Day of the week abbreviation
`%A`	Day of the week
`%b`	Month abbreviation
`%B`	Month
`%c`	`ctime` format: `Sat Nov 19 21:05:57 1994`
`%d`	Numeric day of the month
`%e`	DD
`%D`	MM/DD/YY
`%h`	Month abbreviation
`%H`	Hour, 24-hour clock, leading 0s
`%I`	Hour, 12-hour clock, leading 0s
`%j`	Day of the year
`%k`	Hour
`%l`	Hour, 12-hour clock
`%m`	Month number, starting with `1`
`%M`	Minute, leading 0s
`%n`	Newline
`%o`	Ordinal day of month—1st, 2nd, 25th, and so on
`%p`	AM or PM
`%r`	Time format: `09:05:57 PM`
`%R`	Time format: `21:05`
`%S`	Seconds, leading 0s
`%t`	Tab
`%T`	Time format: `21:05:57`
`%U`	Week number; Sunday as first day of week
`%w`	Day of the week, numerically; `Sunday == 0`
`%W`	Week number; Monday as first day of week
`%x`	Date format: `11/19/94`
`%X`	Time format: `21:05:57`
`%y`	Year (two digits)
`%Y`	Year (four digits)
`%Z`	Time zone in ASCII, such as PST
`echo`	Displays any one of the include variables, listed here. Times are displayed in the time format specified by `timefmt`. The variable to be displayed is indicated with the `var` attribute.

- `DATE_GMT` The current date in Greenwich Mean Time.
- `DATE_LOCAL` The current date in the local time zone.
- `DOCUMENT_NAME` The filename (excluding directories) of the document requested by the user.
- `DOCUMENT_URI` The (%-decoded) URL path of the document requested by the user. Note that in the case of nested include files, this is not the URL for the current document.
- `LAST_MODIFIED`[em]The last modification date of the document requested by the user.

`exec` Executes a shell command or a CGI program, depending on the parameters provided. Valid attributes are `cgi` and `cmd`. Exec will be disabled if `IncludesNOEXEC` is set.

- `cgi` The URL of a CGI program to be executed. The URL needs to be a local CGI, not one located on another machine. The CGI program is passed the `QUERY_STRING` and `PATH_INFO` that were originally passed to the requested document, so the URL specified cannot contain this information. You should really use `include virtual` instead of this directive.
- `cmd` A shell command to be executed. The results will be displayed on the HTML page.

`fsize` Displays the size of a file specified by either the `file` or `virtual` attribute. Size is displayed as specified with the `sizefmt` directive.

- `file` The path (filesystem path) to a file, either relative to the root if the value starts with `/`, or relative to the current directory if not.
- `virtual` The relative URL path to a file.

`flastmod` Displays the last modified date of a file. The desired file is specified as with the `fsize` directive.

`include` Includes the contents of a file. The file is specified with the `file` and `virtual` attributes, as with `fsize` and `flastmod`. If the file specified is a CGI program and `IncludesNOEXEC` is not set, the program will be executed and the results displayed. This is to be used in preference to the `exec` directive. You can pass a `QUERY_STRING` with this directive, which you cannot do with the `exec` directive.

`printenv` Displays all of existing variables. There are no attributes.

Example: `<!--#printenv -->`

`set` Sets the value of a variable. Attributes are `var` and `value`.

Example: `<!--#set var="animal" value="cow" -->`

Note

All defined CGI environment variables are also allowed as include variables.

Note

In your configuration files (or in `.htaccess`), you can specify `Options IncludesNOEXEC` to disallow the `exec` and `include` directives, as this is the least secure of the SSI directives. Be especially cautious when Web users are able to create content (like a guestbook or discussion board) and these options are enabled!

These variables can be used elsewhere with some of the following directives.

Flow Control

Using the variables set with the `set` directive and the various environment and include variables, there is a limited flow control syntax that can be used to generate a certain amount of dynamic content on server-parsed pages.

The syntax of the `if/else` functions is as follows:

```
<!--#if expr="test_condition" -->
<!--#elif expr="test_condition" -->
<!--#else -->
<!--#endif -->
```

`expr` can be a string, which is considered true if non-empty, or a variety of comparisons between two strings. Available comparison operators are `=`, `!=`, `<`, `<=`, `>`, and `>=`. If the second string has the format `/string/`, the strings are compared with regular expressions. Multiple comparisons can be strung together with `&&` (`AND`) and `||` (`OR`). Any text appearing between the `if/elif/else` directives will be displayed on the resulting page. An example of such a flow structure follows:

```
<!--#set var="agent" value="$HTTP_USER_AGENT" -->
<!--#if expr="$agent = /Mozilla/" -->
Mozilla!
<!--#else -->
Something else!
<!--#endif -->
```

This code will display `Mozilla!` if you are using a browser that passes `Mozilla` as part of its `USER_AGENT` string, and `Something else!` otherwise.

Starting and Stopping the Server

At this point, you have your Apache server installed and configured the way you want it. It's time to start it for the first time.

Starting the Server Manually

The Apache server, `httpd`, has a few command-line options you can use to set some defaults specifying where `httpd` will read its configuration directives. The Apache `httpd` executable understands the following options:

```
httpd [-d directory] [-f file]
             [-C "directive"] [-c "directive"]
             [-v] [-V] [-h] [-l] [-L] [-S] [-t]
```

The `-d` option overrides the location of the *`ServerRoot`* directory. It sets the initial value of the *`ServerRoot`* variable (the directory where the Apache server is installed) to whichever path you specify. This default is usually read from the `ServerRoot` directive in `httpd.conf`.

The `-f` flag specifies the location of the main configuration file, `conf/httpd.conf`. It reads and executes the configuration commands found in *`ConfigurationFile`* on startup. If the *`ConfigurationFile`* is not an absolute path (it doesn't begin with a `/`), its location is assumed to be relative to the path specified in the *`ServerRoot`* directive in `httpd.conf`. By default, this value is set to *`ServerRoot`*`/conf/httpd.conf`.

The `-v` option prints the development version of the Apache server and terminates the process.

The `-V` option shows all of the settings that were in effect when the server was compiled.

The `-h` option prints the following usage information for the server:

```
Usage: httpd [-d directory] [-f file]
             [-C "directive"] [-c "directive"]
             [-v] [-V] [-h] [-l] [-L] [-S] [-t]
Options:
  -D name          : define a name for use in <IfDefine name> directives
  -d directory     : specify an alternate initial ServerRoot
  -f file          : specify an alternate ServerConfigFile
  -C "directive"   : process directive before reading config files
  -c "directive"   : process directive after  reading config files
  -v               : show version number
  -V               : show compile settings
  -h               : list available command line options (this page)
```

```
-l              : list compiled-in modules
-L              : list available configuration directives
-S              : show parsed settings (currently only vhost settings)
-t              : run syntax test for configuration files only
```

The `-l` option lists those modules that are compiled into your Apache server

The `-L` option lists all of the configuration directives that are available with the modules that are available to you.

The `-S` option lists the virtual host settings for the server.

The `-t` option is extremely useful. It runs a syntax check on your configuration files. It's a good idea to run this check before restarting your server, once you have made changes to your configuration files.

Note

When you start the server manually from the command line, you need to do so as `root`. There are two main reasons for this:

- If your standalone server uses the default HTTP port (port 80), only the superuser can bind to Internet ports that are lower than 1025.
- Only processes owned by `root` can change their UID and GID as specified by the `User` and `Group` directives. If you start the server under another UID, it will run with the permissions of the user starting the process.

The `/etc/rc.d` or `/etc/init.d` `httpd` Script

Red Hat and Caldera's distributions use scripts in `/etc/rc.d`, and Debian uses a script in `/etc/init.d` to control the startup and shutdown of various services, including the Apache Web server. The main script installed for the Apache Web server is `/etc/rc.d/init.d/httpd` or `/etc/init.d/apache`. The stock `httpd` script from Red Hat is shown in Listing 11.1. If you installed Apache from source, you may want to make a symlink from `/usr/local/apache/apachectl` to `/etc/rc.d/init.d/httpd` or `/etc/init.d/apache`.

Note

`/etc/rc.d/init.d/httpd` or `/etc/init.d/apache` is a shell script and is not the same as the Apache server located in `/usr/sbin`. That is, `/usr/sbin/httpd` is the program executable file, and `/etc/rc.d/init.d/httpd` or `/etc/init.d/apache` is a shell script that helps control that program.

You can use the following options when executing the httpd or Apache script.

`start` The system uses this option to start the Web server during bootup. You, as root, can also use this script to start the server.

`stop` The system uses this option to stop the server gracefully. You should use this script, rather than the kill command, to stop the server.

`reload` You can use this option to send the HUP signal to the httpd server to have it reread the configuration files after modification. (This option is not available with Caldera's script, or the apachectl script.)

`restart` This option is a convenient way to stop and then immediately start the Web server. (This option is not available with Caldera's script.)

`status` This option indicates whether the server is running, and if it is, it provides the various PIDs for each instance of the server. (This option is not available with Caldera's or Debian's script.)

For example, to check on the current status, use the following command:

```
/etc/rc.d/init.d/httpd status
```

That command prints this output:

```
httpd (pid 8643 8642 6510 6102 6101 6100 6099 6323 6322 6098 6097 6096
③ 6095 362 6094 6093) is running...
```

This indicates that the Web server is running; in fact, there are 16 instances of the server currently running.

Tip

Use the reload option if you are making many changes to the various server configuration files. This saves time when you're stopping and starting the server by having the system simply reread the configuration files—without requiring you to remember the PID for the Web server. If you do need to know the PID, the status command can provide that information. Also, the system keeps the PID (and many other PIDs) in a file located in /var/run.

LISTING 11.1 */etc/rc.d/init.d/http*

```
#!/bin/sh
#
# Startup script for the Apache Web Server
#
# chkconfig: 345 85 15
# description: Apache is a World Wide Web server. It is used to serve \
#              HTML files and CGI.
```

```
# processname: httpd
# pidfile: /var/run/httpd.pid
# config: /etc/httpd/conf/access.conf
# config: /etc/httpd/conf/httpd.conf
# config: /etc/httpd/conf/srm.conf

# Source function library.
. /etc/rc.d/init.d/functions

# See how we were called.
case "$1" in
  start)
        echo -n "Starting httpd: "
        daemon httpd
        echo
        touch /var/lock/subsys/httpd
        ;;
  stop)
        echo -n "Shutting down http: "
        [ -f /var/run/httpd.pid ] && {
            kill `cat /var/run/httpd.pid`
            echo -n httpd
        }
        echo
        rm -f /var/lock/subsys/httpd
        rm -f /var/run/httpd.pid
        ;;
  status)
        status httpd
        ;;
  restart)
        $0 stop
        $0 start
        ;;
  reload)
        echo -n "Reloading httpd: "
        [ -f /var/run/httpd.pid ] && {
            kill -HUP `cat /var/run/httpd.pid`
            echo -n httpd
        }
        echo
        ;;
  *)
        echo "Usage: $0 {start|stop|restart|reload|status}"
        exit 1
esac

exit 0
```

Configuration File Listings

What follows are complete listings of the server configuration files for version 1.3.6. If you have a different version of the server installed, or even if you have this version installed, you may notice some differences between your configuration files and the ones listed here. Some of these differences will simply be the differences between my system and yours. Others are places where I have set parameters differently, as I may have indicated earlier.

Listing 11.2 shows the server configuration file.

LISTING 11.2 *conf/httpd.conf*

```
#
# Based upon the NCSA server configuration files
# originally by Rob McCool.
#
# This is the main Apache server configuration file.  It contains the
# configuration directives that give the server its instructions.
# See <URL:http://www.apache.org/docs/> for detailed information about
# the directives.
#
# Do NOT simply read the instructions in here without understanding
# what they do.  They're here only as hints or reminders.
# If you are unsure consult the online docs. You have been warned.
#
# After this file is processed, the server will look for and process
# /etc/httpd/conf/srm.conf and then /etc/httpd/conf/access.conf
# unless you have overridden these with ResourceConfig and/or
# AccessConfig directives here.
#
# The configuration directives are grouped into three basic sections:
#  1. Directives that control the operation of the Apache server process
#     as a whole (the 'global environment').
#  2. Directives that define the parameters of the 'main' or 'default'
#     server which responds to requests that aren't handled by a
#     virtual host.
#     These directives also provide default values for the settings
#     of all virtual hosts.
#  3. Settings for virtual hosts, which allow Web requests to be sent to
#     different IP addresses or hostnames and have them handled by the
#     same Apache server process.
#
# Configuration and logfile names: If the filenames you specify for many
# of the server's control files begin with "/" (or "drive:/" for Win32),
# the server will use that explicit path.  If the filenames do *not*
# begin with "/", the value of ServerRoot is prepended -- so
# "logs/foo.log" with ServerRoot set to "/usr/local/apache" will be
```

```
# interpreted by the server as "/usr/local/apache/logs/foo.log".
#

### Section 1: Global Environment
#
# The directives in this section affect the overall operation of Apache,
# such as the number of concurrent requests it can handle or where it
# can find its configuration files.
#

#
# ServerType is either inetd, or standalone.  Inetd mode is only
# supported on Unix platforms.
#
ServerType standalone

#
# ServerRoot: The top of the directory tree under which the server's
# configuration, error, and log files are kept.
#
# NOTE!  If you intend to place this on an NFS (or otherwise network)
# mounted filesystem then please read the LockFile documentation
# (available at
# <URL:http://www.apache.org/docs/mod/core.html#lockfile>);
# you will save yourself a lot of trouble.
#
# Do NOT add a slash at the end of the directory path.
#
ServerRoot "/etc/httpd"
#
# The LockFile directive sets the path to the lockfile used when Apache
# is compiled with either USE_FCNTL_SERIALIZED_ACCEPT or
# USE_FLOCK_SERIALIZED_ACCEPT. This directive should normally be left at
# its default value. The main reason for changing it is if the logs
# directory is NFS mounted, since the lockfile MUST BE STORED ON A LOCAL
# DISK. The PID of the main server process is automatically appended to
# the filename.
#
#LockFile logs/accept.lock

#
# PidFile: The file in which the server should record its process
# identification number when it starts.
#
PidFile /var/run/httpd.pid
# I usually set put this file in the same location as
# the server log files

#
```

continues

LISTING 11.2 continued

```
# ScoreBoardFile: File used to store internal server process
# information. Not all architectures require this.  But if yours does
# (you'll know because this file will be created when you run Apache)
# then you *must* ensure that no two invocations of Apache share the
# same scoreboard file.
#
ScoreBoardFile logs/apache_runtime_status

#
# In the standard configuration, the server will process this file,
# srm.conf, and access.conf in that order.  The latter two files are
# now distributed empty, as it is recommended that all directives
# be kept in a single file for simplicity.  The commented-out values
# below are the built-in defaults.  You can have the server ignore
# these files altogether by using "/dev/null" (for Unix) or
# "nul" (for Win32) for the arguments to the directives.
#
#ResourceConfig conf/srm.conf
#AccessConfig conf/access.conf
ResourceConfig /dev/null
AccessConfig /dev/null

#
# Timeout: The number of seconds before receives and sends time out.
#
Timeout 300

#
# KeepAlive: Whether or not to allow persistent connections (more than
# one request per connection). Set to "Off" to deactivate.
#
KeepAlive On

#
# MaxKeepAliveRequests: The maximum number of requests to allow
# during a persistent connection. Set to 0 to allow an unlimited amount.
# We recommend you leave this number high, for maximum performance.
#
MaxKeepAliveRequests 100

#
# KeepAliveTimeout: Number of seconds to wait for the next request from
# the same client on the same connection.
#
KeepAliveTimeout 15

#
# Server-pool size regulation.  Rather than making you guess how many
# server processes you need, Apache dynamically adapts to the load it
```

```
# sees --- that is, it tries to maintain enough server processes to
# handle the current load, plus a few spare servers to handle transient
# load spikes (e.g., multiple simultaneous requests from a single
# Netscape browser).
#
# It does this by periodically checking how many servers are waiting
# for a request.  If there are fewer than MinSpareServers, it creates
# a new spare.  If there are more than MaxSpareServers, some of the
# spares die off.  The default values are probably OK for most sites.
#
MinSpareServers 5
MaxSpareServers 10

#
# Number of servers to start initially --- should be a reasonable
# ballpark figure.
#
StartServers 5

#
# Limit on total number of servers running, i.e., limit on the number
# of clients who can simultaneously connect --- if this limit is ever
# reached, clients will be LOCKED OUT, so it should NOT BE SET TOO LOW.
# It is intended mainly as a brake to keep a runaway server from taking
# the system with it as it spirals down...
#
MaxClients 150
#
# MaxRequestsPerChild: the number of requests each child process is
# allowed to process before the child dies.  The child will exit so
# as to avoid problems after prolonged use when Apache (and maybe the
# libraries it uses) leak memory or other resources.  On most systems,
# this isn't really needed, but a few (such as Solaris) do have notable
# leaks in the libraries.
#
MaxRequestsPerChild 30

#
# Listen: Allows you to bind Apache to specific IP addresses and/or
# ports, in addition to the default. See also the <VirtualHost>
# directive.
#
#Listen 3000
#Listen 12.34.56.78:80

#
# BindAddress: You can support virtual hosts with this option. This
# directive is used to tell the server which IP address to listen to.
# It can either contain "*", an IP address, or a fully qualified
# Internet domain name. See also the <VirtualHost> and Listen# directives
```

continues

LISTING 11.2 continued

```
#
#BindAddress *

#
# Dynamic Shared Object (DSO) Support
#
# To be able to use the functionality of a module which was built as
# a DSO you have to place corresponding `LoadModule' lines at this
# location so the directives contained in it are actually available
# before they are used. Please read the file README.DSO in the Apache
# 1.3 distribution for more details about the DSO mechanism and run
# 'httpd -l' for the list of already built-in (statically linked and
# thus always available) modules in your httpd binary.
#
# Note: The order is which modules are loaded is important.  Don't
# change the order below without expert advice.
#
# Example:
# LoadModule foo_module libexec/mod_foo.so

#
# ExtendedStatus controls whether Apache will generate "full" status
# information (ExtendedStatus On) or just basic information
# (ExtendedStatus Off) when the "server-status" handler is called. The
# default is Off.
#
#ExtendedStatus On

### Section 2: 'Main' server configuration
#
# The directives in this section set up the values used by the 'main'
# server, which responds to any requests that aren't handled by a
# <VirtualHost> definition.  These values also provide defaults for
# any <VirtualHost> containers you may define later in the file.
#
# All of these directives may appear inside <VirtualHost> containers,
# in which case these default settings will be overridden for the
# virtual host being defined.
#
#
# If your ServerType directive (set earlier in the 'Global Environment'
# section) is set to "inetd", the next few directives don't have any
# effect since their settings are defined by the inetd configuration.
# Skip ahead to the ServerAdmin directive.
#

#
# Port: The port to which the standalone server listens. For
# ports < 1023, you will need httpd to be run as root initially.
```

```
#
Port 80

#
# If you wish httpd to run as a different user or group, you must run
# httpd as root initially and it will switch.
#
# User/Group: The name (or #number) of the user/group to run httpd as.
#  . On SCO (ODT 3) use "User nouser" and "Group nogroup".
#  . On HPUX you may not be able to use shared memory as nobody, and the
#    suggested workaround is to create a user www and use that user.
#  NOTE that some kernels refuse to setgid(Group) or semctl(IPC_SET)
#  when the value of (unsigned)Group is above 60000;
#  don't use Group #-1 on these systems!
#
User nobody
Group #-1

#
# ServerAdmin: Your address, where problems with the server should be
# e-mailed.  This address appears on some server-generated pages, such
# as error documents.
#
ServerAdmin rbowen@databeam.com

#
# ServerName allows you to set a host name which is sent back to clients
# for your server if it's different than the one the program would get
#(i.e., use "www" instead of the host's real name).
#
# Note: You cannot just invent host names and hope they work. The name
# you define here must be a valid DNS name for your host. If you don't
# understand this, ask your network administrator.
# If your host doesn't have a registered DNS name, enter its IP address
# here. You will have to access it by its address
# http://123.45.67.89/) anyway, and this will make redirections work in
# a sensible way.
#
#ServerName new.host.name
#
# DocumentRoot: The directory out of which you will serve your
# documents. By default, all requests are taken from this directory, but
# symbolic links and aliases may be used to point to other locations.
#
DocumentRoot "/home/httpd/html"

#
# Each directory to which Apache has access, can be configured with
# respect to which services and features are allowed and/or disabled
# in that directory (and its subdirectories).
```

continues

LISTING 11.2 continued

```
#
# First, we configure the "default" to be a very restrictive set of
# permissions.
#
<Directory />
    Options FollowSymLinks
    AllowOverride None
</Directory>
#
# Note that from this point forward you must specifically allow
# particular features to be enabled - so if something's not working as
# you might expect, make sure that you have specifically enabled it
# below.
#

#
# This should be changed to whatever you set DocumentRoot to.
#
<Directory "/etc/httpd/htdocs">

#
# This may also be "None", "All", or any combination of "Indexes",
# "Includes", "FollowSymLinks", "ExecCGI", or "MultiViews".
#
# Note that "MultiViews" must be named *explicitly* --- "Options All"
# doesn't give it to you.
#
    Options Indexes FollowSymLinks

#
# This controls which options the .htaccess files in directories can
# override. Can also be "All", or any combination of "Options",
# "FileInfo", "AuthConfig", and "Limit"
#
    AllowOverride None

#
# Controls who can get stuff from this server.
#
    Order allow,deny
    Allow from all
</Directory>
#
# UserDir: The name of the directory which is appended onto a user's
# home directory if a ~user request is received.
#
UserDir public_html
#
# Control access to UserDir directories.  The following is an example
# for a site where these directories are restricted to read-only.
```

```
#
#<Directory /*/public_html>
#    AllowOverride FileInfo AuthConfig Limit
#    Options MultiViews Indexes SymLinksIfOwnerMatch IncludesNoExec
#    <Limit GET POST OPTIONS PROPFIND>
#        Order allow,deny
#        Allow from all
#    </Limit>
#    <Limit PUT DELETE PATCH PROPPATCH MKCOL COPY MOVE LOCK UNLOCK>
#        Order deny,allow
#        Deny from all
#    </Limit>
#</Directory>

#
# DirectoryIndex: Name of the file or files to use as a pre-written HTML
# directory index.  Separate multiple entries with spaces.
#
DirectoryIndex index.html index.htm index.cgi

#
# AccessFileName: The name of the file to look for in each directory
# for access control information.
#
AccessFileName .htaccess
#
# The following lines prevent .htaccess files from being viewed by
# Web clients.  Since .htaccess files often contain authorization
# information, access is disallowed for security reasons.  Comment
# these lines out if you want Web visitors to see the contents of
# .htaccess files.  If you change the AccessFileName directive above,
# be sure to make the corresponding changes here.
#
<Files .htaccess>
    Order allow,deny
    Deny from all
</Files>

#
# CacheNegotiatedDocs: By default, Apache sends "Pragma: no-cache" with
# each document that was negotiated on the basis of content. This asks
# proxy servers not to cache the document. Uncommenting the following
# line disables this behavior, and proxies will be allowed to cache the
# documents.
#
#CacheNegotiatedDocs

#
# UseCanonicalName:  (new for 1.3)  With this setting turned on,
# whatever Apache needs to construct a self-referencing URL (a URL that
```

continues

LISTING 11.2 continued

```
# refers back to the server the response is coming from) it will use
# ServerName and Port to form a "canonical" name.  With this setting
# off, Apache will use the hostname:port that the client supplied, when
# possible. This also affects SERVER_NAME and SERVER_PORT in CGI# scripts.
#
UseCanonicalName On

#
# TypesConfig describes where the mime.types file (or equivalent) is
# to be found.
#
TypesConfig conf/mime. types
#
# DefaultType is the default MIME type the server will use for a
# document if it cannot otherwise determine one, such as from filename
# extensions. If your server contains mostly text or HTML documents,
# "text/plain" is a good value.  If most of your content is binary, such
# as applications or images, you may want to use
# "application/octet-stream" instead to keep browsers from trying to
# display binary files as though they are text.
#
DefaultType text/plain

#
# The mod_mime_magic module allows the server to use various hints from
# the contents of the file itself to determine its type.  The
# MIMEMagicFile directive tells the module where the hint definitions
# are located. mod_mime_magic is not part of the default server (you
# hvae to add it yourself with a LoadModule [see the DSO paragraph in
# the 'Global Environment' section], or recompile the server and include
# mod_mime_magic as part of the configuration), so it's enclosed in an
# <IfModule> container. This means that the MIMEMagicFile directive will
# only be processed if the module is part of the server.
#
<IfModule mod_mime_magic.c>
    MIMEMagicFile conf/magic
</IfModule>

#
# HostnameLookups: Log the names of clients or just their IP addresses
# e.g., www.apache.org (on) or 204.62.129.132 (off).
# The default is off because it'd be overall better for the net if
# people had to knowingly turn this feature on, since enabling it means
# that each client request will result in AT LEAST one lookup request to
# the nameserver.
#
HostnameLookups Off
#
```

```
# ErrorLog: The location of the error log file.
# If you do not specify an ErrorLog directive within a <VirtualHost>
# container, error messages relating to that virtual host will be
# logged here.  If you *do* define an error logfile for a <VirtualHost>
# container, that host's errors will be logged there and not here.
#
ErrorLog logs/error_log

#
# LogLevel: Control the number of messages logged to the error_log.
# Possible values include: debug, info, notice, warn, error, crit,
# alert, emerg.
#
LogLevel warn

#
# The following directives define some format nicknames for use with
# a CustomLog directive (see below).
#
LogFormat "%h %l %u %t \"%r\" %>s %b \"%{Referer}i\" \"%{User-Agent}i\""
➥ combined
LogFormat "%h %l %u %t \"%r\" %>s %b" common
LogFormat "%{Referer}i -> %U" referer
LogFormat "%{User-agent}i" agent

#
# The location and format of the access logfile (Common Logfile Format).
# If you do not define any access logfiles within a <VirtualHost>
# container, they will be logged here.  Contrariwise, if you *do*
# define per-<VirtualHost> access logfiles, transactions will be
# logged therein and *not* in this file.
#
CustomLog logs/access_log common
#
# If you would like to have agent and referer logfiles, uncomment the
# following directives.
#
#CustomLog logs/referer_log referer
#CustomLog logs/agent_log agent

#
# If you prefer a single logfile with access, agent, and referer
# information (Combined Logfile Format) you can use the following
# directive.
#
#CustomLog logs/access_log combined

#
# Optionally add a line containing the server version and virtual host
# name to server-generated pages (error documents, FTP directory
```

continues

LISTING 11.2 continued

```
# listings, mod_status and mod_info output etc., but not CGI generated
# documents). Set to "EMail" to also include a mailto: link to the
# ServerAdmin. Set to one of:  On ¦ Off ¦ EMail
#
ServerSignature On

#
# Aliases: Add here as many aliases as you need (with no limit). The
# format is
# Alias fakename realname
#
# Note that if you include a trailing / on fakename then the server will
# require it to be present in the URL.  So "/icons" isn't aliased in
# this example, only "/icons/"..
#
Alias /icons/ "/etc/httpd/icons/"

<Directory "/home/httpd/icons">
    Options Indexes MultiViews
    AllowOverride None
    Order allow,deny
    Allow from all
</Directory>

#
# ScriptAlias: This controls which directories contain server scripts.
# ScriptAliases are essentially the same as Aliases, except that
# documents in the realname directory are treated as applications and
# run by the server when requested rather than as documents sent to the
# client. The same rules about trailing "/" apply to ScriptAlias
# directives as to Alias.
#
ScriptAlias /cgi-bin/ "/home/httpd/cgi-bin/"

#
# "/home/httpd/cgi-bin" should be changed to whatever your ScriptAliased
# CGI directory exists, if you have that configured.
#
<Directory "/home/httpd/cgi-bin">
    AllowOverride None
    Options None
    Order allow,deny
    Allow from all
</Directory>
#
# Redirect allows you to tell clients about documents which used to
# exist in your server's namespace, but do not anymore. This allows you
# to tell the clients where to look for the relocated document.
# Format: Redirect old-URI new-URL
```

```
#

#
# Directives controlling the display of server-generated directory
# listings.

#
# FancyIndexing is whether you want fancy directory indexing or standard
#
IndexOptions FancyIndexing

#
# AddIcon* directives tell the server which icon to show for different
# files or filename extensions.  These are only displayed for
# FancyIndexed directories.
#
AddIconByEncoding (CMP,/icons/compressed.gif) x-compress x-gzip

AddIconByType (TXT,/icons/text.gif) text/*
AddIconByType (IMG,/icons/image2.gif) image/*
AddIconByType (SND,/icons/sound2.gif) audio/*
AddIconByType (VID,/icons/movie.gif) video/*

AddIcon /icons/binary.gif .bin .exe
AddIcon /icons/binhex.gif .hqx
AddIcon /icons/tar.gif .tar
AddIcon /icons/world2.gif .wrl .wrl.gz .vrml .vrm .iv
AddIcon /icons/compressed.gif .Z .z .tgz .gz .zip
AddIcon /icons/a.gif .ps .ai .eps
AddIcon /icons/layout.gif .html .shtml .htm .pdf
AddIcon /icons/text.gif .txt
AddIcon /icons/c.gif .c
AddIcon /icons/p.gif .pl .py
AddIcon /icons/f.gif .for
AddIcon /icons/dvi.gif .dvi
AddIcon /icons/uuencoded.gif .uu
AddIcon /icons/script.gif .conf .sh .shar .csh .ksh .tcl
AddIcon /icons/tex.gif .tex
AddIcon /icons/bomb.gif core

AddIcon /icons/back.gif ..
AddIcon /icons/hand.right.gif README
AddIcon /icons/folder.gif ^^DIRECTORY^^
AddIcon /icons/blank.gif ^^BLANKICON^^
#
# DefaultIcon is which icon to show for files which do not have an icon
# explicitly set.
#
DefaultIcon /icons/unknown.gif
```

continues

LISTING 11.2 continued

```
#
# AddDescription allows you to place a short description after a file in
# server-generated indexes.  These are only displayed for FancyIndexed
# directories.
# Format: AddDescription "description" filename
#
#AddDescription "GZIP compressed document" .gz
#AddDescription "tar archive" .tar
#AddDescription "GZIP compressed tar archive" .tgz
#
# ReadmeName is the name of the README file the server will look for by
# default, and append to directory listings.
#
# HeaderName is the name of a file which should be prepended to
# directory indexes.
#
# The server will first look for name.html and include it if found.
# If name.html doesn't exist, the server will then look for name.txt
# and include it as plaintext if found.
#
ReadmeName README
HeaderName HEADER

#
# IndexIgnore is a set of filenames which directory indexing should
# ignore and not include in the listing.  Shell-style wildcarding is
# permitted
#
IndexIgnore .??* *~ *# HEADER* README* RCS CVS *,v *,t

#
# AddEncoding allows you to have certain browsers (Mosaic/X 2.1+)
# uncompress information on the fly. Note: Not all browsers support
# this. Despite the name similarity, the following Add* directives have
# nothing to do with the FancyIndexing customization directives above.
#
AddEncoding x-compress Z
AddEncoding x-gzip gz

#
# AddLanguage allows you to specify the language of a document. You can
# then use content negotiation to give a browser a file in a language
# it can understand.  Note that the suffix does not have to be the same
# as the language keyword --- those with documents in Polish (whose
# net-standard language code is pl) may wish to use "AddLanguage pl .po"
# to avoid the ambiguity with the common suffix for perl scripts.
#
```

```
AddLanguage en .en
AddLanguage fr .fr
AddLanguage de .de
AddLanguage da .da
AddLanguage el .el
AddLanguage it .it
#
# LanguagePriority allows you to give precedence to some languages
# in case of a tie during content negotiation.
# Just list the languages in decreasing order of preference.
#
LanguagePriority en fr de

#
# AddType allows you to tweak mime.types without actually editing it, or
# to make certain files to be certain types.
#
# For example, the PHP3 module (not part of the Apache distribution -
# see http://www.php.net) will typically use:
#
#AddType application/x-httpd-php3 .php3
#AddType application/x-httpd-php3-source .phps

#
# AddHandler allows you to map certain file extensions to "handlers",
# actions unrelated to filetype. These can be either built into the
# server or added with the Action command (see below)
#
# If you want to use server side includes, or CGI outside
# ScriptAliased directories, uncomment the following lines.
#
# To use CGI scripts:
#
#AddHandler cgi-script .cgi
#
# To use server-parsed HTML files
#
#AddType text/html .shtml
#AddHandler server-parsed .shtml
XBitHack on

#
# Uncomment the following line to enable Apache's send-asis HTTP file
# feature
#
#AddHandler send-as-is asis

#
# If you wish to use server-parsed imagemap files, use
```

continues

LISTING 11.2 continued

```
#
#AddHandler imap-file map

#
# To enable type maps, you might want to use
#
#AddHandler type-map var

#
# Action lets you define media types that will execute a script whenever
# a matching file is called. This eliminates the need for repeated URL
# pathnames for oft-used CGI file processors.
# Format: Action media/type /cgi-script/location
# Format: Action handler-name /cgi-script/location
#

#
# MetaDir: specifies the name of the directory in which Apache can find
# meta information files. These files contain additional HTTP headers
# to include when sending the document
#
#MetaDir .web

#
# MetaSuffix: specifies the filename suffix for the file containing the
# meta information.
#
#MetaSuffix .meta
#
# Customizable error response (Apache style)
#  these come in three flavors
#
#    1) plain text
#ErrorDocument 500 "The server made a boo boo.
#  n.b.  the (") marks it as text, it does not get output
#
#    2) local redirects
#ErrorDocument 404 /missing.html
#  to redirect to local URL /missing.html
#ErrorDocument 404 /cgi-bin/missing_handler.pl
#  N.B.: You can redirect to a script or a document using
# server-side-includes
#
#    3) external redirects
#ErrorDocument 402 http://some.other_server.com/subscription_info.html
#  N.B.: Many of the environment variables associated with the original
#  request will *not* be available to such a script.
#
# The following directives modify normal HTTP response behavior.
```

```
# The first directive disables keepalive for Netscape 2.x and browsers
# that spoof it. There are known problems with these browser
# implementations. The second directive is for Microsoft Internet
# Explorer 4.0b2 which has a broken HTTP/1.1 implementation and does not
# properly support keepalive when it is used on 301 or 302 (redirect)
# responses.
#
BrowserMatch "Mozilla/2" nokeepalive
BrowserMatch "MSIE 4\.0b2;" nokeepalive downgrade-1.0 force-response-1.0

#
# The following directive disables HTTP/1.1 responses to browsers which
# are in violation of the HTTP/1.0 spec by not being able to grok a
# basic 1.1 response.
#
BrowserMatch "RealPlayer 4\.0" force-response-1.0
BrowserMatch "Java/1\.0" force-response-1.0
BrowserMatch "JDK/1\.0" force-response-1.0

#
# Allow server status reports, with the URL of
# http://servername/server-status
# Change the ".your_domain.com" to match your domain to enable.
#
#<Location /server-status>
#    SetHandler server-status
#    Order deny,allow
#    Deny from all
#    Allow from .your_domain.com
#</Location>

#
# Allow remote server configuration reports, with the URL of
#  http://servername/server-info (requires that mod_info.c be loaded).
# Change the ".your_domain.com" to match your domain to enable.
#
#<Location /server-info>
#    SetHandler server-info
#    Order deny,allow
#    Deny from all
#    Allow from .your_domain.com
#</Location>
#
# There have been reports of people trying to abuse an old bug from
# pre-1.1 days.  This bug involved a CGI script distributed as a part of
# Apache. By uncommenting these lines you can redirect these attacks to
# a logging script on phf.apache.org.  Or, you can record them yourself,
# using the script support/phf_abuse_log.cgi.
#
```

continues

LISTING 11.2 continued

```
#<Location /cgi-bin/phf*>
#    Deny from all
#    ErrorDocument 403 http://phf.apache.org/phf_abuse_log.cgi
#</Location>

#
# Proxy Server directives. Uncomment the following lines to
# enable the proxy server:
#
#<IfModule mod_proxy.c>
#ProxyRequests On
#
#<Directory proxy:*>
#    Order deny,allow
#    Deny from all
#    Allow from .your_domain.com
#</Directory>
#
# Enable/disable the handling of HTTP/1.1 "Via:" headers.
# ("Full" adds the server version; "Block" removes all outgoing Via:
# headers) Set to one of: Off ¦ On ¦ Full ¦ Block
#
#ProxyVia On

#
# To enable the cache as well, edit and uncomment the following lines:
# (no cacheing without CacheRoot)
#
#CacheRoot "/etc/httpd/proxy"
#CacheSize 5
#CacheGcInterval 4
#CacheMaxExpire 24
#CacheLastModifiedFactor 0.1
#CacheDefaultExpire 1
#NoCache a_domain.com another_domain.edu joes.garage_sale.com

#</IfModule>
# End of proxy directives.

### Section 3: Virtual Hosts
#
# VirtualHost: If you want to maintain multiple domains/hostnames on
# your machine you can setup VirtualHost containers for them.
# Please see the documentation at
# <URL:http://www.apache.org/docs/vhosts/>
# for further details before you try to setup virtual hosts.
# You may use the command line option '-S' to verify your virtual host
# configuration.
```

```
#
# If you want to use name-based virtual hosts you need to define at
# least one IP address (and port number) for them.
#
#NameVirtualHost 12.34.56.78:80
#NameVirtualHost 12.34.56.78

#
# VirtualHost example:
# Almost any Apache directive may go into a VirtualHost container.
#
#<VirtualHost ip.address.of.host.some_domain.com>
#    ServerAdmin webmaster@host.some_domain.com
#    DocumentRoot /www/docs/host.some_domain.com
#    ServerName host.some_domain.com
#    ErrorLog logs/host.some_domain.com-error_log
#    CustomLog logs/host.some_domain.com-access_log common
#</VirtualHost>

#<VirtualHost _default_:*>
#</VirtualHost>
```

Listing 11.3 shows `srm.conf`, which is basically empty.

LISTING 11.3 *conf/srm.conf*

```
#
# This is the default file for the ResourceConfig directive in
# srm.conf. It is processed after httpd.conf but before access.conf.
#
# To avoid confusion, it is recommended that you put all of your
# Apache server directives into the httpd.conf file and leave this
# one essentially empty.
#
```

Listing 11.4 shows the global access configuration file.

LISTING 11.4 *conf/access.conf*

```
#
# This is the default file for the AccessConfig directive in httpd.conf.
# It is processed after httpd.conf and srm.conf.
#
# To avoid confusion, it is recommended that you put all of your
# Apache server directives into the httpd.conf file and leave this
# one essentially empty.
#
```

Summary

There are still some things that you can do to further customize your Web server, but by this point you should at least have a functional server.

There is a plethora of Apache documentation online. For more information about Apache, and the subjects discussed in this chapter, look at some of the following resources.

- Extensive documentation and information about Apache: The Apache Project Web site at `http://www.apache.org/`.
- Breaking news about Apaches, and great technical articles: ApacheWeek at `http://www.apacheweek.com/`.
- HTML, CGI, and related subjects: The HTML Writers Guild at `http://www.hwg.org/`.
- Available add-on modules for Apache: The Apache Module Registry at `http://modules.apache.org/`.

CHAPTER 12

Internet News

In This Chapter

Usenet newsgroups are a fascinating and informative source of information, entertainment, news, and general chat. Usenet is one of the oldest components of the Internet and was popular long before the World Wide Web came on the scene. Usenet is still the most popular aspect of the Internet in terms of user interaction, offering a dynamic and often controversial forum for discussion on any subject.

Usenet newsgroups now number well over 100,000 groups dedicated to many different subjects. A full download of an average day's newsgroup postings takes several hundred megabytes of disk space and associated transfer time. Obviously, if you are going to access Usenet over anything slower than a T1 (1.544Mbps) line, you have to be selective in what you download. An analog modem simply can't download the entire Usenet feeds in a reasonable time. Selective access to newsgroups suits most users because few, if any users actually read all the postings on Usenet every day!

Providing access to the Usenet newsgroups is a natural purpose for Linux because newsgroups evolved under UNIX. To provide Usenet newsgroup access for yourself and anyone else accessing your machine, you need to set up newsgroup software on your system and get access to a source for downloading newsgroups. Any connection to the Internet gives you access to newsgroups, whether through your own gateway, through a news forwarding service, or through a third-party access service. Most Internet service providers (ISPs) can offer news access to you as part of their basic service; you decide which newsgroups you may be interested in from the complete list of all available newsgroups, and those groups are transferred to your machine for reading. If you want to access a newsgroup you didn't download, a quick connection to your ISP lets you sample the postings.

In this chapter you learn how to configure your Linux machine to download newsgroups from your Internet connection. You also see how to configure your machine as a caching news server. Finally, you see how to install and configure one of the most popular common newsreaders, `trn`. There are several alternatives available for Linux access to newsgroups, so I chose the most common method to give you a taste of how to configure your system as a news server.

Linux and Newsgroups

There are three main ways to download newsgroups onto your Linux system: INN, C News, and NNTP Cache. INN implements the NNTP protocol. NNTP stands for the Network News Transfer Protocol, which is widely used over TCP/IP connections to ISPs or the Internet. INN (Internet News) is the most flexible and configurable method of downloading entire newsgroups and works especially well on larger sites that have high-speed connections to the Internet or those sites where a lot of news is transferred (for example, large educational institutions). C News was designed for downloading news through UUCP (UNIX-to-UNIX Copy) connections. NNTP Cache is probably the best choice for most sites, especially those that do not have the bandwidth to download all the news that your organization requires. Because INN is included with most Linux systems, that's the choice discussed first. Following that, this chapter discusses using NNTP Cache as a money-saving alternative method for providing news for your users.

Rich Salz developed INN to provide a complete Usenet package. One of the attractions of INN is that it doesn't care whether you are using TCP/IP or UUCP to transfer your newsgroups. INN handles both methods equally well. INN handles the NNTP protocol for transferring news with the `innd` server process, and provides newsreading services as a separate server, `nntrpd`, which is executed when it detects a connection on the news TCP/IP port (119).

How a News Feed Works

Usenet newsgroup postings are sent from machine to machine across the Internet all the time. To send mail from one system to another, Usenet uses a technique called flooding. *Flooding* happens when one machine connects to another and essentially transfers all the postings in the newsgroups as one big block of data. The receiving machine then connects to another machine and repeats the process. In this way, all the postings in the newsgroups are transferred across the entire Internet. This is much better than maintaining a single source of newsgroup information on a server isolated somewhere on the Internet. Each machine that participates in the flooding has a list of all other machines that can send or receive newsgroup postings. Each connection is called a news feed. When you connect to an ISP and download newsgroup postings, you are creating a news feed between your machine and the ISP's, which in turn has a news feed to another machine somewhere on the Internet.

Every time a new posting is added (or posted) to a newsgroup, the news feeds are used to transfer that posting. Each article has a list of all the machines that have received the posting, so it is easy to avoid transferring the same new posting to every machine on the Internet many times. The list of machines that have received the posting is called the *path*. Each posting also has a unique message ID, which prevents duplicate postings.

Preventing Duplicate News Postings

When you connect to your ISP and request newsgroup updates, one of two methods is usually used to ensure you don't get duplicate postings when you use your *newsreader*, which is what users need to read postings in a newsgroup. The most common technique is called *ihave/sendme*, which informs the machine at the other end of your news feed (such as your ISP's server) which message IDs you have and which ones you lack. Then, only the missing postings are transferred to your Linux machine.

The ihave/sendme protocol is excellent for updating a few newsgroups but starts to bog down dramatically when handling very large volumes of newsgroups. For this reason, a method called batching is used to transfer large newsgroup feeds. With *batching*, everything on one end of the news feed is transferred as a block. Your machine then sorts through the download, discarding any duplicates. Batching adds more overhead to your local Linux machine than ihave/sendme but involves a lot less messaging between the two ends of the news feeds.

Pushing and Pulling the News

Two other terms are used to describe the transfer of newsgroup postings from one machine to another, and these terms apply especially to smaller systems that don't download the entire news feed every day. Your system can download articles from the news feed using the ihave/sendme protocol, a technique called *pushing*. Alternatively, your machine can request specific postings or entire newsgroups from the news feed based on the date of arrival of the posting, a technique called *pulling*.

Alternative Methods to Downloading Newsgroups

Before looking at how to download Usenet newsgroups to your machine, there is one alternative you might want to consider if you don't often utilize Usenet or you have limited connection time to the news feed: interacting with a news server on a remote network, and reading the postings on that server instead of downloading them to your machine. Many ISPs allow you to choose whether to download newsgroups to your machine or to read them on their news server. You obviously must be connected all the time if you are reading on the server, but this might be a better choice if you do not do a lot of Usenet surfing or you have limited disk space on your machine. Another alternative is to read news via the Web at `http://www.deja.com`. This is a very powerful Web site that contains almost all the newsgroups from around the world and offers a very powerful search facility. If you are looking to solve a particular problem that is not necessarily computer related, chances are you will find an answer there.

INN Hardware and Software Requirements

INN doesn't impose too many hardware requirements; most Linux-capable hardware sufficiently runs INN. If you do download a lot of newsgroup postings, however, slow processors will be affected. Because INN often works in background, your foreground tasks get slower while INN crunches away in background. This is usually not a problem with 80486 or better CPUs running Linux.

There are no extra RAM requirements for INN, although to avoid swapping, the more RAM you have, the better. If you download only a dozen newsgroups a day, Linux needs no extra RAM. You should have swap space allocated on your system as a RAM overflow, but there is no need to expand swap space just for INN unless the existing swap space is very small (less than half your physical RAM, for example).

Disk space may be a problem if you don't have a lot to spare. Downloading newsgroups can eat up disk space at an alarming rate, even if you download only a few groups a day. Because newsgroup postings are not automatically deleted after you read them, the effect is cumulative. This is especially a problem with newsgroups that contain binary information such as compiled programs or pictures. A typical newsgroup download can range from a few kilobytes to several megabytes. Some of the binary newsgroups get many megabytes daily, all of which accumulate over a week or so to huge amounts of disk space. It is not unusual for a day's complete download of all the newsgroups to take up quite a few gigabytes of disk space, so you must be careful about which newsgroups you download.

Modems are another issue. Your modem's speed directly impacts how many newsgroups you can download in a reasonable amount of time. Obviously, the faster your modem, the better. A 56Kbps modem downloads much more data in a minute than a 9,600bps modem. That doesn't mean you need to junk your existing slower modems. The determining factor for your connection is the amount of data you will be transferring. A 9,600bps modem is just fine if you download less than a dozen non-binary newsgroups a day. When you start downloading megabytes of data a day, as often happens with binary-laden newsgroups, you need a much faster connection to keep the download time to a minimum. Any of today's 56Kbps modems will suit your purposes for typical Usenet downloads of a few dozen non-binary newsgroups. When you start downloading large amounts of news, you should look at faster connections such as ISDN (128Kbps), T1 (1.544Mbps), or T3 (45Mbps). Fractional use of ISDN and T1 lines are available for a reasonable cost these days (depending on where in the world you live), but the overall expenses of the line and routers are usually more than the newsgroup reading is worth to end users.

Software requirements for INN are simple: You need INN and a configured connection to a news feed source (such as UUCP or TCP/IP to an ISP). INN is supplied with Red Hat Linux or Caldera OpenLinux, and you can also obtain it from most Linux FTP and Web sites.

An Introduction to INN

INN was originally designed for handling news on very large systems with complex connections and configuration problems. INN contains an NNTP component but is noticeably faster when downloading and handling newsgroups than NNTP alone. Luckily, INN can be quickly configured for most basic Linux setups. I look at setting up INN on a typical system using a dial-up connection to an ISP using TCP/IP because this is the most common configuration. One problem with INN is a lack of good documentation. At the time of writing, only the Debian distribution provides a hand with some extra documentation for helping setup your INN server in `/usr/doc`. People running other distributions can find an INN-FAQ amongst other things at the INN home page at `http://www.isc.org/inn.html`.

INN uses a daemon called `innd` to control its behavior. Another daemon, `nnrpd`, is used to provide newsreader services. When you boot your machine, `innd` usually starts right away. A copy of `nnrpd` is started every time a user launches a newsreader.

Installing INN

To install INN, you can start with either the source code (usually obtained from a Web or FTP site) or a precompiled binary included in the INN package for your distribution. Precompiled binaries are much easier because they save the hassle of running a C compiler to produce the binary from source code.

> **Note**
>
> If you are working with INN source code instead of a precompiled binary, you should carefully read any readme files included in the source distribution. They will describe the steps involved in compiling the INN software for your system.

A makefile will accompany the source code and will almost certainly need modification to suit your system. With the latest INN distribution, however, a configure script gets run before compilation; this takes care of most configuration options. The version of INN shipping with Red Hat Linux 6.0 is 2.2 and Caldera Linux 2.2 comes with version 2.1.

To install your precompiled INN binaries on the system and properly configure for secure operation, follow these steps:

1. If you are running Red Hat or Caldera, check your `/etc/passwd` file for a user called `news`. If none exists, create the `news` user. The user `news` should belong to a group called `news`. The home directory can be anything, and the startup command should be `bank` or something like `/bin/false` for security reasons—no one should ever need to actively log in as the `news` user. Neither of these parameters is used by the system. The `news` user is created to allow INN to run as a non-`root` login for better system security. This account should exist by default on Red Hat, Caldera, and Debian systems. Also make sure that the password field is filled by an asterisk (`*`). This makes doubly sure that no one can log in interactively as the `news` user.
2. Check the `/etc/group` file for a group called `news`. If none exists, create it. The `news` login should be the only user in the `news` group. Providing a dedicated group for INN access enhances system security. This group should exist by default on Red Hat, Caldera, and Debian systems.
3. INN often sends mail to the news logins, so you might want to create an alias for the usernames `news` and `usenet` to `root`, `postmaster`, or whatever other login you want these messages to be sent to. The alias file is kept in `/etc/aliases`. When you add aliases, make sure to run the `/usr/bin/newaliases` command afterward so that the added aliases will take effect.
4. On RPM-based systems, check to see if INN is already installed on your system by typing the following:

   ```
   rpm -q inn
   ```

   If no installed package is found, install the INN package from the directory containing RPM files by issuing the following command:

   ```
   rpm -i inn-2.2-8.i386.rpm
   ```

   Caldera

   Caldera users should enter this instead:

   ```
   rpm -i inn-2.1-1.i386.rpm
   ```

Installing the package should cause the creation of two files called /etc/rc.d/init.d/innd and /usr/bin/rc.news. These files will be used by init to start news services each time you boot. Once installed, they are executed automatically during the boot process unless explicitly disabled or removed.

The Caldera files will be /etc/rc.d/init.d/news and /usr/libexec/inn/rc.news.

In Debian, you can ensure that the package is not only installed but installed with the latest version simply by running this code:

```
apt-get install inn
```

Debian will automatically set up and configure the appropriate init scripts based on your choices; they are stored in /etc/init.d/inn and /etc/news/boot.

5. The INN RPM file will install INN under the /usr hierarchy (mainly in /usr/lib and /usr/bin). In previous versions of Red Hat Linux, these files were located under /usr/lib/news.

The Caldera INN RPM file will install INN under various directories. All bundled documentation will be installed under /usr/doc/inn-2.1, and the main INN binaries are in /usr/libexec/inn.

Debian users can find a list of all files installed by the INN package by using dpkg -L inn. Per the standard for Debian packages, the INN package installs user-accessible binaries in /usr/bin, system binaries in /usr/sbin, internal information in /usr/lib/news, configuration information in /etc/news, and the news spool in /var.

6. The INN RPM installs the INN configuration files into the /etc/news directory and adds several files to the /etc/cron.* directories to be run by cron. The /etc/cron.daily/inn-cron-expire file calls the news.daily program once per day to *expire* (remove) old articles and to clean and maintain the INN logs. The /etc/cron.daily/inn-cron-rnews file downloads new articles to your system once per day. The /etc/cron.hourly/inn-cron-nntpsend file sends articles created on your system to your outgoing news server once every hour.

Once the INN package has successfully been installed, you can start news services by typing the following:

```
/etc/rc.d/init.d/innd start
```

The INN RPM installs the INN configuration files into the /etc/news directory. These files generally only need to be changed once during the initial INN setup.

Once the INN package has successfully been installed, you can start news services by typing this:

```
/etc/rc.d/init.d/news start
```

For Debian, the INN package installs the configuration files in `/etc/news`. The installer automatically offers to start the server, but you can do so manually by running `/etc/init.d/inn start`. There are also various `cron` jobs installed in the `crontab` of the `news` user. As with any other user's `crontab`, you can view this with `crontab -l -u news` or modify with `crontab -e -u news`.

7. If you are uncomfortable starting INN on a running system, you can reboot your machine now; INN should start automatically as a part of the boot process.

The INN Startup Files

When the INN RPM is installed, it should automatically install the important INN startup files: `/etc/rc.d/init.d/innd` and `/usr/bin/rc.news`.

In Debian systems, the `cron` scripts can be seen by running `crontab -l -u news`.

Once the INN package is installed and ready to go, you need to check the configuration information to make sure everything will run smoothly when `innd` or `nntpd` (the NNTP daemon) connects to the news feed.

> **Note**
>
> INN is very particular about its user and group setup and file permissions in general. As a general rule, don't modify any INN file permissions at all. If you do so, you may find that the package ceases to work properly.

Configuring INN

Configuring INN can take hours because it is a complex package allowing many news feeds at once. Worried? Don't be. For a simple connection to an ISP through TCP/IP or UUCP, you can configure INN in a few minutes. Most of the work was already done when you installed the package.

Follow these steps to check and configure your INN setup, being careful not to corrupt any files or change permissions as you go:

1. Edit the `/etc/news/incoming.conf` file. This file lists all the news feeds that your system connects to and is read by the INN daemon. Enter the names or IP addresses of the news feed machines using the following as an example:

```
    peer newsfeed {
   hostname:     news.isp.net
}
```

Because most systems will have only a single news feed, you only need one `peer` entry. If your news feed requires a password, add another parameter `password:` with the appropriate password after the colon. There are many other parameters that can be specified on a per news feed basis. For a full list see the manual page `incoming.conf`.

Debian users can simply answer the prompts as INN is installed in order to handle basic configuration needs. Additionally, various examples can be found in `/usr/doc/inn`.

2. If you allow either other machines on your local area network or machines connecting through a remote access server on your machine to read news collected by your system, you need to add their names to the `/etc/news/nnrp.access` file. This file is read when the `nnrpd` daemon starts for each person invoking a newsreader. The `nnrp.access` file contains a list of all the machines that are allowed to read news from your server and follows this syntax:

   ```
   name:perms:user:password:newsgroup
   ```

   name is the address of the machine that you are allowing to read news. (You can use wildcards to allow entire subnets.) *perms* is the permissions and has one of the following values: `Read` (for read-only access), `Post` (to allow posting of messages), or `Read Post` (for both `Read` and `Post`). The *user* field is used to authenticate a username before it is allowed to post, and *password* accomplishes the same task. To prevent a user from posting messages through your server, leave *user* and *password* as spaces so they can't be matched.

   The *newsgroup* field is a pattern of newsgroup names that can be either read or not read, depending on how you set up the contents. Access to newsgroups uses wildcards, so `comp*` allows access to all newsgroups starting with `comp`, whereas `!sex` disables access to any newsgroups starting with the word `sex`. The default setting in the `nnrp.access` file is to prevent all access. To allow all users in the domain `tpci.com` to read and post news with no authentication required, you add this line to `nnrp.access`:

   ```
   *.tpci.com:Read Post:::*
   ```

   To open the news system to everyone on your system regardless of domain name, use an asterisk instead of a domain name.

3. The file `inn.conf` should be in your `/etc/news` directory. You should probably change the line with `organization` in it to the following:

   ```
   organization:    Your company name
   ```

   This specifies the default `organization:` header when your users subscribe to a newsgroup on your server.

The file `inn.conf.sample` will be in your `/etc/news` directory. Rename it **`inn.conf`**. You should probably change the line with `organization` in it as well:

```
organization:    Your company name
```

This specifies the default `organization:` header when your users post to a newsgroup on your server.

Of course, if you are setting up INN to get news from your ISP's news server, your ISP would have to set up his end with the newsgroups that you want your users to be able to access. Remember, news takes up a lot of bandwidth, so try to minimize the amount of news you download.

After setting the `incoming.conf`, `nnrp.access`, and `inn.conf` files and having notified your ISP that you want to access its NNTP service, you should be able to use INN to download news and access it with a newsreader (assuming you've granted yourself permission in the `nnrp.access` file). A lot of complexity can be introduced into INN's configuration file, but keeping it simple tends to be the best method. As your experience grows, you can modify the behavior of the news feeds, but start with as simple an access approach as possible to allow testing of the news system first. After setting up INN, the next step is to provide users with a newsreader.

Introduction to NNTPCache

As mentioned, many companies and individuals run an NNTP cache instead of getting a full news feed themselves; this helps save money. The news feed described here is probably the most popular: NNTPCache. As the time of writing, NNTPCache was not shipping with Red Hat Linux or Caldera OpenLinux, but it is included with Debian GNU/Linux and is downloadable from `http://www.nntpcache.org`.

It should be noted that NNTPCache is free for individuals and non-profit organizations, but should be licensed for commercial environments. See the `LICENSING` file in the distribution for more information.

How NNTPCache Works

NNTPCache was designed to look like a regular NNRP-based server that any newsreader can connect to—but with a difference! In the configuration you specify a default news server that NNTPCache gets its articles from. This would normally be your ISP's news server. For example, if you are reading the newsgroup `comp.os.linux.advocacy`, each article you choose to read is retrieved from your default news server and a copy is kept on your `NNTPCache` server—this is called *caching*.

Not only articles are cached; the news server's active lists are cached as well. An *active* list is the current newsgroup listing for that particular news server. This avoids the listing having to be refetched every time you open your newsreader.

Another useful NNTPCache feature is that it can connect to multiple news servers. There are a number of public news servers on the Internet that are usually related to a particular topic. As an example, Microsoft provide a news server called `msnews.microsoft.com` and has specific newsgroups on Microsoft-related topics. (Newsgroups are named `microsoft.*`.) Similarly, Red Hat has a news server called `news.redhat.com`. (Newsgroups are named `redhat.*`.) To make full use of this neat feature, you configure NNTPCache to talk to specific servers and link newsgroups with these servers. When you are at the newsreader, it makes browsing through all the different groups on all the different news servers transparent—and it caches it all for you!

Obviously, to make full use of NNTPCache's caching capabilities you need a reasonably permanent Internet connection and many people using your `NNTPCache` server. It is still of use even if you use casual dial-up connections. You might, however, want to either configure NNTPCache to use a smaller amount of disk space for its cache or turn off caching altogether.

Downloading and Configuring NNTPCache

Since NNTPCache is notpart of the standard Red Hat Linux 6.0 or Caldera OpenLinux 2.2 distribution, you have to download it. This is a pretty simple process, since there is an RPM at the NNTPCache Web site. Go to `http://www.nntpcache.org` and scroll down to where it mentions the Red Hat RPM package and download it onto your machine. The RPM version is slightly older, but will suffice for explaining the concepts in this section. If you feel adventurous, you can have a go at downloading, compiling, and installing the newer version yourself.

Once you have the NNTPCache RPM downloaded, you need to install it with this command:

```
rpm -i  nntpcache-1.0.7.1-1.i386.rpm
```

This installs the configuration files under `/etc/nntpcache`, some documentation in `/usr/doc/nntpcache-1.0.7.1-1`, and the `NNTPCache` server that does all the work in `/usr/sbin`. Of course, the appropriate startup files are installed in the `/etc/rc.d` tree.

NNTPCache is part of Debian GNU/Linux, and like many packages, it can be installed by simply using this code:

```
apt-get install nntpcache
```

Debian

If you are working from the Debian official CD-ROM set, this package is not installed. It is part of the non-free section. You can find it on the Debian mirror network, however.

Getting up and running should not take very long. Go into the `/etc/nnptcache` directory and enter the **`ls`** command:

```
[root@mycompany /etc/nntpcache]# ls -l
total 26
-rw-r--r--   1 news     news         3584 Apr 27 23:05 access
-rw-r--r--   1 news     news         9315 Apr 27 23:04 config
-rw-r--r--   1 news     news          862 Apr 30 22:11 servers
-rw-r--r--   1 news     news         2612 Jan 21  1998 spam.filter
```

There are three main configuration files: `access`, `config`, and `servers`. Debian comes with the same files, but they are named `nntpcache.access`, `nntpcache.config`, and `nntp.servers`, respectively. There is also another file: `spam.filter`. It contains special search strings that help filter out junk news postings. The default setup for this file should be fine.

The first file to configure is the `access` file. Hosts that are allowed to use the `NNTPCache` are named in here. You can also specify access permissions for the hosts specified here. You generally allow read and post for hosts on your network, but there may be times where you want to give read-only access. An example is if you are running some support newsgroups that can be accessed from the Internet for a particular product you maintain. For now, put an entry in to allow the machines on your LAN to access NNTPCache:

```
*.mycompany.com            *                  read,post
```

The next file to configure is `config`. This is the file read by NNTPCache when it starts. You should probably only need to change the `Organization` field to get up and running:

```
Organization MyCompany Pty Ltd
```

This fills in the `Organization` field when the newsreader does not specify one. You can also force whatever organization you specify to be the organization no matter what the newsreader's client says by changing the next parameter from `no` to `yes`:

```
ReplaceOrganization yes
```

You may find that there are other parameters you need to tweak later on, but this will do for now.

The final file that you need to edit is `servers`. This is where you specify all the news feeds you want to use with your NNTPCache. The `servers` file that came with the NNTPCache distribution has many examples that you might want to refer to later;

I suggest renaming the existing `servers` file **`servers.old`** and creating a new one with the following entries in it:

```
#                 /*                timeouts                        */
# host:port  Interface    Active  Act.tim Newsgrp Group   Xover   Arts
news.myisp.net:119    DEFAULT    10m      12h      12h      10m     60d     60d
msnews.microsoft.com:119 DEFAULT   24h    4d     4d      60m     60d     60d
news.redhat.com:119      DEFAULT   24h    4d     4d      30m     60d     60d
%BeginGroups
# Group pattern Host
*               news.myisp.net:119
microsoft.*     msnews.microsoft.com:119
redhat.*        news.redhat.com:119
```

Make sure this new `servers` file is owned by both the `news` user and the `news` group.

The first three entries specify the news servers to use. Replace *`news.myisp.net`* with the name of the news server that your ISP provides. Notice I have included the Microsoft and Red Hat `news` servers. You can see that there are a few timeout entries in the `servers` file after each `news` server. I will briefly describe what each one is used for. The `Active` parameter directs how long the `active` file will be kept before being retrieved again. `Act.tim` is in regards to the `active.times` file. `Newsgrp` refers to the `newsgroups` file, which has all the newsgroup descriptions contained in it. `Group` indicates the amount of time for which the NNTP `group` command is cached. `Xover` is another NNTP command; it is used to get the subject and other header information of article numbers given as parameters. Finally, `Arts` is the timeout for the `Arts` NNTP command. For full details on any of these NNTP commands or NNTP files, refer to the NNTP RFC, which is included as part of the NNTPCache distribution. It should have been installed into the directory `/usr/doc/nntpcache-1.0.7.1-1` and be called `rfc977.txt`.

Debian users can find RFC 977 as part of the `doc-rfc` package in the `/usr/doc/doc-rfc/all-rfcs/rfc977.txt.gz` file.

You tell NNTPCache to retrieve articles for each set of newsgroups after the `%BeginGoups` line. NNTPCache tries to match the requested newsgroup with all entries listed, and the last match is the one used. I have configured the file so that all Microsoft newsgroups are to use the `msnews.microsoft.com` news server. All Red Hat newsgroup requests go out to `news.redhat.com`, and for every other group NNTPCache goes to. Again, replace `news.myisp.net` with your own.

Now you have NNTPCache configured, you have to start it. You can do this with the command:

```
[root@mycompany /etc/nntpcache]# /etc/rc.d/init.d/nntpcached start
```

Debian

The Debian command follows:

```
/etc/init.d/nntpcache start
```

Also, whenever you restart your Linux server, it should automatically start on bootup. Now that you have NNTPCache running, you can start up your favorite newsreader to read news! If you are using a text-based newsreader such as `tin` or `trn`, set your `NNTPSERVER` environment variable to point to your NNTPCache machine. Here is an example:

```
$ export NNTPSERVER=nntpcache.mycompany.com
```

If you need more information on NNTPCache, read the documents in the `/usr/doc/nntpcache-1.0.7.1-1/` directory or visit the NNTPCache home page.

Introduction to trn

There are many news readers available for Linux systems, but the perennial favorite remains `trn`. This is an old package but is simple, fast, and efficient. You might not need a news reader at all if you have Web services on your system. Many Web browsers allow access to newsgroups either in your own news directory or through a connection to an ISP's news feed.

The primary advantage of `trn` over the earlier `rn` (read news) package is that `trn` lets you follow threads. A *thread* in a newsgroup is a continuing discussion with one primary subject. Before `trn` came along, you had to read news in consecutive order from first to last, trying to assemble several different conversations into logical groups. When `trn` became available, you could start with one thread, read all the postings about that subject, and then move on to another subject, regardless of the chronological order in which the postings were made.

Threads are usually handled automatically, although there is some work performed behind the scenes on your news feed. Some newsgroups do not support threading, but most do. If threads are available, you can follow the thread from start to finish, or jump out and change threads at any time.

Red Hat

Installing and Configuring trn

The `trn` news reader is easy to install as a binary package; an RPM is included with Red Hat Linux. To see if `trn` is already installed on your system, type the following:

```
rpm -q trn
```

If no package by that name is found, you can install the `trn` package from the directory containing RPM files by issuing the following command:

```
rpm -i trn-3.6-12.i386.rpm
```

Debian users can install `trn` with this:

```
apt-get install trn
```

There really is no special configuration required for `trn` to run. When the binary is available on your system, it will check for the newsgroup information in `/usr/lib/news` and present it to you. In the past, `trn` wasn't capable of forming threads on its own. Because of this, external threading utilities such as `mthreads` or `overview` were once popular. As of version 3.0, however, `trn` supports direct threading without the need for external thread utilities, so most users now use `trn` as a standalone program.

Installing and Configuring `tin`

Since Caldera OpenLinux 2.2 does not ship with `trn`, I will describe a different newsreader that does come with Caldera by default, a slightly different newsreader called `tin`.

The `tin` newsreader is easy to install as a binary package; an RPM is included with Caldera OpenLinux. To see if `tin` is already installed on your system, type the following:

```
rpm -q tin
```

If no package by that name is found, you can install the `trn` package from the directory on your CD-ROM containing RPM files by issuing the following command:

```
rpm -i tin-1.3ub-4.i386.rpm
```

There really is no special configuration required for `tin` to run. When the binary is available on your system, it checks for the newsgroup information in `/usr/lib/news` and presents it to you. If you are running it on a system that does not have news locally, you have to set an environment variable telling `tin` from where to read news. If your news server is `news.home.com`, type in this command sequence:

```
$ NNTPSERVER=news.home.com
$ export NNTPSERVER
$ tin -r
```

You can also set the news server in a systemwide file called `/etc/nntpserver`. That way you only have to start the newsreader to read news.

Summary

In this chapter you saw how to install and configure the Internet News Service, INN, and how to set up a caching NNRP server via NNTPCache. The steps involved may seem a little overwhelming, but if you take them slowly and check everything carefully, you'll be surprised how little time it takes to have a functional news feed on your Linux machine. Remember that you do need a connection available to a news feed before you complete and test the INN configuration. Setting up TCP/IP and UUCP connections is explained elsewhere in this book.

CHAPTER 13

IRC, ICQ, and Others

In This Chapter

Back in the dark old days of character-based terminals, when the Internet was used mainly by educational institutions and government organizations, students around the world used to communicate with each other with electronic mail, also known as email. Compared to the alternatives, regular postal mail (slow) or talking on the telephone (expensive), email was effectively free and was relatively fast—email messages only took a few minutes, or at worst a few hours, to reach the destination electronic mailbox. Email was, and still is, a terrific form of communication for both business and pleasure. Despite this, it has a small problem. No matter how fast you trade email messages, it is not like a real-time conversation where there are two or more people in a face-to-face group or gathered for a conference telephone call. Enter the UNIX `talk` client.

The UNIX talk Client

For years, most UNIX systems had some form of a `talk` client installed by default. This method of communicating is great because it allows you to seemingly talk with someone else who is logged on the same computer system. The "talking" is actually typing the conversation on a computer keyboard. To initiate such a talk session, you type in a command at the UNIX shell prompt like this:

```
$ talk bob
```

This causes a message to periodically appear on Bob's screen that looks something like this:

```
Message from Talk_Daemon@curly.latrobe.edu.au at 13:55 ...
talk: connection requested by joe@curly.latrobe.edu.au
talk: respond with:  talk joe@curly.latrobe.edu.au
[Waiting for your party to respond]
```

Bob would then initiate the `talk` command. He could then engage in a typed conversation with Joe. This method of communicating is especially useful if both parties are working on a similar project and need to correspond with each other immediately.

How talk Works

The `talk` client communicates a `talk` protocol with a `talk` daemon (`talkd`) that runs in the background waiting for `talk` requests. It is this `talk` daemon that manages the different `talk` connections that may be going on at once. There are, in fact, two different versions of the `talk` protocol—a BSD-style protocol that listens on UDP port 517, and the SunOS version (called `ntalk`) that listens on UDP port 518. `talkd` is usually managed by `inetd` on all UNIX flavors. You will see a `talkd` entry in the `/etc/inetd.conf` file.

Using either the talk or ntalk client, however, was not limited to talking with people on a single UNIX machine. Notice in the previous talk request example that the domain name of the machine that Joe and Bob are logged in to is part of the command that Bob had to enter. What if another host on the other side of the world had a talk daemon running? It, too, can communicate using the talk protocol. If Joe were in Australia and Bob were located in the United States and they both had UNIX accounts on hosts that were both on the Internet, they could communicate in real time using the talk client—as if they were on the one computer.

talk Limitations

What are the downsides to using the talk command?

One such limitation is that using the stock standard talk or ntalk command allows you to talk with only one other person. With conference calling facilities on the telephone, is there a way to electronically talk with a group of people? There is a freeware implementation of the talk protocol that allows multiple-way conversations. This package is called ytalk and is included with most Linux distributions. On Caldera and Red Hat you will find it in the main packages directory on the CD-ROM called ytalk*.rpm. Even though ytalk addresses one of the main limitations of the original talk client, there is another more important limitation: Most current UNIX systems are firewalled from the Internet. These UNIX systems cannot be seen from the Internet at large. Even some large educational institutions are starting to firewall off parts of their networks. Most incoming traffic in this situation is filtered, which almost certainly includes talk traffic. As with most things, security requirements today take away some of the usefulness of the talk or ytalk commands, so there must be an alternative way for people to chat online.

IRC

A new protocol was developed in the late 1980s and early 1990s called *Internet Relay Chat* (IRC). IRC was developed originally for users on Bulletin Board Systems (BBS) to talk with each other online. It has since grown to massive proportions, with servers all around the world. In May 1993, RFC 1459 was released; it contains the nity-gritty details of the original protocol. You will find it at ftp://ftp.isi.edu/in-notes/rfc1459.txt. Since that time, many other IRC networks have popped up that are based on modifications to this original protocol and that improve various aspects of the IRC experience. These include EFnet (the original IRC network), Undernet, IRCnet, and DALnet, just to name a few.

How IRC Works

As with most chat methods, the IRC protocol is client- and server-based. There are many IRC servers located throughout the world, and you connect to the closest server to you via the IRC client program of your choice. Today there are countless numbers of IRC clients for almost all operating systems. When you start one of these IRC clients, you must provide a nickname. That nickname distinguishes you from any other client also connected to that particular IRC network. Different IRC networks have different requirements for the nickname length, but generally it can be anywhere from 9 to 30 characters. Once your client connects, there are hundreds of chat channels that can then access, each with a specific topic. The channel names usually begin with the hash (#) or ampersand (&) character. Each channel has one or more *channel operators*, also known as *channel ops*. It is these channel ops that control the channel. They have the power to kick people off the channel if they are being disruptive, post a new topic of discussion, and other administrative tasks.

One important point should be made: All the IRC servers throughout the world are connected in a spanning tree-type network. This means that it does not matter which IRC server you connect to; you will generally be able to see all the IRC channels in that particular IRC network. Note that some channels are marked as local—they are to appear only on a single IRC server. All other channels are distributed throughout the IRC network.

Linux IRC Clients

There are many different Linux IRC clients. The most popular is text-based, but there are plenty of IRC clients that can be used with X Windows. Go to `http://www.freshmeat.net` and search for *irc*—you will see just how many different clients there are to choose from! I describe two here, the first being the most popular text IRC client, `ircII`. It is bundled with the Red Hat 6.0 distribution. I also describe an X Windows-based client called `ksirc`. It is bundled with the Caldera OpenLinux distribution.

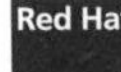

First of all, check to make sure `ircII` is installed with the following command:

```
$ rpm -q ircii
ircii-4.4-7
```

If it is not installed, install it from your Red Hat distribution CD-ROM (assumed to be already mounted under `/mnt/cdrom`):

```
# rpm -i /mnt/cdrom/RedHat/RPMS/ircii-4.4-7.i386.rpm
```

Red Hat

You should be able to enter the following code, which will start your client session:

```
$ irc chat-newbie_us.undernet.org
```

The client session should look something like that displayed in Figure 13.1.

FIGURE 13.1
Starting a command line IRC session.

```
xterm
*** - We reserve the right to bar anyone for any reason from using this
*** - free service. Do not abuse your guest status here. Thank you.
*** - ===================================================================
*** -
*** -     We accept connections on ports 6666, 6667 and 6668.
*** -                 This is an EFNET server.
*** -
*** -     *****************************************************
*** -     * Need help with IRC ? Try http://www.irchelp.org/ *
*** -     *****************************************************
*** -
*** - <><><><><><><><><><><><><><><><><><><><><><><><><><><><><><><><><><>
*** - MCSNet serves the 312, 708, 773, 847, 630, 815 and most of 414 area code
*** -   SLIP/PPP accounts from $10 monthly
*** -   Shell accounts from $5 monthly
*** -   Dedicated service to DS-3 speeds available
*** -   +1 312-803-MCS1 - General office number, 9-5 Monday - Friday
*** -   +1 414-290-5799 - Milwaukee customer service / tech support
*** - <><><><><><><><><><><><><><><><><><><><><><><><><><><><><><><><><><>
*** -
*** -    Riss - Admin, IRCop, Keeper of the K-Lines, and Server Flunky :)
*** -
[1] 16:46 irc-newbi * type /help for help
```

Note

Be sure to check with the channel list on `http://www.irc.net` for the IRC server nearest you for the particular network you want to access. The closer you are to your IRC server, the less lag you experience, which will make your overall chat session much more enjoyable.

Since Caldera does not ship with the text-based `ircII` client, I will give you an introduction to the KDE chat client, `ksirc`. It should be installed as part of your default KDE install under the Applications menu under Internet; it should be called Chat Client. Once you start it, you get a screen similar to that shown in Figure 13.2.

FIGURE 13.2
Opening screen for `ksirc`.

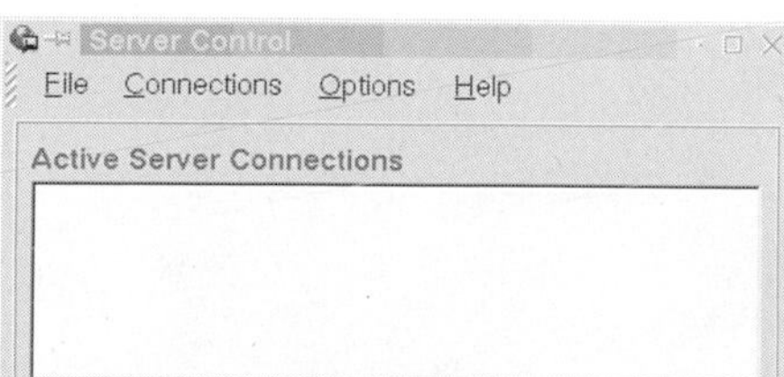

To connect to an IRC server, click Connections, New Server. From there you can select an IRC network and the server to which you want to connect. This example, shown in Figure 13.3, shows a connection to the Undernet.

FIGURE 13.3
Choosing an IRC server to connect to.

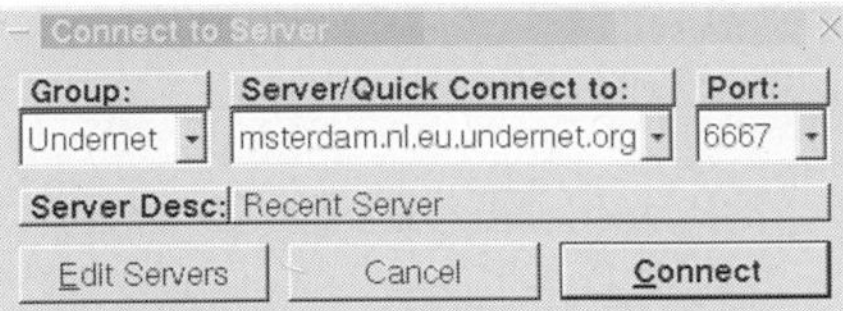

Once you press the Connect button, another window appears. That window contains messages from the server you just connected to. From here you can enter IRC commands. All IRC commands begin with the backslash (/) character. As an example, type in the following:

```
/join #aussies
```

Another window opens and contains the channel you just opened. It will look something like Figure 13.4. The main panel contains the discussion window, and the rectangular panel to the right contains all the clients currently connected to the channel. You can get more information on a particular nickname by right-clicking it and selecting Whois. As shown in the figure, I did a `Whois` on the highlighted nickname JAO. The results of that command are shown in the large display toward the bottom. It shows that particular user's email address, what channels he or she is currently connected to, how long he or she has been idle, and what IRC server he or she is connected to. For a summary of all the commands you can give the server, type `/HELP`.

FIGURE 13.4
Sample active IRC session with `ksirc`.

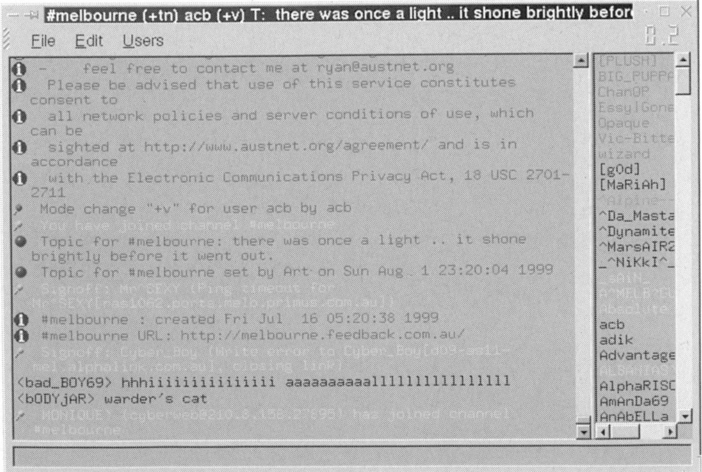

You will also notice that the original window (which came up when you started the IRC client) has a record of the servers you are connected to and a list of all the channels you

have joined on each server. This is quite handy—especially for power users who connect to many servers and channels at once. An example of what it could look like is shown in Figure 13.5.

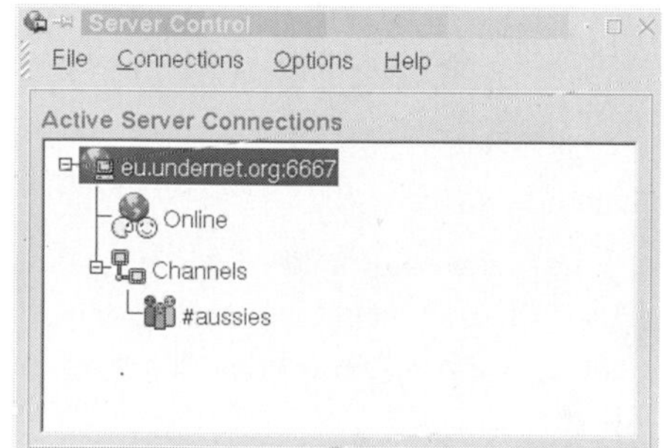

FIGURE 13.5
Listing currently connected IRC sessions with ksirc.

After you initially start either IRC client, some text will display a lot of information. Depending on which IRC network you have chosen to use, this information may include how many channel operators are online, how many channels have been formed, and when the IRC server's message of the day (MOTD) was last modified. This MOTD sometimes contains a lot of important information on such things, such as when the server will be down for maintenance and the server's rules, which is also known as the *Acceptable Usage Policy* (AUP). You can read a server's MOTD at any time with the `/MOTD` command.

First join a channel. You can do this with the `JOIN` command:

```
/JOIN #new2irc
```

When you join a channel, a message similar to this comes up:

```
chat-newbie (newbie@linux.home.com) has joined channel #New2IRC
*** Topic for #New2IRC: Channel for newbies to IRC!
*** #New2IRC W 930919269
*** Users on #ircbar: acb Jaman jackie chat-newbie
*** #New2IRC End of /NAMES list.
*** #New2IRC 830552852
```

As you can see, when you join a new channel, it executes the `/NAMES` command so you can see at a glance who is online. Depending on the time you connect, this channel can have a lot of *IRC newbies* connected. Others you can try are `#newuser` and `#chatback`. If none of these have many people online, try `#ircbar`.

Now that you are connected to a channel, you can join in the current conversation by typing. What you type will appear on the screen similar to this:

```
> What I just typed
```

Other people will see what you typed like this:

```
<your nickname> What I just typed
```

Here are other commands that you might find of use:

- `/WHOIS chat_newbie` gives information on the `chat_newbie` or whatever nickname you specify.
- `/MSG cool-guy your message` sends a one-line message to `cool-guy`. `cool-guy` needn't be on the same channel you're on.
- Any number of `/JOIN #channelname` commands. Each time you issue a `/JOIN` command, the new channel adds to the channels you have already joined. Be careful! If you select busy channels, you may get bombarded with messages and may be unable to keep up with it all!
- Many clients have a `/HELP` command. This gives a list of commands that are valid. From there you can get further help if required.
- `/LEAVE #channelname` disconnects you from the specified channel.

See the following section for resources that help with your first IRC experience.

IRC Resources

For more information on any aspect of IRC, there are plenty of resources on the Internet:

- `http://www.irc.net` is probably the definitive guide to IRC for any platform. It contains information on the history of IRC, some IRC user guides and tutorials, pointers to many different IRC clients, information on all the different IRC networks including server names, and much more.
- `http://www.efnet.net` is the home page for the original IRC network.
- `http://www.irchelp.org` contains many different help files and FAQs.
- `http://ftp.undernet.org/irc` contains servers and clients for many platforms and various IRC-related things.

This should give you a jumpstart. However, if what you need is not listed here, you can find what you need with a well-worded query at your choice of one of the many Internet search engines.

Chatting with ICQ

Over the past couple of years, a new type of chat network has taken the Internet by storm: ICQ. ICQ is a way of communicating with friends and work colleagues, while surfing the Net at the same time. You can send single pop-up messages to other people, play games, send files, or simply chat with people with interests similar to yours. ICQ also has the capability to notify you when someone on your friends list comes online!

Unfortunately, neither Red Hat Linux 6.0 or Caldera OpenLinux 2.2 supply an ICQ client by default; you have to download one. The one I use in this example is `licq`, which you can download from `http://licq.wibble.net/download.html`. I suggest downloading the latest stable release, which at the time of this writing was `licq-0.61.tar.gz`. However, if you want to stay on the bleeding edge, you can grab the latest development version.

Note

Unfortunately, if you are a first-time user, the `licq` client does not lead you through the ICQ registration process. You will have to use a Windows or Macintosh computer because they are the only clients supported; download the applicable client program from there. You can do this by pointing your Web browser to `http://www.icq.net/download`. Scroll down to the section for new users and click your preferred platform. Follow the onscreen instructions to download, install, and then register with ICQ. When all that is complete, you may continue with installing the Linux ICQ client described in the following pages.

Once you have downloaded `licq`, unpack it:

```
$ gunzip -c licq-0.61.tar.gz ¦ tar -xvf -
```

This creates a directory in your current directory called `licq-0.61`. Change into this directory and run the configure script:

```
$ ./configure
```

You may come across a few errors where the configure script will stop. This may be due to you not having the GNU C++ compiler installed; perhaps you do not have the `qt` libraries installed. Make sure that all required library files are installed with the following `rpm` command:

```
$ rpm -q qt qt-devel libstdc++ egcs-c++
qt-1.42-2
qt-devel-1.42-2
libstc++-2.9.0-4
egcs-c++-2.91.60-4
```

The actual version numbers will vary depending on what Linux distribution you have chosen, but this should not matter.

After you have run the `configure` command cleanly, enter the `make` command and wait for `licq` to compile. It should compile with no errors. I suggest that you `su` to the `root` account and install `licq`. By default it will install into `/usr/local/bin`:

```
$ su
Password:
# make install
<...>
# exit
```

The first time you start ICQ, it asks you for some initialization details:

```
$ licq

Before using Licq for the first time, your configuration files must be
set up.

Enter your Alias, UIN and password. These must be obtained by
registering with an official ICQ client - see http://www.mirabilis.com/
for details.

Enter your Alias: my_alias
Enter your UIN: 12345678
Enter your password:
Confirm password:
```

Once you have entered the information relevant to you, the main ICQ window will pop up and should look like Figure 13.6.

FIGURE 13.6
`Licq` opening screen.

Different functions you can now perform with your Linux ICQ client include the following:

- Adding people to your contacts list—System, User Functions, Add User.
- If you don't know the name of the user you want to add, you can search through the ICQ database with System, User Functions, Search for User.
- Changing your status from Offline (the default) to Online, or one of many others—System, Status, and so on.
- If you have added someone to your contacts list, you can right-click here and send an URL, a file, a message, or even a chat request. *Chat requests* allow you to have a one-on-one conversation.

Because the Linux clients are not official ICQ clients, they do not contain all the ICQ capabilities. This is because the coders have reverse-engineered the ICQ protocol and not all the features are figured out yet. However, they are being developed fairly quickly. Before long, you should be able to run a Linux ICQ client that contains all the functions and features of its Windows and Macintosh counterparts.

For the definitive guide to ICQ, `http://www.icq.net` should be added to your bookmark list. It contains FAQs, troubleshooting guides, and heaps of other ICQ-related topics. The other ICQ-related Web site that will interest Linux users is found at `http://www.port-up.com/~gyandl/icq`. Here in one place is a list of the most common ICQ Linux clients.

Installing AOL's Instant Messenger

America Online's Instant Messenger service is another chat-type option available for use. This is quite similar to the ICQ concept, but done in a slightly different way and without some of the bells and whistles of the ICQ service.

Again, none of the Linux distributions actually provide the Instant Messenger client you will have to download it. First go to `http://www.aol.com/aim/home.html`; click the large Sign Up Now graphic toward the bottom of the page.

From this next screen you are asked to enter the screen name you want to use, as well as a password that you will use to access your account. Enter your email address and then click the button that says Click Here!. If your screen name is accepted, you can shortly expect an email that you will have to reply to; that will complete the registration process. This is to ensure that you have given a correct email address.

While you are waiting for the validation email, click the Download button, which should take you to a page that has a list of platforms for which clients are available. Scroll down to the UNIX button and click it; you are taken to the `TiK` Home Page. `TiK` is the name given to the AOL Messenger client for UNIX platforms. Now you just need to click Step 3 of the Download and Install section of the page where `tik-0.73.tar.gz` is mentioned. Note that by the time this book goes to press, the version number may have changed. When it is downloaded, type the following command:

```
$ gunzip -c tik-0.73.tar.gz ¦ tar -xf -
```

This will create a directory called `tik` in your current working directory. Make sure you have `tcl` and `tk` version 8 installed:

```
$ rpm -q tcl tk
tcl-8.0.4-29
tcl-8.0.4-29
```

Typing the following is all you have to do to be up and running:

```
$ cd tik
$ wish tik.tcl &
```

Once it starts, you will get a screen like that shown in Figure 13.7.

FIGURE 13.7
AOL Messenger buddy list.

Tip

Occasionally, the AOL download site for the `TiK` client is down. If this is the case, you can find alternate download locations by going to `http://www.ftpsearch.com` or `http://www.linuxberg.com` and searching for `TiK`.

Enter your selected screen name and password and click the Sign On button. This brings up your Buddies List. This is where you can put all your friends' names so you can tell at a glance if they are online. If any of them happen to be around, you can send messages or engage any number of them in a chat session.

You have only gotten started. There are numerous plug-ins to achieve all sorts of different things (all available from the main `TiK` download page). For a complete list of features and information on what other things AOL Messenger can be used for, see the Web page where I told you to sign up for a Messenger account and click the What Is It? Button at the bottom of the page.

Notice that AOL Messenger bears quite a resemblance to ICQ. Other similar Internet chat-while-you-work applications seem to pop up all the time. Even Yahoo! (`http://www.yahoo.com`) has a similar application!

Other Talk Clients

I have only touched on the most popular talk methods currently available on the Net. There are countless other methods of talking using the Internet! This section is devoted to those other ways.

Teaser and the Firecat

An exciting new chat system on the horizon is known as the Teaser and the Firecat. At the time of this writing it was still in the very early development stages, but it makes big promises. The premise of this new protocol? There are multiple Teasers (the server) around the Internet and users use a client, called the Firecat. This is rather than having an ICQ number, which is mostly meaningless! A user has an account at a particular Teaser; the email address would be something like `username@teaser.whatever.com`. If you would like more information on this, check out `http://www.bowerbird.com.au/teaser`.

Chatting on the Web

There are literally thousands of Web sites devoted to Net chatting. Many provide different chat discussion rooms, where there is something that will appeal to almost anyone! Some Web sites are totally devoted to providing chat discussion areas, whereas others operate at specific times. Some of the most popular Web chat sites include

- `http://login.yahoo.com`
- `http://chat.netcentral.net`
- `http://wbs.net`
- `http://webarrow.net/chatindex` (a large index of other chat-related Web sites)

A lot of television and entertainment Web sites have celebrities online at certain times, fielding questions from everyday people on the Net. This has certainly opened a new way of communicating with your favorite star! Here are some renowned sites:

- `http://chat.lycos.com` has discussion and special interest areas, as well as special events most days of the week.
- `http://www.realhollywood.com` has a lot of special chat events with celebrities and other entertainment chat rooms where you can talk to other fans of your favorite TV shows.
- `http://events.yahoo.com/Entertainment` again has celebrity chats and general chat rooms, entertainment being the theme.
- `http://etonline.com` has both a regular chat room and a celebrity chat room.

I have only highlighted some popular sites—there are heaps of others and they can all be found with your favorite search engine.

The Internet Phone

Something that has really taken off relatively recently is the *Internet phone*. This phone is software that allows you to talk into a microphone connected to your soundcard, which digitizes your voice and transmits it across the Net to the person you are talking with. This obviously could require a large amount of bandwidth; voice is known to be considerably hungry when it comes to soaking up available bandwidth. With the voice-compression algorithms available today, these bandwidth requirements have decreased dramatically; a 56Kbps modem connection should be enough to handle most conversations.

There are countless Internet phone products. Most are for the Windows platform, but more are being developed for Linux. You can find a few by visiting `http://www.freshmeat.net` and searching for *phone* or *Internet phone*.

Summary

You have learned that there are many ways to chat with others on the Internet. People originally used the `talk` program, but then progressed to IRC. Nowadays most people have an ICQ client on their desktop while Web surfing and use a combination of ICQ with IRC. You have also learned that there are many chat Web sites that have discussion rooms, as well as scheduled chats with entertainment celebrities. Finally, you now know that the next generation of Internet chatting utilizes the microphones and speakers attached to your soundcard, allowing you to actually speak with someone rather than typing the conversation.

CHAPTER 14

NIS: Network Information Service

In This Chapter

The *Network Information Service* (NIS) is a simple, generic client/server database system. Under Linux, however, the most common use for it is sharing password and group files across a network. This chapter covers the setup of both master and slave NIS servers, as well as the configuration needed for clients to use them.

NIS, developed by Sun Microsystems as part of its SunOS operating system, was originally known as *The Yellow Pages*, or YP. Unfortunately, the name Yellow Pages had already been trademarked, and the resulting lawsuit forced the name change to NIS. You will soon discover that all the NIS commands are still prefixed with `yp`.

The NIS protocol was made public and implementations of it quickly spread to other variations of UNIX. Linux has supported NIS from its onset. Because Linux follows the NIS standard, it can work with other flavors of UNIX as either the NIS server or client.

Understanding NIS

As you configure your network, you will find that some of your configuration files are not host specific, but they require frequent updating. `/etc/passwd` and `/etc/group` are two that come to mind. NIS enables you to set up a master server where these files are stored and then configure each machine on your network as clients to this server. Whenever a client needs to fetch an entry from the `/etc/passwd` file, it consults the NIS server instead.

Two prerequisites must be met in order for a file to be sharable via NIS. First, the file must be tabular with at least one entry that is unique across the entire file. In the `/etc/passwd` file, this entry is either the login or UID. Second, the file in its raw form must be a straight text file.

With the criteria met, the files are converted into DBM files, a simple database format allowing for quick searches. You must create a separate DBM for each key to be searched. In the `/etc/passwd` file, for instance, you need the database to be searchable by login and by UID. The result is two DBM files, `passwd.byname` and `passwd.byuid`.

The original text file, along with the DBM files created from it, is maintained at the NIS master server. Clients that connect to the server to obtain information do not cache any returned results.

NIS Domains

NIS servers and clients must be in the same NIS domain to communicate with one another. Note that the NIS domain is not the same as a DNS domain, although it is valid for them share the same name.

> **Tip**
>
> You should maintain separate names for your NIS and DNS domains for two reasons. First, it is easier for you to differentiate what you're talking about when discussing problems with anyone else. Second, having separate names makes it more difficult for potential intruders to understand the internal workings of your machines from the outside.

Both the clients and servers bind themselves to a domain; hence, a client can only belong to one NIS domain at a given time. Once bound, clients send a broadcast to find the NIS server for the given domain.

The Different Servers

So far, you might have noticed that I've referenced the NIS server explicitly as the *master* server. The two kinds of NIS servers are master servers and slave servers.

Master NIS servers are the actual truth holders. They contain the text files used to generate the DBM files, and any changes to the database must be made to these files.

Slave NIS servers are designed to supplement master NIS servers by taking some of the load off. When a file is updated on the server, a server push is initiated and the slave NIS server gets an updated copy of the DBM files.

> **Caution**
>
> Like any network service, NIS might have bugs that can allow unauthorized access to your system. It is prudent to keep track of security reports and obtain patches when they become available. The two best places to start are the Computer Emergency Response Team Web site at `www.cert.org` and the comp.os.linux.announce newsgroup. Both provide a moderated source of information that you can use to maintain your system.
>
> Another place to check is with your individual Linux distribution.
>
> Debian GNU/Linux users can visit `http://www.debian.org/` or `http://security.debian.org/`.
>
> 
>
> Red Hat users can visit `http://www.redhat.com`.
>
> 
>
> Finally, Caldera users can visit `http://www.calderasystems.com`.

Installing the Software

If you didn't install the NIS software during the initial setup process, you need to install it now.

For Red Hat, start by mounting the Red Hat CD-ROM. The following assumes that the CD-ROM is mounted on the /mnt/cdrom directory.

Access the /mnt/cdrom/RedHat/RPMS directory:

```
[root@server /root]# cd /mnt/cdrom/RedHat/RPMS
```

Install the RPMS yp-tools-2.2-1.i386.rpm, ypbind-3.3-20.i386.rpm, and ypserv-1.3.6.91-1.i386 with the following commands:

```
[root@server RPMS]# rpm -i yp-tools-2.2-1.i386.rpm
[root@server RPMS]# rpm -i ypbind-3.3-20.i386.rpm
[root@server RPMS]# rpm -i ypserv-1.3.6.91-1.i386.rpm
```

After the software is installed, the next step is configuring the master NIS server.

In Debian, you can install the full suite of tools with this command:

```
apt-get install nis
```

Caldera 2.2 may not have come with the yp distribution tools. Fortunately for you, Caldera uses RPMs. Therefore, mount the Red Hat disk and install the software from there!

Start by mounting the Red Hat CD-ROM. The following assumes that the CD-ROM is mounted on the /mnt/cdrom directory.

Access the /mnt/cdrom/RedHat/RPMS directory:

```
[root@server /root]# cd /mnt/cdrom/RedHat/RPMS
```

Install the RPMS yp-tools-2.2-1.i386.rpm, ypbind-3.3-20.i386.rpm, and ypserv-1.3.6.91-1.i386 with the following commands:

```
[root@server RPMS]# rpm -i yp-tools-2.2-1.i386.rpm
[root@server RPMS]# rpm -i ypbind-3.3-20.i386.rpm
[root@server RPMS]# rpm -i ypserv-1.3.6.  91-1.i386.rpm
```

Configuring a Master NIS Server

Before you configure the server software, you need to decide whether you are going to set up any slave servers. If you are, you need to know their hostnames before continuing. Also, the hostnames must be in the /etc/hosts file. Along with the names of your NIS servers, you need to decide on an NIS domain name at this point. Remember that this domain name is not the same as your DNS domain name and for clarity purposes should be set differently.

With this information, you are ready to begin.

First, you need to set the domain name with the `domainname` command:

```
[root@vestax /etc]# domainname audionet.domain.com
```

Although this will work for the moment, you do need to change a startup configuration file so that this happens every time your system reboots. The `/etc/rc.d/init.d/ypserv` script that was installed as part of the RPM looks for the domain name to be set in the `/etc/sysconfig/network` file. Simply add the following line:

```
NIS_DOMAIN=audionet.domain.com
```

When the Debian package is installed, it prompts you for the NIS domain. Enter the domain at this time; after that, it will not be necessary to take any further action to set it.

If you are running an NIS server on your machine, you need to edit a line in `/etc/init.d/nis`. Look for the `NISSERVER=false` line. If this machine will be a NIS master server, set it to `master`. If it will be a NIS slave server, set it to `slave`. Reload with this:

```
/etc/init.d/nis stop
/etc/init.d/nis start
```

With the domain name set, you can decide what files you want to share via NIS, as well as their filenames. You do this by editing `/var/yp/Makefile`. As the name implies, NIS maintains its maps by using the `make` utility. Although familiarity with how this tool works is useful, it isn't mandatory to configure NIS.

Begin by loading `/var/yp/Makefile` into your favorite editor. Scroll past the lines that read as follows:

```
# These are files from which the NIS databases are built. You may edit
# these to taste in the event that you wish to keep your NIS source files
# separate from your NIS server's actual configuration files.
```

Below this segment of text, you will see lines that resemble the following:

```
GROUP       = $(YPPWDDIR)/group
PASSWD      = $(YPPWDDIR)/passwd
etc...
```

Note

As you scroll down the file, you will notice several parameters you can set to alter the behavior of the NIS server. For the time being, you probably shouldn't alter anything except for those items discussed in this section. If you are feeling adventurous, read the comments associated with each line and have fun with it.

This section tells NIS where your database files are located. The `$(YPPWDDIR)` string is a variable that was set to `/etc` at the top of the `Makefile`. Although it is possible to change this to another directory, you should probably keep it there for consistency. The string that comes after `$(YPPWDDIR)` is the name of the file in `/etc` that will become shared through NIS. Most of these entries can remain the same. The few that you want to change are `GROUP`, `PASSWD`, `SHADOW`, `ALIASES`, and possibly `HOSTS`.

The `GROUP` line shows that the file for controlling group information is at `/etc/group`. You might want to keep your local group file on the server separate from your NIS group file because your local group file could contain server-specific groups that you don't want to share across NIS, such as the `www` group for your Web server.

The same holds true for the other lines as well, especially the `PASSWD` line. A simple convention you can use to indicate that the file is being shared across NIS is to suffix it with a `.yp`. The resulting line looks something like the following:

```
PASSWD          = $(YPPWDDIR)/passwd.yp
```

Note

By default, the NIS server will not distribute any password entries with a UID or GID below 500. To change this, look for the line reading `MINUID=500` in the makefile. Right below it is `MINGID=500`. Changing their values will change the minimum UIDs and GIDs. Unless you already have a UID/GID numbering system that includes values below `500`, you will probably want to keep this setting as is.

With the filenames you want set, you can now determine which files to distribute. Scroll down the makefile past the following block:

```
# If you don't want some of these maps built, feel free to comment
# them out of this list.
```

Your cursor should be at a line like the following:

```
all:  ypservers passwd group hosts rpc services netid protocols mail \
        # shadow publickey # netgrp networks ethers bootparams \
        # amd.home auto.master auto.home
```

This line specifies which maps will be made available via NIS. The # symbol after shadow is the comment symbol. The second and third lines in this example are commented out.

Before making any changes to this line, you should make a copy of it and comment the copy out. The result looks something like the following:

```
#all:  ypservers passwd group hosts rpc services netid protocols mail \
#        # shadow publickey # netgrp networks ethers bootparams \
#        # amd.home auto.master auto.home

all:  ypservers passwd group hosts rpc services netid protocols mail \
        # shadow publickey # netgrp networks ethers bootparams \
        # amd.home auto.master auto.home
```

By commenting out the line, you can retain a copy of it just in case something goes wrong. You can always refer to the copy and see how the line looked before things were changed. With the copy in place, go ahead and begin your changes.

The only files you need to distribute for your network are `ypservers`, `passwd`, `group`, `hosts`, `rpc`, `services`, `netid`, `protocols`, and `mail`. This distribution is already set so you don't need to change anything.

Note

What are those other lines for? Good question! They are other databases that some sites distribute as well. As you need specific entries in that list, you can simply uncomment them and include them for distribution to your clients. At some sites, NIS is used to distribute other kinds of information, so you can create custom entries. You can even use NIS to make a companywide telephone directory.

Unless you are comfortable with makefiles, you should leave the remainder of the file alone. Save the makefile and quit the editor.

You are ready to initialize your NIS database with the `/usr/lib/yp/ypinit` command. When invoked, this command prompts for the name of any NIS slave servers you want to set up. For this example, select `denon` to be the slave NIS server.

Remember that you do not have to set up a slave NIS server. Setting up a slave server is only useful if you have a large number of NIS clients and you need to distribute the load they generate.

If you have not already set your domain name, the following initialization will error out with a message that says `The local host's domain name hasn't been set. Please set it.` To initialize the master server, use the following:

```
 [root@vestax /root]# /usr/lib/yp/ypinit -m
At this point, we have to construct a list of the hosts which will run NIS
servers. vestax is in the list of NIS server hosts. Please continue to add
the names for the other hosts, one per line. When you are done with the
list, type a <control D>.

    next host to add:  vestax
    next host to add:  denon
    next host to add: <CTRL-D>
The current list of NIS servers looks like this:

vestax
denon

Is this correct?  [y/n: y]  y
We need some minutes to build the databases...
Building /var/yp/audionet.domain.com/ypservers...
Running /var/yp/Makefile...
NIS Map update started on Mon May  5 22:16:53 PDT 1997
make[1]: Entering directory '/var/yp/audionet.domain.com'
Updating passwd.byname...
Updating passwd.byuid...
Updating hosts.byname...
Updating hosts.byaddy...
Updating group.byname...
Updating group.bygid...
Updating netid.byname...
Updating protocols.bynumber...
Updating protocols.byname...
Updating rpc.byname...
Updating rpc.bynumber...
Updating services.byname...
Updating mail.aliases...
make[1]: Leaving directory '/var/yp/audionet.domain.com'
NIS Map update completed
```

If anywhere in the middle of the output you receive a message like the following instead, it means that you are missing one of the files you listed in the makefile:

```
make[1]:***No rule to make target '/etc/shadow', needed by 'shadow.byname'.
➥  Stop.
make[1]: Leaving directory '/var/yp/audionet.domain.com'
```

Check that you edited the makefile as you intended, and then make sure that the files you selected to be shared via NIS actually do exist. After you've made sure of these, you do not need to rerun `ypinit` but instead can simply rerun `cd /var/yp;make`.

The hosts that you add are put into the file `/var/yp/ypservers`. As an alternative to running the `ypinit` command, you can manually edit the `/var/yp/ypervers` file and then run `make` using the preceding sequence.

Starting the Daemons on Boot

> **Note**
>
> This section applies to both Caldera and Red Hat. It is not applicable to Debian. All necessary actions for starting on boot are handled automatically or almost automatically at install time.

To start the NIS server automatically at boot time, you need to create a symbolic link from the runlevel 3 startup directory. To do this, type the following:

```
[root@client /root]# cd /etc/rc.d/rc3.d
[root@client rc3.d]# ln -s ../init.d/ypserv S60ypserv
```

The `yppasswdd` daemon allows users from NIS clients to change their passwords on the NIS server. First, make sure that your default runlevel is 3; you can do this be modifying the initdefault line in `/etc/inittab`. To start this program automatically at boot time, you need to type the following:

```
[root@client /root]# cd /etc/rc.d/rc3.d
[root@client rc3.d]# ln -s ../init.d/yppasswdd S61yppasswdd
```

> **Note**
>
> Notice that it says to link to `S61yppasswdd`. Your system may already have something numbered 61, such as `S61rwalld`. If this is the case, use the next available number, such as 64. Therefore, the command would be as follows:
>
> ```
> ln -s ../init.d/yppasswdd s64yppasswdd
> ```

If you want to start the daemons by hand so you don't need to reboot, simply run the following:

```
[root@client /root]# /etc/rc.d/init.d/ypserv start
[root@client /root]# /etc/rc.d/init.d/yppasswdd start
```

You now have a NIS master server. Time to test your work with an NIS client.

Configuring an NIS Client

Compared to configuring an NIS server, NIS clients are trivial. You must deal with only four files, one of which is only one line long.

When you install the NIS services on a Debian machine, the installation script will ask you for this information. You should not have to reconfigure the system after that point unless you have some unusual needs, so this section probably does not apply to you.

Begin by editing the `/etc/yp.conf` file. The entries in this file are used for the initial binding. Use one of the following valid entries:

```
domain NISDOMAIN server HOSTNAME
```

Use server `HOSTNAME` for the domain `NISDOMAIN`. You could have more than one entry of this type for a single domain.

```
domain NISDOMAIN broadcast
```

Use `broadcast` on the local net for domain `NISDOMAIN`.

```
ypserver HOSTNAME
```

Use server `HOSTNAME` for the local domain. The IP address of the server must be listed in `/etc/hosts`.

The next step is to edit the `/etc/sysconfig/network` file to set the NIS domain name for boot time. To do this, simply add this line:

```
NISDOMAIN=domainname
```

`domainname` is the same as specified in the `/etc/yp.conf` file (in this case, `audionet.domain.com`).

The last file that needs to be changed is the `/etc/nsswitch.conf` file. This is slightly more involved than the previous files; however, a default file comes with the Red Hat installation. This file is used to configure which services are used to determine information such as hostnames, password files, and group files.

Begin by opening `/etc/nsswitch.conf` with your favorite editor. Scroll past the comments (those lines beginning with the # symbol). You should see something like this:

```
passwd:    files nisplus nis
shadow:    files nisplus nis
group:    files nisplus nis

hosts:    files nisplus nis dns

services:     nisplus [NOTFOUND=return] files
etc...
```

The first column indicates the file in question. In the first line, this is `passwd`. The next column indicates the source for the file. This can be one of six options:

Option	*Description*
`nis`	Uses NIS to determine this information.
`yp`	Uses NIS to determine this information (alias for `nis`).
`dns`	Uses DNS to determine this information (only applicable to hosts).
`files`	Uses the file on the local machine to determine this information (for example, `/etc/passwd`).
`[NOTFOUND=return]`	Stops searching if the information has not been found yet.
`nisplus`	Uses NIS+.

The order these are placed in the `/etc/nsswitch.conf` file determines the search order used by the system. For example, in the `hosts` line, the order of the entries are files `nis dns`, indicating that hostnames are first searched for in the `/etc/hosts` file, then via NIS in the `map hosts.byname`, and finally by DNS via the DNS server specified in `/etc/resolv.conf`.

In almost all instances, you want to search the local file before searching through NIS or DNS. This allows a machine to have local characteristics (such as a special user listed in `/etc/passwd`) while still using the network services being offered. The notable exception to this is the netgroup file that by its very nature should come from NIS.

Modify the order of your searches to suit your site's needs and save the configuration file.

Now that all the files are in place, set up the client daemon to automatically start at boot time. You do this by creating a symbolic link from `/etc/rc.d/rc.3/S60ypbind` to `/etc/rc.d/init.d/ypbind`. The exact commands are as follows:

```
[root@client /root]# cd /etc/rc.d/rc3.d
[root@client rc3.d]# ln -s ../init.d/ypbind S60ypbind
```

Testing the Client

Because of the way NIS works under Linux, you do not need to reboot to start NIS client functions. To see if you can communicate with the NIS server, try this:

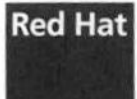

Start by setting the domain name by hand. You can do so with the command:

```
[root@client /root]# domainname nis_domain
```

nis_domain is the NIS domain name. In the test case, it is `audionet.domain.com`. Start the NIS client daemon, `ypbind`, with this command:

```
[root@client /root]# /etc/rc.d/init.d/ypbind start
```

In Debian, you can restart the NIS system and make it reload its configuration with this:

```
/etc/init.d/nis stop
/etc/init.d/nis sart
```

With the NIS client and server configured, you are ready to test your work:

```
ypcat passwd
```

If your configuration is working, you should see the contents of your NIS server's `/etc/passwd.yp` file displayed on your screen (assuming, of course, that you chose that file to be shared via NIS for your `passwd` file). If you receive a message such as

```
No such map passwd.byname.
➥ Reason: can't bind to a server which serves domain
```

you need to double-check that your files have been properly configured.

Tip

As a precautionary measure, you should schedule a reboot while you are with the machine to ensure that it does start and configure the NIS information correctly. After all, your users will not be happy if after a power failure, your machine does not come back up correctly without assistance.

Configuring an NIS Secondary Server

After you've decided to configure a machine as an NIS secondary server, you start by configuring it as an NIS client machine. Verify that you can access the server maps via the `ypcat` command.

Now you are ready to tell the master server that a slave server exists. To do this, edit the `/var/yp/ypservers` file so that the slave server you are setting up is included in the list. If you configured your master server with the name of the slave server during the `ypinit -m` phase, you do not need to do this.

You can now initialize the slave server by running this command:

```
/usr/lib/yp/ypinit -s master
```

master is the hostname for the NIS master server. In this example, it's `vestax`. The output should look something like the following:

```
We will need some minutes to copy the databases from vestax.
Transferring mail.aliases...
Trying ypxfrd ... not running
Transferring services.byname...
Trying ypxfrd ... not running
Transferring rpc.bynumber...
Trying ypxfrd ... not running
[etc...]

denon.domain.com's NIS database has been set up.
If there were warnings, please figure out what went wrong, and fix it.

At this point, make sure that /etc/passwd and /etc/group have
been edited so that when the NIS is activated, the databases you
have just created will be used, instead of the /etc ASCII files.
```

Don't worry about the `Trying ypxfrd...not running` message. This happens because you haven't set the NIS master server to run the YP map transfer daemon `rpc.ypxfrd`. In fact, you never set it up to do so; instead, use a server push method where the NIS master server pushes the maps to all the NIS slaves whenever there is an update.

To set the NIS master to do the actual push, you need to change its makefile a little. On the master server, edit the makefile so that the line `NOPUSH="True"` is changed to read **`#NOPUSH="True"`** and the line that reads `DOMAIN = 'basename \'pwd\''` is changed to **`DOMAIN='/bin/domainname'`**.

Now for the big test: On the NIS master server, run `cd /var/yp;make all` to force all the maps to be rebuilt and pushed. The output should look something like the following:

```
Updating passwd.byname....
Pushed passwd.byname map.
Updating passwd.byuid...
Pushed passwd.byuid map.
Updating hosts.byname...
```

```
Pushed hosts.byname.
Updating hosts.byaddr...
Pushed hosts.byaddr.
[etc...]
```

On the NIS slave server, change the `/etc/yp.conf` file so that the `ypserver` is set to point to the slave server. Run the command `ypcat passwd` and see whether your NIS password file is displayed. If so, you're set. The NIS slave server is configured.

If you're having problems, trace through your steps. Also be sure to reboot the machine to see if your NIS slave server still works correctly. If it doesn't come back up, be sure that the changes you made to the boot sequence when installing `ypserv` were correct.

Tip

If your NIS client or slave server seems to have a hard time finding other hosts on the network, be sure that the `/etc/nsswitch.conf` file is set to resolve hosts by file before NIS. Then be sure that all the important hosts needed for the NIS servers to set themselves up are in their own local `/etc/hosts` file.

Using NISisms in Your `/etc/passwd` File

The most popular use of NIS is to keep a global user database so that it is possible to grant access to any machine at your site to any user. Under Red Hat Linux, this behavior is implicit for all NIS clients. With Debian GNU/Linux, you need to ensure that the special line is in place.

Sometimes, however, you do not want everyone accessing certain systems, such as those used by personnel. You can fix this access by using the special token + in your `/etc/passwd` file. By default, NIS clients have the line `+::::::` at the end of their `/etc/passwd` file, thereby allowing everyone in NIS to log in to the system. To arrange that the host remains an NIS client but does not grant everyone permission, change the line to read `+::::::/bin/false`. This will allow only people with actual entries in the `/etc/passwd` file for that host (for example, `root`) to log in.

To allow a specific person to log in to a host, you can add a line to the `/etc/passwd` file granting this access. The format of the line is `+`*`username`*`::::::` where *`username`* is the login of the user you want to grant access to. NIS will automatically grab the user's `passwd` entry from the NIS server and use the correct information for determining the user information (for example, UID, GID, GECOS, and so on). You can override particular fields by inserting the new value in the `+`*`username`*`::::::` entry. For example, if the user sshah uses /usr/local/bin/tcsh as his shell, but the host he needs to log in to keeps it in /bin/tcsh, you can set his /etc/passwd entry to +sshah:::::/bin/tcsh.

Using Netgroups

Netgroups are a great way to group people and machines into nice, neat names for access control. A good example of using this feature is for a site where users are not allowed to log in to server machines. You can create a netgroup for the system administrators and let in members of the group through a special entry in the /etc/passwd file.

Netgroup information is kept in the /etc/netgroup file and shared via NIS.

The format of a netgroups file is as follows:

groupname member-list

groupname is the name of the group being defined, and the *member-list* consists of other group names or tuples of specific data. Each entry in the *member-list* is separated by a whitespace.

A tuple containing specific data comes in this form:

(*hostname, username, domain name*)

hostname is the name of the machine for which that entry is valid, *username* is the login of the person being referenced, and *domain name* is the NIS domain name. Any entry left blank is considered a wildcard; for example, (technics,,,) implies everybody on the host technics. An entry with a dash in it (-) means that there are no valid values for that entry. For example, (-,sshah,) implies the user sshah and nothing else. This is useful for generating a list of users or machine names for use in other netgroups.

In files where netgroups are supported (such as /etc/passwd), you reference them by placing an @ sign in front of them. If you want to give the netgroup sysadmins consisting of (-,sshah,) (-,heidis,) permission to log in to a server, you add this line to your /etc/passwd file:

```
+@sysadmins:::::
```

An example of a full netgroups file follows:

```
sysadmins     (-,sshah,) (-,heidis,) (-,jnguyen,) (-,mpham,)
servers       (numark,-,) (vestax,-,)
clients       (denon,-,) (technics,-,) (mtx,-,)
research-1    (-,boson,) (-,jyom,) (-,weals,) (-,jaffe,)
research-2    (-,sangeet,) (-,mona,) (-,paresh,) (-,manjari,) (-,jagdish,)
consultants   (-,arturo,)
allusers        sysadmins research-1 research-2 consultants
allhosts        servers clients
```

As a general rule, the line lengths should be no more than 1024 characters. Although the system has no problems with the greater line lengths, it is difficult to edit the file, as vi, view, and perhaps other editors have a 1,024-character line length limitation.

Some Troubleshooting Tips

If the NIS software isn't behaving as you think it should, you can check a few some things:

- Make sure the processes are running. Use `ps auxw` to list all the running processes. Make sure you see the appropriate processes running, regardless of whether the machine is a client, a server, or both.
- Check system logs (in `/var/log`) to see if there are any messages indicating peripheral problems that could be affecting your configuration.
- If the processes appear to be running but are not responsive, kill and restart them. In some rare circumstances, the daemon may be misbehaving and need to be restarted.
- Make sure `/etc/nsswitch.conf` is configured properly. This is a common problem.
- If you are trying to start the daemons by hand, make sure you are logged in as `root`.

When encountering problems, slow down, take a short break, and then retrace your steps. It's amazing how often simply slowing down helps you find problems.

Summary

This chapter covers the installation and configuration of NIS master servers, secondary servers, and clients. In addition to the setup of NIS itself, common "NISisms" and netgroups are discussed. The lessons learned from these sections puts a powerful tool in your hands.

Some key points to remember:

- Use `ypinit` to set up NIS master servers and secondary servers.
- The `/var/yp` directory contains the makefile necessary to update NIS information.
- Consider separating NIS files from your regular system files for clarity.
- NIS servers need the `ypserv` daemon.
- NIS clients need the `ypbind` daemon.

- `yppasswdd` allows users on NIS clients to change their passwords.
- Schedule a reboot to test all your changes.

Although it isn't the most exciting feature to come along in recent history, NIS is one of the most useful of the core network services. In conjunction with other services, NIS gives you the ability to create a seamless system for all of your users.

CHAPTER

NFS: Network Filesystem

In This Chapter

The *Network Filesystem*, or NFS, is the means by which UNIX systems share their disk resources. What makes NFS really useful is its capability to function in a heterogeneous environment. Most UNIX variants, if not all, support NFS, and you can find NFS support for Microsoft Windows inexpensively, making it a good choice for sharing disks.

NFS was originally developed by Sun Microsystems during the 1980s. Sun shared its design and made the protocol a standard, which eliminated any interoperability conflicts with other operating systems. Linux supported NFS before version 1.0 was released.

A key feature of NFS is its robust nature. It is a *stateless protocol*, meaning that each request made between the client and server is complete in itself and does not require knowledge of prior transactions. Because of this, NFS cannot tell the difference between a very slow host and a host that has failed altogether. This allows servers to go down and come back up without having to reboot the clients. If this doesn't make much sense, don't worry about it. Understanding the underlying protocol isn't necessary for you to set up and successfully run an NFS server.

Note

In Chapter 16, "Samba," you'll read about how Linux can share its disks with Windows machines. NFS and Samba are not the same. They are two different protocols with two fundamentally different views on how disks should be shared. One of the many things that makes Linux great is its capability to support both means of sharing disks at the same time. In fact, it's common for Linux servers to share disks with each other through NFS and with Windows-based clients with Samba at the same time.

Caution

Unfortunately, NFS's design is insecure by nature. Although taking some steps to protect yourself from the common user pretending to be an evil hacker provides a moderate level of security, there is not much more you can do. Any time you share a disk with another machine via NFS, you need to give the users of that machine (especially the root user) a certain amount of trust. If you believe that the person you are sharing the disk with is untrustworthy, you need to explore alternatives to NFS for sharing data and disk space.

Keep up with security bulletins from both Red Hat and the Computer Emergency Response Team (CERT). You can find these bulletins on Red Hat's site at `www.redhat.com`, Debian's site at `www.debian.org`, Caldera's site at `www.calderasystems.com`, CERT's site at `www.cert.org`, or the moderated newsgroup `comp.security.announce`.

Installing NFS

Although the NFS software comes preinstalled with some versions of Linux, you need to be aware of what the software is and what each specific program does.

To install on Debian systems, use this code:

```
apt-get install nfs-server
```

This code is important when you are troubleshooting problems and configuring NFS-related tools such as the automounter.

Three programs provide NFS server services:

`rpc.portmapper`	This program does not directly provide NFS services itself; however, it maps calls made from other machines to the correct NFS daemons.
`rpc.nfsd`	This daemon is what translates the NFS requests into actual requests on the local filesystem.
`rpc.mountd`	This daemon services requests to mount and umount filesystems.

Note

The `rpc.nfsd` and `rpc.mountd` programs need only run on your NFS servers. In fact, you might find it prudent not to run them at all on your client machines, for security concerns and to free resources that might otherwise be consumed by them. NFS clients do not need any special NFS software to run. They should run the `rpc.portmapper` program, however, because it provides RPC functionality to programs other than NFS.

By default, these programs are installed and loaded at boot time. To check for this, use the `rpcinfo` command as follows:

```
rpcinfo -p
```

This displays all the registered RPC programs running on your system. To check which RPC programs are registered on a remote host, use `rpcinfo`:

```
rpcinfo -p hostname
```

hostname is the name of the remote host you want to check. The output for a Linux host running NFS appears something like the following:

```
[root@vestax /root]# rpcinfo -p
  program   vers   proto   port
   100000      2     tcp    111   portmapper
   100000      2     udp    111   portmapper
   100005      1     udp    821   mountd
   100005      1     tcp    823   mountd
   100003      2     udp   2049   nfs
   100003      2     tcp   2049   nfs
```

Starting and Stopping the NFS Daemons

You might run across instances when you need to stop NFS and restart it later. You can do this by using the startup scripts that are executed at boot time and shutdown. NFS's scripts are in `/etc/rc.d/init.d/nfs` in Red Hat and Caldera or `/etc/init.d/nfs-server` in Debian.

To start the NFS services, run the following as `root`:

```
[root@vestax /root]# /etc/rc.d/init.d/nfs start
```

To stop NFS services, run the following as `root`:

```
[root@vestax /root]# /etc/rc.d/init.d/nfs stop
```

NFS services are automatically started at package install time or at boot time. However, if you need to start or stop them manually for some reason, you can use the following two lines of code to start or stop the NFS services, respectively:

```
/etc/init.d/nfs-server start
```

```
/etc/init.d/nfs-server stop
```

Status of NFS

There are other options that can be used with NFS to do other tasks. For example, you can get a status of NFS by running the following command:

```
[root@vestax /root]# /etc/rc.d/init.d/nfs status
```

This returns output that is something like this:

```
rpc.statd (pid 965) is runnning…
rpc.mountd (pid 987) is running…
```

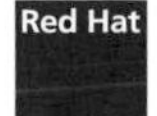

```
rpc.nfsd is stopped
nfsd (pid 366) is running...
rpc.rquotad (pid 976)  is running...
```

Configuring NFS Servers and Clients

The two key files to NFS are `/etc/exports` and `/etc/fstab`. The `exports` file is configured on the server side and specifies which directories are to be shared with which clients and each client's access rights. The `fstab` file is configured on the client side and specifies which servers to contact for certain directories, as well as where to place them in the directory tree.

Setting Up the /etc/exports File

The `/etc/exports` file specifies which directories to share with which hosts on the network. You only need to set up this file on your NFS servers.

The `/etc/exports` file follows this format:

```
/directory/to/export     host1(permissions) host2(permissions)
                ➥host3(permissions) host4(permissions)
#
# Comments begin with the pound sign and must be at the start of
# the line
#
/another/dir/to/export     host2(permissions) host5(permissions)
```

In this example, */directory/to/export* is the directory you want to make available to other machines on the network. You must supply the absolute pathname for this entry. On the same line, you list the hosts and which permissions they have to access. If the list is longer than the line size permits, you can use the standard backslash (\) continuation character to continue on the next line.

You specify the names of the hosts in four ways:

- The direct hostname.
- Using `@`*group*, where *group* is the specific netgroup. Wildcard hosts in the group are ignored.
- Wildcards in the hostname. The asterisk (*) can match an entire network. For example, `*.engr.widgets.com` matches all hosts that end in `.engr.widgets.com`.
- IP subnets can be matched with address/netmask combinations. For example, to match everything in the `192.168.42.0` network where the netmask is `255.255.255.0`, you use `192.168.42.0/24 (i.e. IP/netmask bits)`.

Each host is given a set of access permissions. They are as follows:

`rw`	Read and write access.
`ro`	Read-only access.
`noaccess`	Denies access to all subdirectories below the listed directory. This is useful when you want to export most of a directory tree. You can export high in the tree and set a few exceptions, rather than export a large number of small subdirectories.
`no_root_squash`	Acknowledge and trust the client's `root` account.

If you are familiar with the export file configurations of other flavors of UNIX, you know that this process is not similar. Whether one is better than the other is a holy-war discussion best left to Usenet newsgroups.

After you set up your `/etc/exports` file, run the `exportfs` command with the `-a` option:

```
exportfs -a
```

This sends the appropriate signals to the `rpc.nfsd` and `rpc.mountd` daemons to reread the `/etc/exports` file and update their internal tables.

Tip

It is considered a good convention to place all the directories you want to export in the `/export` hierarchy. This makes the intent clear and self-documenting. If you need the directory to also exist elsewhere in the directory tree, use symbolic links. For example, if your server is exporting its `/usr/local` hierarchy, you should place the directory in `/export`, thereby creating `/export/usr/local`. Because the server itself will need access to the `/export/usr/local` directory, you should create a symbolic link from `/usr/local` that points to the real location, `/export/usr/local`.

Tip

If you have an error in your `/etc/exports` file, it is reported when NFS starts up in `syslog`. Read the section on `syslog` in this book to find out more about this wonderful debugging tool.

Using mount to Mount an Exported Filesystem

To mount a filesystem, use the `mount` command:

```
mount servername:/exported/dir /dir/to/mount
```

servername is the name of the server from which you want to mount a filesystem; */exported/dir* is the directory listed in its `/etc/exports` file; and */dir/to/mount* is the location on your local machine where you want to mount the filesystem. For example, to mount `/export/home` from the NFS server `denon` to the directory `/home`, use this:

```
mount denon:/export/home /home
```

Remember that the directory must exist in your local filesystem before anything can be mounted there.

You can pass options to the `mount` command. The most important characteristics are specified in the `-o` options. These characteristics follow:

`rw` Read/write.

`ro` Read-only.

`bg` Background mount. Should the `mount` initially fail (the server is down, for instance), the `mount` process will place itself in the background and continue trying until it is successful. This is useful for filesystems mounted at boot time because it keeps the system from hanging at that mount if the server is down.

`intr` Interruptible mount. If a process is pending I/O on a mounted partition, it will allow the process to be interrupted and the I/O call to be dropped.

`soft` By default, NFS operations are *hard*, meaning that they require the server to acknowledge completion before returning to the calling process. The `soft` option allows the NFS client to return a failure to the calling process after `retrans` number of retries.

`retrans` Specifies the maximum number of retried transmissions to a soft-mounted filesystem.

`wsize` Specifies the number of bytes to be written across the network at once. The default is `8192` (for example, `wsize=2048`). You shouldn't change this value unless you are sure of what you are doing. Setting this value too low or too high can have a negative impact on your system's performance.

`rsize` Specifies the number of bytes read across the network at once. Like `wsize`, the default is 8,192 bytes. The same warning applies as well: Changing the value without understanding its effect can have a negative impact on your system's performance.

Here's an example of these parameters in use:

```
mount -o rw,bg,intr,soft,retrans=6 denon:/export/home /home
```

Note

There are many more options to the `mount` command, but you will rarely see them. See the man page for `mount` for additional details.

Caution

Solaris NFS clients talking to Linux NFS servers seem to bring out a bug in the Linux NFS implementation. If you suddenly notice normal files being treated as directories or other such unusual behavior, change the `wsize` and `rsize` to `2048` when mounting the directory. This appears to fix the problem without hurting performance too drastically.

Umounting a Filesystem

To umount the filesystem, use the `umount` command:

```
umount /home
```

This will umount the `/home` filesystem.

There is a caveat, of course. If users are using files on a mounted filesystem, you cannot umount it. All files must be closed before the umount can happen, which can be tricky on a large system, to say the least. There are three ways to handle this:

- Use the `lsof` program (available at `ftp://vic.cc.purdue.edu/pub/tools/unix/lsof`) to list the users and their open files on a given filesystem. Then, either wait until they are done, beg and plead for them to leave, or kill their processes. Then you can umount the filesystem. This isn't the most desirable way to achieve an umount, but you'll find that this is often the path you need to take.
- Use `umount` with the `-f` option to force the filesystem to umount. This is often a bad idea because it confuses the programs (and users) who are accessing the filesystem. Files in memory that have not been committed to disk might be lost.

- Bring the system to single-user mode and then umount the filesystem. Although this is the greatest inconvenience of the three, it is the safest way because no one loses any work. Unfortunately, on a large server, you'll have some angry users to contend with. (Welcome to system administration!)

Configuring the `/etc/fstab` File to Mount Filesystems Automatically

At boot time, thesystem will automatically mount the `root` filesystem with read-only privileges. This allows it to load the kernel and read critical startup files. However, it will need guidance after the system has bootstrapped itself. Although it is possible for you to jump in and mount all the filesystems, it isn't realistic because you then have to finish bootstrapping the machine yourself. Even worse, the system might not come back online by itself. (Of course, if you enjoy coming into work at 2 a.m. to bring a system back up, feel free.)

To get around this, Linux uses a special file called `/etc/fstab`. This file lists all the partitions that need to be mounted at boot time and the directory where they need to be mounted. Along with that information, you can pass parameters to the `mount` command.

> **Note**
>
> NFS servers can also be NFS clients. For example, a Web server that exports part of its archive to, say, an FTP server can NFS mount from the server containing home directories at the same time.

Each filesystem to be mounted is listed in the `fstab` file in the following format:

```
/dev/device         /dir/to/mount       ftype parameters fs_freq fs_passno
```

An example of that would look like this:

```
server:/usr/local/pub    /pub    nfs    rsize=8192,wsize=8192,timeo=14,intr
```

The following items make up this line:

`/dev/device` The device to be mounted. In the case of mounting NFS filesystems, this comes in the form of *`servername:/dir/exported`*, where *`servername`* is the name of the NFS server and *`/dir/exported`* is the directory that is exported from the NFS server. For example, `denon:/export/home`, where `denon` is the hostname of your NFS server and `/export/home` is the directory that is specified in the `/etc/exports` directory as being shared.

/dir/to/mount	The location at which the filesystem should be mounted on your directory tree.
ftype	The filesystem type. Usually, this is `ext2` for your local filesystems. However, NFS mounts should use the `NFS` filesystem type.
parameters	These are the parameters you passed to `mount` using the `-o` option. They follow the same comma-delimited format. A sample entry looks like `rw,intr,bg`.
fs_freq	This is used by `dump` to determine whether a filesystem needs to be dumped.
fs_passno	This is used by the `fsck` program to determine the order to check disks at boot time. The root filesystem should be set to `1`, and other filesystems should have a `2`. Filesystems on the same drive will be checked sequentially, but filesystems on different drives will be checked at the same time.

Any lines in the `fstab` file that start with the pound symbol (#) are considered comments and are ignored.

If you need to mount a new filesystem while the machine is live, you must perform the mount by hand. If you want this mount to be active automatically the next time the system is rebooted, you should add it to the `fstab` file.

There are two notable partitions that don't follow the same set of rules as normal partitions. They are the swap partition and `/proc`, which use filesystem types `swap` and `proc`, respectively.

You do not mount the swap partition using the `mount` command. It is instead managed by the `swapon` command. For a swap partition to be mounted, you must list it in the `fstab` file. Once it is there, use `swapon` with the `-a` parameter, followed by the partition on which you've allocated swap space.

The `/proc` filesystem is even stranger because it really isn't a filesystem. It is an interface to the kernel abstracted into a filesystem format. Take a peek into it for a large amount of useful information regarding the inner workings of the kernel.

Tip

If you need to remount a filesystem that already has an entry in the `fstab` file, you don't need to type the `mount` command with all the parameters. Instead, simply pass the directory to `mount` as the parameter, as in the following:

```
mount /dir/to/mount
```

/dir/to/mount is the directory that needs to be mounted. `mount` will automatically look to the `fstab` file for all the details, such as which partition to mount and which options to use.

If you need to remount a large number of filesystems that are already listed in the `fstab` file, you can use the `-a` option in `mount` to remount all the entries in `fstab`:

```
mount -a
```

If it finds that a filesystem is already mounted, no action on that filesystem is performed. If it finds that an entry is not mounted, on the other hand, it will automatically mount it with the appropriate parameters.

Caution

When you are setting up servers that mount filesystems from other servers, be wary of cross mounting. *Cross mounting* happens when two servers mount each other's filesystems. This can be dangerous if you do not configure the `/etc/fstab` file to mount these systems in the background (via the `bg` option) because it is possible for these two machines to deadlock during their boot sequence as each host waits for the other to respond.

For example, say you want `host1` to mount `/export/usr/local` from `host2` and `host2` to mount `/export/home/admin` from `host1`. If both machines are restarted after a power outage, `host1` will try to mount the directory from `host2` before turning on its own NFS services. At the same time, `host2` is trying to mount the directory from `host1` before it turns on its NFS services. The result is that each machine waits forever for the other machine to start.

If you use the `bg` option in the `/etc/fstab` entry for both hosts, they would fail on the initial mount, place the mount in the background, and continue booting. Eventually, both machines would start their NFS daemons and allow each other to mount their respective directories.

Complete Sample Configuration Files

Listing 15.1 contains a complete `/etc/exports` file for a server.

LISTING 15.1 A Complete */etc/exports* File

```
#
# /etc/exports for denon
#
# Share the home dirs:
/export/home        technics(rw) pioneer(rw) vestax(rw)
            ➥atus(rw) rane(rw)

#
# Share local software
#
/export/usr/local    technics(rw,no_root_squash)
             ➥vestax(rw,no_root_squash)
             ➥pioneer(rw,no_root_squash)
             ➥atus(rw,no_root_squash)
             ➥rane(rw,no_root_squash)
```

Listing 15.2 contains a complete `/etc/fstab` file for a client.

LISTING 15.2 A Complete */etc/fstab* File

```
#
# /etc/fstab for technics
#
/dev/hdb2               /                        ext2    defaults       1 1
/dev/hda8               /home                    ext2    defaults       1 2
/dev/hda7               swap                     swap    defaults       0 0
/dev/fd0                /mnt/floppy              ext2    noauto         0 0
/dev/cdrom              /mnt/cdrom               iso9660 noauto,ro      0 0
none                    /proc                    proc    defaults       0 0
none                    /dev/pts                 devpts  mode=0622      0 0
```

You can also manually mount a filesystem. This is especially important if you want to mount a floppy disk as an `msdos` filesystem. The following command will mount a floppy disk to `/mnt/floppy`. Remember to umount the disk before removing it.

```
mount /dev/fd0 /mnt/floppy -t msdos
```

Umounting is just a simple command:

```
umount /mnt/floppy
```

Summary

In this chapter, you learned how to

- Start and stop NFS servers
- Mount and umount directories
- Create and maintain the configuration files for clients and servers

NFS, a rather straightforward tool, is one of the powerful features that lets you work not only with other Linux systems, but with other variants of UNIX as well. From a user's standpoint, it provides a seamless bridge between clients and servers so that they can keep to their tasks instead of trying to remember the drive letter for their home directory.

CHAPTER 16

Samba

In This Chapter

This chapter gives you the information you need to install, configure, and use the Samba suite of Session Message Block (SMB) protocol services under Linux. With Samba, you can share a Linux filesystem with Windows 95, 98, or NT. You can share a Windows 95, 98, or NT FAT filesystem with Linux. You can also share printers connected to either Linux or a system with Windows 95, 98, or NT.

SMB is the protocol used by Microsoft's operating systems to share files and printer services. Microsoft and Intel developed the SMB protocol system in 1987, and later, Andrew Tridgell created an SMB implementation for various UNIX systems and Linux.

The Samba suite of SMB protocol utilities consists of several components. The `smbd` daemon provides the file and print services to SMB clients, such as Windows for Workgroups, Windows NT, LAN Manager, or other Linux and UNIX clients. The configuration file for this daemon is described in `smb.conf`. The `nmbd` daemon provides NetBIOS nameserving and browsing support. You can also run `nmbd` interactively to query other name service daemons.

The SMB client program (`smbclient`) implements a simple FTP-like client on a Linux or UNIX box. The SMB mounting program (`smbmount`) enables mounting of server directories on a Linux or Unix box. The `testparm` utility allows you to test your `smb.conf` configuration file. The `smbstatus` utility tells you who is currently using the `smbd` server.

New for Samba version 2 is the SWAT Web-based interface to the `smb.conf` Samba configuration file. SWAT (Samba Web Administration Tool) is described in this chapter.

In the Red Hat 6.0, Caldera 2.2, and Debian 2.1 distributions, these files can be found in the following directories:

> `smbd` and `nmbd`—`/usr/sbin`
>
> `smbclient`, `smbmount`, `testparm`, `smbstatus`—`/usr/bin`
>
> `smb.conf`—Depends on distribution

Installing Samba

You can install Samba during Linux installation from the CD-ROM or later. This section details the installation of Samba in the Red Hat, Caldera, and Debian distributions.

Installing Samba on Red Hat

Typical Red Hat Linux installs Samba, but in case it doesn't, you can install it by acquiring the `rpm` file from either the distribution CD-ROM or from the Internet.

If you need to install the package, first download the current version from Red Hat's Web site (`http://www.redhat.com`) or locate the package on your CD-ROM in the `RedHat\RPMS` directory. You can then install the package (the current version is `samba-2.0.3-8.i386.rpm`) with the following command:

```
$ rpm -ivh samba-2.0.3-8.i386.rpm
```

Naturally, the exact version number might vary.

Installing Samba on Caldera

To install Samba from your Caldera CD-ROM, navigate to your install CD-ROM's `Packages/RPMS` directory and execute these two commands:

```
$ rpm -ivh samba-2.0.3-0b.i386.rpm

$ rpm -ivh samba-doc-2.0.3-0b.i386.rpm
```

Naturally, the exact version number might vary. You can also get these files (or later versions thereof) from `ftp://ftp.calderasystems.com/pub/OpenLinux/2.2/Packages/RPMS/`.

Installing Samba on Debian

To install Samba from your Debian CD-ROM, run `dselect`, select `Access` to the CD-ROM, select `Update`, then select `Select` and search for the word *Samba*. You'll find a `samba` and a `samba-doc`. Select both for install; press Enter and select `Install`. The installation can also be done with the `apt-get` command.

Note that Debian version 2.1 installs Samba 1.9.18. That version does not have several Samba 2 enhancements, including the SWAT utility. The latest version of Samba contains all the files needed, including the two primary programs (`smbd` and `nmbd`), to run the latest Samba.

Note

Debian 2.2 is dated for Autumn 1999, and is expected to have Samba 2.x. If you have Debian 2.2 or later, your installation CD-ROM should install Samba 2.x with SWAT.

Distribution Dependencies

Samba implementations have more in common than they have differences, so the majority of this chapter addresses Samba issues without regard to distribution. To further that convenience, this section sets forth several concepts, referred to throughout the chapter.

- Samba directory
- `smb.conf`
- Samba `start`, `stop`, and `restart` commands
- The `smbpasswd` file
- Set Samba to `Autostart`

This section identifies the distribution-dependent properties of these concepts so that the concept names can be used independent of distribution throughout the rest of the chapter. If you forget the distribution properties of one of these concepts, you can simply refer to this section.

Samba Directory

The remainder of this chapter refers to the directory containing `smb.conf` and `smbpasswd` as the Samba directory. This directory is vital to Samba configuration. It is not necessarily used by Samba alone.

On Red Hat systems, the Samba directory is `/etc`.

On Caldera systems, the Samba directory is `/etc/samba.d`.

On Debian systems, the Samba directory is `/etc`.

`smb.conf`

File `smb.conf` is Samba's configuration file. It is contained in the Samba directory, which was discussed previously.

Samba `start`, `stop`, and `restart` Commands

This chapter often suggests running the Samba `restart` command. There is also a Samba `stop` command and a Samba `start` command. They are all distribution-dependent.

On Red Hat systems, the Samba `start`, `stop`, and `restart` commands, respectively, are as follows:

```
$ /etc/rc.d/init.d/smb start
$ /etc/rc.d/init.d/smb stop
$ /etc/rc.d/init.d/smb restart
```

On Caldera systems, the Samba `start`, `stop`, and `restart` commands, respectively, are as follows:

```
# /etc/rc.d/init.d/samba start
# /etc/rc.d/init.d/samba stop
# /etc/rc.d/init.d/samba restart
```

Note that this differs from Red Hat in that it's `samba` instead of `smb`.

On Debian systems, the Samba `start`, `stop`, and `restart` commands, respectively, are as follows:

```
# /etc/init.d/samba start
# /etc/init.d/samba stop
# /etc/init.d/samba restart
```

Note that this differs from Caldera and Red Hat in that it's in a different directory. It's also different from Red Hat in that it's `samba` instead of `smb`.

The smbpasswd File

The `smbpasswd` file has the same name in Red Hat, Caldera, and Debian distributions, but as previously explained in the "Samba Directory" section, it's in a different directory on Caldera systems.

Set Samba to Autostart

Using `linuxconf`, navigate `Control:Control panel:Control service activity`, and then make sure the `smb` Enabled radio button is checked.

Run `lisa` and then navigate `System Configuration:System Configuration:Configure daemon/server autostart`; make sure `SMB server processes (samba)` is selected. If you prefer to use COAS, choose `System:Daemons`, and make sure the `SMB server processes (samba)` is selected.

When a package is installed on Debian, it is automatically configured to start on boot, and generally starts at install time as well, so no further action is necessary.

Getting a Simple Samba Setup Running

Samba can be very complex, so it's important to get the simplest possible implementation of Samba running before making major configuration changes.

The main configuration file, `smb.conf`, is located in your Samba server's Samba directory. It is used by the Samba server software (`smbd`) to determine directories and printers, as well as to determine security options for those directories and printers.

> **Note**
>
> Changes to the `smb.conf` file are not recognized until Samba is restarted with your distribution's Samba `restart` command.
>
> The ; character at the beginning of a `smb.conf` line indicates that the line is a comment; it is to be ignored when processed by the Samba server. The # character does the same thing. Customarily, the ; character is used to comment out option lines, while the # is used at the beginning of lines that are truly comments.

The `smb.conf` file layout consists of a series of named sections. Each section starts with its name in brackets, such as `[global]`. Within each section, the parameters are specified by key/value pairs, such as `comment = My Samba Server`.

`smb.conf` consists of three special sections and zero or more custom sections. The special sections are `[global]`, `[homes]`, and `[printers]`. Before describing them in detail, look at acquiring a minimal running Samba.

> **Caution**
>
> Be sure to back up the original `smb.conf` file before making your first modification.

First, make sure whatever username is used on the test client also exists on the Linux box. Add the user and password with the `adduser` and `passwd` commands.

Note

Samba works only on functioning networks. To prevent frustration, always make sure the client and server can ping each other's IP address before attempting any Samba configuration or testing. Also, attempt to ping the server's host name from the client to determine what to expect from `smbclient` or `smbmount` commands using the hostname instead of IP address.

Testing with a Linux Client

The default `smb.conf` installed by Red Hat should be sufficient to run a simple Samba test with a Linux client.

Caldera installations do not create a default `smb.conf`. Instead, they create file `smb.conf.sample`, which is located in the Samba directory. To enable a working simple Samba test, copy that file to `smb.conf` in the Samba directory, and then comment out these two lines:

```
path = %H/Public
only user = yes
```

Your `smb.conf` should now be sufficient to run a simple Samba test with a Linux client.

The default `smb.conf` installed by Debian should be sufficient to run a simple Samba test with a Linux client.

Once your `smb.conf` is sufficient, run the following command:

```
$ smbclient '//192.168.100.1/homes' -U myuid
```

Substitute your Samba server's IP address for *192.168.100.1*. Any name resolving to that same IP address can be used in its place. Substitute whatever username the client is logged in under for *myuid*. `homes` represents the `[homes]` section of `smb.conf`.

You are asked for a password. Type the user's password. If the server password is different from the client password, use the server password. If all is well, you are greeted by the following prompt:

```
smb: \>
```

Type **`ls`** and press Enter. You get a directory listing that includes file `.bash_profile`. You have proven that you have a simple Samba running.

If you get an error message that resembles the following one, it probably indicates that the `smbd` daemon is not running on the server:

```
error connecting to 192.168.100.1:139 (Connection refused)
```

In that case, run the Samba `restart` command for your Linux distribution. When you do, you may see a `"[FAILED]"` on `smbd` shutdown. (It wasn't running in the first place.) You'll see an `"[  OK  ]"` on the subsequent `smb` start. Verify the Set Samba to Autostart procedure discussed in the "Distribution Dependencies" section to make sure the `smb` daemon is enabled on reboot.

Testing with a Windows Client

Samba is what makes a Linux computer show up in a Windows Network Neighborhood. What shows up in Network Neighborhood is the workgroup name attached to `workgroup=` in the `[global]` section of the Samba server's `smb.conf`. Samba works best with workgroup names that are all capital letters, eight characters or fewer, and do not contain spaces.

Next, in the `[global]` section, temporarily uncomment `password level` and `username level`. Make `password level` equal to the longest likely password on this system, and `username level` the longest likely username. These specify how many characters are non–case-sensitive, which is very important with non–case-sensitive SMB clients such as Windows.

Note

The changes to username and password levels are typically not required. The preceding suggestion is simply to temporarily eliminate any possible case-sensitivity problems. Once the system is working perfectly, you'll want to re-comment the password and user levels.

Whenever there's a troubleshooting question involving case sensitivity for users and passwords, you can once again uncomment them and re-comment them upon resolution.

Now decide whether to use clear passwords or encrypted passwords and how to implement that decision. Early Windows SMB clients defaulted to clear text passwords. Beginning with Windows 95 OEM Service Release 2, Windows defaulted to encrypted passwords. All Windows 98 clients default to encrypted passwords. Likewise, the default behavior changed from clear text to encrypted in Windows NT 4.0 Service Pack 3.

Encrypted passwords are typically disabled in most Linux distributions. For Windows versions 95-OSR2 and later and Windows NT 4 Service Pack 3, either each encrypted text client must be changed to clear text passwords, or the server's `smb.conf` must be changed to enable encrypted passwords. In addition, any clear-text clients must be changed to encrypted passwords. A discussion of each technique follows.

Note

The documentation packaged with Linux distributions contains detailed discussions of plain versus encrypted passwords and their ramifications. See these documents:

```
/usr/doc/samba-2.0.3/docs/textdocs/Win95.txt
/usr/doc/samba-2.0.3/docs/textdocs/WinNT.txt
/usr/doc/samba-2.0.3/docs/textdocs/ENCRYPTION.txt
```

Caldera

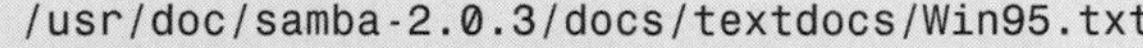

```
/usr/doc/samba-2.0.3/docs/textdocs/Win95.txt
/usr/doc/samba-2.0.3/docs/textdocs/WinNT.txt
/usr/doc/samba-2.0.3/docs/textdocs/ENCRYPTION.txt
```

Debian

```
/usr/doc/samba-doc/Win95.txt.gz
/usr/doc/samba-doc/WinNT.txt.gz
/usr/doc/samba-doc/ENCRYPTION.txt.gz
```

Windows NT users, please note that NT SMB clients present some additional challenges. Be sure to read these three documents carefully if you're having problems with Windows NT SMB clients.

Enabling Encrypted Passwords on the Server

In the `[global]` section, uncomment lines `encrypt passwords = yes` and `smb passwd file = /etc/smbpasswd`.

On Caldera installations the smb passwd file line should read as follows:

```
smb passwd file = /etc/samba.d/smbpasswd.
```

Assuming the client username is `myuid`, perform the following command:

```
smbpasswd -a myuid
```

Type in the password. If the password is not the same as it is on the client, the user is prompted for the password the first time he accesses the Samba server.

Disabling Encrypted Passwords on the Windows Client

If your situationprecludes enabling encrypted passwords on the server, they can also be disabled on the client to match the server.

Cauton

This technique requires editing the Windows Registry, which involves significant risk, including risk of data loss and OS inoperability. If possible, it's preferable to handle this issue on the server, as explained previously.

In `regedit`, navigate to `[HKEY_LOCAL_MACHINE\System\CurrentControlSet\Services\VxD\VNETSUP]`. If it contains an object called `EnablePlainTextPassword`, set that object's value to `1`. If it does not contain that object, create that object as a `DWORD` and give it a value of `1`. Exit `regedit` and reboot the Windows machine.

The Proof: Network Neighborhood

To prove the Samba concept on a Windows computer's network neighborhood, begin by restarting the server's `smb` with the Samba `restart` command for your distribution. Ideally, once you've completed configuration, restarted Samba, and rebooted the Windows client, the server's workgroup (defined in `[global]`, `workgroup=`) should simply appear inside the `Entire Network` folder of Network Neighborhood. Ideally, double-clicking the workgroup should produce an icon for the server, which, if double-clicked, produces an icon for the user directory described in the `[homes]` section. Files in that directory should appear when that directory's icon is double-clicked. Note that files beginning with a dot (such as `.bash_profile`) are considered hidden by Windows and can be viewed only if the folder's Windows Explorer view properties are set to see all files.

The preceding paragraph describes the ideal outcome. Often there are difficulties—even if you've set up everything exactly right. First, it can take Windows more than a minute (sometimes several minutes) to find out that the server's Samba configuration has been changed and restarted. Sites with an NT PDC/Samba combo have been known to take nearly an hour to recognize `smb.conf` Samba server changes. There are often password difficulties resulting from Windows being non–case-sensitive and Linux being case-sensitive. There may be problems with name resolution. Of course, there could be a basic network problem. Perhaps most maddening, the history of when and whether the Windows client has pulled up the share with a particular password can make a difference.

None of this presents a major obstacle. Take a few minutes' break to make sure Windows has gotten the word. You may want to reboot Windows. Make sure you have a network by confirming that the client and server can ping each other's IP address.

It's often helpful to use `Start Button:Find:Computer` to try to find the server's IP address. Note that the capability to find the server is not absolutely essential for complete Samba use; `find` is not equivalent to `ping`. Remember to refresh the various Network Neighborhood screens often (with F5). If problems continue, temporarily set `username level` and `password level` to `128` (overkill) and make sure they're uncommented. Make sure your client and server agree on the use of encrypted or clear-text passwords, as described earlier this chapter. Be sure to execute the Samba `restart` command to see the results of changes to `smb.conf`.

If you can't see a new share you just created, or a share that has just gotten a new password on the server, perhaps it's a history problem. First make sure the proper `smbclient` command accesses the share from a Linux box. (You can even run it on the server itself.) If `smbclient` accesses the share but Windows doesn't, it's likely a Windows history problem. Check to see whether the Samba server is functioning as a WINS server. If not, and if it's practical to do so, temporarily add or set the following line in `smb.conf`:

```
wins support = yes
```

Check that the `workgroup=` line of `smb.conf` matches the workgroup of the Windows client. If it does not, and if it's practical, temporarily change the Samba server to match the Windows client (or vice versa). Determine whether the Windows computer's WINS resolution is set to the IP of the Samba server; if not, temporarily set it there.

Restart Samba with the Samba `restart` command. Reboot the Windows client.

If problems continue, it's time to view the documentation in the `/usr/doc/samba-2.0.3/docs/` or `/usr/doc/samba-doc/` tree. It's important to have a simple Samba working before attempting serious configuration. Once a working Samba has been established, it's a good idea to back up `smb.conf`—but be sure not to overwrite the backup of the original that came with your Linux distribution.

If the preceding WINS and `workgroup=` steps allow the Samba shares to be visible, they can then generally be backed out; they're now registered on the client. It's exactly this type of inconvenience that the Samba servers' WINS server feature is designed to eliminate.

Configuring Samba

Samba has hundredsof configuration options. This chapter discusses those options most likely to be useful. Note that the `smb.conf` file examples in this book are derived from the `smb.conf` file created during Red Hat installation. The other distributions are similar.

Note

Andrew Tridgell has written an excellent diagnostic procedure, called DIAGNOSIS.txt, for Samba. On the Red Hat 6.0 and Caldera 2.2 distributions, it's available at /usr/doc/samba-2.0.3/docs/textdocs/DIAGNOSIS.txt.

On Debian 2.1 machines, this document is contained as a gzipped file at /usr/doc/samba-doc/DIAGNOSIS.txt.gz.

It's excellent for troubleshooting tough Samba problems.

The [global] Section

The [global] section controls parameters for the entire SMB server. This section also provides default values for the other sections:

```
[global]

# workgroup = NT-Domain-Name or Workgroup-Name
   workgroup = MYGROUP
```

workgroup= specifies the workgroup. Try to keep it all uppercase, fewer than nine characters, and without spaces.

```
# server string is the equivalent of the NT Description field
   server string = Samba Server
```

server string= specifies a human-readable string used to identify the server in the client's user interface. server string= goes in the [global] section. Note the similarity to the comment= option, which identifies individual shares in the client's user interface.

```
;   hosts allow = 192.168.1. 192.168.2. 127.
```

If uncommented, the hosts allow= line restricts Samba access to certain subnets—a handy security measure. Multiple subnets are separated by spaces. Class C subnets have three numbers and three dots, class B two numbers and two dots, and class A one number and one dot.

```
# if you want to automatically load your printer list rather
# than setting them up individually then you'll need this
   printcap name = /etc/printcap
   load printers = yes
```

The preceding enables printing without fuss, and is uncommented by default.

```
# It should not be necessary to spell out the print system type unless
# yours is non-standard. Currently supported print systems include:
# bsd, sysv, plp, lprng, aix, hpux, qnx
;   printing = bsd
```

Uncommenting the preceding code on a Red Hat Linux server should be unnecessary.

```
# Uncomment this if you want a guest account, you must add this to /etc/
➥passwd
# otherwise the user "nobody" is used
;  guest account = pcguest
```

The preceding, if uncommented, defines a guest account for clients logged in as a user not known to the Samba server.

```
# Password Level allows matching of _n_ characters of the password for
# all combinations of upper and lower case.
;  password level = 8
;  username level = 8
```

Uncomment these to help troubleshoot problems with connection by Windows clients. Set to the length of the longest likely password and username, respectively. They control non–case-sensitivity. For instance, a value of `8` means the first eight characters of the password will be compared without case sensitivity to the entered password. If the problem goes away, there may be a problem with case sensitivity. Once problems have been corrected, it's best to re-comment these two lines.

```
# You may wish to use password encryption. Please read
# ENCRYPTION.txt, Win95.txt and WinNT.txt in the Samba documentation.
# Do not enable this option unless you have read those documents
;  encrypt passwords = yes
;  smb passwd file = /etc/smbpasswd
```

Note that on Caldera installations the last line will read as follows:

```
;  smb passwd file = /etc/samba.d/smbpasswd
```

Passwords are encrypted by default for Windows 95 OSR2 and beyond, but are clear text for earlier versions. To allow Windows-encrypted passwords to work with Samba, these two lines must be uncommented, and `smb` encrypted passwords added on the server with the `smbpasswd -a` command. Here is an example:

```
# smbpasswd -a valerie
```

The preceding command adds SMB user `valerie` (who should already have a Linux user ID) to the `smb`-encrypted password file, and allows you to give Valerie a password.

```
# Enable this if you want Samba to be a domain logon server for
# Windows95 workstations.
;   domain logons = yes

# if you enable domain logons then you may want a per-machine or
# per user logon script
# run a specific logon batch file per workstation (machine)
;   logon script = %m.bat
# run a specific logon batch file per username
;   logon script = %U.bat
```

The preceding deals with giving users individual login scripts and making Samba a domain server for Windows 9x clients.

The [homes] Section

The [homes] section allows network clients to connect to a user's home directory on your server without having an explicit entry in the smb.conf file. When a service request is made, the Samba server searches the smb.conf file for the specific section corresponding to the service request. If the service is not found, Samba checks whether there is a [homes] section. If the [homes] section exists, the password file is searched to find the home directory for the user making the request. Once this directory is found, the system shares it with the network:

```
[homes]
   comment = Home Directories
   browseable = no
   read only = no
   preserve case = yes
   short preserve case = yes
   path = %H/smbtree
   create mode = 0750
```

The comment entry is a human-readable share identification string to be displayed by the client user interface. Note that comment= is similar to server string=, but the latter is valid only in the [global] section.

The browseable=no entry instructs the SMB client not to list the share in a browser (such as Windows Explorer). However, [homes] is a special case. The user share it represents will be visible in the client browse even if [homes] contains browseable=no. If [homes] were to contain browseable=yes, then a share called homes would actually appear in the client browser.

The read only parameter controls whether a user can create and change files in the directory when shared across the network. The preserve case and short preserve case parameters instruct the server to preserve the case of any new files written to the server. This is important because Windows filename are not typically case-sensitive, but Linux filenames are case-sensitive.

Note the path= entry. Because Samba is primarily a file server, it's probably undesirable to have the user access config files in his home directory (.bash_profile, for instance). %H is a macro indicating the user's home directory, while smbtree is a directory under the user's home directory. To implement this as a policy, the system administrator must of course create a script to create the subdirectory upon addition of each new user.

Caution

Linux and Windows use a different linefeed sequence in text files. When editing a file through Samba, the text file protocol is determined by the OS of the client. This means that if the same file is edited by clients of both operating systems, corruption can result.

The final entry sets the file permissions for any files created on the shared directory.

The `[printers]` Section

There are two ways Samba can make printers available. One is to create a specific share section with a `print ok=yes` line, a specific printcap printer specified by a `printer name=` line, and possibly a list of valid users. The other way is to let the `[printers]` section do most of the work, and list all printcap-defined printers to the client.

Note

This section mentions `/etc/printcap`, *printcap*and *printcap printers* several times. `/etc/printcap` is a file defining all the Linux system's printers. A *printcap printer* is a printer defined by name in `/etc/printcap`.

It is possible to edit `/etc/printcap` with an editor, but `/etc/printcap` has a tricky layout and syntax. The preferred way is to use tools included with your distribution.

The `printtool` works in Red Hat Linux's X environment. Use `printtool &` to access `printtool`.

Configure your printers either with `lisa` or `COAS`. `COAS` runs in the X environment, while `lisa` runs on the console.

Debian contains a package called `magicfilter` that is used to configure your printers. Simply install this package. As part of the setup process, it asks you about your printers. You can modify the configuration later by running `/usr/sbin/magicfilterconfig`.

For further information about Linux printers, printing, and the `/etc/printcap` file, see Chapter 24, "Printing with Linux." For `printcap` specifics, see the `printcap` command man page.

The following two lines sufficiently allow use of all printcap-defined printers on SMB clients, although it's certainly not ideal in terms of security:

```
[printers]
path = /var/spool/samba
```

The simplest case of a dedicated print share follows:

```
[vals_lp]
print ok = yes
printer name = lp_mine
path = /home/everyone
```

In the dedicated print share, `print ok=yes` (or the `printable=yes` synonym) is necessary. It's also necessary to name the printer with the `printer name=` line. The intent of `[printers]` is accessibility to all users with valid IDs. The intent of a special printer is typically to restrict access to a user or group, implying that it would be a good idea to add a `valid users=` line to the dedicated printer share. Beyond that, the `[printers]` section and dedicated print shares function much the same.

The `[printers]` section defines how printing services are controlled if no specific entries are found in the `smb.conf` file. As with the `[homes]` section, if no specific entry is found for a printing service, Samba uses the `[printers]` section (if it's present) to allow a user to connect to any printer defined in `/etc/printcap`:

```
[printers]
   comment = All Printers
   path = /var/spool/samba
   browseable = no
   printable = yes
# Set public = yes to allow user 'guest account' to print
   public = no
   writable = no
   create mode = 0700
```

The `comment`, `browseable`, and `create mode` entries mean the same as those discussed earlier in the `[homes]` section. Note that `browseable=no` applies to the `[printers]` section, not to the printcap printers, which are listed in the SMB client's front end as a consequence of the `[printers]` section. If `browseable=` were `yes`, a share called `printers` would be listed on the client. That's clearly not what's needed.

The `path` entry indicates the location of the spool directory to be used when servicing a print request via SMB. Print files are stored there prior to transfer to the printcap-defined printer's spool directory.

If yes, the printable value indicates that this printer resource can be used to print. It must be set to yes in any printer share, including [printers]. The public entry controls whether the guest account can print. The writable=no entry assures that the only thing written to the spool directory are spool files handled by printing functions.

Samba Printer Troubleshooting Tips

Samba printer shares (including [printers]) usually work the first time. When they don't, it's important to remember a printer share won't work without a working Samba [global] section and a working printcap printer, and Samba won't work without a working network.

> **Note**
>
> The following troubleshooting tips work not only for the [printers] section, but also for any dedicated printer shares. Dedicated printer shares all have print ok=yes, and they have a printer name= option as well.

Therefore, before troubleshooting any printer share including [printers], make sure the client and server machines can ping each other's IP address. If not, troubleshoot the network.

Next, make sure you can see the [global] defined workgroup in the client listing (Network Neighborhood or smbclient -L Ipaddress). If not, troubleshoot Samba as a whole before working on the printer. Use testparm (discussed later this chapter) to verify that smb.conf is internally consistent.

Next, make sure the printcap printer works properly. The printcap name can be deduced from the share's printer name= option. If there's no printer name= in the share, it can be deduced from the client request. Perform the following:

```
$ lpr -P printcap_printer_name /etc/fstab
```

This should print /etc/fstab to the physical printer defined as printcap_printer_name in /etc/printcap. /etc/fstab is an ideal test file because it's short and exists on all Red Hat Linux machines. Once the machines can ping each other, the client can see the workgroup defined in the [global] section, and you can print to the printcap printer, you're ready to troubleshoot the Samba printer share.

Many Samba printer problems occur because the default printer command doesn't work. This is especially true if the printcap printer is a network printer instead of a local printer. First try putting the following line in the printer share:

```
print command = lpr -P %p %s; rm %s
```

The command will print to printer `%p` (the printer name passed from the client) the file `%s` (the spool file passed from the client). You'll notice this is the same command done in the printcap printer test described previously, so it should work.

If it still doesn't work, verify that the `path=` entry points to a directory to which the user has read and write access. Make sure any printer `name=` entry points to a working printer defined in `/etc/printcap`. Make sure the entry has a `printable=yes` or `print ok=yes` entry; otherwise, it's not a Samba printer share. If the printer share has a `valid users=` entry, make sure the user in question is one of those users.

If it still isn't working, it's time to install your own test point. Temporarily create directory **`/home/freeall`** with mode 777 (all can read, write, and execute), comment out any `print command=` line in `smb.conf`, and add the following line:

```
print command = cp %s /home/freeall/%p.tst;rm %s
```

This copies the file to be printed to a file in `/home/freeall` with the same filename as the printcap printer with the extension `.tst`. This gives several pieces of information. First, the filename tells you what printer it's trying to print to. You can check `/etc/printcap` or `printtool` for the existence of that printer. You can print that file and see if it comes out properly.

If the file does not exist, you know something's wrong on the client side of the `print` command. Be sure to check the queue on the client to see if it's getting stuck. Sometimes a single failure on the server can jam the client queue. Also be sure that all users can read, write, and execute directory `/home/freeall`; the print will otherwise bomb on permissions. Once the problem is resolved, be sure to remove the `/home/freeall` test directory you created for security reasons.

Another handy troubleshooting tool is checking the Samba logs. They usually contain useful error messages. If the log file is not defined in the `[global]` section of `smb.conf`, look in the `/var/log/samba` directory.

Beyond these tips, remember that troubleshooting is simply a matter of keeping a cool head and narrowing the scope of the problem.

Sharing Files and Print Services

After configuring your defaults for the Samba server, you can create specific shared directories limited to just certain groups of people or available to everyone. For example, say you want to make a directory available to only one user. To do so, you would create a new section and fill in the needed information. Typically, you need to specify the user, directory path, and configuration information to the SMB server, as shown here:

```
[jacksdir]
comment = Jack's remote source code directory
path = /usr/local/src
valid users = tackett
browseable = yes
public = no
writable = yes
create mode = 0700
```

This sample section creates a shared directory called `jacksdir`. It's best to keep share names to less than nine characters to avoid warnings in the `testparm` utility, and to avoid problems on older SMB clients incapable of using longer share names. The path to the directory on the local server is `/usr/local/src`. Because the `browseable` entry is set to `yes`, `jacksdir` will show up in the client's network browse list (such as Windows Explorer). However, because the `public` entry is set to `no` and the `valid users` entry lists only `tackett`, only the user `tackett` can access this directory using Samba. You can grant access to more users and to groups by specifying them (using an `@` sign prepended to the front of the group name) in the `valid users` entry. Here's the `valid users=` line after giving group `devel` access:

```
valid users = tackett, @devel
```

A printer share is created by placing a `print ok=yes` (or synonym) and a `printer name=` in the share. Here is an example:

```
[vals_lp]
print ok = yes
printer name = lp_mine
path = /home/everyone
valid users = valerie, @devel
browseable = yes
```

Here is a printer that is listed as `vals_lp` on the client because of the `browseable=yes`. It prints out of printcap printer `lp_mine`. Its spool directory is `/home/everyone`, and valid users are `valerie` and the `devel` group.

The primary differences between a printer share like this and the `[printers]` section is that the `[printers]` section displays all printcap printers without being browseable, whereas a printer share such as the preceding displays only the printer whose value appears in the `printer name=` option, and then only if a `browseable=yes` option appears. The `[printers]` section does not have or require a `printer name=` option because its purpose is to display all printers to the client and allow the client access to all printers.

All the same Samba printer troubleshooting tips previously listed in the `[printers]` section of this chapter apply to printer shares.

Optimizing Samba Performance

Samba performs excellently, so performance usually isn't an issue. If performance becomes an issue, there are several options to evaluate.

Note

The author tested all of the following Samba configuration performance enhancement techniques and was unable to attain any significant performance gains on an underloaded Samba server with a Celeron 333, 64MB of ram, a 7200rpm 14.4GB disk, and 100Mb wiring, using a test of copying an 11MB file back and forth. The conclusion is that gains depend on many factors, including but not limited to system load. These techniques will not help if the bottleneck is the wire, which appears to be the case on the author's setup.

Samba's default for option `wide links=` is `yes`. Setting it to `no` gains some security benefits. However, significant performance costs have been reported in certain environments. If you have `wide links=` set to `no` in heavy usage environments, you may want to experiment with changing it to `yes`.

If `wide links=` is set to `yes`, further optimization may be gained by setting `getwd cache=` to `yes` in the `[global]` section. (The default is `no`.)

Tweaks to virtual memory utilization may also improve Samba performance. Two tweaks specifically have been documented.

Caution

Do not attempt the following `bdflush` and `buffermem` tweaks without first consulting and understanding the contents of file `vm.txt`.

```
/usr/doc/kernel-doc-2.2.5/sysctl/vm.txt.
```

```
/usr/src/linux-2.2.5/Documentation/sysctl/vm.txt
```

```
/usr/doc/kernel-doc-2.1.125/Documentation/sysctl/vm.txt.gz
```

This file must be `gunzipped` to be read.

Each of the values are explained in that document. If that file does not exist, install the kernel documentation RPM. It will have a name similar to `kernel-doc-2.2.5-15.i386.rpm`.

```
# echo "80 500 64 64 80 6000 6000 1884 2" >/proc/sys/vm/bdflush
# echo "60 80 80" >/proc/sys/vm/buffermem
```

Some other possible enhancement techniques include faster network hardware and wiring, a better server hard disk, more server memory, or a server CPU upgrade.

The bottom line is that performance is bottleneck-limited, so to improve performance, it's essential to locate the performance bottleneck. A performance enhancement plan can be made once that's done. Until the bottleneck is located, speculation makes little sense.

One of the best bottleneck analysis techniques is deliberately slowing a suspected bottleneck. If system throughput slows by a similar proportion, you've found a bottleneck. If system throughput slows only slightly, continue looking.

Testing Your Configuration

After creating the configuration file, you should test it for correctness. Start by making sure the client and server can ping each others' IP address. Without a functioning network, Samba will not work.

Next use the `testparm` program. `testparm` is a simple test program to check the `smb.conf` configuration file for internal correctness. If this program reports no problems, you can use the configuration file with confidence that `smbd` will successfully load the configuration file.

Caution

Using testparm is not a guarantee that the services specified in the configuration file will be available or will operate as expected. This kind of testing guarantees only that Samba is able to read and understand the configuration file.

testparm has the following command line:

```
# testparm [configfile [hostname hostip]]
```

configfile indicates the location of the smb.conf file if it is not in the default location, or if it is not called smb.conf. The *hostname hostIP* optional parameter instructs testparm to see whether the host has access to the services provided in the smb.conf file. If you specify *hostname*, you must specify the IP number of that host as well. Otherwise, the results will be unpredictable.

The following illustrates sample output from running testparm. If there are any errors, the program reports them, along with a specific error message:

```
[root@ns /etc]# testparm smb.conf ntackett 209.42.203.236
Load smb config files from smb.conf
Processing section "[homes]"
Processing section "[printers]"
Loaded services file OK.
Allow connection from ntackett (209.42.203.236) to homes
Allow connection from ntackett (209.42.203.236) to printers
Allow connection from ntackett (209.42.203.236)  to lp
```

Testing with smbstatus

The smbstatus program reports on current Samba connections. smbstatus has the following command line:

```
# smbstatus [-d] [-p] [-s configfile]
```

configfile is by default smb.conf in the Samba directory. -d provides verbose output, and -p provides a list of current SMB processes. The -p option is useful if you are writing shell scripts using smbstatus. Following is sample output:

```
[root@linuxhost everyone]# smbstatus

Samba version 2.0.3
Service      uid      gid      pid     machine
----------------------------------------------
spec_dir     myuid    myuid     4381   p2300    (192.168.100.201)
➥ Thu May  6 22: 18:31 1999
```

```
No locked files

Share mode memory usage (bytes):
   1048464(99%) free + 56(0%) used + 56(0%) overhead = 1048576(100%) total
```

Running the Samba Server

The Samba server consists of two daemons, `smbd` and `nmbd`. The `smbd` daemon provides the file and print sharing services. The `nmbd` daemon provides NetBIOS name server support.

You can run the Samba server either from the `init` scripts or from `inetd` as a system service. Because Red Hat, Caldera, and Debian by default start SMB services from the `init` scripts each time you boot, rather than as a service from `inetd`, you can use the Samba `start`, `stop`, and `restart` commands previously discussed in the aptly named section.

Using the `init` scripts provides better response to SMB requests than continuously spawning the programs from `inetd`.

Accessing Shares

Samba shares can be accessed by SMB clients on Windows and Linux platforms. Windows access is via Network Neighborhood and Windows Explorer. Linux access is via the `smbclient` and `smbmount` commands.

Using `smbclient` on a Linux Client

The `smbclient` program allows Linux users to access SMB shares on other machines (typically Windows). If you want to access files on other Linux boxes, you can use a variety of methods including FTP, NFS, and the r-commands, such as `rcp`.

`smbclient` provides an FTP-like interface that allows you to transfer files with a network share on another computer running an SMB server. Unlike NFS, `smbclient` does not allow you to mount another share as a local directory. `smbmount`, which is discussed later this chapter, provides the capability to mount `smb` shares.

`smbclient` provides command-line options to query a server for the shared directories available or to exchange files. For more information on all the command-line options, consult the man page for `smbclient`. Use the following command to list all available shares on the machine 192.168.100.1:

```
$ smbclient -L 192.168.100.1
```

If asked for a password, simply press the Enter key; the command contains no user ID. Any name resolving to the IP address can be substituted for the IP address. The `-L` parameter requests the list.

To transfer a file, you must first connect to the Samba server using the following command:

```
$ smbclient '//192.168.100.1/homes' -U tackett
```

The parameter `'//192.168.100.1/homes'` specifies the remote service on the other machine. This is typically either a filesystem directory or a printer. Any name resolving to the IP address can be substituted for the IP address. The `-U` option allows you to specify the username you want to connect with. There are many additional `smbclient` command configurations; see the `smbclient` man page for full details. The `smbclient` utility prompts you for a password if this account requires one. It then places you at this prompt:

```
smb: \
```

The slash indicates the current working directory.

From this command line, you can issue the commands shown in Table 16.1 to transfer and work with files.

TABLE 16.1 *smbclient* Commands

Command	*Parameters*	*Description*
`?` or `help`	`[command]`	Provides a help message on command or in general if no command is specified.
`!`	`[shell command]`	Executes the specified shell command or drops the user to a shell prompt.
`cd`	`[directory]`	Changes to the specified directory on the server machine (not the local machine). If no directory is specified, `smbclient` reports the current working directory.
`lcd`	`[directory]`	Changes to the specified directory on the local machine. If no directory is specified, `smbclient` will report the current working directory on the local machine.
`del`	`[files]`	The specified files on the server are deleted if the user has permission to do so. Files can include wildcard characters.

Command	*Parameters*	*Description*
`dir` or `ls`	`[files]`	Lists the indicated files. You can also use the command `ls` to get a list of files.
`exit` or `quit`	none	Exits from the `smbclient` program.
`get`	`[remotefile]` `[local name]`	Retrieves the specified *`remotefile`* and saves the file on the local server. If *`local name`* is specified, the copied file will be saved with this filename rather than the filename on the remote server.
`mget`	`[files]`	Copies all the indicated files, including those matching any wildcards, to the local machine.
`md` or `mkdir`	`[directory]`	Creates the specified directory on the remote machine.
`rd` or `rmdir`	`[directory]`	Removes the specified directory on the remote machine.
`put`	`[localfile]` `[remotename]`	Copies the specified file from the local machine to the server.
`mput`	`[files]`	Copies all the specified files from the local machine to the server.
`print`	`[file]`	Prints the specified file on the remote machine.
`queue`	none	Displays all the print jobs queued on the remote server.

Mounting Shares on a Linux Client

To make life even easier, the `smbmount` command enables you to mount a Samba share to a local directory. To experiment with this, create an **`/mnt/test`** directory on your local workstation. Now run the following command as user `root`, or quoted in the tail of an `su -c` command:

```
# /usr/sbin/smbmount '//192.168.100.1/homes' '/mnt/test' -U myuid
```

Assume the command is given on the local workstation, and that workstation already contains a `/mnt/test` directory. Further assume a Samba server at 192.168.100.1, accessible to the workstation via the network. Note that any name resolving to the IP address can be substituted for the IP address. Running the preceding command on the local machine mounts to local directory `/mnt/test` the share defined in the `[homes]` section, logged in as user `myuid`.

To unmount it, simply run this command as user `root`, or quoted in the tail of an `su -c` command:

```
# smbumount /mnt/test
```

This capability is not limited to the user's home directory. It can be used on any share in `smb.conf` on the Samba server.

Mounting Shares on a Windows Client

A properly configured Samba share is accessible via Windows Network Neighborhood. This is the path:

```
Network_Neighborhood\Entire_Network\Workgroup\Machine_name\path
```

If there are problems, check the usual suspects: Windows doesn't yet know about the Samba server, user and password case problems, and clear-text versus encrypted passwords. If Windows doesn't yet recognize the Samba server, follow these steps: On the Windows box find the computer, refresh the screen, and wait a couple minutes or reboot the Windows client. In the case of user and password case problems, temporarily set username level and password level in `[global]` to a large value (such as `100`). In the case of clear-text versus encrypted passwords, set `encrypt passwords = yes` and `smb passwd file = /etc/smbpasswd` (or `/etc/samba.d/smbpasswd` for Caldera) in the `[global]` section.

Common smb.conf Configuration Options

There are hundreds of Samba options. For complete documentation, view the `smb.conf` man page with this command:

```
$ man smb.conf
```

Note

An understanding of a few options suffices for most tasks. A discussion of those options and conventions follows. Note that many options are followed by (G) or (S), meaning they are intended for the `[global]` section or a share section, respectively.

Special Conventions

Many options expecting users as the value can also take groups. In these cases the value is the group name preceded by an ampersand. For instance, group `acct` can be represented as `@acct`.

There are several substitution characters that can be used in `smb.conf`. They are all explained on the `smb.conf` man page. Two, `%u` and `%H`, are especially useful. `%u` will be substituted with the username, while `%H` will be substituted with the user's home directory. For instance, here's a share giving a document directory below `/home/everyone` to every user, as long as the sysadmin has created a directory with the user's username below `/home/everyone`:

```
[everyone]
comment = Accessible to everyone
path = /home/everyone/%u
browsable = yes
public = no
writeable = yes
create mode = 700
```

This is not the best way to accomplish this task. It's merely a demonstration of the `%u` substitution.

read Only=, writeable=, writable= and write ok= (S)

`writeable=` , `writable=`, and `write ok=` are synonyms, meaning they completely substitute for each other. `read only=` is an inverted synonym for `writeable=`, `writable=`, and `write ok=`, meaning that a `read only=yes` substitutes for a `writeable=no`, and a `read only=no` substitutes for a `writeable=yes`, and so on. Only one of these four options needs to specify whether a share is writeable. If this option is specified in the `[global]` section, it serves as a default for all shares. (This is true of all options that can be put in share definitions.) Note that these options can be overridden by the `write list=` option.

```
read only=no

writeable=yes

writable=yes

write ok=yes
```

All four mean the same thing and are interchangeable. The default is `read only=yes`.

valid users= (S)

The lack of this option or a blank value following the equal sign in any share makes the share accessible to everyone (probably not what you want). To limit access, place a comma-delimited list of valid users after the equal sign:

```
valid users = myuid, tackett, @acct
```

This option gives access to users `myuid` and `tackett`, and group `acct`. This option is overridden by the `invalid users=` option.

invalid users= (S)

This is a list of users who cannot access this share. This list overrides any users in the valid `users=` option for the share.

```
[ateam]
valid users = myuid,tackett,art
invalid users = myuid,tackett
```

This `smb.conf` snippet allows only `art` to access `[ateam]`.

read list= (S)

The value is a list of users to be given read-only access. This overrides any `read only=`, `writeable=`, and so on, restricting the listed users to read-only access. If any user on the `read list=` list is also on the `write list=` option for the share, `read list=` is overridden and that user can write in the directory.

Does `read list=` override `valid users=`? That's an interesting question. When a user not appearing in an existing `valid users=` list for the share appears in the `read list=` list, that user is prompted for a password. No matter whose password is input, the user is kicked out. This behavior is exactly mirrored by Samba's `smbclient` program and Windows Network Neighborhood. Here is an example:

```
[spec_dir]
path = /home/everyone/spec
valid users = valerie,tackett
writeable = yes
read list = valerie,tackett,myuid
write list = tackett
```

In the preceding example, the `/home/everyone/spec` directory can be read by `valerie` and `tackett`, but not by `myuid` (no `valid users=` entry for `myuid`). User `valerie` cannot write the directory because her entry in `read list=` overrides the `writeable=` option. However, `tackett` can write it because his `write list=` entry overrides his `read list=` entry.

write list= (S)

Any share can have a list of users who can write to that share, no matter what the writeable= or read list= options say. Here's an example giving write access to [billsdir] for bill, tackett, and myuid, in spite of the fact that the directory is optioned to be read-only:

```
[billsdir]
valid users = bill, tackett, myuid
read only = yes
write list = bill, tackett,  myuid
```

path= (S)

This is the directory accessed through the share. In the case of a print share, it's the spool directory. (Spool here before submitting to the printcap printer, which may also have its own spool.) Note that if the [global] section contains a root=, root dir=, or root directory=, the path= will be relative to the directory specified as the root.

create mask= and create mode= (S)

These two are synonyms. They specify the maximum permissions for a newly created file. The DOS permissions (read-only, hidden, and so on) will further restrict it. The default is 744, meaning the user gets all rights, but groups and other users get only read. If the owner later marks the file read-only from DOS, the files' actual mode on the Linux box are changed to 544 to reflect the loss of write permissions.

browseable= (S)

The browseable= entry instructs the SMB client whether to list the share in a SMB client's browse (like Windows Explorer). It does not grant access to users not in the valid users= list, nor does browseable=no deny access to users in the valid users= list.

If set to yes, the existence of the share can be seen even by those without rights to the share. If set to no, it cannot be seen even by those in the valid users= list. However, in clients that allow a user to access a share not listed (smbclient, for instance), browseable=no does not prevent a valid user from accessing the share, as long as the user enters the proper command with the proper share name. For instance, look at the following smb.conf share:

```
[valsdir]
comment = Valerie's special directory
path = /home/everyone/valsdir
browseable = no
valid users = valerie
```

Execute the following command:

```
$ smbclient -L 192.168.100.1 -U valerie
```

This is the yield:

```
Sharename       Type      Comment
        ---------       ----      -------
        everyone        Disk      Accessible to everyone
        IPC$            IPC       IPC Service (Jacks Samba Server)
        jacksdir        Disk      Jack's remote source code directory
        lp              Printer
        myuidx          Disk      Myuid's remote source code directory
        spec_dir        Disk
        valerie         Disk      Home Directories
```

Notice that share `valsdir` is not listed. That's because it's not browseable. However, access is not effected on SMB clients allowing a user to access an unlisted share by name. For instance, in SMB client `smbclient`, user `valerie` can issue the following command:

```
$ smbclient  '//192.168.100.1/valsdir' -U valerie
```

The preceding will bring up an `smbclient` prompt allowing user `valerie` to read and write to `/home/everyone/valsdir`.

In summary, `browseable=` governs the visibility, not the accessibility, of the resource. However, some SMB clients (such as Windows Network Neighborhood and Windows Explorer) make access of unlisted shares extremely difficult.

The default for `browseable=` is `no`. If you are in tight security situations where listing on the client is not desired, you must insert a `browseable=no` line to make it invisible to the client browser.

`printable=` (S)

This allows printing from the share, so it should be used on any share that's a printer, and not used on other shares. In the `[printers]` section, `printable=` defaults to `yes`. Everywhere else it defaults to `no`.

`hosts allow=`, `hosts deny=`, `allow hosts=`, and `deny hosts=` (S)

`hosts allow=` governs which hosts or subnets can access a share. If this option is used in the `[global]` section, it becomes the default for all shares. If this option is used, it denies entry to all hosts or subnets not specifically allowed. Use this code to allow a single host:

```
hosts allow = 192.168.100.201
```

To allow an entire subnet, use its address and subnet mask:

```
hosts allow = 192.168.100./255.255.255.0
```

`hosts allow=` overrides any `hosts deny=` options, which simply deny access to a host or subnet. `allow hosts=` is a synonym to `hosts allow=`, and `deny hosts=` is a synonym to `hosts deny=`.

`public=` and `guest ok=` (S)

These two are synonyms, with `guest ok=` preferred in SWAT. The purpose of this option is to allow those without a login on the server to access a share. This is a security compromise that sometimes makes sense on a printer. Care must be used to avoid the possibility of allowing a hostile exploit. For that reason the default is `no`.

`comment=` (S) and `server string=` (G)

These two are related in that they both provide human-readable strings to identify Samba resources in an SMB client's user interface. `comment=` describes a share, while `server string=` goes in the `[global]` section and describes the entire Samba server.

`domain logons=` (G)

This defaults to `no`, but if set to `yes`, the Samba server is allowed to serve as a domain server for a Windows 95/98 workgroup. This is different from a Windows NT domain.

`encrypt passwords=` and `smb passwd file=` (G)

These options are vital to serving Windows clients, and are discussed extensively earlier this chapter. Defaults are `encrypt passwords=no` and `smb passwd file=/etc/smbpasswd` (`/etc/samba.d/smbpasswd` for Caldera machines).

`hosts equiv=` (G)

This dangerous option points to a file containing hosts and users allowed to log in without a password. This is obviously an extreme security risk. The default is `none`, and the best policy is to leave this option absent from `smb.conf`.

`interfaces=` (G)

This becomes necessary when the server serves multiple subnets. Here's an example:

```
interfaces = 192.168.2.10/24 192.168.3.10/24
```

A /24 is a subnet mask. 24 represents 24 bits of 1a, or 255. 255. 255.0. Thus, the example would serve subnets 192.168.2 and 192.168.3. Normal subnet notations with four dot-delimited numbers can also be used after the slash.

load printers= (G)

This defaults to yes. A yes value loads all printers in printcap for Samba browsing.

null passwords= (G)

This option defaults to no, meaning no user with a zero-length password on the server can log into Samba. Setting this to yes is an obvious security risk.

password level and username level= (G)

These determine the level of non–case-sensitivity of username and password comparisons. The default is 0, meaning the client-provided password or username is first compared case sensitively against the copy on the server, and that the client username or password is converted to lowercase and compared to the copy on the server if that fails.

In troubleshooting Samba connection problems from Windows clients, it's often handy to set these high (like 24), to see if that fixes the problem. Although this represents a minor security problem and also slows initial connection, it often solves the problem. Once problems have been fixed, an attempt should be made to re-comment these two options to beef up security.

Connection problems from Windows clients also are often solved with the encrypt passwords= and smb passwd file = options.

security= (G)

Default is security=user, which enforces security by user and password. This is generally the best choice, with excellent security and predictability.

security=server and security=domain are used primarily when password authentication is actually done by yet another machine. security=domain is used to join Samba to an NT domain. security=share offers less security and less predictable operation, but is sometimes a logical choice in less security intense situations such as if most of the client usernames don't exist on the server, or if most usage is printers not requiring passwords.

This topic is important, and is discussed further in documents /usr/doc/samba-2.0.3/docs/textdocs/security_level.txt and /usr/doc/samba-2.0.3/docs/textdocs/DOMAIN_MEMBER.txt.

workgroup= (G)

This is the workgroup in which the server appears, and also controls the domain name used with the `security=domain` setting. The default is `WORKGROUP`, but Linux-supplied `smb.conf` may set it to another value.

config file= (G)

This is a method of specifying a Samba configuration file other than `smb.conf` in the Samba directory. When Samba encounters this option, it reloads all parameters from the specified file.

Samba Documentation Sources

With Linux installed, you have access to voluminous Samba documentation. Every program has its own man page, available with the Linux command:

```
# man programname
```

programname is `smbtar`, `smbmount`, or the like.

There is also text-based hyperlink help available with the `info` program:

```
# info programname
```

programname is `smbtar`, `smbmount`, or the like.

You can find text format and HTML format Samba documentation on your hard disk. Use the `locate` command to find the documentation for your particular distribution. An excellent SMB HOWTO is located in the following:

`/usr/doc/HOWTO/SMB-HOWTO`

`/usr/doc/HOWTO/other-formats/html/SMB-HOWTO.html`

`/usr/doc/HOWTO/SMB-HOWTO.html`

As of Samba version 2 and later, a great source of documentation is the SWAT (Samba Web Administration Tool). SWAT is discussed later in this chapter. If SWAT is enabled on your server, it's a highly organized source of Samba documentation. Users other than `root` can take advantage of SWAT's documentation, although only user `root` can alter the `smb.conf` configuration through SWAT.

Samba Applications Documentation Sources

Samba is a suite of programs (listed in Table 16.2) designed to give all necessary client and server access to SMB on your Linux-based computer. Each program has a man page and an info page.

TABLE 16.2 Programs Comprising the Samba Suite

Program	*Description*
`smbd`	The daemon that provides the file and print services to SMB clients such as Windows for Workgroups, Windows NT, or LanManager. (The configuration file for this daemon is described in `smb.conf`.)
`nmbd`	The daemon that provides NetBIOS nameserving and browsing support.
`smbclient`	This program implements an FTP-like client that is useful for accessing SMB shares on other compatible servers.
`testparm`	This utility enables you to test the Samba Configuration File.
`smbstatus`	This utility enables you to tell who is currently using the `smbd` server.
`smbpasswd`	This utility changes a user's SMB password in the `smbpasswd` file.
`smbrun`	This is an interface program between `smbd` and external programs.
`smbtar`	This is a shell script for backing up SMB shares directly to a UNIX-based tape drive.
`smbmount`	Use this utility to mount an SMB filesystem.
`smbmnt`	Called by `smbmount` to do the work. Generally not called directly.
`smbumount`	A utility that unmounts an SMB filesystem.

Configuration Option Documentation

Samba has hundreds of configuration options. For complete information, search for these three strings on the `smb.conf` man page: `"COMPLETE LIST OF GLOBAL PARAMETERS"`, `"COMPLETE LIST OF SERVICE PARAMETERS"`, and `"EXPLANATION OF EACH PARAMETER"`. The same information is accessible in the `smb.conf` info page.

Other Documentation

The `smb.conf` file supports a number of variable substitutions. The `%H` and `%u` substitutions are discussed earlier in this chapter. For a complete list and description of these substitutions, search the `smb.conf` man page for the phrase `"VARIABLE SUBSTITUTIONS"`.

The `smb.conf` file has several options related to name mangling. *Name mangling* is a method of interfacing between old DOS 8.3 filename conventions and modern filenaming conventions. It also relates to case sensitivity, default case, and the like. To see a complete treatise on the subject, search for the string `"NAME MANGLING"` in the `smb.conf` man page.

Using SWAT for Web-Based Samba Configuration

SWAT is a Web-based tool to allow remote, password-guarded Samba administration from any browser that can access the server. SWAT is new with Samba 2, and SWAT is now included because Red Hat 6.0 ships with Samba 2.0.3.

> **Caution**
>
> Configuring with SWAT will dramatically change your `smb.conf` file. It will eliminate all comments, eliminate `include=` and `copy=` options, eliminate many options already set to the default, change options to more common synonyms (and in some cases to inverse synonyms, simultaneously reversing the value). SWAT will also eliminate the `[GLOBAL]` line. That is OK because anything appearing at the top of the file, before a bracketed share, is treated as part of `[GLOBAL]` by Samba.
>
> Always back up `smb.conf` before configuring with SWAT. A SWAT-configured `smb.conf` file is much shorter, making it more readable. However, the loss of comments and self-documenting default-configured options can make it less readable. If you've tailored your `smb.conf` for readability and self-documentation, you may want to refrain from using SWAT.

SWAT is a convenience that can improve security by making errors less likely. It dramatically changes `smb.conf`, however, and it can cause a security breach if not used carefully.

Activating SWAT on Your Server

Each Linux distribution has its own requirements for enabling and using SWAT. This section outlines those requirements.

Debian release 2.1 ships with Samba version 1.9.18. Only Samba version 2 and later offer SWAT.

If you are running Debian 2.2, you may install SWAT with the following command:

```
apt-get install swat
```

By default, SWAT is disabled after installation. To enable it, edit `/etc/inetd.conf` and comment out the line for SWAT, which is usually near the end of the file. Restart `inetd` per the following directions.

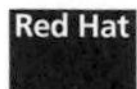

Red Hat 6.0 comes with SWAT disabled. To enable SWAT, follow these steps:

1. Verify that `/etc/services` contains the following line. The line should not be commented:

   ```
   swat            901/tcp
   ```

2. Uncomment the following line in `/etc/inetd.conf`:

   ```
   swat stream  tcp nowait.400 root /usr/sbin/swat swat
   ```

Caldera users: See the note immediately following this list.

3. Find the PID of `inetd`.
4. Issue the following command:

   ```
   # kill -1 PID
   ```

Note

Caldera installs with a functioning SWAT. However, Caldera closes some security holes using `tcpd` in `inetd.conf`. Take a look at the following line:

```
swat stream  tcp nowait.400 root /usr/sbin/swat swat
```

Caldera replaces the `/usr/sbin/swat` with `/usr/sbin/tcpd` as follows:

```
swat stream  tcp nowait.400 root /usr/sbin/tcpd swat
```

Caldera then places the following line in `/etc/hosts.deny`:

```
swat:ALL EXCEPT 127.0.0.2
```

This rejects all SWAT requests from any address except `127.0.0.2`

For the utmost in security, you may want to implement this on distributions other than Caldera.

The procedure should successfully enable SWAT on a typically installed Red Hat 6.0 server. The next step is to access Samba configuration through SWAT.

Configuring `smb.conf` from Your Browser Using SWAT

SECURITY CAUTION!

After completing your SWAT work, you must close all browsers on your workstation. All open browsers will "remember" the password, allowing anyone with physical access to your workstation (or server terminal) access to Samba configuration, including password administration.

Additionally, if SWAT is used on a browser at a remote workstation, passwords are sent across the wire as clear text and can be sniffed.

For best security, use SWAT only on the server's terminal, and when done, close all browsers.

You may want to implement the security precautions described in the preceding note.

From your favorite browser, including Netscape Navigator, Microsoft Internet Explorer, or Lynx, navigate to port 901 of the server's IP address or a valid localhost IP as in the three examples below:

```
#lynx http://192.168.100.1:901

#lynx http://127.0.0.2:901

#lynx http://127.0.0.1:901
```

The browser asks for a username and password. To enable read-write access, use `root` and `root`'s password. Once authenticated, a page appears with links for `HOME`, `GLOBALS`, `SHARES`, `PRINTERS`, `STATUS`, `VIEW`, and `PASSWORD`. Choosing `GLOBALS`, `SHARES`, or `PRINTERS` brings up a page in which you can edit options. Each contains a button that can be toggled between Advanced View and Basic View, with Advanced View showing every possible configuration option. Note that with the `SHARES` and `PRINTERS` pages, you'll need to choose the share or printer from a drop-down list and then click the Choose button before you can edit the share or printer.

Assuming you're logged into SWAT as `root`, a Commit Changes button will be visible. After making changes, clicking this button will write `smb.conf`. If you click the Reset Values button, the options will revert to values in the present `smb.conf` file.

> **Note**
>
> You must restart smbd with the Samba restart command before your changes take effect.

The SWAT page contains voluminous, well-organized documentation, available even to those not logged in as root, and therefore unable to change the configuration.

Summary

Samba enables a Linux computer to act as a secure, sophisticated file and print server. At this point, you should have a properly configured Samba server up and running and have learned the commands and options that make that Samba server practical. You have learned several tips on troubleshooting your Samba setup.

Several advanced options are available for Samba and the various programs that make up the Samba suite. For more information about Samba, read the Samba HOWTO on your Linux system at:

```
/usr/doc/HOWTO/SMB-HOWTO
```

```
/usr/doc/HOWTO/other-formats/html/SMB-HOWTO.html
```

```
/usr/doc/HOWTO/SMB-HOWTO.html
```

Finally, you can find a large amount of information on Samba at http://www.samba.org.

CHAPTER 17

Connecting to the Internet

In This Chapter

Connections from a Linux system to an ISP are usually made through a modem using the now common PPP (Point-to-Point Protocol) or more infrequently currently using SLIP (Serial Line Interface Protocol). Both PPP and SLIP allow you to transfer mail, surf the World Wide Web, use FTP, and access all the other features of the Internet. Both PPP and SLIP use the TCP/IP network protocol, and because TCP/IP and UNIX evolved together, Linux is particularly adept at handling PPP and SLIP.

In this chapter you learn how to easily set up your Linux system to use PPP using manual scripts and graphical interface PPP clients, such as Red Hat's `netcfg` tool and KDE's `kppp` client.

Red Hat users will generally use the `netcfg` tool for their network interface setup. This includes setting up PPP and SLIP interfaces.

If you are using Caldera and the KDE interface, the `kppp` program will be the easiest way to set up PPP.

Debian provides several methods to use to set up PPP. Most people use `pppconfig` or `wvdial`; `pppconfig` is discussed in this chapter. You can find details about `wvdial` at `http://www.worldvisions.ca/wvdial/`.

You will also learn one way to set up your Linux system for dial-in PPP. You probably will not want to set up both PPP and SLIP because these days most ISPs use PPP only, and SLIP seems to be "slipping" into obscurity. PPP is the faster of the two protocols, but you may sometimes need to use SLIP with older systems or legacy software. Before setting up either PPP or SLIP, you need to create a dummy interface so that your machine knows about itself in a networking sense and because most protocols require this dummy interface to work properly.

Setting Up the Dummy Interface

A *dummy interface* is used by TCP/IP to assign an IP address to your machine, which is required for both SLIP and PPP. The reason for a dummy interface is simple: When you connect to an ISP, your IP address is often assigned dynamically and you never know what the IP address will be in advance. This can cause problems for TCP/IP routines in your kernel that need to know an IP address to function properly. TCP/IP is happy when you assign an IP address—the dummy interface IP address—to your machine. The internal IP address is most important when you are not connected to your ISP because many network-aware applications (such as email, news readers, and so on) need to have some IP address to connect to, even if it doesn't lead anywhere. This dummy interface IP address does not conflict with the one assigned by your ISP.

Fortunately, setting up a dummy interface is simple. All that is required are a couple of commands to create the interface and a couple more commands to test that the interface is working, and you're done. The file that Linux uses to store all network IP address information is called `/etc/hosts`, and every system should have one (even if it is empty).

The `/etc/hosts` file is an ASCII file that provides two pieces of information to the TCP/IP drivers and applications: an IP address and the names associated with that IP address. Usually, you will find the `/etc/hosts` file has a single line in it when you install Linux without network support:


```
127.0.0.1        localhost       localhost.localdomain
```

This line essentially tells TCP/IP that a special interface called `localhost` is assigned the IP address `127.0.0.1`. The `localhost` interface is called the *dummy interface* because it is not a real address. This interface is also called the *loopback interface* because it leads back to the same machine.

NOTE

The terms *localhost*, *loopback*, and *dummy interface* all refer to the use of the IP address `127.0.0.1` to refer to the local machine. The term *loopback interface* indicates that, to the networking drivers, it looks as though the machine is talking to a network that consists of only one machine. In internal terms, the kernel sends network traffic out one port and back in to another on the same machine. *Dummy interface* indicates that, to the outside world, the interface doesn't really exist, only to the local machine.

`127.0.0.1` is a special IP address reserved for the local machines on all networks. Every networked Linux machine has this IP address for its `localhost`. If you display the contents of your `/etc/hosts` file and this line already exists, then the dummy interface is set up for you and you can skip this section. If the `/etc/hosts` file doesn't exist or this line is not in the file, you have to set up the interface yourself. If your machine has an IP address other than `127.0.0.1` in your `/etc/hosts` file, and the interface `127.0.0.1` is not there, you do not have the `localhost` interface set up.

NOTE

When you installed Red Hat Linux, you may have chosen to install and support networking. If you did, the dummy interface was probably set up automatically. If you chose a non-networking boot image, you may have to manually add the dummy interface.

To create the dummy interface, your Linux system needs the networking software installed. The installation happens automatically with most `root` and `boot` images, even if the network interfaces are not configured.

Begin the dummy interface setup by editing (or creating, if it doesn't exist) the `/etc/hosts` file, and add the following line:

```
127.0.0.1        localhost        localhost.localdomain
```

The number of spaces between the IP address and the name `localhost` does not matter, as long as there is at least one. Make sure you enter the IP address exactly as shown—with no spaces between the parts of the dotted-quad notation. If you already had an IP address in the `/etc/hosts` file for your local machine but no `localhost` entry with this IP address, you still need to add this line. The `localhost` line is usually the very first line in the `/etc/hosts` file.

After updating the `/etc/hosts` file, you need to tell TCP/IP about the new interface. To set up the dummy interface, issue the following commands when you are logged in as `root`:

```
# ifconfig lo 127.0.0.1
# route add 127.0.0.1 lo
```

The first command tells the system to add an interface called the `localhost` (`lo` is the short form for `localhost`) with an IP address of `127.0.0.1`. The second command adds the IP address `127.0.0.1` to an internal table that keeps track of routes to different addresses.

After you have issued these two commands, the dummy interface should be created and ready to use. A machine reboot usually helps ensure that the proper configurations are read. To test the dummy interface, use the `ifconfig` command again with the name of the interface (`lo` for localhost) to tell you statistics about the interface (or just use `ifconfig` to see all interfaces). The command and a sample output look like this:

```
# ifconfig lo
lo        Link encap:Local Loopback
          inet addr:127.0.0.1  Mask:255.0.0.0
          UP LOOPBACK RUNNING  MTU:3924  Metric:1
          RX packets:60 errors:0 dropped:0 overruns:0 frame:0
          TX packets:60 errors:0 dropped:0 overruns:0 carrier:0
          collisions:0 txqueuelen:0
```

This output shows that the loopback interface is active and running, that it has been assigned the IP address `127.0.0.1`, that the broadcast mask of `255.0.0.0` is used, and that the interface hasn't had much traffic. Don't worry about the errors in the last couple of lines: You haven't used the interface yet so there are no meaningful statistics available.

As a check that your kernel knows about the interface and that your machine responds to the IP address `127.0.0.1` and the name `localhost` (defined in your system's /etc/hosts files), you can use the `ping` command to check that the interface is responding properly:

```
# ping localhost
PING localhost (127.0.0.1): 56 data bytes
64 bytes from 127.0.0.1: icmp_seq=0 ttl=255 time=0.3 ms
64 bytes from 127.0.0.1: icmp_seq=1 ttl=255 time=0.2 ms
64 bytes from 127.0.0.1: icmp_seq=2 ttl=255 time=0.1 ms
64 bytes from 127.0.0.1: icmp_seq=3 ttl=255 time=0.1 ms
64 bytes from 127.0.0.1: icmp_seq=4 ttl=255 time=0.2 ms
64 bytes from 127.0.0.1: icmp_seq=5 ttl=255 time=0.1 ms

--- localhost ping statistics ---
6 packets transmitted, 6 packets received, 0% packet loss
round-trip min/avg/max = 0.1/0.1/0.3 ms
```

To stop the output from the `ping` command, you press Ctrl+C. You should get similar results using either the name `localhost` or the IP address `127.0.0.1` (because they both refer to exactly the same interface according to the `/etc/hosts` file).

If you get the following message, the interface is not set up properly and you should check the `/etc/hosts` file and the `ifconfig` command to make sure you installed the interface properly:

```
# ping localhost
unknown host
```

Repeating the installation steps should correct the problem. After you complete those simple steps and tests, the dummy interface is ready to be used by your system, its applications, and both PPP and SLIP.

Setting Up PPP

Most ISPs today use PPP instead of SLIP. This is good for you because PPP is a faster and more efficient protocol. PPP and SLIP are both designed for two-way networking; in other words, your machine talking to one other machine—usually your ISP—and no other machines at the time (although it is possible to communicate with other computers on your internal network). PPP is not a replacement for a LAN protocol such as TCP/IP, but PPP can coexist with TCP/IP (which provides a transport protocol for data). In fact, PPP is designed to run other protocols over it, not just TCP/IP. SLIP is used only to transport TCP/IP traffic.

One of the major hurdles new Linux users face is setting up PPP and connecting to the Internet. If you're new to Linux, relax! You don't have to understand the intricacies of the protocol in order to use PPP, and setting up PPP on your system is not as scary as you might suspect (although if you want to examine the gritty details, look at the file `ppp.c` under the `/usr/src/linux/drivers/net` directory). You can do it manually from the command line, or by using a graphical interface client. Both approaches produce the same results. However, using the command line offers the advantage that you get to understand what is going on.

PPP uses two components on your system. The first is a daemon called `pppd`, which controls the use of PPP. The second is a driver called the high-level data link control (HDLC), which controls the flow of information between two machines. A third component of PPP is a routine called `chat` that dials the other end of the connection for you when you want it to.

> **Note**
>
> PPP is a complex protocol with many tunable parameters. Fortunately, most of these parameters concern things you will never care about, so you can ignore all those underlying details in the vast majority of installations. Unless you plan to use PPP to connect to the Internet all day (and there are better choices for that), you will do fine using the default settings PPP employs.

Installing PPP

PPP was most likely installed when you installed your Linux distribution. If itPPP;(Point-to-Point Protocol) wasn't, you need to load the package before you can continue to configure the system for PPP use. The PPP library and files are included with practically every CD-ROM distribution of Linux, and you can obtain the most recent versions from the usual Linux Web and FTP sites.

Red Hat

If for some reason PPP is not installed on your system, use Red Hat's `rpm` command to install the PPP package. Mount your Red Hat Linux CD-ROM and then use the following command line:

```
# rpm -ivh /mnt/cdrom/Redhat/RPMS/ppp-2.3.7-2.rpm
```

The path to the PPP `.rpm` file is fully specified in the command line. The full path depends on where you have mounted your CD-ROM (most likely `/mnt/cdrom`). Red Hat Linux 6.0 includes version 2.3.7 of PPP.

If you are using Caldera's OpenLinux and you don't have PPP installed, use the `rpm` command to install the PPP package by mounting your Caldera CD-ROM and then using the following command line:

```
# rpm -ivh /mnt/cdrom/col/install/Rpms/ppp-2.3.5-0b.i386.rpm
```

The path to the PPP `.rpm` file is fully specified in the command line. The full path depends on where you have mounted your CD-ROM (most likly `/mnt/cdrom`). Caldera OpenLinux 2.2 includes version 2.3.5 of PPP.

You can install PPP on your system with this:

```
apt-get install ppp
```

Note

Previous versions of PPP, such as 2.2.0f, will not work with the newer (2.2.X) Linux kernels due to changes in routing code. If you must use older versions of `pppd` (such as 2.2.0f), look for a source code patch file in the file `ppp.txt` under the `/usr/src/linux-2.2.5/Documentation/networking` directory.

Setting Up a PPP User Account

To help protect your system from hackers and break-in attempts from your ISP (remember that if your machine can communicate to the Internet, users on the Internet can communicate with your machine), it is advisable to set up a special user login for PPP. This step is optional but highly recommended.

You can add the new user account for PPP (usually called `ppp` for convenience) using any of the user administration scripts you want, or you can simply edit the `/etc/passwd` file and add the user yourself (only if you do not use password shadowing). Because the PPP login does not have a home directory per se, you don't need to create mailboxes and other paraphernalia that is normally created by a user administration script. The line you want to add to the `/etc/passwd` file looks like this:

```
ppp:*:301:51:PPP account:/tmp:/etc/ppp/pppscript
```

This creates a user called ppp with no password. (The asterisk in the second field can't be matched.) The user ID is 301 in this example, but you can substitute any unused user ID. The group ID is best set to a new group called ppp, although this is not necessary. The fourth field is a comment that describes the account's purpose. The home directory is set to /tmp in this case because you don't want to keep files in the ppp account home directory. The last field in the /etc/passwd entry is used for a startup script. In this case, I've created a new script called /etc/ppp/pppscript, which takes care of starting PPP properly. You will have to create this script yourself. The contents of pppscript should look similar to this:

```
#!/bin/sh
mesg n
stty -echo
exec pppd -detach silent modem crtscts
```

The first line invokes the Bourne SHell to run the script. The second line suppresses messages for this login. The third line stops the remote from echoing everything back. The fourth line invokes the pppd daemon with some options that control its behavior. (You'll look at the pppd daemon in more detail in a few moments.) Make sure the file pppscript is executable by using a command similar to this:

```
# chmod a+x /etc/ppp/pppscript
```

Setting Up chat

Because you are going to use a modem to connect to your ISP, you need to tell PPP about the modem and how to use it. PPP uses a program called chat to handle all these details. (You can use utilities other than chat, but experience has shown that chat is the most foolproof option as well as one of the easiest options to set up quickly.) The chat utility takes a lot of its features from the UUCP program, which makes it familiar for many veteran system administrators.

The chat utility requires a command line that tells it what number to call to connect to your ISP and what types of login responses are required. All of this information is placed on a single-line chat script. These lines are often stored in files to prevent you from having to type the commands every time you want to access the Internet.

Here's a typical chat script for a connection to an ISP:

```
"" ATZ OK ATDT2370400 CONNECT "" ogin: ppp word: guessme
```

In this example, the ISP's phone number is 237-0400, while the username and password to login are `ppp` and `guessme`. `chat` scripts are always set up as a conversation between the `chat` utility and the modem. The script parts are separated by spaces, with the `chat` instruction and the expected reply one after another. This `chat` script tells `chat` the following: Expect nothing from the modem to start (the two quotation marks), then send the string `ATZ` and wait for the reply `OK`. After `OK` is received, `chat` sends the string `ATDT2370400` to dial out to the ISP's number. When a `CONNECT` string is received from the modem, send nothing and wait for the string `ogin:` from the ISP. (This covers all the case types such as `login` and `Login`.) After getting `ogin:`, send the login `ppp` and wait for `word` (the end of `password`) and send the password `guessme`. After that, `chat` terminates and hands control over to `pppd`.

You can see in the script how the conversation goes through with each end (the modem and `chat`) taking turns communicating. You will need to set up a `chat` script like this in a file with your ISP's number and the proper login and password. Place it in an ASCII file. Use the `chat` command to call the file:

```
chat -f filename
```

`filename` is the name of the `chat` script file. The `chat` command has a lot of options for handling error conditions from your modem and the ISP, but these all complicate the script quite a bit. The easiest modifications are to build in handling for both a busy signal from the modem (the ISP's line was busy) and a no-carrier message from the modem (when it couldn't connect properly). To handle both these error conditions in the script and have `chat` terminate when these conditions occur, modify the script to look like this:

```
ABORT BUSY 'NO CARRIER' "" ATZ OK ATDT2370400 CONNECT "" ogin: ppp word: guessme
```

The two `ABORT` sequences in front of the older script tell `chat` to terminate if either the `BUSY` or `NO CARRIER` message is sent by the modem. Make sure you use quotation marks around the two words in `NO CARRIER`; otherwise, `chat` thinks these are two different parts of the script.

Before we go any further, I need to make a clarification with respect to your serial port under Linux. As you know, in DOS your serial ports are named COM1, COM2, COM3, and COM4. Under Linux, you reference your serial ports by their device names. Under most versions of Linux these days, the COM ports map on a one-to-one basis with `/dev/ttyS0`, `/dev/ttyS1`, `/dev/ttyS2`, and `/dev/ttyS3`. The confusing aspect of this is that the Linux device files start numbering at zero, as opposed to the COM ports beginning numbering at one. As an example, COM3 is known as /dev/ttyS2. In some books, and other older Linux references, you will probably find mention of the ports /dev/cua0, /dev/cua1, /dev/cua2, and /dev/cua3. These used to be the standard serial port references, but their use has been depreciated in favor of the `/dev/ttyS{0,1,2,3}` format.

Configuring pppd

As mentioned, most of the PPP functions are controlled by a daemon called pppd. When chat has connected to a remote system and terminates cleanly, it hands control of the connection over to pppd. It is the pppd daemon that handles all the communications from this point forward.

The pppd daemon is usually started with arguments for the modem device and the speed of the connection. If you want to start pppd manually from the command line, your command could look like this:

```
pppd /dev/ttyS0 38400 crtscts defaultroute
```

This line tells pppd to use the serial port /dev/ttyS0 (COM1) to connect at 38,400bps. The crtscts option tells pppd to use hardware handshaking on the connection, and defaultroute tells pppd to use the local IP address for the connection.

Because you'll most likely be assigned a dynamic IP address by your ISP when you connect, you can't hard code the address into the pppd command line. The pppd daemon can accept any IP address the remote connection wants if you modify the command line like this:

```
pppd /dev/ttyS0 38400 crtscts IP_address:
```

You substitute whatever IP address your machine has (even 127.0.0.1) before the colon. The colon with nothing after it tells pppd to accept whatever IP address the remote sends as the other end of the connection.

The pppd daemon accepts options from configuration files if they exist. The most common configuration file for PPP is stored as /etc/ppp/options, although you may use any path and filename you want. The default settings in the /etc/ppp/options file look like this:

```
# /etc/ppp/options: global definitions
domain merlin.com
auth                    # force authentication
usehostname             # use local hostname for authentication
lock                    # use file locking UUCP-style
```

The first line gives the local domain name and you should edit it to suit your domain (if you have one). The second and third lines force authentication to prevent misuse. The fourth line tells pppd to use UUCP-like file locking, which works well to prevent device problems. You can add any other valid pppd options to this file, but these suffice for most setups.

Combining chat and pppd

You have to take two steps to connect to an ISP in light of the way I describe setting up chat and pppd: Use chat to establish the connection and then launch pppd to use PPP over the connection. There is a way to take both steps with one command line, which can be added to the pppscript talked about earlier in this section. By calling chat from the pppd command line, you can simplify the entire process. Here's a modification of the pppd command line that accomplishes this:

```
pppd connect 'chat -v "" ATDT1111111 CONNECT "" ogin: username word: password''
/dev/ttyS0 38400 -detach crtscts modem defaultroute
```

You will need to replace the phone number *1111111* with your ISP access number, and also replace *username* and *password* with whatever your ISP supplied you with for these details. pppd creates the link, and then finishes establishing an active PPP connection. You must have the path to your chat file easily found by chat or specify the full pathname in the command line. As mentioned, you can substitute this line for the pppd line in the pppscript file; the connection will be established in one step.

After these few steps, your system is ready to use PPP to dial out to your ISP. As long as the chat script has all the instructions for connecting to the ISP's modem bank, PPP will start properly once a connection is established.

Setting Up PPP Using the PPP Scripts

While manually creating PPP scripts is one way to set up a PPP user account, when you install your particular Linux distribution and the PPP packages, you'll find a dialer, chat script, and PPP on and off scripts already installed.

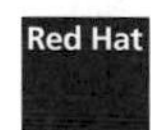

In Red Hat Linux 6.0 they are under the /usr/doc/ppp-2.3.7/scripts directory.

In Caldera OpenLinux 2.2 they are in the /usr/doc/ppp-2.3.5 directory.

Debian users may find these scripts in either /usr/doc/ppp/examples or /usr/doc/ppp/examples/scripts, depending on the version of Debian that they have.

Using these scripts is a lot easier; by performing a few simple edits you'll be connected in a few minutes!

Here are the important script files:

- ppp-on—Contains your ISP's phone number, your username and password, and modem options (such the baud rate).

- `ppp-off` —A utility script that kills the interface and PPP connection.
- `ppp-on-dialer` —A PPP chat script.

To set up these scripts, log in as `root` and copy the scripts to the `/etc/ppp` directory:

```
# cp /usr/doc/ppp*/scripts/ppp-o* /etc/ppp
```

If you are using Caldera, you will need to use this command instead:

```
# cp /usr/doc/ppp*/ppp-o* /etc/ppp
```

Open the `ppp-on` script with your favorite text editor. Look first for the entries for your ISP's phone number and your username and password, like this:

```
TELEPHONE=555-1212        # The telephone number for the connection
ACCOUNT=george            # The account name for logon (as in 'George Burns')
PASSWORD=gracie           # The password for this account (and 'Gracie Allen')
LOCAL_IP=0.0.0.0          # Local IP address if known. Dynamic = 0.0.0.0
REMOTE_IP=0.0.0.0         # Remote IP address if desired. Normally 0.0.0.0
```

Change the values for `TELEPHONE`, `ACCOUNT`, and `PASSWORD`, substituting your ISP's phone number and your username and password. Next, scroll through the script until you find this:

```
exec /usr/sbin/pppd debug lock modem crtscts /dev/ttyS0 38400 \
        asyncmap 20A0000 escape FF kdebug 0 $LOCAL_IP:$REMOTE_IP \
        noipdefault netmask $NETMASK defaultroute connect $DIALER_SCRIPT
```

These lines of the script contain modem options for the `chat` script in the `ppp-on-dialer` script and starts the `pppd` daemon on your computer following a connection to your ISP's computer. Change the modem device (`/dev/ttyS0` in this example) and the baud rate (38,400 in this case) to match your system and desired connection speed. When finished, save the script.

Next, use the `chmod` command to make these scripts executable:

```
# chmod +x /etc/ppp/ppp-o*
```

To debug or check the progress of your modem connection, dialing, and connection to your ISP, use the `tail` command with its `-f` loop forever option:

```
# tail -f /var/log/messages
```

To connect to your ISP, execute the `ppp-on` script (as `root`):

```
# /etc/ppp/ppp-on
```

To stop your PPP connection, use the `ppp-off` script (as `root`):

```
# /etc/ppp/ppp-off
```

You can also move the `ppp-on` and `ppp-off` scripts to a recognized `$PATH`, such as `/usr/local/bin`.

Just a reminder, once you have set up a PPP connection, to look up a DNS name you will need a `/etc/resolv.conf` file configured with your ISP's Domain Name Server (DNS). A basic `/etc/resolv.conf` file will generally look something like this:

```
nameserver 192.168.23.4
```

Remember to replace `192.168.23.4` with your ISP's DNS.

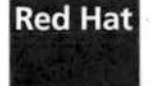

Setting Up PPP with the `netcfg` Client (for Red Hat Users)

Using a manual PPP `chat` script or the PPP connection scripts is an easy way to start and stop a PPP connection. These manual scripts have the advantage of working with or without a graphical interface, such as the X Window System. The disadvantage of using these scripts becomes apparent when you must use or maintain multiple ISP accounts, have security issues for passwords, or want the point-and-click convenience of a graphical interface to PPP setup and connections.

Fortunately, Red Hat Linux 6.0 comes with an easy-to-use network configuration tool, `netcfg`. You must run an X session in order to use `netcfg`. To start it, click the Network Configuration button in the Red Hat `control-panel` client, or type the following from the command line of an X11 terminal window:

```
# netcfg &
```

The `netcfg` window appears after you press Enter. To start your PPP account configuration, click the Interfaces button at the top of the window (as shown in Figure 17.1).

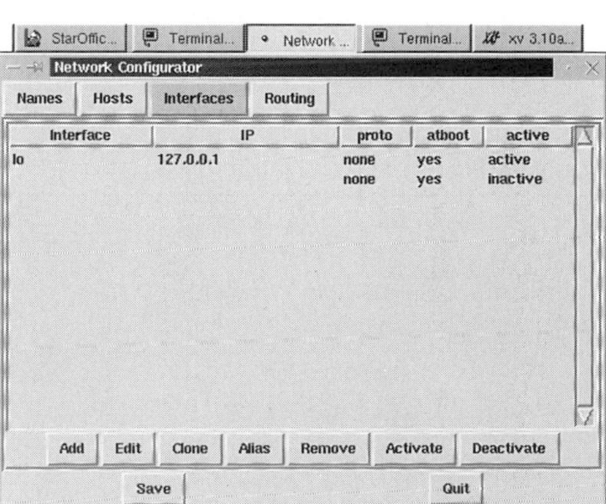

FIGURE 17.1
Red Hat's `netcfg` tool is one way to set up a PPP connection when using Linux.

The first step is to click the Add button at the bottom of the Interfaces dialog box. A small dialog box, shown in Figure 17.2, appears. Click the PPP interface and then click the OK button.

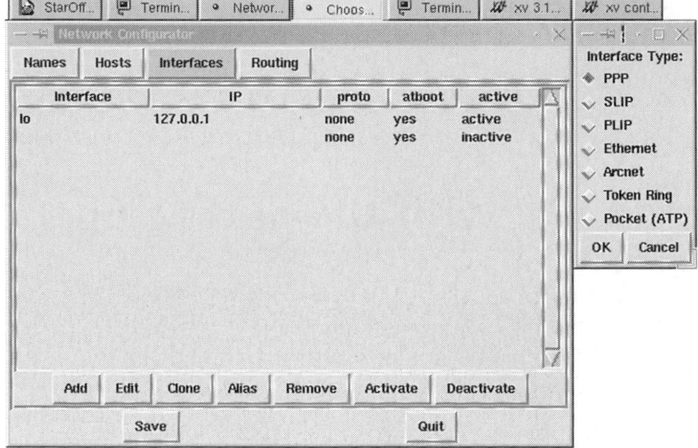

FIGURE 17.2
Select the PPP interface to set up a connection with Red Hat's `netcfg` tool.

A Create PPP Interface dialog box appears, as shown in Figure 17.3. Type in your ISP's phone number, along with your username and password. If these are the only options you need, click the Done button to save your configuration. By default, `netcfg` will use options listed in Table 17.1.

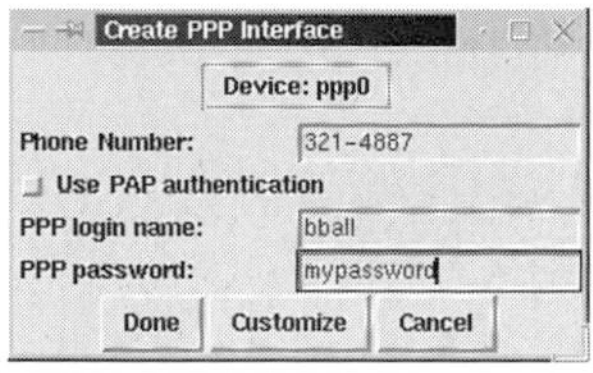

FIGURE 17.3
Configuring a PPP connection with `netcfg` can be as easy as entering a phone number, a username, and a password.

TABLE 17.1 `netcfg` Default PPP Connection Values

Option	*Default Value*
Dialing device	`/dev/modem`
Use hardware flow control	`yes`
Line speed	`115200` baud
Modem `init` string	`ATZ`

Red Hat

Option	*Default Value*
Modem `dial` command	`ATDT`
Expected login string	`ogin:`
Expected password string	`ord:`

If you need to change any default settings, click the Customize button (as shown in Figure 17.3). A dialog box (see Figure 17.4) that you can use to change connection defaults appears.

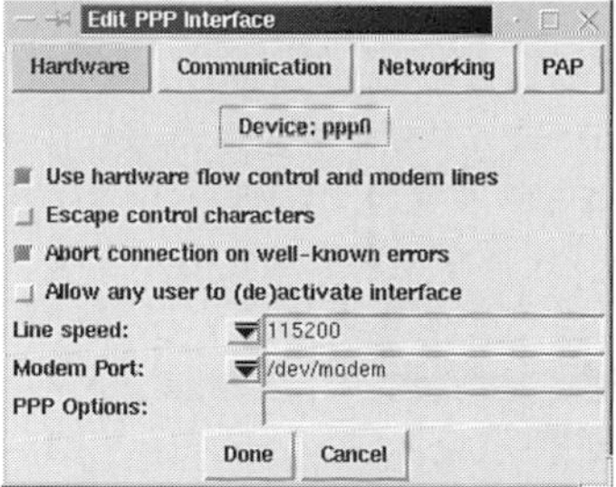

FIGURE 17.4
`netcfg` also offers customized settings for your PPP connection.

Click the Hardware, Communication, Networking, or PAP button to customize your connection. PAP (Password Authentication Protocol)) connections are PPP connections that require authentication packets of information to be transmitted between the client (you) and the server (your ISP's computer).

Note

If you note LCP errors during connection negotiation with your ISP, you may need to use PAP settings for your account.

If your ISP requires a different login procedure prior to starting a PPP connection (a `Login:` and `Password:` prompt are not used), you need to adjust the expected strings in the default `chat` script that the `netcfg` tool will create. Click the Communication button (as shown in Figure 17.4), and a dialog box will appear (as shown in Figure 17.5). In it you can insert, append, edit, or remove expected strings and responses to connect to your ISP.

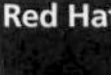

FIGURE 17.5
Change the expected strings and responses, if needed, to set up your PPP connection.

Click the Done button when you've finished setting up your PPP interface. You'll see the interface defined in the main `netcfg` dialog box (as shown in Figure 17.6).

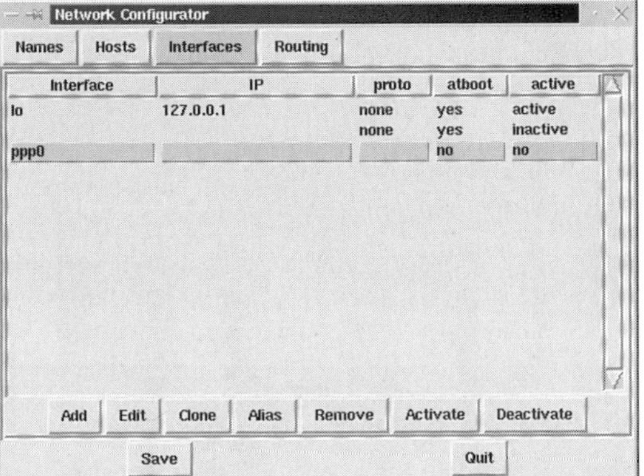

FIGURE 17.6
When you have finished defining your PPP connection, an inactive PPP interface will appear in the `netcfg` *dialog box.*

To start a PPP connection, first click the defined PPP interface and then click the Activate button. To stop an active PPP connection, click the PPP interface and then click the Deactivate button.

Setting Up PPP with the `kppp` Client

Both Red Hat Linux 6.0 and Caldera OpenLinux 2.2 includes the K Desktop Environment and its suite of graphical clients for X. One of these clients is the `kppp` tool, a state-of-the-art PPP and Internet connection utility. This client has the following features:

- Built-in terminal and script generator
- Connection statistics and pppd load monitoring
- Docking of modem send/receive lights in the K desktop panel
- Graphical front end to the pppd daemon
- Multiple account maintenance for different users and ISPs
- Online time tracking and phone-cost accounting

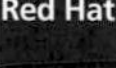

Unfortunately, Red Hat Linux 6.0 does not properly install the kppp client and has a default system-administrative roadblock—but don't worry! These discrepancies are easily fixed. First, the kppp client must be SUID. You can fix this by using the chmod command on the kppp binary:

```
# chmod 4711 /usr/bin/kppp
```

Next, edit the file options under the /etc/ppp directory and remove the keyword lock from the file. You're then ready to launch the kppp client.

If you're using KDE, click the Application Starter button on the K desktop's panel, select Internet, and click the kppp menu item. You can also launch kppp from the command line of a terminal window like this for Red Hat 6.0:

```
# kppp &
```

Do this for Caldera 2.2:

```
# /opt/kde/bin/kppp &
```

The client's main dialog box will appear. It is shown in Figure 17.7.

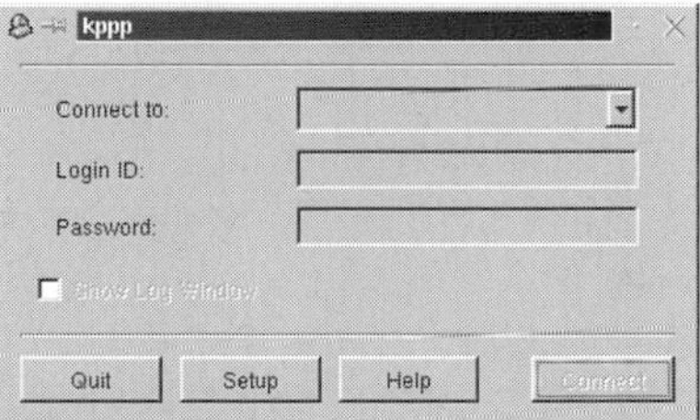

FIGURE 17.7
Click the Setup button to define new PPP accounts.

An Accounts dialog box appears when you click the Setup button. The dialog box is shown in Figure 17.8.

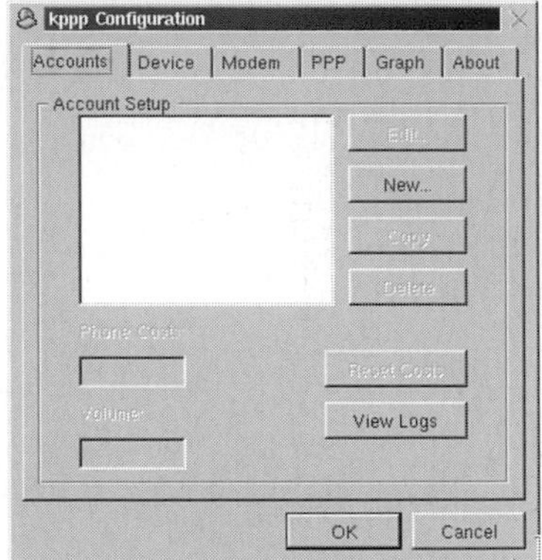

FIGURE 17.8
Click the New button to start configuring a PPP account.

A New Account dialog box appears when you click the New button. Type in a name for your connection, the phone number for your ISP, and select an Authentication protocol (see Figure 17.9). (Most users will choose Script-based, although you can also use PAP.)

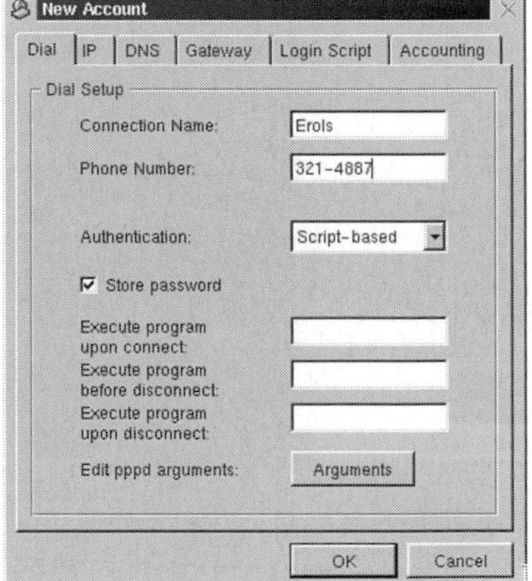

FIGURE 17.9
Enter an account name and ISP phone number in the New Account dialog box.

When finished, click the IP tab at the top of the New Account dialog box. You'll see a dialog box like that shown in Figure 17.10, in which you select the type of Internet Protocol, or IP, address assigned to your computer after establishing a PPP connection with your ISP. (Most ISPs today use *dynamic* addressing, in which you are assigned a different IP from an available pool each time you log in.) If your account provides a *static* (or permanent) IP address, enter this information in the IP dialog box.

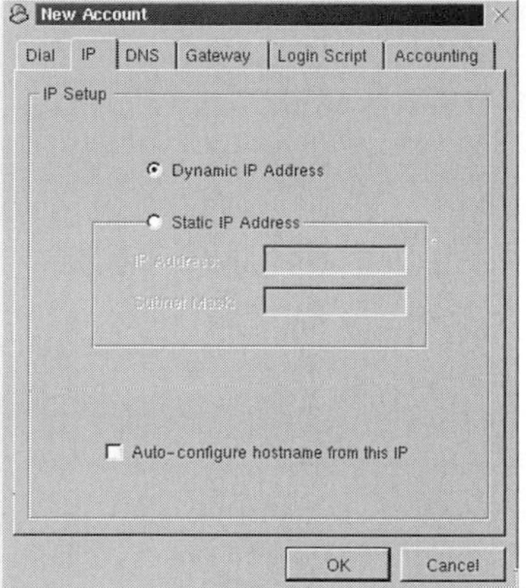

FIGURE 17.10
Set the type of IP address for your PPP connection.

Click the DNS tab in the New Account dialog box. The DNS, or Domain Name Service, dialog box shown in Figure 17.11 is used to specify the domain name and IP address(es) of your ISP's DNS servers. These servers provide translation service of active hostnames to IP numbers and back again.

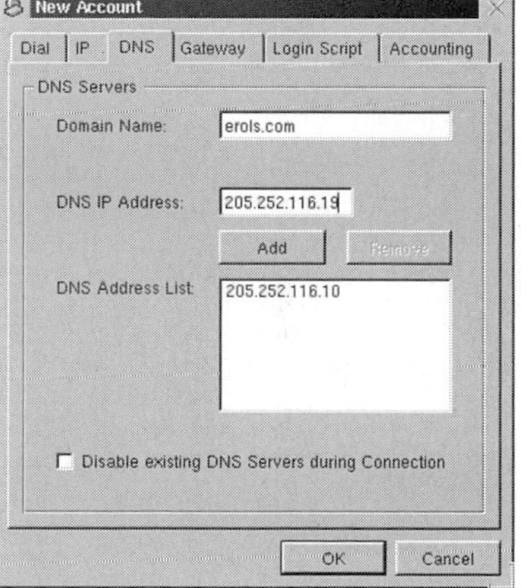

FIGURE 17.11
Enter your ISP's domain name and DNS IP addresses in the dialog box.

To enter a DNS IP address, type in each IP number (provided by your ISP) and then click the Add button. When finished, click the Login Script tab (if you use the common script-based log in procedure). The Login Script dialog box appears; it is shown in Figure 17.12.

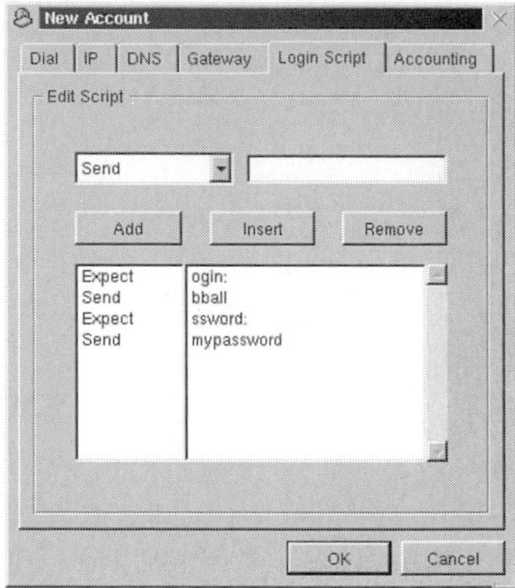

FIGURE 17.12
Login scripts for usernames and passwords are entered in Login Script dialog box.

Scripts are usually in form of *`expect prompt, send prompt`*. For example, many ISPs' computers will first send a `Login:` prompt. Select the `Expect` keyword and then type in a portion of the prompt (such as `ogin:`) and press the Add button. Since your ISP will next expect a username, select the `Send` keyword and then type in your username and click the Add button. Repeat this step for your password. When finished, click the OK button. You'll see the Accounts dialog box shown in Figure 17.13.

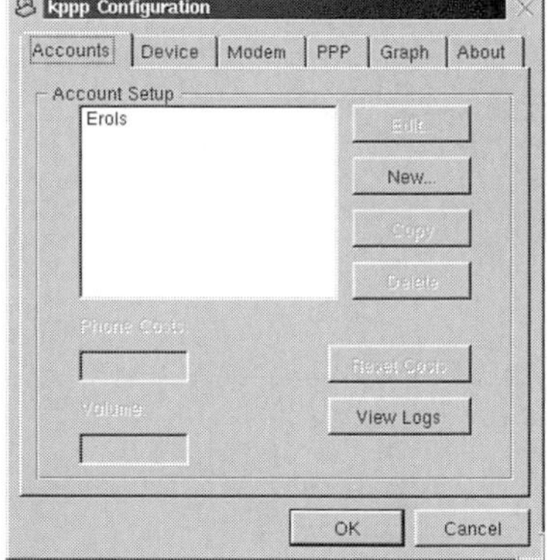

FIGURE 17.13
When you finish defining your PPP account, make sure to check the device, modem, and PPP settings for `kppp`.

Click the Device tab to configure your modem (as shown in Figure 17.14).

FIGURE 17.14
The Device tab in the kppp *Configuration dialog box is used for modem settings.*

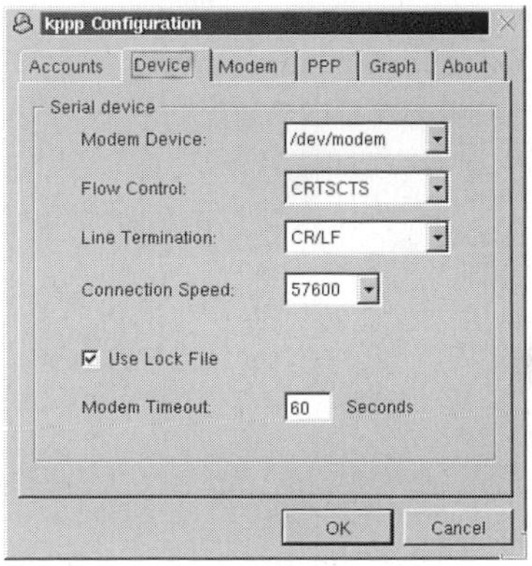

Select the correct device and connection speed for your modem. When finished, click the Modem tab. A dialog box appears, as shown in Figure 17.15.

FIGURE 17.15
The Modem tab in the kppp *Configuration dialog box is used to set default modem commands and to query or test your modem.*

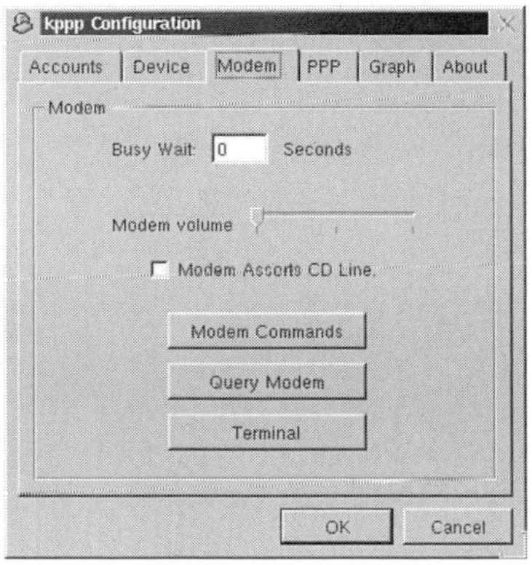

Use the buttons in the dialog box to change the default modem AT commands, to query your modem, or to test your modem by using kppp's built-in terminal program. When finished, click the PPP tab at the top of the dialog box. The PPP options dialog box will appear, as shown in Figure 17.16.

Select or deselect the various options in this dialog box according to your taste. If you click the Dock into Panel on Connect, kppp will display a tiny modem icon with blinking send and receive lights! When finished, click the OK button. You'll see the main kppp window that is shown in Figure 17.17.

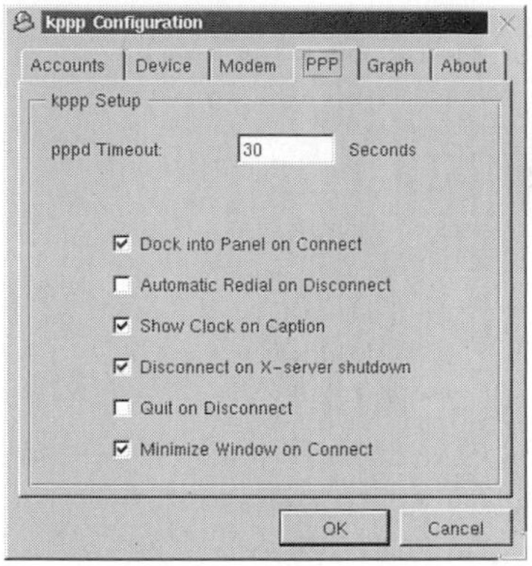

FIGURE 17.16
Use the PPP tab in the kppp Configuration dialog box to set how kppp uses its interface.

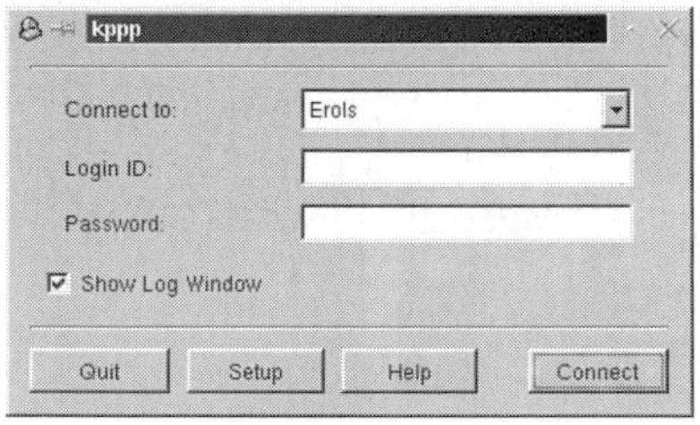

FIGURE 17.17
To start your PPP connection, click the Connect button in the kppp window.

If you click the Show Log Window check box (see Figure 17.17) and then click the Connect button to start your PPP connection, you'll see a login script window (see Figure 17.18).

If you've set `kppp` to dock in your KDE panel, you can then right-click the resulting tiny modem icon in the panel and select Details from the pop-up menu. A `kppp` Statistics dialog box appears, as shown in Figure 17.19. The dialog box shows your PPP connection's IP addresses, modem status lights, various packet information (similar to information returned by the `pppstats` command), and a scrolling load indicator of your PPP activity for the session.

To close your connection, right-click the `kppp` indicator in your panel and then click the Disconnection menu item.

Note

`kppp` also comes with a PPP log utility (`KPPP - Logview`) and another standalone load viewer (KPPPLoad). To launch either tool, click the K desktop panel's Application Starter button and then select Internet.

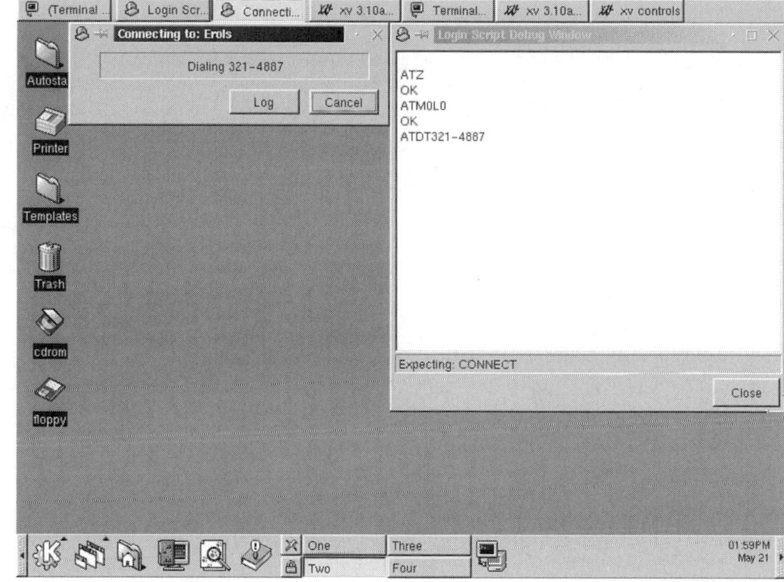

FIGURE 17.18
The kppp login script window shows dialing and connection progress of your connection.

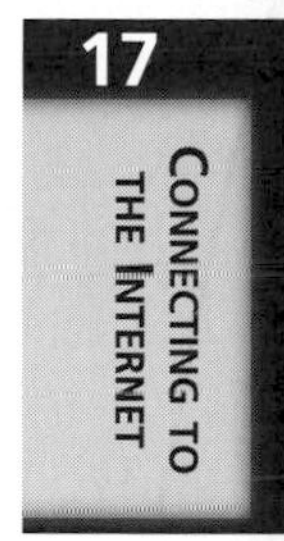

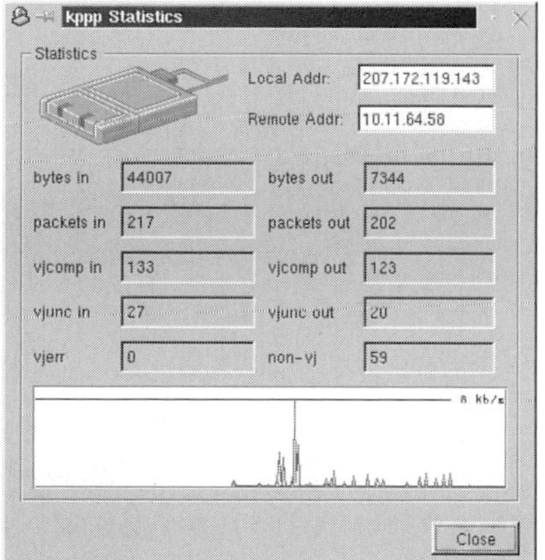

FIGURE 17.19
The kppp Statistics window shows detailed PPP connection information, along with a load progress indicator of your connection.

Debian's `pppconfig`

Debian provides a program called `pppconfig` that is used for setting up your PPP connections. One advantage of this program is that it does not require X11 to run. You need to either log in as `root` on the console or open an `xterm` and then `su` to `root`.

The first thing to do is install `pppconfig`. That is done with this command:

```
apt-get install pppconfig
```

Now you're ready to run `pppconfig`:

```
/usr/sbin/pppconfig
```

You will now arrive at `pppconfig`'s main menu. From here, you can create a connection, change an existing one, delete a connection profile, or exit the utility. Presumably you'll want to create a connection, so just press Enter.

As you proceed through `pppconfig`, you'll notice that it provides you with help every step of the way. For instance, at the screen you should be viewing now (Provider Name), the top third of the screen describes in detail what you are being asked for.

If you have only one Internet provider, you may simply press Enter to accept the default. Otherwise, you may want to enter adifferent name in the box. When done, press Enter to proceed.

You're asked for DNS information. Some `pppconfig` versions ask whether you have static or dynamic DNS. If your ISP can provide you with DNS numbers, select Static. If your ISP provides the DNS numbers as part of the PPP protocol negotiations, select Dynamic.

If you selected Static, the next screen asks for the IP address of the primary nameserver. This is a set of four numbers separated by periods. If you have a secondary nameserver number, you may enter it at the next screen. Otherwise, just leave it blank.

You now need to select an authentication method. If you don't know which method to use, PAP is a good guess. If you have troubles authenticating with your ISP, you may want to try `CHAP` or give the ISP a call to find out what to use in this location.

After this, you need to supply the username. This is part of what is used to authenticate you to the ISP, and is typically also the first part of your email address. The next screen asks for your password, which you can type in now.

You are then asked for your modem port speed. Unless you have a very old modem, use the default of `115200`. On the following screen, select tone dialing unless you have a special need for pulse dialing. Finally, enter the phone number to dial in order to connect to your ISP.

At this point, `pppconfig` offers to try to automatically detect your modem port. This is generally a good idea; select Yes. If `pppconfig` can find it, that option is preselected on the following screen.Otherwise, you need to indicate the value to `pppconfig` yourself.

Now, you arrive at the final properties screen. If all is well, data is saved when you highlight Finished. When you return to the main menu, you can quit.

To establish a PPP connection, simply run the following as `root`:

```
pon
```

If you chose a specific name for the ISP, use this:

```
pon ispname
```

When you're ready to disconnect, use this:

```
poff
```


Setting Up SLIP

SLIP is used (Serial Line Interface Protocol)by some ISPs that don't support PPP (a rarity these days). You may also find SLIP supported by some online services that don't use the Internet, such as bank access programs and stock trading. In the past, SLIP was usually compiled into the Linux kernel, as was a modification of SLIP called CSLIP (Compressed SLIP). With both Red Hat Linux(Serial Line Interface Protocol);setting up 6.0 and Caldera OpenLinux(Serial Line Interface Protocol);setting up 2.2, however, SLIP support is now supplied as a loadable kernel module.

To use SLIP, you need to dedicate a port to it. This means that the port cannot be used by other applications. This is necessary because of the way SLIP handles ports, which causes conflicts if shared with other programs.

Note

Most Linux versions install SLIP by default when the kernel is installed. However, with Red Hat Linux(Serial Line Interface Protocol);kernel 6.0 and (Serial Line Interface Protocol);kernelCaldera OpenLinux 2.2, SLIP support is supplied as a loadable kernel module. If you want SLIP installed permanently into your kernel, you need to rebuild it. See Chapter 23, "Kernel Management" for more information. A quick way to check whether SLIP is installed is to examine the `/proc/net/dev` file for a line starting with `sl0`. If the line exists, SLIP is installed.

Configuring SLIP

The (Serial Line Interface Protocol)fastest way to configure SLIP is to use the `slattach` program. This requires the name of the port that SLIP will use (which has a modem attached for the connection, usually). The command that sets up `slattach` is as follows:

```
slattach /dev/ttyS0 &
```

In this case, I've configured `/dev/ttyS0 port` (COM1) as the SLIP port. You can use any other port attached to your system. The ampersand at the end of the line puts the `slattach` program in the background so you can get your shell prompt back.

When you run `slattach`, the port is renamed `/dev/sl0`, which indicates it is the first SLIP device. It doesn't matter what device name you used for the serial port; the first SLIP device is always called `/dev/sl0`. This can lead to some confusion if you are using `/dev/ttyS2`, for example, which becomes `/dev/sl0`. If more than one SLIP port is created, they are numbered consecutively as `/dev/sl1`, `/dev/sl2`, and so on. Linux usually supports up to eight SLIP lines, but you will almost certainly not need this many!

Linux uses CSLIP by default for most SLIP lines because it packs more information in the same space as SLIP. If the ISP you are connecting to does not support CSLIP, you need to force Linux to use only SLIP. You can do this on the `slattach` line:

```
slattach -p slip /dev/ttyS0 &
```

This tells `slattach` to use only the SLIP protocol. Other valid arguments after the `-p` option are `cslip` (for CSLIP), `adaptive` (which adjusts to whatever is at the other end of the connection), and `slip6` (an older, 6-bit version of SLIP).

Now that the SLIP device has been created, you need to tell the Linux kernel about it, using the `ifconfig` program to set up the dummy interface. The `ifconfig` line that establishes the interface requires the name of the remote system:

```
ifconfig sl0 mymachine-slip pointopoint remotemachine
```

`sl0` is the name of the interface (`/dev/sl0` in this case); *`mymachine`*`-slip` is the local name of the SLIP interface (you should substitute your machine's name, such as `merlin-slip` or `darkstar-slip`); `pointopoint` tells `ifconfig` the interface is a point-to-point connection (not to be confused with PPP); and *`remotemachine`* is the name of the machine at the other end of the connection. For example, if the remote machine's name is `darkstar` and your machine's name is `dogbert`, the `ifconfig` command looks like this:

```
ifconfig sl0 dogbert-slip pointopoint darkstar
```

The next step is to issue the `route` command to add the route to the remote machine to the system databases. The syntax is the same as when you set up the dummy interface:

```
route add default gw darkstar
```

In this case, you are adding a default route to the remote machine called `darkstar`. This means that any packet that is not destined for your local machine (or local network if you have one) will go via this SLIP interface you just set up. You should (Serial Line Interface Protocol)substitute `darkstar` for whatever the remote machine is called.

> **Note**
>
> Many ISPs don't tell you their remote machine's names. That's fine because these machine names are only placeholders. You can substitute the IP address instead to add the default route to your system.

Setting Up a Dial-In PPP Server

You can also set up a simple service on your Linux system to provide PPP for dial-in users. Although commercial ventures, such as ISPs, must necessarily invest in leased lines, switching service, modem pools and routers, you can easily configure a standalone Linux box to answer a modem and start PPP. The general steps may include the following:

- Selecting a phone line, modem, and serial port.
- Properly configuring the modem to answer incoming calls (using `AT` commands and saving the modem profile with `AT&W`).
- Installing a line-monitoring application (such as `getty` or `mgetty`) to watch a serial port (in `/etc/inittab`).
- Possibly configuring a DNS server (see Chapter 8, "The Domain Name Service," for more information).
- Configuring Linux to automatically start the `pppd` daemon after a user logs in.

In general, and for many modems, the `ATE1Q0V1&C1&S0S0=1&W` modem string will set up a modem to autoanswer calls using different terminal monitors. (Some, such as `uugetty`, have configuration files to automatically set up the modem for a particular serial port.) The next step is to make an appropriate entry in the `/etc/inittab` file:

```
3:2345:respawn:/sbin/uugetty ttyS1 38400 vt100
```

This entry assumes you have a modem attached to `/dev/ttyS1`.

Red Hat

If you use the `uugetty` command to monitor your modem's serial port, you'll also need to copy the file `uugetty.autoanswer` from the directory `/usr/doc/getty_ps-2.0.7j/Examples/default` directory to the `/etc/default` directory. You should then edit this file and look for the `ALTLOCK` entry:

```
# alternate lockfile to check... if this lockfile exists, then uugetty is
# restarted so that the modem is re-initialized
ALTLOCK=cua2
```

Change the ALTLOCK entry to match your modem's serial port. Using the previous /etc/inittab entry, the string cua2 would be changed to ttyS1. The file should then be saved in the /etc/default directory with the name uugetty and a suffix to match the serial port (such as uugetty.ttyS0). You should then dial in from a remote computer to check the login process.

The next step is to create a user to test PPP service. Use the adduser command to create a user named **ppp** and then assign a password. Although users can log in to your system and then start pppd from the command line (assuming you've set pppd to SUID), you can have the pppd daemon started automatically by creating a short shell script and then assigning the shell script in the user's /etc/passwd entry like this:

```
ppp:x:501:501::/home/ppp:/usr/local/bin/doppp
```

In this instance, the script doppp (made executable with chmod +x) would contain the following:

```
exec /usr/sbin/pppd -detach
```

Using this approach, pppd will start automatically after the ppp dial-in user connects and logs in (using the ppp-on scripts or other clients, such as netcfg or kppp).

You should also edit the file options under the /etc/ppp directory to include general dial-in options for PPP service on your system, and create specific options files (such as options.ttyS1 for this example) for each enabled dial-in port. For example, /etc/ppp/options could contain the following:

```
asyncmap 0
netmask 255.255.255.0
proxyarp
lock
crtscts
modem
```

There are many approaches to providing PPP service. You may want to assign IP addresses dynamically, or assign static IP addresses for your users. You should probably have DNS enabled, although sharing hostnames via /etc/hosts and providing static address assignment by using options.ttyX files (where X is the serial port). For example, /etc/ppp/options.ttyS1 could contain this:

```
IPofPPPserver:assignedIPofdialinuser
```

After you set up your /etc/ppp/options and /etc/ppp/options.ttyS file, dial in from a remote computer (perhaps using netcfg, kppp, or the ppp-on script). If your chat script uses pppd's debug option, you can watch the progress of your connection by using the tail command on /var/log/messages:

```
...
May 21 17:05:55 aptiva pppd[7761]: Serial connection established.
May 21 17:05:56 aptiva pppd[7761]: Using interface ppp0
May 21 17:05:56 aptiva pppd[7761]: Connect: ppp0 <--> /dev/modem
May 21 17:06:02 aptiva pppd[7761]: local  IP address 198.168.2.36
May 21 17:06:02 aptiva pppd[7761]: remote IP address 198.168.2.34
```


For more information about using PPP, see Robert Hart's PPP HOWTO under /usr/doc/HOWTO.

Summary

In this chapter you learned how to set up PPP and SLIP for use with your Internet connections. You can also use PPP and SLIP for any machine-to-machine connection, so you can create a small network with a friend if you want. PPP and SLIP are mostly transparent to you once the interfaces are properly set up.

System Administration and Management

PART III

IN THIS PART

CHAPTER 18

Managing Filesystems

In This Chapter

One of the simplest and most elegant aspects of Linux design is the way everything is represented as a file. Even the devices on which files are stored are represented as files.

Hardware devices are associated with drivers that provide a file interface; the special files representing hardware devices (or just *devices*) are kept in the directory `/dev`. Devices are either block devices or character devices.

Character Devices

A *character device* is one from which you can read a sequence of characters—for example, the sequence of keys typed at a keyboard or the sequence of bytes sent over a serial line. A *block device* is one that stores data and offers access to all parts of it equally; floppy and hard disks are block devices. Block devices are sometimes called *random access devices,* just as character devices are sometimes called *sequentially accessed devices*. With sequentially accessed devices, you can get data from any random part of a hard disk, but you have to retrieve the data from a serial line in the order it was sent.

When you perform some operation on a file, the kernel can tell that the file involved is a device by looking at its file mode (not its location). Different major and minor device numbers distinguish the device nodes. The *major device number* indicates to the kernel which of its drivers the device node represents. (For example, a block device with major number 3 is an IDE disk drive, and one with the major device number 8 is a SCSI disk.) Each driver is responsible for several instances of the hardware it drives, and these are indicated by the value of the minor device number. For example, the SCSI disk with the minor number 0 represents the whole "first" SCSI disk, and the minor numbers 1 to 15 represent 15 possible partitions on it. The `ls` command prints the major and minor device numbers for you:

```
$ ls -l --sort=none /dev/sda{,?,??} /dev/sdb
brw-rw----   1 root     disk       8,   0 Sep 12  1994 /dev/sda
brw-rw----   1 root     disk       8,   1 Sep 12  1994 /dev/sda1
brw-rw----   1 root     disk       8,   2 Sep 12  1994 /dev/sda2
brw-rw----   1 root     disk       8,   3 Sep 12  1994 /dev/sda3
brw-rw----   1 root     disk       8,   4 Sep 12  1994 /dev/sda4
brw-rw----   1 root     disk       8,   5 Sep 12  1994 /dev/sda5
brw-rw----   1 root     disk       8,   6 Sep 12  1994 /dev/sda6
brw-rw----   1 root     disk       8,   7 Sep 12  1994 /dev/sda7
brw-rw----   1 root     disk       8,   8 Sep 12  1994 /dev/sda8
brw-rw----   1 root     disk       8,   9 Sep 12  1994 /dev/sda9
brw-rw----   1 root     disk       8,  10 Sep 12  1994 /dev/sda10
brw-rw----   1 root     disk       8,  11 Sep 12  1994 /dev/sda11
brw-rw----   1 root     disk       8,  12 Sep 12  1994 /dev/sda12
brw-rw----   1 root     disk       8,  13 Sep 12  1994 /dev/sda13
brw-rw----   1 root     disk       8,  14 Sep 12  1994 /dev/sda14
brw-rw----   1 root     disk       8,  15 Sep 12  1994 /dev/sda15
brw-rw----   1 root     disk       8,  16 Sep 12  1994 /dev/sdb
```

The obscure option (`--sort=none`) with this `ls -l` command ensures that the devices are presented in correct order. If you use only `ls -l`, the entries are sorted alphabetically, and `/dev/sda10` comes before `/dev/sda2`.

The `b` at the far left of the output of this command indicates that each of these entries is a block device. (Character devices are indicated by a `c`.) The major and minor device numbers appear just before the time field, separated by commas. (This is the position normally occupied in `ls -l` output by the file's size.)

Block Devices

If you had just one file of data to store, you could put it directly on a block device and read it back. Block devices have some fixed capacity, however, and you would need some method of marking the end of your data. Block devices behave in most respects just like ordinary files, except that although an ordinary file has a length determined by how much data is in it, the "length" of a block device is its total capacity. If you write a megabyte to a 100MB block device and read back its contents, you get the 1MB of data followed by 99MB of its previous contents. Bearing in mind this restriction, several UNIX utilities encode the amount of data available in the file's data rather than the file's total length and hence are suitable for storing data directly on block devices—for example, `tar` and `cpio`, which are suitable for everybody, and `dump`, which is suitable only for the system administrator (because it requires read access to the block device underlying the data to be backed up). To back up the entire contents of your home directory to floppy disk, you type one of the following:

```
$ tar cf /dev/fd0 $HOME

$ find $HOME -print0 ¦ cpio --create -0 --format=crc >/dev/fd0
```

The `-print0` and `-0` options for `find` and `cpio` ensure that the names of the files to be backed up that `find` sends to `cpio` are separated by ASCII NULLs, rather than newlines. This ensures that any filenames containing a newline are correctly backed up.

> **Note**
>
> The only characters that are illegal in UNIX filenames are the slash and the ASCII NULL.

These backup utilities are written specifically to write their backups to any kind of file; in fact, they were designed for sequentially accessed character devices, such as tape drives.

Filesystems

When you have more than one item of data, it is necessary to have some method of organizing files on the device. These methods are called *filesystems*. Linux enables you to choose any organizational method to marshal your files on its storage device. For example, you can use the MS-DOS filesystem on a floppy or the faster `ext2` filesystem on your hard disk.

Many different filesystems are supported by Linux; the `ext2` filesystem is used most because it is designed for Linux and is very efficient. Other filesystems are used for compatibility with other systems; for example, it's common to use the `msdos` and `vfat` filesystems on floppies; these are the native filesystems of MS-DOS and Windows 95. With Linux, some filesystems are built into the kernel. Several of them are listed below:

```
$ cat /proc/filesystems
        ext2

nodev   proc
nodev    iso9660
    devpts
```

Some filesystems are available as loadable modules:

```
$ ls -x /lib/modules/`uname -r`/fs
autofs.o    binfmt_aout.o    binfmt_java.o    binfmt_misc.o
coda.o    fat.o    hfs.o    hpfs.o
lockd.o    minix.o    msdos.o    ncpfs.o
nfs.o    nfsd.o    nls_cp437.o    nls_cp737.o
nls_cp775.o    nls_cp850.o    nls_cp852.o    nls_cp855.o
nls_cp857.o    nls_cp860.o    nls_cp861.o    nls_cp862.o
nls_cp863.o    nls_cp864.o    nls_cp865.o    nls_cp866.o
nls_cp869.o    nls_cp874.o    nls_iso8859-1.o    nls_iso8859-15.o
nls_iso8859-2.o    nls_iso8859-3.o    nls_iso8859-4.o    nls_iso8859-5.o
nls_iso8859-6.o    nls_iso8859-7.o    nls_iso8859-8.o    nls_iso8859-9.o
nls_koi8-r.o    romfs.o    smbfs.o    sysv.o
ufs.o    umsdos.o    vfat.o
```

Some of these (`nfs`, `ncpfs`, and `smbfs`) are network filesystems that don't depend on block devices. Network filesystems are covered in Chapter 7, "TCP/IP and Network Management." Other filesystems are supported by Linux but are not provided by the standard kernel.

The mount Command

Use the mount command to mount a block device onto the filesystem. You need to specify what device contains the filesystem, what type it is, and where in the directory hierarchy to mount it.

A mount command looks like this:

```
mount [-t type] [-o options] device mount-point
```

device must be a block device; if it contains a colon, it can be the name of another machine from which to mount a filesystem (see Chapter 7). *mount-point* should be an existing directory (or you get an error); the filesystem will appear at this position. (Anything previously in that directory will be hidden.) The filesystem type and options are optional, and the variety and meaning of options depend on the type of filesystem being mounted. If the filesystem you want to mount is specified in the /etc/fstab file, you need to specify only the mount point or the device name; the other details are read from /etc/fstab by mount. Here is an example of the mount command being used:

```
# mount /dev/fd1 -t vfat /mnt/floppy
mount: block device /dev/fd1 is write-protected, mounting read-only
# ls /mnt/floppy
grub-0.4.tar.gz
# umount /mnt/floppy
# ls /mnt/floppy
filesystem not mounted
```


In this example, I mounted a floppy containing a vfat filesystem at the mount point /mnt/floppy (and got an informational message). The directory /mnt/floppy already existed. I used ls to see what was on the disk and unmounted it again. I then ran ls again, and the response I got was simply the name of a file that I leave in the directory /mnt/floppy on my hard disk to remind me that there currently is nothing mounted there. This hint enables me to distinguish a written floppy from an empty floppy that is mounted. I can also use the df command to see what filesystems are mounted.

Mounting a vfat floppy like this causes the Linux kernel to automatically load the vfat driver into the kernel while it was needed. The kernel module handler loads these drivers, and when they become unused after the filesystem is unmounted, they are unloaded to recover the memory that they occupied.

Potential Problems with `mount`

Any one of several things can cause the `mount` command to fail:

- Incorrect device name—It is possible to specify an incorrect device name (that is, a device file that does not exist or one for which a driver is not available in the kernel or for which the hardware is not present).
- Unreadable devices—Devices can be unreadable either because the devices themselves are bad (for example, empty floppy drives or bad media) or because you have insufficient permissions to mount them. Filesystems, other than those sanctioned by the administrator by listing them with the option `user` in `/etc/fstab`, are forbidden to ordinary users and require `root` privilege to mount them.
- Bad mount point—Trying to mount a device at a mount point that does not already exist will not work.
- Other errors—Still more error conditions are possible but unlikely (for example, exceeding the compiled-in limit to the number of mounted filesystems) or self-explanatory (for example, most usage errors for the `mount` command itself). There are some more unlikely error messages that chiefly relate to the loopback devices.

When you mount a filesystem, the point at which it is to be mounted (that is, the *mount point*) must be a directory. This directory doesn't have to be empty, but after the filesystem is mounted, anything underneath it is inaccessible. Linux provides a *singly rooted* filesystem, which is in contrast to those operating systems that give each filesystem a separate drive letter. Although this might seem less flexible, it is more flexible because the size of each block device (hard disk or whatever) is hidden from programs, and things can be moved around. For example, if you have some software that expects to be installed in `/opt/umsp`, you can install it in `/big-disk/stuff/umsp` and make `/opt/umsp` a symbolic link. There is also no need to edit a myriad of configuration files that are using the wrong drive letter after you install a new disk drive, for example.

Many options govern how a mounted filesystem behaves; for example, it can be mounted read-only. There are options for filesystems such as `msdos` that don't have any concept of users. The filesystems enable you to give each file a particular file mode (for security or to allow access by everyone). When you mount an `nfs` filesystem, there is so much flexibility available that the options have a separate manual page (`man nfs` command), although the defaults are perfectly reasonable. The `nfs` filesystem is explained in more detail in Chapter 7.

Table 18.1 contains options useful for `mount` displayed in alphabetical order. Unless otherwise indicated, these options are valid for all filesystem types, although asking for asynchronous writes to a CD-ROM is of no use. Options applicable only to NFS filesystems are not listed here; refer to the `nfs` command manual page for those.

TABLE 18.1 *mount* Options

Option	*Description*
`async`	Write requests for the filesystem normally should wait until the data has reached the hardware; with this option, the program continues immediately instead. This does mean that the system is slightly more prone to data loss in the event of a system crash, but on the other hand, crashes are rare with Linux. This option speeds up NFS filesystems to a startling extent. The opposite of this option is `sync`.
`auto`	Indicates to `mount` that it should mount the device when given the `-a` flag. This flag is used by the startup scripts to make sure that all the required filesystems are mounted at boot time. The opposite of this option is `noauto`.
`defaults`	Turns on the options `rw`, `suid`, `dev`, `exec`, `auto`, `nouser`, and `async`.
`dev`	Allows device nodes on the system to be used. Access to devices is completely determined by access rights to the on-disk device node. Hence, if you mount an `ext2` filesystem on a floppy and you have previously placed a writable `/dev/kmem` device file on the disk, then you've just gained read/write access to kernel memory. System administrators generally prevent this from happening by mounting removable filesystems with the `nodev` `mount` option.
`exec`	Indicates to the kernel that it should allow the execution of programs on the filesystem. This option is more frequently seen as `noexec`, which indicates to the kernel that execution of programs on this filesystem shouldn't be allowed. This is generally used as a security precaution or for NFS filesystems mounted from another machine that contain executable files of a format unsuitable for this machine (for example, intended for a different CPU).
`noauto`	Opposite of `auto`.
`nodev`	Opposite of `dev`.
`noexec`	Opposite of `exec`.
`nosuid`	Opposite of `suid`.
`nouser`	Opposite of `user`.
`remount`	Allows the `mount` command to change the flags for an already-mounted filesystem without interrupting its use. You can't unmount a filesystem that is currently in use, and this option is basically a workaround. The system startup scripts, for example, use the command `mount -n -o remount,ro /` to change the `root` filesystem from read-only (it starts off this way) to read/write (its normal state). The `-n` option indicates to `mount` that it shouldn't update `/etc/fstab` because it can't do this while the `root` filesystem is still read-only.

continues

TABLE 18.1 continued

Option	*Description*
`ro`	Mounts the filesystem read-only. This is the opposite of the option `rw`.
`rw`	Mounts the filesystem read/write. This is the opposite of the option `ro`.
`suid`	Allows the set user ID and set group ID file mode bits to take effect. The opposite of this option is `nosuid`. The `nosuid` option is more common; it is used for the same sorts of reasons that `nodev` is used.
`sync`	All write operations cause the calling program to wait until the data has been committed to the hardware. This mode of operation is slower but a little more reliable than its opposite, asynchronous I/O, which is indicated by the option `async`.
`user`	Allows ordinary users to mount the filesystem. When there is a `user` option in `/etc/fstab`, ordinary users indicate which filesystem they want to mount or unmount by giving the device name or mount point; all the other relevant information is taken from the `/etc/fstab` file. For security reasons, `user` implies the `noexec`, `nosuid`, and `nodev` options.

Note

One of the defaults for filesystems is that they are mounted `async`. This matters in that the operating system will return control before it actually reads or writes a file. Many people have erred by pulling a diskette out of the drive too soon, causing a read or write not to be aborted and errors to occur.

Options are processed by the `mount` command in the order they appear on the command line (or in `/etc/fstab`). Thus, it is possible to allow users to mount a filesystem and then run set user ID executables by using the options `user, suid` in that order. Using them in reverse order (`suid, user`) wouldn't work because the `user` option would turn off the `suid` option again.

Many other options available are all specific to particular filesystems. All the valid options for `mount` are detailed in its manual page. An example is the `umask` flag for the `vfat` and `fat` filesystems, which allows you to make all the files on your MS-DOS or Windows partitions readable (or even writable, if you prefer) for all the users on your Linux system.

Mounting with KDE's User Mount Tool

This graphical tool is good for quickly mounting and unmounting filesystems. This is especially useful for floppy and CD-ROM filesystems. Figure 18.1 shows the user mount tool. You will note that the floppy drive is mounted, but that the CD-ROM is not.

FIGURE 18.1
The user mount tool.

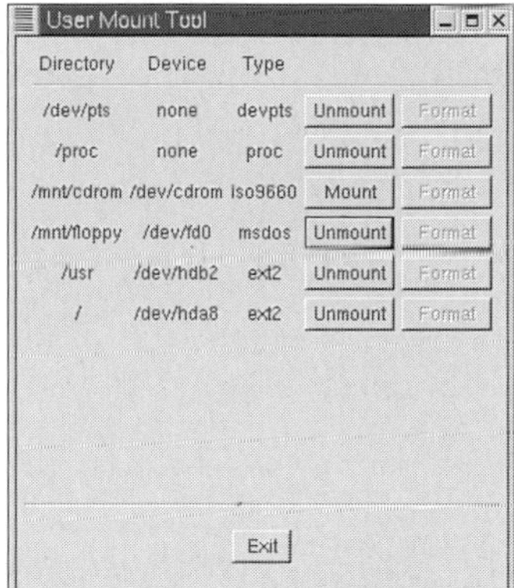

The user mount tool reads `/etc/fstab` to get the information for mounting. This means that by default, the floppy drive is of type `ext2`. This setting is great for Linux, but does not allow it to be used in a DOS setting. I have found that by changing the `/etc/fstab` entry for the floppy drive to the type `msdos`, I gain greater flexibility in the use of my floppy disks as I switch between systems.

Setting Up Filesystems

There are at least two ways of changing the entries in the `/etc/fstab` file. The first is to edit the file manually using your favorite editor. This assumes that you are a flawless typist and know all of the different options. Of course, knowing how to edit the file by hand means you do not have to have X Windows running. The second way I discuss changing the `/etc/fstab` file is through the `fsconf` utility (`/bin/fsconf`). (Note that `fsconf` comes standard with Red Hat. Other utilities—such as `COAS`, discussed in "Using `COAS` to Manipulate Filesystems," later in this chapter—will perform the same tasks in a similar fashion.)

Editing /etc/fstab Manually

The filesystem table /etc/fstab is just a text file; it is designed to have a specific format that is readable by humans and not just computers. It is separated into columns by tabs or spaces. (It doesn't matter which you use.) You can edit it with your favorite text editor; it doesn't matter which. You must take care, however, if you modify it by hand because removing or corrupting an entry will make the system unable to mount that filesystem the next time it boots. For this reason, I make a point of saving previous versions of this file using the Revision Control System (a very useful program; see the manual page for rcs).

A sample /etc/fstab looks like this:

```
#
# /etc/fstab
#
# You should be using fstool (control-panel) to edit this!
#
#<device> <mountpoint> <filesystemtype> <options>    <dump> <fsckorder>

/dev/hda1      /             ext2      defaults          1       1
/dev/hdb5      /home         ext2      defaults,rw       1       2
/dev/hda3      /usr          ext2      defaults          1       2
/dev/hdb1      /usr/src      ext2      defaults          1       3

/dev/hdc       /mnt/cdrom    iso9660   user,noauto,ro    0       0
/dev/sbpcd0    /mnt/pcd      iso9660   user,noauto,ro    0       0
/dev/fd1       /mnt/floppy   vfat      user,noauto       0       0

/proc          /proc         proc      defaults
/dev/hda2      none          swap      sw
```

The first four entries are the ext2 filesystems composing the sample Linux system. When Linux is booted, the root filesystem is mounted first; all the other local (that is, non-network) filesystems are mounted next. Filesystems appear in /etc/fstab in the order they are mounted; /usr must appear before /usr/src, for example, because the mount point for one filesystem exists on the other. The following three filesystems are all removable filesystems (two CD-ROMs and a floppy drive). These have the noauto option set so that they are not automatically mounted at boot time. The removable devices have the user option set so that I can mount and unmount them without having to use su all the time. The CD-ROMs have the filesystem type iso9660, which is the standard filesystem for CD-ROMs, and the floppy drive has the filesystem type vfat because I often use it for interchanging data with MS-DOS and Windows systems.

The last two filesystems are special; the first (`/proc`) is a special filesystem provided by the kernel as a way of providing information about the system to user programs. The information in the `/proc` filesystem is used to make utilities such as `ps`, `top`, `xload`, `free`, `netstat`, and so on work. Some of the "files" in `/proc` are really enormous (for example, `/proc/kcore`). Don't worry; no disk space is wasted. All the information in the `/proc` filesystem is generated on-the-fly by the Linux kernel as you read it. You can tell that they are not real files because, for example, `root` can't give them away with `chown`.

The final "filesystem" isn't a filesystem at all; it is an entry that indicates a disk partition used as swap space. Swap partitions are used to implement virtual memory. Files can also be used for swap space. The names of the swap files go in the first column where the device name usually goes.

The two numeric columns on the right relate to the operation of the `dump` and `fsck` commands. The `dump` command compares the number in column 5 (the *dump interval*) with the number of days since that filesystem was last backed up. This way it can inform the system administrator that the filesystem needs to be backed up. Other backup software—for example, Amanda—can also use this field for the same purpose. (You can find Amanda at `http://www.amanda.org`.) Filesystems without a dump interval field are assumed to have a dump interval of `0`, denoting "never dump." For more information, see the manual page for `dump`.

The sixth column is the `fsck pass` and indicates which filesystems can be checked in parallel at boot time. The root filesystem is always checked first, but after that, separate drives can be checked simultaneously because Linux is a multitasking operating system. There is no point, however, in checking two filesystems on the same hard drive at the same time because this results in a lot of extra disk head movement and wasted time. All the filesystems that have the same pass number are checked in parallel from `1` upward. Filesystems with a `0` or missing pass number (such as the floppy and CD-ROM drives) are not checked at all.

Using COAS to Manipulate Filesystems

Caldera's Open Administration System (`COAS`) provides yet another means of mounting and unmounting filesystems. In Figure 18.2 you see that there are two filesystems not mounted (in the left window) and four filesystems that are mounted (in the right window).

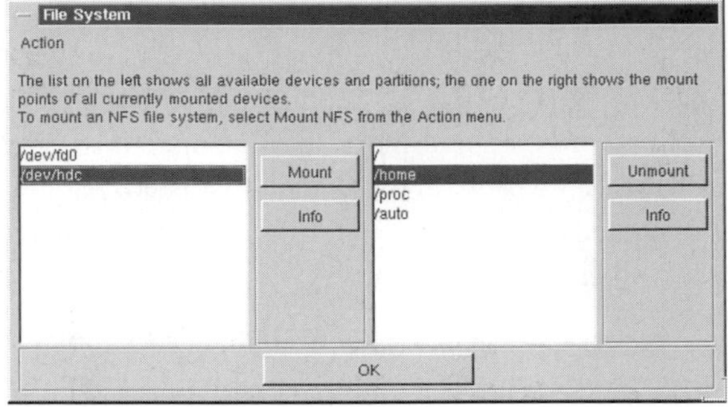

FIGURE 18.2
COAS filesystem tool's initial screen.

In Figure 18.3 you see that I have selected and mounted `/mnt/floppy`.

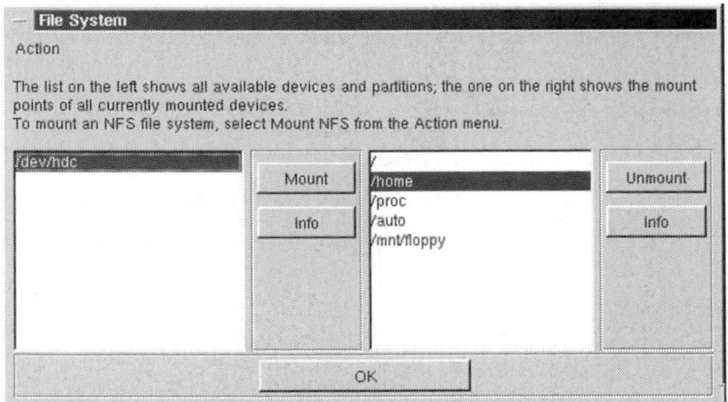

FIGURE 18.3
COAS filesystem tool after mounting `/mnt/floppy`.

The `/mnt/floppy` entry in Figure 18.3 has moved from the left window to the right window. Any filesystem can be mounted or unmounted by simply selecting the entry and clicking the appropriate mount or unmount tab.

Creating New Filesystems

When you install most distributions of Linux, the installation process makes some new filesystems and sets up the system to use them.

Many operating systems don't distinguish between the preparation of the device's surface to receive data (formatting) and the building of new filesystems. Linux does distinguish between the two, principally because only floppy disks need formatting in any case and also because Linux offers as many as half a dozen different filesystems that can be created (on any block device). Separately providing the facility of formatting floppy disks in each of these programs is poor design and requires you to learn a different way of doing it for each kind of new filesystem. The process of formatting floppy disks is dealt with separately. (See "Floppy Disks" later in this chapter for more information.)

Filesystems are initially built by a program that opens the block device and writes some structural data to it so that when the kernel tries to mount the filesystem, the device contains the image of a pristine filesystem. This means that both the kernel and the program used to make the filesystem must agree on the correct filesystem structure.

Linux provides a generic command, `mkfs`, that enables you to make a filesystem on a block device. In fact, because UNIX manages almost all resources with the same set of operations, `mkfs` can be used to generate a filesystem inside an ordinary file! Because this is unusual, `mkfs` asks for confirmation before proceeding. When this is done, you can even mount the resulting filesystem using the loop device. (See the section "Mounting Filesystems on Files" later in this chapter for more information.)

Because of the tremendous variety of filesystems available, almost all the work of building the new filesystem is delegated to a separate program for each; however, the generic `mkfs` program provides a single interface for invoking them all. It's not uncommon to pass options to the top-level `mkfs` (for example, `-V` to make it show what commands it executes or `-c` to make it check the device for bad blocks). The generic `mkfs` program also enables you to pass options to the filesystem-specific `mkfs`. Most of these filesystem-dependent options have sensible defaults, and you normally do not want to change them. The only options you might want to pass to `mke2fs`, which builds `ext2` filesystems, are `-m` and `-i`. The `-m` option specifies how much of the filesystem is reserved for `root`'s use (for example, for working space when the system disk would otherwise have filled completely). The `-i` option is more rarely exercised and is used for setting the balance between inodes and disk blocks; it is related to the expected average file size. As stated previously, the defaults are reasonable for most purposes, so these options are used only in special circumstances:

```
# mkfs -t ext2 /dev/fd0
mke2fs 1.10, 24-Apr-97 for EXT2 FS 0.5b, 95/08/09
Linux ext2 filesystem format
Filesystem label=
360 inodes, 1440 blocks
72 blocks (5.00) reserved for the super user
First data block=1
Block size=1024 (log=0)
Fragment size=1024 (log=0)
1 block group
8192 blocks per group, 8192 fragments per group
360 inodes per group

Writing inode tables: done
Writing superblocks and filesystem accounting information: done
# mount -t ext2 /dev/fd0 /mnt/floppy
# ls -la /mnt/floppy
total 14
```

```
drwxr-xr-x   3 root     root         1024 Aug  1 19:49 .
drwxr-xr-x   7 root     root         1024 Jul  3 21:47 ..
drwxr-xr-x   2 root     root        12288 Aug  1 19:49 lost+found
# umount /mnt/floppy
```

Here, you see the creating and mounting of an `ext2` filesystem on a floppy. The structure of the filesystem as specified by the program's defaults are shown. There is no volume label, and there are 4,096 bytes (4KB) per inode ($360 \times 4 = 1,440$). The block size is 1KB, and 5 percent of the disk is reserved for `root`. These are the defaults (which are explained in the manual page for `mke2fs`). After you have created a filesystem, you can use `dumpe2fs` to display information about an `ext2` filesystem, but remember to pipe the result through a pager such as `less` because this output can be very long.

After creating the filesystem on this floppy, you can include it in the filesystem table by changing the existing line referring to a `vfat` filesystem on `/dev/fd1` to the following:

```
/dev/fd1       /mnt/floppy    ext2   user,sync,errors=continue 0 0
```

The first three columns are the device, mount point, and filesystem type, as shown previously. The options column is more complex than those previous. The `user` option indicates that users are allowed to mount this filesystem. The `sync` option indicates that programs writing to this filesystem wait while each write finishes and only then continue. This might seem obvious, but it is not the normal state of affairs. The kernel normally manages filesystem writes in such a way as to provide high performance. (Data still gets written to the device, of course, but it doesn't necessarily happen immediately.) This is perfect for fixed devices such as hard disks, but for low-capacity removable devices such as floppy disks, it's less beneficial. Normally, you write a few files to a floppy and then unmount it and take it away. The unmount operation must wait until all data has been written to the device before it can finish (and the disk can then be removed). Having to wait like this is off-putting, and there is always the risk that someone might copy a file to the floppy, wait for the disk light to go out, and remove it. With asynchronous writes, some buffered data might not have yet been written to disk. Hence, synchronous writes are safer for removable media.

The `ext2` filesystem has a configurable strategy for errors. If an `ext2` filesystem encounters an error (for example, a bad disk block), there are three possible responses to the error:

Remount the device read-only—For filesystems that contain mostly unessential data (for example, `/tmp`, `/var/tmp`, or news spools), remounting the filesystem read-only so that it can be fixed with `fsck` is often the best choice.

Panic—Continuing regardlessly in the face of potentially corrupted system configuration files is unwise, so a *kernel panic* (a controlled crash—emergency landing, if you prefer) can sometimes be appropriate.

Ignore it—Causing a system shutdown if a floppy disk has a bad sector is a little excessive, so the `continue` option tells the kernel to "carry on regardless" in this situation. If this actually does happen, the best thing to do is to use the `-c` option of `e2fsck`, for example, with `fsck -t ext2 -c /dev/fd1`. This runs `e2fsck`, giving it the `-c` option, which invokes the command `badblocks` to test the device for bad disk blocks. After this is done, `e2fsck` does its best to recover from the situation.

Creating and Editing Filesystems Graphically with `fsconf`

The `fsconf` utility allows you to edit, add, or delete mounts. When you invoke the filesystem configurator, you are given the choice of five tasks (see Figure 18.4).

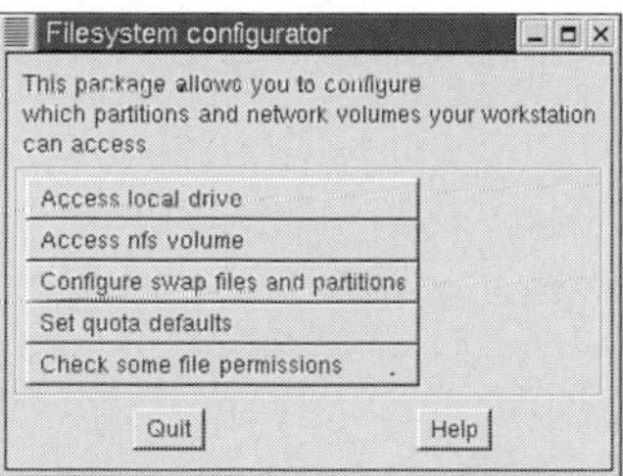

FIGURE 18.4
The `fsconfig` tool—top level.

Each of these choices is detailed here.

Access Local Drive

The first option you see is Access Local Drive. As you can see from Figure 18.5, this option shows the current local filesystems.

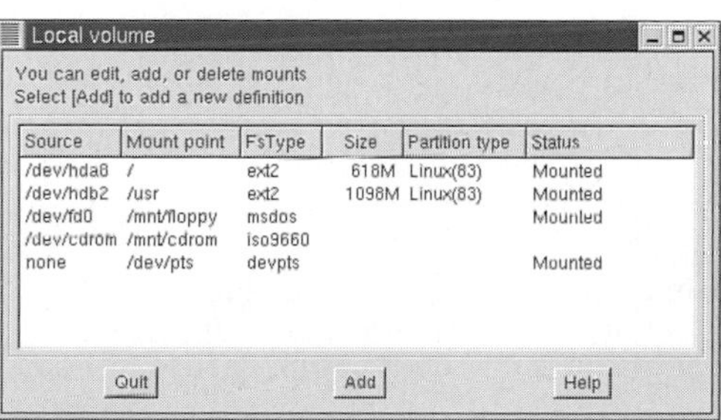

FIGURE 18.5
Accessing the local volume.

You get the Volume Specification window, as seen in Figure 18.6, when you click Add.

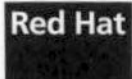

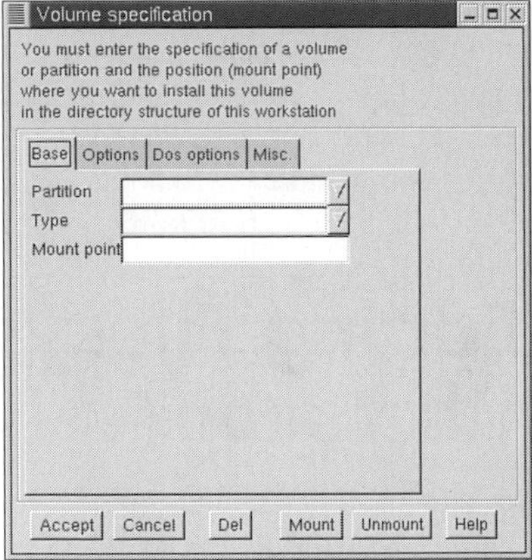

FIGURE 18.6
The Volume Specification window.

You will notice that there is a small arrow pointing down after both the Partition and Type input boxes. Clicking these arrows allows you to select from a list of possible values.

Figure 18.7 shows the screen with the partitions selected. The window gives you a list of all of your current partitions.

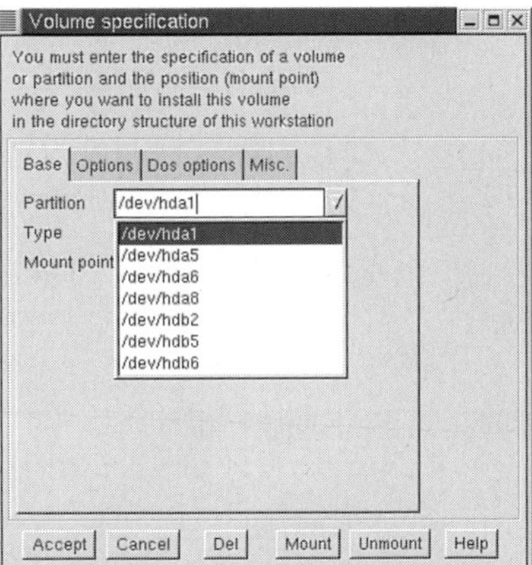

FIGURE 18.7
Volume specification—list of current partitions.

The screen showing the volume type is shown here as Figure 18.8.

As you can see from the list, you have a good set of options to choose from, and you don't have to remember whether it is called MS DOS or just DOS!

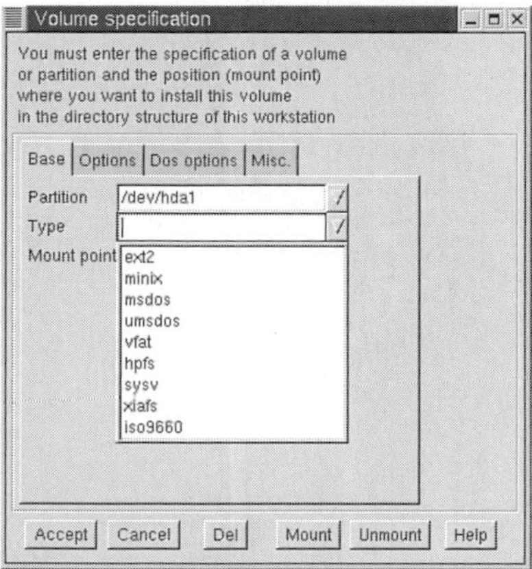

FIGURE 18.8
Volume specification—volume type.

The DOS option is here because DOS and OS/2 are single-user systems, where Linux is a multiuser system. DOS and OS/2, therefore, have no means of assigning ownership of files. To get around this problem, and to keep everyone from seeing everyone else's DOS files, Linux allows entire filesystems to be mounted with the user and group IDs defined with thc default you set here.

Just like many other screens, this one also has drop-down menus that allow you to choose the default user ID, the default group ID, and the translation mode. This can be seen in Figure 18.9.

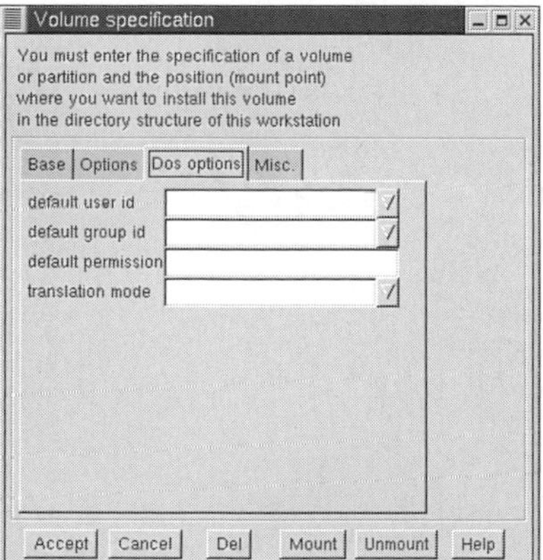

FIGURE 18.9
Volume specification—DOS options.

The translation mode can be a bit confusing. There are three options and they're shown in Figure 18.10.

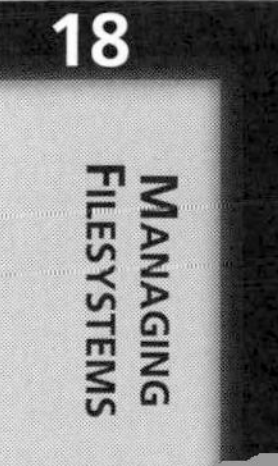

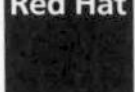

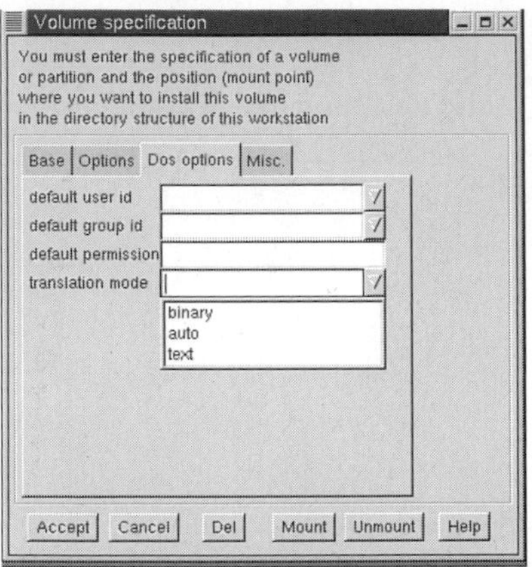

FIGURE 18.10
Volume specification—translation mode.

These options are binary, auto, and text. Text files are stored differently in DOS than in Linux. In Linux, the end-of-file marker is a single line feed. In DOS, the end-of-file marker is an ASCII carriage return followed by an ASCII line feed. The three options listed allow for translation from one type of system to the other. *Binary* indicates no translation. *Auto* means to translate all files that are not named to indicate that they are an executable, program code, graphics, TeX, or an archive file. Executable files have an extension of `BIN`, `COM`, `EXE`, or `SYS`. Program code has an extension of `APP`, `DLL`, `DRV`, `LIB`, `OBJ`, `OVL`, `OVR`, or `PIF`. Graphic files have an extension of `BMP`, `GIF`, `GL`, `JPG`, `PCX`, and `TIF`. TeX files end in `DVI`, `GF`, `PX`, `PXL`, `TFM`, and `VF`. Finally, archive files traditionally have an extension of `ARC`, `ARJ`, `DEB`, `GZ`, `LHA`, `LZH`, `TAR`, `TAZ`, `TPZ`, `TZ`, `TZP`, `Z`, `ZIP`, and `ZOO`. Finally, *text* means to translate all files regardless of type. This third option can cause problems if you accidentally translate a file that should not be translated.

Repairing Filesystems

Some disk data is kept in memory temporarily before being written to disk for performance reasons. (See the previous discussion of the `sync mount` option.) If the kernel does not have an opportunity to actually write this data, the filesystem can become corrupted. This can happen in several ways:

- The storage device (for example, a floppy disk) can be manually removed before the kernel has finished with it.
- The system might suffer a power loss.
- The user might mistakenly turn off the power or accidentally press the Reset button.

As part of the boot process, Linux runs the `fsck` program, whose job it is to check and repair filesystems. Most of the time, the boot follows a controlled shutdown (see the manual page for `shutdown`), and in this case, the filesystems will have been unmounted before the reboot. In this case, `fsck` says that they are "clean." It knows this because before unmounting them, the kernel writes a special signature on the filesystem to indicate that the data is intact. When the filesystem is mounted again for writing, this signature is removed.

If, on the other hand, one of the disasters listed takes place, the filesystems will not be marked "clean;" when `fsck` is invoked, as usual, it will notice this and begin a full check of the filesystem. This also occurs if you specify the `-f` flag to `fsck`. To prevent errors creeping up on it, `fsck` also enforces a periodic check; a full check is done at an interval specified on the filesystem itself (usually every 20 boots or 6 months, whichever comes sooner), even if it were unmounted cleanly.

The boot process checks the root filesystem and then mounts it read/write. (It's mounted read-only by the kernel; `fsck` asks for confirmation before operating on a read/write filesystem, and this is not desirable for an unattended reboot.) First, the `root` filesystem is checked with the following command:

```
fsck -V -a /
```

Executing this command checks all the other filesystems:

```
fsck -R -A -V -a
```

These options specify that all the filesystems should be checked (`-A`) except the `root` filesystem, which doesn't need checking a second time (`-R`), and that operations produce informational messages about what it is doing as it goes (`-V`), but that the process should not be interactive (`-a`). The latter is specified because, for example, there might not be anyone present to answer any questions from `fsck`.

In the case of serious filesystem corruption, the approach breaks down because there are some things that `fsck` will not do to a filesystem without your permission. In this case, it returns an error value to its caller (the startup script), and the startup script spawns a shell to allow the administrator to run `fsck` interactively. When this happens, a message like the following appears:

```
***An error occurred during the file system check.
***Dropping you to a shell; the system will reboot
***when you leave the shell.
Give root password for maintenance
(or type Control-D for normal startup):
```

This is a troubling event, particularly because it might well appear if you have other problems with the system—for example, a lockup (leading you to press the Reset button) or a spontaneous reboot. None of the online manuals are guaranteed to be available at this stage because they might be stored on the filesystem whose check failed. This prompt is issued if the `root` filesystem check failed or the filesystem check failed for any of the other disk filesystems.

When the automatic `fsck` fails, you need to log in by specifying the `root` password and run the `fsck` program manually. When you have typed in the `root` password, you are presented with the following prompt:

```
(Repair filesystem) #
```

You might worry about what command to enter here or indeed what to do at all. At least one of the filesystems needs to be checked, but which one? The preceding messages from `fsck` should indicate which, but it isn't necessary to go hunting for them. You can give `fsck` a set of options that tells it to check everything manually, and this is a good fallback:

```
fsck -A -V ; echo == $? ==
```

This is the same command as the previous one, but the `-R` option is missing, in case the `root` filesystem needs to be checked, and the `-a` option is missing, so `fsck` is in its interactive mode. This might enable a check to succeed just because it can now ask you questions. The purpose of the `echo == $? ==` command is to unambiguously interpret the outcome of the `fsck` operation. If the value printed between the equals signs is less than `4`, all is well. If this value is `4` or more, more recovery measures are needed. The meanings of the various values follow:

`0`	No errors
`1`	Filesystem errors corrected
`2`	System should be rebooted
`4`	Filesystem errors left uncorrected
`8`	Operational error
`16`	Usage or syntax error
`128`	Shared library error

If this does not work, it might be because of a *corrupted superblock*; `fsck` starts its disk check and if this is corrupted, it can't start. By good design, the `ext2` filesystem has many backup superblocks scattered regularly throughout the filesystem. Suppose the command announces that it has failed to clean some particular filesystem—for example, `/dev/fubar`. You can start `fsck` again using a backup superblock by using the following command:

```
fsck -t ext2 -b 8193 /dev/fubar
```

`8193` is the block number for the first backup superblock. This backup superblock is at the start of block group 1. (The first is numbered `0`.) There are more backup superblocks at the start of block group 2 (16385) and block group 3 (24577); they are spaced at intervals of 8,192 blocks. If you made a filesystem with settings other than the defaults, these might change. `mke2fs` lists the superblocks that it creates as it goes, so that is a good time to pay attention if you're not using the default settings. There are further things you can attempt if `fsck` is still not succeeding, but these situations are rare and usually indicate hardware problems so severe that they prevent the proper operation of `fsck`. Examples include broken wires in the IDE connector cable and similar nasty problems. If this command still fails, you might seek expert help or fix the disk in a different machine.

These extreme measures are unlikely; a manual `fsck`, in the unusual circumstance where it is actually required, almost always fixes things. After the manual `fsck` has worked, the `root` shell that the startup scripts provide has done its purpose. Type **`exit`** to exit it. At this point, to make sure that everything goes according to plan, the boot process is started again from the beginning. This second time around, the filesystems should all be error-free and the system should boot normally.

Various Kinds of Hardware

There are block devices under Linux for representing all sorts of random access devices: hard disks (XT, EIDE, and SCSI), floppy disks, CD-ROM drives, loopback devices, ramdisks, and Zip drives.

Hard Disks

Hard disks are large enough to make it useful to keep different filesystems on different parts of the hard disk. The scheme for dividing these disks is called *partitioning*. Although it is common for computers running MS-DOS to have only one partition, it is possible to have several different partitions on each disk. The summary of how the disk is partitioned is kept in its *partition table*.

The Partition Table

A hard disk might be divided like this:

```
$ fdisk -l
Disk /dev/hda: 128 heads, 63 sectors, 970 cylinders
Units = cylinders of 8064 * 512 bytes

   Device Boot    Start       End    Blocks   Id  System
/dev/hda1   *         1       177    713632+   6  FAT16
/dev/hda2           179       970   3193344    5  Extended
/dev/hda3           178       178      4032    a  OS/2 Boot Manager
/dev/hda5           179       696   2088544+   6  FAT16
/dev/hda6           920       970    205600+   6  FAT16
/dev/hda7           697       762    266080+  82  Linux swap
/dev/hda8           763       919    632992+  83  Linux

Disk /dev/hdb: 255 heads, 63 sectors, 523 cylinders
Units = cylinders of 16065 * 512 bytes

   Device Boot    Start       End    Blocks   Id  System
/dev/hdb1   *         2       383   3068415    5  Extended
/dev/hdb2           384       523   1124550   83  Linux
/dev/hdb5             2       192   1534176    6  FAT16
/dev/hdb6           193       383   1534176    6  FAT16
```

Note that the partitions on the first disk have names starting with `/dev/hda` and those on the second have names starting with `/dev/hdb`. The number of the partition follows these prefixes.

Note

All is not quite as simple as it could be in the partition table, however. Early hard disk drives on PCs were quite small (about 10MB), so you were limited to a small number of partitions, and the format of the partition table originally allowed for only four partitions. Later on, this was too great a restriction, and the *extended partition* was introduced as a workaround.

Inside each extended partition is another partition table. This enables the extended partition to be divided, in the same way, into four *logical partitions*. Partitions that aren't inside an extended partition are sometimes referred to as *primary partitions*.

Disk Geometry

The units of the table in the last section are *cylinders*. The partition table allocates a consecutive block of cylinders to each partition. The term *cylinder* itself dates from the days when it was possible to remove a disk pack from a UNIX machine and point to the various parts. That can't be done here, so here's another way of looking at it.

Imagine that a hard disk is in fact a stack of pizzas. Each of the pizzas is a *platter*, a disk-shaped surface with a magnetic coating designed to hold magnetic encodings. Both sides of these platters are used. These platters rotate around the spindle, like the spindle in a record player. The hard disk has a movable arm containing several *disk heads*. Each side of each platter has a separate disk head. If you were to put your fingers between the pizzas while keeping them straight, your fingers are the same as the arrangement of the heads on the arm. All the parts of the platters that the heads pass over in one rotation of the disk is called a *cylinder*. The parts of a single platter that one head passes over in one rotation is called a *track*. Each track is divided into *sectors*, as if the pizzas had been already sliced for you. The layout of a disk, its *geometry*, is described by the number of cylinders, heads, and sectors composing the disk. Another important feature is the rotational speed of the disk; generally, the faster it is, the faster the hard disk can read or write data.

You can discover the geometry of one of your hard disks by using the `hdparm` command (on IDE drives), and typical output might look like this:

```
$ hdparm -g /dev/hda

/dev/hda:
 geometry     = 970/128/63, sectors = 7825932, start = 0

$ hdparm -g /dev/hdb

/dev/hdb:
 geometry     = 523/255/63, sectors = 8406720, start = 0
```

As you can see from the geometry specified in this example, these are the drives discussed previously.

Note

IBM PCs with older BIOSs can have difficulty with large disks; see the Linux Large-Disk mini HOWTO.

Floppy Disks

Floppy disks are removable, low-capacity storage media. As storage devices, they are far slower than hard disks, but they have the advantage of being removable, which makes them good media for transporting modest amounts of data.

The block devices corresponding to the floppy disks begin with the letters `fd`; `/dev/fd0` is the first, and any additional ones have increasing numbers. There are many possible formats for a floppy disk, and the kernel needs to know the format (geometry) of a disk to read it properly. Linux can usually work out the correct format, so the automatic devices `/dev/fd0` (plus `/dev/fd1` and so on for extra floppy drives) are usually sufficient, but if for some reason it is necessary to specify the exact format, further device names are provided. The device `/dev/fd0H1440`, for example, denotes a 1.44MB, high-density floppy. There are many more devices indicating obscure formats, both older lower-capacity formats and other nonstandard, extra–high-capacity formats.

The most common reason to use the specific-format device names is that you are formatting a floppy for the first time. In this situation, the disk is not yet readable, so the kernel will not be able to autoprobe an existing format. You need to use the name `/dev/fd0H1440`, for example, to denote a high-density, 3.5-inch disk in the first floppy drive. For device names representing other formats, refer to the fd manual page. Section 4 of the manual is devoted to devices.

The process of formatting a floppy is completely destructive to the data on it, and because it requires writing to the actual device itself, it requires `root` privileges. It is done like this:

```
# fdformat /dev/fd0H1440
Double-sided, 80 tracks, 18 sec/track. Total capacity 1440 kB.
Formatting ... done
Verifying ... done
```

In Debian, formatting is done with superformat:

```
# superformat /dev/fd0
Measuring drive 0's raw capacity
 Verifying cylinder 79, head 1
```

After you have formatted a floppy, don't forget to use `mkfs` to build a filesystem on it. (See the section "Creating New Filesystems" earlier in this chapter.)

If you have X Windows running, you can use the user mount tool previously discussed in this chapter to accomplish the same tasks by clicking buttons.

CD-ROM Drives

CD-ROM drives are fundamentally another kind of read-only block device. They are mounted in just the same way as other block devices. CD-ROMs almost always contain standard ISO 9660 filesystems, often with some optional extensions. There is no reason, however, why you should not use any other filesystem. Once you have mounted your CD-ROM, it behaves like any other read-only filesystem.

You can set up and mount your CD-ROM drive using the Red Hat File System Manager, as explained previously, or by using the `mount` command:

```
# mount /dev/cdrom -t iso9660 /mnt/cdrom
```

The directory /mnt/cdrom is a common place to mount one's CD-ROM drive under Red Hat Linux because it is where the graphical package manager Glint expects to find the contents of the Red Hat installation CD-ROM, for example. In Debian, you might prefer to use `/cdrom`, although you are free to choose any location you like.

The device name `/dev/cdrom` is commonly used as a symbolic link to the actual device name corresponding to the CD-ROM. This is because at the time the CD-ROM drive became available for the PC, there was no cheap standard interface for these devices. Each manufacturer chose or invented an interfacing scheme that was incompatible with everyone else's. For this reason, there are about a dozen different drivers for CD-ROM drives available in the Linux kernel. SCSI would have been a sensible standard to use, but although SCSI CD-ROM drives are available, they're not particularly popular.

The ATAPI standard arrived in time to ensure that all non-SCSI CD-ROM drives at quad speed or faster use a standard interface, so the situation is far simpler for new CD-ROM drives. Support for ATAPI CD-ROMs is handled by one driver for all drives. The ATAPI standard also provides for very large hard disk drives and tape drives. ATAPI CD-ROM drives are attached to IDE interfaces, just like hard disks, and they have the same set of device names as hard disk devices.

Because CD-ROMs come already written, there is no need to partition them. They are accessed using the device names for whole-disk devices: `/dev/hda`, `/dev/hdb`, and so on.

The ISO 9660 standard specifies a standard format for the layout of data on CD-ROMs. It restricts filenames to no more than 32 characters, for example. Most CD-ROMs are written with very short filenames for compatibility with MS-DOS. To support certain UNIX features such as symbolic links and long filenames, developers created a set of extensions called *Rock Ridge*, and the Linux kernel will automatically detect and use the Rock Ridge extensions.

CD-ROM drives also usually support the playing of audio CDs, and there are many Linux programs for controlling the CD-ROM drive in the same way as you might control a CD player. The multimedia package on the Red Hat 6.0 CD-ROM contains the xplaycd program for playing CDs. To make it work, you need to set the `/dev/cdrom` symbolic link to point to your real CD-ROM device.

If you have X Windows running, you can use the user mount tool previously discussed in this chapter to accomplish the same tasks by clicking buttons.

Loopback Devices

Loopback devices enable you to store new filesystems inside regular files. You might want to do this to prepare an emulated hard disk image for DOSEMU, an install disk, or just to try a filesystem of a new type or an ISO9660 CD-ROM image before writing it to the CD writer.

Mounting Filesystems on Files

Under UNIX, you need `root` permissions to change the system's filesystem structure; even if you own a file and the mount point on which you want to mount it, only `root` can do this, unless the `user` option has been specified in `/etc/fstab` for this filesystem.

When a filesystem is mounted using the loopback driver, the file containing the filesystem plays the role of the block device in the `mount` command and `/etc/fstab`. The kernel talks to the block device interface provided by the loopback device driver, and the driver forwards operations to the file:

```
# mount $(pwd)/rtems.iso -t iso9660 -o ro,loop /mnt/test
# ls -F /mnt/test
INSTALL   LICENSE   README   SUPPORT   c/   doc/   rr_moved/
# mount ¦ grep loop ¦ fold -s
/home/james/documents/books/Sams/Linux-Unleashed-2/ch9/tmp/rtems.iso on
/mnt/test type iso9660 (ro,loop=/dev/loop0)
# umount /mnt/test
```

Once the loopback filesystem is mounted, it's a normal filesystem.

Using Encrypted Filesystems

Loopback filesystems offer even more features—encryption, for example. A loopback filesystem can be configured to decrypt data from the block device on-the-fly so that the data on the device is useless to people even if they can read it—unless they have the password. The `mount` command prompts for the password at the appropriate time. To make this work, first you have to use `mkfs` to generate a filesystem on the encrypted block device; `losetup` is used to associate a loop device and encryption method with the block device you want to use (in the following case, a floppy drive):

```
# /sbin/losetup -e DES /dev/loop0 /dev/fd1
Password:
Init (up to 16 hex digits):
# /sbin/mkfs -t ext2 -m0 /dev/loop0
mke2fs 1.10, 24-Apr-97 for EXT2 FS 0.5b, 95/08/09
Linux ext2 filesystem format
Filesystem label=
360 inodes, 1440 blocks
0 blocks (0.00) reserved for the super user
First data block=1
Block size=1024 (log=0)
Fragment size=1024 (log=0)
1 block group
8192 blocks per group, 8192 fragments per group
360 inodes per group

Writing inode tables: done
Writing superblocks and filesystem accounting information: done
# losetup -d /dev/loop0
```

As shown previously, `losetup`'s `-e` option associates an encryption method and block device with a loopback device. The `-d` option deletes this association and erases the stored encryption key.

When the filesystem has been created on the encrypted device, it can be mounted in a manner similar to the normal case:

```
# /sbin/losetup -d /dev/loop0
# mount /dev/fd1 -t ext2 -o loop=/dev/loop0,encryption=DES /mnt/test
Password:
Init (up to 16 hex digits):
# ls /mnt/test
lost+found
```

Note

Remember, the # used as a prompt indicates a normal user, whereas a $ indicates a `root` authority user.

Usually, the whole process of using an encrypted filesystem can be set up for ordinary users by adding the appropriate line to `/etc/fstab`:

```
$ mount /mnt/test
Password:
Init (up to 16 hex digits):
$ ls -ld /mnt/test
drwxrwxrwx  3 james  root    1024 Sep 14 22:04 /mnt/test
```

In this example, root has enabled users to mount encrypted filesystems by including this line in /etc/fstab:

```
/dev/fd1   /mnt/test   ext2   user,loop,encryption=DES
```

Additionally, ownership of the top-level directory on the floppy disk has been given to the user james because presumably, it is his floppy disk. If root had not done this, james would have been able to mount his filesystem but not read it. It was an essential step, but it turns out that in this example, root has made a fatal mistake. As well as changing the ownership of the filesystem's root directory, root has changed the directory's mode as well. This means that once the unsuspecting james has supplied his secret password, any user on the system can read and write the files on the floppy. This underlines the fact that encryption alone is not sufficient for safety. Careful thought is also essential.

In the previous case, the file ownerships and permissions have turned out to be more of a hindrance than a help. It is probably better to use an MS-DOS filesystem on the encrypted device because ownership is automatically given away to the user mounting the disk and the file modes are set correctly:

```
$ ls -ld  /mnt/floppy/
drwxr-xr-x 2 james  users   7168 Jan  1  1970 /mnt/floppy/
```

However, there are still two problems with this strategy. First, it is not possible to make an encrypted filesystem easily on a floppy because the mkfs.msdos program needs to know the geometry for the device on which it is creating the filesystem and the loopback device drivers don't really have geometries. Second, once your encrypted ext2 filesystem is mounted, the superuser can still read your data.

The encryption methods outlined previously are not available in standard kernels because most useful forms of encryption technology are not legally exportable from the United States. However, they are already available outside the United States at ftp://ftp.replay.com/crypto/linux/all/linux-crypt-kernelpatches.tar.gz.

This site is in Holland. You need to apply these patches to your kernel and recompile it in order to use the DES and IDEA encryption methods with loopback devices. The patches were made against version 2.0.11 of the Linux kernel, but they work perfectly well with the kernel supplied with Red Hat Linux 6.0 (and should work with most other distributions as well).

To summarize, encrypted filesystems can be useful for some kinds of data (for example, for storing digital signatures for important system binaries in such a way that they can't be tampered with), but their usefulness to users other than root is limited. Of course, all the ordinary file encryption mechanisms are still available to and useful for ordinary users.

Other Block Devices

Although hard disks, floppy disks, and CD-ROM drives are probably the most heavily used block devices, there are other kinds of block devices, including ramdisks and Zip drives.

Ramdisks

Ramdisks are block devices that store their data in RAM rather than on a disk. This means they are very fast; nevertheless, ramdisks are rarely used with Linux because Linux has a very good disk-caching scheme, which provides most of the speed benefit of a ramdisk but not the fixed cost in memory.

The most common use for ramdisks is to serve as a `root` filesystem while Linux is being installed. A compressed filesystem image is loaded into a ramdisk, and the installation process is run from this disk. The ramdisk's filesystem can be larger than a single floppy because the image is compressed on the floppy.

Although ramdisks are useful with operating systems lacking effective disk buffering, they offer little performance advantage under Linux. If you want to try a ramdisk, they work just like any other block device. For example, to mount a ramdisk as `/tmp`, you add this line to `/etc/fstab`:

```
/dev/ram    /tmp        ext2    defaults    0 0
```

Then you create and mount an `ext` filesystem with the following:

```
/sbin/mkfs -t ext2 /dev/ram
mount /tmp
```

Any performance benefits from doing this are hard to find, but you might find that this helps in unusual circumstances.

The principal advantage of ramdisks is that they provide great flexibility in the boot process. Although it is possible to recompile a kernel including support for your hardware, it makes the initial installation process difficult. Historically, programmers worked around this problem by providing dozens of different installation boot disks, each with support for one or two items of boot hardware (SCSI cards and CD-ROM drives, for example).

A simpler solution is to exploit loadable kernel modules. Instead of having separate boot disks for each type of hardware, all containing different kernels, it is simple to provide just one boot disk containing a modular kernel and the module utilities themselves.

A compressed filesystem is loaded from the floppy disk into a ramdisk by the kernel loader, LILO, at the same time the kernel is loaded. The kernel mounts this filesystem and runs a program (`/linuxrc`) from it. This program then mounts the "real" `root` filesystem and exits, enabling the kernel to remount the real `root` filesystem on `/`. This system is convenient to set up, and the process of creating initial ramdisks had been automated by Red Hat Software (see the manual page for `mkinitrd`). Red Hat Linux systems whose `root` filesystem is on a SCSI device have a modular kernel and boot by this method.

Zip Drives

Zip drives are drives providing removable 100MB cartridges. They come in three varieties: parallel port (PPA), IDE, and SCSI. All are supported, but the parallel port version is slowest; it is also a SCSI drive but with a proprietary parallel port interface, for which the Linux kernel provides a driver. Hence, both kinds of drive appear as SCSI disks.

Because they're just standard (but removable) SCSI or IDE disks, most aspects of their use are similar to those for other block devices. Red Hat Linux 6.0 comes with support for both the SCSI and PPA varieties. You can find further information in the Zip-Drive mini HOWTO (which explains how to install your Zip drive), and the Zip-Install mini HOWTO, which explains how to install Red Hat Linux onto a Zip drive.

Character Devices

Character devices offer a flow of data that must be read in order. Whereas block devices enable a seek to select the next block of data transferred, for example, from one edge or the other of a floppy disk, character devices represent hardware that doesn't have this capability. An example is a terminal, for which the next character to be read is whatever key you type at the keyboard.

In fact, because there are only two basic types of devices, block and character, all hardware is represented as one or the other, rather like the animal and vegetable kingdoms of biological classification. Inevitably, this means that a few devices don't quite fit into this classification scheme. Examples include tape drives, generic SCSI devices, and the special memory devices such as `/dev/port` and `/dev/kmem`.

Note

Network interfaces are represented differently; see Chapter 7.

Parallel Ports

Parallel ports are usually used for communicating with printers, although they are versatile enough to support other things too—for example, Zip drives, CD-ROM drives, and even networking.

The hardware itself offers character-at-a-time communication. The parallel port can provide an interrupt to notify the kernel that it is now ready to output a new character, but because printers are usually not performance-critical on most PCs, this interrupt is often borrowed for use by some other hardware, often sound hardware. This has an unfortunate consequence: The kernel often needs to poll the parallel hardware, so driving a parallel printer often requires more CPU work than it should.

The good news is that if your parallel printer interrupt is not in use by some other hardware, it can be enabled with the printer driver configuration program `tunelp`. The `-i` option for `tunelp` sets the IRQ for use with each printer device. You might set the IRQ for the printer port to 7 like this:

```
# /usr/sbin/tunelp /dev/lp1 -i 7
/dev/lp1 using IRQ 7
```

If this results in the printer ceasing to work, going back to the polling method is easy:

```
# /usr/sbin/tunelp /dev/lp1 -i 0
/dev/lp1 using polling
```

The best way to test a printer port under Red Hat Linux is from the Control Panel's Printer Configuration tool (`/usr/bin/printtool`). The Tests menu offers the option of printing a test page directly to the device rather than via the normal printing system. This is a good starting point. You can find more information on setting up printers in Chapter 24, "Printing with Linux."

Tape Drives

Tape drives provide I/O of a stream of bytes to or from the tape. Although most tape drives can be repositioned (that is, rewound and wound forward like audio or video tapes), this operation is very slow by disk standards. Although access to a random part of the tape is at least feasible, it is very slow, so the character device interface is workable for using tape drives.

For most UNIX workstations, the interface of choice for tape drives is SCSI because this fits in well with the SCSI disks and so on. SCSI provides the capability to plug in a new device and start using it. (Of course, you can't do this with the power on.) SCSI has traditionally been more expensive than most other PC technologies, so it wasn't used for many tape drives developed for use with PCs. Several interfaces have been used for tape drives for IBM PCs:

Type	*Device Names*	*Major Number*
SCSI	`/dev/st*`	9
Floppy	`/dev/rft*`	27
QIC-02	`/dev/rmt`	12
IDE	`/dev/ht*`	37
Parallel Port	(Currently unsupported)	

All these tape drives have the feature that rewinds the tape when the device is closed. All these drives except the QIC-02 drive have a second device interface with a name prefixed with `n`—for example `/dev/nst0`, `/dev/nst3`, or `/dev/nht0`. All these devices support the magnetic tape control program, `mt`, which is used for winding tapes past files, rewinding them, and so on. Many commands, particularly the more advanced `mt` commands, are only available for SCSI tape drives.

Apart from the `mt` command for the basic control of a tape drive, there are many commands that you can use for storing and retrieving data on tape. Because the character devices are "just files," you could use `cat` to store data on the tape, but this is not very flexible. A great many programs are particularly or partly designed with tape drives in mind:

`tar` — This is widely used for creating archives in regular files but was originally created for making tape backups. In fact, `tar` stands for *tape archiver*. Archives made by `tar` can be read on a wide variety of systems.

`cpio` — Another program principally intended for backups and so on, `cpio` stands for copy in–out. The GNU version of `cpio`, which is used by Linux distributions, supports eight different data formats—some are varieties of its "native" format, two are varieties of `tar` archives, and some are obsolete. If you want to unpack an unknown archive, `cpio`, along with `file` and `dd`, is very useful.

`dump` — The `dump` utility is of use only to system administrators because it backs up an `ext2` filesystem by raw access to the block device on which the filesystem exists. (For this reason, it is better to do this when the filesystem is either not mounted or is mounted read-only.) This has the advantage, among other things, that the access times of the backed-up directories are left unmodified. (GNU `tar` will also do this.) Although tapes written with `dump` are not always readable on other versions of UNIX, unlike those written by `tar` and `cpio`, `dump` is a popular choice.

`dd` — Designed for blockwise I/O, `dd` is a general-purpose tool for doing file manipulations and can often be useful.

`afio` A variant of `cpio`, `afio` compresses individual files into the backup. For backups, this is preferable to `tar`'s compression of the whole archive because a small tape error can make a compressed `tar` archive useless, although a `tar` archive that isn't compressed doesn't have this vulnerability. `afio` isn't widely used outside the Linux world.

`Amanda` `Amanda` is a powerful backup system that schedules, organizes, and executes backups for you. It uses either `tar` or `dump` to do the actual work and will effortlessly allow you to automate all the backups for one machine or a multitude. One of its most useful features is its ability to perform fast backups across the network from several client machines to a single server machine containing a tape drive. More information about `Amanda` is available at the URL `http://www.cs.umd.edu/projects/amanda/`; RPMs of `Amanda` are available on the Red Hat FTP site.

`BRU` `BRU` (Backup and Restore Utility) is a commercial product for making backups.

Terminals

The *terminal* is the principal mode of communication between the kernel and the user. When you type keystrokes, the terminal driver turns them into input readable by the shell or whatever program you are running.

For many years, UNIX ran only on serial terminals. Although most computers now also have video hardware, the terminal is still a useful concept. Each window in which you can run a shell provides a separate *pseudoterminal*, each one rather like a traditional serial terminal. Terminals are often called `ttys` because the device nodes for many of them have names like `/dev/tty*`.

The terminal interface is used to represent serial lines to "real" terminals, to other computers (via modems), mice, printers, and so on. The large variety of hardware addressed by the terminal interface has led to a wide range of capabilities offered by the terminal device driver, and explaining all the facilities offered could easily occupy an entire chapter. This section just offers an overview of the facilities.

For more complete information on terminals and serial I/O, refer to the Linux Documentation Project's excellent HOWTO documents. These are provided on the Red Hat Linux 6.0 CD-ROM and are also available on the Web at `http://metalab.unc.edu/LDP/`. Specific HOWTOs dealing with this are the Serial HOWTO, Section 9 of the Hardware HOWTO, and the Serial Port Programming mini HOWTO. Many documents deal with using modems for networking.

The Terminal Device Driver

The terminal device driver gathers the characters you type at the keyboard and sends them to the program you're working with, after some processing. This processing can involve gathering the characters into batches a line at a time and taking into account the special meanings of some keys you might type.

Some special keys of this sort are used for editing the text that is sent to the program you're interacting with. Much of the time, the terminal driver is building a line of input that it hasn't yet sent to the program receiving your input. Keys that the driver will process specially include the following:

Return (CR) or Line Feed (LF)

CR is usually translated into LF by the terminal driver. (See the `icrnl` option in the manual page for `stty`.) This ends the current line, which is then sent to the application. (It is waiting for terminal input, so it wakes up.)

Backspace/Delete

Only one of these two keys can be selected as the erase key, which erases the previous character typed. For more information, read the Linux Keyboard Setup mini HOWTO.

End-of-File, Usually Ctrl+D

When a program is reading its standard input from the keyboard and you want to let it know that you've typed everything, you press Ctrl+D. ("Usually" indicates that this option is shell dependent and may differ depending upon which shell you are using.)

Word-Erase, Usually Ctrl+W

This combination deletes the last word you typed.

Kill-Line, Usually Ctrl+U

This kills the entire line of input so that you can start again.

Interrupt, Usually Ctrl+C

This kills the current program. Some programs block this at times when the program might leave the terminal in a strange state if it were unexpectedly killed.

Suspend, Usually Ctrl+Z

This key sends a suspend signal to the program you're using. The result is that the program is stopped temporarily, and you get the shell prompt again. You can then put that program (job) in the background and do something else.

Quit, Usually Ctrl+\ (Ctrl+Backslash)

Sends a Quit signal to the current program; programs that ignore Ctrl+C can often be stopped with Ctrl+\, but programs ignoring Ctrl+C are often doing so for a reason.

Stop, Usually Ctrl+S, and Start, Usually Ctrl+Q

These keys stop and restart terminal output temporarily, which can be useful if a command produces a lot of output, although it can often be more useful to repeat the command and pipe it through `less`.

You can examine many other terminal modes and settings with the `stty` command. This command has a built-in set of sensible settings for terminals, and typing `stty` to find the current settings usually shows you only the differences from its "sane" settings:

```
$ stty
speed 9600 baud; line = 0;
```

Tip

If you ever find that your terminal state is messed up, you can usually fix it with the command `$ stty sane` and Ctrl+J. Note that you finish the command Ctrl+J, rather than Enter (which is the same as Ctrl+M). The `icrnl` option might have been turned off. This is fixed again with `stty sane`. GNU `bash` will always cope with CRs that have not been converted to LF anyway, but some other programs won't.

If this still doesn't work, and the screen font appears to have been changed, type **`$ echo`**, press Ctrl+V and Esc, type **`c`**, and press Ctrl+J. You press Ctrl+V to make the terminal driver pass the next key without processing. You can get a similar effect by typing **`$ reset`** and pressing Ctrl+J, but the program `reset` is only available if the `ncurses` package is installed.

Programs can turn off the processing that the line driver does by default; the resulting behavior (raw mode) allows programs to read unprocessed input from the terminal driver (for example, CR is not mapped to LF), and control characters don't produce the signals described in the table earlier in this section. The `stty sane` command will return things to normal.

Serial Communications

Although the terminal interfaces used most commonly under Linux are the console driver and the pseudo-terminals driven by programs such as `xterm`, `script`, and `expect`, the original terminal interface involved serial communications. In fact, this still lingers; a pseudo-`tty` associated with an `xterm` window still has an associated baud rate as shown in the example in the section "The Terminal Device Driver." Changing this baud rate has no actual effect. For real serial ports, however, the baud rate and many other parameters have a direct relevance. The device nodes relating to the serial ports are composed of two "teams," with the names `/dev/cua*` and `/dev/ttyS*`. Starting with version 2.2 of the kernel (which includes the one with this book), `/dev/ttyS*` is the "correct" name to use. `/dev/cua*` will, most likely, disappear from the next version or two. The device nodes allow you to use the same serial hardware for both incoming and outgoing serial connections.

Configuring the Serial Ports

Serial port configuration is mostly done either with the `stty` command or directly by programs using the interface outlined in the `termios` manual page. The `stty` command offers almost all the configuration possibilities provided by `termios`; however, there are configuration issues for serial hardware that are not addressed by `stty`. The `setserial` command allows the configuration of the correct IRQ settings for each serial port and of extra-fast baud rates that the standard `termios` specification doesn't provide. For more detailed information, refer to the Linux Serial HOWTO and the manual page for `setserial`.

Generic SCSI Devices

Not all SCSI devices are hard disks, CD-ROM drives, or tape drives. Some are optical scanners, CD-ROM recorders, or even electron microscopes. The kernel can't possibly abstract the interfaces for all possible SCSI devices, so it gives user programs direct access to SCSI hardware via the generic SCSI devices. These enable programs to send arbitrary SCSI commands to hardware. Although this arrangement offers the opportunity of wreaking havoc by mistake, it also offers the capability of driving all sorts of interesting hardware, of which the principal examples are CD-ROM recorders. The SCSI device nodes all have names starting with `/dev/sg`. SCSI commands are sent to the devices by writing data to the device, and the results are read back by reading from the device.

CD-ROM Recorders

CD-ROM recorders are devices for recording data on special media that can be read in ordinary CD-ROM drives. There are two stages in the writing of a CD: generating the CD image and writing that image to the media.

The surface of a CD-R (recordable CD) is only writable once, so if `mkisofs` worked like the other `mkfs` tools, it would always generate image files representing empty CDs. For this reason, `mkisofs` populates the filesystem with files as it generates the image file.

The CD image file is produced by the mkisofs program, which generates the structures for an ISO 9660 filesystem and populates it with the files from a directory tree. CDs are not writable in the same sense as block devices; this is why they are not actually block devices. The image file must be written to the CD-R with a specialized program, `cdwrite`, which understands all the various proprietary schemes used for driving CD writers. All the CD writers supported by Linux (as of version 2.0.30 of the kernel) are SCSI devices, so the kernel accommodates this by providing access to the generic SCSI device interface that enables a program to send SCSI commands to these devices.

While *burning* (writing) a CD, it is usually important that the flow of data to the writer keeps up with the speed at which the writer is going; otherwise, if the writer runs out of data to write, the CD-R is ruined. For this reason, it is usual to use `mkisofs` to generate an image file and then separately use `cdwrite` to write this image file to the CD writer.

It is possible to use a pipe to send the data from `mkisofs` directly to `cdwrite`. This often works either because a fast machine can ensure that `mkisofs` supplies the data fast enough to keep the CD writer busy or because the CD writer is not sensitive to data underruns. (Some of the more expensive ones have internal hard disks to which the data is written during an intermediate stage.) This technique is not recommended, however, because the generation of the intermediate image file has other benefits; it enables you to test your CD image before the final writing of the data takes place.

Testing CD Images

Just as you can use `mkfs` to create a filesystem inside an ordinary file, you can mount filesystems contained in ordinary files by using the loopback device driver described previously. The first example of mounting a loopback filesystem is a demonstration of how you can test a CD image.

Other Character Devices

Several other varieties of character devices, such as /dev/null, are used frequently.

The Controlling Terminal Device—/dev/tty

Most processes have a controlling terminal, particularly if they were started interactively by a user. The *controlling terminal*, which I refer to as simply /dev/tty, is used for initiating a conversation directly with the user (for example, to ask him something). An example is the crypt command:

```
$ fmt diary.txt ¦ crypt ¦ mail -s Diary confidant@linux.org
Enter key:
$
```

Here, the crypt command has opened /dev/tty to obtain a password. It was not able to use its own standard output to issue the prompt and its standard input to read the password because they are being used for the data to be encrypted.

Note

Of course, it's unusual to send email encrypted with crypt. A better choice is probably PGP. PGP is available in RPM format from ftp://ftp.replay.com//pub/linux/redhat.

More useful examples are commands that need to ask the operator something even if the input and output are redirected. A case in point is the cpio command, which prompts the operator for the name of a new tape device when it runs out of space. See the section "/dev/null and Friends" later in this chapter for another example.

Nonserial Mice

Many computers have bus or PS/2 mice instead of serial mice. This arrangement has the advantage of keeping both of the two standard serial ports free, but the disadvantage of using up another IRQ. These devices are used by gpm and the X Window system, but most other programs don't interact with them directly. Setting up your system with these mice is easy; the Red Hat and Caldera installation processes pretty much take care of it for you, whereas Debian's does not. If you have problems with your mouse, however, you should read the manual page for gpm and the Linux BusMouse HOWTO.

Audio Devices

There are several audio-related device nodes on Linux systems, and they include the following:

`/dev/sndstat`	Indicates the status of the sound driver
`/dev/audio*`	Sun-compatible audio output device
`/dev/dsp*`	Sound sampling device
`/dev/mixer`	For control of the mixer hardware on the sound card
`/dev/music`	A high-level sequencer interface
`/dev/sequencer*`	A low-level sequencer interface
`/dev/midi*`	Direct MIDI port access

Setting up the sound driver under Linux can sometimes be difficult, but the Linux Sound HOWTO provides useful advice.

Random Number Devices

Many program features require the generation of apparently random sequences. Examples include games, numerical computations, and various computer-security–related applications. Numerical computing with random numbers requires that the sequence of random numbers be repeatable but also that the sequence "look" random. Games require apparently random numbers, but the quality of the random numbers is not quite as critical as for numerical computation programs. The system libraries produce repeatable sequences of "pseudo-random" numbers that satisfy these requirements well.

On the other hand, in many aspects of computer security, it is advantageous to generate numbers that really are random. Because you can assume that an attacker has access to the same sorts of random number generators that you do, using them is not very safe; an attacker can use these generators to figure out what random number you'll use next. Sequences that are genuinely random must, in the end, be produced from the real world and not from the internals of some computer program. For this reason, the Linux kernel keeps a supply of random numbers internally. These numbers are derived from very precise timings of the intervals between "random" external events—for example, the user's key presses on the keyboard, mouse events, and even some interrupts (such as from the floppy disk drive and some network cards). These "real" random numbers are used in security-critical contexts—for example, the choosing of TCP sequence numbers.

> **Note**
>
> The Linux kernel uses these methods to produce TCP sequence numbers that are more difficult to guess than those of any other implementation at the time of writing. This improves the security of TCP connections against "hijacking."

The two random number devices differ in what happens when the rate of reading exceeds the rate at which random data is collected inside the kernel. The `/dev/random` device makes the calling program wait until some more randomness arrives, and the `/dev/urandom` device falls back on the difficult-to-guess MD5 hash to produce a stream of random data. When more random information arrives later, it is added to the randomness of `/dev/urandom`. To summarize, `/dev/random` doesn't sacrifice quality in favor of speed, but `/dev/urandom` does.

`/dev/null` and Friends

In the following segment, the special devices `/dev/full` and `/dev/null` first simulate a tape-full condition and then discard the output:

```
$ echo diary.txt ¦ cpio -o >/dev/full
Found end of tape.  To continue, type device/file name when ready.
/dev/null
52 blocks
```

In the real world, when the tape on `/dev/st0` becomes full, you probably just change the tape in the drive and type `/dev/st0` a second time. However, `/dev/full` is occasionally useful for testing purposes, and `/dev/null` is used all the time for discarding unwanted output. The device `/dev/full` produces a stream of zero bytes when read. (`/dev/null`, on the other hand, produces no output at all.)

Memory Devices

The memory devices have the same major device number as `/dev/null` and `/dev/full` but are used differently. They are as follows:

`/dev/mem`	Provides access to physical memory
`/dev/kmem`	Provides access to the kernel's virtual memory
`/dev/port`	Provides access to I/O ports

These devices are not frequently used in many programs; the X Window system's X server uses memory mapping on `/dev/mem` to access the video memory, and many programs use `/dev/port` to access I/O ports on those architectures that have a separate I/O space. (Many modern processors do not.)

Virtual Console Screen Devices

The virtual console screen devices exist to provide screen capture capabilities for virtual consoles (VCs). They are not readable by ordinary users; hence, other users cannot eavesdrop on your session.

There are two sets of device nodes for this purpose:

```
$ ls -l /dev/vcs[012] /dev/vcsa[012]
crw--w----    1 root     tty        7,   0 Sep 27  1995 /dev/vcs0
crw--w----    1 root     tty        7,   1 Sep 27  1995 /dev/vcs1
crw--w----    1 root     tty        7,   2 Sep 27  1995 /dev/vcs2
crw--w----    1 root     tty        7, 128 Sep 27  1995 /dev/vcsa0
crw--w----    1 root     tty        7, 129 Sep 27  1995 /dev/vcsa1
crw--w----    1 root     tty        7, 130 Sep 27  1995 /dev/vcsa2
```

Each set is numbered from 0 to 63, corresponding to the numbering system for the `/dev/tty*` console devices. The device `/dev/vcs0`, like the device `dev/tty0`, always refers to the currently selected VC.

The `/dev/vcs*` files provide a snapshot of what is in view on the corresponding VC. This snapshot contains no newlines because there are none actually on the screen; after all, a newline character just moves the cursor. To make the captured data into the kind of thing you usually see in text files or send to printers, you need to add newlines in the appropriate places. This can be done with `dd`:

```
$ dd cbs=80 conv=unblock </dev/vcs1 ¦ lpr
```

This command works only if the screen is 80 columns wide. This is not always true; the kernel can set up a different video mode at boot time, and you can use the `SVGATextMode` command to change it at any time.

You can overcome this problem by using the other set of devices, `/dev/vcsa*`. Reading from these devices gives a header, followed by the screen data with attribute bytes. The header consists of two bytes indicating the screen size (height first), followed by two bytes indicating the cursor position. The screen data is provided at a rate of two bytes per character cell, the first containing the attribute byte and the second containing the character data (as with `/dev/vcs*`). You can use this data to provide full-color screen dumps and so on. The following script uses `/dev/vcsa1` to determine the width of the VC and to get the conversion of `/dev/vcs1` right:

```
#! /bin/sh

# Insist on exactly one argument (the VC number to dump)
[ $# -eq 1 ] ¦¦ { echo "usage: $0 [vc-number]" >&2; exit 1; }

vc=$1 # Which VC to dump.
```

```
# Extract the VC's width from the second byte of the vcsa device.
# Th "unpack" expression extracts the value of the second
# character of the input (the vcsa device).
width='perl -e 'print unpack("x%C",<>);' < /dev/vcsa${vc}'

# Use dd(1) to convert the output now that we know the width.
dd cbs=${width} conv=unblock </dev/vcs${vc}
```

Summary

This chapter introduced the topics of character and block devices and filesystem administration and gave an overview of the hardware accessed via the special files in the directory /dev.

The difficulty in writing a chapter like this is that things are constantly changing. For example, soon we will be using `ext3` instead of `ext2` for the standard filesystem type. The various standards committees are trying to keep things in line enough so that consumers (you and I) can use this stuff, but at the same time allow flexibility for new and improved "stuff" can be designed. Many of the areas that the Linux community has focused on throughout the years have fallen under the section devices and filesystems. Therefore, as the standards switch from using `/dev/cua*` devices to using `/dev/ttyS*` devices, programmers are working their penguins to the wing tip trying to design easier tools to help remove some of the difficulty with using and configuring Linux. They have come a long way with tools such as `usermount` and `fsconf`, but they have a long way to go before they are finished.

You can find further information from the Linux Documentation Project material at `http://metalab.unc.edu/LDP`.

CHAPTER 19

Software Management

In This Chapter

This chapter covers the basics of getting started with Red Hat, Caldera OpenLinux, and Debian software administration. This refers to how to install, remove, and upgrade optional parts of the system, whether from the distribution vendor or elsewhere. Red Hat and Caldera both use the same underlying text-based package manager, the Red Hat Package Manager (`rpm`), whereas Debian uses `dpkg`.

This chapter begins with a tour of the file trees of the three systems, which are quite similar, but with important differences. Then the Red Hat Package Manager is discussed, followed by high-level RPM interface tools available in Red Hat and Caldera environments. Finally, the Debian package manager and associated graphical tools are covered.

Organization of the Linux File Hierarchy

As you may recall from Chapter 18, "Managing Filesystems," the UNIX and Linux environments use a single hierarchy of directories no matter how many separate physical volumes or partitions might be involved. This sets Linux apart from such operating systems as DEC VMS or Microsoft MS-DOS. The latter has lettered volume names (A:, C:, and so on). The primary or root partition is mounted at the root of the tree `/`, while other partitions are grafted onto the tree at *mount points*. It has become customary for certain basic directories, such as `/home`, to be placed in separate filesystems (*partitions*) if possible. The reasons for this vary quite a bit. Perhaps the most telling reasons are the following:

- Disk capacity—Disks can be extremely limited in storage capacity. Using a single disk for multiple purposes might consume too much space.
- Performance—The `root` directory has to be searched linearly every time any pathname in UNIX/Linux is accessed. If the `root` directory is cluttered, this will impede performance of the entire system.
- Backup—It's better to concentrate important and frequently changing data (such as the contents of user home directories) into a single place so that this relatively small amount of data can be backed up more often than the massive but seldom changing system data.
- User convenience—It's easier to find things if there are clear guidelines on where to look.

From the point of view of navigating the Linux file hierarchy, it is irrelevant (for the most part) whether a directory is a mount point (so that it is on a different disk than its parent directory), an ordinary subdirectory, or a *symbolic link* (pointer) elsewhere in the file tree.

However, a worthwhile holdover from the days of small disks has been well-established customs about the logical organization of UNIX-like filesystems. In fact, the accumulated wisdom of assorted UNIX and Linux administrators over the years has been distilled into something called the Filesystem Hierarchy Standard (FSSTND), which can be found at `http://www.pathname.com/fhs/`.

One of the objectives of the standard is continuity with the past, even when it's slightly counterintuitive. For instance, as you guess from its name, the important `/usr` top-level directory contained, among other things, user home directories on early UNIX systems. Now, however, `/usr` contains mostly system files, and user home directories are found in `/home`, except for the home directory of the user `root`, whose home directory must be in the root partition.

A feature of FSSTND is that the `root` directory (`/`) should be very clean and only hold the most essential items, preferably no files at all—only directories. The command `ls -p /` for a freshly installed Red Hat 6.0 system looks like the following:

```
bin/   dev/  home/  lost+found/  proc/  sbin/  usr/
boot/  etc/  lib/   mnt/         root/  tmp/   var/
```

For a freshly installed OpenLinux 2.2 system, it looks more like the following:

```
bin/   bru/  etc/   initrd/   lib/         mnt/  proc/  sbin/  usr/  vmlinuz
boot/  dev/  home/  install/  lost+found/  opt/  root/  tmp/   var/
```

The file `vmlinuz` in the OpenLinux root directory is the compressed Linux kernel. It is hard linked to `/boot/vmlinuz-2.2.5-modular`. Apart from this, both systems have no ordinary files in the `root` directory.

A typical Debian root directory listing is very similar, but contains empty directories /mnt, `/cdrom`, and `/floppy` as mount points for removable devices. Here is a sample:

```
bin   cdrom  floppy  home    lib         mnt   root  tmp  var      vmlinuz.old
boot  etc    ftp     initrd  lost+found  proc  sbin  usr  vmlinuz
```


The directory `lost+found` contains files salvaged by the `fsck` utility after an improper dismount or system shutdown/failure. If this directory is not present, salvaged files are simply deleted. Therefore, a directory of this name should be present at the root of every modifiable filesystem (except NFS and Samba partitions) or data may be lost. The directories `/boot`, `/dev`, and `/proc` have special roles.

The `/dev` directory normally contains only device nodes, with names like `/dev/hda` for the first IDE hard disk, although the `root` user can in fact create ordinary files there. So for instance, the following command generates a directory listing, and throws the output away by sending it to the device node `/dev/null`.

```
#ls -l >/dev/null
```

Sending output to `/dev/null` is a very standard technique to discard unwanted output. However, the following very similar command does *not* throw the output away, but creates an ordinary file called `/dev/nul`.

```
# ls -l > /dev/nul
```

Of course, such a command would normally be just a typing mistake, but the system would not issue an error message.

> **Tip**
>
> If the second command were executed by an ordinary user, then permission to create or modify `/dev/nul` would be denied and the error would be caught. This illustrates the principle never to use root privilege unless you really need it. The `su` (1) system command is available to temporarily acquire root privilege.

The `/proc` directory is best-described as a pseudo-filesystem, which is used to view and modify system information. For instance, each running process has a directory in this filesystem. Inside this directory is a lot of information about the process, including its entire memory state. Writing to this filesystem is generally not done directly but through various utilities.

Finally, `/boot` generally contains information used during the earliest stages of the system boot, such as the system kernel image itself.

In the early stages of the boot sequence, only the root filesystem is available, and therefore nothing outside the root partition should be necessary to start a session for the `root` user. This sometimes influences the choice of where to put files.

Essentials of `/bin` and `/sbin`

Most of the essential programs for using and maintaining Linux are stored in the `/bin` and `/sbin` directories. The `bin` in the names of these directories comes from the fact that executable programs are binary (not human readable) files.

The `/bin` directory most often holds the commonly used essential user programs:

- login
- Shells (`bash`, `ksh`, `csh`)
- File manipulation utilities (`cp`, `mv`, `rm`, `ln`, `tar`)

- Editors (ed, vi)
- Filesystem utilities (dd, df, mount, umount, sync)
- System utilities (uname, hostname, arch)

In addition to these types of programs, the /bin directory also contains GNU utilities such as gzip and gunzip.

The /sbin directory holds essential maintenance or system programs:

- fsck
- fdisk
- mkfs
- shutdown
- lilo
- init

The main difference between the programs stored in /bin and /sbin is that nearly all of the programs in /sbin are executable only by root (one exception is the ifconfig command). By default, the /sbin and /usr/sbin directories are not included in normal users' PATH.

Tip

Also, they are not automatically added when an ordinary user executes the su (superuser/substitute user) command. After a su command, you will see the # prompt, but many root-only commands will be apparently unavailable; they are simply not in your PATH. The following command will add these two directories to the beginning of your PATH for the duration of the current shell session:

```
#PATH="/sbin:/usr/sbin:${PATH}"
```


Configuration Files in /etc

The /etc directory is normally used to store system-wide configuration files required by many programs. Some of the important files in /etc are as follows:

- passwd
- shadow
- fstab
- hosts

- inittab
- motd
- profile
- shells
- services
- lilo.conf

The first two files in this list, /etc/passwd and /etc/shadow, define the authorized users for a system (which may be supplemented by NIS; see Chapter 14, "NIS: Network Information Service"). The /etc/passwd file contains all of the information about a user except the encrypted password, which is contained in /etc/shadow for security reasons. The password information in /etc/shadow was previously incorporated into /etc/passwd, which is a world-readable file. This was reasonably safe because the passwords are irreversibly encrypted. Nevertheless, a number of unfortunate incidents, especially the Morris Internet Worm, convinced people that even encrypted passwords should be kept in the separate file /etc/shadow, readable only by root.

Manually editing these files is not recommended. To add or change user information, use one of the tools described in Chapter 6, "System Service Tools," or the underlying command-line tools useradd(8), userdel(8), and usermod(8), as described in Appendix B and the on-line manual pages

The next file on the list, /etc/fstab, contains a list of devices the system knows how to mount automatically. This file is known as the filesystem table. A line from this file looks something like the following:

```
/dev/sdb3            /                  ext2    defaults        1 1
/dev/sdb7            /boot              ext2    defaults        1 2
/dev/sda5            swap               swap    defaults        0 0
/dev/sda6            swap               swap    defaults        0 0
/dev/sda7            swap               swap    defaults        0 0
/dev/sdb5            swap               swap    defaults        0 0
/dev/sdb6            swap               swap    defaults        0 0
/dev/fd0             /mnt/floppy        ext2    noauto          0 0
/dev/cdrom           /mnt/cdrom         iso9660 noauto,ro       0 0
none                 /proc              proc    defaults        0 0
none                 /dev/pts           devpts  mode=0622       0 0
```

Each line defines a complete entry, always beginning with the root filesystem. The entries are split into fields, separated by whitespace, as with many other Linux and UNIX configuration files. For the first entry, the first field (/dev/sdb3) indicates the device to mount (in this case the third partition on my second SCSI hard disk (/dev/sdb). The second part (/) indicates the *mount point*—where to mount the device in the filename hierarchy. Next, the field ext2 indicates what type of filesystem the device contains, while the rest of the line contains mount options, whose meaning depends on the particular type of filesystem being mounted. In the case of `ext2` entries, the numbers following the word `defaults` indicate the priorities for performing the potentially time-consuming file system check (`fsck`) during system boot. The option `noauto` means not to mount the system automatically during system boot. This option is important for removable media, such as floppy disks and CD-ROMs. See the `mount` command's man page for further details.

This `/etc/fstab` table also contains five swap entries because this machine has two CPUs and a respectable amount of memory. Previous Linux kernels had a maximum effective swap partition size of 128MB, and I need 640MB of swap space.

A minimal `/etc/fstab` contains three entries: one for the root (only) partition, one swap partition, and an entry for the `/proc` pseudo-filesystem.

On many systems, `/etc/fstab` also contains entries for CD-ROMs, floppy disks, Zip disks, and other mountable media. To add, delete, or change mount information, use a high-level tool such as Red Hat's `linuxconf` or Caldera's `COAS`, as described in Chapter 6. Alternatively, you can edit the file directly. With some distributions, such as Debian, this is the preferred—and sometimes only—way to make changes.

The file `/etc/hosts` contains a list of IP addresses and the corresponding hostnames (and aliases). This list is used to resolve the IP address of a machine when its name is given. A sample entry might look like the following:

```
# IP address     the hostname          host alias
192.168.1.34     presario.home.org     presario
```

Note

The extremely important file `/etc/inittab`, which controls the entire operation of the Linux system from just after the kernel boot to just before shutdown, is described in detail in Chapter 6.

`/etc/motd` is the file in which the system administrator puts the *m*essage *o*f *t*he *d*ay (hence the `motd`). Usually it contains information related to the system, such as scheduled downtime or upgrades of software, but it can contain anything. The contents of this file are usually displayed at login.

/etc/profile is the default initialization file for users whose shell is either sh, ksh, or bash (the default shell for Red Hat, Debian, and Caldera OpenLinux). Mostly it is used for setting variables such as PATH and PS1, along with such things as the initial user permissions mask (see the umask man page and the discussion of the umask command in the bash documentation). The /etc/profile file is not meant to be used in place of personal initialization files and should be kept small because it is used by scripts as well as users.

The file /etc/shells also pertains to shells. It is a list of "approved" shells for users. One of its primary uses is to prevent people from accidentally changing their shells to something unusable.

/etc/services contains a list of the symbolic names of well-known ports used by various system services, and is closely related to /etc/protocols which contains symbolic names of various network protocols. The entries will look something like the following:

```
telnet          23/tcp
ntalk           518/udp
```

Each line constitutes an entry. The first field is the name of the service; the second field, is divided into two subfields by a /, into the port number and the protocol. Additional information may appear, but it is ignored, except by humans. The first line above shows the format for the telnet service, which listens on tcp port 23. The second line indicates that the ntalk chat service listens on udp port 518. The server programs that implement these services typically do not hard-code the numeric ports they listen on, but interrogate /etc/services. This is particularly true for the super-server inetd. While this file sets port numbers for "well-behaved" applications, the presence of an entry in this file does not necessarily mean that any actual implementation of the service exists on the system or is currently running. Nor does it prevent other applications from grabbing the port for other purposes.

The last file on the list is /etc/lilo.conf. This file contains a description of the system's behavior at boot time, along with a list of all of the bootable images on the system.

Two important subdirectories are also in /etc: X11 and rc.d.

On Debian systems and classic System V UNIX systems (such as Solaris), there is no rc.d directory; instead directories such as rc2.d or init.d are found directly in the /etc directory instead of in rc.d. For instance, whereas RedHat and OpenLinux have /etc/rc.d/init.d, Debian and Solaris have /etc/init.d. The purpose of the directory in each instance is identical. In RedHat and OpenLinux, the /etc/init.d and the various /etc/rcX.d directories were consolidated into the single /etc/rc.d directory to reduce the somewhat notorious clutter in /etc, which is a dumping ground for practically anything that doesn't belong anywhere else.

The /etc/X11 subdirectory contains the configuration files for the X server, X display managers (such as xdm, gdm, and kdm), and the various window managers (such as fvwm2, fvwm, mwm, and twm). Most window manager packages add their configuration files into a directory located under /etc/X11. OpenLinux looks for the crucial XFree86 file XF86Config in /etc instead of in /etc/X11. The display and window managers themselves are generally located elsewhere; only their configurations are stored in /etc/X11. User-specific configuration is stored in various hidden directories and files in their home directories. For more information on display managers see Chapter 4, "The X Window System," and for more information on window managers, see Chapter 5, "Window Managers."

The rc.d subdirectory contains subdirectories with initialization scripts that are run when Linux is loaded or shut down. Some of the scripts contain commands to load modules; others handle general boot behavior. These directories are described in more detail in Chapter 6.

As noted above, Debian has no /etc/rc.d directory, but it *does* have directories directly under /etc with identical names and purposes to those under /etc/rc.d in Red Hat and OpenLinux systems.

In addition to the files discussed, many other configuration files are found in the /etc directory, such as smb.conf (see Chapter 16, "Samba") or mailcap (see the metamail(1) manual page). There has been a trend to move these files to subdirectories or out of /etc completely. For instance, the Apache Web server uses multiple configuration files, which the Red Hat 6 version of Apache keeps in the directory /etc/httpd/conf (see Chapter 11, "Apache Server"). In addition, sometimes configuration files are actually kept elsewhere, but a symbolic link to them is placed in /etc.

/home

The /home directory is where all home directories for all users on a system are stored. This includes home directories for actual users (people) and for users such as ftp or httpd.

/mnt

By convention, the /mnt directory is the directory under which other filesystems—such as DOS, network-mounted NFS filesystems, or removable media such as CD-ROMs, floppy disks, Zip disks, or Jaz disks—are mounted. Sometimes the /mnt directory contains a number of subdirectories, each of which is a mount point for a particular device. The /mnt directory on my Red Hat 6.0 system looks like the following:

```
caldera/  cdrom/  floppy/
```

In a system with multiple CD-ROM drives, the names might be modified to include cdrom0, cdrom1, and so on. By using subdirectories under /mnt to house all of your mounted media, you keep the / directory clean. Judicious use of symbolic links may be very useful to disguise the actual mount point of disks, so that for instance, /home/smith is really /mnt/home/smith.

> **Note**
>
> If something is mounted onto a directory inside /mnt and then something else is mounted on /mnt, this is not an error, but the directories inside /mnt will be hidden by those from the newly mounted device until it is unmounted (using the umount command), after which they will reappear!

/tmp

The /tmp and /var directories are used to hold temporary files or files with constantly varying content.

The /tmp directory is usually a dumping ground for files that only need to be used briefly and can be deleted at any time. It usually is quite unstructured. On a multi-user system, most users abide by the convention of creating a personal directory (given the same as their username) in /tmp for storing their temporary files. The most common use of /tmp (other than as a location for throwaway files) is as a starting point for building and installing programs.

Some versions of UNIX used to place logic in the boot sequence to clean out /tmp every time a system was booted. This is no longer common, but some systems do have periodic cron jobs (see Chapter 22, “Automating Tasks”). These discard items in /tmp and /usr/tmp which have not been accessed or modified recently, with the term *recently* at the discretion of the local site administrator.

/var

The /var directory is used by various core system services to store constantly changing, and sometimes constantly growing files.

A prime example is the spool subdirectory, which contains various types of queues, such as the unsent mail queue, the print job queue, pending batch and scheduled jobs, and UUCP traffic. Another important subdirectory is /var/run, which contains the process IDs of various running system services. It is sometimes better to look in /var/run than to fish through the process table if you’re in a hurry to kill a rogue process.

Finally, all Linux users should become familiar with the purpose of /var/log and examine its contents from time to time. This directory, and various subdirectories thereof, contain various system logs—especially syslog, which can grow without bound over time. With today's huge disks, this isn't the problem it used to be, but it is still a good idea to look in this area once in a while for uncontrolled file growth. Apache Web server logs are kept, by default, in /var/log/httpd.

Here's a ls -p /var/log listing from a typical Red Hat system:

```
boot.log  htmlaccess.log  maillog.1    samba/        spooler    xferlog
cron      httpd/          messages     secure        spooler.1  xferlog.1
cron.1    lastlog         messages.1   secure.1      uucp/
dmesg     maillog         netconf.log  sendmail.st   wtmp
```

Of these files, the following are very helpful when attempting to diagnose system problems:

- dmesg contains kernel messages displayed when the system was last booted.
- messages contains all system messages since the system was first booted.

For example, one helpful way to diagnose problems, such as establishing a Point-to-Point Protocol connection, is to use the tail command to continuously display the last few lines of /var/log/messages:

```
# tail -f /var/log/messages
```

/usr

By convention, the /usr directory is where most programs and files directly relating to users of the system are stored. It is in some ways a mini-version of the / directory. The /usr directory on my system looks like this:

```
X11R6/    doc/                 i386-redhat-linux/  lib/      sbin/
bin/      etc/                 i486-linux-libc5/   libexec/  share/
cgi-bin/  games/               include/            local/    src/
dict/     i386-glibc20-linux/  info/               man/      tmp@
```

The contents of several of these directories are briefly described in the following paragraphs.

The /usr/bin and /usr/sbin directories hold the vast majority of the executables available on a system. The function and type of the executables placed into these directories follow the same general convention as for /bin and /sbin. However, unless you are logged in as the root operator, you won't often be able to run commands from the /usr/sbin or /sbin directories. These programs might act on important system files.

The /usr/X11 and /usr/X11R6 directories and subdirectories contain nearly all of the X Window-related files, such as man pages, libraries, and executables. Red Hat Linux systems contain only /usr/X11R6, the sixth revision of the X Window version 11, although for some unknown reason, Red Hat Linux 6.0 has the majority of the KDE and GNOME clients installed under /usr/bin.

The /usr/local directory is where local programs, man pages, and libraries are installed. At many sites, most of the directories in /usr are kept the same on every computer, but anything that needs to be installed on a particular machine is placed in /usr/local, thus identifying these files as local files and making maintenance of large numbers of systems easier.

Finally, one of the most useful directories under /usr is /usr/dict, where the local dictionary for the system, called /usr/dict/words, is stored. Most versions of /usr/dict/words contain about 45,000 words, but some can be as large as 100,000 or more. In Red Hat Linux, the words file is a symbolic link to the file linux.words. The main dictionary for Red Hat's default spelling checker, ispell, resides under the /usr/lib/ispell directory, but you can force ispell to use /usr/dict/words with the -l command-line option.

/opt

The /opt subdirectory is designed to hold optional packages. This directory is well-populated in commercial versions of UNIX such as Solaris or SCO UnixWare. A basic install of Red Hat or Debian does not have this directory, whereas Caldera puts a few products there. This is where fully commercial products, such as Star Office or WordPerfect, belong. However, practices vary.

Consider some examples.

Caldera OpenLinux puts the KDE in /opt/kde, whereas Red Hat puts it in /usr/share/apps/kde.

OpenLinux puts Netscape Communicator in /opt/netscape/communicator, whereas Red Hat puts it in /usr/bin. For convenience, Caldera has a symbolic link at /usr/bin/netscape, which points to /opt/netscape/communicator/netscape, whereas Red Hat has a script at /usr/bin/netscape to hunt down Netscape's real hiding place at run-time.

In general, each directory in /opt should be of the form vendor/product, with other directories below that with names like bin (for the principal executables), man (for the manual pages in troff/groff format), doc (for other forms of documentation), and lib (for libraries and control files). This concentrates all files from a single vendor into a single directory. In practice, the *vendor* part is frequently dropped, as in Caldera's name for the KDE directory.

The Red Hat Package Manager (RPM)

One of the most powerful and innovative utilities available in Red Hat Linux is RPM, the Red Hat Package Manager. It can be used to install, uninstall, upgrade, query, verify, and build software packages. The Red Hat Package Manager has been adopted by other Linux and UNIX vendors, including Caldera, so this section is just as applicable to OpenLinux as to Red Hat Linux installation. Although many high-level software installation and management tools exist (including some described later in this chapter), they are all interfaces to RPM, either curses or X Windows-based. Multiple high-level interfaces don't cause any trouble; multiple low-level tools can, however, because they build separate databases that are opaque to each other.

A software package built with RPM is an archive of files and some associated information, such as a name, a version, and a description. Following are a few of the advantages of RPM packages over the traditional `tar.gz` method of software distribution:

- The presence of necessary other software packages can be checked.
- A permanent record is kept of all installation and removal activity.
- The installation can be coupled with an install script to properly install all the various pieces of the software in common directories.
- The removal of the software can be blocked pending the removal of other software that depends on it.
- Installation will be prevented (without override action) if a later version of a package is already installed.
- A new version of the software can be installed without losing site-specific customization files.
- A software package that installs files in several locations can be cleanly removed.
- After installation, a package can be verified to be in working order.
- Information about what package a file belongs to can be easily obtained.
- Installation can be made dependent upon a particular kernel version or other packages. Unfortunately, this can also have an adverse cascade effect. For instance, an RPM for `egcs` and a different Linux distribution may be extremely difficult to use.

A minor caveat to using RPM is that its installation database can be sizable, although this is scarcely a problem with today's enormous disk drives. The RPM database is located in `/var/lib/rpm`, at least on Red Hat and Caldera systems.

RPM has command options for installing a software package wherever you want, provided that the packager of the software has provided this flexibility. All too often, however, the packager has taken the easy way out and forbidden this.

RPM also has provision for using a directory as the `root` directory for the purposes of installation. This is done using the `chroot` utility, and you should refer to both the RPM documentation and the chroot man page for details. The main application is for building an embedded `root` filesystem for a new Linux system while it is temporarily mounted somewhere on your development system. Embedded systems have no installation media (floppy disks, network cards, CD-ROMs) or even a keyboard, and so the only way to install software is to temporarily mount the disk on another system.

In addition to these features, RPM is available for many flavors of Linux and UNIX, making it one of the emerging utilities for distributing software packages. Red Hat Linux 6.0 includes version 3.0 of the `rpm` command.

The majority of the `rpm` command's files, which includes an indexed database of installed software, are found under the `/var/lib/rpm` directory. This directory contains these files:

```
conflictsindex.rpm  nameindex.rpm      requiredby.rpm
fileindex.rpm       packages.rpm       triggerindex.rpm
groupindex.rpm      providesindex.rpm
```

The largest of these files, `packages.rpm`, contains a database of information regarding installed packages, and may grow to more than 12MB in a large system. Other components of the `rpm` system are found under the `/usr/lib/rpm` directory, which contains these files:

```
config.guess      find-lang.sh  freshen.sh  mkinstalldirs
config.sub       find-provides getpo.sh    rpmpopt
convertrpmrc.sh  find-requires macros      rpmrc
```

This directory contains utility shell scripts, an empty directory of macros, and two systemwide configuration files, `rpmopt` and `rpmrc`. The current configuration options may be displayed by using the `--showrc` command-line option:

```
# rpm --showrc
```

Major Modes and Common Options

The major modes in which RPM can be run are the following:

- Install (`rpm -i`)
- Uninstall (`rpm -e`)
- Query (`rpm -q`)
- Verify (`rpm -V`)

The options for invoking the major modes are given in parentheses. These major modes are covered in detail in subsequent sections.

All of these major modes understand the following options:

`-vv`	Prints out all debugging information; useful to see what exactly RPM is doing
`--quiet`	Prints out very little information, only error messages

In addition to these, a few "minor" modes are useful. These are as follows:

Version (`rpm --version`)

Help (`rpm --help`)

Showrc (`rpm --showrc`)

Rebuilddb (`rpm --rebuilddb`)

The `Version` mode is invoked as follows:

```
# rpm –version
```

The mode prints out a line containing version information, similar to this:

```
RPM version 3.0
```

The `Help` mode prints out an extensive help message and is invoked as follows:

```
# rpm –help
```

Because the message is long, it is handy to have a large `xterm` or to pipe the output to `more`. To get a shorter help message, just type this:

```
# rpm
```

This prints out a usage message. The `Showrc` mode prints out a list of variables that can be set in the files `/usr/lib/rpm/rpmrc` and `$HOME/.rpmrc`.

```
# rpm –showrc
```

The default values are adequate for most installations.

The `Rebuilddb` option is used to rebuild the database RPM uses to keep track of which packages are installed on a system. It is invoked as follows:

```
# rpm –rebuilddb
```

The database files are usually stored in `/var/lib/rpm/`. In most cases, the database files do not need to be rebuilt very often.

Installing Packages

One of the major uses of RPM is installing software packages. The general syntax of an `rpm` install command is as follows:

```
rpm -i [options] [packages]
```

`options` can be one of the common options given earlier or one of the install options covered in the following list, and *`packages`* is the name of one or more RPM package files. Some of the install options are as follows:

`-v`	Prints out what RPM is doing.
`-h` or `--hash`	Prints out 50 hash marks (#) as the package is installed.
`--percent`	Prints out percentages as files are extracted from the package.
`--test`	Goes through a package install, but does not install anything; mainly used to catch conflicts.
`--excludedocs`	Prevents the installation of files marked as documentation, such as man pages.
`--includedocs`	Forces files marked as documentation to be installed; this is the default.
`--nodeps`	No dependency checks are performed before installing a package.
`--replacefiles`	Allows for installed files to be replaced with files from the package being installed.
`--replacepkgs`	Allows for installed packages to be replaced with the packages being installed.
`--oldpackage`	Allows for a newer version of an installed package to be replaced with an older version.
`--noscripts`	Used in dire emergencies to prevent the running of the package-specific installation or removal scripts. This usually means the package isn't installed properly, but is at least deposited on the disk.
`--force`	Forces a package to be installed.

When giving options to RPM, regardless of the mode, all of the single-letter options can be lumped together in one block. For example, the first command given here is equivalent to the second:

```
# rpm -i -v -h kernel-2.2.5-15.i386.rpm
```

```
# rpm -ivh kernel-2.2.5-15.i386.rpm
```

All options starting with `--` must be given separately, however.

Now look at a couple of examples of installing RPM packages. The first example installs enscript, a program for generating postscript versions of text files. The Red Hat 6.0 CD provides the following package file for `enscript`:

```
enscript-1.6.1-8.i386.rpm
```

This package follows the standard naming convention for RPM packages, which is this:

```
name-version-release.arch.rpm
```

name is the package's name, *version* is the package's version, *release* is the package's release level, *arch* is the hardware architecture the package is for, and `rpm` is the default extension. This naming scheme is quite handy because some of the essential information about a particular package can be determined from just looking at its name.

For the `enscript` package, say you are installing `enscript` version 1.6,1, release 8, for a computer with the i386 architecture. Go ahead and install this package. With the Red Hat CD-ROM on `/mnt/cdrom`, the package you want is `/mnt/cdrom/RedHat/RPMS/enscript-1.6.1-8.i386.rpm`.

First, **cd** into the directory containing the archive, which is `/mnt/cdrom/RedHat/RPMS` when the Red Hat CD is mounted in the usual place. To install `enscript`, type the following at the prompt (#):

```
# rpm -ivh  enscript-1.6.1-8.i386.rpm
```

As the package is installed, the output looks like the following:

```
enscript                        ################
```

The `h` option above makes `rpm` generate the hash marks as a sign of progress (50 of them when the install is finished). Otherwise, it works silently. If you try to install this package as a user other than `root`, an error similar to the following is generated:

```
failed to open //var/lib/rpm/packages.rpm
error: cannot open //var/lib/rpm/packages.rpm
```

This is for security reasons. Normally, no other user except `root` has write access to the system's `rpm` database.

If you try to install a package already installed on your system, you will get the following (or a similar) error:

```
error: package enscript-1.6.1-8 is already installed
```

To install this package, use the `--replacepkgs` option:

```
# rpm -ivh –replacepkgs  enscript-1.6.1-8.i386.rpm
```

Occasionally, the files install by one package conflict with the files of a previously installed package. This is illustrated by considering a second example, trying to install VIM 4.5-2 when VIM 4.2-0 is already installed if you have vim version 4.2 installed:

```
/bin/vim conflicts with file from vim-4.2-8
/usr/share/vim/vim_tips.txt conflicts with file from vim-4.2-8
error: vim-4.5-2.i386.rpm cannot be installed
```

If you want to install these files anyway, the `--replacefiles` option can be added to the command. Note: VIM has since been greatly expanded, and is now divided into 4 separate packages.

A dependency conflict is sometimes encountered when a package you are installing requires certain other packages to function correctly. Although it is usually not a good idea to ignore dependency problems, using the `--nodeps` option causes RPM to ignore these errors and install the package.

Sometimes even this is not sufficient, because the install script may still detect the absence of needed resources (such as shared libraries) and block the installation. This is a frequent occurrence when installing RPM's built for a different environment. This sometimes creates an insurmountable obstacle. Package A cannot be installed without Package B. Package B cannot be installed because it conflicts with package C. By ignoring dependencies, `rpm` can be convinced to at least try to install Package A, but the install script of Package A may block the install. In cases like this, the `--noscripts` option (see above) may be of some use but will usually leave some degree of chaos to be cleaned up by hand.

Upgrading Packages

RPM's `Upgrade` mode provides an easy way to upgrade existing software packages to newer versions. `Upgrade` mode is similar to `Install` mode:

```
rpm -U [options] [packages]
```

`options` can be any of the install options or any of the general options.

Here is an example of how to upgrade packages. On my system I am currently running `emacs` version 19.31, but I want to upgrade to the newer `emacs` version 19.34. To upgrade, I use the following command:

```
# rpm -Uvh emacs-19.34-4.i386.rpm
```

The Upgrade mode is a combination of two operations, uninstall and install. First, RPM uninstalls any older versions of the requested package, and then it installs the newer version. If an older version of the package does not exist, RPM simply installs the requested package.

An additional advantage of using upgrade over manually installing and uninstalling is that upgrade automatically saves configuration files. For these reasons, some people prefer to use upgrade rather than install for all package installations.

Uninstalling Packages

RPM's Uninstall mode provides for a clean method of removing files belonging to a software package from many locations.

Many packages install files in /etc, /usr, and /lib, so removing a package can be confusing. An entire package can be removed, however, with RPM:

```
rpm -e [options] [package]
```

options is one of the options listed later in this section, and *package* is the name of the package to be removed. For example, if I want to remove the package for DOSEMU, the command is as follows:

```
# rpm -e dosemu
```

The name specified here for the package is just the name of the package, not the name of the file that was used to install the package. Assume I had asked for this:

```
# rpm -e dosemu-0.99.10-4.i386.rpm
```

The following error would have been generated:

```
package dosemu-0.99.10-4.i386.rpm is not installed
```

Another common error encountered while trying to uninstall packages is a dependency error when a package that is being uninstalled has files required by another package. For example, when I try to remove DOSEMU from my system, I get the following error:

```
removing these packages would break dependencies:
dosemu = 0.99.10 is needed by dosemu-freedos-0.99.10-4
dosemu = 0.99.10 is needed by xdosemu-0.99.10-4
```

This means the package XDOSEMU will not function properly if the package DOSEMU is removed. If I still want to remove this package, I can give RPM the --nodeps option to make it ignore dependency errors.

The other useful option is the --test option, which causes RPM to go through the motions of removing a package without actually removing anything. Usually there is no output from an uninstall, so the -vv option is given along with the --test option to see what would happen during an uninstall. For example, the given input (in bold) produces the following output on my system:

```
# rpm -e -vv --test xdosemu

D: opening database mode 0x0 in //var/lib/rpm/
D: will remove files test = 1
D:     file: /usr/man/man1/xtermdos.1 action: remove
D:     file: /usr/man/man1/xdos.1 action: remove
D:     file: /usr/bin/xtermdos action: remove
D:     file: /usr/bin/xdos action: remove
D:     file: /usr/X11R6/lib/X11/fonts/misc/vga.pcf action: remove
D: removing database entry
```

As you can see, the files that would have been removed are clearly indicated in the output.

Querying Packages

The `Query` mode in RPM allows for determining the various attributes of packages. The basic syntax for querying packages is this:

```
rpm -q [options] [packages]
```

`options` is one or more of the query options listed later in this section. The most basic query is one similar to this:

```
# rpm -q kernel
```

On my system, this prints out the following line for the kernel package:

```
kernel-2.2.5-15
```

In a manner similar to `uninstall`, RPM's `Query` mode uses the name of the package, not the name of the file in which the package came.

Now for a few more sample queries: You can use the `-l` option if you want to get a list of all files "owned" by the kernel package:

```
# rpm -ql kernel
```

This outputs the following (partial) list of files on my system:

```
/boot/System.map-2.2.5-15
/boot/module-info-2.2.5-15
/boot/vmlinux-2.2.5-15
/boot/vmlinuz-2.2.5-15
/lib/modules
/lib/modules/2.2.5-15
/lib/modules/2.2.5-15/.rhkmvtag
...
```

Not all the output is shown here (as the kernel package also owns all the installed kernel modules). In addition to getting a list of the files, you can determine their state by using the -s option:

```
# rpm -qs kernel
```

This option gives the following information about the state of files in my kernel package:

```
normal        /boot/System.map-2.2.5-15
normal        /boot/module-info-2.2.5-15
normal        /boot/vmlinux-2.2.5-15
normal        /boot/vmlinuz-2.2.5-15
normal        /lib/modules
normal        /lib/modules/2.2.5-15
normal        /lib/modules/2.2.5-15/.rhkmvtag
```

If any of these files reported a state of `missing`, there would probably be problems with the package.

In addition to the state of the files in a package, the documentation files and the configuration files can be listed. To list the documentation that comes with the `efax` package, use the following:

```
# rpm -qd efax
```

This produces the following list:

```
/usr/doc/efax-0.8a/COPYING
/usr/doc/efax-0.8a/README
/usr/man/man1/efax.1
/usr/man/man1/efix.1
/usr/man/man1/fax.1
```

To get the configuration files for the same package, you use the following query:

```
# rpm -qc efax
```

This results in the following list:

```
/usr/bin/fax
```

In addition to these queries, complete information about a package can be determined by using the `info` option. For example, this bold input gives the following information about the installed kernel package:

```
# rpm -qi kernel
Name        : kernel                         Relocations: (not relocateable)
Version     : 2.2.5                               Vendor: Red Hat Software
Release     : 15                              Build Date: Mon Apr 19 22:39:52 1999
Install date: Sat May  8 07:38:34 1999        Build Host: porky.devel.redhat.com
```

```
Group       : System Environment/Kernel     Source RPM: kernel-2.2.5-15.src.rpm
Size        : 9947601                          License: GPL
Packager    : Red Hat Software <http://developer.redhat.com/bugzilla>
Summary     : The Linux kernel (the core of the Linux operating system).
Description :
The kernel package contains the Linux kernel (vmlinuz), the core of your
Red Hat Linux operating system.  The kernel handles the basic functions
of the operating system:  memory allocation, process allocation, device
input and output, etc.
```

Here is a summary of the query options:

`-l`	Lists all files in a package
`-s`	Lists the state of files in a package
`-d`	Lists all files in a package that are marked as documentation
`-c`	Lists all files in a package that are marked as configuration
`-i`	Lists the complete information for a package

If any of these options (except `-i`) are given along with a `-v` option, the files are listed in `ls -l` format. Take this command line as an example:

```
# rpm -qlv enscript
```

It outputs the following, in part:

```
# ¦ more
-rw-r--r--     root     root       4975 Mar 29 15:20 /etc/enscript.cfg
-rwxr-xr-x     root     root       4631 Mar 29 15:20 /usr/bin/diffpp
-rwxr-xr-x     root     root     166168 Mar 29 15:20 /usr/bin/enscript
-rwxr-xr-x     root     root      61096 Mar 29 15:20 /usr/bin/mkafmmap
-rwxr-xr-x     root     root     166168 Mar 29 15:20 /usr/bin/nenscript
-rwxr-xr-x     root     root        104 Mar 29 15:20 /usr/bin/over
-rwxr-xr-x     root     root       2006 Mar 29 15:20 /usr/bin/sliceprint
-rwxr-xr-x     root     root      74940 Mar 29 15:20 /usr/bin/states
drwxr-xr-x     root     root       1024 Mar 29 15:20 /usr/doc/enscript-1.6.1
```

In addition to the preceding, RPM understands the following query options:

`-a`	Lists all installed packages
`-f` *`file`*	Lists the package that owns the specified file
`-p` *`package`*	Lists the package name of the specified package

Verifying Packages

Verifying packages is an easy way to determine any problems with an installation. In verification mode, RPM compares information about an installed package against information about the original package, which is stored in the package database at install time.

The basic syntax for verifying a package is as follows:

```
rpm -V [package]
```

If a package is verified correctly, RPM does not output anything. If RPM detects a difference between the installed package and the database record, it outputs an 8-character string, in which tests that fail are represented by a single character and tests that pass are represented by a period (.). The characters for failed tests are as follows:

Character	*Failed Test*
5	MD5 Sum
S	File size
L	Symlink
T	Mtime
D	Device
U	User
G	Group
M	Mode (permissions and file type)

For example, assume you verify the `bash` package on my system by using this code:

```
# rpm -V bash
```

It fails as follows:

```
.M..L...   /bin/bash
....L...   /bin/sh
```

This indicates that the size of my `bash` is different from the information stored in the database. This is okay on my system because I have recompiled `bash`.

In addition, you can use the query option `-f` to verify a package containing a particular file, which is helpful when diagnosing problems with programs. For example, if `ksh` is behaving peculiarly, the following will verify that the package `ksh` came in:

```
# rpm -Vf /bin/ksh
```

If any of the tests fail, you will be closer to understanding the source of the problems.

Red Hat Software Tools

Red Hat's `rpm` is a powerful but text-based tool. Since there should only be one central software installation manager, various graphical front ends for RPM have been developed.

The most common way users interacted with RPM using previous versions of Red Hat Linux was with `glint`. However, starting with Red Hat 6.0, `glint` has been replaced with another X-based interface for RPM—`gnorpm`—that like `glint` requires X11, but allows for installing, uninstalling, querying, and verifying packages via a graphical "file manager" interface (with GNOME enhancements).

`gnorpm` is accessible from the command line of an X11 terminal window or the GNOME panel's System menu. To launch `gnorpm` from the command line, simply type this:

```
# gnorpm
```

The main window will appear, as shown in Figure 19.1. Unlike `glint`, `gnorpm` accepts numerous command-line options (including X Toolkit geometry settings), with several options similar to the `rpm` command.

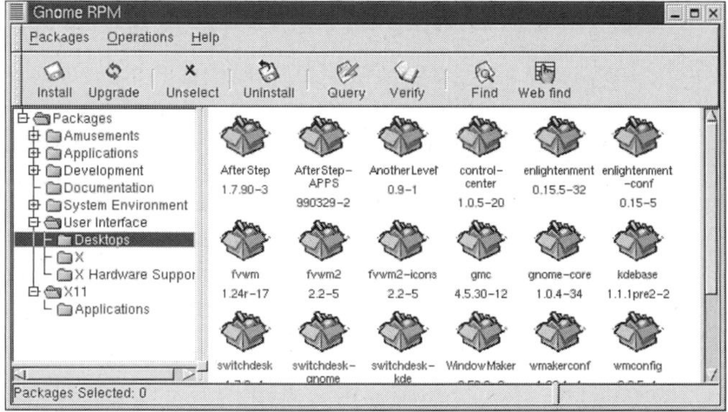

FIGURE 19.1
The primary `gnorpm` window offers point-and-click convenience for system software management.

These options include queries (`-q` or `--query`), installation (`-i` or `--install`), and upgrading (`-U or --upgrade`). You can view a quick summary of available options by using the `-?` or `--help` option:

```
# gnorpm --help
```

Help is also available by clicking the Help menu item (as shown in Figure 19.1).

From the main `gnorpm` window, packages can be selected and queried, verified, uninstalled, or installed. To install a package, click the Install toolbar button. An Install dialog box will appear. To add packages to install, click the Install dialog box's Add button. An Add Packages dialog box appears (as shown in Figure 19.2). Next, navigate to the directory where the `.rpm` file or files are located, click the name of the `.rpm` file in the Files list, and click the Add Packages's Add button. The name of the `.rpm` file will appear in the Install dialog box. You can then query, install, or verify the PGP signature of the `.rpm` file (provided you have PGP installed).

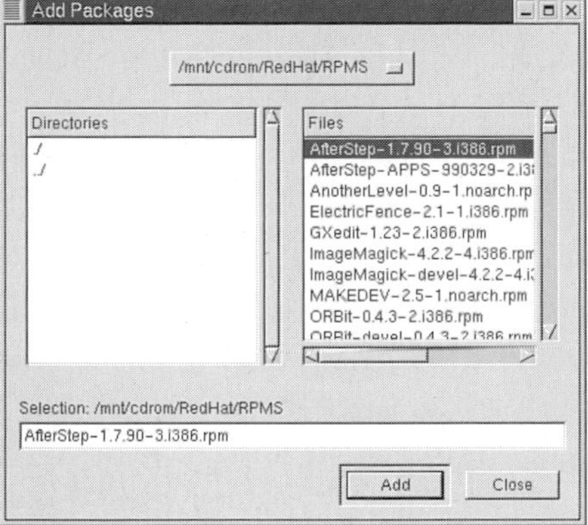

FIGURE 19.2
Packages to be installed must be added to the Install dialog box through the Add Packages dialog box.

If you click the Query button, a dialog box (as shown in Figure 19.3) provides details about the package, such as a description and list of files to be installed. You can then click an Install, Upgrade, Check Sig, or Close button.

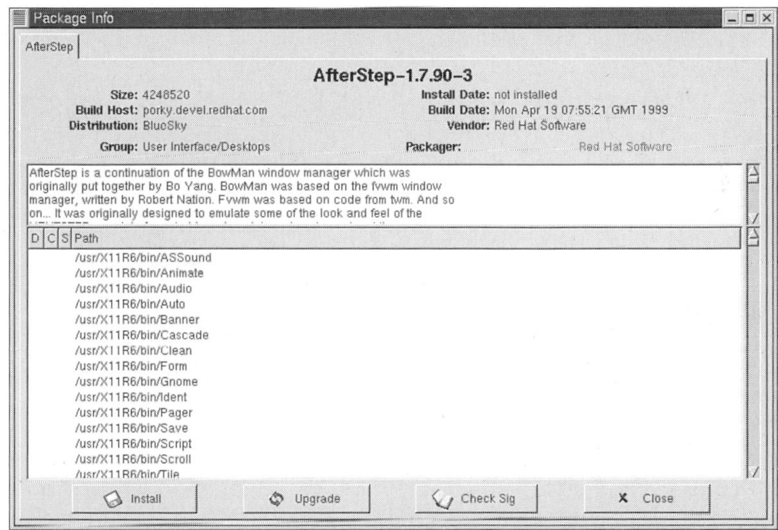

FIGURE 19.3
The Package Info dialog box shows RPM query information about a package, and offers installation, upgrade, and further query information.

Default directories containing `.rpm` files—such as the path `/mnt/cdrom/RedHat/RPMS` for a mounted Red Hat Linux 6.0 CD-ROM—may be specified through the Preferences menu item of `gnorpm`'s Operations menu. Click Preferences; a Preferences dialog box will appear. Next, click the Interface tab and click the Browse button. An RpmPath dialog box will appear (as shown in Figure 19.4), through which you can browse your file system. Navigate to the `.rpm` file directory. When finished, click OK, then click the OK button in the Preferences dialog box to set the default directory. `gnorpm` will use the default path setting until you change it.

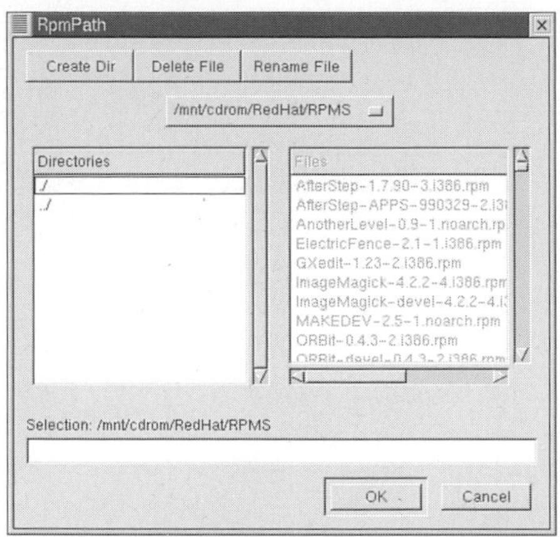

FIGURE 19.4
You can set the default location of .rpm files through gnorpm's Preferences dialog box.

The gnorpm client also takes advantage of the network download capability built in to the rpm command. If you have an active Internet connection, you can search the Web and then install packages via FTP by using gnorpm's Web Find menu. According to the default Rpmfind setting in gnorpm's Preferences, package information is retrieved from a metadata server located at http://www.redhat.com/RDF. The default download location is set to the path /root/rpms. (Obviously you should run gnorpm as root when searching, downloading, installing, or upgrading packages despite the stern warning that GNOME gives when you attempt to do so.) Any preference changes will be saved in the file gnorpmrc under the .gnome directory in your homedirectory.

Caldera OpenLinux Tools

The Caldera OpenLinux distribution contains three graphical tools that provide front ends to the Red Hat Package Manager and, in the case of kpackage, to the Debian package manager as well, although the Debian package manager does not ship with OpenLinux 2.2.

Each of these tools has its strengths and weaknesses. The COAS tool seems to be Caldera's future, and with some caveats, is the easiest to use, at least with the packages on the first (main) OpenLinux CD-ROM. In particular, COAS can automatically mount a CD-ROM for you; kpackage cannot. On the other hand, COAS only looks in one installation source at a time, whereas kpackage can take a lengthy list of both RPM and DPM sources.

In the past, the principal software installation tool for Caldera was lisa, but that part of lisa seems nonfunctional at the time of this writing. Caldera will undoubtedly repair this at some point and make the updates available on its Web site, but COAS and kpackage are better tools. (See Chapter 6 about lisa updates.)

COAS

As explained in Chapter 6, COAS is being developed in cooperation with Caldera as a multimodal universal administration framework for Linux. The present discussion concentrates on final COAS Loadable Administration Module: software, meaning software installation, updating, and removal. At its present development stage, the COAS software module is only useful for examining software already installed and for browsing the OpenLinux CD-ROM. For this one task, however, it is quite useful, and definitely a worthy alternative to kpackage, which is the tool that Caldera presently recommends for this purpose in the printed manual that comes with OpenLinux 2.2.

Launching the COAS Software Module

As discussed in Chapter 6, COAS can be launched from the KDE panel, and Software is one of the items on the first pop-up COAS menu. Alternatively, this module can be by the following command line:

```
$ kdesu root 'coastool software'
```

Notice that the prompt is the $. You don't have to be logged in as the root user to do this, although you will be asked for the root password.

This method of launch can be very useful when you are performing remote system administration, especially since Linux forbids you to log in as root remotely. If you want root privilege across a network, first log in remotely as yourself and then use su; even better, use the Secure SHell (ssh) as explained in Chapter 17, "Internet Connections."

Selecting a Software Source

When the COAS software module is first launched, COAS will first display a greeting modal dialog box. After closing that box, you see a dialog box resembling Figure 19.5.

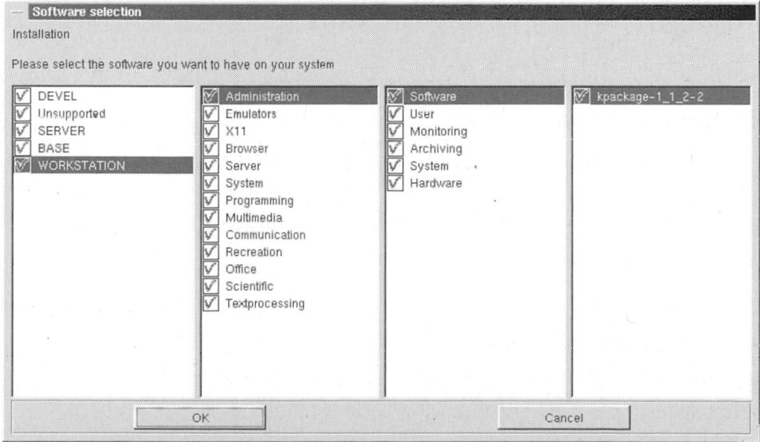

FIGURE 19.5
Initial COAS Software dialog box.

The display is organized into four levels. The first column selects what type of installation (server, base, workstation, or the like); the second gives general application areas (programming, communication, and the like); the third lists specific application areas (mail, news, and so on); the final column gives names of specific packages. In each case, the highlighted item in a column determines the contents of the columns to the right.

`COAS` can also operate in Text Mode, in which case the display is imitated with text columns.

Note that the check boxes to the left of each item are color-coded. Blue means that all available items are installed. Green mean that some are installed. An empty check box means none are installed.

With the initial display, all the checks in the boxes are blue, indicating that there is nothing you haven't installed yet. That's not because every conceivable package is installed, but because `COAS` has not yet been told where to look for additional packages. To do that, click the word Installation at the top of the dialog box. A tiny pop-up menu with the single item Source appears. The dialog box shown in Figure 19.6 appears when you click Source.

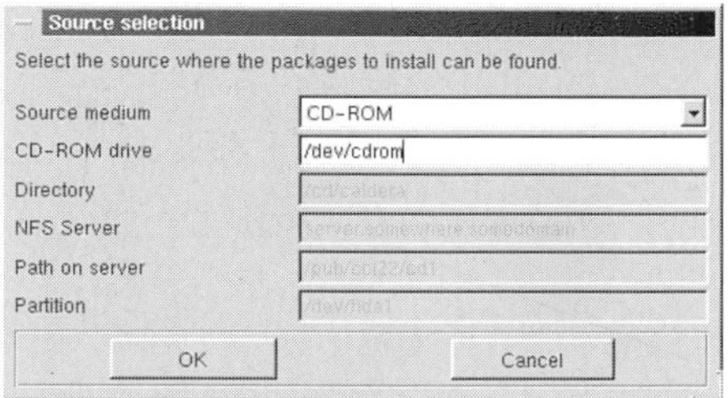

FIGURE 19.6
Selecting the source of additional packages in `COAS`.

The dialog box offers a wide variety of package sources, but the present discussion is confined to the choice shown in the figure, CD-ROM. After clicking OK, `COAS` automatically attempts to mount your CD-ROM onto `/mnt` for the duration of the `COAS` session only. Read earlier in this chapter about the normal purpose of the `/mnt` directory for a discussion of the possible mysterious side-effects.

After closing the Source Selection dialog box, you are asked for confirmation of your choice with the dialog box shown in Figure 19.7.

FIGURE 19.7
Confirming the choice of software source in COAS.

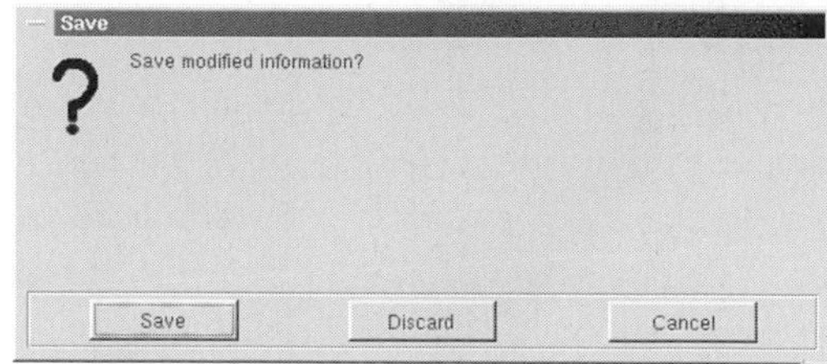

It is crucial that you click Save in order to view the additional packages on the CD-ROM.

Selecting Software to Install

After you've told `COAS` where to look for additional packages, you see a selection dialog box similar to the one shown in Figure 19.8.

FIGURE 19.8
Typical COAS *combination display of additional and installed packages.*

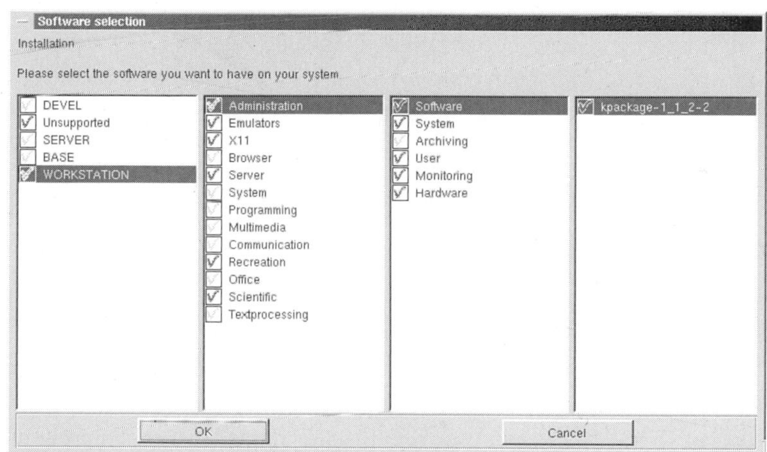

As you can see, you can at least tell that `kpackage` is installed!

To install or remove packages, simply toggle the check boxes to the left of their names in various places in the tree. After clicking OK, `COAS` attempts to install the additional packages you have selected and removes the packages you deselected.

You should not to try to install or remove more than one package at a time, unless they are closely related (such as the group of various X servers for different video cards) and clearly independent.

kpackage

The kpackage tool is part of KDE and is available by default in OpenLinux (but not Red Hat 6.0). Updates are available from http://www.kde.org/. In most respects, kpackage is a tool superior to COAS at the present. However, you need to have your installation directories already mounted to use kpackage. On most systems, assuming that an empty directory /mnt/cdrom exists, the following command can usually be used to mount the CD-ROM:

```
# mount -r /dev/cdrom /mnt/cdrom
```

Similarly, the following command can be used to dismount it:

```
#umount /mnt/cdrom
```

In addition, other tools (such as lisa and other parts of COAS) can be used to mount both CD-ROM drives and remote NFS filesystems.

On another note, kpackage will not fish around a drive looking for RPM files; you have to do that for yourself. Fortunately, this is quite easy and convenient using the K File Manager (kfm), which can be launched using the house symbol on the KDE panel. Just browse anywhere, including the Net, and if you click an RPM file—whether on a Web site or on a local filesystem—an instance of kpackage will be launched.

Alternatively, the following command can be used to hunt for RPM files:

```
# find /mnt/cdrom -type f -name '*.rpm' | less
```

The purpose of issuing this command is just to find *directories* with RPM files in them. What it actually finds is the names of the RPM archives in them. While there may be hundreds of RPM files available, they will be found in relatively few places, usually less than four. The kfm tool can then be used to conveniently browse them. As powerful as find is, there is no way to use find for directories that contain a file with a certain name pattern.

The kpackage utility can also be launched directly from the KDE main menu under Utilities, Package. When kpackage is launched this way for the first time, you will see the greeting screen shown in Figure 19.9

kpackage and many modern graphical tools benefit greatly from large amounts of screen real estate. The screen captures here were done with a screen resolution of 800×600. Use at least 1,280×1,024 if your hardware supports it—but don't overdrive your monitor! You can blow your monitor that way.

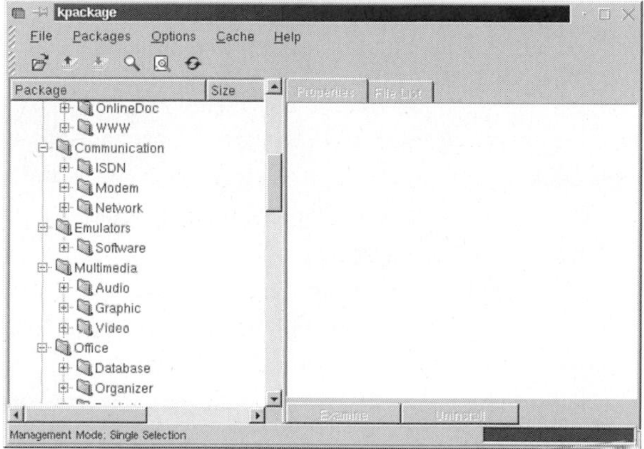

FIGURE 19.9
Greeting screen when `kpackage` *is run for the first time on a Caldera system.*

Another important point to understand is that initially `kpackage` only reports the software packages already installed. In order to see new and updated software packages not yet installed, you first tell `kpackage` where to look for them by pulling down the Options menu and selecting Location of Uninstalled Packages: RPM. This brings up the dialog box shown in Figure 19.10

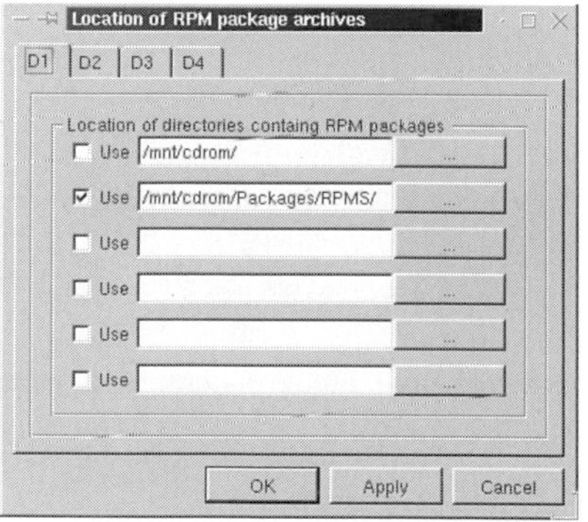

FIGURE 19.10
Telling `kpackage` *where to look for uninstalled packages.*

You can use the thumbtack to keep this dialog box up permanently, or push OK to have it take effect and go away. If you want to leave it up, use Apply.

The dialog box allows you to select many different locations (directories) in which to look for RPMs. They can also be dynamically enabled and disabled. In the example given, the path `/mnt/cdrom` is disabled and the path `/mnt/cdrom/Packages/RPMS` is enabled.

After you have selected one or more sources of RPM files, click OK or Apply. Although stored, these choices do not take immediate effect. To have `kpackage` search these paths for new packages, pull down the File menu and select Reload.

You may not notice much of a change. until you pull down the Packages menu and select Expand Tree! After you've done all that, unless you've already installed everything under the sun, you'll see something akin to Figure 19.11 after some window resizing.

The big red Ns indicate new packages. A U represents a package for which an update is available. When you click a package name in the tree, the right panel shows information about that package. There are two tabs available: Properties and File List. Properties include the crucial Unsatisfied Dependencies and Vendor. If you are interested in installing a package, click the Examine button at the bottom of the right panel. A dialog box resembling that shown in Figure 19.12 will appear.

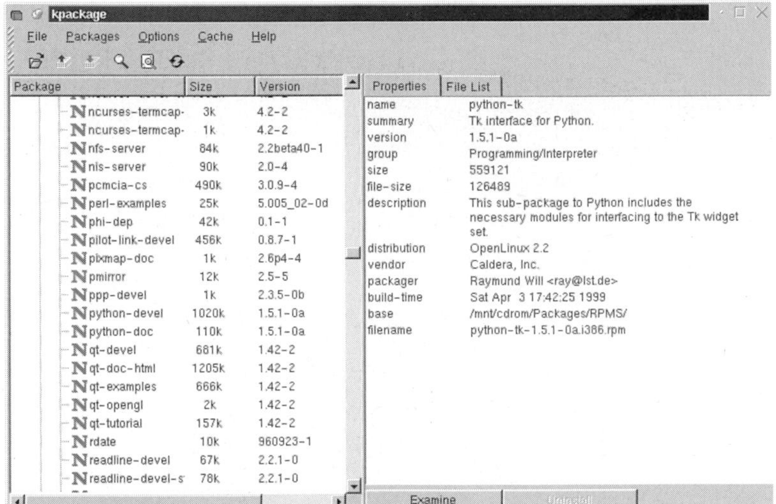

FIGURE 19.11
Resized kpackage *display of new packages available to be installed.*

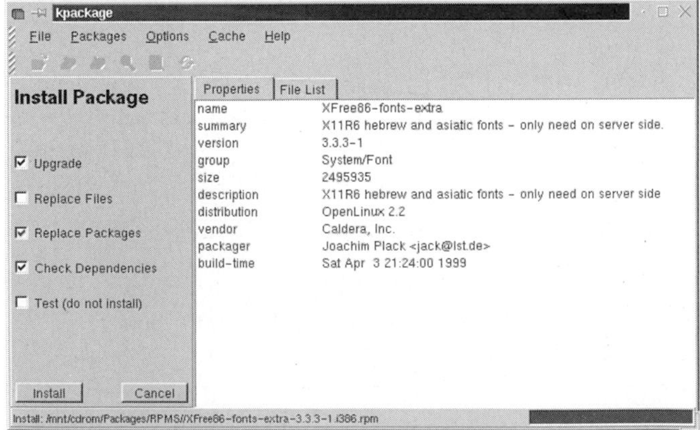

FIGURE 19.12
Typical kpackage *display of information about selected package file.*

The check boxes on the left side of the dialog box correspond to RPM options explained earlier. For instance, deselecting the Check Dependencies check box, which is abnormal procedure, causes the `—nodeps` option to be passed to RPM. This can be used to defeat dependencies on particular versions of share libraries (`/usr/lib/lib`*`something`*`.so.NN`). These dependencies are frequently irrelevant when a later version of the library is available.

Also, the Test option allows you to test what would happen if you tried to install the software. The package may apparently disappear from its place in the tree! This happens because `kpackage` doesn't bother to classify new software it finds, but simply puts it under a gigantic tree node called `NEW`. When it opens the package for testing, it reads information from the package, which allows it to put it in its proper place in the tree.

Fortunately, there is a feature available from the File pull-down menu. Find Package looks for a package, not in the world at large, but in the package tree. You can use a substring search. If you lose a package in the forest, you can find it again.

Debian Package Management

Package management responsibilities in Debian are divided among three main tools. The first is `dpkg`, which is the program that does actual package installation and removal. The other two are front ends for `dpkg`. The most powerful of these is also the newest: `apt`. The current interface to `apt` is a command-line tool called `apt-get`, although both X-based and curses-based interfaces are in development. Another interface is `dselect`, which has been a mainstay of Debian installations since the very first release, but may be phased out in favor of an `apt` system.

dpkg

`dpkg` is the low-level tool for installing, removing, and getting information about packages. You can invoke it directly if you prefer. For instance, you can use `dpkg -i` to install a given package on your system. Packages in Debian come in the `.deb` form. The `dpkg` tool can install these packages on your system. As part of this process, `dpkg` verifies that all the dependencies are met and that everything went well with the installation; it then runs the post-installation programs for the package, if any.

`dpkg` does not concern itself with finding or downloading packages—just with dealing with them once they're available. For finding and downloading packages, many people turn to `apt` or `dselect`.

Querying Package Information

You can get information about packages in several ways. If you want to see a detailed display of information about a package installed on your system, use `dpkg -s`. For instance, use this command to get information about the `bash` package:

```
# dpkg -s bash
```

`dpkg` will print out a screenful of information, indicating the version number of the installed package, whether it is installed, what its dependencies are, which files provided by the package are configuration files, and a package description.

You can also ask `dpkg` for information about which package provides a file on your system. For instance, if you want to know where `/etc/profile` came from, you could use this command:

```
# dpkg -S /etc/profile
```

`dpkg` will indicate that the `bash` package provides that file.

Another option is to get a summary of package status information. The `-l` command is used for this. For instance, you might run this command:

```
# dpkg -l bash tcsh csh ksh
```

You'll get a screen with information on each of these packages, including the name, version number, description, and installation status. If a given package isn't installed, `dpkg` tells you about that as well.

Installing a Package

If you have a `.deb` file that you'd like to install on your system, you need to use the `dpkg -i` command. Its syntax is simple: Just give it the name of the `.deb` file. Here is an example:

```
# dpkg -i someprogram.deb
```

This code installs the program contained in `someprogram.deb`. `dpkg` will automatically get the correct name of the package from inside the package itself, so don't worry about the filename here.

Removing or Purging Packages

When you want to remove software from your system, there are two things you can do: You can either use the `remove` or the `purge` option. The `remove` option gets rid of all parts of the package except for its configuration files. This way, if you later decide to reinstall the package, its configuration files will remain and the package will be ready to use. This option is recommended for most situations, especially since the configuration files are usually quite small.

The other option is a purge, which removes absolutely all files provided by a package, leaving no remnants behind.

The options to dpkg are the package name (as installed on the system), along with a --remove or --purge command.

Examples of these commands follow:

```
# dpkg --purge taper

# dpkg --remove telnetd
```

Dependencies and Conflicts

Debian provides a sophisticated mechanism for managing data that is shared between different packages. This mechanism allows packages to be split into smaller pieces, so that you don't need to have anything on your system that you don't actually require. Thus, you get space savings and more finely grained control over your system.

To do this, the parts of packages that are shared between different programs are often placed in a separate package. All the programs that require this separate package then contain special information that informs the system that they depend on this package. dpkg will then refuse to install other programs if the package depends upon is not already installed, and it will refuse to remove a package if other installed programs depend on it.

Conflicts can occur when installing multiple packages from the distribution that perform the same task. The system has room for any number of text editors, because multiple text editors do not step on each others' toes. Any sort of network service is generally more contentious. Two instances of a network service, will likely try to reserve the name well-known port, such as port 80 for HTTP (Web) servers. Such conflicts can sometimes be overcome by installing additional servers on non-standard ports. However, subtler problems may arise. For instance, for a long time sendmail was practically the only mail transfer agent in use, so much so that many other programs that automatically generate mail messages explicitly call sendmail by name. Therefore, each mail server you install takes over the name /usr/lib/sendmail even though it may in fact be a completely different program. Presently, in fact, there are quite a few replacements for sendmail, some of which are included on in the Debian distribution in addition to sendmail itself. dpkg is aware of this and similar issues, and will prevent you from installing two conflicting packages, since doing so could damage your system. Naturally, the conflict prevention is only as good as the information supplied by the packagers of the software and so this is no substitute for proper planning.

The `dselect` program provides an interface to dependency and conflict resolution, allowing you to see which packages have outstanding dependency or conflict issues, and available candidates to resolve these issues. You then indicate what you want done; `dselect` will do it.

`apt` provides Debian's most advanced tool in this area, complete with a built-in dependency and conflict resolution algorithm to sort out how to resolve any dependency or conflict situations automatically. While you may occasionally want tighter control similar to what you get with `dselect`, `apt`'s algorithm is just the right thing for almost all cases.

When you ask `apt` to install a program, it automatically figures out what needs to be done in order to allow a successful installation. This may include the installation or upgrading of packages your new program depends upon, or the removal of packages it conflicts with. After `apt` figures this out, it can tell you what it plans to do, and let you confirm that you want it to continue. If you say yes, `apt` automatically installs everything necessary for your new program to run. Your software is fully functional when `apt` exits. Because it is so fast and easy to use, `apt` is used in this book as the example tool for installing packages in Debian.

apt: A Package Tool

As you've seen, `apt` has tremendously powerful algorithms for resolving package conflict and dependency issues. It's much more than that, though. You can also tell `apt` where your favorite Debian mirror is (even if it's a local CD-ROM), and it can do things such as automatically install packages from your own CD-ROM in most cases, or download a copy from the Internet if a newer version has appeared since your CD-ROM was pressed.

To make `apt` work, you need to configure it. This is done with `/etc/apt/sources.list` file. You can get details on that file by typing **`man sources.list`** at a shell prompt. The main format of the file follows:

```
deb location distribution components
```

For instance, you could use this line to tell `apt` to automatically fetch information from the `ftp1.us.debian.org` site:

```
# deb http://ftp1.us.debian.org/debian stable main contrib non-free
```

You tell it to get packages from `ftp1.us.debian.org`, that you want the stable distribution, and that you want the main, contrib, and non-free sections to be available.

After you set up your `sources.list` file, you need to let `apt` get a listing of all the packages available for installation, their versions, and some other details about them. You need to do this now, whenever you update sources.list, and whenever you want to upgrade to newer packages. The command that does this follows:

```
apt-get update
```

After you run the update command, you're ready to use apt to install packages. Assume that you want to install the xcalc package, which depends on portions of the X Windows System to work. If you already have them installed, apt has only to install xcalc. However, if those items are not already installed, apt needs to install xcalc as well as the required components from X.

To do this, just run this code:

```
# apt-get install xcalc
```

dselect

dselect is another front end for dpkg that's used for package maintenance. dselect's main interface is a full screen designed to allow you to make interactive changes to the package list and to then apply them.

dselect allows many different methods to get packages to your system. Most people use the apt method since it is the most powerful available. After you select a method with the access command, you must run an update. Running the update essentially does the same thing as an apt-get update does for apt. The next step is select, which is where you can make changes to the list of packages. After that, you can move on to install, which adds any new packages needed to make the set of packages on the system reflect those you requested to be installed. If your method is apt, this is the last thing to do; otherwise, move on to the configure and remove steps.

From here, you can go to the detailed dselect tutorial, which will walk you through dselect usage. This tutorial is available online at http://www.debian.org/releases/stable/i386/dselect-beginner.html.

Summary

The advent of advanced tools such as gnorpm, COAS, and kpackage has greatly reduced the need to install software using command-line tools. They are contributing greatly to the taming of Linux administration. This chapter has introduced you to the fundamentals of these tools, as well as the older text-based management tools. This opens the door to experimentation with all sorts of tools from third parties, which can greatly improve your Linux system's value.

CHAPTER 20

Backup and Restore

In This Chapter

Data is important, made valuable by both the time it took to create it and the uniqueness of the data. Therefore, you should take care not to lose that data.

Data can be lost several ways. The first is through carelessness. I do not know how many times I have restored data for people who have been in the wrong directory when they issued an `rm-r` command. The second way data can be lost is via hardware failure. Although newer hard drives are more reliable than older ones, they still fail, and data is lost. A third way data is lost is through faulty software. Too many times I have programmed a tool to perform a task, only to have the tool destroy my data instead of manipulating it. These days, programs are often released before they are ready. If there is a bug, the people who developed the software put out a patch; still, the data—and the time it took to enter—are both gone. Finally, the earth can just swallow up entire buildings, or there can be earthquakes, or tornadoes, or volcanoes, or hurricanes, or aliens from outer space.

This chapter covers what the qualities of a good backup are and the process of selecting a good backup medium and a backup tool. Finally, backup strategies are considered, including incremental and full backups and when to perform each.

Successful Backup Considerations

Backups can protect your investment in time and in data, but only if you are successful in backing up and keeping the information; therefore, part of a successful backup procedure is a test strategy to spot-check backups. The easiest way to spot-check your backups is to perform a restore with them, which you should attempt before it is actually needed.

Backups can take many forms. I worked for a company that had six servers. Their backup method was to tar servers and store a copy of that tar on another server. In addition, they did tape backups of the servers, which included the online version of the backups. These tape backups were used for disaster recovery purposes and kept off site. This example shows a couple of different ways to perform backups—storing tarred copies on other machines and storing copies on tape backup (and keeping the copies off site). The combination of these methods provides a fairly reliable way of doing backups, covering everything from the simple "Oops, I accidentally deleted your database" to "Godzilla just stepped on our building, and we need the data back in less than two days!"

The Difference Between Backup and Archive

You need to understand the difference between a backup and an archive. A good backup strategy involves both forms of data protection. Backups are file operations that save your data at regular intervals, either in whole or incrementally (see "Backup Strategies and Operations," later in this chapter). Archives are file operations that save your data for long periods of time.

Qualities of a Good Backup

Obviously, in the best of all possible worlds, backups would be perfectly reliable, always available, easy to use, and really fast. In the real world, trade-offs must be made. For example, backups stored offsite are good for disaster recovery, but are not always available.

Above all, backups need to be reliable. A reliable backup medium will last for several years. Of course, if the backups are never successfully written to the backup medium, it does not matter how good the medium is.

Speed is more or less important, depending on the system. If a time window is available when the system is not being used and the backup can be automated, speed is not an issue. On the other hand, restoration might be an issue. The time it takes to restore the data is as important as the need to have the data available.

Availability is a necessary quality. Performing regular backups does no good if, when they are needed, they are unavailable. Backups for disaster recovery may not be available locally and don't always include data timely enough to restore a single file accidentally deleted by a user. A good backup and recovery scheme includes both a local set of backups for day-to-day restores and an offsite set of backups for disaster recovery purposes.

Fast, available, reliable backups are no good if they are not usable. The tools used for backup and restoration need to be easy to use. This is especially important for restoration. In an emergency, the person who normally performs the backup and restores might be unavailable, and a nontechnical user might have to perform the restoration. Obviously, documentation is a part of usability.

Selecting a Backup Medium

Today, many backup media choices exist, although the three most common types for a long time were floppy disks, tapes, and hard drives. Table 20.1 rates these media—and newer ones such as CD-ROM read-only and CD-ROM read-write—in terms of reliability, speed, availability, and usability.

TABLE 20.1 Backup Media Comparison

Medium	*Reliability*	*Speed*	*Availability*	*Usability*
Floppy disks	Good	Slow	High	Good with small data; bad with large data
CD-ROM RO	Good	Slow	High	Read-only media; okay for archives
CD-ROM RW	Good	Slow	Medium	Read-write media; economical for medium-sized systems
Iomega Zip	Good	Slow	High	100MB storage; okay for small systems
Flash ROM	Excellent	Fast	Low	Very expensive; currently limited to less than 200MB
Tapes	Good	Medium to fast	High	Depending on the size of the tape, can be highly usable; tapes cannot be formatted under Linux
Removable HD	Excellent	Fast	High	Relatively expensive, but available in sizes of 1GB or larger
Hard drives	Excellent	Fast	High	Highly usable

Writable CDs are good for archival purposes, and some formats can be overwritten; however, the expense in time tends to be high if a large number of regular archives or backups must be made. Flopticals, with attributes of both floppy and optical disks, tend to have the good qualities of floppy disks and tapes and are good for single file restoration. Flopticals can hold a lot of data, but have not captured the consumer market; they are popular in high-end, large-scale computing operations. More popular removable media are Iomega Zip and Jaz drives, which come in 100MB and 250MB Zip and 1–2GB Jaz form factors.

Selecting a Backup Tool

Many tools are available for making backups. In addition to numerous third-party applications, Linux distributions come with some standard tools for performing this task. This section examines two of them, `tar` and `cpio`. (`cpio` has nothing to do with Star Wars and was called this way before the golden android originally made it to the silver screen.)

Note

If you're looking for more sophisticated backup software, you can also try AMANDA, the Advanced Maryland Automatic Network Disk Archiver. This free software, from the University of Maryland at College Park, can be used over a network to back up multiple computer filesystems to a single, large-capacity tape drive. Some features include graceful error recovery, compression, scheduling, encryption, and high-speed backup operation. For more information, see `http://www.amanda.org`.

`tar` and `cpio` are very similar. Both are capable of storing and retrieving data from almost any media. In addition, both `tar` and `cpio` are ideal for small systems, which Red Hat Linux systems often are. For example, the following `tar` command saves all files under `/home` to the standard output (which can then be redirected to your system's tape device):

```
$ tar -c /home
```

The `-c` option tells `tar` to create a new archive, and the specified directory is used to gather the files. Of course, to really make the `tar` command useful, you would want the information to go somewhere other than the screen. This can be done with the `-f` option.

```
$ tar -cvf /tmp/home.tar /home
```

The `v` stands for verbose. Following the `f` must be the name of the file where you want the output to go. The file can be named anything you want, but the convention is to name it *something*`.tar` so that you (and others) will know that it is a `tar` file.

Although similar to the `tar` command, `cpio` has several advantages. First, it packs data more efficiently. Second, it is designed to back up arbitrary sets of files. (`tar` is designed to back up subdirectories.) Third, `cpio` is designed to handle backups that span over several tapes. Finally, `cpio` skips over bad sections on a tape and continues, but `tar` crashes and burns.

Note

The GNU version of `tar` included with Red Hat Linux has several options useful for file compression and multivolume backup operations. If you use the `z` option in the `tar` command line, `tar` uses `gzip` compression or decompression. To perform a multivolume backup or restore, use `tar`'s `M` option on the command line. For example, to create a compressed backup of the `/home` directory via multiple floppy disks, use `tar -cvzMf /dev/fd0 /home`.

Backup Strategies and Operations

The simplest backup strategy is to copy every file from the system to a tape. This is called a full backup. Full backups by themselves are good for small systems, such as those typically used by Linux users.

The downside of a full backup is that it can be time-consuming. Restoring a single file from a large backup such as a tape archive can be almost too cumbersome to be of value. Sometimes a full backup is the way to go, and sometimes it is not. A good backup and recovery scheme identifies when a full backup is necessary and when incremental backups are preferred.

Note

If you use your Linux system for business, you should definitely have a backup strategy. Creating a formal plan to regularly save critical information, such as customer accounts or work projects, is essential to avoid financial disaster. Even more important: After you devise your backup plan, stick to it!

Incremental backups tend to be done more frequently. With an incremental backup, only those files that have changed since the last backup are backed up. Therefore, each incremental builds upon previous incremental backups.

Linux uses the concept of a backup level to distinguish different kinds of backups. A full backup is designated as a level 0 backup. The other levels indicate the files that have changed since the preceding level. For example, on Sunday evening you might perform a level 0 backup (full backup). Then on Monday night you would perform a level 1 backup, which backs up all files changed since the level 0 backup. Tuesday night would be a level 2 backup, which backs up all files changed since the level 1 backup, and so on. This gives way to two basic backup and recovery strategies. Here is the first:

Sunday	Level 0 backup
Monday	Level 1 backup
Tuesday	Level 1 backup
Wednesday	Level 1 backup
Thursday	Level 1 backup
Friday	Level 1 backup
Saturday	Level 1 backup

The advantage of this backup scheme is that it requires only two sets of backup media. Restoring the full system from the level 0 backup and the previous evening's incremental can perform a complete restore. The negative side is that the amount backed up grows throughout the week, and additional media might be needed to perform the backup. Here is the second strategy:

Sunday	Level 0 backup
Monday	Level 1 backup
Tuesday	Level 2 backup
Wednesday	Level 3 backup
Thursday	Level 4 backup
Friday	Level 5 backup
Saturday	Level 6 backup

The advantage of this backup scheme is that each backup is relatively quick. Also, the backups stay relatively small and easy to manage. The disadvantage is that it requires seven sets of media. Also, you must use all seven sets to do a complete restore.

When deciding which type of backup scheme to use, you need to know how the system is used. Files that change often should be backed up more often than files that rarely change. Some directories, such as `/tmp`, never need to be backed up.

Performing Backups with `tar` and `cpio`

A full backup with `tar` is as easy as this:

```
$ tar -c /
```

An incremental backup takes a bit more work. Fortunately, the `find` command is a wonderful tool to use with backups to find all files that have changed since a certain date. It can also find files that are newer than a specified file. With this information, it is easy to perform an incremental backup. The following command finds all files that have been modified today and backs up those files with the `tar` command to an archive on `/dev/rmt1`:

```
$ tar c `find / -mtime -1 ! -type d -print`
```

`! -type d` says that if the object found is a directory, don't give it to the tar command for archiving. This is done because `tar` follows the directories, and you don't want to back up an entire directory unless everything in it has changed. Of course, the find command can also be used for the `cpio` command. The following command performs the same task as the preceding `tar` command:

```
$ find / -mtime -1 ¦ cpio -o >/dev/rmt1
```

As mentioned, the `find` command can find files that are newer than a specified file. The `touch` command updates the time of a file; therefore, it is easy to `touch` a file after a backup has completed. Then, at the next backup, you simply search for files that are newer than the file you touched. The following example searches for files that are newer than the file /tmp/last_backup and performs a cpio to archive the data:

```
$ find / -newer /tmp/last_backup -print ¦ cpio -o > /dev/rmt0
```

With `tar`, the same action is completed this way:

```
$ tar c1 `find / -newer /tmp/last_backup -print`
```

Note

You will want to touch the file before you start the backup. This means you have to use different files for each level of backup, but it ensures that the next backup gets any files modified during the current backup.

Performing Backups with `taper`

The `taper` script (`/usr/sbin/taper` on Red Hat and `/sbin/taper` on Debian, and unavailable with Caldera) is a backup and restore program you can use to maintain compressed or uncompressed archives on tapes or removable media (even over a network!). Using `taper` is easy; the format of a `taper` command line looks like this:

```
# taper <-T tape-type> <option> <device>
```

You first need to decide what type of device (or media) you'd like to use with `taper`. This program supports a number of devices, which are listed in Table 20.2 along with the command lines to use.

TABLE 20.2 Device Support by *taper*

Device	*Type*	*Command Line*
/dev/zftape	Floppy tape driver	`# taper -T z`
/dev/ht0	IDE tape driver	`# taper -T i`
file	File on hard disk	`# taper -T l`
/dev/ftape	Floppy tape driver	`# taper -T f`
/dev/fd0	Removable floppy drive	`# taper -T r`
/dev/sda4	Removable Zip drive	`# taper -T r -b /dev/sda4` (-b denotes the device and archive file)
/dev/sda	SCSI tape drive	`# taper -T s`

After you start taper from the command line of your console or an X11 terminal window (you must be the root operator), you'll see a main menu of options to back up, restore, re-create, verify, set preferences, or exit, as shown in Figure 20.1.

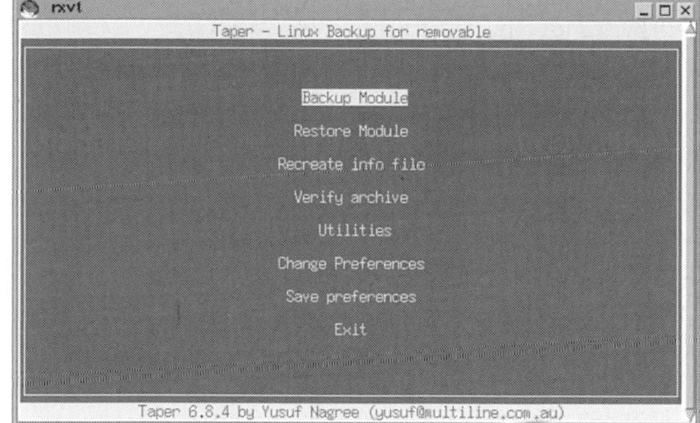

FIGURE 20.1
The taper *script offers a graphical interface (of sorts) to back up and restore operations for Linux.*

Navigate through taper's menus with your up or down arrow keys and press the Enter key to make a selection. If you're not sure what keys to use, press the question mark (?) to have **taper** show a concise Help screen.

Start the backup process by selecting files or directories for your backup. First, highlight the Backup Module menu item and then press the Enter key. The taper script checks the status of the device you've specified on the command line and then looks for an existing tape archive on the device. If none is found, taper asks you to name the volume and then give a name for the new archive. You'll then see a directory listing similar to that in Figure 20.2.

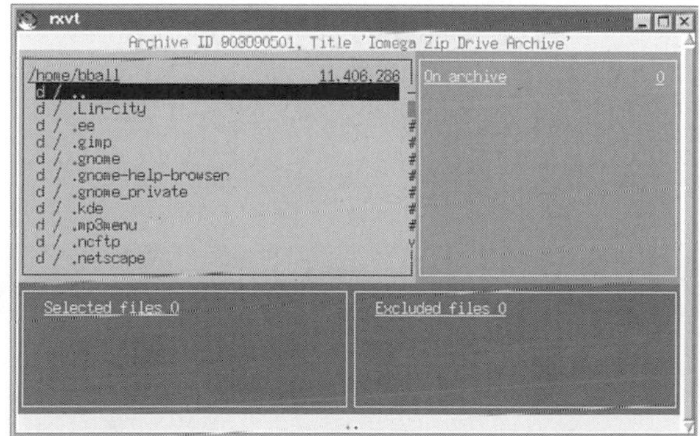

FIGURE 20.2
The taper program offers selective backup and restoration of your directories or files.

Next, navigate through the listings or directories, using the i or I key to select files or directories to back up. When you finish, press the f or F key to start backing up your files. The taper program has many features and can be customized through preference settings in its main menu. For detailed information, see its documentation under the `/usr/doc/taper` directory.

Performing Backups with BRU-2000

Linux users (including Red Hat and Caldera) will find a copy of Enhanced Software Technologies' BRU-2000-PE on an Enhanced Linux Application CD-ROM. BRU-2000-PE is a personal edition of a more complete, commercial network backup and restore program that features the following things:

- Command-line or graphical interface for X11
- Error detection during backup
- Data integrity verification following backup operations
- Backup and restore operations of live filesystems
- Built-in help
- Automatic recognition of compressed files (so archives don't become larger by trying to compress already compressed files or directories)
- Background mode (so backups can be scheduled)

This software includes two commands: `bru` for backing up from the console and `xbru` for a graphical interface during X11 sessions. BRU-2000 uses several files and directories on your Linux filesystem. Much of the graphical interface support is found under the `/usr/lib/bru` directory, and the support file `/etc/brutab` is used to specify different backup devices.

The BRU-2000-PE software is installed by using the rpm or glint command (or during an initial installation of the commercial version of Red Hat Linux).

To do a full or incremental backup of your system, you must run BRU-2000 as the root operator. To use the graphical interface version, start the program by typing **`xbru`** at the command line of an X11 terminal window. This opens the main dialog box, as shown in Figure 20.3.

Note

Updated software of the X11 BRU-2000 interface is available at `ftp://ftp.estinc.com/pub/X11` or through `http://www.estinc.com`.

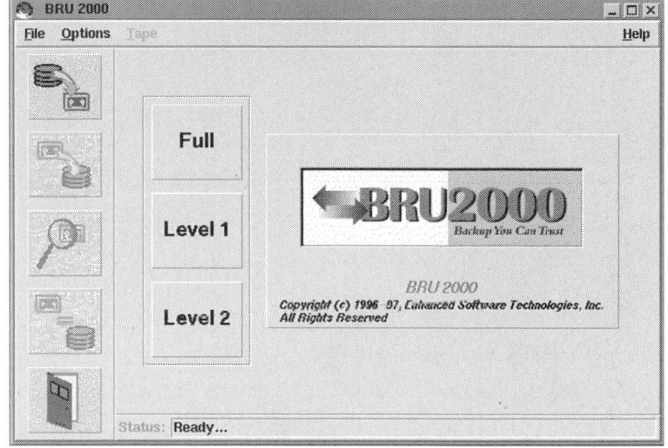

FIGURE 20.3
The BRU-2000 program is a commercial backup and restore program for nearly 20 operating systems, including Linux.

The program first checks the status of the default backup device, but you can configure the program to use one of more than 37 different devices for backup. You can also define new devices, such as Iomega Zip drives, to use for storing tape archives. To configure BRU-2000 to use a Zip disk as a backup device, select the Configure BRU menu item from the File menu. A new dialog box appears, as shown in Figure 20.4.

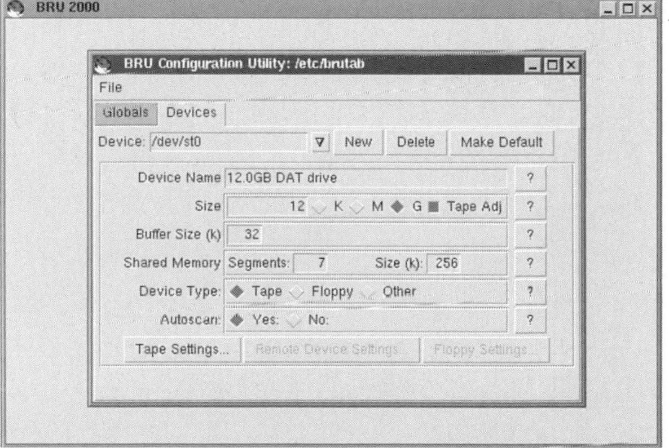

FIGURE 20.4
To configure a new backup device for BRU-2000, select the Devices tab in its Configuration dialog box.

> **Note**
>
> If you have an older version of BRU-2000, check `http://www.estinc.com/brutabs.html` for important updated device table files such as `jaz.bt` and `zip.bt`. You'll need them to use an Iomega Zip or Jaz disk with BRU-2000. First, you should add the following lines to the file `/usr/lib/bru/unmounttape.tcl`:
>
> *continues*

```
    if [string match "/dev/hd*" $device] {
    exit 0
}
if [string match "/dev/sd*" $device] {
    exit 0
}
```

Select the Devices tab and then the New button. A New Device window appears, as shown in Figure 20.5. Type in the name of your Zip disk's device (for example, `/dev/sda4`), select the Device Type OTHER, and press the Create button. You can then type in a description of your Zip drive in the Device Name field and set the size of the device as 95MB. Press the Save button, followed by the Exit button.

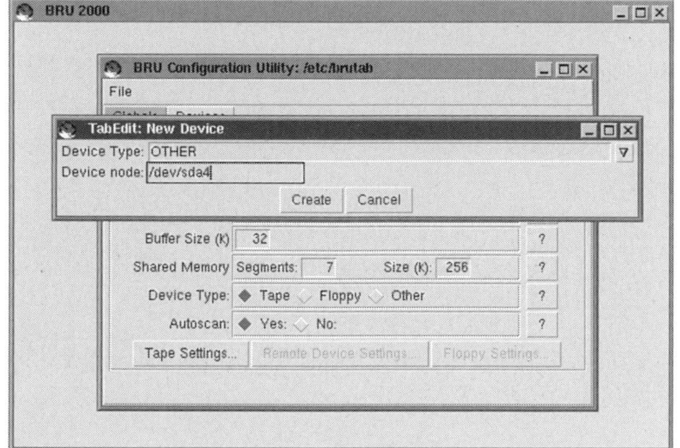

FIGURE 20.5
The New Device dialog box is used to select a new backup device or create a new one for BRU-2000.

To select which files or directories to back up, either select Backup from the File menu or press the top button in BRU-2000's main dialog box (as shown in Figure 20.3). A directory and file selection dialog appears, as shown in Figure 20.6. You can then choose the files or directories by highlighting the name and then pressing the Add button. When finished, press the Start Backup button to begin operation. If you want to use file compression or set other options, use the Options button before backing up.

BRU-2000 has many options and features. After you finish your backup, you can restore your archive, test its integrity, and even view the contents of your archives. For more details, read BRU-2000's `bru` command man page, check the `/bru` directory after installation, or browse to `http://www.estinc.com`.

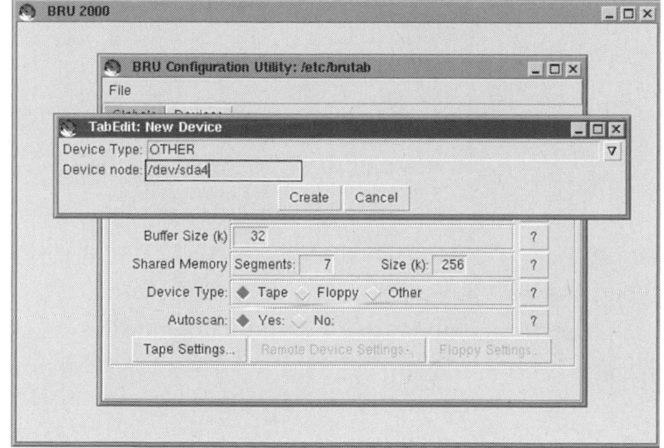

FIGURE 20.6
BRU-2000 offers numerous backup options and a selective file and directory backup dialog box.

Restoring Files

Backing up files is a good thing, but backups are like an insurance policy. When it is time for them to pay up, you want it all, and you want it now! To get the files, you must restore them. Fortunately, it is not difficult to restore files with either `tar` or `cpio`. The following command restores the file `/home/alana/bethany.txt` from the current tape in the drive:

```
$ tar -xp /home/alana/bethany.txt
$ cpio -im `*bethany.txt$` < /dev/rmt0
```

The `-p` in `tar` and the `-m` in `cpio` ensure that all of the file attributes are restored along with the file. By the way, when you restore directories with `cpio`, the `-d` option creates subdirectories. The `tar` command creates subdirectories automatically.

What Is on the Tape?

When you have a tape, you might not know what is on it. Perhaps you are using a multiple-level backup scheme and you don't know which day the file was backed up. Both `tar` and `cpio` offer a way of creating a table of contents for the tape. The most convenient time to create this TOC file, of course, is during the actual backup. The following two lines show how to perform a backup and at the same time create a table of contents file for that tape:

```
$ tar -cv / > /tmp/backup.Monday.TOC
$ find / -print ¦ cpio -ov > /dev/rmt0 2> /tmp/backup.Monday.TOC
```

The `cpio` backup automatically sends the list to standard error; therefore, this line just captures standard error and saves it as a file. By the way, if the > in the `tar` command is replaced with the word `tee`, the table of contents is not only written to the file; it is also printed to standard output (the screen).

Summary

Backups are important, but being able to restore the files is more important. Nothing will cause a lump in the throat to appear faster than trying to restore a system, only to find that the backups failed. As with any administrative task performed on a system, backups require a good plan, proper implementation, good documentation, and lots of testing. An occasional spot-check of a backup could save hours, if not days, of time.

CHAPTER 21

System Security

In This Chapter

Security is one of the hottest topics in any system debate. How do you make your site more secure? How do you keep the hackers out of your system? How do you make sure your data is safe from intruders? How do you keep your company's secrets a secret?

Your system is as secure as its weakest point. This is an old saying, and one that is still true. I am reminded of an episode of *The Andy Griffith Show* in which the town drunk (Otis) is sleeping off another episode in the jail. After he is sober, Otis looks around at the bars on the windows, the barred walls, and the gate. "A pretty secure jail," I thought, until he pushed open the door, said good-bye to Barney, and left. So much for the security!

Many times, systems are as secure as that jail. All the bars and locks are in place, but the door is left open. This chapter takes a look at some of the bars and locks and explains how to lock the door. More importantly, though, it explains how to conduct a security audit and where to get more information.

Security comes in many forms. Passwords and file permissions are your first two lines of defense. After that, things get difficult. Security breaches take many forms. To understand your particular system and the security issues relevant to your system, you should first develop a security audit.

Thinking About Security—An Audit

A security audit has three basic parts, each with many things to think about. First, develop a plan, a set of security aspects to be evaluated. Second, consider the tools available for evaluating the security aspects and choose those suitable to your system. The third part of a security audit is knowledge-gathering—not only how to use the system, but what the users are doing with the system, break-in methods for your system, physical security issues, and much more. The following sections look at each of these three pieces of the audit and offer some direction about where to go for more information.

A Security Plan

The plan can be as complex as a formal document or as simple as a few notes scribbled on the back of a Java receipt. Regardless of the complexity, the plan should at least list what aspects of the system you are going to evaluate and how. This means asking two questions:

- What types of security problems could we have?
- Which ones can we (or should we) attempt to detect or fix?

To answer these questions, a few more questions might be necessary concerning the following areas:

- Accountability
- Change control and tracking
- Data integrity, including backups
- Physical security
- Privacy of data
- System access
- System availability

A more detailed plan can be developed based on discussion of these topics. As always, there will trade-offs; for example, privacy of data could mean that only certain people can log on to the system, which affects system access for the users. System availability is always in conflict with change control. For example, when do you change that failing hard drive on a 7×24 system? The bottom line is that your detailed plan should include a set of goals, a way of tracking the progression of the goals (including changes to the system), and a knowledge base of what types of tools are needed to do the job.

Security Tools

Having the right tools always makes the job easier—especially when you are dealing with security issues. A number of tools are available on the Internet, including tools that check passwords, check system security, and protect your system. Some major UNIX-oriented security organizations assist the UNIX/Red Hat Linux user groups in discussing, testing, and describing tools available for use. CERT, CIAC, and the Linux Emergency Response Team are excellent sources of information for both the beginning and advanced system administrator.

The following list introduces many of the available tools. This should be a good excuse, however, to surf the Net and see what else is available:

`Cops` — A set of programs; each checks a different aspect of security on a UNIX system. If any potential security holes do exist, the results are either mailed or saved to a report file.

`crack` — A program designed to find standard UNIX eight-character DES-encrypted passwords by standard guessing techniques.

`deslogin` — A remote login program that can be used safely across insecure networks.

`findsuid.tar.Z`	Finds changes in `setuid` (set user ID) and `setgid` (set group ID) files.
`freestone`	A portable, fully functional firewall implementation.
`gabriel`	A `satan` detector. `gabriel` gives the system administrator an early warning of possible network intrusions by detecting and identifying satan's network probing.
`ipfilter`	A free packet filter that can be incorporated into any of the supported operating systems, providing IP packet-level filtering per interface.
`ipfirewall`	An IP packet-filtering tool, similar to the packet-filtering provided by most commercial routers.
`kerberos`	A network authentication system for use on physically insecure networks. It allows entities communicating over networks to prove their identities to each other while preventing eavesdropping or replay attacks.
`merlin`	Takes a popular security tool (such as `tiger`, `tripwire`, `Cops`, `crack`, or `spi`) and provides it with an easy-to-use, consistent graphical interface, simplifying and enhancing its capabilities.
`npasswd`	`passwd` replacement with password sanity check.
`obvious-pw.tar.Z`	An obvious password detector.
`opie`	Provides a one-time password system for POSIX-compliant, UNIX-like operating systems.
`pcheck.tar.Z`	Checks format of `/etc/passwd`; verifies `rootdefault` shell and `passwd` fields.
`Plugslot Ltd.`	PCP/PSP UNIX network security and configuration monitor.
`rsaeuro`	A cryptographic toolkit providing various functions for the use of digital signatures, data encryption, and supporting areas (PEM encoding, random number generation, and so on).
`rscan`	Allows system administrators to execute complex (or simple) scanner scripts on one (or many) machines and create clean, formatted reports in either ASCII or HTML.
`satan`	The security analysis tool for auditing networks. In its simplest (and default) mode, `satan` gathers as much information about remote hosts and networks as possible by examining such network services as `finger`,

	NFS, NIS, `ftp`, `tftp`, and `rexd`.
`ssh`	Secure SHell—a remote login program.
`tcp wrappers`	Can monitor and control remote access to your local `tftp`, `exec`, `ftp`, `rsh`, `telnet`, `rlogin`, `finger`, and `systat` daemon.
`tiger`	Scans a system for potential security problems.
`tis` firewall toolkit	Includes enhancements and bug fixes from version 1.2 and new proxies for HTTP/Gopher and X11.
`tripwire`	Monitors system for security break-in attempts.
`xp-beta`	An application gateway of X11 protocol. It is designed to be used at a site that has a firewall and uses SOCKS or CERN WWW Proxy.
`xroute`	Routes X packets from one machine to another.

As you can see, a few tools exist for your use. If you want a second reason for looking at these tools, keep in mind that people trying to break into your system know how to—and do—use these tools. This is where the knowledge comesin.

Knowledge Gathering

Someone once said a little knowledge goes along way. As stated in the chapter opening, all the bells and whistles can be there, but they do no good if they are not active. It is therefore important that the system staff, the users, and the keepers of the sacred `root` password all follow the security procedures put in place—and that they gather all the knowledge necessary to adhere to those procedures.

I was at the bank the other day, filling out an application for a car loan. The person assisting me at the bank was at a copy machine in another room (I could see her through the window). Another banking person, obviously new, could be heard from his office, where he was having problems logging in to the bank's computer. He came out and looked around for the bank employee helping me. When he did not see her, I got his attention and pointed him toward the copy area. He thanked me and went to her and asked for the system's password because he could not remember it. She could not remember the password. He went back to his desk, checked a list of telephone numbers hanging on the wall by his phone, entered something into the computer, and was in. About that time, my bank person came out of the copy area, stuck her head in his office, and said that she recalled the password. He said he had it. She asked if he had done with the password what they normally do. He looked at his phone list and said yes. She left and returned to me at her desk.

This scenario is true. The unfortunate thing about it, besides the fact that at least two customers—the person with the employee trying to log in to the system and I—saw the whole thing is that they didn't know, nor did they care, that others might be listening. To them it was business as usual. What can be learned from this? Don't write down passwords!

Not only should passwords not be written down, they should not be easily associated with the user. I'll give you two examples that illustrate this point. The first involves a wonderful man from the Middle East with whom I worked on a client site. He has three boys. As a proud father, he talks about them often. When referring to them individually, he uses their first names. When referring to them cumulatively, he calls them "three boys." His password (he uses the same password for all his accounts) is `threeboys`.

The second example comes from one of the sweetest people I have met in the industry. On this woman's desk is a little stuffed cow named Chelsea. I do not remember the significance of the name, but I remember that she really likes dairy cows. Her password is—you guessed it—`chelsea`. These peoples' passwords are probably still `threeboys` and `chelsea`.

File security is another big issue. The use of `umask` (file creation masks) should be mandated. It should also be set to the maximum amount possible. Changing a particular file to give someone else access to it is easy. Knowing who is looking at your files is difficult, if not impossible. The sensitivity of the data, of course, would certainly determine the exact level of security placed on the file. In extremely sensitive cases, such as employees' personnel records, encryption of the files might also be necessary.

After an audit has been done, you should have an excellent idea of what security issues you need to be aware of and which issues you need to track. The next section shows you how to trackintruders.

"Danger, Will Robinson, Danger!"

I used to love watching *Lost in Space*. On that show was a life-sized robot that would declare, "Danger, Will Robinson, danger!" Unfortunately, no such robot warns of danger on our systems. (Although some tools exist, they are nowhere near as consistent as that robot was!)

If you have a lot of extra disk space, you can turn on auditing, which records all user connects and disconnects from your system. If you don't rely on auditing, you should scan the logs often. A worthwhile alternative might be to write a quick summary script that gives an account of the amount of time each user is on the system.

Unfortunately, there are too many holes to block them all. Measures can be placed to plug the biggest, but the only way to keep a system secure is by locking a computer in a vault, allowing no one access to it and no connectivity outside the vault. The bottom line is that users who want into your system and are good enough, can get in. What you have to do is prepare for the worst.

Preparing for the Worst

The three things that can happen to a system—short of it physically being removed, are data being stolen, data being destroyed (which includes making it inaccessible), and easier access being provided for next time. Physically, an intruder can destroy or remove equipment or, if very creative, even add hardware. Short of chaining the system to the desk, retinal scans, card readers, and armed guards, there is not much you can do to prevent theft. Physical security is beyond the scope of this book. What is within the scope of this book is dealing with the data and dealing with additional access measures.

Data should be backed up on a regular basis. The backed-up information, depending on how secure it needs to be, can be kept on a shelf next to the system or in a locked vault at an alternate location. A backup is the best way for retrieving data that has been destroyed.

Most of the time, though, data is not just destroyed. A more common problem is that the data is captured. This could include actual company secrets or system configuration files. Keeping an eye on the system files is very important. Another good idea is to occasionally search for programs that have `suid` or `sgid` capability. It might be wise to search for `suid` and `sgid` files when the system is first installed, so that later searches can be compared to this initial list.

`suid` and `sgid`

Many people talk about `suid` (set user ID) and `sgid` (set group ID) without clearly understanding them. The concept behind these powerful and dangerous tools is that a program (not a script) is set to run as the owner or group set for the program—not as the person running the program. For example, if you have a program with `suid` set and its owner is `root`, users run that program with the permissions of the owner instead of their own permissions. The `passwd` command is a good example of this. The `/etc/passwd` file is writable by `root` and readable by everyone. The `passwd` program has `suid` turned on; therefore, anyone can run the `passwd` program and change her password. Because the program is running as the user `root`, not as the actual user, the `/etc/passwd` file can be written to.

The same concept holds true for `sgid`. Instead of the program running with the permissions and authority of the group associated with the person calling the program, the program is run with the permissions and authority of the group associated with the program.

How to Find `suid` and `sgid` Files

The `find` command once again comes in handy. You can search the entire system with the following command, looking for programs with their `suid` or `sgid` turned on:

```
find / -perm -2000 -o -perm -4000 -print
```

Running the preceding `find` command when you first load a system is probably best, saving its output to a file readable only by `root`. Future searches can be performed and compared to this "clean" list of `suid` and `sgid` files to ensure that only the files that are supposed to have these permissions really do. With the current release of Red Hat Linux 6.0, there are approximately 30 files that have either `suid` or `sgid` set and have either the owner or group of `root`.

In Debian, the number of files varies depending on which programs you have installed.

Setting `suid` and `sgid`

`suid` and `sgid` can be powerful tools for giving users the ability to perform tasks without the other problems that could arise if a user has the actual permissions of that group or user. However, these can be dangerous tools as well. When considering changing the permissions on a file to be either `suid` or `sgid`, keep in mind these two things:

- Use the lowest permissions needed to accomplish the task.
- Watch for back doors.

Using the lowest permissions means not giving a file an `suid` of `root` if at all possible. Often, a less privileged person can be configured to perform the task. The same goes for `sgid`. Many times, setting the group to the appropriate non-sys group accomplishes the same task whilelimiting other potential problems.

Back doors come in many forms. A program that allows a shell is a *back door*. Multiple entrances and exits to a program are back doors. Keep in mind that if a user can run an `suid` program set to `root` and the program contains a back door (users can get out of the program to a prompt without actually exiting the program), the system keeps the effective user ID as what the program is set to (`root`). The user now has `root` permissions.

With that said, how do you set a file to make the effective user the owner of the file? How do you set a file to make the effective group the group of the file, instead of running as the user ID or the user's group ID of the person invoking the file? The permissions are added with the `chmod` command, as follows:

```
chmod u+s file(s)
chmod g+s file(s)
```

The first example sets `suid` for the file(s) listed. The second example sets `sgid` to the file(s) listed. Remember, `suid` sets the effective ID of the process to the owner associated with the file, and `sgid` sets the effective group's ID of the process to the group associated with the file. These cannot be set on nonexecutables.

File and Directory Permissions

As stated in this chapter's introduction, file and directory permissions are the basics for providing security on a system. These, along with the authentication system, provide the basis for all security. Unfortunately, many people do not know what permissions on directories mean, or it's assumed they mean the same thing they do on files. The following section describes the permissions on files; after that, the permissions on directories are described.

Files

The *permissions* for files are split into three sections: the owner of the file, the group associated with the file, and everyone else (the world). Each section has its own set of file permissions, which provide the ability to read, write, and execute (or, of course, to deny the same). These permissions are called a file's *filemode*. Filemodes are set with the `chmod` command.

The object's permissions can be specified in two ways—the numeric coding system or the letter coding system. Using the letter coding system, the three sections are referred to as `u` for user, `g` for group, `o` for other, or `a` for all three. The three basic types of permissions are `r` for read, `w` for write, and `x` for execute. Combinations of `r`, `w`, and `x` with the three groups provide the permissions for files. In the following example, the owner of the file has read, write, and execute permissions, and everyone else has read access only:

```
shell:/home/dpitts$ ls -l test
-rwxr--r--    1 dpitts    users          22 Sep 15 00:49 test
```

The command `ls -l` tells the computer to give you a long (`-l`) listing (`ls`) of the file (`test`). The resulting line is shown in the second code line and tells you a number of things about the file. First, it tells you the permissions. Next, it tells you how many links the file has. It then tells you who owns the file (`dpitts`) and what group is associated with the file (`users`). Following the ownership section, the date and timestamp for the last time the file was modified is given. Finally, the name of the file is listed (`test`). The permissions are actually made up of four sections. The first section is a single character that identifies the type of object listed. Check Table 21.1 to determine the options for this field.

TABLE 21.1 Object Type Identifier

Character	*Description*
-	Plain file
b	Block special file
c	Character special file
d	Directory
l	Symbolic link
p	Named pipe
s	Socket

Following the file type identifier are the three sets of permissions: `rwx` (owner), `r--` (group), and `r--` (other).

Note

A small explanation needs to be made as to what read, write, and execute actually mean. For files, a user who has *read* permission can see the contents of the file; a user who has *write* permission can write to it; a user who has *execute* permission can execute the file. If the file to be executed is a script, the user must have read and execute permissions to execute the file. If the file is a binary, just the execute permission is required to execute the file.

Directories

The permissions on a directory are the same as those used by files: read, write, and execute. The actual permissions, however, mean different things. For a directory, read access provides the capability to list the names of the files in the directory but does not allow the other attributes to be seen (owner, group, size, and so on). Write access provides the capability to alter the directory contents. This means the user could create and delete files in the directory. Finally, the execute access enables the user to make the directory the current directory.

Table 21.2 summarizes the differences between the permissions for a file and those for a directory.

TABLE 21.2 File Permissions Versus Directory Permissions

Permission	*File*	*Directory*
`r`	View the contents.	Search the contents.
`w`	Alter file contents.	Alter directory contents.
`x`	Run executable file.	Make it the current directory.

Combinations of these permissions also allow certain tasks. For example, I previously mentioned that it takes both read and execute permissions to execute a script. This is because the shell must first read the file to see what to do with it. (Remember that `#! /local/bin/perl` tells the shell to execute the `/local/bin/perl` executable, passing the rest of the file to the executable.) Other combinations allow certain functionality. Table 21.3 describes the combinations of permissions and what they mean, both for a file and for a directory.

TABLE 21.3 Comparison of File and Directory Permission Combinations

Permission	*File*	*Directory*
`---`	Cannot do anything with it.	Cannot access it or any of its subdirectories.
`r--`	Can see the contents.	Can see the contents.
`rw-`	Can see and alter contents.	Can see and alter the contents.
`Rwx`	Can see and list the contents, change the contents, as well as execute the file.	Can add or remove files, and make the directory the current (`cd` to it).
`r-x`	If a script, can execute it. Otherwise, provides read and execute permission	Provides capability to change to directory and list contents, but not to delete or add files to directory.
`--x`	Can execute if a binary.	Users can execute a binary they already know about.

As stated, the permissions can also be manipulated with a numeric coding system. The basic concept is the same as the letter coding system. As a matter of fact, the permissions look exactly alike—the difference is the way the permissions are identified. The numeric system uses binary counting to determine a value for each permission and sets them. Also, the `find` command can accept the permissions as an argument, using the `-perm` option. In that case, the permissions must be given in their numeric form.

You count from right to left with binary. Therefore, if you look at a file, you can easily come up with its numeric coding system value. The following file has full permissions for the owner and read permissions for the group and the world:

```
shell:/home/dpitts$ ls -la test
-rwxr--r--   1 dpitts   users          22 Sep 15 00:49 test
```

This would be coded as `744`. Table 21.4 explains how this number was achieved.

TABLE 21.4 Numeric Permissions

Permission	*Value*
Read	4
Write	2
Execute	1

Permissions use an additive process; therefore, a person with read, write, and execute permissions to a file would have a `7` (`4+2+1`). Read and execute would have a value of `5`. Remember, there are three sets of values, so each section has its own value.

Table 21.5 shows both the numeric system and the character system for the permissions.

TABLE 21.5 Comparison of Numeric and Character Permissions

Permission	*Numeric*	*Character*
Read-only	4	r--
Write-only	2	-w-
Execute-only	1	--x
Read and write	6	rw-
Read and execute	5	r-x
Read, write, and execute		7rwx

Permissions can be changed by using the `chmod` command. With the numeric system, the `chmod` command must be given the value for all three fields. Therefore, you would issue the following command to change a file to read, write, and execute by everyone:

```
$ chmod 777 <filename>
```

To perform the same task with the character system, you would issue the following command:

```
$ chmod a+rwx <filename>
```

Of course, more than one type of permission can be specified at one time. The following command adds write access for the owner of the file and adds read and execute access to the group and everyone else:

```
$ chmod u+w,og+rx <filename>
```

The advantage that the character system provides is that you do not have to know the previous permissions. You can selectively add or remove permissions without worrying about the rest. With the numeric system, each section of users must always be specified. The downside of the character system is apparent when complex changes are being made. Looking at the preceding example (`chmod u+w,og+rx <filename>`), an easier way might have been to use the numeric system and replace all those letters with three numbers: `755`.

How suid and sgid Fit into This Picture

The special-purpose access modes `suid` and `sgid` add an extra character to the picture. Before looking at what a file looks like with the special access modes, check Table 21.6 for the identifying characters for each of the modes and for a reminder of what they mean.

TABLE 21.6 Special-Purpose Access Modes

Code	*Name*	*Meaning*
s	suid	Sets process user ID on execution
s	sgid	Sets process group ID on execution

`suid` and `sgid` are used on executables; therefore, the code is placed where the code for the executable would normally go. The following file has `suid` set:

```
$ ls -la test
-rwsr--r--   1 dpitts   users          22 Sep 15 00:49 test
```

The difference between setting the suid and setting the sgid is the placement of the code. The same file with sgid active would look like this:

```
$ ls -la test
-rwxr-sr--   1 dpitts   users          22 Sep 15 00:49 test
```

To set the suid with the character system, you execute the following command:

```
$ chmod u+s <filename>
```

To set the sgid with the character system, you execute the following command:

```
$ chmod g+s <filename>
```

To set the suid and the sgid using the numeric system, use these two commands:

```
$ chmod 2### <filename>
```

```
$ chmod 4### <filename>
```

In both instances, you replace ### with the rest of the values for the permissions. The additive process is used to combine permissions; therefore, the following command adds suid and sgid to a file:

```
$ chmod 6### <filename>
```

Note

A sticky bit is set by using chmod 1### *<filename>*. If a *sticky bit* is set, the executable is kept in memory after it has finished executing. The display for a sticky bit is a t, placed in the last field of the permissions. Therefore, a file that has been set to 7777 would have the following permissions: -rwsrwsrwt.

The Default Mode for a File or Directory

The default mode for a file or directory is set with umask, which uses the numeric system to define its value. To set the umask, you must first determine the value you want the files to have. For example, a common file permission set is 644, with which the owner has read and write permission and the rest of the world has read permission. After the value is determined, you subtract it from 777. Keeping the same example of 644, the value would be 133. This value is the umask value.Typically, this value is placed in a system file that is read when a user first logs on. After the value is set, all files created will set their permissions automatically, using this value.

Passwords—A Second Look

The system stores the user's encrypted password in the /etc/passwd file. If the system is using a shadow password system, the value placed in this field is x. A value of * blocks login access to the account, as * is not a valid character for an encrypted field. This field should never be edited by hand (after it is set up). Instead, a program such as passwd should be used so that proper encryption takes place. If this field is changed, the old password is no longer valid and more than likely will have to be changed by root.

> **Note**
>
> If the system is using a shadow password system, a separate file, /etc/shadow, contains passwords (encrypted, of course).

A *password* is a secret set of characters set up by the user and known only by the user. The system asks for the password, compares the input to the known password, and if there is a match, confirms the user's identity and lets the user access the system. It cannot be said enough: Do not write down your password! A person who has a user's name and password is, from the system's perspective, that user—and has all of that user's rights and privileges.

Related WWW Sites

Table 21.7 shows the more standard locations to find some of the tools discussed in this chapter. Other Web sites have these tools as well, but these were chosen because they will probably still be around when this book is published. As a matter of fact, I checked these sites a year after originally putting them here for the second edition, and only two entries needed to be changed for the third edition.

A good place for information on security problems can be found at http://support.redhat.com/errata.

The Caldera folks put a lot of effort in keeping up with security, so it is a good habit to check out their security-related portion of their Web site on a regular basis: http://www.calderasystems.com/news/security/.

Like every other major distribution, the people who take care of Debian have a security Web site. You can find all the relevant and up-to-date information here: http://www.debian.org/security/.

TABLE 21.7 WWW Sites for Tools

Tool	*Address*
Cops	ftp://ftp.cert.org/pub/tools/cops
crack	ftp://ftp.cert.org/pub/tools/crack
deslogin	ftp://ftp.uu.net/pub/security/des
findsuid.tar.Z	ftp://isgate.is/ pub/unix/sec8/findsuid.tar.Z
freestone	ftp.soscorp.com/pub/sos/freestone
gabriel	ftp://ftp.best.com/pub/lat
ipfilter	http://cheops.anu.edu.au/~avalon/
ipfirewall	ftp://ftp.nebulus.net/pub/bsdi/
kerberos	http://www.contrib.andrew.cmu.edu/ usr/db74/kerberos.html
merlin	http://ciac.llnl.gov/
obvious-pw.tar.Z	ftp://isgate.is /pub/unix/sec7/obvious-pw.tar.Z
pcheck.tar.Z	ftp://isgate.is/pub/unix/sec8/pcheck.tar.Z
Plugslot Ltd.	http://www.plusglot.com
rsaeuro	ftp://ftp.ox.ac.uk /pub/crypto/misc/rscan http://www.umbc.edu/rscan/
satan	http://www.fish.com/satan
Secure Telnet	ftp://idea.sec.dsi.unimi.it/cert-it/stel-b5.tar.gz
ssh	http://www.cs.hut.fi/sshprotocols2/tcp wrappersftp.porcupine.org/pub/security
telnet (encrypted)	ftp.tuchemnitz.de/pub/Local/informatik/sec_tel_ftp/
tiger	ftp://wuarchive.wustl.edu/packages/security/TAMU/
tis firewall	ftp://ftp.tis.com/pub/firewalls/toolkit toolkit/
tripwire	ftp://wuarchive.wustl.edu/packages/security/tripwire/
xp-beta	ftp://ftp.mri.co.jp/pub/XpBETA/
xroute	ftp://ftp.x.org/contrib/utilities/

Summary

Security is only as good as the users' willingness to follow policy. On many systems and in many companies, this is where the contention comes in. The users just want to get their jobs done. The administrators want to keep undesirables out of the system. The corporate management wants to keep the corporate secrets secret. Security is, in many ways, the hardest area in which to get users to cooperate. It is, in fact, the most important.

Users who write down or share passwords, poorly written software, and maliciousness are the biggest security problems.

For the administrator in charge of the system, I can only offer this advice: The best user will only follow the policies you follow. If you have poor security habits, they will be passed along. On the other hand, people generally rise to the minimum level they see exhibited or expected. The administrator's job is to go beyond the call of duty and gently point out improvements, while at the same time fighting the dragons at the back gate trying to get into the system.

CHAPTER 22

Automating Tasks

In This Chapter

"[T]he three great virtues of a programmer: *laziness*, *impatience*, and *hubris*."

—Wall and Schwartz, in *Programming Perl*

Automation enlists a machine—a Linux computer, in the present case—to perform jobs. What makes this definition live, however, and the true subject of this chapter, is *attitude*. The most important step you can take in understanding mechanisms of automation under Linux is to adopt the attitude that the computer works for you. After you've done that, when you realize you're too lazy to type a telephone number that the machine should already know or too impatient to wait until midnight to start backups, and when you have enough confidence in your own creativity to teach the machine a better way, the technical details will work themselves out. This chapter offers more than a dozen examples of how small, understandable automation initiatives make an immediate difference. Let them lead you to your own successes.

First Example—Automating Data Entry

How can the details work out? Look at an example from the day before I started to write this chapter.

Problem and Solution

A client wanted to enhance an online catalog to include thumbnail pictures of the merchandise. After a bit of confusion about what this really meant, I realized that I needed to update a simple database table of products to include a new column (or attribute or value) that would specify the filenames of the thumbnails. The database management system has a couple of interactive front ends, and I'm a swift typist, so it probably would have been quickest to point and click my way through the 200 picture updates. Did I do that? Of course not—what happened later proved the wisdom of this decision. Instead, I wrote a shell script to automate the update, which is shown in Listing 22.1.

LISTING 22.1 A Shell Script That Updates a Database

```
# picture names seem to look like {$DIR/137-13p.jpg,$DIR/201-942f.jpg,...}
# The corresponding products appear to be {137-13P, 201-942F, ...}
DIR=/particular/directory/for/my/client

     # Will we use .gif-s, also, eventually?  I don't know.
for F in $DIR/*.jpg
do
       # BASE will have values {137-13p,201-942f, ...}
```

```
BASE=`basename $F .jpg`
     # The only suffixes I've encountered are 'p' and 'f', so I'll simply
     #     transform those two.
     # Example values for PRODUCT:  {137-13P, 201-942F, ...}
PRODUCT=`echo $BASE ¦ tr pf PF`
     # one_command is a shell script that passes a line of SQL to the DBMS.
one_command update catalog set Picture = "'$DIR/$BASE.jpg'" where Product = "'$PRODUCT'"
done
```


As it turned out, the team decided within a couple days that the pictures needed to be in a different directory, so it was only a few seconds' work to update the penultimate line of the script, add a comment such as the following, and rerun it:

```
    ...
    # Do *not* include a directory specification in Picture; that will be known
    #     only at the time the data are retrieved.
    one_command update catalog set Picture = "'$BASE.jpg'" where
       Product = "'$PRODUCT'"
done
```

It's inevitable we'll someday have more pictures to add to the database or will want reports on *orphaned pictures* (those that haven't been connected yet to any product), and this same script—or a close derivative of it—will come into play again.

Analysis of the Implementation

Now work through the example in Listing 22.1 in detail to practice the automation mentality.

Do you understand how the script in Listing 22.1 works? Chapter 25, "Shell Programming," explains shell processing, and Appendix B, "Top Linux Commands and Utilities," presents everything you're likely to need about the most commonly used UNIX utilities. You can always learn more about these by reading the corresponding man pages or any of the fine books available on shell programming. The most certain way to learn, of course, is to experiment on your own. For example, if you have any question about what `man tr` means by "translation," it's an easy matter to experiment. Try using this:

```
# tr pf PF <<HERE
abcopqOPQ
FfpPab
HERE
```

You can easily conclude that you're on the right track when you see the following:

```
abcoPqOPQ
FFPPab
```

This is one of the charms of relying on shells for automation; it's easy to bounce between interaction and automation, which shapes a powerful didactic perspective and a check on understanding.

The sample product catalog script in Listing 22.1 is written for `sh` processing. I strongly recommend this be your target for scripts, rather than `ksh`, `csh`, or `bash`. I much prefer any of the latter for interactive command-line use. In automating, however, when I'm often connecting to hosts that don't use Linux, availability and esoteric security issues have convinced me to code using constructs that `sh`—and therefore all the shells—recognize. Default Linux installations use a link named `/bin/sh` that points to `/bin/bash`. All the work in this chapter is written so that the scripts will function properly no matter what the details of your host's configuration. Chapter 25 gives more details on the differences among shells.

Did I really include the inline comments, the lines that begin with `#`, when I first wrote the script in Listing 22.1? Yes. I've made this level of source-code documentation a habit, and it's one I recommend to you. If your life is at all like mine, telephones ring, co-workers chat, and power supplies fail; I find it easier to type this much detail as I'm thinking about it, rather than risk having to re-create my thoughts in case of an interruption. Also, it's much easier to pick up the work again days or weeks later. Writing for human readability also eases the transition when you pass your work on to others.

Listing 22.1 begins by assigning a shell variable `DIR` in Line 3. It's good practice to make such an assignment, even for a variable (apparently) used only once. It contributes to self-documentation and generally enhances maintainability; it's easy to look at the top of the script and see immediately on what magic words or configuration in the outside environment (`/particular/directory/for/my/client`, in this case; see line 3) the script depends.

Many of the jobs you'll want to accomplish involve a quantifier: "change all...," "correct every," and so on. The shell's looping constructs, `for` and `while`, are your friends. You'll make almost daily use of them.

`basename` and `tr` are universally available and widely used. `tr`, like many UNIX utilities, expects to read standard input. If you have information in shell variables, you can feed `tr` the information you want either one of two ways. This is through a pipe from `echo`:

```
echo $VARIABLE ¦ tr [a-z] [A-Z]
```

This is as an equivalent, or with a so-called `HERE` document:

```
tr [a-z] [A-Z] <<HERE
$VARIABLE
HERE
```

You can also perhaps create a temporary file:

```
echo $VARIABLE >$TMPFILE
tr [a-z] [A-Z] <$TMPFILE
```

`one_command`, as invoked in Line 15 of Listing 22.1, is a two-line shell script written earlier in the day to process SQL commands. Why not inline the body of that script here? Although technically feasible, I have a strong preference for small, simple programs that are easy to understand and correspondingly easy to implement correctly. `one_command` already has been verified to do one small job reliably, so the script lets it do that job. This fits with the UNIX tradition that counsels combining robust toolkit pieces to construct grander works.

In fact, notice that the example in Listing 22.1 shows the shell's nature as a "glue" language. There's a small amount of processing within the shell in manipulating filenames, and then most of the work is handed off to other commands; the shell just glues together results. This is typical and is the correct style you should adopt for your own scripting.

Certainly, it was pleasant when the filenames changed and I realized I could rework one word of the script, rather than retype the 200 entries. As satisfying as this was, the total benefit of automation is still more profound. Even greater than saving my time are the improvements in quality, traceability, and reusability this affords. With the script, I control the data entering the database at a higher level and eliminate whole categories of error: mistyping, accidentally pushing a wrong button in a graphical user interface, and so on. Also, the script in Listing 22.1 records my procedure, in case it's later useful to audit the data. Suppose, for example, that next year it's decided I shouldn't have inserted any of these references to the database's `Picture` attribute. How many will have to be backed out? Useful answers—at most, the count of `$DIR/*.jpg`—can be read directly from the script; there's no need to rely on memory or speculation.

Tips for Improving Automation Technique

You're in charge of your career in automation. Along with everything else this chapter advises, you'll go furthest if you do the following:

- Improve your automation technique.
- Engineer well.

These tips have specific meaning in the rest of this chapter. Look for ways to apply them in all that follows.

Continuing Education

There are three important ways to improve your skill with automation techniques, which apply equally well whether you're using Perl, `cron`, Expect, or another mechanism:

- Scan the documentation.
- Read good scripts.
- Practice writing scripts.

Documentation has the reputation of being dry and even unreadable. It's important you learn how to employ it. All the tools presented here have man pages, which you need to be comfortable using. Read these documents and reread them. Authors of the tools faced many of the challenges you do. Often, reading through the lists of options or keywords, you'll realize that particular capabilities apply exactly to your situation. Study the documentation with this in mind; look for the ideas that you can use. Give particular attention to commands you don't recognize. If some of them—`cu`, perhaps, or `od`—are largely superannuated, you'll realize in reading about others—such as `tput`, `ulimit`, `bc`, `nice`, or `wait`—that earlier users were confronted with just the situations that confound your own work. Stand on their shoulders and see farther.

> **Note**
>
> Want to know more about a command? There may be two other sources of information besides its man page. Linux users should also check the `/usr/doc` directory, where programs have individual directories of additional information. You may also find more detailed information about a command if its man page indicates the program is part of the GNU software distribution; the command may be documented with a GNU info page. Information documents reside under the `/usr/info` directory, and you'll find hundreds of information documents installed on your system. Use the info command in this way:
> `info` *<command>*.

It's important to read examples of good programming. Aspiring literary authors find inspiration in Pushkin and Pynchon, not grammar primers; similarly, you'll go furthest when you read the best work of the best programmers. Look in the columns of computer magazines and, most importantly, the archives of software with freely available source. Good examples of coding occasionally turn up in Usenet discussions. Prize these; read them and learn from the masters.

All the examples in this chapter are written for easy use. They typically do one small task completely; this is one of the best ways to demonstrate a new concept. Although exception handling—and argument validation in particular—is important, it is beyond the scope of this chapter.

Crystallize your learning by writing your own scripts. All the documents you read will make more sense after you put the knowledge in place with your own experience.

Good Engineering

The other advice for those pursuing automation is to practice good engineering. This always starts with a clear, well-defined goal. Automation isn't an absolute good; it's only a method for achieving human goals. Part of what you'll learn in working through this chapter is how much, and how little, to automate.

When your goal is set, move as close to it as you can with components that are already written. "Glue" existing programs together with small, understandable scripting modules. Choose meaningful variable names. Define interfaces carefully. Write comments.

Shell Scripts

Although Chapter 25 covers the basic syntax and language of shell programming, look at a few additional examples of scripts that are often useful in day-to-day operation.

Changing Strings in Files with `chstr`

Users who maintain source code, client lists, and other records often want to launch a find-and-replace operation from the command line. It's useful to have a variant of `chstr` on UNIX hosts. Listing 22.2 gives one example.

LISTING 22.2 *chstr*—A Simple Find-and-Replace Operation

```
########
#
# See usage() definition, below, for more details.
#
# This implementation doesn't do well with complicated escape
#     sequences. That has been no more than a minor problem in
#     the real world.
#
########
usage() {
     echo \
"chstr BEFORE AFTER <filenames>
     changes the first instance of BEFORE to AFTER in each line of
➥ <filenames>,
     and reports on the differences.
```

continues

LISTING 22.2 continued

```
Examples:
     chstr TX Texas */addresses.*
     chstr ii counter2 *.c"
     exit 0
}

case $1 in
     -h¦-help)     usage;;
esac

if test $# -lt 3
then
     usage
fi

TMPDIR=/tmp
     # It's OK if more than one instance of chstr is run simultaneously.
     #     The TMPFILE names are specific to each invocation, so there's
     #     no conflict.
TMPFILE=$TMPDIR/chstr.$$

BEFORE=$1
AFTER=$2

     # Toss the BEFORE and AFTER arguments out of the argument list.
shift
shift

for FILE in $*
do
     sed -e "s/$BEFORE/$AFTER/" $FILE >$TMPFILE
     echo "$FILE:"
     diff $FILE $TMPFILE
     echo ""
     mv $TMPFILE $FILE
done
```

Most interactive editors permit a form of global search-and-replace, and some even make it easy to operate on more than one file. Perhaps that's a superior automation for your needs. If not, `chstr` is a minimal command-line alternative that is maximally simple to use.

Note

Of course, experienced Perl hackers may find Listing 22.2 a bit longer than necessary when nearly the same changes can be accomplished from the command line like this:

```
# perl -p -i.tmp -e s/beforestr/afterstr/g file(s)
```

See Chapter 28, "Perl Programming," for more information.

WWW Retrieval

A question that arises frequently is how to automate retrieval of pages from the World Wide Web. This section shows the simplest of many techniques.

FTP Retrieval

Create a shell script, `retrieve_one`, with the contents of Listing 22.3 and with execution enabled: command `chmod +x retrieve_one`.

LISTING 22.3 *`retrieve_one`*—Automating FTP Retrieval

```
# Usage:  "retrieve_one HOST:FILE" uses anonymous FTP to connect
#     to HOST and retrieve FILE into the local directory.

MY_ACCOUNT=myaccount@myhost.com
HOST=`echo $1 ¦ sed -e "s/:.*//"`
FILE=`echo $1 ¦ sed -e "s/.*://"`
LOCAL_FILE=`basename $FILE`

     # -v:  report all statistics.
     # -n:  connect without interactive user authentication.
ftp -v -n $HOST << SCRIPT
     user anonymous $MY_ACCOUNT
     get $FILE $LOCAL_FILE
     quit
SCRIPT
```

`retrieve_one` is useful for purposes such as ordering a current copy of a FAQ into your local directory. Start experimenting with it by making a request with the following:

```
# retrieve_one rtfm.mit.edu:/pub/usenet-by-hierarchy/comp/os/linux/answers/
➥linux/info-sheet
```

Linux comes with other utilities you can use for FTP retrieval. See Chapter 10, "FTP," for information about the `ncftp` and Red Hat's GNOME-enabled `gftp` commands.

HTTP Retrieval

For an HTTP interaction, let the text-only lynx Web browser do the bulk of the work. The lynx browser that typically accompanies your GNU/Linux distribution is adequate for all but the most specialized purposes. You can obtain the latest version at `http://lynx.browser.org`. Although most lynx users think of lynx as an interactive browser, it's also handy for dropping a copy of the latest headlines, with live links, in a friend's mailbox with this:

```
# lynx -source http://www.cnn.com ¦ mail someone@somewhere.com
```

To create a primitive news update service, script this:

```
NEW=/tmp/news.new
OLD=/tmp/news.old
URL=http://www.cnn.com
while true
do
     mv $NEW $OLD
     lynx -dump -nolist $URL >$NEW
     diff $NEW $OLD
          # Wait ten minutes before starting the next comparison.
     sleep 600
done
```

Launch it in the background (using the ampersand, `&`). Any changes in the appearance of CNN's home page will appear onscreen every 10 minutes. This simple approach is less practical than you might first expect because CNN periodically shuffles the content without changing the information. It's an instructive example, however, and a starting point from which you can elaborate your own scripts.

Conclusions on Shell Programming

Shells are glue; if there's a way to get an application to perform an action from the command line, there's almost certainly a way to wrap it in a shell script that gives you power over argument validation, iteration, and input-output redirection. These are powerful techniques and well worth the few minutes of study and practice it takes to begin learning them.

Even small automations pay off. My personal rule of thumb is to write tiny disposable one-line shell scripts when I expect to use a sequence even twice during a session. For example, although I have a sophisticated set of reporting commands for analyzing World Wide Web server logs, I also find myself going to the trouble of editing a disposable script such as `/tmp/r9`, to do quick, ad hoc queries on recent hit patterns. This particular example reports on the number of requests for pages that include the string `claird` and exclude the first argument to `/tmp/r9`, in the most recent log:

```
grep claird `ls -t /usr/cern/log/* ¦ head -1` ¦ grep -v $1 ¦ wc -l
```

Scheduling Tasks with cron and at Jobs

Every Linux distribution comes with several utilities that manage the rudiments of job scheduling. at schedules a process for later execution, and cron (or crontab—it has a couple of interfaces, and different engineers use both these names) periodically launches a process.

The crond daemon is started by the crond script under the /etc/rc.d/init.d directory when you boot Red Hat Linux. On Debian systems, the script resides in /etc/init.d/cron. This daemon checks your system's /etc/crontab file and /var/spool/cron directory every minute, looking for assigned tasks at assigned times. Under Caldera OpenLinux, scheduling is administered by the cron script under the /etc/rc.d/init.d directory, which launches the cron daemon. This script uses the ssd, or start-stop-daemon, command to launch or stop scheduling of the cron daemon (which, like Red Hat's crond, also checks /etc/crontab every minute).

As a system administrator, you'll schedule system tasks in /etc/crontab. Under Red Hat Linux, this file initially contains four entries:

```
01 * * * * root run-parts /etc/cron.hourly
02 4 * * * root run-parts /etc/cron.daily
22 4 * * 0 root run-parts /etc/cron.weekly
42 4 1 * * root run-parts /etc/cron.monthly
```

Scripts set to run on an hourly, daily, weekly, or monthly basis will be found under the /etc directory as shown earlier. Caldera OpenLinux has an initial crontab with similar entries:

```
# run-parts
03  3  1  *  * root [ -x /usr/sbin/cronloop ] && /usr/sbin/cronloop Monthly
04  4  *  *  6 root [ -x /usr/sbin/cronloop ] && /usr/sbin/cronloop Weekly
05  5  *  *  * root [ -x /usr/sbin/cronloop ] && /usr/sbin/cronloop Daily
42  *  *  *  * root [ -x /usr/sbin/cronloop ] && /usr/sbin/cronloop Hourly
```

With the Caldera Linux distribution, a shell script named cronloop is used to execute regular tasks defined in the Monthly, Weekly, Daily, or Hourly directories under the /etc/cron.d directory. Personal cron tasks, created by using the crontab command, are saved under the /var/spool/cron directory. To allow system users to schedule personal cron tasks under Caldera OpenLinux, the root operator must first create two files—/etc/cron.allow and /etc/cron.deny—and then insert the root operator name (root), and the names of allowed users in the /etc/cron.allow file.

Note

When the crontab command is used with the -e option to create a personal crontab file, crontab uses the vi editor, or an editor defined with the EDITOR environment variable. Under Caldera OpenLinux 2.2, users should install the pico editor (part of the pine mail RPM package, found on CD-ROM under the col/contrib directory) and define pico as the default editor in the .profile file in their home directory, like this:

```
EDITOR=/usr/bin/pico; export EDITOR
```

For some obscure reason, no other editor—including me, vim, gvim, and kedit—will work with Caldera's crontab command. Alternatively, create your crontab entries as shown in the section "Tracking System Core Files."

Personal at jobs under Red Hat Linux are saved under the /var/spool/at directory and will have group and file ownership of the creator, like this:

```
-rwx------    1 bball    bball        1093 Apr 19 17:47 a0000200eb209c
```

With Caldera OpenLinux, at jobs are stored under the /var/spool/atjobs directory with a default users group membership. The difference between crontab and at is that crontab should be used to schedule and run periodic, repetitive tasks on a regular basis, while at jobs are usually meant to run once at a future time.

Note

The /etc/cron.allow and /etc/cron.deny files control who may use crontab on your system. For details, see the crontab man page. You can also control who can use the at command on your system with the /etc/at.allow and /etc/at.deny files. By default, some Linux distributions let anyone use the at and crontab commands.

cron and find—Exploring Disk Usage

One eternal reality of system administration is that there's not enough disk space. The following sections offer a couple expedients recommended for keeping on top of what's happening with your system.

Tracking System Core Files

cron use use always involves a bit of setup. Although Appendix B gives more details on cron's features and options, I'll go carefully through an example here that helps track down core clutter.

You need at least one external file to start using the cron facility. Practice cron concepts by commanding this first:

```
# echo "0,5,10,15,20,25,30,35,40,45,50,55 * * * * date > `tty`"
➥>/tmp/experiment
```

Then command this:

```
# crontab /tmp/experiment
```

Finally, command this:

```
# crontab -l
```

The last of these gives you a result that looks something like the following:

```
0,5,10,15,20,25,30,35,40,45,50,55 * * * * date > /dev/ttyxx
```

The current time will appear in the window every five minutes from which you launched this experiment.

For a more useful example, create a /tmp/entry file with this single line:

```
0 2 * * * find / -name "core*" -exec ls -l {} \;
```

Next, use this command:

```
# crontab /tmp/entry
```

The result is that each morning at 2:00, cron launches the core-searching job and emails you the results when finished. This is quite useful because Linux creates files core under certain error conditions. These core images are often large and can easily fill up a distressing amount of space on your disk. With the preceding sequence, you'll have a report in your email inbox each morning, listing exactly the locations and sizes of a collection of files that are likely doing you no good.

Monitoring User Space

Suppose you've experimented a bit and accumulated an inventory of cron jobs to monitor the health of your system. Now, along with your other jobs, you want your system to tell you every Monday morning at 2:10 which 10 users have the biggest home directory trees (/home/*). Enter this first to capture all the jobs you've scheduled:

```
# crontab -l >/tmp/entries
```

Append this line to the bottom of /tmp/entries:

```
10 2 * * 1 du -s /home/* | sort -nr | head -10
```

Make the following request and cron will email the reports you seek:

```
# crontab /tmp/entries
```

at: Scheduling Future Events

Suppose you write a you write a weekly column on cycles in the material world, which you deliver by email. To simplify legal ramifications involving financial markets, you make a point of delivering it at 5:00 Friday afternoon. It's Wednesday now, you've finished your analysis, and you're almost through packing for the vacation you're starting tonight. How do you do right by your subscribers? It only takes three lines of at scripting using the shell's here (<<) operator:

```
# at 17:00 Friday << COMMAND
   mail -s "This week's CYCLES report." mailing_list <
➥ analysis.already_written
COMMAND
```

This schedules the mail command for later processing. You can log off from your session, and your Linux host will still send the mail at 17:00 Friday, just as you instructed. In fact, you can even shut down your machine after commanding it at ..., and as long as it's rebooted in time, your scheduled task will still be launched on the schedulelaunched on the schedule you dictated. you dictated.

Other Mechanisms: Expect, Perl, and More

Are you ready to move beyond the constraints of the UNIX shell? Several alternative technologies are free, easy to install and to learn, and more powerful—that is, with richer capabilities and more structured syntax—than the shell. A few examples will suggest what they have to offer.

Expect

Expect, by Don Libes, is a scripting language that works with many different programs,and can be used as a powerful software tool for automation. Why? Expect automates interactions, particularly those involving terminal control and time delays, that no other tool has attempted. Many command-line applications have the reputation for being unscriptable because they involve password entry and refuse to accept redirection of standard input for this purpose. That's no problem for the `expect` command, however. Many Linux distributions offer `expect`; it's typically installed in `/usr/bin`, and you'll find documentation in its manual page.

> **Note**
>
> The `expect` interpreter is not included with Caldera OpenLinux 2.2, but you can download an RPM archive of the latest version from `http://rpmfind.net/linux/RPM/Programming_Interpreter.html`.

Create a script `hold` with the contents of Listing 22.4.

LISTING 22.4 *hold*—A "Keep-Alive" Written in Expect

```
#!/usr /bin/expect

# Usage:  "hold HOST USER PASS".
# Action:  login to node HOST as USER.  Offer a shell prompt for
#     normal usage, and also print to the screen the word HELD
#     every five seconds, to exercise the connection periodically.
#     This is useful for testing and using WANs with short time-outs.
#     You can walk away from the keyboard, and never lose your
#     connection through a time-out.
# WARNING:  the security hazard of passing a password through the
#     command line makes this example only illustrative.  Modify to
#     a particular security situation as appropriate.
set hostname [lindex $argv 0]
set username [lindex $argv 1]
set password [lindex $argv 2]

     # There's trouble if $username's prompt is not set to "...} ".
     #     A more sophisticated manager knows how to look for different
     #     prompts on different hosts.
set prompt_sequence "} "

spawn telnet $hostname

expect "login: "
send "$username\r"
expect "Password:"
send "$password\r"

     # Some hosts don't inquire about TERM.  That's another
     #     complexification to consider before widespread use
     #     of this application is practical.
```

continues

LISTING 22.4 continued

```
     # Note use of global [gl] pattern matching to parse "*"
     #     as a wildcard.
expect -gl "TERM = (*)"
send "\r"

expect $prompt_sequence
send "sh -c 'while true; do echo HELD; sleep 5; done'\r"
interact
```

I work with several telephone lines that are used with short timeouts, as a check on out-of-pocket expenses. I use a variant of the script in Listing 22.4 daily, for I often need that to hold one of the connections open.

Expect is an extension to `tcl`, so it is fully programmable with all the `tcl` capabilities that Chapter 30, "`tcl` and `tk` Programming," presents. For information about `tcl` and `tk` from its author, Dr. John Ousterhout, visit `http://www.sun.com/960710/cover/ousterhout.html`. For more information about Expect, visit `http://www.expect.org`.

Tip

You'll also find the `autoexpect` command included with expect. This command watches an interactive session at the console and then creates an executable program to execute the console session. See Chapter 10 for an example of how to use `autoexpect` to automate an FTP session.

Perl

Chapter 28 presents Perl as the most popular scripting language for Linux, apart from the shell. Its power and brevity take on particular value in automation contexts.

Note

For more information about Perl and to get the latest release, browse `http://www.perl.com` or `http://www.perl.org`.

For example, assume `/usr/local/bin/modified_directories.pl` contains the following:

```
#!/usr/bin/perl
# Usage:  "modified_directories.pl DIR1 DIR2 ... DIRN"
# Output:  a list of all directories in the file systems under
```

```
#     DIR1 ... DIRN, collectively.  They appear, sorted by the
#     interval since their last activity, that is, since a file
#     within them was last created, deleted, or renamed.
# Randal Schwartz wrote a related program from which this is
#     descended.
use File::Find;
@directory_list = @ARGV;
# "-M" abbreviates "time since last modification", while
#      "-d" "... is a directory."

find ( sub {
$modification_lapse{$File::Find::name} = -M if -d },
@directory_list );

for ( sort {
$modification_lapse{$a} <=> $modification_lapse{$b}} keys
%modification_lapse ) {

    # Tabulate the results in nice columns.
    printf "%5d:  %s\n", $modification_lapse{$_}, $_;
}
```


Assume also that you adjoin an entry such as this to your `crontab`:

```
20 2 * * * /usr/local/bin/modified_directories.pl /
```

In this case, each morning you'll receive an email report on the date each directory on your host was last modified. This can be useful both for spotting security issues when read-only directories have been changed (they'll appear unexpectedly at the top of the list) and for identifying dormant domains in the filesystem (at the bottom of the list) that might be liberated for better uses.

Other Tools

Many other general-purpose scripting languages effectively automate operations. Apart from Perl and `tcl`, Python deserves the most attention for several reasons, such as its portability and extensibility.

The next sections describe Python and two other special-purpose tools important in automation: `Emacs` and `procmail`.

Python

Python can be of special interest to Linux users since several tools, such as `printtool`, are supported by Python. Python is object-oriented, modern, clean, portable, and particularly easy to maintain. If you are a full-time system administrator looking for a scripting language that will grow with you, consider Python. See Chapter 31, "Programming in Python," for more information. The official home page for Python is `http://www.python.org`.

Emacs

Emacs is one of the most polarizing lightning rods for religious controversy among computer users. Emacs has many intelligent and zealous users who believe it the ideal platform for all automation efforts. Its devotees have developed what was originally a screen editor into a tool with capabilities to manage newsgroup discussion, Web browsing, application development, general-purpose scripting, and much more. For the purposes of this chapter, what you need to know about Emacs follows:

- It's an editor that you ought to try at some point in your career.
- Emacs is included with nearly every Linux distribution (although different distributions may use variations, such as xemacs included with Caldera OpenLinux, or GNU's emacs included with Red Hat Linux).
- If you favor integrated development environments, Emacs can do almost anything you imagine. As an editor, it emulates any other editor, and its developers ensure that it always offers state-of-the-art capabilities in language-directed formatting, application integration, and development automation.

Even if the *weight* of Emacs (it may seem slow on startup and can require quite a bit of education and configuration) sways you against its daily use, keep it in mind as a paragon of how sophisticated programming makes common operations more efficient.

Note

The Emacs editor is included with many Linux distributions, and you can use Emacs with or without the X Window system. Type the word **emacs** on the command line of your console or an X11 terminal window, and press the Enter key. Run its built-in tutorial by pressing Ctrl+H and typing the t key.

procmail

Computer use has exploded in the Internet era. The most indispensable, most-used Internet function is email. Can email be automated?

Yes, of course, and it's perhaps the single best return on your invested time to do so. Along with aliases, distribution lists, startup configurations, and the plethora of mail agents or clients with their feature sets, you'll want to learn about procmail. Suppose that you receive a hundred messages a day; a fifth of them can be handled completely automatically, and it takes at least three seconds of your time to process a single piece of email. Those are conservative estimates, from the experience of the computer workers I know. A bit of procmail automation will save you at least a minute a day, or six hours a year. Even conservative estimates make it clear that an hour of setting up procmail pays for itself many times over.

Along with the man procmail* pages, serious study of procmail starts with the page found at http://www.faqs.org/faqs/mail/filtering-faq—Nancy McGough's Filtering Mail FAQ. This gives detailed installation and debugging directions. You'll also find information about procmail in the mail HOWTO, found under the /usr/doc/HOWTO directory included with most Linux distributions. Because your Linux machine will almost certainly have a correctly configured procmail if you install your distribution's procmail package you can immediately begin to use it. As a first experiment, create the file ~/.procmailrc, with these contents:

```
VERBOSE=on
MAILDIR=$HOME/mail
PMDIR=$HOME/.procmail
LOGFILE=$PMDIR/log
INCLUDERC=$PMDIR/rc.testing
```

Create ~/.procmail/rc.testing, which should hold this:

```
:0:
* ^Subject:.*HOT
SPAM.HOT
```

Create ~/.forward, including this:

```
"¦IFS=' ' && exec /usr/bin/procmail -f ¦¦ exec 75 #YOUR_EMAIL_NAME"
```

After you create these three, set necessary permissions with the following:

```
# chmod 644 ~/.forward
# chmod a+x ~/.
```

Now, exercise your filter with the following (substituting your email name, of course):

```
# echo "This message 1." ¦ mail -s "Example of HOT SPAM." YOUR_EMAIL_NAME
# echo "This message 2." ¦ mail -s "Desired message." YOUR_EMAIL_NAME
```

What you now see in your mailbox is only one new item—the one with the subject Desired message. You also have a new file in your home directory, SPAM.HOT, holding the first message.

procmail is a robust, flexible utility you can program to achieve even more useful automations than this. When you gain familiarity with it, it will become natural to construct rules that, for example, automatically discard obvious spam, sort incoming mailing-list traffic, and perhaps even implement pager forwarding, remote system monitoring, or FAQ responding. This can save you considerable time each day.

Internal Scripts

One more element of the automation attitude is to be on the lookout for opportunities within every application you use. Scripting has become a pervasive theme, and almost all common applications have at least a rudimentary macro or scripting capability. IRC users know about bots, Web browsers typically expose at least a couple of scripting interfaces, all modern PPP clients are scriptable, and even such venerable tools as `vi` and `ftp` have configuration, shortcut, and macro capabilities that enormously magnify productivity. If you use a tool regularly, take a few minutes to reread its presentation in this volume; chances are, you'll come up with a way to make your work easier and more effective.

Concluding Challenge for an Automater—Explaining Value

You've become knowledgeable and experienced in scripting your computer so that it best serves you. You know how to improve your skills in script writing. You've practiced different approaches enough to know how to solve problems efficiently. The final challenge in your automation career is this: How do you explain how good you have become?

This is a serious problem, and as usual, the solution begins with attitude. You no longer pound at the keyboard to bludgeon technical tasks into submission; you now operate in a more refined way and achieve correspondingly grander results. As an employee, you're much more valuable than the system administrators and programmers who reinvent wheels every day. In your recreational or personal use of Linux, the computer is working for you, not the other way around, as it might have been when you started. Your attitude needs to adjust to the reality you've created by improving your productivity. Invest in yourself, whether by attending technical conferences where you can further promote your skills, negotiating a higher salary, or simply taking the time in your computer work to get things right. It's easy in organizations to give attention to crises and reward those visibly coping with emergencies. It takes true leadership to plan ahead, organize work so emergencies don't happen, and use techniques of automation to achieve predictable and manageable results on schedule.

One of the most effective tools you have in taking up this challenge is *quantification*. Keep simple records to demonstrate how much time you put into setting up backups before you learned about `cron`, or run a simple experiment to compare two ways of approaching an elementary database maintenance operation. Find out how much of your online time goes just to the login process and decide whether scripting that is justified. Chart a class of mistakes that you make and see whether your precision improves as you apply automation ideas.

In all cases, keep in mind you are efficient, perhaps extraordinarily efficient, because of the knowledge you apply. Automation feels good!

Summary

Automation offers enormous opportunities for using your Linux computer to achieve the goals you set. The examples in this chapter have demonstrated that every Linux user can begin immediately to exploit the techniques and attitude of automation. Some of the major automation mechanisms provided by Linux include background processes, scheduling, and sophisticated software tools. As you gain experience by overcoming required administrative tasks, you'll build your own approaches to system administration automation.

CHAPTER 23

Kernel Management

IN THIS CHAPTER

There is a popular conception that kernel tuning is no place for the average user. In reality, this is both true and false. Like any other feature of Linux, the configuration possibilities are endless and deep, but you don't necessarily need to understand arcane PCI chipset mantras or the gory details of virtual memory to tailor a better Linux for your computer. Armed with nothing more than your computer manuals, you should be able to zero in on those features you need and leave the more technical tuning for some day down the road. If you do know all these technical details, Linux will not stand in your way. If all you know is how to run a shell command, this section will show you how you can build a better Linux for your computer.

Linux is a UNIX-like system, and the core of a UNIX system is the *kernel*, the innermost layer of the operating system that provides a uniform interface to the local hardware. When your computer starts, the boot loader hands control to the kernel. The kernel then identifies your hardware, initiates the boot scripts, and launches your network and terminal daemons. After the boot, the kernel becomes the gateway to the local hardware, supplying applications with a standard interface to basic services such as task switching, signaling, device I/O, and memory management.

Although the default kernel installed by your distribution CD-ROM stands a very good chance of running on your hardware, one kernel cannot be all things to all people. At some point, you will want to harness the real power of UNIX—the power of choice. In Linux, kernel tweaking can be as simple as adding a few command parameters to modify the kernel at boot time, picking and choosing from the ever-growing list of modules and kernel options; as in-depth as tuning memory and filesystem behavior; or as deep as directly modifying or creating driver C code. The Linux kernel can be adapted for low-memory machines, optimized as a router or firewall, or extended to support new hardware, alien filesystems, and a wide array of network protocols.

This chapter describes what makes the Linux kernel so special, even among UNIX-like systems, and includes tips and tutorials on configuring your Linux iron. This chapter covers

- An overview of the Linux kernel architecture
- Obtaining and patching Linux kernel sources
- Compiling a kernel for multiple machines
- Configuring modules and the new kmod auto-loader
- How to configure the kernel for alien filesystems and arbitrary binary executables
- Optimizing Linux as a router versus as a workstation
- Virtual memory and filesystem tuning

- RAID support and software RAID
- Adding network services such as IP masquerading and port forwarding, IPv6, Packet Radio, ISDN, and firewalls
- Installing MS-DOS National Language Support (NLS)
- Supporting special devices such as video/radio/TV cards, joysticks, and infrared controls
- Configuring the OpenSoundSystem driver and the new software-based MIDI Wave Table
- Kernel troubleshooting

After reading this chapter, you will be well equipped to create a custom kernel for your particular machine. The size of this chapter may be a little daunting, but this only illustrates the flexibility of the Linux kernel. You may only need to consult those few sections on installing your sound or special device. On the other hand, for those difficult kernel optimization problems, advanced networking, or tailoring the kernel for embedded and other special situations, this chapter should give you a full overview of what is possible.

Caution

The worst that can happen while reconfiguring your kernel is boot failure. It happens to the best of us, usually because of incompatible settings or forgetting to run `LILO` after changing a kernel. There are few things as frightening as the dread `LI-` boot prompt.

Before you reboot a new kernel, you should take a few precautions to ensure a backup boot method. If your hardware has a floppy drive, keep your distribution install/rescue disks handy. Also, production machines should always keep a boot-floppy with their current stable kernel. Your `LILO` configuration should also include at least one backup kernel image.

Although many people have a penchant for reinstalling from scratch, a habit unfortunately instilled by another popular operating system, in Linux this a rarity. As the South African proverb goes, "If you hear hoofbeats in the street, it is probably not a zebra." With Linux, your darkest hour still probably does not require reinstalling the entire system. Even in seemingly hopeless situations, it is far more likely that your system can be safely rescued and repaired.

When the worst happens, use your rescue disks to boot your system, manually `fsck` and mount the hard drive, restore order, rerun `LILO`, and breathe easier. You can also find a number of rescue disks and tools in the Metalab archive at `ftp://metalab.unc.edu/pub/Linux`.

An Introduction to the Linux Kernel

Linux is one of the fastest-growing OS platforms, already rivaling the installed base of MacOS and giving NT something to worry about. There are millions of users and countless developers deploying Linux in Web servers, edge servers, routers, and embedded systems. Linux has been used on the space shuttle, for telerobotics, and in Hollywood. The reason for this success is not simply the low price tag. Linux has succeeded because it is based on a solid design that's friendly to open source development and portability. Put succinctly, Linux succeeds because it works.

Linux is UNIX-like. It's not a version of UNIX, but rather a new OS highly reminiscent of UNIX. This heritage has freed Linux from legacy code: Linux is designed to be UNIX-compatible, but has been developed from scratch. This freedom allowed Linus Torvalds and the kernel authors to develop a core framework that is highly portable. In the years since the first 68KB rewrite for the Amiga, Linux has been ported to platforms from the PalmPilot to the Dec Alpha, proving the portability of the core design.

Linux is an extremely large and complex piece of software. The kernel contains 1.7 million lines of source code, and by commercial standards, we could expect the development of Linux to take 5 to 10 years and require up to a 500 programmers. The development process of open source has also been proven through the kernel project; Richard Gooch's Kernel FAQ (`http://www.tux.org/lkml/`) observes that Linux is a little more than eight years old, placing it right on track compared to those commercial standards, while harnessing the talents of as many as a thousand programmers spread around the world under the peer-review of many thousands more.

Microkernels Versus Monoliths

"We should do smart things with stupid technology before we do stupid things with smart technology."—Bill Buxton l, Alias Research

A successful operating system must weigh performance and portability to compete in the real world, and the choices made in the Linux project are often a focus of debate. Linux is a *monolithic* kernel, meaning that it places many core services inside the non-swappable memory space of the core program, but to some this also means it is "old technology." When Linus began working on the kernel in 1991, *microkernels*, small and simple core programs that move most processing out in layers of abstraction, were the darling of academia and deemed to be the Holy Grail of portability. Microkernels were thought to be the thoroughly modern path.

Inside the kernel, memory must be divided into kernel space (non-swappable RAM) and user space (virtual memory, that is to say, everywhere else). The monolithic approach keeps most basic machine services in kernel space for efficiency, but having these inside the kernel binds them to the local hardware, impeding portability. In the early '90s, the conventional wisdom on compilers believed that a simple set of core services could abstract the host machine in a small, machine-dependent package, and only this one package would require porting to move the system to a new platform. This approach may sound familiar to Java programmers, and the microkernel model also somewhat influenced the design of Microsoft's NT. Microkernel thinking also later formed the basis of Apple's MkLinux and the GNU HURD.

Linus was not convinced. Microkernels seemed too complex and prone to performance bottlenecks. For Linux, he chose to take the optimization knowledge from microkernel research and apply it to a monolithic design. He reasoned that in the real world, computer architecture will follow certain "best" designs, and by accommodating those patterns, Linux would be essentially portable. By designing for the lowest common denominator of many different architectures, he could harness monolithic kernel research while keeping Linux portable on real-world machines. This LCD philosophy is one of the basic pillars that guides Linux kernel development.

Another pillar is the interfaces. A small number of simple interfaces allowed other developers to extend Linux with minimal danger to other parts of the project. Also, a process was set up to limit adding new interfaces: Although any number of developers could freely build new drivers to plug into the disk-driver interface, adding a new service such as video4linux (cameras and radio/TV cards) would bring the risk of including a bad interface, and such an error could haunt the project later. Linus cites the example of the 11-character filename interface imposed on NT by the DOS legacy; NT must now duplicate all file services for longer filenames.

Although Linux does carry some similar baggage by being UNIX-compatible, its interface-based design is a major force behind its popularity. Rather than having a free-for-all or a design by committee, Torvalds can exercise control over the project by guarding the interfaces. Yet Linux can also accommodate a staggering and ever-increasing number of new devices. With the newer kernels and the notion of dynamically loaded modules, Linux has been opened even more to the development of third-party modules from outside developers and vendors.

Kernel Modules

For most purposes, building a Linux kernel means selecting the devices and services that you need and omitting those that don't apply to your situation. Starting with Linux 2.0, a new design feature was introduced into the kernel to provide a middle ground: Components can be dynamically loaded and unloaded from the kernel, as needed, at runtime.

Kernel modules are services that are included in the kernel as needed and are removed from memory when done. This can include support for filesystems or network protocols that are needed only for certain applications, or dynamically adding support for a network interface such as PPP without carrying around this code while offline. Modules are very convenient for adding many services under tight memory constraints, such as in laptops or embedded systems. A quick look at `/lib/modules` will show many extraneous components your default installation has included just in case you need them.

Modules have one other important use. In certain situations, the configuration of the hardware may not be known at boot time, and loading the drivers as modules allows you to first query (or set) the hardware before loading the code. One example is with plug-and-play sound cards, where the boot process must initialize the interrupts before the module can be invoked.

The introduction of modules to the Linux kernel also has a political implication. Because module system calls are not considered "linking against the kernel," modules are not bound by the GPL that governs the rest of the Linux kernel. Developers are free to create binary modules and to distribute them without needing to release their source code. This shift has opened the door for commercial vendors to create proprietary modules and is one of the reasons for the current commercial interest in Linux as a viable enterprise platform.

Tip

As you will see in the sections that follow, there are many ways to modify the performance and default behavior of Linux. Only one of these ways is to set values in the kernel configuration and recompile from sources.

With all versions of Linux, many parameters, such as sound card ports, hard drive geometries, and IRQ assignments, can be set using *boot command-line options*. Also, many characteristics of the running kernel, even delicate issues such as virtual memory and filesystem behaviors, can be queried and set through the `/proc` filesystem (if `/proc` is enabled in your kernel).

For example, if all you need to do is set the proper address for an old SoundBlaster CD-ROM, you can add this line to your /etc/lilo.conf and rerun LILO.

```
append="sbpcd=0x230,SoundBlaster"
```

For testing purposes, most options can also be added manually after the LILO: prompt when your system boots:

```
LILO: linux sbpcd=0x230,SoundBlaster
```

In the sections on kernel options, many will allow for overriding default settings through boot command-line options. Others will accept new settings by echoing some value to a /proc file. For example, to enable defense against Syn-Cookie attacks, the following line could be appended to /etc/rc.d/rc.local:

```
echo 1 >/proc/sys/net/ipv4/tcp_syncookies
```

Before you do a complete recompile, you can save a lot of time and bother by investigating these alternate tuning methods.

Kernel Version Numbers

Linux kernel version numbers identify the base design and the revision, and they also identify whether you are running an experimental or production release. The version in use by any Linux system can be queried with `uname -a`:

```
>uname -a
Linux psitta.dyndns.org 2.2.5 #2 Thu Apr 15 18:34:07 EDT 1999 i586 unknown
```

This line identifies my kernel as version 2.2.5 and gives the date when the kernel was compiled. A version number contains three parts:

- The major number
- The minor number
- The current revision

The first of these is easy: It is either 1 or 2. Although there are enough of the old edition to be impressive, there are not many 1.x kernels around. For most practical purposes, the major number of the Linux kernel is 2. The last number has some special significance as well, especially with the experimental kernels. But for the moment, the important portion of the kernel version number is the middle digit: the minor number.

Some time ago, Torvalds decreed that odd-minor numbers would denote experimental kernels, while even-minor numbers would carry a stamp of respectability and be considered production editions. Today, although many Linux distributions still carry a 2.0 kernel as the default, it is the newer 2.2 kernel that has generating most of the public and commercial interest in Linux, with the impending advances building to 2.4 carrying the momentum even higher. Upgrading from 2.0 to 2.2, or from 2.2 to 2.3, is very likely the reason you are reading this chapter.

On the experimental side, the 2.1 series kernels have been supplanted by 2.2, which is now stabilizing as a worthy successor to the two-year-old workhorse of 2.0. The work continues with 2.3 as the kernel continues to refine on the infrastructure introduced in the new production kernel toward new models and methods, for example, in improved network and SMP performance. A successful software project must mature at some point, and the legendary development pace of Linux has slowed somewhat. Torvalds himself has stated that there aren't a lot of innovations left, other than to take advantage of the current architecture to port Linux to new systems and to continue to create new modules for new devices and services. He isn't always right, of course, but it does seem likely that the 2.4 kernel will follow relatively quickly compared to the jump up from 2.0, and this new Linux will be largely transparent except to enterprise and performance users. Of course, I am not always right, either.

Caution

During the rapid development of the odd-minor kernels, it is important that you don't simply jump in and expect to join the other kernel surfers. Although the development group endeavors to only release stable code, very often a core change can create havoc for other users. These troubles are often traced to needing specific libraries, modules, or compiler tools, and sometimes the development can inadvertently strand whole communities of developers. When you're surveying the patches, the best practice is to first check the Linux kernel changes Web site, and then watch the Linux kernel development mailing list for trouble reports. Only then should you dive in at a development kernel revision that has been stable for at least a few days.

The official Web site of the kernel development team is found at `http://www.tux.org`.

Obtaining the Kernel Sources

Your Linux distribution should contain the sources for some version of the 2.2 series kernels, or at least the last revision to 2.0. For most people, this will be sufficient for creating a new kernel that's more in tune with their computer hardware. Since the current Linux distributions include the 2.2 series kernels, this chapter will concentrate on the configuration and installation of the newer production release. The 2.2 kernel includes many options for devices and protocols that were unknown in 2.0, but the process of obtaining, configuring, building, and installing the kernel will be identical regardless of your version.

Your Red Hat installation provides options to include the kernel headers, and also to include the kernel sources. You must install the kernel headers if you plan to compile any software (that is, build your own binaries from source code), but you must also install the kernel sources RPM to build the kernel. After you install the kernel source RPM, you will find the source tarball in `/usr/src/redhat`.

Debian systems have several kernel options available as packages. Debian 2.1 ships with kernel 2.0.x, but the 2.2 kernel as downloaded from a kernel site will work just fine as well.

If you wish, you may use Debian's kernel-package program, which will make a `.deb` out of a kernel and its modules. This is optional, but it can make sense if you want to proceed that way.

Alternatively, you can compile your kernels the "standard" way, as described in this chapter.

If you want to upgrade to the newer development or production kernels, you can obtain the sources from many sites, and it is good nettiquette to seek out a mirror site that's as close to you as possible. Although famous sites such as `ftp://ftp.redhat.com` and `ftp://ftp.kernel.org` will have the files you need, you should first check with `http://www.kernel.org` to find an appropriate mirror site. If you need to download your tarball from an official mirror, you will find the files partitioned by version numbers. For example, 2.2 sources will be in the `/pub/linux/kernel/v2.2` directory on that FTP site.

A kernel mirror FTP site will list two types of files: the source tarballs and compressed patch files. If you are making the jump from a 2.0 or 2.1 kernel or want to start fresh, you will need the complete sources, which are in a file with a name such as `linux-2.2.10.tar.gz`. Although this is can be tedious over a modem connection, once you have a relatively recent source tree, you can later update your sources incrementally by only downloading the much smaller patch files. The system I use now has been patched to 2.2.10 from 2.1.103!

Before you open any `tar` file, the first thing you should do is list the contents to see if the file is complete and to get an overview of the directory structure it will install:

```
tar -tzf linux-2.2.5.tar.gz
```

This will show a long list of files, including directories for device drivers, modules, and architecture-depended code for all the current Linux ports. The salient detail right now is that the `tar` is based in a directory simply called `linux/`.

Tip

You should always manually create a directory for your kernel sources and symlink (`ln -s`) this directory to the generic `/usr/src/linux` location. For example, if you obtained `linux-2.2.7.tar.gz`, you should manually create `/usr/src/linux-2.2.7` and alias that to `/usr/src/linux`:

```
cd /usr/src
mkdir linux-2.2.7
ln -s linux-2.2.7 linux
```

This has two benefits. First, if your kernel include directory `/usr/include/linux` is also symlinked to `/usr/src/linux/include`, your include files will always belong to your current kernel. Second, you can keep several versions of the kernel, each in its own `/usr/src/linux-X.X.X` directory. Then, when you update your sources using the patch utility, the patch will be applied to the appropriate kernel sources. This allows you to experiment with one version and then quickly return to another version later.

After you have created the new `/usr/src/linux-2.2.7` directory and symlinked it to `/usr/src/linux`, unpack the tarball from your `/usr/src` directory:

```
cd /usr/src
tar xzf /home/garym/incoming/linux-2.2.7.tar.gz
```

Tip

Building and running the kernel depends on many different software components, which are all listed in `linux/Changes`. Before you attempt to run your new kernel, you must ensure that your system is running at least the version numbers listed in the `Changes` file.

Similarly, the drivers provided with the Linux kernel may not be the latest. If you have problems with a particular device, or with very state-of-the-art hardware such as new video or sound cards, you may want to search for an update before building your kernel.

Kernel changes may also require changes to your boot scripts, to /etc/lilo.conf, or to other configuration options elsewhere on your machine, such as the /etc/conf.modules file. The linux/Documentation collection contains many short readme files for many different parts of the kernel, and each driver subdirectory may also contain additional information on installing or configuring difficult devices. Most kernel modules accept parameters through the boot command line, through the append line of /etc/lilo.conf, or for dynamically loaded modules, on the /sbin/insmod command line or in /etc/conf.modules.

If you give options both in lilo.conf and at the boot prompt, the option strings are concatenated, with the boot prompt options coming last. This allows you to override your installed options at the command line to preempt unwanted settings, and this is also why many modules also include options to restore their default behavior.

LinuxHQ is a good starting place for all your kernel needs, for build and module tool updates, and for new packages and device drivers. You can find the LinuxHQ at http://www.kernelnotes.org.

Tip

Version numbers of software pertinent to the kernel should always be checked against the Documentation/Changes file. But checking each and every package can be tedious, especially if you can't remember the command syntax for all those commands. The following shell script generates a simple list of packages typically included in the Changes list. I originally wrote this as a poor man's version of the versions command available on SiliconGraphics IRIX machines:

```
#!/bin/sh
echo Versions 0.1 c.1999 by Gary Lawrence Murphy
echo ==========================================================
/sbin/insmod -V 2>&1 ¦ grep version ¦ grep insmod
echo -n GCC:
gcc --version
ld -v
ls -l /lib/libc.so.* ¦ gawk '{print $9 $10 $11;}'
ldd --version  2>&1 ¦ grep ldd
ls -l /usr/lib/libg++.so.* ¦ gawk '{print $9 $10 $11;}'
ps --version
procinfo -v
mount --version
hostname -V
basename --v
```

continues

```
/sbin/automount --version
/sbin/showmount --version
bash -version
ncpmount -v
pppd --version
chsh -v
echo=============================================================
```

Patching the Source Tree

Even if your Linux distribution includes the 2.2 kernel, you may need to upgrade your system to the more recent version of this kernel to take advantage of improvements in performance, security, or device support. Updates to the Linux kernel are always available on the standard mirror sites as patch files named for the version that will result from the patch. For example, the upgrade from 2.2.4 to 2.2.5 will be called `patch-2.2.5.gz`. Patch files are simply context `diffs`; that is, the output of the `diff` command (see `man diff`) lists the differences between the prior version and the new version. A patch is applied by running the output generated by `diff` through the GNU `patch` utility. `patch` will be given the lines of context around the change and told to delete, add, or replace lines in the source files.

Patch files only upgrade your sources by one revision number. If you need to upgrade from 2.2.1 to 2.2.6, you will need to obtain all of the patches for the intermediate releases. Also, unless you have some experience in kernel building, it is a good practice to follow all of these instructions to compile and test each revision before applying the next patch. Once a patch is applied, there is no way to undo the changes.

Patch files are also created by comparing the sources of totally clean Linux distributions. Before you run the patch, it is very important that you back up your `.config` file and then clean your kernel source tree to the most pristine state using `make mrproper`:

```
cd /usr/src/linux
cp .config /usr/src/config-old
make mrproper
```

This ensures that there are no residual generated files that could hinder the patch or interfere with your subsequent kernel build. Saving your old `config` (which would be removed by `mrproper`) allows you to bootstrap your next kernel `config` with the `oldconfig` option.

Two things you should know about patch files: They are typically much smaller than the source tarball (at most, a few hundred kilobytes) and they do not always work.

Tip

After you use the `patch` program to patch your sources, you should search your kernel tree for any reject files (`.rej`). These files will contain the diffs that haven't been applied, and are most often the result of some innocuous difference in whitespace or tab stops between the sources owned by the creator of the `diff` and your own sources.

If you find any `*.rej` files, you must manually correct the associated source file before you compile.

Once you have patched your sources, you can bootstrap your configuration by copying your backup config file to `.config` and running the following:

```
cp /usr/src/config-old .config
make oldconfig
```

This will set all the options that were present in your previous installation, preserving all those options that are so easy to forget, such as the IRQ of your sound card. But it will stop and prompt for any new options that have been added by the new sources. Once the `oldconfig` has run, the kernel can be configured and compiled.

About Modules

Modules are services of the kernel that are dynamically inserted and removed from the system as required. With the current kernels, almost all devices and services can be configured to load as modules.

The loading of a module is done by the `/sbin/insmod` program, and `/sbin/rmmod` removes the module. Other utilities in this suite include `/sbin/depmod` to compute module dependencies and `/sbin/modprobe` to query a module for those modules upon which it depends.

There are three things that can go wrong with a module when you upgrade to a newer kernel:

- Module version numbers are mismatched.
- Module utilities are incompatible.
- Module dependencies conflict.

The first issue occurs when the kernel has been compiled with the option to check module version numbers and those numbers do not exactly match (including the build number). When this happens, the modules are rejected and your system may not come up if it depends on some critical module to function. This is not an issue with the 2.2 kernel because this test is no longer part of the configuration.

The second situation is more likely to happen, although at the time of this writing, the kernel module tools have not changed in months. You will have no problem if your module utilities meet the requirements spelled out in `linux/Documentation/Changes`, but you may hang if you do happen to boot a kernel with old module utilities.

The third problem can hit anyone, and once you figure out what has happened, you realize the solution is just common sense. For example, you might compile Windows VFAT filesystem support as a module, but then your boot scripts try to use some file from your windows partition prior to the module loading. Or, more likely, you configure your network support as a module, forgetting that the `httpd` will hang the boot scripts while trying to resolve the hostname.

The best plan is to use dynamic modules only where they are appropriate. There will be some overhead in loading and unloading, and some overhead in coding the driver as a module. If the code is needed frequently or continuously, or if it is critical to the boot process, perhaps it should not be compiled as a module.

Caution

When building kernel systems as modules, keep in mind that modules are not loaded until fairly late in the system boot. While you can insert modules during your system `init` scripts, you need to be mindful of including all the systems you will need to get to that point. If you set a critical system as a module, the boot sequence may hang. An obvious caveat is to avoid compiling your boot partition filesystem or bootp network drivers as modules.

New Features in 2.2

Linux 2.2 adds a number of new facilities to the suite of kernel options, including kernel-level read-only support for the NT filesystem and experimental support for the distributed CODA filesystem. Many performance optimizations have also been added, including support for MTRR registers, finer-grain locking on SMP systems, user buffer checks, and directory entry caching.

Also new with the 2.2 kernel is the ability for kernel programmers to mark sections of their code as being for initialization only. Kernel memory is not swappable, and after the kernel has initialized, the marked code is jettisoned and the memory is freed. This makes the new kernel actually leave a smaller footprint in memory than the 2.0 kernel.

Another advance with the 2.2 kernel is the change over from `kerneld` to the more secure `kmod` system of module loading. `init` scripts that depended on the `kerneld` system should be updated to the new methods.

The 2.2 kernel will work on a system installed for a 2.0 kernel, but it will require the upgrading of some of the dependent utilities, such as the modules package and net-tools. Older systems will also need to run the `MAKEDEV` script to ensure that obsolete devices are replaced by the current set. For developers of third-party kernel modules, the kernel interface has changed between 2.0 and 2.2. If you want to port code, you can find more information at `http://www.atnf.csiro.au/~rgooch/linux/docs/`.

Tip

One thing is true of any software project with 1.7 million lines of code that is intended to run on such a wide array of platforms and combinations: There will be bugs. If you encounter problems, your first stop should be to check Richard Gooch's Kernel Newsflash page (`http://www.atnf.csiro.au/~rgooch/linux/docs/kernel-newsflash.html`) for reports and patches on the latest kernel release.

Your second stop should be the Linux kernel FAQ and the Linux kernel mailing list archives at `http://www.tux.org/lkml/`.

Configuring Linux Kernel

Is your `lilo.conf` file prepared to find the new kernel? Do you have a backup kernel and a boot disk? Do you have enough drive space? These may seem trivial questions, but they are important. An error in any of these items can leave your system in an inoperable state and entirely devour your weekend. Even if all you are doing is to set a few `/proc` values or add a network interface on the boot prompt, it is good defensive driving to consider the recovery plan.

If you need to add or remove modules, set parameters such as your soundcard IRQs or if you are upgrading to a new kernel version, the next step is to run one of the kernel configuration program. The Linux makefile provides four methods of setting your configuration options:

- `make config` A command-line terminal program
- `make menuconfig` An `ncurses`-based console program
- `make xconfig` A `tk/tcl`-based X11 GUI program
- `make oldconfig` A semi-automatic update program

Tip

Before you begin, double-check your system against the requirements in `linux/Documentation/Changes`.

You should also create an entry in your `/etc/lilo.conf` to keep your current kernel installed as a backup. For example, in addition to adding a few seconds delay on the boot prompt with the `LILO delay` parameter (so you can interrupt), you should add a section for the last stable kernel. Try the original Linux kernel image:

```
image = /boot/vmlinuz
  label = stable
```

If all else fails, you can enter **`stable`** at the `LILO:` prompt and boot your original Linux kernel.

I also add the following lines into my `lilo.conf` to accommodate the `make bzlilo` kernel compile option:

```
image = /vmlinuz
  label = linux
  root=/dev/hdc1
  read-only
image = /vmlinuz.old
  label = old
```

The `zlilo` and `bzlilo` compile commands automatically back up the previous kernel from `/vmlinuz` to `/vmlinuz.old` and then run the `LILO` command to install the new kernels. The preceding `lilo.conf` sections give you one more line of defense against a kernel that cannot boot. A fourth section, labeled `backup`, allows you to make periodic backups of particularly stable development kernels, in case repeated compiles leave you with both `/vmlinuz` and `/vmlinuz.old` as unstable kernels. Such caution is fortunately (or sadly) no longer as necessary now that Linux has stabilized with 2.2, but it may still be a good practice when you're experimenting with delicate kernel tuning.

Caution

If you are experimenting with kernel options, remember to set the `LILO delay` parameter to provide some grace time while selecting an alternate kernel. If your production system has a delay of zero seconds, you will not have the opportunity to preempt loading the default kernel. If that kernel is faulty, your only option is to boot from a floppy disk. For more dangerous experiments, the delay parameter also accepts a value of `-1`, which will cause the boot process to wait indefinitely for a boot parameter.

I remember sitting in a Linux user group meeting one evening and complaining about wanting to set some kernel option one way but letting it slip by or setting it wrong, and then having to abort the program and start again. Everyone looked at me rather strangely. I had been using the command-line interface for so long that I hadn't even considered that other methods might have been introduced in the intervening years.

Why have a command-line interface? Suppose? Suppose you had an autonomous robot submarine, or perhaps a space probe, that was in the midst of maneuvers and needed a fast kernel `reconfig`. Simple dumb terminal interfaces can go places that other interfaces cannot go. Keep this in mind if you plan to read your email or news from some GUI-only package!

That said, other than using the `oldconfig` option for generating an updated configuration from a previous `.config` file, I don't think I have used the command-line interface since that day. Without a doubt, the X11/`tk` interface is the most elegant and appealing, although it does require that `tk` and X11 are both working. X11 sometimes isn't practical to use, such as if you're doing remote administration over a slow Telnet connection.

This leaves the Linux console `ncurses` configuration as the main workhorse of Linux configuration, with the X11 interface as the vehicle of choice when possible. Both the X11 and the `ncurses` configuration tools offer the same options in the same order, and they have roughly the same capability to navigate backwards and forwards through the configuration options.

To start the configuration, simply go to the `/usr/src/linux` directory and enter one of the first three configuration commands. If you choose either of the `ncurses` or X11 methods, you will see a brief flurry of compiler activity while the user-interface programs compile. You will then be greeted by an overview screen with all the categories of kernel options.

If you recoil in horror at the thought of a command line, you can now rest easy for a bit. From this point on, if you are using the `xconfig` method, you will be in carpal-tunnel land until the configuration is done.

Configuration Options

Figure 23.1 shows the initial screen in the `xconfig` display for the 2.2.6 kernel. 2.0.x kernels are very much the same, with fewer options and minor cosmetic differences. In all of the configuration methods, most kernel options can be set to be included, included as a module, or left out of the compile. On the `xconfig` and `menuconfig` screens, there are also options to include or exclude certain sections of the configuration, and disabling these sections will gray out any dependent options (the dumb-terminal `config` option will silently skip these sections).

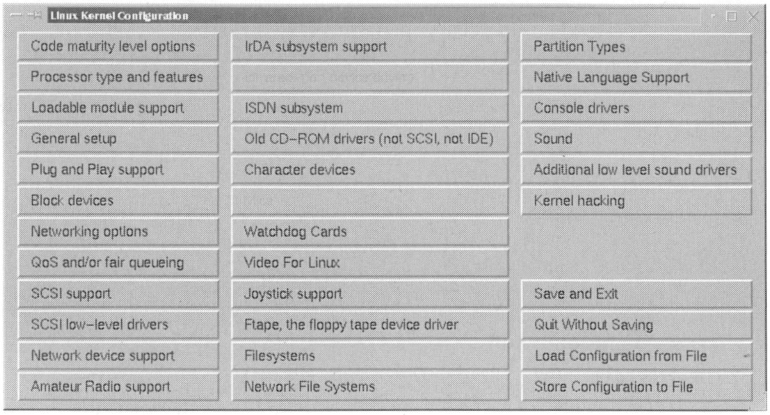

FIGURE 23.1
The `xconfig` *kernel configuration panel.*

I'm not going to hold your hand during this process. You can figure out 90 percent of what you need to know without my help. This guide will not attempt to describe every one of the 407 options in the Linux kernel, but instead will focus on options of interest to specific applications and explain some of the implications and configuration options for relevant modules. Some of these sections will be more interesting to new Linux users, and I will outline these in some detail. Other sections will be of interest only to seasoned network or systems administrators and may appear bogged down in acronyms to the more novice readers.

The important feature on all the kernel configuration screens, whether you use the dumb-terminal, `ncurses`, or X11 method, is the HELP option. Almost all kernel features are well documented right in the configuration screen. Whether you are looking at beginner options for installing network support or expert options for setting filesystem caching, most options carry this very reassuring advice: "If you are in doubt, choose Y" (or N).

Tip

Before you can answer many of the questions about your new kernel configuration, you may need to know about the insides of your computer. Kernel configuration will ask about your network card, your PCI chipset, your IDE and SCSI controllers, and a host of other highly personal questions.

For your first time through, you can use the defaults or the recommended option in the associated HELP page. Or, if you're feeling zealous, keep your computer manuals nearby or run through your first configuration with the panels taken off your computer and a flashlight in hand.

Take heart—it is not absolutely essential that you match your computer chipset perfectly on your first kernel configuration. The defaults have served you well so far.

Code Maturity Level

Although a stable kernel release such as the 2.2 series is considered to be ready for prime time, the kernel will still offer some features that are deemed experimental. These features may support new technology for which the standard is not yet been resolved, or may offer new techniques that were considered essential enough to include but were not thought to be stable at the time of the release.

All these features are clearly marked as experimental so Linux users won't use them without knowing what they are doing. Users are invited to try these new features, report on their results, and file proper bug reports, but are asked not to flood the mailing lists and newsgroups with complaints.

Alpha-release drivers should not be considered to be only for the brave or the foolish. In some cases, "experimental" code may be essential to your purpose, such as Amiga filesystem support or enhanced support for certain PCI subsystems. It is the real-world testing of these features that is worth most to the developers. The main caveat here is that if your kernel fails to load or crashes midstream, you should remove all experimental modules before you suspect you have found a bug among the stable modules.

Processor Type and Features

Most distributions are preset for the safest setting: the old Intel 386 computer. This may be the first kernel option you will change.

When you're selecting the processor type, keep in mind that compiling for an advanced CPU may mean your kernel will not boot or will fail on an older machine. This is also true for excluding the floating-point coprocessor emulation. A 386-SX may not run if the emulator is missing. Table 23.1 shows the recommended mapping of processor types to processor options.

TABLE 23.1 CPU Kernel Options

Kernel Option	*Recommended CPU*
386	AMD/Cyrix/Intel 386DX/DXL/SL/SLC/SX, Cyrix/TI. 486DLC/DLC2 and UMC 486SX-S. Only 386 kernels will run on an i386 machine.
486	For the AMD/Cyrix/IBM/Intel DX4 or 486DX/DX2/SL/SX/SX2, AMD/Cyrix 5x86, NexGen Nx586 and UMC U5D or U5S.
586	Generic Pentium, possibly lacking the timestamp counter register.
Pentium	Intel Pentium/Pentium MMX, AMD K5, K6 and K63D.
PPro	Cyrix/IBM/National Semiconductor 6x86MX, MII and Intel Pentium II/Pentium Pro.

MTRR and SMP

For Pentium II and Pentium Pro machines, Linux includes optional support for the Memory Type Range Register (MTRR). When this option is supported by the hardware and software, it can double the performance of video transfers. To use MTRR, you will need an X-Server that is aware of the interface either through `ioctl()` calls or through the `/proc/mtrr` pseudo-file. You can query your MTRR system through `cat /proc/mtrr`, and code for manipulating the interface is provided in `linux/Documentation/mtrr.txt`. An initialization bug on some Symmetric Multi-Processor (SMP) machines can also be corrected by including MTRR support.

The last processor feature option enables support for SMP. With the 2.2 kernels, SMP support for up to 16 processors on Intel x86 machines is now a standard feature and is not experimental—support for up to 64 processors is expected soon and may be in general release by the time this book is published. While Intel-platform SMP is fairly well defined in the 2.2 kernels, it is much more refined in the 2.3 versions and the support for other architectures is still considered experimental. For many enterprise applications, SMP support will be a primary reason for upgrading to Linux 2.3 or 2.4.

Tip

If you require SMP support, you will also need to include the RealTime Clock option under Character Devices.

On machines with only one CPU, SMP support can degrade performance and may not run on some hardware. Deselecting this option for machines that have more than one CPU will cause Linux to use only the primary processor. To complete the configuration for SMP, you will also need to include the RealTime Clock option, and you may need to set your BIOS options for Unixware. For more information on SMP support, look up the SMP FAQ at `http://www.irisa.fr/prive/mentre/smp-faq/`.

Loadable Module Support

It is hard to imagine a circumstance in which you would not want to include module support and enable the kernel module loader. For most situations, module support allows the kernel to support many devices and filesystems without incurring the overhead of including this support at all times. In some situations, incompatible devices can share ports through the loading and unloading of modules, such as using a single parallel port for both a printer and a parallel-port SCSI drive.

Keeping the module version information is also a fairly rare situation. Without version details, the kernel will use the `modprobe` utility to determine whether modules are compatible with the current kernel (and will fail to compile if the modules' utility package is missing or out of date). A kernel with the version symbols enabled will be able to load binary modules from third-party sources, but may run into trouble when modules are of the same kernel version but belong to a different build.

Modules are usually loaded by `init` scripts or other shell scripts that explicitly call the `insmod` and `rmmod` utilities to load and unload modules as needed. The 2.2 kernel now includes support for automagically loading modules as needed. When the kernel detects a missing module, it will use the program specified in `/proc/sys/kernel/modprobe` (usually `/sbin/modprobe`) to load the module. To clear out unused modules, you will need to call `rmmod -a` yourself or schedule it periodically through the root `crontab` entry:

```
0-59/5 * * * * /sbin/rmmod -a
```

General Setup

General setup includes enabling networking, PCI hardware, Microchannel and Parallel ports, Advanced Power Management, and support for ELF, `aout`, and other binary executables. For most new Linux systems, the important details here will be the `parport` and PCI options. Advanced administrators will probably want to pay close attention to the PCI options and the new `sysctl` interface.

Networking Support

Unless you have a very good technical reason (such as that you know what you're doing), you will need to include networking support. Many applications require this module even on non-networked machines and will not run if this option is not included. For the 2.2 kernel, you must also ensure that your net-tools package understands the new `/proc/dev/net`. net-tools-1.50 is also required to accommodate IPv6 protocol.

BSD Accounting

BSD accounting is of most interest to ISPs and other organizations that need to trace and track the use of their systems for billing or other accounting purposes. Adding BSD accounting will create a special file that logs and measures each process, allowing compatible software to gather detailed usage information.

SysV IPC (DOSEMU)

Interprocess Communications (IPC) is a protocol for synchronizing and exchanging data between separate programs. If you plan on running the DOSEMU MS-DOS Emulator, you will need to include IPC. However, now that `kmod` has replaced `kerneld`, there is no longer any need to include IPC in the main kernel. The 2.2 kernel now offers IPC as a loadable module, and removing `kerneld` support from the IPC module has reduced its size by 40 percent.

`sysctl` Support

Adding `sysctl` provides a means for controlling the running kernel either through system calls or, if the `/proc` filesystem is enabled, by writing to pseudo-files in the `/proc/sys` directory. This directory is partitioned into several areas that govern different aspects of the kernel:

`dev/`	Device-specific information (`dev/cdrom/info`)
`fs/`	Control of specific filesystems, such as setting the number of file-handles and inodes, dentry and quota tuning, and configuring the support for arbitrary binaries (see "Support for Misc Binaries" later in this chapter)
`kernel/`	Kernel status and tuning
`net/`	Networking parameters
`sunrpc/`	SUN Remote Procedure Call (NFS)
`vm/`	Virtual memory and buffer and cache management

These services are both powerful and dangerous. Make sure you know what you are getting into before you fiddle with them! Kernel parameters include the interpretation of Ctrl+Alt+Del, the time delay for a reboot after a kernel panic, your system host and domain name, and a number of architecture-dependent features for the Sparc and Macintosh platforms. The `sunrpc` directory includes debug flags for kernel hacking of remote procedure calls.

Virtual memory tuning allows for hand-optimizing the machine for disk activity. For example, if you set the system's tolerance for dirty memory pages to a higher value, the kernel will have less disk activity (which saves power and improves speed, although it increases the risk of thrashing if real memory becomes scarce). On a machine with a lot of memory, the default behavior of the caching algorithm could be modified with the following:

```
echo "80 500 64 64 80 6000 6000 1884 2" >/proc/sys/vm/bdflush
```

This would restrict the flushing of the dirty buffers until memory was 80 percent full; the other values set the maximum numbers for dirty blocks, the number of free buffers to allocate on a refill, the threshold to trigger a flush and the buffer and superblock age limits (see `linux/Documentation/sysctl/vm.txt`). For a single-purpose machine that had to run many processes, other options could be modified, making the buffer cache claim a major chunk of the total memory and then restricting the pruning of this cache until nearly all of this memory was consumed:

```
echo "60 80 80" >/proc/sys/vm/buffermem
```

The `"80"` values are arbitrary since the kernel currently ignores them, with the initial `"60"` setting the percentage of memory which may be allocated to buffers. Keep in mind that these changes may improve file or process performance for one purpose, but they might upset this machine terribly for many other purposes. Be certain you know what you are doing before you install any optimization.

Other tunable `vm` parameters include setting the number of pages that can be read in one transaction and removing the pagetable caching for single-CPU machines with limited memory (such as embedded systems and older machines).

Tip

The First Rule of Optimization: Don't.

The Second Rule of Optimization (for experts only): Don't (yet).

The most common use of the `sysctrl` files will be in the filesystem (`fs`) directory. This holds a collection of diagnostic pseudo-files for reading the number of file handles, inodes, and superblock and quota entries, with corresponding files for setting maximum values for these items. For example, systems that require many open files (such as very busy Web servers) may see a flurry of file-handle messages in the logs. You can query the current number of files though `cat file-nr`, and you can set a new limit by echoing a higher number to the `sysctrl file-max`.

Detailed information on using and interpreting all these features can be found in `linux/Documentation/sysctl/`.

Support for Misc Binaries

Long before other operating systems provided for running Java applications from the command line, binary executable support for Java class files was added to the Linux kernel. Later, this feature was generalized to all binary and interpreter types. Using the sysctrl pseudo-files, Linux will integrate Java, MS-DOS programs, Windows programs, tk/tcl, Perl, or any other strange executable as seamlessly as an ELF binary or a shell script.

To use the misc binaries support, you need to register the *magic cookie* of the file type and the corresponding interpreter through the sysctr pseudo-files in /proc/sys/fs/binfmt_misc. You can derive the magic cookie from the first few bytes of the file or from the filename (such as .com or .exe), and you can register it by echoing a string to /proc/sys/fs/binfmt_misc/register, where the format of the string specifies the following:

```
:name:type:offset:magic:mask:interpreter:
```

- name is an arbitrary identifier for this executable type.
- type specifies M or E, depending on whether the cookie is by mask or extension.
- offset is the count in bytes from the front of the file. If omitted, a default of 0 is used.
- magic is the sequence of bytes to match. Hex codes may be specified as \x0A or \xFF. (Be careful to escape the slash character if you set the binfmt through a shell statement.) For extension matching, the magic pattern is the extension that follows the last dot in the filename.
- mask is also optional and, if included, must be the same length as the magic sequence. The bits in the mask are applied against the file contents before comparison to the magic cookie sequence.
- interpreter is the program that is used to run the executable.

To use misc binaries support, you could create a script in /etc/rc.d/init.d (/etc/init.d in Debian) to echo the control strings to the binfmt_misc file, or add these statements to your rc.local (bootmisc.sh in Debian) script. For example, to emulate the original Java support, you might add the following line to the end of /etc/rc.d/rc.local or bootmisc.sh:

```
echo ':Java:M::\xca\xfe\xba\xbe::/usr/local/jdk/bin/javawrapper:' >  \
  /proc/sys/fs/binfmt_misc/register
```

This would create a new /proc/sys/fs/binfmt_misc/Java entry in the sysctl directories, and would allow running a Java application by simply using the full filename. Support for running applets through appletviewer might be added by the following:

```
echo ':Applet:E::html::/usr/local/jdk/bin/appletviewer:'  > \
```

```
/proc/sys/fs/binfmt_misc/register
```

Note that for this to work, you need to create a special wrapper script to run the Java interpreter. Brian Lantz provides a sample script in `linux/Documentation/java.txt` (see sidebar). Once it's installed and the `binfmt_misc` is registered, Java applications and applets can be run from the command line. Use `chmod +x` to set the `.class` or `.html` file as executable and then simply call it from the command line either one of these two ways:

```
./HelloWorld.class
```

```
./HelloApplet.html
```

Lantz's Java a Wrapper Script for *binfmt_misc java* Support

```
#!/bin/bash
# /usr/local/jdk/bin/javawrapper - the wrapper for binfmt_misc/java
CLASS=$1

# if classname is a link,
# we follow it (this could be done easier - how?)
if [ -L "$1" ] ; then
        CLASS=`ls --color=no -l $1 ¦\
               tr -s '\t ' '  ' ¦ cut -d ' ' -f 11`
fi
CLASSN=`basename $CLASS .class`
CLASSP=`dirname $CLASS`

FOO=$PATH
PATH=$CLASSPATH
if [ -z "`type -p -a $CLASSN.class`" ] ; then
        # class is not in CLASSPATH
        if [ -e "$CLASSP/$CLASSN.class" ] ; then
                # append dir of class to CLASSPATH
                if [ -z "${CLASSPATH}" ] ; then
                        export CLASSPATH=$CLASSP
                else
                        export CLASSPATH=$CLASSP:$CLASSPATH
                fi        else
                # uh! now we would have to
                # create a symbolic link - really
                # ugly, i.e. print a message
                # that one has to change the setup
                echo "Hey! This is not a good setup to run $1 !"
                exit 1
        fi
fi
PATH=$FOO

shift
/usr/local/jdk/bin/java $CLASSN "$@"
```

To run Windows applications via the Wine emulator, you could add the following line:

```
echo ':DOSWin:M::MZ::/usr/local/bin/wine:' > /proc/sys/fs/binfmt_misc/register
```

You can read the status of a `binfmt_misc` file by using `cat` on the filename. For example, `cat /proc/sys/fs/binfmt_misc/Java` might produce the following:

```
enabled
interpreter /usr/local/jdk/bin/javawrapper
offset 0
magic cafebabe
```

Caution

When you're configuring `binfmt_misc` support, the register control string cannot exceed 255 characters, the magic cookie must be within the first 128 bytes of the file, `offset+size(magic)` must be less than 128, and the interpreter string cannot exceed 127 characters.

For more information about `binfmt_misc` and creating the magic cookie patterns, see Richard Günther's `binfmt_misc` home page at `http://www.anatom.uni-tuebingen.de/~richi/linux/binfmt_misc.html`.

Parallel Ports (parport)

One major change between the 2.0 and 2.2 kernels is the introduction of the `parport` module, an abstract representation of the parallel ports. This separates architecture-dependent code from the parallel interface and allows you to share the same physical parallel port between many devices. For example, you can use the same port for both a printer and a Zip drive or Qcam video camera.

Parallel ports are often dangerous beasts to probe, especially when many onboard ports may be fixed at IRQ numbers that can conflict with sound and network cards. It is best to avoid probing and to specify the port addresses and IRQ settings of the parallel port hardware, either by appending the parameters to the boot command or by loading the `parport` as a module and specifying the parameters on the `insmod` command line. By default, the `parport` module does not probe for IRQs and will initialize all parallel ports in polling mode.

The new `parport` modules also split parallel port control into two modules: the basic `parport` to manage port sharing and an architecture-dependent layer (such as the `parport_pc` module). Either one can be compiled into the kernel or built as a module and loaded as needed, but in both cases you will probably need to add port configuration details to the boot or insmod command line. For example, to load parport and parport_pc as modules, you might use the following command lines:

```
# insmod parport.o
# insmod parport_pc.o io=0x3bc,0x378,0x278 irq=none,7,auto
```

This would install three parallel ports: the first in polling mode, the second on IRQ7, and the third probed for the current values.

Once the modules are installed, the parport_probe module can be inserted to query IEEE1284-compliant devices. This will output a status report to the system messages and to /proc/parport/x/autoprobe. Other files in /proc/parport/x include the devices file where parport will record the attached devices and flag those currently using the port, as well as the irq file. irq can be used to query the IRQ number of the port and also to set this value by echoing either the number or "none" to that file.

To use parport, modules that require the parallel port can be given options to direct the module to a particular port

```
# insmod lp.o parport=0,2
```

This will install the printer module only on ports 0 and 2, rather than the default action of installing the module on all available ports. You can also do this by adding lp=parport0 lp=parport2 to the boot prompt or in /etc/lilo.conf.

A common use of parport modules is to share a parallel port between several devices by dynamically inserting device support and then removing that device before inserting the module for an alternate device. For example, you could share the printer port with a parallel port camera, a Zip drive, or PLIP (parallel port-based network connection) by scripting each facility to first remove the other module before installing itself.

Tip

In most instances, you can assign many modules to a parport simultaneously without needing to first remove the prior module. When conflicts occur, however, modules can be removed and inserted as needed.

Advanced Power Management (APM) Support

Advanced Power Management (APM) does does not power down hard drives or trigger "green" monitors to go into sleep mode. The Linux APM system is almost exclusively restricted to battery-powered computers such as laptops. Although APM is a very good idea in principle, there are many different interpretations of the standard among laptop manufacturers. As a result, APM support is a prime suspect when you're debugging laptop kernel problems. When in doubt, turn off all APM options and enable each one only after you've verified that it is either useful or benign.

Watchdog Support

Detailed support for hardware-based watchdog systems is set further down, but the general options also allow for a software-based watchdog. With this option, the kernel will monitor and periodically update `/dev/watchdog`, and will force a reboot if the updates fail to occur. This can be useful for small ISPs and other applications where the machine may be unattended and must be rebooted if any sort of crash occurs. This support is embedded in the kernel, so there's a slightly better chance that it will do its job, even if all other processes have been halted or are being blocked. If you are using the software watchdog, you may also want to append `panic=60` as a boot argument (such as in `/etc/lilo.conf`).

Alan Cox has included information on watchdog hardware manufacturers and source code for creating a software watchdog update program, which can be found in `Documentation/watchdog.txt`.

Plug-and-Play Support

This contains options to enable kernel support of generic plug-and-play devices, and to enable probing of devices attached to the parallel ports for mapping parallel port peripherals to the `parport` modules. In general, probing parallel ports for IRQ numbers can cause problems. A better option is to explicitly specify your `parport` options through the append line in `/etc/lilo.conf` (see "Parallel Ports (`parport`)").

Block Devices

The Block Devices dialog box contains options for disks, from ancient MFM and RLL IDE drives through modern IDE/ATAPI devices to Parallel-Port IDE and ATAPI and RAID systems.

Floppy Disk Driver

Because of its use for other devices (such as tape backup units) and its capability to run multiple disk controllers, the floppy disk driver is worth some attention. This driver can also be configured through boot commands by using the following options:

> `floppy=daring` for well-behaved (usually all-modern Pentium systems) controllers. This option allows for optimizations that can speed up floppy access, but may fail on incompatible systems.

`floppy=one_fdc` tells the driver that only one controller is available. This is the default setting for the FDC driver.

`floppy=two_fdc` or `floppy=<address>,two_fdc` tells the driver to use two controllers, with the second located at the specified address. The default address is 0x370, or will be taken from CMOS memory if the `cmos` option is selected.

`floppy=thinkpad` alerts the driver to the inverted convention for the disk change line that's used in some ThinkPad laptops.

`floppy=omnibook` or `floppy=nodma` prevents the use of DMA for data transfers. You will need this option if you get frequent `"Unable to allocate DMA memory"` messages or if you are using an HP Omnibook. DMA is also not available on 386 computers or if your FDC does not have a FIFO buffer (8272A and 82072). When you're using `nodma`, the FIFO threshold should also be set to `10` or lower to limit the number of data transfer interrupts.

`floppy=yesdma` can be used to force DMA mode. When you're using a FIFO-enabled controller, the driver will fall back to `nodma` mode if it cannot find the contiguous memory it needs. The `yesdma` option will prevent this. This option is the default setting.

`floppy=nofifo` is required if you receive `"Bus master arbitration"` errors from the Ethernet card (or any other devices) while using your floppy controller. The default is the `fifo` option.

`floppy=<threshold>,fifo_depth` sets the FIFO depth for DMA mode. A higher setting will tolerate more latency but will trigger more interrupts and impose more load on the system. A lower setting will generate fewer interrupts but will require a faster processor.

Tip

If the floppy driver is compiled as a module, you can experiment with the `floppy=<threshold>,fifo_depth` driver option to find the optimum settings. To do this, you will need the `floppycontrol` utility with the `--messages` flag to log controller diagnostics. After you've inserted the `floppy.o` module and run `floppycontrol --messages`, access the floppy disk. A rush of `"Over/Underrun - retrying"` messages will indicate that your FIFO threshold is too low. You can then find an optimum value by unloading the module and trying again with higher values until these messages are very infrequent.

`floppy=<drive>,<type>,cmos` sets the CMOS type of the specified drive to the given type and is a required option on systems with more than two floppy drives. Codes for the CMOS types can be found in `drivers/block/README.fd`.

`floppy=L40SX` prevents the printing of messages when unexpected interrupts are received, and it is required on IBM L40SX laptops to prevent a conflict between the video and floppy disk controllers.

`floppy=broken_dcl` avoids using the disk change line and assumes that the disk may have been changed whenever the device is reopened. In most situations, this symptom can be traced to other physical causes, such as loose or broken cables and mistaken jumper settings, but it can be a real issue on older floppy drives and some laptop computers.

`floppy=<nr>,irq` and `floppy=<nr>,dma` set the IRQ and DMA for the given device. The defaults are `6` and `2`, respectively.

`Floppy=slow` is required on some PS/2 machines that have a dramatically slower step rate.

The full list of FDC module options can be found in `drivers/block/README.fd` and the `fdutils` package. A set of floppy driver utility programs, including an enhanced `mtools` kit, can be downloaded from `ftp://metalab.unc.edu/pub/Linux/system/Misc/`.

Tip

Floppy driver options are specified using the `floppy=` syntax, but unlike some kernel drivers, the device expects only one such declaration. For example, to set both `daring` and `two_fdc`, both options should be included in one command, separated by a space, as shown in the following:

```
insmod floppy 'floppy="daring two_fdc"'
```

You can pass options to the Linux floppy disk driver by using the usual `/etc/lilo.conf` append line on the boot prompt, or by using `/sbin/insmod` when compiled as a module, and also through using the older environment variable syntax.

Enhanced IDE Support

Linux will support up to eight IDE drives. Many options for tuning the runtime performance of the IDE drives can be set using the `hdparm` utility. With Linux 2.1/2.2, support has also been added for IDE ATAPI floppy drives, tape drives, and CD-ROM drives with auto-detection `of` interfaces, IRQs, and disk geometries. The new driver also adds support for PIO modes on OPTi chipsets, SCSI host adapter emulation, and PCI Bus-master DMA, as well as experimental support for many PCI chipsets.

The driver also detects buggy PCI IDE systems, such as the prefetch feature of the RZ1000 or “IRQ unmasking” on the CMD640. Full details of the IDE driver and supported systems can be found in `linux/Documentation/ide.txt`.

While the driver automatically probes for disk drives, geometries, and IRQs, these interfaces can be specified using kernel command-line options. For example, enter the following to set the ioport addresses and the IRQ for controller 3:

```
ide3=0x168,0x36e,10
```

If the IRQ number is omitted, the driver will probe for it. Any number of interfaces can share an IRQ, although this will degrade performance. The driver will detect and account for this situation, but your controller cards may suffer damage in the process (theoretically).

Disk geometry can also be specified on the command line as three numbers for sectors, cylinders, and head, as in hdc=768,16,32. And if your CD-ROM is not being detected, you can give the kernel an extra nudge by using the hdd=cdrom option.

IDE interfaces on sound cards may require initialization before they can be used. The program to initialize the driver is most often among the software that comes with the card and is usually part of the MS-DOS driver. The only alternative for using these devices is to boot your computer under MS-DOS, allowing the drivers to initialize the device, and then to use loadin to switch to Linux.

Older hard drives may not be compatible with the newer IDE driver, and in this situation you can include both interfaces in the kernel. The older driver will command the primary IDE interface while still allowing newer hardware to be used on the other interfaces.

Caution

When you're passing IDE driver options to loadable modules using /sbin/insmod, substitute ; for any for any commas in the command line:

```
insmod ide.o options="ide0=serialize ide2=0x1e8;0x3ee;11"
```

Loopback Disk Devices

Loopback disks allow you to treat a normal file as a separate filesystem. For example, you can mount and test a CD-ROM or floppy disk image before committing the image to the physical disk. Loopback also allows you to use cryptographic methods to secure a filesystem. Before you use the loopback disk devices, you will need to ensure that your util-linux package is up to date with the requirements of linux/Documentation/Changes.

Network Block Devices

Using Network Block Devices allows the client to transparently use a remote block device over TCP/IP. This is very different from NFS or Coda. For example, a thin client could use an NBD disk for any filesystem type, including as a swap disk.

This code is considered very experimental.

Multiple Devices and Software-RAID

If you need reliable and reasonably efficient redundant filesystems on a tight budget, Linux now includes a Software-RAID package that can bind several disks as one RAID unit. MD support can be used to append, stripe, or mirror partitions together to form one logical partition.

More information on Software-RAID can be found in the Software-RAID HOWTO at `ftp://metalab.unc.edu/pub/Linux/docs/HOWTO/mini`.

PARIDE and `parport`

For the Parallel-IDE support (PARIDE), you can safely combine both `parport` and `paride` devices on the same physical parallel port. However, if `parport` is included as a loadable module, the `paride` driver must also be included as a module. Also, if `paride` is included directly in the kernel, individual protocols for disks, tapes, and CD-ROM drives may still be included as modules and loaded dynamically as needed.

Networking Options

UNIX is a networking operating system, and Linux follows in this tradition. In the UNIX world, computers are not thought of as isolated personal possessions, but as nodes, mere portals into the whole network. Building a workstation without network services is not unlike building an office with no windows or doors.

For most single-networked or SOHO workstations, networking options will only be a matter of choosing TCP/IP network support, and perhaps including IPX support to coexist with Windows machines or to run the DOSEMU MS-DOS emulator. Some people may add the Coda or NFS network filesystems as a means to share their local disk resources, or they may configure Linux as a firewall and dial-up gateway for a home office or small enterprise. Small Novell shops might also use the Linux IPX support en route to using Linux as a high-powered Netware file server. The standard Linux kernel supports all of these application features through the Network Options.

For the enterprise network administrator, however, this dialog box is a playground of protocols, options, system diagnostics, and controls that position Linux as the glue holding the enterprise together. Linux can be optimized for routing or forwarding between interfaces, and set as a secure WAN router for a virtual private network over the Internet. Linux speaks IPX, Appletalk, Acorn Econet, and Ipv6. It can log attacks, perform multicast (MBONE) routing, encapsulate IP over IP, do IP masquerading (to give machines inside the firewall access to services without using a proxy server), provide ARP services over huge networks, and boot a diskless client. It's pretty darn amazing, and it keeps getting better.

Kernel Netlink Socket

Netlink is a communication channel between kernel services and user programs through a special character device in the `/dev` directory. This interface can be used by the Routing Messages package to log network behavior, or by the IP Firewall Netlink device to log information about possible attacks. Netlink is also required when you're using the `arpd` daemon to map IP numbers to local network hardware addresses outside of kernel space, or when you're using `ethertap` (user programs using raw Ethernet frames).

Network Firewall

The head of network services for Bell Global Solutions once confirmed my suspicion: The only firewall that is impervious is one that's implemented with scissors. That said, we all do what we can to be as secure as we need to be. It is all a matter of cost and necessity. High security systems can and are built from Linux machines, but for the modest requirements of the masses, the stock kernel firewall provides decent protection with a minimum of fuss.

The Network Firewall is a packet-based protection that can be configured to accept or deny incoming or outbound packets based on the port, the protocol, and the originating and/or destination network IP addresses. Proxy-based firewalls can expand this protection and use knowledge about the protocols to provide additional security, but this most often requires modified software and is a great deal more work to install. Even if you plan to use a proxy-based system, most often such systems also require including the packet-based firewall. For a gateway firewall for a small or medium-sized enterprise or a home office, packet-based protection is simple, easy to install, and offers pretty good security.

To set up a TCP/IP firewall, you will need to include the Network Firewall option and the IP: Firewalling option. Many installations will also include the IP: Masquerading option to give inside machines access to services outside the firewall. Using

IP: Masquerading, the remote computer perceives these connections as originating from the firewall machine, and thereby removes the need to register IP addresses for all local network hosts that require these outside connections.

Let's say your office LAN includes a workstation that needs HTTP and ICQ access. Using IP: Masquerading, this workstation can run Netscape or ICQ without any proxy and can connect directly to the Web site or Mirablis servers. Because their packets will appear to come from the firewall, remote ICQ users can't call in directly. An extra level of security can be added to this scheme by enabling the IP: Transparent Proxy support, which silently redirects traffic from local machines to a predesignated proxy server address.

Caution

Network firewall support is not compatible with the Fast Switching ultra-fast network option.

Basic IP: Masquerading will only redirect UDP and TCP traffic. This prevents some Windows applications that depend on ICMP packets, such as `ping` and `tracert`. Support for these applications can be enabled through the IP: ICMP Masquerading option.

Inside hosts also can't receive connections unless port forwarding is enabled using the Special Modules options. Through the external port administration utilities `ipautofw` and `ipportfw`, the Linux firewall can provide a gateway for outside machines to reach services on inside machines by forwarding packets for predefined ports. For example, if the gateway machine is not using X11, port 6001 can be forwarded to another machine that will then be able to run remote X11 applications. Port forwarding support is considered experimental.

Optimize as Router

In the current Linux kernel, this switch only prevents some checksum operations on incoming packets that are not required when using the machine exclusively as a router. In the future, this option may contain other router-only optimizations.

IP Tunnelling

IP tunnelling is a technique for connecting two LANs across another network while staying under the same network address. An example application might be to allow machines at a trade show to use services only available inside the corporate firewall, or to give a roaming user in a hotel room full access to their office files. The basic support for IP tunnelling wraps plain IPv4 inside IPv4. The GRE tunnel support is more useful if you are connecting through Cisco routers, and it can also encode IPv6 inside IPv4.

GRE/IP can also be used to create what appears to be a normal Ethernet network, but that can be distributed all over the Internet. For example, this would allow all branch offices of a global enterprise to use the same LAN IP numbers and to appear to be within the overall firewall. This feature requires the GRE Tunnelling option with the GRE Broadcast and the IP: Multicast option.

Webmasters and IP Aliasing

This option is of most interest to Webmasters who need *multi-homing*, or to provide different documents or services to outside hosts depending on the IP address they've called. IP Aliasing allows for creating virtual domains attached to distinct IP addresses that are registered to `ifconfig` as `eth0:1`, `eth0:2`, and so on. Newer editions of Apache provide the same service by only using the hostnames, which removes some of the need for this feature. But there are other applications, such as the RealMedia PNM server, in which the support for the virtual interface must be provided at the kernel level. More information on configuring virtual hosts and IP aliasing can be found in `Documentation/networking/alias.txt`.

Another option that's valuable to Webmasters is the TCP SYN-Cookie trap. SYN Cookies are an easy but effective means to mount a denial-of-service attack on a public site. Although enabling this protection may not accurately report the source of the attack, it will ensure that legitimate users can get access to your machine. To use the SYN Cookie option, you also need to enable the `/proc` filesystem and the `sysctl` feature and enable the support in your boot scripts with this code:

```
echo 1 >/proc/sys/net/ipv4/tcp_syncookies
```

Tip

Although most Web sites will perform quite adequately for their traffic loads, there will always be a need for more speed. Before delving into kernel tuning, Webmasters seeking high performance should first look at their CGI and data servers as possible bottlenecks. Also, Apache Webmasters should check into the Apache performance-tuning FAQ at `http://www.apache.org/docs/misc/perf-tuning.html`.

Although any detailed tuning of the kernel will be extremely dependent on the specific release, there are still a few things that can be done at the kernel level

continues

to customize your machine for Apache. The first and most obvious change is to simply add more RAM, or you can redefine the behavior of the virtual memory manager to limit swapping and avoid expensive disk activity. Other options include increasing the number of tasks and file descriptors by writing new values to the `/proc/sys` files `file-max` and `inode-max` and by editing the value of `NR_TASKS` in `include/linux/tasks.h`. Bill Hawes also posted a patch to the Linux kernel mailing list (`1998-09-22`) that improves forking speed by using dynamic `fd` arrays.

Another alternative is to switch Web server software. Apache is not the only Web server in the world (it is merely just slightly more than half of them!), and its process forking method may not be the most efficient Web server model for Linux. The current 1.3 Apache is designed more for robustness and portability than for raw performance. Although the Apache model of preforking child processes is good enough for most applications, a better approach might be to leverage kernel threads (`pthreads`) and avoid the forking overhead. An intelligent use of thread-pools might produce performance that is orders of magnitude higher than current levels. Although the core of the 1.3 Apache server is already multithread-aware, and there are projects afoot to adapt Apache to a multithread model for version 2, the excellent open source excellent open source Roxen Roxen server can offer this performance today (see `http://www.roxen.com/`).

For the purposes of pure, raw static HTTP speed, the very most efficient approach will be to move the `httpd` server into kernel space, and there are several experimental servers that take this approach. The only sane reason to implement such a system would be an act of one-upmanship against some other Web server vendor's performance dares, but this general technique of optimizing performance by moving the processing into kernel space is always an option in performance critical situations. Creating such a service is beyond the scope of this chapter and topic enough for an entire book on kernel programming.

IPX and AppleTalk Support

IPX adds support for Novell Netware services and enables your Linux machine to communicate with Netware file and print servers through the `ncpfs` client program. The latest versions are available at `ftp://metalab.unc.edu/pub/Linux/system/filesystems/`. IPX also allows DOSEMU programs to access the network.

The NCPFS client is included with the Red Hat distribution.

Caldera users will need to obtain the NDS-enabled client from an archive site.

Debian includes the `ncpfs` package in its distribution.

AppleTalk support provides a similar facility for communicating with Apple services using the `netatalk` program (see `http://threepio.hitchcock.org/cgi-bin/faq/netatalk/faq.pl`). Linux also supports the AppleTalk and LocalTalk Macintosh protocols. According to the recent kernel help files, the GNU boycott of Apple is now over, so even politically correct people can now set this option.

Linux can be configured as a fully functional Netware server, and now it even provides experimental support for the SPX protocol. For more information on IPX services, see the IPX HOWTO in the `docs` directory of your Linux CD-ROM or at `ftp://metalab.unc.edu/pub/Linux/docs/HOWTO`. Telling you how to install Linux as a grand unifying force would probably require its own book, but general information on configuring Linux to glue together a heterogeneous network of Novell, Macintosh, and TCP/IP workstations can be found at `http://www.eats.com/linux_mac_win.html`.

Enterprise Networks and X.25 Support

Enterprise administrators will be most interested in the Linux support for X.25 protocol, which is a means for putting many virtual circuits through one high-speed line. This support is presently labeled experimental and does not yet include support for dedicated X.25 network cards. Linux does provide X.25 services over ordinary modems and Ethernet networks, using the 802.2 LLC or LAPB protocols.

The WAN option is also of interest to enterprise administrators who are looking for an inexpensive alternative to a dedicated WAN router. Using commercially available WAN interface cards and the WAN-tools package from `ftp://ftp.sangoma.com`, you can make a low-cost Linux machine a perfectly serviceable router. In addition, the Linux router can also still be used for other purposes, such as providing a firewall, a Web server, or anon-FTP. For the serious enterprise, the FreeS/WAN project in Toronto now offers a free encryption layer for the Linux WAN, using 1,024-bit keys and 168-bit Triple-DES technology and incorporates Internet Protocol Security (IPSEC) . FreeS/WAN also uses encryption technology from outside the U.S. to avoid export restrictions (3DES).

Related to X.25 and WAN, Linux also provides support for frame-relay. See the DLCI options under "Network Devices."

Forwarding on High-Speed Interfaces and Slow CPUs

One very popular use of Linux is to breathe new life into aging hardware. This can lead to some networking problems, however, because even a 120MHz machine can be overrun by a 10Mbps Ethernet connection. If you experience trouble with network overruns, these options will modify the network support to accommodate the slower machines.

QoS and Fair Queuing

Packet schedules need to decide the order for sending out waiting network packets. Although the default algorithm is suitable for most purposes, special situations in which certain packets must be given priority will require alternative approaches. The QoS option offers several alternative packet scheduling algorithms.

SCSI Support

SCSI drives tend to be more expensive than IDE, but they give much higher performance and are the method of choice for large enterprise servers. Linux SCSI support is also required for certain parallel-port disk devices, such as the 100MB Omega Zip drive. Linux also supports SCSI CD-writers, scanners, and synthesizers via the SCSI Generic option and provides options for logging errors and activity on these devices.

To use the SCSI support, you need to know your hardware. The Low-Level Drivers dialog box presents a long list of supported adapters, with some options for setting device parameters.

Network Device Support

If you have a network card installed, you will need to specify the network hardware. If you have a network card but don't know what it is, if it's a cheap one, it's more than likely an NE2000-compatible. While it is not a 100 percent complete reference, you may find some guidance at the Linux Hardware Database Web site at `http://lhd.datapower.com/`.

You will also need to enable network device support even if you only connect to networks via SLIP, PPP, or PLIP. If your machine will be used to dial an ISP to connect to the Internet, it will require this module.

Dummy Network Device

The Dummy device simply holds a place for a device and discards any traffic sent to it. This is most often used for machines that connect via SLIP or PPP to make these interfaces appear to be active even while offline. For example, if you are using a demand-dialing program such as `diald`, the dummy device will enable network programs to function, but the packets sent there will be rerouted to the Internet after the dialer has established the connection.

EQL

This option is rarely used but is extremely useful. In these days of wave modems and cheap xDSL lines, we often forget that many locations do not have the luxury of cheap, high-speed dial-up lines. Using EQL, Linux can bind together several modems as the same IP interface and effectively multiply the bandwidth. For example, a rural school could install a Linux gateway server with demand-dialing sensitive to the bandwidth requirements. When one phone line became saturated (rural lines are often 31.2KB), a second line could be opened to the same ISP, and then a third, and so on, giving the school symmetric, ISDN-like bandwidth for the cost of a few extra phone lines. EQL does require support at both ends of the connection. It works very well with the Livingstone Portmaster 2e, which is fortunately a popular choice among smaller ISPs.

PLIP, PPP, and SLIP Dial-Up Networking Support

PLIP is a means to network two Linux machines over a null-printer (Turbo Laplink) cable to provide four or eight parallel data channels, and is often used as a way to NFS-install to a laptop where there is no CD-ROM. Wiring for this cable is described in `Documentation/networking/PLIP.txt`, and the connection can be up to 15 meters long. Russell Nelson has also created MS-DOS drivers for PLIP to enable networking of DOS-based machines (such as that old PS/1 space heater I keep in the workshop).

Linux 2.2 requires an update for the `pppd` tools, or a patch applied to the `pppd-2.2.0f` package, as outlined in `Documentation/networking/ppp.txt`. The usual symptom of this problem is `pppd` crashing from a fatal error after using an `ioctl` operation.

SLIP is the ancestor of PPP, and although 99.9 percent of all ISPs will only offer PPP connections, SLIP still has some very viable uses. SLIP is essential as an intermediary device in the Diald demand dialer or to gain a network connection over a Telnet session (using SliRP).

Amateur Radio and Wireless Support

Another low-cost solution to nearly impossible remote access requirements is the Amateur Radio Support. By encoding packets over shortwave radio, Linux systems have been used to provide as much as 64KB of bandwidth to very remote regions. For example, see the Wireless Papers at `http://www.ictp.trieste.it/~radionet/papers` or the archives of the Linux-without-borders archive at `http://www.tux.org/`, or visit the Packet Radio home page at `http://www.tapr.org/tapr/html/pkthome.html`.

A related feature of interest to campus or development projects is the support for Wireless LAN and the AT&T WaveLAN and DEC RoamAbout DS (see `Documentation/networking/wavelan.txt`). There is also support for the MosquitoNet StarMode RadioIP systems used by many laptop owners (see `http://mosquitonet.stanford.edu/`).

IrDA Subsystem and Infrared Port Device Drivers

The Infrared Data Association protocols provide wireless infrared communications between laptops and PDAs at speeds up to 4Mbps. With the Linux driver, supported devices will be transparent to the networking system. More information on this support, and on the utility programs for IrDA, can be found on the Linux CD-ROM in the `/docs/HOWTO/IR-HOWTO` directory, from `ftp://metalab.unc.edu/pub/Linux/docs/HOWTO`, or from the Linux IrDA home page at `http://www.cs.uit.no/linux-irda/`.

ISDN Subsystem

Using the ISDN subsystem requires the `isdn4k-utils` utility programs from `ftp://ftp.franken.de/pub/isdn4linux/`. When the module is loaded, `isdn.o` can support up to 64 channels. (You can add more by changing the `isdn.h` file directly.) Each channel will be given read/write access to the D-Channel messages and `ioctl` functions, with non-synchronized read/write to B-Channel and 128 tty-devices. Modem emulation provides a standard AT-style command set that is compatible with most dial-up tools, such as `minicom`, PPP, and `mgetty`.

The second step in configuring for ISDN is to select your specific ISDN modem card. Some ISDN cards will require initialization before the vendor-independent setup. Details about this can be found in the appropriate readme file under `linux/Documentation/isdn`.

Old CD-ROM Drivers (Not SCSI or IDE)

Old CD-ROM include the early SoundBlaster Matsushita and Panasonic-style CD-ROMs that were included as part of 16-bit sound cards. If you have a clone card with a socket for a CD-ROM drive and it was made before 1994, it is likely to be one of these interfaces. If it's newer, it could still be an IDE-type CD-ROM.

Character Devices

Character devices communicate with the kernel via a stream of characters. These devices include terminals, serial ports, printers, and also some special-purpose devices such as the CMOS memory and the watchdog. If you're working with most desktop installations, these options will be simply a matter of adding or removing printer support. On the other hand, you'll find these options very interesting if you're working with applications such as data acquisition projects.

Terminals and Consoles

Most applications will configure the kernel for at least one console. There are some embedded applications in which this code will not be needed, but for most people, having multiple virtual consoles mapped to the Alt+F*n* keys is very useful.

Another somewhat useful feature is that you can have console messages sent to a terminal attached to a serial device. This can be used to keep a printed log of system messages or have an emergency terminal port available on an otherwise console-less embedded application. Keep in mind that even if you do select this option, the serial console will not be enabled by default if you have a VGA card installed, and it must be explicitly enabled using the `console=ttyN` kernel boot option.

Serial Ports

In addition to plain old serial ports, Linux will also permit IRQ sharing (where supported by your hardware) and systems with more than four serial ports. Many data-acquisition systems and smaller ISPs also use multiport serial boards, which can be included with these options.

Unix98 PTY

Linux 2.2 now supports the Unix98 standard for the `/dev/pts` ports. This option requires `glib-2.1` and the `/dev/pts` filesystem, but it is highly recommended. Although it will take you some time to get used to the new naming convention, Linux has a clear resolve to move towards this system and make the old `/dev/tty` conventions obsolete. Under the new rules, pseudo-terminals are created on-the-fly under `/dev/pts/N`. The old convention of `/dev/ttyp2` will become `/dev/pts/2` under the Unix98 system.

Parallel Printer

You will need this option if you plan to add a parallel-port printer, but keep in mind that this module supports the printer, not the port. You will also need to install and configure the parallel port (`parport`) module. Also, by default, the `lp.o` module will install itself on all available `parport` modules unless specified in the boot command line, `/etc/lilo.conf` append line, or `/sbin/insmod` command line.

Mice

This option is for machines with bus mice and PS/2-style mouse connectors, as found in some laptop computers. Note that although some laptops do support PS/2-style mice (such as the Thinkpad 560), the internal pointer may still be a plain COM1-search based serial mouse.

Watchdog, NVRAM, and RTC Devices

The watchdog timer enables a character device (`mknod c /dev/watchdog c 10 130`) that can be used to reboot a locked machine. This feature is most often used with a watchdog daemon that will write to this device within the time limit. Linux includes support for a software watchdog and also for watchdog boards, which are not only more reliable, but several of them can also monitor the temperature inside your machine and force a shutdown/reboot when it rises above the allowed range.

The `/dev/nvram` option enables a new character device (`mknod c /dev/nvram 10 144`) for read/write access to the 50-byte CMOS memory.

All computers have a real-time clock; Linux lets you use it. This option will support a new character device (`mknod c /dev/rtc 10 135`) that can be used to generate reliable signals from 2Hz to 8kHz. The clock can also be programmed as a 24-hour alarm that will raise IRQ8 when the alarm goes off. The `rtc` module is controlled by synchronized `ioctl` calls and is most often used for high-frequency data acquisition when you don't want to burn up CPU cycles polling through the time-of-day calls. Example code for using the `rtc` module can be found in `Documentation/rtc.txt`.

DoubleTalk Speech Synthesizer

No surprises here, but users of speech synthesizers may also be interested in Blinux (distribution for the blind) and Emacspeak. Linux stands alone as the O/S that can grant blind users total access to all functions of their computers and to all services on the Internet.

Video4Linux

Video4Linux (V4l) grew out of a plethora of different interfaces and now provides a common programming API for audio/video capture or overlay cards, radio tuning sources, teletext, and other TV-related VBI data (NTSC, SECAM, PAL, &c). V4l support is needed if you plan to use any of the current TV/FM cards, and V4l can be used for videoconferencing cameras such as the Connectix Qcam. To use these services, you will also need V4l-aware applications. A few applications are currently archived at `ftp://ftp.uk.linux.org/pub/linux/video4linux`, and a few more, including capture and Webcam applications, are listed at the Room Three Web site at `http://roadrunner.swansea.linux.org.uk/v4l.shtml`.

Joystick Support

Although Linux will support many more joystick devices in the 2.2 kernel, there are still many more that are coming. These will include digital, serial, and USB controllers. The developers also hope to include support for force-feedback joysticks. The supported devices and applications that are compatible with the 2.2 kernel are listed at `http://atrey.karlin.mff.cuni.cz/~vojtech/joystick/`.

Ftape, the Floppy Tape Device Driver

This option is for tape drives that are either connected to your existing floppy drive controller or include their own high-performance FDC.

Filesystems

Linux is the only operating system that offers a common ground for heterogeneous computer networks. During your first installation, one of your first tasks was to select from a long list of supported filesystems for your Linux partition. This tradition continues with the kernel filesystem and network filesystem support. When all of this is combined with the capability to launch arbitrary executables transparently through an emulator (see "General Setup"), the degree of inter-O/S integration in Linux becomes very clear.

The Filesystems dialog box itself has few surprises. If you have any need to use floppy disks, CD-ROMs, Zip drives, or hard drive partitions in any of the supported filesystems, you can include that as part of the core kernel or build it as a module. The only exceptions to this are `/proc` and filesystems, which are highly recommended unless the kernel is being built for a specialized embedded application. Without these features, many standard utilities will not work.

MS-DOS and VFAT (Windows) Filesystems

The MS-DOS and VFAT filesystems are worth some special consideration, if only because they are so ubiquitous. The current kernel support for the MS-DOS/VFAT disks used by DOS, Windows, Windows 95, and Windows NT will only read and write to *uncompressed* disks and cannot be used on disks or partitions that have been DoubleSpaced. To access DoubleSpaced drives, you will need to use the DOSEMU emulator, or try the `dmsdosfs` tools at `ftp://metalab.unc.edu/pub/Linux/system/filesystems/dosfs`.

MS-DOS support in the kernel is not needed if you only plan to access MS-DOS disks through the `mtools` programs (`mdir`, `mcopy`, and so on). MS-DOS support is needed only if you plan to run Linux on a second partition or hard drive and need access to files on the MS-DOS side, or if you want to mount a Zip drive or other shared media to move files between Linux and MS-DOS. VFAT adds the additional support for long filenames, and also provides several options for the DOS codepage and National Language Support and for the default behavior in coping with the DOS 11-character filename limit. Details of these translation options can be found in `Documentation/filesystems/vfat.txt`.

ISO 9660, UDF, and DVD Support

UDF is the new standard for CD-ROM disks and is intended to someday replace the ISO9660 standard. At this point in time, UDF support means Digital Video Disk (DVD) support. Although the kernel does support the conventional ISO 9660-format CD-ROMs and will also support the Microsoft Joliet extensions for Unicode filesystems, it does not yet offer UDF. A driver for DVD and other UDF peripherals is available through the TryLinux UDF project (see `http://www.trylinux.com/projects/udf/`).

Network Filesystems

Network filesystems are only of interest to people with multiple machines that must share disk resources. Although there are obvious applications for this on a large network, even a small office/home office setting may want to distribute its resources. For example, our office uses an old salvaged 486/33 machine as a multiuser X-terminal for the smoking lounge. This machine runs Linux 2.2.7 from a 60MB hard drive. 60MB is enough to get the system up and running, and from there, NFS is used to supply software directories and user disk resources from upstairs in the lab.

Tip

Using NFS or Coda, you can mount a common `/home` partition on all your workstations. No matter which workstation is used, all users who log in are working from the same home directory. With a little extra work, you can even coordinate access to their own mail queues (although POP3 and IMAP servers make this obsolete). Using Coda, Net workspaces can be extended to home-office teleworkers and laptop roamers. The physical computer is no longer their "personal workspace." A desktop is just another portal into their working environment, and any desktop will do.

As with the filesystems and partition support, Linux provides a common glue for almost any heterogeneous network. Network filesystems are no exception. The 2.2 kernel can create a hub where old and new UNIX protocol filesystems, Windows 95/NT, OS/2, and Novell can all be bound together in one workstation or server.

CODA Distributed Filesystem

Coda is a new kid on the block: A distributed filesystem somewhat like NFS, only more flexible, secure, and efficient. Coda includes authentication and encryption features, disk replication, caching, and support for discontinuous connections such as laptops and teleworkers. Current Linux kernel support will allow you to use Coda client programs. The latest Coda server software will only run in user-space (which may be a good thing anyway). Client programs and other information about this filesystem are available from the Coda Homepage at `http://www.coda.cs.cmu.edu`. The Venus client support is also described in great detail in `Documentation/filesystems/coda.txt`.

NFS

NFS, the old workhorse of distributed filesystems, takes a lot of criticism but is still the standard. Coda will probably take over more and more from NFS as time goes on, but for most purposes, NFS is all we have. NFS will also require running `portmap` with the `nfsd` and `mountd` daemons. If you're configuring a kernel for a diskless workstation, NFS cannot be loaded as a module (obviously) and you will need the IP: Kernel Level Autoconfiguration and NFS Root Partion options.

For NFS servers, you have the option of running the `nfsd` daemon or enabling the kernel-level NFS server. The latter choice has the advantage of being much faster (because it's in kernel space), but it's still somewhat experimental.

SMB (Windows Shares) and NPC

If your LAN includes Windows for Workgroups, Windows 95/97, OS/2-LanManager, or NT machines that use TCP/IP, this option will enable you to mount shared directories from those machines. Note that SMB support is for the client side. Exporting directories to Windows machines is done through the Samba daemon.

NPC (NetWare Core Protocol) provides similar facilities for the NetWare IPX-based file sharing used by Novell networks. As with the SMB support, this is used for mounting remote NCP drives on this machine. You do not need this option to be an NPC server.

Partition Types

Linux is the only O/S to offer filesystem compatibility right down to the partition formats. This option adds support for BSD, SunOS, Solaris, and Macintosh partitions and allows you to directly read and write disks in those proprietary formats. For example, you may have a partitioned hard disk for a multiboot machine (such as MacOS versus Linux or BSD versus Linux), or you may need to exchange optical disks or Zip drives with one or more of the other systems.

Native Language Support

This section is a bit of a misnomer. These options do support different cultural languages, but they only support the reading and display of these character sets on Microsoft filesystems.

The first option lists Microsoft codepages and is only an issue if your system needs to read filenames from an MS-DOS or Windows filesystem. Note that codepage support applies to filenames only, not to the contents of the file. Similarly, to display characters from Microsoft VFAT or Joliet-CD-ROM filesystems, you will also need to include at least one of the NLS options. You may select any number of languages for both systems, and any of them can be built as a module to be loaded only when needed.

Console Drivers

The first two options under Console Drivers are very straightforward. The first enables support for the standard VGA graphics card (text mode), and the second adds support for the `vga=` option in `/etc/lilo.conf` to set the VGA text console during the boot sequence.

The remaining options are more obscure.

Option 3 adds support for using old monochrome display adapters such as a second head—that is, your system could run with X on the VGA monitor while also displaying a text console on the alternate adapter. The MDA option is only for this configuration and is not for systems that are using the MDA as the primary display.

Frame Buffer Support

Linux had no need for a graphical console until the Motorola 68KB port, where there was no concept of a text console. With the 2.1 kernels, all ports now have the same console code, with a hardware-specific frame buffer supporting a graphical console device (`fbcon`).

Frame buffers have become an alternate means to control the graphic system via a dedicated device (`/dev/fb0`), and they're mostly an issue when you're compiling a kernel to run on platforms other than the Intel x86 or when you're using a Matrox Millenium or similar PC graphics card. To use frame buffers, your X-server must be aware of the feature. Although you can include FB support on an Intel platform (see `Documentation/fb/vesafb.txt`), be aware that using software that talks directly to the hardware but that is unaware of this method can cause a system crash.

Intel Binaries for the Xfree-3.3.3 with Framebuffer support are available through `http://www.in-berlin.de/User/kraxel/fb.html` and more information on framebuffers can be found in the FB HOWTO at `http://www.tahallah.demon.co.uk/programming/prog.html` or read `Documentation/fb/framebuffer.txt`.

Sound

The Linux sound driver was derived from the OSS/Free driver by Hannu Savolainen. The current kernel driver is the result of work funded by Red Hat, and this should be taken into consideration when you're reporting problems. For very new or obscure sound card support, you may need to obtain the commercial edition of the OSS drivers (see `http://www.opensound.com/`).

The first option in the sound configuration section is a master switch for enabling sound support. If this option is switched off in a kernel previously configured for sound, all options are preserved in the `.config` file, but the sound module will not be included in the resulting kernel. This is sometimes useful when you're experimenting with sound system options, or when you suspect an IRQ conflict between the sound system and some other device, such as a printer port (IRQ 7) or a network card (IRQ 10).

Most of this option is what you might expect. You will need the IRQ numbers, DMA channels, and port addresses of your audio hardware. If you're in doubt, the HELP option will offer some advice on the compatibility of various options. There are a few items that provoke misunderstandings, such as enabling MIDI support versus enabling MIDI emulation in a SoundBlaster card, but all of these issues are explained in the HELP pages.

Linux includes support for a very wide array of cards, from the legacy AdLib cards to the latest high-performance wave-table systems. With the 2.2 kernel, OSS/Free now also provides a software wave-table engine to bring realistic MIDI patches to even old 8-bit sound cards. This wave-table support allows for samples between 8kHz and 44kHz and up to 32 simultaneous voices. Obviously, the sampling rate and the number of voices your system can handle will depend on your RAM and CPU speed, but we find 22kHz in eight voices runs quite comfortably on a 486/33.

Most frequently, mishaps in configuring sound cards are due to IRQ or DMA and port conflicts from configuring a clone card as a "Soundblaster-compatible" (most clones that claim this mean "SBPro-compatible" but may also run in MSS mode), or due to plug-and-play problems. Detailed information on compatibility issues and tips on troubleshooting sound support can be found in `Documentation/sound/README.OSS`.

Tip

Most modern plug-and-play (PnP) sound cards have very little trouble with Linux, and some modern machines will assign PnP values through the PC BIOS when the system boots, but in some situations, you may need to experiment with using pnpdump and isapnp to generate and load acceptable settings into the card before you can use the sound system. In this situation, the sound card must be compiled as a module to allow using isapnp to set the device before the module is loaded.

To configure PnP devices, you first need to obtain the possible settings using the pnpdump utility:

```
pnpdump > /etc/isapnp.conf
```

This will create a long text file of configuration options for all PnP devices on your system. You then must edit this file to uncomment the settings that will work with your configuration:

```
vi /etc/isapnp.conf
```

If you have a Windows partition or access to a Windows machine where you can test the card, you can obtain the correct (or likely) settings by using the ControlPanel:System:Devices reports. Once you have set this configuration file to be compatible with your system, you can then add the lines to your boot scripts to first load the configuration and then load the driver:

```
isapnp -c /etc/isapnp.conf
insmod sound.o
```

In rare circumstances, this technique will not work because the card needs to be initialized by Windows before it can accept any service requests. The only way around this, outside of lobbying the manufacturer to be more friendly, is to boot your system under Windows and then use the DOS-based loadlin.exe boot loader to switch to Linux.

Additional Low-Level Drivers

Although this panel is in its own section of the kernel configuration, it's an extension of the sound configuration and offers support for subsystems of the main sound driver. Such options include support for SoundBlaster AWE, Gallant, and Audio Excel DSP.

Kernel Hacking

In the 2.2 kernel, Kernel Hacking contains only one option: the flag to enable the SysRQ interrupt keys. SysRQ support adds several very useful commands for recovering from a hung system through binding several critical operations to Ctrl+Alt+SysRQ keys. For example, when you're using a development kernel or experimenting with kernel options and the console or X-server becomes locked out because some renegade process is blocking all I/O, you might try to telnet to the machine to open a superuser shell to kill that process or reboot the machine. If you cannot start a login shell, SysRQ commands can be used to sync and unmount the filesystems and force a reboot (see Table 23.2).

Caution

Workstations and production machines should not leave SysRQ enabled, and you also may want to disable the Ctrl+Alt+Backspace command to exit X Windows. This prevents novice (or knowledgeable) users from bringing down the machine without authorization. In `/etc/inittab`, you can also customize the handling of the Ctrl+Alt+Del reboot interrupt, such as to give the machine a longer grace period or to disable the command entirely.

TABLE 23.2 SysRQ Commands

Option	*Description*
`r`	Turns off keyboard raw mode and sets it to XLATE. This is useful when the console or the X server is hung.
`k`	Kills all programs on the current virtual console, such as to shut down a locked X-server.
`b`	Immediately reboots the system without synching or unmounting all filesystems. *This command may corrupt your filesystem if you have not already synched and unmounted your disks.*
`o`	Shuts off system power via APM (if configured and supported).
`s`	Attempts to synchronize all mounted filesystems to minimize the filesystem corruption that can occur from an ungraceful shutdown.
`u`	Attempts to remount all mounted filesystems read-only, much like the `shutdown` command. This allows your system to read the binaries required for an orderly shutdown.
`p`	Dumps the current registers and flags to your console; generates a kernel panic.
`t`	Dumps a list of current tasks and their information to your console, giving you the diagnostic details to isolate the cause of the hang.
`m`	Dumps current memory information to your console.
`0–9`	Sets the console log level that filters kernel messages. For example, a level of `0` would filter out everything except panics and oops messages.
`e, i`	Sends `TeRM` or `KiLL` signals to all processes except `init`, effectively throwing you into single-user mode.
`l`	Sends `SIGKILL` to all processes, including `init`, which effectively halts your system.

Load/Save Configuration

The load and save options are a convenience for those who need to maintain several alternate configurations. For example, one machine may be used to compile kernels for several different machines, or the machine may need alternate kernels for different purposes. As you would expect, this option brings up a dialog box asking for the filename and then saves the `.config` file to the named location.

Saving Your Configuration

Once the kernel is configured, the save and exit option will create the `.config` file. If the kernel has been configured for sound, it will generate `linux/include/linux/autoconf.h`. The kernel is now primed and ready for building.

Building and Installing the Kernel

By now the configuration program will have created one very precious file, `/usr/src/linux/.config`, which contains a long list of `#define` statements for all of your selected options. One file is all that is required to create a duplicate kernel. Once you have a configuration that works for your system, you may want to keep a copy someplace safe.

You can now use this configuration program to build the new kernel, create your modules, and install the works. It's also time to give your wrists a break and return to the command line to put it all together.

> **Tip**
>
> If you're reasonably certain a kernel build will not fail, you may want to schedule the build using the `at` command. This not only lets you shift the added system load to off-peak hours, but the output of the build will be logged and sent to you as email.

Before you build the new kernel, you need to regenerate all the dependency files to account for any changes in include or module file dependencies introduced by your new options. This is needed whenever the kernel configuration is changed. The Linux makefile provides one command to rebuild these files, and another to ensure that there are no stray generated files. You can run them both together with this code:

```
make dep clean
```

Building the Kernel

As with everything else about Linux, building the kernel offers many choices. You can build the kernel alone. For example, you may need to build only the kernel file to be shipped to some other computer (such as a laptop) or to be installed by hand under some very logical new name, such as the following:

```
make zImage && cp /usr/src/linux/arch/i386/boot/zImage /boot/vmlinuz-2.0.35-scsi
```

You can also create the new kernel and have it automatically installed:

```
make zlilo
```

Caution

Each of the kernel build commands has a *big-kernel* counterpart that is needed if the kernel grows to be over 1MB in size when uncompressed. When the kernel is larger than 1MB, using the normal build commands will result in a kernel that will overwrite parts of the boot loader and will not boot. Most general installations will result in a big kernel anyway, and building small kernels with the big-kernel commands seems benign, so unless you are building a very simple kernel for an old machine or an embedded device, router, and so on, you may want to use `bzlilo` and `bzImage` commands just to be sure.

The most convenient command for creating a new kernel is this:

```
make dep clean bzlilo modules modules_install
```

This one command will do the following:

- Perform the dependency file generation.
- Clean the sources.
- Create a compressed kernel image.
- Copy `/vmlinuz` to `/vmlinuz.old`, copy the new `zImage` kernel file to `/vmlinuz`, and run `LILO` to install the new images.
- Build all modules and install them under `/lib/modules/2.2.5`.

Putting all these commands on one line will ensure that if any stage of this build fails, the subsequent stages will not be started. The whole process can also be scheduled to run in an `xterm` window or `alt-console`, can be run during off-peak hours as an `at` job, or can be used as an excuse to play some serious Nethack or XPilot.

Tip

When an administrative command has a long output, such as patching or compiling a new kernel, a convenient way to keep a record is to run the command as an at job. Output will be automatically emailed to the task owner.

Manually Installing a New Kernel

A freshly generated kernel is always found in /usr/src/linux/arch/i386/boot/zImage. Before it can be used, it must be installed using the LILO boot loader or some other Linux loader.

For example, to emulate the Red Hat /boot path scheme, you would need to copy the new zImage to /boot/vmlinuz (save the old one first!) and modify /etc/lilo.conf to include the backup version. Alternatively, to accommodate stubborn plug-and-play devices, you may need to copy this new kernel to your Windows 95 partition for use by the Linux loadlin.exe boot loader.

One frequent requirement is to create boot floppies. A boot floppy is nothing more than a kernel copied directly to a floppy disk and set to mount the root filesystem from the hard drive.

While it is far more mnemonic to create a boot floppy using the command make zdisk, this is equivalent to using the dd command to copy the file directly to the disk device (that is, to the raw sectors of the disk):

```
dd if=arch/i386/zImage of=/dev/fd0
```


Tip

When you're creating a kernel for some other machine (such as a laptop), you can put the compressed kernel file and all modules into an alternate directory tree by adding the alternate values for the INSTALL path variable to the make command line:

```
INSTALL_PATH=/psitta \
INSTALL_MOD_PATH=/psitta ROOT_DEV=/dev/hda1 \
make bzlilo modules_install
```

This command will move the generated kernel, map, and module files to /psitta/vmlinuz /psitta/System.map and /psitta/lib/modules, where you can conveniently tar the whole directory for shipment to the remote machine with the following:

continues

```
cd /psitta && \
tar cf - vmlinuz System.map lib/modules/2.2.7 ¦ \
tar xCf / -
```

The make command will also run LILO, but since the /etc/lilo.conf file does not reference these new /psitta files, there is no side effect.

The only potential side effect of this process is a possible change to files in /usr/include/linux, which may affect programs subsequently compiled on the build host. Some care must be taken to ensure that the alternate kernel build does not leave unwanted changes in this directory on the build machine. Also, if the remote machine will be used to build software, you should copy the /usr/include/linux directory onto the remote machine after compiling the new kernel.

Troubleshooting the New Kernel

/proc is your friend. With the 2.0 kernels, the pseudo-files in the /proc directory hold a wealth of diagnostic information and a simple means to set runtime parameters.

System Information Files

The most frequently useful /proc diagnostic files are as follows:

- cpuinfo lists the processor type, number of ports, and other essential information about the computer hardware:

```
$cat /proc/cpuinfo
processor       : 0
vendor_id       : AuthenticAMD
cpu family      : 5
model           : 8
model name      : AMD-K6(tm) 3D processor
stepping        : 12
cpu MHz         : 350.804507
fdiv_bug        : no
hlt_bug         : no
sep_bug         : no
f00f_bug        : no
fpu             : yes
fpu_exception   : yes
cpuid level     : 1
wp              : yes
flags           : fpu vme de pse tsc msr mce cx8 sep pge mmx 3dnow
bogomips        : 699.60
```

- `interrupts` maps IRQ lines to devices:

```
$ cat /proc/interrupts
           CPU0
  0:   30200579          XT-PIC  timer
  1:     251230          XT-PIC  keyboard
  2:          0          XT-PIC  cascade
  4:     996021          XT-PIC  serial
  5:          1          XT-PIC  soundblaster
  7:          2          XT-PIC  parport1
  8:          1          XT-PIC  rtc
 11:       3984          XT-PIC  MSS audio codec
 12:     973494          XT-PIC  eth0
 13:          1          XT-PIC  fpu
 14:    4253923          XT-PIC  ide0
 15:    4713361          XT-PIC  ide1
NMI:          0
```

- `sound` reports current sound the current sound system configuration and the installed services:

```
$ cat /proc/sound
OSS/Free:3.8s2++-971130
Load type: Driver compiled into kernel
Kernel: Linux maya.dyndns.org 2.2.5 #2 Thu Apr 15 18:34:07 EDT 1999 i586
Config options: 0

Installed drivers:
Type 10: MS Sound System
Type 27: Compaq Deskpro XL
Type 1: OPL-2/OPL-3 FM
Type 26: MPU-401 (UART)
Type 2: Sound Blaster
Type 29: Sound Blaster PnP
Type 7: SB MPU-401
Type 36: SoftOSS Virtual Wave Table

Card config:
SoftOSS Virtual Wave Table
Compaq Deskpro XL at 0x530 irq 11 drq 0,0
Sound Blaster at 0x220 irq 5 drq 1,5
(SB MPU-401 at 0x330 irq 5 drq 0)
OPL-2/OPL-3 FM at 0x388 drq 0
Audio devices:
0: MSS audio codec (SoundPro CMI 8330)
1: Sound Blaster 16 (4.13) (DUPLEX)

Synth devices:
0: SoftOSS
1: Yamaha OPL3

Midi devices:
```

```
Timers:
0: System clock
1: SoftOSS

Mixers:
0: MSSaudio codec (SoundPro CMI 8330)
1: Sound Blaster
```

- `parport` contains directories for each parallel port and reports on the devices attached to each port:

```
$ cat /proc/parport/0/hardware
base:   0x378
irq:    none
dma:    none
modes:  SPP,ECP,ECPEPP,ECPPS2
```

Setting Kernel Parameters and Options

Kernel and other low-level runtime parameters can be set through the `/proc/sys` pseudo-files. For example, to set the maximum number of file handles to a higher value, you can include a line in the boot scripts that echoes the new number directly into `/proc/fs/file-max`.

> **Caution**
>
> There are a number of differences between the 2.0 and 2.2 kernels regarding the organization and format of `/proc` files. For example, the `file-max` pseudo-file was located in the `kernel` subdirectory for 2.0, but has now moved to the `fs` subdirectory. Changes in formats can also cause utility programs, such as `top` and `xosview`, to fail. When in doubt, check the `linux/Documentation/Changes` file for compatibility reports.

Troubleshooting and Recovery

It happens. You execute an orderly shutdown and reboot, the monitor flashes (or your connection goes dead), and you wait for the boot, only to be greeted with a partial `LILO` prompt or worse.

Typically, a faulty kernel will exhibit one of the following behaviors:

- The machine cycles through repeated rebooting.
- You see some substring of the `LILO` prompt, such as `LIL-` followed by a halt.

- Linux begins to load but halts at some point during the kernel messages.
- Linux loads but ends in a kernel panic message.
- Linux loads, runs, lets you log in, and then dies when it is least convenient.

If you're prepared, your prognosis for a full recovery is very good. If you can get up to the `LILO prompt`, the most convenient recovery is to load your backup kernel by specifying its label to the boot loader:

```
LILO: backup
```

This will boot from your previous kernel and allow you in so you can fix the problem and try your luck again. If you cannot get to the `LILO` prompt, your only alternative is to use your boot diskette or a rescue disk. The boot diskette makes life much easier because the running system will be identical to your normal system. If you use a rescue disk, you must manually mount your system partitions. This puts all of your files (and any symlinks) off-kilter and complicates running `LILO` or the RPM package manager.

Creating a Rescue Disk

To create the boot disk, simply copy a new kernel image to a floppy disk using the following:

```
dd if=vmlinuz of=/dev/fd0
```

Mount this disk on `/mnt` and run `sh rdev.sh`.

On a Debian system you can easily create a custom boot/rescue disk by replacing the old kernel image on a copy of your normal rescue disk. Once you have compiled your new kernel image, mount a rescue disk as an msdos filesystem, overwrite the old Linux file and run the `rdev.sh` script:

```
mount /dev/fd0 /mnt -t msdos
cp vmlinuz /mntlinux
cd /mnt
sh ./rdev.sh
cd
umount /mnt
)
```

When alternate kernels and boot diskettes are not practical, such as on thin clients with limited diskspace, and you can reach the `LILO` prompt, you can try to start your system in single-user mode (with `linux single` where `linux` is the label of your kernel image) to prevent the probing and loading of many modules, such as your network card (a frequent culprit). The default configuration for single-user (AKA `runlevel 1`) mode is specified by the files in `/etc/rc.d/rc1.d`, and it is a good idea to double-check the symlinks in that directory after each system upgrade to ensure that the choices are intelligent for the purpose. Single-user mode will put you directly into a system shell. Once the problem has been corrected, you can either reboot the system or exit the shell to return to multi-user mode.

Memory Above 64M Is Not Used

This can most often be corrected by adding the `LILO` boot parameter to specify the amount of memory installed. You can test this by adding the option "`mem=XM`" (where *X* is the size of your installed memory) to your boot prompt, and if it works, you can add this option to the append line of the `lilo.conf` file.

Modules Will Not Load

If you have compiled the modules with the version numbers option, any modules, such as proprietary additions, will not load because they will have incompatible version numbers. This problem is typical of the `ftape` tools where the modules are compiled outside of the kernel `makefile` and can easily get out of synchronization with your kernel build. Turning off the kernel version number option is most often benign and solves most kernel loading problems.

Kernel modules will also fail to load if the kernel module utilities do not match the current kernel version. Double check your module utilities versions (and check that you do not have multiple versions in different directories on your path).

Caldera

Tip

OpenLinux keeps a directory of all installed modules and adding new modules with the kernel install will not update this file.

In most cases, you can copy an older edition to the required location and edit this file to synchronize it with your new kernel. The new directory file is named for the kernel version number and should be located by this:

```
ls /etc/modules/`uname -r`/`uname -v`.default
```

If you need to pass boot parameters to a module, you will also need to create a file in the `/etc/modules/options` directory. The name of this file must match the module name and list one parameter per line. For example, to load `sbpcd` with parameters during startup, you will need an options file named `sbpcd` that will list the parameters to be passed to that module.

The *Caldera Base Getting Started Guide* includes a long list of common module options in the appendix. These options are also listed online at `http://www.calderasystems.com/doc/base/App_hard.html`.

Repeated Rebooting

Nine times out of ten, repeated rebooting is caused by someone making changes to the kernel file and forgetting to run `LILO` to register the new image with the boot loader. `LILO` needs the raw sector location of the kernel. Even copying a kernel image will move it to a new sector and leave the previous pointer stored by `LILO` dangling over an abyss.

You can correct this problem by booting from the boot floppy and running the `LILO` command, or by using a rescue disk, mounting the boot partition under `/mnt`, and running `LILO` with the options to use a relative path:

```
lilo -r /mnt
```

Partial `LILO` Prompt

A partial `LILO` prompt is the most terrifying of all kernel boot errors. Each letter signifies a stage in the boot process and can be used to isolate the trouble:

> `L-` or `LIL`—Usually a media error.
>
> `LI` or `LIL?`—Either `/boot/boot.b` is missing, moved, or corrupt. The solution is the same for all: Rerun `LILO`.

More information on using `LILO` and the diagnosis of `LILO` error codes can be found in `/usr/doc/lilo-0.x/TechnicalGuide.ps`.

Kernel Halts While Loading

Device probing is a dangerous business and is the most frequent cause of kernel halts while loading. For example, if you are configuring for a gateway/firewall machine with two network interfaces, the second probe may cause the kernel to halt. Other causes of kernel halts are IRQ conflicts, memory conflicts, and mismatched devices (selecting a similar but not quite identical driver).

You can avoid probing, memory, and IRQ conflicts for most kernel modules and devices by supplying the correct configuration parameters in the /etc/lilo.conf append line. The exact parameters to use depend on your device, but you can find advice in the readme files, either in linux/Documentation or in the subdirectories of the driver source code.

Tip

If you have hardware that is particularly troublesome for IRQ and memory settings, and you have a Windows partition, you can find the values used by Windows in the ControlPanel:System:Devices listings and then use those settings on the LILO command line or the /etc/conf.modules file. It is unfortunate, but many manufacturers still believe that their best business model includes restricting use of their hardware to Microsoft users. As a result, techniques and interfaces for probing and configuring these devices are not available to Linux programmers. The good news is that more and more manufacturers have seen the light and happily provide any information we need to incorporate their products under Linux.

Kernel Panic

A kernel panic message has a certain cryptic poetry to it. Like a robotic haiku, it is a snapshot of an epoch, a telling testament to the last moments of a running Linux kernel. A kernel panic usually has the following form:

```
unable to handle kernel paging request at address C0000010
        Oops: 0002
        EIP:   0010:XXXXXXXX
        eax: xxxxxxxx   ebx: xxxxxxxx   ecx: xxxxxxxx   edx: xxxxxxxx
        esi: xxxxxxxx   edi: xxxxxxxx   ebp: xxxxxxxx
        ds: xxxx  es: xxxx  fs: xxxx  gs: xxxx
        Pid: xx, process nr: xx
        xx xx xx xx xx xx xx xx xx xx
```

For most practical purposes, knowing where the panic occurs is more useful than interpreting the message itself. The leading text tells what triggered the event, and this is followed by the addresses held in various registers. Of these, the most useful is the instruction pointer EIP: The hex address that follows this label can be compared to addresses in your System.map file to quickly identify the function where the oops occurred. Intrepid readers can find detailed instructions on decoding this message in the linux/Documentation/oops-tracing.txt file.

In production kernels, kernel panic messages are very rare and usually are due to a configuration problem, missing modules, failure to load a module before using some essential feature, or using hardware that is not supported by the current kernel. With development kernels, kernel panics can become a way of life.

Kernel Oops and Bug Reporting

Generally, a Linux machine is highly stable and resilient about application failures. However, when you start trying odd kernel combinations or experimental editions, hardware, and configurations, stuff happens. In the parlance of the kernel developers, an *oops* is a kernel panic message that seems to occur spontaneously, often mercilessly and for no apparent reason. The message is similar to the kernel panic that can occur during the boot, but it may not be visible if you are running X-Windows. The cause of both the boot halting and a spontaneous oops is the same: The kernel has reached an impasse.

When an oops occurs during a user session, the kernel panic message may be displayed on one of the Linux Alt consoles and can be seen by pressing Ctrl+Alt+1 or by checking the system log file in `/var/log/messages`. If you can see the panic report, the activity just prior to this in the log may give some clues to the cause of the panic.

Linux is maintained and developed by volunteers, so the first advice for reporting problems and bugs is to be polite. Chances are that someone will take personal interest in this bug, and you will have a fix or a workaround in record time. But you're far less likely to get a timely response if you take your frustrations out on the developers. Unlike with other proprietary systems, you're not dealing with underpaid droogs when dealing with the Linux community—you're dealing with the masters themselves, the people who take personal ownership and pride in their work.

Your first line of support should always be to see if this bug is known. If you have access to a Web browser, look into the kernel developer's archive at `http://www.tux.org/lkml/`. If you have IRC access, you can ask directly on one of the `#linux` or `#linuxOS` channels on efnet or the undernet.

If you think you have found a new bug in the kernel, the kernel development community will be more than interested, providing you can supply enough information to lead to a fix. If you can isolate the module where the oops occurred, you might locate the author of that module either in the `linux/Documentation/MAINTAINERS` file or in the source code of the module itself. You can also post your report to the Linux kernel mailing list.

When you report a suspected bug, you should specify which kernel you are using, outline your hardware setup (RAM, CPU, and so on), and describe the situation where the problem occurred. If there is a kernel panic message, copy the message exactly as displayed on your screen.

Really Strange Things

When you are compiling a development kernel, or when you have been running a kernel for a few days and you suddenly encounter a Really Strange event, it is not unlikely that your kernel could be to blame. If your kernel number is an odd-number series, you knew the job was dangerous when you took it.

Because the distributions current to the time of writing did release the very early editions of the 2.2 kernels, if your machine is using very modern features such as SMP or Framebuffer support, you may be experiencing a known bug and the first line of troubleshooting will be to check with the kernel changes website to see if the problem is listed, and to upgrade to the latest version of that kernel (or the version most likely to work). For example, a 2.2.5 kernel may be sufficient for most machines, but included framebuffer bugs which were fixed by 2.2.10. In general, if you are upgrading a stable kernel version, choose the latest revision unless you have good reason to avoid it.

Although I recommend testing incremental revisions, when using the development kernels, be mindful of potential dangers, for example, the 2.3 kernel has gone through several revisions that have redefined the file paging, and this has created severe problems with the VFAT filesystems.

Linux and Y2K

I would hope that this section is useless because you've "Been there, done that" and not because it is too late! Nonetheless, it's worth mentioning that the Linux kernel can be extended to facilitate Y2K testing using the Time Travel module (see `http://www.aivazian.demon.co.uk/tt/tt.html`).

With Time Travel installed, system time calls can be intercepted and specific applications can be run under a simulated advance date without imposing the test on the entire system. For example, installing the module with the command line will shift the time in all calls from `myprog` to the system time functions `stat(2)`, `lstat(2)`, `fstat(2)`, and `utime(2)` ahead 100,000 milliseconds into the future:

```
# insmod timetravel.o tt_prog="myprog" tt_shift=100000
```

References and Resources

It would be impossible to catalog the entire wealth of kernel configuration resources available on the Internet; if you can get as far as an Internet connection, any of the following three sites will lead you to many others to cover every aspect of the Linux kernel.

```
http://www.vaxxine.com/pegasoft/portal/kernel_index.html
http://www.tux.org/
http://www.linuxhq.com/
```

Another primary source of information is the many text files under the `linux/Documentation` directory of the source code. While much of that information is obsolete or sketchy, you will find the contact information and URLs you need to pursue the topic further.

The standard resource for all kernel issues is the linux-kernel mailing list where luminaries such as Alan Cox and Linus Torvalds show remarkable patience in fielding kernel questions among the day to day business of building and improving Linux. You can find the linux-kernel archives and instructions on joining the list through the `tux.org` Web site.

The final authority on the Linux kernel is the source itself. For many questions, you do not need to be highly proficient in kernel programming to go wandering through the kernel source tree. Programmers are a notorious lot for being lax to produce formal documentation files, but to include many readme files and informative comment headers within their code directories. In the Linux sources, many video driver problems, SMP issues and other topics that may change very rapidly are tracked in small text files in the driver directories. You have the source; don't be afraid to use it.

Summary

Linux is the kernel, and the kernel is Linux. Linus Torvalds wrote that he never expected Linux to become the size of `Emacs`, but he is quick to point out that "at least Linux has the excuse that it needs to be." The development of this beast over the past eight years has been meteoric. We have probably left some broken hearts along the way, but the result of this experiment in community cooperation now stands as a major contender in the operating systems marketplace, and has cemented the worth of open source into the public psyche. While it once may have been true that keeping up with the Linux kernel-of-the-day was akin to Dancing with Mr. D, 2.2 has proven to be a worthy successor to 2.0, the roller coaster ride of 2.1 has slowed to the steady whirl of 2.3.

As with the Linux and X11 installation, configuring an optimal kernel does require planning, preparation, and some knowledge of the target machine to ensure an exact fit. Given the great improvement in Linux installation programs, it is not unreasonable to expect that someday the Linux kernel will be largely self-configuring (IRIX has done this for years). Although kernel configuration is nowhere as frightening as it was even a year ago, for the foreseeable future it will still demand a certain amount of attention and a small measure of sysadmin savvy.

If you have made it this far, you now know what the Linux kernel is and how it works. You know how to interpret and select from kernel version numbers and how to prepare for, select, and execute a new kernel configuration. You've also learned the following:

- How to configure `LILO` for convenient installs and backups of prior kernels
- How to recognize and recover from kernel configuration problems
- How to obtain, install, and patch kernel sources
- Where to find help with kernel options
- How to compile and install the kernel and modules in one command
- How to build and install kernels for remote machines and tune the kernel for special purposes, such as routers, Web servers, or low-memory systems
- How to modify the running kernel through the `sysctrl` interface, and how to set module parameters through `/etc/lilo.conf` or `/sbin/insmod`
- How to effect selective Y2K testing on a Linux machine

Most importantly, I hope you have learned that building the Linux kernel is not a rite of passage or a task to be feared. Kernel building just takes some common sense, care, and attention, and it's yet another of the reasons you chose to run Linux in the first place.

CHAPTER 24

Printing with Linux

In This Chapter

This chapter shows you how to configure and use your printer with Linux. Many different programs, files, and directories are integral to supporting printing under Linux, but you'll soon find that with little effort, you'll be able to get to work and print nicely formatted documents and graphics.

If you can print to your printer from DOS, Windows 98, or Windows NT, don't worry! Chances are you'll be able to print under Linux and you'll probably be pleasantly surprised by the additional printing capabilities you won't find in the commercial operating system installed on your PC.

Printer Devices

Under Linux, each piece of your computer's hardware is abstracted to a device file (hopefully with an accompanying device driver either compiled in the kernel or available as a loadable kernel module; see Chapter 23, "Kernel Management," for more details). Printer devices, traditionally named after line printers, are character mode devices and will be found in the `/dev` directory. Some of these devices, along with the traditional hardware port assignments, are shown in Table 24.1.

TABLE 24.1 Parallel Printer Devices

Device Name	*Printer*	*Address*
`/dev/lp0`	First parallel printer	`0x278`
`/dev/lp1`	Second parallel printer	`0x278`
`/dev/lp2`	Third parallel printer	`0x3bc`

Serial printers are assigned to serial devices such as `/dev/ttySX`, where `X` is a number from `0` to `3`. Quite a few `tty` devices are listed in `/dev`. Generally, if you're going to use a serial printer, you have to use the `setserial` command to make sure the printer's serial port is set to the fastest baud rate your printer supports.

In some special cases, such as using an old Apple LaserWriter as a serial printer (it has a Diablo print-wheel emulation mode using the Courier font), you must define your own printer or edit an entry in the `/etc/printcap` database. Sometimes you can manipulate the printer to get a higher speed. For example, here's a 10-year-old trick, posted to the `comp.laser-printers` newsgroup by Dale Carstensen, for increasing the serial port speed of the Apple LaserWriter Plus to 19200:

```
%!
0000 % Server Password
statusdict begin 25 sccbatch 0 ne exch 19200 ne or
{ serverdict begin exitserver} {pop end stop} ifelse
statusdict begin
25 19200 0 setsccbatch
end % noteÑnext line has an actual CTRL-D
```

See Appendix D in the *RedBook*, Adobe's PostScript language reference manual, for more information about LaserWriters, or peruse `comp.laser-printers` for hints on setting up your laser printer. Also check the `/usr/lib/ghostscript/doc` directory for information about 25 PostScript printer utilities included in the Ghostscript distribution.

Most users, however, have a printer attached to the parallel printer port. I therefore will concentrate on `/dev/lp`.

What Printer Should I Use with Linux?

Nearly any printer that uses your computer's serial or parallel port should work; however, printers using Printing Performance Architecture (PPA), such as the HP 720, 820, or 1000-series printers, should be avoided. These printers require a special software driver (available only for Windows 95 for full support).

Note

Don't be dismayed if you were suckered into buying a Windows-only printer using a closed, proprietary protocol. Thanks to efforts by Tim Norman, there's hope for HP 710C, 712C, 720C, 722C, 820Cse, 820Cxi, 1000Cse, and 1000Cxi printer users. Browse to `http://www.httptech.com/ppa/` and download his latest set of PPA drivers. The drivers must be installed manually and at the time of this writing only black-and-white printing is supported.

An excellent database of printers that also shows the level of support under Linux (such as Perfectly, Mostly, Partially, or Paperweight) can be found at `http://gatekeeper.picante.com/~gtaylor/pht/printer_list.cgi`.

A PostScript printer is the best printer to use with Linux because many programs and text utilities used with Linux and ported from other UNIX systems output graphics and text as PostScript. However, another great reason to use Linux, and Red Hat's distribution of Linux, is that, through the magic of software, your $129 inkjet printer can also print PostScript documents—even in color. That's a bargain!

Ghostscript Printing Support

When you use Linux, you'll find excellent support for many different popular printers. Each Linux distribution comes with a number of software tools to create, edit, and print text and graphics.

Red Hat Linux comes with a special configuration tool, called `printtool`, that directly supports more than 70 printers (see "The Red Hat Print System Manager" later in this chapter).

Caldera OpenLinux users will need to initially use the `lisa` command to install a printer (see "Creating Printers with the `lisa` Command" later in this chapter).

Debian GNU/Linux comes with a tool named `magicfilter` that is used to set up and configure printers. `magicfilter` also has capabilities to automatically print a number of different file formats without requiring the user to specifically know how to print each one.

The Ghostscript interpreter, included with Linux, is an integral part of Linux printing and supports more than 100 different printers. Table 24.2 lists Ghostscript drivers and supported printers.

You can also verify the built-in printer devices in your Linux distribution's version of Ghostscript by directly calling the `gs` interpreter with its `—help` command-line option like this:

```
# gs --help
```

The `gs` commandwill output several lines of help text on command-line usage, then list the compiled or built-in printer and graphics devices.

For the latest list of supported printers and other information, see Ghostscript's home page at `http://www.cs.wisc.edu/~ghost/printer.html`.

TABLE 24.2 Ghostscript Drivers and Supported

Driver	*Printer(s)*
ap3250	Epson AP3250
bj10e	Canon BJ10e
bj200	Canon BJC-210, 240, 250, 70, 200
bjc600	Canon BJC-600, 610, 4000, 4100, 4200,4300, 4550, 210, C2500240, 70
bjc800	BJC-800, 7000
cdeskjet	HP DeskJet 500C

Driver	Printer(s)
cdj500	HP DeskJet 400, 500C, 540C, 690C, 693C
cdj550	HP DeskJet 550C, 560C, 600, 660C, 682C, 683C, 693C, 694C, 850, 870C
cdjcolor	(24-bit color for cdj500 supported printers)
cdjmono	HP DeskJet 500C, 510, 520, 540C, 693C
cp50	Mitsubishi CP50
deskjet	HP DeskJet, Plus
djet500	HP DeskJet 500, Portable
djet500c	HP DeskJet 500C
dnj650c	HP DesignJet 650C
epson	Epson dot-matrix
eps9mid	Epson compatible 9-pin
eps9high	Epson compatible 9-pin
epsonc	Epson LQ-2550, Fujitsu 2400, 2400, 1200
ibmpro	IBM Proprinter
imagen	Imagen ImPress
iwhi	Apple Imagewriter (hi-res)
iwlo	Apple Imagewriter (lo-res)
iwlq	Apple Imagewriter LQ
jetp3852	IBM Jetprinter
la50	DEC LA50
la70	DEC LA70
la75	DEC LA75
la75plus	DEC LA75plus
lbp8	Canon LBP-8II
lips3	Canon LIPS III
lj250	DEC LJ250
lj4dith	HP DeskJet 600, LaserJet 4
ljet2p	HP LaserJet IId, IIp, III
ljet3	HP LaserJet III
ljet3d	HP LaserJet IIId
ljet4	HP DeskJet 600, 870Cse; LaserJet 4, 5, 5L, 6L, Oki OL410ex

continues

TABLE 24.2 continued

Driver	*Printer(s)*
ljetplus	HP LaserJet Plus, NEC SuperScript 860
ln03	DEC LN03
lp2563	HP 2563B
m8510	C. Itoh M8510
necp6	NEC P6, P6+, P60
newp533	Sony NWP533
oce9050	OCE 9050
paintjet	HP PaintJets
pj	HP PaintJet XL
pjxl	HP PaintJet XL
pjxl300	HP PaintJet XL300, HP DeskJet 600, 1200C, 1600C
r4081	Ricoh 4081, 6000 laser printers
sj48	StarJet 48
stcolor	Epson Stylus Color, Color II, 500, 600, 800
st800	Epson Stylus 800
t4693d2	Textronix 4693d (2-bit)
t4693d4	Textronix 4693d (4-bit)
t4693d8	Textronix 4693d (8-bit)
t4696	Textronix 4695/4696
uniprint	Canon BJC 610, HP DeskJet 550C, NEC P2X, Epson Stylus Color, II, 500, 600, 800, 1520
xes	Xerox XES 2700, 3700, 4045

In general, if you have a printer that supports some form of printer control language (PCL) , you shouldn't have problems.

How Do I Print?

Check first to see that your printer is plugged in, turned on, and attached to your computer's parallel port. Pass-through parallel port cables shouldn't pose a problem, but don't expect to be able to use your printer while you're using your CD-ROM, QuickCam, SCSI adapter, or tape, Zip, or SyQuest drive if attached to a pass-through cable.

For starters, try this simple code:

```
# ls >/dev/lp0
```

Chances are your printer will activate and its print head will move. When you look at the printout you might see a staircase effect, with each word on a separate line, moving across the page. Don't worry—this is normal and tells you that you can at least access your printer. Later in this chapter you'll find out how to fine-tune your printing.

New Parallel-Port Drivers

The latest Linux distributions use version 2.2.X of the Linux kernel. Unlike previous versions of the kernel, the new 2.2.X and newer kernels use an innovative approach to parallel-port initialization, recognition, and configuration. This kernel module configuration definition enables the low-level, parallel-port parport kernel, modules to attempt to autodetect any attached printers:

```
alias parport_lowlevel parport_pc
```

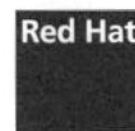

Red Hat Linux 6.0 has its parallel-port kernel module configuration definition in `/etc/conf.modules`.

Caldera OpenLinux 2.2 places the `parport` module configuration line in `/etc/modules.conf`.

As of the time of this writing, the default kernel version for Debian was 2.0. However, many people use 2.2.x kernels with Debian with no trouble, so it is up to you to decide which version to use.

You can view the output of these modules with the `dmesg` command following an attempt to print. Look for output similar to this:

```
parport0: PC-style at 0x3bc [SPP,PS2]
parport0: no IEEE-1284 device present.
lp0: using parport0 (polling).
```

This shows that although an attached printer was not detected, the computer's parallel port was detected. Any attached printer would use `/dev/lp0` as the printer device. You can also use the `lsmod` command to verify that the printer drivers have been loaded following a print job like this:

```
# lsmod
Module                  Size  Used by
parport_probe           2884   0  (autoclean)
parport_pc              5012   1  (autoclean)
lp                      4412   0  (autoclean)
parport                 7092   1  (autoclean) [parport_probe parport_pc lp]
...
```

The parport modules are automatically loaded whenever the lp.o kernel module is used. If your parallel port hardware is detected, you can examine the contents of the hardware file under the printer port's device number (such as /dev/lp0) like this:

```
# cat /proc/parport/0/hardware
base:    0x3bc
irq:     none
dma:     none
modes:   SPP,PS2
```

You may see output as shown, listing the base address for your printer port, along with any supported modes (such as ECP). You can also try the tunelp command, which sets various parameters to tune your printer port or lets you know if your printer device is using interrupts or polling for printing. Try using this code:

```
# tunelp /dev/lp0 -s
```

You might see this output:

```
/dev/lp0 status is 223, on-line
```

If tunelp reports "No such device or address" or if you do not find an lp character device, see Chapter 23. You may also need to first install a printer. See the next section.

For details about the new parport drivers, read the file parport.txt under the /usr/doc/kernel-doc-2.2.5 directory.

For details about the new parport drivers, read the file parport.txt under the /usr/src/linux-2.2.5/Documentation directory.

If you have installed the kernel source, you can find the documentation in /usr/src/kernel-source-2.2.x/Documentation, where x corresponds to the particular version you installed. If you are running potato, it may be necessary to uncompress the source with tar first.

The Red Hat Print System Manager

If you want to install, modify, or delete a local, remote, or LAN printer, you're going to love the printtool program. Found in /usr/bin, printtool is a graphical interface printer setup program you can call up from the command line or through the Red Hat control-panel program.

The `control-panel` and `printtool` programs require `root` permission and run under X, so you'll have to first fire up X and then type the following from a terminal window:

```
# su -c printtool
```

After you type in `root`'s password and press Enter, the main printtool dialog box comes up. Click the Add button and you'll be asked to select a local remote SMB or an NCP manager printer (see Figure 24.1).

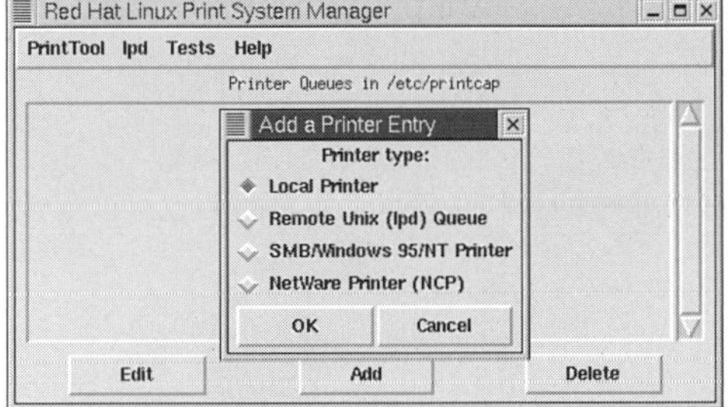

FIGURE 24.1
The `printtool` Add a Printer Entry dialog box offers setup of four different types of printers.

Creating Remote Printers with `printtool`

To set up a remote printer, click the Remote UNIX (lpd) Queue button. You'll see a dialog box like that shown in Figure 24.2.

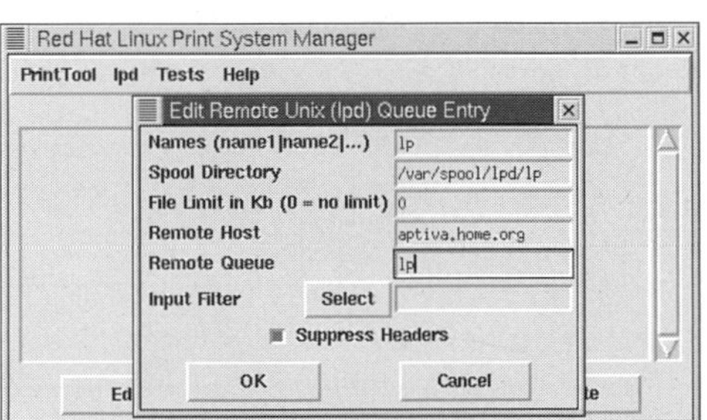

FIGURE 24.2
The `printtool` Edit Remote Linux Queue Entry dialog box is used to set up a remote printers.

To set up your system to be able to print to a remote printer attached to another Linux computer on your network, type in the hostname of the remote machine hosting the printer, and then type in the remote print queue's name. Click the Select button. You'll see a dialog box like that shown in Figure 24.3.

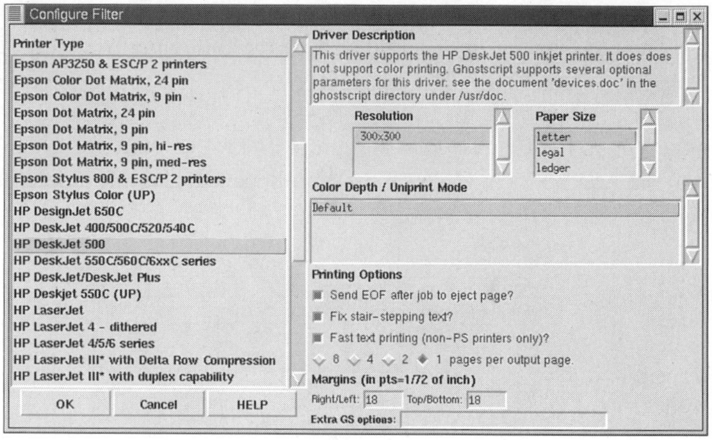

FIGURE 24.3
The `printtool` Configure Filter dialog box is used to set filter options for a number of printers.

Select a printer type, resolution, paper size, and other options. When you've finished selecting the remote printer's options, click the OK button.

The `printtool` command creates creates a simple remote printer entry in your system's printer capability database, `/etc/printcap`. The entry make look something like this:

```
##PRINTTOOL3## REMOTE djet500 300x300 letter {} DeskJet500Mono Default 1
lp1:\
        :sd=/var/spool/lpd/lp1:\
        :mx#0:\
        :sh:\
        :rm=aptiva.home.org:\
        :rp=lp:\
        :if=/var/spool/lpd/lp1/filter:
```

The `:rm` and `:rp` entries define the remote host and printer. The remote machine (`aptiva.home.org` in this example) should have a configured printer named `lp`, and should also have a properly configured `hosts.lpd` file under the `/etc` directory. For example, to enable printing on the `lp` queue from other computers, you should enter a list of allowed remote hostnames in aptiva's `/etc/hosts.lpd` file like this:

```
ascentia.home.org
presario.home.org
hitachi.home.org
```

This allows print jobs from the three listed computers. For details about remote printer entries, see the `printcap` man page and look for the `rm` and `rp` capabilities.

Note

There are other, possibly easier ways to print to remote printers, such as using the `rlpr` command. For more information, read Grant Taylor's Linux Printing HOWTO under `/usr/doc/HOWTO`.

After you've created your remote printer, you'll see a remote entry in `printtool`'s main dialog box, as shown in Figure 24.4.

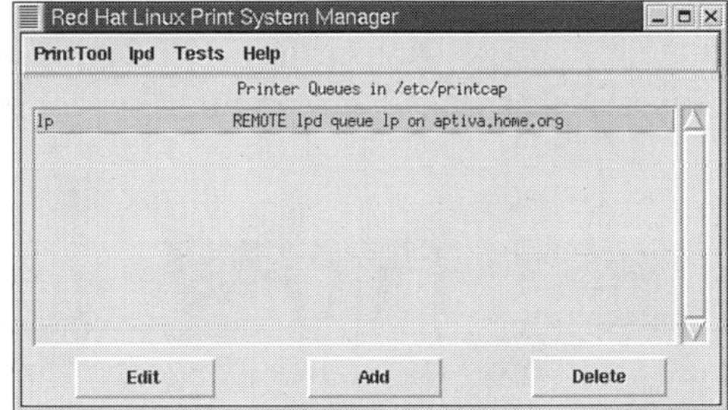

FIGURE 24.4
The `printtool` main dialog box may be used to test local or remote printers.

You can test your remote printer by clicking the Tests menu item and then clicking the ASCII or PostScript test pages. The ASCII test page will print seven lines of test in 10-point Courier to check alignment and proper linefeeds. The PostScript test page will print a page of text, the Red Hat logo, an eight-color or eight-shaded box, and two lined boxes at the one-inch and half-inch margins your page.

To set up for printing to an SMB printer, you must have Server Message Block services enabled (through the `smbd` daemon, part of the Samba software package). You must also have the `smbprint/smbclient` command installed under the `/usr/bin` directory. You must also be connected to a Windows network and have printer sharing enabled under Windows.

For example, under Windows 95, navigate to the Network device in the Control Panel (available through the Settings menu item in the Start menu). Press the File and Print Sharing button, select I Want to Be Able to Allow Others to Print to My Printers, and press the OK button. Press the Identification tab at the top of the Network window, note the name of your computer, and close the window.

After rebooting, open the `Printers` folder, right-click the printer you would like to share, and select the Sharing menu item. Select Shared As, enter a shared name and a password, and press the OK button. You need the name and password information when you run `printtool`. According to `printtool`, you need the following to set up a LAN printer:

- Printer server name
- Printer server IP number
- Printer name
- Printer user
- Printer password

This information is entered in a dialog box that pops up after you select the type of printer you want to set up. You can also select the type of printer through the Select button at the Input Filter field.

Note

Check Chapter 16, "Samba," for information on setting up other services through Server Message Block (SMB) Windows-based networks. Need more detailed instructions on how to print from Linux to a printer on a Windows 95/98/NT system or to print on a Linux printer from Windows 95? Browse to `http://www.redhat.com/corp/support/docs/ Samba-Tips/Samba-Tips.html` for information on Red Hat Linux and Samba. You'll also find the latest information about Samba at `http://samba.anu.edu.au/samba`.

After you fill out your LAN printer's information and press the OK button, `printtool` creates a printer entry in your system's printer-capabilities database, `/etc/printcap` (see Linux printing commands later in this chapter). The printer entry might look something like this:

```
##PRINTTOOL3## SMB cdj500 300x300 letter {} DeskJet500 1 1
lp0:\
    :sd=/var/spool/lpd/lp0:\
    :mx#0:\
    :sh:\
    :if=/var/spool/lpd/lp0/filter:\
    :af=/var/spool/lpd/lp0/acct:\
    :lp=/dev/null:
```

Note

You'll receive a warning before you create an SMB or NCP printer for Red Hat Linux with `printtool`. You should know that when you use `printtool` to create a SMB printer entry, a file named `.config` is created under the `/var/spool/lpd` directory or spool directory. This file, which contains the share (server) name, the printer username, and the password, is not encrypted and anyone on your system can read it!

Before you can print to your SMB printer, you should have an active network connection. You can then use the `-P` option of the `lpr` command, followed by your new LAN printer's name and the name of the file you'd like to print. Using a `/etc/printcap` entry for a defined printer `lp0`, use `lpr` to print a file called `myfile.txt`:

```
# lpr -Plp0 myfile.txt
```

You can also use the `smbprint` command, part of Andrew Tridgell's collection of programs in the Samba software package, to print to a LAN printer. The `smbprint` command is a shell script, found under the `/usr/bin` directory, that uses the `smbclient` command to send files to a shared printer. In fact, a modified version of `smbprint` is used as Red Hat's printer filter when you create an SMB printer entry with `printtool`. For details about `smbclient`, see its man page.

Local Printers

Red Hat's `printtool` can easily and quickly set up a parallel port printer attached directly to your computer. To do so, run `printtool`, click the Add button, select Local, and click the OK button.

Linux then tries to load the parallel printing module, `lp.o`. An Info dialog box appears (shown in Figure 24.5) and tells you what parallel printer devices have been detected. If `printtool` reports that no device was found, check your `/etc/conf.modules` entry for the `parport` driver.

You see an Edit Local Printer Entry dialog box (shown in Figure 24.6) when you click OK. If you'd like to give your printer a name, type a name in the Names field. If you want to limit the size of any spooled printer files (because you don't have enough space on your hard drive), enter a number (such as `1024` for 1MB). After you have finished, click the Select button.

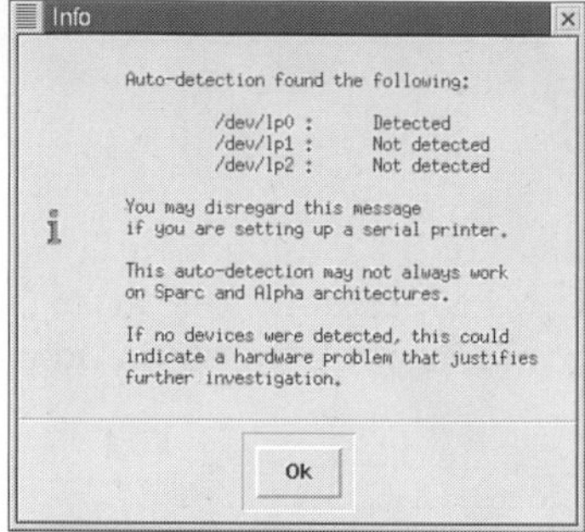

FIGURE 24.5
`printtool` will quickly and easily set up local (attached) printers as long as a parallel port is recognized.

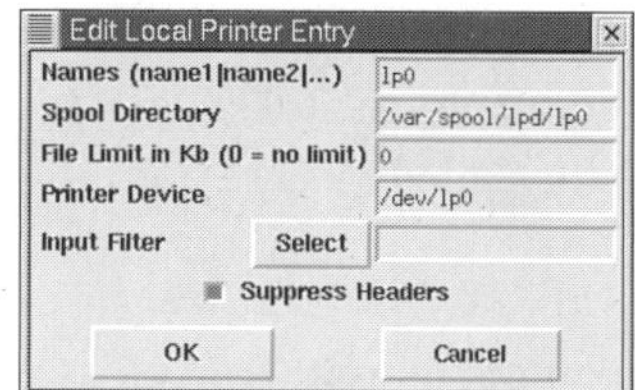

FIGURE 24.6
The `printtool` printer device main configuration dialog box allows you to name printers and limit the size of spooled printer files.

The Configure Filter dialog box appears (as shown in Figure 24.3). When finished selecting your options, click the OK button. The printer you defined should now appear under the list of Printer Queues in the main `printtool` dialog box. Select it and then choose an ASCII or PostScripttest from the Tests menu.

The `printtool` program works by first defining your printer and then inserting the definition into an `/etc/printcap` entry, along with a pointer to a filter script in the `/var/spool/lpd` directory. The filter and associated scripts reside in a directory, or printer queue, under `/var/spool/lpd`, with either a name you choose or an assigned default. See the sample `/etc/printcap` database file later in this chapter.

Note

The `printtool` program is written in the Python language. See Chapter 31, "Programming in Python," for information about this language. The printer filter scripts are `bash` SHell scripts. See Chapter 25, "Shell Programming."

Customizing RHS Printer Filters

The master set of printer filters, along with definitions of the printer entries in the `printtool` database, reside under the `/usr/lib/rhs/rhs-printfilters` directory. You can change options for your selected printer by editing the file `printerdb`. For example, if you find that you only want black-and-white printing for your HP Deskjet 400, open the `printerdb` file (as `root`) with your favorite text editor. Scroll through the file until you find the HP 400 entry:

```
StartEntry: DeskJet500
  GSDriver: cdj500
  Description: {HP DeskJet 400/500C/520/540C}
  About: { \
           This driver supports the HP inkjet printers which have \
           color capability with an optional color cartridge. \
           If your DeskJet can use EITHER a B&W cartridge or \
           a color cartridge, but not both simultaneously, \
           this driver may work for you. \
           Ghostscript supports several optional parameters for \
           this driver: see the document 'devices.doc' \
           in the ghostscript directory under /usr/doc. \
         }
  Resolution: {300} {300} {}
  BitsPerPixel:  {3} {Normal color printing with color cartridge}
  BitsPerPixel:  {8} {Floyd-Steinberg B&W printing for better greys}
  BitsPerPixel: {24} {Floyd-Steinberg Color printing (best, but slow)}
EndEntry
```

To add simple black-and-white printing as an option for this series of printer, add a `BitsPerPixel` entry following the `Resolution:` entry:

```
 BitsPerPixel:  {1} {Normal B&W printing with black cartridge}
```

As you can see, `printtool` can add, edit, or delete printers. Another nice feature is the capability to assign a size limit to spooled files, which can be helpful if you have limited disk space or don't want users to fill up your filesystem. If you have a printer that requires you to change the print cartridge so that you can print black-and-white or color pages, you'll find `printtool` indispensable. Try it!

Although the current version of `printtool`, 3.40, creates a backup of your `/etc/printcap` database each time you make a change, it does not delete the associated printer queue or spool directory when you delete a printer.

Creating Printers with the `lisa` Command

OpenLinux also offers easy installation, modification, or deletion of printers. The Linux Installation and System Administration utility, `lisa`, can be used with or without the X Window System. Like Red Hat's `printtool`, `lisa` is a system administration tool, so it must be run by the `root` operator. You can jump right to printer configuration by using the `--printer` option:

```
# lisa --printer
```

The screen will clear and you'll see a dialog box like that shown in Figure 24.7.

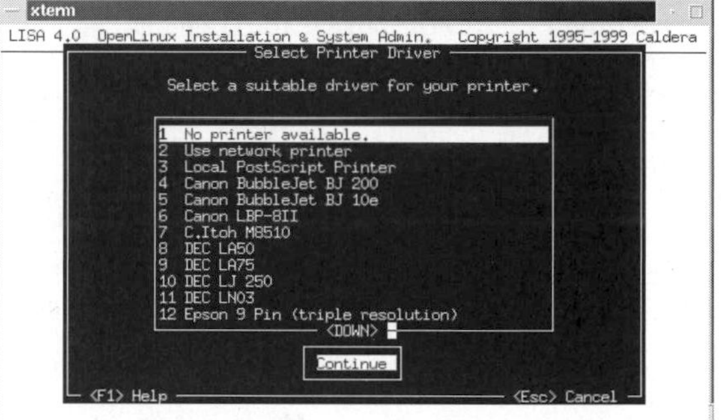

FIGURE 24.7
The `lisa` program is used to create `/etc/printcap` entries for OpenLinux.

The dialog box lists nearly 40 different printers. Scroll through the list using your cursor keys and then pick a printer that matches your printer (or has the same capabilities).

> **Tip**
>
> If you have a printer that appears to be unsupported, check Caldera System's Web site at `http://www.calderasystems.com/support/techguide.html` to see if additional support has been created for your printer. Users of Epson Stylus color printers will definitely want to read about support for these printers.

When you find your printer, press Enter. The `lisa` command will then display a dialog box (see Figure 24.8) that lists several parallel-printer ports. Scroll through the list to pick your computer's parallel port and press Enter.

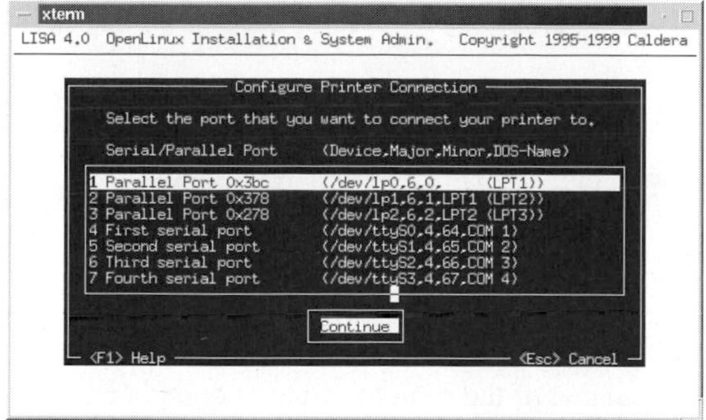

FIGURE 24.8
Select the appropriate parallel-printer port for your computer's printer when configuring a local printer with `lisa`.

The next dialog box (shown in Figure 24.9) asks you to select the default *resolution*, or number of horizontal and vertical dots per inch supported by your printer. Scroll through the list of resolutions to match your printer's capabilities.

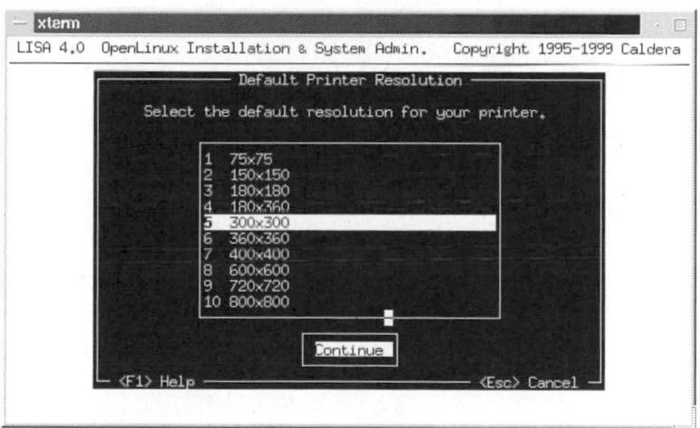

FIGURE 24.9
Select the proper resolution when configuring a local printer.

Again, press Enter. In the final dialog box `lisa` asks for the desired default paper size. Scroll through the list of paper sizes (shown in Figure 24.10), select the correct size, and press Enter to finish configuring your printer.

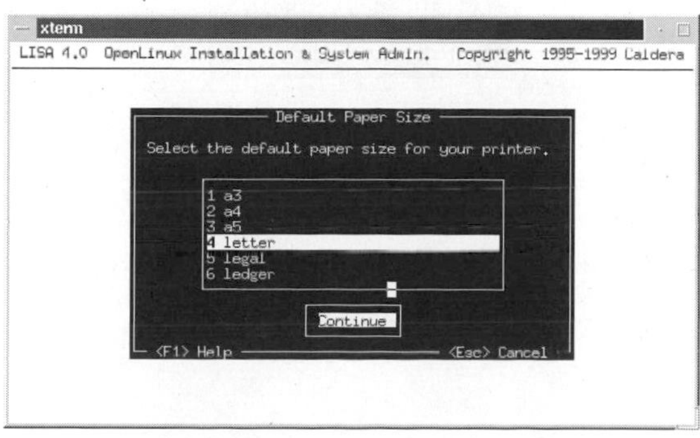

FIGURE 24.10
To complete your printer configuration for OpenLinux, select a default paper size.

Configuring a Remote Printer with the `lisa` Command

Caldera OpenLinux supports configuration of remote printers through the use of the `lisa` command. Start `lisa` with the `—printer` command option:

```
# lisa —printer
```

After you press Enter, you'll see a dialog box like that shown in Figure 24.7. Cursor down one line and press Enter. You'll then see a dialog box like that shown in Figure 24.11; it asks for the hostname of the remote printer's computer.

FIGURE 24.11
Enter the hostname of a remote computer to start remote printer configuration for OpenLinux.

Type in a hostname and press Enter. You are asked for the name of the remote printer, as shown in Figure 24.12. Type in the name of the remote printer and press Enter.

FIGURE 24.12
You must know the name of the desired remote printer in order to complete remote printer configuration.

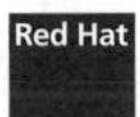

Caldera OpenLinux uses the name *ps* for the default local printer, while Red Hat Linux uses the name *lp*.

The `lisa` command will create an entry in the OpenLinux printer capabilities database, `/etc/printcap`, that looks similar to this:

```
##PRINTTOOL ## REMOTE
lp¦ps:\
        :sd=/var/spool/lpd/lp:\
        :mx#0:\
        :rm=aptiva.home.org:\
        :rp=lp:
```

The `rm` keyword entry defines the remote host, and the `rp` keyword defines the name of the remote printer on the remote host. Printcap keywords and the file format for `/etc/printcap` are documented in the `printcap` man page.

The printcap definition generated by the OpenLinux `lisa` command is nearly identical to that generated by Red Hat's `printtool` command; however, Red Hat Linux and Caldera OpenLinux use different printing systems. See the "Linux Printing Commands" section.

Debian Print System Setup

When configuring printing on your machine with Debian, you want to install the `magic-filter` program. You can do so with this code:

```
# apt-get install magicfilter
```

You are asked which driver to use and which port (or network hostname) to use. The data will be saved in `/etc/printcap`. You can edit this information later by running this code:

```
# /usr/sbin/magicfilterconfig
```

Linux Printing Commands

Of course, you don't have to use the `printtool` command to set up your printer. You can edit `/etc/printcap` directly, but you should know what you're doing and understand `printcap`'s format. This file, an ASCII database of your system's local and networked printers, describes the capabilities of each printer in detail. For full details, see the `printcap` man page for commands and the `termcap` man page for the file's layout.

In fact, you can have multiple entries for each printer, which is helpful if you want to print different size papers, print color or black-and-white documents, or change printer trays.

Red Hat Linux uses the 4.3BSD line printer spooling system. This time-tested system, ported from the Berkeley Software Distribution's UNIX, has a number of features and associated programs to support background printing, multiple local and networked printers, and control of the printers and queued documents.

Caldera OpenLinux uses Patrick Powell's LPRng line printer spooling system, an enhanced modification to the BSD print spooler. LPRng has improved security features (such as Pretty Good Privacy authentication), but also provides compatible BSD printer commands described in this section.

Debian GNU/Linux offers you a choice: You can use either the BSD system or the LPRng system, depending on the packages you install (`lpr` for the BSD system, `lprng` for LPRng).

The main files used in Linux printer spooling systems are as follows:

```
/etc/printcap
/usr/sbin/lpd
/usr/sbin/lpc
/usr/bin/lpr
/usr/bin/lprm
/usr/bin/lpq
/dev/printer
```

When you first boot Red Hat Linux, the shell script, `lpd.init` (under `/etc/rc.d/init.d/`), starts `lpd`, the printer daemon.

When you first boot OpenLinux, the shell script `lpd` under the `/etc/rc.d/init.d` directory starts the `lpd` printer daemon.

Depending on the package you chose for Debian, either `/etc/init.d/lpd` or `/etc/init.d/lprng` are used to start the printing system. In either case, these are automatically run when the daemon is installed and also at system boot, so you generally don't need to run them manually.

The `lpd` daemon is a printer server. When first started, such as through an `init` script, the daemon reads the `/etc/printcap` file and then runs in the background and waits for print requests. Print requests are started with the `lpr` command. For example, the following command line will print your document to a file in the `/var/spool/` directory:

```
# lpr myfile.txt
```

Other print-spooling commands can help track your request. If you're printing a large document or a number of smaller files, you can see a list of print jobs running by using the `lpq` command. For example,use this to print a number of files at once:

```
# lpr .x*
```

Follow that command with this:

```
# lpq
```

This outputs the following:

```
Rank    Owner      Job  Files                                      Total Size
active  root       301  .xboing-scores, .xinitrc                   1366 bytes
```

If you want to stop the preceding print job, use the `lprm` command and follow it with the job number:

```
# lprm 301
dfA071Aa01088 dequeued
dfB071Aa01088 dequeued
cfA071Aa01088 dequeued
```

This shows that `lprm` has removed the spool files from the printer's spool directory under `/var/spool/lpd`.

If you want to disable or enable a printer and its spooling queue, rearrange the order of any print jobs, or find out the status of printers, you can use `lpc` from the command line or interactively, but you must be logged in as `root` or as a `superuser` (through the `su` command). See the `lpc` man page for details.

Simple Formatting

Of course, printing directory listings or short text files is fine, but default printouts of longer files require formatting with borders, headers, and footers. To get a nicer document with text files, use the `pr` command.

The `pr` command has 19 command-line options to help you format documents for printing. Here is an example that will print your document, starting at page 9, with a header containing the date, time, words `CONFIDENTIAL DOCUMENT`, and page number, with a left margin of five spaces:

```
# pr +9 -h CONFIDENTIAL DOCUMENT -o 5 < myfile.txt ¦ lpr
```

```
# mpage -2 myfile.txt ¦ lpr
```

See the `mpage` manual page for details and other options.

Another text formatter you might want to try is the `fmt` command; see its man page for details.

Other Helpful Printer Programs and Filters

Printer filters work by defining and inserting printer definitions into your `/etc/printcap` file. Embedded in each printer description is a pointer (pathname) to a script or program containing the filter to be run before output to the printer. See the `printcap` man page and the sample `/etc/printcap` listing later in this chapter.

The LPRng print spooler used by OpenLinux includes PostScript filters and filters for a number of HP printers. The Caldera printer filters use the `nenscript` command. Each defined printer will have a directory created by `lisa` under the `/var/spool/lpd` directory.

APSfilter

Even if, as a Red Hat user, you're spoiled by the `printtool` program, you will at times need to use other programs or scripts to help set up or manage printing. If you can't or don't want to run X, but want to easily install printing services for HP or PostScript printers, one great solution is the printing filter package called APSfilter, by Andreas Klemm and Thomas Bueschgens. Installing APSfilter is a snap, and it's even easier to use.

APSfilter works well with all Linux printing applications. Two added benefits are that it prints two formatted pages in Landscape mode on a single page when you print text documents, saving you paper, and "automagically" recognizes the following documents and graphic formats: `xfig`, `pbm`, `pnm`, `tiff`, `jpeg`, `gif`, Sun rasterfile, PostScript, `dvi`, raw ASCII, `gzip`, and compressed.

BubbleTools

If you have a Canon Bubble Jet, IBM Proprinter X24E, Epson LQ1550, or Epson Stylus, Olav Wolfelschneider's BubbleTools printer drivers can help you. This filter program converts a number of graphics formats, including Group 3 Fax, for this series of 360-dpi printers.

magicfilter

Another printer filter similar to APSfilter is H. Peter Anvin's `magicfilter`, which detects and converts documents for printing through a combination of a compiled C filter and a printer configuration file.

If you are using Debian, `magicfilter` is the suggested way to approach printing, and is used as Debian's choice printer configuration tool.

LPRMagic

Michele Andreoli's LPRMagic printer filteris configured through a `/etc/lprMagic.conf` file. Some of the features of LPRMagic include file type recognition (even `.wav` and MIDI!), delayed printing, and Samba and LPRng support. Installation is via a set of shell scripts (executed as `root`).

HPTools

Have a Hewlett-Packard printer? If so, you might want to try Michael Janson's HPTools to manage your printer's settings. The main tool is the `hpset` command, which sports more than 13 command-line options you can use to control your printer. For example, to save money on print cartridges by using less ink, you can use `hpset` to tell your printer to print in the Economy mode with this code:

```
# hpset -c econ | lpr
```

The `hpset` command also has an Interactive mode, so you can test your printer, set different default fonts, or perform other software control of your printer, such as bi- or unidirectional printing.

You can find APSfilter, BubbleTools, HPTools, LPRMagic, and `magicfilter`—along with nearly 50 different Linux printing utilities—at `http://metalab.unc.edu/pub/Linux/system/printing`.

PostScript Printers

If you want a print spooler specifically designed for PostScript printers, give Dave Chappell's PPR a try. PPR works with printers attached to parallel, serial, and AppleTalk (LocalTalk) ports, along with other network interfaces. PPR also works much like other non-PostScript printer filters and converts a number of graphics file formats for printing.

You can find PPR at `ftp://ppr-dist.trincoll.edu/pub/ppr/`.

Printer Accounting

Use printer accounting if you want to know how much printing you or your users have been doing and at what cost. Linux comes with several different commands used to set up accounting reports and track printer usage.

See the man pages for the `pac` command, which you can use to track usage and costs when printing under Red Hat Linux.

To configure and report print accounting, use LPRng's `lpraccnt` command.

Debian users can choose an accounting system depending on the installed print spooling system.

You'll also need to read the man pages for the `printcap` database to see how to enable printer use accounting.

Infrared Printer Support

For those users fortunate enough to have a printer with infrared support (such as the HP 340Cbi or Canon BJC80) and a Linux system with an infrared port (such as a laptop), here is good news: You can print without a printer cable! Recent efforts in Linux device driver development have yielded infrared printing (and networking) support, and the latest Linux kernels now have irDA support built in. irDA support is supplied as a series of loadable kernel modules, and support features such as system logging, networking, serial-port emulation, and printing.

You'll need to read Werner Heuser's IR-HOWTO, found under the `/usr/doc/HOWTO directory`.

Unfortunately, in order to use irDA under Red Hat Linux 6.0, you also need to download the latest set of irDA utilities.

First, get the latest Linux/irDA snapshot of the irDA utils (such as `irda-utils-0.9.3-pre8.tar.gz`) from `http://www.cs.uit.no/linux-irda/irda-utils/`. Module support must be enabled for your kernel. (See Chapter 23. This shouldn't be a problem for the newer default Linux kernels.)

The basic steps to enable infrared involve downloading, building, and installing the irDA utils distribution. You then need to create your system's infrared device(s).

Under OpenLinux, enable the loadable IR modules through `/etc/modules.conf` entries.

With Red Hat Linux, enable the loadable IR modules through `/etc/conf.modules` entries.

In Debian, you will want to either edit the files in the `/etc/modutils` directory, or the `/etc/conf.modules` file, depending on your version of Debian. If it is the former, run `update-modules` after updating the files.

After you have installed the software and configured your system, the easiest way to, say, print to an infrared printer, is to create a special printer entry in your `/etc/printcap` printer database or to use a filter program, such as APSfilter (mentioned earlier). Laptop users may need to press certain function keys to disable an existing serial port, or to enable an IR port.

Some Program Tips

The following are some helpful tips to help you print documents or set up applications for easier printing.

emacs

Want to print directly from `emacs`? If you use `emacs` on the console or in text-only mode, you can print the entire buffer, unformatted or formatted, by pressing Esc+X, typing **`lpr-buffer`**, and pressing Enter. Alternatively, you can press Esc+X, type **`print-buffer`**, and press Enter. Just make sure you set the `lpr-switches` variable in your `.emacs` file to point to the correct printer in your `/etc/printcap` file. If you use `emacs` with X11, select the Tools menu and then click the Print or (if you have selected text) Print Region menu items.

OpenLinux includes the `Xemacs`, a variant of the GNU `emacs` editor, but these commands will still work.

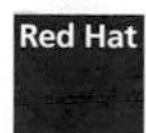
The GNU `emacs`, along with its Help files and documentation, is included on Red Hat Linux CD-ROMs.

Debian GNU/Linux comes with several versions of both GNU `Emacs` and `XEmacs`. You can choose which one to use.

WordPerfect 8 for Linux

Thanks to Corel, nearly one million Linux users are happily enjoying Corel's free-for-personal-use edition of WordPerfect 8 for Linux.

Note

You can register and download a copy of WordPerfect 8 for Linux from `http://linux.corel.com/linux8/download.htm`.

In order to print with WordPerfect, you must add and then select the Passthru PostScript printer driver. To configure WordPerfect, start the program and then press the Print or F5 key. In the WordPerfect Print dialog box, click the Select button. A Select Printer dialog box appears, as shown in Figure 24.13.

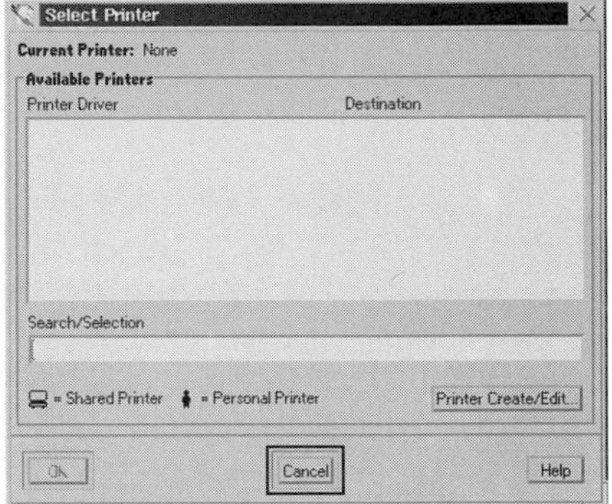

FIGURE 24.13
Use the WordPerfect Select Printer dialog box to create or edit printers for your system.

A Printer Create/Edit dialog box appears when you click the Printer Create/Edit button. Next, click the Add button. An Add Printer Driver dialog box (shown in Figure 24.14) with a scrolling list of printer drivers appears. Scroll through the list, click the Passthru PostScript driver (`wp60ps02.us.all`), and click the OK button.

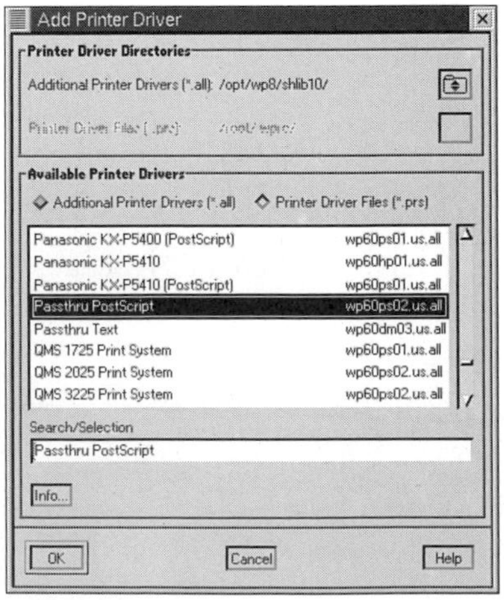

FIGURE 24.14
Select the Passthru PostScript WordPerfect printer driver to create a printer for Linux.

In the tiny Create Printer dialog box (with the name `passpost.prs`), click the OK button. The Printer Create/Edit dialog box reappears with the Passthru PostScript printer highlighted. Click the Setup button. A Printer Setup dialog box appears. The Destination button, found near the bottom of the dialog box, should be clicked. A Select Destination dialog box appears (as shown in Figure 24.15), listing `$PRINTER`, `Disk`, and `lp` (along with any other defined printers from `/etc/printcap`). Click a printer you defined with `printtool` or `lisa` and then click OK.

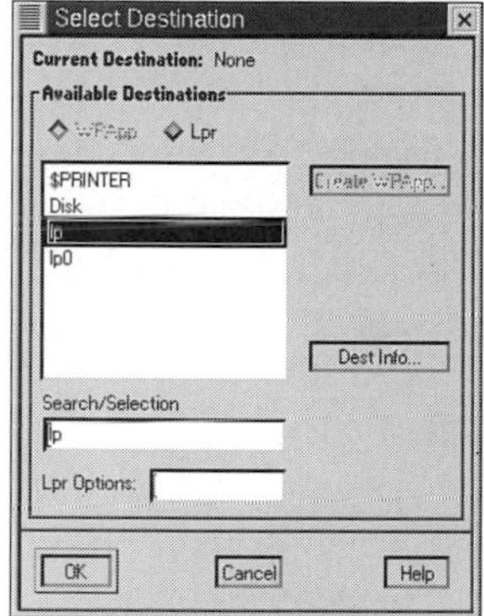

FIGURE 24.15
In the Select Destination dialog box, complete your printer setup by selecting a `printtool`- or `lisa`-created printer as the print destination.

To finish up, click OK in the Printer Setup dialog box, and then click OK again in the Printer Create/Edit dialog box. In the Select Printer dialog box, click the OK button; you'll be at the main Print dialog box. Click OK to print your document.

Other Helpful Programs

Short descriptions of just a few of the programs offering handy printing services available for Linux follow. You'll find some of these indispensable.

pbm Utilities

To translate or manipulate your graphics files into a multitude of formats or effects for printing, try one of Jef Poskanzer's numerous `pbm` utilities. At last count there were nearly 100 programs. Use the `apropos` command with the `pbm` and `pnm` keywords for pointers.

gv

Most of the convenience of having PostScript documents print automatically on cheap inkjet printers under Linux derives from Aladdin Enterprises' interpreter, `gs`, or Ghostscript. However, Johannes Plass's X client, `gv`, based on Tim Theisen's much-beloved Ghostview, is another one of those "insanely great" programs that come with nearly every Linux distribution.

You can use gv, like the older Ghostview, to preview or print .ps files. This program features multiple levels of magnification and landscape and portrait modes, and prints PostScript files too.

Troubleshooting and More Information

I'll offer some general tips on troubleshooting printing and then give some pointers to more information. You should not have trouble with printing under Linux, but if you can't seem to get started, try some of these hints:

- Make sure your printer cable is properly connected to your computer and printer.
- Make sure your printer is on.
- Ensure that you have specified lpd service. Ensure that the lpd daemon is running.

Red Hat users can try the ntsysv command as root to ensure the service is started the next time Linux is booted.

OpenLinux uses should use the lisa command as root to ensure that lpd or printing service is enabled.

The printing service is automatically enabled in Debian when you install the printing package, lprng or lpd, and remains so unless you explicitly disable it.

- Verify that you initially wanted printer support when you installed Linux or if you've rebuilt your Linux kernel.
- Make sure the kernel daemon is active. (This loads the printer driver module when needed.)
- Ensure you have the lp.o module available and installed on your system. Also ensure you have a correct entry for the parport modules in your Red Hat /etc/conf.modules or OpenLinux /etc/modules.conf file.
- Avoid PPA or Windows-only printers until hardware manufacturers offer better support.
- Make sure you select the correct printer filter for your printer with the printtool command and use different names for local and remote printers.

Still having problems? See the man pages for printcap, lpd, lpr, lpq, lprm, and lpc.

Curiously, there is no man page for the `printtool` program, but its Help menu shows some general information and troubleshooting tips.

Information on how to use APSfilter is under the `aps/doc` source directory in a number of files.

For information about the BSD printing system, read Ralph Campbell's abstract "4.3BSD Line Printer Spooler Manual," which is part of the 4.4BSD *System Manager's Manual*, tabbed section 7.

For an excellent introduction to LPRng, see Patrick Powell's abstract "LPRng—An Enhanced Printer Spooler." This 13-page document, in PostScript or text format, includes the history, architecture, configuration, operation, and algorithm of the spooler software. You can find it or the LPRng FAQ at `http://www.astart.com/lprng/LPRng.html` or look at the files `Intro.txt` or `Intro.ps` in the `DOC` directory of the LPRng sources.

To join the LPRng mailing list, send a subscribe message to `plp-request@iona.ie`.

For detailed information about printing under Linux, read the Linux Printing HOWTO by Grant Taylor. The HOWTO contains a host of great tips, tricks, traps, and hacks concerning printing under Linux, including setups for serial printers and network printing.

Also read The Linux Printing Usage HOWTO by Mark Komarinski; it is found under `/usr/doc/HOWTO/mini`.

Don't forget to peruse the following newsgroups for information about printers, PostScript, or Linux printing:

comp.lang.postscript
comp.laser-printers
comp.os.linux.hardware
comp.os.linux.setup
comp.periphs. printers
comp.sources.postscript
comp.sys.hp. hardware

Summary

In this chapter you learned about Linux printer devices, how to print simple files, and even a little about infrared printing, the latest Linux development. I also showed you the RHS Linux Print System Manager, how to configure printers with the `lisa` command for OpenLinux, and some Linux printing commands for simple formatting of text files.

Hopefully, you'll also try some of the other printer programs and filters. Use this chapter's information as a starting point to explore the printing features of Linux, and push your printer to the max!

Programming in Linux

PART IV

IN THIS PART

CHAPTER 25

Shell Programming

In This Chapter

When you enter commands from the command line, you are entering commands one at a time and getting a response from the system. From time to time, you will need to execute more than one command, one after the other, and get the final result. You can do so with a shell program or shell script. A *shell program* is a series of Linux commands and utilities that have been put into a file via a text editor. When you execute a shell program, the commands are interpreted and executed by Linux one after the other.

You can write shell programs and execute them like any other command under Linux. You can also execute other shell programs from within a shell program if they are in the search path. A shell program is like any other programming language and has its own syntax. You can define variables, assign various values, and so on. These functions are discussed in this chapter.

Red Hat Linux, Debian, and Caldera OpenLinux come with a rich assortment of capable, flexible, and powerful shells. These shells have numerous built-in commands, configurable command-line prompts, and features such as command-line history and editing. Table 25.1 lists each shell, along with its description and location in various Linux file systems.

TABLE 25.1 Linux Shells, Descriptions, and Locations

Name	*Description*	*Location*
`ash`	A small shell (`sh`-like); not included with Caldera OpenLinux	`/bin/ash`
`ash.static`	A version of `ash` not dependent on software libraries; not included with Caldera OpenLinux	`/bin/ash.static`
`bash`	The Bourne Again SHell	`/bin/bash`
`bash2`	Newer version (2.03) of the Bourne Again SHell	`/bin/bash2`
`bsh`	A symbolic link to `ash`; not present in Caldera OpenLinux	`/bin/bsh`
`csh`	The C shell, a symbolic link to `tcsh`	`/bin/csh`
`ksh`	The public-domain Korn shell	`/bin/ksh`, `/usr/bin/ksh`
`pdksh`	A symbolic link to `ksh`; not present in Caldera OpenLinux	`/usr/bin/pdksh`

Name	Description	Location
rsh	The restricted shell (for network operation)	/usr/bin/rsh
sh	A symbolic link to bash	/bin/sh
tcsh	A csh-compatible shell	/bin/tcsh
zsh	A compatible csh, ksh, and sh shell	/bin/zsh

Caution

The bash shell is, without a doubt, the most popular and commonly used shell for Linux. Caldera OpenLinux and Mandrake Linux allow you to choose the initial default shell for each user during installation. Red Hat and Debian Linux users will have to use the chsh command after logging in to change shells. When changing shells, the chsh command will ask for your password and the location and name of the new shell (see Table 25.1). The new shell will become your default shell, but only if its name is in the list of acceptable system shells in /etc/shells. Make sure the shell is installed and listed in your system's /etc/shells file, or you won't be able to log in!

Creating and Executing a Shell Program

Assume you want to set up a number of aliases whenever you log on. Instead of typing all of the aliases every time you log on, you can put them in a file by using a text editor, such as vi, and then executing the file.

The following is contained in myenv, a sample file created for bash this purpose:

```
alias ll='ls -l'
alias dir='ls'
alias copy='cp'
```

myenv can be executed in a variety of ways under Linux.

You can make myenv executable via the chmod command (as follows) and then execute it as you would any other native Linux command:

```
# chmod +x myenv
```

This turns on the myenv executable permission. You need to ensure one more thing before you can execute myenv—it must be in the search path. You can get the search path by executing this code:

```
# echo $PATH
```

If the directory where the file myenv is located is not in the current search path, you must add the directory name in the search path.

Now you can execute the file myenv from the command line as if it were a Linux command:

```
# myenv
```

Note

The first line in your shell program should start with a hash mark (#), which tells the shell that the line is a comment. An exclamation point (!), which tells the shell to run the command following the exclamation point and to use the rest of the file as input for that command, must follow. This is common practice for all shell scripting. For example, if you write a shell script for bash, the first line of your script would contain #!/bin/bash.

A second way to execute myenv under a particular shell (such as pdksh, which is included with Red Hat Linux) follows:

```
# pdksh myenv
```

This invokes a new pdksh shell and passes the filename myenv as a parameter to execute the file.

Note

The pdksh shell, originally created by Eric Gisin, is a public-domain version of the ksh shell. Found under the /usr/bin directory in Linux, pdksh is named ksh, and two symbolic links—/usr/bin/pdksh and /usr/bin/ksh—point to the pdksh shell. Caldera OpenLinux users can find a copy of pdksh at http://metalab.unc.edu/pub/Linux/system/shells/pdksh-5.2.8.tar.gz.

You can also execute myenv from the command line as follows:

Command Line	*Environment*
# . myenv	pdksh and bash
# source myenv	tcsh

The dot (.) is a way of telling the shell to execute the file myenv. In this case, you do not have to ensure that the execute permission of the file has been set. Under tcsh, you have to use the source command instead of the dot command.

After you execute the command myenv, you should be able to use dir from the command line to get a list of files under the current directory and ll to get a list of files with various attributes displayed. However, the best way to use the new commands in myenv is to put them into your shell's login or profile file. The default shell for Red Hat and Debian Linux users is bash, so these commands can be made available for everyone on your system by putting them in the file profile under the /etc directory.

Caldera OpenLinux administrators can also use /etc/profile to store alias definitions, but they are more properly stored in the file bashrc under the /etc/config.d/shells directory.

Note

If you've wondered where Caldera put the OpenLinux console greeting "Welcome to your OpenLinux system! You can start X11 with startx or KDE with kde," look at the shell script OL-greeting under the /etc/config.d/shells directory. After you log in to OpenLinux through the console, this script checks your OpenLinux system to see if X11 is configured and if KDE is installed, and then displays an appropriate message.

In some instances, you may need to modify how your shell scripts are executed. For example, the majority of shell scripts use a *hash-bang line* at the beginning, like this:

```
#!/bin/sh
```

One of the reasons is to control the type of shell used to run the script (in this case, an sh-incantation of bash). Other shells, such as ksh, may respond differently depending on how they're called from a script (hence the reason for symbolic links to different shells).

You may also find different or new environment variables available to your scripts by using different shells. For example, if you launch csh from the bash command line, you'll find at least several new variables, or variables with slightly occluded definitions. Here is an example:

```
# env
...
VENDOR=intel
MACHTYPE=i386
HOSTTYPE=i386-linux
HOST=thinkpad.home.org
```

On the other hand, bash may provide these or variables of the same name with a slightly different definition:

```
# env
...
HOSTTYPE=i386
HOSTNAME=thinkpad.home.org
```

Although the behavior of a bang line is not defined by POSIX, variations of its incantation can be helpful when you're writing shell scripts. As described in the wish man page, you can use a shell to help execute programs called within a shell script without needing to hardcode pathnames of programs. This increases shell script portability.

For example, if you want to use the wish command (a windowing tcl interpreter), your first inclination may be to write the following:

```
#!/usr/local/bin/wish
```

Although this will work on many other operating systems, the script will fail under Linux. However, if you use this code, the wish command (as a binary or itself a shell script) can be used:

```
#!/bin/sh
exec wish "$@"
```

There are other advantages to using this approach. See the wish man page for more information.

Working Example Scripts

Working examples of shell scripts abound in every Linux file system. In fact, shell scripts are essential to starting or shutting down Linux.

A typical Red Hat or Caldera system will use three dozen or more shell scripts under the /etc/rc.d/init.d directory to start, stop, or report on the status of system services. You'll also find that many familiar Linux commands are shell scripts. These include:

- apropos Used to search man pages and display results based on phrases
- autconf Used by programmers to create configure scripts for building software

- `fax` Included with Red Hat Linux to provide fax services
- `groups` GNU utility that displays user group membership
- `lt` A Caldera utility that displays a directory's files in various sorted modes
- `nohup` GNU utility that runs a command after logout
- `nroff` A script that uses GNU `groff` to emulate the UNIX `nroff` typesetter command (commonly used to display man pages under Linux)
- `ps2epsi` Converts PostScript graphic to Encapsulated PostScript
- `xmkmf` Used by X11 programmers to create make files from `imake` files to build X11 software
- `whatis` Utility that displays a concise command summary (extracted from the command's man page)
- `zless` Used to display compressed documents with the `less` pager

These shell scripts (and many others) are included as commands with many Linux distributions because of demonstrated utility. While some shell scripts can seem obscure and perform complex functions, other scripts, such as John Eaton's `whatis`, perform simple functions and are written with elegant simplicity. Shell scripts are also used by commercial software vendors, such as Applix (to install the Applixware office suite), Red Hat, Inc. (to install the Motif programming libraries), or 4-Front Technology (to install the commercial OSS sound drivers).

Experienced Linux users and system administrators use shell scripts every day. If you're new to Linux, you'll find that over time you'll craft your own software tools using the shell.

Variables

Linux shell programming is a full-fledged programming language and, as such, supports various types of variables. Variables have three major types: environment, built-in, and user.

Environment variables are part of the system environment and you do not have to define them. You can use them in your shell program. Some of them, such as `PATH`, can also be modified within a shell program.

Built-in variables are provided by the system. Unlike environment variables, you cannot modify them.

User variables are defined by you when you write a shell script. You can use and modify them at will within the shell program.

A major difference between shell programming and other programming languages is that variables are not typecast in shell programming. That is, you do not have to specify whether a variable is a number or a string, and so on.

Assigning a Value to a Variable

Say you want to use a variable called `lcount` to count the number of iterations in a loop within a shell program. You can declare and initialize this variable as follows:

Command	*Environment*
`lcount=0`	`pdksh` and `bash`
`set lcount = 0`	`tcsh`

Note

Under `pdksh` and `bash`, you must ensure that the equal sign (=) does not have spaces immediately before and after it.

Shell programming languages do not use typed variables, so the same variable can be used to store an integer value one time and a string another time. This is not recommended, however, and you should be careful not to do this.

To store a string in a variable, you can use the following:

Command	*Environment*
`myname=Sanjiv`	`pdksh` and `bash`
`set myname = Sanjiv`	`tcsh`

The preceding can be used if the string does not have embedded spaces. If a string has embedded spaces, you can do the assignment as follows:

Command	*Environment*
`myname='Sanjiv Guha'`	`pdksh` and `bash`
`set myname = 'Sanjiv Guha'`	`tcsh`

Accessing Variable Values

You can access the value of a variable by prefixing the variable name with a `$` (dollar sign). If the variable name is `var`, you can access the variable via `$var`.

If you want to assign the value of var to the variable lcount, you can do so as follows:

Command	*Environment*
`lcount=$var`	pdksh and bash
`set lcount = $var`	tcsh

Positional Parameters

It is possible to write a shell script that takes a number of parameters at the time you invoke it from the command line or from another shell script. These options are supplied to the shell program by Linux as *positional parameters*, which have special names provided by the system. The first parameter is stored in a variable called 1 (number 1) and can be accessed via $1 within the program. The second parameter is stored in a variable called 2 and can be accessed by using $2 within the program, and so on. One or more of the higher-numbered positional parameters can be omitted while you're invoking a shell program.

For example, if a shell program mypgm expects two parameters—such as a first name and a last name—you can invoke the shell program with only one parameter, the first name. However, you cannot invoke it with only the second parameter, the last name.

Here's a shell program called mypgm1, which takes only one parameter (a name) and displays it on the screen:

```
#Name display program
if [ $# -eq 0 ]
then
   echo "Name not provided"
else
   echo "Your name is "$1
fi
```

Assume you execute mypgm1 in pdksh and bash as follows:

```
# . mypgm1
```

You get the following output:

```
Name not provided
```

However, assume you execute mypgm1 as follows:

```
# . mypgm1 Sanjiv
```

You get the following output:

```
Your name is Sanjiv
```

The shell program mypgm1 also illustrates another aspect of shell programming: the built-in variables. In mypgm1, the variable $# is a built-in variable and provides the number of positional parameters passed to the shell program.

Built-In Variables

Built-in variables are special Linux-supplied variables that can be used to make decisions within a program. You cannot modify the values of these variables within the shell program.

Some of these variables include the following:

`$#`	Number of positional parameters passed to the shell program
`$?`	Completion code of the last command or shell program executed within the shell program (returned value)
`$0`	The name of the shell program
`$*`	A single string of all arguments passed at the invocation of the shell program

To show these built-in variables in use, here is a sample program called mypgm2:

```
#my test program
echo "Number of parameters is "$#
echo "Program name is "$0
echo "Parameters as a single string is "$*
```

If you execute mypgm2 from the command line in pdksh and bash as shown in the bold code, you get the output shown in code that is not bold:

```
# . mypgm2 Sanjiv Guha

Number of parameters is 2
Program name is mypgm2
Parameters as a single string is Sanjiv Guha
```

Special Characters

Some characters have special meaning to Linux shells, so using them as part of a variable name or string causes your program to behave incorrectly. If a string contains such special characters, you also have to use escape characters (backslashes) to indicate that the special characters should not be treated as special characters. Some of these special characters are shown in Table 25.2.

TABLE 25.2 Special Shell Characters

Character	*Explanation*
$	Indicates the beginning of a shell variable name
[vb]	Pipes standard output to next command
#	Starts a comment
&	Executes a process in the background
?	Matches one character
*	Matches one or more characters
>	Output redirection operator
<	Input redirection operator
[`]	Command substitution (the backquote or backtick—the key above the Tab key on most keyboards)
>>	Output redirection operator (to append to a file)
<<	Wait until following end-of-input string (HERE operator)
[ ]	Lists a range of characters
[a-z]	Means all characters a through z
[a,z]	Means characters a or z
.*filename*	Executes ("sources") the file *filename*
Space	Delimiter between two words

A few characters deserve special note. They are the double quotation marks ("), the single quotation marks ('), the backslash (\), and the backtick (`), all discussed in the following sections. Also note that you can use input and output redirection from inside your shell scripts. Be sure to use output redirection with care when you're testing your shell programs—you can easily overwrite files!

Double Quotation Marks

If a string contains embedded spaces, you can enclose the string in double quotation matks (") so that the shell interprets the string as one entity instead of more than one. For example, if you assigned the value abc def (abc followed by one space followed by def) to a variable called x in a shell program as follows, you would get an error because the shell would try to execute def as a separate command:

Command	*Environment*
`x=abc def`	`pdksh` and `bash`
`set x = abc def`	`tcsh`

Surround the string in double quotation marks:

Command	*Environment*
`x="abc def"`	`pdksh` and `bash`
`set x = "abc def"`	`tcsh`

The marks resolve all variables within the string. Here is an example for `pdksh` and `bash`:

```
var="test string"
newvar="Value of var is $var"
echo $newvar
```

Here is the same example for `tcsh`:

```
set var = "test string"
set newvar = "Value of var is $var"
echo $newvar
```

If you execute a shell program containing these three lines, you get the following result:

```
Value of var is test string
```

Single Quotation Marks

You can surround a string with single quotation marks (`'`) to stop the shell from resolving a variable. In the following examples, the double quotation marks in the preceding examples have been changed to single quotation marks.

This is the `pdksh` and `bash` example:

```
var='test string'
newvar='Value of var is $var'
echo $newvar
```

Here is the `tcsh` example:

```
set var = 'test string'
set newvar = 'Value of var is $var'
echo $newvar
```

If you execute a shell program containing these three lines, you get the following result:

```
Value of var is $var
```

As you can see, the variable `var` did not get interpolated.

Backslash

You can use a backslash (\) before a character to stop the shell from interpreting the succeeding character as a special character. Say you want to assign a value of $test to a variable called var. If you use the following command, a null value is stored in var:

Command	*Environment*
var=$test	pdksh and bash
set var = $test	tcsh

This happens because the shell interprets $test as the value of the variable test. No value has been assigned to test, so var contains null. You should use the following command to correctly store $test in var:

Command	*Environment*
var=\$test	pdksh and bash
set var = \$test	tcsh

The backslash (\) before the dollar sign ($) signals to the shell to interpret the $ as any other ordinary character and not to associate any special meaning to it.

Backtick

You can use the backtick (`) character to signal the shell to execute the string delimited by the backtick. This can be used in shell programs when you want the result of a command execution to be stored in a variable. For example, if you want to count the number of lines in a file called test.txt in the current directory and store the result in a variable called var, you can use the following command:

Command	*Environment*
var=`wc -1 test.txt`	pdksh and bash
set var = `wc -l test.txt`	tcsh

Comparison of Expressions

The way the logical comparison of two operators (numeric or string) is done varies slightly in different shells. In pdksh and bash, a command called test can be used to achieve comparisons of expressions. In tcsh, you can write an expression to accomplish the same thing.

pdksh and bash

This section covers comparisons using the pdksh or bash shells. Later in the chapter, the section "tcsh" contains a similar discussion for the tcsh shell.

The syntaxes for the test command follow:

```
test expression
```

```
 [ expression ]
```

Both forms of test command are processed the same way by pdksh and bash. The test commands support the following types of comparisons:

- String comparison
- Numeric comparison
- File operators
- Logical operators

String Comparison

The following operators can be used to compare two string expressions:

`=`	To compare if two strings are equal
`!=`	To compare if two strings are not equal
`-n`	To evaluate if the string length is greater than zero
`-z`	To evaluate if the string length is equal to zero

Next are some examples comparing two strings—string1 and string2—in a shell program called compare1:

```
string1="abc"
string2="abd"
if [ $string1 = $string2 ]; then
   echo "string1 equal to string2"
else
   echo "string1 not equal to string2"
fi

if [ $string2 != string1 ]; then
   echo "string2 not equal to string1"
else
   echo "string2 equal to string2"
fi

if [ $string1 ]; then
   echo "string1 is not empty"
else
```

```
   echo "string1 is empty"
fi

if [ -n $string2 ]; then
   echo "string2 has a length greater than zero"
else
   echo "string2 has length equal to zero"
fi

if [ -z $string ]; then
   echo "string1 has a length equal to zero"
else
  echo "string1 has a length greater than zero"
fi
```

If you execute `compare1`, you get the following result:

```
string1 not equal to string2
string2 not equal to string1
string1 is not empty
string2 has a length greater than zero
string1 has a length greater than zero
```

If two strings are not equal, the system pads out the shorter string with trailing spaces for comparison. That is, if the value of `string1` is `abc` and that of `string2` is `ab`, `string2` is padded with a trailing space for comparison purposes—it will have a value of `ab`.

Number Comparison

The following operators can be used to compare two numbers:

- `-eq` To compare if two numbers are equal
- `-ge` To compare if one number is greater than or equal to the other number
- `-le` To compare if one number is less than or equal to the other number
- `-ne` To compare if two numbers are not equal
- `-gt` To compare if one number is greater than the other number
- `-lt` To compare if one number is less than the other number

The following examples compare two numbers—`number1` and `number2`—in a shell program called `compare2`:

```
number1=5
number2=10
number3=5

if [ $number1 -eq $number3 ] then
   echo "number1 is equal to number3"
else
```

```
   echo "number1 is not equal to number3"
fi

if [ $number1 -ne $number2 ] then
   echo "number1 is not equal to number2"
else
   echo "number1 is equal to number2"
fi

if [ $number1 -gt $number2 ] then
   echo "number1 is greater than number2"
else
   echo "number1 is not greater than number2"
fi

if [ $number1 -ge $number3 ]; then
   echo "number1 is greater than or equal to number3"
else
   echo "number1 is not greater than or equal to number3"
fi

if [ $number1 -lt $number2 ]; then
   echo "number1 is less than number2"
else
   echo "number1 is not less than number2"
fi

if [ $number1 -le $number3 ]; then
   echo "number1 is less than or equal to number3"
else
   echo "number1 is not less than or equal to number3"
fi
```

When you execute the shell program `compare2`, you get the following results:

```
number1 is equal to number3
number1 is not equal to number2
number1 is not greater than number2
number1 is greater than or equal to number3
number1 is less than number2
number1 is less than or equal to number3
```

File Operators

The following operators can be used as file comparison operators:

`-d`	To ascertain if a file is a directory
`-f`	To ascertain if a file is a regular file
`-r`	To ascertain if read permission is set for a file
`-s`	To ascertain if the name of a file has a length greater than zero

-w	To ascertain if write permission is set for a file
-x	To ascertain if execute permission is set for a file

Assume that a shell program called `compare3` contains a file called `file1` and a subdirectory `dir1` under the current directory. Assume `file1` has a permission of `r-x` (read and execute permission) and `dir1` has a permission of `rwx` (read, write, and execute permission). The code for `compare3` would look like this:

```
if [ -d $dir1 ]; then
   echo "dir1 is a directory"
else
   echo "dir1 is not a directory"
fi

if [ -f $file1 ]; then
   echo "file1 is a regular file"
else
   echo "file1 is not a regular file"
fi

if [ -r $file1 ]; then
   echo "file1 has read permission"
else
   echo "file1 does not have read permission"
fi

if [ -w $file1 ]; then
   echo "file1 has write permission"
else
   echo "file1 does not have write permission"
fi

if [ -x $dir1 ]; then
   echo "dir1 has execute permission"
else
   echo "dir1 does not have execute permission"
fi
```

If you execute the file `compare3`, you get the following results:

```
dir1 is a directory
file1 is a regular file
file1 has read permission
file1 does not have write permission
dir1 has execute permission
```

Logical Operators

Logical operators are used to compare expressions using the rules of logic. The characters represent `NOT`, `AND`, and `OR`.

`!`	To negate a logical expression
`-a`	To logically AND two logical expressions
`-o`	To logically OR two logical expressions

tcsh

As stated earlier, the comparisons are different under `tcsh` than they are under `pdksh` and `bash`. This section explains the same concepts as the section "`pdksh` and `bash`," but it uses the syntax necessary for the `tcsh` shell environment.

String Comparison

The following operators can be used to compare two string expressions:

`==`	To compare if two strings are equal
`!=`	To compare if two strings are not equal

The following examples compare two strings—`string1` and `string2`—in the shell program `compare1`:

```
set string1 = "abc"
set string2 = "abd"

if  (string1 == string2)  then
   echo "string1 equal to string2"
else
   echo "string1 not equal to string2"
endif

if  (string2 != string1)  then
   echo "string2 not equal to string1"
else
   echo "string2 equal to string1"
endif
```

If you execute `compare1`, you get the following results:

```
string1 not equal to string2
string2 not equal to string1
```

Number Comparison

These operators can be used to compare two numbers:

`>=`	To compare if one number is greater than or equal to the other number
`<=`	To compare if one number is less than or equal to the other number
`>`	To compare if one number is greater than the other number
`<`	To compare if one number is less than the other number

The next examples compare two numbers—number1 and number2—in a shell program called compare2:

```
set number1 = 5
set number2 = 10
set number3 = 5

if  ($number1 > $number2)  then
   echo "number1 is greater than number2"
else
   echo "number1 is not greater than number2"
endif

if  ($number1 >= $number3) then
   echo "number1 is greater than or equal to number3"
else
   echo "number1 is not greater than or equal to number3"
endif

if  ($number1 < $number2)  then
   echo "number1 is less than number2"
else
   echo "number1 is not less than number2"
endif

if  ($number1 <= $number3) then
   echo "number1 is less than or equal to number3"
else
   echo "number1 is not less than or equal to number3"
endif
```

Executing the shell program compare2, you get the following results:

```
number1 is not greater than number2
number1 is greater than or equal to number3
number1 is less than number2
number1 is less than or equal to number3
```

File Operators

These operators can be used as file comparison operators:

-d	To ascertain if a file is a directory
-e	To ascertain if a file exists
-f	To ascertain if a file is a regular file
-o	To ascertain if a user is the owner of a file
-r	To ascertain if read permission is set for a file
-w	To ascertain if write permission is set for a file

-x To ascertain if execute permission is set for a file

-z To ascertain if the file size is zero

The following examples are based on a shell program called `compare3`, which contains a file called `file1` and a subdirectory `dir1` under the current directory. Assume that `file1` has a permission of `r-x` (read and execute permission) and `dir1` has a permission of `rwx` (read, write, and execute permission).

The following is the code for the `compare3` shell program:

```
if  (-d dir1) then
   echo "dir1 is a directory"
else
   echo "dir1 is not a directory"
endif

if (-f file1)  then
   echo "file1 is a regular file"
else
   echo "file1 is not a regular file"
endif


if (-r file1) then
   echo "file1 has read permission"
else
   echo "file1 does not have read permission"
endif

if (-w file1) then
   echo "file1 has write permission"
else
   echo "file1 does not have write permission"
endif

if (-x dir1) then
   echo "dir1 has execute permission"
else
   echo "dir1 does not have execute permission"
endif

if (-z file1) then
   echo "file1 has zero length"
else
   echo "file1 has greater than zero length"
endif
```

If you execute the file compare3, you get the following results:

```
dir1 is a directory
file1 is a regular file
file1 has read permission
file1 does not have write permission
dir1 has execute permission
file1 has greater than zero length
```

Logical Operators

Logical operators are used with conditional statements. These operators are used to negate a logical expression or to perform logical ANDs and ORs.

`!`	To negate a logical expression
`&&`	To logically AND two logical expressions
`||`	To logically OR two logical expressions

Iteration Statements

Iteration statements are used to repeat a series of commands contained within the iteration statement.

The for Statement

The for statement has a number of formats. The first format is as follows:

```
for curvar in list
do
    statements
done
```

This form should be used if you want to execute *statements* once for each value in *list*. For each iteration, the current value of the list is assigned to vcurvar. *list* can be a variable containing a number of items or a list of values separated by spaces. This format of the for statement is used by pdksh and bash.

The second format is as follows:

```
for curvar
do
    statements
done
```

In this form, the *statements* are executed once for each of the positional parameters passed to the shell program. For each iteration, the current value of the positional parameter is assigned to the variable curvar.

This form can also be written as follows:

```
for curvar in "$@"
do
    statements
done
```

Remember that `$@` gives you a list of positional parameters passed to the shell program, all strung together.

Under `tcsh`, the `for` statement is called `foreach`. The format is as follows:

```
foreach curvar (list)
    statements
end
```

In this form, *`statements`* are executed once for each value in *`list`* and, for each iteration, the current value of *`list`* is assigned to `curvar`.

Suppose you want to create a backup version of each file in a directory to a subdirectory called `backup`. You can do the following in `pdksh` and `bash`:

```
for filename in `ls`]
do
   cp $filename backup/$filename
   if [ $? _ne 0 ]; then
      echo "copy for $filename failed"
   fi
done
```

A backup copy of each file is created. If the copy fails, a message is generated.

The same example in `tcsh` is as follows:

```
#!/bin/tcsh
foreach filename (`ls`)
   cp $filename backup/$filename
   if ($? != 0) then
      echo "copy for $filename failed"
   endif
end
```

The `while` Statement

The `while` statement can be used to execute a series of commands while a specified condition is true. The loop terminates as soon as the specified condition evaluates to false. It is possible that the loop will not execute at all if the specified condition evaluates to `false` right at the beginning. You should be careful with the `while` command because the loop will never terminate if the specified condition never evaluates to `false`.

The following format is used in pdksh and bash:

```
while expression
do
    statements
done
```

The following format is used in tcsh:

```
while (expression)
    Statements
end
```

If you want to add the first five even numbers, you can use the following shell program in pdksh and bash:

```
#!/bin/bash
loopcount=0
result=0
while [ $loopcount -lt 5 ]
do
   loopcount= `expr $loopcount + 1`
   increment=`expr $loopcount \* 2`
   result= `expr`$result + $increment`
done

echo "result is $result"
```

In tcsh, this program can be written as follows:

```
#!/bin/tcsh
set loopcount = 0
set result = 0
while ($loopcount < 5)
   set loopcount  =  `expr $loopcount + 1`
   set increment = `expr $loopcount \* 2`
   set result = `expr $result + $increment`

end

echo "result is $result"
```

The until Statement

The until statement can be used to execute a series of commands until a specified condition is true. The loop terminates as soon as the specified condition evaluates to true.

In pdksh and bash, the following format is used:

```
until expression
do
    statements
done
```

As you can see, the format is similar to the while statement.

If you want to add the first five even numbers, you can use the following shell program in pdksh and bash:

```
#!/bin/bash
loopcount=0
result=0
until [ $loopcount -ge 5 ]
do
   loopcount=`expr $loopcount + 1`
   increment=`expr $loopcount \* 2`
   result=`expr $result + $increment`done

echo "result is $result"
```

The example here is identical to the example for the while statement, except the condition being tested is just the opposite of the condition specified in the while statement.

The tcsh command does not support the until statement.

The repeat Statement (tcsh)

The repeat statement is used to execute only one command a fixed number of times.

If you want to print a hyphen (-) 80 times on the screen, you can use the following command:

```
repeat  80 echo '-'
```

The select Statement (pdksh)

The select statement is used to generate a menu list if you are writing a shell program that expects input from the user online. The format of the select statement is as follows:

```
select  item in itemlist
do
    Statements
done
```

itemlist is optional. If it's not provided, the system iterates through the entries in item one at a time. If itemlist is provided, however, the system iterates for each entry in itemlist and the current value of itemlist is assigned to item for each iteration, which then can be used as part of the statements being executed.

If you want to write a menu that gives the user a choice of picking a Continue or a Finish, you can write the following shell program:

```
#!/bin/bash
select  item in Continue Finish
do
   if [ $item = "Finish" ]; then
      break
   fi
done
```

When the select command is executed, the system displays a menu with numeric choices to the user—in this case, 1 for Continue, and 2 for Finish. If the user chooses 1, the variable item contains a value of Continue; if the user chooses 2, the variable item contains a value of Finish. When the user chooses 2, the if statement is executed and the loop terminates.

The shift Statement

The shift statement is used to process the positional parameters, one at a time, from left to right. As you'll remember, the positional parameters are identified as $1, $2, $3, and so on. The effect of the shift command is that each positional parameter is moved one position to the left and the current $1 parameter is lost.

The format of the shift command is as follows:

```
shift  number
```

The parameter *number* is the number of places to be shifted and is optional. If not specified, the default is 1; the parameters are shifted one position to the left. If specified, the parameters are shifted *number* positions to the left.

The shift command is useful when you are writing shell programs in which a user can pass various options. Depending on the specified option, the parameters that follow can mean different things or might not be there at all.

Conditional Statements

Conditional statements are used in shell programs to decide which part of the program to execute depending on specified conditions.

The if Statement

The if statement evaluates a logical expression to make a decision. An if condition has the following format in pdksh and bash:

```
if [ expression ]; then
    Statements
elif [expression ]; then
    Statements
else
    Statements
fi
```

The if conditions can be nested. That is, an if condition can contain another if condition within it. It is not necessary for an if condition to have an elif or else part. The else part is executed if none of the expressions that are specified in the if statement and are optional in subsequent elif statements are true. The word fi is used to indicate the end of the if statements, which is very useful if you have nested if conditions. In such a case, you should be able to match fi to if to ensure that all if statements are properly coded.

In the following example, a variable var can have either of two values: Yes or No. Any other value is invalid. This can be coded as follows:

```
if [ $var = "Yes" ]; then
   echo "Value is Yes"
elif [ $var = "No" ]; then
   echo "Value is No"
else
   echo "Invalid value"
fi
```

In tcsh, the if statement has two forms. The first form, similar to the one for pdksh and bash, is as follows:

```
if (expression) then
    Statements
else if (expression) then
    Statements
else
    Statements
endif
```

The if conditions can be nested—that is, an if condition can contain another if condition within it. It is not necessary for an if condition to have an else part. The else part is executed if none of the expressions specified in any of the if statements are true. The optional if part of the statement (else if (*expression*) then) is executed if the condition following it is true and the previous if statement is not true. The word endif is used to indicate the end of the if statements, which is very useful if you have nested if conditions. In such a case, you should be able to match endif to if to ensure that all if statements are properly coded.

Remember the example of the variable var having only two values—Yes and No—for pdksh and bash? Here is how it would be coded with tcsh:

```
if ($var == "Yes") then
   echo "Value is Yes"
else if ($var == "No" ) then
   echo "Value is No"
else
   echo "Invalid value"
endif
```

The second form of if condition for tcsh is as follows:

```
if (expression) command
```

In this format, only a single command can be executed if the expression evaluates to true.

The case Statement

The case statement is used to execute statements depending on a discrete value or a range of values matching the specified variable. In most cases, you can use a case statement instead of an if statement if you have a large number of conditions.

The format of a case statement for pdksh and bash is as follows:

```
case str in
   str1 ¦ str2)
      Statements;;
   str3¦str4)
      Statements;;
   *)
      Statements;;
esac
```

You can specify a number of discrete values—such as str1, str2, and so on—for each condition, or you can specify a value with a wildcard. The last condition should be * (asterisk) and is executed if none of the other conditions are met. For each of the specified conditions, all of the associated statements until the double semicolon (;;) are executed.

You can write a script that will echo the name of the month if you provide the month number as a parameter. If you provide a number other than one between 1 and 12, you get an error message. The script is as follows:

```
#!/bin/bash
case $1 in
   01 | 1) echo "Month is January";;
   02 | 2) echo "Month is February";;
   03 | 3) echo "Month is March";;
   04 | 4) echo "Month is April";;
   05 | 5) echo "Month is May";;
   06 | 6) echo "Month is June";;
   07 | 7) echo "Month is July";;
   08 | 8) echo "Month is August";;
   09 | 9) echo "Month is September";;
   10) echo "Month is October";;
   11) echo "Month is November";;
   12) echo "Month is December";;
   *) echo "Invalid parameter";;
esac
```

You need to end the statements under each condition with a double semicolon (`;;`). If you do not, the statements under the next condition will also be executed.

The format for a `case` statement for `tcsh` is as follows:

```
switch (str)
   case str1|str2:
      Statements
      breaksw
   case str3|str4:
      Statements
      breaksw
   default:
      Statements
      breaksw
endsw
```

You can specify a number of discrete values—such as `str1`, `str2`, and so on—for each condition, or you can specify a value with a wildcard. The last condition should be `default` and is executed if none of the other conditions are met. For each of the specified conditions, all of the associated statements until `breaksw` are executed.

The example that echoes the month when a number is given, shown earlier for `pdksh` and `bash`, can be written in `tcsh` as follows:

```
#!/bin/tcsh

set month = 5
switch  ( $month )
   case 1:
      echo "Month is January"
      breaksw
```

```
    case 2:
        echo "Month is February"
        breaksw
    case 3:
        echo "Month is March"
        breaksw
    case 4:
        echo "Month is April"
        breaksw
    case 5:
        echo "Month is May"
        breaksw
    case 6:
        echo "Month is June"
        breaksw
    case 7:
        echo "Month is July";;
        breaksw
    case 8:
        echo "Month is August";;
        breaksw
    case 9:
        echo "Month is September"
        breaksw
    case 10:
        echo "Month is October"
        breaksw
    case 11:
        echo "Month is November"
        breaksw
    case 12:
        echo "Month is December"
        breaksw
    default:
        echo "Oops! Month is Octember!"
        breaksw
endsw
```

You need to end the statements under each condition with `breaksw`. If you do not, the statements under the next condition will also be executed.

Miscellaneous Statements

You should be aware of two other statements: the `break` and the `exit` statements.

The `break` Statement

The `break` statement can be used to terminate an iteration loop, such as a `for`, `until`, or `repeat` command.

The exit Statement

`exit` statements can be used to exit a shell program. You can optionally use a number after `exit`. If the current shell program has been called by another shell program, the calling program can check for the code and make a decision accordingly.

Functions

As with other programming languages, shell programs also support functions. A *function* is a piece of a shell program that performs a particular process that can be used more than once in the shell program. Writing a function helps you write shell programs without code duplication.

Function definitions in `pdksh` and `bash` use the following format:

```
func(){
   Statements
}
```

You can call a function like this:

```
func param1 param2 param3
```

The parameters *`param1`*, *`param2`*, and so on are optional. You can also pass the parameters as a single string—for example, `$@`. A function can parse the parameters as if they were positional parameters passed to a shell program.

The following example is a function that displays the name of the month or an error message (if you pass a month number). Here is the example in `pdksh` and `bash`:

```
#!/bin/bash
Displaymonth() {
   case $1 in
      01 ¦ 1) echo "Month is January";;
      02 ¦ 2) echo "Month is February";;
      03 ¦ 3) echo "Month is March";;
      04 ¦ 4) echo "Month is April";;
      05 ¦ 5) echo "Month is May";;
      06 ¦ 6) echo "Month is June";;
      07 ¦ 7) echo "Month is July";;
      08 ¦ 8) echo "Month is August";;
      09 ¦ 9) echo "Month is September";;
      10) echo "Month is October";;
      11) echo "Month is November";;
      12) echo "Month is December";;
      *) echo "Invalid parameter";;
   esac
}
Displaymonth $1
```

Name the script testme, and pass the number 8, like this:

```
# . testme 8
```

The preceding program displays the following:

```
Month is August
```

Summary

In this chapter you were introduced to the syntax of shell programming and you have learned how to write a shell program. Shell programs can be used to write programs that do simple things, such as setting a number of aliases when you log on, or complicated things, such as customizing your shell environment and performing system administration tasks.

CHAPTER 26

C and C++ Programming

In This Chapter

UNIX shells support a wide range of commands that can be combined, in the form of scripts, into reusable programs. Command scripts for shell programs (and utilities such as gawk and Perl) are all the programming that many UNIX users need to customize their computing environments.

Script languages have several shortcomings, however. To begin with, the commands a user types into a script are read and evaluated only when the script is being executed. Interpreted languages are flexible and easy to use, but they are inefficient because the commands must be reinterpreted each time the script is executed. Interpreted languages are also ill-suited to manipulating the computer's memory and I/O devices directly. Therefore, programs that process scripts (such as the various UNIX shells, the awk utility, and the Perl interpreter) are themselves written in the C and C++ languages, as is the UNIX kernel.

Many users find it fairly easy to learn a scripted, interpreted language because the commands usually can be tried out one at a time, with clearly visible results. Learning a language such as C or C++ is more complex and difficult because you must learn to think in terms of machine resources and the way actions are accomplished within the computer, rather than in terms of user-oriented commands.

This chapter introduces you to the basic concepts of C and C++ and demonstrates how to build some simple programs. Even if you don't go on to learn how to program extensively in either language, you will find that the information in this chapter helps you understand how kernels are built and why some of the other features of UNIX work the way they do. Additional resources are listed at the end of the chapter.

Background on the C Language

C is the programming language most frequently associated with UNIX. Since the 1970s, the bulk of the UNIX operating system and its applications have been written in C. Because the C language doesn't directly rely on any specific hardware architecture, UNIX was one of the first portable operating systems. In other words, the majority of the code that makes up UNIX doesn't know and doesn't care which computer it is actually running on. Machine-specific features are isolated in a few modules within the UNIX kernel, which makes it easy for you to modify them when you're porting to a different hardware architecture.

C was first designed by Dennis Ritchie for use with UNIX on DEC PDP-11 computers. The language evolved from Martin Richard's BCPL, and one of its earlier forms was the B language, which was written by Ken Thompson for the DEC PDP-7. The first book on C was *The C Programming Language* by Brian Kernighan and Dennis Ritchie, published in 1978.

In 1983, the American National Standards Institute (ANSI) established a committee to standardize the definition of C. The resulting standard is known as *ANSI C*, and it is the recognized standard for the language, grammar, and a core set of libraries. The syntax is slightly different from the original C language, which is frequently called K&R for Kernighan and Ritchie. This chapter will primarily address ANSI C.

Programming in C: Basic Concepts

C is a compiled, third-generation procedural language. *Compiled* means that C code is analyzed, interpreted, and translated into machine instructions at some time prior to the execution of the C program. These steps are carried out by the C compiler and, depending on the complexity of the C program, by the `make` utility. After the program is compiled, it can be executed over and over without recompilation.

The phrase *third-generation procedural* describes computer languages that clearly distinguish the data used in a program from the actions performed on that data. Programs written in third-generation languages take the form of a series of explicit processing steps or procedures. These procedures manipulate the contents of data structures by means of explicit references to their locations in memory and manipulate the computer's hardware in response to hardware interrupts.

Functions in C Programs

In the C language, all procedures take the form of functions. Just as a mathematical function transforms input data, a C function is typically a procedure that transforms some value (or input values, known as *arguments*) or performs some other action and returns the results. The act of invoking the transformation is known as *calling* the function.

Mathematical function calls can be nested, as can function calls in C. When function calls are nested, the results of the innermost function are passed as input to the next function, and so on. Table 26.1 shows how nested calls to the square root function are evaluated arithmetically.

TABLE 26.1 Nested Operations in Mathematics

Function	*Value*
`sqrt(256)`	16
`sqrt( sqrt(256) ) = sqrt(16)`	4
`sqrt( sqrt( sqrt(256) ) ) = sqrt(4)`	2

Figure 26.1 shows the way function calls are nested within C programs. In the figure, the `Main` function calls `Function 1`, which calls `Function 2`. `Function 2` is evaluated first, and its results are passed back to `Function 1`. When `Function 1` completes its operations, its results are passed back to the `Main` function.

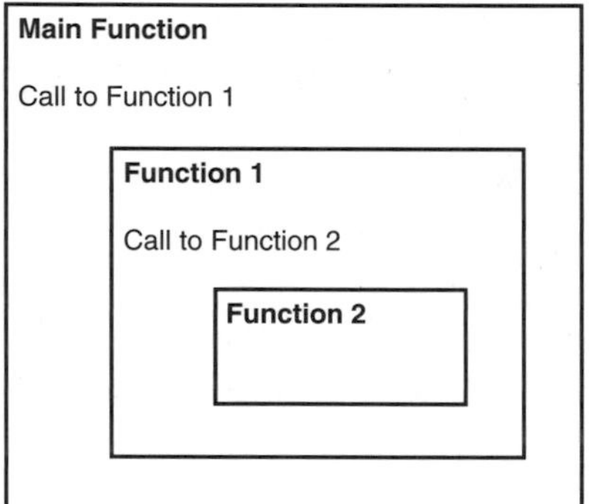

FIGURE 26.1
Nesting function calls within C programs.

Nonfunctional procedures in other languages often operate on data variables that are shared with other code in the program. For instance, a nonfunctional procedure might update a programwide `COUNT_OF_ERRORS` whenever a user makes a keyboard mistake. Such procedures must be carefully written, and they are usually specific to the program for which they were first created because they reference particular shared data variables within the wider program.

A function, however, receives all the information it needs when it is called (including the location of data variables to use in each instance). The function neither knows nor cares about the wider program context that calls it. It simply transforms the values found within the input variables (parameters), whatever they might be, and returns the results to whichever other function invokes it.

Because procedures written in C are implemented as functions, they don't need to know whether (or how deeply) they will be nested inside other function calls. This enables you to reuse C functions in many different programs without modifying them. For example, `Function 2` in Figure 26.1 might be called directly by the `Main` logic in a different C program.

An entire C program is itself a function that returns a result code, when executed, to the program that invokes it. This is usually a shell in the case of applications, but it might also be any other part of the operating system or any other UNIX program. Because C programs are all structured as functions, they can be invoked by other programs or nested inside larger programs without needing to be rewritten in any way.

Note

C's featuring of structuring programs as functions has heavily shaped the look and feel of UNIX. More than in most other operating environments, UNIX systems consist of many small C programs that call one another, are combined into larger programs, and are invoked by the user as needed. Instead of using monolithic, integrated applications, UNIX typically hosts many small, flexible programs. Users can customize their working environments by combining these tools to do new tasks.

Data in C Programs

The two kinds of data that are manipulated within C programs are *literal values* and *variables*. Literal values are specific, actual numbers or characters, such as `1`, `4.35`, or `a`. Variables are names associated with a place in memory that can hold data values. Each variable in C is typed; it can hold only one kind of value. The basic datatypes include integers, floating-point (real) numbers, characters, and arrays. An *array* is a series of data elements of the same type; the elements are identified by the order in which they appear (in other words, by their place within the series).

You can define complex data structures as well. Complex data structures are used to gather a number of related data items together under one name. A terminal communications program, for example, might have a *terminal control block* (TCB) associated with each user who is logged on. The TCB typically contains data elements identifying the communications port, the active application process, and other information associated with that terminal session.

All the variables in a C program must be explicitly defined before they can be used.

Creating, Compiling, and Executing Your First Program

The development of a C program is an iterative procedure. Many UNIX tools familiar to software developers are involved in this four-step process:

1. Using an editor, write your code into a text file.
2. Compile the program.
3. Execute the program.
4. Debug the program.

Repeat the first two steps until the program compiles successfully. Then begin the execution and debugging.

When I explain each of these steps in this chapter, you might find that some of the concepts seem strange, especially if you're a nonprogrammer. Remember that this chapter serves as only an introduction to C as a programming language. For more in-depth coverage of C, check out one of the resources listed at the end of this chapter in the section "Additional Resources."

Before you can begin compiling programs for Linux, you must install the required development software tools (such as the `egcs` compiler suite, the GNU `as` assembler, and `ld` linker), and software development libraries (such as `glibc-devel*`).

Linux software development archives for Red Hat Linux may be installed from the Red Hat CD-ROM by using the `gnorpm` or `rpm` command.

Linux software development archives may be installed from the OpenLinux CD-ROM by using the `lisa` or `rpm` command (or the `kpackage` client if you're running X11 and KDE has been installed).

You may install the Debian software with `dpkg`, `dselect`, or `apt-get`. Installing `gcc` to begin brings along its related tools if they aren't yet installed.

The typical first C program is almost a cliché—the `Hello, World` program, which prints the simple line `Hello, World`. Listing 26.1 contains the source code of the program.

LISTING 26.1 Source Code of the *Hello, World* Program

```
main()
{
printf("Hello, World\n");
}
```

This program can be compiled and executed as follows:

```
$ gcc hello.c
$ ./a.out
Hello, World
$
```

Note

If the current directory is not in your path, you must execute `a.out` by typing the following:

```
# ./a.out
```

The `Hello, World` program is compiled with the `gcc` command, which creates an `a.out` file if the code is correct. Just typing **`a.out`** will run it. Notice that Listing 26.1 includes only one function: `main`. Every C program must have a `main` function, which is where the program's execution begins. The only statement in Listing 26.1 is a call to the `printf` library function, which passes the string `Hello, World\n`. (Functions are described in detail later in this chapter, in the "Functions" section.) The last two characters of the string, `\n`, represent the newline character.

> **Note**
>
> `a.out` is the default filename for executables (binaries) created by the C compiler under UNIX. This can be changed through the use of a command-line switch (see "GNU C/C++ Compiler Command-Line Switches" later in this chapter).

Elements of the C Language

As with all programming languages, C programs must follow certain rules, including how a program should appear and what the words and symbols mean. Together, these rules are called the *syntax* of a programming language. Think of a program as a story. Within the story, each sentence must have a noun and a verb, put together with a particular syntax. Sentences form paragraphs, and the paragraphs tell the story. Similarly, C statements constructed with the correct syntax can form functions and programs.

Elementary C Syntax

Like all languages, C deals primarily with the manipulation and presentation of data. The language that C evolved from, BCPL, dealt with data only as data. C goes one step further, however, by using the concept of *datatypes*. The three basic datatypes are integers, floating-point numbers, and characters. Other datatypes are built from these.

Integers are the basic mathematical datatype. They can be classified as `long` and `short` integers, and their size is implementation-dependent. With a few exceptions, integers are four bytes in length, and they can range from -2,147,483,648 to 2,147,483,647. In ANSI C, these values are defined in a header (`limit.h`) as `INT_MIN` and `INT_MAX`. The qualifier `unsigned` moves the range one bit higher to the equivalent of `INT_MAX` minus `INT_MIN`.

Floating-point numbers are used for more complicated mathematics, whereas integer mathematics is limited to integer results. For example, with integers, 3/2 equals 1. Floating-point numbers give a greater amount of precision to mathematical calculations than integers can; with floating-point numbers, 3/2 equals 1.5. Floating-point numbers can be represented by a decimal number, such as 687.534, or with scientific notation, such as 8.87534E+2. For larger numbers, scientific notation is preferred. For even greater precision, the datatype `double` provides a greater range. Again, specific ranges are implementation-dependent.

Characters are usually implemented as single bytes, although some international character sets require two bytes. One common set of character representations is ASCII, which is found on most U.S. computers.

You use arrays for sequences of values that are often position-dependent. An array is particularly useful when you need a range of values of a given type. The *pointer* is related to the array. Variables are stored in memory, and the pointer is the physical address of that memory. In a sense, pointers and arrays are similar, except when a program is invoked. The space needed for an array's data is allocated when the routine that needs the space is invoked. For a pointer, the space must be allocated by the programmer, or the variable must be assigned by dereferencing a variable. The ampersand (`&`) is used to indicate dereferencing, and the asterisk (`*`) is used to indicate when the value pointed at is required. Here are some sample declarations:

`int i;`	Declares an integer
`char c;`	Declares a character
`char *ptr;`	Declares a pointer to a character
`double temp[16];`	Declares an array of double-precision floating-point numbers with 16 values

Listing 26.2 shows an example of a program with pointers.

LISTING 26.2 A Program with Pointers

```
int i;
int *ptr;

i=5;
ptr = &i;
printf("%d %x %d\n", i,ptr,*ptr);
```

The output of this program follows:

```
5 f7fffa6c 5
```

Note

The middle value, `f7fffa6c`, is an address. This might be different on your system because the pointer variable changes from version to version of the libraries.

A pointer is just a memory address and will tell you the address of any variable.

There is no specific type for a string. An array of characters is used to represent strings. They can be printed using an `%s` flag instead of `%c`.

Simple output is created by the `printf` function, which takes a format string and the list of arguments to be printed. A complete set of format options is presented in Table 26.2. Format options can be modified with sizes. Check the `gcc` documentation (man page or info file) for the full specification and the `printf` man page for details.

TABLE 26.2 Format Conversions for *printf*

Conversion	*Meaning*
`%%`	Percentage sign
`%E`	Double (scientific notation)
`%G`	Double (format depends on value)
`%X`	Hexadecimal (letters are capitalized)
`%c`	Single character
`%d`	Integer
`%e`	Double (scientific notation)
`%f`	Double of the form `mmm.ddd`
`%g`	Double (format depends on value)
`%i`	Integer
`%ld`	Long integer
`%n`	Count of characters written in current `printf`
`%o`	Octal
`%p`	Print as a pointer
`%s`	Character pointer (string)
`%u`	Unsigned integer
`%x`	Hexadecimal

Some characters cannot be included easily in a program. Newlines, for example, require a special escape sequence because there cannot be an unescaped newline in a string. Table 26.3 contains a complete list of escape sequences.

TABLE 26.3 Escape Characters for Strings

Escape Sequence	*Meaning*
`\"`	Double quotation mark
`\'`	Single quotation mark
`\?`	Question mark
`\\`	Backslash
`\a`	Audible bell
`\b`	Backspace
`\f`	Form feed (new page)
`\n`	Newline
`\ooo`	Octal number
`\r`	Carriage return
`\t`	Horizontal tab
`\v`	Vertical tab
`\xhh`	Hexadecimal number

A *full program* is a compilation of statements. Statements are separated by semicolons and can be grouped in blocks of statements surrounded by braces (curly brackets). The simplest statement is an assignment, in which a variable on the left side is assigned the value of an expression on the right.

Expressions

At the heart of the C programming language are *expressions*. These are techniques for combining simple values into new values. The three basic types of expressions are comparison, numerical, and bitwise.

Comparison Expressions

The simplest expression is a comparison, which evaluates to a true or false value. In C, true is a nonzero value and false is a zero value. Table 26.4 contains a list of comparison operators.

TABLE 26.4 Comparison Operators

Operator	*Meaning*
<	Less than
>	Greater than
==	Equal to
<=	Less than or equal to
>=	Greater than or equal to
||	Logical OR
&&	Logical AND
!	Logical NOT

You can combine simple comparisons with ANDs and ORs to make complex expressions. For example, consider the definition of a leap year. In plain English, it is any year divisible by 4 except a year divisible by 100, unless that year is divisible by 400. Using year as the variable, you can define a leap year with the following expression:

```
((((year%4)==0)&&((year%100)!=0))||((year%400)==0))
```

This code might look complicated on first inspection, but it isn't. The parentheses group the simple expressions with the ANDs and ORs to make a complex expression.

Mathematical Expressions

One convenient aspect of C is that expressions can be treated as mathematical values, and mathematical statements can be used in expressions. In fact, any statement—even a simple assignment—has values that can be used in other places as expressions.

The mathematics of C are straightforward. Barring parenthetical groupings, multiplication and division have higher precedence than addition and subtraction. The operators are standard and are listed in Table 26.5.

TABLE 26.5 Mathematical Operators

Operator	*Meaning*
+	Addition
-	Subtraction
*	Multiplication
/	Division
%	Integer remainder

There are also *unary* operators, which affect a single variable. These are ++ (increment by 1) and – (decrement by 1) and are shorthand for `var = var + 1` and `var = var - 1`, respectively. Postfix and prefix notation with these operators will also affect a variable's value and when the operation is applied. In general, when used before a variable, the operation is performed before using the variable's value (and after in postfix form).

Shorthand can be used for situations in which you want to change the value of a variable. For example, if you want to add an expression to a variable called `a` and assign a new value to `a`, the shorthand `a += expr` is the same as `a=a+expr`. The expression can be as complex or as simple as required.

Note

Most UNIX functions take advantage of the truth values and return `0` for success. This enables a programmer to write code such as

```
if (function())
        {
        error condition
        }
```

The return value of a function determines whether the function worked.

Bitwise Operations

Because a variable is just a string of bits, many operations work on those bit patterns. Table 26.6 lists the bit operators.

TABLE 26.6 Bit Operators

Operator	*Meaning*
&	Bitwise AND
¦	Bitwise OR
~	Negation (1's complement)
<<	Bit shift left
>>	Bit shift right

A bitwise AND compares the individual bits in place. If both are `1`, the value `1` is assigned to the expression. Otherwise, `0` is assigned. For a logical OR, `1` is assigned if either value is a `1`. Bit shift operations move the bits a number of positions to the right or left.

Mathematically, this is the same as multiplying or dividing by 2, but there are circumstances in which the bit shift is preferred.

Bit operations are often used for masking values and for comparisons. A simple way to determine whether a value is odd or even is to perform a bitwise AND with the integer value 1. If it is true, the number is odd.

Statement Controls

With what you've seen so far, you can create a list of statements that are executed only once, after which the program terminates. To control the flow of commands, three types of loops exist in C. The simplest is the `while` loop. The syntax follows:

```
while (expression)
        statement
```

As long as the expression between the parentheses evaluates as nonzero—or `true` in C—the statement is executed. *`statement`* actually can be a list of statements blocked off with braces. If the expression evaluates to zero the first time it is reached, the statement is never executed. To force at least one execution of the statement, use a `do` loop. The syntax for a `do` loop follows:

```
do
         statement
         while (expression);
```

The third type of control flow is the `for` loop. This is more complicated. The syntax follows:

```
for(expr1;expr2;expr3) statement
```

When this statement is reached for the first time, *`expr1`* is evaluated and then *`expr2`* is evaluated. If *`expr2`* is nonzero, *`statement`* is executed, followed by *`expr3`*. Then *`expr2`* is tested again, followed by the statement and *`expr3`*, until *`expr2`* evaluates to zero. Strictly speaking, this is a notational convenience because a `while` loop can be structured to perform the same actions, as in the following:

```
expr1;
while (expr2) {
         statement;
         expr3
         }
```

Loops can be interrupted in three ways. A `break` statement terminates execution in a loop and exits it. A `continue` statement terminates the current iteration and retests the loop before possibly reexecuting the statement. For an unconventional exit, you could use `goto`, which changes the program's execution to a labeled statement. According to many programmers, `goto` is poor programming practice, and you should avoid using it.

Statements can also be executed conditionally. Again, there are three different formats for statement execution. The simplest is an `if` statement. The syntax follows:

```
if (expr) statement
```

If the expression *expr* evaluates to nonzero, *statement* is executed. You can expand this with an `else`, the second type of conditional execution. Here is the syntax for `else`:

```
if (expr) statement else statement
```

If the expression evaluates to zero, the second statement is executed.

> **Note**
>
> The second statement in an `else` condition can be another `if` statement. This situation might cause the grammar to be indeterminate if the following structure is not parsed cleanly:
>
> ```
> if (expr) if (expr) statement else statement
> ```
>
> As the code is written, the `else` is considered applicable to the second `if`. To make the `else` applicable to the first `if`, surround the second `if` statement with braces, as in the following:
>
> ```
> if (expr) {if (expr) statement} else statement
> ```

The third type of conditional execution is more complicated. The `switch` statement first evaluates an expression. Then it looks through a series of `case` statements to find a label that matches the expression's value and executes the statements following the label. A special label `default` exists if no other conditions are met. If you want only a set of statements executed for each label, you must use the `break` statement to leave the `switch` statement.

This covers the simplest building blocks of a C program. You can add more power by using functions and by declaring complex datatypes.

If your program requires different pieces of data to be grouped on a consistent basis, you can group them into structures. Listing 26.3 shows a structure for a California driver's license. Note that it includes integer, character, and character array (string) types.

LISTING 26.3 An Example of a Structure

```
struct license {
        char name[128];
        char address[3][128];
        int zipcode;
        int height, weight, month, day, year;
        char license_letter;
        int license_number;
        };

struct license newlicensee;
struct license *user;
```

Because California driver's license numbers consist of a single character followed by a seven-digit number, the license ID is broken into two components. Similarly, the new licensee's address is broken into three lines, represented by three arrays of 128 characters.

Accessing individual fields of a structure requires two different techniques. To read a member of a locally defined structure, you append a dot to the variable and then the field name, as in the following example:

```
newlicensee.zipcode=94404;
```

When using a pointer to a structure, you need `->` to point to the member (to reference the individual members):

```
user->zipcode=94404;
```

Interestingly, if the structure pointer is incremented, the address is increased not by 1, but by the size of the structure.

Functions

Functions are an easy way to group statements and to give them a name. These are usually related statements that perform repetitive tasks such as I/O. `printf`, described earlier, is a function that is provided with the standard C library. Listing 26.4 illustrates a function definition, a function call, and a function.

> **Note**
>
> The three-dot ellipses simply means that some lines of sample code are not shown here to save space.

LISTING 26.4 An Example of a Function

```
int swapandmin( int *, int *);          /* Function declaration */

...

int i,j,lower;

i=2; j=4;
lower=swapandmin(&i, &j);              /* Function call */

...

int swapandmin(int *a,int *b)          /* Function definition */
{
int tmp;

tmp=(*a);
(*a)=(*b);
(*b)=tmp;
if ((*a)<(*b)) return(*a);
return(*b);
}
```

ANSI C and K&R differ most in function declarations and calls. ANSI C requires that function arguments be prototyped when the function is declared. K&R required only the name and the type of the returned value. The declaration in Listing 26.4 states that a function `swapandmin` will take two pointers to integers as arguments and that it will return an integer. The function call takes the addresses of two integers and sets the variable named `lower` to the return value of the function.

When a function is called from a C program, the values of the arguments are passed to the function. Therefore, if any of the arguments will be changed for the calling function, you can't pass only the variable—you must pass the address, too. Likewise, to change the value of the argument in the calling routine of the function, you must assign the new value to the address.

In the function in Listing 26.4, the value pointed to by `a` is assigned to the `tmp` variable. `b` is assigned to `a`, and `tmp` is assigned to `b`. `*a` is used instead of `a` to ensure that the change is reflected in the calling routine. Finally, the values of `*a` and `*b` are compared, and the lower of the two is returned.

If you include the following line after the function call, you will see `2 4 2` as output:

```
printf("%d %d %d",lower,i,j);
```

This sample function is quite simple, and it is ideal for a macro. A *macro* is a technique used to replace a token with different text. You can use macros to make code more readable. For example, you might use `EOF` instead of `(-1)` to indicate the end of a file. You can also use macros to replace code. Listing 26.5 is the same as Listing 26.4, except that it uses macros.

LISTING 26.5 An Example of Macros

```
#define SWAP(X,Y) {int tmp; tmp=X; X=Y; Y=tmp; }
#define MIN(X,Y) ((X<Y) ? X : Y )

...

int i,j,lower;

i=2; j=4;
SWAP(i,j);
lower=MIN(i,j);
```

When a C program is compiled, macro replacement is one of the first steps performed. Listing 26.6 illustrates the results of the replacement.

LISTING 26.6 An Example of Macro Replacement

```
int i,j,lower;

i=2; j=4;
{int tmp; tmp=i; i=j; j=tmp; };
lower= ((i<j) ? i : j );
```

The macros make the code easier to read and understand.

Caution

Macros can have side effects, which occur because the programmer expects a variable to be evaluated once when it is actually evaluated more than once. Replacing the variable `i` with `i++` changes things dramatically:

```
lower=MIN(i++,j);
```

This is converted to this:

```
lower= ((i++ < j) ? i++ : j );
```

As a result, the variable `i` can be incremented twice instead of once, as the programmer expects.

Creating a Simple Program

For the next example, you'll write a program that prints a chart of the first 10 integers and their squares, cubes, and square roots.

Writing the Code

Using the text editor of your choice, enter all the code in Listing 26.7 and save it in a file called `sample.c`.

LISTING 26.7 Source Code for *sample.c*

```
#include <stdio.h>
#include <math.h>

main()
{
int i;
double a;

for(i=1;i<11;i++)
        {
        a=i*1.0;
        printf("%2d. %3d %4d %7.5f\n",i,i*i,i*i*i,sqrt(a));
        }
}
```

The first two lines are header files. The `stdio.h` file provides the function definitions and structures associated with the C input and output libraries. The `math.h` file includes the definitions of mathematical library functions. You need it for the square root function.

The `main` loop is the only function you need to write for this example. It takes no arguments. You define two variables: One is the integer `i` and the other is a double-precision floating-point number called `a`. You don't have to use `a`, but you can for the sake of convenience.

The program is a simple `for` loop that starts at `1` and ends at `11`. It increments `i` by 1 each time through. When `i` equals `11`, the `for` loop stops executing. You also could have written `i<=10` because the expressions have the same meaning.

First, you multiply `i` by 1.0 and assign the product to `a`. A simple assignment would also work, but the multiplication reminds you that you are converting the value to a double-precision floating-point number.

Next, you call the `print` function. The format string includes three integers of widths `2`, `3`, and `4`. After the first integer is printed, you print a period. After the next integer is printed, you print a floating-point number that is seven characters wide, with five digits following the decimal point. The arguments after the format string show that you print the integer, the square of the integer, the cube of the integer, and the square root of the integer.

Compiling the Program

To compile this program using the GNU C compiler, enter the following command:

```
$ gcc sample.c -lm
```

This command produces an output file called `a.out`. This is the simplest use of the C compiler. `gcc` is one of the most powerful and flexible commands of a UNIX system.

A number of different flags can change the compiler's output. These flags are often dependent on the system or compiler. Some flags common to all C compilers are described in the following paragraphs.

The `-o` flag tells the compiler to write the output to the file named after the flag. The `gcc -o sample sample.c -lm` command puts the program in a file named `sample`.

> **Note**
>
> The output discussed here is the compiler's output, not the sample program. Compiler output is usually the program, and in every example here, it is an executable program. Also, avoid using the name *test* for a sample program. Unless you explicitly run the program like this, you will end up running the command `test`, found under the `/usr/bin` directory:
>
> ```
> # ./test
> ```

A `-g` flag tells the compiler to save the symbol table (the data used by a program to associate variable names with memory locations) in the executable, which is necessary for debuggers. Its opposite is the `-O` flag, which tells the compiler to optimize the code—that is, to make it more efficient. You can change the search path for header files with the `-I` flag, and you can add libraries with the `-l` and `-L` flags. The preceding example command line adds math library (`libm`) support for the `sqrt()` function in the `sample` program.

The compilation process takes place in several steps:

1. First, the C preprocessor parses the file. To do so, it sequentially reads the lines, includes header files, and performs macro replacement.

2. The compiler parses the modified code for correct syntax. This builds a symbol table and creates an intermediate object format. Most symbols have specific memory addresses assigned, although symbols defined in other modules, such as external variables, do not.
3. The last compilation stage, linking, ties together different files and libraries and then links the files by resolving the symbols that hadn't previously been resolved.

Executing the Program

The output from this program appears in Listing 26.8.

LISTING 26.8 Output from the *sample.c* Program

```
$ sample
 1.   1    1 1.00000
 2.   4    8 1.41421
 3.   9   27 1.73205
 4.  16   64 2.00000
 5.  25  125 2.23607
 6.  36  216 2.44949
 7.  49  343 2.64575
 8.  64  512 2.82843
 9.  81  729 3.00000
10. 100 1000 3.16228
```

Note

To execute a program, just type in its name at a shell prompt. The output will immediately follow.

Building Large Applications

C programs can be broken into any number of files, as long as no single function spans more than one file. To compile this program, you compile each source file into an intermediate object before you link all the objects into a single executable. The `-c` flag tells the compiler to stop at this stage. During the link stage, all the object files should be listed on the command line. Object files are identified by the `.o` suffix.

Making Libraries with `ar`

If several different programs use the same functions, they can be combined into a single library archive. The `ar` command is used to build a library. When this library is included on the compile line, the archive is searched to resolve any external symbols. Listing 26.9 shows an example of building and using a library.

LISTING 26.9 Building a Large Application

```
$ gcc -c sine.c
$ gcc -c cosine.c
$ gcc -c tangent.c
$ ar c libtrig.a sine.o cosine.o tangent.o

$ gcc -c mainprog.c
$ gcc -o mainprog mainprog.o libtrig.a
```

Large applications can require hundreds of source code files. Compiling and linking these applications can be a complex and error-prone task of its own. In the next section you'll read about the `make` utility, a tool that helps developers organize the process of building the executable form of complex applications from many source files.

Project Management Tools

This section introduces some of the programming and project management tools included with Linux. If you have some previous UNIX experience, you'll be familiar with most of these because they are traditional complements to a programmer's suite of software.

If you have programming experience on other software platforms, you'll find that these programs are easy to learn. However, mastery will come with experience!

Building Programs with make

The `make` command is only one of several programming automation utilities included with Linux. You'll find others, such as `pmake` (a parallel make), `imake` (a dependency drive makefile generator, usually for building X11 applications), `automake`, and one of the latest tools, `autconf` (which builds shell scripts used to configure program source code packages).

Note

For a bit more information about `imake` and building makefiles when developing Motif clients for the X Window System, see Chapter 27, "Motif Programming."

The pmake command is not included with Caldera OpenLinux. The make command will be installed from the make-3.77-1.i386.rpm archive.

Debian's default make tool also has parallel capabilities; no special package is required.

The make command's roots stem from an early version of System V UNIX. The version included with Red Hat Linux is part of the GNU utilities distribution. make is used to automatically handle the building and install of a program, which can be as simple as this:

```
# make install
```

The magic of make is that it will automatically update and build applications. You create this magic through a default file named Makefile. However, if you use make's -f option, you can specify any makefile, such as MyMakeFile, like this:

```
# make -f MyMakeFile
```

A *makefile* is a text file that can contain instructions about which options to pass on to the compiler preprocessor, the compiler, and the linker. The makefile can also specify which source code files need to be compiled (and the compiler command line) for a particular code module, and which code modules are needed to build the program—a mechanism called *dependency checking*.

Using make can also aid in the portability of your program through the use of macros. This allows users of other operating systems to easily configure a program build by specifying local values, such as the names and locations, or *pathnames*, of any required software tools. In the following example, macros define the name of the compiler (CC), the installer program (INS), where the program should be installed (INSDIR), where the linker should look for required libraries (LIBDIR), the names of required libraries (LIBS), a source code file (SRC), the intermediate object code file (OBS), and the name of the final program (PROG):

```
# a sample makefile for a skeleton program
CC= gcc
INS= install
INSDIR = /usr/local/bin
LIBDIR= -L/usr/X11R6/lib
LIBS= -lXm -lSM -lICE -lXt -lX11
SRC= skel.c
OBJS= skel.o
PROG= skel

skel:  ${OBJS}
        ${CC} -o ${PROG} ${SRC} ${LIBDIR} ${LIBS}

install: ${PROG}
        ${INS} -g root -o root ${PROG} ${INSDIR}
```

Using this approach, you can build the program with this:

```
# make
```

To build a specified component of your makefile, use a *target* definition on the command line. To build just the program, use `make` with the `skel` target like this:

```
# make skel
```

If you make any changes to any element of a target object, such as a source code file, `make` will rebuild the target. To build and install the program in one step (using the example), specify the `install` target:

```
# make install
```

Larger software projects may have any number of traditional targets in the makefile:

- `test`—To run specific tests on the final software.
- `man`—To process an `include troff` document with the `-man` macros.
- `clean`—To delete any remaining object files.
- `archive`—To clean up, archive, and compress the entire source code tree.
- `bugreport`—To automatically collect and then mail build or error logs.

The beauty of the `make` command is in its flexibility. You can use `make` with a simple makefile, or write complex makefiles containing numerous macros, rules, or commands that work in a single directory or transverse your filesystem recursively to build programs, update your system, and even function as a document management system. The `make` command will work with nearly any program, including text processing systems such as TeX!

Managing Software Projects with RCS and CVS

Although `make` can be used to manage a software project, larger software projects requiring document management, source code controls, security, and tracking usually use the Revision Control System (RCS) or the Concurrent Versions System (CVS).

The RCS and CVS systems are used to track changes to multiple versions of files, and they can be used to backtrack or branch off versions of documents inside the scope of a project. The systems are also used to prevent or resolve conflicting entries or (sometimes simultaneously) changes to source code files by numerous developers.

Although RCS and CVS aim to provide similar features, the main difference between the two systems is that RCS uses a locking and unlocking scheme for access, while CVS provides a modification and merging approach to working on older, current, or new versions of software. While RCS uses different programs to check in or out of a revision under a directory, CVS uses a number of administrative files in a software *repository* of source code *modules* to merge and resolve change conflicts.

RCS uses at least eight separate programs, including these:

- `ci`—Check in revisions.
- `co`—Check out revisions.
- `ident`—Keyword utility for source files.
- `rcs`—Change file attributes.
- `rcsclean`—Clean up working files.
- `rcsdiff`—Revision comparison utility.
- `rcsmerge`—Merge revisions.
- `rlog`—Logging and information utility.

Source code control with CVS requires the use of at least six command options on the `cvs` command line. Some of these commands require additional fields, such as the names of files:

- `checkout`—Check out revisions.
- `update`—Update your sources with changes by other developers.
- `add`—Add new files in `cvs` records.
- `import`—Add new sources into the repository.
- `remove`—Eliminate files from the repository.
- `commit`—Publish changes to other repository developers.

RCS and CVS may be used for more than software development projects. These tools may also be used for document preparation and workgroup editing of documents, and will work with any text files. Both systems use registration and control files to accomplish revision management. Both systems also offer the opportunity to revisit any step or branch in a revision *history*, and to restore previous versions of a project. This mechanism is extremely important in cross-platform development or for software maintenance.

Tracking information is usually contained in separate control files, and each document within a project may contain information automatically updated with each change to a project using a process called *keyword substitution*. CVS can use keywords similar to RCS, which are usually included inside C comment strings (`/* */`) near the top of a document. A sample of the available keywords includes these:

- `$Author$`—Username of person performing last check-in.
- `$Date$`—Date and time of last check-in.
- `$Header$`—Insert the pathname of the document's RCS file, revision number, date and time, author, and state.
- `$Id$`—Same as `$Header$`, but without full pathname.
- `$Name$`—A symbolic name (see the `co` man page).
- `$Revision$`—The assigned revision number (such as 1.1).
- `$Source$`—RCS file's full pathname.
- `$State$`—The state of the document, such as `Exp` for experimental, `Rel` for released, or `Stab` for stable.

These keywords may also be used to insert version information into compiled programs by using character strings in program source code. For example, take this extremely short C program named `foo.c`:

```
/* $Header$ */
#include <stdio.h>
static char rsrcid{} = "$Header$";
main() {
    printf("Hello, Linus!\n");
}
```

The resulting `$Header$` keyword may expand (in an RCS document) to this:

```
$Header: /home/bball/sw/RCS/foo.c,v 1.1 1999/04/20 15:01:07 root Exp Root $
```

Getting started with RCS is as simple as creating a project directory and an RCS directory under the project directory, and then creating or copying initial source files in the project directory. You then use the `ci` command to check in documents. Getting started with CVS requires you to initialize a repository by first setting the `$CVSROOT` environment variable with the full pathname of the repository and then using the `init` command option with the `cvs` command, like this:

```
# cvs init
```

You'll find documentation for RCS in various man pages and under the `/usr/doc/rcs-5.7` directory.

The CVS system is documented in the cvs man page, the /usr/doc/cvs-1.10.5 directory, and a number of GNU information documents.

Caldera OpenLinux provides an older version of CVS. Documentation is found under the /usr/doc/cvs-1.9.28 directory.

Debian GNU/Linux users can find the documentation in /usr/doc/cvs.

Debugging Tools

Debugging is a science and an art unto itself. Sometimes, the simplest tool—the code listing—is best. At other times, however, you need to use other tools. Three of these tools are `lint`, `gprof`, and `gdb`. Other available tools include `escape`, `cxref`, and `cb`. Many UNIX commands have debugging uses.

`lint` is a traditional UNIX command that examines source code for possible problems, but it is not included with most Linux distributions. The code might meet the standards for C and compile cleanly, but it might not execute correctly. `lint` checks type mismatches and incorrect argument counts on function calls. `lint` also uses the C preprocessor, so you can use command-like options similar to those you would use for `gcc`. The GNU C compiler supports extensive warnings (through the `-Wall` and `-pedantic` options) that might eliminate the need for a separate `lint` command.

Note

If you'd like to explore various C syntax-checking programs (along with memory trace, profiling, and other debugging tools), navigate to `http://metalab.unc.edu/pub/Linux/devel/lang/c`. One program that closely resembles the traditional `lint` program is `lclint`, found in the `lclint-2.2a-src.tar.gz` file.

The `gprof` command is used to study where a program is spending its time. If a program is compiled and linked with `-p` as a flag, a `mon.out` file is created when it executes, with data on how often each function is called and how much time is spent in each function. `gprof` parses and displays this data. An analysis of the output generated by `gprof` helps you determine where performance bottlenecks occur. Whereas using an optimizing compiler can speed up your program, taking the time to use `gprof`'s analysis and revising bottleneck functions will significantly improve program performance.

The third tool is `gdb`—a symbolic debugger. When a program is compiled with `-g`, the symbol tables are retained and a symbolic debugger can be used to track program bugs.

The basic technique is to invoke `gdb` after a core dump and get a stack trace. This indicates the source line where the core dump occurred and the functions that were called to reach that line. Often, this is enough to identify the problem. It is not the limit of `gdb`, though.

`gdb` also provides an environment for debugging programs interactively. Invoking `gdb` with a program enables you to set breakpoints, examine variable values, and monitor variables. If you suspect a problem near a line of code, you can set a breakpoint at that line and run the program. Execution is interrupted when the line is reached. You can check variable values, examine the stack trace, and observe the program's environment. You can single-step through the program, checking values. You can resume execution at any point. By using breakpoints, you can discover many of the bugs in your code that you've missed.

There is an X Window version of `gdb` called `xxgdb`.

Note

If you browse to `http://metalab.unc.edu/pub/Linux/devel/debuggers`, you'll find at least a dozen different debuggers, including the Data Display Debugger, or `ddd`, a graphical interface to `gdb`. Debian also offers a `ddd` package.

`cpp` is another tool that can be used to debug programs. It performs macro replacements, includes headers, and parses the code. The output is the actual module to be compiled. Normally, though, `cpp` is never executed by the programmer directly. Instead, it is invoked through `gcc` with either an `-E` or `-P` option. `-E` sends the output directly to the terminal; `-P` makes a file with an `.i` suffix.

Elements of the C++ Language

If C is the language most associated with UNIX, C++ is the language that underlies most graphical user interfaces available today.

C++ was originally developed by Dr. Bjarne Stroustrup at the Computer Science Research Center of AT&T's Bell Laboratories (Murray Hill, NJ), also the source of UNIX itself. Dr. Stroustrup's original goal was an object-oriented simulation language. The availability of C compilers for many hardware architectures convinced him to design the language as an extension of C, allowing a preprocessor to translate C++ programs into C for compilation.

After the C language was standardized by a joint committee of the American National Standards Institute and the International Standards Organization (ISO) in 1989, a new joint committee began the effort to formalize C++ as well. This effort has produced several new features and has significantly refined the interpretation of other language features.

Programming in C++: Basic Concepts

C++ is an object-oriented extension to C. Because C++ is a superset of C, C++ compilers will compile C programs correctly, and it is possible to write non–object-oriented code in C++.

The distinction between an object-oriented language and a procedural one can be subtle and hard to grasp, especially with regard to C++, which retains all of C's characteristics and concepts. One way to describe the difference is to say that when programmers code in a procedural language, they specify actions that process the data, whereas when they write object-oriented code, they create data objects that can be requested to perform actions on or with regard to themselves.

Thus, a C function receives one or more values as input, transforms or acts on them in some way, and returns a result. If the values that are passed include pointers, the contents of data variables can be modified by the function. As the standard library routines show, it is likely that the code calling a function won't know, and won't need to know, what steps the function takes when it is invoked. However, such matters as the datatype of the input parameters and the result code are specified when the function is defined and remain invariable throughout program execution.

Functions are associated with C++ objects as well. But as you will see, the actions performed when an object's function is invoked can automatically differ, perhaps substantially, depending on the specific type of the data structure with which it is associated. This is known as *overloading* function names. Overloading is related to a second characteristic of C++—the fact that functions can be defined as belonging to C++ data structures, an aspect of the wider language feature known as *encapsulation*.

In addition to overloading and encapsulation, object-oriented languages allow programmers to define new abstract datatypes (including associated functions) and then derive subsequent datatypes from them. The notion of a new class of data objects, in addition to the built-in classes such as integer, floating-point number, and character, goes beyond the familiar capability to define complex data objects in C. Just as a C data structure that includes an integer element inherits the properties and functions applicable to integers, so too a C++ class that is derived from another class *inherits* the parent class's functions and properties. When a specific variable or structure (instance) of that class's type is defined, the class (parent or child) is said to be *instantiated*.

The remainder of this chapter will look at some of the basic features of C++ in more detail, along with code listings that provide concrete examples of these concepts. To learn more about the rich capabilities of C++, see the additional resources listed at the end of the chapter.

File Naming

Most C programs will compile with a C++ compiler if you follow strict ANSI rules. For example, you can compile the `hello.c` program shown in Listing 26.1 with the GNU C++ compiler. Typically, you will name the file something like `hello.cc`, `hello.C`, or `hello.cxx`. The GNU C++ compiler will accept any of these three names.

Differences Between C and C++

C++ differs from C in some details apart from the more obvious object-oriented features. Some of these are fairly superficial, including the following:

- The capability to define variables anywhere within a code block rather than always at the start of the block.
- The addition of an `enum` datatype to facilitate conditional logic based on case values.
- The capability to designate functions as `inline`, causing the compiler to generate another copy of the function code at that point in the program rather than a call to shared code.

Other differences have to do with advanced concepts such as memory management and the scope of reference for variable and function names. Because the latter features especially are used in object-oriented C++ programs, they are worth examining more closely in this short introduction to the language.

Scope of Reference in C and C++

The phrase *scope of reference* is used to discuss how a name in C, C++, or certain other programming languages is interpreted when the language permits more than one instance of a name to occur within a program. Consider the code in Listing 26.10, which defines and then calls two different functions. Each function has an internal variable called `tmp`.

The `tmp` that is defined within `printnum` is *local* to the `printnum` function—that is, it can be accessed only by logic within `printnum`. Similarly, the `tmp` that is defined within `printchar` is local to the `printchar` function. The scope of reference for each `tmp` variable is limited to the `printnum` and `printchar` functions, respectively.

LISTING 26.10 Scope of Reference Example 1

```
#include <stdio.h>                /* I/O function declarations */

void printnum  ( int );           /* function declaration      */
void printchar ( char );          /* function declaration      */

main ()
{
   printnum (5);                  /* print the number 5        */
   printchar ('a');               /* print the letter a        */
}

/* define the functions called above                           */
/* void means the function does not return a value             */

   void printnum (int inputnum)
{
   int tmp;
   tmp = inputnum;
   printf ("%d \n",tmp);
}

void printchar (char inputchar)
{
   char tmp;
   tmp = inputchar;
   printf ("%c \n",tmp);
}
```

When this program is executed after compilation, it creates the following output:

```
5
a
```

Listing 26.11 shows another example of scope of reference. There is a `tmp` variable that is *global*—it is known to the entire program because it is defined outside the `main` function—in addition to the two `tmp` variables that are local to the `printnum` and `printchar` functions.

LISTING 26.11 Scope of Reference Example 2

```
#include <stdio.h>

void printnum  ( int );         /* function declaration             */
void printchar ( char );        /* function declaration             */
double tmp;                     /* define a global variable         */

main ()
{
   tmp = 1.234;
   printf ("%f\n",tmp);         /* print the value of the global tmp */
   printnum (5);                /* print the number 5               */
   printf ("%f\n",tmp);         /* print the value of the global tmp */
   printchar ('a');             /* print the letter a               */
   printf ("%f\n",tmp);         /* print the value of the global tmp */
}

/* define the functions used above                                  */
/* void means the function does not return a value                  */

void printnum (int inputnum)
{
   int tmp;
   tmp = inputnum;
   printf ("%d \n",tmp);
}

void printchar (char inputchar)
{
   char tmp;
   tmp = inputchar;
   printf ("%c \n",tmp);
}
```

The global `tmp` is not modified when the local `tmp` variables are used within their respective functions, as shown by the output:

```
1.234
5
1.234
a
1.234
```

C++ provides a means to specify a global variable even when a local variable with the same name is in scope. The operator `::` prefixed to a variable name always resolves that name to the global instance. Thus, the global `tmp` variable defined in `main` in Listing 26.11 could be accessed within the `print` functions by using the label `::tmp`.

Why would a language such as C or C++ allow different scopes of reference for the same variable?

Allowing variable scope of reference also allows functions to be placed into public libraries for other programmers to use. Library functions can be invoked merely by knowing their calling sequences, and no one needs to check to be sure the programmers didn't use the same local variable names. This, in turn, means library functions can be improved, if necessary, without affecting existing code. This is true whether the library contains application code for reuse or is distributed as the runtime library associated with a compiler.

Note

A runtime library is a collection of compiled modules that perform common C, C++, and UNIX functions. The code is written carefully, debugged, and highly optimized. For example, the `printf` function requires machine instructions to format the various output fields, send them to the standard output device, and check to see that there were no I/O errors. Because this takes many machine instructions, it would be inefficient to repeat that sequence for every `printf` call in a program. Instead, a single, all-purpose `printf` function is written once and placed in the standard library by the developers of the compiler. When your program is compiled, the compiler generates calls to these prewritten programs rather than re-creating the logic each time a `printf` call occurs in the source code.

Variable scope of reference is the language feature that allows small C and C++ programs to be designed to perform standalone functions, yet also to be combined into larger utilities as needed. This flexibility is characteristic of UNIX, the first operating system to be built on the C language. As you'll see in the rest of the chapter, variable scope of reference also makes object-oriented programming possible in C++.

Overloading Functions and Operators in C++

Overloading is a technique that allows more than one function to have the same name. In at least two circumstances, a programmer might want to define a new function with the same name as an existing one:

- When the existing version of the function doesn't perform the exact desired functionality, but it must otherwise be included with the program (as with a function from the standard library).

- When the same function must operate differently depending on the format of the data passed to it.

In C, a function name can be reused as long as the old function name isn't within scope. A function name's scope of reference is determined in the same way as a data name's scope: A function that is defined (not just called) within the definition of another function is local to that other function.

When two similar C functions must coexist within the same scope, however, they cannot bear the same name. Instead, two different names must be assigned, as with the `strcpy` and `strncpy` functions from the standard library, each of which copies strings but does so in a slightly different fashion.

C++ gets around this restriction by allowing overloaded function names—the C++ language allows programmers to reuse function names within the same scope of reference, as long as the parameters for the function differ in number or type.

Listing 26.12 shows an example of overloading functions. This program defines and calls two versions of the `printvar` function, one equivalent to `printnum` in Listing 26.11 and the other to `printchar`.

Listing 26.12 An Example of an Overloaded Function

```
#include <stdio.h>
void printvar (int tmp)
{
   printf ("%d \n",tmp);
}

void printvar (char tmp)
{
   printf ("a \n",tmp);
}

void main ()
{
   int  numvar;
   char charvar;
   numvar = 5;
   printvar (numvar);
   charvar = 'a';
   printvar (charvar);
}
```

The following is the output of this program when it is executed:

```
5
a
```

Overloading is possible because C++ compilers can determine the format of the arguments sent to the `printvar` function each time it is called from within `main`. The compiler substitutes a call to the correct version of the function based on those formats. If the function being overloaded resides in a library or in another module, the associated header file (such as `stdio.h`) must be included in this source code module. This header file contains the prototype for the external function, thereby informing the compiler of the parameters and parameter formats used in the external version of the function.

Standard mathematical, logical, and other operators can also be overloaded. This is an advanced and powerful technique that allows the programmer to customize exactly how a standard language feature will operate on a specific data structure or at certain points in the code. Great care must be exercised when overloading standard operators such as `+`, `MOD`, and `OR` to ensure that the resulting operation functions correctly, is restricted to the appropriate occurrences in the code, and is well documented.

Functions within C++ Data Structures

A second feature of C++ that supports object-oriented programming, in addition to overloading, is the capability to associate a function with a particular data structure or format. Such functions can be *public* (able to be invoked by any code), can be *private* (able to be invoked only by other functions within the data structure), or can allow limited access.

Data structures in C++ must be defined by using the `struct` keyword and become new datatypes added to the language (within the scope of the structure's definition). Listing 26.13 revisits the structure of Listing 26.3 and adds a display function to print out instances of the license structure. Note the alternative way to designate comments in C++, using a double slash. This tells the compiler to ignore everything that follows on the given line only.

Also notice that Listing 26.13 uses the C++ character output function `cout` rather than the C routine `printf`.

Listing 26.13 Adding Functions to Data Structures

```
#include <iostream.h>
//              structure = new datatype
struct license {
        char name[128];
        char address[3][128];
        int zipcode;
        int height, weight, month, day, year;
        char license_letter;
        int license_number;
```

```
        void display(void)
➥// there will be a function to display license type structures
        };

// now define the display function for this datatype

void license::display()
{
   cout << "Name:     "  << name;
   cout << "Address: "  << address[0];
   cout << "          "  << address[1];
   cout << "          " << address[2] << " " << zipcode;
   cout << "Height:   " << height << " inches";
   cout << "Weight:   " << weight << " lbs";
   cout << "Date:     " << month << "/" << day  << "/" << year;
   cout << "License: " <<license_letter <<license_number;
}


main()
{
   struct license newlicensee;      // define a variable of type license
   newlicensee.name = "Joe Smith";  //  and initialize it
   newlicensee.address(0) = "123 Elm Street";
   newlicensee.address(1) = "";
   newlicensee.address(2) = "Smalltown, AnyState";
   newlicensee.zipcode = "98765";
   newlicensee.height = 70;
   newlicensee.weight = 165;
   license.month = 1;
   newlicensee.day = 23;
   newlicensee.year = 97;
   newlicensee.license_letter = A;
   newlicensee.license_number = 567890;


   newlicensee.display;   // and display this instance of the structure
}
```

Note that there are three references to the same `display` function in Listing 26.13. First, the `display` function is prototyped as an element within the structure definition. Second, the function is defined. Because the function definition is valid for all instances of the datatype `license`, the structure's data elements are referenced by the `display` function without naming any instance of the structure. Finally, when a specific instance of `license` is created, its associated `display` function is invoked by prefixing the function name with that of the structure instance.

Listing 26.14 shows the output of this program.

LISTING 26.14 Output of the Function Defined Within a Structure

```
Name:     Joe Smith
Address: 123 Elm Street

         Smalltown, AnyState  98765
Height:  70 inches
Weight:  160 lbs
Date:    1/23/1997
License: A567890
```

Note that the operator << is the bitwise shift-left operator except when it is used with `cout`. With `cout`, << is used to move data to the screen. This is an example of operator overloading, because the operator can have a different meaning depending on the context of its use. The >> operator is used for bitwise shift right except when used with `cin`; with `cin`, >> is used to move data from the keyboard to the specified variable.

Classes in C++

Overloading and associating functions with data structures lays the groundwork for object-oriented code in C++. Full object orientation is available through the use of the C++ class feature.

A C++ class extends the idea of data structures with associated functions by binding (or *encapsulating*) data descriptions and manipulation algorithms into new abstract datatypes. When a class is defined, the class type and methods are described in the public interface. The class can also have hidden private functions and data members.

Class declaration defines a datatype and format, but does not allocate memory or in any other way create an object of the class's type. The wider program must declare an instance, or object, of this type in order to store values in the data elements or invoke the public class functions. A class is often placed into libraries for use by many different programs, each of which then declares objects that instantiate that class for use during program execution.

Declaring a Class in C++

Listing 26.15 contains an example of a typical class declaration in C++.

LISTING 26.15 Declaring a Class in C++

```
#include <iostream.h>
// declare the Circle class
class Circle   {
private:
   double rad;                    // private data member
public:
   Circle (double);               // constructor function
   ~Circle ();                    // deconstructor function
   double area (void);            // member function - compute area
};

//  constructor function for objects of this class
Circle::Circle(double radius)
{
   rad = radius;
}

//  deconstructor function for objects of this class
Circle::~Circle()
{
   // does nothing
}

// member function to compute the Circle's area
double Circle::area()
{
    return rad * rad * 3.141592654;
}

//        application program that uses a Circle object
main()
{
    Circle mycircle (2);     // declare a circle of radius = 2
    cout << mycircle.area();     // compute & display its area
}
```

The example in Listing 26.15 begins by declaring the `Circle` class. This class has one private member: a floating-point element. The `Circle` class also has several public members, consisting of three functions—`Circle`, `~Circle`, and `area`.

The *constructor function* of a class is a function called by a program to construct or create an object that is an instance of the class. In the case of the `Circle` class, the constructor function (`Circle(double)`) requires a single parameter, namely the radius of the desired circle. If a constructor function is explicitly defined, it has the same name as the class and does not specify a return value, even of type `void`.

Note

When a C++ program is compiled, the compiler generates calls to the runtime system, which allocates sufficient memory each time an object of class `Circle` comes into scope. For example, an object that is defined within a function is created (and goes into scope) whenever the function is called. However, the object's data elements are not initialized unless a constructor function has been defined for the class.

The *deconstructor function* of a class is a function called by a program to deconstruct an object of the class type. A deconstructor takes no parameters and returns nothing. In this example, the `Circle` class's deconstructor function is `~Circle`.

Note

Under normal circumstances, the memory associated with an object of a given class is released for reuse whenever the object goes out of scope. In such a case, the programmer can omit defining the deconstructor function. However, in advanced applications or where class assignments cause potential pointer conflicts, explicit deallocation of free-store memory might be necessary.

In addition to the constructor and deconstructor functions, the `Circle` class contains a public function called `area`. Programs can call this function to compute the area of `Circle` objects.

The main program (the `main` function) in Listing 26.15 shows how an object can be declared. `mycircle` is declared to be of type `Circle` and is given a radius of 2.

The final statement in this program calls the function to compute the area of `mycircle` and passes it to the output function for display. Note that the area computation function is identified by a composite name, just as with other functions that are members of C++ data structures outside of class definitions. This usage underscores the fact that the object `mycircle`, of type `Circle`, is being asked to execute a function that is a member of itself and with reference to itself. The programmer could define a `Rectangle` class that also contains an `area` function, thereby overloading the `area` function name with the appropriate algorithm for computing the areas of different kinds of geometric entities.

Inheritance and Polymorphism

A final characteristic of object-oriented languages, and of C++, is support for class inheritance and polymorphism.

New C++ classes (and hence datatypes) can be defined so that they automatically *inherit* the properties and algorithms associated with their parent classes. This is done whenever a new class uses any of the standard C datatypes. The class from which new class definitions are created is called the *base class*. For example, a structure that includes integer members will also inherit all the mathematical functions associated with integers. New classes that are defined in terms of the base classes are called *derived classes*. The `Circle` class in Listing 26.15 is a derived class.

Derived classes can be based on more than one base class, in which case the derived class inherits multiple datatypes and their associated functions. This is called *multiple inheritance*.

Because functions can be overloaded, it is possible that an object declared as a member of a derived class might act differently than an object of the base class type. For example, the class of positive integers might return an error if the program attempts to assign a negative number to a class object, although such an assignment would be legal with regard to an object of the base integer type.

This capability of different objects within the same class hierarchy to act differently under the same circumstances is referred to as *polymorphism*. This is the object-oriented concept that many people have the most difficulty grasping; however, it also provides much of the power and elegance of object-oriented design and code. For instance, a programmer who's designing an application using predefined graphical user interface (GUI) classes is free to ask various window objects to display themselves appropriately without having to concern herself with how the window color, location, or other display characteristics are handled in each case.

Class inheritance and polymorphism are among the most powerful object-oriented features of C++. Together with the other, less dramatic extensions to C, these features have made possible many of the newest applications and systems capabilities of UNIX today, including GUIs for user terminals and many of the most advanced Internet and World Wide Web technologies—some of which will be discussed in subsequent chapters of this book.

GNU C/C++ Compiler Command-Line Switches

Many options are available for the GNU C/C++ compiler, and many of them match the C and C++ compilers available on other UNIX systems. Table 26.7 shows the important switches. Look at the man page for `gcc` or the information file on the CD-ROM for the full list and description.

TABLE 26.7 GNU C/C++ Compiler Switches

Switch	*Description*
`-x` *`language`*	Specifies the language (C, C++, and assembler are valid values).
`-c`	Compiles and assembles only (does not link).
`-S`	Compiles (does not assemble or link); generates an assembler code (`.s`) file.
`-E`	Preprocesses only (does not compile, assemble, or link).
`-o` *`file`*	Specifies the output filename (`a.out` is the default).
`-l library`	Specifies the libraries to use.
`-I directory`	Searches the specified directory for include files.
`-w`	Inhibits warning messages.
`-pedantic`	Strict ANSI compliance required.
`-Wall`	Prints additional warning messages.
`-g`	Produces debugging information (for use with `gdb`).
`-ggdb`	Generates native-format debugging info (and `gdb` extensions).
`-p`	Produces information required by `prof`.
`-pg`	Produces information for use by `gprof`.
`-O`	Optimizes.

New Features of the GNU egcs Compiler System

The egcs (pronounced *eggs*) program suite originally was an experimental version of the gcc compiler whose development was first hosted by Cygnus Support (http://www.cygnus.com).

Starting with Red Hat 5.1 for Intel, egcs was made available for installation as part of your Red Hat Linux system.

Caldera OpenLinux 2.2 includes version 1.1.1 of the egcs compiler suite for C and C++ in the egcs*2.91.60-4.i386.rpm archives.

Debian distributions offer egcs as well. For some platforms, egcs is installed as the default compiler; for others, it is just another option.

According to Cygnus, egcs initially was an experimental step in the development of gcc. Since its first release in late summer 1997, egcs has incorporated many of the latest developments and features from *parallel* development of gcc with many new developments of its own, such as a built-in Fortran 77 front end. At the time of this writing, egcs also includes compiler support for the Java language.

Note

You'll need to use the gcj front end to the egcs compiler in order to compile Java language classes. The front-end software and related packages are not included with most Linux distributions, but you can find out more about egcs Java support by browsing to http://sourceware.cygnus.com/java/compile.html.

Intrepid Linux developers can jump right to the source code tree for the latest egcs and Java support software by hopping to ftp://egcs.cygnus.com/pub/egcs/snapshots/index.html.

Although some Linux developers may have felt that development of egcs represented a fork (or split) in gcc compiler development, Cygnus stated that cooperation between the developers of gcc and egcs would prevent this. The hope, according to Cygnus, was that the new compiler architecture and features of egcs will help gcc be the best compiler in the world.

In April 1999, egcs officially became part of future GNU gcc software, and according to Cygnus, the egcs team will be responsible for rolling out future GCC releases. The egcs compiler system, as distributed with Red Hat Linux 6.0 and Caldera OpenLinux 2.2, is now the default C and C++ compiler.

In Red Hat 5.1 and 5.2, egcs was different from gcc in several ways and could have prevented you from properly building programs in several instances (see the next section, "egcs Considerations for Red Hat 5.2").

egcs Considerations for Red Hat 5.2

Under Red Hat 5.2 and earlier, if you choose not to install egcs either during your initial Red Hat Linux installation or later via rpm or glint, your gcc and any legacy (read *older*) C++ makefile scripts will function as expected. However, expect at least one or two important changes if you install egcs alongside gcc.

Have you installed gcc and egcs? If so, the traditional gcc compiler and the egcs compiler are installed, but components, such as cc, gcc, g++, c++, egcs, or g77, point to a different compiler. Table 26.8 lists the components, compilers, and locations for Red Hat Linux 5.1 for Intel. (A similar table can be found at the URL given earlier for Red Hat.)

TABLE 26.8 *gcc* and *egcs* Software Links and Locations for Red Hat 5.1 and 5.2

Command	*Compiler*	*Location*
c++	egcs	/usr/bin/c++
cc	gcc	/usr/bin/cc->gcc (symbolic link)
egcs	egcs	/usr/bin/egcs
g++	egcs	/usr/bin/g++
g77	egcs	/usr/bin/g77 (built-in Fortran 77)
gcc	gcc	/usr/bin/gcc

Under Red Hat Linux 5.2, components of both the older gcc and the newer egcs are located under the /usr/lib/gcc-lib/i386-redhat-linux directory, in the directories named 2.7.2.3 (gcc) and egcs-2.90.29 (egcs). Table 26.8 shows the names and locations of the primary front ends for both versions, but if you have trouble or want to confirm the version of gcc or egcs installed on your system, use the name of the command followed by the -version command-line option, like this:

```
$ g77 -version
egcs-2.90.27 980315 (egcs-1.0.2 release)
$ gcc -version
```

```
2.7.2.3
$ cc —version
2.7.2.3
$ g++ —version
egcs-2.90.27 980315 (egcs-1.0.2 release)
$ c++ —version
egcs-2.90.27 980315 (egcs-1.0.2 release)
```

Problems might occur when you're using `egcs` if you try to build a software package written in C++ that references `gcc` in its makefile. For example, trying to compile Chris Cannam's wmx X11 window manager (see Chapter 5, "Window Managers," for details about X window managers) results in an error and a barf on the build like this:

```
$ make
gcc -c -g -O2 Border.C
gcc: installation problem, cannot exec `cc1plus': No such file or
directory
make:***[Border.o] Error 1
```

The makefile script contains names and locations of programs and files used during the build process. The `wmx Makefile` contained the following two definitions:

```
CC    = gcc
CCC    = gcc
```

While this will work if you have only `gcc` installed, youl need to change the name of the designated C++ compiler in your makefile to `g++` if you install the `egcs` suite:

```
CC    = gcc
CCC    = g++
```

Be aware that if you use `egcs` to compile C++ source files (files ending in `.C`, `.cc`, or `.cxx`), you might have to fix the software's makefile first. However, because `egcs` is new, here are some other caveats of which you should be aware:

- Because of certain problems with assembler language constructs, `egcs` cannot be used to rebuild your Linux kernel. Use `gcc` instead.
- Because of changes in the way the `egcs` g++ handles the new keyword in array declarations in C++, `egcs` might not build the K Desktop Environment, or KDE (see Chapter 5 for more information about KDE). This might be fixed by the time you read this.
- `egcs` does not work with GNU Pascal.

For more information about `egcs`, see your system's `/usr/doc/egcs` directory or the `egcs` man page. For the latest updates, versions, or feature news about `egcs`, browse to `http:// www.gnu.org/software/gcc/gcc.html`. You'll find an `egcs` FAQ and pointers to the latest stable `egcs` release, or snapshots of the most recent development version.

Additional Resources

If you are interested in learning more about C and C++, you should look for the following books:

- *Sams Teach Yourself C in 21 Days*, by Peter Aitken and Bradley Jones, Sams Publishing.
- *C How to Program* and *C++ How to Program*, by H. M. Deitel and P. J. Deitel, Prentice-Hall.
- *The C Programming Language*, by Brian Kernighan and Dennis Ritchie, Prentice-Hall.
- *The Annotated C++ Reference Manual*, by Margaret Ellis and Bjarne Stroustrup, Addison-Wesley.
- *Sams Teach Yourself Linux Programming in 24 Hours*, by Warren W. Gay, Sams Publishing.
- *Programming in ANSI C*, by Stephen G. Kochan.

Summary

UNIX was built on the C language. C is a platform-independent, compiled, procedural language based on functions and the capability to derive new, programmer-defined data structures.

C++ extends the capabilities of C by providing the necessary features for object-oriented design and code. C++ compilers such as `gcc` correctly compile ANSI C code. C++ also provides some features, such as the capability to associate functions with data structures, that don't require the use of full, class-based, object-oriented techniques. For these reasons, the C++ language allows existing UNIX programs to migrate toward the adoption object orientation over time.

CHAPTER 27

Motif Programming

In This Chapter

This chapter introduces you to the OSF/Motif programming libraries. You'll learn about the different versions of Motif; how to install Red Hat's Motif 2.1 distribution or the free alternative; how Motif programs, or clients, work; how to write and compile a simple Motif client; how to use the programming utilities `imake` and `xmkmf`; and how you might save money by using a Motif clone, LessTif.

You need to have the GNU `gcc` compiler and associated headers, libraries, and associated headers, libraries, and utilities installed on your system. You also need X and Motif installed on your system if you want to run any Motif clients, including `mwm`. You do not have to run X to program with Motif, although compiling, running, and seeing a program in action is a lot more fun with it.

What Is Motif?

First of all, you should understand that unlike the XFree86 distribution of X, Motif is not free—you must pay for a distribution. Motif has distributions for Linux on the Intel, SPARC, or Alpha platforms. If you want to build Motif clients and distribute them, you must purchase a version for your computer and operating system. If you want other people to run your clients, you can build the clients in either shared library or static versions, for people who either have or don't have Motif (see "Shared and Static Libraries" later in this chapter).

If your budget is tight, or if you object to paying for a client license for Motif, don't despair. Later in this chapter, you'll learn about LessTif, a free alternative to Motif.

Motif is a toolkit of source headers, libraries, a window manager, `mwm`, demonstration programs, and manual pages. Originally announced in 1988 and designed by the Open Software Foundation (OSF) in 1989, Motif is now owned and updated by The Open Group. Motif provides a rich selection of tools to build cross-platform, graphical interface applications or clients.

The idea behind Motif is to provide the tools to build consistent, usable, and portable programs for the X Window System. Motif provides functions and system calls—as well as almost anything you need to craft graphical interface programs—to build client interfaces with the following:

- Arrow buttons
- Cascade buttons
- Check boxes
- Draw buttons
- File selection dialog boxes

- List widgets
- Menu bars
- Pushbuttons
- Radio boxes
- Scrollbars
- Toggle buttons
- Dialog boxes
- Icons
- Drop-down menus
- Pull-down menus
- Tear-off menus

In fact, more than 600 man pages are included with each Motif distribution, documenting its clients, function calls, libraries, and window manager. Although you can use X functions to build clients with a Motif look, why not take advantage of all the work put into Motif?

Where Do I Get Motif?

Several vendors supply Motif for Linux. Because the object, or philosophy, of OSF/Motif is to provide cross-platform, source-code–level compatibility, you should be able to develop Motif clients on your Intel Linux system that will compile and run on any other computer with a Motif distribution installed.

Of the Linux vendors and distributions discussed in this book, only Red Hat, Inc. markets a matching Motif distribution. This chapter concentrates on the Red Hat distribution, but other Motif distributions may be installed and used to build Motif clients, even if you use Red Hat Linux.

Several distributors sell Motif for Linux. These include the following:

- Xi Graphics, Inc. (`http://www.xig.com`)
- Metro Link Incorporated (`http://www.metrolink.com`)
- InfoMagic (`http://www.infomagic.com`)

What Version of Motif Should I Use?

To make an intelligent decision regarding which version of Motif to get, you should know a little about the history and direction of the standard. In 1996, The Open Group

(TOG) acquired the X Window System from the X Consortium, with the aim of integrating X, Motif, and the Common Desktop Environment (CDE). CDE represents the future of Motif, according to TOG, and offers graphical interface improvements, support for multiuser applications, and new networking features (see Chapter 5, "Window Managers," for more information).

The X Consortium acquired the X Window System from the MIT X Consortium in 1993 and was responsible for the past several releases, the most recent of which is X11R6.4. Broadway, which was the code name for X11R6.3, includes improvements in network communications to support graphics, and audio for use in Web browsers.

The historic versions of Motif in use at many computer sites around the world are 1.2, 2.0, and the current version of Motif, 2.1.20. TOG's aim is to merge X, Motif, and CDE. What does this mean to the user and what does this mean to the programmer?

The Linux user should choose one of the latest versions. If you want the Motif 1.2.5 libraries, a drag-and-drop, industry-standard interface, and many other improvements, you can also try Xig's or TriTeal's CDE. The Motif window manager, `mwm`, is replaced in CDE by new terminal managers (based on a window manager called `dtwm`).

The choice may not be as clear for the programmer. According to The Open Group, Motif 2.0 and CDE can be used together and Motif 2.0 is binary-compatible with Motif 1.2, but all of the important Motif 2.0 developer features are now available in CDE 2.1 and Motif 2.1. This means programmers can use the developers version of CDE 2.1 or the Motif 2.1 libraries to get the latest programming features. However, you should know that support for C++ programmers was dropped with Motif 2.1 (see Chapter 26, "C and C++ Programming," for details about this language), along with support for "platform-independent uid files" and the "`CSText` widget."

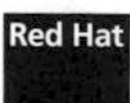

One bonus of the Red Hat Motif 2.1 release is that you get eight critical TOG Motif programming and style documents on CD-ROM—nearly 142MB of documentation! These documents, in PostScript format and compressed, include the following:

- Motif Programmer's Guide
- Motif Programmer's Reference
- Motif and CDE Style Guide
- Motif and CDE Style Guide Reference
- Motif and CDE Style Guide Certification Checklist
- Motif Widget Writer's Guide
- Motif User's Guide (also provided in paperback form with your CD-ROM)
- Motif Glossary

This is a bargain, considering that most Motif 1.2 and 2.0 distributions included only a user's guide. The original Motif style guide was nearly $24 (for a 120-page paperback).

The files can be copied from your Red Hat Motif CD-ROM and decompressed on your hard drive. Alternatively, you can read the standalone PostScript files with the gv client during an X session. For example, to read the Motif and CDE Style Reference Guide, type **gv** on the command line of a terminal window, followed by the pathname to the file:

```
# gv /mnt/cdrom/docs/mot-cdesgr.ps.gz
```

A minimal install of Caldera OpenLinux installs the X Window System, but does not include the gv client. However, gv may be installed using the lisa or rpm command. Install gv and its documentation with the rpm command after mounting the OpenLinux CD-ROM like this:

```
# rpm -ivh /mnt/cdrom/Packages/RPMS/gv-3.5.8*rpm
```

The gv client will be copied to the /usr/X11R6/bin directory, and the documentation will be found under the /usr/doc/gv-3.5.8 directory.

Other OSF titles, such as the Motif Programmer's Reference, are PostScript documents in a compressed tar archive. They must be copied and decompressed to your hard drive.

Red Hat Motif Installation

As mentioned before, this chapter concentrates on the specifics of Red Hat's Motif distribution. Installing Red Hat Motif 2.1 is easy. First, make sure you have enough room on your hard drive. You'll need about 20MB for a full software installation. If you want to run just the Motif window manager (mwm) and other Motif clients, you can save about 15MB by installing only the Motif libraries and mwm.

Software Development Preliminaries

Minimal Linux installations rarely include the necessary development software tools, libraries, and header files required for software development. Your first step should be to install the necessary glibc-based archives containing basic Linux development tools, libraries, and files, and then install the XFree86 software development archives in order to develop programs for X11.

There are two ways to install Motif from the Red Hat CD-ROM, but both require you to mount the disk to a convenient directory with one of the following:

```
#mount /dev/cdrom
```

or

```
# mount -t iso9660 /dev/cdrom /mnt/cdrom
```

Next, navigate to your CD-ROM's directory with this:

```
# cd /mnt/cdrom
```

You can then launch the installation script:

```
# ./install-motif
```

The installation script automatically determines the type of Linux software libraries installed on your computer, and then installs the correct RPM files (libc5-based or the latest glibc). Another way to install the software is to use the `rpm` command.

Note

All recent Linux distributions (using the Linux 2.2.X+ kernels) now use the new glibc libraries. Programmers who need to develop libc-based software for backwards compatibility with older Linux distributions will also need to install the libc development packages.

You can also use the `rpm` command to uninstall Motif from your system. To avoid dependency problems, remove the Motif development libraries first:

```
# rpm -e motif-devel
```

You can then remove the `mwm` client, followed by manual pages and other documentation, like this:

```
# rpm -e motif-mwm
# rpm -e motif-2.1
```

The Red Hat folks have assembled the Motif software into the RPM (Red Hat Package Manager) packages discussed in the following sections.

Motif 2.1 Development `rpms`

These packages contain the static libraries and `#include` files, or headers, needed to build Motif clients. You'll also find the Motif User Interface Language compiler, `uil`, and the Motif function-call manual pages.

Motif 2.1 `rpms`

If you just want to run `mwm` or the Motif Workspace Manager (`Wsm`), you'll need the shared libraries in this package. More than 800 icons are also installed from this file under the `/usr/X11R6/include/X11/icons` directory.

Motif 2.1 `Mwm` `rpms`

Here's where you'll find not only the window manager (`mwm`), but the `Wsm`, which demonstrates some of the features of Motif 2.0. Also included are `panner`, `pixmap`, and a handy bitmap browser (`xbmbrowser`) that transverses directories and shows what `.xpm` or `.xbm` graphics look like, one directory at a time.

Motif Demonstration Source `rpms`

Install this package if you're interested in exploring features of Motif 2.1, if you need source-code examples to help you learn about Motif programming, or if you want to read the source to the example clients. Before you can build the examples, you must install the development libraries. Some of the concepts these programs demonstrate are discussed later in this chapter, but here's a list of the examples included:

- `Exm`—An example program that shows how to write a Motif widget
- `airport`—Demonstrates Motif drag-and-drop
- `animate`—Animates pixel maps in an X window
- `drag_and_drop`—A thorough demonstration of drag-and-drop features
- `draw`—A simple graphics application
- `earth`—The classic rotating earth
- `filemanager`—A simple, graphical file manager
- `fileview`—A Motif "more" program
- `getsubres`—A Motif widget resources viewer
- `hellomotif`—The classic "Hello, world!"
- `hellomotifi18n`—A better "Hello, world!" in different languages
- `i18ninput`—Shows how to handle text input in different languages
- `periodic`—Demonstrates displayable Motif widgets
- `piano`—A simple Motif MIDI application (You'll need MIDI support.)
- `popups`—Shows pop-up menu improvements in Motif 2.0
- `sampler2_0`—A fairly complete demonstration of Motif 2.0 features
- `setdate`—Sets the system's date and demonstrates the Motif SpinBox widget

Along with these programs, you'll find 10 other examples in a separate directory.

Motif Demos rpms

Install this package if you don't want to spend the time building the sample clients from the source code and prefer to try some of the features of Motif. Before you can run these clients, you must install the shared libraries.

A Simple Example of Motif Programming Concepts

This section presents an extremely simple example of a Motif program—just enough to get you started. Before getting into the details, I'll cover the basic concepts in an overview of Motif programming.

Writing programs for the Linux command line in C is fairly simple, but if you're familiar with programming for X, you know there's a lot more involved in writing a windowing program. You have to consider labels, dialog boxes, windows, scrolling, colors, buttons, and many other features of how a program works—besides the internal algorithms that make a program unique. Along with this unique functionality, you should consider consistency and ease of use for the user when programming for X.

This is where Motif can help you. By providing a rich variety of functions, Motif can help programmers build attractive and easy-to-use programs. A lot of the program code in Motif, especially for smaller programs, is devoted to the graphical interface.

When you write C programs for the Linux command line, you'll generally use the `glibc` libraries. If you write programs for X, you'll generally use the `Xlib` libraries. When you program for Motif, you'll use X as the window system and the X Toolkit or `Xt` libraries (and others) for the interface.

After you install Motif 2.1, you'll find a number of libraries under the `/usr/X11R6/lib` directory:

```
/usr/X11R6/lib/libMrm.a
/usr/X11R6/lib/libUil.a
/usr/X11R6/lib/libXm.a
/usr/X11R6/lib/libXmCxx.a
/usr/X11R6/lib/libMrm.so
/usr/X11R6/lib/libMrm.so.2
/usr/X11R6/lib/libMrm.so.2.0
/usr/X11R6/lib/libXm.so
/usr/X11R6/lib/libXm.so.2
/usr/X11R6/lib/libXm.so.2.0
```

The Motif #include files are located under the /usr/X11R6/include/Mrm, /usr/X11R6/include/Xm, and /usr/X11R6/include/uil directories. The location of these libraries and headers is mostly standard across all computer systems, but if they are located in a different place, this difference will be documented in configuration files and rules files for imake and xmkmf. (For more information on these utilities, see the "Using imake and xmkmf" section later in this chapter.)

Widgets and Event-Driven Programming

An important concept to consider when programming for X and Motif is that these programs usually do not just run and quit. These programs are driven by events such as mouse clicks, button pushes, mouse drags, other programs, and keystrokes. Apple Macintosh programmers will feel right at home in programming for Motif. Some of the interface elements that intercept these events are built with Motif routines called *widgets*, and as you become more proficient, you'll even write some of your own.

If you're just starting off with Motif programming, don't be put off by the new terms and concepts. You'll learn about callbacks, children, classes, composites, coupled resources, gadgets, hierarchies, initiators, instantiation, modality, properties, receivers, and subclasses. Although there's not enough room in this book to cover all of these subjects, Listing 27.1 contains a simple example to get you started.

The Simple Motif Program

Listing 27.1 creates a small window with File, Edit, and Help menus. The application window is resizable, can be minimized or maximized, and generally responds like any Motif application. This program demonstrates how to create a window, a menu bar, a pull-down menu, buttons, and a pop-up dialog box.

It's not a perfect example because the interface is in the main() part of the program, it doesn't use resources, and it really doesn't do anything. I'll leave the internals of how the program might work up to you.

LISTING 27.1 motif_skeleton.c

```
/* a simple skeleton Motif program */
#include <Xm/RowColumn.h>
#include <Xm/MainW.h>
#include <Xm/CascadeB.h>
#include <Xm/MessageB.h>
#include <Xm/SeparatoG.h>
#include <Xm/PushBG.h>
```

continues

LISTING 27.1 continued

```
Widget skeleton;    /* our application */
/* what happens when user selects Exit */
void skel_exit_action() {
exit(0);
    }

/* destroy a dialog */
void skel_dialog_handler(skel_dialog)
Widget skel_dialog;
{
XtUnmanageChild(skel_dialog);
}

/* create a Help action dialog*/
void skel_help_action()
{
    Arg      args[10];
    Widget   skel_dialog;
XmString skel_string;

    /* store help string */
    skel_string =
XmStringCreateLocalized("This is Skeleton v0.1, a simple Motif client.");

/* build dialog */
skel_dialog = XmCreateMessageDialog (skeleton, "dialog", args, 0);
XtVaSetValues(skel_dialog, XmNmessageString, skel_string, NULL, NULL);

/* call skel_dialog_handler() after OK button is pushed */
XtAddCallback(skel_dialog, XmNokCallback, skel_dialog_handler, NULL);

    /* free storage */
    XmStringFree(skel_string);

    /* display the dialog */
    XtManageChild(skel_dialog);
};

/* main program begins here */
main (argc, argv)
int argc;
char *argv[];
{
    /* declare our widgets, including menu actions */
    Widget    skel_window,              /* main window */
              skel_menubar,             /* main window menu bar */
              skel_filepulldown,        /* File menu */
                  skel_new,
                  skel_open,
```

```
                skel_close,
                skel_save,
                skel_exit,
            skel_editpulldown,      /* Edit menu */
                skel_cut,
                skel_copy,
                skel_paste,
            skel_helppulldown,      /* Help menu */
                skel_version;
    XmString  skel_string;          /* temporary storage */
    XtAppContext skel_app;

XtSetLanguageProc (NULL, NULL, NULL);

/* give the app a name and initial size */
skeleton = XtVaAppInitialize(&skel_app, "Skeleton", NULL, 0, &argc, argv,
NULL, XmNwidth, 320, XmNheight, 240, NULL);

/* create the main window */
skel_window = XtVaCreateManagedWidget("skel", xmMainWindowWidgetClass, skeleton,
XmNscrollingPolicy, XmAUTOMATIC, NULL);

/* build a menu bar across main window */
skel_menubar = XmCreateMenuBar(skel_window, "skel_menubar", NULL, 0);

/* build the File pull-down menu */
skel_filepulldown = XmCreatePulldownMenu (skel_menubar, "File", NULL, 0);
➥skel_string = XmStringCreateLocalized ("File");

/* create the menu, assign ALT+F as mnemonic key */
XtVaCreateManagedWidget ("File", xmCascadeButtonWidgetClass, skel_menubar,
XmNlabelString, skel_string, XmNmnemonic, 'F', XmNsubMenuId,
➥skel_filepulldown, NULL);

    /* release storage */
    XmStringFree(skel_string);

/* now add File pull-down menu elements */
skel_new = XtVaCreateManagedWidget("New", xmPushButtonGadgetClass,
skel_filepulldown, NULL);
skel_open = XtVaCreateManagedWidget("Open", xmPushButtonGadgetClass,
skel_filepulldown, NULL);
XtVaCreateManagedWidget("separator", xmSeparatorGadgetClass, skel_filepulldown,
        NULL);
skel_close = XtVaCreateManagedWidget("Close", xmPushButtonGadgetClass,
skel_filepulldown, NULL);
skel_save = XtVaCreateManagedWidget("Save", xmPushButtonGadgetClass,
skel_filepulldown, NULL);
XtVaCreateManagedWidget("separator", xmSeparatorGadgetClass, skel_filepulldown,
        NULL);
```

continues

LISTING 27.1 continued

```
skel_exit = XtVaCreateManagedWidget("Exit", xmPushButtonGadgetClass,
skel_filepulldown, NULL);

/* add what to do when user selects Exit */
XtAddCallback(skel_exit, XmNactivateCallback, skel_exit_action, NULL);

/* build Edit menu */
skel_editpulldown = XmCreatePulldownMenu(skel_menubar, "Edit", NULL, 0);
skel_string = XmStringCreateLocalized ("Edit");
XtVaCreateManagedWidget ("Edit", xmCascadeButtonWidgetClass, skel_menubar,
XmNlabelString, skel_string, XmNmnemonic, 'E', XmNsubMenuId,
➥skel_editpulldown, NULL);

    /* release storage */
    XmStringFree(skel_string);

/* add Edit pull-down menu elements */
skel_cut = XtVaCreateManagedWidget("Cut", xmPushButtonGadgetClass,
skel_editpulldown, NULL);
skel_copy = XtVaCreateManagedWidget("Copy", xmPushButtonGadgetClass,
skel_editpulldown, NULL);
skel_paste = XtVaCreateManagedWidget("Paste", xmPushButtonGadgetClass,
skel_editpulldown, NULL);

/* build Help menu */
skel_helppulldown = XmCreatePulldownMenu(skel_menubar, "Help", NULL, 0);
➥skel_string = XmStringCreateLocalized ("Help");
XtVaCreateManagedWidget ("Help", xmCascadeButtonWidgetClass, skel_menubar,
XmNlabelString, skel_string, XmNmnemonic, 'H', XmNsubMenuId,
➥skel_helppulldown, NULL);

    /* release storage */
    XmStringFree(skel_string);

/* now move the Help pull-down to right side - thanks, Motif FAQ! */
XtVaSetValues(skel_menubar, XmNmenuHelpWidget, XtNameToWidget(skel_menubar,
"Help"), NULL);

/* now label, create, and assign action to Help menu */
skel_version = XtVaCreateManagedWidget ("Version", xmPushButtonGadgetClass,
skel_helppulldown, NULL);
XtAddCallback(skel_version, XmNactivateCallback, skel_help_action, NULL);

    XtManageChild(skel_menubar);
    XtRealizeWidget(skeleton);
    XtAppMainLoop (skel_app);
    return (0);
}
```

If you have an older version of Motif, such as 2.01, use the following command line to build the client:

```
# gcc -o skel skeleton.c -L/usr/X11R6/lib -lXm -lXpm -lXt -lXext -lX11
```

To compile this program for Motif 2.1, you need to add a new library and linker directive:

```
# gcc -o skel skeleton.c -L/usr/X11R6/lib -lXp -lXm -lXpm -lXt -lXext -lX11
```

These lines direct the GNU linker to look in the `/usr/X11/lib` directories for needed libraries. The program is then linked, using the shared `Xp`, `Xm`, `Xpm`, `Xt`, `Xext`, and `X11` libraries. The final size of the program is fewer than 16,000 characters.

You must run this Motif client during an X Window session (as all Motif clients are built with software libraries that still depend upon X11 graphics support). Type the following at the command line of terminal window and press Enter:

```
# skel
```

If you select the Help menu item after the program starts, a small dialog box appears, as shown in Figure 27.1.

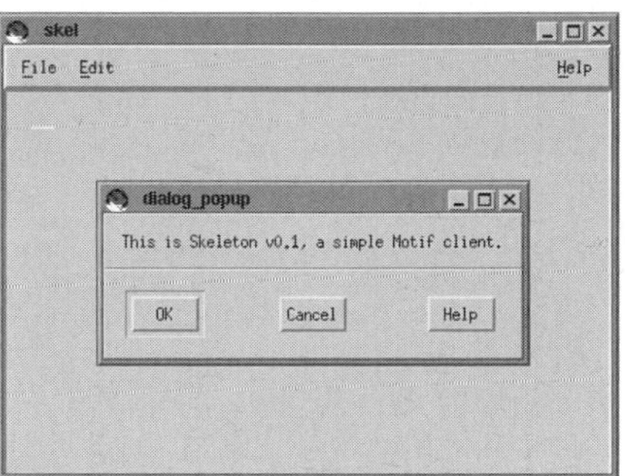

FIGURE 27.1
The sample Motif client also provides a small Help dialog box.

How the Program Works

If you've programmed in C to build Linux command-line or X programs, you know that if you use certain routines or functions, you must tell the compiler which `#include` files contain definitions needed by the functions in your program. Our sample program starts by listing the needed `#include` files for the Motif functions used in `skeleton.c`.

Next, the declaration of skeleton as a top-level widget makes information about our program available outside `main()`. This is because `skel_help_action()`, which creates a Motif dialog box, needs to know to whom the dialog box belongs. The next two routines, `skel_exit_action()` and `skel_dialog_handler()`, are known as *callback routines*.

Callback routines make your program work. These routines are called when you push buttons or select menu items, and when your program receives information from other programs or the operating system. If you look at `skel_dialog_handler()`, you see the following line:

```
XtAddCallback(skel_dialog, XmNokCallback, skel_dialog_handler, NULL);
```

This function tells the program what to do after the dialog box appears, what to do when you click the OK button, and what to do when you press the Enter key—all without a lot of extra code.

`skel_help_action()` is also a callback routine, called in response to the `main()` program line:

```
XtAddCallback(skel_version, XmNactivateCallback, skel_help_action, NULL);
```

In this instance, `skel_help_action()` is run when you choose Version from the program's Help menu. The routine `skel_exit_action()` is called when you choose Exit from the program's File menu. After creating room for the text string that contains the version information to be displayed, the `skel_help_action()` routine then creates the dialog box with this code:

```
skel_dialog = XmCreateMessageDialog (skeleton, "dialog", args, 0);
```

Required information is filled in with this routine:

```
XtVaSetValues(skel_dialog, XmNmessageString, skel_string, NULL, NULL);
```

The callback routine designation follows. Finally, it displays the dialog box with this code:

```
XtManageChild(skel_dialog);
```

The `main()` routine starts with declarations for various widgets and widget elements. The call to `XtVaAppInitialize()` declares the application name, indicates whether the program should read any command-line arguments, and assigns an initial size in pixel width and height.

Sample Program Resources

By using resources, you can set the initial window size (and many other default actions of all other Motif and many X11 programs). One way to do this is to open your `.Xdefaults` file in your home directory and type the following:

```
Skeleton.height: 480
Skeleton.width:  640
```

Save the file. Next, look for this program line:

```
skeleton = XtVaAppInitialize(&skel_app, "Skeleton", NULL, 0, &argc,
argv, NULL, XmNwidth, 320, XmNheight, 240, NULL);
```

Replace it with this:

```
skeleton = XtAppInitialize(&skel_app, "Skeleton",NULL,0, &argc, argv,
        NULL, NULL,0);
```

Rebuild the program and run it. You should see a much larger window than the earlier version. Finally, yet another way to feed resources to this program is to create a file called `Skeleton`, type in the resource strings for width and height mentioned earlier, and save the file into the `/usr/X11R6/lib/X11/app-defaults` directory. This way, the program will start with a default window size for everyone on your system.

Continuing with the example, the client's main window as a managed widget is created next with `XtVaCreateManagedWidget()`; then a menu bar is built across the top of the window with `XmCreateMenubar()`. After that, a pull-down menu is created with `XmCreatePulldownMenu()`, and a File button is built on the menu. This button will respond not only to a mouse click, but to Alt+F.

Building the rest of the File menu is easy. Note the callback routine to tell the program what to do when the Exit menu item is selected. After the File menu, the Edit menu is created the same way, along with the Help menu.

Note

Thanks are due to Ken Lee's Motif FAQ for the tip on moving the Help menu string to the end of the main window's menu bar. You can get a copy in various document formats at `http://www.rahul.net/kenton/faqs/mfaq_index.html`.

Finally, the menu bar is displayed along with the application, and the program starts waiting for keystrokes, clicks, and other events in `XtAppMainLoop()`.

As you can see, even a simple Motif program has a lot of code devoted to handling the user interface. Using Motif can save you a lot of time and effort because a lot of the code required to build, display, and handle the interface is hidden in the Motif routines, freeing you to concentrate on the internals of what your program does and what gives your programs a consistent look and feel.

The UIL Compiler

Although there isn't enough room to discuss the User Interface Language (UIL), if you want to quickly and easily build your program's interface, you might want to learn this language and its compiler, `uil`. For details on using the compiler and language, read the `uil` and UIL man pages. A number of the Motif demonstration programs use UIL, so you can read source code examples.

Many commercial graphical interface builders enable you to draw, design, and test your interface and then—with the click of a button—write out the Motif source code. See the Motif FAQ for more information. (Pointers for the FAQ are provided later in this chapter, in the section titled "For More Information.")

Tutorials and Examples

If you're serious about learning Motif programming, you'll need several good books and lots of program examples. If you want a basic introduction, you can also try some of the online tutorials, or you can peruse code examples. Try one of these sites:

- `http://www.motifzone.com`

  This is a great place to visit and read *The Motif Developer*, an online magazine for Motif programmers, with loads of tips and articles about Motif.

- `http://www.cen.com/mw3/code.html`

  This site includes several useful links to Motif programming code examples, lectures, and tutorials.

- `http://devcentral.iftech.com/learning/tutorials`

  This site features a Motif programming tutorial you might find helpful when getting started.

- `ftp://ftp.x.org`

  At this site, look under `/contrib/docs/` for a copy of Jan Borchers' `xmtutor`, an interactive tutorial on Motif programming.

Using `imake` and `xmkmf`

If you've created or built programs for the X Window System, you'll be familiar with Todd Brunhoff's `imake` utility and Jim Fulton's `xmkmf` command. Like the `make` command, these commands help you save time, limit errors, and organize your programming tasks by automating the building process.

`imake`, a C preprocessor interface to `make`, uses configuration files found under the `/usr/X11R6/lib/X11/config` directory. These files include `linux.cf`, `lnxLib.rules`, `lnxLib.tmpl`, `lnxdoc.rules`, and `lnxdoc.tmpl`.

Note

Nearly all Linux distributions also include template and configuration files for Motif (found under the `/usr/X11R6/lib/X11/config` directory with names beginning with `Motif*`).

The `xmkmf` command, which creates a makefile from an imakefile, is a simple shell script that runs `imake`, telling it where to find the specifics about your system and which command-line parameters need to be passed to your compiler, assembler, linker, and even man-page formatter. Note that you should never run `imake` by itself; always use the `xmkmf` script instead.

Typically, after unpacking the source for an X or Motif program, you use the `xmkmf` command and then the `make` command to build your program. Another of the reasons many programmers use `imake` is to ensure portability. Assuming the `imake` file is written properly, the `xmkmf` command will work on nearly any UNIX system, and that includes Linux.

Note

Many Linux programmers now include a `configure` shell script to be used when building a program for the Linux console, a client for X11, other collections of software, especially the K Desktop Environment (or the `LessTif` libraries - see "LessTif - An Alternative Motif Clone" below). The `configure` script is built with the GNU Autoconf package and creates scripts to automagically configure source code packages prior to using the `make` command. This approach has several advantages, one of which is that the `configure` script is independent of `autoconf` (meaning that `autoconf` does not need to be installed). On the other hand, Imakefiles are more compact and work well with a properly configured distribution. All Linux distributions now include `autoconf`. For more information, see the `autoconf` GNU info file.

`imake` works by reading an imakefile. In turn, the imakefile contains directions for the `cpp` compiler preprocessor, whose output is then fed back into `imake`, which generates the makefile for your program. The magic of imake is that it simplifies the job of creating makefiles for every possible computer or operating system your program could be built on or run under.

For example, here's a simple imakefile for the sample skeleton.c program:

```
       INCLUDES = -I.
DEPLIBS = XmClientDepLibs
LOCAL_LIBRARIES = XmClientLibs
SRCS= skeleton.c
OBJS= skeleton.o
PROGRAMS = skel
NormalLibraryObjectRule()
MComplexProgramTarget(skeleton,$(LOCAL_LIBRARIES),$(SYSLIBS))
```

To use this listing, type it in your favorite text editor (such as pico or nedit) and save the text as Imakefile. Use these two commands to build the program:

```
# xmkmf
```

```
# make
```

This also saves you a lot of time if you use the edit-compile-run-edit cycle of programming—you won't have to retype the compiler command line shown earlier in this chapter (# gcc -o skel skeleton.c -L/usr/X11R6/lib -lXm -lXpm -lXt -lXext -lX11).

LessTif—An Alternative Motif Clone

Much of the success of Linux is a direct result of the generosity of the thousands of programmers who chose to distribute their software either for free or under the GNU General Public License. Motif, as you already know, is not freeware, nor is it distributed under the GPL. As Red Hat Linux users, we're spoiled by the ability to examine program source code or make changes as we see fit.

The source code to Motif 2.1 for your computer's operating system has a price tag of $17,000 at the time of this writing. If you're interested in lifetime, full-distribution rights to Motif 2.1, be prepared to fork over $6 million. If you're interested in building a distribution of Motif for Linux, you can get the price list by browsing http://www.opengroup.org/tech/desktop/ordering.

There is an alternative for those of us who like source code but are on more limited budgets and want to build Motif-compliant clients without paying for a distribution: LessTif. LessTif is a Motif clone designed to be compatible with Motif 1.2. Distributed under the terms of the GNU GPL, LessTif currently builds more than 70 Motif clients (probably many more by the time you read this). Those of you running Debian GNU/Linux can find LessTif included with the distribution; furthermore, many programs in Debian have been built with LessTif, so you can see that it is usable for production work.

Building, Installing, and Testing LessTif

Those people running Debian GNU/Linux can install LessTif and its development libraries by using this command:

```
apt-get install lesstif-bin lesstifg lesstifg-dev
```

After running this, the full LessTif development and runtime environment will be installed.

Those people not running Debian can find a copy of the current LessTif distribution for Linux through `http://www.lesstif.org` (probably at `ftp.hungry.com` or a mirror). Follow the directions and download either the source code or binary archives for your system. The source code is a little more than 3MB in compressed form and expands to more than 15MB when decompressed. Use the `tar` command to decompress the LessTif archive, followed by the archive name, like this:

```
# tar xvzf lesstif-0.88.0.tar.gz
```

Next, navigate into the `lesstif` directory and configure the software build to your system with the `configure` command, like this:

```
# ./configure
```

You can then build the software with the `make` command:

```
# make
```

About 15 minutes later (on a 64MB, 300MHz Pentium computer) the build will finish.

Tip

Before you install LessTif, change the directory into the test directory and then configure and make the LessTif test suite:

```
# ./configure
# make
```

This creates nearly 200 programs and provide lots of sample source code!

To install the LessTif libraries and documentation, again use the make command, followed by install, like this:

```
# make install
```

The LessTif files and libraries will install under the /usr/local directory. You can then test the LessTif installation by compiling and running the sample Motif file in this chapter:

```
# gcc -o lesstifskel skel.c -L/usr/local/lib -lXm -L/usr/X11R6/lib -lSM
-lICE -lXt -lX11 -I/usr/X11R6/include
```

Note that the -L linker option is used with the /usr/local/lib pathname. This tells the linker to look under the /usr/local/lib directory for any required libraries. You may use this option several times. After the program builds and links, try to run the resulting client:

```
# ./lesstifskel
```

You'll probably get an error about the Motif shared library not being found:

```
./lesstifskel: error in loading shared libraries:
libXm.so.1: cannot open shared object file: No such file or directory
```

The program cannot find the LessTif library. One solution is to define and store the environment variable LD_LIBRARY_PATH and have it point to the installed LessTif libraries:

```
# LD_LIBRARY_PATH=/usr/local/lib;export LD_LIBRARY_PATH
```

You can then run the compiled program. Another solution is to put the /usr/local/lib path in your system's /etc/ld.so.conf file and then run the run-time linker utility ldconfig:

```
# /sbin/ldconfig
```

The current distribution doesn't require that you use imake or xmkmf and it comes with shared and static libraries. If you're a real Motif hacker and are interested in the internals of graphical interface construction and widget programming, you should read the details of how LessTif is constructed. You can get a free copy of Harold Albrecht's book, *Inside LessTif*, at http://www.igpm.rwth-aachen.de/~albrecht/hungry.html.

For More Information

If you're interested in finding answers to common questions about Motif, read Ken Lee's Motif FAQ, which is posted regularly to the newsgroup comp.windows.x.motif. Without a doubt, this is the best source of information on getting started with Motif, but it won't replace a good book on Motif programming. You can find the FAQ on the newsgroup, or at `ftp://ftp.rahul.net/pub/kenton/faqs/Motif-FAQ`. An HTML version can be found at `http://www.rahul.net/kenton/faqs/Motif-FAQ.html`.

For information on how to use `imake`, read Paul DuBois' *Software Portability with* `imake` from O'Reilly & Associates.

For Motif 1.2 programming and reference material, read Dan Heller and Paula M. Ferguson's *Motif Programming Manual* and Paula M. Ferguson and David Brennan's *Motif Reference Manual*, both from O'Reilly & Associates.

For the latest news about Motif or CDE, check The Open Group's site at `http://www.opengroup.org`.

For the latest information, installation, or programming errata about Red Hat's Motif distribution, see `http://www.redhat.com`.

For the latest binaries of LessTif, programming hints, and a list of Motif 1.2-compatible functions and Motif clients that build under the latest LessTif distribution, see `http://www.lesstif.org`.

For official information on Motif 1.2 from OSF, the following titles (from Prentice Hall) might help, but they're unnecessary if you've purchased Motif 2.1:

- *OSF/Motif Programmers Guide*
- *OSF/Motif Programmers Reference Manual*
- *OSF/Motif Style Guide*

For learning about `Xt`, you should look at Adrian Nye and Tim O'Reilly's *X Toolkit Intrinsics Programming Manual, Motif Edition*, and David Flanagan's *X Toolkit Intrinsics Reference Manual*, both from O'Reilly.

Other books about Motif include the following:

- *Motif Programming: The Essentials... and More*, by Marshall Brain, Digital Press.
- *The X Toolkit Cookbook*, by Paul E. Kimball, Prentice Hall, 1995.
- *Building OSF/Motif Applications: A Practical Introduction*, by Mark Sebern, Prentice Hall, 1994.

Summary

In this chapter you learned about Motif, a commercial software library add-on for Linux that is available from several vendors. Although you'll have to decide which version of

Motif is best for you, it's difficult to overlook some of the benefits of using Motif to write programs for the X Window System.

- By following the sample program in Listing 27.1, you learned a little about how Motif programs work and how to incorporate some of Motif's features into your programs.
- By using `imake` and `xmkmf`—two programming tools included in your Linux distribution—you witnessed how you can save time and effort when writing your own programs for Motif or X11.
- Finally, I gave you some tips on a Motif alternative, LessTif.

I hope you'll explore more topics concerning graphical interface programming for X.

CHAPTER 28

Perl Programming

In This Chapter

Perl (Practical Extraction and Report Language) was developed in the mid 1980s by Larry Wall, who was already responsible for a number of rather important UNIX utilities. Larry claims that Perl really stands for "Pathologically Eclectic Rubbish Lister." With the birth of the WWW in the early 1990s, Perl took off as the language of choice for CGI programming. With the recent burst of interest in the Open Source movement, Perl has gotten almost as much press as Linux.

Perl, according to Larry, is all about "making easy things easy, and hard things possible." So many programming languages make you spend an undue amount of time doing stuff to keep the language happy before you ever get around to making it do what you want. Perl lets you get your work done without worrying about things like memory allocation and variable typing.

Perl contains the best features of C, Basic, and a variety of other programming languages, with a hearty dollop of `awk`, `sed`, and shell scripting thrown in. One advantage of Perl over the other UNIX tools is that it can process binary files (those without line terminators or that contain binary data), while `sed` and `awk` cannot.

In Perl, "there is more than one way to do it." This is the unofficial motto of Perl and it comes up so often that it is usually abbreviated as TIMTOWTDI. If you are familiar with some other programming language, chances are you can write functional Perl code.

A version of Perl comes with most Linux distributions, but it is typically several versions out of date. This makes sense when you consider the time required to produce a distribution and actually distribute it. As of this writing, the current production version of Perl is 5.005_03 (which is Perl version 5 point 5, patch level 3). Version 5.005_57 is available as a developer release (generally considered experimental). You can determine what version of Perl you have installed by typing **`perl -v`** at a shell prompt.

This chapter focuses on version 5. Many of the examples shown will fail if you try them with version 4 of Perl. If you have version 4, you should get one of the newer versions. If you are installing a recent Linux distribution, you should have version 5.

Perl is an interpreted language. The interpreter has been ported to just about every operating system that is known. For UNIX and UNIX-like (Linux, for example) operating systems, you can just download the code from `http://www.perl.com/` and build it yourself.

A Simple Perl Program

To introduce you to the absolute basics of Perl programming, Listing 28.1 illustrates a trivial Perl program.

LISTING 28.1 A Trivial Perl Program

```
#!/usr/bin/perl
print "Look at all the camels!\n";
```

That is the whole program. Type that in, save it to a file called **`trivial.pl`**, **`chmod +x`** it, and execute it.

The `#!` line is technically not part of the Perl code at all (the # character is the comment character in Perl), but is instead a message to the shell, telling it where it should go for the executable to run this program. That is standard practice in shell programming, as is discussed in Chapter 25, "Shell Programming."

Note

`#!` is often pronounced *she-bang*, which is short for *sharp*, the musical name for the # character, and *bang*, which is another name for the exclamation point. Another pronunciation is *pound-bang* because most people refer to the # character on a telephone keypad as *pound*.

If for some reason Perl is not located at `/usr/bin/perl` on your system, you can locate the correct location of Perl by using the `which` command:

```
which perl
```

If you do not have Perl installed, you might want to skip to "For More Information" in this chapter to find out where you can obtain the Perl interpreter. Since a version of Perl comes with most Linux distributions, this should not be the case.

The second line does precisely what you would expect—it prints the text enclosed in quotation marks. `\n` is the escape sequence for a newline character.

Perl statements are terminated with a semicolon. A Perl statement can extend over several actual screen lines. Alternatively, you can have Perl statements in one line. Perl is not particularly concerned about whitespace.

The # character indicates that the rest of the screen line is a comment. That is, there is a comment from the # character until the next newline and it is ignored by the interpreter. Exceptions to this include when the # character is in a quoted string and when it is being used as the delimiter in a regular expression.

A block of code, such as what might appear inside a loop or a branch of a conditional statement, is indicated with curly braces (`{}`).

Included with the Perl installation is a document called *perlfunc*, which lists all of the available Perl functions and their usage. You can view this document by typing **`perldoc perlfunc`** at the command line. You can also find this document online at `http://www.cpan.org/doc/manual/html/pod/perlfunc.html`.

> **Tip**
>
> You can use the `perldoc` and `man` commands to get more information on the version of Perl installed on your system.
>
> To get information on the `perldoc` command, enter the following:
>
> ```
> perldoc perldoc
> ```
>
> To get introductory information on Perl, you have a choice of two different commands:
>
> ```
> perldoc perl
> man perl
> ```
>
> The documentation is extensive and is well organized to help you find what you need.

Perl Variables and Data Structures

Perl is a *weakly typed* language, meaning that it does not require that you specify what datatype will be stored in a particular variable. C, for example, makes you declare that a particular variable is an integer, a character, a pointer, or whatever the case may be. Perl variables are whatever type they need to be, and can change type when you need them to.

Perl Variable Types

There are three variable types in Perl—scalars, arrays, and hashes. In an attempt to make each data type visually distinct, a different character is used to signify each variable type.

Scalar Variables

Scalar variables are indicated with the `$` character, as in `$penguin`. Scalars can be numerical and can be strings, and they can change type from one to the other as needed. If you treat a number like a string, it's a string. If you treat a string like a number, it will be translated into a number if it makes sense to do so; otherwise, it will probably evaluate as `0`. For example, the string `"76trombones"` will evaluate as the number `76` if used in a numerical calculation, but the string `"polar bear"` will evaluate to `0`.

Arrays

Arrays are indicated with the @ character, as in @fish. An *array* is a list of values that are referenced by index number, starting with the first element numbered 0, just like C and awk. Each element in the array is a scalar value. Because scalar values are indicated with the $ character, a single element in an array is also indicated with a $ character. For example, $fish[2] refers to the third element in the @fish array. This tends to throw some people off, but is completely consistent.

Hashes

Hashes are indicated with the % character, as in %employee. A *hash*, which used to go by the cumbersome name *associative arrays*, is a list of name, value pairs. Individual elements in the hash are referenced by name, rather than by index. Again, because the values are scalars, the $ character is used for individual elements. For example, $employee{name} gives you one value from the hash. Two rather useful functions for dealing with hashes are *keys* and *values*. The keys function returns an array containing all of the keys of the hash, and values returns an array of the values of the hash. The code in Listing 28.2 displays all of the values in your environment, much like typing the env command.

LISTING 28.2 Displaying the Contents of the *env* Hash

```
foreach $key (keys %ENV)  {
    print "$key = $ENV{$key}\n";
} languages;Perl;variables>
```

Special Variables

Perl has a wide variety of special variables. These usually look like punctuation—such as $_, $!, and $]—and are extremely useful for shorthand code. ($_ is the default variable, $! is the error message returned by the operating system, and $] is the Perl version number.)

$_ is perhaps the most useful of these, and you use that some more within this chapter. $_ is the Perl default variable, which is used when no argument is specified. For example, the following two statements are equal:

```
chomp;

chomp($_);
```

The following loops are equal:

```
for $cow (@cattle) {
        print "$cow says moo.\n";
}

for (@cattle)       {
        print "$_ says moo.\n";
}
```

For a complete listing of these special variables, you should see the `perlvar` document that comes with your Perl distribution, or you can jump online at `http://www.cpan.org/doc/manual/html/pod/perlvar.html`.

Operators

Perl supports a number of operators to perform various operations. There are comparison operators (used, as the name implies, to compare values), compound operators (used to combine operations or multiple comparisons), arithmetic operators (to perform math), and special string constants.

Comparison Operators

The comparison operators used by Perl are similar to those used by C, `awk`, and the UNIX shells. They are the notation used to specify and compare values (including strings). Most frequently, a comparison operator is used within an `if` statement or loop.

Perl has comparison operators for numbers and strings.

Table 28.1 shows the numeric comparison operators and their behavior.

TABLE 28.1 Numeric Comparison Operators in Perl

Operator	*Meaning*
`==`	Is equal to
`<`	Less than
`>`	Greater than
`<=`	Less than or equal to
`>=`	Greater than or equal to
`!=`	Not equal to
`..`	Range of >= first operand to <= second operand
`<=>`	Return `-1` if less than, `0` if equal, and `1` if greater than

Table 28.2 shows the string comparison operators and their behaviors.

TABLE 28.2 String Comparison Operators in Perl

Operator	*Meaning*
`eq`	Is equal to
`lt`	Less than
`gt`	Greater than
`le`	Less than or equal to
`ge`	Greater than or equal to
`ne`	Not equal to
`cmp`	Return `-1` if less than, `0` if equal to, and `1` if greater than
`=~`	Matched by regular expression
`!~`	Not matched by regular expression

Compound Operators

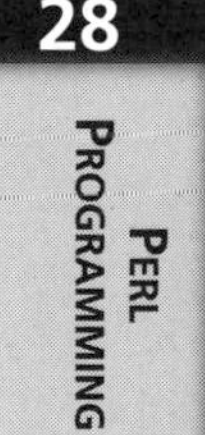

The compound operators used by `Perl` are similar to those used by C, `awk`, and the UNIX shells. They are the notations used to combine other operations into a complex form of logic.

Table 28.3 shows the compound pattern operators and their behavior.

TABLE 28.3 Compound Pattern Operators in Perl

Operator	*Meaning*
`&&`	Logical AND
`||`	Logical OR
`!`	Logical NOT
`()`	Parentheses; used to group compound statements

Arithmetic Operators

Perl supports a wide variety of math operations. Table 28.4 summarizes these operators.

TABLE 28.4 Perl Arithmetic Operators

Operator	*Purpose*
x**y	Raises x to the y power (same as x^y)
x%y	Calculates the remainder of x/y
x+y	Adds x to y
x-y	Subtracts y from x
x*y	Multiplies x times y
x/y	Divides x by y
-y	Negates y (switches the sign of y); also known as the *unary minus*
++y	Increments y by 1 and uses value (prefix increment)
y++	Uses value of y and then increments by 1 (postfix increment)
—y	Decrements y by 1 and uses value (prefix decrement)
y—	Uses value of y and then decrements by 1 (postfix decrement)
x=y	Assigns value of y to x. Perl also supports operator-assignment operators (+=, -=, *=, /=, %=, **=, and others)

You can also use comparison operators (like == or <) and compound pattern operators (&&, ¦¦, and !) in arithmetic statements. They evaluate to the value 0 for false and 1 for true.

Other Operators

Perl supports a number of operators that do not fit any of the prior categories. Table 28.5 summarizes these operators.

TABLE 28.5 Other Perl Operators

Operator	*Purpose*
~x	Bitwise not (changes 0 bits to 1 and 1 bits to 0).
x & y	Bitwise and.
x ¦ y	Bitwise or.
x ^ y	Bitwise exclusive or (XOR).

Operator	Purpose
`x << y`	Bitwise shift left (shift x by y bits).
`x >> y`	Bitwise shift right (shift x by y bits).
`x . y`	Concatenate y onto x.
`a x b`	Repeat string a for b number of times.
`x , y`	Comma operator—evaluate x and then y.
`x ? y : z`	Conditional expression—if x is true, then y is evaluated, otherwise z is evaluated. Provides the capability of an `if` statement anywhere you want (in the middle of a `print`, for instance).

Except for the comma operator and conditional expression, these operators can also be used with the assignment operator (similar to the way addition (+) can be combined with assignment (=) giving `+=`).

Special String Constants

`Perl` supports string constants that have special meaning or cannot be entered from the keyboard.

Table 28.6 shows most of the constants supported by Perl.

TABLE 28.6 Perl Special String Constants

Expression	Meaning
`\\`	The means of including a backslash
`\a`	The alert or bell character
`\b`	Backspace
`\cC`	Control character (like holding the Ctrl key down and pressing the C character)
`\e`	Escape
`\f`	Formfeed
`\n`	Newline
`\r`	Carriage return
`\t`	Tab
`\v`	Vertical tab
`\xNN`	Indicates that NN is a hexadecimal number
`\0NNN`	Indicates that NNN is an octal (base 8) number

Conditional Statements: `if/else` and `unless`

Perl offers two conditional statements, `if` and `unless`, which function opposite one another. `if` allows you to execute a block of code only if certain conditions are met, and so control the flow of logic through your program. Conversely, `unless` performs the statements when certain conditions are not met.

if

The syntax of the Perl `if/else` structure is as follows:

```
if (condition) {
     statement or block of code
     }
elsif (condition) {
     statement or block of code
     }
else {
     statement( or block of code
     }
```

`condition` can be a statement that returns a true or false value.

> **Note**
>
> Truth is defined in Perl in a way that might be unfamiliar to you, so be careful. Everything in Perl is true except `0` (the digit zero), `"0"` (the string containing the number `0`), `""` (the empty string), and an undefined value. Note that even the string `"00"` is a true value because it is not one of those four cases.

The statement or block of code is executed if the test condition returns a true value.

For example, Listing 28.3 uses the `if/else` structure.

LISTING 28.3 *`if/elsif/else`*

```
if ($favorite eq "chocolate") {
      print "I like chocolate too.\n";
} elsif ($favorite eq "spinach") {
      print "Oh, I don't like spinach.\n";
} else {
    print "Your favorite food is $favorite.\n";
}
```

Note

Larry is a linguist, and so Perl contains a lot of idiomatic ways of saying things that correspond with spoken English. The `if` statement is one of the good examples. For example, you can say the following:

```
if ($name eq "Rich") {
  print "Hello, Rich!\n";
}
```

Alternatively, you can write it as you would more likely say it:

```
print "Hello Rich!\n" if $name eq "Rich";
```

Larry designed Perl as a natural language. In this respect, it is rather different from most other programming languages. The traditional computer science way of doing things is to have a minimal set of keywords, from which all other concepts are built. Perl, on the other hand, provides you with more than one way to say the same thing (TIMTOWTDI) like a human language would.

Also like human language, Perl evolved as it was used. If people saw a need for a particular function or new syntax, Larry threw it in the next version. If nobody used a particular feature, or everyone hated a particular construct, it was thrown out. As Larry put it, "I picked the feature set of Perl because I thought they were cool features. I left the other ones behind because I thought they sucked."

unless

`unless` works justlike `if`, only backward. `unless` performs a statement or block if a condition is false.

```
unless ($name eq "Rich")        {
        print "Go away, you're not allowed in here!\n";
}
```

Note

You can restate the preceding example in more natural language, like you did in the `if` example.

```
print "Go away!\n" unless $name eq "Rich";
```

Although it is not a rule, you should try to put the more important part of the statement (think of it as a sentence) on the left, so that it is easier to read.

Looping

A *loop* is a way to do something multiple times. A very simple example is a countdown timer that performs a task (waiting for one second) 300 times before telling you that your egg is done boiling.

Looping constructs can either perform a block of code as long as certain conditions apply, or while they step through a list of values, perhaps using that list as arguments.

Perl has four looping constructs: `for`, `foreach`, `while`, and `until`.

for

The `for` construct performs a *statement* (block of code) for a set of conditions defined as follows:

```
for (start condition; end condition; increment function) {
     statement(s)
}
```

The start condition is set at the beginning of the loop. Each time the loop is executed, the increment function is performed until the end condition is achieved. This looks much like the traditional `for/next` loop. The following code is an example of a `for` loop:

```
for ($i=1; $i<=10; $i++) {
      print "$i\n"
}
```

foreach

The `foreach` construct performs a statement block for each element in a list or array:

```
foreach $name (@names) {
     print "$name\n"
}
```

The loop variable (`$name` in the example) is not merely set to the value of the array elements; it is aliased to that element. This means that if you modify the loop variable, you are actually modifying the array.

If no loop array is specified, as in the following example, the Perl default variable `$_` is used:

```
for (@names)        {
        print "$_ was here\n";
}
```

This syntax can be very convenient, but can also lead to unreadable code. Give a thought to the poor person who will be maintaining your code. It will probably be you.

Note

foreach is frequently abbreviated as for.

while

while performs a block of statements as long as a particular condition is true:

```
while ($x<10) {
     print "$x\n";
     $x++;
}
```

Remember that the condition can be anything that returns a true or false value. For example, it could be a function call:

```
while ( InvalidPassword($user, $password) )        {
        print "You've entered an invalid password. Please try again.\n";
        $password = GetPassword;
}
```

until

until is the exact opposite of the while statement. It performs a block of statements as long as a particular condition is false—or, rather, until it becomes true:

```
until (ValidPassword($user, $password))  {
        print "You've entered an invalid password. Please try again.\n";
        $password = GetPassword;
}
```

last and next

You can force Perl to end a loop early by using the last statement. last is similar to the C break command—the loop is exited. If you decide you need to skip the remaining contents of a loop without ending the loop itself, you can use next, which is similar to the C continue command. Unfortunately, these do not work with do_..._while.

do ... while and do ... until

The while and until loops evaluate the conditional first. The behavior is changed by applying a do block before the conditional. With the do block, the condition is evaluated last, which results in the contents of the block always executing at least once (even if the condition is false). This is similar to the C language `do ... while (conditional)` statement.

Regular Expressions

Perl's greatest strength is in text and file manipulation, which are accomplished by using the regular expression (regex) library. Regexes allow complicated pattern matching and replacement to be done efficiently and easily.

For example, the following line of code replaces every occurrence of the string `bob` or the string `mary` with `fred` in a line of text:

```
$string =~ s/bob¦mary/fred/gi;
```

Without going into too many of the details, Table 28.7 explains what the preceding line says.

TABLE 28.7 Explanation of *$string =~ s/bob¦mary/fred/gi;*

Element	*Explanation*
`$string =~`	Performs this pattern match on the text found in the variable called `$string`.
`s`	Substitute.
`/`	Begins the text to be matched.
`bob¦mary`	Matches the text `bob` or `mary`. You should remember that it is looking for the text `mary`, not the word `mary`; that is, it will also match the text `mary` in the word `maryland`.
`/`	Ends text to be matched; begins text to replace it.
`fred`	Replaces anything that was matched with the text `fred`.
`/`	Ends replace text.
`g`	Does this substitution globally; that is, replaces the match text wherever in the string you match it (and any number of times).
`i`	The search text is non–case-sensitive. It matches `bob`, `Bob`, or `bOB`.
`;`	Indicates the end of the line of code.

If you are interested in the details, you can get more information using the regex (5) section of the manual.

Although replacing one string with another might seem a rather trivial task, the code required to do the same thing in another language (for example, C) is rather daunting.

Access to the Shell

Perl is useful for administrative functions because, for one thing, it has access to the shell. This means Perl can perform for you any process you might ordinarily perform by typing commands to the shell. You do this with the `` syntax. For example, the following code in Listing 28.4 prints a directory listing:

LISTING 28.4 Using Backticks to Access the Shell

```
$curr_dir = `pwd`;
@listing = `ls -la`;
print "Listing for $curr_dir\n";
foreach $file (@listing) {
     print "$file";
}
```

Note

The `` notation uses the backtick found above the Tab key (on most keyboards), not the single quotation mark.

You can also use the `Shell` module to access the shell. `Shell` is one of the standard modules that comes with Perl. It gives an even more transparent access to the shell. Look at the following code for an example:

```
use Shell qw(cp);
cp ("/home/httpd/logs/access.log", "/tmp/httpd.log");
```

It almost looks like it is importing the command-line functions directly into Perl, and while that is not really happening, you can pretend that it is and use it accordingly.

A third method of accessing the shell is via the `system` function call:

```
$rc = 0xffff & system('cp /home/httpd/logs/access.log /tmp/httpd.log');
if ($rc == 0) {
        print "system cp succeeded \n";
}
else {
        print "system cp failed $rc";
}
```

The call can also be used with the `or die` clause:

```
system('cp /home/httpd/logs/access.log /tmp/httpd.log') == 0
        or die "system cp failed: $?"
```

However, you cannot capture the output of a command executed through the `system` function.

Access to the command line is fairly common in shell scripting languages, but is less common in higher-level programming languages.

Switches

Perl has a variety of command-line options (*switches*) that subtly change Perl's behavior. These switches can appear on the command line, or can be placed on the `#!` line at the beginning of the Perl program.

The following are all the available command-line switches.

> **Note**
>
> Several command-line switches can be stacked together, so that `-pie` is the same as `-p -i -e`.

`-0[digits]`

Specifies the input record separator (`$/`) as an octal number. `$/` is usually a newline, so you get one line per record. For example, if you read a file into an array, this gives you one line per array element. The value `00` is a special case and causes Perl to read in your file one paragraph per record.

`-a`

Turns on Autosplit mode when used with a `-n` or `-p`. That means that each line of input is automatically split into the `@F` array.

`-c`

Tells Perl to perform syntax checking on the specified Perl program without executing it. This is invaluable, and the error messages given are informative, readable, and tell you where to begin looking for the problem, which is a rarity in error messages.

`-d`

Runs the script under the Perl debugger. See `perldebug` for more information.

> **Note**
>
> The Perl documentation is referred to a few times in this section. `perldebug`, `perlrun`, `perlmod`, and `perlmodlib`, for example, are documents from the Perl documentation. To see these documents, just type **`perldoc perlmodlib`** at the shell prompt. You can also see all of the Perl documents online at `http://www.cpan.org/doc/index.html` or on any CPAN site. (CPAN is the Comprehensive Perl Archive Network. See "Modules and CPAN" later in this chapter.)
>
> Perl documentation is written in POD (Plain Old Documentation) format and can be converted into any other format, such as tex, ASCII, or HTML, with the `pod2*` tools that ship with Perl. For example, to produce HTML documentation on the `Fubar` module, you would type **`pod2html Fubar.pm > Fubar.html`**.

`-d:foo`

Runs the script under the control of a debugging or tracing module installed as `Devel::foo`. For example, `-d:Dprof` executes the script using the `Devel::DProf` profiler. See `perldebug` for additional information on the Perl debugger.

`-D`*`flags`*

Sets debugging flags. See `perlrun` for more details.

`-e commandline`

Indicates that what follows is Perl code. This allows you to enter Perl code directly on the command line, rather than running code contained in a file.

```
perl -e 'print join " ", keys %ENV;'
```

`-Fpattern`

Specifies the pattern to split on if `-a` is also in effect. This is `" "` by default, and `-F` allows you to set it to whatever works for you, such as `','` or `';'`. The pattern may be surrounded by `//`, `""`, or `''`.

`-h`

Typing `perl -h` lists all available command-line switches.

`-i[extension]`

This indicates that files are to be edited in place. If the extension is provided, the original is backed up with that extension. Otherwise, the original file is overwritten.

`-Idirectory`

Directories specified by `-I` are prepended to the search path for modules (`@INC`).

-l[octnum]

Enables automatic line-ending processing, which means that end-of-line characters are automatically removed from input and put back on to output. If the optional octal number is unspecified, this is just the newline character.

-m[-]module or **-M[-]module**

Loads the specified module before running your script. There is a subtle difference between `m` and `M`. See `perlrun` for more details.

-n

Causes Perl to loop around your script for each file provided to the command line. Does not print the output. The following example, from `perlrun`, deletes all files older than a week:

```
find . -mtime +7 -print ¦ perl -nle 'unlink;'
```

-p

This is just like `-n`, except that that each line is printed.

-P

This causes your script to be run through the C preprocessor before compilation by Perl.

-s

This performs some command-line switch parsing and puts the switch into the corresponding variable in the Perl script. For example, the following script prints `'1'` if run with the `-fubar` switch. Your Perl code might look like:

```
#!/usr/bin/perl -s
print $fubar;
```

When you execute it, you would enter

```
myperl -fubar
```

-S

This searches for the script using the `PATH` environment variable.

-T

This enables *taint* checking. In this mode, Perl assumes that all user input is tainted, or insecure, until the programmer tells it otherwise. This helps protect you from people trying to exploit security holes in your code and is especially important when writing CGI programs.

-u

This tells Perl to dump core after compiling this script. You could presumably, with much time and patience, use this to create an executable file.

-U

This allows you to do unsafe things in your Perl program, such as unlinking directories while running as `superuser`.

-v

This prints the version and patchlevel of your Perl executable.

```
% perl -v
This is perl, version 5.005_03 built for i586-linux

Copyright 1987-1999, Larry Wall

Perl may be copied only under the terms of either the
Artistic License or the GNU General Public License,
which may be found in the Perl 5.0 source kit.

Complete documentation for Perl, including FAQ lists,
should be found on this system using `man perl' or
`perldoc perl'.  If you have access to the Internet,
point your browser at http://www.perl.com/, the Perl
Home Page.
```

-V

This prints a summary of the major Perl configuration values and the current value of `@INC`.

`-V:names`

This parameter displays the value of the names configuration variable.

-w

This tells Perl to display warning messages about potential problems in the program, such as variables used only once (might be a typo), using = instead of == in a comparison, and the like. This is often used in conjunction with the `-c` flag to do a thorough program check.

```
perl -cw finalassignment.pl
```

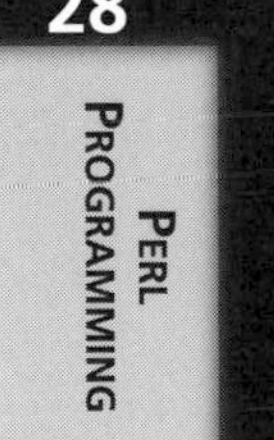

-x directory

This tells Perl that the script is embedded in something larger, such as an email message. Perl throws away everything before a line starting with `#!`, containing the string `'perl'`, and everything after `__END__`. If a directory is specified, Perl changes to the directory before executing the script.

Modules and CPAN

A great strength of the Perl community (and the Linux community) is the fact that it is an Open Source community. Perl expresses this via CPAN (Comprehensive Perl Archive Network), which is a network of mirrors of a repository of code—Perl code, to be more precise.

Most of CPAN is made up of *modules*, which are reusable chunks of code that do useful things, so that you do not have to reinvent the wheel every time you try to build a bicycle.

There are thousands of Perl modules, which do everything from send email to maintain your Cisco router access lists to tell you whether a name is masculine or feminine to printing the time in some fancy format. There are modules for CGI programming and modules that access the socket libraries and modules that post to Usenet for you. If you can think of doing something, chances are pretty good that there is a module to help you. If there is no module that helps, you are encouraged to write one and share it with the rest of the community.

At `http://www.perl.com/CPAN/` you will find the CPAN Multiplex Dispatcher, which will attempt to direct you to the CPAN site closest to you.

Perl comes with a set of standard modules installed. Those modules contain much of the function that you will want. You can use the CPAN module (which is one of the standard modules) to download and install other modules onto your system. Typing the following command will put you into an interactive shell that gives you access to CPAN. You can type **`help`** at the prompt to get more information on how to use the CPAN program.

```
perl -MCPAN -e shell
```

Once you have installed a module from CPAN (or written one of your own), you can load that module into memory where you can use it with the `use` function.

```
use Time::CTime;
```

use looks in the directories listed in the variable @INC for the module. In this example, use looks for a directory called Time, which contains a file called CTime.pm, which in turn is assumed to contain a package called Time::CTime. The distribution of each module should contain documentation on using that module.

For a list of all the standard Perl modules (those that come with Perl when you install it), see perlmodlib in the Perl documentation. You can read this document by typing **perldoc perlmodlib** at the command prompt.

Code Examples

Over the last few years a lot of people have picked up the notion that Perl is a CGI language, as though it is not good for anything else. Nothing could be further from the truth. You can use Perl in every aspect of your system administration and as a building block in whatever applications you are planning to run on your shiny new Linux system.

The following sections contain a few examples of things you might want to do with Perl. Perl is versatile enough that you can make it do about anything.

Sending Mail

There are several ways to get Perl to send email. One method that you see frequently is opening a pipe to sendmail and sending data to it (shown in Listing 28.5). Another method is using the Mail::Sendmail module, which uses socket connections directly to send mail (shown in Listing 28.6). The latter method is faster because it does not have to launch an external process.

LISTING 28.5 Sending Mail Using Sendmail

```
open (MAIL, "| /usr/sbin/sendmail -t"); # Use -t to protect from users
print MAIL <<EndMail;
To: dpitts\@mk.net
From: rbowen\@mk.net
Subject: Email notification

David,
 Sending email from Perl is easy!
Rich
.
EndMail
close MAIL;
```

Note

Note that the `@` sign in the email addresses needs to be escaped so that Perl does not try to evaluate an array of that name.

The syntax used to print the mail message is called a *here document*. The syntax is as follows:

```
print <<EndText;
.....
EndText
```

The `EndText` value must be identical at the beginning and at the end of the block, including any whitespace.

LISTING 28.6 Sending Mail Using the *`Mail::Sendmail`* Module

```
use Mail::Sendmail;
%mail = ('To' => 'dpitts@mk.net',
        'From' => 'rbowen@mk.net'
        'Subject' => 'Email notification',
        'Message' => 'Sending email from Perl is easy!',
        );
sendmail(%mail);
```

Perl ignores the comma after the last element in the hash. It is convenient to leave it there; if you want to add items to the hash, you do not need to add the comma. This is purely a style decision.

Note also that the `@` sign did not need to be escaped within single quotation marks (`''`). Perl does not *interpolate* (evaluate variables) within single quotation marks, but does within double quotation marks and here documents.

Purging Logs

Many programs maintain some variety of logs. Often, much of the information in the logs is redundant or just useless. The program shown in Listing 28.7 removes all lines from a file that contain a particular word or phrase, so that lines you know are not important can be purged. For example, one might want to remove all of the lines in the Apache error log that originate with your test client machine because you know that these error messages were produced during testing.

LISTING 28.7 Purging Log Files

```
#!/usr/bin/perl
#       Be careful using this program!!
#       This will remove all lines that contain a given word
#       Usage:  remove <word> <file>
$word=@ARGV[0];
$file=@ARGV[1];
if ($file)  {
     # Open file for reading
     open (FILE, "$file") or die "Could not open file: $!";      @lines=<FILE>;
     close FILE;
     # Open file for writing
     open (FILE, ">$file") or die "Could not open file for writing: $!";
     for (@lines)  {
          print FILE unless /$word/;
     } # End for
     close FILE;
}  else  {
     print "Usage:  remove <word> <file>\n";
}  #  End if...else
```


The code uses a few idiomatic Perl expressions to keep the code brief. It reads the file into an array using the `<FILE>` notation; it then writes the lines back out to the file unless they match the pattern given on the command line.

The `die` function kills program operation and displays an error message if the open statements fail. `$!` in the error message, as mentioned in the section on special variables, is the error message returned by the operating system. It will likely be something like `'file not found'` or `'permission denied'`.

Posting to Usenet

If some portion of your job requires periodic postings to Usenet—a FAQ listing, for example—the following Perl program can automate the process for you. In the sample code, the posted text is read in from a text file, but your input can come from anywhere.

The program shown in Listing 28.8 uses the `Net::NNTP` module, which is a standard part of the Perl distribution. You can find more documentation on the `Net::NNTP` module by typing **`'perldoc Net::NNTP'`** at the command line.

LISTING 28.8 Posting an Article to Usenet

```
#!/usr/bin/perl
open (POST, "post.file");
@post = <POST>;
close POST;
use Net::NNTP;
$NNTPhost = 'news';
$nntp = Net::NNTP->new($NNTPhost)
       or die "Cannot contact $NNTPhost: $!";
# $nntp->debug(1);
$nntp->post()
   or die "Could not post article: $!";
$nntp->datasend("Newsgroups: news.announce\n");
$nntp->datasend("Subject: FAQ - Frequently Asked Questions\n");
$nntp->datasend("From: ADMIN <root\@rcbowen.com>\n");
$nntp->datasend("\n\n");
for (@post)     {
     $nntp->datasend($_);
} #  End for
$nntp->quit;
```

One-Liners

Perl has the rather undeserved reputation of being unreadable. The fact is that you can write unreadable code in any language. Perl allows for more than one way to do something, and this leads rather naturally to people trying to find the most arcane way to do things.

One medium in which Perl excels is the one-liner. Folks go to great lengths to reduce tasks to one line of Perl code. Some examples of one-liners that might make your life easier follow.

Tip

Just because you can do something is not a particularly good reason for doing it. I will frequently write somewhat more lengthy pieces of code for something that could be done in just one line, just for the sake of readability. It is very irritating to go back to a piece of code in which I reduced something to one line for efficiency, or just because I could, and have to spend 30 minutes trying to figure out what it does.

The Schwartzian Transform

Named for Randal Schwartz, the *Schwartzian transform* is a way of sorting an array by something that is not obvious. The sort function sorts arrays alphabetically; that's pretty obvious. What if you want to sort an array of strings alphabetically by the third word? Perhaps you want something more useful, such as sorting a list of files by file size? The Schwartzian transform creates a new list that contains the information that you want to sort by, referencing the first list. You then sort the new list and use it to figure out the order that the first list should be in. Here's a simple example that sorts a list of strings by length:

```
@sorted_by_length =
  map { $_ => [0] }               # Extract original list
  sort { $a=>[1] <=> $b=>[1] } # Sort by the transformed value
  map { [$_, length($_)] }      # Map to a list of element lengths
  @list;
```

Because each operator acts on the thing immediately to the right of it, it helps to read this from right to left (or bottom to top, the way it is written here).

The first thing that acts on the list is the map operator. It transforms the list into a hash, in which the keys are the list elements and the values are the lengths of each element. This is where you put in your code that does the transformation by which you want to sort.

The next operator is the sort function, which sorts the list by the values.

Finally, the hash is transformed back into an array by extracting its keys. The array is now in the desired order.

Command-Line Processing

Perl is great at parsing the output of various programs. This is a task for which a lot of people use tools such as awk and sed. Perl gives you a larger vocabulary for performing these tasks. The following example is very simple, but illustrates how you might use Perl to chop up some output and do something with it. In the example, Perl is used to list only those files that are larger than 10KB.

```
ls -la ¦ perl -nae 'print "$F[8] is $F[4]\n" if $F[4] > 10000;'
```

The -n switch indicates that I want the Perl code run for each line of the output. The -a switch automatically splits the output into the @F array. The -e switch indicates that the Perl code is going to follow on the command line. (See "Switches" earlier in this chapter.)

Perl-Related Tools

There are a number of tools that are related to Perl or are included with the Perl distribution. The most common of these follow:

- `perldoc`—Displays Perl documentation.
- `pod2html`—Converts Perl documentation to HTML format.
- `pod2man`—Converts Perl documentation to man (`nroff`/`troff`) format.
- `a2p`—Converts `awk` scripts to Perl.
- `s2p` —Converts `sed` commands to Perl.

For More Information

The first place to look is in the Perl documentation and Linux man pages.

Perl, all of its documentation, and millions of lines of Perl programs are all available on the Internet for free. There are also a number of Usenet newsgroups devoted to Perl, shelves of books, and a quarterly journal.

Books

While your local bookstore may have dozens of titles on Perl, the following are some of the more highly recommended of these. You might also look at the *Camel Critiques* (Tom Christiansen; `http://language.perl.com/critiques/index.html`) for reviews of other Perl books that are available.

- *Programming Perl*, Second Edition, by Larry Wall, Randall Schwartz, and Tom Christiansen. O'Reilly & Associates.
- *Effective Perl Programming: Writing Better Programs with Perl*, by Joseph Hall. Addison-Wesley Publishing Company.
- *Mastering Regular Expressions*, by Jeffrey Friedl. O'Reilly & Associates.

Usenet

Check out the following on Usenet:

- `comp.lang.perl.misc`

  Discusses various aspects of the Perl programming language. Make sure your questions are Perl-specific, not generic CGI programming questions. The regulars tend to flame folks who do not know the difference.

- `comp.infosystems.www.authoring.cgi`

  Discusses authoring of CGI programs, so much of the discussion is Perl-specific. Make sure your questions are related to CGI programming, not just Perl. The regulars are very particular about staying on-topic.

WWW

Check these sites on the World Wide Web:

- `http://www.perl.com/`

  The Perl language home page is maintained by Tom Christiansen. This is the place to find all sorts of information about Perl, from its history and culture to helpful tips. This is also the place to download the Perl interpreter for your system.

- `http://www.perl.com/CPAN/`

  This is part of the site just mentioned, but it merits its own mention. CPAN (Comprehensive Perl Archive Network) is the place for you to find modules and programs in Perl. If you end up writing something in Perl that you think is particularly useful, you can make it available to the Perl community here.

- `http://www.perlmonth.com/`

  A monthly e-zine dedicated to Perl. This is a fairly new venture, but already has an impressive line-up of contributors.

- `http://www.hwg.org/`

  The HTML Writers Guild is a non-profit organization dedicated to assisting Web developers. One of their services is a plethora of mailing lists. The hwg-servers mailing list and the hwg-languages mailing list are great places for asking Perl-related questions.

- `http://www.pm.org/`

  The Perl Mongers are local Perl users groups. There might be one in your area.

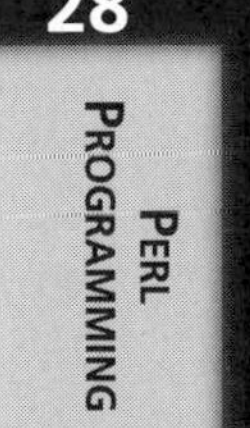

Other

There is another valuable resource not falling into any of the preceding categories:

- *The Perl Journal* (`http://www.tpj.com/`)

  The Perl Journal is a quarterly publication devoted to the Perl programming language. Orchestrated by Jon Orwant, *TPJ* is always full of excellent, amusing, and informative articles, and is an invaluable resource to the new, and experienced, Perl programmer.

Summary

Perl, in the words of its creator, "combines the best elements of C, `sed`, `awk`, and `sh`," and is also a great language for folks who have no experience with these languages.

Perl's powerful regex (regular expression) library and ease of use have made it one of the preferred scripting languages in use today, particularly in the realm of CGI programming. Many people even think of Perl as exclusively a CGI language, when in fact, it is capable of so much more.

Perl is often referred to as a glue language for its capability to stick together a variety of disparate applications into something coherent. Perl can make your job as a system administrator easier by taking some of the work off your hands and by making your various applications work together.

CHAPTER 29

gawk Programming

IN THIS CHAPTER

gawk, or GNU awk, is one of the newer versions of the awk programming language created for UNIX by Alfred V. Aho, Peter J. Weinberger, and Brian W. Kernighan in 1977. The name awk comes from the initials of the creators' last names. Kernighan was also involved with the creation of the C programming language and UNIX; Aho and Weinberger were involved with the development of UNIX. Because of their backgrounds, you will see many similarities between awk and C.

Several versions of awk exist: the original awk, nawk, POSIX awk, and—of course—gawk. nawk was created in 1985 and is the version described in *The awk Programming Language*. POSIX awk is defined in the *IEEE Standard for Information Technology, Portable Operating System Interface, Part 2: Shell and Utilities Volume 2*, ANSI-approved, April 5, 1993. (IEEE is the Institute of Electrical and Electronics Engineers, Inc.) GNU awk is based on POSIX awk.

Linux users should find the awk command, under both the /bin and /usr/bin directories, is actually a symbolic link to the /bin/gawk program. In addition to a short manual page for (g)awk included under the /usr/man/man1 directory, a wealth of information about (g)awk programming can be found under the /usr/doc/gawk directory. The info gawk command (or C-h i gawk in emacs) are other ways to get more information.

Tip

The Caldera distribution includes the new awk version (nawk) as mawk. The Red Hat distribution does **not** include nawk or mawk.

The awk language (in all of its versions) is a pattern-matching and processing language with a lot of power. It will search a file (or multiple files) for records that match a specified pattern. A specified action is performed when a match is found. As a programmer, you do not have to worry about opening, looping through the file reading each record, handling end-of-file, or closing the file when done. These details are handled automatically for you.

Creating short awk programs is easy because of this functionality—many of the details are handled by the language automatically. Its many functions and built-in features handle many of the tasks of processing files.

Applications of awk

You'll find many possible uses for awk, including extracting data from a file, counting occurrences within a file, and creating reports.

The basic syntax of the awk language matches the C programming language; if you already know C, you know most of awk. In many ways, awk is an easier version of C because of the way it dynamically handles strings and arrays. If you do not know C yet, learning awk will make learning C a little easier.

awk is also very useful for rapid prototyping or trying out an idea that will be implemented in another language, such as C. Instead of having to worry about some of the minute details, you can let the built-in automation take care of them, and you can worry about the basic functionality.

Tip

awk works with text files, not binary. Because binary data can contain values that look like the newline character —or not have any values at all—awk gets confused. If you need to process binary files, look into Perl or use a traditional programming language such as C.

Features of the awk Language

Like the UNIX environment, awk is flexible, contains predefined variables, automates many of the programming tasks, provides the conventional variables, supports the C-formatted output, and is easy to use. awk lets you combine the best of shell scripts and C programming.

Because there are usually many ways to perform the same task within awk, programmers get to decide which method is best suited to their applications. Many of the common programming tasks are automatically performed with awk's built-in variables and functions. awk automatically reads each record, splits it into fields, and performs type conversions whenever needed. The way a variable is used determines its type—you have no need (or method) to declare variables of any type.

Of course, the "normal" C programming constructs such as `if-else`, `do-while`, `for`, and `while` are supported. awk supports C's `printf()` for formatted output and also has a `print` command for simpler output. awk does not support the C `switch/case` construct.

awk Fundamentals

Unlike some of the other UNIX tools (shell, grep, and so on), awk requires a program (known as an *awk script*). This program can be as simple as one line or as complex as several thousand lines. (I once developed an awk program that summarizes data at several levels with multiple control breaks; it is just short of 1,000 lines.)

The awk program can be entered a number of ways—on the command line or in a program file. awk can accept input from a file, piped in from another program, or even directly from the keyboard. Output normally goes to the standard output device, but that can be redirected to a file or piped into another program. Output can also be sent directly to a file instead of standard output.

Using awk from the Command Line

The simplest way to use awk is to code the program on the command line, accept input from the standard input device, and send output to the standard output device (screen). Listing 29.1 shows this in its simplest form; it prints the number of fields, or words, in the input record or individual line, along with the record itself, for the text from file.txt.

LISTING 29.1 Simplest Use of *awk*

```
$ cat file.txt ¦ gawk '{print NF ": " $0}'
6: Now is the time for all
7: Good Americans to come to the Aid
3: of Their Country.
16: Ask not what you can do for awk, but rather what awk can do for you.
$ _
```

Note

The entire awk script is contained within single quotation marks (') to prevent the shell from interpreting its contents. The single quotation marks are a requirement of the operating system or shell, not the awk language.

NF is a predefined variable set to the number of fields on each record. $0 is that record. The individual fields can be referenced as $1, $2, and so on.

You can think of each line in a file as being a record and each word in that line as being a field.

You can also store your awk script in a file and specify that filename on the command line by using the -f flag. If you do that, you don't have to contain the program within single quotation marks.

Note

gawk and other versions of awk that meet the POSIX standard support the specification of multiple programs through the use of multiple -f options. This enables you to execute multiple awk programs on the same input. I tend to avoid this just because it gets a bit confusing.

You can also use the normal UNIX shell redirection, as in the following first line of code, or just specify the filename on the command line to accept the input from a file instead of the keyboard, as in the second line of code:

```
$ gawk '{print NF ": " $0}' < inputs
```

```
$ gawk '{print NF ": " $0}' inputs
```

Multiple files can be specified by just listing them on the command line:

```
$ gawk '{print NF ": " $0}' input1 input2 input3
```

Output can be redirected through the normal UNIX shell facilities to send it to a file, as in the following first line of code or pipe it into another program, as done in the second line of code:

```
$ gawk '{print NF ": " $0}' inputs > outputs
```

```
$ gawk '{print NF ": " $0}' inputs | more
```

Of course, both input and output can be redirected at the same time.

Note

If you omit the input file name, awk looks to stdin, which is the keyboard by default. Of course, you can always redirect stdin to get input from a file.

One of the ways I use awk most commonly is to process the output of another command by piping its output into awk. For example, if I wanted to create a custom listing of files containing only the filenames and then the permissions, I would execute a command like this:

```
$ ls -l ¦ gawk '{print $NF, " ", $1}'
```

$NF is the last field (which is the filename—I didn't want to count the fields to figure out its number). $1 is the first field. The output of ls -l is piped into awk, which processes it for me.

If I put the awk script into a file (named lser.awk) and redirected the output to the printer, I would have a command that looks like this:

```
$ ls -l ¦ gawk -f lser.awk ¦ lp
```

I tend to save my awk scripts with the suffix of .awk just to make them obvious when I'm looking through a directory listing. If the program is longer than about 30 characters, I make a point of saving it because there is no such thing as a "one-time only" program, user request, or personal need.

Caution

If you forget the -f option before a program filename, your program will be treated as if it were data.

If you code your awk program on the command line but place it after the name are of your data file, it will also be treated as if it were data.

What you will get are odd results.

See "Commands On-the-Fly" later in this chapter for more examples of using awk scripts to process piped data.

Patterns and Actions

Each awk statement consists of two parts: the pattern and the action. The pattern decides when the action is executed and, of course, the action is what the programmer wants to occur. Without a pattern, the action is always executed (the pattern can be said to "default to true"). Without an action, nothing happens.

Two special patterns (also known as *blocks*) are `BEGIN` and `END`. The `BEGIN` code is executed before the first record is read from the file and is used to initialize variables and set up such things as control breaks. The `END` code is executed after end-of-file is reached and is used for any cleanup required (for example, printing final totals on a report). The other patterns are tested for each record read from the file.

The general program format is to put the `BEGIN` block at the top, then any pattern/action pairs, and finally, the `END` block at the end. This is not a language requirement—it is just the way most people do it (mostly for readability reasons).

`BEGIN` and `END` blocks are optional; if you use them, you should have a maximum of one each. Don't code two `BEGIN` blocks, and don't code two `END` blocks.

Examples with BEGIN/END blocks are shown later in this chapter.

The pattern is specified before the action. It can be a regular expression (contained within a pair of slashes [`/ /`]) that matches part of the input record or an expression that contains comparison operators. It can also be compound or complex patterns that consist of expressions and regular expressions combined or of a range of patterns.

The action is contained within braces (`{ }`) and can consist of one or many statements. If you omit the pattern portion, it defaults to true, which causes the action to be executed for every line in the file. If you omit the action, it defaults to `print $0` (print the entire record).

Regular Expression Patterns

The regular expressions used by `awk` are similar to those used by `grep`, `egrep`, `sed`, and the UNIX editors `ed`, `ex`, and `vi`. They are the notations used to specify and match strings. A regular expression consists of *characters* (such as the letters *A*, *B*, and *c* that match themselves in the input) and metacharacters. *Metacharacters* are characters that have special (meta) meaning; they do not match themselves but perform some special function.

Table 29.1 shows the metacharacters and their behavior.

TABLE 29.1 Regular Expression Metacharacters in *awk*

Metacharacter	*Meaning*
`\`	Escape sequence (next character has special meaning, `\n` is the newline character and `\t` is the tab). Any escaped metacharacter will match to that character (as if it were not a metacharacter).
`^`	Starts match at beginning of string.
`$`	Matches at end of string.
`/^$/`	Matches a blank line.
`.`	Matches any single character.
`[ABC]`	Matches any one of `A`, `B`, or `C`.
`[A-Ca-c]`	Matches any one of `A`, `B`, `C`, `a`, `b`, or `c` (ranges).
`[^ABC]`	Matches any character other than `A`, `B`, and `C`.
`Desk¦Chair`	Matches any one of `Desk` or `Chair`.
`[ABC][DEF]`	Concatenation. Matches any one of `A`, `B`, or `C` that is followed by any one of `D`, `E`, or `F`.
`*`	`[ABC]*`—Matches zero or more occurrences of `A`, `B`, or `C`.
`+`	`[ABC]+`—Matches one or more occurrences of `A`, `B`, or `C`.
`?`	`[ABC]?`—Matches zero or one occurrences of `A`, `B`, or `C`.
`()`	Combines regular expressions. For example, `(Blue¦Black)berry` matches to `Blueberry` or `Blackberry`.

All of these can be combined to form complex search strings. Typical search strings can be used to search for specific strings (`Report Date`) or strings in different formats (`may`, `MAY`, `May`) or as groups of characters (any combination of upper- and lowercase characters that spell out the month of May). These look like the following:

```
/Report Date/  { print "do something" }

/(may)¦(MAY)¦(May)/ { print "do something else" }

/[Mm]„[Yy]/ { print "do something completely different" }
```

Comparison Operators and Patterns

The comparison operators used by `awk` are similar to those used by C and the UNIX shells. They are the notation used to specify and compare values (including strings). A regular expression alone will match to any portion of the input record. By combining a comparison with a regular expression, you can test specific fields.

Table 29.2 shows the comparison operators and their behavior.

TABLE 29.2 Comparison Operators in *awk*

Operator	*Meaning*
`==`	Equal to
`<`	Less than
`>`	Greater than
`<=`	Less than or equal to
`>=`	Greater than or equal to
`!=`	Not equal to
`~`	Matched by regular expression
`!~`	Not matched by regular expression

This enables you to perform specific comparisons on fields instead of the entire record. Remember that you can also perform comparisons on the entire record by using `$0` instead of a specific field.

Typical search strings can be used to search for a name in the first field (`Bob`) and compare specific fields with regular expressions:

```
$1 == "Bob"    { print "Bob stuff" }

$2 ~ /(may)¦(MAY)¦(May)/ { print "May stuff" }

$3 !~ /[Mm]„[Yy]/ { print "other May stuff" }
```

Compound Pattern Operators

The compound pattern operators used by `awk` are similar to those used by C and the UNIX shells. They are the notations used to combine other patterns (expressions or regular expressions) into a complex form of logic.

Table 29.3 shows the compound pattern operators and their behavior.

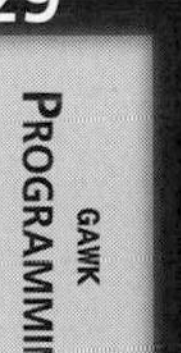

TABLE 29.3 Compound Pattern Operators in *awk*

Operator	*Meaning*
`&&`	Logical AND
`¦¦`	Logical OR
`!`	Logical NOT
`()`	Parentheses; used to group compound statements

If I wanted to execute some action (print a special message, for instance) if the first field contained the value "Bob" and the fourth field contained the value "Street", I could use a compound pattern that looks like this:

```
$1 == "Bob" && $4 == "Street" {print"some message"}
```

Range Pattern Operators

The range pattern is slightly more complex than the other types—it is set true when the first pattern is matched and remains true until the second pattern becomes true. The catch is that the file needs to be sorted on the fields that the range pattern matches; otherwise, it might be set true prematurely or end early.

The individual patterns in a range pattern are separated by a comma (,). If you have 26 files in your directory with the names A to Z, you can show a range of the files as shown in Listing 29.2.

LISTING 29.2 Range Pattern Example

```
$ ls ¦ gawk '$1 == "B", $1 == "D"'
B
C
D
$ ls ¦ gawk '$1 == "B", $1 <= "D"'
B
$ ls ¦ gawk '$1 == "B", $1 > "D"'
B
C
D
E
$ _
```

The first example is obvious—all of the records between B and D are shown. The other examples are less intuitive, but the key to remember is that the pattern is completed when the second condition is true. The second gawk command only shows the B, because C is less than or equal to D (making the second condition true). The third gawk shows B through E, because E is the first one that is greater than D (making the second condition true).

Handling Input

As awk reads each record, it breaks the record into fields and then searches for matching patterns and the related actions to perform. It assumes that each record occupies a single line (the newline character, by definition, ends a record). Lines that are just blanks or are empty (just the newline) count as records, but with very few fields (usually zero).

You can force awk to read the next record in a file (cease searching for pattern matches) by using the next statement. next is similar to the C continue command—control returns to the outermost loop, which, in awk, is the automatic read of the file. If you decide you need to break out of your program completely, you can use the exit statement, which acts as though the end-of-file was reached and passes control to the END block (if one exists). If exit is in the END block, the program immediately exits.

By default, fields are separated by spaces. It does not matter to awk whether there is one space or many spaces—the next field begins when the first nonspace character is found. You can change the field separator by setting the variable FS to that character. To set your field separator to the colon (:), which is the separator in /etc/passwd, code the following:

```
BEGIN { FS = ":" }
```

The general format of the /etc/passwd file looks something like the following:

```
david:!:207:1017:David B Horvath,CCP:/u/david:/bin/pdksh
```

If you want to list the names of everyone on the system, use the following:

```
$ gawk --field-separator=: '{ print $5 }' /etc/passwd
```

You will then see a list of everyone's name. In this example, I set the field separator variable (FS) from the command line, using the gawk format command-line options (--field-separator=:). I could also use -F :, which is supported by all versions of awk.

The first field is $1, the second is $2, and so on. The entire record is contained in $0. You can get the last field (if you don't want to count) by referencing $NF. NF is the number of fields in a record.

Coding Your Program

The nice thing about awk is that, with a few exceptions, it is free format—like the C language. Blank lines are ignored. Statements can be placed on the same line or split up in any form you like. awk recognizes whitespace, much as C does. The following two lines are essentially the same:

```
$1=="Bob"{print"Bob stuff"}

$1     ==     "Bob"       {      print     "Bob stuff"      }
```

Spaces within quotation marks are significant because they appear in the output or are used in a comparison for matching. The other spaces are not. You can also split up the action, but you have to have the left brace on the same line as the pattern:

```
$1     ==     "Bob"       {
                             print     "Bob stuff"
                          }
```

You can have multiple statements within an action. If you place them on the same line, you need to use semicolons (;) to separate them (so awk can tell when one ends and the next begins). Printing multiple lines looks like the following:

```
$1      ==      "Bob"         {
                                 print     "Bob stuff"; print     "more stuff";
                                 ③print     "last stuff";
                              }
```

You can also put the statements on separate lines. When you do that, you don't need to code the semicolons, and the code looks like the following:

```
$1      ==      "Bob"         {
                                 print     "Bob stuff"
                                 print     "more stuff"
                                 print     "last stuff"
                              }
```

I am in the habit of coding the semicolon after each statement because that is the way it has to be done in C. To awk, the following example is just like the previous. Here you can see the semicolons:

```
$1      ==      "Bob"         {
                                 print     "Bob stuff";
                                 print     "more stuff";
                                 print     "last stuff";
                              }
```

Another thing you should make use of is comments. Anything on a line after the pound sign or octothorpe (#) is ignored by awk. These are notes designed for the programmer to read and aid in the understanding of the program code. In general, the more comments you place in a program, the easier it is to maintain.

Actions

The *actions* of your program are the part that tells awk what to do when a pattern is matched. If there is no pattern, it defaults to true. A pattern without an action defaults to {print $0}.

All actions are enclosed within braces ({ }). The left brace should appear on the same line as the pattern; other than that, there are no restrictions. An action consists of one or many actions.

Variables

Except for simple find-and-print types of programs, you are going to need to save data, which is done through the use of variables. Within awk, the three types of variables are field, predefined, and user-defined. You have already seen examples of the first two—$1 is the field variable that contains the first field in the input record, and FS is the predefined variable that contains the field separator.

User-defined variables are ones you create. Unlike many other languages, awk doesn't require you to define or declare your variables before using them. In C, you must declare the type of data contained in a variable (such as int—integer, float—floating-point number, char—character data, and so on). In awk, you just use the variable; awk attempts to determine the data in the variable by how it is used. If you put character data in the variable, it is treated as a string; if you put a number in, it is treated as numeric.

awk also performs conversions between the data types. If you put the string "123" in a variable and later perform a calculation on it, it is treated as a number. The danger of this is, what happens when you perform a calculation on the string "abc"? awk attempts to convert the string to a number, gets a conversion error, and treats the value as a numeric 0! This type of logic error can be difficult to debug.

Tip

Initialize all variables in a BEGIN action like this:

```
BEGIN {total = 0.0; loop = 0; first_time = "yes"; }
```

Like the C language, awk requires that variables begin with an alphabetic character or an underscore. The alphabetic character can be upper- or lowercase. The remainder of the variable name can consist of letters, numbers, or underscores. It would be nice to make the variable names meaningful. Make them descriptive.

You can have the variables APPLE, Apple, and apple—which are all different variables. Case is significant.

Although you can make your variable names all uppercase letters, that is a bad practice because the predefined variables (such as NF or FS) are in uppercase. A common error is to type the predefined variables in lowercase—you will not get any errors from awk, and this mistake can be difficult to debug. The variables won't behave like the proper, uppercase spelling, and you won't get the results you expect.

Predefined Variables

gawk provides you with a number of predefined (also known as *built-in*) variables. These are used to provide useful data to your program and can also be used to change the default behavior of gawk (by setting them to a specific value).

Table 29.4 summarizes the predefined variables in gawk. Earlier versions of awk don't support all of these variables.

TABLE 29.4 *gawk* Predefined Variables

Variable	*Meaning*	*Default Value (If Any)*
ARGC	The number of command-line arguments	
ARGIND	The index within ARGV of the current file being processed	
ARGV	An array of command-line arguments	
CONVFMT	The conversion format for numbers (more information on conversion formats in the printf section)	%.6g
ENVIRON	The UNIX environmental variables	
ERRNO	The UNIX system error message	
FIELDWIDTHS	A whitespace-separated string of the width of input fields	
FILENAME	The name of the current input file	
FNR	The current record number in the current file	
FS	The input field separator	Space
IGNORECASE	Controls the case sensitivity	0 (case-sensitive)
NF	The number of fields in the current record	
NR	The number of records already read (does not reset to zero when reading multiple files)	
OFMT	The output format for numbers	%.6g
OFS	The output field separator	Space
ORS	The output record separator	Newline
RS	The input record separator	Newline
RSTART	Start of string matched by match function	
RLENGTH	Length of string matched by match function	
SUBSEP	Subscript separator	\"

The ARGC variable contains the number of command-line arguments passed to your program. ARGV is an array of ARGC elements that contains the command-line arguments themselves. The first one is ARGV[0], and the last one is ARGV[ARGC-1]. ARGV[0] contains the name of the command being executed (gawk). The gawk command-line options won't appear in ARGV—they are interpreted by gawk itself. ARGIND is the index within ARGV of the current file being processed.

The default conversion (input) format for numbers is stored in CONVFMT (conversion format) and defaults to the format string "%.6g". See the section "printf" for more information on the meaning of the format string.

The ENVIRON variable is an array that contains the environmental variables defined to your UNIX session. The subscript is the name of the environmental variable for which you want to get the value.

If you want your program to perform specific code depending on the value in an environmental variable, you can use the following:

```
ENVIRON["TERM"] == "vt100"  {print "Working on a Video Tube!"}
```

If you are using a VT100 terminal, you will get the message Working on a Video Tube! Note that you only put quotes around the environmental variable if you are using a literal. If you have a variable named VARTYPE that contains the string "TERM", you leave the double quotations off as shown below:

```
BEGIN {VARTYPE = "TERM"}
ENVIRON[VARTYPE] == "vt100"  {print "Working on a Video Tube!"}
```

The ERRNO variable contains the UNIX system error message if a system error occurs during redirection, read, or close.

The FIELDWIDTHS variable provides a facility for having fixed-length fields instead of using field separators. To specify the size of fields, you set FIELDWIDTHS to a string that contains the width of each field, separated by a space or tab character. After this variable is set, gawk splits up the input record based on the specified widths. To revert to using a field-separator character, you assign a new value to FS.

The variable FILENAME contains the name of the current input file. Because different (or even multiple files) can be specified on the command line, this provides you a means of determining which input file is being processed.

The FNR variable contains the number of the current record within the current input file. The variable is reset for each file that is specified on the command line and always contains a value that is less than or equal to the variable NR.

The character used to separate fields is stored in the variable FS with a default value of space or tab. You can change this variable with a command-line option or within your program. If you know your file will have some character other than a space as the field separator (for example, the /etc/passwd file in earlier examples, which uses the colon), you can specify it in your program with the BEGIN pattern or on the command line by using the -F option, followed by a different delimiter character, as in -F":" to use a colon).

You can control the case sensitivity of gawk regular expressions with the IGNORECASE variable. When set to the default (0), pattern-matching checks the case in regular expressions. If you set it to a nonzero value, case is ignored. (Thus, the letter A matches to the letter a.)

The variable NF is set after each record is read and contains the number of fields. The fields are determined by the FS or FIELDWIDTHS variables.

The variable NR contains the total number of records read. It is never less than FNR, which is reset to 0 for each file.

The default output format for numbers is stored in OFMT and defaults to the format string "%.6g". See the section "printf" for more information on the meaning of the format string.

The output field separator is contained in OFS with a default of space. This is the character or string that is output whenever you use a comma with the print statement, as in the following:

```
{print $1, $2, $3;}
```

This statement prints the first three fields of a file, separated by spaces. If you want to separate them by colons (like the /etc/passwd file), you simply set OFS to a new value: OFS=":".

You can change the output record separator by setting ORS to a new value. ORS defaults to the newline character (\n).

The length of any string matched by the match() function call is stored in RLENGTH. This is used in conjunction with the RSTART predefined variable to extract the matched string using the substr function.

You can change the input record separator by setting RS to a new value. RS defaults to the newline character (\n).

The length of any string matched by the match() function call is stored in RLENGTH. This is used in conjunction with the RSTART predefined variable to extract the matched string using the substr function.

The SUBSEP variable contains the value used to separate subscripts for multidimension arrays. The default value is the double quotation mark character (").

Note

If you change a field ($1, $2, and so on) or the input record ($0), you will cause other predefined variables to change. If your original input record had two fields and you set $3="third one", NF will be changed from 2 to 3.

Strings

awk supports two general types of variables: *numeric* (which can consist of the characters 0 through 9, + or -, and the decimal [.]) and *character* (which can contain any character). Variables that contain characters are generally referred to as *strings*. A character string can contain a valid number, text such as words, or even a formatted phone number. If the string contains a valid number, awk can automatically convert it and use it as if it were a numeric variable; if you attempt to use a string that contains a formatted phone number or contains numbers and letters ("123abc" for example) as a numeric variable, awk attempts to convert and use it as a numeric variable—containing the value zero. The automatic conversion occurs when you use a string in an arithmetic operation.

String Constants

A string constant is always enclosed within double quotation marks ("") and can be from zero (an *empty* string) to many characters long. The exact maximum varies by version of UNIX; personally, I have never hit the maximum. The double quotation marks aren't stored in memory. A typical string constant might look like the following:

```
"Linux Unleashed, Fourth Edition"
```

You have already seen string constants used earlier in this chapter—with comparisons and the print statement.

String Operators

There is really only one string operator, and that is *concatenation*. You can combine multiple strings (constants or variables in any combination) by just putting them together. Listing 29.1 does this with the print statement, where the string ": " is prepended to the input record ($0).

Listing 29.3 shows a couple of ways to concatenate strings.

LISTING 29.3 Concatenating Strings Example

```
$ gawk 'BEGIN{x="abc""def"; y="ghi"; z=x y; z2 =
➥ "A"x"B"y"C"; print x, y, z, z2}'
abcdef ghi abcdefghi AabcdefBghiC
```

Variable `x` is set to two concatenated strings; it prints as `abcdef`. Variable `y` is set to one string for use with the variable `z`. Variable `z` is the concatenation of two string variables printing as `abcdefghi`. Finally, the variable `z2` shows the concatenation of string constants and string variables printing as `AabcdefBghiC`.

If you leave the comma out of the `print` statement, all of the strings will be concatenated and will look like the following:

```
abcdefghiabcdefghiAabcdefBghiC
```

Built-In String Functions

In addition to the one-string operation (concatenation), `gawk` provides a number of functions for processing strings.

Table 29.5 summarizes the built-in string functions in `gawk`. Earlier versions of `awk` don't support all of these functions.

TABLE 29.5 *gawk* Built-In String Functions

Function	*Purpose*
`gsub(`*`reg`*`, `*`string`*`, `*`target`*`)`	Substitutes *`string`* in *`target`* string every time the regular expression *`reg`* is matched.
`index(`*`search`*`, `*`string`*`)`	Returns the position of the *`search`* string in *`string`*.
`length(`*`string`*`)`	The number of characters in *`string`*.
`match(`*`string`*`, `*`reg`*`)`	Returns the position in *`string`* that matches the regular expression *`reg`*.
`printf(`*`format`*`, `*`variables`*`)`	Writes formatted data based on *`format`*; *`variables`* is the data you want printed.
`split(`*`string`*`, `*`store`*`, `*`delim`*`)`	Splits *`string`* into array elements of *`store`* based on the delimiter *`delim`*.
`sprintf(`*`format`*`, `*`variables`*`)`	Returns a string containing formatted data based on *`format`*; *`variables`* is the data you want placed in the string.

Function	*Purpose*
strftime(*format*, *timestamp*)	Returns a formatted date or time string based on *format*; *timestamp* is the time returned by the systime() function.
sub(*reg*, *string*, *target*)	Substitutes *string* in *target* string the first time the regular expression *reg* is matched.
substr(*string*, *position*, *length*)	Returns a substring beginning at *position* for *length* number of characters.
tolower(*string*)	Returns the characters in *string* as their lowercase equivalent.
toupper(*string*)	Returns the characters in *string* as their uppercase equivalent.

The gsub(*reg*, *string*, *target*) function enables you to globally substitute one set of characters for another (defined in the form of the regular expression *reg*) within *string*. The number of substitutions is returned by the function. If *target* is omitted, the input record, $0, is the target. This is patterned after the substitute command in the ed/ex/vi text editors.

The index(*search*, *string*) function returns the first position (counting from the left) of the *search* string within *string*. If *string* is omitted, 0 is returned.

The length(*string*) function returns a count of the number of characters in *string*. If no *string* is given, then the length of $0 is returned. awk keeps track of the length of strings internally.

The match(*string*, *reg*) function determines whether *string* contains the set of characters defined by *reg*. If there is a match, the position is returned and the variables RSTART and RLENGTH are set.

The printf(*format*, *variables*) function writes formatted data converting *variables* based on the *format* string. This function is very similar to the C printf() function. More information about this function and the formatting strings is provided in the section "printf" later in this chapter.

The split(*string*, *store*, *delim*) function splits *string* into elements of the array *store* based on the *delim* string. The number of elements in *store* is returned. If you omit the *delim* string, FS is used. To split a slash-delimited (/) date into its component parts, code the following:

```
split("08/12/1962", results, "/");
```

After the function call, `results[1]` contains `08`, `results[2]` contains `12`, and `results[3]` contains `1962`. When used with the `split` function, the array begins with the element one. This also works with strings that contain text.

The `sprintf(format, variables)` function behaves like the `printf` function except it returns the result string instead of writing output. This function produces formatted data, converting `variables` based on the `format` string, and is very similar to the C `sprintf()` function. More information about this function and the formatting strings is provided in the "`printf`" section of this chapter.

The `strftime(`*`format, timestamp`*`)` function returns a formatted date or time based on the *`format`* string; *`timestamp`* is the number of seconds since midnight on January 1, 1970. The `systime` function returns a value in this form. The format is the same as the C `strftime()` function.

The `sub(`*`reg, string, target`*`)` function enables you to substitute one set of characters for the first occurrence of another (defined in the form of the regular expression *`reg`*) within *`string`*. The number of substitutions is returned by the function. If *`target`* is omitted, the input record, `$0`, is the target. This is patterned after the `substitute` command in the `ed/ex/vi` text editors.

The `substr(`*`string, position, length`*`)`function enables you to extract a substring based on a starting *`position`* and *`length`*. If you omit the *`len`* parameter, the remaining string is returned.

The `tolower(`*`string`*`)` function returns the uppercase alphabetic characters in *`string,`* converted to lowercase. Any other characters are returned without any conversion.

The `toupper(`*`string`*`)` function returns the lowercase alphabetic characters in *`string`*, converted to uppercase. Any other characters are returned without any conversion.

Special String Constants

`awk` supports special string constants that have special meaning or cannot be entered from the keyboard. If you want to have a double quotation mark (`"`) character as a string constant (`x = """`), how would you prevent `awk` from thinking the second one (the one you really want) is the end of the string? The answer is by escaping, or telling `awk` the next character has special meaning. This is done through the backslash (`\`) character, as in the rest of UNIX.

Table 29.6 shows most of the constants supported by `gawk`.

TABLE 29.6 *gawk* Special String Constants

Expression	*Meaning*
`\\`	The means of including a backslash
`\a`	The alert or bell character
`\b`	Backspace
`\f`	Formfeed
`\n`	Newline
`\r`	Carriage return
`\t`	Tab
`\v`	Vertical tab
`\"`	Double quotation
`\xNN`	Indicates that *NN* is a hexadecimal number
`\0NNN`	Indicates that *NNN* is an octal (base 8) number

Arrays

When you have more than one related piece of data, you have two choices—you can create multiple variables or you can use an array. An array enables you to keep a collection of related data together.

You access individual elements within an array by enclosing the subscript within brackets (`[ ]`). In general, you can use an array element anyplace you can use a regular variable.

Arrays in `awk` have special capabilities lacking in most other languages—they are dynamic, they are sparse, and the subscript is actually a string. You don't have to declare a variable to be an array, and you don't have to define the maximum number of elements—when you use an element for the first time, it is created dynamically. Because of this, a block of memory is not initially allocated. If you want to accumulate sales for each month in a year, in normal programming practice 12 elements are allocated—even if you are only processing December at the moment. `awk` arrays are sparse; if you are working with December, only that element exists—not the other 11 (empty) months.

In my experience, the last capability is the most useful—that the subscript is a string. In most programming languages, if you want to accumulate data based on a string (for example, totaling sales by state or country), you need to have two arrays—the state or country name (a string) and the numeric sales array. You search the state or country name for a match and then use the same element of the sales array. `awk` performs this for you. You create an element in the sales array with the state or country name as the subscript and address it directly, as in the following:

```
total_sales["Pennsylvania"] = 10.15
```

This requires much less programming and is much easier to read and maintain than the "search one array and change another" method. The `awk` version is known as an *associative array*.

However, `awk` does not directly support multidimension arrays.

Array Functions

`gawk` provides a couple of functions specifically for use with arrays: `in` and `delete`. The `in` function tests for membership in an array. The `delete` function removes elements from an array.

If you have an array with a subscript of states and want to determine whether a specific state is in the list, put the following within a conditional test:

```
"Delaware" in total_sales
```

You can read more about conditional tests in this chapter's "Conditional Flow" section. You can also use the `in` function within a loop to step through the elements in an array (especially if the array is sparse or associative). This is a special case of the `for` loop and is described in the section "The `for` Statement," later in the chapter.

Code the following to delete an array element. The state of Delaware is used in this example:

```
delete total_sales["Delaware"]
```

Caution

When an array element is deleted, it has been removed from memory. The data is no longer available.

Deleting elements in an array, or entire arrays, when you are finished with them is always good practice. Although memory is cheap and large quantities are available (especially with virtual memory), you will eventually run out if you don't clean up.

Note

You must loop through all loop elements and delete each one. You cannot delete an entire array directly; therefore, the following is valid:

```
delete total_sales
```

Multidimension Arrays

Although awk doesn't directly support multidimension arrays, it does provide a facility to simulate them. The distinction is fairly trivial to you as a programmer. You can specify multiple dimensions in the subscript (within the brackets) in a form slightly unfamiliar to C programmers:

```
array[5, 3] = "Mary"
```

This is stored in a single-dimension array with the subscript actually stored in the form 5 SUBSEP 3. The predefined variable SUBSEP contains the value of the separator of the subscript components. The variable defaults to the double quotation mark (" or \034) because it is unlikely to appear in the subscript itself. Remember that the double quotation marks are used to contain a string; they are not stored as part of the string itself. You can always change SUBSEP if you need to have the double quotation mark in your multidimension array subscript.

Caution

In general, you don't want to change SUBSEP!

If you want to calculate total sales by city and state or country, you use a two-dimension array:

```
total_sales["Philadelphia", "Pennsylvania"] = 10.15
```

You can use the in function within a conditional:

```
("Wilmington", "Delaware") in total_sales
```

You can also use the in function within a loop to step through various cities.

Built-In Numeric Functions

gawk provides several numeric functions that calculate special values.

Table 29.7 summarizes the built-in numeric functions in gawk. Earlier versions of awk don't support all of these functions.

TABLE 29.7 *gawk's* Built-In Numeric Functions

Function	*Purpose*
`atan2(x, y)`	Returns the arctangent of y/x in radians
`cos(x)`	Returns the cosine of x in radians
`exp(x)`	Returns e raised to the x power
`int(x)`	Returns the value of x truncated to an integer. int(1.5) returns 1, int(-1.5) returns -1.
`log(x)`	Returns the natural log of x
`rand()`	Returns a random number between 0 and 1
`sin(x)`	Returns the sine of x in radians
`sqrt(x)`	Returns the square root of x
`srand(x)`	Initializes (seeds) the random number generator; `systime()` is used if x is omitted
`systime()`	Returns the current time in seconds since midnight, January 1, 1970

Arithmetic Operators

gawk supports a wide variety of math operations. Table 29.8 summarizes these operators.

TABLE 29.8 *gawk* Arithmetic Operators

Operator	*Purpose*
`x^y`	Raises x to the y power (this is the one operator in awk that C does not directly support—in C you have to use the `pow()` function).
`x**y`	Raises x to the y power (same as x^y).
`x%y`	Calculates the remainder of x/y. The C remainder function only supports integers; awk supports integers and reals.
`x+y`	Adds x to y.
`x-y`	Subtracts y from x.
`x*y`	Multiplies x times y.

Operator	Purpose
`x/y`	Divides `x` by `y`.
`-y`	Negates `y` (switches the sign of `y`); also known as the unary minus.
`++y`	Increments `y` by 1 and uses value (prefix increment).
`y++`	Uses value of `y` and then increments by 1 (postfix increment).
`--y`	Decrements `y` by 1 and uses value (prefix decrement).
`y--`	Uses value of `y` and then decrements by 1 (postfix decrement).
`x=y`	Assigns value of `y` to `x`. `gawk` also supports operator-assignment operators (`+=`, `-=`, `*=`, `/=`, `%=`, `^=`, and `**=`).

Note

All math in `gawk` uses floating point, even if you treat the number as an integer.

You can also use comparison operators (like `==` or `<`) and compound pattern operators (`&&`, `||`, and `!`) in arithmetic statements. They evaluate to the value zero for false and one for true.

Conditional Flow

By its very nature, an action within a `gawk` program is conditional—executed if its pattern is true. You can also have conditional programs flow within the action through the use of an `if` statement.

The general flow of an `if` statement is as follows:

```
if (condition)
   statement to execute when true
else
   statement to execute when false
```

`condition` can be any valid combination of patterns shown in Tables 29.2 and 29.3. `else` is optional.

If you have more than one statement to execute, you need to enclose the statements within braces (`{ }`), just as in the C syntax.

You can also stack `if` and `else` statements as necessary:

```
if ("Pennsylvania" in total_sales)
   print "We have Pennsylvania data"
```

```
else if ("Delaware" in total_sales)
   print "We have Delaware data"
else if (current_year < 2010)
   print "Uranus is still a planet"
else
   print "none of the conditions were met."
```

The null Statement

By definition, `if` requires one (or more) statements to execute; in some cases, the logic might be straightforward when coded so the code you want executed occurs when the condition is false. I have used this when it would be difficult or ugly to reverse the logic to execute the code when the condition is true.

The solution to this problem is easy: Just use the `null` statement: the semicolon (`;`). The `null` statement satisfies the syntax requirement that `if` requires statements to execute; it does nothing.

Your code will look something like the following:

```
if (($1 <= 5 && $2 > 3) || ($1 > 7 && $2 < 2))
   ;         # The Null Statement
else
```

  the code I really want to execute

The Conditional Operator

`gawk` has one operator that actually has three parameters: the conditional operator. This operator allows you to apply an if-test anywhere in your code.

The general format of the conditional expression follows:

```
condition ? true-result : false-result
```

Although this might seem like duplication of the `if` statement, it can make your code easier to read. If you have a data file that consists of an employee name and the number of sick days taken, for example, you can use the following:

```
{ print $1, "has taken", $2, "day" $2 != 1 ? "s" : "", "of sick time" }
```

This prints `day` if the employee only took one day of sick time and prints `days` if the employee took zero or more than one day of sick time. The resulting sentence is more readable. To code the same example using an `if` statement would be more complex and would look like the following:

```
if ($2 != 1)
   print $1, "has taken", $2, "days of sick time"
else
   print $1, "has taken", $2, "day of sick time"
```

Looping

By their very nature, awk programs are one big loop—reading each record in the input file and processing the appropriate patterns and actions. The need for repetition often occurs within an action. awk supports loops through the do, for, and while statements that are similar to those found in C.

As with the if statement, you must contain multiple statements in braces if you want to execute them.

Tip

Forgetting the braces around multiple statements is a common programming error with conditional and looping statements.

The do Statement

The do statement (sometimes referred to as the do while statement) provides a looping construct that will be executed at least once. The condition or test occurs after the contents of the loop have been executed.

The do statement takes the following form:

```
do
   statement
while (condition)
```

statement can be one statement or multiple statements enclosed in braces. *condition* is any valid test like those used with the if statement or the pattern used to trigger actions.

In general, you must change the value of the variable in the condition within the loop. If you don't, you have a loop-forever condition because the test result (*condition*) never changes to become false.

The for Statement

The for statement provides a looping construct that modifies values within the loop. It is good for counting through a specific number of items.

The for statement has two general forms:

```
for (loop = 0; loop < 10; loop++)
   statement

for (subscript in array)
   statement
```

The first form initializes the variable (`loop = 0`), performs the test (`loop < 10`), and then performs the loop contents (*`statement`*). Then it modifies the variable (`loop++`) and tests again. As long as the test is true, *`statement`* will execute.

In the second form, *`statement`* is executed with `subscript` being set to each of the subscripts in *`array`*. This enables you to loop through an array even if you don't know the values of the subscripts. This works well for multidimensional arrays.

`statement` can be one statement or multiple statements enclosed in braces. The condition (`loop < 10`) is any valid test like those used with the `if` statement or the pattern used to trigger actions.

In general, you don't want to change the loop control variable (`loop` or `subscript`) within the loop body. Let the `for` statement do that; you might otherwise get behavior that is difficult to debug.

For the first form, the modification of the variable can be any valid operation (including calls to functions). In most cases, it is an increment or decrement.

Tip

This example shows the postfix increment. It doesn't matter whether you use the postfix (`loop++`) or prefix (`++loop`) increment—the results will be the same in our example.

The `for` loop is a good method of looping through data of an unknown size:

```
for (i=1; i<=NF; i++)
     print $i
```

Each field on the current record will be printed on its own line. As a programmer, I don't know how many fields are in a particular record when I write the code. The variable `NF` lets me know as the program runs.

The `while` Statement

The final loop structure is the `while` loop. It is the most general because it executes while the condition is true. The general form is as follows:

```
while(condition)
   statement
```

statement can be one statement or multiple statements enclosed in braces. *condition* is any valid test like those used with the `if` statement or the pattern used to trigger actions.

If the condition is false before the `while` is encountered, the contents of the loop are not executed. This is different from `do`, which always executes the loop contents at least once.

In general, you must change the value of the variable in the condition within the loop. If you don't, you have a loop-forever condition because the test result (*condition*) never changes to become false.

Loop Control

You can exit or return to the conditional test in any loop early if you need to (without assigning some bogus value to the variable in the condition). `awk` provides two facilities to do this: `break` and `continue`.

`break` causes the current (innermost) loop to be exited. It behaves as if the conditional test were performed immediately, with a false result. None of the remaining code in the loop (after the `break` statement) executes, and the loop ends. This is useful when you need to handle some error or early-end condition.

`continue` causes the current loop to return to the conditional test. None of the remaining code in the loop (after the `continue` statement) is executed, and the test is immediately executed. This is most useful when there is code you want to skip (within the loop) temporarily. The `continue` is different from the `break` because the loop is not forced to end.

Advanced Input and Output

In addition to the simple input and output facilities provided by `awk`, you can take advantage of a number of advanced features for more complicated processing.

By default, `awk` automatically reads and loops through your program, but you can alter this behavior. You can force input to come from a different file or cause the loop to recycle early (read the next record without performing any more actions) or even just read the next record. You can even get data from the output of other commands.

On the output side, you can format the output and send it to a file (other than the standard output device) or as input to another command.

Input

You do not have to program the normal input loop process in awk. It reads a record and then searches for pattern matches and the corresponding actions to execute. If multiple files are specified on the command line, they are processed in order. It is only if you want to change this behavior that you have to do any special programming.

next and exit

The next command causes awk to read the next record and perform the pattern match and the corresponding action execution immediately. Normally, it executes all of your code in any actions with matching patterns. next causes any additional matching patterns to be ignored for this record.

The exit command in any action except END behaves as if the end of file was reached. Code execution in all pattern/actions is ceased, and the actions within the END pattern are executed. exit appearing in the END pattern is a special case—it causes the program to end.

getline

The getline statement is used to explicitly read a record. This is especially useful if you have a data record that looks like two physical records. It performs the normal field splitting (setting $0, the field variables, FNR, NF, and NR). It returns the value 1 if the read was successful and 0 if it failed (end of file was reached). If you want to explicitly read through a file, you can code something like the following:

```
{ while (getline == 1)
  {
      # process the inputted fields
  }
}
```

You can also have getline store the input data in a field instead of taking advantage of the normal field processing by using the form getline *variable*. When used this way, NF is set to 0, and FNR and NR are incremented.

Input from a File

You can use getline to input data from a specific file instead of the ones listed on the command line. The general form is getline < "*filename*". When coded this way, getline performs the normal field splitting (setting $0, the field variables, and NF). If the file doesn't exist, getline returns -1; it returns 1 on success and 0 on failure.

You can read the data from the specified file into a variable. You can also replace *filename* with `stdin` or a variable that contains the filename.

Note

If you use `getline < "filename"` to read data into your program, neither `FNR` nor `NR` is changed.

Input from a Command

Another way of using the `getline` statement is to accept input from a UNIX command. If you want to perform some processing for each person signed on the system (send him or her a message, for instance), you can code something like the following:

```
{ while ("who -u" | getline)
  {
      # process each line from the who command
   }
}
```

The `who` command is executed once and each of its output lines is processed by `getline`. You could also use the form `"command" | getline variable`.

Ending Input from a File or Command

Whenever you use `getline` to get input from a specified file or command, you should close it when you have finished processing the data. The maximum number of open files allowed to `awk` varies with the operating system version or individual account configuration (a command output pipe counts as a file). By closing files when you have finished with them, you reduce the chances of hitting the limit.

The syntax to close a file follows:

```
close ("filename")
```

filename is the one specified on the `getline` (which could also be `stdin`, a variable that contains the filename, or the exact command used with `getline`).

Output

A few advanced features are available for output: pretty formatting, sending output to files, and piping output as input to other commands. The `printf` command is used for pretty formatting—instead of seeing the output in whatever default format `awk` decides to use (which is often ugly), you can specify how it looks.

printf

The print statement produces simple output for you. If you want to be able to format the data (producing fixed columns, for instance), you need to use printf. The nice thing about awk printf is that it uses syntax that is very similar to the printf() function in C.

The general format of the awk printf follows. The parentheses are only required if a relational expression is included:

```
printf format-specifier, variable1,variable2, variable3,..variablen
printf(format-specifier, variable1,variable2, variable3,..variablen)
```

Personally, I use the second form because I am so used to coding in C.

The variables are optional, but format-specifier is mandatory. Often you will have printf statements that only include format-specifier (to print messages that contain no variables):

```
printf ("Program Starting\n")
printf ("\f")        # new page in output
```

format-specifier can consist of text, escaped characters, or actual print specifiers. A print specifier begins with the percent sign (%), followed by an optional numeric value that specifies the size of the field and then by the format type (which describes the type of variable or output format). If you want to print a percent sign in your output, you use %%.

The field size can consist of two numbers separated by a decimal point (.). For floating-point numbers, the first number is the size of the entire field (including the decimal point) and the second number is the number of digits to the right of the decimal. For other types of fields, the first number is the minimum field size and the second number is the maximum field size (number of characters to actually print); if you omit the first number, it takes the value of the maximum field size. If you omit the second number, there is no defined maximum (it will be however big it needs to be to hold the data).

The print specifiers determine how the variable is printed; there are also modifiers that change the behavior of the specifiers. Table 29.9 shows the print format specifiers.

TABLE 29.9 Format Specifiers for *awk*

Format	*Meaning*
`%c`	ASCII character
`%d`	An integer (decimal number)
`%i`	An integer, just like `%d`
`%e`	A floating-point number using scientific notation (1.00000E+01)
`%f`	A floating-point number (10.43)
`%g`	`awk` chooses between `%e` or `%f` display format (whichever is shorter), suppressing nonsignificant zeros
`%o`	An unsigned octal (base 8) number (integer)
`%s`	A string of characters
`%x`	An unsigned hexadecimal (base 16) number (integer)
`%X`	Same as `%x` but using ABCDEF instead of abcdef

Note

If you attempt to print a numeric value or variable using `%c`, it is printed as a character. (The ASCII character for that value will print.)

The format modifiers change the default behavior of the format specifiers. Listing 29.4 shows the use of various specifiers and modifiers.

LISTING 29.4 *printf* Format Specifiers and Modifiers

```
printf("%d %3.3d %03.3d %.3d %-.3d %3d %-3d\n", 64, 64, 64, 64, 64, 64, 64)
printf("%c %c %2.2c %-2.2c %2c %-2c\n", 64, "abc", "abc", "abc", "abc",
➥ "abc")
printf("%s %2s %-2s %2.2s %-2.2s %.2s %-.2s\n",
       "abc", "abc", "abc", "abc", "abc", "abc", "abc")
printf("%f %6.1f %06.1f %.1f %-.1f %6f\n",
       123.456, 123.456, 123.456, 123.456, 123.456, 123.456)

64 064 064 064 064  64 64
@ a ab ab  a a
abc abc abc ab ab ab ab
123.456000  123.5 0123.5 123.5 123.5 123.456000
```

Note

The second line of output may appear as

```
@ a  a a   a a
```

in non-gawk versions of awk like nawk and mawk.

When using the integer or decimal (%d) specifier, the field size defaults to the size of the value being printed (two digits for the value 64). If you specify a field maximum size that is larger than that, you automatically get the field zero filled. All numeric fields are right-justified unless you use the minus sign (-) modifier, which causes them to be left-justified. If you specify only the field minimum size and want the rest of the field zero filled, you have to use the zero modifier (before the field minimum size).

When using the character (%c) specifier, only one character prints from the input, no matter what size you use for the field minimum or maximum sizes and no matter how many characters are in the value being printed. Note that the value 64 printed as a character shows up as @.

When using the string (%s) specifier, the entire string prints unless you specify the field maximum size. Strings are left-justified unless you use the minus sign (-) modifier, which causes them to be right-justified.

When using the floating (%f) specifier, the field size defaults to .6 (as many digits to the left of the decimal and 6 digits to the right). If you specify a number after the decimal in the format, that many digits print to the right of the decimal and awk rounds the number. All numeric fields are right-justified unless you use the minus sign (-) modifier, which causes them to be left-justified. If you want the field zero filled, you have to use the zero modifier (before the field minimum size).

The best way to determine printing results is to work with them. Try the various modifiers and see what makes your output look best.

Output to a File

You can send your output (from print or printf) to a file. The following creates a new (or empties out an existing) file containing the printed message:

```
printf ("hello world\n") > "datafile"
```

If you execute this statement multiple times or other statements that redirect output to *datafile*, the output remains in the file. The file creation/emptying out only occurs the first time the file is used in the program.

To append data to an existing file, you use the following:

```
printf ("hello world\n") >> "datafile"
```

Output to a Command

In addition to redirecting your output to a file, you can send the output from your program to act as input for another command. You can code something like the following:

```
printf ("hello world\n") ¦ "sort -t`,`"
```

Any other output statements that pipe data into the same command will specify exactly the same command after the pipe character (¦) because that is how awk keeps track of which command is receiving which output from your program.

Closing an Output File or Pipe

Whenever you send output to a file or pipe, you should close it when you have finished processing the data. The maximum number of open files allowed to awk varies with the operating system version or individual account configuration (a pipe counts as a file). By closing files when you have finished with them, you reduce the chances of hitting the limit.

The syntax to close a file follows:

```
close ("filename")
```

filename is the one specified on the output statement (which can also be stdout, a variable that contains the filename, or the exact command used with a pipe).

Functions

In addition to the built-in functions (for example, gsub or srand), gawk allows you to write your own. User-defined functions are a means of creating a block of code that is accessed in multiple places in your code. These functions can also be used to build a library of commonly used routines so you do not have to recode the same algorithms repeatedly.

User-defined functions are not a part of the original awk—they were added to nawk and are supported by gawk.

Using a function includes two parts: the definition and the call. The function definition contains the code to be executed (the function itself), and the call temporarily transfers from the main code to the function. The command execution is transferred back to the main code in two ways: implicit and explicit returns. When gawk reaches the end of a function (the right brace [}]), it automatically (implicitly) returns control to the calling routine. If you want to leave your function before the bottom, you can explicitly use (i.e., code in your program) the return statement to exit early.

Function Definition

The general form of a gawk function definition looks like this:

```
function functionname(parameter list) {
     the function body
}
```

You code your function just as if it were any other set of action statements, and you can place it anywhere you would put a pattern/action set. If you think about it, the function *functionname(parameter list)* portion of the definition could be considered a pattern and *the function body* the action.

> **Note**
>
> gawk supports another form of function definition where the `function` keyword is abbreviated to `func`. The remaining syntax is the same:
>
> ```
> func functionname(parameter list) {
>      the function body
> }
> ```

Listing 29.5 shows the defining and calling of a function.

LISTING 29.5 Defining and Calling Functions

```
BEGIN { print_header() }

function print_header( ) {
   printf("This is the header\n");
   printf("this is a second line of the header\n");
}

This is the header
this is a second line of the header
```

The code inside the function is executed only once—when the function is called from within the BEGIN action. This function uses the implicit return method.

Caution

When working with user-defined functions, you must place the parentheses that contain the parameter list immediately after the function name when calling that function. When you use the built-in functions, this is not a requirement.

Function Parameters

Like C, gawk passes parameters to functions by value. In other words, a copy of the original value is made and that copy is passed to the called function. The original is untouched, even if the function changes the value.

Any parameters are listed in the function definition, separated by commas. If you have no parameters, you can leave the parameter list (contained in the parentheses) empty.

Listing 29.6 is an expanded version of Listing 29.5; it shows the pass-by-value nature of gawk function parameters.

LISTING 29.6 Passing Parameters

```
BEGIN { pageno = 0;
        print_header(pageno);
        printf("the page number is now %d\n", pageno);
}

function print_header(page ) {
   page++;
   printf("This is the header for page %d\n", page);
   printf("this is a second line of the header\n");
}

This is the header for page 1
this is a second line of the header
the page number is now 0
```

The page number is initialized before the first call to the print_header function and incremented in the function. It remains at the original value when it is printed after the function call.

Caution

gawk does not perform parameter validation. When you call a function, you can list more or fewer parameters than the function expects. Any extra parameters are ignored, and any missing ones default to zero or empty strings (depending on how they are used).

Tip

You can take advantage of the lack of function parameter validation. It can be used to create local variables within the called function—just list more variables in the function definition than you use in the function call. I strongly suggest you comment the fact that the extra parameters are really being used as local variables.

A called function can change variables in the calling routines in several ways—through explicit return or by using the variables in the calling routine directly. (These variables are normally global.)

The `return` Statement (Explicit Return)

If you want to return a value or leave a function early, you need to code a `return` statement. If you don't code one, the function ends with the right brace (`}`). I prefer to code them at the bottom even though they are not really needed.

If the calling code expects a returned value from your function, you must code the `return` statement in the following form:

`return` *`variable`*

Expanding on Listing 29.6 to let the function change the page number, Listing 29.7 shows the use of the `return` statement.

LISTING 29.7 Returning Values

```
BEGIN { pageno = 0;
        pageno = print_header(pageno);
        printf("the page number is now %d\n", pageno);
}

function print_header(page ) {
```

```
    page++;
    printf("This is the header for page %d\n", page);
    printf("this is a second line of the header\n");
    return page;
}
```

```
This is the header for page 1
this is a second line of the header
the page number is now 1
```

The updated page number is returned to the code that called the function.

Note

The `return` statement allows you to return only one value back to the calling routine.

Writing Reports

Generating a report in `awk` entails a sequence of steps, with each step producing the input for the next step. Report-writing is usually a three-step process: pick the data, sort the data, and make the output pretty.

Complex Reports

Using `awk`, you can quickly create complex reports. Performing string comparisons, building arrays on-the-fly, and taking advantage of associative arrays is much easier than coding in another language (such as C). Instead of having to search through an array for a match with a text key, that key can be used as the array subscript.

I have produced reports using `awk` with three levels of control breaks, multiple sections of reports in the same control break, and multiple totaling pages. The totaling pages were for each level of control break plus a final page; if the control break did not have a particular type of data, the totaling page did not have it either. If there were only one member of a control break, the totaling page for that level wasn't created. (This saved a lot of paper when there was really only one level of control break—the highest.)

This report ended up being more than 1,000 lines of `awk` code (`nawk` to be specific). It takes a little longer to run than the equivalent C program, but it took a lot less programmer time to create. Because it was easy to create and modify, it was developed by using prototypes. The users briefly described what they wanted, and I produced a report. They decided they needed more control breaks, and I added them; then they realized a lot of paper was wasted on totaling pages, so the report was modified as described.

Being easy to develop incrementally without knowing the final result made it easier and more fun for me. Because I could be responsive to user changes, the users were happy!

Extracting Data

As mentioned early in this chapter, many systems do not produce data in the desired format. When working with data stored in relational databases, two main ways are available for getting data out: Use a query tool with SQL or write a program to get the data from the database and output it in the desired form. SQL query tools have limited formatting ability but can provide quick and easy access to the data.

One technique I have found very useful is extracting the data from the database into a file that is then manipulated by an awk script to produce the exact format you need. When required, an awk script can even create the SQL statements used to query the database (specifying the key values for the rows to select).

The following example is used when the query tool places a space before a numeric field that must be removed for a program that will use the data in another system (mainframe COBOL):

```
{   printf("%s%s%-25.25s\n", $1, $2, $3);   }
```

awk automatically removes the field separator (the space character) when splitting the input record into individual fields, and the formatting %s string format specifiers in printf are *contiguous* (do not have any spaces between them).

Commands On-the-Fly

The capability to pipe the output of a command into another is very powerful because the output from the first becomes the input that the second can manipulate. A frequent use of one-line awk programs is the creation of commands based on a list.

The find command can be used to produce a list of files that match its conditions, or it can execute a single command that takes a single command-line argument. You can see files in a directory (and subdirectories) that match specific conditions with the following:

```
$ find . -name "*.prn" -print
```

This is the output:

```
./exam2.prn
./exam1.prn
./exam3.prn
```

You can alternatively print the contents of those files with the following:

```
$ find . -name "*.prn" -exec lp {} \;
```

The `find` command inserts the individual filenames it locates in place of the `{}` and executes the `lp` command. If you want to execute a command that requires two arguments (to copy files to a new name) or execute multiple commands at once, you cannot do it with `find` alone. You can create a shell script that will accept the single argument and use it in multiple places, or you can create an `awk` single-line program:

```
$ find . -name "*.prn" -print ¦ awk '{print "echo bak" $1;
➥print "cp " $1 " " $1".bak";}'
```

Here is the output:

```
echo bak./exam2.prn
cp ./exam2.prn ./exam2.prn.bak
echo bak./exam1.prn
cp ./exam1.prn ./exam1.prn.bak
echo bak./exam3.prn
cp ./exam3.prn ./exam3.prn.bak
```

To get the commands to actually execute, you need to pipe the commands into one of the shells. The following example uses the Public Domain Korn SHell (pdksh):

```
$ find . -name "*.prn" -print ¦
    awk '{print "echo bak" $1; print "cp " $1 " " $1".bak";}' ¦
    pdksh
```

This is the output:

```
bak./exam2.prn
bak./exam1.prn
bak./exam3.prn
```

Before each copy takes place, the message is shown. This is also handy if you want to search for a string (using the `grep` command) in the files of multiple subdirectories. Many versions of the `grep` command will not show the name of the file searched unless you use wildcards (or specify multiple filenames on the command line). The following uses `find` to search for C source files, `awk` to create `grep` commands to look for an error message, and the shell `echo` command to show the file being searched:

```
$ find . -name "*.c" -print ¦
    awk '{print "echo " $1; print "grep error-message " $1;}' ¦
    pdksh
```

The same technique can be used to perform `lint` checks on source code in a series of subdirectories. I execute the following in a shell script periodically to check all C code:

```
$ find . -name "*.c" -print ¦
     awk '{print "lint " $1 " > " $1".lint"}' ¦
     pdksh
```

The `lint` version on one system prints the code error as a heading line and then the parts of code in question as a list below. `grep` shows the heading but not the detail lines. The `awk` script prints all lines from the heading until the first blank line (end of the `lint` section).

Note

Although you won't find the `lint` program included with your Linux distribution, you can find a similar (and in many ways much more powerful) C syntax checker from the Massachusetts Institute of Technology (MIT) called `lclint`. Look at `http://sunsite.unc.edu/pub/Linux/devel/lang/c` where you will find `lclint`, along with numerous other programming utilities that you can install on your system.

When in doubt, pipe the output into `more` or `less` to view the created commands before you pipe them into a shell for execution.

Tip

`pdksh` (Public Domain Korn SHell) was used in the preceding examples. You can replace it with your preferred shell. If your shell does not recognize any of the commands in the examples (like `echo`), you will have to replace them with the proper command for your shell when trying the example.

One Last Built-In Function: `system`

One more built-in function, which does not fit in the character or numeric categories, is `system`. The `system` function executes the string passed to it as an argument, allowing you to execute commands or scripts on-the-fly when your `awk` code has the need.

You can code a report to automatically print to paper when it is complete. The code looks something like Listing 29.8.

LISTING 29.8 Using the *system* Function

```
BEGIN { pageno = 0;
        pageno = print_header(pageno);
        printf("the page number is now %d\n", pageno);
}

# The production of the report would be coded here

END { close ("report.txt");
      system ("lpr -Pmyprinter report.txt");
}

function print_header(page ) {
   page++;
   printf("This is the header for page %d\n", page) > "report.txt";
   printf("this is a second line of the header\n")  > "report.txt";
}

This is the header for page 1
this is a second line of the header
the page number is now 0
```

The output is the same as that of Listing 29.6 except that this shows up on the printer instead of the screen. You have to close the program before printing it.

> **Note**
>
> Ideally, the code in Listing 29.8 would be executed on a file. Be careful when using input or output redirection or requiring direct user input in your awk scripts.

Summary

This chapter provided an introduction to the awk programming language and the GNU awk—gawk—a very powerful and useful language that enables you to search for data, extract data from files, create commands on-the-fly, or even create entire programs.

gawk is very useful as a prototyping language—with it you can create reports very quickly. After showing the reports to the user, you can make changes quickly, also. Although less efficient than a comparable program written in C, gawk is not so inefficient that you cannot create production programs. If efficiency is a concern with an awk program, it can be converted into C.

There is also an awk-to-C translator available. Eric S. Raymond wrote the awk2c program. Although it does not support all awk features, you might find it useful. It is available in the file awk2c050.tgz at http://sunsite.unc.edu/pub/Linux/utils/text.

For further information, see the following:

The awk Programming Language. Aho, Alfred V., Brian W. Kernighan, and Peter J. Weinberger. Addison-Wesley, 1988 (copyright AT&T Bell Lab).

A short quick-reference guide to gawk is available in the file awkcard.ps (created by Specialized Systems Consultants, Inc. SSC, the publishers of *Linux Journal).*

Gawk *User Manual* by Arnold D. Robbins is available in the file gawk.ps.

Both awkcard.ps and gawk.ps are in PostScript format and can be read online or printed by using the gv X11 PostScript viewer from the command line of an X11 terminal window like this:

```
# gv /usr/doc/gawk*/*.ps
```

Tip

If you experience problems with this command (with the wildcards), you will have to specify the specific path and file names.

Of course, you can also check the man pages or info for gawk on your system.

CHAPTER 30

`tcl` and `tk` Programming

IN THIS CHAPTER

The tcl (pronounced *tickle*) scripting language and the tk toolkit are programming environments for creating graphical user interfaces for the X Window system. tcl, which stands for Tool Command Language, and tk are easy to learn and use, and with them, you can construct user interfaces much faster than with traditional X Window programming methods.

tcl/tk was written by John K. Ousterhout while he was a professor of electrical engineering and computer science at the University of California at Berkeley. It was originally designed to provide a reusable command language for interactive tools, but it has expanded far beyond that and is used in a wide range of software products.

The true power of tcl/tk is that complex graphical applications can be written almost entirely in the tcl scripting language, thus hiding many of the complexities of interface programming encountered in writing interfaces using the C language.

The official tcl/tk Web site is located at http://www.scriptics.com/.

According to its Web site, Scriptics Corporation is the tcl platform company. Formed by John Ousterhout, tcl creator and industry visionary, Scriptics is focused on bringing the tcl scripting language into the corporate mainstream. Scriptics will provide development tools, technology extensions, and commercial support services for tcl while continuing to develop the open source tcl and tk packages.

The site also has links for downloading and installing the latest versions of tcl/tk. Presently, the newest available stable version of tcl/tk is 8.1.1.

tcl binaries tcl, tclsh, wish, and tclhelp are installed by Red Hat's RPM in /usr/bin. Voluminous help on both tcl and tk is available by running the tclhelp command. There are also man pages for tclsh and wish.

The programs discussed in this chapter are compatible with most versions of tcl and tk and should work fine for the current version.

Installing tcl/tk

As this is being written, the newest available stable version of tcl/tk is 8.1.1, available for download at http://www.scriptics.com/. It's likely, however, that your Linux distribution came with tcl/tk. The first step is to verify whether tcl/tk has already been installed. From the command prompt, issue this command:

```
# tclsh
```

If you receive the % tcl prompt, command-line tcl is installed. Next, issue this command from a command window in an X environment:

```
# wish
```

If you receive the tcl prompt and a little GUI window opens on your screen, GUI tcl/tk is installed.

Even if you don't get the prompts, these programs could still be installed. Check to see if command files tclsh and wish are installed in directory /usr/bin.

If tcl or tk are not installed, you can install them from your Linux distribution installation CD-ROM or from the Internet.

Installing tcl/tk from Your Red Hat Install CD-ROM

In the /RedHat/RPMS directory on your installation CD-ROM are files tcl-8.0.4-27.i386.rpm and tclx-8.0.4-27.i386.rpm. You can (as root) install them by mounting the CD-ROM, navigating to that directory, and running the following commands:

```
rpm -ivh tcl-8.0.4-27.i386.rpm
rpm -ivh tclx-8.0.4-27.i386.rpm
```

Note

The exact filenames of the .rpm files on the CD-ROM will vary with exact Linux distribution and version.

Installing tcl/tk from Your Caldera Install CD-ROM

These files are in the /Packages/RPMS directory on your installation CD-ROM:

- tcl-8.0.4-1.i386.rpm
- tcl-devel-8.0.4-1.i386.rpm
- tcl-devel-static-8.0.4-1.i386.rpm
- tclX-8.0.4-1.i386.rpm
- tclX-devel-8.0.4-1.i386.rpm
- tclX-devel-static-8.0.4-1.i386.rpm

You can (as `root`) install them by mounting the CD-ROM, navigating to that directory, and running the following commands:

```
rpm -ivh tcl-8.0.4-1.i386.rpm
rpm -ivh tcl-devel-8.0.4-1.i386.rpm
rpm -ivh tcl-devel-static-8.0.4-1.i386.rpm
rpm -ivh tclX-8.0.4-1.i386.rpm
rpm -ivh tclX-devel-8.0.4-1.i386.rpm
rpm -ivh tclX-devel-static-8.0.4-1.i386.rpm
```

Note

The exact filenames of the `.rpm` files on the CD-ROM will vary with exact Linux distribution and version.

Installing `tcl/tk` from Your Debian Install CD-ROM

You can install the full `tcl/tk` development environment in Debian with this command:

```
apt-get install tcl8.0 tcl8.0-dev tk8.0 tk8.0-dev
```

If you have configured your `apt` to use the Internet for installing packages, `apt-get` will automatically download `tcl` from there instead of from your CD-ROM.

Installing `tcl/tk` from the Internet

Since Web URLs can change from time to time, start by accessing the Scriptics Web site at `http://www.scriptics.com/`. Navigate to the download page, which at the time of this writing is at `http://www.scriptics.com/software/download.html`. Be sure to choose the UNIX release, which works for Linux. Since the UNIX release is a source release, you'll need to compile it. Be sure to read the compilation instructions, which at this writing are at `http://www.scriptics.com/support/howto/compile.html`.

At this writing you can purchase the Scriptics TCL Blast! CD-ROM, which contains a Linux binary release (Windows also) and an installer. If you are willing to part with a little money and to accept a slightly less up-to-date version of `tcl/tk`, this option can save you some time and trouble.

`tcl` Basics

`tcl` is an interpreted language similar to Perl or the UNIX shell, which means `tcl` commands are first read and then evaluated. `tk` is a windowing toolkit that uses the tcl syntax for creating GUI components such as buttons, scrollbars, dialog boxes, and windows.

To run tcl, the tcl shell (tclsh) or the windowing shell (wish) is required. Both tclsh and wish are similar to standard UNIX shells such as sh or csh, in that they allow commands to be executed interactively or read in from a file. In practice, these shells are seldom used interactively because their interactive capabilities are quite limited.

The main difference between tclsh and wish is that tclsh only understands tcl commands, while wish understands both tcl and tk commands.

Interactive Use of tcl

This section briefly covers the interactive use of the tcl shells to illustrate one of their hazards.

To start using tcl interactively, type **tclsh** at the UNIX shell's prompt (or **wish**, which works only in a graphical environment). The following prompt should appear:

```
%
```

In this chapter, interactive commands start with the percent character (%). Type the following at the prompt:

```
% echo "hello world"
```

The words hello world should appear, followed by a new prompt. Now try this code:

```
% puts "hello world"
```

The same output appears, but there is a big difference between the two outputs. The first command ran the echo binary to echo the string "hello world", whereas the second command uses the puts (put string) tcl command. The echo version of "hello world" works only when tclsh is run interactively, which is one of the hazards of using tclsh and wish interactively. For example, assume you put the following command into the file helloworld.tcl:

```
echo "hello world"
```

Now assume you source that file from tclsh:

```
% source helloworld.tcl
```

You get the following error:

```
invalid command name "echo"
```

This executes the command with its arguments in a UNIX shell. This is only one example of things that work differently in the interactive mode of the tcl shells.

Noninteractive Use of tcl

Commonly, `tclsh` and `wish` are used *noninteractively*, which means they are invoked on scripts from the UNIX prompt ($), such as the following:

```
$ tclsh myprog.tcl
$ wish myprog.tcl
```

They are also called from within a script that has, as its first line, something like the following:

```
#!/usr/bin/tclsh
```

Usually this first line must be changed for each installation of the script because `wish` or `tclsh` will be in different places. To avoid the need to edit the script for each installation, the man page for `tclsh` recommends that the following three lines be used as the first three lines of all `tcl/tk` scripts:

```
#!/bin/sh
# the next line restarts using tclsh \
exec wish "$0" "$@"
```

This means users only need to have `tclsh` in their path to use the script. Individual results with this approach could vary, depending on the version of `sh` on the system.

The real advantage of noninteractive `tcl` use is the same as for noninteractive use of the UNIX shell. Noninteractive use allows for many commands to be grouped together and executed by simply typing the name of the script It also allows for faster development and debugging of large programs.

The tcl Language

This section contains an introduction to the `tcl` language syntax and its use in scripts. The code in the following section can be run interactively or from a script. The spacing of the output will vary slightly in interactive mode. It is likely you will find it easier to edit and run scripts.

Command Structure

The basic structure of a `tcl` command is as follows:

```
commandname arguments
```

`commandname` is the command that `tcl` is to execute, and *`arguments`* is the optional arguments to give to that command. The entire line (*`commandname`* and *`arguments`*) is called

the *command*. Commands are separated by *newlines* (\n) or by a semicolon (;). If only one command is given on a line, the semicolon is not required. As an illustration, the two commands can be written one per line:

```
set foo 0
set bar 1
```

They can also be written on the same line:

```
set foo 0; set bar 1;
```

Sometimes you need to use the value of one expression in another. You use brackets to do that:

```
puts [expr 1000 / 4];
```

This prints out the number `250`. These brackets can be nested as necessary.

Comments

Other than commands, the only other lines in a `tcl` script are comments. As in UNIX shells and Perl, a *comment line* is a line that begins with a pound symbol (#):

```
# this is a comment
```

Unlike in a shell, the following is not a comment:

```
set foo 0 # initialize foo
```

This will result in an error because the `tcl` parser thinks a command is terminated either by a newline or a semicolon. To include comments on the same line as a command, the command needs to be terminated by a semicolon:

```
set foo 0;# initialize foo
```

It is probably a good idea to terminate all commands with a semicolon, although it is not required.

Datatypes

`tcl` doesn't support variable types such as `int`, `float`, `double`, or `char`. This means a variable can be set to a number, a character, or a string at different times in the same program.

Internally, however, `tcl` treats all variables as strings. When a variable needs to be manipulated, `tcl` allows numbers (real and integer) to be given in all the forms that are

understood by ANSI C. The following are examples of valid numeric values for variables:

`74`	Integer
`0112`	Octal, starts with `0`
`0x4a`	Hexadecimal, starts with `0x`
`74.`	Real
`74.0`	Real
`7.4e1`	Real
`7.4e+1`	Real

Other values are treated as strings and will generate errors if used in mathematical expressions.

Variables

`tcl` defines two types of variables—*scalars* and *arrays*. To create a scalar variable and assign it a value, use the `set` command. For example, the following creates the variable `banana` and gives it a value of `1`:

```
set banana 1;
```

To set the value of `banana` to something different, simply use `set` again:

```
set banana "Fresh from Brazil";
```

Now the variable `banana` has the value `"Fresh from Brazil"`. The double quotation marks tell `tcl` that all the characters, including the spaces, make up the value of the variable. (Quoting and substitution are covered later in this chapter's "Quoting and Substitution" section.)

To print out the value of `banana`, use the `puts` command:

```
puts $banana;
```

This prints the value of the variable `banana` to the standard output (sometimes referred to as `STDOUT`). Putting `$` before the name of the variable tells `tcl` to access the value assigned to that variable. This convention, known as *variable substitution*, is similar to conventions used in UNIX shells.

Note

Use the dollar sign when looking at or using the contents of the variable. Do not use the dollar sign when setting or changing the variable.

To create a one-dimensional array, enter the following:

```
set fruit(0) banana;
set fruit(1) orange;
```

This creates the array `fruit` and assigns the values `banana` and `orange` to the first and second elements, `0` and `1`.

Note

Remember, computers start counting with the number `0`, not `1`.

The assignments to array indexes need not be in order. The following commands create only three items in the array `fruit`:

```
set fruit(100) peach;
set fruit(2) kiwi;
set fruit(87) pear;
```

Arrays in `tcl` are like associative arrays, which associate a key with a value. Arrays in `tcl` associate a given string with another string. This makes it possible to have array indexes that are not numbers. This command sets the value of item `banana` in the array `fruit` to `100`:

```
set fruit(banana) 100
```

The assigned values need not be numeric:

```
set food(koala) eucalyptus;
set food(chipmunk) acorn;
```

Use the `$` convention to access the value stored in a one-dimensional array variable:

```
puts $food(koala);
```

This prints out the value stored in the array `food` at index `koala`. The array `index` can also be a variable:

```
set animal chipmunk;
puts $food($animal);
```

These commands will output `acorn`, given the previous assignments.

Multidimensional arrays are a simple extension of one-dimensional arrays and are set as follows:

```
set myarray(1,1) 0;
```

This sets the value of the item at `1,1` in the array `myarray` to `0`. By separating the indexes by commas, you can make arrays of three, four, or more dimensions:

```
set array(1,1,1,1,1,1) "foo";
```

In addition to setting array values, `tcl` provides the `array` command for getting information about arrays and the `parray` command for printing out information about arrays. First, take a look at the `parray` command. Assume you have these declarations:

```
set food(koala) eucalyptus;
set food(chipmunk) acorn;
set food(panda) bamboo;
```

Assume you have this command:

```
parray food
```

That command produces the following output:

```
food(chipmunk) = acorn
food(koala)   = eucalyptus
food(panda)   = bamboo
```

Now look at the `array` command and its arguments, which are used to get information about an array and its elements. The basic syntax for an `array` command is as follows:

```
array option arrayname
```

The supported options are discussed later in this section.

One of the most frequently used pieces of information about an array is its size. Assume these declarations:

```
set fruit(0) banana;
set fruit(1) peach;
set fruit(2) pear;
set fruit(3) apple;
```

Assume this command:

```
array size fruit;
```

`4` is returned. This number is often useful in loops.

Because arrays can have nonsequential or nonnumeric indexes, the `array` command provides an option for getting elements from an array. Assuming that the `food` array has been defined as presented earlier, the first thing you need to do to start getting elements is to use `startsearch` through the array. This is accomplished by first getting a search ID for the array:

```
set food_sid [array startsearch food];
```

The array startsearch food command inside the brackets returns a string, which is the name of the search (see the section "Quoting and Substitution"). You need this for future reference, so you assign its value to that of a variable; in this case, food_sid.

To get the first element (and every subsequent element) of the food array, use the following:

```
array nextelement food $food_sid;
```

When the array search is done, terminate the search for the array by using this code:

```
array donesearch food $food_sid;
```

One other option to the array command that is frequently in use while iterating through an array is the anymore option. It returns true (a value of 1) if there are any more items in the search. For example, the following returns 1 the first two times it is used with the food array declared earlier:

```
array anymore food $food_sid;
```

Use the unset command to dispose of a variable (scalar or array):

```
unset banana;
```

This unsets the variable banana. If you use unset $banana (assuming that banana was set to the value shown earlier) instead of just banana, you get an error like this:

```
can't unset "0": no such variable
```

This occurs because when $ precedes a variable's name, the value of the variable is substituted in before the command is executed.

Manipulating String Values

The simplest form of string manipulation is the append command, which concatenates multiple strings and variables together. The following commands are examples:

```
set str1 ""Begin"";
append str1 "" a String"";
set str2 " even more text";
append str1 " with some text" " and add" $str2 " to it.";
puts $str1;
```

They give this output:

```
Begin a String with some text and add even more text to it.
```

You can achieve the same results by using the following commands:

```
set str1 "Begin";
```

```
set str1 "$str1 a String";
set str2 " even more text";
set str1 "$str1 with some text and add$str2 to it.";
```

This will be slower than using `append` because it does not do character copying as `set` does.

For more advanced string manipulation, `tcl` provides the `string` command, which understands a whole host of options. The basic syntax of the `string` command is as follows:

`string` *`option string1 string2`*

`string1` and *`string2`* can either be literal strings (`"this is a string"`) or variables, and *`option`* is one of the following:

`compare`	Returns `-1`, `0`, or `1`, depending on whether *`string1`* is lexographically less than, equal to, or greater than *`string2`* (similar to the C library function `strcmp`).
`first`	Returns the index of the first occurrence of *`string1`* in *`string2`*, or `-1` if *`string1`* does not occur in *`string2`*.
`last`	Returns the index of the last occurrence of *`string1`* in *`string2`*, or `-1` if *`string1`* does not occur in *`string2`*.

The following options to the `string` command interpret *`string2`* as a list of characters to trim from *`string1`*:

`trim`	Removes any leading and trailing characters present in *`string2`* from *`string1`*.
`trimleft`	Removes any leading characters present in *`string2`* from *`string1`*.
`trimright`	Removes any trailing characters present in *`string2`* from *`string1`*.

The following options to the `string` command only take *`string1`* as an argument:

`length`	Returns the number of characters in *`string1`*.
`tolower`	Returns a new string with all of the characters in *`string1`* converted to lowercase.
`toupper`	Returns a new string with all of the characters in *`string1`* converted to uppercase.

Now look at a few examples. First, make a string and get its length:

```
set str " Here Is A Test String ";
string length $str;
```

This gives a length of 23 (the length option counts whitespace characters). Now get the location of the first and last occurrences of the string "st" in $str:

```
string first "st" $str;
string last "st" $str
```

This gives a value of 13 for the first occurrence of "st" (corresponding to the occurrence in Test) and a value of 13 for the last occurrence of "st" (Test again). What about the "st" in String? Well, most of the string comparison functions are case- and whitespace-sensitive, so temporarily convert $str to lowercase and try again:

```
string last "st" [string tolower $str];
```

This gives a value of 16, which corresponds to the "st" in String. Finally, strip off the leading and trailing spaces and get a length for the string:

```
string length [string trim $str " "];
```

The value 21 is returned, which means the first and last spaces were stripped off.

Manipulating Numeric Values

tcl provides two commands for manipulating numeric variables and constants: incr and expr.

The incr command gives tcl an equivalent to the C language operators +=, -=, ++, and --. The basic syntax is as follows:

```
incr variable integer
```

variable must be an integer. The incr command adds the given *integer* to the *variable*; thus, decrementing is handled by giving negative integers. We can demonstrate its usage. First, create a variable and do an incr on it:

```
set a 81;
incr a;
puts $a;
```

$a has a value of 82. By default, incr is the same as ++; if it is not given an integer argument, it adds one to the named variable. Now decrement $a by 3:

```
incr a -3
puts $a
```

Note that `$a` has a value of `79`. One last point is that the integer can be the value of a variable:

```
set a 6;
set b 9;
incr a $b;
puts $a;
```

`$a` has a value of `15`.

For more complex mathematical operations, `tcl` provides the `expr` command, which works with all standard ANSI C operators. Operator precedence is mostly the same as in ANSI C.

When any mathematical operations are required, they must be preceded by the `expr` command. For example, look at these commands:

```
set a 20;
set b 4;
set c $a/$b;
puts $c;
```

Instead of the desired result of `5`, the preceding code outputs:

```
20/4
```

Use the `expr` command to get the right answer:

```
set c [expr $a / $b];
```

In addition to the standard operators `+`, `-`, `*`, and `/`, the `expr` command can be given several options that enable it to perform mathematical operations. The basic syntax is this:

```
expr function number
```

`expr` understands some of the following functions, along with the values they return:

`abs(x)`	Absolute value of `x`
`round(x)`	The integer value resulting from rounding `x`
`cos(x)`	Cosine of `x` (`x` in radians)
`cosh(x)`	Hyperbolic cosine of `x`
`acos(x)`	Arccosine of `x` (0 to pi)
`sin(x)`	Sine of `x` (`x` in radians)
`sinh(x)`	Hyperbolic sine of `x`
`asin(x)`	Arcsine of `x` (–pi/2 to pi/2)
`tan(x)`	Tangent of `x` (`x` in radians)

`tanh(x)`	Hyperbolic tangent of x
`atan(x)`	Arctangent of x (–pi/2 to pi/2)
`exp(x)`	e raised to the power of x
`log(x)`	Natural log of x
`log10(x)`	Log base 10 of x
`sqrt(x)`	The square root of x

The following math function takes two number arguments:

`pow(x,y)`	x raised to the power of y

This is used as follows:

```
set a 2;
set b [expr pow($a,3)];
puts $b;
```

The output is `8.0`, the value of `2` raised to the third power.

Quoting and Substitution

Quoting and substitution are both used heavily in relation to variables. You saw the most basic version of quoting (using double quotation marks to make strings) and substitution earlier in this chapter. `tcl` supports one more type of quoting—brace quoting—and one more type of substitution—command substitution.

To review, the most common use of double quotation marks is to create strings with embedded whitespace:

```
set kiwi "Fresh from New Zealand";
```

Double quotation marks can also be used to make multiline strings:

```
set kiwi "Fresh from
New Zealand 3 for a dollar";
```

In addition to making multiline strings, the standard ANSI C language escape sequences can be used in `tcl` strings:

```
set kiwi "Fresh from New Zealand\n\t3 for a dollar."
```

This outputs the following:

```
Fresh from New Zealand
   3 for a dollar.
```

The two types of substitution can also be applied within double quotation–marked strings. The first type of substitution—variable substitution—is explained in the

"Variables" section earlier in this chapter. In a double quotation–marked string, you can access the value of a variable by preceding the variable's name with `$`. Look at the following commands:

```
set fruit kiwi;
set place "New Zealand";
set how_many 3;
puts "$fruit, fresh from $place, $how_many for a dollar";
```

They output this:

```
kiwi, fresh from New Zealand, 3 for a dollar
```

The other type of substitution is command substitution. A *command substitution* block begins with a left bracket (`[`) and ends with a right bracket (`]`):

```
set len_in 2;     puts "$len_in inches is [expr $len_in*2.54] cm";
```

The preceding code produces the following output:

```
2 inches is 5.08 cm
```

The `5.08` is the result of the `expr $len_in*2.54` command:

Because this command is in brackets, the value it returns is substituted in. In this case, the `tcl` command `expr` is used, but any `tcl` command can be placed between brackets. Command substitution can be used in most commands and is not limited to double quotation–marked commands. For example, the following three commands produce the same output as the single line of code below them:

```
set len_in 2;
set len_cm [expr $len_in*2.54];
puts "$len_in inches is $len_cm cm";
```

```
set len_in 2;     puts "$len_in inches is [expr $len_in*2.54] cm";
```

The other type of quoting available in `tcl` is *brace quoting*, which is similar to using single quotation marks in UNIX shells. Brace quoting creates a string with the given characters, no substitution (command or variable) takes place, and the C language escape sequences are not interpreted:

```
puts "This\nis a\nmulti-line\nstring"
```

The preceding code produces the following output:

```
This
is a
multi-line
string
```

Contrast the previous example with the following code, which uses braces instead of quotation marks:

```
puts {This\nis a\nmulti-line\nstring}
```

The preceding code produces the following output.

```
This\nis a\nmulti-line\nstring
```

To get tabs, newlines, and other special characters in a brace quotation–marked string, they must be entered physically, like this:

```
puts {This
is a
multi-line
string}
```

This will produce the desired output. The real use for brace quotation–marked strings comes when certain characters with special meanings need to be given as values for variables. For example:

```
set price 1.00;
puts "Pears, $$price per pound";
```

The preceding code produces the following output:

```
Pears, $1.00 per pound
```

Because `$$price` has the potential to be confusing, it is better if the variable `price` has the value `$1.00`. You could use brace quotations to achieve the following:

```
set price {$1.00};
puts "Pears, $price per pound";
```

Brace quoting is also used to defer evaluation in control structures and procedure definitions. In such cases, the values of variables are substituted in after the entire block is read.

Flow Control—`if` and `switch`

`tcl` provides several commands for flow control and supports all the standard ANSI C comparison operators for both string and numeric data.

This section starts with the `if/elseif/else` commands. The simplest `if` statement is one like the following:

```
if {$x < 0} {
   set x 10;
}
```

Caution

tcl is very picky about braces and spaces. The beginning brace of an `if`, `elseif`, or `else` statement must be on the same line as the `if`, `elseif`, or `else`. The outside of braces must always border on a space. An `else` or `elseif` statement must always be on the same line as the closing brace of the previous `if` or `elseif`.

This example has only one line in the body of the `if` clause, but any number of lines and subblocks can be added. If additional tests need to be performed, each test is given in parentheses as follows:

```
if { ($x == "SJ") || ($x == "LA") } {
   puts "You Live in California!";
}
```

Tests can be nested as in the following example:

```
if { ( ($arch == "ppc") || ($arch == "intel") ) && ($os != "Linux") } {
   puts "Get Linux!";
}
```

Adding an `else` clause to an `if` statement is done like this:

```
if {$x <= 0} {
   set x 10;
} else {
   set x 0;
}
```

You can also add as many `elseif` statements as desired:

```
if {$x == 0} {
   set x 10;
} elseif {$x == 10} {
   incr x -1;
} elseif {$x == 100} {
   set x 50;
} else {
   set x 0;
}
```

In many cases, adding extra `elseif` statements becomes cumbersome and makes the code difficult to understand. To provide a more compact way of expressing the same logic, `tcl` implements the `switch` command. `switch` works by associating a value (string or number) with a block. The preceding `if` statement, when written as a `switch` statement, becomes this:

```
switch $x {
   0 {set x 10;}
   10 {incr x -1;}
   100 {set x 50;}
}
```

By default, only the block corresponding to the matched valuc is executed, but a `switch` statement can implement *fallthrough* (the execution of everything after the first matching value) if the block is designated as a single minus sign (-). The `switch` statement is shown here:

```
switch $x {
   0 -
   10 -
   100 {incr x -1}
}
```

The `switch` statement is equivalent to the following `if` statement:

```
if { ($x == 0) ¦¦ ($x == 10) ¦¦ ($x == 100) } {
   incr x -1;
}
```

Loops

`tcl` provides three loop commands:

- `for`
- `foreach`
- `while`

`tcl` also provides two loop control commands:

- `break`
- `continue`

The `while` loop executes its body while its test condition is `true`. The structure can be `thought` of as this:

```
while {condition} {block}
```

The following is a simple `while` loop that counts to `10`:

```
set x 0;
while {$x < 10} {
   incr x;
   puts $x;
}
```

Caution

The beginning brace of a `for`, `foreach`, or `while` statement must be on the same line as the `for`, `foreach`, or `while`. The outside of braces must always border on a space.

The `foreach` loop iterates over a set of arguments and executes its body each time. The `foreach` loop has the following structure:

```
foreach variable {items} {block}
```

`variable` is the name of the variable to which each item in the set *`items`* is assigned in turn. Here is an example:

```
foreach element {o c n p li} {
   switch $element {
      o -
      n {puts gas;}
      c -
      p -
      li {puts solid;}
   }
}
```

In this case, the list of items to check is specified, but a variable can be used also:

```
set elements "o c n p li";
foreach element $elements {
   switch $element {
      o -
      n {puts gas;}
      c -
      p -
      li {puts solid;}
   }
}
```

If a variable instead of a list of items is given, braces should not be used because the braces would be treated as if used for quoting.

The for loop allows the most control while looping. It can be broken down like this:

```
for {initialization} {condition} {increment} {body}
```

A simple for loop example that counts to 10 is this:

```
for {set i 0} {$i <= 10} {incr i} { puts $i; }
```

You have seen simple initialization statements, but the initialization and increment parts of the for loop can be as complicated as required.

Now for a look at the break and continue loop control commands: The break command terminates execution of loop and executes the next line of code after the loop's block; the continue command skips to the next iteration of the loop.

The continue command is handy for reading in initialization files where comment lines need to be allowed. If the following statement is included in a loop that reads in a file, all lines that start with a pound sign (#) will be skipped.

```
if { [regexp {^#} [string trim $line] ]} {continue;}
```

File I/O and File Information

tcl provides a simple and effective method for file input and output similar to the methods in the C-standard I/O library. The first step in file I/O is to open a file and get a file handle or file ID. As an example, the following command opens the file /etc/host.conf with mode r and returns a file handle assigned to the variable f:

```
set f [ open /etc/host.conf r];
```

Caution

Be sure to use r for the mode. Other letters could corrupt or delete information in /etc/host.conf.

tcl supports the following file open modes:

r	Open for reading only; the file must exist.
r+	Open for reading and writing; the file must exist.
w	Open for writing. The file will be created if it does not exist; otherwise, it is truncated.
w+	Same as w, except the file is opened for reading also.

a	Open the file for appending text; the file will be created if it does not exist.
a+	Same as a, except the file is opened for reading also.

The open command can also be overloaded to run subprocesses with more control than the exec command provides. To open a process instead of a file, replace the filename with a brace quotation–marked string beginning with a pipe character (¦) and containing the command to run. For example, the following command opens a ps for reading:

```
set f [ open {¦ ps } r ];
```

For processes opened in this manner, the tcl command pid returns the process ID of the file handle associated with a process. For the preceding example, this code returns the pid associated with $f, the file handle for the ps command that was opened:

```
pid $f
```

If a file (or process) is opened in a mode that supports reading, you can read from the file by using the gets command. The following while command is often used to process all the lines of a file:

```
while { [ gets $f line ] >= 0 }
```

This works because the gets command returns -1 when EOF is reached. In this case, the gets command reads in a line from the file handle $f and assigns the value to the variable line. $line can be accessed and manipulated in the body of the loop.

If a file is opened for writing, the puts command can be used to write output to the file. If the file handle $f corresponds to a file opened for writing, the following command writes the string "This is a line of text" to the open file:

```
puts $f "This is a line of text";
```

The only other file I/O command is the close command, which takes as its argument a file handle. You would simply use this to close the file you opened earlier:

```
close $f;
```

It is probably a good idea to close any file handles that are open at the end of a program. Also, if the same file handle variable is to be reused several times in a program, it is a good idea to close it before the next open.

In addition to reading and writing from files, it is sometimes necessary to obtain information about files. tcl provides the file command to accomplish this. The file command's syntax follows:

```
file option filename
```

filename is the name of the file to run the tests on and *option* is one of the following options, which return true (1) or false (0) information about files:

executable	True if the file is executable by the current user
exists	True if the file exists
isdirectory	True if the file is a directory
isfile	True if the file is a regular file
owned	True if the current user owns the file
readable	True if the file is readable by the current user
writable	True if the file is writable by the current user

The following options return additional information about a file:

atime	Returns the time the file was last accessed in seconds since January 1, 1970.
mtime	Returns the time the file was last modified in seconds since January 1, 1970.
size	Returns the size of the file in bytes.
readlink	Returns the value of a symbolic link if the given file is a symbolic link.
type	Returns a string giving the type of file.

Procedures

Procedures are the tcl equivalent of functions in the C language. The proc command creates a procedure, which has the following syntax:

```
proc procedure_name {arguments} {body}
```

The number of arguments is variable, and an empty argument list is specified by {}. *body* can contain any valid tcl statement and can be as long as required.

A simple procedure that takes no arguments is as follows:

```
proc test_proc {} { puts "procedure test"; }
```

To invoke this procedure, simply give its name (test_proc;) to get the output:

```
procedure test
```

A more realistic example is a file output procedure, which takes in as an argument a filename:

```
proc cat {filename} {
   set f [open $filename r];
```

```
    while { [ gets $f line ] >= 0 } {
        puts $line;
    }
    close $f;
}
```

Caution

The beginning brace of the procedure must be on the same line as the `proc` keyword. The outside of braces must always border a space.

To invoke this procedure with `/etc/host.conf` as its argument, use the following:

```
cat /etc/host.conf
```

This prints out the contents of `/etc/host.conf`.

Three important commands for use in procedures are `return`, `global`, and `catch`. The `global` command gives a procedure access to global variables, and the `return` command returns a value from a procedure. The `catch` command is useful for detecting errors and returning a failure value.

You can rewrite the `cat` procedure to be a little more robust by doing the following:

```
proc cat {filename} {
    set ret_code 0;
    catch {
        set f [open $filename r];
        while { [ gets $f line ] >= 0 } {
            puts $line;
        }
        close $f;
        set ret_code 1;
    }
return $ret_code;
}
```

This code demonstrates the use of both `catch` and `return`. If any parts of the procedure fail, it returns `0` (false). If the `cat` is successful, it returns `1` (true). This information is useful if `cat` is called with a process to execute as its argument.

The tk Toolkit

The `tk` toolkit enables X Window GUIs to be written via the `tcl` scripting language. The `tk` toolkit adds to the `tcl` language by enabling the creation of GUI components called *widgets*. This section looks briefly at the available tk widgets and shows how to create them.

Introduction to Widgets

The basic method for creating a widget is as follows:

```
widget_type path option
```

widget_type is one of the widget types given in the following list; *path* is a window pathname (usually starting with a dot, which is the name of the root window); and *option* is any option the widget understands.

The tk toolkit defines the following widget types:

canvas	Allows for drawing objects
entry	Allows for the input of a single line of text
frame	Used to contain other widgets
listbox	Displays a set of strings and allows for choosing one or more of them
menu	Displays a menu bar and menu items
text	Displays multiple lines of text
label	Displays a single line of static text
button	A widget that displays a clickable button
checkbutton	Displays a checkable box
radiobutton	Displays several mutually exclusive checkable boxes
scale	Similar to a slider that sets a value

To create and manipulate widgets, the windowing shell, wish, must be used. To invoke wish interactively, type **wish** at the UNIX prompt. The following wish prompt appears:

```
%
```

An empty window pops up on the screen along with this prompt. This window is the wish root window (called .) and all the widgets that are created will appear within it.

Creating Widgets

This section shows how to create a widget and manipulate it. First, create a button:

```
button .button;
```

What did that do?

The widget type is specified as `button`, so `tk` created a button. The path is `.button`, so `tk` created the button in the `root` window (`.` is the `root` tk window) and named it `button`.

Where is the button, anyway?

The button isn't displayed right now; `tk` simply created it. To display the button, you need to tell `tk` how to display the widget. For this, use the `pack` command and give it the `path` to the widget you want to display:

```
pack .button;
```

Now the button is showing, but it's blank (see Figure 30.1). This is where the widget's options come into play.

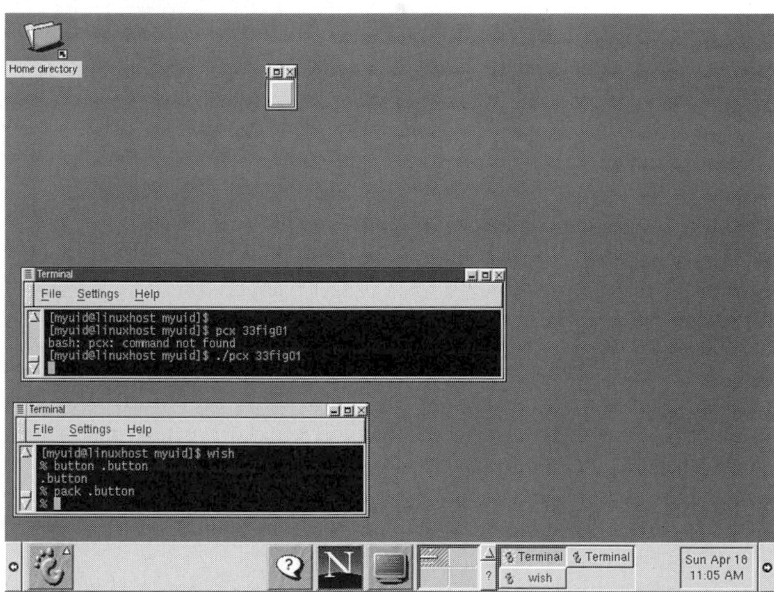

FIGURE 30.1
The widget starts as a plain button.

Note

Your output may look slightly different from the figures in this chapter. The appearance of `tk` graphical output varies slightly between distributions and desktops.

Widget Options

All tk widgets use standard options that control appearance and function. Most widgets understand the following options:

`-background color, -bg color`	The background color of the widget. Valid values are of the form #RRGGBB, #RRRGGGBBB, or one of the names defined in /usr/lib/X11/rgb.txt.
`-foreground color, -fg color`	The foreground color of the widget. Valid values are of the form #RRGGBB, #RRRGGGBBB, or one of the names defined in /usr/lib/X11/rgb.txt.
`-height pixels`	The widget's height in pixels.
`-width pixels`	The widget's width in pixels.
`-borderwidth pixels, -db pixels`	The width of the widget's border in pixels.
`-padx pixels`	Extra space required by the widget in the x direction.
`-pady pixels`	Extra space required by the widget in the y direction.
`-relief type`	The 3D effect of the widget, where *type* is one of these strings: flat, raised, groove, ridge, or sunken.
`-text string`	The string to display in the widget.
`-font font`	The font to be used for the text displayed in a widget; valid font definitions are given by the command xlsfonts.
`-command command`	The tcl command to execute when the widget is used; usually this is the name of a procedure or an exec statement.

In addition to these options, the pack command understands the following options of its own:

`-side type`	Controls the order in which widgets are placed. Valid types are left, right, top, or bottom. For example, left indicates that new widgets should be placed to the left of existing widgets.
`-fill type`	Controls whether widgets are stretched to fill open space in the window. Valid values are none, x, y, or both. For example, both indicates that widgets should fill all open space.
`-expand value`	Controls whether widgets expand if the window's size increases. *value* is either 0 or 1, with 1 indicating true.

A tcl/tk Widget Programming Example

Now that you know about the options for widgets and for `pack`, you can start using them. `reliefs` are an interesting widget feature. The widgets get their 3D look from a `relief`. To get an idea of how each `relief` looks, make some labels using the following:

```
foreach i {raised sunken flat groove ridge} {
   label .$i -relief $i -text $i;
   pack .$i
}
```

This example iterates through the set of relief types, creating one `label` for each type, along with setting each label's `text` to be the `relief` type. The layout will look similar to Figure 30.2.

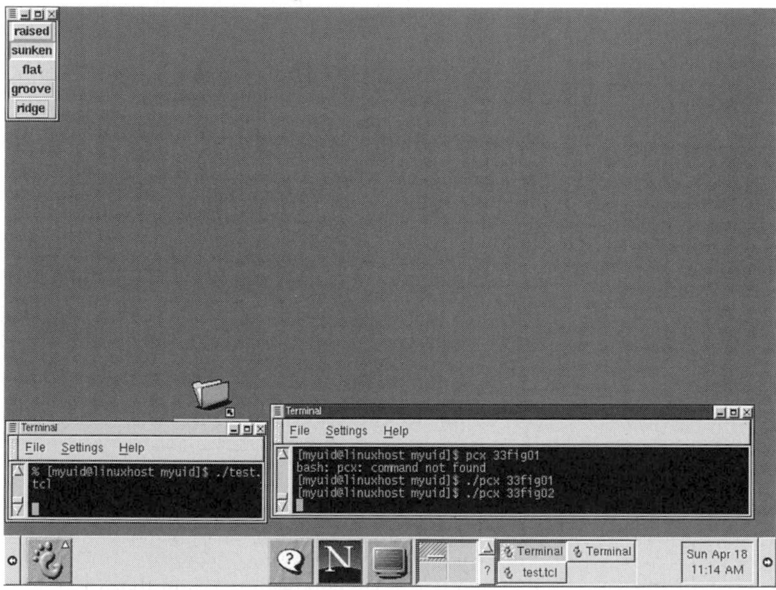

FIGURE 30.2
Labels of varying `relief`.

There are two things to notice here. First, the labels are not all the same size. Second, the labels are stacked one on top of the other. This is an example of the `pack` command's default behavior; it determines the size of each widget automatically and then places each widget below the previously placed widget.

Now make all the labels the same size and pack them next to each other, instead of one on top of the other. There are two ways to do this. The first is to rewrite the loop:

```
foreach i {raised sunken flat groove ridge} {
   label .$i -relief $i -text $i -height 10 -width 10;
   pack .$i -side left;
}
```

The second way is to reconfigure the labels by using the `configure` option, which has the following syntax:

```
widget configure option
```

In this case, you could use the following loop (after the labels are created):

```
foreach i {raised sunken flat groove ridge} {
   .$i configure -height 10 -width 10;
   pack .$i -side left;
}
```

Why use `configure`?

If `wish` is run interactively and one version of the loop is given, modifying and running it again produces the following error:

```
window name "raised" already exists in parent
```

This is how `wish` tells the programmer that the program has attempted to re-create an existing widget (this time, with the label raised). You need to use `configure`; in fact, `configure` is required anytime an existing widget needs to be changed.

In this case, the only way to use the new version of the loop is to destroy the existing labels via the `destroy` command:

```
foreach i {raised sunken flat groove ridge} { destroy .$i }
```

The new result will be similar to Figure 30.3.

Now back to the example. Two things in Figure 30.3 need to be fixed. First, it is difficult to tell the labels apart. Second, most of the window is blank.

You can make the labels easier to distinguish by padding them when they are packed and by increasing their borderwidths. To have the labels take up all of the available space, give `pack` the `fill` option for both `x` and `y` and set the `expand` option to `true`:

```
foreach i {raised sunken flat groove ridge} {
   label .$i -relief $i -text $i;
   .$i configure -height 5 -width 5 -borderwidth 5;
   pack .$i -side left -padx 5 -pady 5 -fill both -expand 1;
}
```

The result will be similar to Figure 30.4.

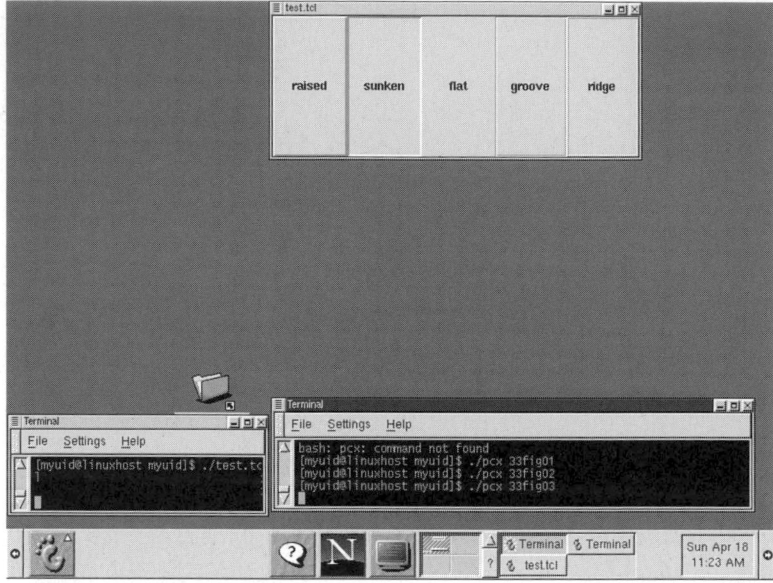

FIGURE 30.3
Labels of varying `relief`*, packed next to each other.*

FIGURE 30.4
The labels here are padded.

Note

To see the effect of the fill and expand options, you need to resize the window (see Figure 30.4) and watch the labels expand and contract to fit the window.

This example can be easily changed to use any of the widget types by replacing `label` with a different type of widget.

A tcl/tk Interface to xsetroot

This section introduces some of the other capabilities of the `tk` toolkit by applying them to the development of a GUI front end for the X Window program `xsetroot`.

Most X Window users will be familiar with the X Window program `xsetroot`, which can be used to set the background color of the `root` window, under X11. The actual command is as follows:

```
xsetroot -solid color
```

`color` can be given in the form `#RRGGBB`. The front end allows for colors to be previewed and then applied.

Note

On systems with 8-bit or less color (256 or fewer colors), many colors will cause an error similar to this:

```
xsetroot: unable to allocate color for "#590000".
```

This is not a problem with your program, but instead is a property of your video. Running the `xsetroot` command with that same color as its argument would produce the same result. Here is an example:

```
#xsetroot -solid "#590000"
#xsetroot: unable to allocate color for "#590000".
```

On limited color monitors, always test your program with each slider either all the way up or all the way down.

You can get started now. The first thing you need is a variable that holds the color. You then need to create two basic frames, one for the application's main area and another in which to put messages. You also need a third frame for the controls.

Frames are handy because they can be used to pack items of a particular type or function together. Also, they are useful in partitioning a window into sections that don't change.

Create the frames and the color globally:

```
set color "#000000";
frame .main_frame;
```

```
frame .message_frame;
frame .control_frame;
```

Now pack the frames:

```
pack .control_frame -in .main_frame -expand 1 -fill both;
pack .main_frame -anchor c -expand 1;
pack .message_frame -anchor s -padx 2 -pady 2 \
-fill x -expand 1;
```

You also need to create a label to handle messages. This is done here as a procedure, so it will be easy to modify and execute:

```
proc make_message_label {} {
   label .message_label -relief sunken;
   pack .message_label -anchor c \
   -in .message_frame -padx 2 \
   -pady 2 -fill both -expand 1;
}
```

Pack the message label into the `.message_frame` so it is at the bottom of the window at all times.

Now make the scales. You need three scales—one each for red, blue, and green, with each one going from `0` to `255`. You also need to pack the scales and their corresponding labels in their own frame:

```
proc make_scales {} {
   frame .scale_frame;
   foreach i {red green blue} {
      frame .scale_frame_$i -bg $i;
      label .label_$i -text $i -bg $i \
      -fg white;
      scale .scale_$i -from 0 -to 255 \
      -command setColor;
      pack .label_$i .scale_$i \
      -in .scale_frame_$i;
      pack .scale_frame_$i -in .scale_frame \
      -side left -padx 2 -pady 2;
   }
   pack .scale_frame -in .control_frame \
   -side left -expand 1;
}
```

This procedure is a good example of using frames. In all, this example creates four frames, one for each slider and label pair and overall frame. Adding the labels and sliders to their own frames simplifies the overall layout strategy.

Another example in this procedure is the use of the -command option for a widget. Each time the scales change, the command specified by the -command option is executed. In this case, the setColor command, which sets the global variable color, is executed:

```
proc setColor {value} {
   global color;
   foreach i {red green blue} {
      set $i [format %02x [.scale_$i get]];
   }
   set color "#$red$green$blue";
   .preview_label configure -bg $color;
   .message_label configure -text "$color";
}
```

You can preview the color change by setting the background color of the widget, .preview_label. Use the following procedure to create .preview label:

```
proc make_preview {} {
   global color;

   frame .preview_frame;
   label .preview_label -bg $color \
   -height 5 -width 5;
   pack .preview_label -in .preview_frame \
   -padx 2 -pady 2 -fill both \
   -anchor c -expand 1;
   pack .preview_frame -in .control_frame \
   -side bottom -fill both -expand 1 \
   -padx 2 -pady 2;
}
```

Now you need to add a few buttons—one to apply the changes and another to quit the program. Use the following procedure:

```
proc make_buttons {} {
   frame .button_frame;
   button .apply -text "apply" \
   -command setRootColor;
   button .quit -text "quit" -command exit;
   pack .apply .quit -in .button_frame \
   -fill both -expand 1 -padx 2 \
   -pady 2 -side left;
   pack .button_frame -in .main_frame \
   -fill both;
}
```

You also need the following procedure, which sets the root color:

```
proc setRootColor {} {
   global color;
```

```
    catch {
        exec xsetroot -solid $color;
    } msg;

    if {$msg != {}} {
        set msg "An ($msg) error occurred";
    } else {
        set msg "$color";
    }

    .message_label configure -text $msg;
}
```

Now that you are done with the procedures, invoke them:

```
make_message_label;
make_scales;
make_preview;
make_buttons;
```

You are now ready to test your little `tcl` application. When the application is run, the resulting window should look like Figure 30.5.

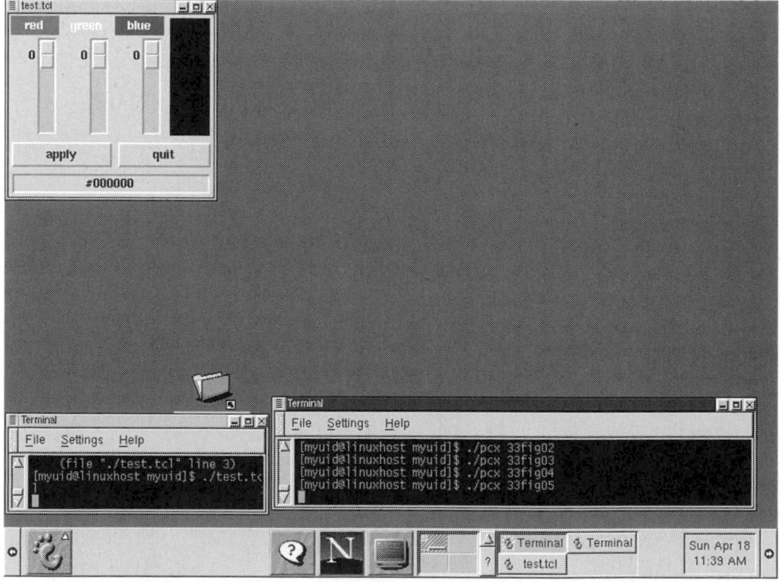

FIGURE 30.5
The `tksetroot` application window with buttons and colors.

Listing 30.1 contains the complete source code of the `tksetroot` application.

LISTING 30.1 *tksetroot*

```
set color "#000000";
frame .main_frame;
frame .message_frame;
frame .control_frame;

pack .control_frame -in .main_frame -expand 1 -fill both;
pack .main_frame -anchor c -expand 1;
pack .message_frame -anchor s -padx 2 -pady 2 \
-fill x -expand 1;

proc make_message_label {} {
   label .message_label -relief sunken;
   pack .message_label -anchor c -in .message_frame \
   -padx 2 -pady 2 -fill both -expand 1;
}

proc make_scales {} {
   frame .scale_frame;
   foreach i {red green blue} {
      frame .scale_frame_$i -bg $i;
      label .label_$i -text $i -bg $i -fg white;
      scale .scale_$i -from 0 -to 255 \
      -command setColor;
      pack .label_$i .scale_$i -in .scale_frame_$i;
      pack .scale_frame_$i -in .scale_frame -side left \
      -padx 2 -pady 2;
   }
   pack .scale_frame -in .control_frame -side left -expand 1;
}

proc setColor {value} {
   global color;
   foreach i {red green blue} {
      set $i [format %02x [.scale_$i get]];
   }
set color "#$red$green$blue";
   .preview_label configure -bg $color;
   .message_label configure -text "$color";
}

proc make_preview {} {
   global color;

   frame .preview_frame;
   label .preview_label -bg $color \
   -height 5 -width 5;
   pack .preview_label -in .preview_frame \
   -padx 2 -pady 2 -fill both -anchor c \
```

continues

LISTING 30.1 continued

```
   -expand 1;
   pack .preview_frame -in .control_frame \
   -side top -fill both -expand 1 \
   -padx 2 -pady 2;
}

proc make_buttons {} {
   frame .button_frame;
   button .apply -text "apply" -command setRootColor;
   button .quit -text "quit" -command exit;
   pack .apply .quit -in .button_frame -fill both \
   -expand 1 -padx 2 -pady 2 -side left;
   pack .button_frame -in .main_frame -fill both;
}

proc setRootColor {} {
   global color;

   catch {
      exec xsetroot -solid $color;
   } msg;

   if {$msg != {}} {
      set msg "An ($msg) error occurred";
   } else {
      set msg "$color";
   }

   .message_label configure -text $msg;
}

make_message_label;
make_scales;
make_preview;
make_buttons;
```

Summary

This chapter was an introduction to programming in `tcl/tk`. The examples demonstrated the power of `tcl/tk`, which lies in its capability to make user interfaces within a short amount of time and with little code. Although this chapter covered many `tcl/tk` features, there are many more. This chapter was a stepping stone, and you will hopefully enjoy many years of developing `tcl/tk` applications.

CHAPTER 31

Programming in Python

IN THIS CHAPTER

Python is a public domain, object-oriented, dynamic language. Developed in 1990 by Guido van Rossum and named after the Monty Python troop, Python has become popular as both a scripting language and a rapid-development tool. Python is true freeware because there are no rules about copying the software or distributing any applications developed with it. When you obtain a copy of Python, you get all of the source code, a debugger, a code profiler, and a set of interfaces for most GUIs in use today. Python runs on practically any operating system platform, including Linux.

Python, which has quickly become one of the most popular languages in use, is often referred to as a bridging language between compiled languages such as C and scripting languages such as Perl and `tcl/tk`. What makes Python so popular? The language lends itself to scripting, but several aspects of Python make it much more than a simple scripting tool. For example, Python is extensible, allowing the language to adapt and expand to meet your requirements. Python code is simple to read and maintain. Python is also object-oriented, although you do not need to use OO features as part of your developments. Sounds powerful, doesn't it? At the same time, Python is remarkably easy to use, with no type declarations to worry about and no compile-link cycles to go through. As you will see in this chapter, you can quickly learn to use Python, and the language grows with you as your programming abilities increase.

Note

The Python Software Activity (PSA) group was group was formed to provide a development center forformed to provide a development center for Python. A Web site devoted to Python is at `http://www.python.org`. This Web site contains voluminous Python documentation, and should be consulted whenever this chapter recommends looking at Python documentation.

To support the Python language, the Usenet `newsgroup comp.lang.python` sees lots of traffic. Distributions of Python are available from many Web and FTP sites. Red Hat, Caldera, and Debian all offer Python as part of their CD-ROM bundle.

Getting Ready to Run Python

If you want to play with Python as we go through the programming language in more detail, you need to install the Python programming tools on your Linux system if they aren't there already. You also need to set up your environment so it knows about Python and the directories to search for Python files.

Red Hat installs Python by default because Red Hat writes many of its tools in Python. Caldera also installs Python by default. Python may or may not be installed for you if you run Debian; whether it is installed depends upon how you installed your system and which installation options you chose. You can determine if it is installed by verifying the existence of the file `/usr/bin/python`. You can install Python on a Debian system by searching for the string *python* in the `dselect` program, and installing all such instances. You can install a minimal Python by installing only python-base.

Installing Python

If for some reason you don't have the CD-ROM, or you want to check for more recent versions, the easiest place to find the code is through the Python FTP site (`ftp://ftp.python.org/pub/python/src`). You can use anonymous FTP to obtain the source code.

Python source files are usually supplied as C source code, which you need to compile and link, using any C compiler on your system. The FTP site also contains precompiled binaries for many target hardware and operating system combinations, making compilation unnecessary. Make sure you download the binary that's appropriate for your machine.

Tip

To make obtaining the proper binaries or source code even simpler, the Python Web site has been updated to allow you to choose the proper platform and operating system. The appropriate binaries are then transferred for you. Even if you have the binaries, you might want to obtain the source code. This is especially true if you plan to add any C extensions to Python. Anytime Python is extended, the entire binary has to be recompiled and relinked; the source code is necessary.

At the time of writing, the 1.5.2 release of Python was available on the FTP and Web sites. Versions of Python for several UNIX versions, Linux, Windows, and Macintosh are all available.

If you download just the source code, Python is usually supplied as a gzipped file that requires `gzip -d` to unpack. The packed file usually shows the version number as part of the name, such as python1.3, which means version 1.3 of the system. The file extension is usually `.tar.gz` or `.tgz`., both of which are unpacked using the same commands.

One or more README files are usually included with the Python distribution, often containing the compilation process and hints for your operating system. To begin the installation process, use a command similar to this to unpack the gzipped file:

```
gzip -d python1.X.tar.gz
```

The preceding command is an example. You must substitute your filename for `python1.X.tar.gz` in the command, of course. Then, use this command to untar the file:

```
tar xvf python1.X.tar
```

Again, use the proper filename. Note that this command works with both `.tar.gz` and `.tgz` extensions. Note also that you can use both the `gzip -d` and the `tar` commands with the `-z tar` option, as illustrated in the following example:

```
tar xvzf python1.X.tar.gz
```

In either case, the Python files will be untarred in the current directory.

The next step is to run the auto-configuration routine by issuing the following command:

```
./configure
```

Start the compilation of the executables with this command:

```
make
```

This compiles and links the Python files. You can also run a self-test program to ensure everything is completed properly and all files are accounted for by issuing this command:

```
make test
```

Finally, complete the installation process by copying the compiled executables and all support files to the proper Linux directories with this command:

```
make install
```

Following that, Python is ready to roll. Of course, all these steps are unnecessary if you use the precompiled RPM version of Python.

Note

The Python FAQ is posted at regular intervals to the Usenet `comp.lang.python` newsgroup and is available through several FTP and Web sites, including `http://www.python.org`. The FAQ contains up-to-date information about the language and its versions, as well as hints on building the Python executables on many platforms.

Setting Python Environment Variables

You will most likely need to set up several shell environment variables to allow Python to work properly. This doesn't take very long and you don't need to be a Linux guru. Python needs two environment variables—PATH and and PYTHONPATH. The PATH variable already exists for you; it is set when you log in to a shell. If you use the included RPM or DEB package to install Python, you won't have to modify the PATH variable at all, as the Python file will be placed in /usr/bin, which is in your path by default.

A quick way of making sure Python is installed in your path is to execute the python command and watch the output:

```
python
```

If you get an error message, the PATH environment variable might not be properly set. If Python launches properly, you will see three right-angle brackets. This means the executable is in your search path. You can exit Python with Ctrl+D. You can confirm your current path with this command:

```
echo $PATH
```

This command displays your default search path like this:

```
/bin:/usr/bin:$HOME/bin:.
```

If the Python executables are in the /usr/bin directory, this path finds them without a problem. If your path does not have the Python executable location in it, you need to modify the startup file for your shell (.cshrc, .login, .profile, or .kshrc, depending on the shell). Simply add the executable location to the existing PATH setting, using colons to separate entries. If there is no PATH statement in your startup files, add one, using the existing default path $PATH as one of the directory names.

The PYTHONPATH environment variable needs to be set for each user who will use Python. This path is used to locate files during runtime, and because many of the files are not kept in the default path, you will need to set this variable in your startup files in most cases. The PYTHONPATH variable is usually set to include the current directory, the library location for the Python files (set during installation and usually /usr/lib), and any other directories Python needs, such as tcl/tk directories. Here is an example of a command to set PYTHONPATH:

```
$ PYTHONPATH="./:/usr/lib:"
```

Finally, you can create an initialization file for Python to read when it launches (like the shell startup files). The name of the file is given in an environment variable called PYTHONSTARTUP and should be set to the absolute pathname of the startup file. The startup file can contain any valid Python commands you want running.

If you are using tcl/tk to integrate GUIs with Python, you will also need to make sure environment variables such as TK_LIBRARY and TCL_LIBRARY are set. Python uses these variables to find the tcl/tk files it needs.

Python Command-Line Interpreter

The Python executable can be used as both a line-by-line and a command-line interpreter (just as the Linux shells can be). To use the command-line interpreter, you need to start the Python program, called python (lowercase). When you do, you'll see a line of three right-angle brackets that represent the Python prompt:

```
$ python
>>>
```

You can exit the python program by using Ctrl+D.

Typing any valid Python command line at the prompt results in the execution of the action (if there is one):

```
>>> print "Hello World!"
Hello World!
```

As you can see, the print command acts like the UNIX echo statement. Double quotation marks help prevent interpretation of the string and should be used with all print statements. Single quotation marks can also be used to enclose a string, but do not use the single back quotation marks (back ticks). By default, the print statement sends output to the standard output (usually the screen).

You can use the command-line interpreter as a calculator. If you use variables, they are set automatically to the proper type and can be used later in the program. Don't use an assignment operator to generate output from Python:

```
>>> a = 2
>>> b = 5
>>> a * b
10
>>> bigvar = 37465
>>> smallvar = a / 2
>>> bigvar / smallvar
37465
>>>
```

The variables were set by using the equal sign. Spaces on either side of the equal sign are ignored, so you can adopt whichever style you want. The following statements are identical:

```
A = 2
```

```
A=2
```

Case is important to Python, as it is to most UNIX-based languages, so the variables A and a are different. You can use long variable names to help differentiate variables and their purposes, with mixed case if you want. To display the current value of a variable, type its name at the prompt; any assigned value is shown. An error message is displayed if the variable has no value set.

Standard mathematical order of precedence applies. Division and multiplication are carried out before addition and subtraction. So the following statement results in 8 (4 + 4), not 6 (4 + 8 divided by 2):

```
>>> 4 + 8 / 2
```

You can assign numeric and string values to variables and print them both out at the same time, like this:

```
>>> a = "Python"
>>> b = "1"
>>> c = "statements"
>>> print b, a, c
1 Python statements
```

You can also set multiple values at once, like this, which sets all three variables to 19:

```
>>> a = b = c = 19
```

You could, of course, do them separately, but setting multiple values often saves time during coding.

> **Note**
>
> In Python, a variable's type is set by the operations performed on it. If any of the variables in any mathematical operation are floating point, all are converted to floating point automatically.

If you are typing a compound expression, such as an `if` or `for` loop, the command-line interpreter switches the prompt to a set of three dots, allowing you to complete the expression:

```
>>> if b < 10:
...
```

After the three dots, you can complete the compound expression. Be sure to indent the compound expression.

To start Python executing a file, supply the name as an argument. If the program needs any arguments, they can be specified on the command line too. For example, the following command starts the Python executable running the program `big_prog`, using the three arguments following the program name in the program:

```
python big_prog 12 24 36
```

You'll see how these arguments are read later in this chapter.

Python supports unlimited precision numbers. By default, numbers are tracked only to a considerable number of significant digits, but appending an `L` to the number switches to unlimited precision mode, as the following example shows:

```
>>> 123456789 * 123456789
Traceback (innermost last):
  File "<interactive input>", line 0, in ?
OverflowError: integer multiplication
>>> 123456789L * 123456789L
15241578750190521L
>>>
```

The first multiplication overflowed the allowed number of digits and generated an error message. By appending the `L` to the end of the numbers (with no spaces between the number and the `L`), you can impose unlimited precision.

Python Programs

A *Python program* is a straightforward ASCII file that can be created with any text editor. You can also use any word processor, if it can save files in ASCII format. By convention, Python files end in the extension `.py` (such as `primes.py` and `sort.py`). This filetype convention is not strictly necessary because Python can open any type of file and execute it, but it does help identify the files.

Each Python script file is called a module. A *module* is the largest program unit in Python and can be thought of as the main or master file. A module can import other modules. Lines of a Python module can contain comments, statements, and objects.

As with any programming language, Python has a number of statements. The majority of Python statements will be familiar to programmers, such as `if` and `for` loops and the equal sign for assignments. Python does add a few statements for functions and object-oriented tasks, but these are not difficult to learn (especially if you have programmed in other languages). If you do not feel comfortable with these more advanced statements, you have the option to code without them. After all, not all programs are suited to object-oriented approaches.

Python objects are handled by statements and define the types of data being handled. If you have done any OO programming before, you will be familiar with Python's use of objects. For non–object-oriented programmers, *objects* define simple things, such as the type of variable (string, integer, and so on), as well as other entities, such as module and filenames.

If you have never seen a Python module before, you'll be surprised to see how simple it is. Python is similar to the UNIX languages `awk` and Perl in that you don't have to define variable types before assigning them. When you assign a value to a variable, the variable is dynamically created, removing the need for declaring and typing statements at the top of the module. This makes Python an ideal language for rapid programming. It also makes Python programs much shorter and easier to read. Python's excellent object implementation makes it an ideal candidate for substantial software development.

The first line in a Python program usually looks like this:

```
#!/usr/bin/python
```

This tells the shell to use the `python` executable to run the script. The full path might be different on your system, depending on where you installed your Python files. Any number of valid Python commands can follow this line. Python ignores whitespace, so you can use blank lines to separate sections of the program, making your code more readable.

Python comment lines start with a # sign. You can embed as many comments as you want in your code; the Python interpreter ignores any line with a pound sign at the beginning. A comment can also be placed anywhere on a line, with everything after the comment symbol ignored by Python:

```
Var1 = 6     # sets Var1
```

At the top of most Python programs, you may see `import` statements. The `import` statement is used to read in another module (similar to an `include` in C). The most often used module for Python code is called `sys`. The `sys` module contains a set of system-level components. If you don't use any of these components in your code, you don't need to have the following statement at the top of your program, but it also doesn't cause any harm:

```
import sys
```

Command-Line Arguments and Environment Variables

Command-line arguments are accessed in Python through the `sys` module's `argv` list. The number of arguments, including the program name as one of those arguments, (comparable to `argc` in C or C++) is available as `len(sys.argv)`. `sys.argv[0]` is the program name, while `sys.argv[1]` to `sys.argv[len(sys.argv)-1]` are the rest of the arguments. To shed more light on the subject, assume the following code is saved as `test.py`:

```
#!/usr/bin/python

import sys
print "Args are:", sys.argv
print "Counting program name,",
print "number of args is", len(sys.argv)
print "Program name is", sys.argv[0]
print "Final arg is", sys.argv[len(sys.argv)-1]
```

Run with the following command from the command line (after `chmod a+x test.py`):

```
$ ./test.py one two three
```

The output is as follows:

```
Args are: ['./test.py', 'one', 'two', 'three']
Counting program name, number of args is 4
Program name is ./test.py
Final arg is three
```

Environment variables are accessed in Python through the `os` module's `environ` dictionary. Because it's a dictionary, lookups are done with the `os.environ[VARNAME]` syntax, with the environment variable's name in quotation marks. That syntax throws a `KeyError` exception if `VARNAME` isn't in the environment. Unfortunately, an uncaught `KeyError` exception will clumsily terminate the program. To prevent that, the `try`, `except`, `else` syntax is used to handle any `KeyError` exception. Note the following code:

```
#!/usr/bin/python
import os

def printenv(s):
   try:
      x = os.environ[s]
   except KeyError:
      print "No such environment var:", s
   else:
      print "Env var", s, "has value:", x


printenv("SHELL")
printenv("OSTYPE")
printenv("JUNK")
```

> **Note**
>
> The code must be indented as shown. Python decides where the blocks of code to be executed start and end by the statement's indents (when executing a script) or blank lines (when running interactively). The `def:`, `try:`, `except KeyError:`, and `else:` statements each have subservient blocks of code.

Try this code on your system. You'll almost certainly have environment variables `SHELL` and `OSTYPE`, and probably will not have `JUNK`. With those assumptions, here is the output you can expect:

```
Env var SHELL has value: /bin/bash
Env var OSTYPE has value: Linux
No such environment var: JUNK
```

Environment variables can be added, changed, and deleted in `os.environ` with standard dictionary manipulation:

```
os.environ["JUNK"] = "added"
printenv("JUNK")
os.environ["JUNK"] = "changed"
printenv("JUNK")
del os.environ["JUNK"]
printenv("JUNK")
```

The preceding code added environment variable `JUNK`, and then changed and deleted its value, calling the `printenv()` function defined previously. The output is predictable:

```
Env var JUNK has value: added
Env var JUNK has value: changed
No such environment var: JUNK
```

This is useful because any such environment changes are available in subprocesses started with the `os.system()`, `os.popen()`, `os.fork()`, and `os.execv()`.

Control Statements

Like many programming languages, Python has the usual assortment of control statements. The most commonly used statements are the `if` conditional test and the `for` and `while` loops. If you have programmed any other language before, or if you are familiar with shell scripts, you'll find little new about these statements. If you are new to programming, you will probably find the use of these statements a little confusing at first. That's not Python's fault; all languages are like this. A little practice quickly makes their usage clear.

The if Statement

The Python `if` statement syntax uses the condition to be tested on the `if` line, followed by any statements to be executed if the test is true. An `else` can be used to execute statements if the test is negative. The syntax for the Python `if` statement looks like this:

```
if <condition>:
   statements
else:
   statements
```

The `else` section and its following statements are optional. Notice the use of colons at the end of the `if` and `else` lines, indicating to Python that there is a continuation of the section on the next line. There is no termination statement for the `if` statement, such as an `endif` or `fi`.

Note

Python decides where the blocks of code to be executed start and end by the statement's indents (when executing a script) or blank lines (when running interactively). This is different from most programming languages that use braces or some special statement or symbol to terminate each block. The number of spaces or tabs you use to indent statements in a block doesn't matter, as long as you are consistent.

Here's a simple `if` statement:

```
var1 = 5

if var1 < 10:
  var2 = 0
  print "the value is less than ten"
else:
  var2 = 1
  print "the value is ten or more"
```

The condition allows all the usual mathematical comparisons (==, !=, >, >=, <, and <=). Note that you can't use the single equal sign in the `if` statement for a condition test. The single equal sign is used for assignment, not comparison. The double equal sign is used to indicate "exactly equal to."

As with the C programming language, the Python `if` statement doesn't test for actual values but determines a simple true or false. If the condition is true, it has a return code of non-zero, while a false has a return code of zero. The value of the return code dictates whether the statements below the `if` or the `else` are executed. You can show this with a simple Python program:

```
X = 4
Y = 5
A = X > Y
print A
```

The zero result shows that the test of `X` being greater than `Y` was false, assigning the return value of zero to the variable `A`.

Python also allows the `elif` (`else if`) structure in the `if` statement. There can be many cascaded `elifs`, which might be necessary for multiple branching tests because Python does not offer a `switch` or `case` statement. An example of using `elifs` follows:

```
if var2 >= 10:
  print "The value is greater than or equal to ten"
elif var2 <= 5:
  print "The value is less than or equal to five"
else:
  print "The value is between five and ten"
```

Python allows a virtually unlimited number of nests in its `if` statements, although your code will start to bog down after too many nests. If you need to nest more than three or four levels deep, you should probably try to find a better way to code the section.

When any section of the `if` statement has been completed as the result of a condition's being true or false, the Python interpreter jumps to the end of the `if` statement. This means the second part of a nested `if` might never be executed. For example, when the first test proves true in the following program, the first print is executed:

```
x = 6
if x > 5:
   print "X is greater than 5"
elif x > 2:
   print "X is greater than 2"
else:
   print "X is less than 2"
```

Even though the second test (where the `elif` is) is also true, it does not get executed because the Python interpreter jumps to the statements after the end of the `else` section.

The `if` statement can contain Booleans, as you might expect; however, you should write out Booleans in Python instead of using symbols as you do in C and shell scripts. The Boolean statements are `and`, `or`, and `not`. The following are all legal statements in Python:

```
if a < 5 and b > 6:
if a < b or c > d:
if not a < b:
if a < b or ( a > 5 and b < 10):
```

The use of `not` negates the test, so the third example shown is the same as testing `a >= b`. The last example uses parentheses to add another layer of testing, at which Python excels. As long as the conditions and Booleans are used properly, you can construct very long, complex statements in Python that would be almost impossible to construct in a few lines with other programming languages.

If you are reading Python programs written by others, you will often see the `if` condition and statement compressed onto a single line, like this:

```
if x < 5: print "X is less than five"
```

This is perfectly legal. Another common sight in code is comparisons run together, like this:

```
if 3 < X < 5: print "X is four"
```

The preceding code is the same as writing this:

```
if x > 3 and x < 5:  print "X is four"
```

The `while` Loop

The Python `while` loop continues to loop as long as some condition is true. The general syntax for the `while` loop follows:

```
while <condition>:
  statements
```

As you can guess, the block of statements to be executed when the condition is true is indicated by indenting. Here is a simple `while` loop:

```
a = 0
while a < 10:
  print "a is currently set at ", a
  a = a + 1
print "all done!"
```

The last `print` statement is executed after the `while` loop condition tests false, or even if the `while` loop is not executed at all. This happens because it is not indented to match the rest of the statements in the `while` block.

Note

You can use C-like formatting operations in print functions to produce the results you want, like this:

```
>>> print "The result of %d times %d is %d. %s!"
➥% (2, 3, 2*3, "Excellent")
The result of 2 times 3 is 6. Excellent!
```

The condition is always tested and assigned a return code, and the `while` loop executes as long as the return code is non-zero. You could use this fact to abort the loop when a value hits zero:

```
a = 10
while a:
  print "a is currently set at ", a
  a = a - 1
print "all done!"
```

This starts counting with a set to `10`, and because `10` is non-zero, the `while` loop is true. When the decrement results in a value of `0` for a, the `while` loop stops. This type of syntax might look confusing but is quite common.

Python allows a `break` statement to be used to exit from a `while` statement at any time. Whenever a `break` is encountered, the interpreter immediately assumes the `while` condition is false and carries on execution after the last line of the `while` block. Take a look at the following program:

```
a = 10
while a:
  print "a is currently set at ", a
  a = a - 1
  if a == 4:
     break
print "all done!"
```

The countdown proceeds as you would expect until the value of a is set to `4`, at which point the `if` condition is true and the break executes. The `"all done!"` message is printed right after the break is reached because it is the first statement after the `while` block. Usually a break is used in an `if` block as a way of escaping the `while` loop if certain conditions are met. You can save a lot of coding in the `while` condition by using the break.

The for Loop

The for loop is used to iterate through a list or a string. The statements subservient to the for statement must not alter the list or string in any way. The syntax for the for loop under Python follows:

```
for var in <list or string>:
  statements
```

As with the if statement, Python knows where the body of the for loop is by the indentation. The colon at the end of the for statement also indicates a continuation to the interpreter. The var in the preceding assumes individual values in the list or string.

The following simple for loop iterates the string:

```
for ltr in "Hello World":
  print ltr,
```

The preceding code prints each letter of the string, followed by a space:

```
H e l l o   W o r l d
```

Note

A comma on the end of a print statement eliminates the newline from the output, instead inserting a single space.

The "Lists and the range() Function" section examines for loops in greater detail.

Lists and the range() Function

A list is any sequence of zero or more items. You can specify a list in Python by using brackets. A simple list using numbers looks like this:

```
A = [1, 2, 3, 4, 5]
```

This list, called A, has five elements. You can recall the entire list by using the variable name, as this code example shows:

```
A = [1, 2, 3, 4, 5]
print A
```

The preceding code simply prints the list in brackets, as shown in the output:

```
[1, 2, 3, 4, 5]
```

To recall any single element from the list, use the variable name and the subscript of the element number in brackets. Remember that Python is a zero-origin subscripting language, meaning the counting of elements starts at `0`:

```
A = [1, 2, 3, 4, 5]
print A[2]
print A[0]
```

The preceding code prints **3** on one line and **1** on the next. If you try to access an element that doesn't exist, you usually get an error message from the interpreter.

Note

Even though Python performs some bounds checking for elements in a list, you should not expect Python to ensure that your code uses list elements correctly. For example, while Python will reject a reference to `A[10]` if the list `A` has only five elements, Python will allow a reference to the same list using `A[-4]`. The uses of negative list elements aren't discussed here, but you should be careful when using list elements in your code.

You can create lists with strings just as easily, separating each string with a comma and using quotation marks to surround each string:

```
A = ["Python", " powerful", "is", "language", "a"]
print A[0], A[2], A[4], A[1], A[3]
```

The preceding code prints list `A` as elements, in the order invoked in the `print` statement, outputting the sentence `Python is a powerful language`. Lists can be mixed between strings and numeric values just as easily. If you define each element properly, Python lets you manipulate them however you prefer:

```
Z = [ 5, "good", "is", 6, "This", 2]
print Z[4], Z[2], Z[1]
print Z[0] + Z[3] / Z[5]
```

Once again, the elements are printed according to the `print` statement, yielding this output:

```
This is good
8
```

Note that the order of precedence in the last statement resulted in the value `8` and not `5.5`.

To find the number of elements in a list, use Python's built-in `len()`function as follows:

```
a = [1,3,5,7]
print len(a)
```

The preceding code yields `4`—the number of elements in the list. We can also add and delete members from a list. Please remember in this discussion that element numbers start at `0`. The following insertion and deletion examples assume the following list string:

```
a = ["zero","one","two","three","four"]
To delete a[2] ("two"), we do this:
a[2:3] = []
```

The `"two"` is now missing from the list. The following code reinserts it:

```
a[2:2] = ["two"]
```

A good way to remember where the preceding syntax chooses to insert is to remember that you're adding a new element `2`, thus pushing the present element `2` out to element `3`.

Here's an example of a multiple deletion (delete elements `2` and `3`):

```
a[2:4] = []
```

A multiple insertion can be done by placing multiple elements in the right side of the equal sign. Consider this code, which reinserts elements `2` and `3`, deleted previously:

```
a[2:2] = ["two", "three"]
```

The `for` loop is ideal for stepping through a list. In the following code, a list is displayed one element at a time:

```
A = [1, 2, 3, 4, 5, 6, 7, 8, 9, 10]
for x in A:
   print x
```

The preceding code creates a new variable, `x`, which holds the value of the indexes in `A`, one after another. You can do exactly the same with string lists, as the following example shows:

```
A = ["a", "b", "c", "d", "e", "f", "g"]
print A
for x in A:
   print x
```

The preceding code prints list `A`, then steps through the list, assigning each element to `x` and printing `x`, as shown in the following output:

```
['a', 'b', 'c', 'd', 'e', 'f', 'g']
a
b
```

```
c
d
e
f
g
```

To print all the elements, one after another on a single line and with a single space between them (instead of in a column), you need to place a comma after the `print` statement at the end of the `for` statement. Note that the `print` statement is ended with a comma:

```
A = ["a", "b", "c", "d", "e", "f", "g"]
for x in A:
   print x,
```

Here's the resulting output:

```
a b c d e f g
```

You can test for the inclusion of a particular value as an element, which yields a return code of `0` (false) or non-zero (true). For example, look at the following code:

```
A = [1, 2, 3, 4, 5]
print "This should be 1:", 3 in A
print "But this should be 0:", 8 in A
```

The tests performed cause a search of all the elements to check for a match, and the proper return code is then displayed. This could be handy for some `if` or `for` loops when you need to make sure particular elements exist before continuing processing.

Individual elements in a list can be changed by using the element subscript, as the following example shows:

```
A = [1, 2, 3, 4, 5]
print A
A[3] = 7
print A
```

The preceding code changes `A[3]` from `4` to `7`, as shown by the following output:

```
[1, 2, 3, 4, 5]
[1, 2, 3, 7, 5]
```

Lists spanning a contiguous range can be created using the `range()` command, which comes in a one-argument and two-argument syntax:

```
#This is the one argument syntax:
mylist = range(4)
print "range(4) is:", mylist
```

```
#This is the two argument syntax:
mylist = range(5,10)
print "range(5,10) is:", mylist
```

Here are the rather surprising results:

```
range(4) is: [0, 1, 2, 3]
range(5,10) is: [5, 6, 7, 8, 9]
```

In the one-argument `range()` call, the argument represents the number of elements in the `0`-based list. In the two-argument `range()`, the first argument is the first element in the list, while the last number is 1 greater than the last element.

You can use `range()` anywhere you could place a list. It can be assigned to variables or used as part of a command structure.

Upper and lower limits may be positive or negative:

```
print "range(-10, -5) is: ", range(-10, -5)
print "range(-5, 5) is: ", range(-5, 5)
print "range(-5, -10) is: ", range(-5, -10)
```

The preceding code's output follows:

```
range(-10, -5) is:  [-10, -9, -8, -7, -6]
range(-5, 5) is:  [-5, -4, -3, -2, -1, 0, 1, 2, 3, 4]
range(-5, -10) is:  []
```

Notice the last range in the code. It's perfectly legal to specify a lower limit higher than the upper limit (although it is a little silly). The result is a list with no elements.

Using Tuples

This brings you to the slightly more complicated issue of tuples. A *tuple* is a Python data structure that works like a list but is more efficiently stored and managed. A tuple's elements cannot be moved around and extracted with the same ease as a list's elements.

The difference between lists and tuples, at least as far as Python's interpreter is concerned, is that a *list* is a variable-sized array of elements that might need to grow in size. A tuple has a fixed size; hence, it is more efficiently stored and managed by the interpreter. A tuple's element values can't be changed without redefining the entire tuple, but a list's elements can be easily changed. This leads to the use of tuples for defining invariant constants in Python, much as the `#define` statement does in C. Tuples are also returned by many Python functions.

To define a tuple, you set it up much the same as a list, but with parentheses instead of brackets. Python isn't that fussy about the parentheses, as long as there is no ambiguity.

Still, it is advisable to always use parentheses when defining a tuple, as it helps make clear in your mind that you are working with a tuple. Here is an example defining and displaying the value of a numeric tuple and a text tuple:

```
a = (1,2,3,4)
print "This is a numerical tuple:", a
a = ("This", "is", "a", "tuple", "of", "strings")
print a
```

We've set variable a to a numerical tuple, then a string tuple, as shown by the following output:

```
This is a numerical tuple: (1, 2, 3, 4)
('This', 'is', 'a', 'tuple', 'of', 'strings')
```

Why bother with tuples? They are useful when you want to use either the full tuple value or specific elements out of a tuple as a complete set of information. Each element in a tuple can be assigned to a specific variable, as long as the number of variables matches the number of elements in the tuple. The following code assigns the elements of a tuple to variables `w`, `x`, `y`, and `z`, changes the value of `y`, and then creates a new tuple from `x` and `y`:

```
w, x, y, z = (1, 2, 3, 4)
y = 7
mytuple = (x, y)
print mytuple
```

The preceding code assigned element `0` (`1`) to variable `w`, element `1` (`2`) to `x`, and so on. It then changes `y` to `7`, producing the following output:

```
(2, 7)
```

To convert between lists and tuples, you need to do a little coding that assembles each structure from the other. Often, the easier way is to simply redefine the variable as either a list or a tuple instead of performing a conversion in your program code.

Dictionaries

Python is a high-level language and, as such, has some special datatypes designed to take advantage of some aspects of the language's features. One of these special datatypes is the dictionary. *Dictionaries* are associative arrays. In plainer English, it means data is referred to by a key, similar to a variable. Perl programmers will recognize Python dictionaries as similar to Perl hashes. To Python, a dictionary is a simple hash table that can grow at any time.

To create a one-element dictionary, specify both a key and the value to which that key refers. These *key:value pairs* (in Python-speak) are enclosed in braces, with the key and value separated by a colon. Python allows almost any kind of data to be used as a key or a value. Any number of key:value pairs can be in a dictionary. An example of setting up a dictionary is a good place to start. This code creates a dictionary, called `a`, that uses the key `"python"` to refer to a value `"language"` (two strings for key and value in this case):

```
a = {"python": "language"}
```

Brackets are used to refer to the value, either in whole or in part. Using the given definition, you can recall the whole value with this command-line sequence:

```
a = {"python": "language"}
print a["python"]        #prints the word "language"
```

As you can see, referring to the element `"python"` in the dictionary `a` brings up the value assigned to `"python"`, which is `"language"`. Note, however, that only the key—not the value—may be used inside the brackets. The following code fails:

```
a = {"python": "language"}
print a["language"]        #Aborts with a KeyError"
```

So far this is rather unexciting and it is hard to see why you would want to use dictionaries. The advantage of dictionaries comes when you start using multiple values. Here's an example of a dictionary set up to hold computer languages and their categories:

```
a = {"C": "Compiler", "C++": "Compiler", "Python": "Interpreter"}
b = "Python"
print b, "is a", a[b]
```

Here, `a[b]` produces the word `"Interpreter"`, as shown in the following output:

```
Python is a Interpreter
```

Note that when defining multiple key:value pairs, they are separated in the braces by commas. Note also that values can be duplicates (both C and C++ are `"Compiler(s)"` according to the preceding code), but the keys must never duplicate.

It is an error to try to access a nonexistent key in a dictionary. Thus, the following program will abort with a `KeyError` exception:

```
a = {"python": "language"}
print a["perl"]
```

This can be handled gracefully with the `try`, `except`, `else` syntax:

```
def printelement(dict,key):
   try:
      x = dict[key]
   except KeyError:
```

```
        print "No key", key, "in dictionary."
    else:
        print "Key", key, "has value:", x + "."


a = {"python": "language"}
printelement(a, "perl")
printelement(a, "python")
```

Here the KeyError exception is handled and processing continues. The output looks like this:

```
No key perl in dictionary.
Key python has value: language.
```

Dictionary elements can be added, changed, and deleted as follows:

```
a = {"SIZE": "BIG", "WEIGHT": "HEAVY"}
a["STATUS"] = "added"
printelement(a, "STATUS")
a["STATUS"] = "changed"
printelement(a, "STATUS")
del a["STATUS"]
printelement(a, "STATUS")
```

Given the previous definition of function `printelement()`, the output of the preceding code is exactly as expected:

```
Key STATUS has value: added.
Key STATUS has value: changed.
No key STATUS in dictionary.
```

Dictionaries bestow immense power because their values can be class instances (which are discussed later this chapter). When used this way, dictionaries can eliminate huge sections of `if:elif:else` code, and are excellent for lookups.

Console I/O

As mentioned, console output in Python is done with the `print` statement. Each `print` statement prints a newline (linefeed) after the desired output, unless the `print` statement is ended with a comma (`,`). In that case the output is ended with a single space, as demonstrated in the following code:

```
#!/usr/bin/python
print "This is a complete line."
print "This is the first half of a line, and",
print "this is the final half."
```

The second line of the preceding code does not linefeed, but instead appends a single space. The first and third lines linefeed, to produce the following output:

```
This is a complete line.
This is the first half of a line, and this is the final half.
```

If the space inserted by the ending comma isn't desired, strings (but not numbers) can be concatenated with the plus sign:

```
a="Python"
b="is"
c="great"
print a+b+c
```

The preceding code concatenated three string variables without spaces, producing the following output:

```
Pythonisgreat
```

Note that numbers cannot be concatenated without first converting them to strings. String conversions are covered later in this chapter.

You can use C-like formatting operations in `print` functions to produce the results you want, like this:

```
print "The result of %d times %d is %d. %s!" % (2, 3, 2*3, "Excellent")
```

The arguments inside the parentheses are assigned the substitution strings inside the format string, as shown in the following output:

```
The result of 2 times 3 is 6. Excellent!
```

Console input is done with the `raw_input()` command. This function takes a single string argument, which is used as a prompt, and accepts a single line of keyboard input. It does not read individual keystrokes, but rather accepts the entire line when the Enter key is pressed. Here is an example:

```
x = raw_input("Please type your name==>")
print x
```

The preceding code prints out whatever you type at the prompt. Note that the input is always interpreted as a string; the `eval()` function must be used to acquire numbers. The following code prints double the number you type in:

```
x = raw_input("Please type number to be doubled==>")
x = 2 * eval(x)
print x
```

Typing a non-number causes an error, so a real program checks to see that the variable contains a number before invoking the `eval()` function.

With the inclusion of the `readline` module, `raw_input()` becomes much more powerful, including line editing and history. To demonstrate its power, run the following program:

```
import readline
x = "Anything but q to ensure first iteration"
while(x != "q"):
   x = raw_input("Please type your name==>")
   print x
```

The preceding code repeatedly asks for your name (until a single lowercase `q` is typed at the prompt), and prints whatever is typed at the prompt. The addition of the import readline statement enables command-line editing and history, which can be explored using the keyboard's arrow keys. This capability is enabled even inside GUI Telnet sessions.

File I/O

A major portion of programming involves reading and writing files. Python has a rich variety of file functions. This section discusses the basic file I/O functions: `open()`, `close()`, `read()`, `readline()`, `readlines()`, and `write()`.

File Output

File output is done with the `write()` function on a file that has been opened for output with the `open()` function. The command that opens file `test.tst` for output follows:

```
outfile = open("test.tst", "w")
```

The first argument is the name of the file to open, while the second is the mode in which it is open. Frequent modes are `r` for read, `w` for write (delete any existing file), and `a` for append (write to the end of any existing file).

Note

An optional third argument, the buffer size, can be used with `open()`. In its absence, file I/O operations buffer according to the system default. A test conducted on an unloaded Celeron 333 with a 7200 RPM 14.4GB disk wrote a 4.5MB file in 12 seconds using the two-argument version. A buffer size of a million did not appreciably decrease that time, leading to the conclusion that the two-argument form is sufficient for most work.

On a loaded system with a busy CPU, larger buffers can improve performance significantly. If file performance appears to bottleneck, experiment with this third argument.

Also note that when writing to a device where the character should be immediately written out (a serial port, for example), this third argument should be set to `0`.

The `open()` statement can fail for any number of reasons: the filename is a directory, the disk is full, the user lacks the proper permissions in the directory, and more. Function `open()` for read fails if the file does not exist. When an `open()` statement fails, the program terminates with an error message. If you want to gracefully handle such failures, use the `try`, `except`, `else` syntax for `IOError` exceptions:

```
try:
   outfile = open("test.tst", "w")
except IOError:
   print "Failed to open test.tst for write."
else:
   #place  file writes and close statement in this block
```

The preceding code gracefully prints an error message if the open fails. On success, however, the code continues executing after the `else` statement. You place the code to write to and eventually close the file in the block subservient to the `else` statement.

This syntax also works on files open for read. If this syntax becomes obfuscated due to excessive nesting of multiple files, each open file's `except IOError` block can set a variable to be evaluated by subsequent code.

For simplicity's sake, the remainder of this chapter's sample code does not include error-handling code. However, real programs should handle their own file errors.

Once the file is opened, it is written with the `write()` function:

```
outfile.write("Hello World\n")
```

When the preceding code is run, assuming `outfile` has been successfully opened for write, a single line containing the text `Hello World` is written to the file. Only strings can be written to the file. Numbers must be converted using the `str()` or `repr()` functions.

As soon as all data has been written to the file, the file should be closed with the `close()` function. Although the file will be closed on normal termination of the Python program, it remains subject to change or corruption while open. The following is a short program to create a four-line file called `test.tst`:

```
outfile = open("test.tst", "w")
for x in ["Spring", "Summer", "Fall", "Winter"]:
   outfile.write(x + "\n")
outfile.close()
```

The preceding code opens file `test.tst`, iterates through the seasons printing one per line, and then closes the file. Please save the resulting file, as it will serve as the input files in file input examples that follow.

File Input

File input is accomplished with the `read()`, `readline()`, and `readlines()` functions, operating on a file that has been opened for input with the `open()` function. The command to open a file for input follows:

```
outfile = open("test.tst", "r")
```

The first argument is the name of the file to be opened, and the second is a string containing a lowercase `r`, which stands for read.

Function `readline()` is used to read a single line from a file. It returns a single line, complete with newline. If the line is blank, it returns only the newline. At *end of file* (EOF), it returns the null string (`""`). After testing for EOF, the newline can be removed from string `x` using the following syntax:

```
x = x[:-1]
```

Following is the Python code necessary to read file `test.tst`, surround each line with angle brackets, and print it:

```
infile = open("test.tst", "r")
x = infile.readline()
while x != "":
   x = x[:-1]
   print "<" + x + ">"
   x = infile.readline()
infile.close()
```

The preceding code uses a priming read and a loop-bottom read to simulate a test-at-bottom loop, thereby avoiding `if` statements inside the loop and (technically unstructured) break statements.

When the filesize is known to be consistently tiny compared to system memory, the file can be read straight into a list using the `readlines()` function:

```
infile = open("test.tst", "r")
xl = infile.readlines()          #note readlines is plural
infile.close()
for x in xl:
   x = x[:-1]
   print "<" + x + ">"
```

The preceding syntax closes the file faster, eliminates the priming and bottom reads, and is much more readable. However, the results become undefined (and likely unpleasant) if memory is ever insufficient to hold list `xl`.

`read()` is the function of choice for non–line-oriented input. Assuming an open file called `infile`, here is the syntax:

```
x = read(numbytes)
```

Function `read()` is used for fast file input, reading fixed-length, sequential record files, file copy operations, translations, and the like. The following code copies file `test.tst` to file `test2.tst`:

```
infile = open("test.tst", "r")
outfile = open("test2.tst", "w")
x = infile.read(10)
while x != "":
   outfile.write(x)
   x = infile.read(10)
outfile.close()
infile.close()
```

The preceding code reads `test.tst`, 10 bytes at a time, into variable `x`, then writes variable `x` to file `test2.tst`. After running this code, you can verify its success by running this command at the command line:

```
$ diff test.tst test2.tst
```

If the files are identical, the command produces no output. A message prints if there's a difference, or if either file doesn't exist. Note that the byte argument of `10` would result in snail-like performance in a real program. For general file input, use a large number (such as `5000`) as the byte argument. For fixed-length record operations, use the record length or a multiple of the record length.

File I/O Example

The following is a Python program that converts text file `test.tst` to a numbered listing in an HTML-formatted file called `o.html`:

```
#!/usr/bin/python

fname = "test.tst"
ouf = open("o.html", "w")
ouf.write("<html><body><P><H1>\n")
ouf.write(fname + " Listing</H1><PRE>\n")

inf=open(fname, "r")
line = inf.readline()
n=10001
while line != "":
   line = line[0:-1]
   ouf.write(str(n) + "     " + line + "\n")
   n = n + 1
   line = inf.readline()
inf.close()
```

```
ouf.write("</PRE></body></html>\n");
ouf.close()
```

Note how easily this code can be made powerful. Assigning `sys.argv[1]` to `fname` makes it a general program.

Caution

Make sure `fname` is opened for read and not for write. otherwise, you will overwrite the file described on the command line!

If all the `ouf.write()` statements are changed to `print` statements, this code becomes a handy CGI script. (Once again, be careful of security.) Make no mistake about it—Python is an extremely powerful language.

Functions and Modules

Like many high-level languages, Python uses functions and modules to break large programs into smaller functional blocks.

Functions

The use of functions also leads directly to code reuse, allowing you to write functions for specific tasks that can be incorporated with little or no change into any future programs you write. Defining a function is straightforward. Here's an example of a simple function with a single input:

```
def simplefunction(name):
   print name
```

The keyword `def` identified the code as a function to Python, followed by the name of the function and the variable names to be assigned to any incoming data (in this case, a single object), followed by a colon signifying that the following indented text is part of the function. Indenting indicates the body of the function.

As the following code demonstrates, the function executes when called, using whatever data object is passed:

```
def simplefunction(name):
   print name

simplefunction("Python")
```

The call to `simplefunction()` leads to the execution of function `simplefunction()`, using argument `"Python"`, to print the word `"Python"` to the screen.

You can use local variables in a function, as you can with most other languages. A local variable is valid only inside the function and has no meaning when tried outside that function. Here's a function that computes the average of any numbers passed to it:

```
def average(array):
  numvars = 0
  total = 0
  for a in array:
    numvars = numvars + 1
    total = total + a
  print "There are ", numvars, " numbers"
  print "The total is ", total
  print "The average is ", total/numvars
```

The variables `numvars` and `total` are valid only inside the function average. If a global variable conflicts with a local variable, the local variable takes precedence inside the function. When this function is called with a list containing `1` through `5` inclusive, the following output is generated:

```
There are 5 numbers
The total is 15
The average is 3
```

Caution

Any variable used outside of all functions is global and is accessible inside all functions. Since global variables represent a modularity breach, it is best in all but the simplest programs to place all top-level procedural code inside a function (typically called `main()`). Thus, the only code existing outside all functions would be the path to `python`, the import statements (covered later in this chapter), and a single call to function `main()`. If the imported modules do not declare global variables, such a construction prevents accidental creation of global variables in your program.

If you want to pass a result back to the calling function (which will often be the case), the `return` statement is used. The modification of the `average` function returns a numeric average value because of the `return` statement:

```
def average(array):
  numvars = 0
  total = 0
  for a in array:
    numvars = numvars + 1
```

```
     total = total + a
   return total/numvars
```

A handy Python feature is the capability to pass back multiple objects, as demonstrated by the following code:

```
#!/usr/bin/python

def getLocation():
   return("USA", "Indiana", "Indianapolis")

(country, state, city) = getLocation();
print "Location is", city + ",", state +",", country
```

The function `getLocation()` in the preceding code returns three values, resulting in the following output:

```
Location is Indianapolis, Indiana, USA
```

Multiple `return` works only when the variable list on the left of the equal sign has the same number of variables as returned by the function on the right. Otherwise, a runtime error will occur.

Modules

Modules, as mentioned at the beginning of this chapter, are files or scripts of Python code, usually ending with `.py`. Again, modules are designed to allow code reuse, so you can write self-contained modules that can be dropped into future applications. Modules are written with any ASCII editor and are called from another module with the `import` statement. The main module in Python (and the module into which all your command-line interpreter statements are entered) is called `__main__`.

To show how modules work, put the `average` function demonstrated earlier into a module called `average.py`. This is saved to disk and must be in either the current directory (which must also contain the main module) or the search path of the Python interpreter, defined by the environment variable `PYTHONPATH`. To use the `average.py` file in either the command-line interpreter or another module, embed the line as shown in this short program:

```
import average

a = [1,2,3,4,5]
average.average(a)
```

The code imports module `average` and calls the `average` function inside module `average`. The module name need not be identical to the function name.

To call a specific function inside a module, use the module name and the function name separated by a period. For example, if you have a file called `mymath.py` that includes functions called `average()`, `mean()`, and `deviation()`, you would call each from another module (after the `import` statement) as `mymath.average()`, `mymath.mean()`, and `mymath.deviation()`. This prevents conflicts with function names that are identical in different modules.

Strings and Regular Expressions

To a great extent, the productivity of a computer language depends on how easily the programmer can modify and parse strings. It is precisely these qualities that have contributed to the recent popularity of both Python and Perl.

Strings

Python has a rich variety of string-handling features. Features such as appending with the plus sign, string slicing, and conversion functions `str()` and `num()` are built in to the language. If those aren't enough, Python's string module offers most of the C language's `string.h` functionality.

Appending with the Plus Sign

The plus (+) sign allows concatenation of strings, as shown in the following source code:

```
fname = "resolv.conf"
dname = "/etc"
fullpath = dname + "/" + fname
print fullpath
```

The preceding code concatenates the directory, a slash, and the filename, resulting in the following output:

```
/etc/resolv.conf
```

String Slices

String slices are Python's ultra-flexible, built-in method of extracting substrings from larger strings. They can slice off the beginning or the end relative to either the beginning or end, or slice out the middle, relative to either the beginning or end. When using string slices, remember that the first character is element `0`. Perhaps the simplest string slice is grabbing a single character. This could also be considered *subscripting*:

```
a="ABCDEFGHIJKLMNOPQRSTUVWXYZ"
print a[2]
```

The preceding prints the letter `C`, which is element 2. Remember that Python has zero-origin arrays, so element 2 is the third element. Consider the following code, which prints the first five characters of the string:

```
a="ABCDEFGHIJKLMNOPQRSTUVWXYZ"
print a[0:5]
```

The preceding prints `"ABCDE"`. Often you want to remove a certain number of characters from the end of the string. Most often this is done to remove a newline from the end of the string. Using a `0` before the colon and a negative number after trims off characters numbering the absolute value of the negative number, from the end of the string:

```
a="ABCDEFGHIJKLMNOPQRSTUVWXYZ"
print a[0:-1]
```

The preceding code trims the `Z` off the end of the string. Often you need just a portion from the middle of the string:

```
a="ABCDEFGHIJKLMNOPQRSTUVWXYZ"
print a[2:5]
```

The preceding code prints elements `2`, `3`, and `4`; the string `"CDE"`. The best way to remember this is that the number of elements in the slice is the difference between the second and first numbers. Unless, of course, the second number goes past the end of the string, in which case the effect is simply to trim off the characters before the element corresponding to the first number. Here is an example:

```
a="ABCDEFGHIJKLMNOPQRSTUVWXYZ"
print a[2:1000]
```

The preceding prints `"CDEFGHIJKLMNOPQRSTUVWXYZ"`. It stripped from elements `0` and `1`, printing element `2` (`C`) as the first character. To print the last three characters of the string, you can combine a huge second number with a negative first number:

```
a="ABCDEFGHIJKLMNOPQRSTUVWXYZ"
print a[-3:1000]
```

The preceding code prints the last three characters, `"XYZ"`. If you find providing an arbitrarily large number unappealing, you can use the `len()` function to get the exact string length and accomplish the same thing, as illustrated in the following example:

```
a="ABCDEFGHIJKLMNOPQRSTUVWXYZ"
print a[-3:len(a)]
```

Once again, the output is `"XYZ"`. Occasionally you may want to extract a substring from `"almost"` the end. In that case, both numbers are negative. For instance, use the following to get the fourth-to-last, third-to-last, and second-to-last characters of the string:

```
a="ABCDEFGHIJKLMNOPQRSTUVWXYZ"
print a[-4:-1]
```

The preceding code prints "WXY". Remember that the number of characters returned is the difference between the numbers, assuming the original string contains enough characters.

String slicing is a versatile tool built in to the Python language. There are more uses of string slicing, but the preceding discussion gives you a strong foundation.

Converting with str(), repr(), and eval()

Python is more strongly typed than some languages (Perl, for instance), so strings and numbers can't be mixed without conversion. The `str()` and `repr()` functions convert a number to a string, while the `eval()` function converts a string to a number. The difference between `str()` and `repr()` is that `repr()` attempts to return a string that can be converted back to a number by `eval()`, while `str()` attempts to return a printable string. In practice, both `repr()` and `str()` usually do an excellent job of returning a string convertible to a number. Consider this example:

```
pi_string = "3.14159"
r = 2.0
area = eval(pi_string) * r * r
print "Area = " + repr(area)
print "Area = " + str(area)
print "Area =",
print 3.14159 * 2 * 2
```

The preceding code prints the area of a radius 2 circle three times. The first two times, it converts a string representation of pi to a number before doing the calculation; the third time, it calculates from numeric constants. The first and second time differ only in that the first uses `repr()`, while the second uses `str()`. All three produce these identical results:

```
Area = 12.56636
Area = 12.56636
Area = 12.56636
```

Rearranging a String

String slicing and appending can be used to rearrange strings. Consider the following function to convert a `MM/DD/YYYY` represented date to `YYYYMMDD`:

```
def yyyymmdd(d):
   return(d[-4:1000] + d[0:2] +d[3:5])

print yyyymmdd("07/04/1999")
print yyyymmdd("12/25/1999")
print yyyymmdd("01/01/2000")
```

Function yyyymmdd returns the last four characters, then the first two, then the fourth and fifth (elements 3 and 4), to produce this output:

```
19990704
19991225
20000101
```

This simplistic function assumes an exact format for the input date. Later in this chapter you build a "smarter" converter using string and number conversions and regular expressions.

The String Module

The previously described string capabilities occasionally aren't enough. Python's string module is used for those cases. Some functions included in the string module are explained in this section.

`atof()`, `atoi()`, and `atol()` are sophisticated alternatives for the capabilities yielded by `eval()`, capable of working with number systems other than decimal.

Various case conversions return copies of their arguments, rather than change the string in place. `capitalize()` capitalizes the first character of a string; `capwords()` capitalizes`()` the first letter of each word (but has the side effect of removing redundant whitespace and leading and trailing whitespace). `upper()` completely capitalizes its argument. `lower()` converts every letter to lowercase. `swapcase()` converts all lowercase to uppercase, and vice versa.

Functions `lstrip()`, `rstrip()`, and `strip()` return copies of their argument with whitespace stripped from the left, the right, and both, respectively.

`split(s[, sep[,` and `maxsplit]])` return a list of substrings from string `s`. The default for `sep` is one or more contiguous whitespace characters. (In other words, it splits the string into space-delimited words.) Used with a `sep` argument, this function becomes a powerful aid in parsing delimited data files. `maxsplit]])` defaults to `0`, but if positive, declares the maximum number of `split`, with any remainder becoming the last entry in the list. The following can split a quotation- and comma-delimited record into fields. Note that the actual parsing is accomplished in two lines:

```
import string
s="\"Smith\",\"John\",\"developer\""

s = s[1:-1]                   #strip first and last quote
z = string.split(s,'","')     #split by ","

for x in z:                   #print fields
   print x
```

`join(list[, sep])` is the inverse of `split()`. It joins the list into a single string, with each separated by `sep` if it's used. If `sep` is not used, it defaults to a single space. Thus, `string.join(string.split(s))` removes extra whitespace from string `s`, while `string.join(string.split(s),"")` removes all whitespace, and `string.join(string.split(s),"¦")` pipe character delimits the former whitespace-delimited words.

`find()` and `rfind()` are used to find substrings from the left and right, respectively. The `count()` function counts the number of substring occurrences that don't overlap in the string.

`zfill(s, width)` left, fills a string with zeros.

There are several more functions in the `string` module. They can be found in the module documentation. To use the string module, remember these two requirements:

1. The `import string` command must appear at the program's top.
2. Each function must be preceded by the word `string` and a dot.

Regular Expressions

Regular expressions enable the programmer to complete parsing tasks in a few lines of code instead of the 20 to 100 lines required in the C language. Regular expressions are flexible, wildcard-enabled strings used to match, pick apart, and translate other strings.

Regular Expressions: Python and Perl

The Perl language's success can be attributed partially to its inclusion of regular expressions. Python also supports regular expressions with the new, Perl-compatible `re` module, as well as the obsolete `regex` module. (Don't use this module.) The syntax for invoking regular expressions and retrieving groups between the two languages is as different as can be, but the regular expressions themselves are identical. If you can construct a Perl regular expression, you can do the same in Python. Here is a Perl example to find the seven characters before the word `Linux` in a string:

```
#!/usr/bin/perl

my($a) = "I like Linux for development.";
$a =~ m/(.{4})Linux /;
my($b) = $1;   #group 1
print "<$b>\n";
```

Here's the same code written in Python:

```
#!/usr/bin/python
import re
```

```
a = "I like Linux for development."
m = re.search("(.{4})Linux", a)
b = m.group(1)
print "<" + b + ">"
```

Each prints the string `<ike >`. The syntax is completely different, but the regular expression, in this case `"(.{4})Linux"`, remains the same.

The preceding code uses the `re` module's `search` function. The `re` module also contains a `match` function, which is not covered in this chapter.

Note the line `import re` line. This must be done in every module using the `re` module's regular expressions.

Simple Matches

The simplest use of regular expression is to determine whether a string conforms to the specified regular expression. Perhaps the simplest is simply searching the string for the existence of a substring:

```
import re
a = "I like Linux for development."
m = re.search("Linux", a)
if m == None:
   print "Not found"
else:
   print "Found"
```

Function `re.search()` returns a match object. The *match object*, which was assigned to variable `m` in the preceding code, contains all information concerning the application of the regular expression against the string. If nothing in the string matched the regular expression, `re.search()` returns special value `None`.

There are several wildcards. Here are the most important:

`.`	Any character
`^`	Beginning of the string
`$`	End of the string
`\s`	Whitespace character
`\S`	Non-whitespace character
`\d`	Digit character
`\D`	Non-digit character

There are several repetition specifiers. These can be placed after a character or wildcard to indicate repetition of the character or wildcard. Here are the most important:

`*`	0 or more repetitions
`+`	1 or more repetitions
`?`	1 or 0 repetitions
`{n}`	Exactly *n* repetitions
`{n,}`	At least *n* repetitions
`{n,m}`	At least *n* but not more than *m* repetitions

Several flags can be used to modify the behavior of the regular expression search. These flags are numeric constants used as an optional third argument to the `re.search()` function. These flags can be `OR`ed using the pipe symbol to accomplish multiple modifications. By far the most common flag is `re.IGNORECASE`, which ignores case during searches. There are several others, which can be found in Python's documentation.

Here's a comparison of a search with and without `re.IGNORECASE`:

```
m = re.search("Linux", a, re.IGNORECASE)
m = re.search("Linux", a)
```

The first search finds `"Linux"`, `"LINUX"`, `"linux"`, `"lInUx"`, and any other combination of upper- and lowercase spelling `"Linux"`. The second search finds only the exact string `"Linux"`.

To demonstrate wildcards and repetitions, here is a simplified regular expression that identifies whether a date exists in a line:

```
a = "Valentines is 2/14/2000. Don\'t forget!"
m = re.search("\D\d{1,2}/\d{1,2}/\d{2,4}\D", a)
if m == None:
   print "No date in string."
else:
   print "String contains date."
```

The preceding code checks for the existence anywhere in the string of a non-digit followed by one or two digits, followed by a slash, followed by one or two digits, followed by another slash, followed by two, three, or four digits, followed by a non-digit.

Note

There is an alternative syntax that precompiles the regular expression for faster use in tight loops. In the author's experiments it improved regular expression performance roughly 15 percent. It is not covered in this chapter. If you need better regular expression performance in loops, look up `re.compile()` in your Python documentation.

Simple Parsing with Groups

Classifying strings is nice, but the real power comes from the capability to parse strings. Perhaps the simplest example is changing a file extension. Consider this:

```
src = "myfile.conf"
m = re.search("(\S+)\.conf", src)
dst = m.group(1) + ".bak"
print dst
```

The preceding code searches the source string for a group of one or more non-whitespace characters, followed by `".conf"`, and creates a match object, which is assigned to variable *m*. The group, which is specified by the parentheses around the `\S+`, is available as `m.group(1)`, to which is appended `".bak"` to complete the destination name.

Here's an example that parses dates. Note that this example is not complete enough for use in applications:

```
a = "11/21/1999"
m = re.search("^([01]?\d)[/-]([0123]?\d)[/-](\d{2,4})$", a)
print m.groups()
month = m.group(1)
day = m.group(2)
year = m.group(3)
print year, month, day
```

Carefully consider the `search` statement in the preceding code sample. It looks for a string consisting of a date as a one- or two-digit number, with the tens place being `0` or `1` if existing, followed by either a slash or hyphen, followed by another one- or two-digit number—this one with the tens place being `0`, `1`, `2`, or `3`. This second one- or two-digit number is followed by another slash or hyphen, followed by any number of two to four digits. Note that this is about as much validation as can be performed without integer arithmetic.

Each number in the regular expression is surrounded by parentheses so that each is accessible as a group in the match object. The groups are then evaluated and assigned to month, day, and year. The sample code prints the following:

```
1999 11 21
```

Another way to accomplish the same objective is to use the `groups()` function to return a tuple, which can then be assigned the groups, as shown here:

```
a = "11/21/1999"
m = re.search("^([01]?\d)[/-]([0123]?\d)[/-](\d{2,4})", a)
month,day,year = m.groups()
print year, month, day
```

Note that the assignment of the `m.groups()` to three variables works only if the number of variables equals the number of elements in the tuple returned by `m.group`. You know in advance how many elements there will be by the number of parentheses pairs inserted in the regular expression. You can also access the number of elements in the tuple with the `len()` function.

Regular Expression Example

The following complete program takes a file called `test.tst`, searches it for lines containing text inside square brackets, and returns that text minus any left or right space:

```
#!/usr/bin/python
import re

infile = open("test.tst", "r")
x = infile.readline()
while x != "":
   x = x[:-1]
   m = re.search("\[\s*(.*)\s*\]", x)
   if m:
      print m.group(1)
   x = infile.readline()
infile.close()
```

The preceding code reads every line of file `test.tst`, checks it for text between brackets, and if such text exists, prints it. Since many types of configuration files use brackets for headers, this can be molded into useful code.

Strings and Regular Expressions Example

The example in Listing 31.1 illustrates many features of strings and regular expressions. It repeatedly queries the user to type in dates, evaluating, checking, and printing those dates until the user enters a single lowercase `q`.

LISTING 31.1 *ex31_1.py* Prints Dates in Different Formats

```
#!/usr/bin/python

############################################
# Sample Only. Do not use in production.
############################################

import re          #regular expressions
import string      #string manipulation
import readline    #command line editing
def std(s):
   m=re.search("^([01]?\d)[/-]([0123]?\d)[/-](\d{2,4})",s)
```

```
   if m:
      mm =   eval(m.group(1))
      dd =   eval(m.group(2))
      yyyy = eval(m.group(3))
      if yyyy < 40:
         yyyy = yyyy + 2000
      elif yyyy < 100:
         yyyy = yyyy + 1900
      rv = (yyyy,mm,dd)
   else:
      rv = None
   return(rv)

def mdy(t):
   if t:
      mstring = string.zfill(t[1],2)
      dstring = string.zfill(t[2],2)
      return(mstring + "/" + dstring + "/" + str(t[0]))
   else:
      return("bad date")

def ymd(t):
   if t:
      mstring = string.zfill(t[1],2)
      dstring = string.zfill(t[2],2)
      ystring = string.zfill(t[0],4)
      return(ystring +  mstring  + dstring)
   else:
      return("bad date")

def printdates(s):
   print std(s);
   print mdy(std(s))
   print ymd(std(s))

def main():
   x = raw_input("Please type a date, q to quit==>")
   while(x != "q"):
      printdates(x)
      print
      x = raw_input("Please type a date, q to quit==>")

main()
```

Function `std()` creates a standard `ymd` tuple from its string argument, returning `None` if the string is not a date. Function `mdy()` formats a standard `ymd` tuple as a `mm/dd/yyyy` string, while function `ymd()` formats a standard `ymd` tuple as a `yyyymmdd` string. Both `mdy()` and `ymd()` return the string `"bad date"` if passed `None`.

Classes

Python is an object-oriented language and, as such, has features such as classes. If you are unfamiliar with object-oriented programming (OOP), this might all seem confusing and you can skip the use of classes without reducing the utility of Python for simple and moderate programs. However, classes do add OOP capabilities to Python that, when properly used, extend the language considerably.

Class Definition and Instantiation

Python treats classes much as C++ does. To define a class, you use a modification of the function syntax, defining the class that holds the functions:

```
class myclass:
   def printout(self, string):
      print string
```

The first line defines a class called `myclass`. The `myclass` class contains a single function, called `printout`. In OOP terms, `myclass` is the *class* and `printout` is the *method.*

To use the class you create an *instance* of the class. Another word often used for a class instance is the word *object*. The process of creating this instance is called *instantiation.* The following code creates an instance of the `myclass` class, assigning that instance to variable `my`, and operating that instance:

```
my = myclass()
my.printout("This is a string")
```

The first line creates the object (instance). The second line invokes the my object's `printout()` method, as defined in the class. This code prints out the phrase `"This is a string"`.

You might wonder why the function definition has two arguments, `self` and `string`. The variable `string` is whatever is being passed in to the function. The `self` keyword is required for classes because when an instance's method is called, the instance passes itself as the first argument. The use of the word `"self"` takes care of this method pass. If you were calling a function that had no input, you would have only the single `self` name in the function definition. The word `self` is used by convention, but it could be anything.

```
class yourclass:
def printit(self):
   print "This is a function string!"
```

Tip

A good way to describe the relationship between a class and an instance of that class (an object), is that the class is a blueprint. Instances are built from that blueprint like a housing developer builds houses from a blueprint. The houses are the thing of value, but they're defined by the blueprint. In the same way that houses designed the same have different colors and swimming pools, objects from the same class can have different properties.

Encapsulation and Private Identifiers

The more modular the design of a system, the easier it is to build and troubleshoot the system, and the less likely it is to contain design flaws. Consider a home audio system: Almost any pair of speakers will connect to almost any receiver via speaker wires. Almost any CD player will connect almost any receiver via patch cords. Likewise for tapedecks and equalizers. A car is another example. The only knowledge the driver requires is the operation of the gas pedal, brake, and steering wheel.

Imagine driving a car with driver-controlled spark timing, driver control of each of the four brake calipers, and driver control of each wheel's angle. How many crashes would result? Imagine an audio receiver requiring tapedeck inputs and outputs for head angle, bias, and tape speed. How many people could make good recordings on such a system?

The same principle applies to computer programs. Programs are separated into parts. The less each part needs to know about other parts, the more modular the program, and the more reliably the program works.

This is what's so exciting about OOP. Instead of simply dividing a program into tasks (functions), the OOP programmer divides the program into distinct parts, called *classes*, each with its own tasks, behaviors, properties, and most important, public methods.

A *public method* is a function contained by the class and publicized to other classes as well as to the program in general. Public methods are the equivalent of the patch cord jacks on the back of a CD player. Every CD player has them, and everyone knows it.

Consider the following simple class describing a person:

```
class person:
   def getFirstname(self):
      return(self.__fname)
   def getLastname(self):
      return(self.__lname)
   def putFirstname(self, s):
```

```
        self.__fname = s
    def putLastname(self, s):
        self.__lname = s
    __fname = ""
    __lname = ""
```

The rest of the program knows instances of the person class by four public functions: `getFirstname()`, `getLastname()`, `putFirstname()`, and `putLastname()`. The rest of the program need know nothing else about the person class.

Note

Python defines any function or variable inside a class as private if the name of that function or variable begins with at least two underscores, and ends with no more than one underscore. Private variables are inaccessible to code outside the class definition.

Python provides a "back door" for accessing private variables outside the class definition. This chapter does not discuss that method, as doing so would defeat the purpose of object-oriented programming and defeat your program's modularity. That back door should never be used.

To the programmer using instances of the `person` class, it is of absolutely no interest that the person's name happens to be kept in private class variables `__fname` and `__lname`. In fact, those two variables cannot be accessed outside the class code. Consider this attempt to access `__fname` directly:

```
p = person()
print p.__fname
```

The preceding code errors out with an attribute error. Because `__fname` is private, it can't be accessed as `p.__fname`. It cannot be seen or changed anywhere outside the class definition. `__fname` and `__lname` are the equivalents of a tapedeck's bias circuit or a car's timing. They're internally necessary to the class, but the other code operating class instances needn't—and definitely shouldn't—know about them. Thus, `__fname` and `__lname` are said to be *encapsulated*. The process of encapsulating all variables and methods except those intended to be accessed is called *encapsulation*. Good encapsulation requires each class to offer the minimum necessary public functions necessary for other program parts to operate that classes objects. Such a *thin interface* makes an OOP program ultra modular, reliable, easy to modify, and easy to troubleshoot—and yes, it makes the program's classes reusable.

The person class previously defined provides for any necessary access to __fname via the getFirstname() and putFirstname() methods, in the same way the car provides any necessary access to the brake calipers via the brake pedal. The working of the person class is fairly obvious. A call to putFirstname() changes __fname, and a call to getFirstname() retrieves __fname. The same is true for methods and variables for the last name.

Now add the following code to exercise the person class code:

```
p = person()
print "*", p.getFirstname(), p.getLastname(), "*"
p.putFirstname("John")
p.putLastname("Smith")
print "*", p.getFirstname(), p.getLastname(), "*"
```

The preceding code instantiates a person object called p, prints the (presently empty) first and last names, sets the first and last names, and then prints them again. The output looks like this:

```
*  *
* John Smith *
```

Now add a class constructor. Class constructors are always called __init__()—the word init preceded and followed by two underscores. There can be only one defined class constructor. You've made your class constructor so the person's name is defined on instantiation:

```
class person:
   def __init__(self, lname, fname):
      self.__lname = lname
      self.__fname = fname
   def getFirstname(self):
      return(self.__fname)
   def getLastname(self):
      return(self.__lname)
   def putFirstname(self, s):
      self.__fname = s
   def putLastname(self, s):
      self.__lname = s
   __fname = ""
   __lname = ""

p = person("Jones", "Paul")
print "*", p.getFirstname(), p.getLastname(), "*"
```

The person's name is set upon instantiation by the __init__() method, so the print statement prints the correct name:

```
* Paul Jones *
```

Modularity has been the basis of cost-effective, reliable, easy-to-repair systems since the dawn of the Industrial Revolution. OOP's potential for encapsulation enables those advantages in software. Tight encapsulation makes programs scalable, meaning they can grow without reaching a point where the interaction combinations grow geometrically and prevent further growth. The road to tight encapsulation is deciding what each class represents and creating very few public functions to allow other software entities to control its behavior and query it for information.

Inheritance

Object orientation allows construction of programs in parts rather than tasks. Often these parts represent tangible objects or business entities. At such times it's handy to classify these objects or entities the way we do in English.

Note

Inheritance is an advanced OOP topic, of concern primarily to those doing serious development. If you're doing small-to-moderate projects, you may safely choose to skip this section.

Here is an example:

```
Animal
  |--Bird
  |     |--Duck
  |     |--Robin
  |     `--Owl
  `--Fish
        |--Trout
        `--Catfish
```

The relationships of this hierarchy can be thought of as an "is a" relationship. In other words, a bird *is a* animal with wings. A robin *is a* bird. The robin "inherits" traits from birds (wings), and traits from animals (movement).

Here's another example:

```
Person
  '--Employee
```

An employee *is a* person. Look at some code:

```
class person:
   def getFirstname(self):
      return(self.__fname)
```

```
   def getLastname(self):
      return(self.__lname)
   def putFirstname(self, s):
      self.__fname = s
   def putLastname(self, s):
      self.__lname = s
   __fname = ""
   __lname = ""

class employee(person):
   def getNumber(self):
      return(self.__number)
   def putNumber(self, n):
      self.__number = n
   __number = -99999
```

In the physical world, an employee is a person (who works for the employer). Here we've created a class called `employee`, which *inherits* traits from class `person`. `employee` is said to be a *subclass* of `person`, while `person` is said to be the *superclass*, and an *ancestor*, of `employee`. The act of creating a new class that inherits from another class is sometimes called *subclassing* or *deriving*. In the preceding code, the fact that `person` is in parentheses after `employee` designates this inheritance relationship.

The `employee` class has not only the `getNumber()` and `putNumber()` methods, but also `getFirstname()`, `getLastName()`, `putFirstname()`, and `putLastName()`. The latter four methods are inherited from the `person` class. Thus, assuming the preceding coding of the `person` and `employee` classes, the following code instantiates and exercises an object of the `employee` class:

```
e = employee()
e.putFirstname("Maria")
e.putLastname("Garcia")
e.putNumber("1234")
print "Employee", e.getFirstname(), e.getLastname(),
print "has employee #", e.getNumber()
```

The output prints as follows:

```
Employee Maria Garcia has employee # 1234
```

Notice the benefits we've obtained. Creating the new class was trivial, because we merely added the trait (employee number) that makes a person an employee. If the `person` class is changed later, those changes will *filter down* to the employee class.

Inheritance can greatly simplify the creation and maintenance of large programs. Consider using inheritance in large programs when you observe program entities that have an is a relationship.

Additional Python Capabilities

Python ships with several modules, giving it additional capabilities. A module is enabled by placing an `import` statement for the module at the top of the program.

The sys module enables access to command-line arguments via `sys.argv`. The sys module also provides `exit()` for exiting the program, in addition to several other useful functions.

The os module enables execution of shell commands via the `exec()` and `system()` functions. It provides for directory navigation and manipulation, environment variable access and manipulation, file descriptor I/O, file manipulation, pathname manipulation, and date and time functions.

The `os.path` module, which is enabled by importing the os module, contains various file information such as file time and whether it's a directory, file, link, and so on. Functions from the `os.path` module must be prefaced with `os.path`, not just `os`.

The `glob` module is used for filename expansion. Programs scanning multiple files or walking directory trees use this. Here's a 15-line program using the `sys`, `os`, `os.path` (imported automatically with `os`), and `glob` modules to walk a directory tree and print out the files:

```
#!/usr/bin/python
import sys
import os
import glob

def do1dir(s):
   s = s + "/*"
   files = glob.glob(s)
   for x in files:
      if os.path.isfile(x):
         print x
      elif os.path.isdir(x):
         do1dir(x)

if len(sys.argv[1]) > 2:  # prevent /,. or ..
   do1dir(sys.argv[1])
else:
   print "Cannot do:", sys.argv[1], "-- too short."
```

Note

Recursion is obviously alive and well in Python.

The `math` module provides trig functions, logarithmic functions, square root, raising to powers, and other math functions expected from a full-featured language. The `cmath` (complex math) module provides most of those same functions for complex numbers.

If you need a nice GUI front end to your Python program, import the `Tkinter` module, which provides a nice interface to the TK widgets of the `tcl` programming language. Documentation on the `Tkinter` module is available at `http://www.python.org/topics/tkinter/doc.html`.

Python's built-in functions are sufficient for CGI (Web programming). However, various included modules greatly ease complex CGI tasks. When considering what language to use for Web programming, investigate Python's `cgi` module to ease forms handling, `urllib` for opening Web resources, and `urlparse` for splitting and building URLs.

Going deeper, investigate the `xmllib`, `htmllib`, `ftplib`, `poplib`, `SocketServer`, `socket`, `thread`, `threading`, `Queue`, `zlib`, and `gzip` modules.

Summary

In this chapter you've seen the primary programming features of the Python language. For more information about Python's more advanced features, look for programming guidelines in the Python distributions on the `http://www.python.org` Web site or in a dedicated Python book.

Python is easy to learn, making it a great first language. Yet its power, features, add-ons, and object orientation make Python ideal for large-scale application development. Add the spectacular programmer productivity gained through Python's concise command set, and it's clear why Python is increasingly the language of choice for challenging software projects.

CHAPTER 32

Network Programming

In This Chapter

Networking and Linux are a natural combination. After all, Linux is a product of the Internet itself because most of the developers collaborated (and still do collaborate) across the world over email, the World Wide Web, and Usenet news. In addition, Linux is based on UNIX, one of the operating systems on which many common computer networking technologies were developed.

Linux's mature and fully functional networking features make it an excellent platform for networking programming. Because Linux provides full support for the sockets interface, most programs developed on other version of UNIX will build and run on Linux with little or no modification. Textbooks and documentation about UNIX networking are fully applicable to Linux.

This chapter uses Perl examples to introduce network programming concepts and shows how to create functioning network programs for Linux quickly and easily. Perl was selected because it enables you to focus on network programming concepts instead of application development issues and programming environments. Note that when these scripts were developed, the emphasis was on illustrating key network programming concepts, not programming style, robustness, or how to program in Perl. Only a basic knowledge of Perl is required to understand the examples, and they are certainly clear enough for C or C++ programmers to follow. For detailed information on the Perl language and how to use it for a wide variety of tasks, see Chapter 28, "Perl Programming."

This chapter is by no means exhaustive because concepts such as protocol layering and routing could fill entire books themselves. This chapter is intended to serve as an introductory tutorial to network programming, with an emphasis on hands-on exercises.

Networking Concepts

This section covers the fundamentals of networking, including the necessary components of network communication. You will learn how these components are used to build a connection by following a simple program that retrieves networking information and uses it to connect to another program. By the end of this section, you should have a good understanding of network addresses, sockets, and the differences between TCP (Transmission Control Protocol) and its counterpart UDP (User Datagram Protocol).

Listing 32.1 contains a Perl function that creates a connection to a server by using TCP. This code will not run by itself, it is a function to be called by other Perl routines.

LISTING 32.1 *makeconn()*—Creating a TCP Connection

```
sub makeconn
{
   my ($host, $portname, $server, $port, $proto, $servaddr);

   $host = $_[0];
   $portname = $_[1];

    #
    # Server hostname, port and protocol
    #
   $server = gethostbyname($host) or
       die "gethostbyname: cannot locate host: $!";
   $port = getservbyname($portname, 'tcp') or
       die "getservbyname: cannot get port : $!";
   $proto = getprotobyname('tcp') or
       die "getprotobyname: cannot get proto : $!";

    #
    # Build an inet address
    #
  $servaddr = sockaddr_in($port, $server);


    #
    # Create the socket and connect it
    #
  socket(CONNFD, PF_INET, SOCK_STREAM, $proto);
  connect(CONNFD, $servaddr) or die "connect : $!";

  return CONNFD;
}
```


Tip

When you type in the `network.pl` file, make sure that the last line of the file is 1; otherwise it will trigger an error and it will take forever to figure out.

This procedure can be summarized to three essential steps:

1. Build an address.
2. Create a socket.
3. Establish a connection.

The network address is built by retrieving address information in lines 11 and 13 and then assembling it in line 21. In line 27, you create the socket by way of protocol information retrieved in line 15. (The protocol information, however, can actually be considered part of the address, as you will see.) In line 28, you finally establish the connection.

Building Network Addresses

The steps involved in building a network address and connecting to it provide a framework for observing how network communication works. Each part of this process is covered to better prepare for the hands-on tutorials. For a more in-depth look at TCP/IP and networking, see Chapter 7, "TCP/IP and Network Management."

If you ever configured a PC or workstation for Internet connectivity, you have probably seen an *Internet address* (or *IP address*) similar to `192.9.200.10` or `10.7.8.14`. This is called *dotted-decimal format* and, like many things in computing, it is a representation of network addresses that are intended to make things easier for humans to read. Computers, routers, and other internet devices actually use a 32-bit number, often called a *canonical address*, to communicate. When this number is evaluated, it is broken down into four smaller, 8-bit (1 byte) values, much the way the dotted-decimal format consists of four numbers separated by decimals.

An *internetwork*, or *internet* for short, consists of two or more networks that are connected. In this case, the word *internet* refers to any two networks, not the *Internet*, which has become a proper name for the network that encompasses most of the world. The *Internet Protocol* (IP) was designed with this sort of topography in mind. For an internet address to be useful, it has to be capable of identifying not only a specific node (computer), but also the network on which the node resides. Both bits of information are provided in the 32-bit address. Which portion of the address is related to each component is decided by the *netmask* that is applied to the address. Depending on an organization's needs, a network architect can decide to have more networks or more addresses. For details on *subnetting* networks, see Chapter 7. For the sake of network programming, you only need to know what information is stored in an internet address and that individual workstation netmasks have to be correct for a message to be successfully delivered.

Dotted-decimal format is easier to read than 32-bit values (especially because many of the possible values are not printable or would work out to some pretty ponderous numbers). Even so, most people would rather use names than numbers, finding `gandalf` or `www.yahoo.com` a lot easier to remember than `12.156.27.4` or `182.250.2.178`. For this reason, the notion of hostnames, domain names, and the domain name system was devised. You can get access to a database of name-to-number mappings through a set of *network library functions*, which provide host (node) information in response to names or numbers. For example, in line 11 of Listing 32.1, you retrieve the address associated with a name by using one of these functions, `gethostbyname()`.

Depending on the host configuration, `gethostbyname()` can retrieve the address associated with a name from a file (`/etc/hosts`), from the Domain Name System (DNS), or from the Network Information System (NIS or Yellow Pages). DNS and NIS (see Chapters 8, "The Domain Name Service," and 14, "NIS: Network Information Service") are networkwide services administrators used to simplify network configuration. Adding and updating network address numbers from a central location (and maybe a backup location) is obviously a lot easier than updating files on every workstation in an organization. These systems are also useful for internetworks because the address of a remote host can be determined by making a DNS request when it is needed, instead of exchanging configuration files in advance.

One other advantage of using names is that the address associated with a name can be changed without affecting applications. The application only needs to know the name; the address can be discovered at runtime.

To illustrate the use of the `gethostbyname()` function and the difference between dotted-decimal formatted addresses and canonical addresses, try the script in Listing 32.2.

LISTING 32.2 *resolv*

```
1:#!/usr/bin/perl
2: use Socket;
3:   $addr = gethostbyname($ARGV[0]);
4:   $dotfmt = inet_ntoa($addr);
5:   print "$ARGV[0]: numeric: $addr dotted: $dotfmt\n";
```

Line 2 uses the `Socket` module included with Perl 5 distributions. This module is required for all the sample code in this chapter, including Listing 32.1.

When you run this program, passing it a hostname for which you want information, you see something like the following:

```
$ ./resolv www.redhat.com
www.redhat.com: numeric: Çwy´ dotted: 199.183.24.140
```

Line 3 passes the name specified on the command line to `gethostbyname()`, which places the canonical address in `$addr`. This address is then passed to `inet_ntoa()`, which returns the same address in dotted-decimal format. (`inet_ntoa` is an abbreviation for "internet number to ASCII.") You then print both values out in line 5. As you can see, the 32-bit address looks rather strange when printed.

Note

If your Linux system is not connected to the Internet, simply specify your own hostname to resolve or another hostname that is in your own `/etc/hosts` file or available to your workstation via DNS or NIS.

If your workstation is on the Internet and you see a different address for `http://www.redhat.com`, it just means the address has changed—after all, that is one of the reasons DNS was developed!

Network Services

Being able to locate a computer is a fundamental part of network communication, but it is not the only necessary component in an address. Why do you want to contact a specific host? Do you want to retrieve an HTML document from it? Do you want to log in and check mail? Most workstations, especially those running Linux or any other version of UNIX, provide more than one service to other nodes on a network.

In line 13 of Listing 32.1, you called the `getservbyname()` function, which provides the other value used to form the complete network address. This value, referred to as a *service port number*, is the portion of the address that specifies the service or program with which you want to communicate. The port number is a 16-bit integer that becomes part of the source and target (client or server) IP address your applications use to form a *connection endpoint*. If you execute the `netstat -a` command, you see multiple IP address pairs with their associated port numbers. (The numbers might actually be replaced by the service port name from the `/etc/services` file.) This combination of an IP address and a port number is called a *socket*.

Like host addresses, service ports can be referred to by name instead of number. `getservbyname()` retrieves the number associated with the specified name from the file `/etc/services`. (If NIS is available, the number can also be retrieved from a network database.) Port numbers listed in this database are called *well-known ports* (0 through 1023). In theory, any host can connect to one of these services on any machine because the port numbers customarily remain consistent. (For example, Telnet uses port 23 whether you use UNIX or Windows NT.) Even though this is true 99 percent of the time, the `/etc/services` file can easily be altered—watch out for corruption. Applications that do not rely on the well-known ports use what are called *ephemeral ports*, considered available for any application to use. The port numbers used by applications do not have to be listed in or retrieved from this database; it is considered a good idea to list them in `/etc/services` and share them in an effort to prevent conflicts.

Tip

Some of the common ports are 21 for FTP, 23 for telnet, 25 for SMTP, and 69 for TFTP. Look in `/etc/services` for your system.

After you have retrieved the two components necessary to build a fully qualified address, you provide them to the `sockaddr_in` function, which builds a `SOCKADDR_IN` structure for you. `SOCKADDR_IN` is the programmatic representation of a network address needed for most socket system calls.

Sockets and Portability

Before you can use your addressing information, you need a socket. The `socket()` function in line 27 of Listing 32.1 illustrates how to create one. Some explanation of what sockets are and the types first available to a program will help explain the function.

Sockets are an Application Programming Interface (API) used for network communication. This API was first available with BSD UNIX for the VAX architecture in the early 1980s, and has become prevalent in almost all UNIX versions and recently on Windows, along with a variety of other operating systems. System V Release 4 UNIX supports a different interface, called the Transport Layer Interface (TLI) , and a TLI superset called X/Open Transport Interface (XTI), but even most system V Release 4 versions, such as Solaris 2.x and AT&T SVR4 UNIX, provide socket interfaces. Linux provides a full implementation of the socket interface.

Socket applications treat network connections (or to be more exact, connection endpoints) the same way most UNIX interfaces are handled—as file handles. The reason for the endpoint qualification is simple: Not all network sessions are connected, and referring to all network streams as connections can be incorrect and misleading. As a matter of fact, after a network endpoint is created and bound or connected, it can be written to, read from, and destroyed by using the same functions as files. Because of this interface, socket programs tend to be portable between different versions of UNIX and frequently many other operating systems.

Protocols and Socket Types

The socket API is designed to support multiple protocols, called *domains* or *families*. Most UNIX versions support at least two domains: UNIX and Internet. (Two of the other domains are the Xerox Network system and the ISO protocol suite.) UNIX domain sockets use the local workstation file system to provide communication between programs running on the same workstation only. Internet domain sockets use the Internet Protocol (IP) suite to communicate over the network (as well as on the same machine). As you might guess, you will be concerned with Internet domain sockets.

In the following call to `socket()`, you specify the scalar variable in which you want to have the socket descriptor stored and three values that describe the type of socket you want to have created—the protocol family, the socket type, and the protocol. In this example, the protocol family is specified as `PF_INET`, which is for the Internet.

```
socket(CONNFD, PF_INET, SOCK_STREAM, $proto);
```

The possible socket types are `SOCK_STREAM`, `SOCK_DGRAM`, `SOCK_RAW`, `SOCK_RDM`, and `SOCK_SEQPACKET`. The last three are used for low-level, advanced operations and are beyond the scope of this chapter.

`SOCK_STREAM` sockets are connected at both ends, they are reliable, and the messages between them are sequenced. The terms *reliable* and *sequenced* have special meanings in networking. *Reliability* refers to the fact that the network guarantees delivery: An application can write a packet with the understanding that it will arrive at the other end unless the connection is suddenly broken by a catastrophic event, such as the unexpected shutting down of a host or a literal break in the network. *Sequencing* means that all messages are always delivered to the other application in the order in which they are sent. (It does not mean they will arrive at the client or server machine in the order sent.)

Note

A client application can mysteriously disappear (if a client machine is restarted or crashes) without performing an orderly shutdown of the connection. In this situation, your server could still be hanging around waiting for messages to be sent from the client. These are called *half-connections* because your server believes the client is still there. If you think this could be a problem in your environment, try using the `keepalive` option, which periodically probes the client to see if it is still there. If the client is not found, the connection is shut down.

`SOCK_DGRAM` sockets support connectionless and unreliable datagrams. A *datagram* is typically a fixed-length, small message. Applications have no guarantees that datagrams will be delivered or in what order if delivered. On the surface, it seems no application would ever want to use `SOCK_DGRAM`, but as you will see, many applications do and for good reasons.

The type of socket is very closely related to the protocol being used. In the case of the Internet suite, `SOCK_STREAM` sockets always implement TCP, and `SOCK_DGRAM` sockets implement UDP.

The characteristics of the TCP protocol match the characteristics of `SOCK_STREAM`. TCP packets are guaranteed to be delivered, barring a network disaster. (The workstation on the other end of the connection drops out or the network itself suffers a serious, unrecoverable outage.) Packets are always delivered to the application in the same order in which they were written by the sending application. Obviously, these properties make the job of a network developer easy because a message can be written and essentially forgotten. There is, however, a cost: TCP messages are much more expensive (demanding) in terms of both network and computing resources than UDP messages. The systems at both ends of a session have to confirm that they have received the correct information, which results in more work for the operating system and more network traffic. Both systems also have to track the order in which messages were sent, and quite possibly have to store messages until others arrive, depending on the state of the network "terrain" between the two workstations. (New messages can arrive while others are being retransmitted because of an error.) In addition, the fact that TCP connections are just that—connections—has a price. Every conversation has an endpoint associated with it, so a server with more than one client has to arbitrate between multiple sockets, which can be very difficult. (See "I/O Multiplexing with TCP" later in this chapter for details.)

UDP, like `SOCK_DGRAM`, is connectionless, which means the Transport Layer does not guarantee that every packet sent will make it to the destination machine. Try to envision UDP as a "Fire and Forget" protocol. It was considered unreliable in the past, but with today's Local Area Networks (LANs), UDP is usually considered very reliable. Using UDP in a Wide Area Network (WAN) is usually more prone to error because you have no idea of the reliability of the networks and machines your packets will pass through in a WAN.

With UDP, applications have to provide whatever reliability mechanisms are necessary for the job they are performing. For some applications, this is an advantage because all the mechanisms provided by TCP are not always needed. For example, DNS, which uses UDP, simply sends a message and waits for a response for a predetermined interval; because DNS is a one-to-one message-to-response protocol, sequencing between client and server is not necessary. UDP is connectionless, so a server can use one socket to communicate with many clients. All clients write to the same address for the server, and the server responds individually by writing to specific client addresses. If DNS does not get a response before the interval expires (known as *timing out*), it tries again. At some point, it will report a failure and give up.

UDP messages can also be broadcast to entire networks—a blessing to an application that needs to communicate one message to many users, but a curse for systems that do not need the message but have to read it to figure out it is not destined for them. Because UDP does not require a connection to be set up in advance, it is considered much quicker than TCP; however, vendors are getting better at speeding up TCP, so in the future this might not always be true.

Making a Connection

Logically, if you are creating a connection like that of the `makeconn()` function in Listing 32.1, you need to create a `SOCK_STREAM` socket with the TCP protocol information retrieved by `getprotobyname()` in line 15. Take a look at lines 27 and 28 from Listing 32.1, repeated here:

```
27:  socket(CONNFD, PF_INET, SOCK_STREAM, $proto);
28:  connect(CONNFD, $servaddr) or die "connect : $!";
```

After creating the socket in line 27, you then pass it to `connect()` with the address structure created by `sockaddr_in()`. The `connect()` function actually contacts the address specified in the structure and establishes the virtual circuit supported by TCP.

A TCP Client Example

Listing 32.3 puts `makeconn()` to work in a sample program.

LISTING 32.3 *client1*

```
#!/usr/bin/perl
use Socket;
require "./network.pl";

$NETFD = makeconn($ARGV[0], $ARGV[1]);

#
# Get the message
#
sysread $NETFD, $message, 32768 or die "error getting message : $!";
print "$message \n";
close $NETFD;
```

Run this program with two command-line arguments—the name of a Linux host that is running `sendmail` and the `smtp` mail port name:

```
$ ./client1 iest smtp
220 iest.home.mxn.com ESMTP Sendmail 8.8.5/8.8.5;
 Sat, 4 Oct 1997 18:25:08 -0400
```

This program uses `makeconn()` to connect to the `sendmail` program running on the named host and uses the `sysread()` function to read the greeting the host sends to a new client when it first connects.

`sysread()` is one of the functions used for extracting network messages from sockets. It is a wrapper for the UNIX `read()` system call. You cannot use the Perl `read()` function because it is designed for standard I/O, which uses buffering and other high-level features that interfere with network communications. In a real-world application, you would probably read messages with `sysread()` in and out of a buffer of your own, keeping careful track of what you had just read because you could be interrupted in a read call by a signal. (You would also install signal handlers.) As this example demonstrates, establishing a client connection and retrieving some data is pretty simple.

Tip

One of the benefits of using Perl for network programming is that it hides the issue of byte ordering between different architectures. Intel *x*86 chips and Sun SPARC chips, for example, represent values differently. The creators of the Internet introduced a concept of *network byte order*, in which programs are supposed to place values prior to transmission and then translate back to their network format when they read in messages. Perl does this for us.

A TCP Server Example

Now you can write your own server to which `client1` will connect. First, you have to place a socket in the listen state by using `makelisten()`, another function defined in `network.pl`. `makelisten()` is shown in Listing 32.4.

LISTING 32.4 *`makelisten()`*

```
sub makelisten {

    my ($portname, $port, $proto, $servaddr);
    $portname = $_[0];

    #
    #  port and protocol
    #
    $port = getservbyname($portname, 'tcp') or
    die "getservbyname: cannot get port : $!";
```

continues

LISTING 32.4 continued

```
11:      $proto = getprotobyname('tcp') or
12:      die "getprotobyname: cannot get proto : $!";
13:
14:      #
15:      # Bind an inet address
16:      #
17:      socket(LISTFD, PF_INET, SOCK_STREAM, $proto);
18:      bind (LISTFD, sockaddr_in($port, INADDR_ANY)) or die "bind: $!";
19:      listen (LISTFD, SOMAXCONN) or die "listen: $!";
20:      return LISTFD;
21: }
```

The `makelisten()` function creates a TCP socket, binds it to a local address, and then places the socket in the listen state.

Lines 9 and 11 retrieve the same information `makeconn()` retrieves to create a connection, with the exception of an internet address. `makelisten()` then creates an internet family `SOCK_STREAM` socket, which by definition is a TCP socket, but you specify this explicitly, as in `makeconn()`.

In line 18, the socket is bound to a local address. This tells the system that any messages sent to the specified service port and internet address should be relayed to the specified socket. You use `sockaddr_in()` to build an address from the service port retrieved with `getportbyname()` and with a special address that corresponds to all addresses on the workstation. In this way, connections can be made to all network interfaces and even over any dial-up interfaces on the workstation. This function shows a little laziness, in that it passes the `sockaddr_in()` function to `bind()` instead of calling it separately and saving the results.

There are some restrictions on what service ports can be bound. For historical reasons, only programs executing with superuser (`root`) access can bind service ports numbered lower than 1024. Even if you find yourself on an operating system that bypasses this restriction, resist the temptation to use ports below 1024. You might find yourself needing to change your code when you either upgrade your OS level or port your application to an environment that enforces this restriction.

After the socket is bound, you can execute `listen()`, which notifies the system that your program is ready to accept client connections.

`server1`, the program that uses `makelisten()`, is just as simple as the client and is shown in Listing 32.5.

LISTING 32.5 *server1*

```
#!/usr/bin/perl
  use Socket;
  require "./network.pl";

  $hello = "Hello world!";

  $LISTFD = makelisten("test");

  LOOP: while (1) {
    unless ($paddr = accept(NEWFD, $LISTFD)) {
    next LOOP;
    }
    syswrite(NEWFD, $hello, length($hello));
    close NEWFD;
}
```


In Listing 32.5, you simply place a socket in the listen state by using `makelisten()` and then enter a `while` loop that centers on the function `accept()`. The purpose of `accept()` is exactly as it sounds, to accept client connections. You pass two arguments to `accept()`: a new variable (`NEWFD`) that contains the socket identifier for the accepted connection and the socket (`$LISTFD`) that has been set up with `listen()`.

Whenever `accept()` returns a connection, you write a string to the new socket and immediately close it.

Before you can test your server, you need to add the entry for the test service it uses. Add the following three lines to the `/etc/services` file. You will have to be `root` to edit this file.

```
test            8000/tcp
test            8000/udp
test1           8001/udp
```

You have added three entries for your test programs, one for TCP and two others for UDP that you will use later.

Now, to test your server, you need to execute the following commands:

```
$ ./server1&
$./client1 iest test
Hello world!
```

`iest` is the hostname of your system. The server writes back your greeting and exits. Because the server is executing inside a `while` loop, you can run `./client1` repeatedly. When the test is finished, use `kill` to stop the server:

```
$ ps ax¦ grep server1 ¦ awk '{ print $1 }'
pid
$ kill pid
```

A UDP Example

To implement the same test in UDP, you have to set up a SOCK_DGRAM socket for both a client and a server. This function, makeudpcli(), can also be found in network.pl and is shown in Listing 32.6.

Listing 32.6 *makeudpcli()*

```
sub makeudpcli {

    my ($proto, $servaddr);

    $proto = getprotobyname('udp') or
    die "getprotobyname: cannot get proto : $!";

    #
    # Bind a UDP port
    #
    socket(DGFD, PF_INET, SOCK_DGRAM, $proto);
    bind (DGFD,  sockaddr_in(0, INADDR_ANY)) or die "bind: $!";

    return DGFD;
}
```

In Listing 32.6, you retrieve the protocol information for UDP and then create a SOCK_DGRAM socket. You then bind it, but you tell the system to bind to any address and any service port; in other words, you want the socket named but do not care what that name is.

The reason for this extra bind() is quite straightforward. Because UDP is connectionless, special attention has to be made to addresses when you are sending and receiving datagrams. When datagram messages are read, the reader also receives the address of the originator so it knows where to send any replies. If you want to receive replies to your messages, you need to guarantee they come from a unique address. The call to bind() ensures that the system allocates a unique address for you.

Now that you have created a datagram socket, you can communicate with a server, using the program in Listing 32.7, client2.

LISTING 32.7 *client2*

```
1: #!/usr/bin/perl
2:
3: use Socket;
4: require "./network.pl";
5:
6: $poke = "yo!";
7:
8:  $NETFD = makeudpcli();
9:
10: #
11: # Work out server address
12: #
13:  $addr = gethostbyname($ARGV[0]);
14:  $port = getservbyname($ARGV[1], 'udp');
15:
16:  $servaddr = sockaddr_in($port, $addr);
17:
18: #
19: # Poke the server
20: #
21:  send $NETFD, $poke, 0, $servaddr;
22:
23: #
24: # Recv the reply
25: #
26:  recv $NETFD, $message, 32768, 0 or die "error getting message : $!";
27:  print "$message \n";
28:  close $NETFD;
```

After you create the socket, you still have to resolve the server address, but instead of providing this address to the `connect()` function, you have to provide it to the `send()` function in line 21 so it knows where to, well, send the message. But why are you sending anything to the server at all? After all, in the TCP example in Listing 32.3, the communication is one way.

In the TCP example, the server sends a message as soon as you connect and then closes the session. The act of connecting is, in effect, a message from the client to the server. Because UDP lacks connections, you have to use a message from the client as a trigger for the conversation.

The server creates a UDP socket in a slightly different manner because it needs to bind a well-known port. It uses `getservbyname()` to retrieve a port number and specifies it as part of the call to `bind()`. Look at `makeudpserv()` in `network.pl` for details.

The server's main loop is actually pretty close to that of the TCP server and is shown in Listing 32.8.

LISTING 32.8 *server2*

```
#!/usr/bin/perl
#
#
use Socket;
require "./network.pl";

$hello = "Hello world!";

$LISTFD = makeudpserv("test");

while (1) {
    $cliaddr = recv $LISTFD, $message, 32768, 0;
    print "Received $message from client\n";
    send $LISTFD, $hello, 0, $cliaddr;
}
```

Instead of waiting for a client by looping on the `accept()` function, the server loops on the `recv()` function. There are also no new sockets to close after the reply is sent to the client.

You see the following when these programs are run:

```
$ ./server2&
$./client2 iest test
Received yo! from client
Hello world!
```

You see that from a programmer's standpoint, the differences between UDP and TCP affect not only the socket functions you use and how you use them, but also how you design your programs. Differences such as the lack of a connection and the lack of built-in reliability mechanisms must be seriously considered when you design an application. There is no guarantee, for example, that the server in this section ever receives your poke message. For that reason, a mechanism such as a timer would be employed in a real-world application.

Blocking Versus Nonblocking Descriptors

Most input/output operations that you perform take advantage of *blocking* where your program waits (or is *blocked* from processing) until the operation is complete. The program issues the request to the operating system and once the data is available, the operating system lets the program continue. This block may be for milliseconds (waiting for a hard disk platter to rotate to the correct sector) or almost forever (waiting for keyboard input).

All the examples to this point in this chapter have relied on blocking I/O. Certain operations, such as reading, writing, and connecting or accepting connections, are set to block when they wait for completion, which brings a program (or thread) to a halt. After `server1` sets up a listen, for example, it enters the `while` loop and calls `accept()`. Until a client connects to the listening socket, the program is halted. It just waits and does not repeatedly call `accept()`; it calls it once and blocks. This condition is also true for `client2`, which blocks on the `recv()` call until the server replies. If the server is unavailable, the program will block forever. This is especially unwise for an application that uses UDP, but how can a timer be implemented if the call to `recv()` will never return?

Writing can also block on TCP connections when the receiver of the data has not read enough data to allow the current write to complete. To maintain reliability and proper flow control, the systems on both ends of a connection maintain buffers, usually about 8,192 bytes. TCP utilizes a “sliding window” mechanism to manage the transfer of data. Look at it as a byte stream with a fixed size “window” sliding over the data stream. As packets are acknowledged from either the client or the server, the “window” moves forward until the data has been transmitted. If the buffers fill up from either connection (that is, window size equals 0), communications in that direction cease until data has passed from the buffer(s), up the protocol stack, and into the applications buffers. This is yet another concern for servers writing large messages to clients that are not running on very powerful systems or that are on remote networks with low bandwidth links. In these scenarios, one client can slow things down for everyone. Keep in mind, slow internet equipment can slow down your application as well. As a rule, the less data you must transfer via your application, the better.

Blocking I/O is acceptable for programs that do not have to maintain GUI interfaces and only have to maintain one communications channel. Needless to say, many programs cannot afford to use blocking communications.

I/O is said to be *nonblocking* when an operation returns an error or status code without waiting for the operation to complete.

`nonblock`, shown in Listing 32.9, is a modified version of `client2`, which is shown in Listing 32.7. The changes needed to `client2` to remove blocking are shown here.

LISTING 32.9 *nonblock*

```
1: #!/usr/bin/perl
2: use Socket;
3: use Fcntl;
4: require "./network.pl";
5: $poke = "yo!";
6: $NETFD = makeudpcli();
7: fcntl $NETFD, &F_SETFL, O_NONBLOCK or die "Fcntl failed : $!\n";
8: (rest of file remains the same)
```

A new module, `Fcntl`, is added to the program in line 3, which provides an interface to the `fcntl(2)` system call. It is used to alter file descriptor properties, such as blocking and how certain signals are handled. In line 7, the last line of the modifications to `client2`, you set the `O_NONBLOCK` flag for the UDP socket. The rest of the program is unchanged.

To demonstrate this, run `client2` without running the server. It will start and not return until you halt it by pressing Ctrl+C.

Now run `nonblock`:

```
$ ./nonblock
error getting message : Try again at ./nonblock line 30
```

You receive the `Try again` message from the `recv()` function.

When nonblocking I/O is used, the application designer has to be very careful when handling errors returned from `recv()`, `send()`, and other I/O-related functions. When no more data is available for reading or no more data can be written, these functions return error codes. As a result, the application has to be prepared to handle some errors as being routine conditions. This is also true of the C/C++ interfaces.

I/O Multiplexing with UDP

Frequently, applications need to maintain more than one socket or file descriptor. For example, many system services, such as Telnet, `rlogin`, and FTP, are managed by one process on Linux. To do this, the process `inetd` listens for requests for these services by opening a socket for each one. Other applications, such as Applix, Netscape, and Xemacs, monitor file descriptors for the keyboard, mouse, and perhaps the network.

Now set up an example that monitors the keyboard and a network connection. Listing 32.10 is contained in the file `udptalk`.

LISTING 32.10 *updtalk*

```
#!/usr/bin/perl

use Socket;
require "./network.pl";

 $NETFD = makeudpserv($ARGV[2]);

 $addr = gethostbyname($ARGV[0]);
 $port = getservbyname($ARGV[1], 'udp');

 $servaddr = sockaddr_in($port, $addr);

 $rin = "";
 vec($rin, fileno(STDIN), 1) = 1;
 vec($rin, fileno($NETFD), 1) = 1;

 while (1) {

    select $ready = $rin, undef, undef, undef;

    if (vec($ready, fileno(STDIN), 1) == 1) {
      sysread STDIN, $mesg, 256;
       send $NETFD, $mesg, 0, $servaddr;
    }
    if (vec($ready, fileno($NETFD), 1) == 1) {
        recv $NETFD, $netmsg, 256, 0;
       print "$netmsg";
       $netmsg = "";
    }
}
  close $NETFD;
```

To test this program, you must run it either in two windows on the same system or on two different systems. At one command-line session, execute the following command, where *`iest`* is the host on which the second command will be run:

`$ ./udptalk` ***`iest`*** **`test test1`**

On the second host, run the following command, where *`iest`* is the host where the first command was run:

`$ ./udptalk` ***`iest`*** **`test1 test`**

Each session waits for keyboard input. Each line typed at one program is printed by the other, after you press Enter.

To perform the two-way communication required for this exercise, both instances of udptalk have to bind a well-known port. To permit this on a single workstation, the program accepts two port names as the second and third command-line arguments. For obvious reasons, two programs cannot register interest in the same port.

In line 6 of Listing 32.10, udptalk uses makeudpserv() to create a UDP socket and bind it to a well-known port. For the examples here, I used 8000 for one copy and 8001 for the other.

In lines 8–11, you perform the usual procedure for building a network address. This will be the address to which the keyboard input is written.

Lines 13–15 build bit vectors in preparation for the select() function. In Perl, a *bit vector* is a scalar variable that is handled as an array of bits; in other words, instead of being evaluated as bytes that add up to characters or numbers, each individual bit is evaluated as a distinct value.

In line 13, you create a variable ($rin) and tell the Perl interpreter to clear it. You then use the vec() and fileno() functions to determine the file number for STDIN (the keyboard) and set that bit in $rin. Then you do the same for the socket created by makeudpcli(). Therefore, if STDIN uses file descriptor 1 (which is generally the case), the second bit in $rin is set to 1. (Bit vectors, like other arrays, start numbering indexes at zero.) Fortunately, the vec() function can also be used to read bit vectors, so you can treat these data structures as opaque (and sleep a lot better at night for not knowing the details).

select() is a key function for systems programmers. Unfortunately, it suffers from an arcane interface that is intimidating in any language. System V UNIX has a replacement, poll(), that is a little easier to use, but it is not available on Linux or within Perl. The following is the function description for select():

```
select readfds, writefds, exceptfds, timeout;
```

Like most of the UNIX system interface, this is virtually identical to select() in C/C++. select() is used for discovering which file descriptors are ready for reading, are ready for writing, or have an exceptional condition. An exceptional condition usually corresponds with the arrival of what is called *out-of-band*, or urgent, data. This sort of data is most frequently associated with TCP connections. When a message is sent out-of-band, it is tagged as being more important than any previously sent data and is placed at the top of the data queue. A client or server can use this to notify the process on the other end of a connection that it is exiting immediately.

The first three arguments are bit vectors that correspond to the file descriptors that you are interested in reading or writing to or that you are monitoring for exceptional conditions. If your program is not interested in a set of file descriptors, you can pass `undef` instead of a vector. In Listing 32.10, your program is not interested in writing or exceptions, so you pass `undef` for the second and third arguments.

When `select` returns, only the bits that correspond to files with activity are set; if any descriptors are not ready when `select` returns, their settings are lost in the vector. For that reason, you have `select()` create a new vector and copy it into `$ready`. This is done by passing an assignment to `select()` as the first argument in line 19.

The last parameter is the time-out interval in seconds. `select()` waits for activity for this interval. If the interval expires with no activity occurring, `select()` returns with everything in the vector cleared. Because `undef` is supplied for *`timeout`* in line 19, `select()` blocks until a file is ready.

Inside the `while` loop entered in line 17, you call `select()`, passing it the bit vector built earlier and the new one to be created. When it returns, you check the vector by using `vec()` with pretty much the same syntax as you used to set the bits; however, because you are using == instead of =, `vec()` returns the value of the bit instead of setting it.

If the bit for `STDIN` is set, you read from the keyboard and send it to the other instance of `udptalk`. If the bit for the socket is set, you read from it and print it to the terminal. This sequence illustrates a very important advantage of the sockets interface—the program is extracting data to and from the network by using the same functions as the keyboard and screen.

This process is called *multiplexing* and is the loop at the core of many network-aware applications, although the actual mechanics can be concealed by sophisticated dispatchers or notifiers that trigger events based on which connection is ready to be read from or written to. Something else lacking in Listing 32.10 is the minimum amount of error checking and signal handling that cleans up connections when a quit signal is received.

I/O Multiplexing with TCP

To demonstrate TCP multiplexing, it is necessary to create different programs for the client and server. The server, `tcplisten`, is shown in Listing 32.11 and is the one that requires the most scrutiny. The client, `tcptalk`, and is not reprinted here because it resembles the server so closely. The explanation on how the client works appears as the server is covered.

LISTING 32.11 *tcplisten*

```
 1: #!/usr/bin/perl
 2:
 3: use Socket;
 4: require "./network.pl";
 5:
 6:  $NETFD = makelisten($ARGV[0]);
 7:
 8:  while (1) {
 9:
10:     $paddr = accept(NEWFD, $NETFD);
11:
12:     ($port, $iaddr) = sockaddr_in($paddr);
13:
14:     print "Accepted connection from ", inet_ntoa($iaddr),
15:     " on port number ", $port, "\n";
16:
17:     $rin = "";
18:     vec($rin, fileno(STDIN), 1) = 1;
19:     vec($rin, fileno(NEWFD), 1) = 1;
20:
21:     while (1)
22:
23:      select $ready = $rin, undef, undef, undef;
24:
25:      if (vec($ready, fileno(STDIN), 1) == 1) {
26:         sysread STDIN, $mesg, 256;
27:         syswrite NEWFD, $mesg, length($mesg);
28:      }
29:      if (vec($ready, fileno(NEWFD), 1) == 1) {
30:         $bytes = sysread NEWFD, $netmsg, 256;
31:         if ($bytes == 0) { goto EXIT; }
32:         print "$netmsg";
33:         $netmsg = "";
34:      }
35:     }
36:     EXIT: close NEWFD;
37:     print "Client closed connection\n";
38:  }
39:
40:  close $NETFD;
```

The server creates a listening socket in line 6 and then immediately enters a `while` loop. At the top of the loop is a call to `accept()`. Because you place this in a loop, the server can repeatedly accept client connections, like our other TCP server. The listen socket, `$NETFD`, can accept more than one connection, regardless of the state of any file descriptors cloned from it by using `accept()`.

accept() returns the address of the connecting client. You use this address in lines 12 and 14 to print out some information about the client. In line 12, you use sockaddr_in() to reverse-engineer the fully qualified address back into a network address and a service port. Then you use print to display it on the terminal. Note the call to inet_ntoa() embedded in the print command.

You set up for a select() loop, using almost the same code as in Listing 32.10. There is, however, a key difference in the way the network connection is handled. You are reading with sysread() again, but you are saving the return value.

When a peer closes a TCP connection, the other program receives an end-of-file (EOF) indication. This is signified by marking the socket as ready for reading and returning zero bytes when it is read. By saving the number of bytes returned by sysread(), you are able to detect a closed connection and record it and then return to accept() at the top of the outer while loop.

The following is a server session, followed by the client session that is communicating with it. The client is tcptalk.

```
$ ./tcplisten test
Accepted connection from 10.8.100.20 on port number 29337
Hello, world.
Goodbye, cruel....
Client closed connection
```

```
$ ./tcptalk iest test
Hello, world.
Goodbye, cruel....
^C
```

Advanced Topics in Network Programming

This chapter provides an introduction to network programming. At this point the chapter touches on a few more advanced topics.

One of the biggest issues for TCP applications is queuing messages. Depending on the nature of the data being transferred, the network bandwidth available, and the rate at which clients can keep pace with the data being delivered, data can queue up. Experienced application designers generally specify a queuing mechanism and the rules associated with it as part of the initial product description.

UDP applications have to wrestle with data reliability, and some schemes rely on message sequence numbers. All nodes involved in a transaction (or a series of transactions) keep track of a numbering scheme. When a node receives a message out of order, it sends a negative acknowledgment for the message it missed. This sort of scheme greatly reduces traffic when everything goes well but can become very expensive when things fall out of sequence.

Some applications can use asynchronous I/O to service network traffic and other tasks in a single application. This scheme registers interest in a signal that can be delivered whenever a file descriptor has data ready to be read. This method is not recommended, though, because only one signal can be delivered for all file descriptors (so `select()` would still be needed) and because signals are not reliable.

Security is always a big issue, regardless of the protocols being used. For that reason, applications that require a high level of security do not just rely on TCP to keep them secure. They tend to use encryption and authentication technologies as a means of securing data transmissions, including user IDs and passwords, over a LAN or WAN.

Summary

This chapter covered a lot of material in few pages, introducing essential networking concepts such as the components of a network address and how an application can form an address from symbolic host and service names by looking them up with the resolver functions.

Sockets, the most commonly used network programming interface, are used throughout the chapter. This API enables you to treat network connections and data streams like files, which shortens the network programming learning curve and also makes applications easy to design and maintain.

The two most commonly used protocols on the Internet—TCP and UDP—were discussed here as well. TCP, a connection-oriented protocol, has very robust reliability mechanisms that allow an application to use the network without worrying too much about whether the messages it is sending are reaching the other end. This reliability does carry a price, however, because TCP comes with a certain degree of overhead in terms of speed and bandwidth. TCP also supports only two-way communication, so clients and servers that need to communicate with more than one node have to maintain multiple connections, which can be expensive.

UDP, on the other hand, is a connectionless, datagram-oriented protocol. By itself, UDP comes with virtually no overhead. A possible downside is that the applications themselves have to provide their own reliability mechanisms. UDP also supports broadcast, which can be convenient but also represents a potential problem for some networks.

This chapter introduced some of the fundamental concepts behind network applications. Using these concepts, you will be able to create some simple tools, or you can build on this information by utilizing some of the advanced information available on the Internet and in advanced texts.

The concepts and examples presented here can all be easily applied to C programming because Perl essentially provides "wrappers" to the same system calls C uses for socket programming. All the functions used here have C equivalents and their own manual pages.

For more information on network programming, see the UNIX socket programming FAQs at `http://www.ibrado.com/sock-faq/`. This page includes a wealth of information, as well as pointers to other resources. You can also check the man pages on your system for the various function calls.

CHAPTER 33

Java Programming

IN THIS CHAPTER

This chapter is intended as a short introduction to the Java programming language and platform. Here you learn about what Java is and how it can help you build applications for your Linux system. You also learn a little about how you can use Java and the Web to build applications for your intranet or the Internet.

What Is Java?

Java is a programming language originally developed by Sun Microsystems, Inc. Java started as another project called Green and then later changed to Oak, inspired by the tree outside the window of one of the designer's office windows. Java's original intent was to be used to develop software for consumer electronics. The original idea was that VCRs and microwaves used many different microprocessors and embedded operating systems. The designers felt there had to be an easier way to develop software for these appliances and to ultimately make them talk to one another.

These solutions eventually became known as Java. Java found a new use once the Internet craze hit and somebody realized that Internet applications had the same problem as consumer appliances. Many different platforms were connected via the Internet and World Wide Web—Java connected them even more by allowing them to share and execute the same programming instructions.

Sure, HTML was platform independent. It did not matter what machine, operating system, or Web browser you had—but, the Web out grew its hyperlink text and there was a need for more sophisticated uses of the World Wide Web: to deliver dynamic real-time data and applications. The Java designers embedded Java in a Web browser and the rest is history: The Java applet was born. You can now load a Web page embedded with a small, platform-independent program written in the Java language.

Uses of Java

Java has many uses. It provides many features that other languages provide. Java also contains the Java base API, designed as a common set of APIs for Java. They consist of reusable objects that most developers would need to develop applications.

This set of common libraries extends Java's uses even further. The Java base API includes libraries for networking, distributing objects, and database connectivity. The base API also includes a platform-independent windowing toolkit called the Java Abstract Windowing Toolkit for writing graphical user interfaces.

Java's biggest momentum right now seems to stem from the enterprise. Big corporations seem to be embracing its platform independence and easy integration with other environments. Java is quickly growing as a solution to complex business problems. Some of the new APIs and specifications that are being developed for Java make it ideal. Java makes it easy to integrate with existing enterprise databases via the JDBC (Java Database Connectivity) API, and new specifications such as Enterprise Java Beans are built around standards such as CORBA (Common Object Request Broker) that can integrate with existing systems. Enterprise Java Beans is an extension of Java's component architecture, Java Beans. Enterprise Java Beans enhances Java Beans by making it distributed and persistent.

Note

JavaScript is a scripting language developed by Netscape. JavaScript is normally used as script embedded in HTML, which Web browsers interpret. Java and JavaScript are completely different.

Java is also finding many uses for Web applications. Java was originally touted as little applets that could be run in your Web browser, but more and more people are finding Java can be used on the server side via servlets. These servlets are replacing Web server CGI scripts that were traditionally written in languages such as Perl, C, and C++.

The Java Virtual Machine

To run compiled code for the Java platform requires a piece of software that is commonly referred to as the *Java Virtual Machine*. This piece of software adds an abstraction layer to the underlying operating system and hardware of a particular platform.

Many languages are compiled into machine code that can be executed directly on the machines hardware. This kind of compilation is specific to the platform and consequently can only be run on that hardware. For example, a C program compiled for Windows can only run under the Windows platform.

Byte Code

What sets Java apart from many other technologies? Java is not compiled into machine code for a specific platform. Java is compiled into platform-independent *byte codes*, which are instructions for a platform that does not physically exist as a computer. These byte codes are designed to run for a virtual machine.

How the JVM Protects the Underlying Operating Environment

Each platform has a different implementation of the Java Virtual Machine and all implementations should be able to run the architectural neutral byte codes per the Java specifications. This makes the portability of Java possible by hiding the underlying system specifics in the Virtual Machine and making it possible to run Java applications on other platforms without even recompiling. Developers can write and compile their Java applications under one platform, then deploy and run them on a totally different one. Some platforms that support Java are shown in this incomplete list:

Linux
UNIX (Solaris, AIX, HP UX, UnixWare, IRIX, and so on…)
Windows 95/98/NT
IBM OS/390, OS/400, OS/2
MacOS

Applications Versus Applets

Applications and applets are the two basic types of programs you can write in Java. Java *applications* are very similar to other applications that are written in C++, or Visual Basic, or any other language Java. They are typically installed on your workstation and executed via a command-line command and run as standalone programs; not too much magic here.

On the other hand, Java *applets* are small programs that are designed to be run within in a Web browser and dynamically loaded over the network to be executed on your workstation. Java applets are typically seen embedded in Web pages that perform some small task.

When a user writes a Java applet, he or she adds functionality to `java.applet.Applet` object. The `java.applet.Applet` object is a generic applet that the Web browser recognizes. Extending the generic Java applet gives your applet the advantage of running in a feature-rich environment.

Security is a very important applet feature; that security makes it different from applications. Java applets run within a restricted environment within the Web browser. This environment prevents the applet from performing any malicious acts on your workstation, such as removing all the files from your hard disk.

Cross-Platform Development Versus Proprietary Development

Cross development is more important than ever since the evolution of the Internet. Overnight, we have the ability to do our banking from our personal computer, which just a few years ago would have seemed only feasible if you were a banker. We can trade stocks, find out what the current weather is, and even track the packages we have shipped.

Let's say you log on to the Internet to transfer some money into your checking account. The computers, software, and architecture that your bank uses for its information systems is almost always far different from those you use at home. Can you imagine having to purchase a mainframe to transfer some money from your savings to your checking account? Could you imagine the bank having to write a different application for every type of platform available so you could do so?

As depicted in the bank example, proprietary development can be very costly by duplicating effort and adding complexity to integration. The Internet age is dependent on information and the technology it is built on changes very rapidly. In addition, huge corporations have a wide range of hardware and software they need to integrate.

Sun has been relatively open to input on the Java specification, even going as far as trying to get the Java language standardized. Since the Java specifications are available, anyone can implement a Virtual Machine or compiler.

You can find out more about Sun's continued Java specifications development at `http://www.javasoft.com/aboutJava/communityprocess/`.

Java Support in Linux

Linux has support for Java, similar to other UNIX systems. Various distributions include software for Java. Red Hat Linux 6.0, Caldera, SuSE, and Debian GNU/Linux include some packages that ship with the distributions of Open Source software for Java. The distributions contain Kaffe, which is a grounds-up implementation of the Java Virtual Machine. Both distributions also contain Guavac, which is a Java byte code compiler for compiling your Java programs. Both Kaffe and Guavac are clean room, Open Source implementations of the Java Virtual Machine and compiler, whereas the JDK is a port of Sun's implementation. This chapter focuses on the Java Development Kit available for the Linux platform. SuSE 6.x and Debian GNU/Linux distributions also include packages of the Java Development Kit. See the section on RPMs for further information on installation for SuSE. Debian GNU/Linux includes deb-format packages of the JDK in its non-free section. Debian 2.1 includes JDK 1.1.7.

The Blackdown port of Java 1.2 JDK was only available as a beta release. At the time of this writing, a pre-release copy was available. This chapter therefore focuses on Java 1.1. There are not very many fundamental changes in the language itself.

The biggest addition to Java 1.2 was the introduction of the JFC (Java Foundation Classes) as part of the Java base API. New JFC features are the Swing GUI toolkit, Java 2D API, Application Services, Accessibility, and Drag & Drop. Some other enhancements include policy-based security, weak references, the Java IDL API, and an array of performance enhancements.

Software Development Kits (Java Development Kits)

A good place for every Java developer to start off with is Sun's Java Development Kit. This is the basic toolkit with which to start your Java development; it is available on almost every other platform. The JDK contains the software and tools that developers need to compile, debug, and run applets and applications written using Java. The JDK also contains documentation and samples to help get you started. The Linux port is done by the Blackdown team. At the time of this writing, version 1.2 of the Java Development Kit was still in beta. A great deal of information can be found on the Blackdown Web site, including the latest version of the port, which you can download from `http://www.blackdown.org`.

Java development tools are still on the lean side on the Linux platform compared with other platforms, but the Linux operating system is quickly gaining momentum. New development tools are popping up every day, including IDEs (Integrated Development Environments). Sun Microsystems has its own Java IDE—Java Workshop—which runs under Linux, including Red Hat, with a patch. IBM is in the process of porting its IBM Visual Age for Java IDE to Linux.

IBM research has also ported its Open Source Java byte code compiler (Jikes) to Linux. Sun's JDK byte code compiler, javac, is written in Java itself. Jikes, on the other hand, is written in native C++. Jikes promises to be a much faster and accurate compiler according to the Java language specification. More information on that project can be found at `http://www.ibm.com/research/jikes`.

You can also get IBM's port of the JDK at `http://www.alphaWorks.ibm.com/tech/linuxJVM`.

Interpreters

The Blackdown port of the Java Development Kit also includes a port of Sun Microsystems Java byte code interpreter. There are several JITs available for the Blackdown port. The newer port of JDK 1.2 will include JIT. Just In Time compilation is a technique used to speed up byte code execution of the virtual machine. Instead of interpreting the Java byte code, the JIT directly translates byte code to native machine code on-the-fly, making execution of the code much faster.

The TYA Just In Time compiler is the "100 percent inofficial" JIT for the Linux port of the JDK and can be used with the Blackdown port of JDK 1.1. The TYA JIT can be found on the Blackdown Web site.

There also exist several Open Source Java Virtual Machines written from the ground up that include JIT technology. One of the implementations is called Kaffe. More information can be found at `http://www.kaffe.org`.

An Overview of the Java Language

According to an early Sun Microsystems, Inc., white paper, *The Java Language: An Overview*, the Java language is "a simple, object-oriented, network-savvy, interpreted, robust, secure, architecture neutral, portable, high-performance, multithreaded, dynamic language." There are a lot of buzzwords there, but it is a good description of what Java is.

Java is simple. It is syntactically very similar to C++ but omits many features that are rarely used or that seem to bring more complexity than benefit to the language.

Java is object-oriented. Object-oriented programming has been around since the 1960s and is finally making its way into mainstream programming. Object-oriented programming languages use techniques for focusing design around data and the operations that can be performed on that data. Java provides these object-oriented techniques, including concepts of building software from building blocks referred to as *objects*. Java also supports encapsulation to provide simple interfaces and hide implementation details.

Java is network-savvy. Java was designed for network environments with an extensive library of APIs built around standard Internet protocols such as TCP/IP and HTTP. The designers had the foresight to build distributed application using Java.

Java is robust. Java facilitates in writing more reliable applications and has strong type checking at compile time to aid in early detection of possible developer errors. Java has automatic garbage collection, which eliminates the need for the developer to manager his own memory. Many languages such as C and C++ leave memory management to the developer. Improper memory management can lead to data being overwritten or corrupted, and the failure to free memory can introduce memory leaks.

Java is secure. The robustness of Java's memory management also plays a role in security by preventing memory access to private data in objects that other parts of the application should not have access to. Java applets are designed to run in a sandbox to protect your workstation from malicious applets.

Java is architecturally neutral. Java programs are compiled into platform-independent byte codes rather than architecture-specific machine code. These byte codes are then run on an appropriate Java Virtual Machine, which runs on the native hardware. This gives the developer the opportunity to develop and compile applications on one platform and run them, without recompiling, on many other platforms. Sun touts Java as being write once, run anywhere.

Java is portable. Compiling to platform-independent byte codes is just one part of being portable. Unlike many other languages, there are no implementation-dependent aspects of the languages. For example, `int` always indicates a signed 32-bit integer, and `float` always indicates a 32-bit IEEE 754 floating-point number. Because Java is common across all platforms, Java programs will work the same way anywhere you run your program.

Java is multi-threaded. *Multi-threading* is a way of performing multiple tasks at the same time. Many modern operating systems such as Linux support multi-threading, but not all of these platforms perform multi-threading the same way. Java provides a platform-independent means of multi-threading without having knowledge of threading for a specific platform.

Objects, Classes, and Object-Oriented Programming

Java is an object-oriented programming language. With the exception of the primitive Java datatypes, everything in Java is an object. Most of the object-oriented concepts known today were introduced during the late 1960s with a language called Simula. Later, new object-oriented languages such as Smalltalk and C++ emerged. Many of these languages inspired Java and you may notice that Java implemented the best features of all of them.

An object can be defined as a software building block that contains data and a defined set of operations that can be performed on the data. What makes this type of programming different is that the design is focused around the data itself. Often times the data is encapsulated in the object and the object provides interfaces via the operations to manipulate that data indirectly. These objects utilize information hiding and the only way to access the data is through the objects' interfaces. This is also a way for the objects to provide an abstraction as to how the data is actually represented.

Objects are meant to mimic real-life objects. For example, you can define a `Car` object. The `Car` has operations that can be performed on it, such as brake, accelerate, turn left, and turn right. The `Car` can also be defined to have *state*, such as speed and location. It's important to note that the operation you perform on the car affects the state, or the data, of the `Car`. If you accelerate, you change the speed of the `Car`. You do not, however, directly change the speed of the car.

Objects in Java are described by classes. *Classes* define the *methods*, which are operations that can be performed on the object, and the *variables*, or the data, that make up an object. Here is an example of writing a Java class:

```
public class GreetWorld {
   String greeting = "HelloWorld!";
```

```
    public void sayGreeting() {
        System.out.println( greeting );
    }
}
```

The class `GreetWorld` defines objects with a variable `greeting` and the methods, or operations, that can be performed on the object, the method `sayGreeting`. An object defined by the `GreetWorld` class is not created until you instantiate and allocate space for it. Often times you will hear the words *class* and *object* used interchangeably. That is incorrect; they are different.

You can have many objects of the defined type `GreetWorld` and they each have their own, separate variables; they do not share data. To create objects in Java, you need to use the `new` operator to allocate space and create an instance. Here is an example:

```
myGreetWorld = new GreetWorld();
```

The `new` operator allocates space for your object, instantiates it, and returns a reference to that object so that you can access its methods and variables. When you instantiate an object, any variables that have not been initialized are automatically initialized to `null`, meaning no object.

Class visibility is more related to packages. *Packages* are simply a way to group classes together within a common namespace. The syntax for packages follows:

```
package Identifier;
```

This statement must be placed at the beginning of your source file. Here is an example:

```
package mypackage.businessObjects;
```

You can import package namespaces with the `import` statement. If a class `Account` were part of `mypackage.businessObjects`, you would have to refer to this class using its full name: `mypackage.businessObjects.Account`. If you use the `import` statement, you can use just the class name:

```
import mypackage.businessObjects.Account;
```

Alternatively, you can add all the objects within that package to your namespace using a wildcard:

```
import mypackage.businessObjects.*;
```

Classes have visibility similar to methods. Classes that are public are visible to all packages. Classes that do not have a modifier will default to visibility within their own package.

Datatypes

Java has defined a set of basic datatypes. They exist for performance reasons, allowing developers to use basic datatypes without the overhead of objects. There are also objects in the base library package, `java.lang`, which encapsulates these datatypes. The datatype objects also have nifty utility methods for operation-like conversion and precision. Table 33.1 lists the Java datatypes.

TABLE 33.1 Java Datatypes

Type	*Size*
`byte`	8-bit
`char`	16-bit
`short`	16-bit
`int`	32-bit
`long`	64-bit
`float`	32-bit
`double`	64-bit
`boolean`	1-bit

Integers are 8-bit `byte`, 16-bit `short`, 32-bit `int`, and 64-bit `long`. The `byte` datatype replaces the old C convention of the 8-bit `char`. Java has a different interpretation of the `char` datatype.

Real numeric types are `float` and `double`. The `float` type reserves storage for a 32-bit, single-precision number. The `double` type reserves storage for a 64-bit, double-precision number. Real datatypes are defined by the IEEE 754 specification.

The `char` type in Java is different from the traditional C `char` datatype. Java uses Unicode characters stored as a 16-bit, unsigned integer. This gives Java the added advantage of internationalization and localization, greatly expanding world market potential. This also helps make Java suitable for the Internet because of its broad geographic audience—in other words, the world.

Java arrays are first class language objects. An *array* is a real object with a runtime representation. You can create an array of any datatype including arrays of Java objects. Multi-dimensional arrays are achieved by creating arrays of arrays.

Take, for example, an array declaration of a `Banana` class, which you declared somewhere else within your code. The declaration of the array may look something like this:

```
Banana[] bunchOfBananas;
```

This declaration would allocate a reference handle for an array of `Bananas`, although you must still allocate the amount of storage you need for the array of `Bananas`. You would get an error if you tried to index the array. You can do something like this to allocate space for an array:

```
bunchOfBananas = new Banana[10];
```

You can also declare arrays with initializers if you already know the values you want in the array. The compiler will automatically return an instance of an array with initial values and size.

```
char alphabet[] = { 'a', 'b', 'c', 'd' };
```

This will return an allocated array of size `four` with values `a`, `b`, `c`, and `d`. The compiler is performing the equivalent of allocating space and setting the array's values.

Note

Be aware when you declare an array of objects that you are really creating an array of references and not allocating space for the objects. These references are initialized to `null`. When you declare an array of primitive types, you are allocating space for the datatypes since they do not have references.

Now you are required to allocate space for `bunchOfBananas`. You created an array that contains a `bunchOfBanana` references. The `bunchOfBananas` array will be initialized to `null` references since the `Bananas` themselves have not been created. You may want to create some `Bananas` for the array. You can do that with a simple `for` loop.

```
for( int i=0; i<10; i++ ) {
   bunchOfBananas[i] = new Banana();
}
```

Now you have an array full of `Bananas`. As said, arrays are objects. Since arrays are fixed length, the array object provides index bounds checking. No longer can you walk off the end of an array, corrupting memory by accessing an index that does not exist. An exception error is thrown if the index is out of the array's bounds.

The length of an array is stored in the `length` instance variable. For example, because at creation time we specified the size as 10, this code assigns the value `10` to `howManyBananas`:

```
howManyBananas = bunchOfBananas.length;
```

This length variable is very useful when iterating through the array in a loop. You do not have to hang on to the size of the array for whenever you want to iterate through it.

```
for ( int i = 0; i < howManyBananas; i++ ) {
   bunchOfBananas[i].eatBanana();
}
```

Expressions

Once you create some variables in Java, you may want to evaluate some expressions on them. Expressions are mostly used with the primitive datatypes but also can involve objects. You may assign one object reference to another, for instance, which would make both references point to the same object.

Expressions consist of a combination of operators and operands. *Operators* enable you to perform operations such as multiplication or assignment on the operands.

```
result = 3 * y;
```

The operators being used in this example are multiplication (*) and assignment (=). The operands are `3`, `y`, `result`, and the evaluated expression of `3 * y`. The multiplication takes precedence over the assignment; `3 * y` is therefore evaluated first.

Comparison Operators

Java supports almost all the standard C comparison operators and the operators have the same precedence. Table 33.2 lists these operators.

TABLE 33.2 Comparison Operators

Operator	*Description*
==	Determines whether two primitives or objects references are equal
!=	Determines whether two primitives or objects references are not equal
<=	Determines whether one primitive is less than or equal to another
>=	Determines whether one primitive is greater than or equal to another
&&	Conditional AND of two comparisons
||	Conditional OR of two comparisons
?:	Conditional ternary `instanceof`; checks the instance of an object

Note

The `instanceof` operator is a special operator that returns `true` if an object is an instance of a particular class. It also returns `true` if the object is an instance of a subclass of the type specified. This operator can be very useful in casting.

Caution

When used with objects, the operator == will determine whether object references are equal. It normally will not compare the content of the objects themselves. It is best to compare object content with the `equals()` method, although it will work when comparing strings. Java strings are special objects and Java maintains a string table. Do not get in the habit of using the == for strings.

Mathematical Operators

Java provides many operators that you can use to evaluate a wide range of complex mathematical expressions. Table 33.3 lists those operators.

TABLE 33.3 Mathematical Operators

Operator	*Description*
++	Increment
--	Decrement
!	Negation
*	Multiplication
/	Division
%	Modulus
+	Addition
-	Subtraction
<<	Left shift
>>	Right shift
>>>	Zero fill right shift
&	Bitwise AND
|	Bitwise OR
^	Bitwise XOR

continues

TABLE 33.3 continued

Operator	*Description*
~	Bitwise complement
=	Assignment
+=, =, *=, /=, %=, &=, |=, ^=, <<=, >>=, <<<=, >>>=	Assignment with operation

The Java API also provides a `Math` class, `java.lang.Math`, for performing other common mathematical functions. You do not instantiate a `Math` class. The object is more of a utility class with static methods for performing common math functions. The `Math` class is also defined as final so that it cannot be overloaded. You would not want anyone to change the behavior of the sin function, for instance. The most useful methods in the `Math` class follow:

Common `Math` class common methods:

`static int abs( int a )`	`static double atan( double a )`
`static long abs( long a )`	`static double cos( double a )`
`static float abs( float a )`	`static double sin( double a )`
`static double abs( double a )`	`static double tan ( double a )`
`static double acos( double a )`	`static double sqrt( double a )`
`static double asin( double a )`	

Control Statements: (`if else`, `while`, `for`)

The `if else`, `while`, `do while`, `switch`, and `for` control statements are exactly the same in Java as they are in C/C++—not really too much magic to learn if you are a programmer familiar with either language. In Java, however, these conditional expressions must evaluate to the Java `boolean` type. Examples of these expressions follow.

The `if-else` structure is used to choose alternatives based on a given condition:

```
if( Condition ) {
   Statment
else
   Statement
```

The `switch` statement is similar to an `if-else`, but you can define a number of alternatives for an evaluated expression:

```
switch( Expression ) {
   case Constant1
```

```
      Statement1
   case Constant2
      Statement2
   default:
      DefaultStatement
}
```

The while loop is a repetitive structure that allows the program to specify based on the condition of how many times a code block will repeat:

```
while( Condition ) {
  Statement1
  Statement2
}
```

The do-while loop is similar to the while loop, but the code block is executed before the condition is checked:

```
do {
   Statement1
   Statement2
} while( Condition );
```

The for loop is a repetitive structure with indexing:

```
for( InitializerExpression; Condition; StepExpression ) {
   Statement1
   Statement2
}
```

Here is an example of a control statement:

```
for ( int i = 0; i < arrayOfStrings.length; i++ ) {
   String s = arrayOfStrings[i];
   if( s.equals( "hi" ) ) {
      System.out.println( "It says hi" );
   }
}
```

This simple example iterates through a list of strings and determines whether there are strings equivalent to hi. If a string match is found, the program will print It says hi to the output stream.

Writing Your Own Methods

Methods are an object-oriented language's version of functions, but the result can be unique to a particular instance on an object. Each instance has its own copy of local variables and they are not shared. Methods are also actions that can be performed on a specific object and that belong to that object. You can define a new method rather simply:

```
public void sayGreeting( String greeting ) {
   System.out.println( greeting );
}
```

Every method signature—how we define methods—has an accessibility modifier assigned to it. In this example, the method is assigned to be `public`. This means that any class has visibility to this method and can perform a method call. If you had an instance of the object and this class were defined in a class called `greetObject`, you could simply access this method with this code:

```
greetObject.sayGreeting( "HelloWorld" );
```

The method visibility modifiers are `public`, `package`, `protected`, and `private`. Table 33.4 describes each of these modifiers.

TABLE 33.4 Method Visibility Modifiers

Modifier	*Description*
`public`	Any object can access the method.
`package`	Method access is restricted to the package that contains the class.
`protected`	Method access is restricted to subclasses.
`private`	Method access is restricted to the class it is defined in.

Method calls are normally performed on an instance of an object unless the method is defined as `static`. In this case the method call is performed on the class. Only one static method exists for every instance of the class. You can define the `sayGreeting` method as static with the `static` modifier:

```
public static void sayGreeting( String greeting )
   System.out.println( greeting );
}
```

An instance of the object is not required. Here is an example:

```
GreetWorld.sayGreeting( "Hello World!" );
```

Table 33.5 lists these modifiers.

TABLE 33.5 Other Java Modifiers

Modifier	*Description*
`abstract`	The class or method does not have a complete implementation and cannot be instantiated.
`final`	The class, method, or variable cannot be subclassed or have its value changed.
`native`	The method is not implemented in Java and is platform dependent.
`static`	The class, method, or variable has only one instance, regardless of the number of class instances.

Java Compared to C and C++

Java is syntactically similar to C and C++. This was done by the developers of the language to keep it familiar to programmers and to shorten the learning curve of the language. There are quite a few features from C++ that Java did not adopt, as well as a few concepts it added.

Operation overloading is one feature that Java left out of the language. C++ allows you to define and redefine your own operators for the classes you write. This is a nice feature that can be very useful. For example, you would use operation overloading if the developer has a matrix class and wants to overload the + operator to be able to add matrices. After much debate, though, the designers decided to leave operator overloading out of the language due to the confusion it can cause. The developers did leave in method overloading, which is often used in Java programming.

C++ supports multiple inheritance. This allows a developer to inherit from multiple superclasses. Java only supports single inheritance. Java designers decided to use multiple interfaces that do not inherit method implementations. This was done to avoid complexity and the restriction was also intended to encourage good object-oriented design.

C++ method calls are, by default, called by value and can be specified calls by reference with an `&` on the parameter. Java objects are always called by reference. If you modify an object parameter in Java within a method, the change will propagate outside. The datatypes are always called by value.

Java has no pointers. The referencing is handled for you automatically via Java object references. You cannot do any kind of pointer arithmetic in Java nor can you do any funky casting. This makes debugging in Java much simpler. Memory management errors are often times very hard to locate. For example, the compiler does not let you know when you access some other data's memory segment.

Note

Java object references differ from C pointers. Pointers can "point" anywhere in memory that you want to. Java is a very strongly typed language. A reference of type `String` can only refer to an object of type `String`.

Java has no support for templates; it is a very object-oriented language. Much of the templates' functionality in C++ is replaced with Java interfaces.

Java has no `goto` statement. To avoid confusion, however, it is a reserved keyword. Having `goto` statements in your code has often been regarded as poor design—especially, in object-oriented design.

Exception Handling

Java includes a way of handling errors that is probably not too familiar to many programmers. An exception is an event that occurs when there is an error or abnormal condition. You may notice that some methods *throw* an exception. The process of creating the event for the error is known as *throwing an exception*.

An exceptions will propagate its way up your code until it is caught. This is done with a `try-catch` block. It looks something like this:

```
try {
  call some method that throws an exception
}
catch( the exception to be caught ) {
  code that will handle this error
}
```

Exceptions are Java objects that are instances of some subclass `java.lang.Throwable`. These Java object exceptions contain some runtime when the exception was thrown. The idea is to recover from an error.

Here is an example of catching an `IOException` from the `readLine()` method of `BufferedInputStream`. The `try-catch` block simply prints an error. A real application may try to take some steps to recover from this error.

```
try  {
  file.readLine();
}
catch( IOException ioe ) {
   ioe.printStackTrace();
   System.err.println( "Couldn't read from file" );
}
finally {
   file.close();
}
```

The `finally` code block is optional. Normally this is used to do some clean-up work and this code block is always executed, regardless of whether an exception is thrown.

Java Object Packages

Here is a list of all the packages included as part of the Java 1.1 base API. Only a couple of the packages are mentioned in this chapter. There a quite a few and the group is growing. You can find complete documentation with the JDK API documentation.

```
java.applet
java.awt
java.awt.datatransfer
java.awt.event
java.awt.image
java.beans
java.io
java.lang
java.lang.reflect
java.math
java.net
java.rmi
java.rmi.dgc
java.rmi.registry
java.rmi.server
java.security
java.security.acl
java.security.interfaces
java.sql
java.text
java.util
java.util.zip
```


Thc `java.lang` package contains classes for the Java language. This package includes object wrappers for all the datatypes, the `String` class, and a `System` class. This package also contains classes for exception handling and internationalization.

The `java.io` package contains all the necessary classes required to I/O in Java, including objects for streaming and objects to read and write to files.

The `java.util` package contains some very common utility classes and data structures. Some of these data structures include a `Hashtable`, `Vector`, and a `Stack`.

The `java.awt` package contains objects for Java's Abstract Windowing toolkit. The toolkit is built on top of the native platforms windowing toolkit.

Abstract Windowing Toolkit

Most applications these days have graphical user interfaces (GUIs), which make the applications easier to use and more appealing to the eye. The Java base API provides a library of classes for creating GUIs. This library is referred to as the AWT and can be located as part of the Java base API. The package is named `java.awt`.

AWT is an abstraction layer for the platforms's native windowing toolkit. When you run a graphical application under Linux, it will look like it was developed with Motif. All the buttons, text fields, and check boxes will look familiar to any Motif developer. In contrast, if you run the same application under Windows, it will look as if it was built using the native Windows GUI toolkit.

The base class for AWT objects is `Component`. A `Component` is an object having a graphical representation that can be displayed on the screen and that can interact with the user. Most `Components` consist of buttons, list boxes, text fields, and the like.

There are special `Components` called `Containers`. These `Containers` can contain other AWT `Components`. `Containers` are a way of grouping other `Components` and making it easier to build a GUI layout.

To help aid in `Component` layout even more, `Containers` are associated with a `LayoutManager`, which defines a policy of how the `Components` should be layed out within that `Container`. Common components are

```
Frame

Panel

Canvas

Checkbox

Choice

Dialog

Menu

TextField

TextArea
```

Table 33.6 shows the available layout managers.

TABLE 33.6 Available Layout Managers

Layout Manager	*Description*
`BorderLayout`	A `BorderLayout` lays out a container, arranging and resizing its components to fit in five regions: `North`, `South`, `East`, `West`, and `Center`.

Layout Manager	*Description*
`CardLayout`	`CardLayout` treats each component in the container as a card. Only one card is visible at a time, and the container acts as a stack of cards.
`FlowLayout`	A `FlowLayout` arranges components in a left-to-right flow, much like lines of text in a paragraph.
`GridLayout`	The `GridLayout` class is a layout manager that lays out a container's components in a rectangular grid.
`GridBagLayout`	The `GridBagLayout` class is a flexible layout manager that aligns components vertically and horizontally, without requiring that the components be of the same size.

Tip

The `GridBagLayout` is by far the most difficult layout manager to get the hang of. You can create a GUI just as nicely with a combination of the other layout managers with different panels.

Here is an example using AWT `HelloWorldAWT.java`:

```
import java.awt.Frame;
import java.awt.Panel;
import java.awt.Label;
import java.awt.Button;
import java.awt.GridLayout;
import java.awt.event.ActionListener;
import java.awt.event.ActionEvent;

public class HelloWorldAWT implements  ActionListener {
   private Frame frame;
   private Panel panel;
   private Label label;
   private Button pushme;

   public static void main( String args[] ) {
      // Create a new Instance of the object
      new HelloWorldAWT();
   }

   public HelloWorldAWT() {
      // Create a frame for the GUI and all of its components
      frame = new Frame();
      pushme = new Button( "Push Me!" );
```

```
        panel = new Panel();
        label = new Label();

        frame.setSize( 100, 100 );
        frame.add( panel );

        // Set the layout manager to a grid style layout
        panel.setLayout( new GridLayout( 2, 1 ) );
        panel.add( pushme );
        panel.add( label );

        // Delegate the even to a listener that implements the ActionListener
        // Interface.  We make our HelloWorldAWT the listener.
        pushme.addActionListener( this );
        frame.setVisible( true );
    }

    public void actionPerformed( ActionEvent e ) {
        label.setText( "Hello World!" );
    }
}
```

This is a simple AWT application that contains a `Button` and a `Label`. When an action event is received by the `Button`, the text on the `Label` is changed to `"Hello World!"`. Notice that I registered a `listener` with the `Button` class, telling it that the class is interested in receiving its events. This is know as *event delegation*. Only classes that implement the `ActionListener` interface can be registered as `listeners`. When implementing this interface, you need to implement an `actionPerformed()` method .

Java I/O

The `java.io` package contains all the necessary classes required to I/O in Java, including objects for streaming and objects to read and write to files.

The `java.io` package handles input and output. This package contains all the classes necessary for streaming data on the system console as well as files. Common `java.io` classes are listed in Table 33.7.

TABLE 33.7 Common *java.io* Classes

Class	*Description*
`InputStream`	This abstract class is the superclass of all classes representing an input stream of bytes.
`OutputStream`	This abstract class is the superclass of all classes representing an output stream of bytes.

Class	Description
`Reader`	Abstract class for reading character streams. This class uses a Unicode representation.
`Writer`	Abstract class for writing to character streams.
`PrintWriter`	Print formatted representations of objects to a text output stream.
`File`	Instances of this class represent the name of a file or directory on the host file system.
`FileInputStream`	A file input stream is an input stream for reading data from a file or from a `FileDescriptor`.
`FileOutputStream`	A file output stream is an output stream for writing data to a file or to a `FileDescriptor`.

Here is a small example of how to read a line from a file when using Java. It is file input example `HelloWorldFile.java`:

```
import java.io.FileReader;
import java.io.BufferedReader;
import java.io.IOException;

// This is a class that reads Hello World from a file and prints it out
public class HelloWorldFile {
   public static void main( String args[] ) {
      try {
         // Here we create a new FileReader giving it the filename and
         // then create a BufferedReader for buffered input
         BufferedReader in = null;
         in = new BufferedReader( new FileReader("HelloWorld.txt") );

  // Read a line from the input stream
         String line = in.readLine();
         System.out.println( "This file contains the line: " + line );
      }
      catch( IOException e ) {
         System.err.println( "There was an error reading the file" );
         e.printStackTrace();
      }
    }
}
```

This example creates a `FileReader` and passes the filename to the constructor so it knows the name and path of what file to open. The `FileReader` creates a `BufferedReader` object so that I can get buffered input. This `BufferedReader` allows me to read the file one line at a time using the `readLine()` method.

Note

Remember that Java uses Unicode to represent its character set. A character stream is different from a regular I/O stream. The former streams 16-bit Unicode characters where normal, and the latter streams `byte` characters.

Writing Java Programs

Unlike some languages, writing Java programs is fun. Nothing takes the fun out of programming more than compiling and executing your program, and then getting back a message that says `Segmentation Fault`.

Creating the Code

The simplest program you can write for Java is probably the `Hello World` program. This snippet of code consists of a class called `HelloWorld`, since Java is an object-oriented language. Also, Java applications require an entry point for execution, so, you must define a main method. This lets the virtual machine knows where to start execution.

```
class HelloWorld {
   static public void main(String args[]) {
   System.out.println("Hello World!");
}
```

This snippet of Java code obviously produces the output `"Hello World!"`.

To make your code a little easier to write with just a little documentation, Java allows comments in your source code that are moved by the compiler when the code is compiled (see Table 33.8). Comments can be defined three ways and are very similar in C and C++.

TABLE 33.8 Java Comments

Comment Type	*Description*
`/* comment */`	This is a C–style comment. Everything between `/*` and `*/` is ignored by the compiler.
`//`	This is a C++–style comment. Everything after the `//` up to the end of line is ignored by the compiler.
`/** comment */`	Same as the C-style comment but can be used with the `javadoc` tool provided with the JDK to create useful documentation from your source code.

Editing

Editing Java code can be done with any editor, much like C or C++ can be. The most common editor available on UNIX-like platforms is the `vi` editor. `Emacs` is another popular editor among UNIX/Linux programmers. A nifty `Emacs` feature is a special Java mode to help format your code. The `vi` editor is normally part of a required package when you install most Linux distributions. You do not have to worry about installing it. `Emacs` is available as an optional package on most Linux distribution. There also exists a nicer graphical version of `Emacs` called `XEmacs`. You can find more information on `Emacs` and `XEmacs` at `http://www.emacs.org` and `http://www.xemacs.org`.

Tip

You can get help on using the `vi` editor by reading the man pages available. Just type **`man vi`** on your Linux shell.

The Java compiler recognizes Java source files by the extension `.java`. Several different Java classes can go into one `.java` file, but only one public class can be contained per file. This filename must be the same name as the public class within that file.

Required Sections (Methods)

When instantiated, every class does some initialization and a special method is designated for classes that allows you to initialize values for your class. This method is called a *constructor*. There is a default constructor for Java classes, but you can define one of your own or multiple constructors. The only requirement is that they have different method signatures—take a different number or set of parameters, in other words.

The Java application `GreetWorld.java` shows an example of using a constructor:

```
public class GreetWorld {
   String greeting;
   public GreetWorld( String g ) {
      greeting = g;
   }

   public void sayGreeting() {
      System.out.println( greeting );
   }

   public static void main( String args[] ) {
      GreetWorld gw = new GreetWorld( "Hello World!" );
      gw.sayGreeting();
   }
}
```

You do not specify a return type for a constructor because the return type is always understood to be a reference to an instance of the class. Also, constructors always have the same name as the class.

Compiling

Java source code is a compiled for the Java platform. The source code needs to be translated into Java byte code by a Java byte code compiler. This is most commonly performed with the Sun JDK with the javac byte code compiler. Others, such as Jikes, are available. IDEs like Java Workshop also perform byte code compilation for you.

The javac byte code compiler included in the JDK takes in input files with the `*.java` extension. To compile the `HelloWorld` example, you would type on your Linux shell command line:

```
javac HelloWorld.java
```

The compiler will produces a file called `HelloWorld.class` in the same directory as the `HelloWorld.java` file. These are the byte code compiled classes. Java creates a `.class` file for every class, even if one file contains multiple classes or inner classes. You can type the following on your Linux command line shell for quick commandline help on the javac compiler:

```
javac  h
```

Creating and Running an Application

Java applications require a special entry point for a class. This entry point is the main method. The Java interpreter calls this method first and passes an array of command-line arguments.

```
public static void main( String args[] ) {
   ..._
}
```

The Java interpreter (`java`) runs standalone Java-executable programs. Applications are normally run from a command line as follows:

```
java Options Classname
```

To run the `HelloWorld` class, run the Java interpreter and indicate the class name of the program you want to run. The Linux kernel can also be configured to automatically run the interpreter for you.

```
java HelloWorld
```

Note

The Java interpreter requires classes with a main method defined. Any class can contain a main method.

Creating and Running an Applet

Applets are where Java tends to get most of its visibility. A Java *applet* is a small program that is embedded in a Web browser and contains a Java applet engine. These applets are dynamically loaded from the network and executed on your local workstation.

Some people are concerned about a program dynamically loaded and executing on their workstation. This is why applets have an extra layer of security referred to as the applet's *sandbox*. The sandbox restricts applets from system features, such as your filesystem, and gives them a safe space to play in. As a developer, this may quickly get annoying because it limits what an applet can actually do. This problem has introduced newer security models, including trusted applets that are digitally signed and are required to ask the user permission to access your filesystem, for example.

Applets have a different structure than do Java applications. One big thing you will notice is that applets do not have a `main()` method. Applets are invoked by an applet engine within your Web browser rather than running alone. Instead, applets are subclassed from the `java.applet.Applet` class. This class provides the entry point for the applet engine.

The Java applet class has four major methods you need to know: `init()`, `start()`, `stop()`, and `destroy()`. Because applets are instantiated by the applet engine and contain no `main()` method, your main entry point for an applet is the `init()` method. Keep in mind you never call these methods yourself.

Any initialization should be performed in the `init()` method. This method is called when the applet first starts. Initialization normally includes obtaining or creating any resource that the applet may need, such as images or audio clips.

After the applet engine does calls the `init()` method, your applet is ready to be started. This is when the `start()` method is called. Often times a new thread is created and is started when the `start()` method is called; it stops when the `stop()` method is called because the applet is hidden or not visible. Lastly, the `destroy()` method is called when the applet is about to be permanently stopped. You should do any clean up of resources in this method.

For the most part, Java applets are graphical since the `Applet` class itself inherits from an AWT `Panel`. If you perform any I/O to the system console, it will most likely go to a log window in most browsers. Figure 33.1 illustrates this process, and Listing 33.1 shows how to write a simple Hello World applet.

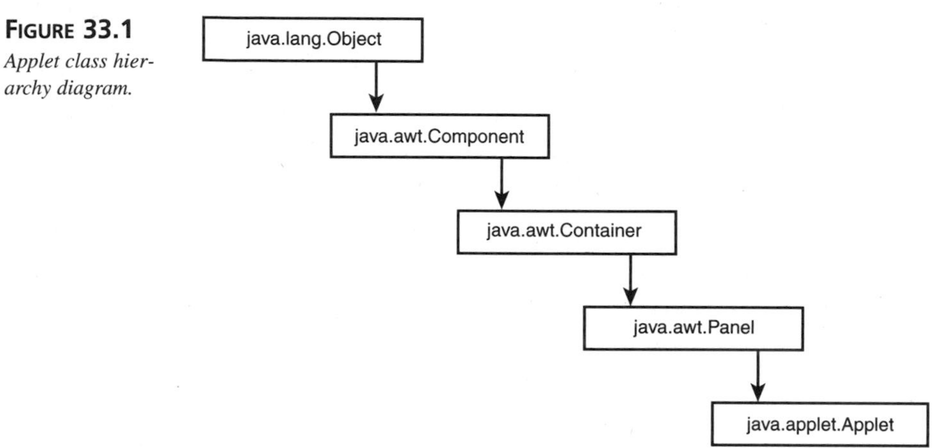

FIGURE 33.1
Applet class hierarchy diagram.

LISTING 33.1 Hello World Applet *HelloWorldApplet.java*

```
import java.applet.Applet;
import java.awt.Label;

public class HelloWorldApplet extends Applet {
   public void init() {
      add( new Label("Hello World!") );
   }
}
```

Since Java applets are normally embedded within a Web browser, there exists an HTML `<APPLET>` tag to tell the browser a bit about the applet it has to load and execute. The tag tells the browser which class file to load as the applet, from where to load the applet, the size of the applet on the screen, and any parameters to pass to the applet.

The HTML code for this applet looks something like this. This example is the Hello World Applet HTML `HelloWorldApplet.html`:

```
<HTML>
   <HEAD>
      <TITLE>Hello World Applet</TITLE>
   </HEAD>
   <BODY>
      <APPLET HEIGHT=100 WIDTH=100 CODE=HelloWorldApplet.class></APPLET>
   </BODY>
</HTML>
```

You can test your applet using a Web browser, or you can use the `appletviewer` tool that is part of the JDK. To run the applets, simply type this code:

```
appletviewer HelloWorldApplet.html
```

Java and the Internet

Java and the Internet complement each other very well. The Internet launched Java into the mainstream and made the benefit of distributed cross-platform applications a necessity. Since Java's introduction, several new Java APIs have been developed to help bring the Internet and enterprise computing closer to Java. These APIs are discussed next.

JDBC

JDBC stands for Java Database Connectivity. The JDBC API provides a generic high-level interface for database connectivity to an DBMS (DataBase Management System). The JDBC class library is released as part of the JDK in a package called `java.sql`.

JDBC is implemented in two layers: the JDBC API database abstraction layer and the driver layer. The JDBC layer consists of the JDBC `DriverManager` and classes provided to connect to a particular database. The driver layer contains a database-specific driver that knows how to communicate with the database. With this abstraction, when the database changes, the driver can be switched with very few changes to the Java code.

The JDBC interfaces in the `java.sql` package are listed here:

```
CallableStatement
Connection
DatabaseMetaData
Driver
PreparedStatement
ResultSet
ResultMetaData
Statement
```

JDBC classes in the `java.sql` package are listed here:

```
Date
DriverManager
DriverPropertyInfo
Time
Timestamp
Types
```

The most important JDBC class is `DriverManager`. This class is used to load the appropriate driver for the DBMS that you are using for your application. The `DriverManger` also provides a basic service for managing JDBC drivers.

JDBC drivers can be split into four categories: JDBC ODBC drivers, native API drivers, Java-Net, and drivers and native protocol. The native protocol drivers are best suited for Internet use because they do not rely on a DBMS client to interact on your workstation.

Most major DBMSs have support for 100 percent Java driver implementations.

RMI

RMI stands for Remote Method Invocation. RMI can be thought of as similar to RPC (Remote Procedure Call), where its RMI uses a skeleton/stub approach for distributed applications to communicate with one another. That is where the similarities stop. RMI also introduces the idea of remote objects and not just remote procedures.

Many developers are using CORBA to build their distributed systems in large heterogeneous environments. CORBA is a specification held by a consortium called the Object Management Group. This consortium exists to fill the need for interoperability among the constantly increasing number of hardware and software products available today. CORBA defines an IDL (Interfaces Definition Language) and APIs that enable client/server object interaction within a specific implementation of an Object Request Broker (ORB). More information on CORBA can be found at `http://www.omg.org`.

CORBA is platform and language independent. The IDL is translated into a specific language for the chosen implementation. There even are several implementations for the Java platform.

Note

Work is being done to implement RMI using the OMG's IIOP (Internet Inter-ORB Protocol). More information can be found at the Java Developer Connection at `http://developer.java.sun.com/developer/earlyAccess/rmi-iiop/index.html`.

Why use RMI? RMI has some advantages over CORBA. RMI does not require an IDL but instead is only implemented for the Java language. This can be a plus if you are dealing with only Java in your distributed system. RMI also utilizes Java object serialization to marshal and unmarshal parameters, which is relatively lightweight on the network. *Marshalling* is the process of converting an object to a format that can be sent over the network.

RMI has some added security features. RMI uses the security manager defined to protect systems from hostile applets to protect your systems and network from potentially hostile downloaded code.

Java RMI is included with the Java base API under the `java.rmi` package. Table 33.9 shows some of the most important.

TABLE 33.9 Import RMI Classes

Class	*Description*
`Remote`	`Remote` is an interface defined in the `java.rmi` package. The `Remote` interface serves to identify interfaces whose methods may be invoked from a remote virtual machine.
`Naming`	`Naming` is a the bootstrap mechanism, a class located in `java.rmi` for obtaining references to remote objects based on Uniform Resource Locator (URL) syntax.
`RemoteServer`	`RemoteServer`, located in `java.rmi.server`, is a superclass for all server implementations and provides the interface for functions needed to create and export remote objects.

Note

More information on RMI, including sample code and tutorials, can be found on the JavaSoft Web site at `http://www.javasoft.com/products/jdk/1.1/docs/guide/rmi/index.html`.

The JDK also includes a couple of tools for RMI, `rmic`, and the `rmiregistry`. The `rmic` compiler generates stub and skeleton class files for remote objects from the names of compiled Java classes that contain remote object implementations. (A *remote object* is one that implements the interface `java.rmi.Remote`.)

The `rmiregistry` is a tool that creates a remote object registry, which is a naming service used by RMI servers on a host to bind remote objects to names.

`java.net`: Networking Techniques

A language that touts itself as being network-savvy requires a good network library. This is why the Java base API contains the `java.net` package. The `java.net` package contains an extensive library of classes for networking. The Java networking package is based on widely accepted Internet protocols such as TCP/IP and HTTP to specify network resources.

Some common networking classes include the following:

`Socket`

`ServerSocket`

`DatagramSocket`

`InetAddress`

`URL`

`MulticastSocket`

The two most important classes in this package are `Socket` and `ServerSocket`. These two classes can be used to create client/server connections via a TCP/IP streamed connection. Streamed TCP/IP connections work similarly to input/output streams. In fact, you need to obtain a stream from the socket class in order to communicate across a socket.

The `WebSocket` Web client example demonstrates how to write a simple Java client using the `Socket` class to connect to a Web server:

```
import java.net.Socket;
import java.net.URL;
import java.net.MalformedURLException;
import java.io.PrintWriter;
import java.io.BufferedReader;
import java.io.InputStreamReader;
import java.io.IOException;

// WebSocket class will connect to a webserver and receive a webpage
// Try it by typing: java WebSocket http://www.mcp.com
public class WebSocket {
   private PrintWriter sockout;
   private BufferedReader sockin;
   private Socket sock;

   public static void main( String args[] ) {
      // Create our WebSocket class and give a URL object formed from
      // the command line arg
      try {
         new WebSocket( new URL(args[0]) );
      }
      catch( MalformedURLException mfu ) {
         System.err.println( "Invalid URL format..." );
         System.err.println( "Usage: java WebSocket [url]" );
      }
   }

   public WebSocket( URL webadd ) {
      try {
```

```
        // Open up a new socket connection to the host on the HTTP port 80
        sock = new Socket( webadd.getHost(), 80 );

        // Create the Reader and Writer for the Socket
        sockout = new PrintWriter( sock.getOutputStream() );
        sockin = new BufferedReader(
           new InputStreamReader(sock.getInputStream()) );

        // Tell the webserver what file you want
        sockout.println( "GET " + webadd.getFile() );
        sockout.flush();

        // Print out the HTML the webserver returned to the console
        for( String line = sockin.readLine(); line != null;
             line = sockin.readLine() )
           System.out.println( line );
        }
        catch(IOException ioe) {
           System.err.println( "Error connecting to host " +
                               webadd.getHost() );
        }
     }
}
```

This is a simple Web client application written in Java that makes a socket connection to a Web server on port 80, the HTTP port where the server listens for requests. After a connection has been made, the `WebSocket` Web client asks the server to serve the HTML document you entered. This is exactly what your Web browser does, although most Web browsers have complex parsing and graphics engines to format and display the HTML in a more interesting fashion.

Servlets

You have seen how to do programming with Java on the Web browser client using Java applets. Sometimes applets can be a little fat and slow loading over the network due to limited bandwidth. It may suit your need best to have dynamically loaded HTML on the Web browser. Since the Web's creation, the most common way of doing this was to use CGI (Common Gateway Interface) with Perl or C/C++. What if you still wanted to utilize the advantages Java offers?

The answer is Java servlets. Java *servlets* provide a mechanism for extending the functionality of a Web server in much the same way that CGI scripts do. In addition, servlets provide all the advantages that Java provides, such as portability and multi-threading.

The servlet model is similar to the applet model. There is a servlet engine that runs as part of your Web server. This engine may come embedded as part of your Web server or may be sold as an add-on referred to as an *application server*. Application servers provide servlet engine capabilities plus added features that help you build dynamic Web sites. Some popular add-on servlet engines or application servers follow:

- The Java-Apache project's JServ module. This is an open source servlet engine by the Apache Group for the popular Apache Web server. `http://java.apache.org`.
- IBM's WebSphere Application Server. This is IBM's application server which supports many popular Web servers. `http://www.software.ibm.com/webservers`.
- BEA Weblogic Application Server. This is Weblogic's application server for Java servlets. `http://www.beasys.com/linux/`.
- Live Software's JRun Servlet Engine. JRun is a servlet engine for Java servlets available with the Red Hat 6.0 distribution. `http://www.jrun.com`.

Servlet engines load servlets that extend the servlet base class `HTTPServlet`, which is located in the servlet package `javax.servlet`. When you have a Web page that calls a servlet, the request is formatted into a `HttpServletRequest`, which contains the parameters and other information about the request. The servlet engine then loads and calls either the `doPost` or `doGet` method. The following `Hello There` servlet code demonstrates a simple Java servlet:

```
import javax.servlet.*;
import javax.servlet.http.*;

public class HelloThereServlet extends HttpServlet {
   public void doGet( HttpServletRequest req, HttpServletResponse res )
    throws ServletException, IOException
{
      // Get the parameter pass in
      String name = req.getParameters("name")[0];
      PrintWriter servout = res.getWriter();

      // Set the content type
      res.setContentType("text/html");

      servout.println( "<HTML>" );
      servout.println( "<HEAD>" );
      servout.println( "<TITLE>Hello There Servlet</TITLE>" );
      servout.println( "<BODY>" );
      servout.println( "Hello There, " + name );
      servout.println( "</BODY>" );
      servout.println( "</HTML>" );
   }
}
```

Here is the HTML code that invokes the servlet:

```
<HTML>
   <HEAD>
      <TITLE>Hello There Servlet</TITLE>
   </HEAD>
   <BODY>
      <FORM METHOD=GET ACTION="/servlet/HelloThereServlet">
      What is your name? <INPUT TYPE=TEXT NAME="name" SIZE=25>
      <INPUT TYPE=SUBMIT VALUE= "Say Hello There!">
      </FORM>
   </BODY>
</HTML>
```

Other References

There are an endless amount of books, magazines, and Web sites devoted to using programming with Java. Listed here are just a few references you can use to become more familiar with Java. This chapter has just been an introduction to the Java programming language and shows you how to get started programming under Linux. For more information, you may want to read some of these books that go into much greater detail.

Books

- *Object-Oriented Technology: A Manager's Guide*. Taylor.
- *Java 2 Platform Unleashed*. Jamie Jaworski, Sams Publishing.
- *Java Distributed Objects*. Bill McCarty, Sams Publishing.
- *Developing Java Servlets*. James Goodwill, Sams Publishing.
- *Java 1.1 Unleashed*. Michael Morrison, Sams Publishing.
- *The Java Programming Language*. Ken Arnolds and James Gosling, Addison-Wesley.
- *Java In A Nutshell*. David Flanagan, O'Reilley & Associates, Inc.

Web Sites

- `http://www.javasoft.com` This Web site is the JavaSoft division of Sun Microsystems, Inc.
- `http://www.gamelan.com` This is a well-known Web site containing a wide variety of useful Java information.
- `http://www.blackdown.org` For more information on the Blackdown team and the Blackdown port of the Sun Java Development Kit.

- `http://www.kaffe.org` Gives information on the Open Source Java Virtual Machine.
- `http://www.beasys.com/linux/` See this site for more information on the BEA Weblogic application server for Linux.
- `http://www.software.ibm.com/webservers` See this site for information on the IBM Websphere application server for Linux.
- `http://java.apache.org` For more information on the Java Apache JServ Servlet Engine.
- `http://www.jrun.com` Browse here for more information on Live Software's JRun Java servlet engine.
- `http://www.ibm.com/research/jikes` This site has information on the Jikes Open Source native Java compiler with IBM Research.
- `http://www.omg.org` This is the Web site for the Object Management Group, a consortium for the CORBA specification.

Summary

This chapter introduced you to the Java programming language and showed you how to begin utilizing Linux to develop your own Java applications, applets, and servlets. You gained knowledge about tools available for Red Hat Linux for developing applications and where to obtain more information about Java. You also saw basics of the Java programming language and platform and how to compile and run simple Java programs.

Advanced Topics

Part V

In This Part

CHAPTER 34

Linux Graphics Applications

In This Chapter

The interesting thing about graphics applications is that they have a broader marketplace than many other Linux applications. The graphics tools range from a straightforward paint program to a highly sophisticated graphics program that rivals or exceeds commercial packages for other operating systems.

This means that the Linux graphics environment can provide a tool for children learning about colors and simple painting tools, the small business that needs a tool to produce graphics layouts and brochures, and the serious graphics artist who needs state-of-the-art tools to produce complex works and will not compromise on quality.

This chapter covers converting, editing, and creating graphics using popular tools available under Linux. Other tools, such as office suites, are covered only from the perspective of generating a presentation or slideshow.

There is special mini-HOWTO on graphics maintained by Michael J. Hammel; it is available at `http://www.graphics-muse.org/linux/lgh.html`. It is not included with most HOWTO distributions because it is very graphic-intensive.

Graphics File Formats

Linux supports most of the popular graphics formats. The following is a representative list of supported formats:

- GIF (various formats of GIF)
- JPEG and MPEG
- BMP
- PCX
- Photo CD (PCD)
- XCF (`GIMP` native format)
- MIFF (`ImageMagick` native format)
- TIFF
- TARGA or TGA format
- PostScript and Encapsulated PostScript (EPS)
- PNG
- PPM
- PGM

Converting Graphics

One of the sure bets in the graphics world is that you will have one format and need another to complete the task. Many Web sites use GIF format, while others prefer JPEG format. Linux graphics tools can help convert the image from one format to another. There are both command-line tools and Graphical User Interface (GUI) tools to convert graphics.

The main issue with converting is that there may or may not be a loss in resolution or clarity when files are converted. This mainly stems from the fact that some image formats are lossy. *Lossy* means that some of the data is lost as an image is compressed or converted. This lost data usually has no effect on the image's display if you have 100,000 data points in a solid blue box. If 100 data points are lost, it will still look like a solid blue box. The advantage of a lossy format is that it will compress and you will actually save space. A *lossless* image will not drop data points. The advantage of a lossless image is that every data point is still there. The bad side is that it will be a larger image.

The other conversion issue is the size of the final image. What stated out as a small image in one format may grow into an almost 0.5MB image when you convert to another format. A good example is converting a JPEG file to a PostScript file—it is possible that a 25K JPEG file would convert into a 421KB PostScript file.

Using `convert`

`convert` is a command-line utility that transforms one graphical format to another. `convert` supports most major types of images, including GIF, JPEG, Photo CD, TIFF, and so on. If you have a file called `snapshot1.gif` and want to convert it to a JPEG file, use the following command:

```
# convert snapshot1.gif snapshot1.jpg
```

`convert` is part of the `ImageMagick` toolset along with `display`. `display` can be used to display the converted image.

```
# display snapshot1.jpg
```

`display` will bring up the `snapshot1.jpg` image in a full-screen window.

Using `xv`

`xv` is one of the standard UNIX tools for converting and viewing graphical images. The `xv` RPM is approximately 1.1Mb in size; the latest update is available at `http://www.trilon.com/xv/`. `xv` is released under a shareware arrangement, in which the suggested fee for commercial or business use is $25. Additional information about `xv` is available at `http://www.trilon.com/xv/`.

`xv` is an excellent tool for the display and conversion of images. Its best feature is that `xv` runs under numerous UNIX and PC platforms. This allows portability between platforms and the ability to utilize the same tool under different environments.

Command-Line Utilities

`Giftrans` is a good tool for converting GIF87 to GIF89 images. Its main purpose is to make one color in the GIF file transparent. One example is changing the background color of a GIF file to match the background color of the web page. This would make the box around the GIF "transparent" or blend into the Web page and highlight the contents of the GIF image.

Editing Graphics

There are many tools that can be used to edit graphics—some allow basic functionality such as crop and rotate, while others can transform the image using special filters or effects.

GQView

`GQView` provides the ability to see and organize existing images. One feature allows you to see a thumbnail sketch of each image in a file list (see Figure 34.1) and you can display the image on the screen (see Figure 34.2) while also looking at other images in thumbnail format. `GQView` can also zoom in and out to focus on certain portions of the image.

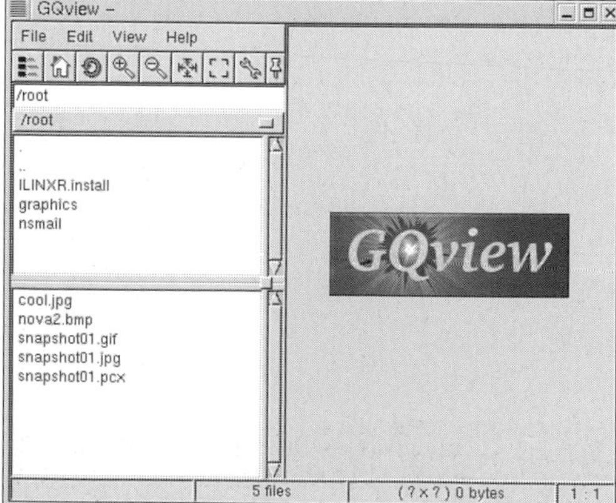

FIGURE 34.1
The initial `GQView` dialog box.

GQView works in conjunction with other tools such as xv, GIMP, Electric Eyes, and paint for the editing of images. These tools are on a default menu and additional tools can be added. The editing tool is launched from a pull-down menu and GQView is still active in the background.

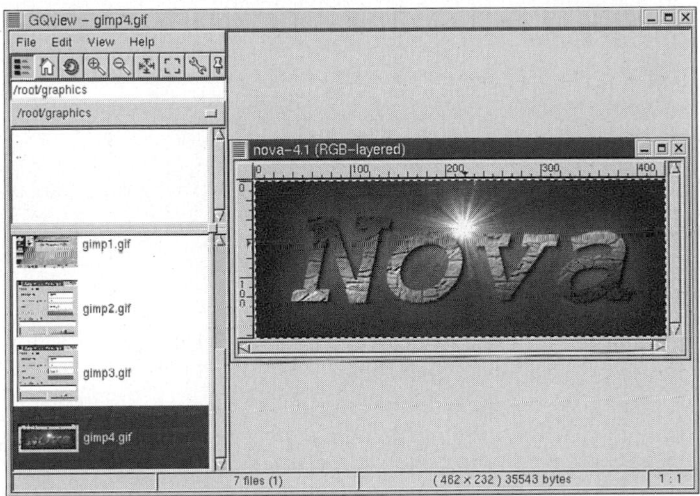

FIGURE 34.2
The initial GQView dialog box with thumbnail sketches.

ImageMagick

ImageMagick is an X11 package that can display, convert, and edit images. It supports most standard image formats such as JPEG, TIFF, PNM, XPM, Photo CD, and GIF. ImageMagick also has a native format known as .miff. Most graphics tools have a native format that keeps layer or configuration information about the image. The RPM package for version 4.2.2 is 3MB. Information about ImageMagick can be found at http://www.wizards.dupont.com/cristy/ImageMagick.html.

The main tools for ImageMagick include display, import, animate, montage, convert, mogrify, identify, combine, and xtp. These tools are invoked using the command line, for example, by using convert to display the file snapshot01.gif.

```
# display snapshot01.gif
```

This will bring up a full-screen rendering of the snapshot01.gif image file as shown in Figure 34.3.

> **Tip**
>
> Bring up an image using the display command and then right-click the mouse; select Short Cuts. This displays a floating toolbar with most of the common elements such as File, Edit, View Transform, and Help.

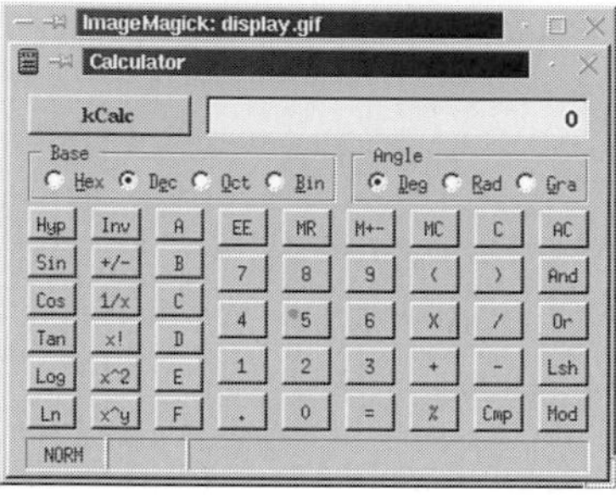

FIGURE 34.3
snapshot01.gif.

The following is an extract of the man page describing the functions of `ImageMagick`:

`ImageMagick(1)` `ImageMagick(1)`

Display

Display is a machine architecture independent image and display program. It can display an image on any workstation display running an X server. Display can read and write many of the more popular image formats (e.g. JPEG, TIFF, PNM, Photo CD, etc.). You can perform these functions on the image:

- load an image from a file
- display the next image
- display the former image
- display a sequence of images as a slideshow
- write the image to a file
- print the image to a PostScript printer
- delete the image file
- create a Visual Image Directory
- select the image to display by its thumbnail rather than name
- undo last image transformation
- copy a region of the image
- pastc a region to the image
- restore the image to its original size
- refresh the image
- half the image size
- double the image size
- resize the image
- crop the image

- cut the image
- flip image in the horizontal direction
- flip image in the vertical direction
- rotate the image 90 degrees clockwise
- rotate the image 90 degrees counter-clockwise
- rotate the image
- shear the image
- trim the image edges
- invert the colors of the image
- vary the color brightness
- vary the color saturation
- vary the image hue
- gamma correct the image
- sharpen the image contrast
- dull the image contrast
- perform histogram equalization on the image
- perform histogram normalization on the image
- negate the image colors
- toggle the colormap type: Shared or Private
- reduce the speckles within an image
- eliminate peak noise from an image
- detect edges within the image
- emboss an image
- oil paint an image
- convert the image to grayscale
- set the maximum number of unique colors in the image
- segment the image by color
- apply image processing techniques to a region of interest
- annotate the image with text
- draw on the image
- edit an image pixel color
- edit the image matte information
- composite an image with another

- add a border to the image
- surround image with an ornamental border
- add an image comment
- display image centered on a backdrop
- display image to background of a window
- display information about the image
- display information about this program
- discard all images and exit program
- change the level of magnification
- display images specified by a World Wide Web (WWW) uniform resource locator (URL)

Import

Import reads an image from any visible window on an X server and outputs it as an image file. You can capture a single window, the entire screen, or any rectangular portion of the screen. You can use the display (see display(1)) utility for redisplay, printing, editing, formatting, archiving, image processing, etc. of the captured image.

The target window can be specified by id, name, or may be selected by clicking the mouse in the desired window. If you press a button and then drag, a rectangle will form which expands and con- tracts as the mouse moves. To save the portion of the screen defined by the rectangle, just release the button. The keyboard bell is rung once at the beginning of the screen capture and twice when it completes.

Animate

Animate imports a sequence of images on any work- station display running an X server. Animate first determines the hardware capabilities of the workstation. If the number of unique colors in an image is less than or equal to the number the work-station can support, the image is displayed in an X window. Otherwise the number of colors in the image is first reduced to match the color resolution of the workstation before it is displayed.

This means that a continuous-tone 24 bits/pixel image can display on a 8 bit pseudo-color device or monochrome device. In most instances the reduced color image closely resembles the original. Alternatively, a monochrome or pseudo-color image sequence can display on a continuous-tone 24 bits/pixels device.

Montage

Montage creates acomposite image by combining several separate images. The images are tiled on the composite image with the name of the image optionally appearing just below the individual tile.

Convert

Convert converts an input file using one image for- mat to an output file with a differing image format. By default, the image format is determined by it's magic number. To specify a particular image format, precede the filename with an image format name and a colon (i.e. ps:image) or specify the image type as the filename suffix (i.e. image.ps). Specify file as - for standard input or output. If file has the extension .Z, the file is decoded with uncompress.

Mogrify

Mogrify transforms an image or a sequence of images. These transforms include image scaling, image rotation, color reduction, and others. The transmogrified image overwrites the original image.

Identify describes the format and characteristics of one or more image files. It will also report if an image is incomplete or corrupt. The information displayed includes the scene number, the file name, the width and height of the image, whether the image is colormapped or not, the number of colors in the image, the number of bytes in the image, the format of the image (JPEG, PNM, etc.), and finally the number of seconds it took to read and process the image.

Combine

Combine combines images to create new images.

Xtp

Xtp is a utility for retrieving, listing, or printing files from a remote network site, or sending files to a remote network site. Xtp performs most of the same functions as the ftp program, but does not require any interactive commands. You simply specify the file transfer task on the command line and xtp performs the task automatically.

AUTHORS

John Cristy, E.I. du Pont de Nemours and Company Incorporated

Electric Eyes

`Electric Eyes`, or `ee`, is part of the GNOME Distribution and was created by Rasterman. It is loaded during the initial install of Red Hat with the graphics option. The RPM for version 0.3.8 is 450KB. It features the capability to crop, rotate, and enhance images. Figure 34.4 shows the opening screen for `Electric Eyes`. The normal toolbar includes Exit Electric Eyes, Open a New File, Save as Original Filename, Save as New File, Print Image, View the File Image in the List, View the Previous Image in the List, View the Next Image in the List, View the Last Image in the List, and Crop the Current Selection. Figure 34.5 shows a thumbnail sketch of an image along with relevant file and image information.

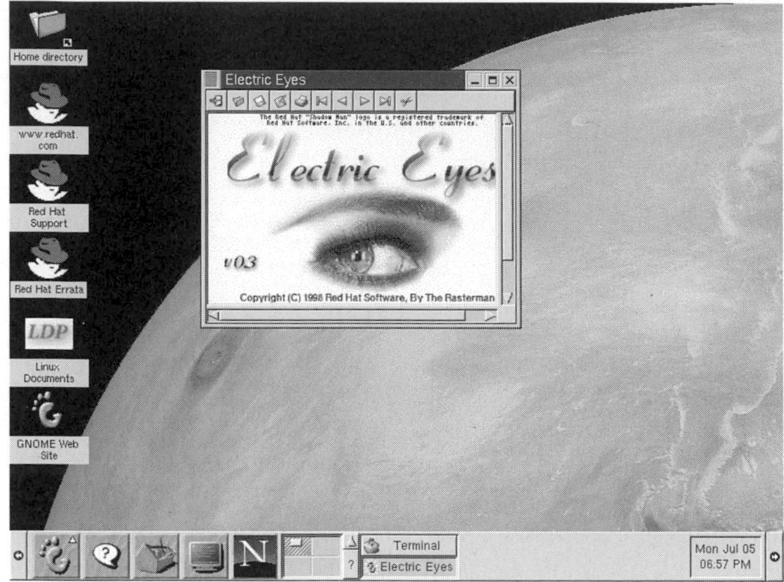

FIGURE 34.4
The opening dialog box of `Electric Eyes`.

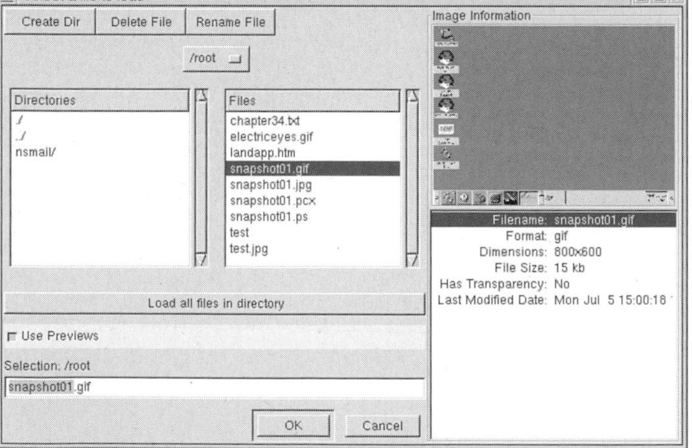

FIGURE 34.5
`Electric Eyes`, *showing a thumbnail image.*

Creating Graphics

One of the strong features of Linux graphics tools is its capability to not only manipulate existing graphics, but to create original graphics. One way to generate graphics is to take a snapshot of existing screens using a screen capture facility. The other way is to generate original graphics using the digital equivalent of a brush and canvas.

Linux graphics tools will not make you an instant artist—you still need to understand the basics: perspective, lighting, color renditions, and all the other good things that are taught in art class. Linux graphics tools, like any other electronic graphic tool, are good for adding special effects and automating repetitive tasks. The bottom line, however, is that you must have the creative vision to create a good product. The key is to experiment with the tools, start with a simple project, and progress as time and your ability allow.

Creating Screenshots

One of the handier graphics utilities is a screenshot tool, especially if you are developing documentation or training material. A screenshot tool allows you to take "pictures" of what is on the video display. This can be the whole display, including toolbars and all the windows within a display, or a single window, such as a terminal session or a dialog box from an application. Figure 34.6 shows the `Ksnapshot` dialog box.

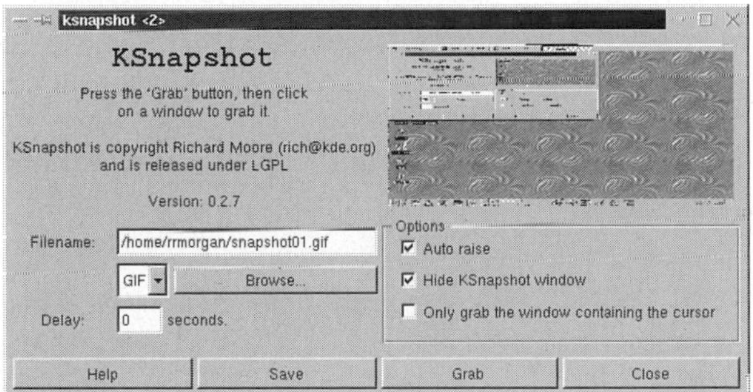

FIGURE 34.6
The `Ksnapshot` dialog box.

The KDE tool, `Ksnapshot`, is part of the graphics RPM from an initial Red Hat or Caldera Systems setup. The `kdegraphics` RPM is 2.8MB and includes `kdvi` (TeX display), `kfax` (for fax display), `kfract` (a fractical generator), `kghostscript` (displays PostScript files), `kiconedit` (icon editor), `kpaint` (simple drawing program), `ksnapshot`, and `kview` (image viewer).

A nice feature of `Ksnapshot` is that it can save the file in many different formats and has the capability to pick one window or the whole screen.

> **Tip**
>
> If you are trying to capture a single window and your screen-capture tool takes the snapshot before you can position your cursor over the correct window, try changing the default time from `0` to `2` seconds. That should give you enough time to position the cursor and get the shot.

`xv` has a screenshot facility that allows you to grab and manipulate images. `ImageMagick` has a tool (`image`) that allows you to capture a screen or a selected portion of the screen. `GIMP` also has a grab or screenshot capability.

GIMP

GNU Image Manipulation Program (`GIMP`) has the potential to be a killer graphics application for Linux. This open source package rivals most $500+ graphics packages and can be as powerful as a specialized graphics workstation costing three or four times the cost of a high-end PC. `GIMP` is a good package for both the beginner and the expert graphics artist. The keys with `GIMP` are the flexibility to start with basic functionality, work up to very sophisticated add-on features, and then utilize a macro-like feature called Script-Fu. Figure 34.7 shows the toolbar and a `GIMP` Tip of the Day.

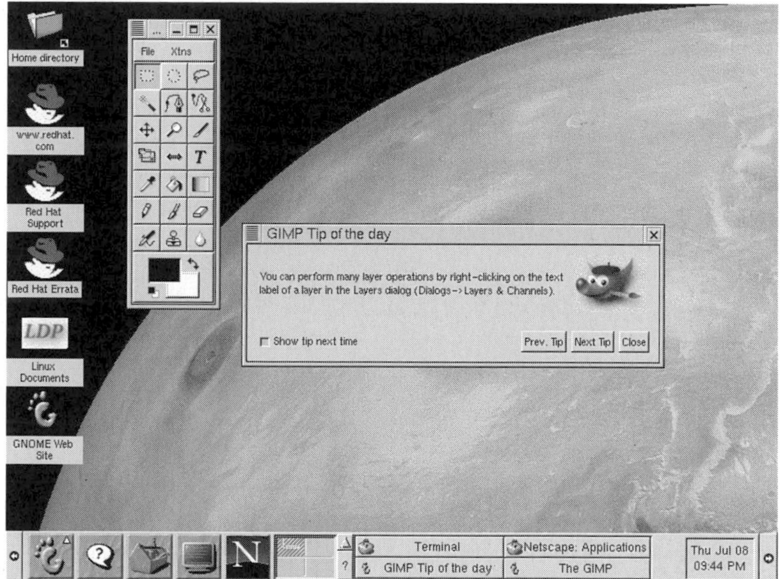

FIGURE 34.7
GIMP toolbar and Tip of the Day.

The `GIMP` home page provides the latest software updates, tips on usage, manuals, and features such as newsletters. Most distributions have `GIMP` as an RPM or it is readily available from the `GIMP` home page (`http://www.gimp.org`). Version 1.0.4 RPM of `GIMP` is 6.5MB. Some of the distributions do not include fonts. Additional fonts can be found at the `GIMP` home page. The RPM `gimp-data-extras` includes additional tools for `GIMP` and is 7.8MB. The fully installed `GIMP` can take more than 50MB of disk space. The *`GIMP` User's Manual*, or *GUM*, is more than 500 pages and starts with the basics and goes through advanced functionality. The book, *The Artists' Guide to the GIMP* (Michael Hammel, SSC, 1999), is another good source of information on `GIMP`.

Tip

GIMP is a very powerful tool—the trick is to realize that you cannot learn all its functionality in one sitting. Master a few of the tools and then add tools as you feel comfortable.

GIMP can import most graphics formats and is essentially a combination of an electric darkroom and a special effects studio. One of GIMP's strong points is taking photographic images in most standard graphics formats and manipulating the image by cropping, lightening, darkening, and using filters to overlay patterns, blurring, reverse imaging, and most standard darkroom techniques. GIMP can also be used to remove red-eye from photographs and even remove that dreaded family member from the picture. Other GIMP applications include creating magazine covers and flyer layouts, and developing complex freehand graphics for Web pages. GIMP can save using most popular graphics formats, but also has a native format called `.xcf`.

The next level of intensity is the capability to produce special effects beyond what is possible with a camera, and to move into the world that is limited only by the imagination of the artist. GIMPs capability to combine photos, drawings, gradients, and overlays can make an image as robust as any other package on the market can. It is also possible to create animated GIFs for Web pages using GIMP.

The following is an example of using the available Script-Fu tools that were installed with the initial package. The goal is to create a sample logo.

If the environment is GNOME, the first step is to bring up GIMP: Click the GNOME Icon, Graphics, the GIMP. This will bring up two items (refer to Figure 34.7), a GIMP toolbox and a GIMP Tip of the Day.

The next step is to click Xtns, Script-Fu, Logos, Starscape. Starscape is one of many logo templates. Figure 34.8 shows the initial dialog box for the Starscape Script-Fu.

FIGURE 34.8
Initial Starscape Script-Fu dialog box.

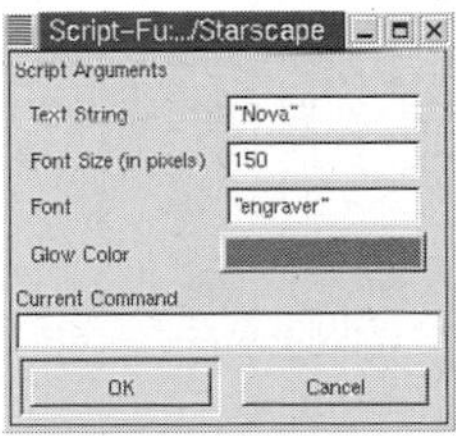

If you loaded the complete font set, you can click OK at this point. The complete font set is not loaded as a default, and Figure 34.9 shows how to change the font from Engraver to Courier. Since Courier is a basic system default font, the Starscape Script-Fu can start executing using Courier.

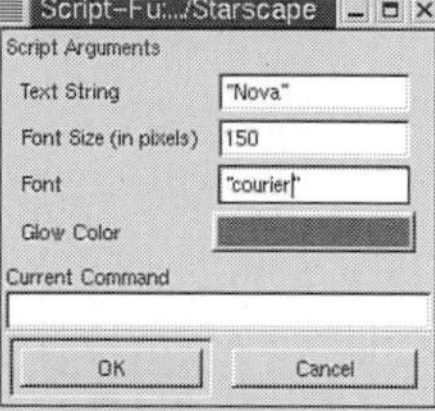

FIGURE 34.9
Changing the font in dialog box Starscape Script-Fu.

A series of dialog boxes will appear and disappear as the script continues executing functions. The end result, shown in Figure 34.10, is a Nova logo in 150-point font size.

FIGURE 34.10
End result of Starscape dialog box Script-Fu.

The last step is to right-click in the image box and save the image. This is accomplished by choosing File, Save under selection. Pick a filename such as **`nova.xcf`** and change the Determine File Type pull-down box to **`.xcf`** to save the image as a native `GIMP` file. The file will be saved when you click OK.

Other Clients

Other clients for creating graphics include `xpaint`. `xpaint` is a straightforward tool that provides basic functionality such as shapes, coloring, and shading and can generate an image quickly and efficiently. `xpaint` runs on many platforms such as Sun Solaris and HP HP-UX. The 234KB zipped tar `xpaint` package is available at `http://metalab.unc.edu/pub/linux/apps/graphics/draw/` and is also part of the 2.8MB `kdegraphics` RPM package.

`xpaint` is a simple applications tool and is great for kids to use as a first tool. Figure 34.11 shows the initial dialog box and Figure 34.12 shows a simple design capability.

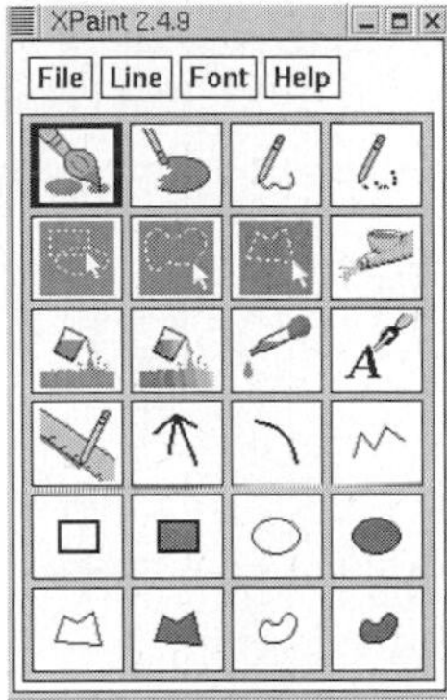

FIGURE 34.11
The initial `xpaint` *dialog box.*

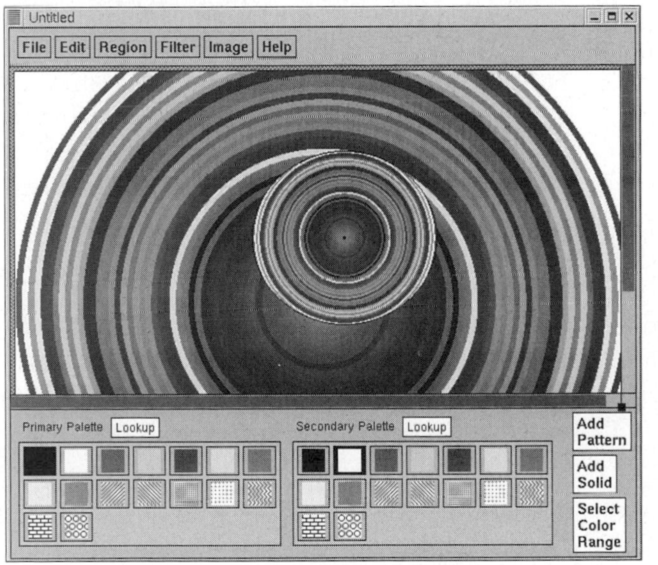

FIGURE 34.12
A simple design in `xpaint`*.*

Scanners and tablets are other devices that assist in creating graphics. There are numerous scanners that work under Linux. The first preference is SCSI scanners, since SCSI can be used for other purposes (such as connecting disk drives and tapes). Other scanners can connect via the USB or parallel port, but Linux support is on a case-by-case basis. Consulting the scanner hardware list is the best thing to do. Scanner software is available at the Scanner Access Now Easy (SANE) site at `http://www.mostang.com/sane/`. SANE is a project that generates a standard scanning interface that works on additional platforms such as FreeBSD, SUN Solaris, Compaq/DEC UNIX, and SGI Irix. The SANE plug-in `xscanimage` will work with `GIMP`. Various scanners have Linux software ports; it's best to pick a scanner that has both a separate driver and is also supported under SANE.

Linux supports most tablets and specialized graphic input boards via the serial port. This is another area in which you may have to search the HOWTOs and the Internet. You can find tips there on how to install and fully utilize these devices.

Displaying and Printing Graphics

Graphical packages like `GIMP` can actually take advantage of additional hardware, such as memory, graphics cards, top-quality monitors, and CPU speed. Graphics is one of the few applications where is there is a direct relationship between memory and CPU cycles and the capability to complete complex projects. The recommendation for occasional graphics generation is 64MB of memory and at least 128MB for the generation of large or multi-layered graphics.

The recommendation is to buy the best video card and monitor that you can afford. It is tough to look at a 14-inch, 800×600–resolution monitor driven by a 2MB graphics card for more then a few hours a day. If you are serious about graphics, the first thing to buy is a good video card. The cards that are good for games also work very well for displaying graphics. If you buy one revision or model back from the top of the line or latest fanciest card, you should be able to get one at a fair price. The second benefit of buying an established video card is that there will most likely be a video driver available that has the bugs worked out and can take advantage of the card's features. If you buy the latest card, there is a chance that the video driver may not be optimized or that it will be an experimental video driver. There is nothing wrong with experimental drivers; you need to understand that if you are interested in pushing the edge. However, if you want something that is rock solid and time tested, experimental drivers are not the place for you.

Monitor prices follow a pattern: If you bought a 15-inch monitor last year, 17-inch monitors are available this year at a similar price point. Monitors are like audio speakers in that different monitors appeal to different people. There usually is no one "best" monitor for everyone. The best advice is to research monitors using the Internet to get reviews and then narrow your choices to a few. The next step is to visit a store that has all the monitors on display and look at each one under similar lighting conditions. Some of the video distribution systems may not push the monitor to the maximum—try to find a couple of the top choices hooked up directly to a computer for additional clarity. The last step is to find a store or vendor that will let you try your monitor in your home or business under the lighting conditions and with the graphic applications that you normally use.

It might be nice to have a 21-inch monitor for your workstation, but realize that they cost a significant amount of money and take up a significant amount of desk space. That old cardtable or small computer table may not work with a large monitor. Large monitors also tend to be very heavy and bulky. Flat-screen monitors have made significant strides in the past year; they are becoming affordable and are approaching the quality of glass monitors. The bottom line on flat-screen monitors is that they are expensive and offer other advantages, such as taking less desk space and offering clearer images.

Tip

If you are in the market for a printer, check the Linux printer HOWTO to see which printers are on the list. While it is possible to connect many of the latest printers, the problem is that not all of the printer's features will be supported unless a good print driver is available. `GIMP` also has a printer plug-in that supports a wide range of printers.

Everyone wants the latest color laser printer, but the fiscal reality is that a good inkjet printer will work for most people on a tight budget. Not only will the initial purchase work, but the replacement cartridges are also less expensive than a laser printer's. Using an inkjet printer with specially treated paper and photographic paper currently available in the marketplace is a viable alternative that can produce results that rival many laser printers.

Most graphics artists will send their work out to be printed at specialty shops and most packages support the export of images for these shops. The one exception, Pantone, is generally not available due to licensing issues.

One thing that you should be aware of is that most large graphic images will not fit on a floppy drive and require the use of something such as a zip or similar drive or the capability to perform high-speed transfers over the Internet. Even with high-speed Internet connections, the larger images will take a significant amount of time, bandwidth, and patience to transmit.

Creating Presentations and Slideshows

There are two main ways to create a presentation using Linux: Generate an `.html` file and view it using a Web browser or use an integrated package such as Applixware or StarOffice that contains a presentation package.

There are many tools for generating HTML code for a presentation to a business or organization. One simple way to present graphics is to use a Web browser and create a slideshow. The great thing is that `.html` files are portable and can be either viewed over the Web or as a local file.

Applixware has a feature called Present that offers standard templates suitable for most office or organizational briefs. A slideshow can be generated using individual slides. Figure 34.13 is a screenshot of Present with a standard template shown.

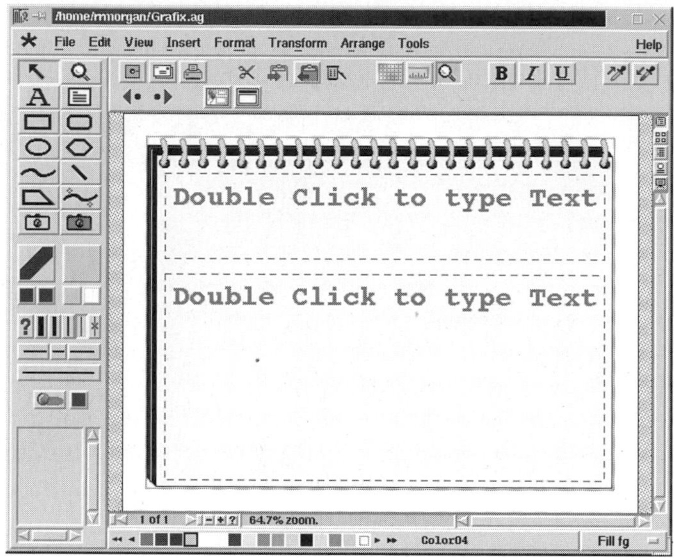

FIGURE 34.13 *A standard template in Applixwares's Present.*

The StarOffice package offers the following features as part of its presentation tool:

- Date, time, and slide numbers
- Free-floating test
- Templates
- Outlining feature
- Graphics (clip-art) that can be edited
- Sound clips
- Outliner or rapid production feature

There is also a drawing function that can be used to generate graphics and 3D objects.

Portable Document Format Clients

One of the more popular formats on the Web is `.pdf`, or Portable Document Format (PDF), by Adobe Systems. The Acrobat Reader is available for most platforms and is a good cross-platform document distribution system. The recommended system requirement for version 4.0 is 32MB of RAM and 12MB of available hard disk space. The Linux client is freely available from the Adobe Web site (`http://www.adobe.com`) and version 4.0 is 5.7MB. Figure 34.14 shows the Adobe Acrobat Reader running under Linux.

The Acrobat Reader can be configured with a Web browser such as Netscape using MIME types. This allows the reader to click a `.pdf` document and have the option of displaying the document or saving it for later viewing.

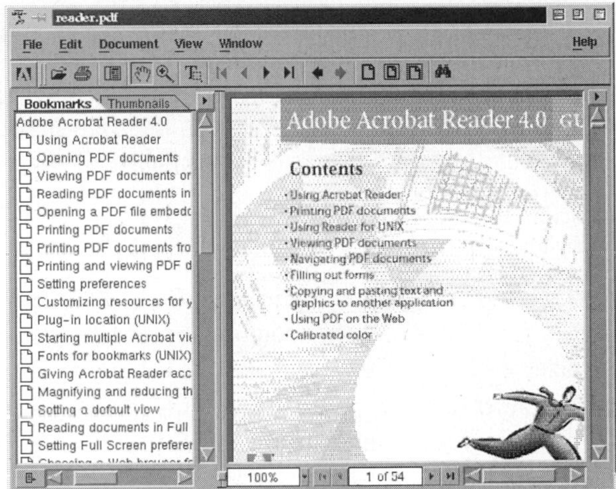

FIGURE 34.14
Adobe Acrobat Reader displaying a .pdf file.

As of this writing, the Acrobat Writer for version 4.0 was unavailable for Linux.

`xpdf` is an X Windows-based PDF viewer that is smaller in disk size and memory requirements then other PDF viewers. The version 0.80 RPM is 1.4MB.

Tip

There is a patch to `xv` and `Ghostscript` that can read PDF files. It is available at `http://www.trilon.com/xv/`.

PostScript

PostScript is one of the most popular printer types in the marketplace. PostScript (PS) is a language of its own and is independent of client hardware and software platforms, making it possible to have a heterogeneous network of PCs, Macintoshes, and UNIX platforms all printing to the same printer.

The other PS advantage is that you can program in it—it is a language. You can write code that produces complex graphics, shapes, and text. If you are familiar with `nroff` and `troff`, PS provides another alternative to generating and controlling output.

Tip

Since PS is a portable language, it is possible to generate a PS file by redirecting the printer output to a file, transporting that file using a floppy or network connection, and printing or manipulating the file on a Linux machine. Examine the first few lines to make sure that the line containing `PS` or `PostScript` is the first line.

The alternative is to use `Ghostscript` for printing and display PostScript on the monitor. The `Ghostscript` RPM is 3.33MB and also requires the 1.5MB `ghostscript-fonts` RPM. It essentially takes the place of PS functionality and allows you to print to non-PostScript printers. The other nice feature is the capability to view the interpretation of the PostScript code on the screen and not just in a text file.

Summary

Linux is a very powerful platform for graphics and will continue to gain marketshare because its applications are solid and because there are tools that allow beginners to create images and movie companies to do complex image rendering.

Linux has many tools that can convert images and will save the user from having to buy custom conversion software or send out the image to a graphics shop for a simple conversion. This conversion feature will save time and money, and allow the user control, as opposed to having to depend on someone else to assist in the conversion.

There are simple, straightforward tools, such as `xpaint`, that can be used without a significant learning curve. There are other tools, such as `GIMP`, that take time to master. `GIMP` has an initial learning curve, but the additional functionality is well worth the time invested. If you are a graphics artist by profession or are involved in major graphics projects, you owe it to yourself to install and tinker with this application.

There are good tools like `xv`, `Electric Eyes`, `GQView`, and `ImageMagick` that can assist in the editing, viewing, creation, and conversion of graphics images. Each tool has its strengths and limitations, but is worth investigating—you can find out how each can be best utilized on projects.

The downside of doing intensive graphics work is that it is very hardware- and software-intensive. It is unreasonable to expect to edit a multi-megabyte file on a 486 class machine. No matter what CPU, memory, and disk space you have, you will want to upgrade hardware as your images grow in complexity and size. The best thing about using Linux is that the total cost of ownership is lower than most other platforms. The high-end Linux systems can effectively compete with specialized graphics workstations without compromising the end product.

CHAPTER 35

Linux Multimedia

In This Chapter

Sound Card Configuration

One of the most complex subsystems to install on any PC is the multimedia subsystem, which normally includes a number of components such as sound cards, MIDI ports, game ports, and CD-ROM drives. The key to a successful Linux multimedia subsystem installation and configuration is the initial planning, starting with the purchase of a sound card. Linux supports a wide range of sound cards from inexpensive Plug-and-Play (PnP) to the latest 3-D sound cards. One of the best sources of information on Linux sound implementations is Jeff Tranter's Linux sound HOWTO (v1.20, 24 March 1999; `jeff_tranter@pobox.com`). The Linux sound HOWTO is located on most distributions and can be found at the Red Hat site under the `HOWTO` directory (`http://www.redhat.com/LDP/HOWTO`). Table 35.1 is a representative list of sound cards and corresponding kernel modules. Table 35.1 is not exhaustive, but represents a sample of the cards supported by Linux under 2.2.x.

Tip

There are a number of good sources of information on sound card installation and hardware compatibility:

- The sound HOWTOs.
- Local Linux User Groups (LUGs).
- `http://www.redhat.com`—Search for the Red Hat Linux Hardware Compatibility List for Intel/6.0.
- `http://www.debian.org/doc/`—Look for the Linux Hardware Compatibility List.
- `http://www.calderasystems.com/products/openlinux/hardware.html`
- `http://www.suse.de/e/`—Look for the Hardware database.
- `http://www.turbolinux.com/support`—Look for the Turbo Linux Compatible Hardware Systems List.
- `http://www.linux-mandrake.com`—Look for the Supported Hardware link.
- `http://www.slackware.com/install`—Look for the Checking System Requirements link.

Some of the LUGS hold an installfest, during which experienced users install or help with the installation of Linux.

TABLE 35.1 Representative Soundcard Support Through the Linux Kernel Drivers

Sound Card	*Module*
6850 UART MIDI Interface	`uart6850.o`
AdLib (no longer manufactured)	`adlib_card.o`
Audio Excel DSP 16	`aedsp.o`
Corel Netwinder WaveArtist	`waveartist.o`
Crystal CS423x	`cs4232.o`
ESS1688 sound chip	`sb.o`
ESS1788 sound chip	`sb.o`
ESS1868 sound chip	`sb.o`
ESS1869 sound chip	`sb.o`
ESS1887 sound chip	`sb.o`
ESS1888 sound chip	`sb.o`
ESS688 sound chip	`sb.o`
ES1370 sound chip	`es1370.o`
ES1371 sound chip	`es1371.o`
Ensoniq AudioPCI (ES1370)	`es1370.o`
Ensoniq AudioPCI 97 (ES1371)	`es1371.o`
Ensoniq SoundScape	`sscape.o`
Gravis Ultrasound	`gus.o`
Gravis Ultrasound ACE	`gus.o`
Gravis Ultrasound Max	`gus.o`
Gravis Ultrasound with 16 bit	`gus.o`
Logitech SoundMan Wave	`sb.o`
MAD16 Pro (OPTi 82C928, 82C929, 82C930, 82C924 chipsets)	`mad16.o`
Media Vision Jazz16	`sb.o`
MediaTriX AudioTriX Pro	`trix.o`
Microsoft Windows Sound System (MSS/WSS)	`ad1848.o`
Mozart (OAK OTI-601)	`mad16.0`
Personal Sound System (PSS)	`pss.o`
Pro Audio Spectrum 16	`pas2.o`

continues

TABLE 35.1 Continued

Sound Card	*Module*
Roland MPU-401 MIDI interface	`mpu401.o`
SoundBlaster 1.0	`sb.o`
SoundBlaster 2.0	`sb.o`
SoundBlaster 16	`sb.o`
SoundBlaster 16ASP	`sb.o`
SoundBlaster 32	`sb.o`
SoundBlaster 64	`sb.o`
SoundBlaster AWE32	`sb.o`
SoundBlaster AWE64	`sb.o`
SoundBlaster PCI	`sb.o`
SoundBlaster Pro	`sb.o`
SoundBlaster Vibra	`sb.o`
Turtle Beach Maui	`maui.o`
Turtle Beach MultiSound Classic	`msnd.o`, `msnd_classic.0`
Turtle Beach MultiSound Fiji	`msnd.o`
Turtle Beach MultiSound Hurricane	`msnd.o`
Turtle Beach MultiSound Monterey	`msnd.o`
Turtle Beach MultiSound Pinnacle	`msnd.o`, `msnd_pinnacle.o`
Turtle Beach MultiSound Tahiti	`msnd.o`
Turtle Beach WaveFront Maui	`maui.o`
Turtle Beach WaveFront Tropez	`maui.o`
Turtle Beach WaveFront Tropez+	`maui.o`
VIDC 16-bit sound	`v_midi.o`
Yamaha OPL3 sound chip	`op13.o`
Yamaha OPL3-SA1 sound chip	`op13sa.o`
Yamaha OPL3-SA2 sound chip	`op13sa.o`
Yamaha OPL3-SA3 sound chip	`op13sa.o`
Yamaha OPL3-SAx sound chip	`op13sa.o`

Choosing a sound card is the key to an easy installation. There are typically three types of sound card installations: installing a new sound card, utilizing an existing sound card, and on-board sound cards. The easiest and cleanest sound card to install and configure is a PCI-based sound card, which simplifies the configuration of DMA, I/O channels, and IRQs, and utilizes the faster PCI bus as opposed to the ISA bus.

The next step is finding a card that has hardware jumpers. It may be hard to find new cards that have jumpers, but it might be possible to find a good used one from a friend who has upgraded hers to the latest card or you could find one in a used computer store. The third choice is a Plug-and-Play(PnP) card. The tool, `isapnp`, is used to configure PnP cards. The challenge with PnP cards is that the card settings are dynamically allocated. If you add a new PnP card, it has the potential to move card settings. This is good because you do not have to know how to configure the settings; it is bad because it is not always predicable. This creates the potential for reconfiguration of existing cards each time you add a new card.

The second type of installation is configuring an existing sound card either in a system that is being converted from another operating system or an older system that may not have a PCI bus. The first step is to check the Linux sound HOWTO list to see if the exact card is listed. SoundBlaster-compatible cards may or may not work utilizing the SoundBlaster driver. The next step is ascertaining whether the card is working under an existing operating system and then writing down the IRQ, I/O port, DMA address, MIDI port, game port address, and any other configuration parameters that are required for card installation.

Tip

The Advanced Linux Sound Architecture (ALSA) drivers, located at `http://www.alsa-project.org`, are an alternative to the standard OSS sound drivers. There is a separate ALSA mini-HOWTO that can answer questions about installation and why ALSA is a viable alternative to the stock drivers.

The third type of sound card installation is an on-board sound card/chip; it already resides on the motherboard. At first glance, the concept of an integrated motherboard that contains video, sound, serial, parallel, and game ports is an interesting concept. This is initially attractive because these motherboards tend to cost less than other motherboards and it is appealing to have everything in one package. Many major manufacturers sell PCs and laptops that also have integrated chips. Table 35.1 lists some on-board chips that are supported under Linux.

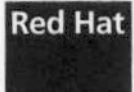

Using Red Hat's sndconfig

The first step is to install the sound card in the PC. This involves opening the case and installing the card in the appropriate slot following the computer manufacturer's instructions and the sound card manufacturer's instructions. This step is not necessary for PCs that contain on-board sound chips.

> **Caution**
>
> If you are unfamiliar with opening a PC case and installing cards, either seek the advice of someone who is familiar or take the PC to a reputable computer repair shop and have them perform the installation.

During the initial Red Hat 6.0 installation you have the option of picking multimedia support, as well as GNOME or KDE window environments. This provides the software to utilize the sound card, but does not configure the sound card.

If you did not load the multimedia RPM(s) during installation, you have to load them after the sound card is installed. The multimedia files are located on the distribution CD-ROM or the RPM CD-ROM and the following are representative sizes: `kdemultimedia-version_#` is approximately 999K, the stock multimedia file used by AnotherLevel is 165K, and the GNOME-media is 118K. The use of RPMs is covered in another section, but briefly type the **`rpm`** command using the **`–ivv`** arguments (install and optional verbose mode) on the file, in this case `multimedia_file.rpm`:

```
# rpm –ivv multimedia.rpm
```

This installs the multimedia options and also indicates if there are any dependencies required to install the multimedia tools.

The last step is the configuration of the sound card and making it known to the kernel as a loadable module. The *sound drivers* are modules that do not require rebooting the computer or recompiling the kernel. Sound card configuration is accomplished by utilizing Red Hat's `sndconfig` command. `sndconfig` detects the sound card and configures ISA PnP, if required, using the `isapnp` tool.

To start `sndconfig`, open a terminal window and type in the following command:

```
# sndconfig
```

A series of blue dialog boxes appear. Here are the basic steps in utilizing `sndconfig`; they're accompanied by figures showing the dialog boxes.

- `sndconfig` probes your machine for a sound card.
- `sndconfig` returns a dialog box indicating that it found sound card *X*.
- The file, `/etc/config.module`, is backed up to `/etc/config.module.bak`.
- `sndconfig` returns a dialog box to play a sample sound.
- If the sample sound is played successfully, you are finished.
- If the sample sound did not play correctly, you need to manually configure the sound card.
- After the reconfiguration of the sound card parameters, the sample sound should now play.

See Figure 35.1 for information and select OK.

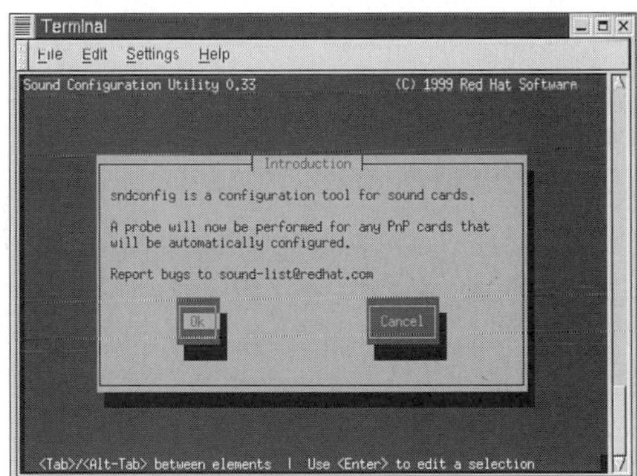

FIGURE 35.1
The initial `sndconfig` screen.

`Sndconfig` probes for a sound card and returns a dialog box like that shown in Figure 35.2; select OK.

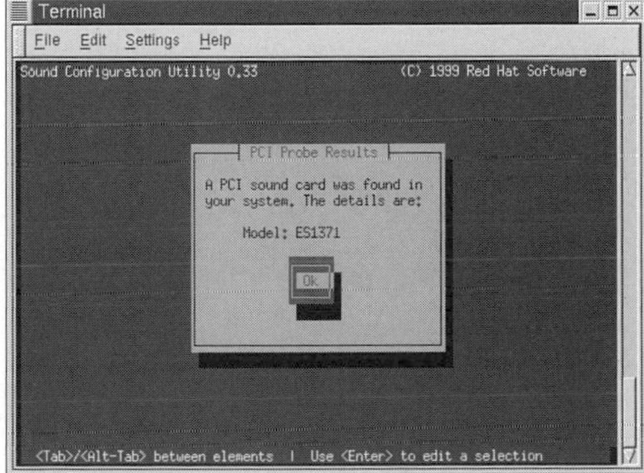

FIGURE 35.2
The results from PCI card.

Any existing `/etc/config.module` file is backed up to `/etc/config.module.`

If the configuration is successful, a sample sound of Linus Torvalds speaking is played (see Figure 35.3).

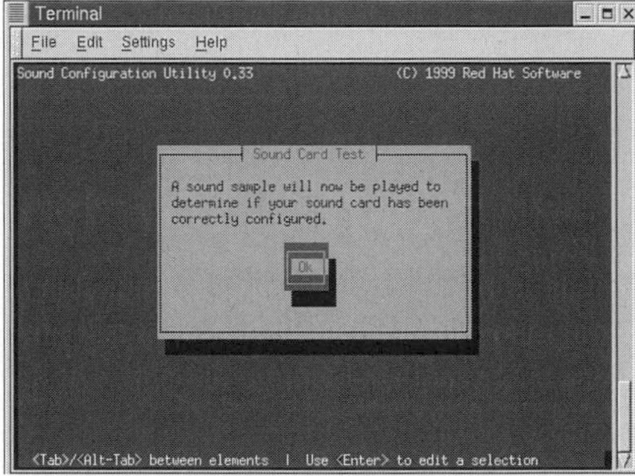

FIGURE 35.3
A sample sound dialog box.

> **Tip**
>
> Make sure that either external speakers or headphones are plugged in to the correct connection and the sound volume is turned up so that you can hear the sound.

If you heard a sample sound, you are finished; if you did not hear it, select No, as shown in Figure 35.4.

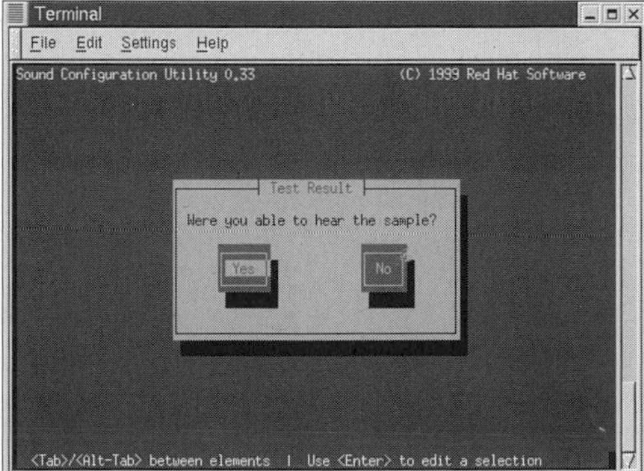

FIGURE 35.4
Did you hear the sample sound?

If `sndconfig` cannot detect your card, you are placed in a manual configuration option (see Figure 35.5). The reader has the option to pick the sound card from a dialog box as shown in Figure 35.6. As discussed earlier in the chapter, this is where having the settings written down will save hours of work. The dialog box will ask for I/O, DMA, and so on (see Figure 35.6 for a screen shot of the dialog box). The sample sound is played if you have correctly configured the PnP card (see Figure 35.7) or jumper card.

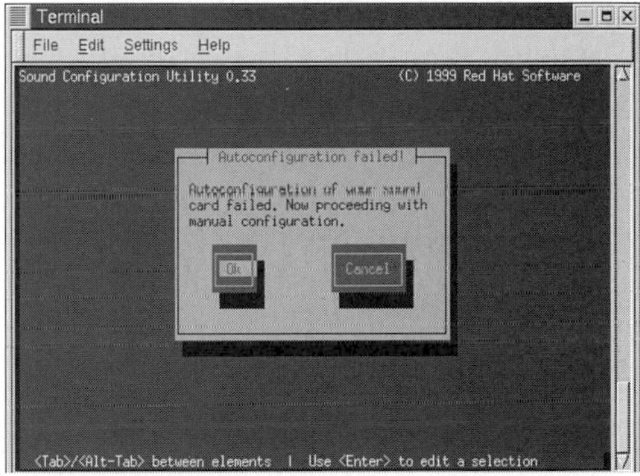

FIGURE 35.5
The manual configuration dialog box.

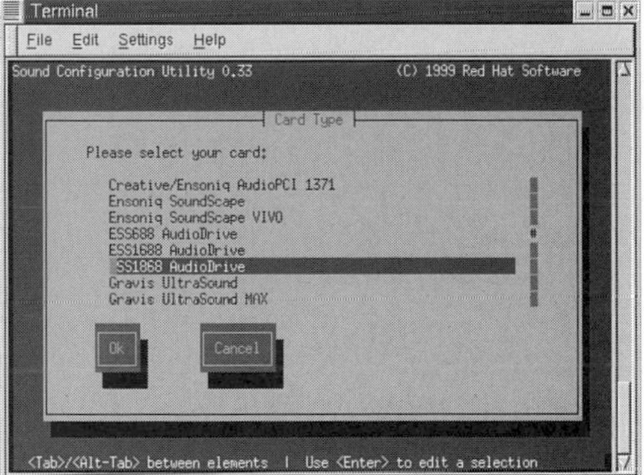

FIGURE 35.6
Selecting a sound card dialog box.

You are returned to the command window after you have pressed OK; the sound card configuration under Red Hat is complete.

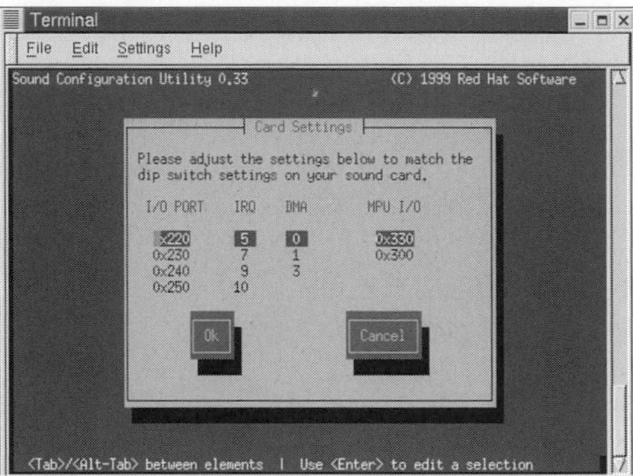

FIGURE 35.7
A PnP Card sample.

Using Caldera Systems Caldera Open Administration System (COAS)

The reader needs to install the sound card and run `isapnp` to configure the card if it is a PnP. Caldera Systems's approach is to utilize `COAS` to load the sound modules. `COAS` does not provide a sound probe mechanism. Instead, it relies on the reader to load the correct module. The interface lists all loadable modules where Ethernet cards are mixed in with sound drivers. Table 35.1 provides a representative sample of the sound cards matched with the `.o`, or object, file. Most of the common sound modules are available under the Caldera Systems distribution. The reader may need to obtain the source code, compile the source code, and install the module, if it is not supplied with the distribution. The recommendation is that the reader obtain the exact sound card model and configuration parameters before starting sound configuration. The reader should check Caldera Systems' Web site, `http://www.calderasystems.com`, for a list of supported cards.

Invoke the `COAS` either from the icon on the bottom tray that comes with the stock Caldera KDE install or by using the KDE program launcher. Then launch `COAS`.

The next step is to pick the Kernel option; the result is a list of loadable modules. Highlight the sound module (on the left side as, shown in Figure 35.8) that corresponds with your sound card and click Load.

A Kernel Module Configuration dialog box (see Figure 35.9) appears. Fill in the parameters that match the sound card. When in doubt, take the defaults and adjust the parameters in a subsequent session.

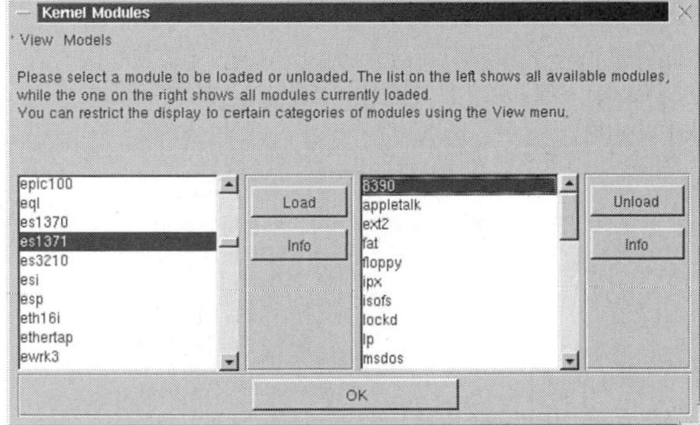

FIGURE 35.8
The COAS *initial screen.*

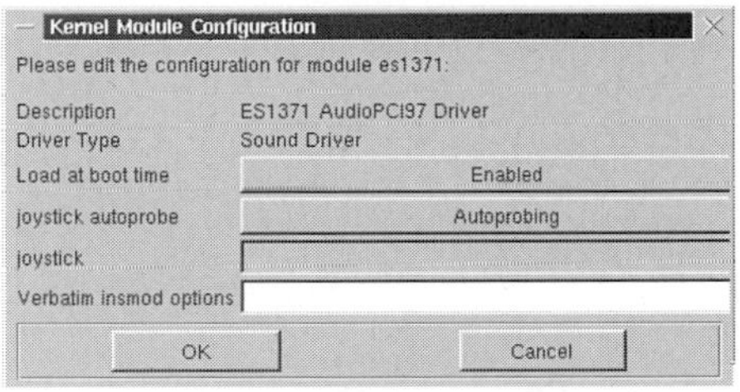

Kernel Module Configuration
Please edit the configuration for module es1371:
Description ES1371 AudioPCI97 Driver
Driver Type Sound Driver
Load at boot time Enabled
joystick autoprobe Autoprobing
joystick
Verbatim insmod options
OK Cancel

FIGURE 35.9
The Kernel Module Configuration dialog box.

After the module is loaded, it will appear on the right side of the dialog box, as shown in Figure 35.10. Some soundcards have an initial module, and may have dependencies on other modules, such as a secondary sound module, MPU module or joystick module. When the reader tries to utilize the function, a dialog box may pop up and indicate that an additional module is required. The reader should use `COAS` and load the required driver.

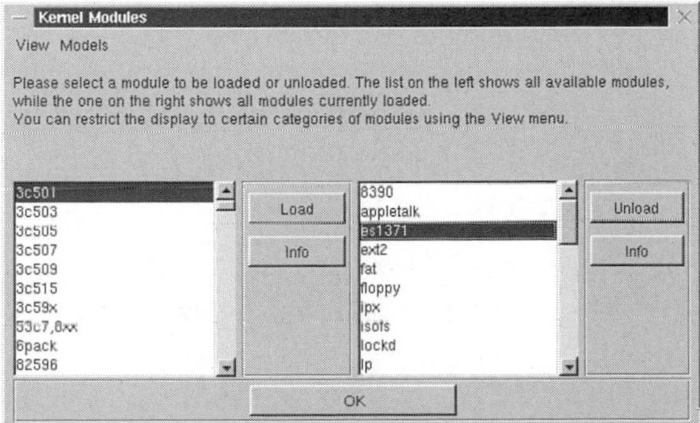

FIGURE 35.10
The sound card configuration dialog box.

The next step is to test sound utilizing the standard KDE sounds. Open the KDE Control Center; the button's right side is sound. Two options appear when you click the Sound button: bell and system sounds. Clicking the Enable System Sounds check box enables the stock KDE system sounds (see Figure 35.11).

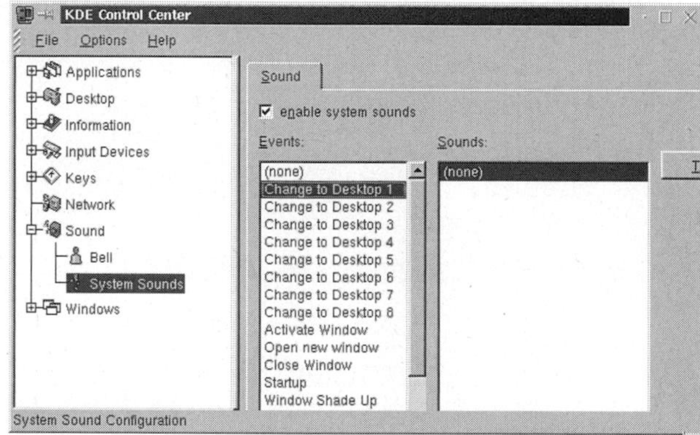

FIGURE 35.11
Enabling KDE sound.

> **Tip**
>
> After you enable system sounds, log out and then log back in to the system. This is one way to make sure the changes take effect during subsequent logins.

Playing Audio CDs

There are two ways to listen to music CDs: through the jack on the CD-ROM drive itself and through the sound card. Either way provides an enjoyable experience while working on the PC. This process describes how to play audio CDs through the sound card in your system.

Initial Configuration

The initial configuration of the CD-ROM and sound card has two parts: The physical cabling between the devices needs to be connected and the software to run the audio CD needs to be installed. There's often a single audio cable between CD-ROMs and sound cards. The audio cable is about the size of a typical mouse cable, normally with a four-pin plastic connector on each end. Consult the sound card and CD-ROM manuals for exact connection instructions. The audio cable on motherboards with built-in sound cards is typically connected to a socket or set of pins directly on the motherboard.

Tip

When installing the audio cable and CD-ROM hardware, double-check to see that all other connections are still secure. In the process of connecting the cables, other cables may come loose, causing other problems such as disk drives becoming unavailable.

Once the physical connections between the sound card and the CD-ROM are complete, a CD-ROM software player and a mixer facilitate listening to audio CDs. A CD-ROM software player is a graphical representation of an audio CD player, similar to one in a home or a car. The CD-ROM player typically shows how long the CD-ROM runs, current track, number of tracks, time in the particular song/audio track, and a graphical representation of stop, pause, eject, replay, fast forward, and reverse buttons. These controls are pushed using the mouse or keyboard. There are command-line versions of CD players, and in many cases the Graphical User Interface (GUI) is a front end for the command-line version.

A mixer is a software representation of a mixer board used in audio studios. It controls the sound volume for the output speakers/headphones; the input volume for things like CD-ROM players, microphones, audio input devices; and line-in and line-out features. High-end mixers also allow the control of the audio signal for video inputs.

gmix

`gmix` is part of the GNOME toolset, installed as part of the Red Hat 6.0 installation and as an option on other distributions. Further information on GNOME multimedia functions is located at `http://www.gnome.org`. Figure 35.12 shows the `gmix` interface. `gmix` is a good, easy-to-use mixer in which each function is labeled and clearly marked.

FIGURE 35.12
The `gmix` *mixer.*

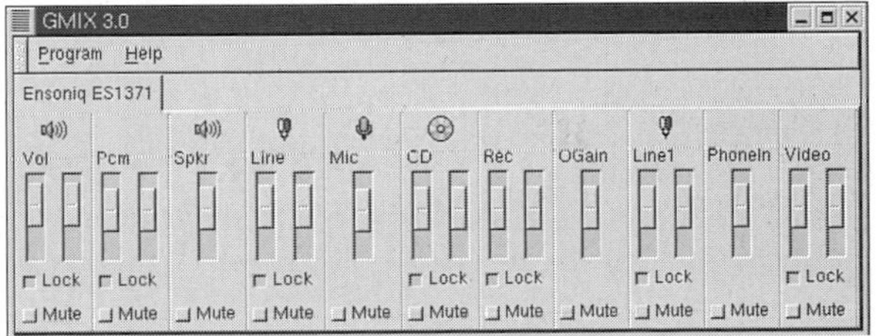

kmix

`kmix` is a KDE family mixer. It is more icon-oriented than `gmix`. `kmix` is installed as part of the Red Hat multimedia initial installation and the selection of the KDE window manager. If you have KDE and did not install the multimedia package, the installation steps are described earlier in this chapter and the files are located on the distribution disk or at `http://www.kde.org`. Figure 35.13 shows the `kmix` interface.

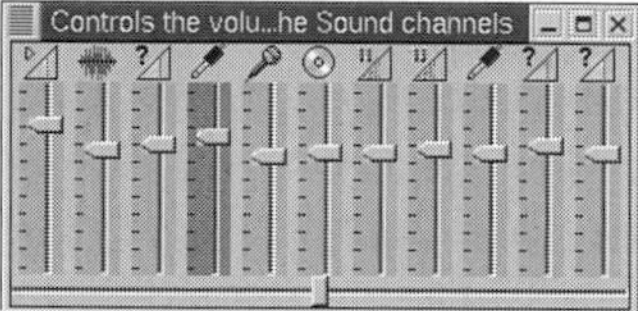

FIGURE 35.13
The `kmix` KDE mixer.

`kmix` has icons instead of labels. It also features context-sensitive help accessed by placing the mouse over a given function; there is a banner that shows additional functionality.

> **Tip**
>
> To obtain a listing of the kmix icons, right-click the mouse in the kmix panel over one of the icons, select Options, and select channels for a listing of functions.

`xmixer`

`xmixer` is an X-11 mixer package that is standard across a number of platforms and operating systems. It combines both icons and labels to identify the functions within the mixer. `xmixer` is part of the Red Hat 6.0 AnotherLevel menu and is part of the Debian menu if installed on a Debian system. It is found under AnotherLevel's Utilities and Sound Program tabs. Figure 35.14 shows the `xmixer` interface.

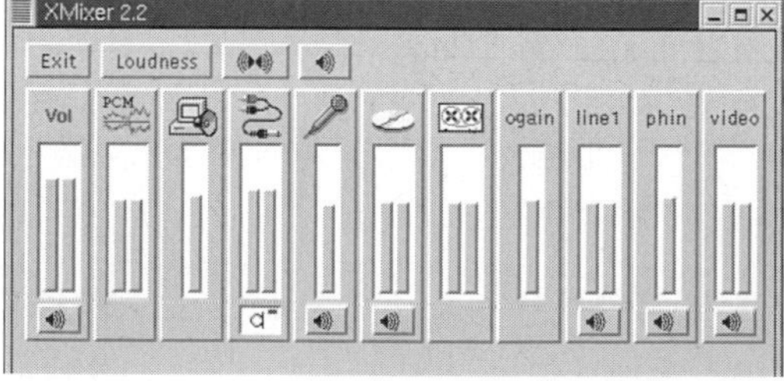

FIGURE 35.14
The `xmixer` interface.

`gtcd`

`gtcd` is a graphical representation of a CD-ROM player that controls the functionality of the audio CD-ROM. `gtcd` originally was called `tcd` and turned into `gtcd` with the addition of a GTK interface. Figure 35.15 shows the `gtcd` interface.

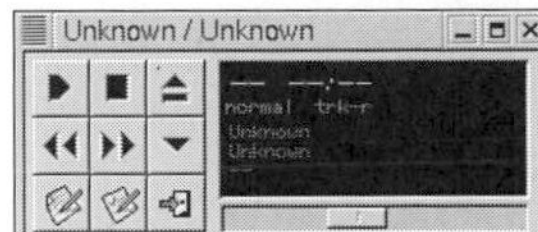

FIGURE 35.15
The gtcd *interface.*

Perhaps gtcd's and kscd's most interesting feature is the capability to connect to an Internet CD database (www.cddb.com) and pull down information such as artist, title, and tracks and to graphically display this information as the songs are played. The information can be stored locally or updated from the database.

kscd

kscd is the KDE CD-ROM player that is part of the KDE window manager. It is installed as part of the multimedia and KDE initial installs under Red Hat 6.0 or Caldera Systems. If you have KDE and did not install the multimedia package, instruction on how to install the package is located in this chapter and the files are located on the distribution disk and at http://www.kde.org. Figure 35.16 shows the kscd interface.

FIGURE 35.16
The kscd *interface.*

Interesting features include CDDB access. CDDB is a database on the Internet that has track and title information on a vast array of music. kscd can be configured to utilize an http proxy to download the CD-ROM information.

xplaycd

xplaycd is part of the standard multimedia package. The instructions are located earlier in this chapter, and the file is part of the standard Red Hat 6.0 distribution. xplaycd is a standard X-11 CD-ROM player. It is part of Afterstep package and can be found under the utilities and sound tab. The interesting thing about xplaycd is that it is utilized under a number of different platforms and not just Linux. Figure 35.17 shows the xplaycd interface.

xplaycd does not include the CDDB feature found in gtcd and kscd.

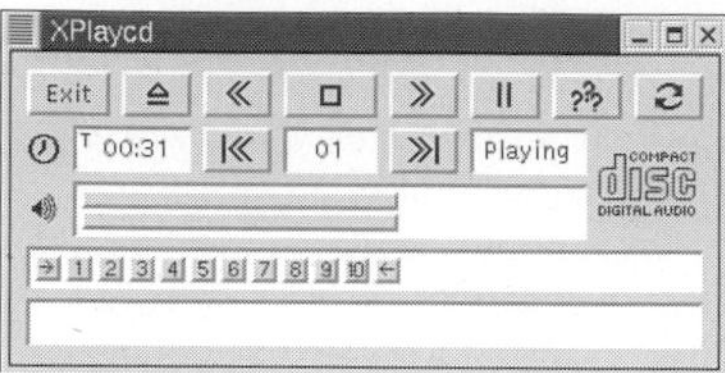

FIGURE 35.17
The `xplaycd` *player.*

Animations

One of the emerging Linux and Web features is the utilization of animation, video, and television tools. Animation tools such as `xanim` can make animated GIFs and play numerous video clips.

`xanim`

`xanim` is one of the more popular tools for viewing video clips and creating animated GIFs under Linux created by Mark Podlipec. `xanim` utilizes a command-line interface (CLI) and has spawned a number of graphical interfaces and toolsets that utilize `xanim` and add features. Figure 35.18 shows the `xanim` screenshot. It is utilizing the following command using the sample filename `xanim.gif`:

```
# xanim xanim.gif
```

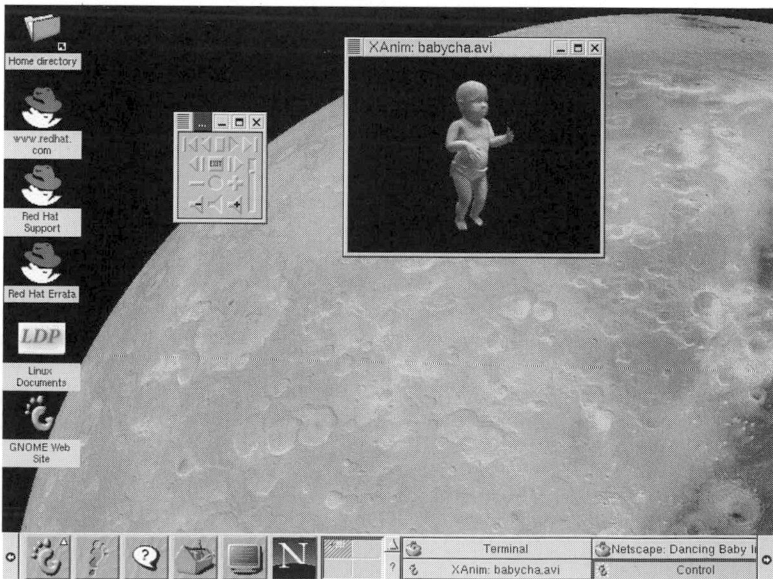

FIGURE 35.18
Ron Lussier's `babycha.avi` *file using* `xanim`.

Table 35.2 is a list of the help features invoked by the following command:

```
# xanim -h
```

Usage:

```
xanim [+V#] [ [+¦-]opts ...] animfile [ [ [+¦-opts] animfile] ... ]
```

A + turns an option on and a - turns it off.

TABLE 35.2 List of the Help Features Invoked by `# xanim -h`

Options	*Feature*
`A[aopts]`	Audio submenu.
`Addev`	AIX audio only. `dev` is audio device.
`Ae`	Enables audio.
`Ak`	Enables video frame skipping to keep in sync with audio.
`Ap#`	Plays audio from output port # (sparc only).
`Av#`	Sets audio volume to #; range `0` to `100`.
`C[copts]`	Color submenu.
`C1`	Creates `cmap` from first TrueColor frame. Maps the rest to this first `cmap` (could be slow).
`Ca`	Remaps all images to single new `cmap`. Default is `off`.
`Cd`	Uses floyd-steinberg dithering (buffered only). Default is `off`.
`CF4`	Better color mapping for TrueColor anims. Default is `off`.
`Cg`	Converts TrueColor anims to grayscale. Default is `off`.
`Cn`	Be Nice: Allocates colors from default `cmap`. Default is `on`.
`G[gopts]`	Gamma submenu.
`Ga#`	Sets animation gamma. Default `1.000000`.
`Gd#`	Sets display gamma. Default `1.000000`.
`S[sopts]`	Scaling and Sizing submenu.
`Si`	Reduces the height of `IFF` anims by half if interlaced. Default is `off`.
`Sn`	Prevents X11 window from resizing to match anim's size. Default is `off`.
`Sr`	Allows user to resize anim on-the-fly. Default is `off`.
`Ss#`	Scales size of anim by # before displaying.
`Sh#`	Scales width of anim by # before displaying.
`Sv#`	Scales height of anim by # before displaying.

continues

TABLE 35.2 Continued

Options	*Feature*
Sx#	Scales anim to have width # before displaying.
Sy#	Scales anim to have height # before displaying.
Sc	Copies display scaling factors to buffer scaling factors.
SS#	Scales size of anim by # before buffering.
SH#	Scales width of anim by # before buffering.
SV#	Scales height of anim by # before buffering.
SX#	Scales anim to have width # before buffering.
SY#	Scales anim to have height # before buffering.
SC	Copies buffer scaling factors to display scaling factors.
W[wopts]	Window submenu.
W#	X11 Window ID of window to draw into.
Wd	Don't refresh window at end of anim.
Wnx	Uses property x for communication.
Wp	Prepares anim, but don't start playing it.
Wr	Resizes X11 Window to fit anim.
Wx#	Positions anim at x coordinate #.
Wy#	Positions anim at y coordinate #.
Wc	Positions relative to center of anim.
	Normal Options
b	Uncompresses and buffers images ahead of time. Default is off.
B	Uses X11 shared memory extension if supported. Default is on.
c	Disables looping for nonlooping IFF anims. Default is off.
d#	Debugs. 0 (off) to 5 (most) for level of detail. Default is 0.
F	Enables dithering for certain video codecs only. See readme for monochrome displays. Default is on.
f	Doesn't load anims into memory, but allows reading from file as needed. Default is off.
j#	# is number of milliseconds between frames. If 0, then default depends on the animation. Default is 0.
l#	Loops anim # times before moving on. Default is 1.

Options	Feature
lp#	Ping-pongs anim # times before moving on. Default is 0.
N	No display. Useful for benchmarking.
o	Turns on certain optimizations. See readme. Default is on.
p	Uses Pixmap instead of image in X11 (buffered only). Default is off.
q	Quiet mode.
r	Allows color cycling for IFF single images.
+root	Tiles video onto root window. Default is on.
R	Allows color cycling for IFF anims. Default is off.
T#	Title option. See readme.
v	Verbose mode. Default is off.
V#	Uses visual #. # is obtained by +X option.
X	X11 Verbose mode. Display visual information.
Ze	Have XAnim exit after playing cmd line.
Zp#	Pauses at specified frame number.
Zpe	Pauses at end of animation.
	Window Commands
q	Quits.
Q	Quits.
g	Stops color cycling.
r	Restores original colors. Useful after g.
<space>	Toggles. Starts/stops animation.
,	Single step back one frame.
.	Single step forward one frame.
<	Go back to start of previous anim.
>	Go forward to start of next anim.
m	Single step back one frame staying within anim.
/	Single step forward one frame staying within anim.
-	Increases animation playback speed.
=	Decreases animation playback speed.
0	Resets animation playback speed to original values.
1	Decreases audio volume 5 percent.

continues

TABLE 35.2 Continued

Options	*Feature*
2	Decreases audio volume 1 percent.
3	Increases audio volume 1 percent.
4	Increases audio volume 5 percent.
8	Sends audio to headphones.
9	Sends audio to speakers.
s	Mutes audio.
	Mouse Buttons
`<Left>`	Single step back one frame.
`<Middle>`	Toggles. Starts/stops animation.
`<Right>`	Single step forward one frame.

RealPlayer for Linux

Would you like to sit at home and watch a live concert or an internationally broadcast radio show? Would you like to provide a method for your corporation or non-profit organization to stream live video to remote locations? One answer is the RealPlayer for Linux.

One of the key players in the streaming video technology is Real Networks, Inc. (see Figure 35.19). RealPlayer supports both RealAudio and RealVideo. RealPlayer normally comes in two varieties—the first is a free version that provides basic functionality; the second is a $29.99 version that includes additional functionality.

Tip

At the time of this writing, the only version that worked on 2.2.x kernels was alpha version of RealPlayer G2 and a patch to the RealPlayer 5.0 for UNIX (Real Networks # RAP-001014-03) done by a user at this URL: `http://www.i2k.com/~jeffd/rpopen/`. As with all alpha and user patches, your results may vary. Try the free or alpha version to see if your Internet connection and hardware can support streaming audio and video. It is possible to watch streaming video using a 28.8 modem, but you might want to upgrade your connection if you plan on viewing a significant number of broadcasts.

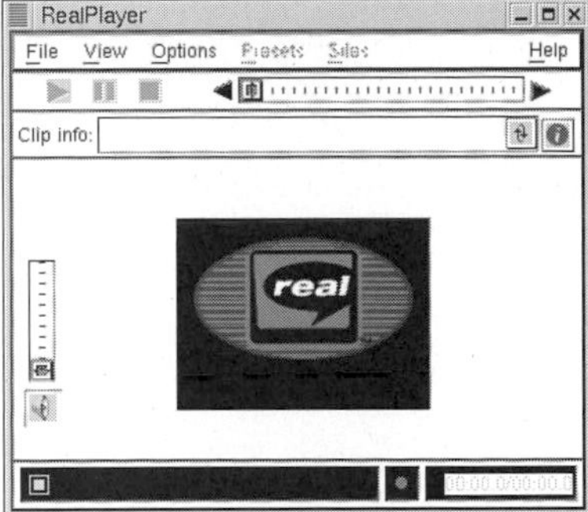

FIGURE 35.19
The RealPlayer dialog box.

Download and Configuration

`http://www.real.com` is the location for both the free and enhanced version of RealPlayer. The alpha version at `http://www.real.com/products/player/linux.html` is about 7.7MB and comes as an `rpm` or `tar` file. The typical information required to download RealPlayer includes name, email address, country, OS selection, machine class/processor family selection, language, and Internet connection speed.

Tip

The minimum suggested configuration for the alpha version of RealPlayer G2 is a Pentium 200Mhz or equivalent; 64MB memory; 65,000-color video display capability; and a 14.4KB Internet connection for audio and 28.8KB Internet connection for video.

The other configuration issue that applications like RealPlayer make you consider is the purchase of a better video card, more memory, or a higher-speed Internet connection.

The alpha version is downloaded as a `.bin` file, which is a Linux executable file. The following is an example of how to change the permissions of a file called `realplayer.bin` and execute the file. The filename will vary between alpha, beta, and general release versions of RealPlayer.

```
# chmod 744 realplayer.bin
# ./realplayer.bin
```

A dialog box appears and asks where to place the files. Unless you have a reason to override the default selection, select the default `/usr/local/RealPlayerG2`.

Once the files have been placed in the RealPlayer directory, you need to modify your path by including the following in your startup profile. An example is shown here for the `bash` shell:

```
# REALPLAYER_HOME=/usr/local/RealPlayerG2
# export REALPLAYER_HOME
```

Once you have the RealPlayer installed, you need to make the browser aware of the `.ra`, `.rv`, and `.ram` RealPlayer MIME types. The following is an example for the Netscape browser.

Bring up the Netscape browser, then choose View, Preferences, and Application Preferences tab. Use the following parameters:

Description	*RealPlayer G2*
MIMEType	**`audio/x-pn-realaudio`**
Suffixes	**`ra,rm,ram`**
Handled By	**`realplayer %s`**

Tip

The configuration of the application preferences is dependent on RealPlayer being in the user's path.

Please consult the latest RealPlayer instructions for configuration information. The instructions here were based on the alpha version and may change with later releases.

RealPlayer can be used by clicking a Web page that has a RealPlayer icon and then executing the command in an X Window terminal, clicking an icon representation, or using the application menus:

```
# realplayer
```

RealPlayer has the following parametersthat may need to be modified, depending on the speed of your connection to the Internet or things like firewall proxies:

- Performance (see Figure 35.20)
- Transport (see Figure 35.21)
- Proxy (see Figure 35.22)
- Connection (see Figure 35.23)

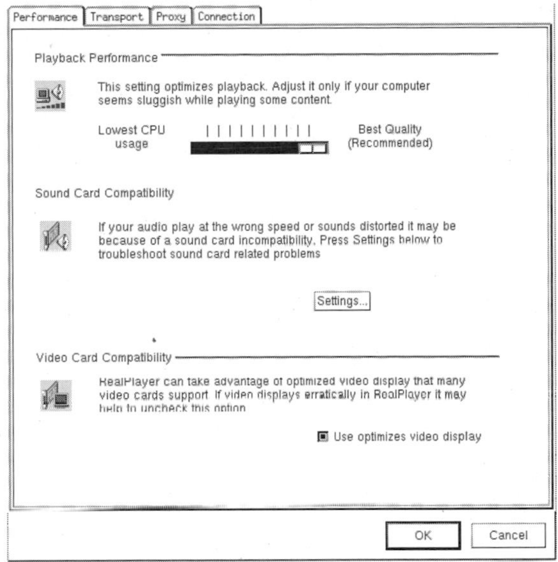

FIGURE 35.20
The Performance dialog box.

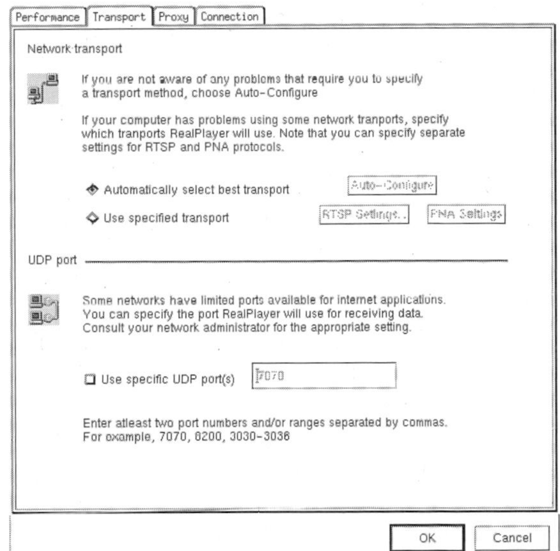

FIGURE 35.21
The Transport dialog box.

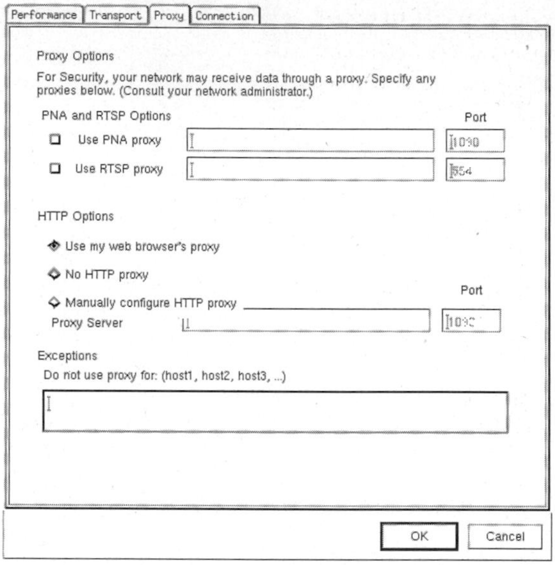

FIGURE 35.22
The Proxy dialog box.

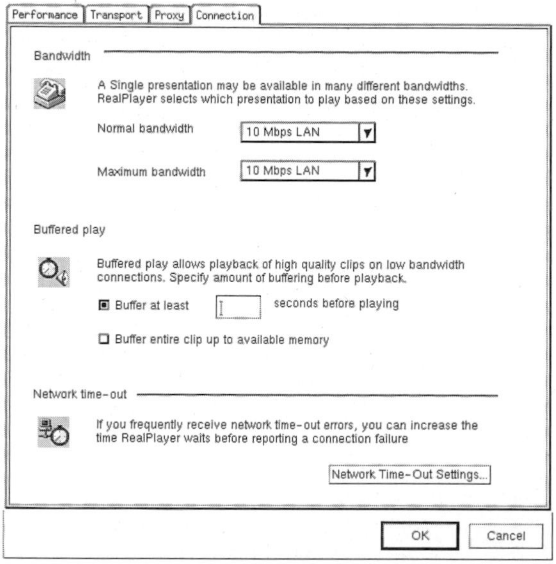

FIGURE 35.23
The Connection dialog box.

RealPlayer requires an URL with a Real Server in order to stream audio or video. The best place to start is somewhere such as `http://www.realguide.real.com`. The size of the Internet connection will determine the clarity of the audio stream. Many popular radio stations are not only offering normal over-the-air broadcasts, but have streaming audio sites. The advantage is that the RealAudio sites are not dependent on how close one is to the radio station, and it is possible to hear a radio broadcast across the world. Some major college basketball teams stream the audio so that fans around the country or world can catch the game without having to buy a ticket.

Since the playing of audio and video is dependent on the Internet connection, the download stream may have to *buffer*, which means that the video or audio may have to pause while downloading. You should expect this if you are utilizing a modem or an ISDN connection. The solution is to find a faster Internet connection.

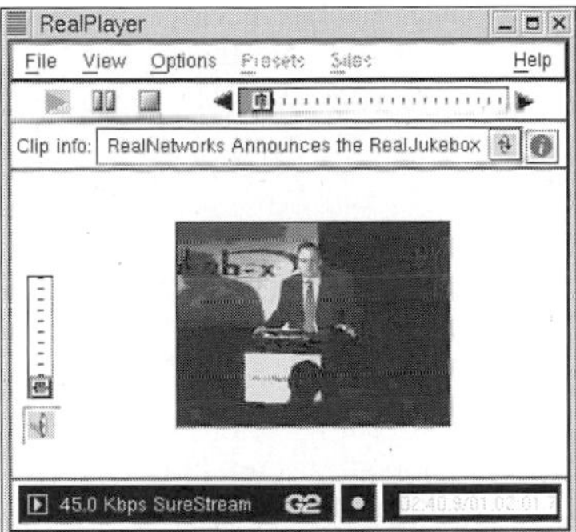

FIGURE 35.24
RealPlayer in action.

The Real networks site has many interesting videos, including one that describes its recent product introduction Real Jukebox (see Figure 35.24), a feature that allows you to track, mix, and download audio using the jukebox analogy. At the time of this publication, it was not ported to Linux.

The minimum system requirements are

- Windows 95 w/Service pack 1 on Windows 98 or Windows NT 4.0 with Service Pack 4
- Intel® Pentium® 200MHz MMX, Cyrix® 6x86MX PR233, or AMD® K5 PR-200
- 32MB of RAM
- 200MB of free hard-disk space
- Full duplex sound card and speakers
- 16-bit color video card
- Internet connection and Web browser (IE3 or later)
- CD-ROM drive

Note

It is also possible to utilize a medium-sized PC to produce streaming audio and a high-end PC to produce streaming video on Linux. The RealPlayer site (`http://www.real.com`) has additional information on configuration and pricing information for servers.

Summary

Linux is a strong platform for entertainment and for cutting-edge features such as streaming video and audio. The advantage that Linux brings to the table is that a 486 with a 2x CD-ROM and an old 16-bit soundcard can be turned into a CD-ROM player and mixer. This allows older hardware to be given a second life and allows you to learn about multimedia installations at the same time.

Pick an initial window manager such as GNOME, KDE, AnotherLevel, or any other favorite window manager and match the packages such as `gmix` and `gtcd` for GNOME or `kmix` and `kscd` for KDE. The point is to pick one manager and its tools, get it running, and then experiment with other managers and tools.

Linux also covers the high end and can stream video just as well as other platforms and operating systems. Linux has an attractive total cost of ownership for streaming video or audio system.

MP3 is a hot format, but the final disposition is not clear at this time. The issues of compensation for the artist and recording companies were not settled at publication time. MP3 does, however, represent a unique opportunity for the average home user to download digital audio, and either play it on his machine or buy a $200 to $300 device and record the music on a portable device.

It is possible to view TV and video capture utilizing the TV tuner card and something like `video4linux`. There are also a number of applications that provide the graphical representation of a TV tuner and allow the viewer to channel surf.

The one area that needs work under Linux is DVD technology. Currently there are drives to utilize DVDs that read ISO 9660 format. The problem is that some DVD implementations utilize proprietary MPEG devices and interfaces. There are currently efforts to develop a DVD kit for Linux, but detailed information is not available at this time. DVD drives and writers are also expensive for home users. DVD prices should follow the pricing curve similar to the CD-ROM's.

CHAPTER 36

Productivity Clients and Suites for Linux

In This Chapter

Computers are supposed to help us be more productive and make things easier. One way the computer can help is by doing our office and administrative work. The computer doesn't forget to remind us that we have an appointment. The computer makes it really easy to reprint a document that your bone-head cube-mate just spilled coffee on.

This chapter covers Linux-based software that can help you increase your productivity, make your work look snazzy, create databases, and help you do all this as quickly as possible.

A Note about Software Packaging

As discussed earlier, many programs come in a package format. This packaging allows you to install a binary version of the software and not worry with many of the details of compiling and linking a program. Typically, you may find these programs in the RPM format. RPM is the Red Hat Package Manager, a format made popular by Red Hat Software and included with its distribution of Linux. Several other distributions have begun to use this system. You might also find `.deb` packages if you happen to be using the Debian distribution.

Tip

Check out `http://www.rpm.org` or *Maximum RPM* (ISBN 0-672-31105-4) for further details on the Red Hat Package Manager.

In other cases, such as with WordPerfect 8, the software may provide its own installation program and provide binary software only in a proprietary format.

Advantages of Packages

Using packaged software can remove the difficulties of finding, downloading, and compiling software. Often, example configuration files and documentation are included in the package, making installation a breeze. The package manager program can unpack the software, place the necessary files in the proper location, and keep a record of its transactions. RPM and `dpkg` actually keep track of all of your software (that it installs) and help you avoid deleting programs that may be needed by other programs (*dependencies*).

Also, for the hard-core hacker, the source code to many Open Source software programs is available in the RPM or `deb` format. This option allows you to get all the pieces that you need, review the source code, and still have full control of compiling and linking the program. What a deal!

Disadvantages of Packages

One of the main disadvantages of using packaged binary software is security. Not all binaries are riddled with Trojan horse programs or will leave gaping security holes in your system, but when you download and install a packaged binary program, there is a level of trust that must exist between you and the software packager.

Assume that Corel, distributor of WordPerfect, decides to distribute its software or updates in a packaged format. You can be fairly certain that they have the quality control procedures in place to prevent their software from being maliciously insecure.

However, suppose you decide to download a program (a packaged binary) from an obscure Web site. Without actually looking at the code to verify the contents, you place your system at risk for Trojan-horse programs or other security holes, simply because you have no idea what is inside the program you just installed!

Be aware of who created and packaged the software and keep up-to-date on system security patches and news. Just being careful can save you lots of grief and lost work, but don't forget to do backups!

Now that you are sufficiently aware (don't be frightened), move on to the good stuff.

Office Suites

Having grown up using BASIC, clunky MS-DOS, and later moving into Microsoft Windows before becoming a Linux guy, I am inclined to be a fan of a well-written and useful graphical user interface (GUI) when I can find one for office and productivity applications.

This chapter looks at "office" applications that have text and GUI interfaces (or both). For your normal office worker, being able to use a word processor and spreadsheet takes care of much of the day. Spreadsheets must be created to calculate profits or keep track of items. Word processors must be used to create letters and other correspondence and write reports for the boss.

The next section looks at two office suites: Applixware and Star Office.

Applixware

Applix, Inc., makes a very capable office suite that retails for between $80 and $100. Applixware was one of the first graphical "office" programs for UNIX platforms and the Linux versions show that depth of experience.

The office suite includes a WYSIWYG word processor (Words), a spreadsheet program (Spreadsheets), a presentation manager (Presents), a data interface (Data) for accessing ODBC-compliant databases, a very basic graphics editor (Graphics), and a fairly nice electronic mail client. Newer versions include a WYSIWYG HTML Author and the Applix Builder. The Builder is a rapid-application development environment that allows the user to create her own applications. Languages in addition to English, such as French and German, are supported.

Applixware is available for numerous platforms, including Linux (of course), Solaris, and many other flavors of UNIX.

I began using Applixware for Linux at version 4.3. This version included filters for Microsoft Office 95 documents. The latest version, 4.4.1, boasts filters that will import and export Office 97 documents, and you can expect to see filters for Microsoft Office 2000 documents in upcoming versions. This interoperability is important in an office where the Microsoft Office suite may be a de facto standard.

Installation

The installation is fairly straightforward. I simply mounted the CD and logged in as `root` in an X-Terminal window. I typed this:

```
# ./setup
```

If you will be installing Applixware in a place that requires `root` access, you will probably want to briefly log in to X as `root`. Alternatively, you may use `xhost +localhost`, but this is not recommended.

If you happen to be upgrading from version 4.37, this is the command:

```
# ./install-applix
```

As with most of my other applications, I chose to have Applix install into the `/opt` directory. We'll call this the install-dir. Applixware also creates a number of its own directories, as in Figure 36.1.

When you begin using Applixware, it creates a directory named `axhome` in your home directory (see Figure 36.2). Configurations specific to the user are stored here in a number of files. Although configuration files may be stored here as text files, it is highly advisable to use the graphical configuration screens contained in Applix to make changes, as the files are often not clearly understandable or well-documented.

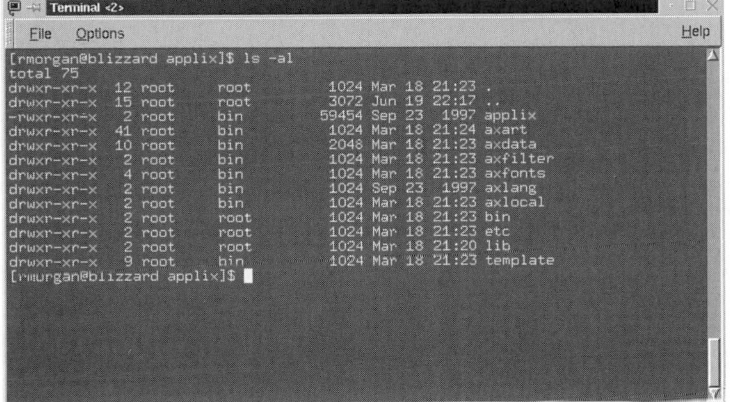

FIGURE 36.1
The Applix directory after installation.

```
[rmorgan@blizzard axhome]$ pwd
/home/rmorgan/axhome
[rmorgan@blizzard axhome]$ ls -al
total 36
drwxrwxr-x   5 rmorgan  rmorgan      1024 Jun 21 23:04 .
drwx------  41 rmorgan  rmorgan      5120 Jun 21 23:04 ..
drwxrwx---   4 rmorgan  rmorgan      1024 Mar 29 23:19 axMail
-rw-rw-r--   1 rmorgan  rmorgan      1024 Mar 18 21:29 ax_eng.dct
-rw-rw-r--   1 rmorgan  rmorgan      1030 Jun 13 18:51 ax_prof4
-rw-r--r--   1 rmorgan  rmorgan     22913 Mar 29 23:34 ax_wp4
drwxr-xr-x   2 rmorgan  rmorgan      1024 Jun 13 18:51 backup
drwxrwx---   2 rmorgan  rmorgan      1024 Mar 29 23:22 macros
[rmorgan@blizzard axhome]$
```

FIGURE 36.2
User-specific Applix files.

To make accessing Applixware simple, I added a desktop icon in my KDE window manager. Applixware allows you to launch applications from a central dialog box or individually via command-line options. To launch the Applixware dialog box, simply execute this code:

```
install-dir/applix
```

To launch a specific Applixware tool, such as `Spreadsheets`, use this:

```
install-dir/applix -ss
```

The program documentation provides the options for launching each program.

Besides using the command-line options, Applixware allows you to specify a filename that causes the proper Applixware tool to be opened. You'd use the following to open a Words document:

```
install-dir/applix report34.aw
```

These features make creating desktop shortcuts to specific tools or documents a simple task under most window managers.

Configuration

Out-of-the-box Applixware possesses a basic and sensible configuration. Changes to configurations can be made in two places. Suite wide changes are made by choosing the applicable area from a central menu box called Applixware Preferences.

From the Applix menu box, choose * then Applixware Preferences.

The box shown in Figure 36.3 is displayed.

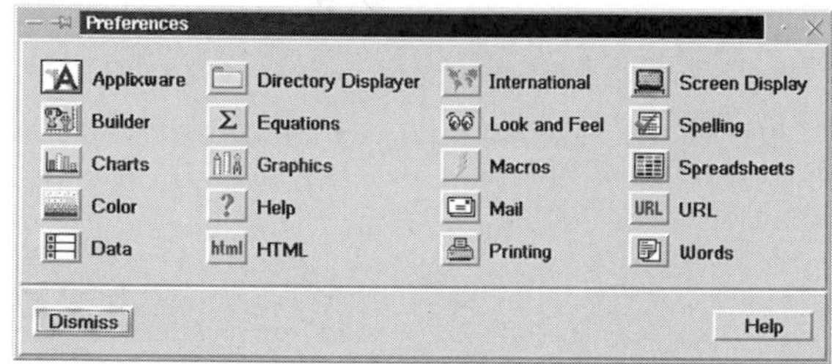

FIGURE 36.3
The Applixware Preferences menu.

As you can see, you may make changes to configurations for the entire suite or to configurations for specific applications such as Words or Spreadsheets. These application-specific configurations are also accessible inside the application.

One of the first things I changed was the option to create backup copies of documents as I work with them. I prefer to have automatic backup copies of documents made as I work on them; this removes the need for me to manually save things as I go. In the event of a power outage, the most work I might lose would be about three minutes' worth. Figure 36.4 shows the preferences for Applixware Words.

The second thing I changed were the keystrokes used for cut, copy, and paste—they now match the Control+C, Control+X, and Control+V used by Microsoft Word. I use Microsoft Word and Excel at work and have found that these keystrokes are burned into my brain from years of use. Rather than fight with my word processor every day, I chose to change the Applixware key mappings.

This is rather easy to do: From the Words menu bar, choose *, then Customize Menu Bar.

Choose the corresponding menu item and change the Accelerator Key. I changed the Accelerator Key for cut from F3 to Ctrl+X, which is represented by ^X.

FIGURE 36.4
Words preferences.

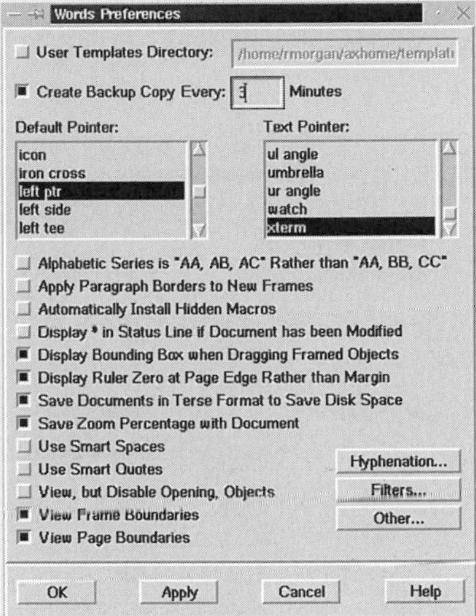

Tip

Applixware has a few quirks. For example, seemingly normal keystrokes like End and Home did not work quite as I expected. A substantial discussion of this topic occurred on the Applixware mailing lists, where I also found lots of other tips. Check the Applix Web site at `http://www.applix.com` for details on support mailing lists.

Interoperability

One of the nicer Applixware features is its capability to import and export files in the formats of other popular programs, such as WordPerfect and Microsoft Excel. This allows the user to exchange files with others, while maintaining the use of his versatile and stable Linux workstation.

Applixware also offers a few international options, as well as allowing you to choose from up to 16 foreign language dictionaries at installation. You may even change the language used during your work.

Using Applixware

The Applixware interface is straightforward and closely resembles most of the mass-market office suites available. Using Applixware is as simple as opening the proper application by clicking the icon and typing. Cursor movement is accomplished with the

Enter key and with the arrow keys. Text may be highlighted with the mouse or a combination of Shift+arrow keys. The toolbar symbols are clear and easily understandable. Figure 36.5 shows the Words toolbar and a sample document.

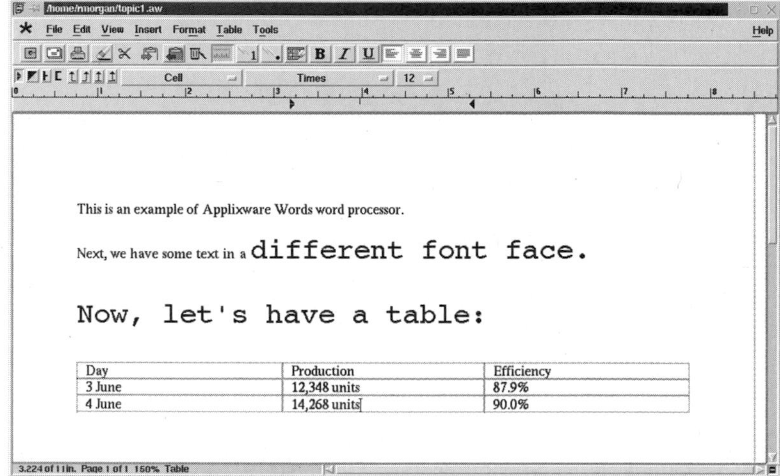

FIGURE 36.5
The Words user interface.

Star Office

Star Office is very full-featured suite of office applications. It can be described as "Microsoft Office-like" in that it is a huge program that provides many of the same features and functionalities as the popular office suite. Like that old television commercial for spaghetti sauce said, "It's in there!" Star Office has many features:

- Word processor
- Spreadsheet program
- HTML editor (WYSIWYG)
- Graphics editor
- Presentation editor
- Electronic mail capabilities
- Calendar
- To-Do List Manager
- Palm Pilot Hot-Sync interface
- Web browser

Where Can I Get Star Office?

Star Office can be had from a number of sources. It is available for free for noncommercial use via download from the Star Division Web site at `http://www.stardivision.com`. Be aware that version 5.1 is a download of over 70MB, which might be tough to get on a dial-up line from home. You can also purchase Star Office on CD-ROM from the same Web site.

Occasionally, programs such as Star Office or Applixware are bundled with a Linux distribution. Star Office 5.1 Personal Edition can be found bundled in this manner. Star Office is available only in a binary format because it is not Open Source software.

Installing and Configuring Star Office

You should follow the instructions provided with your copy of Star Office during the installation of the program files. The instructions or pointers, as with most other Linux programs, are contained in a file called `readme`.

Star Office 5.1 then provides an installation Auto Pilot (similar to a wizard), which guides you through the process of installing the program for a user workstation. The result is the creation of an `Office51` subdirectory in the user's home directory. This directory and its subdirectories contain literally hundreds of files. Here you will find configuration files, fonts, scripts, filters, and templates.

As with Applixware, there is little or no need for editing text configuration files manually. All of the necessary configuring may be done inside of Star Office using the graphical interface (Tools, Options). Choosing Tools, Configure option allows you to customize your working environment by allowing changes to toolbars, keyboard mappings, and other functionality. The different types of customization are chosen by clicking the representative tab.

Using Star Office

One of the design goals in creating the Star Office was to let the user accomplish everything in one program—or so it appears. The Star Office environment creates its own desktop complete with a Start button and taskbar.

To make launching Star Office easier, I created a desktop (my desktop, KDE) icon to launch Star Office. The icon contained the following command-line entry:

```
/opt/Office51/bin/soffice
```

This launches Star Office and the desktop. The desktop provides links to the individual applications and sets up the menu bar controls for the entire suite of programs. Figure 36.6 shows the Star Office desktop.

FIGURE 36.6
Star Office desktop.

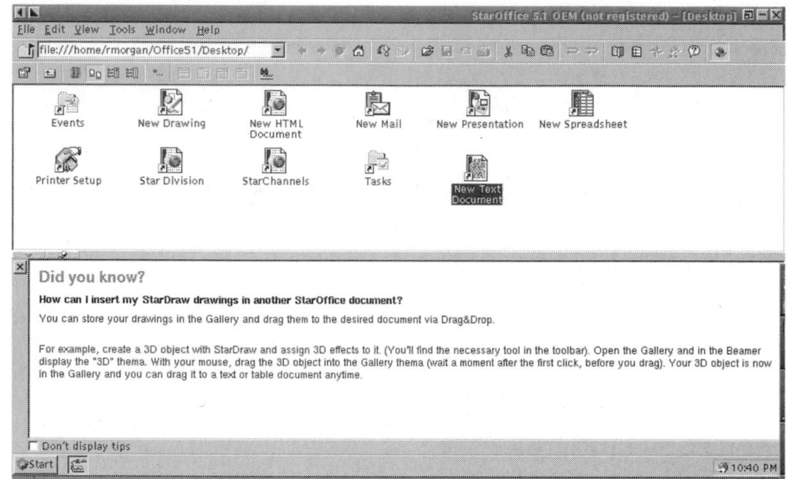

Cursor movement and functions such as cut and paste use fairly standard keystrokes. Ctrl+C performs a copy of a selection, while Ctrl+V performs a paste of the Clipboard contents. All of these functions are reminiscent of Microsoft Word, Excel, and the like, so users familiar with these products should have little problem adjusting to Star Office.

Switching Between Applications

As mentioned, Star Office creates its own desktop environment and provides a taskbar. The taskbar icon lets the user move easily among the open documents; alternatively, you may use Ctrl+Tab to cycle through the open documents.

To create a new document, choose File, New, Document-Type. You can also click the desktop icon (a desk lamp) available on the taskbar to move back to your desktop, which has links to the individual applications.

Importing and Exporting Microsoft Documents

Star Office provides an Auto Pilot that assists you with importing Microsoft Office documents. You may import Word, Excel or PowerPoint files.

Choose File, Auto Pilot, Microsoft Import.

There is not a function labeled Export. When working with a document, you have the choice of saving it in several formats, including the native Star Office format, plain text, and so on. Star Office 5.1 also allows you to save documents in Microsoft Office 95/97 formats.

Choose File, Save As to save your document in a format other than the native Star Office Format.

Use the File Type drop-down box to specify the format.

Text and Document Processing

The tools reviewed are probably a bit too much to be used to edit text files throughout the system. Starting an entire office suite to change an item in a configuration file is not very efficient, especially if you are in a console environment. With that said, we will now review a few text and document tools that can help you when you are not creating office documents.

Emacs

`Emacs` is the Swiss-Army knife of text editors. It has numerous add-on modules that allow the intrepid user to read email and Usenet news, code and check syntax in several programming languages, and even edit some plain old text file. `vi` is another UNIX editor. The `Emacs` versus `vi` war rages on among users who espouse their choice of editors with almost religious conviction.

`Emacs` was written in the mid-1980s by Richard Stallman, who also founded the Free Software Foundation and wrote much of the GNU software.

`Emacs` is somewhat more complex than `vi`, which can be found on most machines by default. However, `Emacs` provides extensive capabilities and multiple modes. Many of the functions are written in a special version of `Emacs` LISP.

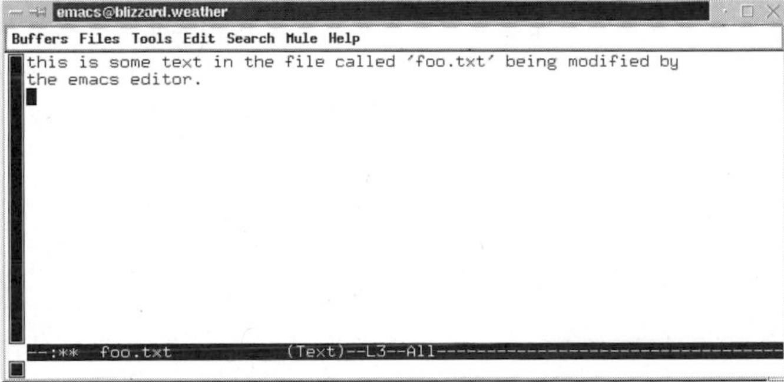

FIGURE 36.7
The `Emacs` *editor.*

You can obtain directions to downloading `Emacs` and documentation for the editor at `http://www.emacs.org/`.

Even the Web site for `Emacs` conveys its no-nonsense character (see Figure 36.8).

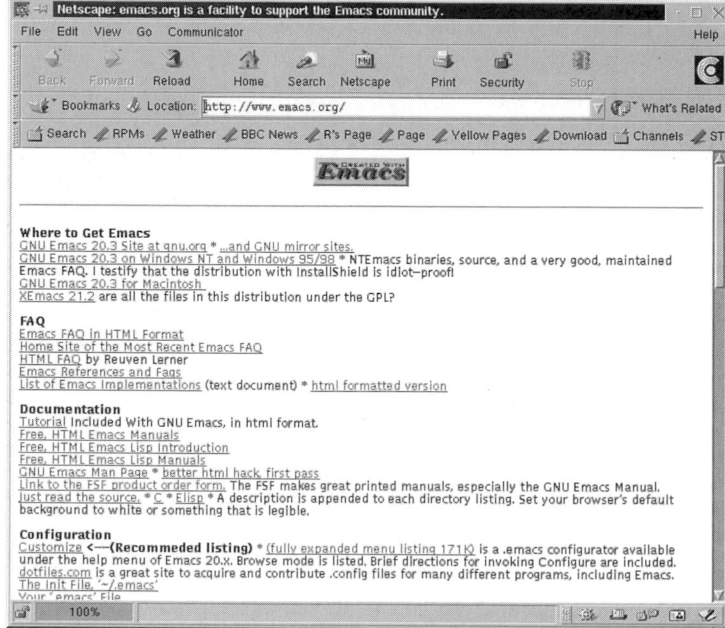

FIGURE 36.8
The Emacs Web site.

Installing `Emacs`

`Emacs` is included as part of the Red Hat Linux distribution, and you may choose to install `Emacs` as part of your system installation. Red Hat also ships `Emacs` as an RPM package for easy installation as well as providing the ever-popular source code (Open Source!) for you to compile. As with most other Linux software, the choice and freedom is yours.

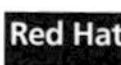

Installing `Emacs` (binary version) via RPM is as simple as this:

1. Become the `superuser` (`root`).
2. Mount the CD-ROM.
3. Change to the proper CD-ROM directory. Here is an example: `cd mount-point/RedHat/RPMS/`.
4. Use RPM to install the pieces you need:

```
rpm -ivh package-name
```

Refer to the RPM documentation for a full explanation of its usage.

To install on Debian, you need to first choose which version you prefer. Then you can install with a command such as this:

```
apt-get install emacs20
```

Installing `Emacs` by compiling from source is a bit more involved. You need to get the source code files from your distribution CD-ROM or download them from the Internet. Downloading from the Internet ensures you have the latest version of the source code.

Compiling a program allows you the fullest control possible over where files are placed and what compiler options are chosen. Compiling a program from source code requires a basic understanding of configuration files and use of a C language compiler. None of this is terribly hard to get started with, but it can become quite involved quickly, especially if something goes awry.

Although these steps may vary, always follow the instructions enclosed with the source code. It is a good idea to generally start by reviewing a file called `readme`.

These are the general steps you will follow:

1. Obtain copies of the source files.
2. Unpack them (using the `tar` and/or `gzip` commands).
3. Review the enclosed documentation for instructions.
4. "Make" and install the source files following the instructions contained in the `readme` or `install` files included with the source code package.

Using `Emacs`

One way or another, you now have `Emacs` installed. Fire it up:

```
$ emacs file-name
```

`file-name` can be a new file that you are creating or an existing file that you want to modify.

Keystrokes

The keystrokes required to perform many functions can appear incomprehensible at first glance. For example, the keystrokes for opening a new file once you are using `Emacs` are C+X C+F. This sequence indicates that you should press Ctrl+X and then Ctrl+F.

Before striking out into `Emacs` territory, take a few minutes to run through the `Emacs` tutorial included in the `Emacs` Help area. This handy tutorial gives you an introduction to different `Emacs` modes and demystifies cursor control and command key sequences. `Emacs` is complex, but that is mostly due to its depth of flexibility.

Most of the functions can be accessed using the toolbar, which also displays the necessary keystrokes. As you use `Emacs`, you will begin to learn and use the keystrokes to speed your work.

Be aware, the Meta key is usually Alt. The keystroke M+% corresponds to Alt+% (Shift+5). A keystroke like C+W indicates you should hold down the Ctrl key and press W at the same time.

Some Helpful `Emacs` and Keystrokes

Cut	C+w	Ctrl + W
Paste	C+y	Ctrl + Y
Undo	C+_	Ctrl + underscore
Search (use regular expressions)	M+C+s	Meta + Control + S
Search (incremental as you type)	C+S	Ctrl + S
Replace	M+%	Meta + %
Previous Line (or up arrow key)	C+P	Control + P
Next Line (or Down arrow key)	C+N	Ctrl + N

As you make changes to your `Emacs` environment, the customizations are stored in a file called `.emacs` in your home directory.

Tip

Though I might be flamed by the `Emacs` zealots for committing this act, I suggest also trying out a couple of other text editors such as `pico` or `jed` as a beginner.

If you are comfortable with these or other text editors, by all means try `Emacs`. Its numerous features and options will spoil you!

kedit and gEdit

Two of today's popular window managers, KDE and Gnome, each offer their own text editor as part of the deal. These two programs are covered in relatively light detail.

kedit

As a regular KDE user, I use `kedit` regularly. The program is included as part of the KDE package, thus, it requires no compilation or installation time. I find that `kedit` provides simplicity in a fast, lightweight editor that performs many necessary functions such as cut and paste, spell checking, and a limited integration with email. `kedit` is also customizable. I prefer a dark green background with white text (see Figure 36.9) and `kedit` allows me to do this.

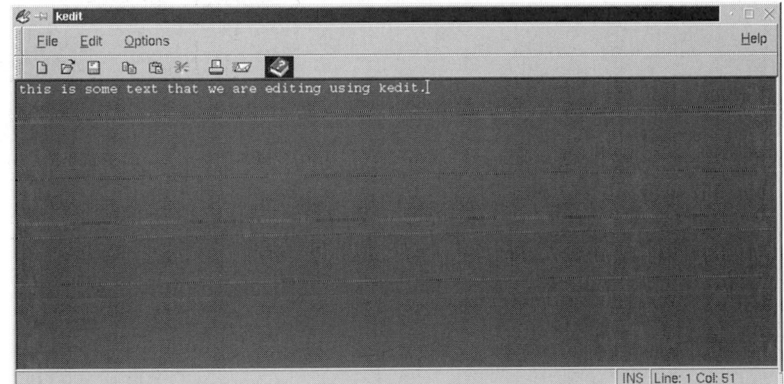

FIGURE 36.9
Editing text in `kedit`.

Tailoring kedit

`kedit` has a pleasantly limited number of configuration options that may be changed directly within the program without editing text files by hand. Figure 36.10 shows the dropdown menu options for customizing `kedit`. Font colors and sizes may be changed, and you have a measure of control over how the spellchecker will operate. Other than that, `kedit` gets out of your way and lets you type.

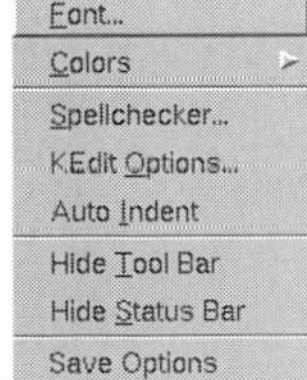

FIGURE 36.10
`kedit` *options.*

Using kedit

`kedit` provides the normal highlighting and cut/copy/paste functionality that many have come to associate with GUI environments. Using the mouse, or a combination of Shift+arrow keys, you may highlight sections of text. After the text is highlighted, you may use Ctrl+C to copy, Ctrl+X to cut, and Ctrl+V to paste text. This familiarity seems to be an almost purposeful attempt to ease the transition of Windows users to KDE and Linux.

Other functions such as save (Ctrl+S) and open file (Ctrl+O) follow this structure. The `kedit` toolbar also possesses the familiar icons for frequently used functions such as New File, Save File, Open File, Print, Copy, Cut, Paste, Help, and email.

The `kedit` email functionality is rather limited. When you choose the Email button, you are prompted for the recipient's address and a subject for the email (see Figure 36.11). The text is inserted into an email and sent using your system's `mail` command, by default. This `mail` command can be changed in Options, `kedit` Options, Mail Command. No other email functionality (such as an address book) is available at this time.

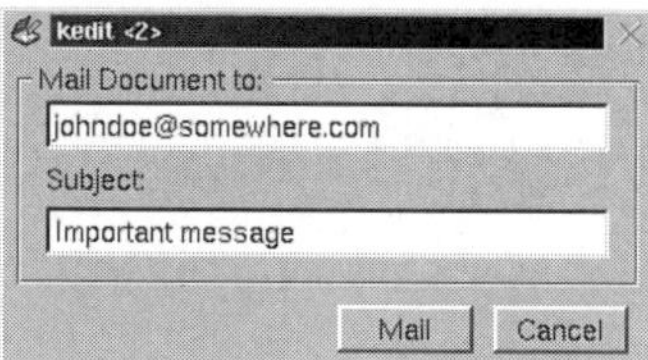

FIGURE 36.11
`kedit`*'s email function.*

Help!

We all need an occasional bump in the right direction, but computer Help facilities historically leave us unsatisfied. The KDE team seems to have made a great effort to provide thorough help files, all formatted in a logical manner, for most of the KDE tools and applications. An example of the `kedit` help is shown in Figure 36.12.

Really, the only downside of using `kedit` is getting attached to it and then moving on to another environment where it is unavailable. I have found it to be a quick and efficient tool when working in KDE. I could use an X-terminal and another text editor such as `vi` or `Emacs`, but simply clicking the `kedit` icon on my desktop and typing away seems to do just fine for me.

The KDE can be found on the Internet at `http://www.kde.org`.

gEdit

According to Help, About, "gEdit is a small and lightweight text editor for GNOME/Gtk+". That doesn't quite say it all though: `gEdit` provides a number of additional functions beyond basic text editing that really add to its usefulness. You'll take a look at those in just a bit.

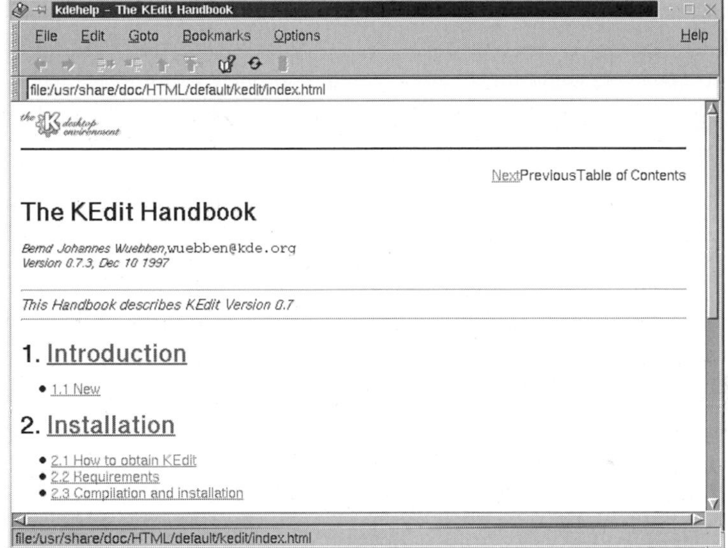

FIGURE 36.12
Getting help in `kedit`.

Getting and Installing `gEdit`

There are several ways to get `gEdit`. It may be included with the Gnome (GNU Network Object Model Environment) desktop environment, which provides a lot of the neat functions such as drag and drop. `gEdit` can be also downloaded as a packaged binary from `http://www.gnome.org` and installed. For the hacker in all of us, the source code is available; you can then compile and customize the program yourself.

Configuring `gEdit`

Freshly installed, `gEdit` needs no tweaking to be useful as a text editor. The default settings are sensible. If you need to change things, choose Settings, Preferences. (See Figure 36.13.)

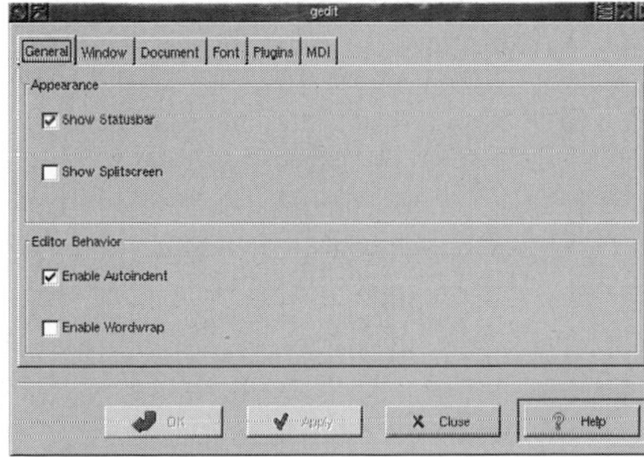

FIGURE 36.13
`gEdit` *preferences.*

Figure 36.13 shows a screenshot of the configuration window. The tabs at the top direct you to configurations for general operation, print command, default font, and plug-in controls. The plug-in controls allow you to add plug-ins to `gEdit`, which extends it capabilities while keeping the core of the program small and fast. You'll take a look at plug-ins in just a bit.

The font controls are one of the most useful interfaces. Handling fonts in Linux can be a bit scary, especially with font names like -adobe-courier-medium-r-normal-*-*-140-*-*-m-*-iso8859-1.

Gnome makes it easy by decoding that long string into a nice interface where you can choose a font by font name (Courier) and then make further selections for font style (bold, italic), and finally a size (10-, 12-, 14-point). This makes things a bit easier on the user who is unfamiliar with decoding long strings of font specifications. See Figure 36.14.

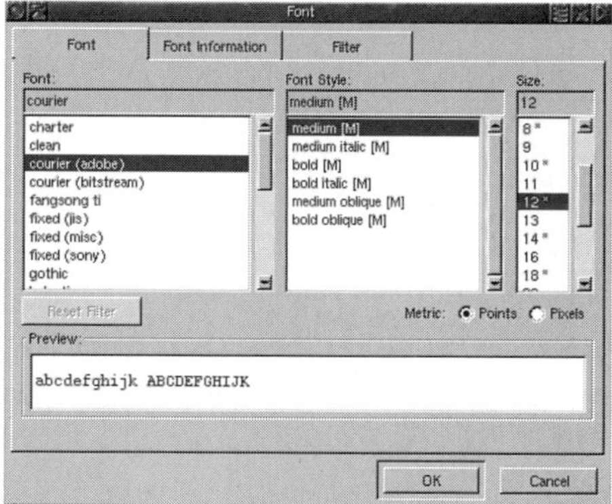

FIGURE 36.14
Handling fonts in `gEdit`.

Using `gEdit`

As with `kedit`, using `gEdit` is very straightforward. The key bindings follow those of `kedit` (Ctrl+C to copy, Ctrl+V to paste, and so on) and cursor movement works with the arrow keys. Highlighting areas of text with the mouse is supported, as is highlighting using Shift+an arrow key.

Familiar toolbar icons (Figure 36.15) provide expected functionality with a mouse click needed for opening, saving, or printing a document. The toolbar icons also provide *ToolTips*, which give a name or short description of the icon's functionality. For example, hold the pointer over the Save icon. A small text box pops up that reads "Save the current file."

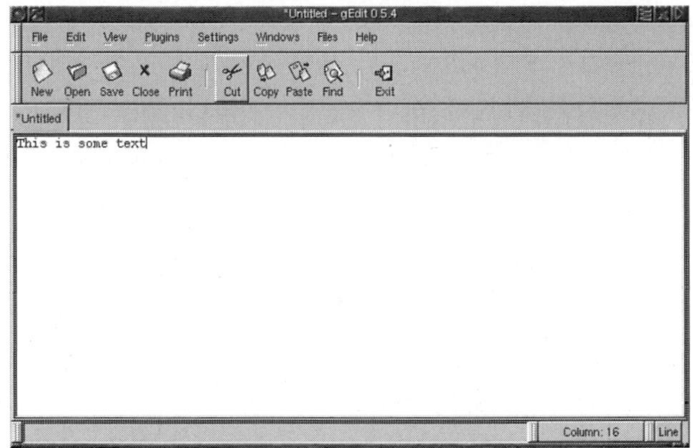

FIGURE 36.15
`gEdit` *toolbar and work area.*

One handy feature of `gEdit` is having multiple documents open at once and moving between them using a tab mechanism. The tabs appear around the edge of the interface and represent open documents. The tabs may be clicked to change your view to a new file and edit it. Settings, Document tabs control the physical location of the tabs in the editor. Cut and paste is supported between documents, thus allowing you to transfer text between files easily. Cursor position is displayed at the bottom-right of the editor screen in the taskbar.

Plug-Ins

Much of `gEdit`'s power lies in its use of different plug-in modules, which provide options for customization and extra functionality. The capability to load exactly the plug-ins you need is rather refreshing in today's world of bloated programs with an excess of features.

When installed with GNOME from a Red Hat 6.0 installation, `gEdit` has several plug-in modules already installed. You can add or remove plug-ins with Settings, Preferences, Plugins.

To use a plug-in, choose Plugins, Plugin Name.

Plug-In Examples

A number of handy plug-ins exist. The View in Browser plug-in allows you to edit a file (perhaps in HTML) and view that same file in a Web browser. Thus, writing HTML pages in `gEdit` allows you to quickly open a browser and view the results of your edits (Plugins, View in Web Browser).

Like `kedit`, the capability to send document text as an email is available (Plugins, Email). Choosing the Email plug-in provides you with a dialog box for specifying the email subject line and the recipient's email address. One plug-in (Plugins, Reverse) even provides the functionality to reverse the text of an entire document!

`Kilroy was here` becomes `ereh saw yorliK`.

If you are a programmer editing code in `gEdit`, you may need the plug-ins that are available to convert numbers (Decimal to Hex, Hex to Decimal, and Decimal to Octal) and to perform a diff on two files to show differences. *Diff* is a command-line Linux/Unix utility that compares the contents of two files and shows the differences in the two files.

Check the GNOME home page for new `gEdit` versions and plug-ins (GNU Network Object Model Environment at `http://www.gnome.org0`.

Lyx

Lyx is a publishingenvironment that provides a graphical interface for user input and a facility for feeding a user-created document to LaTeX for typesetting. Lyx is a rather different way of doing things but does create quite nice documents.

Lyx should be called a document processor rather than a word processor. It allows you to concentrate on the structure of your document rather than worrying with the niggling details of appearance. The appearance is defined by a number of rulesets. *Rulesets* already exist for most popular writing formats, such a scientific papers, letters, conference proceedings, and technical journals.

Obtaining Lyx

As with other programs, Lyx can be obtained on the Internet. See `http://www.lyx.org` for the latest release. Lyx is Open Source software, you may thus download and build from source code for the installation. It is rumored that a packaged version (RPM format) of Lyx exists, but it is not officially supported by the Lyx team.

Debian does include a packaged version that you can install. The command to do so follows:

```
apt-get install lyx
```

You should be aware that in order to use Lyx, you need to have LaTeX installed on your computer. Lyx passes its contents to LaTeX for typesetting. LaTeX can be found bundled with your Linux distribution.

Using Lyx

Lyx has a number of basic features that you come to expect in using GUI software. There is a toolbar that controls much of the functionality. Functions such as cut, paste, undo/redo, and spellchecking are all included.

Rules

You can spend a lot of time formatting a document with a traditional word processor such as Microsoft Word. With Lyx, that aggravation is removed.

Basically, you define the elements of your document and let Lyx do the rest. Say you have one element: a section title. Once you have defined an element as a section title, Lyx consults the rules and sees what formatting and other actions should be taken for section titles. The rules for your type of document (perhaps a technical manual) specifies that a section title should appear in bold font and should also be recorded in the table of contents.

All of this is done behind the scenes. All you had to do was define the element in your document. The time saved on this formatting can be quite substantial on a large project.

WordPerfect for Linux

When Corel announced that it would be releasing WordPerfect for Linux, there was quite a buzz in the Linux community. A well-known, extremely capable commercial piece of software, WordPerfect was well received and has been a boon to Linux well-wishers. The very fact that a respected company like Corel would release a Linux port of this popular program seemed to indicate that Linux had arrived.

During the late 1990s, throughout corporate America, Microsoft Word unseated WordPerfect as the de facto standard and Corel has been playing catch-up ever since. This version of WordPerfect seems to have all of the features that allows it to compete fairly with Word. Corel did a good job on the Linux version. Take a look.

Obtaining and Installing WordPerfect

WordPerfect is a bit different than some of the other programs you have looked at so far in this chapter, mainly because it is not Open Source. Your choices for installation are limited to a binary release. Corel allows a free download of WordPerfect for non-commercial usage from its Web site (`http://www.corel.com`). The download for version 8.0 was approximately 23MB, which may take a couple of hours on a dial-up line.

Your other option is to buy a full-version of WordPerfect, which arrives with a nice manual and provides a quick installation from a CD-ROM.

The installation scripts provide a straightforward set of screens and options that guide you through the installation process. The last step, just prior to the installation actually beginning to copy files, is a confirmation screen that gives you one final chance to change things such as the installation directory. This is a nice feature because it allows you to see the options you have chosen and to change them if necessary. This indicates a well thought out installation process.

WordPerfect requires the X Windows environment and sufficient RAM and processor speed to operate. Check the exact details on the Corel Web site or in the program documentation.

Configuring WordPerfect

As do most other GUI editors, WordPerfect provides GUI configuration tools that remove the need for editing text configuration files by hand. The WordPerfect configuration tool provides a nice menu (see Figure 36.16) of the different areas you can change, such as fonts, colors, and keyboard and display options.

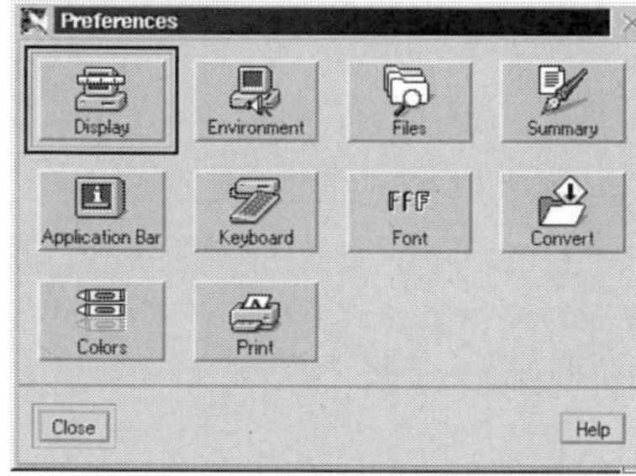

FIGURE 36.16
WordPerfect Preferences Menu.

Not each area is described here. Suffice it to say that the options are pretty self-explanatory and there are good help resources available with each screen.

Figure 36.17 shows the Files Preferences configuration screen.

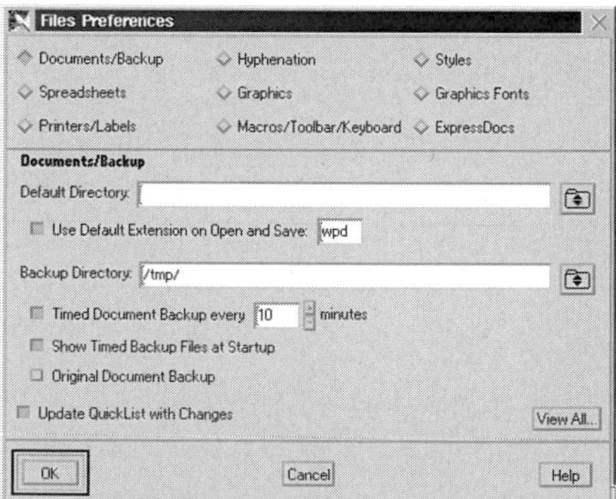

FIGURE 36.17
WordPerfect Preferences.

Make sure to set the timed document backup to something smaller than the default 10 minutes; I suggest 3 minutes. This option causes WordPerfect to automatically make periodic backups of your document. This can be handy if you happen to lose power during your work and haven't formally saved in a while.

Figure 36.18 shows the Display Preferences configuration. By clicking each of the topics in the top portion of the screen (Document, Show, View/Zoom, and so on), you are presented with a set of options for that topic. Show is chosen, which lets you control what formatting symbols—such as tabs and returns—are displayed while you are typing the document. Having these symbols displayed can be handy if you are adding some complex formatting to your document. You can also turn some or all of them off.

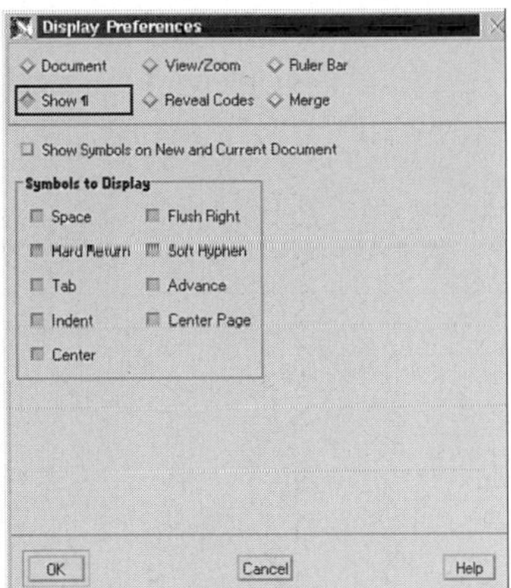

FIGURE 36.18
WordPerfect Display Preferences.

Using WordPerfect

Now that WordPerfect is configured, start using it. I created a desktop icon that calls the `xwp` WordPerfect executable. `xwp` is found in the `install-directory/wordperfect/wpbin` directory. You could also call this program from the command line, as long as you are in an X Windows environment.

The keybindings and cursor movement keys are fairly standard: Ctrl+C copies highlighted text, Ctrl+V pastes text, arrow keys move the cursor around, and so on. The toolbar and layout are similar to those in Microsoft Word, which would make for an easy transition from Word to WordPerfect for most users.

One feature that is really well done in WordPerfect is the undo/redo function. By choosing Edit, Undo, you can reverse some text or formatting changes you have made. There is even a feature that allows you to see a history of changes and undo and redo changes from the history of your document.

Saving Files

WordPerfect allows you to save a file in many different formats. To save a file, choose File, Save from the toolbar or simply press Ctrl+S. This saves the file in WordPerfect format. To save a file in a format other than WordPerfect, choose File, Save As, or simply press the F3 key.

Here are the available file formats:

- Ami Pro
- Applixware
- ASCII text
- FrameMaker
- PostScript
- RTF
- WordPerfect

Saving a page in HTML requires the use of a simple tool called Internet Publisher (see Figure 36.19), which is included. Choose File, Internet Publisher and then follow the directions. I reviewed the HTML code that WordPerfect created, and while not perfect, it was acceptable. This has potential for use as a WYSIWYG Web page creation tool by people who don't use HTML.

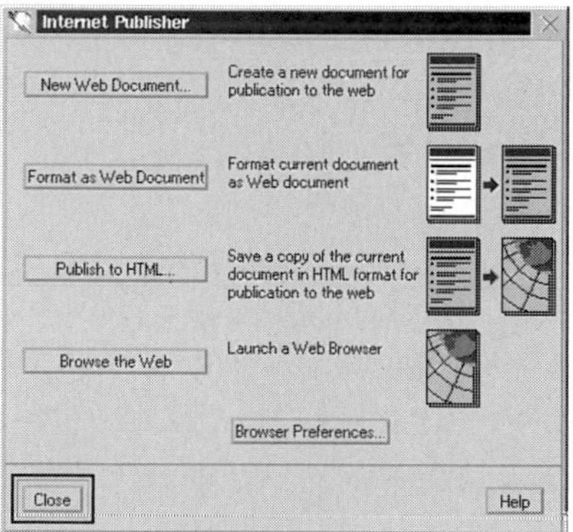

FIGURE 36.19
WordPerfect Internet Publisher.

Quite a bit of material has been covered so far. The office suites and text editors used allow you to perform a range of tasks. You can go from doing quick edits on text files all the way to HTML publishing and creating complex spreadsheets and wonderfully rich documents. Now take a look at available Linux databases.

Databases

Almost every day we hear the names of database vendors—Oracle, Sybase, Informix—whose popularity and sales are growing like wildfire. However, you don't have to run an expensive, proprietary database system to handle data on Linux. A number of solid, SQL-compliant databases exist for Linux. You look at one of them: PostgreSQL. You also take a quick side trip to look at Gnomecard, a nifty address database.

Note

SQL stands for Structured Query Language. Although SQL is a standard language for accessing databases, don't think of it as a programming language.

SQL is a *Data Definition Language* (DDL) used for defining database structures. It is also a *Data Manipulation Language* (DML) used for accessing and modifying data stored in SQL-compliant databases.

SQL varies in implementation, usually on the side of functionality being added by database vendors. Additional functions such as program control or other programming language constructs are often added to create a new product, such as Oracle's PL/SQL.

There are several standards, but you should endeavor to choose a database that is SQL-92 compliant. The 92 indicates the year the standard was created. Newer standards are sure to emerge. Always be aware of functionality to ensure backwards compatibility. This helps maintain the usefulness of older database applications.

PostgreSQL

PostgreSQL is a full-blown relational database management system. It has all of the features that you would expect of a professional RDMS, such as full-SQL compliance and transaction support. PostgreSQL has shown itself to be another wonder of the Open Source world, supporting multi-gigabyte databases and high transaction loads without a problem. It is also under active development and version 6.5 was recently released.

Postgres, PostgreSQL's forerunner, was developed at the University of California, Berkeley, with the guidance of professor Michael Stonebraker. The name has changed and features have been added, all through the work of hundreds of volunteers throughout the world using the Internet.

One of the nicer features provided by PostgreSQL is transaction support. The concept of a transaction is important to understand because it provides a level of error-handling that is important when dealing with important things such as payments, credits, and charges, for example, in a financial application.

Obtaining and Installing PostgreSQL

PostgreSQL ships with many Linux distributions and is also available on the Internet at `http://www.postgresql.org`. PostgreSQLis an Open Source product and is available in source code and as packaged binaries. The Red Hat distribution ships these in the RPM format and Debian ships in `.deb` format, making the installation a breeze.

Here are the pieces you will need:

- `postgresql`—This is the base package that provides most of the functionality including the back-end database services.
- `postgresql-clients`—This is a group of utilities that allow you to interact with the back-end database server in the client/server model. It provides libraries for C, C++, and Perl interfaces.
- `postgresql-devel`—This packages provides the libraries and header files that allow you to compile applications that communicate directly with the database server.
- `postgresql-data`—This package provides an initial database structure, allowing a user to quickly begin using PostgreSQL.

How Does It All Fit Together?

PostgreSQL uses the client/server model. A back-end database server runs on the server machine. You have to keep your server types straight here. It is easy to get confused! The database server processes all the SQL queries provided by the various front-end interfaces.

The front-end interface can be psql (formerly called the *monitor*) or a program written in various languages that support the PostgreSQL API. The monitor is an interactive environment, similar to a shell, that allows you to execute SQL commands and PostgreSQL commands from a command line. You may also administer the database from this area. The PostgreSQL API supports C, C++, Perl, Python, `tcl`, and of course, SQL. Connectivity via ODBC and JDBC is also supported.

Communications between the two areas (back end and front end) are controlled by the postmaster. The *postmaster* is a daemon process that runs constantly and manages the connections and memory allocation and also performs the necessary initializations when connections are made. Basically, the front end indicates to the postmaster that it needs a database connection. The postmaster then makes the necessary preparations and connects to the back-end server.

Configuring PostgreSQL for First Use

There is a bit of configuration that must be done after installing the necessary pieces. You need to make sure the postmaster daemon is running and set yourself up as a PostgreSQL user. You can then go about the business of creating databases and manipulating data.

The installation should have placed a copy of the extensive documentation on your system, possibly at `/usr/doc/postgres-x.x.x`, where `x.x.x` is the version number you are using. All of the common startup problems are well detailed there.

Initialization and Starting the Postmaster

The first thing to do is initialize things. Figure 36.20 shows some of the messages.

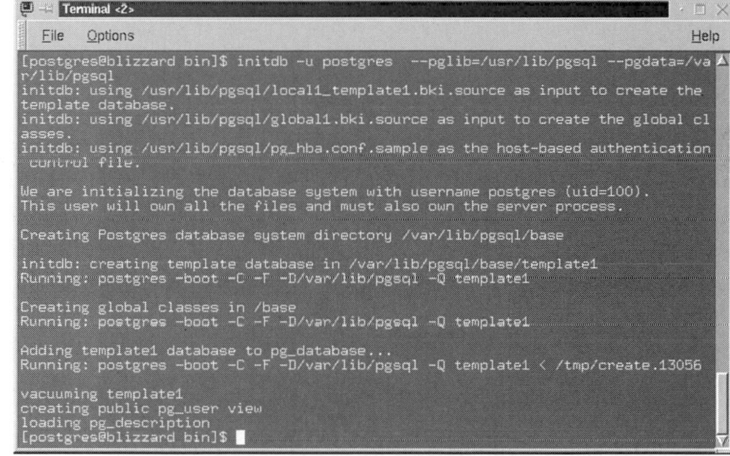

FIGURE 36.20
Intializing PostgreSQL.

After initialization, you can use the following command to start the postmaster daemon process:

```
$ postgresql start
```

The postmaster is automatically invoked with Debian; there is no need to manually start it.

Creating a User

Set yourself up as a user with the `/usr/bin/createuser` command and respond to the questions:

```
$ createuser johndoe
Enter user's postgres ID or RETURN to use unix user ID: 501 ->  <return>
Is user "johndoe" allowed to create databases (y/n) y
Is user "johndoe" allowed to add users? (y/n) y
createuser: johndoe was successfully added
```

Creating a Database

Now, create a database. Call it `vegetable` for fun:

```
$ createdb vegetable
```

Now that you have a database, get into the psql monitor and interact with your `vegetable` database:

```
$ psql vegetable
Welcome to the POSTGRESQL interactive sql monitor:
  Please read the file COPYRIGHT for copyright terms of POSTGRESQL

   type \? for help on slash commands
   type \q to quit
   type \g or terminate with semicolon to execute query
 You are currently connected to the database: vegetable

vegetable=>
```

At this point, you can begin interacting with your database using SQL commands to create tables and fields. After tables and fields are created, you can then add and manipulate data using SQL commands from the psql monitor or from the other interfaces that PostgreSQL supports. psql also uses a number of *slash commands*, which are simply a backslash (\) followed by a keystroke.

Tip

If you get stuck for a command and need help, try `\?`. This gives you a list of the available slash commands.

SQL is a topic that can fill books (and it often does). There are numerous SQL tutorials on the Internet as well as a number of fine books available. If you are unfamiliar with SQL, try one of those resources.

Using PostgreSQL psql

Although describing SQL syntax is far beyond the scope of this book, look at a couple of entries in the psql monitor and their results.

The psql monitor environment acts like a shell or command line to the user. Rather than a regular shell prompt, you have a prompt like this:

```
vegetable=>
```

A Short Exercise

In this short exercise, we will create a table (PostgreSQL calls this a *class*). This presents the use of the slash commands and SQL statements while using the psql monitor.

First list the databases:

```
vegetable=> \l

datname   ¦datdba¦datpath
---------+------+---------
template1¦   100¦template1
vegetable¦   501¦vegetable
(2 rows)
```

Try some SQL. Use the `CREATE SQL` statement to create a table called `names`, where you will store records of your vegetables. The class will have attributes (also called *fields*).

```
vegetable=> CREATE TABLE names (veggie_name varchar(40), quantity int);
CREATE
```

The `CREATE` response lets you know the statement completed, but take a look at the result of that statement by listing the tables:

```
vegetable=> \d

Database    = vegetable
 +------------------+----------------------------------+----------+
 ¦  Owner           ¦             Relation             ¦  Type    ¦
 +------------------+----------------------------------+----------+
 ¦ johndoe          ¦ names                            ¦ table    ¦
 +------------------+----------------------------------+----------+
```

Next, find out the structure of the table called `names`:

```
vegetable=> \d names

Table    = names
+----------------------------+----------------------------------+-------+
¦            Field           ¦               Type               ¦ Length¦
+----------------------------+----------------------------------+-------+
¦ veggie_name                ¦ varchar()                        ¦    40 ¦
¦ quantity                   ¦ int4                             ¦     4 ¦
+----------------------------+----------------------------------+-------+
```

Now that you have created a database and a class, I will leave populating it with data to you.

Again, an Internet search will yield great results in searching for *SQL tutorial* or a similar phrase. The PostgreSQL documentation should also be found on your system (try `/usr/doc/`) and is freely downloadable from `http://www.postgresql.org`.

Note

In addition to the full-featured PostgreSQL, you might consider MySQL. MySQL is a robust, SQL-compliant database with lots of features. You can get it at `http://www.mysql.org`.

MySQL's best feature is its sheer speed. The database is designed to handle data quickly and efficiently and to minimize overhead processing when possible.

Many Web sites use MySQL as a database back end, even the highly popular `http://slashdot.org`. There are a number of modules available to directly embed SQL calls into popular programming languages such as Perl and C.

GnomeCard

GnomeCard is a basic, but rather handy, address book program that displays contact information in a configurable list format, with a sidebar showing detailed information about a highlighted item. It is provided as part of the GNOME desktop environment.

Obtaining and Installing GnomeCard

You can find the latest release of GnomeCard on the GNOME Web site (`http://www.gnome.org`). GnomeCard is also part of the stock GNOME installation shipped with Red Hat 5.2 and later. Install the GnomeCard applicable to the format you obtained. If it is a packaged binary, such as RPM, use the Red Hat Package Manager.

Configuration

GnomeCard is quite usable initially and provides little in the way of customization. The only real change you can make is to the columnar display. Choose Settings, Preferences to make changes.

Using GnomeCard

GnomeCard has a nice toolbar (see Figure 36.21) that controls most of its functions. These functions also have specific keystrokes, allowing you to speed your use. The functions include opening and saving a GnomeCard file, adding, modifying, and deleting a card, and navigating through existing cards. A simple Find function provides a limited search capability.

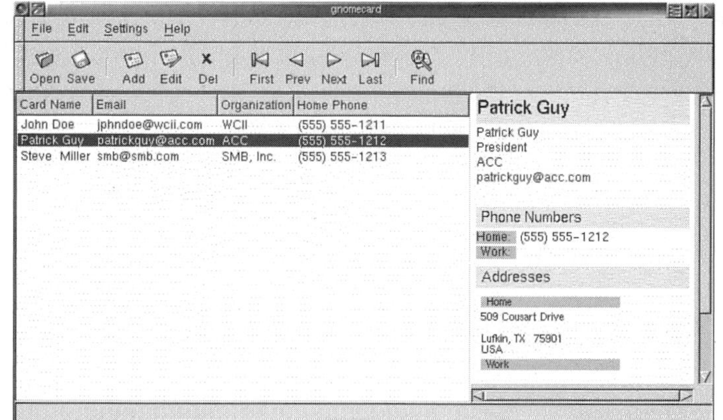

FIGURE 36.21
The GnomeCard address book.

Appointments and Scheduling Clients

Even if you have great-looking reports and reliable data, you still have to make it to meetings on time. This section takes a look at a few appointment and scheduling tools available for Linux.

KPilot

The PDA (Personal Digital Assistant) had quite a rocky start in corporate America. Hokey interfaces, tiny screens, and miniscule storage capacities all kept the PDA from realizing its true potential as a portable information tool.

Enter the 3Com Palm Pilot.

The Palm Pilot has revolutionized the use of the PDA and made it almost as indispensable as the cellular telephone for busy people. Since the Palm Pilot is widely used and vastly popular, it only makes sense that there exist tools that allow you to back up the data on your PDA and synchronize its files with your laptop or desktop computer. KDE offers the `KPilot` utility to perform these functions.

Obtaining `KPilot`

`KPilot` comes as part of the standard KDE distribution. You don't really have much to do to get it. Check out `http://www.kde.org` for new versions or other updates.

Configuring `KPilot`

`KPilot` has two simple configuration screens (see Figure 36.22) that are displayed during its first use and they can also be found by choosing File, Settings.

You really only need be concerned with the first tab—General. It allows you to define very basic options for communication with your Palm Pilot, such as who you are, what connection speed to use, and how to connect. The second tab may be ignored for now. It is mainly used for importing and exporting addresses from text files.

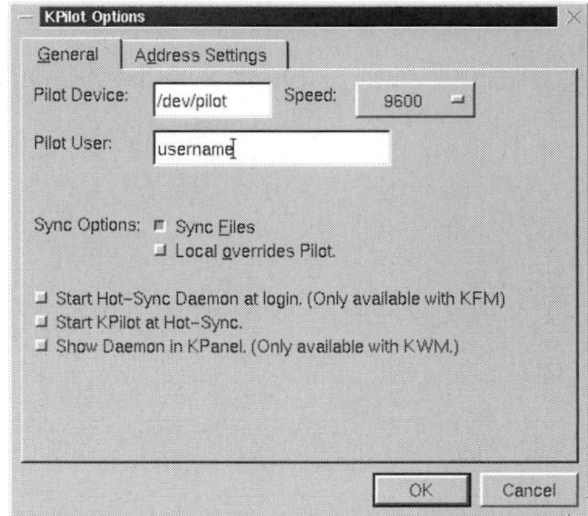

FIGURE 36.22
Kpilot Options.

`KPilot` uses a daemon program that allows the `KPilot` GUI to be started by simply inserting it into its cradle and pressing the Hot Sync button. This process synchronizes your files.

Tip

One important item that you want to think about: the Local Overrides Pilot option. When the same record has been modified on both the Palm Pilot and your desktop machine, only one version can be used when synchronizing files. Choosing this option causes the local copy of the record to override the copy of the record residing on your Palm Pilot.

Your Palm Pilot cradle should be attached to a serial port on your computer. As the `root` user, add a symbolic link called `/dev/pilot`; it points you to the proper serial port. The permissions for the serial port should be read/write for all (666). Use the `chmod` command to do this.

Use this code to add a link. The Palm Pilot cradle is attached to `/dev/cua0`:

```
# ln -s /dev/cua0 /dev/pilot
```

Use this code to change permissions. Read/write permissions are for all.

```
# chmod 666 /dev/pilot
```

Using `KPilot`

On your first use of `KPilot`, you should perform a full backup (File, Backup) of your Palm Pilot. This copies files into a directory on your local machine and provides a baseline of files for future synchronization. This may take some time, depending on the amount of data you have in your Palm Pilot.

During your regular use of `KPilot`, you will simply pop the Palm Pilot in its cradle and press the Hot Sync button—it's that easy.

`KPilot` also has a couple of application screens that allow you to move specific items between your local machine and the Palm Pilot. Choose the specific application from the list; files for the specific application are shown. You can then choose to import, export, delete, or edit records.

Gnome Calendar

Gnome Calendar is a very basic calendar program with one notable feature: It supports the vCalendar standard. That allows the interchange of calendar information on the Internet. Gnome Calendar even uses the vCalendar format as the file format to store its data on your hard disk. According to the Gnome Web site, Gnome Calendar is in its infancy. In the future, look for many new features. See Figure 36.23.

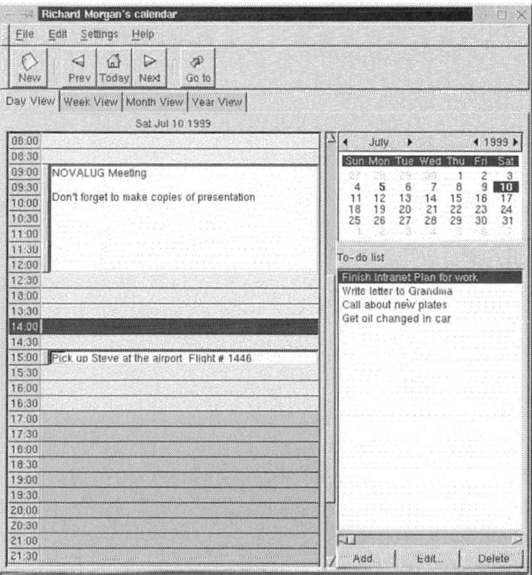

FIGURE 36.23
Gnome Calendar.

Obtaining and Configuring Gnome Calendar

Gnome Calendar arrived as part of my Gnome desktop package. It may also be obtained at the Gnome Web site (`http://www.gnome.org`). You can obtain the latest version of this program there.

There is little configuration available. Figure 36.24 shows the simple configuration tool. Use Settings, Preferences to get there.

FIGURE 36.24
Gnome Calendar Preferences.

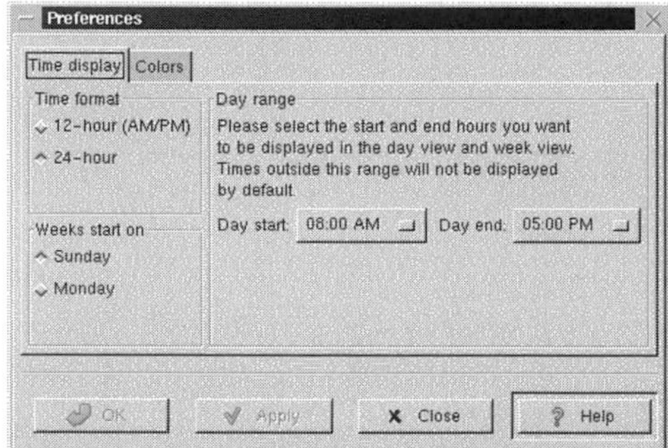

> **Note**
>
> See the Web site of the Internet Mail Consortium (`http://www.imc.org`) for further details about the vCalendar standard.

Using the Calendar

Adding entries tothe calendar is fairly straightforward—just click the appointment time and start typing. To add a new entry and use more Gnome Calendar features, either click the New icon on the toolbar or choose Edit, New Appointment. Figure 36.25 shows a new appointment being created.

When viewing your calendar, use the tabs below the toolbar to change your view. You can view the calendar for a day, a week, a month, or a year.

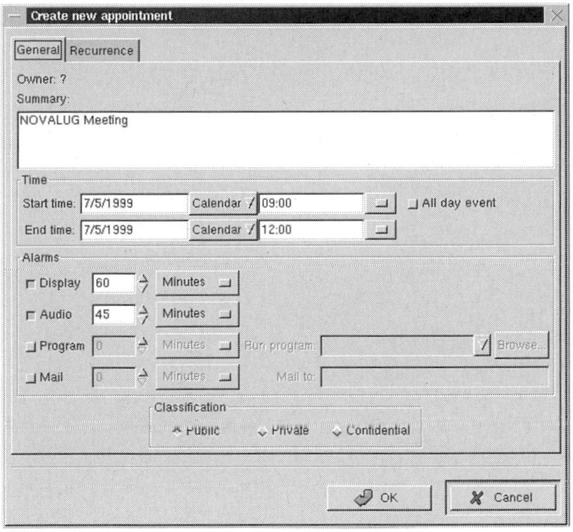

FIGURE 36.25
Creating an appointment in Gnome Calendar.

Ical

`Ical` is a calendar/appointment tool very similar to the Gnome Calendar program. `Ical` is implemented in C++ using `tcl` libraries. The user interface (see Figure 36.26) is very easy to use and works well.

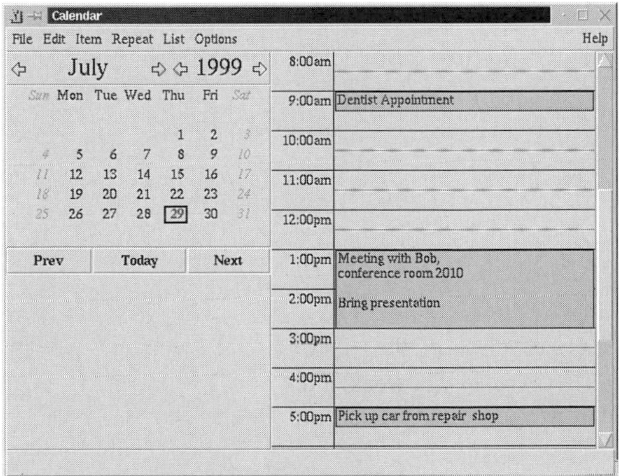

FIGURE 36.26
The `Ical` *Calendar.*

Configuration is a snap using the Option menu choice. See Figure 36.27. One neat item is the use of a slider in many of the configuration screens. Use the slider to make numeric adjustments.

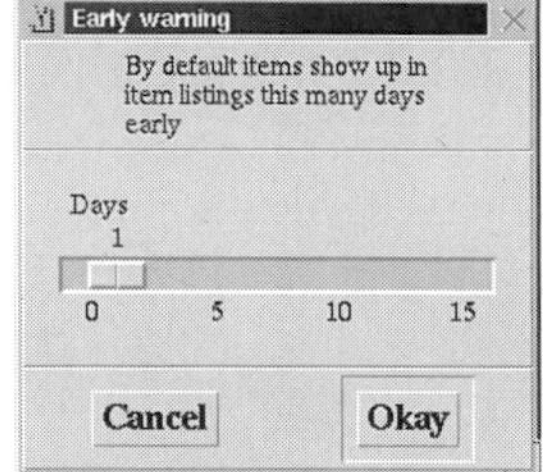

FIGURE 36.27
`Ical` *configuration.*

rclock

`rclock` is a very simple clock (see Figure 36.28) that can be used in an X Windows environment. Most modern window managers or desktops include some type of clock, but `rclock` can also be used. It is available on many Linux systems and can be installed as part of a standard distribution.

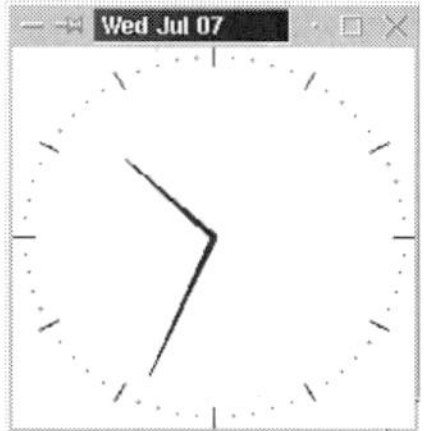

FIGURE 36.28
`rclock` *for X Windows*

As with many Linux programs, at the command line you may type the name of the program followed by `--help` to see a list of program options:

```
$ rclock —help
Usage v2.4.7:
  rclock [options]

where options include:
    -display displayname        X server to contact
    -geometry geom              size (in pixels) and position
    -bg color                   background color
    -fg color                   foreground color
    -fn fontname                normal font for messages
    -iconic                     start iconic
    -adjust +/-ddhhmm           adjust clock time
    -update seconds             clock update interval
    -mail seconds               check $MAIL interval
    #geom                       icon window geometry
```

Summary

In this chapter, we covered some of the Linux products and tools that can help you become more productive and also prepare professional documents.

Expect to see an explosion of this kind of software being written for Linux as companies realize the size and value of the Linux market. As companies begin using Linux as a desktop operating system, the market for "office" applications will surely grow.

CHAPTER 37

Emulators

In This Chapter

Linux supports a wealth of software you can use to extend the operating system's capabilities. This means that you can run software from other operating systems, run other operating systems under Linux, or even simulate other, often wildly different, computers on your Linux box. This chapter discusses various GPL'd software packages included with Red Hat, Caldera, and Debian, along with GPL'd and commercial software you can use to

- Create and run virtual networks, enabling you to operate your Linux desktop from Windows, or to work in Windows from your Linux desktop.
- Easily transfer files between different media (such as floppies)
- Emulate different computers under Linux
- Install, configure, and run different operating systems under Linux
- Install, configure, and run Linux under different operating systems
- Run a DOS session under the Linux console or X11
- Run applications from Windows on your Linux desktop

Why Use an Emulator?

Emulators have been used since the early days of computing. An *emulator* is a software program designed to mimic a Central Processing Unit (CPU), computer language, or entire operating system on a foreign computer platform. Emulators are used to test CPUs, hardware devices, programs, and operating systems. They are also used to enable the *porting*, or building of applications on one computer when the programs are destined for other—and usually quite dissimilar—computing platforms. Emulators are also useful for running old applications for which there is no source code (yet another good reason to support Open Source).

Many of the early emulators under UNIX were assembler language macros that translated the low-level code for foreign CPUs into native code on the computer. In this way, programs could be transferred from one computer system to the next. This chapter doesn't go into the details of how modern-day emulators work, nor does it cover all the emulators available for Linux (such as those used to run read-only memory, or ROM programs, from arcane machines under X11, or older emulators, such as those for CP/M), but you'll find that Linux supports some very useful and ingenious emulators.

Emulating DOS with DOSEMU

DOSEMU, based on the early work of Matthias Lautner and currently maintained by Hans Lermen, is not—according to its author—an emulator, but a virtual machine for

DOS. This means that the program creates a virtual computer in your system's memory. Do you have to buy MS-DOS to use DOSEMU? Of course not! A copy of Pat Vallani's FreeDOS kernel (actually a DOS filesystem under the `/var/lib/dosemu` directory) is included. You'll find most of the familiar DOS programs included.

DOSEMU may be used from the command line of a Linux console or launched in its own window during an X session. The main configuration file, `global.conf`, is located under the `/var/lib/dosemu` directory in Red Hat. In Debian, it is in `/usr/lib/dosemu`. However, to configure most systemwide settings edit the file `/etc/dosemu.conf` or `/etc/dosemu/conf` in Debian. You'll find nearly 80 different settings through which you can configure how DOSEMU works.

Under Red Hat Linux 6.0, DOSEMU (version dosemu-0.99.10.0, located under the `/usr/bin` directory) may only be launched by the `root` operator. If you first try launching the program, you'll see this:

```
# dos
Sorry bball. You are not allowed to use DOSEMU. Contact System Admin.
```

On the other hand, both Caldera OpenLinux's DOSEMU (version dosemu-0.98.5.0) and Debian's DOSEMU (0.98.7) allow a limited launch of DOSEMU by any user. In COL, DOSEMU is a symbolic link under the `/usr/bin` directory that points to the `dos` executable under the `/usr/lib/dosemu/bin` directory. To allow other users to launch and use DOSEMU on Red Hat Linux, edit the file `/etc/dosemu.users` (as `root`) with your favorite text editor. Look for this entry:

```
# If you want to allow limited dosemu to all users, uncomment the line below
# all nosuidroot restricted # all other users have normal user restrictions
```

One way to enable your system's users is to remove the leading pound sign (#) from the word `all`:

```
all nosuidroot restricted # all other users have normal user restrictions
```

Note

To give yourself access to all features, such as writing to disk, sending through serial ports, or formatting floppies, create an entry that mimics the root operator's entry:

```
yourusername c_all
```

Save the file. Next, under Red Hat Linux, use the `cp` command to create a copy of DOSEMU:

```
# cp /usr/bin/dos /usr/bin/dodos
```

Finally, use the `chmod` command to remove the program's SETUID bit like this:

```
# chmod 755 /usr/bin/dodos
```

Your users can then start a DOS session (with restrictions on storage and hardware access).

To enable your Red Hat Linux 6.0 users to start a DOS session in an X11 window, make a copy of the `xdos` command and also change its permissions. To start a DOS session on the console or inside an X11 terminal window, type the new DOSEMU command's name like this:

```
# dodos
```

You'll then see a DOS session start, as shown in Figure 37.1.

```
DOS in a BOX
 This program is free software; you can redistribute it and/or modify
 it under the terms of the GNU General Public License as published by
 the Free Software Foundation; either version 2 of the License, or
 (at your option) any later version.

 This program is distributed in the hope that it will be useful,
 but WITHOUT ANY WARRANTY; without even the implied warranty of
 MERCHANTABILITY or FITNESS FOR A PARTICULAR PURPOSE.  See the
 GNU General Public License for more details.

 You should have received a copy of the GNU General Public License
 along with this program; if not, write to the Free Software
 Foundation, Inc., 675 Mass Ave, Cambridge, MA 02139, USA.

FreeDOS Command Line Interface version 0.72b

developed by: Tim Norman
              Matt Rains
              Evan Jeffrey
              Steffen Kaiser
              Svante Frey
              Oliver Mueller
              Aaron Kaufman
              Marc Desrochers

C:\>
```

FIGURE 37.1
Use DOSEMU to run a DOS session from the console or during an X11 session.

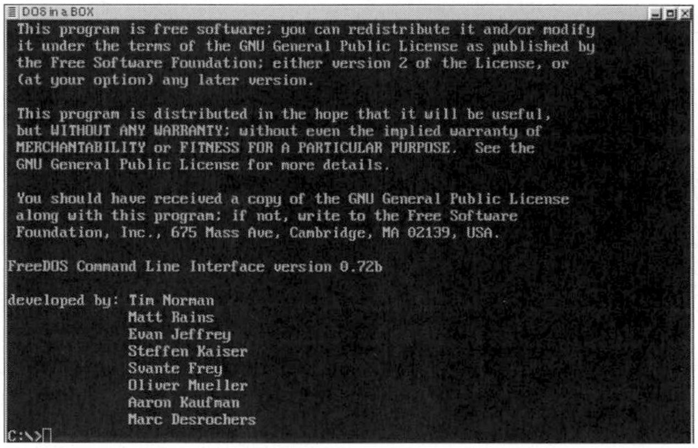

When DOSEMU starts, it will use the hard drive image file specified in the `/etc/dosemu.conf` (or `/etc/dosemu/conf`). To custom configure DOSEMU for your system, edit this file (as `root`) with your favorite text editor. This is the default hard drive image defined in `/etc/dosemu.conf` under COL:

```
$_hdimage = "hdimage.drdos703.eval"
```

This is a 7.7MB hard drive image (used as a virtual filesystem by DOSEMU) located under the `/var/lib/dosemu` directory, and it contains a feature-limited copy of Caldera's DR-DOS (formerly known as OPEN-DOS). This hard drive image has more then seven megabytes of free disk space, and by default has restricted write permissions of 644. This means that only the `root` operator may copy or delete files on the image or C drive. You can change this by using the `chmod` command on the image.

According to Caldera, you can download a free, fully functional hard drive image (or different tryout versions of DR-DOS) from `http://www.lineo.com/products/download.html`.

Red Hat Linux 6.0 and Debian GNU/Linux both define the DOSEMU hard drive image as shown here:

```
$_hdimage = "hdimage.first"
```

This is the name of an 8.4MB hard drive image with Red Hat, or a 360k image with Debian. It is found under the `/var/lib/dosemu` directory (with Red Hat, it's actually a symbolic link to the file `hdimage.freedos`). This drive image, also with limited write permissions, contains a copy of FreeDOS, that unlike DR-DOS, is licensed under the GNU GPL. You can get more information and updates, such as a mini-distribution of the latest version on two diskettes, or a full archive of 20MB of software through `http://www.freedos.org`.

Running Windows Clients with Wine

The Wine emulator, supported by programmers contributing the Wine project, allows you to run many DOS, Window 3.1, or Win32 programs. This emulator may be downloaded from `http://www.winehq.com` in binary or source archives.

Note

Corel Corporation, the same kind folks who made a free, for-personal-use-only version of WordPerfect 8 available for Linux in 1998, announced at the March 1999 Linuxworld Conference that it would make version of its WordPerfect Office 2000, CorelDRAW, and Corel PHOTO PAINT available for Linux. As part of this effort, Corel also pledged active support and development of Wine "to speed the process of moving our office suite applications to Linux."

Corel also said that the results of development work on Wine would be returned to the Wine project. This means that you can expect better program support as this effort continues. Stay tuned!

The easiest way to install Wine is to download a pre-built `.rpm` or `.deb` file, then install the program with the following code:

```
# rpm -ivh Wine*rpm
```

In Debian, you can automaticallydownload (or fetch off the CD-ROM) and install Wine with this code:

```
apt-get install wine
```

If you want additional documentation, you can also run

```
apt-get install wine-doc
```

To build Wine from scratch, download the 3.1MB archive, then decompress the archive like this:

```
# tar xvzf Wine*gz
```

Change directory into the resulting `Wine` directory and use the `configure` command:

```
# cd wine*
# ./configure
```

Finally, use the `make` command to build `Wine`:

```
# make depend && make
```

After `Wine` build finishes, use the `make` command to install Wine as `root`:

```
# make install
```

This copies the file `wine` into the `/usr/local/bin` directory. By default, debugging symbols are compiled into the binary, resulting in a 13MB file! You can reduce `wine`'s size by using the `strip` command:

```
# strip /usr/local/bin/wine
```

This leaves `wine` as a 3MB binary file. As a final step, copy the file `wine.ini` from the `Wine` directory to the `/usr/local/etc` directory with the name `wine.conf`. You must be `root` to do this.

```
# cp wine.ini /usr/local/etc/wine.conf
```

If you are using the Debian pre-built `.deb` package, the relevant file is `/etc/wine.conf`.

Open this file with your favorite text editor, and then change the line designating the path to drive C, which looks something like this:

```
[Drive C]
Path=/c
```

Change the pathname following the `Path` entry to the path of your Windows `root` partition (mount point). Because `Wine` is used to run programs and application for DOS, Windows 3.1, and Win32, you must have a copy of Windows installed on your system. For example, assume you mount your Windows partition like this:

```
# mount -t vfat /dev/hda1 /mnt/dos
```

You would need to change the path entry to your mount point like this:

```
Path=/mnt/dos
```

If you have your Windows partition mounted, you can then try to play a game of solitaire by typing this:

```
# wine /mnt/dos/window/sol.exe
```

The game window will appear, as shown in Figure 37.2.

FIGURE 37.2
The Wine emulator allows you to run DOS or Windows programs during your Linux X11 sessions.

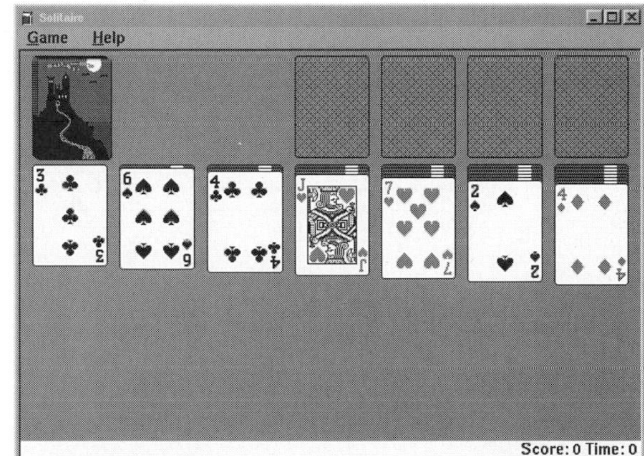

> **Note**
>
> If you'd like to learn more about Wine, or exchange tips and hints with other users or developers, read the Usenet newsgroup `comp.emulators.ms-windows.wine`. You'll also find nearly 30 newsgroups focused on discussions about emulators if you do a search at `http://www.dejanews.com`.

VMware for Linux and Windows

VMware from VMware, Inc. is a software package for Linux, Win32 operating systems, and others that you can use to install and run an operating system into a virtual filesystem on your computer. This approach, similar to the hard drive image used by DOSEMU, can be used to install and run Linux under a Win32 operating system without partitioning the hard drive, or to install and run a Win32 operating system under Linux.

At the time of this writing, VMware for Linux was still in beta testing, and available in various versions for download on a limited-trial basis. Unlike the free AT&T Laboratories Cambridge virtual network software (discussed in "Windowing Clients" in this chapter), VMware is a commercial software package. This section discusses installing and running VMware under Linux, although VMware is available for other platforms. For details, browse to `http://www.vmware.com`.

The beta VMware software for Linux is distributed at a 1.9MB compressed archive, and requires at least a 266Mhz processor and the X Window System.

Installing VMware for Linux

To install VMware under Linux, download the package and then decompress the archive with the `tar` command:

```
# tar xvzf vmware*gz
```

Next, navigate to the `vmware` directory, and run (as `root`) the file `install.pl`:

```
# ./install.pl

-----------------------------------------
         VMware for Linux  installer

    Copyright (C) 1998,1999 VMware, Inc.
-----------------------------------------

Perform default installation? (yes/no/help) [yes]
```

The installation script starts and you are asked to read a license agreement file and answer questions. The script will check your system, build any required software modules, and then ask whether you'd like a closed or working networking configuration (whether to allow the installed operating system to communicate with other computers). If you need networking support for your intended operating system, answer the script to enable networking support. If you choose a host-only configuration, the VMware install script will pick an unreachable network number for its configuration.

After you choose your configuration, the script installs the VMware software under the `/usr/local/bin` directory, and will exit. In order to run VMware, you must have a license file from VMware, Inc. This license may be obtained by registering at the VMware home page, and will be emailed to you. When you receive the license, save the email message as a text file named `license`.

Next, use the `mkdir` command to create a directory in your home directory named `.vmware`; then copy the license into the `.vmware` directory like this:

```
# mkdir .vmware ; cp license .vmware
```

Starting and Configuring VMware

To first start VMware, type **`vmware`** at the command line of your terminal window. You do not need to be logged in as the `root` operator, but you will need read and write permission for the device `/dev/zero`. The VMware configuration window and configuration dialog box appears, as shown in Figure 37.3.

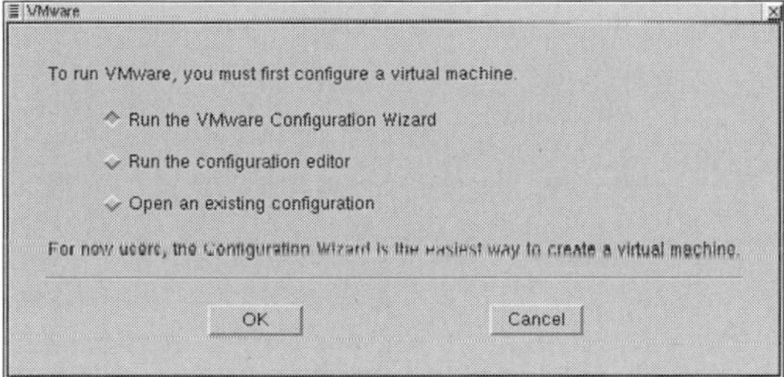

FIGURE 37.3
Before you can install another operating system, you must first configure VMware.

Click the OK button to continue. You'll then see the Configuration Wizard screen, as shown in Figure 37.4.

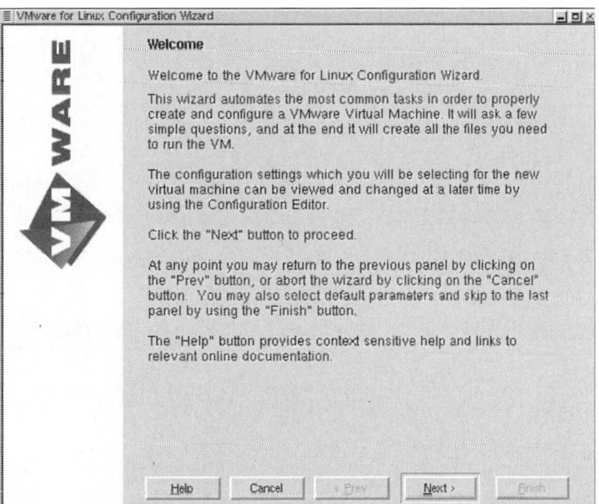

FIGURE 37.4
Configure VMware through its Configuration Wizard.

To start your configuration, click the Next button. Throughout the configuration process, you can step forwards or backwards to change settings. The next screen, shown in Figure 37.5, will ask you to select the Guest Operating System. Note that you can even install another Linux distribution, or if you click Other, another UNIX variant, such as FreeBSD!

Note

You can also use VMware to install and run several different operating systems on your computer. In fact, it is possible to install and run multiple operating systems at the same time on a single computer, and to then network the different operating systems. I guess this would be called a "LAN-in-a-box"?

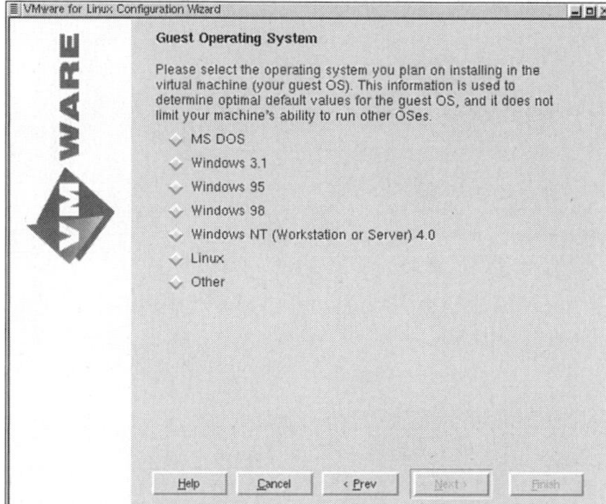

FIGURE 37.5
Select the type of operating system you'd like to use with VMware.

After you select the operating system, you are asked to select the location of the virtual filesystem, a file size for the new operating system, the CD-ROM and floppy device, and the type of networking, as shown in Figure 37.6.

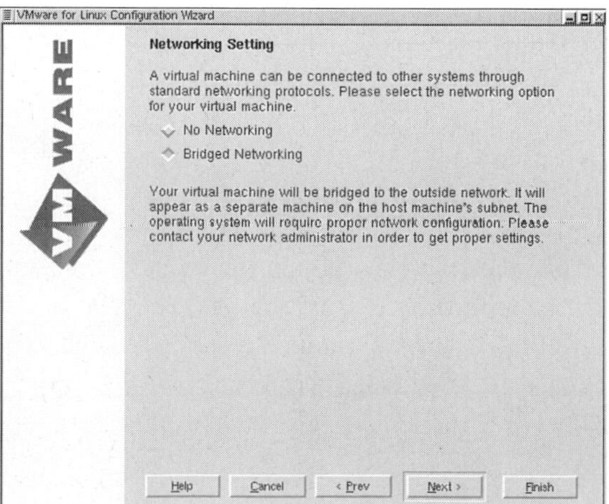

FIGURE 37.6
Select networking to allow your new operating system to communicate over a network.

You are then asked to confirm your settings, as shown in Figure 37.7.

FIGURE 37.7
Confirm your configuration settings before using VMware.

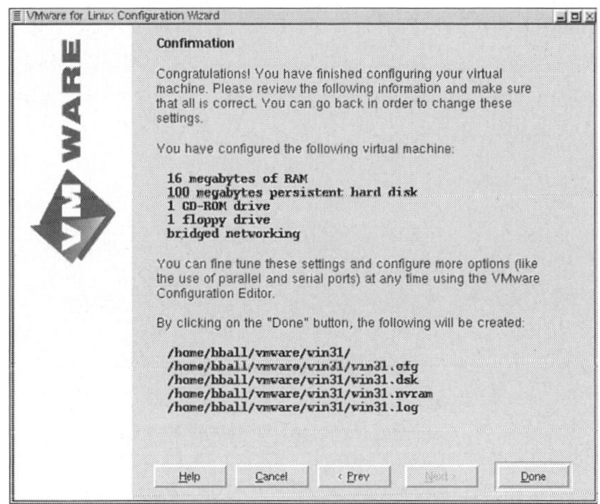

After you click the Done button, you're ready to install an operating system.

Installing Your Operating System

To start the installation process, insert a diskette or CD-ROM into your computer and then click the Power On button in the VMware window. The software boots, as shown in Figure 37.8.

FIGURE 37.8
Power on VMware with an inserted floppy or CD-ROM operating system installation disk to install your new operating system.

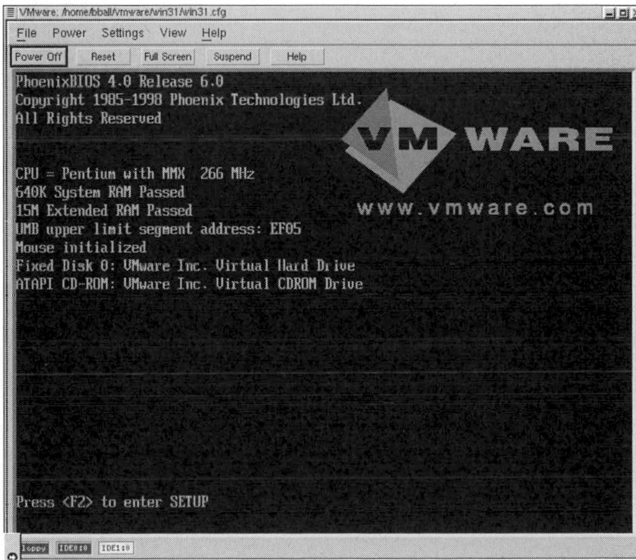

Continue through and finish your operating system installation. The next time you start VMware, you are asked to select a desired configuration, usually found under the directory you designated when you configured your virtual machine. The configuration file will have a name ending in `.cfg` in the directory (usually under the `vmware` directory in your home directory). To start your session, select the file and then click the Power On button. Your operating system will boot, as shown in Figure 37.9.

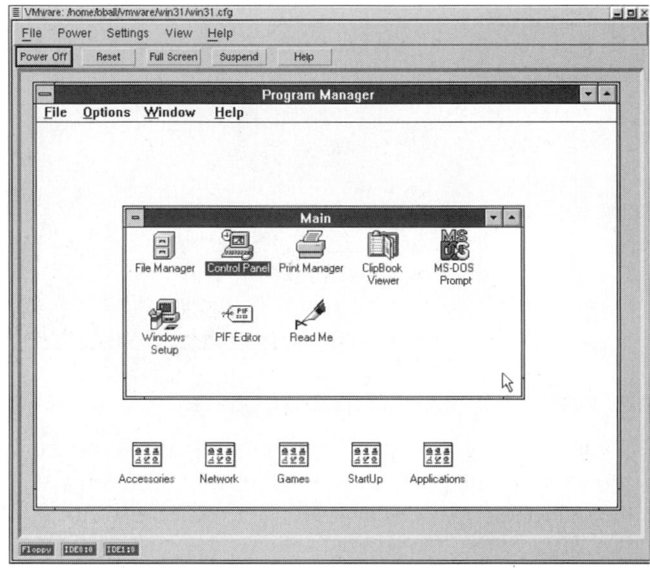

FIGURE 37.9
The VMware software support many different types of operating systems.

When you click in the VMware window, your mouse becomes "attached" to the operating system's window. To release your mouse, press Ctrl+Alt+Esc. When you've finished working with VMware, make sure to properly shut down the running operating system, and then click the Power Off button in the VMware window.

For tips and hints on troubleshooting problems, or to learn more about VMware for other operating systems, browse to `http://www.vmware.com`.

The `mtools` Package

The `mtools` package, originally by Emmet P. Gray and now maintained by Alain Knaff and David Niemi, is a public-domain set of programs you can use in just about any operation on MS-DOS floppies. These commands are useful because you don't need to mount the floppy in order to read, write, or make changes to the floppy's contents. Table 37.1 lists the tools included in the package.

Debian users should note that this package may not be installed by default. It can be installed with `apt-get install mtools`.

TABLE 37.1 *mtools* Package Contents

Program Name	*Function*
`mattrib`	Changes file attributes
`mbadblocks`	Floppy testing program
`mcd`	Changes directory command
`mcheck`	Checks a floppy
`mcopy`	Copies files to and from diskette
`mdel`	Deletes files on diskette
`mdeltree`	Recursively deletes files and directories
`mdir`	Lists contents of a floppy
`mformat`	Formats a floppy
`minfo`	Categorizes, prints floppy characteristics
`mkmanifest`	Restores Linux filenames from floppy
`mlabel`	Labels a floppy
`mmd`	Creates subdirectory
`mmount`	Mounts floppy
`mmove`	`mv` command for floppy files, directories
`mpartition`	Makes DOS filesystem as partition
`mrd`	Deletes directories
`mren`	Renames a file
`mtoolstest`	Tests `mtools` package installation
`mtype`	Types (lists) a file
`mzip`	Zip/Jaz drive utility

The most often used are the `mformat`, `mdir`, `mcopy`, and `mdel` commands. The `mformat` command formats nearly any type of floppy device. One of this software package's nice features is that you don't have to remember the specific names of floppy devices, such as

/dev/fd0, and can use the (possibly) familiar A or B drive designators. This is possible because of mtool's use of the /etc/mtools.conf configuration file.

Entries for different disk devices are listed in the file. You can edit the file (as root) to configure mtools for your system without having to rebuild the software (although if you need the source, you can readily find a copy on your favorite Linux site, or at ftp://ftp.tux.org/pub/knaff/mtools, along with numerous add-ons and utilities). If you examine the /etc/mtools.conf file, you'll see entries for different devices, and configurations for other operating systems. For example, the floppy device entries look like this:

```
# Linux floppy drives
drive a: file="/dev/fd0" exclusive
drive b: file="/dev/fd1" exclusive
```

These entries allow you to easily format a floppy in drive A without mounting the disk, like this:

```
# mformat a:
```

Note

In most Linux distributions, such as Red Hat's, strict read and write permissions are enforced on your system's devices. This default configuration will force you to use mtools as root. Although this is the safest and most secure approach, you can use the chmod command with 666 permissions to enable anyone to manipulate floppies, like this:

```
# chmod 666 /dev/fd0
```

Tip

If you receive the error mformat: Non-removable media is not supported, you need to fix the entry for your floppy drive in /etc/mtools.conf. You must tell the complete geometry of the disk, either in /etc/mtools or on the command line.

Log in as the root operator and then use your favorite text editor to change your floppy's /etc/mtools.conf entry from

```
drive a: file="/dev/fd0" exclusive
```

to

```
drive a: file="/dev/fd0" fat_bits=12 tracks=80 heads=2 sectors=18
```

Save the /etc/mtools.conf file. Details about creating custom device entries can be found in the mtools man page in section 5 of your Linux manuals. Read the man page like this:

```
# man 5 mtools
```

After the mformat command has finished, you can copy files to and from the diskette with the mcopy command:

```
# mcopy *.txt a:
```

This copies all files ending in .txt to your diskette. To copy files from your diskette, just reverse the arguments (in DOS form) to the mcopy command:

```
# mcopy a:*.txt
```

This copies all files ending in .txt to the current directory, or to a directory you specify. Use the mdir command to see what is on the diskette:

```
# mdir a
 Volume in drive A has no label
 Volume Serial Number is 4917-9EDD
Directory for A:/
launch   gif     62835 04-09-1999  13:43  launch.gif
vmware   gif     10703 04-09-1999  13:44  vmware.gif
vnc      gif     21487 04-09-1999  13:44  vnc.gif
        3 files             95 025 bytes
                         1 362 432 bytes free
```

To label the diskette, you can use the mlabel command:

```
# mlabel a:
 Volume has no label
Enter the new volume label : LINUX
```

You can also use special shell command-line quoting to label the diskette from the command line:

```
# mlabel a:'DOS DISK'
```

This is a handy way to use spaces in a diskette's label. If you want to delete files on your diskette, use the mdel command:

```
# mdel a:*.txt
```

This deletes all files ending in .txt on the diskette in the A drive. You can also mount your diskette. For details, see the mmount manual page, along with the mount command manual page.

Note

Interestingly, Caldera's OpenLinux has a misconfigured entry for drive N in /etc/mtools.conf. Under COL, the entry is listed as this:

```
drive n: file="/var/lib/dosemu/hdimage.first" offset=3840
```

continues

Red Hat Linux lists the entry as this:

```
drive n: file="/var/lib/dosemu/hdimage" offset=8832
```

That listing works correctly when using a command such as `mdir N:`.

Debian has these entries:

```
      # # dosemu hdimage.
drive m: file="/var/lib/dosemu/hdimage.first" partition=1 offset=128

# # dosemu floppy image
drive n: file="/var/lib/dosemu/fdimage"
```

The effect of this is that you can access a DOSEMU hard disk image with drive M and a floppy disk image with drive N.

Windowing Clients

While software and hardware emulators can ease many computing tasks, the demands on system resources such as memory or storage can be tremendous. If you have extra computers or work in a networked environment, an easier approach is to use the X Window System and networking protocols to communicate with other systems and run other clients.

Thanks to AT&T Laboratories Cambridge, Linux users can now enjoy working on the desktops of foreign operating systems with relative ease through virtual networking computing. Even better news is that the software, called vnc, is available under the GNU Public License with source code for Linux, and readily builds and installs under Red Hat Linux.

The vnc Linux software consists of several major components: an X server named Xvnc, a server named `vncserver`, a password utility named `vncpasswd`, and a network communication viewer named `vncviewer`. The vnc software is also available for many other computers and operating systems, such as (but not limited to):

- DEC Alpha OSF1 3.2
- Macintosh OS
- Solaris
- Win32
- Windows CE 2

The software is available at `http://www.uk.research.att.com/vnc`. A compressed archive of binaries for Linux is available, and you can download the 2.1MB UNIX source code tarball.

Debian users can find vnc included with the distribution. You can install the entire system with this command:

```
apt-get install xvncviewer vncserver svncviewer vnc-doc
```

Building and Installing the vnc Software

If you download the binaries, decompress the file with the `tar` command:

```
# tar xvzf vnc-3.3.2r3_x86_linux_2.0.tgz
```

This creates a `vnc` directory. Read the included readme file in the directory, or copy the files `Xvnc`, `vncserver`, `vncviewer`, and `vncpasswd` to the `/usr/local/bin` directory.

If you download the `vnc` source, decompress the archive with the `tar` command:

```
# tar xvzf vnc-3.3.2r3_unixsrc.tgz
```

This creates the `vnc_unixsrc` directory. Navigate into the directory and then start the build with the `xmkmf` command:

```
# xmkmf
# make World
```

Navigate into the `Xvnc` directory and build the vnc `X` server like this:

```
# cd Xvnc
# make World
```

Finally, install the vnc software (as `root`) with the included installation script, specifying an installation directory like this:

```
# ./vncinstall /usr/local/bin
```

This completes your Linux software installation. However, if you want to work on the desktops of other computers, you need to download and install the vnc software for the desired platform. For example, if you want to work with a Windows 95 or Windows 98 desktop, download the Win32 vnc software onto the desired computer.

Enabling Virtual Network Service

The vnc server software must be started on a remote computer in order to work on the remote computer's desktop. This can be done through a Telnet session or by sitting at the console and starting the software. To start the server for Linux, use the `vncserver` script from the command line:

```
# vncserver
You will require a password to access your desktops.

Password:
```

Enter a password used to allow remote access and press Enter. The script loads and starts the `Xvnc X11` server (a customized `X11R6.3` server based on XFree86 3.3.2). If you want to work on the remote desktop of a networked Win32 computer, the vnc software for Win32 must be downloaded and copied onto the remote computer. The Win32 software must then be extracted with an archive utility, such as WinZip.

Decompress the Win32 vnc software and install the software using the vnc Setup. To start the server, click the Install Default Registry Settings menu item from the `vnc` folder on your desktop's Start menu. Next, click the WinVNC 3.3.2 menu item, as shown in Figure 37.10.

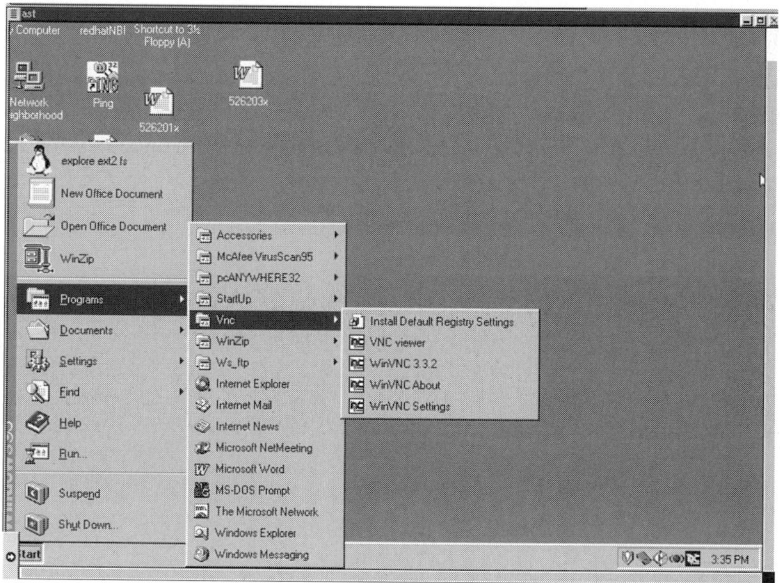

FIGURE 37.10
The Win32 vnc software provides easy-to-use menu items from the Start menu on the Windows desktop.

That's all there is to do! If you need to customize your settings or change the password for access to the Win32 desktop, click the WinVNC settings menu item. You'll see a dialog box like that shown in Figure 37.11, which you can use to change the network or password settings.

To view the remote Win32 desktop from Linux, use the `vncviewer` command, followed by the hostname or IP address of the Win32 computer, and the desktop number (which, according to the vnc readme) will always be `0`. Type the command in an X11 terminal window like this:

```
# vncviewer ascentia.home.org:0
```

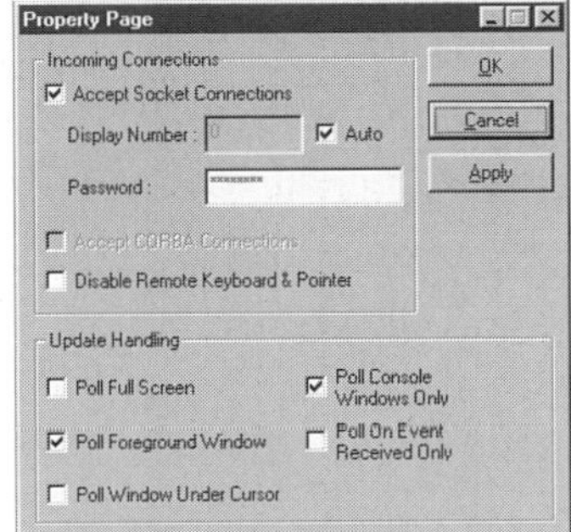

FIGURE 37.11
Use the WinVNC settings dialog to configure WinVNC for your Win32 desktop.

You are then prompted for the password of the remote vnc server like this:

```
vncviewer: VNC server supports protocol version 3.3 (viewer 3.3)
Password:
```

After you type in the password and press Enter, an X11 window appears with the remote desktop (as shown in Figure 37.12). You can then launch remote applications and work on the computer as if it were your own!

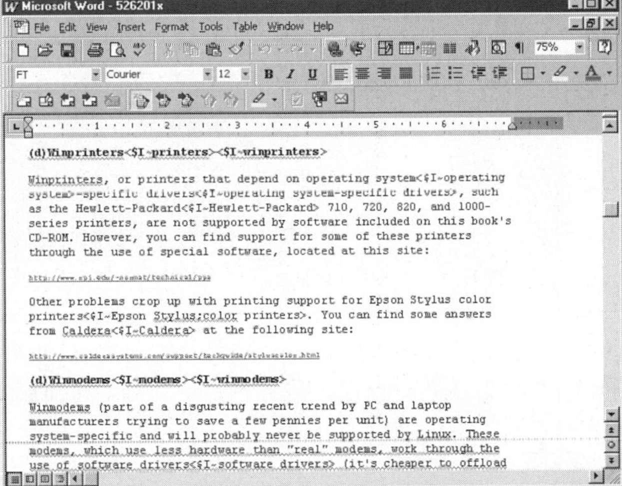

FIGURE 37.12
The Linux `vncviewer` client is used to launch and work a remote desktop session.

You can also use the `vncviewer` client on remote computers to view the Linux desktop. The settings and X resource files for the Linux vnc desktop may be quite different from your normal X session! Look in the `.vnc` directory for the file `xstartup`, which will look like this:

```
#!/bin/sh

xrdb $HOME/.Xresources
xsetroot -solid grey
xterm -geometry 80x24+10+10 -ls -title "$VNCDESKTOP Desktop" &
twm &
```

Note that only a single X terminal and the `twm` window manager are used! Edit this file to suit your needs. Of course, with all this flexibility, remote sessions can get a little confusing. For example, Figure 37.13 shows a Windows 95 desktop remotely viewed through a remote computer using KDE for its X11 session, which itself is being remotely run from a Red Hat Linux GNOME Enlightenment X session.

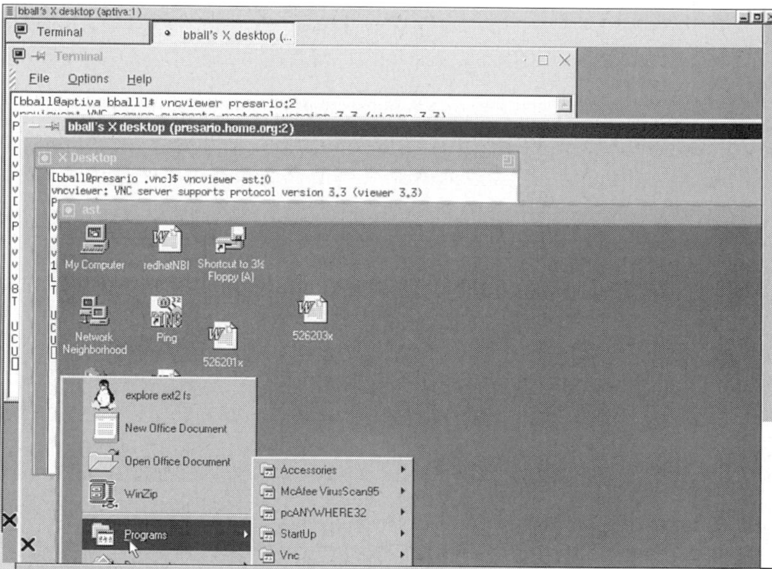

FIGURE 37.13
A chain of three remote virtual network sessions can get a bit confusing, but works quite well thanks to the vnc software.

Emulating the Apple Macintosh with Executor

Executor, by ARDI, is a commercial software emulator you can use to run Macintosh applications under Linux (although a Windows version is also available). According to ARDI, Executor on a 90-megahertz Pentium can run most applications almost as fast as a 50-megahertz 68040. The Executor software is distributed in a series of `.rpm` archives, and a demo version is available through `http://www.ardi.com`.

Although this software may help you run one of nearly 340 legacy Macintosh applications, the software emulation of the Apple Macintosh is not perfect and does have some limitations. The default emulated MacOS is System 6.0.7, although some System 7.0 applications may work. More importantly though, other exclusions include

- Access to serial ports
- AppleTalk (LocalTalk)
- CDEVs
- INITs
- Internationalization
- Modem usage

There is limited sound support, and the software can read and write 1.44MB Macintosh-formatted floppy disks. According to ARDI, "Desk Accessory support is very weak; most will not run."

Install the software as `root` with the `rpm` command, or your favorite installer, such as `gnorpm` if you're using Red Hat Linux 6.0, or the `kpackage` client if you're using COL. After installation, the main executable (in this case, for the demo version) is found under the `/opt/executor/bin` directory. Although an SVGA version is included, the easiest way to run the `executor` command is during an X11 session. Start X; type the following at the command line of a terminal to start the demo:

```
# /opt/executor/bin/executor-demo
```

A splash screen appears and then the main window appears, as shown in Figure 37.14

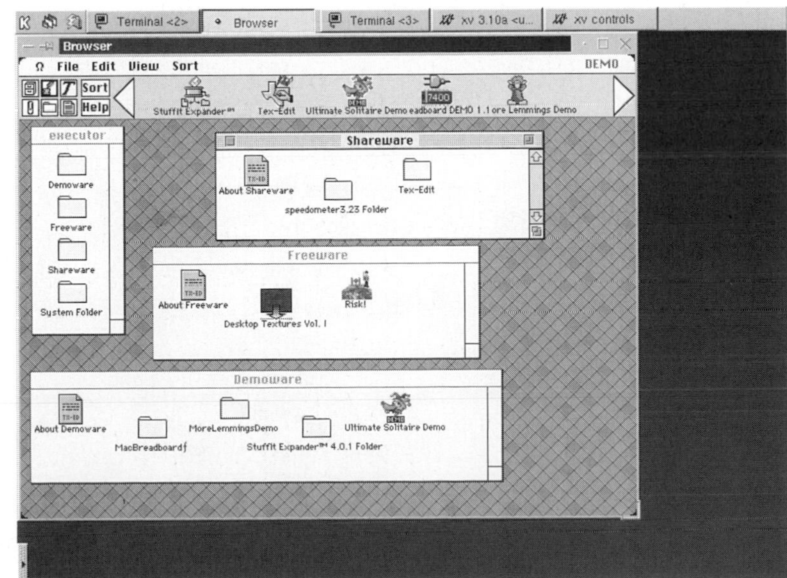

FIGURE 37.14
ARDI's Executor emulates a legacy Apple Macintosh and runs more then 300 different Macintosh applications.

The default screen size of the emulation window is 640×480, but you can alter this by using one of Executor's command-line switches, as shown in Table 37.2.

TABLE 37.2 Executor Command-Line Switches

Option	*Action*
`applzone` *n*`[k]`	Uses *n* kilobytes of memory for an application
`applzone` *n*`[MB]`	Uses *n* megabytes of memory for an application
`bpp` *n*	Uses *n* bits per pixel (1 or 8)
`desparate`	Minimalist mode (only for DOS)
`geometry` *heightxwidth*	Standard X geometry settings
`grayscale`	Uses grayscale when running
`help`	Prints help message on options and quits
`info`	Prints system information
`keyboard` *keyboard*	Uses specified *keyboard*
`keyboards`	Prints available keyboard maps
`memory` *n*	Creates *n* megabytes of use for system memory
`nobrowser`	Disables file browser when starting
`nodiskcache`	Disables internal disk cache
`nodotfiles`	Doesn't list filenames beginning with a period
`nosound`	Disable sound
`privatecmap`	Uses a private colormap for X
`refresh` *n*	Refreshes screen every *n* 60th of a second
`size` *heightxwidth*	Uses initial window of *height* and *width* pixels
`stack` *n*`[k]`	Uses *n* kilobytes of stack memory for the system

Option	*Action*
`stack` *n*`[MB]`	Uses *n* megabytes of stack memory for the system
`sticky`	Uses sticky menus
`syszone` *n*`[k]`	Uses *n* kilobytes of memory for the system
`syszone` *n*`[MB]`	Uses *n* megabytes of memory for the system

To help use traditional Macintosh keys, such as the Command and Option keys, Executor uses the left Alt key as Command and the right Alt key as the Option key. If you press Cmd+Shift+5 (left Alt+Shift+5), a preferences dialog box appears. The dialog box, which is shown in Figure 37.15, is used to set compatibility options.

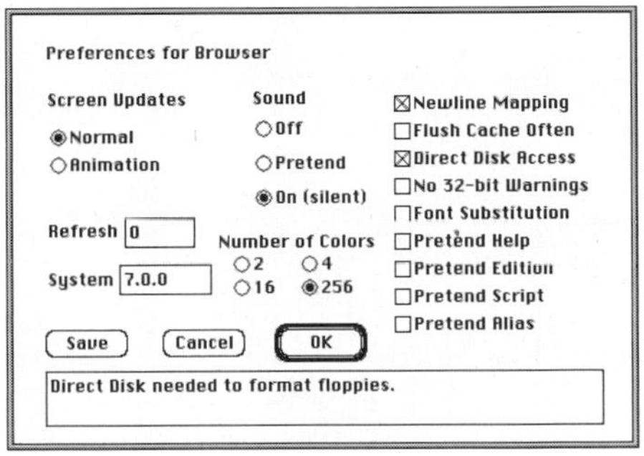

FIGURE 37.15
You can set System 7 compatibility options by using the left Alt+Shift+5 key combination.

Printing under Linux is supported through configuration of the `printers.ini` file found under the `/opt/executor` directory. The default output is PostScript, which prints through the Red Hat print filter system using the `lpr` command, or under COL, which uses `lprNG`.

Summary

This chapter introduced software emulators and other programs for Linux. These software tools extend the capabilities of Linux to provide a much richer computing environment, and add support for legacy hardware and software. The virtual network software can also be used to link widely disparate computing systems, and provides a useful medium to continue work, even over a remote distances. Though computers and software continue to evolve at a rapid pace, there will always be a need to extend the life of older systems, and operating system emulators can help. You'll find these tools to be indispensable when faced with having to provide extra life to the timeline of older hardware and software.

CHAPTER 38

Games for Linux

IN THIS CHAPTER

Games are included with nearly every Linux distribution, and game playing can be an important part of the computing experience by teaching new users how Linux works. Many computer games for Linux use the mouse, keyboard, or other input device (such as a joystick), provide visually stimulating graphics, and play various sounds or music. Although corporate business environments may frown on users whiling away spare minutes on a game of chess. This chapter introduces you to the different types of games included with Linux and highlights several of the best in different categories.

Introduction to Games

Games have been part of computing since computers first hit the industrial marketplace, well before the era of the PC. Indeed, although UNIX's official history may state that the operating system was developed to support in-house text processing and typesetting, hackers know that the real reason UNIX came into being was to support a multi-player version of a game named Space War. Although I'll leave the rest of UNIX to history, you'll soon see that Linux has inherited a number of games from the UNIX tree, including the venerable and distinguished Berkeley Software Distribution, or BSD UNIX.

This section first introduces you to some of the more popular games for the Linux console, then moves on to graphic games for X11. You'll also learn how to start the games with example command lines.

Games for the Console

Just because you don't use X11 doesn't mean you won't have fun at the console. Most Linux distributions come with an assortment of 40 or more classic UNIX games (many from BSD UNIX). Many of these games are listed in Table 38.1.

TABLE 38.1 Console Games for Linux

Name	*Description*
adventure	Classic cave adventure.
arithmetic	Timed and scored 20-question arithmetic quiz.
atc	Play air traffic control.
backgammon	Backgammon and game tutorial.
banner	Create banner printouts.
battlestar	Another text-based bed game.

Name	Description
bcd	Create punched cards from input text.
caesar	Simple cryptography utility.
canfield	A solitaire card game.
cribbage	A card game.
dm	System administrator game control utility.
factor	Factor numbers, generate prime numbers.
fish	Play the Go Fish! card game.
gomoku	Play Five in a Row in solitaire or competitively.
hangman	Classic guessing game.
hunt	An early networked multi-player game.
mille	Classic card game.
monop	Classic board game.
morse	Produce Morse code from input text.
number	Convert numbers to English.
phantasia	Role-playing character generator.
pig	Generate pig Latin from input text.
pom	Tongue-in-cheek moon phase calculator.
ppt	Create punched cards from input text.
primes	Generate prime numbers.
quiz	Random, interactive quiz game.
rain	Console screensaver.
random	Random number/line/file generator.
robots	Robot console game.
rot13	Simple encryption utility.
sail	A nautical adventure game.
snake	Snake console game.
tetris-bsd	Classic falling blocks game.
trek	*Star Trek* console game.
wargames	Game launcher script.
worm	Classic Worm console game.
worms	Console screensaver.
wump	Classic Hunt the Wumpus game.

Caldera OpenLinux does not include the traditional collection of games for the console (except for the `banner` command). You can download the BSD games from `http://metalabl.unc.edu/pub/Linux/games`. Look for the file `bsd-games-2.7.tar.gz`.

Most Linux distributions install these games in the filesystem under the `/usr/games` directory. Each game is usually accompanied by a man page installed under section 6 of the man pages. Some of these games are quite complex and use cursor addressing and positioning to simulate animation and scrolling. Others, such as number, are so simple that the game seems more like a utility. For example, to translate the number 202,340,239,424,935 to English, use the `number` command like this:

```
# number 202340239424935
two hundred two trillion.
three hundred forty billion.
two hundred thirty-nine million.
four hundred twenty-four thousand.
nine hundred thirty-five.
```

One of the classic games is adventure, an early example of the first generation of interactive text games. Simple commands—`n`, `w`, `e`, `s`, `look`, or `inventory`—are used to try to delve into a cave, retrieve treasures, and escape in one piece. Start adventure by typing its name or the full pathname to the program:

```
# /usr/games/adventure

Welcome to Adventure!! Would you like instructions?
yes

Somewhere nearby is Colossal Cave, where others have found fortunes in
treasure and gold, though it is rumored that some who enter are never
seen again.  Magic is said to work in the cave.  I will be your eyes
and hands.  Direct me with commands of 1 or 2 words.  I should warn
you that I look at only the first five letters of each word, so you'll
have to enter "northeast" as "ne" to distinguish it from "north".
(Should you get stuck, type "help" for some general hints.  For
information on how to end your adventure, etc., type "info".)
                              - - -
This program was originally developed by Will Crowther.  Most of the
features of the current program were added by Don Woods.  Address
complaints about the UNIX version to Jim Gillogly (jim@rand.org).

You are standing at the end of a road before a small brick building.
Around you is a forest.  A small stream flows out of the building and
down a gully.
```

Type `quit` to exit the game.

For the challenge of a good chess game, try gnuchess. You'll generally find several versions of this game included in your Linux distribution:

- gnuchess—Uses cursor addressing to provide a basic graphic display.
- gnuchessr —Scrolls each board after successive moves and uses reverse video and cursor addressing for a fancier display.
- gnuchessx —A version compatible with the `xboard` client (see this chapter's "Playing Chess with thc `xboard` Clicnt").
- gnuchessn —Uses fancy cursor addressing and reverse video for its graphic display.

Moves are entered by specifying the column and row as a letter and number, as in the following example:

```
# gnuchess
Enter [moves] minutes[:sec] [increment][+]:
Computer                                 GNU Chess
```

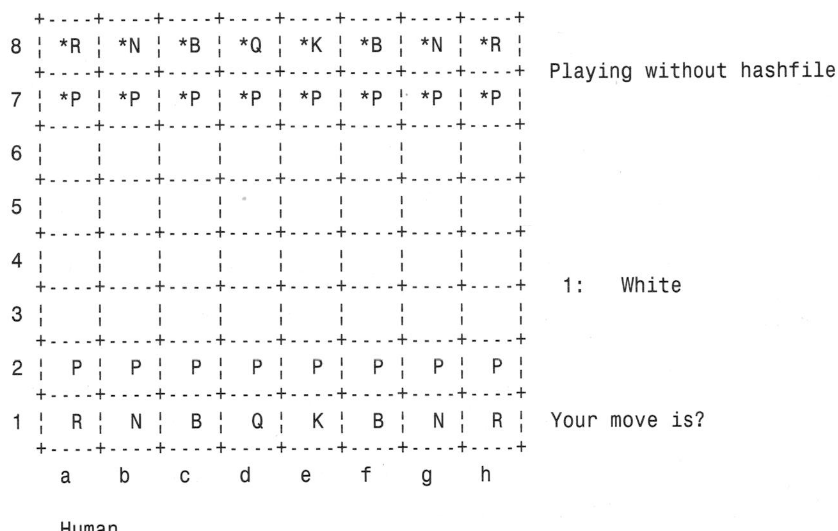

```
   +----+----+----+----+----+----+----+----+
 8 | *R | *N | *B | *Q | *K | *B | *N | *R |
   +----+----+----+----+----+----+----+----+  Playing without hashfile
 7 | *P | *P | *P | *P | *P | *P | *P | *P |
   +----+----+----+----+----+----+----+----+
 6 |    |    |    |    |    |    |    |    |
   +----+----+----+----+----+----+----+----+
 5 |    |    |    |    |    |    |    |    |
   +----+----+----+----+----+----+----+----+
 4 |    |    |    |    |    |    |    |    |
   +----+----+----+----+----+----+----+----+   1:    White
 3 |    |    |    |    |    |    |    |    |
   +----+----+----+----+----+----+----+----+
 2 |  P |  P |  P |  P |  P |  P |  P |  P |
   +----+----+----+----+----+----+----+----+
 1 |  R |  N |  B |  Q |  K |  B |  N |  R |  Your move is?
   +----+----+----+----+----+----+----+----+
     a    b    c    d    e    f    g    h

    Human
```

If you don't want to specify a timer, just press Enter after starting the game. To move the pawn up two squares from the lower rank, enter **`e2e4`** and press the Enter key. The computer makes its move and new piece positions are updated on your display. To quit, type the word `quit` and press Enter. The program has more than 23 command-line options and features displaying play modes, hints, and timed games.

Playing Games with the emacs Editor

The venerable GNU `emacs` editor not only edits text, reads mail, and handles your appointments, but also comes with 18 wacky games and modes that you can use to pass the time, such as doctor, dunnet, psychoanalyze-pinhead, and yow.

To play dunnet, a text adventure, use `emacs` from the command line:

```
# emacs -batch -l dunnet
Dead end
You are at a dead end of a dirt road.  The road goes to the east.
In the distance you can see that it will eventually fork off.  The
trees here are very tall royal palms, and they are spaced equidistant
from each other.
There is a shovel here.
>
```

This command line starts the game. At the > prompt, enter commands such as `inventory`, `look`, or `go east`. To end the adventure, enter the word `quit`. Other games are listed in Table 38.2. Many of these games may be started by pressing Esc, then X, and then typing the name of the game and pressing Enter.

TABLE 38.2 Games for the GNU *emacs* Editor

Name	*Description*
blackbox	The blackbox game in `emacs` Lisp.
bruce	`bruce phrase` utility for overloading the Communications.
decipher	Cryptanalyze monoalphabetic substitution ciphers.
dissociate	Scramble text in current buffer.
doctor	Eliza-like psychological help.
dunnet	A text adventure for `emacs`.
gomoku	The Gomoku game for `emacs`.
hanoi	The Towers of Hanoi puzzle game.
life	John Horton Conway's Life game.
mpuz	A multiplication puzzle.
snake	The snake game for `emacs`.
solitaire	Solitaire in `emacs` Lisp.
spook	Generate phrase lines to overload National Security Agency computer monitoring of Internet message traffic.
tetris	Implementation of Tetris for `emacs`.
yow	Generate random Zippy quotes.

Strategy Games for X11

This section introduces you to some popular strategy games for X11. Many games are graphic renditions of classic games, such as chess, backgammon, or Mah-jongg, while others are unique and original puzzle games.

Play Chess with the `xboard` Client

Chess is a classic game and one of the major challenges you can face is playing chess against your computer. Use the `xboard` client to play chess in X11. This program uses the GNU chess engine and can play chess over the Internet or through electronic mail.

The `xboard` client (shown in Figure 38.1) recognizes many X11 toolkit options, such as geometry settings, and has 54 different command-line options. If you have a display smaller than 1,024×768 pixels, use the `-size` or `-boardSize small` command-line option to fit the board on your screen.

```
# xboard -size small &
```

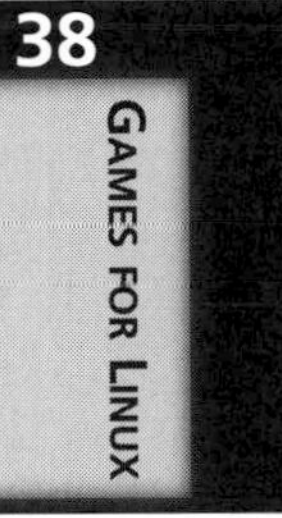

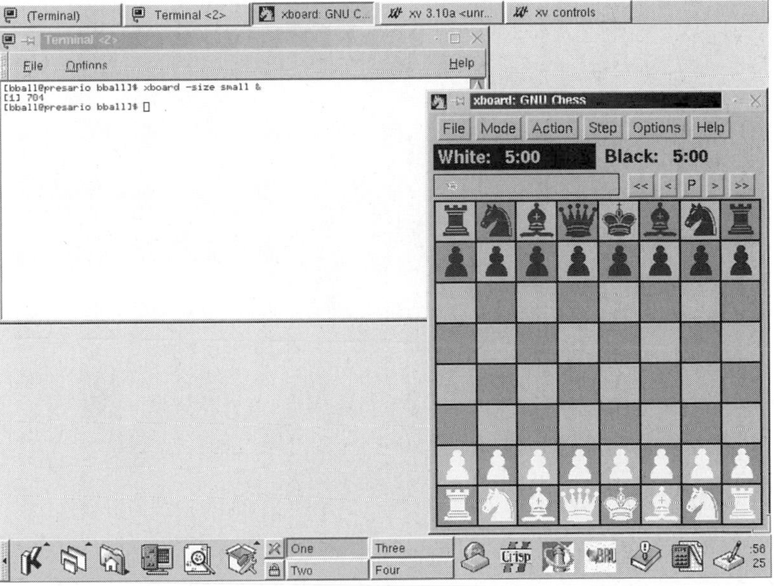

FIGURE 38.1
The `xboard` X11 client plays chess on your display, over the Internet, or through email.

The chess board window appears and sports controls for using a timer, switching players and positions, or controlling other aspects of the match.

Play Solitaire with xpat2

Although there are many different solitaire card games for X11, one of the best is the xpat2 X11 client, created by Heiko Eissfeldt and Michael Bischoff. This program (shown in Figure 38.2) features 14 different solitaire games with scoring, hints, built-in help, and sound. Start the game from the command line of a terminal window:

```
# xpat2 &
```

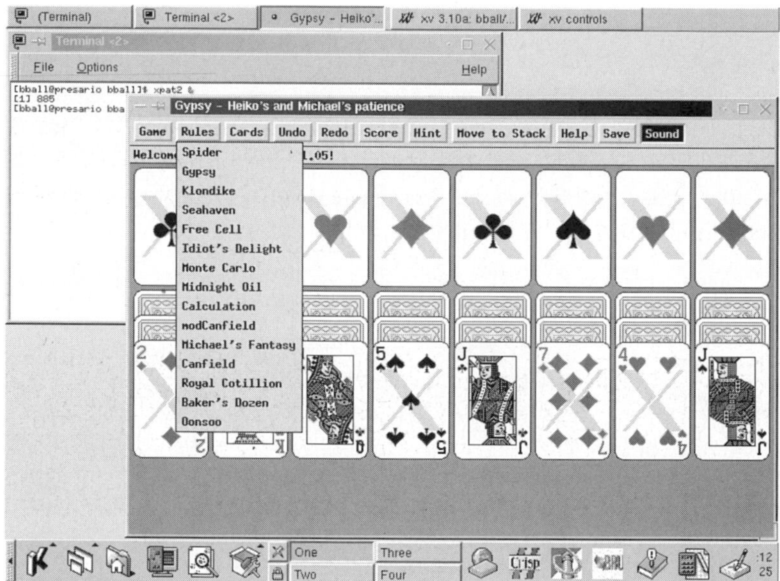

FIGURE 38.2
The xpat2 solitaire game for X11 features 14 different card games.

If Linux is configured to work with your computer's sound card, you'll hear whooping when you win, and goodbye when you quit.

Although the xpat2 client is not part of the OpenLinux distribution, you can find a copy at http://metalab.unc.edu/pub/Linux/games/solitaires/xpat2-1.06.tar.gz.

Playing Backgammon with xgammon

The xgammon client, by Lambert Klasen and Detlef Steuer (shown in Figure 38.3) provide hours of backgammon fun and practice. This game (unlike other X11 games) runs comfortably on an 800×600 pixel display.

Start xgammon from the command line of a terminal window:

```
# xgammon&
```

FIGURE 38.3
The xgammon *game provides a challenging game and features various types of play.*

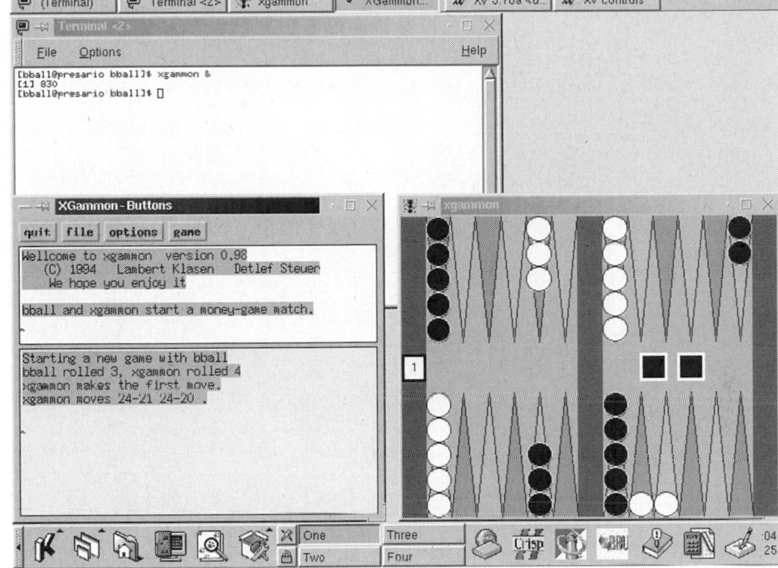

Note

If the xgammon client is not included with your favorite Linux distribution, you can find the `xgammon-0.98-14.i386.rpm` archive on a Red Hat Linux mirror site (start at `http://www.redhat.com`), or try the GNU backgammon client, available at `http://www.gnu.org/software/gnubg/gnubg.html`.

The `xgammon` client has 21 different command-line options. For an interesting variation, try watching your computer play itself:

```
# xgammon -g cvc &
```

Other challenging games may be created by editing the board and placing backgammon stones in different positions before play.

Playing Mah-jongg with `kmahjongg`

The `kmahjongg` client, included with the popular KDE is a beautiful rendition of the tile solitaire game. This game, by Mathius Mueller, also runs comfortably on an 800×600 pixel display. Although most users will start the game by clicking the K desktop panel's

Application Starter button, selecting Games, and then clicking the Mah-jongg menu item, `kmahjongg` may be launched from the command line of a terminal window like this:

```
# kmajonng&
```

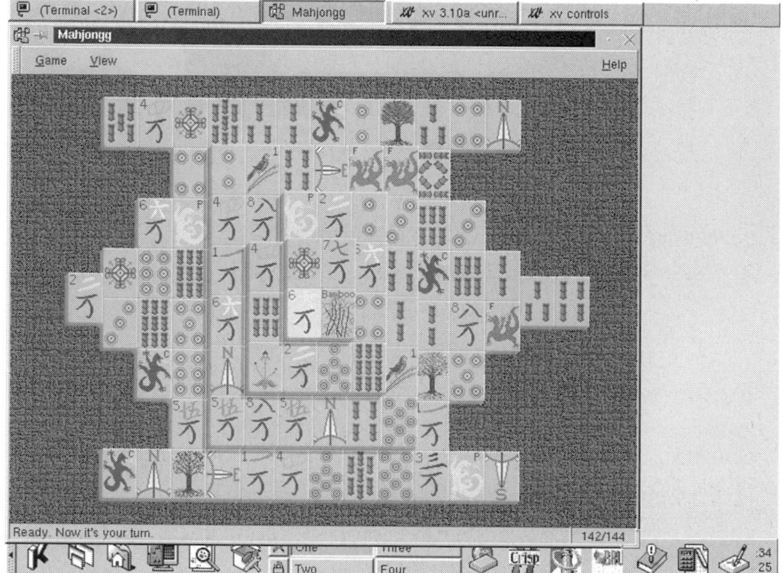

FIGURE 38.4
The `kmahjongg` game is a colorful and easy to play game of tile solitaire.

The game board will appear (as shown in Figure 38.4) in a 640×480 pixel window, and you can start the game using one of four different random tile patterns: classic, tower, triangle, or pyramid. The game features a demo mode, a chance to undo moves, and different backgrounds (loaded through the View menu).

Games for the K Desktop Environment

The `kmahjongg` client is only one of the many different games included with or coded for KDE. You do not have to use KDE as your desktop environment during your X11 sessions to play these games (listed in Table 38.3), but you must have the KDE and accompanying QT software libraries installed on your system. These software libraries provide a consistent look and feel for KDE clients, and feature floating, tear-off, or configurable menu and toolbars, along with documentation through a Help menu. For a more thorough discussion about the features of KDE, see Chapter 5, "Window Managers."

TABLE 38.3 Various Games for the K Desktop Environment

Name	*Description*
kabalone	Two-player board game.
kasteroids	KDE rendition of the classic shoot-em-up.
katchit	Single-player board game.
kblackbox	Single-player hide-and-seek board game.
kblackjack	Point-and-click card game of 21.
kgo	KDE rendition of GNU Go.
kjewel	Single-player falling blocks game.
kjumpingCube	Two-player board game.
kmahjongg	KDE rendition of tile solitaire.
kmaster	Single-player board game.
kmines	A Minesweeper-type game.
konquest	KDE rendition of the multi-player Gnu-Lactic Konquest.
kpacman	Faithful rendition of the classic arcade game.
kpat	Multi-game card solitaire.
kpipe	Connect-the-pipes timed board game.
kplumber	Connect-the-pipes timed board game.
kpoker	Simple point-and-click draw poker.
krepton	KDE rendition of the BBC Micro Repton game (similar to sokoban).
kreversi	Two-player capture-the-board game.
krossword	Crossword puzzle client.
ksame	Single-player piece elimination board game.
kshisen	Similar to kmahjongg.
ksirtet	Another KDE rendition of the falling blocks game.
ksmiletris	Yet another rendition of the falling blocks game.
ksnake	KDE rendition of the snake game.
ksokoban	KDE rendition of xsokoban (similar to krepton).
kspaceduel	Two-player arcade game.
ktron	KDE rendition of moving line game.
kzacman	A maze-like board game.

Games for the GNU Network Object Model Environment

There are also many different games included with or coded for GNOME. As with KDE, you do not have to use a GNOME-aware desktop manager during your X11 sessions to play these games (only some of which are listed in Table 38.3), but you must have the GNOME software libraries installed on your system. These software libraries provide a consistent look and feel for GNOME clients, such as menus and toolbars.

Note

For a more thorough discussion about GNOME's features, see Chapter 5.

TABLE 38.3 Various Games for the GNOME

Name	*Description*
GnomeScott	Game interpreter.
freecell	GNOME version of the FreeCell card game.
gnibbles	Single-player game.
gnobots	GNOME version of Robot Attack.
gnobots2	Another version of Robot Attack.
gnome-stones	Single-player board game.
gnomine	Minesweeper-like game.
mah-jongg	Tile solitaire game.
same-gnome	Similar to KDE's `same` game.
sol	Solitaire card game.

Hack, Rogue-Type, and Simulation Games

Veteran UNIX gamers will recall the classic game of rogue, in which you navigate through a series of mazes on varying levels, trying to stay alive as long as possible. The original version of this game used a variety of keyboard characters for movement, quaffing potions, doffing armor, and wielding weapons. Play was displayed by using cursor positioning to draw crude rooms, tunnels, and monsters. Later versions, such as hack, and later still, nethack, added the choice of characters and a dog as a partner-in-crime.

You'll find several newer versions with various improvements for Linux. Two of these are nethack and crossfire. The `crossfire` client for X11 (shown in Figure 38.5) features a host of improvements, including a scrolling display of your character as it moves through levels of the maze.

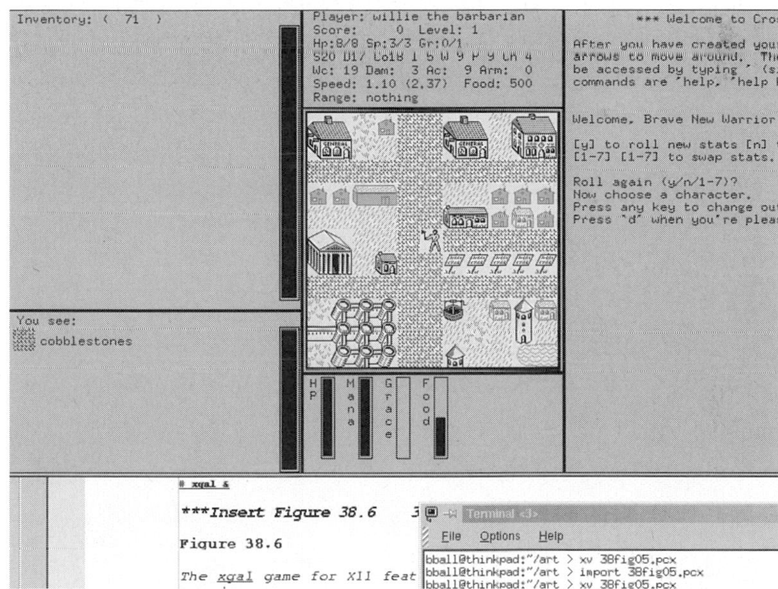

FIGURE 38.5
The crossfire game for X11 features an improved display to the classic rogue-type UNIX game.

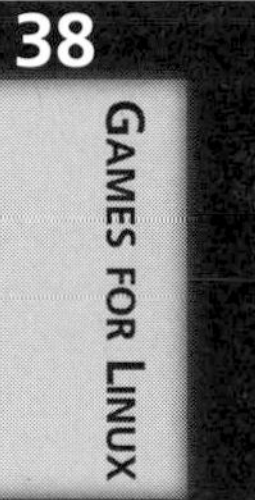

Simulators are another interesting genre of computer games, and you'll find a number (including older versions of SimCity) for Linux. One of the newest and most popular free simulation games is LinCity by I. J. Peters. This simulation game has numerous features (such as time/speed control), a plethora of simulation objects (such as factories, housing, windmills, rivers, and roads), and you can either launch built-in scenarios or build your own cities or region.

FIGURE 38.6
The xlincity simulation game can provide hours of fun as you watch your created village grow into a city.

Arcade Games for X11

For more action, try some of the video arcade games available for X11. Many provide plenty of action and stereo sounds. The following is a list of just a few of the more popular titles:

- abuse—Futuristic combat game.
- acm —Aerial combat simulator.
- battalion —A MESA library-enhanced 3D game.
- doom —Cult classic destroy-them-all game.
- koules —Smash-balls-into-the-wall game.
- Maelstrom —X11 port of an asteroid-like game for the Apple Macintosh.
- paradise —A networked combat game.
- quake —Successor to Doom (see "Quake II for Linux" in this chapter).
- rocksndiamonds —Collect objects while navigating a maze.
- scavenger —Lode-runner for X11.
- xboing —Classic break-out game.
- xchomp —Classic Pac-Man–like game.

- xjewel, xtrojka, xbl—Falling blocks games.
- xlander —A lunar lander game.
- xpilot —Networked combat game.

Playing Galaga for X11

A video action arcade game can be a lot of fun if it has great graphics and sound. One of the favorite shoot-em-ups is the xgal game by Joe Rumsey, which uses a simple keyboard interface. The xgal game (shown in Figure 38.6) can be started at a terminal window by typing this code:

```
# xgal &
```

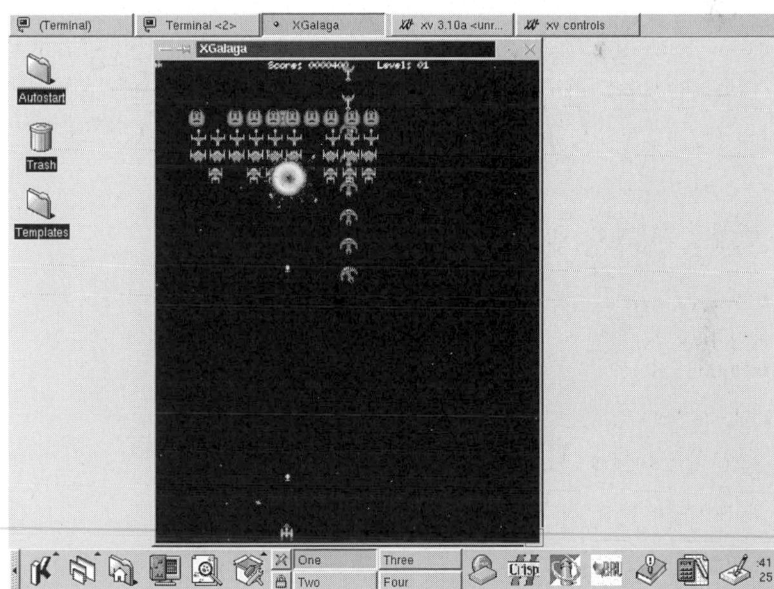

FIGURE 38.7
The xgal game for X11 features spiffy arcade action and good sound.

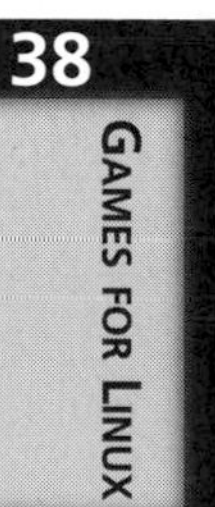

Press your spacebar to start the play. Use the right and left cursor keys to move your ship across the screen and use your spacebar to fire.

Quake II for Linux

Quake, by id Software, was the follow-up game to Doom, one of the most popular arcade games to hit the personal computer scene in the last 10 years. Beginning in mid-1999, the first of a wave of commercial games for Linux appeared on the market: Quake II (by id Software and distributed by Macmillan Digital Software).

> **Note**
>
> Original Quake fans can install and play a full or demo version for Linux. You'll need to download the `quake106.zip` shareware resource file (unless you own a copy of Quake) from `http://www.planetquake.com/linux`.
>
> Follow the installation instructions to install this version of Quake for your version of Linux. Linux users interested in setting up a Quake server for Internet or network games can check out the `xqf` Quake server browser and launcher. Browse to `http://www.linuxgames.com/xqf/`.

Installing Quake II for Linux

Graphics and sound-intensive applications such as games can tax even the most powerful PCs today, and Quake II is no exception. Quake II for Linux requires the following minimum hardware requirements:

- Intel Pentium 166Mhz or better equivalent CPU
- Linux kernel version 2.0.24 or higher
- 206–386MB of hard drive space
- 16–24MB of RAM
- A double-speed or better CD-ROM drive

Quake II is distribution in a series of `.rpm` archives on CD-ROM. To install Quake II, mount the CD-ROM, navigate to the CD-ROM base directory, and then execute a script named `setup`.

The Quake II system is distributed in RPM format only, with no Debian-format `.deb` packages. However, you can still install it on your Debian system. First, you need to install RPM for Debian:

```
apt-get install rpm
```

Now follow the instructions given here.

```
# sh setup
This will install Quake II (Colossus) to your system.

Please enter the location where RPM is installed. If you do not have
```

```
RPM installed, please enter "none" and this script will use cpio for
installation instead.

Location of RPM binary?  [/bin/rpm]
```

Press Enter if the default pathname (in brackets) is correct, or retype the path to the specified command.

```
Quake II (Colossus) will be installed in /usr/local/games/quake2

If you wish to install Quake II into another directory, please exit this
script now and place a symlink that points /usr/local/games/quake2
to your desired location.

Please select your installation option:

   Installation Type                         Size
1. Full Installation (game, CTF and videos)  386MB
2. Minimal Installation (game only)          206MB
3. Minimal with CTF                          226MB

Your choice? [1]
```

Press Enter to do a default, full installation. If hard drive space is a consideration, type a **2** and press Enter.

```
Installing....
Installating Quake II Binaries...
quake2
##################################################
Installating Quake II Game files...
quake2-data
##################################################
Installating Quake II Video files...
quake2-video
##################################################
Installating Quake II CTF files...
quake2-ctf
##################################################
Installation completed
```

As you can see, the `rpm` command will print hash marks (#) to show the progress of installation for each component of the game system. To get started right away, navigate to the `/usr/local/games/quake2` directory and type this:

```
# ./quake2
```

The main window will appear, as shown in Figure 38.8.

FIGURE 38.8
Quake II for Linux has many different features and includes a server mode for sponsoring network matches.

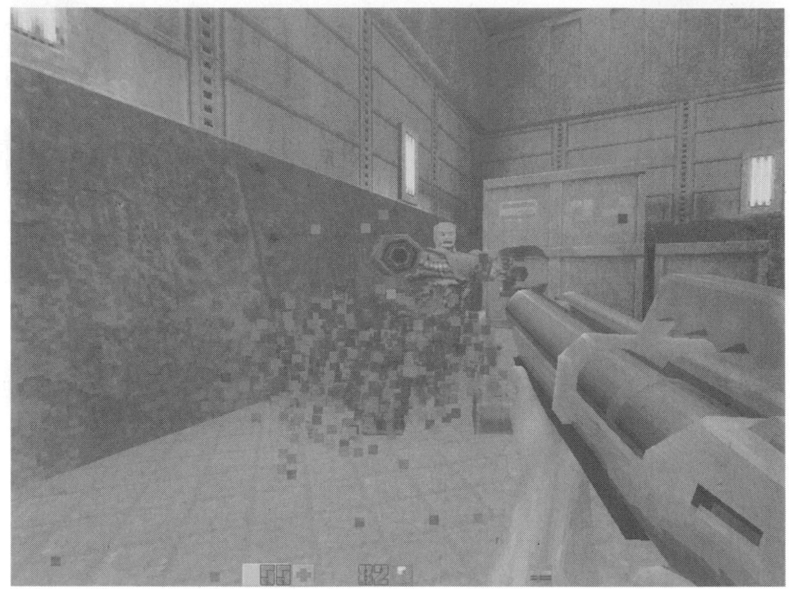

Resizing the Quake II Window and Customizing Controls

The default screen size of the Quake II window is 320×200 pixels. To enlarge the screen, press Esc, then scroll down to the video settings. Press the right or left cursor keys to enlarge the screen in increments from 320×200 to 640×480 or 800×600 pixels. When finished, scroll down to the Apply menu item and press Enter. The screen will then resize.

> **Note**
>
> Even with a fast (300Mhz or better) computer, you may find diminished performance when using a larger window during play. The optimum size for most computers will probably be 640×480 pixels. Increasing the brightness (through the Video submenu) may help improve clarity of the game.

By default, basic motion is accomplished by using the cursor keys. The default keyboard controls are listed in Table 38.4.

TABLE 38.4 Quake II Default Keyboard Controls

Action	*Keystroke*
Change weapon	Forward slash (/)
Crouch	c
Fire weapon	Ctrl or mouse button 1
Help	F key 1
Jump	Spacebar
Look down	z or Del
Look up	a or PgDn
Move backward	Down cursor
Move forward	Up cursor or mouse button 3
Run	Shift
Show inventory	Tab
Sidestep	Alt or mouse button 2
Step left	Comma (,)
Step right	Period (.)
Turn left	Left cursor
Turn right	Right cursor

If you're an experienced X11 user, you may be familiar with a common problem when playing games that use the mouse: loss of focus, in which you lose control of the game controls by moving the mouse outside of the active game window. Many X11 games provide for a grab option to tie the X11 pointer to the active game window. If you use the mouse or a joystick to play Quake II, you can set the mouse to be tied to the Quake II window through the Video menu's Windowed Mouse option. You can also use *key bindings*, or definitions entered through the Quake II console to define keyboard controls to bind or unbind the mouse. See the file `readme` in the `/usr/local/games/quake2` directory (or wherever you've installed the Quake II binaries and files).

You can also set various options, such as those for video and sound for game play through `quake2`'s `set` command-line option. For example, to try to use better sound quality (if your soundcard supports it), you can specify a higher sampling rate (such as 11025, 22051, or 44100) with the `set` option:

```
# ./quake2 +set sndspeed 22051
```

Finally, for those Quake fanatics who want to set up and run a Quake server to support network gaming, you can start Quake II in a server mode by using the set option, followed by a server command or specifications. Here's an example:

```
# ./quake2 +set dedicated 1
```

There are a number of other server settings, and you can also save settings in various configuration files. Again, see the `readme` file in the installed Quake II directory for details.

Summary

Linux has a wealth of available games. Many of these games were inherited by default from early UNIX operating systems. It is a credit to these early games programmers that these games remain popular and can still amuse and enchant today's Linux users. New Linux users will be able to rediscover the joys of playing older challenging games and will also enjoy the fruits of the growing popularity of Linux: Commercial quality games are being developed, marketed, and sold for Linux.

CHAPTER 39

Linux on Laptops

In This Chapter

Notebook computers (or *laptops*, as they're sometimes called) can be both liberating and frustrating. The liberating aspect is easy to understand—it's very handy to be able to whip out a full-fledged computer at a moment's notice, whether for important tasks or wasting time.

At the same time, getting a notebook completely configured and working to its full potential can be quite a daunting task. Notebooks are complex; many of the features required to make them useful also make them difficult to work with. Installing any operating system is a bit of a challenge since most operating systems aim themselves at the large desktop market and see notebooks as secondary.

The good news is that it is possible to get Linux running on a notebook, and most distributions make it as easy as possible. Moreover, Linux can in many cases bring new life to older notebooks, as its hardware requirements are much lower than most traditional notebook OSs.

Getting Installed

Installation is always the first step in getting Linux working. In general, this installation process isn't much different from the regular one. The best approach to installing Linux, therefore, is to keep in mind some important factors discussed in the following sections before installation or while installing.

Selecting a Notebook Computer for Linux

The best way to avoidinstallation headaches is, of course, to buy with Linux in mind. This can be accomplished two ways: buying a notebook from a Linux vendor or researching. Several vendors sell Linux preinstalled on notebooks. Usually, these are extensively tested for compatibility, and most (if not all) of the features they provide will work. You should make sure that all of the drivers for all of the hardware are free, and get a list of any hardware drivers that are not; this will allow you to reinstall the system (or install it, if the notebook comes with a different Linux distribution).

If you do not buy from a Linux vendor, the next best thing is to research your options extensively. Make sure you know what hardware to avoid and then look around at machines. When you see one you like, look for drivers for all its hardware. If it doesn't have some critical drivers, continue shopping. Stop when you find a model that has full hardware support (or at least enough hardware support that you can live with it).

Tip

Probably the most comprehensive Linux notebook site is the Linux laptop home page at `http://www.cs.utexas.edu/users/kharker/linux-laptop/`.

This page has a semi-complete database of links to pages for specific models of notebooks, several links to important tech issues, and other information. If you have a Linux notebook, bookmark it!

The Tecra Problem

Some computers have a problem when booting the Linux kernel. All PC-style computers start in a mode called *real mode*; while in this mode, the computer can use only 640K of memory at a time. The kernel is responsible for switching the computer into *protected mode*, where the full amount of memory is available. Computers with the *Tecra problem* have a bug in their circuitry, which causes the computer to hang the moment Linux attempts to switch the computer into full-blown protected mode under certain circumstances.

While the problem has been seen in desktop machines, it is far more common in notebooks. Its name, in fact, comes from the Toshiba Tecra line of notebooks, which was particularly prone to this problem. The problem is not exclusive to Toshiba notebooks, however.

Debian GNU/Linux addresses the problem by providing a special version of the Debian rescue disk for starting the installation. The kernel compiled on that disk includes a patch that will fix the problem. The images are located in the same location as the regular rescue disk images, with the word *tecra* in the name, such as `resc1440tecra.bin`.

If your computer has the Tecra problem, you should not install the standard Debian kernel packages (`kernel-image-x.x.xx-xxx.deb`) to upgrade your kernel. These kernels will, most likely, not have the Tecra patch. You can build your own kernel for this purpose; you can get away without applying the patch if you only build zImage kernels instead of bzImage kernels.

Fortunately, the recently released Linux 2.2 kernel included with most Linux distributions has incorporated the Tecra patch. Thus, any 2.2 kernel will build and boot properly with or without the patch, no matter how it is built.

Handling Media

Many notebooks have limited installation media options; many do not have CD-ROMs and some do not allow you to use the CD and floppy drives at the same time.

If your notebook has a CD-ROM drive and can boot from it, you will have no problem; simply boot from the first CD in the official set and continue from there. The same is true of a system that includes both a CD-ROM and a floppy and allows you to use them at the same time. These systems will install in the normal way.

If you cannot install this way (you don't have a CD-ROM or it shares a docking bay with the floppy drive or you have the Tecra problem and must boot from the floppy), boot from the floppy drive. You can then install the base system from floppy, hard disk, or NFS.

Most Linux distributions are capable of a floppyless install of the base system from a DOS partition on a hard drive. While it might seem wasteful to lose the space for the DOS partition, it makes more sense on a notebook.

Most modern notebooks support a suspend mode where the BIOS writes the contents of memory to disk, restoring it when the system is revived. This typically requires a small DOS partition for the BIOS to write to; the same partition should have enough room to hold the installation files for the floppyless install. After installation, you can delete the install files from the partition and configure the notebook to support suspend-to-disk; read on for details.

Tip

You can usually enable the use of PCMCIA devices during a Linux installation. This is not necessary, but is useful when you need a PCMCIA device to install (such as a network card for network installations, or a PCMCIA adapter for a CD-ROM). You can find a list of cards and the drivers they need in the file `SUPPORTED.CARDS`, available from David Hinds (author of Card Services for Linux) at `http://hyper.stanford.edu/HyperNews/get/pcmcia/home.html`.

Once the base system has been installed, the issues concerning shared docking bays, the Tecra bug, and the like, should be resolved. Installing the rest of the system can be done in the usual ways. If you configured PCMCIA during the install, it should still work on the base system. If you have a modem, one possibility is to install the rest of the base system over PPP using your Internet connection; it will likely be slow, but do-able.

Laptop Support

Hardware issues tend to be more important on notebooks than they typically are on desktop machines. Full-size machines usually install extra hardware into expansion slots, making them easy to replace if necessary, and most of the work on desktop systems involves issues such as speed and capacity. By contrast, notebooks usually have all extra hardware hardwired into the motherboard, and replacing or expanding it usually involves giving up a precious PCMCIA slot. Also, size is as important (if not more so) as speed or capacity; this tends to cause notebook hardware to be more or less incompatible with each other.

PCMCIA

PCMCIA stands as a notable exception to the chaos of notebook hardware. It is a robust, mature standard, supported by most OSs and most notebook computers, and has been until recently the only way to add capabilities to a notebook. At its core, PCMCIA is a specification for the physical and logical connections between a computer and expansion hardware. Most notebooks (but not all) include two PCMCIA slots, usually located one above the other on the side of your computer. The "cards" that fit in it are about the size of some of the smallest pocket calculators or smart cards.

From a software perspective, the PCMCIA bus is driven by a chip on the motherboard. A master set of PCMCIA drivers controls the chip. When the chip detects a PCMCIA card in a slot, it notifies the drivers, giving them specific instructions about the card. The drivers can then load additional drivers to talk to the card itself, as well as trigger the OS to set up the card and begin using it. When a card is removed, the reverse happens; the drivers signal the OS to shut down support of the card and unload any drivers necessary.

Under Linux, the `cardmgr` user-space process performs all of the active tasks—watching for insertions and removals, loading and unloading drivers, and configuring and unconfiguring devices. Assisting in this work are a set of shell scripts in the `/etc/pcmcia` directory, which are run in similar fashion to the boot scripts when cards are added or removed.

Red Hat

Card Services for Red Hat Linux is enabled through settings in the file named `pcmcia` under the `/etc/sysconfig` directory. If you install or overlay a new version of Card Services on your Red Hat system, please read David Hinds' PCMCIA HOWTO (found under the `/usr/doc/HOWTO` or `/usr/doc/pcmcia` directory) for details about proper boot configuration.

PCMCIA is a *hot-swap protocol*; generally speaking, it's not necessary to start a card after inserting it, or shut down a card after removing it. However, the fact that PCMCIA devices are hot-swappable does not imply that the services they provide are hot-swappable. For example, if you mount a disk over a PCMCIA SCSI card, you can pop out the card anytime without the PCMCIA subsystem having problems, but if you don't unmount the filesystem before popping out the card, you're likely to have serious problems with your machine.

If necessary, you can shut down a card through software before ejecting it to ensure that all drives are unmounted and all references to the drive are closed; this is done with the `cardctl` command.

```
# cardctl eject <socket number>
```

`<socket number>` is most likely `0` or `1`.

OpenLinux laptop users running X11 can use the `cardinfo` client from the command line of a terminal window to graphically control PC cards.

Caution

PCMCIA IDE cards cards must be shut down manually before they can be ejected.

Installing PCMCIA Support

There are two packages that provide PCMCIA support: `pcmcia-cs` and `pcmcia-modules-x.xx.xx`, where `x.xx.xx` represents a kernel version.

If you use one of Debian's provided kernel packages for your kernel, you should be able to install the proper `pcmcia-modules` package for your kernel version. Each `pcmcia-modules` package recommends a corresponding kernel package; you should install the corresponding kernel package unless there is a good reason not to, such as if you have the Tecra problem.

If you build your own custom kernel, you need to build a custom `pcmcia-modules` package that matches the kernel. Here are the basic steps:

1. Install the `pcmcia-source` package.
2. Change to the `/usr/src` directory as `root` and locate the `pcmcia-cs.tar.gz` file there. Unpack it with this command:

   ```
   # tar xvzf pcmcia-cs.tar.gz
   ```

   This installs the module source in the right directory.
3. Install the Linux kernel source code and build the kernel package as normal. For more information about building a custom kernel, please read Chapter 23, "Kernel Management." A tool named `make-kpkg` is used at this point to compile the kernel and modules and create a kernel package to hold them.

4. After the kernel package has been built, you must execute `make-kpkg` again from the same directory (typically `/usr/src/linux` or `/usr/src/kernel-source-x.xx.xx`). This time, however, `modules-image` is the final argument instead of `kernel-image`. As an example, assume you built your kernel package with this command line:

   ```
   # make-kpkg --revision=custom.1.0 kernel-image
   ```

   In that case, you should run this command line next:

   ```
   # make-kpkg --revision=custom.1.0 modules-image
   ```

   This builds all of the add-on module source packages, including `pcmcia-source`. You will find these packages with the custom kernel package in `/usr/src`.

After you have located or compiled the proper `pcmcia-modules` package for your system, you can then install `pcmcia-modules` and `pcmcia-cs`. Don't forget to install your custom kernel package as well; the drivers are unlikely to work if the proper kernel isn't running.

Default initialization of Card Services for Red Hat Linux is controlled by a shell script named `pcmcia` under the `/etc/rc.d/init.d` directory, while boot options are contained in another file named `pcmcia` under the `/etc/sysconfig` directory. This script recognizes and uses the keywords `start`, `stop`, `restart`, and `status`.

At this point, `cardmgr` should be running and it should have at least tried to configure any devices in the notebook's slots. If it hasn't, look at the log files to see what might have gone wrong. The most common problem is a version mismatch between the running kernel and the PCMCIA modules; to fix this, simply either make sure you're running a matched pair of `kernel-package` and `pcmcia-modules` or build a custom kernel.

Note

You can use the `dmesg` command or examine the contents of your system log (usually `/var/log/messages`) for output from Card Services. This information looks somewhat like the following. Note that not all the output is shown:

```
Linux PCMCIA Card Services 3.0.9
  kernel build: 2.2.7 unknown
  options:  [pci] [cardbus]
Intel PCIC probe:
...
```

This information can be invaluable in diagnosing problems related to PCMCIA recognition and initialization.

Understanding the Setup Files

As mentioned, `cardmgr` is notified whenever a card is inserted or removed. When a new card is inserted, a description of the card is given to `cardmgr`. This description is matched with a description given in /etc/pcmcia/config; the device type and driver filename are read from the config file, the device driver is loaded, and a script associated with the device type is run with some options passed.

Typically, each script has a file with a name ending in .opts associated with it, such as network and network.opts. The script itself is considered a part of the system code and should not be changed. However, the .opts file is run by the standard scripts to provide local configuration. If you need to make adjustments to the system's configuration, don't edit the .opts file unless you know what you're doing.

The cardmgr program has the concept of named *schemes* that can be chosen with the cardctl program. Schemes are persistent across reboots and are in effect until changed. The scheme is always passed to the .opts file when it is executed; by testing for the scheme name, it is possible to generate hardware profiles for the different circumstances the notebook may find itself in: docked or undocked, at work or at home, attached to different networks, and so on. These profiles can then be switched on-the-fly by switching schemes; since the cards are reconfigured when the scheme is switched, the scheme switch takes effect immediately.

Setting Up Network Cards

Because of the dynamic nature of PCMCIA and the mobility notebooks provide, configuring PCMCIA networking is probably the most complicated part of PCMCIA configuration. Besides having to handle all the different devices that might be plugged in, the configuration must also take into account the different networks, with different IP adresses, gateways, and name servers that may be connected.

Configuration of PCMCIA network cards should not be done with the standard network configuration scripts; PCMCIA cards cannot be set up through the standard network configuration because of their ability to disappear and reappear literally at any time. Rather, PCMCIA network configuration should be done in /etc/pcmcia/network.opts.

Red Hat

The default Card Services set up under Red Hat Linux does not require a network.opts; network PCMCIA setup is contained in a file named network under the /etc/pcmcia directory. According to David Hinds in his PCMCIA HOWTO, you can use a network.opts file with these contents:

```
if [ -f /etc/sysconfig/network-scripts/ifcfg-eth0 ] ; then
     start_fn () {
          /sbin/ifup $1
     }
     stop_fn () {
          /sbin/ifdown $1
     }
fi
```

The default Card Services set up for Caldera OpenLinux is similar to Red Hat Linux.

The pcmcia-cs package provides a pcnetconfig script for simple network configuration. Through this script, you can set the interface to use DHCP or BOOTP, or you can set the configuration manually. This works best when you can guarantee that you will be able to autoconfigure with DHCP or BOOTP wherever you happen to plug in, or if you know you will only be plugging in to a single network. As a convenience, the pcmcia-cs package runs this as part of the post-installation process; thus, you should be ready to go if you configured the network device properly when you installed this package.

For more complicated network configurations, you need to edit network.opts to get it to do what you need. The environment for network.opts contains a variable called ADDRESS, with all of the information for the current setup. It contains four fields, separated by commas—the current scheme, the socket the card was inserted into, the interface instance (used when a card provides multiple devices), and the hardware MAC address of the network card. By using standard shell script syntax, it is possible to set various environment variables which will affect how the device is configured. These variables can be set:

- IF_PORT—The transceiver type. This can be set to auto, 10baseT, 10base2, aui, or 100baseT.
- BOOTP DHCP—These take a y or n, for yes or no, respectively. This indicates that the particular auto-configuration system (BOOTP or DHCP) should be used. You should only set one of these to y. Note that both BOOTP and DHCP can provide many of the other options.
- IPADDR NETMASK BROADCAST NETWORK GATEWAY—These options together set up a manually configured interface.
- DOMAIN SEARCH—Only one of these should be set. The former sets the current domain name, and the other sets up a domain search list for DNS name lookups.
- DNS_1 DNS_2 DNS_3—Hostnames or IP addresses of DNS name servers, in order of preference. If you use hostnames for these, you need to make sure that the hostnames can be resolved—by adding their names to /etc/hosts, for example.
- MOUNTS—A list of mount points to automount when this device is configured, and to unmount when the device is removed. Each mount point should be configured in /etc/fstab; usually, you will want these to have the noauto flag since you only want them to mount when PCMCIA is configured. If you use this, you should be careful when removing the network card, as it will usually be impossible to unmount the filesystem properly if the network card is removed without warning.
- IPX_FRAME IPX_NETNUM—These options configure IPX support, corresponding to the IPX frame type and network number. They are passed directly to

ipx_interface to configure the interface; see documentation on IPX networking (such as Kevin Thorpe's IPX HOWTO under the /usr/doc/HOWTO directory) for details.

A sample network.opts is shown in Listing 39.1. This setup uses both the hardware interface and the socket number to configure each interface. It assumes that any card inserted into socket 0 will configure itself with DHCP. It sets up two different manual setups for two different hardware addresses if the card is inserted into socket 1, falling back to DHCP if neither of those two cards is found.

LISTING 39.1 Sample Card Services *network.opts*

```
case "$ADDRESS" in
*,0,*,*)
    DHCP="y"
    ;;
*,1,*,00:00:12:34:56:78)
    IPADDR="192.168.1.25"
    NETMASK="255.255.255.0"
    NETWORK="192.168.1.0"
    BROADCAST="192.168.1.255"
    GATEWAY="192.168.1.1"
    DOMAIN="tech.example.com"
    DNS_1="192.168.1.1"
    ;;
*,1,*,00:00:87:65:43:21)
    IPADDR="10.3.14.6"
    NETMASK="255.255.0.0"
    NETWORK="10.3.0.0"
    BROADCAST="10.3.255.255"
    GATEWAY="10.3.2.1"
    DOMAIN="financial. example.com"
    DNS_1="10.3.16.221"
    ;;
*,1,*,*)
    DHCP="y"
    ;;
esac
```

Setting Up Modems

Modem devices usually configure themselves; there is usually no need to change the delivered defaults in /etc/pcmcia/serial.opts. As with network cards, you should not set up PCMCIA modems in the regular setup scripts; reserve that for permanent devices, such as built-in serial ports or modems.

There are several options available if you want to change the default setup for any reason. They work in the same way as the network options; set them in environment variables in `serial.opts`. You can also look at the `ADDRESS` environment variable (just as with `network.opts`) to detect various conditions. Three fields are passed: the PCMCIA scheme, socket number, and device instance. The options follow:

- `LINK`—This option tells the system to provide a symbolic link to the real serial device at this location. This is useful especially with PCMCIA modems since there is no guarantee that a particular modem will be configured as the same device each time it is inserted. The default is the symbolic link `/dev/modem` (pointing to the pertinent serial device, such as /dev/ttySX), which allows most Debian software to locate the modem easily with the default configurations. You may need to change this if you ever need to have more than one modem installed. That way the PCMCIA system will not overwrite any symbolic links when modems are added or removed.
- `SERIAL_OPTS`—This allows you to pass options directly to `setserial` when the serial port is being configured.
- `INITTAB`—This option allows you to add a program to `/etc/inittab` whenever the modem is inserted; it removes the program when the card is removed. This allows you to run a `getty` process on the modem when it's installed, creating an instant dial-in machine. Set this to the command line for the process you want to run; the script will add the device name to the end of the command line before adding it to the `inittab` file.

Setting Up Other Devices

Most other devices are configured as storage devices. They can be partitioned, formatted, and mounted just like hard disks. Some of them can also be read from and written to like an arbitrary file if necessary. Usually, the default settings will work fine for these devices; you should only need to change them if you want to do something interesting (such as automount a device at insertion time).

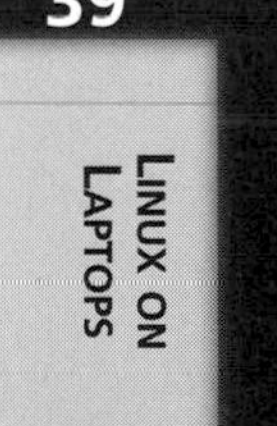

The `ADDRESS` variable, when passed to the `.opts` file, contains at least two parameters separated by commas: the PCMCIA scheme and the socket number. Cards that are not standard memory cards will add a third parameter; this is the instance number for flash memory cards and the serial number for the drive being configured for IDE adapters. If there are partitions present on the device, the fourth number will be the partition number.

The options that can be set by the `.opts` file are as follows:

- `DO_FSTAB DO_FSCK DO_MOUNT`—These options all take a `y` or `n` for yes or no, respectively. These specify whether an `fstab` entry should be created, whether the device should have its filesystem checked on insertion, and whether the device should be mounted on insertion.

- FSTYPE OPTS MOUNTPT—These parameters tell the system what kind of disk device this device is. This is used for the DO_* options, so cardmgr knows what parameters to use.

SCSI devices other than disks should simply become available when the card is plugged in, using the normal SCSI device files. You should ensure that issues with termination and so on are taken care of on the SCSI bus before inserting the card. All connected devices should be powered on before insertion and not powered off until after the card is removed.

The ADDRESS field for SCSI devices is quite different. There are six required fields, one optional: the PCMCIA scheme, the device type (sd, st, sr, or sg, for disk, tape, CD, or generic devices, respectively), the socket number, the SCSI channel, the SCSI ID, the logical unit number, and (optionally) the partition number. As with the rest of the scripts, each field is separated by a space, and you can use the information in scsi.opts to specify different options.

Memory cards are treated either as block or character devices. If used as a character device, it is possible to write to arbitrary parts of the device. Most people will want to use memory cards to increase the available memory of the system; this can be done by formatting the device as a swap partition and adding the swap partition to the available swap space. If you do this, you should increase the priority of the memory card's swap space to be higher than disk swap, as the memory card will be much faster.

Flash memory cards are treated as a different device class than regular memory cards; for these, you may need to use the ftl_format utility before working with the card. Some cards use the Microsoft Flash File System instead of the industry-standard FTL format; these memory cards cannot yet be used with Linux.

Advanced Power Management

When you're on a battery-powered computer, it stands to reason that minimizing power consumption is an important issue. While better technology—lower-power components, idle detection, spin-down disks, and the like—help immensely, there is also much to gain from letting the computer actively assist in preserving power. To this end, many computers provide a standard interface to the system that allows it to learn where the power is coming from and how much time may be left, as well as turn off portions of itself when not needed and alert otherwise unnecessary power-hungry applications to stop running. This interface is the Advanced Power Management specification (APM).

APM provides more features that have uses outside a notebook. For example, it allows the OS to tell the PC to shut off the power completely as part of a shutdown script, and it can trigger or respond to a request to put the machine into a low- or zero-power mode (Standby or Suspend mode). These features are sometimes handy on desktop machines as well as notebooks, and are often provided with newer PCs for conservation or management purposes.

All of these options are supported under Linux. Most are supported transparently by the kernel; once it's turned on, it works without any intervention. User-level software is also included, which allows even greater savings. If you're willing to tweak your system a bit, even more savings can be found.

APM support is compiled into the default Red Hat Linux kernel; notebook users will only have to rebuild the kernel if special options or patches are required.

The default Caldera OpenLinux kernel does not support APM; you will have to recompile the OpenLinux kernel to enable power-saving features for your notebook.

Debian users must also recompile the kernel for APM support.

Understanding APM

The interface to APM is provided through a series of BIOS calls. Besides returning information, these calls also allow the system to receive APM events and command APM to do something. The underlying operations to actually do everything are proprietary to each model, but they are hidden beneath the APM BIOS.

The kernel provides a standard character device for the APM BIOS, which is installed on Debian as `/dev/apm_bios`. This device allows user-mode software to watch for APM events and control the driver. The file `/proc/apm` is also provided for reporting status to user-mode programs.

The Suspend mode feature is handled entirely within the APM BIOS. When Suspend mode is requested, the BIOS writes the entire contents of memory to a disk file, as well as some status information, and then turns the computer off. When the computer is turned on again, the APM BIOS recognizes this, reloads memory from the backup file, and restarts everything exactly as it was before.

Kernel Options for APM

The standard Debian and OpenLinux kernels come with APM disabled, so you must build a custom kernel in order to take advantage of it. When configuring, make sure you say Yes to Advanced Power Management BIOS Support when configuring the kernel.

The kernel has several settings that control how APM support is configured:

- Ignore `USER SUSPEND` This option exists to compensate for a bug in the BIOS of some NEC notebooks. Only use it if you have a problem notebook.
- Enable APM at Boot Time This option allows many APM features (such as auto-standby and CPU idle) to turn themselves on at boot instead of when the OS turns them on. Generally, it's okay to turn this off, since APM boots early enough in the boot sequence for this to make little difference.
- Make `CPU IDLE` Calls When Idle This features allows Linux to tell the CPU that it is idle. Some computers will see these calls and slow the CPU down during idle times, which draws less power. Turn this on by default. On some machines, you may notice problems with the machine hanging after being idle for a time; recompile with this option off if you see this.
- Enable Console Blanking Using APM The internal console screensaver usually turns the screen to black when it activates. With this selected, the screensaver will call APM to shut off the display. This can save lots of power, so turn it on if you can.
- Power Off on Shutdown Enables Linux to turn the power off after shutting down the system. Turn this on unless you have problems with it.
- Ignore Multiple Suspend Some IBM notebooks cannot handle multiple suspend requests that come in at the same time. This option will block suspend requests that come in while a suspend request is being processed.

APM Software

The user-mode software for controlling APM is provided in the Debian `apmd` package or the Red Hat `apmd-3.0beta507 .rpm` file. It includes `apmd` itself, a command-line status program called `apm`, and `xapm`, a simple X battery meter.

You may not find APM support or software `.rpm` files included on your OpenLinux 2.2 CD-ROM! Browse to `ftp://ftp.caldera.com` and search for updated or contributed APM support files.

`apmd` is a program that runs in the background, watching the current power status and listening for APM events. It logs interesting information to the standard log files, can send alerts when battery power runs low, and allows Linux to handle suspend and resume events properly.

Under Debian, you can specify any number of arbitrary scripts to run at suspend or resume time by placing the script in `/etc/apm/suspend.d` or `/etc/apm/resume.d`, respectively. Several packages (`pcmcia`, for example) place scripts in this directory to handle the most common problems, so you do not need to put a script here. The `init`

script also handles reloading the system time from the CMOS clock properly, consulting the standard Debian configuration files to determine whether the time is stored as Universal Time.

You may want to change some of the other `apmd` settings. This can be done by editing the Debian `init` script (`/etc/init.d/apmd`) and setting the `APMD` variable in the script to contain the options you want, separated by spaces.

The `apmd` settings file is located under the `/etc/sysconfig` directory.

The options available follow:

`-p` *`<percent>`*

Set the logging change percentage. This tells `apmd` by what percentage the power must change before `apmd` logs the information. The default is `5`, or 5 percent.

`-w` *`<percent>`*

Set the warning percentage. `apmd` begins logging warnings when the power drops below this level. The default is `10`, or 10 percent.

`-W`

In addition to logging any problems, send a message to every logged-in user about the problem. This can alert you to a problem without you having to constantly monitor a log file.

Getting X Running

Notebooks present several unique problems for running XFree86. First, while XFree86 is designed for the wild world of standard analog SVGA, most notebooks use fixed-resolution LCD screens. Additionally, many notebooks include an external VGA connector for attaching an external monitor; these external monitors can often be driven at resolutions far beyond what are available on the built-in screen. What's worse, many manufacturers of laptop VGA chipsets refuse to release documentation or drivers for XFree86; this is curious, considering how most desktop vendors have given up on secrecy.

Note

While most Linux laptop users will choose XFree86, there are also commercial alternative servers available from at least two vendors: Metrolink, Inc.'s Metro-X (`http://www.metrolink.com`), and Xi-Graphic's Accelerated-X (`http://www.xig.com`).

The details of getting X configured are covered in Chapter 4, "The X Window System." This section deals with issues unique to notebook computers.

Selecting the Right X Server

The first step in configuring XFree86 is to select and install the proper X server. The server installed should be able to talk to and drive the graphics chipset.

The notebook manual should describe the hardware in the machine and should include information on the chipset used. If it doesn't, or if you don't have the monitor, you can use the `SuperProbe` utility to determine what chipset you have or look on the Web for the information you need. The Linux laptop home page lists notebook models it knows about, and the manufacturer's site will often list the information as well.

Once you have figured out what chipset you have, you can install the proper server. See Chapter 4 for more details on this process.

Tip

Notebook graphics chipsets are notorious for being unsupported. If the chipset supports the VESA BIOS 2.0 standard, however, you may still be able to run X on it, if you don't mind running the 2.2 kernel and don't mind running it unaccelerated.

Linux 2.2.x includes a new console driver—the framebuffer console. This allows the kernel to drive the display in graphics mode instead of relying on the VGA text mode support on the card. The supplied driver works with any VESA 2.0 BIOS.

Layered on top of this is a new X server, provided in the package `xserver-fbdev`, which uses the framebuffer console to draw to the screen instead of talking directly to the graphics chipset. This X server will work on any system that is using the framebuffer console, no matter what card or driver is underneath. For more information on setting up and using the framebuffer console, see the files in `Documentation/fb` under the Linux 2.2.x kernel source.

Setting Up for Running the LCD Screen

As mentioned, XFree86 is designed to control analog CRT monitors. These monitors are typically capable of running at multiple resolutions and color depths, and even parameters such as the refresh rate are available to tweak. By contrast, LCD screens are, in most respects, fixed: one standard resolution, one standard refresh rate. Some even have limitations regarding color depth they can display.

Most notebook chipsets handle this gracefully, providing a mostly standard SVGA interface, but translating all settings into the settings that the LCD can be driven at. For this reason, the actual settings that are normally vital for SVGA aren't as important.

The important thing is to set up the default resolution and color depth to something that the LCD can handle. Since the LCD will most likely be the primary monitor on the machine, it should be the first resolution to come up.

Handling External Monitors

If you will be attaching external monitors to the VGA connector on the notebook, configure X to drive those monitors. Since the chipset mostly handles driving the LCD display, the settings for the external monitor won't interfere with using the LCD. In fact, many laptops can enable you to drive both monitors at the same time; since this is usually handled through hardware, Debian will support running in that mode. This is especially handy when doing product demonstrations or presentations on a projector screen.

In some notebooks, the chipset can drive an external monitor at higher resolutions than the LCD can handle. This is okay, as long as the LCD is not being used (either exclusively or in dual mode). The default resolution should always be set to one the LCD can handle; after this, use Ctrl+Alt+Plus and Ctrl+Alt+Minus to switch modes once the LCD is shut off. (The Ctrl+Alt+Plus and Ctrl+Alt+Minus key sequences may require the keypad plus and minus keys to work. Most notebooks provide this through a special shift or lock key.)

Note

Certain notebook chipsets may also need to have external display capabilities enabled by the X server. For example, NeoMagic users may need to insert this in the Device section of the `XF86Config` file in order to enable external display:

```
Option    extern_disp
```

You also need to add the following option to enable an external and LCD display:

```
Option    intern_disp
```

See the pertinent readme file for your notebook's chipset under the `/usr/X11R6/lib/X11/doc` directory for more information.

Other Built-In Hardware

Most other hardware for notebooks have the same issues as hardware on regular computers. Notebooks tend to be more prone to new and strange hardware, mostly because of the size and power consumption issues.

Some notebooks come with *multimedia chipsets*. These chipsets usually provide sound and modem support at a minimum; others may also put their video support on them. Unfortunately, most of these chipsets are not well documented, and some rely on software drivers to do most of their work; this makes them mostly unsupported by Linux. A few (notably the MWave chipset found on some IBM ThinkPad notebooks) will work under Linux if a DOS driver is first allowed to configure the chip. You can accommodate these notebooks by booting them first into DOS, configuring the chipset, and using `LOADLIN` to load Linux from DOS.

Sound

Until the advent of loadable kernel modules, configuring sound for Linux meant recompiling the kernel and hoping that the limited support under Linux would work with your notebook's sound system. The great news is that sound support has been much improved for notebooks in the last two years, and users now have at least three different options for configuring sound.

Sound support included with most distributions is included with the Linux kernel under the `/usr/src/linux/drivers/sound` directory. A number of loadable kernel modules will usually be included by default after you install Linux. Configuring sound can be accomplished in a number of ways, such as manually loading kernel sound modules from the command line as `root`, using the `modprobe` command after editing the system's modules configuration files, or using a freeware or commercial sound driver system to install and configure support.

For example, OpenLinux notebook users with a SoundBlaster-compatible system could enable sound with earlier Linux 2.0.X kernels by manually loading the modules like this:

```
# insmod sound
# insmod uart401
# insmod sb io=0x220 irq=5 dma=1,0 mpu_io=0x330
```

Red Hat Linux includes the `sndconfig` command, which can be used from the console or the command line of an X11 terminal window to configure sound. After probing for your system's card, you can also set different options through a graphical interface and then test your configuration. Configuration will be saved in a file named `sound` under the `/etc/sysconfig` directory.

OpenLinux now includes the COAS administration tool. Select the kernel administration module to load and configure sound for OpenLinux using the default sound modules included with your distribution.

If you have trouble using the default sound modules, you can try a commercial alternative: the Open Sound System drivers. (A "lite" version is included with the Linux kernel.) These drivers support more than 200 different sound cards/chipsets and install via a shell script. A demo version is available online at `http://www.opensound.com`.

The newest set of sound drivers for Linux is from the Advanced Linux Sound Architecture (ALSA) project at `http://www.alsa-project.org/`. The drivers, support libraries, and sound utilities are contained in three source tarballs. To install the drivers, follow these steps:

1. Download and decompress the ALSA drivers, library, and utilities tarballs.
2. Navigate to the resulting `alsa-drivers` directory and then build and install the drivers (as `root`) with the following:

   ```
   # ./configure --with-debug=full
   # make
   # make install
   # ./snddevices
   ```

   If you have a Plug-and-Pray sound system, use the following `./configure` script command line instead of the one preceding:

   ```
   # ./configure --isapnp=yes --with-debug=full
   ```

   The `./snddevices` script creates sound devices and links under your `/dev/directory`.
3. Navigate to the `alsa-lib` directory and do this:

   ```
   # ./configure
   # make
   # make install
   ```
4. Navigate to the `alsa-utils` directory and do this:

   ```
   # ./configure
   # make
   # make install
   ```
5. Edit your Red Hat `/etc/conf.modules` or OpenLinux `/etc/modules.conf` file and add appropriate lines for your notebook. This example is for an IBM i1720 ThinkPad:

   ```
   # ALSA config for IBM i1720
   # uses the opl3sa driver
   alias char-major-116 snd
   options snd snd_major=116 snd_cards_limit=1
   alias snd-card-0 snd-opl3sa
   #
   ```

```
# the following should be one line! broken here with '\'s
#
options snd-opl3sa snd_port=0x120 snd_sb_port=0x220 snd_wss_port=0x530 \
        snd_midi_port=0x300 snd_fm_port=0x388 snd_irq=5 snd_dma1=0 \
        snd_dma1_size=128 snd_dma2=1 snd_dma2_size=128
#
# defines for OSS-lite compatibility
#
alias char-major-14 soundcore
alias sound-slot-0 snd-card-0
alias sound-service-0-3 snd-pcm1-oss
alias sound-service-0-12 snd-pcm1-oss
```

6. Save the file and exit your editor. Configure your modules dependencies with this:

   ```
   # depmod -a
   ```

   Load the drivers with this:

   ```
   # modprobe snd
   ```

7. You must then "unmute" your notebook's sound devices with this:

   ```
   # amixer -c 1 master 125:125 unmute
   # amixer -c 1 pcm 125:125 unmute
   # amixer -c 1 cd 125:125 unmute
   # amixer -c 1 fm 125:125 unmute
   ```

The ALSA drivers represent an excellent alternative if you have trouble configuring your notebook for sound. The unmuting may be put into a shell script and then executed when booting Linux. The ALSA distribution also includes utilities such as `amixer`, `alsamixer`, and `alsactl` for controlling sound devices, input and output levels, and recording.

Infrared

Many notebooks today include infrared sensors that conform to the Infrared Data Association (IrDA) specifications. These can be used to "beam" data back and forth between two notebooks, communicate with smaller devices such as the Palm, print to IrDA-enabled printers, allow your computer to be controlled with a remote control, and even control other remote-control devices such as a TV, VCR, or stereo.

Debian GNU/Linux does not officially support IrDA at this time. It is possible, however, to add IrDA support to Debian. You need to build a 2.2 kernel with IrDA support turned on, as well as download and compile the utilities needed for IrDA yourself.

For more Linux IR information, please look at the Linux-IrDA project site at `http://www.cs.uit.no/linux-irda/`.

USB and FireWire

Universal Serial Bus (USB) and FireWire (also known as i.share or IEEE 1394) are specifications for hot-plugging devices into a special port on a computer with a cable. USB is slower, has been around longer, and is supported by more devices, while FireWire is newer and not as well supported. USB, in particular, has become very popular on notebooks recently as an easy way to connect external mice and keyboards.

At this time, neither of these is supported by Debian GNU/Linux. Projects are under way to support them in Linux, and some support for USB should be available in the next Debian release.

Tip

If you must have USB support, you can get it in the 2.2.7 or later versions of the Linux kernel. It is still somewhat experimental, but there are several reports of success. Currently, Linux supports USB keyboards, mice, printers, modems, and some digital cameras, and will work with USB hubs as well as directly connected devices.

A HOWTO has been posted, although it is still in the preliminary stages as of this writing. You can find a copy at `http://lwn.net/1999/0617/a/howto-usb.html`.

Tips on Running Your Laptop

Once you have Linux installed and configured on your notebook, and all of the possible hardware is working, running a notebook is mostly like running a desktop machine. However, there are some tricks and tips that, while not strictly essential, can assist greatly in keeping your notebook up to speed.

Using `anacron`

Because of its heritage on large minicomputers and high-end servers, Linux tends to assume that it will be running on a more or less continuous basis, with only occasional outages. This is reflected in the scheduled periodic maintenance jobs, performing tasks like updating various databases, cleaning out log files, running system checks, running backups, and the like.

Notebooks, on the other hand, are usually only turned on when needed, spending the rest of the time turned off to preserve battery life. As a result, some of these housekeeping tasks will not run when they should, and the system can start to run out of disk space or lose information about the system that isn't being updated.

The anacron package solves this. Like cron, anacron runs jobs at certain times. Unlike cron, anacron decides whether to run jobs by looking at the interval since the job was last run. Since this interval is stored on the filesystem, anacron can remember the last job even across reboots. It also accepts a delay parameter; this makes sure that many pending jobs don't run simultaneously, bogging down the system in the process.

anacron reads information about the jobs it needs to perform from /etc/anacrontab. When it runs (usually at boot time), it reads anacrontab and figures out which jobs need to be run. If no jobs need to be run, it exits. Otherwise, it runs each job, delayed by the number of minutes configured for each job, and exits when the last job completes. By default, cron is set to run anacron once per day, to ensure that its tasks are completed even if the system does run for a longer period of time.

Generally, you should not need to configure anacron; it should simply do its work without intervention. If you want to add jobs that run on a regular basis, you should create scripts to perform those jobs and put them in cron.daily, cron.weekly, or cron.monthly; anacron (and cron) will pick them up on the next scheduled run.

Lengthening Battery Life

The default APM setup allows you to extend battery life considerably. Nevertheless, there are ways to conserve power even further. Generally, the default configuration for Linux is optimized for a standard desktop or server configuration, where power is not a major issue. Thus, it is often useful to make a few changes to tune the system for power consumption.

Altering Setup When on Battery

With APM enabled, the apm command-line tool will report on the status of the power system: the power source (wall outlet or battery), the state of the battery, and the remaining time left. This information can be incorporated into system scripts such that certain tasks are avoided when on battery, or when the battery reaches a certain level.

One way to do this is to create two scripts that test for certain conditions and report true or false; these are easy to incorporate into shell scripts or the like. One, which is called isbatt here, determines whether the system is on battery. The other, pwrlevel, takes a percentage as an argument and returns whether the battery's power level (reported by apm as a percentage) is below that threshold.

Here is a sample script for isbatt:

```
#!/bin/sh

# isbatt: Test whether we're on battery power.
```

```
# Written by Jeff Licquia.

# [Insert copyright here.]

if [ ! -f /proc/apm ]; then
    exit 0
fi

test `apm ¦ fgrep -c "AC off-line"` -gt 0
```

And here is pwrlevel:

```
#!/bin/sh

# pwrlevel: Test whether the battery is below a certain percentage.
#           Takes the percentage as the first argument.
# Written by Jeff Licquia.

# [Insert copyright here.]

if [ ! -f /proc/apm ]; then
    exit 0
fi

test `apm ¦ awk '{print $5}' ¦ sed 's/%//'` -lt $1
```

Install these under the /usr/local/bin directory, if you use them. Now, you can change various scripts that run to disable themselves when running on battery, or when the battery is below a certain percentage.

For example, /etc/cron.daily/man-db automatically finds old formatted man pages and deletes them once per day. To disable it when the battery is running, add this line to the file before the first real command, but after the first comment line:

```
if [ /usr/local/bin/isbatt ]; then exit; fi
```


Minimizing Hard Disk Power Usage

The hard disk is another major power drain. Generally, most notebook hard drives will spin down when idle to save power. This can be helpful, but with an unoptimized system, it can actually hurt power consumption if some running process wakes up the disk regularly, causing the disk to repeatedly spin up and down.

Changing `update`

update is one process that can cause hard drive spin. This process is started at boot time; its job is to force the kernel to write cached information to disk every so often. By default, this happens every 5 seconds for data, with metadata information, such as directory or permission information, written every 30 seconds. Normally, this is not a problem, but some drives will interpret every call to write flushed data as a reason to keep the disk spun up, even if no data has changed.

Tip

Nearly every Linux distribution includes the `hdparm` command. This utility can be used to query your notebook's hard drive and to set power modes and spin-down timeouts. You must be `root` in order to use this program.

If this is a problem for you, you can change `update` to force the write less frequently. The problem is that more information will be lost in the event of a crash. Values of several more seconds to several minutes are safe, but not very helpful; in fact, they could make the problem worse by repeatedly spinning the drive up and down. Values as long as an hour are reported, but are obviously much more dangerous. Strike a happy medium between these two, depending on your comfort level.

To change update's timeouts, edit `/etc/rcS.d/S10checkroot.sh`.

Find the line that runs `update` and change the `update` command:

```
# update -s <sync-seconds> -f <flush-seconds>
```

`sync-seconds` corresponds to the time interval to write all data (including directory and permission information) and *`flush-seconds`* corresponds to the time interval to write cached data to disk.

Changing syslogd

The `syslogd` process handles the collection and writing of log information from many places on the system. When a log entry is created, `syslogd`'s default behavior is to flush the disk cache immediately after writing the entry. If entries are created every few seconds, this amounts to essentially constant writing to disk.

You can disable this behavior for any log entry by editing `/etc/syslog.conf` and placing a dash (`-`) before the filename of the log file. If this is done for log files that receive regular writes, then the writes are cached instead of being written immediately to disk. This option is also a bit of a give-and-take, as the same caching problems mentioned under update apply here—if the system crashes, recent log information may be lost.

suspend/resume

Some notebooks give you the option of suspending the system. This involves stopping all processes, dumping the contents of memory to disk, and turning off the power. On `resume`, the APM BIOS reloads memory from the dump and restores the system to the exact state it was in before. This allows for a quick shutdown if battery power runs low; it also allows you to pick up where you left off once power can be found. Some systems will force a `suspend` if battery power becomes too low.

Typically, the APM BIOS can only write to a FAT filesystem (the filesystem used by DOS and Windows 95). Therefore, to use this feature, you should create a partition for holding this information. The partition can be useful for other purposes, such as booting and initializing DOS-only hardware or holding the installation files for installing from hard disk. Generally, this partition should be as large or larger than the amount of RAM on your notebook; for more accurate information, look in your notebook documentation for the amount of free space you need to be able to suspend.

The `apmd` process should be running in order for `suspend` to work; `apmd` takes care of the details involved in cleanly disabling and enabling devices, shutting down and restarting programs, and resetting the system time.

Docking Station Tips

Some notebooks can attach to a *docking station* or *port replicator* device. This device will usually provide AC power and several other extended features, such as a full-fledged expansion bus for standard devices and extra ports. Besides allowing a notebook to have the expandability of a desktop in some cases, these devices are convenient ways of attaching a full-size monitor, keyboard, mouse, and other devices to a notebook without dealing with multiple cables.

Linux does not support docking stations directly, but it does support multiple configurations through the concept of runlevels. When the system is booted, the initial process (`init`) uses the starting runlevel as a key to start the system, only running startup scripts that are associated with the current runlevel. It is possible to switch runlevels after booting; when this happens, certain processes can be shut down and others started to reflect the new state. In fact, single-user mode, shutting down, and rebooting are all implemented by switching to special runlevels (1, 0, and 6, respectively) that switch the system to the desired state.

For more information on configuring runlevels, see Chapter 6, "System Service Tools." By selecting a runlevel as the docked runlevel, and writing an `init` script to initialize and shut down the docking hardware, it's possible to associate a runlevel with being docked. It's then possible to pass the startup runlevel to the kernel at boot time by simply passing the runlevel as a kernel parameter. For example, enter the following at the `LILO` prompt:

```
linux 3
```

This starts the image configured as `linux` at run level 3.

Summary

This chapter introduced a number of concepts and configurations to choose when installing and using a laptop with Linux. If you're in the market for a notebook and want to run Linux, choose carefully. Research as much as possible ahead of time to reduce the possibility of purchasing incompatible hardware. Although Linux will run on nearly any laptop, some models can pose special problems, especially with the X Window System or sound configuration.

Appendixes

Part VI

In This Part

APPENDIX

The Linux Documentation Project

IN THIS APPENDIX

This is the Linux Documentation Project "Manifesto,"
Last Revision 21 September 1998, by Michael K. Johnson

This file describes the goals and current status of the Linux Documentation Project, including names of projects, volunteers, FTP sites, and so on.

Overview of the Linux Documentation Project

The Linux Documentation Project is working on developing good, reliable docs for the Linux operating system. The overall goal of the LDP is to collaborate in taking care of all of the issues of Linux documentation, ranging from online documents (man pages, textinfo documents, and so on) to printed manuals covering topics such as installing, using, and running Linux. The LDP is essentially a loose team of volunteers with little central organization; anyone who is interested in helping is welcome to join. We think that working together and agreeing on the direction and scope of Linux documentation is the best way to go, to reduce problems with conflicting efforts; two people writing two books on the same aspect of Linux wastes someone's time along the way.

The LDP is set out to produce the canonical set of Linux online and printed documentation. Because our documents are freely available (like software licensed under the terms of the GNU GPL) and distributed on the Net, we are able to easily update the documentation and stay on top of the many changes in the Linux world. If you are interested in publishing any of the LDP works, see "Publishing LDP Manuals" in this chapter.

Getting Involved

Send mail to `mailto:linux-howto@metalab.unc.edu` Of course, you also need to get in touch with the coordinator of whatever LDP projects you're interested in working on; see the next section.

Current Projects

For a list of current projects, see `http://metalab.unc.edu/LDP/`. The best way to get involved with one of these projects is to pick up the current version of the manual and send revisions, editions, or suggestions to the coordinator. You probably want to coordinate with the author before sending revisions so that you know you are working together.

FTP Sites for LDP Works

LDP works can be found on `metalab.unc.edu` in the directory /pub/Linux/docs. LDP manuals are found in /pub/Linux/docs/LDP, HOWTOs and other documentation found in /pub/Linux/docs/HOWTO.

Documentation Conventions

This appendix contains the conventions currently used in LDP manuals. If you are interested in writing another manual using different conventions, please let us know of your plans first.

The man pages—the UNIX standard for online manuals—are created with the UNIX standard nroff man (or BSD mdoc) macros.

The guides, full books produced by the LDP, have historically been done in LaTeX, as producing printed documentation has been the primary goal. However, guide authors have been moving toward SGML with the DocBook DTD because it allows them to create more different output types: both printed and online. If you use LaTeX, we have a style file you can use to keep your printed look consistent with other LDP documents. We suggest its use.

The HOWTO documents are all required to be in SGML format. Currently, they use the linuxdoc DTD, which is quite simple. There is a move afoot to switch to the DocBook DTD over time.

LDP documents must be freely redistributable without fees paid to the authors. It is not required that the text be modifiable, but it is encouraged. You can come up with your own license terms that satisfy this constraint, or you can use a previously prepared license. The LDP provides a boilerplate license that you can use; some people like to use the GPL, and others write their own.

The copyright for each manual should be in the name of the head writer or coordinator for the project. "The Linux Documentation Project" isn't a formal entity and shouldn't be used to copyright the documents.

Copyright and License

Here is a boilerplate license you can apply to your work. It has not been reviewed by a lawyer; feel free to have your own lawyer review it (or your modification of it) for its applicability to your own preferences. Remember that in order for your document to be part of the LDP, you must allow unlimited reproduction and distribution without fee.

This manual may be reproduced and distributed in whole or in part, without fee, subject to the following conditions:

The copyright notice and this permission notice must be preserved complete on all complete or partial copies.

Any translation or derived work must be approved by the author in writing before distribution.

If you distribute this work in part, instructions for obtaining the complete version of this manual must be included and a means for obtaining a complete version provided.

Small portions may be reproduced as illustrations for reviews or quotes in other works without this permission notice if proper citation is given.

Exceptions to these rules may be granted for academic purposes: Write to the author and ask. These restrictions are here to protect authors, not to restrict you as learners and educators.

All source code in this document is placed under the GNU General Public License, available via anonymous FTP from `prep.ai.mit.edu:/pub/gnu/COPYING`.

Publishing LDP Manuals

If you're a publishing company interested in distributing any of the LDP manuals, read on.

By the license requirements given previously, anyone is allowed to publish and distribute verbatim copies of the Linux Documentation Project manuals. You don't need our explicit permission for this. However, if you would like to distribute a translation or derivative work based on any of the LDP manuals, you may need to obtain permission from the author, in writing, before doing so.

You may, of course, sell the LDP manuals for profit. We encourage you to do so. Keep in mind, however, that because the LDP manuals are freely distributable, anyone can photocopy or distribute printed copies free of charge.

We do not require to be paid royalties for any profit earned from selling LDP manuals. However, we suggest that if you do sell LDP manuals for profit, that you either offer the author royalties, or donate a portion of your earnings to the author, to the LDP as a whole, or to the Linux development community. You may also want to send one or more free copies of the LDP manuals that you are distributing to the authors. Your show of support for the LDP and the Linux community will be appreciated.

We would like to be informed of any plans to publish or distribute LDP manuals. This lets us know how they're becoming available. If you are publishing or planning to publish any LDP manuals, please send mail to `ldp-l@linux.org.au`. It's nice to know who's doing what.

We encourage Linux software distributors to distribute the LDP manuals (such as the *Installation* and *Getting Started Guide*) with their software. The LDP manuals are intended to be used as the "official" Linux documentation, and we are glad to see mail-order distributors bundling the LDP manuals with the software. As the LDP manuals mature, hopefully they will continually fulfill this goal more adequately.

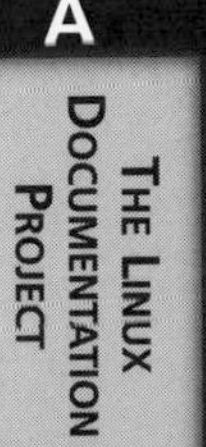

Top Linux Commands and Utilities

In This Appendix

This appendix is not designed to replace the man pages and does not detail all of the options for each command. You'll find most of the information you need in the man pages for these programs or, in the case of a shell operator such as > or <, in the man pages for the shell commands. This appendix is designed to give you a feel for the commands and a brief description of what they do. In most cases, more parameters are available than are shown here.

Many descriptions also have examples. If these examples aren't self-evident, an explanation is provided. This is not an exhaustive list—Linux comes with many more commands—but these are the most common, and you will find yourself using them over and over again.

To keep things simple, the commands are listed in alphabetical order; however, I do want to summarize by listing what are, at least for me, the 10 most common commands—also alphabetically:

- `cat`
- `cd`
- `cp`
- `find`
- `grep`
- `ls`
- `more`
- `rm`
- `vi`
- `who`

General Guidelines

Many of the programs distributed with Linux descended from counterparts in the UNIX world and have inherited the terse, sometimes cryptic naming style. If you want to change something that already exists, the command usually begins with `ch`. If you want to do something for the first time, the command usually begins with `mk`. If you want to undo something completely, the command usually begins with `rm`. For example, to make a new directory, you use the `mkdir` command; to remove a directory, you use the `rmdir` command.

The List

The commands listed in this appendix are some of the most common used in Linux. An example is provided in cases where the command seems ambiguous. With each of these commands, the man pages can provide additional information, as well as more examples.

.

The `.` shell commandtells the shell to execute all of the commands in the file that are passed an argument to the command. This works in `bash` or `pdksh`. The equivalent in `tcsh` is the `source` command. The following example executes the command `adobe`:

```
. adobe
```

&

The `&` shell operator after any other command tells the computer to run the command in the background. By placing a job in the background, the user can then continue using that shell to process other commands. If the command is run in the foreground, the user cannot continue using that shell until the process finishes.

¦

The ¦ (pipe) shell operator is used between separate programs on the command line to "pipe" the output of one command to another. This type of operation is one of the principal strengths of Linux and the shell and can be used to construct complex commands from a series of simple programs. For example, to sort the contents of a file, you can pipe the output of the `cat` command through the `sort` command like this:

```
# cat long_list.txt ¦ sort
```

>

The > (standard output) shell operator is used to send the output of a program to a file or other device. Use this operator with caution, as it will overwrite an existing file! To save a listing of the current directory to a text file, use the > operator like this:

```
# ls > dir.txt
```

Note that if the file `dir.txt` exists, it will be erased and overwritten with the new contents! Because Linux works much like other versions of UNIX, you can also send the contents of programs directory to a device:

```
# cat welcome.au >/dev/audio
```

This plays a sound file by sending it directly to a Linux audio device.

<

The < (standard input) shell operator is used to feed a program the contents of a file or input from another device or source. For example, you can use this operator like the `cat` command to sort a file and save the results:

```
# sort < unsorted.txt > sorted.txt
```

>>

The >> (append) shell operator will not replace a designated file, but appends the output of a program onto the end of a specified file. This can be used, for example, to build log files:

```
# cat newfile.txt >> oldfile.txt
```

The contents of `newfile.txt` will not overwrite `oldfile.txt`, but will append to the end of it.

<<

The << (here) shell operator is used to tell a program when end-of-input is reached. For example, to use the shell as a text editor, tell the shell to stop accepting input when the word `end` is used like this:

```
# > document.txt << end
This is a line of text.
end
```

After you type the word `end`, the shell saves your text into the file document text because you've told the shell that the word `end` terminates input.

adduser

The `adduser` command is used by `root` (or someone else who has the authority) to create a new user. The `adduser` command is followed by the account name to be created:

```
# adduser dpitts
```

alias

The `alias` command is used to make aliases or alternative names for commands. Typically, these aliases are abbreviations of the actual commands. In the following example, the user (probably a DOS user) is adding an alias of `dir` for a directory listing:

```
alias dir=ls
```

Typing `alias` by itself gives you a list of all your current aliases. Such a list might look like this:

```
svr01:/home/dpitts$ alias
alias d='dir'
alias dir='/bin/ls $LS_OPTIONS --format=vertical'
alias ls='/bin/ls $LS_OPTIONS'
alias v='vdir'
alias vdir='/bin/ls $LS_OPTIONS --format=long'
```

apropos *<parameter>*

The `apropos` command literally means appropriate or regarding (others). When followed by a parameter, `apropos` searches the man pages for entries that include the parameter, performing a keyword search on all of the man pages. This is the equivalent of the `man -k` *`<parameter>`* command.

ash

`ash` is a simple shell with features much like the `sh`, or Bourne SHell. The `ash` shell is run by the symbolic link `bsh`, which is found under the `/bin` directory.

at

`at` runs a program at a specified time. You can use the `at` command to schedule a task or job to run at a time you specify on the command line or in a file.

atq

Use `atq` to list the queue of waiting jobs. The `atq` command prints a list of waiting jobs or events for the `at` command (usually found under the `/var/spool/at` directory).

atrm

Use `atrm` to remove a specified job. The `atrm` command removes one or several jobs waiting in the `at` queue. The `atrm` command can be used by users or the `root` operator to delete pending events (stop `at` commands from running).

banner

banner prints a large, high-quality banner to the standard output. If the message is omitted, banner prompts for and reads one line from the standard input. For example, enter $ banner hi to create the following banner:

```
##                                                    ###
##                                                    ###
#########################################################
#########################################################
#########################################################
#########################################################
#########################################################
##                         ###
                             ###
                             ###
                             ####
                             ####
                             ####
##                        #######
#################################
#################################
################################
#############################
##########################
##
##                             ##
##                             ##          ####
#################################        ########
#################################        ########
#################################        ########
#################################         ######
#################################          ####
##
```

bash

bash is the GNU Bourne Again SHell. The default shell for Red Hat Linux, bash has many features, such as command-line editing, built-in help, and command history. The bash shell is run by the symbolic link sh, which is found under the /bin directory.

batch

The batch command runs jobs according to load average. This program is used to run events when the computer reaches a certain load average, as determined by real-time values found in the loadavg file in the /proc directory. batch also has other options; read the at command manual pages for details.

bc

`bc` is an interpreter and language for building calculator programs and tools. You can use this interpreter and language to program custom calculators.

bg

The `bg` command is used to force a suspended process to run in the background. For example, say you have started a command in the foreground (without using the `&` after the command) and realize it is going to take a while, but you still need your shell. You can use Ctrl+Z to place the current process on hold. You can either leave it on hold—just as if you called your telephone company—or you can type **bg** to place that process in the background and free your shell to allow you to execute other commands.

bind

Used in `pdksh`, the `bind` command enables the user to change the behavior of key combinations for the purpose of command-line editing. Many times people bind the up, down, left, and right arrow keys so they work the way they would in the Bourne Again SHell (`bsh`). This is the syntax used for the command:

```
bind <key  sequence>  <command>
```

The following examples are the `bind` commands to create bindings for scrolling up and down the history list and for moving left and right along the command line:

```
bind `^[[`=prefix-2
bind `^XA`=up-history
bind `^XB`=down-history
bind `^XC`=forward-char
bind `^XD`=backward-char
```

cat

`cat` does not call your favorite feline; instead, it tells the contents of (typically) the file to scroll its contents across the screen. If that file happens to be binary, the cat gets a hairball and shows it to you on the screen. Typically, this is a noisy process as well. The `cat` command is scrolling the characters of the file, and the terminal is doing all it can to interpret and display the data in the file. This interpretation can include the character used to create the bell signal, which is where the noise comes from. As you might have surmised, the `cat` command requires something to display and has the following format:

```
cat <filename>
```

cd

`cd` stands for change directory. You will find this command extremely useful. The three typical ways of using this command follow:

`cd ..`	Moves one directory up the directory tree.
`cd ~`	Moves to your home directory from wherever you currently are. This is the same as issuing `cd` by itself.
`cd` *directory name*	Changes to a specific directory. This can be a directory relative to your current location or can be based on the `root` directory by placing a forward slash (`/`) before the directory name.

These examples can be combined. For example, suppose you are in the directory `/home/dsp1234` and you want to go to `tng4321`'s home account. You can perform the following command to move back up the directory one level and then down into the `tng4321` directory:

```
cd ../tng4321
```

chfn

The `chfn` command changes finger information. You can use this command to enter or update information used by the finger networking tool from the `/etc/passwd` entry for your Linux system. You can enter full names, offices, and office and home phone numbers. Follow `chfn` with a user's name:

```
# chfn willie
```

chgrp

The `chgrp` command is used to change the group associated with the permissions of the file or directory. The owner of the file (and `root`) has the authority to change the group associated with the file. The format for the command is simple:

```
chgrp <new group> <file>
```

chmod

The `chmod` command is used to change the permissions associated with the object (typically a file or directory). What you are really doing is changing the file mode. You can specify the permissions of the object in two ways: by the numeric coding system or the letter coding system. As you recall, three sets of users are associated with every object: the owner of the object, the group for the object, and everybody else. Using the letter coding system, they are referred to as u for user, g for group, o for other, and a for all. The three basic types of permissions you can change are r for read, w for write, and x for execute. These three permissions can be changed by using the plus (+) and minus (-) signs. For example, to add read and execute permissions to owner and group of the file test1, you would issue the following command:

```
chmod ug+rx test1
```

To remove the read and execute permissions from the user and group of the test1 file, you would change the plus (+) sign to a minus (-) sign:

```
chmod ug-rx test1
```

This is called making *relative changes* to the mode of the file.

When using the numeric coding system, you always have to give the absolute value of the permissions, regardless of their previous permissions. The numeric system is based on three sets of base 2 numbers—one set for each category of user, group, and other. The values are 4, 2, and 1, where 4 equals *read*, 2 equals *write*, and 1 equals *execute*. These values are added together to give the set of permissions for that category. With numeric coding, you always specify all three categories. Therefore, you would use the value 700 to give read, write, and execute permissions to the owner of the file test1, and no permissions to anyone else:

```
chmod 700 test1
```

To make the same file readable and writable by the user, and readable by both the group and others, you would use the following mathematical logic. For the first set of permissions—the user—the value for readable is 4 and the value for writable is 2. The sum of these two is 6. The next set of permissions—the group—only gets readable, so that is 4. The setting for others, as for the group, is 4. Therefore, the command would be as follows:

```
chmod 644 test1
```

The format for the command, using either method, is the same. You issue the chmod command followed by the permissions, either absolute or relative, followed by the objects for which you want the mode changed:

```
chmod <permissions> <file>
```

chown

This command is used to change the user ID (owner) associated with the permissions of the file or directory. The owner of the file (and, of course, root) has the authority to change the user associated with the file. The format for the command is as follows:

```
chown <new user id> <file>
```

chroot

The `chroot` command makes the `/` directory (called the *root directory*) be something other than `/` on the filesystem. For example, when working with an Internet server, you can set the root directory to equal `/usr/ftp`. Anyone who logs on using FTP (which goes to the root directory by default) will actually go to the directory `/usr/ftp`. This protects the rest of your directory structure from being seen or even changed by this anonymous guest to your machine. If someone were to enter `cd /etc`, the `ftp` program would try to put her in the root directory and then in the etc directory off of that. Because the root directory is `/usr/ftp`, the `ftp` program will actually put the user in the `/usr/ftp/etc` directory (assuming there is one).

The syntax for the command follows:

```
chroot <original filesystem location> <new filesystem location>
```

chsh

You can use this program to change the type of shell you use when you log in to your Linux system. The shell must be available on the system and must be allowed by the `root` operator by having its name listed in the `/etc/shells` file. Type the name of a shell, following the `chsh` command:

```
# chsh zsh
```

control-panel

The `control-panel` command is one of several Red Hat Linux system administration tools. This command is an X11 client (actually a Python language script) used to display several system administration tools, such as `timetool`, `netcfg`, and `modemtool`.

cp

The `cp` command is an abbreviation for copy; therefore, this command enables you to copy objects. For example, to copy the `file1` to `file2`, issue the following command:

```
cp file1 file2
```

As the example shows, the syntax is very simple:

```
cp <original object name> <new object name>
```

cpio

The `cpio` command copies files in and out of file archives. `cpio` works much like the `tar` (tape archive) command, but with a slightly different syntax. Many Linux users are more familiar with the `tar` command.

crond

This is the `cron` daemon. This program, started when you first boot Linux, scans the `/etc/crontab` file and the `/var/spool/cron` directory. It looks for regularly scheduled jobs entered by the `root` operator or other system users. It is started when you first boot Linux.

crontab

The `crontab` command, not to be confused with the `/etc/crontab` file, is used by your system's users to schedule personal `cron` events. The `cron` files are stored under the `/var/spool/cron` directory. System administrators can control whether this facility exists on the system through the `/etc/cron.allow` and `/etc/cron.deny` files. All current jobs are listed when the `crontab` command is used with the `-l` option. Use the `-e` option to create or edit a job, and the `-r` option to delete a job.

cu

`cu` is a communications program used to call up other computers. This program is text-based and is not as user friendly as the `minicom` or `seyon` communications programs for Linux.

cut

This program cuts specified columns or fields from input text. The `cut` command, a text filter, can be used to manipulate the output of other text utilities or contents of your files by selectively displaying fields of text.

dc

`dc` is a command-line desk calculator. This calculator, which does not have a graphical interface, uses reverse-polish notation to perform calculations entered from the command line or a file.

dd

The `dd` command converts file formats. For example, to copy a boot image to a disk (assuming the device name for the disk is `/dev/fd0`), you issue this command:

```
dd if=<filename> of-/dev/fd0 obs=18k
```

`filename` might be `BOOT0001.img`; `of` is the object format (what you are copying to); and `obs` is the output block size.

df

Use the `df` command to show the amount of free disk space on any currently mounted filesystem. This information is useful in determining whether you have available storage for programs or data.

dir

`dir` lists the contents of directories. This command has many of the same command-line options as the `ls` command.

display

This program requires X11 and is part of the `ImageMagick` package. This is a menu-driven application you can use to create, edit, change, print, and save graphics during your X11 session. `ImageMagick` is typically started in the background from the command line of a terminal window like this:

```
# display &
```

dmesg

The `dmesg` command prints a system boot log, `dmesg`, found in the `/var/log` directory. This program is handy to diagnose system problems, listing software services and hardware devices found while your system is starting.

du

The `du` command shows how much disk space is used by various files or directories, and can show where the most or least disk space is used on your system.

dump

The `dump` command, most often used by the `root` operator, creates a backup of either the whole filesystem or selected directories. The companion program to the `dump` command is the `restore` command, which extracts files and directories from a dump backup.

echo

`echo` echoes a string to the display. The `echo` command is generally used to print lines of text to your display console or—through redirection—to files, devices, programs, or the standard output of your shell. The `-e` option lets you use certain control characters in your output string.

ed

`ed` is a bare-bones line editor.

edquota

The `edquota` program, meant to be used by the `root` operator, is used to change the amount of disk space available to a user. It is used in conjunction with the `quota`, `quotaon`, or `quotaoff` commands.

efax

This is a communications program for sending and receiving faxes under Linux. This command is part of the `efax` software package and does the actual sending and receiving when called by the shell script `fax`.

efix

`efix` is used to convert files between text and fax graphics formats. The `efix` program is called by the shell script `fax` to convert sent or received fax documents.

elm

`elm` is a mail-handling program you can use to create, compose, edit, and send mail. You can organize your mail into different folders and also organize how your want your incoming mail to be filed. This program is similar to the `pine` mail program.

emacs

emacs is the GNU text (edit macros) editor. It can be used not only to edit text files but also as a calendar, diary, and appointment scheduler (and much more). emacs is also a complete environment to support programming and electronic mail.

emacs-nox

emacs-nox is the non-X11 version of the emacs editor.

env

The env command is used to see the exported environment variables. The result of the command is a two-column list in which the variable's name is on the left and the value associated with that variable is on the right. The command is issued without any parameters. Hence, typing env might get you a list similar to this one:

```
svr01:/home/dpitts$ env
HOSTNAME=svr01.mk.net
LOGNAME=dpitts
MAIL=/var/spool/mail/dpitts
TERM=vt100
HOSTTYPE=i386
PATH=/usr/local/bin:/usr/bin:/bin:.:/usr/local/java/bin
HOME=/home2/dpitts
SHELL=/bin/bash
LS_OPTIONS=--8bit --color=tty -F -b -T 0
PS1=\h:\w\$
PS2=>
MANPATH=/usr/local/man:/usr/man/preformat:/usr/man:/usr/lib/perl5/man
LESS=-MM
OSTYPE=Linux
SHLVL=1
```

ex

ex is a symbolic link to the vim editor. In this mode, the vim editor emulates the ex line editor.

fax

Use fax to create, transmit, receive, display, or print a fax. This complex shell script is the driver program for the efax software package and provides an easy-to-use way to send or receive fax documents under Linux.

faxq

Use faxq to list faxes in the fax-sending queue. This program is part of the mgetty+sendfax software package for allowing Linux logins and fax transmission and reception.

faxrm

Use faxrm to delete faxes in the sending queue. You can use this program, part of mgetty+sendfax, to delete faxes waiting to be sent.

faxrunq

faxrunq sends spooled faxes from the fax queue. This program, run by the root operator or process, sends faxes waiting in the fax queue—usually the /var/spool/fax directory.

faxspool

faxspool prepares and sends fax documents to the fax queue. This shell script is a driver program for the mgetty+sendfax program and recognizes nine different file formats when converting and sending documents.

fc

The fc command is used to edit the history file. The parameters passed to it, if there are any, can be used to select a range of commands from the history file. This list is then placed in an editing shell. Which editor fc uses is based on the value of the variable FCEDIT. If no value is present for this variable, the command looks at the EDITOR variable. If it is not there, the default (vi) is used.

fdformat

This command only performs a low-level format of a floppy disk. You must then use the mkfs command to place a specified filesystem on the disk.

fetchmail

This program gets your mail from your ISP and can handle a number of electronic mail protocols besides the Post Office Protocol, or POP. You use this program by itself or in a shell script to get your mail after you've established a Point-to-Point, or PPP connection.

fg

Processes can be run in either the background or the foreground. The `fg` command enables you to take a suspended process and run it in the foreground. This is typically used when you have a process running in the foreground and need to suspend it for some reason (thus allowing you to run other commands). The process will continue until you either place it in the background or bring it to the foreground.

file

The `file` command tests each argument passed to it for one of three things: the filesystem test, the magic number test, or the language test. The first test to succeed causes the file type to be printed. If the file is text (an ASCII file), it attempts to guess which language. The following example identifies the file `nquota` as a text file that contains Perl commands. A *magic number file* is a file that has data in particular fixed formats. Here is an example for checking the file `nquota` to see what kind of file it is:

```
file nquota
nquota: perl commands text
```

find

Did you ever say to yourself, "Where did I put that file?" Instead of talking to yourself, you can ask the computer. All you have to do is ask the computer to find the file.

The `find` command looks in whatever directory you indicate, as well as all subdirectories. After it finds this list, it follows your instructions about what to do with the list. Typically, you just want to know where it is; ask it to print out the list. The command's syntax is the command itself, followed by the directory you want to start searching in, followed by the filename (metacharacters are acceptable), and what you want done with the list. In the following example, the `find` command searches for files ending with `.pl` in the current directory (and all subdirectories). It then prints the results to standard output.

```
find . -name *.pl -print
./public_html/scripts/gant.pl
./public_html/scripts/edit_gant.pl
./public_html/scripts/httools.pl
./public_html/scripts/chart.no.comments.pl
```

finger

Use the `finger` command to look up user information (usually found in the `/etc/passwd` file) on your computer or other computer systems.

fmt

The `fmt` program formats input text into page and line sizes you specify on the command line.

free

The `free` commands shows how memory is being used on your system.

ftp

This is the File Transfer Protocol program. You can use the `ftp` command to send and receive files interactively from your computer's hard drive or other remote computer systems. The `ftp` command features built-in help. To see the latest offerings from Macmillan Publishing, try `# ftp ftp.mcp.com`.

glint

This X11 client can be called from the command line or the `control-panel` and uses the `rpm` command, or Red Hat package manager, to control the software installed on your system. The `glint` presents a graphical interface for software installation, maintenance, or removal. It is usually started in the background, like this:

```
# glint &
```

gnuplot

The `gnuplot` program, which can generate graphic displays of mathematical formulas or other data under the X Window System, supports a variety of displays and printers. You can use this program to visualize equations and other data.

grep

The `grep` (global regular expression parse) command searches the object you specify for the text you specify. The command's syntax is `grep <text> <file>`. In the following example, I am searching for instances of the text `httools` in all files in the current directory:

```
grep httools *
edit_gant.cgi:require 'httools.pl';
edit_gant.pl:require 'httools.pl';
gant.cgi:   require 'httools.pl';  # Library containing reusable code
gant.cgi:        &date;     # Calls the todays date subroutine from httools.pl
gant.cgi:         &date;   #  Calls the todays date subroutine from httools.pl
gant.cgi:   &header;  # from httools.pl
```

Although this is valuable, the `grep` command can also be used in conjunction with the results of other commands. For example, the following command calls for the `grep` command to take the output of the `ps` command and take out all instances of the word *root* (the `-v` means everything but the text that follows):

```
ps -ef ¦grep -v root
```

The same command without the `-v` (`ps -ef ¦grep root`) returns all instances that contain the word *root* from the process listing.

groff

`groff` is the front end to the `groff` document-formatting program. This program, by default, calls the `troff` program.

gs

This is the Ghostscript interpreter. This program can interpret and prepare PostScript documents and print on more three dozen displays and printers.

gunzip

Use this program to decompress files compressed with the `gzip` command back to their original form.

gv

A PostScript and PDF document previewer, this X11 client previews and prints PostScript and portable document files and is handy for reading documentation or previewing graphics or documents before printing. Start the `gv` client by itself in the background, or specify a file on the command line like this:

```
# gv myPostScriptdoc.ps &
```

gvim

This program is a graphical version of the `vim` editor and is used under the X Window System.

gzip

`gzip` is GNU's version of the zip compression software. The syntax can be as simple as this:

```
gzip <filename>
```

Many times, however, the syntax also contains some parameters between the command and the filename to be compressed.

halt

The `halt` command tells the kernel to shut down. This is a `superuser`-only command—you must be `root`.

head

The `head` command is a text filter, similar to the `tail` command, but prints only the number of lines you specify from the beginnings of files.

hostname

`hostname` is used to either display the current host or domain name of the system or to set the hostname of the system. Here is an example:

```
svr01:/home/dpitts$ hostname
svr01
```

ical

This is an X11 calendar program. The `ical` client can be used to create and maintain personal or group calendars and to schedule alarms or reminders of important dates or appointments. The calendar files can be printed, along with custom versions of multiday calendars.

ifconfig

This is one of several programs you can use to configure network interfaces. Although usually used by the `root` operator, the `ifconfig` command can be handy to use as a check on currently used network interfaces and lists a snapshot of the interfaces and traffic on the interface at the time the program is run.

irc

This is the Internet Relay Chat program. You can use `irc` to communicate interactively with other persons on the Internet. The `irc` program has built-in help and features a split-window display so you can read ongoing discussions and type in your own messages to other people.

ispell

This flexible, interactive spelling checker is used by `emacs` and other text editors under Linux to check the spelling in text documents. You can also use `ispell` like the traditional UNIX spell command by using the `-l` command line option:

```
# ispell -l < document.txt
```

jed

This editor can emulate the `emacs`, Wordstar, and Brief editors. The X11 version is called `xjed`.

jmacs

This `jmacs` version of the `joe` editor emulates the `emacs` editor and uses its keyboard commands.

joe

`joe` is a recursive acronym, in the GNU tradition, for *Joe's own editor*. It is a very small (160k) and very fast full-screen editor; `joe` is a popular alternative to `vi`.

This editor features online help, multiple document editing in split screen, fast search and replace, keystroke macros, book marks and hooks to allow running external filters—for compiling projects or for running ispell, as examples.

jpico

This version of the `joe` editor emulates the `pico` editor included in the `pine` mail program distribution.

jstar

A Wordstar-compatible version of the `joe` editor. This editor uses keyboard commands, such as the famous Control-key diamond (e, s, d, x) for cursor movement and emulates most other keyboard commands.

kill

`kill` sends the specified signal to the specified process. If no signal is specified, the `TERM` (15) signal is sent. The `TERM` signal kills processes that do not process that. For processes that do process the `TERM` signal, you might need to use the `KILL` (9) signal; it cannot be caught. The syntax for the `kill` command is `kill <option> <pid>`, and an example is as follows:

```
svr01:/home/dpitts$kill -9 1438
```

less

`less` is a program similar to `more`, but allows backward as well as forward movement in the file. `less` also doesn't have to read the entire input file before starting, so with large input files it starts faster than text editors such as `vi`.

ln

The `ln` command is used to make a copy of a file that is either a shortcut (symbolic link) or a duplicate file (hard link) to a file. Use the `ls` command's `-l` option to see which files in a directory are symbolic links.

locate

The `locate` program prints locations of files. You can use this command to quickly find files on your system because it uses a single database of file locations in the `locatedb` database under the `/var/lib` directory.

login

`login` is used when signing on to a system. It can also be used to switch from one user to another at any time.

logout

`logout` is used to sign off of a system as the current user. If it is the only user you are logged in as, you are logged off the system.

look

The `look` command is used to search text files for matching lines for a given string. You can also use this command to quickly look up the spelling of a word, as the default file it searches is the system dictionary, words, found under the `/usr/dict` directory.

lpc

`lpc` is used by the system administrator to control the operation of the line printer system. `lpc` can be used to disable or enable a printer or a printer's spooling queue, to rearrange the order of jobs in a spooling queue, to determine the status of printers, to determine the status of the spooling queues, and to determine the status of the printer daemons. The `lpc` command can be used for any of the printers configured in `/etc/printcap`.

lpd

`lpd` is the line printer daemon and is normally invoked at boot time from the `rc` file. `lpd` makes a single pass through the `/etc/printcap` file to find out about the existing printers and prints any files left after a crash. It then uses the system calls `listen` and `accept` to receive requests to print files in the queue, transfer files to the spooling area, display the queue, or remove jobs from the queue.

lpq

`lpq` examines the spooling area used by `lpd` for printing files on the line printer and reports the status of the specified jobs or all jobs associated with a user. If invoked without any arguments, `lpq` reports on any jobs currently in the print queue.

lpr

The line printer command uses a spooling daemon to print the named files when facilities become available. If no names appear, the standard input is assumed. The following is an example of the `lpr` command:

```
lpr /etc/hosts
```

lprm

The `lprm` command removes a print job from the document queue. This program is used to stop a print job by specifying its job number on the command line. The following example stops print job 28, which was shown by the `lpq` command:

```
# lprm 28
```

ls

The `ls` command lists the contents of a directory. The format of the output is manipulated with options. The `ls` command with no options lists all *nonhidden files* (a file that begins with a dot is a hidden file) in alphabetical order, filling as many columns as fit in the window. Probably the most common set of options used with this command is the `-la` option. The `a` means list all (including hidden files) files, and the `l` means make the output a long listing. Here is an example of this command:

```
svr01:~$ ls -la
total 35
drwxr-xr-x   7 dpitts   users          1024 Jul 21 00:19 ./
drwxr-xr-x 140 root     root           3072 Jul 23 14:38 ../
-rw-r--r--   1 dpitts   users          4541 Jul 23 23:33 .bash_history
-rw-r--r--   1 dpitts   users            18 Sep 16  1996 .forward
-rw-r--r--   2 dpitts   users           136 May 10 01:46 .htaccess
-rw-r--r--   1 dpitts   users           164 Dec 30  1995 .kermrc
-rw-r--r--   1 dpitts   users            34 Jun  6  1993 .less
-rw-r--r--   1 dpitts   users           114 Nov 23  1993 .lessrc
-rw-r--r--   1 dpitts   users            10 Jul 20 22:32 .profile
drwxr-xr-x   2 dpitts   users          1024 Dec 20  1995 .term/
drwx------   2 dpitts   users          1024 Jul 16 02:04 Mail/
drwxr-xr-x   2 dpitts   users          1024 Feb  1  1996 cgi-src/
-rw-r--r--   1 dpitts   users          1643 Jul 21 00:23 hi
-rwxr-xr-x   1 dpitts   users           496 Jan  3  1997 nquota*
drwxr-xr-x   2 dpitts   users          1024 Jan  3  1997 passwd/
drwxrwxrwx   5 dpitts   users          1024 May 14 20:29 public_html/
```

lynx

The lynx browser is a fast, compact, and efficient text-only Web browser with nearly all the capabilities of other Web browsers. Start lynx from the command line of your console or an X11 terminal window, specifying a Web address like this

```
# lynx http://www.mcp.com
```

mail

This program provides a bare-bones interface to sending, handling, or reading mail, but can be very handy when sending one-line mail messages from the command line. You'll probably prefer to use the pine mail program instead.

make

The purpose of the make utility is to automatically determine which pieces of a large program need to be recompiled and then to issue the commands necessary to recompile them.

makewhatis

The makewhatis command builds the whatis command database, located in the /usr/man directory.

man

The `man` command is used to format and display the online manual pages. The *manual pages* are the text that describes, in detail, how to use a specified command. In the following example, I have called the man page that describes the man pages:

```
svr01:~$ man man
man(1)                                                          man(1)


NAME
       man - format and display the on-line manual pages
       manpath - determine user's search path for man pages
SYNOPSIS
       man  [-adfhktwW]  [-m system] [-p string] [-C config_file]
       [-M path] [-P pager] [-S section_list] [section] name  ...

DESCRIPTION
       man  formats  and displays the on-line manual pages.  This
       version knows about  the  MANPATH  and  PAGER  environment
       variables, so you can have your own set(s) of personal man
       pages and choose whatever program you like to display  the
       formatted  pages.  If section is specified, man only looks
       in that section of the manual.  You may also  specify  the
       order to search the sections for entries and which prepro-
       cessors to run  on  the  source  files  via  command  line
       options  or  environment  variables.  If name contains a /
       then it is first tried as a filename, so that you  can  do
```

mcopy

The `mcopy` command is part of the `mtools` software package and copies file to and from DOS-formatted disks without having to mount the disk drive first.

mdel

This command, part of the `mtools` package, deletes files from a DOS disk without mounting the disk drive.

mdir

The `mdir` command lists files on a DOS disk and is part of the `mtools` disk drive support package.

mesg

The `mesg` utility is run by a user to control the write access others have to the terminal device associated with the standard error output. If write access is allowed, programs

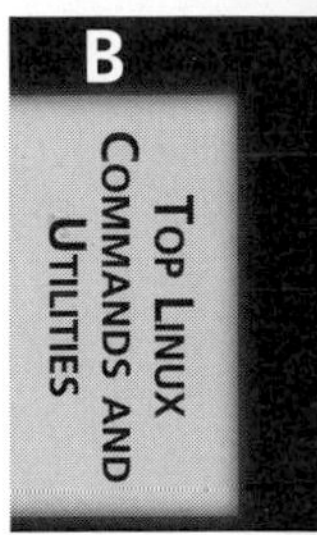

such as `talk` and `write` have permission to display messages on the terminal. Write access is allowed by default.

mformat

The `mformat` command performs a low-level format of a floppy disk with a DOS filesystem. This command is part of the `mtools` software package.

mgetty

Use the `mgetty` program to monitor incoming logins to set terminal speed, type, and other parameters. This command is part of the `mgetty+sendfax` package.

minicom

`minicom` is a serial communications program. The `minicom` program provides an easy-to-use interface with menus and custom colors and is a capable, flexible communications program used to dial out and connect with other computers.

mkdir

The `mkdir` command is used to make a new directory.

mke2fs

The `mke2fs` command is used to make a second extended Linux filesystem on a specified hard drive or other device, such as a floppy disk. This command does not format the new filesystem, but does make it available for use. `mke2fs` can also be used to label a partition and to specify a mount point or directory where the partition can be accessed after it's mounted.

mkfs

`mkfs` is used to build a Linux filesystem on a device, usually a hard disk partition. The syntax for the command is `mkfs` *`<filesystem>`*, where *`<filesystem>`* is either the device name (such as `/dev/hda1`) or the mount point (for example, `/`, `/usr`, `/home`) for the filesystem.

mkswap

`mkswap` sets up a Linux swap area on a device (usually a disk partition).

The device is usually of the following form:

```
/dev/hda[1-8]
/dev/hdb[1-8]
/dev/sda[1-8]
/dev/sdb[1-8]
```

mlabel

The `mlabel` command, part of the `mtools` package, is used to *label* (name) a DOS floppy disk.

more

`more` is a filter for paging through text one screen at a time. This command can only page down through the text, as opposed to `less`, which can page both up and down though the text.

mount

`mount` attaches the filesystem specified by `specialfile` (which is often a device name) to the directory specified as the parameter. Only the `superuser` can mount files. If the `mount` command is run without parameters, it lists all currently mounted filesystems. The following is an example of the `mount` command:

```
svr01:/home/dpitts$ mount
/dev/hda1 on / type ext2 (rw)
/dev/hda2 on /var/spool/mail type ext2 (rw,usrquota)
/dev/hda3 on /logs type ext2 (rw,usrquota)
/dev/hdc1 on /home type ext2 (rw,usrquota)
none on /proc type proc (rw)
```

mpage

The `mpage` command formats multiple pages on a single sheet, saving money and a number of trees your printer would otherwise eat. After you've installed your printer, try printing a document with two sheets per page, like this:

```
# mpage -2 myfile.txt ¦ lpr
```

mt

`mt` is a magnetic tape command. You can use this command to erase, rewind, or re-tension tapes in your tape drive. You can perform nearly 40 different actions with this command.

mv

The mv command is used to move an object from one location to another. If the last argument names an existing directory, the command moves the rest of the list into that directory. If two files are given, the command moves the first into the second. It is an error to have more than two arguments with this command unless the last argument is a directory.

netcfg

This is a Red Hat Linux network configuration tool. The netcfg command is an X11 client used to configure Linux networking hardware, interfaces, and services.

netstat

netstat displays the status of network connections on either TCP, UDP, RAW, or UNIX sockets to the system. The -r option is used to obtain information about the routing table. The following is an example of the netstat command:

```
svr01:/home/dpitts$ netstat
Active Internet connections
Proto Recv-Q Send-Q Local Address          Foreign Address        (State)
User
tcp        0  16501 www.mk.net:www         sdlb12119.sannet.:3148 FIN_WAIT1
root
tcp        0  16501 auth02.mk.net:www      sdlb12119.sannet.:3188 FIN_WAIT1
root
tcp        0      1 www.anglernet.com:www  ts88.cctrap.com:1070   SYN_RECV
root
tcp        0      1 www.anglernet.com:www  ts88.cctrap.com:1071   SYN_RECV
root
udp        0      0 localhost:domain       *:*
udp        0      0 svr01.mk.net:domain    *:*
udp        0      0 poto.mk.net:domain     *:*
udp        0      0 stats.mk.net:domain    *:*
udp        0      0 home.mk.net:domain     *:*
udp        0      0 www.cmf.net:domain     *:*
Active UNIX domain sockets
Proto RefCnt Flags      Type          State          Path
unix  2      [ ]        SOCK_STREAM   UNCONNECTED    1605182
unix  2      [ ]        SOCK_STREAM   UNCONNECTED    1627039
unix  2      [ ]        SOCK_STREAM   CONNECTED      1652605
```

newgrp

newgrp is used to enter a new group. You can use this command to temporarily become a member of a different group so you can access or work on different files or directories.

nxterm

nxterm is a color-capable xterm terminal emulator for X11. This client is used as a console window during X sessions, and can change features on-the-fly through pop-up menus.

passwd

For the normal user (non-superuser), no arguments are used with the passwd command. The command asks the user for the old password. Following this, the command asks for the new password twice, to make sure it was typed correctly. The new password must be at least six characters long and must contain at least one character that is either uppercase or a nonletter. Also, the new password cannot be the same password as the one being replaced, nor can it match the user's ID (account name).

If the command is run by the superuser, it can be followed by either one or two arguments. If the command is followed by a single user's ID, the superuser can change that user's password. The superuser is not bound by any of the restrictions imposed on the user. If there is an argument after the single user's ID, that argument becomes that user's new password.

pdksh

This public domain Korn shell is a workalike shell with features nearly compatible to the commercial Korn shell, and is found on your Linux system with the name ksh.

pico

The pico command is a handy, virtually crash-proof text editor that is part of the pine mail program's software distribution. One handy command-line option is -w, which disables line wrapping. (This is useful when you're manually configuring system files.) pico performs spell-checking of text files, but does not print.

pine

pine is the program for Internet news and email. Though normally thought of as a mail-handling program, pine can also be used to read Usenet news. This mail program also comes with a handy editor, called pico. You can organize your incoming mail and file messages into different folders.

ping

This command requests packet echoes from network hosts. The ping command sends out a request for an echo of an information packet from a specific computer on a network. It can be used to check communication links or to check whether the specific host exists or is running. ping is used from the command line, followed by an Internet Protocol (IP) number or domain name, like this:

```
# ping staffnet.com
```

ping continues to send requests until you stop the program with Ctrl+C.

pppd

The Point-to Point Protocol, or PPP, daemon. This program runs in the background in your Linux system while you have a PPP connection with your ISP and handles the transmission and format of data into and out of your computer.

pppstats

pppstats prints PPP network statistics. This program prints a variety of information about a current PPP network connection. It can be useful for determining if the PPP connection is active and how much information is being transferred.

pr

The pr command performs basic formatting of text documents for printing and can also be used to convert input text into different formats through 19 command-line options. One is-h, or header option, which puts specified text at the top of each page. Try this code:

```
# ls ¦ pr -h "TOP SECRET DOCUMENT" ¦ lpr
```

printtool

This is the Red Hat Linux printer configuration tool. This X11 client can be run from the command line of a terminal window or through the control-panel, and is used to install, set up, and configure printers for Linux.

procmail

The procmail command processes incoming mail by searching messages for specified strings and either discards, files, or replies to messages according to filters or recipes you specify. This is a handy way to handle unwanted incoming mail or organize vast amounts of incoming mail.

ps

ps gives a snapshot of the current processes. An example follows:

```
svr01:/home/dpitts$ ps -ef

PID TTY STAT  TIME COMMAND
10916  p3 S     0:00 -bash TERM=vt100 HOME=/home2/dpitts PATH=/usr/local/bin:/us
10973  p3 R     0:00  \_ ps -ef LESSOPEN=¦lesspipe.sh %s ignoreeof=10 HOSTNAME=s
10974  p3 S     0:00  \_ more LESSOPEN=¦lesspipe.sh %s ignoreeof=10 HOSTNAME=svr
```

pwd

pwd prints the current working directory. It tells you what directory you are in currently.

quota

The quota command reports on disk quota settings. This command, most often used by the root operator, shows how much disk space users can use by individual or group.

quotacheck

Gives a report on disk-quota usage. This command, most often used by the root operator, scans a specified or current filesystem, reporting on disk usage if disk quotas for users are turned on.

quotaoff

quotaoff turns off disk quotas. This command is used by the root operator to disable disk-quota checking for users.

quotaon

quotaon turns on disk quotas. This command is used by the root operator to enable or enforce disk quotas for users and can be helpful in limiting how much disk space a user can take up with programs or data.

rclock

This is an X11 clock client and appointment reminder. Besides displaying a variety of clock faces in different colors, the rclock program can also be used as an appointment or reminder system and features pop-up notes.

red

Red is the restricted `ed` editor. With this version of the `ed` command, you can only edit files in the current directory. `red` does not have a shell escape command.

repquota

This command gives a report on disk usage. It scans different filesystems and reports on usage and quotas if disk quotas are enabled.

restore

Restore a dump backup with `restore`. The `restore` command features built-in help and an interactive mode for restoring files and directories of a backup created by the `dump` command.

rjoe

The restricted `joe` editor is `rjoe`. With this version of the `joe` editor, you can only edit files specified on the command line.

rm

`rm` is used to delete specified files. With the `-r` option—which can be dangerous!—`rm` recursively removes files. If as `root` you type the command `rm -r /`, you had better have a good backup—all of your files are now gone. This is a good command to use in conjunction with the `find` command to find files owned by a certain user or in a certain group and delete them. By default, the `rm` command does not remove directories.

rmdir

`rmdir` removes a given *empty* directory; the word *empty* is the key word. The syntax is simply `rmdir` *<directory name>*.

route

Use `route` to show or configure the IP routing table. This is another network utility you can use to monitor communication through interfaces on your computer. Although normally used by system administrators, you can use this command to monitor your PPP connection while you're online.

rxvt

`rxvt` is a color-capable, memory-efficient terminal emulator for X11 with nearly all of the features of the `xterm` client. This client is usually started in the background:

```
# rxvt &
```

sed

This is the stream editor, a noninteractive text editor designed to change or manipulate streams of text. The `sed` command can be used to quickly perform global search-and-replace operations on streams of text—through pipes, for example:

```
# cat employees.txt ¦ sed 's/Bill/William/g' >newemployees.txt
```

This changes all instances of `Bill` to `William` in the original file and creates a new file.

sendfax

Use this to send fax documents. The `sendfax` program, part of the `mgetty+sendfax` software package, dials out and sends prepared fax-format graphics documents. This program is usually run by the `faxspool` shell script.

set

The `set` command is used to temporarily change an environment variable. In some shells, the `set -o vi` command allows you to bring back previous commands you have in your history file. It is common to place the `set` command in your `.profile`. Some environment variables require an equal sign, and some, as in the example `set -o vi`, do not.

setfdprm

`setfdprm` sets floppy drive parameters. This command, usually run by the `root` operator, is used to set the current floppy device, usually in preparation for a low-level format.

setserial

The `setserial` command is used to configure or fine-tune specific serial ports in your computer. This command can also be used to report on a serial port's status or identity.

seyon

`seyon` is an X11 serial communications program. The program only runs under X11, but offers a scripting language and point-and-click setup of communications parameters.

shutdown

One time during *Star Trek: The Next Generation*, Data commanded the computer to "Shut down the holodeck!" Unfortunately, most systems don't have voice controls, but systems can still be shut down. This command happens to be that one. Technically, the `shutdown` call, shown here, causes all or part of a full-duplex connection on a socket associated with `s` to be shut down, but who's being technical?

```
int shutdown(int s, int how));
```

The `shutdown` command can also be used to issue a "Vulcan Neck Pinch" (Ctrl+Alt+Del) and restart the system.

slrn

A news reading program, the `slrn` newsreader provides an easy-to-use interface for reading Usenet news. It has some advantages over the `tin` newsreader by providing custom colors for different parts of messages and support for mouse clicks and function keys.

sort

The `sort` command comes in handy whenever you need to generate alphabetical lists of the information from your files. Information can also be listed in reverse order. See the `sort` manual page for more information.

stat

Use this to print file information. The `stat` command prints a variety of information about a specified file and can also be used to check for the validity of symbolic links.

statserial

Use the `statserial` command to print serial port statistics. This command, run only by the `root` operator, shows the current condition of a specified serial port and can be helpful in diagnosing serial port problems.

strings

The `strings` command outputs all text strings found inside binary programs. This can be useful to view the contents of files when you don't have a viewer program for a file's format or for looking at the contents of a binary program (such as to search for help text). For example, use the following code to look at all strings inside the `pico` editor:

```
# strings /usr/bin/pico ¦ less
```

su

`su` enables a user to temporarily become another user. If a user ID is not given, the computer thinks you want to be either the `superuser` or `root`. In either case, a shell that makes you the new user—complete with that user ID, group ID, and any supplemental groups of that new user—is spawned. If you are not `root` and the user has a password (and the user should!), `su` prompts for a password. `root` can become any user at any time without knowing passwords. Technically, the user needs only to have a user ID of `0` (which makes a user a `superuser`) to log on as anyone else without a password.

swapoff

No, `swapoff` is not a move from *The Karate Kid*. Instead, it is a command that stops swapping to a file or block device.

swapon

Also not from the movie *The Karate Kid*, `swapon` sets the swap area to the file or block device by path. `swapoff` stops swapping to the file and is normally done during system boot.

tail

`tail` prints to standard output the last 10 lines of a given file. If no file is given, it reads from standard input. If more than one file is given, it prints a header consisting of the file's name enclosed in left and right arrows (==> and <==) before the output of each file. The default value of 10 lines can be changed by placing `-###` in the command. The syntax for the command follows:

```
tail [-<# of lines to see>] [<filename(s)>]
```

talk

The `talk` command is used to have a "visual" discussion with someone else over a terminal. The basic idea behind this visual discussion is that your input is copied to the other person's terminal, and the other person's input is copied to your terminal. Thus, both people involved in the discussion see the input from both themselves and the other person.

taper

A tape archiving and backup program, the `taper` command features a friendly interface to the `tar` and `gzip` programs to provide archive backups and compression.

tar

`tar` is an archiving program designed to store and extract files from an archive file. A tarred file (called a *tar file*) can be archived to any medium, including a tape drive or a hard drive. The syntax of a `tar` command is `tar <action> <optional functions> <file(s)/directory(ies)>`. If the last parameter is a directory, all subdirectories are also tarred.

tcsh

This enhanced `csh` shell has all of the features of the `csh` shell, with many improvements, such as command-line editing, job control, and command history. This shell is run by the symbolic link (`csh`) found under the `/bin` directory.

telnet

Start and run a Telnet session with `telnet`. You can use the `telnet` command to log in to remote computer systems, to run programs, or to retrieve data.

tin

This is a Usenet news reading program. The `tin` newsreader, like the `slrn` newsreader, provides a menu system for reading Usenet news, allowing you to quickly browse, save, post, or reply to messages found in a specific Usenet newsgroup. The `tin` reader looks for a list of desired newsgroups in the file `.newsrc` in your home directory and can be started like this from the command line of your console or terminal window:

```
# tin -nqr
```

top

You can display CPU processes with the `top` command. This command can be used to print the most active or system resource-intensive processes or programs.

touch

You can use the `touch` command to quickly create a file or update its timestamp.

tput

Change or reset terminal settings. The `tput` command, found under the `/usr/bin` directory, uses terminal capabilities found in the `terminfo` database under the `/usr/lib` directory. This database contains character sequences recognized by different terminals. You can use `tput` in a variety of ways. One handy feature is the `reset` option, which can help you clear up a terminal window if your display becomes munged because of spurious control codes echoed to the screen.

tr

Used to transliterate characters. The `tr` command, a text filter, translates sets of characters you specify on the command line. The classic example is to translate a text file from all uppercase to lowercase:

```
# cat uppercase.txt ¦ tr A-Z a-z > lowercase.txt
```

tree

Use `tree` to print a visual directory. If you'd like to see how your directories are organized, you can use this command to print a graphic tree.

twm

This is the Tab window manager for X11, from which the `fvwm` window manager and others are descended. Although this window manager does not support virtual desktops, you can customize its menus and windows. The `twm` window manager is usually started from the contents of your `.xinitrc` in your home directory.

ulimit

Show resource limit settings with `ulimit`. This is a built-in command for the `bash` or `ksh` shell and can be used to set limits on a number of system resources. This command is similar to the limit command of the `tcsh` or `csh` shells.

umount

Just as the cavalry soldiers dismount from their horses, filesystems dismount from their locations. The `umount` command performs this action. The syntax of the command follows:

```
umount <filesystem>
```

unalias

`unalias` is the command that undoes an alias. In the `alias` command section earlier in this appendix, I aliased `dir` to be the `ls` command. To unalias this command, you would simply type **`unalias dir`**.

unzip

The `unzip` command lists, tests, or extracts files from a zipped archive. The default is to extract files from the archive. The basic syntax is `unzip <filename>`.

updatedb

This command builds `locate` command's database, called `locatedb`, in the `/var/lib` directory.

uptime

You can show how long your system has been running (in case you want to brag to your NT friends). The `uptime` command shows how long your Linux system has been running, who is currently logged on, and what the average system load has been for the last 5, 10, and 15 minutes. Linux system uptimes are generally measured in years (and almost always end due to hardware failure)!

uugetty

Set login parameters, such as terminal type, speed, and protocol. You can use `uugetty` to monitor incoming connections to your Linux system. This program can display login messages or run programs when you log in.

vdir

List the contents of directories with `vdir`. This command is the same as using the `ls` command with the `-l` option to get a detailed directory listing.

vi

Normally known as the `vi` (visual) editor under Red Hat Linux, `vi` is a symbolic link to the `vim` editor. In this mode, the `vim` editor closely emulates the classic `vi` editor, originally distributed with the Berkley Software Distribution.

view

This is a symbolic link to the `vim` editor.

vim

`vim` stands for *VIsual editor iMproved*. This editor is an improvement of the `vi` editor and can also emulate the `ex` line-oriented editor. The X11 version of this editor is called `gvim`.

vimx

This is a symbolic link to the `gvim` X11 editor.

vmstat

`vmstat` prints virtual memory statistics. This command shows how much disk space has been used by your system, usually on the swap file partition.

w

Show who is logged on by using the `w` command, which shows not only who is currently logged in to your system but also the same information as does the `uptime` command.

wall

`wall` displays the contents of standard input on all terminals of all currently logged-in users. Basically, the command writes to all terminals; hence, its name. The contents of files can also be displayed. The `superuser`, or `root`, can write to the terminals of those who have chosen to deny messages or are using a program that automatically denies messages.

wc

This is a word-count program. The `wc` command counts the number of characters, words, and lines in your file and prints a small report to your display. The default is to show all three, but you can limit the report by using the `-c`, `-w`, or `-l` options.

whatis

This command searches the `whatis` database (located under the `/usr/man` directory) for command names and prints a one-line synopsis of what each command does. Use the `whatis` command, followed by the name of another command:

```
# whatis emacs
```

whereis

Use `whereis` to find commands, command sources, and manual pages. This program searches a built-in list of directories to find and then print matches of the command name you specify.

who

Either the who command calls an owl (which it doesn't) or it prints the login name, terminal type, login time, and remote hostname of each user currently logged in. The following is an example of the who command:

```
svr01:/home/dpitts$ who
root     ttyp0    Jul 27 11:44 (www01.mk.net)
dpitts   ttyp2    Jul 27 19:32 (d12.dialup.seane)
ehooban  ttyp3    Jul 27 11:47 (205.177.146.78)
dpitts   ttyp4    Jul 27 19:34 (d12.dialup.seane)
```

If two nonoption arguments are passed to the who command, the command prints the entry for the user running it. Typically, this is run with the command who am I, but any two arguments will work. For example, the following gives information on my session:

```
svr01:/home/dpitts$ who who who
svr01!dpitts   ttyp2    Jul 27 19:32 (d12.dialup.seane)
```

The -u option is nice if you want to see how long it has been since that session has been used, such as in the following:

```
svr01:/home/dpitts$ who -u
root     ttyp0    Jul 27 11:44 08:07 (www01.mk.net)
dpitts   ttyp2    Jul 27 19:32   .   (d12.dialup.seane)
ehooban  ttyp3    Jul 27 11:47 00:09 (205.177.146.78)
dpitts   ttyp4    Jul 27 19:34 00:06  (d12.dialup.seane)
```

whoami

To show your current user identity, the whoami command prints the username of who you currently are. It is useful for checking who you are if you're running as the root operator.

xclock

xclock is an X11 clock client that can be run with a standard clock face or as a digital clock.

xcutsel

This is an X11 client that provides a buffer for copy and paste operations. This program is handy for copying and pasting information between programs that may not support direct copying and pasting.

xdaliclock

An X11 digital clock client that features melting digits, transparent backgrounds, and extensive customized features and keyboard commands.

xdm

This X11 Display Manager provides a log-in interface, called the *chooser*, that when properly configured on your system can manage several X displays.

xfig

`xfig` is an X11 drawing program. The `xfig` client is an interactive drawing program that uses objects rather than pixel images to display figures. You can use this program to develop blueprints or other technical drawings.

xhost +

The `xhost +` command allows `xterms` to be displayed on a system. Probably the most common reason a remote terminal cannot be opened is that the `xhost +` command has not been run. To turn off the capability to allow `xterms`, use the `xhost -` command.

xjed

This is the X11 version of the `jed` editor. This version runs under the X Window System and offers keyboard menus.

xload

This is the X11 system load reporting client. This X11 command is used to show a graphic of the system load average, a combination of memory, CPU, and swap-file space usage. This program, like may X11 clients, is started in the background:

```
# xload &
```

xloadimage

An X11 client that can load, translate, and display graphic images or window dumps created by the `xwd` client on your display or desktop. You can also use the `xloadimage` command to provide slide shows of graphics.

xlock

`xlock` is an X11 terminal-locking program that provides password protection and more than 50 screensavers.

xlsfonts

This X11 client displays and searches for fonts recognized by the current X11 server and is useful for finding a specific font or for getting detailed font reports.

xmessage

An X11 client that displays messages on your display. You can also program your own custom messages with labels, buttons, and other information. Although this client is often used with other programs to provide appointment reminders, an `xmessage` can also be used as a sticky-note reminder.

xminicom

Runs the `minicom` program in an X11 terminal window. This is the preferred way to run the `minicom` communications program under the X Window System.

xmkmf

The `xmkmf` command (a shell script) is used to create the Imakefiles for X sources. It actually runs the `imake` command with a set of arguments.

xmodmap

A utility for modifying keyboards or mouse buttons during an X session. You can use `xmodmap` to remap your keyboard or rearrange your mouse buttons.

xscreensaver

A screensaver for X11, this client is usually run in the background to blank your screen and run a screensaver program after a preselected time. The `xscreensaver` client is usually controlled with the `xscreensaver-command` client.

xscreensaver-command

This X11 client is used to control the `xscreensaver` program to turn screensaving on or off or to cycle through various screensaving displays.

xset

The `xset` command sets some of the options in an X Window session. You can use this option to set your bell (`xset b` *<volume> <frequency> <duration in milliseconds>*), your mouse speed (`xset m` *<acceleration> <threshold>*), and many others.

xsetroot

This X11 client changes how the `root` window or background of your display appears, as well as how the cursor looks. You can use this client to add background patterns, colors, or pictures, or to change your root window cursor. Want a blue background for your X11 desktop? Try this:

```
# xsetroot -solid blue
```

xtop

Similar to the `top` command, `xtop` displays graphically the most active or system resource-intensive processes or programs.

xv

You can display images in X11 with `xv`. This X11 client provides many controls for capturing, changing, saving, and printing images and comes with extensive documentation.

xwd

This is an X11 window-dumping client. You can use this client to take pictures of windows or the entire display. Don't forget to specify an output file like this:

```
# xwd >myscreendump.xwd
```

xwininfo

This X11 information client gathers available information about a window and prints a short report. You can use the `xwininfo` utility to determine a window's size and placement.

xwud

This is an X11 graphics utility client that displays window dumps created by the `xwd` X11 client.

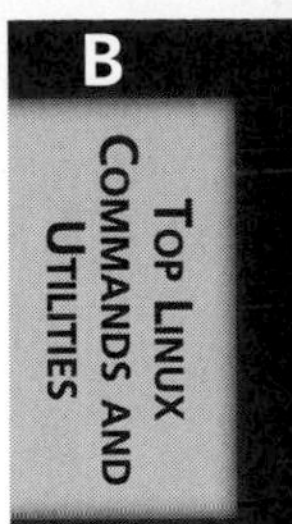

zip

The `zip` command lists, tests, or adds files to a zipped archive. The default is to add files to an archive.

zsh

The `z` shell is the largest shell for Linux, with many, many features and lots of documentation. This shell has features derived from the `csh` and `tcsh` shells and can emulate the `ksh` (Korn) SHell and `sh` (Bourne) SHells.

Summary

If you read this entire appendix, you noticed two things. First, this appendix contains more than 200 commands. The second thing you should have noticed is that you have way too much time on your hands—go out and program some new Linux drivers or something!

I hope this appendix has helped you gain an understanding of some of the commands available for your use, whether you are a user, a systems administrator, or just someone who wants to learn more about Linux. I encourage you to use the man pages to learn about the many details left out of this appendix. Most of the commands have arguments that can be passed to them and, although this appendix attempts to point out a few of them, an entire book would be needed just to go into the detail provided in the man pages.

APPENDIX

Working with Other Systems

In This Appendix

One of the many wonderful things about Linux is the wealth of software extending the operating system's capabilities. When you use Linux, you'll find a wealth of software tools at your fingertips. This appendix discusses several included, GPLd, and commercial software packages you can use to

- Easily transfer files between different media (such as floppies).
- Run a DOS session under the Linux console or X11.
- Run applications from Windows on your Linux desktop.
- Install, configure, and run different operating systems under Linux.
- Install, configure, and run Linux under different operating systems.
- Create and run virtual networks, enabling you to operate your Linux desktop from Windows or work in Windows from your Linux desktop.

Emulators

Emulators have been used since the early days of computing. An *emulator* is a software program designed to mimic a Central Processing Unit (CPU), computer language, or entire operating system on a foreign computer platform. Emulators are used to test CPUs, hardware devices, programs, and operating systems. They are also used to enable the porting or building of applications on one computer when the programs are destined for other, usually quite dissimilar, computing platforms.

Many of the early emulators under UNIX were assembler language macros that translated the low-level code for foreign CPUs into native code on the computer. In this way, programs could be transferred from one computer system to the next. This appendix does not detail how modern-day emulators work or cover all the emulators available for Linux (such as those used to run read-only memory programs from arcade machines under X11), but you'll find that Linux supports some very useful and ingenious emulators.

Emulating DOS with DOSEMU

DOSEMU, based on the early work of Matthias Lautner and currently maintained by Hans Lermen, is not (according to its author) an emulator. Instead, Lautner claims it is a virtual machine for DOS. This means that the program creates a virtual computer in your system's memory. Do you have to buy MS-DOS to use DOSEMU? Of course not! A copy of Pat Vallani's FreeDOS kernel (actually an 8MB DOS filesystem named under the /var/lib/dosemu directory) is included. You'll find most of DOSEMU's documentation under the /usr/doc/dosemu directory.

DOSEMU may be used from the command line of a Linux console or launched in its own window during an X session. The main configuration file, global.conf, is located under the /var/lib/dosemu directory. However, to configure most systemwide settings, you'll edit the file /etc/dosemu.conf. You'll find nearly 80 different settings through which you can configure how DOSEMU works.

By default, DOSEMU may only be launched by the root operator. If you first try launching the program, you'll see this:

```
# dos
Sorry bball. You are not allowed to use DOSEMU. Contact System Admin.
```

To allow other users to launch and use DOSEMU, edit the file /etc/dosemu.users as root with your favorite text editor. Look for this entry:

```
# If you want to allow limited dosemu to all users, uncomment the line below
# all nosuidroot restricted # all other users have normal user restrictions
```

One way to enable your system's users is to remove the leading pound sign (#) from the word all:

```
all nosuidroot restricted # all other users have normal user restrictions
```

Save the file. Next, use the cp command to create a copy of DOSEMU:

```
# cp /usr/bin/dos /usr/bin/dodos
```

Finally, use the chmod command to remove the program's SETUID bit:

```
# chmod 755 /usr/bin/dodos
```

Your users can start a DOS session (with restrictions on storage and hardware access). To enable your users to start a DOS session in an X11 window, make a copy of the xdos command and also change its permissions. To start a DOS session on the console or inside an X11 terminal window, type the new DOSEMU command's name:

```
# dodos
```

You'll then see a DOS session start, as shown in Figure C.1.

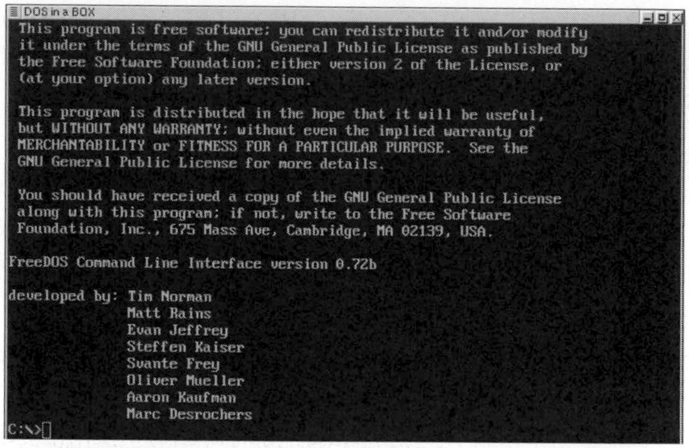

```
DOS in a BOX
This program is free software; you can redistribute it and/or modify
it under the terms of the GNU General Public License as published by
the Free Software Foundation; either version 2 of the License, or
(at your option) any later version.

This program is distributed in the hope that it will be useful,
but WITHOUT ANY WARRANTY; without even the implied warranty of
MERCHANTABILITY or FITNESS FOR A PARTICULAR PURPOSE.  See the
GNU General Public License for more details.

You should have received a copy of the GNU General Public License
along with this program; if not, write to the Free Software
Foundation, Inc., 675 Mass Ave, Cambridge, MA 02139, USA.

FreeDOS Command Line Interface version 0.72b

developed by: Tim Norman
              Matt Rains
              Evan Jeffrey
              Steffen Kaiser
              Svante Frey
              Oliver Mueller
              Aaron Kaufman
              Marc Desrochers
C:\>
```

FIGURE C.1
Use DOSEMU to run a DOS session from the console or during an X11 session.

When DOSEMU starts, it uses the hard drive image file specified in `/etc/dosemu.conf`. To custom configure DOSEMU for your system, edit the file `/etc/dosemu.conf` (as `root`) with your favorite text editor.

Running Windows Clients with Wine

The Wine emulator, supported by programmers contributing to the Wine project, allows you to run many DOS, Window 3.1, or Win32 programs. This emulator may be downloaded from `http://www.winehq.com` in binary or source archives.

> **Note**
>
> Corel Corporation, the same company that made a free, for-personal-use-only version of WordPerfect 8 available for Linux in 1998, announced at the March 1999 Linuxworld Conference that it would make versions of its WordPerfect Office 2000, CorelDRAW, and Corel PHOTO PAINT available for Linux. As part of this effort, Corel also pledged active support and development of Wine "to speed the process of moving our office suite applications to Linux."
>
> Corel also said that the results of development work on Wine would be returned to the Wine project. This means that you can expect better program support as this effort continues. Stay tuned!

The easiest way to install Wine is to download a prebuilt `.rpm` file and to then install the program with this code:

```
# rpm -ivh Wine*rpm
```

To build Wine from scratch, download the 3.1MB archive and then decompress the archive:

```
# tar xvzf Wine*gz
```

Change the directory into the resulting **wine** directory and use the **configure** command:

```
# cd wine*
# ./configure
```

Finally, to build Wine, use the **make** command:

```
# make depend && make
```

After the Wine build finishes, use the make command to install Wine as root:

```
# make install
```

This copies the file wine into the /usr/local/bin directory. By default, debugging symbols are compiled into the binary, resulting in a 13MB file! You can reduce wine's size by using the strip command:

```
# strip /usr/local/bin/wine
```

This leaves wine as a 3MB binary file. As a final step, copy the file wine.ini from the wine directory to the /usr/local/etc directory with the name **wine.conf**. You must be root to do this.

```
# cp wine.ini /usr/local/etc/wine.conf
```

Open this file with your favorite text editor and then change the line designating the path to drive C, which looks like this:

```
Drive C
Path=/c
```

Change the pathname following the Path entry to the path of your Windows root partition (mount point). Because Wine runs programs and applications for DOS, Windows 3.1, and Win32, you must have a copy of Windows installed on your system. For example, assume you mount your Windows partition like this:

```
# mount -t vfat /dev/hda1 /mnt/dos
```

You must change the path entry to your mount point like this:

```
Path=/mnt/dos
```

If you have your Windows partition mounted, you can then try to play a game of solitaire by typing this:

```
# wine /mnt/dos/window/sol.exe
```

The game window appears, as shown in Figure C.2.

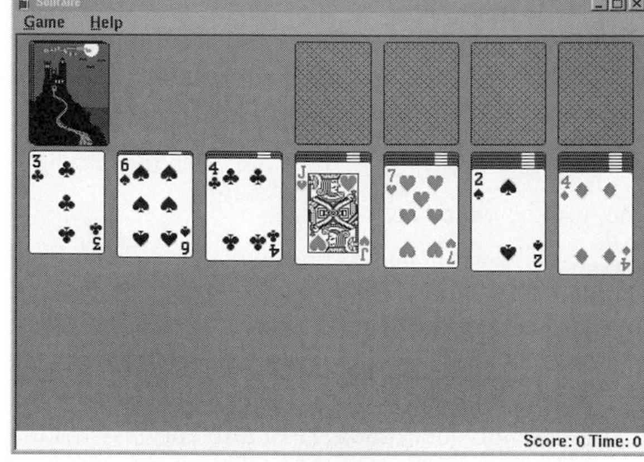

FIGURE C.2
The Wine emulator allows you to run DOS or Windows programs during your Linux X11 sessions.

> **Note**
>
> If you'd like to learn more about Wine or exchange tips and hints with other users or developers, read the Usenet newsgroup `comp.emulators.ms-windows.wine`. You'll also find nearly 30 newsgroups focused on discussions about emulators if you search at `http://www.dejanews.com`.

VMware for Linux and Windows

VMware from VMware, Inc., is a software package for Linux, Win32 operating systems, and others that you can use to install and run an operating system into a virtual filesystem on your computer. This approach, similar to the hard drive image used by DOSEMU, can be used to install and run Linux under a Win32 operating system without partitioning the hard drive. It can also be used to install and run a Win32 operating system under Linux.

At the time of this writing, VMware for Linux was still in beta testing and available for download on a limited-trial basis. Unlike the free At&T Laboratories Cambridge virtual network software (discussed in this appendix's "Windowing Clients" section), VMware is a commercial software package. This section discusses installing and running VMware under Linux, although VMware is available for other platforms. For details, browse to `http://www.vmware.com`.

The beta VMware software for Linux is distributed as a 1.9MB compressed archive, and requires at least a 266Mhz processor and the X Window System.

Installing VMware for Linux

To install VMware under Linux, download the package and then decompress the archive with the **tar** command:

```
# tar xvzf vmware*gz
```

Navigate to the vmware directory and run the file install.pl as root:

```
# ./install.pl

-----------------------------------------
        VMware for Linux  installer

   Copyright  1998,1999 VMware, Inc.
-----------------------------------------

Perform default installation? (yes/no/help) yes
```

The installation script starts and you are asked to read a license agreement file and answer questions. The script checks your system, builds any required software modules, and asks whether you'd like a closed or working networking configuration. (This helps determine whether to allow the installed operating system to communicate with other computers.) If you need networking support for your intended operating system, allow the script to enable networking support. If you choose a "host only" configuration, the VMware install script will pick an unreachable network number for its configuration.

After you choose your configuration, the script installs the VMware software under the /usr/local/bin directory, and exits. In order to run VMware, you must have a license file from VMware, Inc. This license may be obtained by registering at the VMware home page, and will be emailed to you. When you receive the license, save the email message as a text file named **license**.

Next, use the **mkdir** command to create a directory in your home directory named **.vmware**. Copy the license into the .vmware directory:

```
# mkdir .vmware ; cp license .vmware
```

Starting and Configuring VMware

To first start VMware, type **vmware** at the command line of your terminal window. (You do not need to be logged in as the root operator, but you will need read and write permission for the device /dev/zero.) The VMware configuration window and configuration dialog box appears, as shown in Figure C.3.

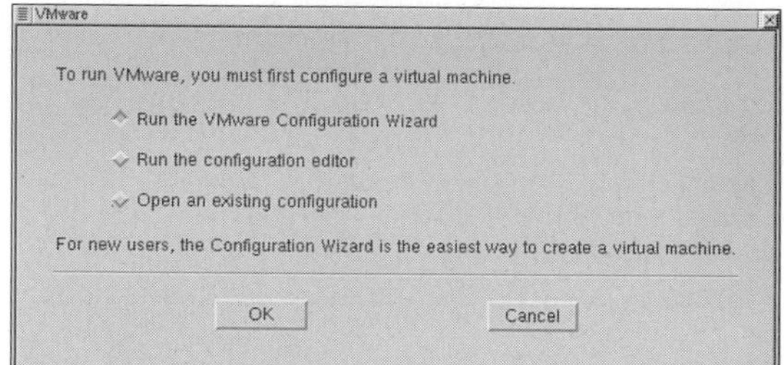

FIGURE C.3
Before you can install another operating system, you must first configure VMware.

Click the OK button to continue. You'll see the Configuration Wizard screen, as shown in Figure C.4.

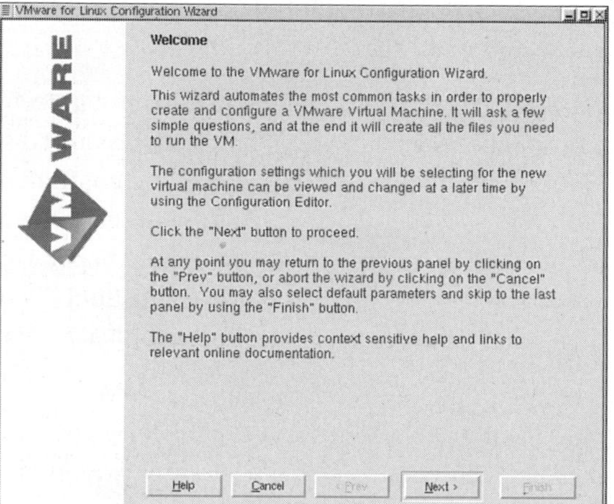

FIGURE C.4
Configure VMware through its Configuration Wizard.

To start your configuration, click the Next button. Throughout the configuration process, you can step forward or backward to change settings. The next screen, shown in Figure C.5, asks you to select the guest operating system. Note that you can even install another Linux distribution, or if you click Other, another UNIX variant, such as FreeBSD!

> **Note**
>
> You can also use VMware to install and run several different operating systems on your computer. In fact, it is even possible to install and run multiple operating systems at the same time on a single computer and then network the different operating systems. I guess this would be called a "LAN-in-a-box."

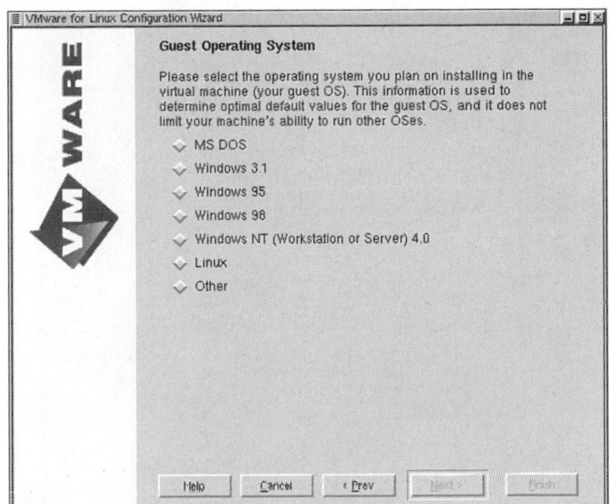

FIGURE C.5
Select the type of operating system you'd like to use with VMware.

After you select the operating system, you are asked to select the location of the virtual filesystem, a file size for the new operating system, the CD-ROM and floppy device, and the type of networking, as shown in Figure C.6.

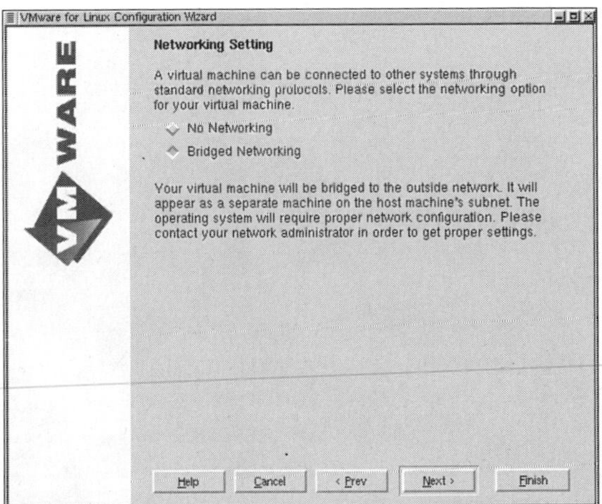

FIGURE C.6
Select networking to allow your new operating system to communicate over a network.

You are then asked to confirm your settings, as shown in Figure C.7.

After you click the Done button, you're ready to install an operating system.

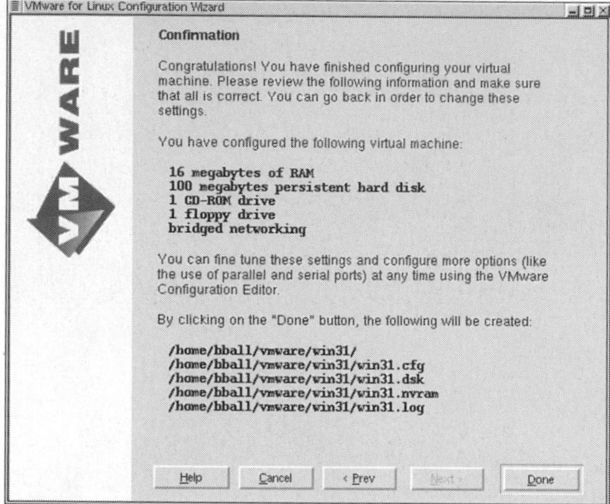

FIGURE C.7
Confirm your configuration settings before using VMware.

Installing Your Operating System

To start the installation process, insert a disk or CD-ROM into your computer and then click the Power On button in the VMware window. The software boots, as shown in Figure C.8.

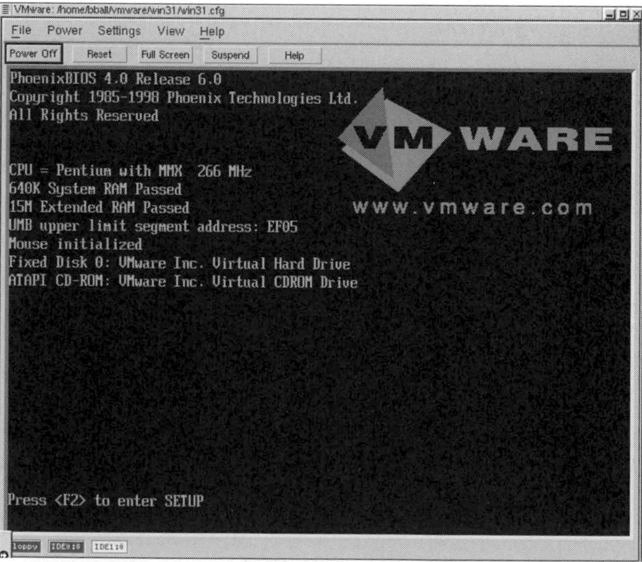

FIGURE C.8
Power on VMware with an inserted floppy or CD-ROM operating system installation disk to install your new operating system.

Continue through and finish your operating system installation. The next time you start VMware, you'll be asked to select a desired configuration, usually found under the directory you designated when you configured your virtual machine. The configuration file will have a name ending in `.cfg` in the directory (usually under the `vmware` directory in your home directory). To start your session, select the file and then click the Power On button. Your operating system will boot, as shown in Figure C.9.

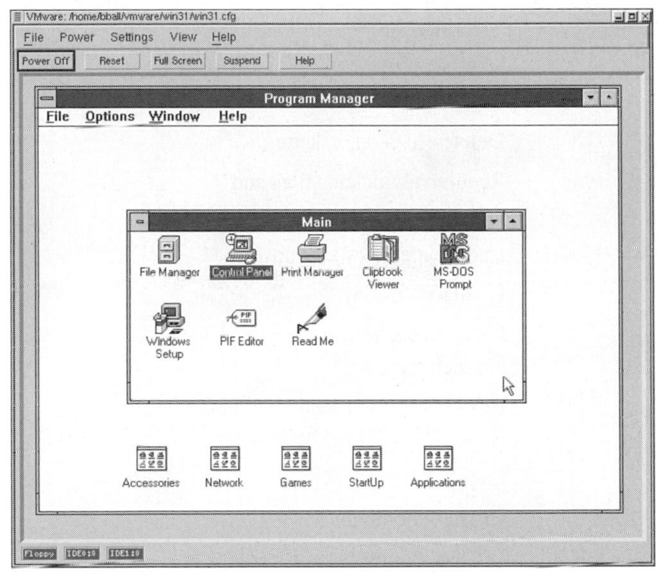

FIGURE C.9
The VMware software supports many different types of operating systems, including legacy software such as the now-defunct Windows for Workgroups.

When you click in the VMware window, your mouse will become "attached" to the operating system's window. To release your mouse, press Ctrl+Alt+Esc. When you've finished working with VMware, make sure to properly shut down the running operating system and then click the Power Off button in the VMware window.

For tips and hints on troubleshooting problems, or to learn more about VMware for other operating systems, browse to `http://www.vmware.com`.

The `mtools` Package

The `mtools` package, originally created by Emmet P. Gray and now maintained by Alain Knaff and David Niemi, is a public-domain set of programs you can use in just about any operation on MS-DOS floppies. These commands are useful because you don't need to mount the floppy in order to read, write, or make changes to the floppy's contents. Table C.1 lists the tools included in the package.

TABLE C.1 `mtools` Package Contents

Program Name	*Function*
`mattrib`	Changes file attributes
`mbadblocks`	Floppy testing program
`mcd`	Changes directory command
`mcheck`	Checks a floppy
`mcopy`	Copies files to and from diskette
`mdel`	Deletes files on diskette
`mdeltree`	Recursively deletes files and directories
`mdir`	Lists contents of a floppy
`mformat`	Formats a floppy
`minfo`	Categorizes, print floppy characteristics
`mkmanifest`	Restores Linux filenames from floppy
`mlabel`	Labels a floppy
`mmd`	Creates subdirectory
`mmount`	Mounts floppy
`mmove`	`mv` command for floppy files and directories
`mpartition`	Makes DOS filesystem as partition
`mrd`	Deletes directories
`mren`	Renames a file
`mtoolstest`	Tests mtools package installation
`mtype`	Types (lists) a file
`mzip`	Zip/JAZ drive utility

The most often used commands will be `mformat`, `mdir`, `mcopy`, and `mdel`. The `mformat` command formats nearly any type of floppy device. One of this package software's nice features is that you don't have to remember the specific names of floppy devices, such as

/dev/fd0, and can use the (possibly) familiar A or B drive designators. This is possible because of mtool's use of the configuration file, /etc/mtools.conf.

Entries for different disk devices are listed in the file. You can edit the file (as root) to configure mtools for your system without having to rebuild the software. (If you need the source, however, you can readily find a copy on your favorite Linux site, or at ftp://www.tux.org/pub/knaff/mtools, along with numerous add-ons and utilities.) If you examine the /etc/mtools.conf file, you'll see entries for different devices and configurations for other operating systems. For example, the floppy device entries look like this:

```
# Linux floppy drives
drive a: file="/dev/fd0" exclusive
drive b: file="/dev/fd1" exclusive
```

These entries allow you to easily format a floppy in drive A without mounting the disk:

```
# mformat a:
```


Note

In most Linux distributions, such as Red Hat's, strict read and write permissions are enforced on your system's devices. This default configuration will force you to use mtools as root. Although this is the safest and most secure approach, you can use the chmod command with 666 permissions to enable anyone to manipulate floppies, like this:

```
# chmod 666 /dev/fd0
```

Tip

The mtools distribution may also be broken! If you receive the error mformat: Non-removable media is not supported (You must tell the complete geometry of the disk, either in /etc/mtools or on the command line), you'll need to fix the entry for your floppy drive in /etc/mtools.conf.

Log in as the root operator and then use your favorite text editor to change your floppy's /etc/mtools.conf entry from this

```
drive a: file="/dev/fd0" exclusive
```

to this

```
drive a: file="/dev/fd0" fat_bits=12 tracks=80 heads=2 sectors=18
```

Save the /etc/mtools.conf file. Details about creating custom device entries may be found in the mtools man page in section 5 of your Linux manuals. Read the man page like this:

```
# man 5 mtools
```

After the `mformat` command has finished, you can copy files to and from the disk with the `mcopy` command. Here is an example:

```
# mcopy *.txt a:
```

This copies all files ending in `.txt` to your disk. To copy files from your disk, reverse the arguments (in DOS form) to the `mcopy` command:

```
# mcopy a:*.txt
```

This copies all files ending in `.txt` to the current directory, or to whatever directory you specify. To see what is on the disk, use the `mdir` command. Here is an example:

```
# mdir a

 Volume in drive A has no label
 Volume Serial Number is 4917-9EDD
Directory for A:/
launch   gif     62835 04-09-1999  13:43  launch.gif
vmware   gif     10703 04-09-1999  13:44  vmware.gif
vnc      gif     21487 04-09-1999  13:44  vnc.gif
        3 files             95 025 bytes
                         1 362 432 bytes free
```

You can use the `mlabel` command to label the diskette:

```
# mlabel a:
 Volume has no label
Enter the new volume label : LINUX
```

You can also use special shell command-line quoting to label the diskette from the command line:

```
# mlabel a:'DOS DISK'
```

This is a handy way to use spaces in a diskette's label. If you want to delete files on your diskette, use the `mdel` command:

```
# mdel a:*.txt
```

This deletes all files ending in `.txt` on the diskette in the A drive. You can also mount your diskette. For details, see the `mmount` command manual page, along with the `mount` command manual page.

Windowing Clients

While software and hardware emulators can ease many computing tasks, the demands on system resources such as memory or storage can be tremendous. If you have extra computers or work in a networked environment, an easier approach is to use the X Window System and networking protocols to communicate with other systems and run other clients.

Thanks to AT&T Laboratories Cambridge, Linux users can now enjoy working on the desktops of foreign operating systems with relative ease through virtual networking computing. Even better news is that the software, called `vnc`, is available under the GNU Public License with source code for Linux, and readily builds and installs under Red Hat Linux 6.0.

The `vnc` Linux software consists of several major components: an X server named `Xvnc`, a server named `vncserver`, a password utility named `vncpasswd`, and a network communication viewer name `vncviewer`. The `vnc` software is also available for other computers and operating systems, such as these:

- DEC Alpha OSF1 3.2
- Macintosh OS
- Solaris
- Win32
- Windows CE2

The software is available at `http://www.uk.research.att.com/vnc`. A compressed archive of binaries for Linux is available, and you can download the 2.1MB UNIX source code tarball.

Building and Installing the vnc Software

If you download the binaries, decompress the file with the `tar` command:

```
# tar xvzf vnc-3.3.2r3_x86_linux_2.0.tgz
```

This creates a `vnc` directory. Either read the included `readme` file in the directory or copy the files `Xvnc`, `vncserver`, `vncviewer`, and `vncpasswd` to the `/usr/local/bin` directory.

If you download the `vnc` source, decompress the archive with the `tar` command:

```
# tar xvzf vnc-3.3.2r3_unixsrc.tgz
```

This creates the `vnc_unixsrc` directory. Navigate into the directory and then start the build with the `xmkmf` command:

```
# xmkmf
# make World
```

Note

The xmkmf command (actually a shell script) is installed from your CD-ROM when you install development software for the X Window System. You'll find xmkmf, along with other software tools such as imake, in the RPM archive XFree86-devel-3.3.3.1-49.rpm. For more information about xmkmf, see Chapter 27, "Motif Programming."

Navigate into the Xvnc directory and build the vnc X server like this:

```
# cd Xvnc
# make World
```

Finally, install the vnc software (as root) with the included installation script, specifying an installation directory:

```
# ./vncinstall /usr/local/bin
```

This completes your Linux software installation. However, if you want to work on the desktops of other computers, you need to download and install the vnc software for the desired platform. For example, if you want to work with a Windows 95 or Windows 98 desktop, download the Win32 vnc software onto the desired computer.

Enabling Virtual Network Service

The vnc server software must be started on a remote computer in order to work on the remote computer's desktop. This may be done through a Telnet session or by sitting at the console and starting the software. To start the server for Linux, use the vncserver script from the command line:

```
# vncserver
You will require a password to access your desktops.

Password:
```

Enter a password used to allow remote access and press Enter. The script then loads and starts the Xvnc X11 server (a customized X11R6.3 server based on XFree86 3.3.2). If you want to work on the remote desktop of a networked Win32 computer, the vnc software for Win32 must be downloaded and copied onto the remote computer. The Win32 software must then be extracted with an archive utility such as WinZip.

Decompress the Win32 vnc software and install the software using the vnc Setup. To start the server, click the Install Default Registry Settings menu item from the vnc folder on your desktop's Start menu. Click the WinVNC 3.3.2 menu item that is shown in Figure C.10.

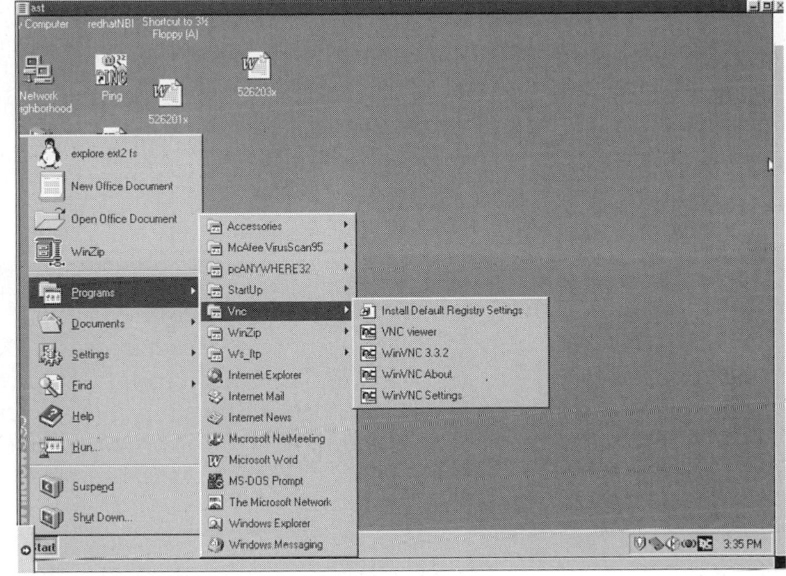

FIGURE C.10
The Win32 vnc software provides easy-to-use menu items from the Start menu on the Windows desktop.

That's all there is to do! If you need to customize your settings or change the password for access to the Win32 desktop, click the WinVNC settings menu item. You'll see a dialog box, as shown in Figure C.11, that you can use to change the network or password settings.

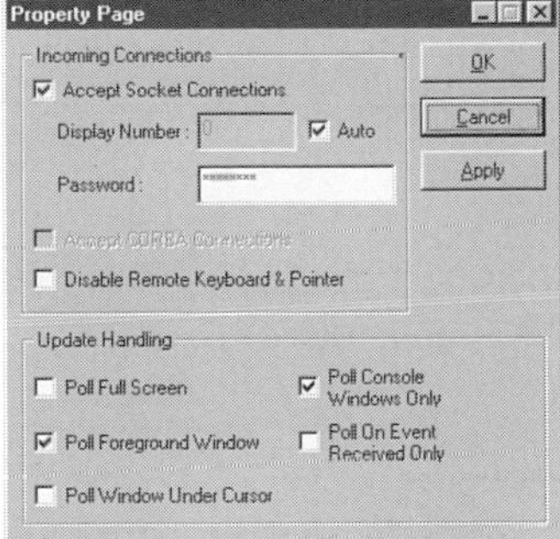

FIGURE C.11
Use the WinVNC settings dialog box to configure WinVNC for your Win32 desktop.

To view the remote Win32 desktop from Linux, use the `vncviewer` command, followed by the hostname or IP address of the Win32 computer and the desktop number (which, according to the `vnc readme`, will always be `0`). Type the command in an X11 terminal window:

```
# vncviewer ascentia.home.org:0
```

You are prompted for the password of the remote vnc server:

```
vncviewer: VNC server supports protocol version 3.3 (viewer 3.3)
Password:
```

After you type in the password and press Enter, an X11 window appears with the remote desktop (as shown in Figure C.12). You can then launch remote applications and work on the computer as if it were your own!

> **Note**
>
> The `vncviewer` client and `vncserver` script also recognize several X11 Toolkit options, such as geometry settings. For example, if you start the `vncserver` on a remote Linux computer (such as through a Telnet session), you can specify the size of remotely viewed desktops with the `-geometry` option, followed by the size of the desktop in horizontal and vertical pixels. To start an 800×600-pixel server desktop, use `vncserver` like this:
>
> ```
> # vncserver -geometry 800x600 hostname:displaynumber
> ```
>
> When this desktop is viewed remotely from another computer, the desktop will use an 800×600 display. (The default size of a vnc desktop is 1,024×768 pixels.) For more information about X11 Toolkit options, see the X man page.

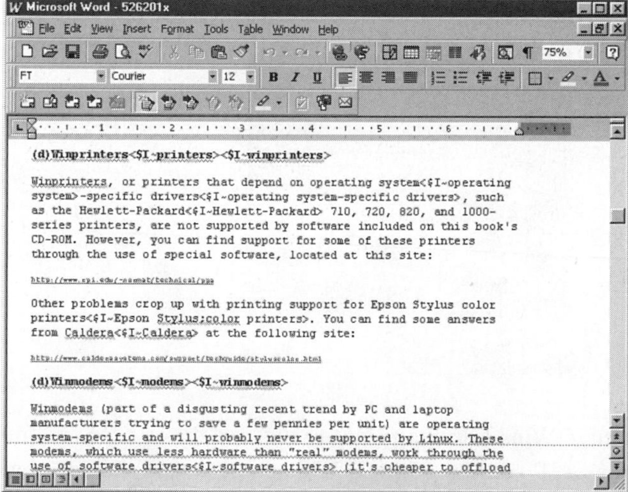

FIGURE C.12
The Linux `vncviewer` client launches and works a remote desktop session.

You can also use the `vncviewer` client on remote computers to view the Linux desktop. The settings and X resource files for the Linux vnc desktop may be quite different from your normal X session! Look in the .vnc directory for the file xstartup, which will look like this:

```
#!/bin/sh

xrdb $HOME/.Xresources
xsetroot -solid grey
xterm -geometry 80x24+10+10 -ls -title "$VNCDESKTOP Desktop" &
twm &
```

Note that only a single X terminal and the twm window manager are used! Edit this file to suit your needs. Of course, with all this flexibility, remote sessions can get a little confusing. For example, Figure C.13 shows a Windows 95 desktop remotely viewed through a remote computer using KDE for its X11 session, which itself is being remotely run from a Red Hat Linux GNOME Enlightenment X session.

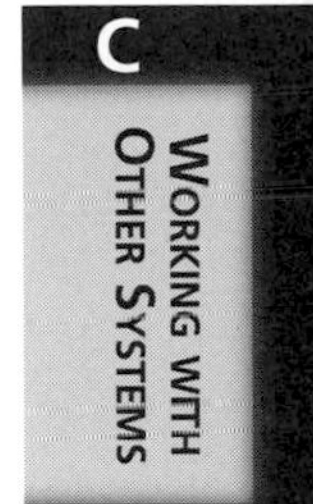

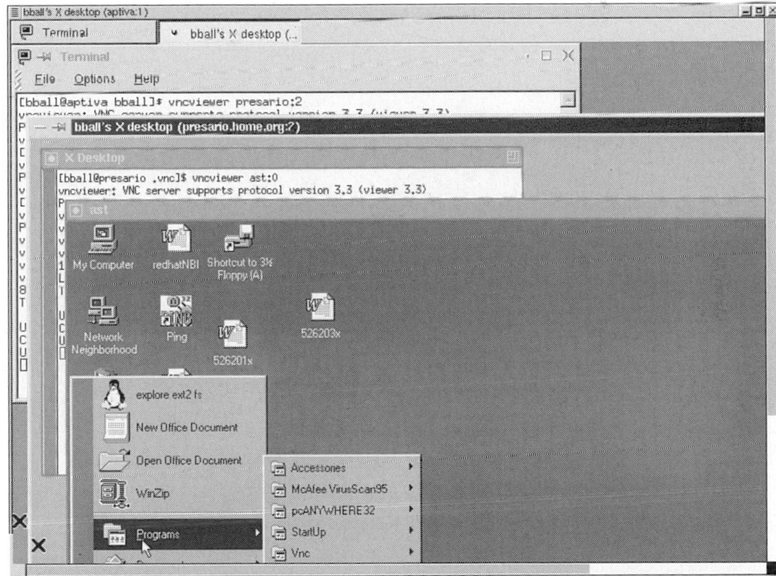

FIGURE C.13
A chain of three remote virtual network sessions can get a bit confusing, but works quite well thanks to the vnc *software.*

Summary

This appendix introduced you to a number of useful software applications that can be used to extend the Linux computing experience. Emulators or virtual networks can be used to add flexibility to your computing environment or to breathe new life into legacy operating systems and applications. As you can see, there are quite a few programs and suites of software available for Linux. It is up to you to explore the networking limits of these applications or to find new uses for older software through emulators.

APPENDIX D

The Linux Documentation Project Copyright License

IN THIS APPENDIX

Last modified: 6 January 1997

The following copyright license applies to all works by the Linux Documentation Project.

Read the license carefully; it is somewhat like the GNU General Public License, but several conditions in it differ from what you might be used to. If you have any questions, email the LDP coordinator at `mdw@metalab.unc.edu`.

Copyright License

The Linux Documentation Project manuals may be reproduced and distributed in whole or in part, subject to the following conditions:

All Linux Documentation Project manuals are copyrighted by their respective authors. They are not in the public domain.

- The copyright notice and this permission notice must be preserved completely on all complete or partial copies.
- Any translation or derivative work of *Linux Installation and Getting Started* must be approved by the author in writing before distribution.
- If you distribute *Linux Installation and Getting Started* in part, instructions for obtaining the complete version of this manual must be included and a means for obtaining a complete version provided.
- Small portions may be reproduced as illustrations for reviews or quotes in other works without this permission notice if proper citation is given.
- The GNU General Public License may be reproduced under the conditions given within it.

Exceptions to these rules may be granted for academic purposes: Write to the author and ask. These restrictions are here to protect us as authors, not to restrict you as educators and learners. All source code in *Linux Installation and Getting Started* is placed under the GNU General Public License, available via anonymous FTP from `ftp://prep.ai.mit.edu/pub/gnu/COPYING`.

Publishing LDP Manuals

If you're a publishing company interested in distributing any of the LDP manuals, read on.

By the license given in the previous section, anyone is allowed to publish and distribute verbatim copies of the Linux Documentation Project manuals. You don't need our explicit permission for this. However, if you would like to distribute a translation or derivative work based on any of the LDP manuals, you must obtain permission from the author, in writing, before doing so.

All translations and derivative works of LDP manuals must be placed under the Linux Documentation License given in the previous section. That is, if you plan to release a translation of one of the manuals, it must be freely distributable by the above terms.

You may, of course, sell the LDP manuals for profit. We encourage you to do so. Keep in mind, however, that because the LDP manuals are freely distributable, anyone may photocopy or distribute printed copies free of charge, if they wish to do so.

We do not require to be paid royalties for any profit earned from selling LDP manuals. However, we would like to suggest that if you do sell LDP manuals for profit, that you either offer the author royalties, or donate a portion of your earnings to the author, the LDP as a whole, or to the Linux development community. You may also wish to send one or more free copies of the LDP manual that you are distributing to the author. Your show of support for the LDP and the Linux community will be very appreciated.

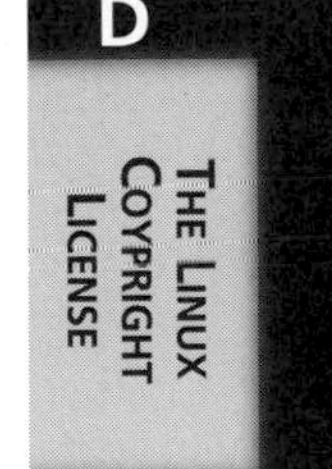

We would like to be informed of any plans to publish or distribute LDP manuals, just so we know how they're becoming available. If you are publishing or planning to publish any LDP manuals, please send email to Matt Welsh at `mdw@metalab.unc.edu`.

We encourage Linux software distributors to distribute the LDP manuals (such as the *Installation and Getting Started* guide) with their software. The LDP manuals are intended to be used as the "official" Linux documentation, and we'd like to see mail-order distributors bundling the LDP manuals with the software. As the LDP manuals mature, hopefully, they will fulfill this goal more adequately.

sendmail.cf: The Configuration File

With the advent of V.8, `sendmail` has shipped with a quick and easy way to automatically create a `sendmail.cf` file for you. In fact, it is highly recommended that you do not create or modify any `sendmail.cf` files manually. This section can be safely skipped if you aren't interested in the gory details regarding the `sendmail.cf` file. (I discuss the easy way to configure `sendmail` in the next section.)

The `sendmail.cf` file provides `sendmail` with its brains, and because it's so important, this section covers it in fairly excruciating detail. Don't worry if you don't understand everything the first time through. It will make more sense upon re-reading and after you've had a chance to play with some configuration files of your own.

`sendmail`'s power lies in its flexibility, which comes from its configuration file, `sendmail.cf`. `sendmail.cf` statements compose a cryptic programming language that at first glance doesn't inspire much confidence. (C code probably didn't, either, the first time you saw it.) However, learning the `sendmail.cf` language isn't very hard, and you won't have to learn the nitty-gritty details unless you plan to write a `sendmail.cf` from scratch—a bad idea at best.

General Form of the Configuration File

Each line of the configuration file begins with a single command character that indicates the function and syntax of that line. Lines beginning with a # are comments; blank lines are ignored. Lines beginning with a space or tab are continuations of the preceding line, although you should usually avoid continuations.

Table E.1 shows the command characters and their functions as well as an example of their usage. This table is split into three parts, corresponding to the three main functions of a configuration file, which are covered later in this chapter in the section called "A Functional Description of the Configuration File."

TABLE E.1 *`sendmail.cf`* **Command Characters**

Command Character	*Command Syntax and Example*	*Function*
#	# comments are ignored.	The character signifies a comment line. Always use lots of comments.
	# Standard RFC822 parsing	
D	*DX string*	Defines a macro `X` to have the string value *`string`*.
	`Mmailhub.gonzo.gov`	

Command Character	Command Syntax and Example	Function
D	`D{MacroName}value`	Defines long macro `{MacroName}` to have the value, *value*, then referenced later with `${MacroName}`.
	`D{Relay}mailhub.gonzo.gov`	
	`DMmailhub.gonzo.gov`	
C	`CX word1`, *word2*, and so on	Defines a class *X* as *word1*, *word2*, and so on.
	`Cwlocalhost myuucp name`	
F	`FX/path/to/a/file`	Defines a class `X` by reading it from a file.
	`Fw/etc/mail/host_aliases`	
H	`H?mailerflag?name:template`	Defines a mail header.
	`H?F?From: $q`	
O	`OX option arguments`	Sets option `X`. Most command-line options can be set in `sendmail.cf`.
	`OL9` # sets the log level to 9.	
P	`Pclass=nn`	Sets mail delivery precedence based on the class of the mail.
	`Pjunk=-100`	
V	`Vn`	Tells V.8 `sendmail` the version level of the configuration file.
	`V3`	
K	`Kname` class arguments	Defines a key file (database map).
	`Kuucphosts dbm hash /etc/mail/uucphsts`	
M	`Mname,field_1=value_1,...`	Defines a mailer.
	`Mprog,P=/bin/sh,F=lsD,A=sh -c $u`	
S	`Snn`	Begins a new rule set.
	`S22`	
R	`Rlhs rhs comment`	Defines a matching/rewriting rule.
	`R$+ $:$>22 call ruleset 22`	

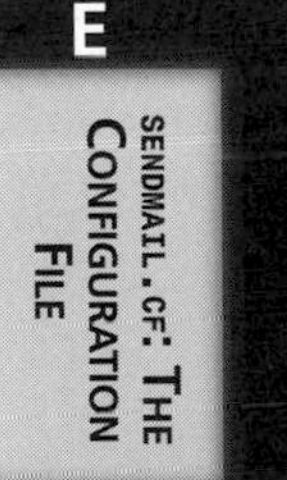

A Functional Description of the Configuration File

A configuration file does three things. First, it sets the environment for `sendmail` by telling it what options you want set and the locations of the files and databases it uses.

Second, a configuration file defines the characteristics of the mailers (delivery agents or MTAs) that `sendmail` uses after it decides where to route a letter. All configuration files must define local and program mailers to handle delivery to users on the local host. Most of them also define one or more SMTP mailers, and sites that must handle UUCP mail define UUCP mailers.

Third, a configuration file specifies rulesets that rewrite sender and recipient addresses and select mailers. All rulesets are user-defined, but some have special meaning to `sendmail`. Ruleset 0, for example, is used to select a mailer. Rulesets 0, 1, 2, 3, and 4 all have special meaning to `sendmail` and are processed in a particular order. (See "The `S` and `R` Operators: Rulesets and Rewriting Rules" later in this chapter.)

The following sections cover the operators in more detail, in the order in which they appear in Table 9.1.

The `D` Operator: Macros

Macros are like shell variables. After you define a macro's value, you can refer to it later in the configuration file and its value will be substituted for the macro. For example, a configuration file might have many lines that mention the hypothetical mail hub, `mailer.gonzo.gov`. Rather than type that name over and over, you can define a macro `R` (for relay mailer) as follows:

```
DRmailer.gonzo.gov
```

When `sendmail` encounters an `$R` in `sendmail.cf`, it substitutes the string `mailer.gonzo.gov`.

Macro names can be more than one character. You could, for example, define the following:

```
D{Relay}mailer.gonzo.gov
```

Refer to it later with this:

```
${Relay}
```

Quite a few macros are defined by `sendmail` and shouldn't be redefined except to work around broken software. `sendmail` uses lowercase letters for its predefined macros. Uppercase letters can be used freely. V.8 `sendmail`'s predefined macros are fully documented in section 5.1.2 of the *Sendmail Installation and Operation (SIOG)*.

The C and F Operators: Classes

Classes are similar to macros but are used for different purposes in rewriting rules. (See "The S and R Operators: Rulesets and Rewriting Rules" later in this chapter.) As with macros, classes are named by single characters. Lowercase letters are reserved for sendmail and uppercase letters for user-defined classes. A class contains one or more words. For example, you could define a class H containing all the hosts in the local domain as follows:

```
CH larry moe curly
```

For convenience, large classes can be continued on subsequent lines. The following definition of the class H is the same as the preceding one:

```
CH larry
CH moe
CH curly
```

You can also define a class by reading its words from a file:

```
CF/usr/local/lib/localhosts
```

If the file /usr/local/lib/localhosts contains the words larry, moe, and curly (one per line), this definition is equivalent to the preceding two.

Why use macros and classes? The best reason is that they centralize information in the configuration file. If you decide in the preceding example to change the name of the mail hub from mailer.gonzo.gov to mailhub.gonzo.gov, you have to change only the definition of the $R macro remedy for the configuration file to work as before. If the name mailer.gonzo.gov is scattered throughout the file, you might forget to change it in some places. If important information is centralized, you can also comment it extensively in a single place. Because configuration files tend to be obscure at best, a liberal dose of comments is a good antidote to that sinking feeling you get when, six months later, you wonder why you made a change.

The H Operator: Header Definitions

You probably won't want to change the header definitions given in the V.8 sendmail configuration files because they already follow accepted standards. Here are some sample headers:

```
H?D?Date: $a

H?F?Resent-From: $q

H?F?From: $q

H?x?Full-Name: $x
```

Note that header definitions can use macros, which are expanded when inserted into a letter. For example, the `$x` macro used in the preceding `Full-Name:` header definition expands to the full name of the sender.

The optional `?mailerflag?` construct tells `sendmail` to insert a header only if the chosen mailer has that mailer flag set. (See "The `M` Operator: Mailer Definitions" later in this chapter.)

Suppose the definition of your local mailer has a flag `Q`, and `sendmail` selects that mailer to deliver a letter. If your configuration file contains a header definition like the one following, `sendmail` inserts that header into letters delivered through the local mailer, substituting the value of the macro `$F`:

```
H?Q?X-Fruit-of-the-day: $F
```

Why would you use the `?mailerflag?` feature? Different protocols can require different mail headers. Because they also need different mailers, you can define appropriate mailer flags for each in the mailer definition and use the `?mailerflag?` construct in the header definition to tell `sendmail` whether to insert the header.

The `O` Operator: Setting Options

`sendmail` has many options that change its operation or inform it of the location of the files it uses. Most of them can be given either on the command line or in the configuration file. For example, you can specify the location of the aliases file in either place. Use the `-o` option to specify the aliases file on the command line:

```
$ /usr/sbin/sendmail -oA/etc/aliases [other arguments...]
$ /etc/mta/sendmail -oA/etc/aliases [other arguments...]
```

To do the same thing in the configuration file, you include a line like this:

```
OA/etc/aliases
```

The uses are equivalent, but options such as the location of the aliases file rarely change, and most people set them in `sendmail.cf`. The V.8 `sendmail` options are fully described in the SIOG.

The `P` Operator: Mail Precedence

Users can include mail headers indicating the relative importance of their mail, and `sendmail` can use those headers to decide the priority of competing letters. Precedences for V.8 `sendmail` are given as follows:

```
Pspecial-delivery=100
Pfirst-class=0
Plist=-30
```

```
Pbulk=-60
Pjunk=-100
```

If users who run large mailing lists include the header `Precedence: bulk` in their letters, `sendmail` gives them a lower priority than letters with the header `Precedence: first-class`.

The `V` Operator: `sendmail.cf` Version Levels

As V.8 `sendmail` evolves, its author adds new features. The `V` operator tells V.8 `sendmail` which features it should expect to find in your configuration file. Older versions of `sendmail` don't understand this command. The SIOG explains the configuration file version levels in detail.

> **Note**
>
> The configuration file version level does not correspond to the `sendmail` version level. V.8 `sendmail` understands versions 1 through 5 of configuration files, and no such thing as a version 8 configuration file exists.

The `K` Operator: Key Files

`sendmail` has always used keyed databases—for example, the aliases databases. Given the key `postmaster`, `sendmail` looks up the data associated with that key and returns the names of the accounts to which the postmaster's mail should be delivered. V.8 `sendmail` extends this concept to arbitrary databases, including NIS maps (Sun's Network Information Service, formerly known as Yellow Pages or YP; see Chapter 14, "NIS: Network Information Service," for details). The `K` operator tells `sendmail` the location of the database, its class, and how to access it. V.8 `sendmail` supports the following classes of user-defined databases: `dbm`, `btree`, `hash`, and `NIS`. The default used when compiling under Linux is the `btree` format. See the SIOG for the lowdown on key files.

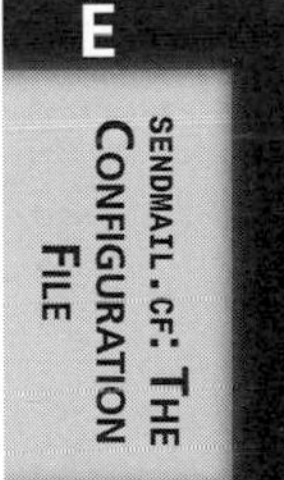

The `M` Operator: Mailer Definitions

Mailers are either MTAs or final delivery agents. Recall that the aliases file enables you to send mail to a login name (which might be aliased to a remote user), a program, or a file. A special mailer can be defined for each purpose, and even though the SMTP MTA is built in, it must have a mailer definition to tailor `sendmail`'s SMTP operations.

Mailer definitions are important because all recipient addresses must resolve to a mailer in ruleset 0. Resolving to a mailer is just another name for `sendmail`'s main function, mail routing. For example, resolving to the local mailer routes the letter to a local user via the final delivery agent defined in that mailer (such as `/bin/mail`), and resolving to the SMTP mailer routes the letter to another host via `sendmail`'s built-in SMTP transport, as defined in the SMTP mailer.

A concrete example of a mailer definition will make this information clearer. Because `sendmail` requires a local mailer definition, look at the following:

```
Mlocal, P=/bin/mail, F=lsDFMfSn, S=10, R=20, A=mail -d $u
```

All mailer definitions begin with the `M` operator and the name of the mailer—in this case, `local`. Other fields follow, separated by commas. Each field consists of a field name and its value, separated by an equal sign (=). The allowable fields are explained in section 5.1.4 of the SIOG.

In the preceding local mailer definition, the `P=` equivalence gives the program's pathname to run to deliver the mail, `/bin/mail`. The `F=` field gives the `sendmail` flags for the local mailer. (See "The `H` Operator: Header Definitions" earlier in this chapter.) These flags are not passed to the command mentioned in the `P=` field but are used by `sendmail` to modify its operation, depending on the mailer it chooses. For example, `sendmail` usually drops its `superuser` status before invoking mailers, but you can use the `S` mailer flag to tell `sendmail` to retain this status for certain mailers.

The `S=` and `R=` fields specify rulesets for `sendmail` to use in rewriting sender and recipient addresses. Because you can give different `R=` and `S=` flags for each mailer you define, you can rewrite addresses differently for each mailer. For example, if one of your UUCP neighbors runs obsolete software that doesn't understand domain addressing, you might declare a special mailer just for that site and write mailer-specific rulesets to convert addresses into a form its mailer can understand.

The `S=` and `R=` fields can also specify different rulesets to rewrite the envelope and header addresses. (See "Header and Envelope Addresses" earlier in this chapter.) A specification such as `S=21/31` tells `sendmail` to use ruleset 21 to rewrite sender envelope addresses and ruleset 31 to rewrite sender header addresses. This capability comes in handy for mailers that require addresses to be presented differently in the envelope than in the headers.

The `A=` field gives the argument vector (command line) for the program that will be run—in this case, `/bin/mail`. In this example, `sendmail` runs the command as `mail -d $u`, expanding the `$u` macro to the name of the user to whom the mail should be delivered:

```
/bin/mail -d joe
```

You could type this same expanded command to your shell at a command prompt.

You might want to use many other mailer flags to tune mailers—to limit the maximum message size on a per-mailer basis, for example. These flags are all documented in section 5.1.4 of the SIOG.

The S and R Operators: Rulesets and Rewriting Rules

A configuration file is composed of a series of rulesets, which are somewhat like subroutines in a program. *Rulesets* are used to detect bad addresses, to rewrite addresses into forms that remote mailers can understand, and to route mail to one of sendmail's internal mailers. (See the section called "The M Operator: Mailer Definitions," earlier in this chapter.)

sendmail passes addresses to rulesets according to a built-in order. Rulesets also can call other rulesets not in the built-in order. The built-in order varies, depending on whether the address being handled is a sender or receiver address and which mailer has been chosen to deliver the letter.

Rulesets are announced by the S command, which is followed by a number to identify the ruleset. sendmail collects subsequent R (rule) lines until it finds another S operator or the end of the configuration file. The following example defines ruleset 11:

```
# Ruleset 11
S11
R$+        $: $>22 $1      call ruleset 22
```

This ruleset doesn't do much that is useful. The important point to note is that sendmail collects ruleset number 11, which is composed of a single rule.

sendmail's Built-In Ruleset Processing Rules

sendmail uses a three-track approach to processing addresses: one to choose a delivery agent, another to process sender addresses, and another for receiver addresses.

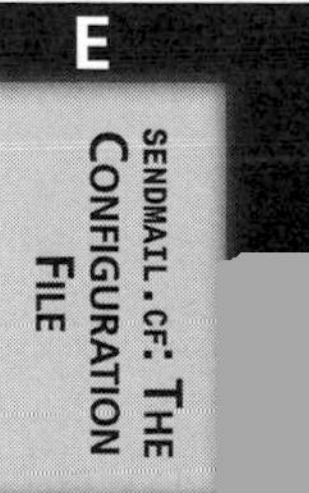

All addresses are first sent through ruleset 3 for preprocessing into a canonical form that makes them easy for other rulesets to handle. Regardless of the complexity of the address, ruleset 3's job is to decide the next host to which a letter should be sent. Ruleset 3 tries to locate that host in the address and mark it within angle brackets. In the simplest case, an address such as joe@gonzo.gov becomes joe<@gonzo.gov>.

Ruleset 0 then determines the correct delivery agent (mailer) to use for each recipient. For example, a letter from betty@whizzer.com to joe@gonzo.gov (an Internet site) and pinhead!zippy (an old-style UUCP site) requires two different mailers: an SMTP mailer for gonzo.gov and an old-style UUCP mailer for pinhead. Mailer selection determines later processing of sender and recipient addresses because the rulesets given in the S= and R= mailer flags vary from mailer to mailer.

Addresses sent through ruleset 0 must resolve to a mailer. This means that when an address matches the `lhs`, the `rhs` gives a triple of the mailer, user, and host. The following line shows the syntax for a rule that resolves to a mailer:

```
Rlhs      $#mailer $@host $:user   your comment here...
```

The mailer is the name of one of the mailers you've defined in an `M` command—for example, `smtp`. The host and user are usually positional macros taken from the `lhs` match. (See "The Right-Hand Side (`rhs`) of Rules" later in this chapter.)

After `sendmail` selects a mailer in ruleset 0, it processes sender addresses through ruleset 1 (often empty) and then sends them to the ruleset given in the `S=` flag for that mailer.

Similarly, `sendmail` sends recipient addresses through ruleset 2 (also often empty) and then to the ruleset mentioned in the `R=` mailer flag.

Finally, `sendmail` post-processes all addresses in ruleset 4, which (among other things) removes the angle brackets inserted by ruleset 3.

Why do mailers have different `S=` and `R=` flags? Consider the previous example of the letter sent to `joe@gonzo.gov` and `pinhead!zippy`. If `betty@whizzer.com` sends the mail, her address must appear in a different form to each recipient. For Joe, it should be a domain address, `betty@whizzer.com`. Because `pinhead` expects old-style UUCP addresses, the return address for Zippy should be `whizzer!betty`. Joe's address must also be rewritten for the `pinhead` UUCP mailer, and Joe's copy must include an address for Zippy that his mailer can handle.

Processing Rules Within Rulesets

`sendmail` passes an address to a ruleset and then processes it through each rule, line by line. If a rule's `lhs` matches the address, it is rewritten by the `rhs`. If it doesn't match, `sendmail` continues to the next rule until it reaches the end of the ruleset. At the end of the ruleset, `sendmail` returns the rewritten address to the calling ruleset or to the next ruleset in its built-in execution sequence.

If an address matches the `lhs` and is rewritten by the `rhs`, the rule is tried again—an implicit loop. However, see "`$:` and `$@`: Altering a Ruleset's Evaluation" section later in this chapter for exceptions to this rule.

As shown in Table 9.1, each rewriting rule is introduced by the `R` command and has three fields—the left-hand side (`lhs`, or matching side); the right-hand side (`rhs`, or rewriting side); and an optional comment (which must be separated from one another by tab characters). Look at this example:

```
Rlhs      rhs       comment
```

Parsing: Turning Addresses into Tokens

sendmail parses addresses and the lhs of rules into tokens and then matches the address and the lhs, token by token. The macro $o contains the characters that sendmail uses to separate an address into tokens. It's often defined like this:

```
# address delimiter characters
Do.:%@!^/[]
```

All the characters in $o are both token separators and tokens. sendmail takes an address such as rae@rainbow.org and breaks it into tokens according to the characters in the o macro, like this:

```
"rae"    "@"    "rainbow"    "."    "org"
```

sendmail also parses the lhs of rewriting rules into tokens so they can be compared, one by one, with the input address to see whether they match. For example, the lhs $-@rainbow.org is parsed as follows:

```
"$-"    "@"    "rainbow"    "."    "org"
```

(Don't worry about the $- just yet. It's a pattern-matching operator, similar to a shell wildcard, that matches any single token and is covered later in this chapter in the section "The Left-Hand Side (lhs) of Rules.") Now you can put the two together to show how sendmail decides whether an address matches the lhs of a rule:

```
 "rae"    "@"    "rainbow"    "."    "org"
"$-"    "@"    "rainbow"    "."    "org"
```

In this case, each token from the address matches a constant string (for example, rainbow) or a pattern-matching operator ($-). This way, the address matches and sendmail will use the rhs to rewrite the address.

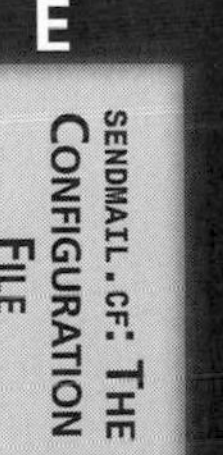

Consider the (usually bad) effect of changing the value of $o. As shown previously, sendmail breaks the rae@rainbow.org address into five tokens. However, if the @ character were not in $o, the address would be parsed quite differently, into only three tokens:

```
"rae@rainbow"    "."    "org"
```

You can see that changing $o has a drastic effect on sendmail's address parsing, and you should leave it alone until you know what you're doing. You probably won't want to change it even then because the V.8 sendmail configuration files already have it correctly defined for standard RFC 822 and RFC 976 address interpretation.

The Left-Hand Side (lhs) of Rules

The lhs is a pattern against which sendmail matches the input address. The lhs can contain ordinary text or any of the pattern-matching operators shown in Table E.2.

TABLE E.2 *lhs* Pattern-Matching Operators

Operator	*Function*
$-	Match exactly one token
$+	Match one or more tokens
$*	Match zero or more tokens
$@	Match the null input; used to call the error mailer

The values of macros and classes are matched in the lhs with the operators shown in Table E.3.

TABLE E.3 *lhs* Macro and Class-Matching Operators

Operator	*Function*
$X	Match the value of macro X
$=C	Match any word in class C
$~C	Match if token is not in class C

The pattern-, macro-, and class-matching operators are necessary because most rules must match many different input addresses. For example, a rule might need to match all addresses that end with gonzo.gov and begin with one or more of any character.

The Right-Hand Side (rhs) of Rules

The rhs of a rewriting rule tells sendmail how to rewrite an address that matches the lhs. The rhs can include text, macros, and positional references to matches in the lhs. When a pattern-matching operator from Table 9.2 matches the input, sendmail assigns it to a numeric macro $n, corresponding to the position it matches in the lhs. For example, suppose the address joe@pc1.gonzo.gov is passed to the following rule:

```
R$+ @ $+        $: $1 < @ $2 >              focus on domain
```

In this example, joe matches $+ (one or more of anything), so sendmail assigns the string joe to $1. The @ in the address matches the @ in the lhs, but constant strings are not assigned to positional macros. The tokens in the string pc1.gonzo.gov match the second $+ and are assigned to $2. The address is rewritten as $1<@$2>, or joe<@pc1.gonzo.gov>.

$: and $@: Altering a Ruleset's Evaluation

Consider the following rule:

```
R$*  $: $1 < @ $j > add local domain
```

After rewriting an address in the rhs, sendmail tries to match the rewritten address with the lhs of the current rule. Because $* matches zero or more of anything, what prevents sendmail from going into an infinite loop on this rule? After all, no matter how the rhs rewrites the address, it will always match $*.

The rhs $: preface comes to the rescue; it tells sendmail to evaluate the rule only once.

Sometimes you might want a ruleset to terminate immediately and return the address to the calling ruleset or the next ruleset in sendmail's built-in sequence. Prefacing a rule's rhs with $@ causes sendmail to exit the ruleset immediately after rewriting the address in the rhs.

$>: Calling Another Ruleset

A ruleset can pass an address to another ruleset by using the $> preface to the rhs. Consider the following rule:

```
R$*        $: $>66 $1          call ruleset 66
```

The lhs $* matches zero or more of anything, so sendmail always does the rhs. As you learned in the preceding section, the $: prevents the rule from being evaluated more than once. The $>66 $1 calls ruleset 66 with $1 as its input address. Because the $1 matches whatever was in the lhs, this rule simply passes the entirety of the current input address to ruleset 66. Whatever preface> ruleset 66 returns is passed to the next rule in the ruleset.

Testing Rules and Rulesets: The -bt, -d, and -C Options

Debugging sendmail.cf can be a tricky business. Fortunately, sendmail provides several ways to test rulesets before you install them.

> **Note**
>
> The examples in this section assume that your system has a working sendmail. If your system does not, try running these examples again after you have installed V.8 sendmail.

The -bt option tells sendmail to enter its rule-testing mode:

```
$ /usr/sbin/sendmail -bt
$ /etc/mta/sendmail -bt
ADDRESS TEST MODE (ruleset 3 NOT automatically invoked)
Enter <ruleset> <address>
>
```

Note

Notice the ruleset 3 NOT automatically invoked warning. Older versions of sendmail ran ruleset 3 automatically when in address test mode, which made sense because sendmail sends all addresses through ruleset 3 anyway. V.8 sendmail does not, but invoking ruleset 3 manually is a good idea because later rulesets expect the address to be in canonical form.

The > prompt means sendmail is waiting for you to enter one or more ruleset numbers, separated by commas, and an address. Try your login name with rulesets 3 and 0. The result should look something like this:

```
> 3,0 joe
rewrite: ruleset  3   input: joe
rewrite: ruleset  3 returns: joe
rewrite: ruleset  0   input: joe
rewrite: ruleset  3   input: joe
rewrite: ruleset  3 returns: joe
rewrite: ruleset  6   input: joe
rewrite: ruleset  6 returns: joe
rewrite: ruleset  0 returns: $# local $: joe
>
```

The output shows how sendmail processes the input address joe in each ruleset. Each line of output is identified with the number of the ruleset processing it, the input address, and the address that the ruleset returns. The > is a second prompt indicating that sendmail is waiting for another line of input. When you're done testing, just press Ctrl+D.

Indentation and blank lines better show the flow of processing in this example:

```
rewrite: ruleset  3   input: joe
rewrite: ruleset  3 returns: joe

rewrite: ruleset  0   input: joe

     rewrite: ruleset  3   input: joe
     rewrite: ruleset  3 returns: joe
```

```
    rewrite: ruleset  6   input: joe
    rewrite: ruleset  6 returns: joe

rewrite: ruleset  0 returns: $# local $: joe
```

The rulesets called were 3 and 0, in that order. Ruleset 3 was processed and returned the value `joe`, and then `sendmail` called ruleset 0. Ruleset 0 called ruleset 3 again and then ruleset 6, an example of how a ruleset can call another one by using `$>`. Neither ruleset 3 nor ruleset 6 rewrote the input address. Finally, ruleset 0 resolved to a mailer, as it must.

Often you need more detail than `-bt` provides—usually just before you tear out a large handful of hair because you don't understand why an address doesn't match the `lhs` of a rule. But you need not worry, because `sendmail` has verbose debugging built in to most of its code.

You use the `-d` option to turn on `sendmail`'s verbose debugging. This option is followed by a numeric code that indicates which section of debugging code to turn on and at what level. The following example shows how to run `sendmail` in one of its debugging modes and the output it produces:

```
$ /usr/sbin/sendmail -bt -d21.12
$ /etc/mta/sendmail -bt -d21.12
ADDRESS TEST MODE (ruleset 3 NOT automatically invoked)
Enter <ruleset> <address>
> 3,0 joe
rewrite: ruleset  3   input: joe
--trying rule: $* < > $*
-- rule fails
--trying rule: $* < $* < $* < $+ > $* > $* > $*
-- rule fails
[etc.]
```

The `-d21.12` in the preceding example tells `sendmail` to turn on level 12 debugging in section 21 of its code. The same command with the option `-d21.36` gives more verbose output (debug level 36 instead of 12).

Note

You can combine one or more debugging specifications separated by commas, as in `-d21.12,14.2`, which turns on level 12 debugging in section 21 and level 2 debugging in section 14. You can also give a range of debugging sections, as in `-d1-10.35`, which turns on debugging in sections 1 through 10 at level 35. The specification `-d0-91.104` turns on all sections of V.8 `sendmail`'s debugging code at the highest levels and produces thousands of lines of output for a single address.

The -d option is not limited for use with sendmail's address testing mode (-bt). You can also use it to see how sendmail processes rulesets while sending a letter, as the following example shows:

```
$ /usr/sbin/sendmail -d21.36 joe@gonzo.gov < /tmp/letter
$ /etc/mta/sendmail -d21.36 joe@gonzo.gov < /tmp/letter
[lots and lots of output...]
```

Unfortunately, the SIOG doesn't tell you which numbers correspond to which sections of code. Instead, you should look at the code itself to discover the correct debugging formulas.

The function tTd() is the one to look for. For example, suppose you want to turn on debugging in sendmail's address-parsing code. The source file parseaddr.c contains most of this code, and the following command finds the allowable debugging levels:

```
$ egrep tTd parseaddr.c
        if (tTd(20, 1))
[...]
        if (tTd(24, 4))
        if (tTd(22, 11))
[etc.]
```

The egrep output shows that debugging specifications such as -d20.1, -d24.4, -d22.11, and others will make sense to sendmail.

If perusing thousands of lines of C code doesn't appeal to you, *sendmail*, second edition, (O'Reilly) documents the debugging flags for sendmail. Note the book only covers up to sendmail 8.8; there could be small differences in detail, but it remains a good reference.

The -C option enables you to test new configuration files before you install them, which is always a good idea. If you want to test a different file, use -C*/path/to/the/file*. You can combine it with the -bt and -d flags. For example, here is a common invocation for testing new configuration files:

```
/usr/sbin/sendmail -Ctest.cf -bt -d21.12
/etc/mta/sendmail -Ctest.cf -bt -d21.12
```

Caution

For security, sendmail drops its superuser permissions when you use the -C option. You should perform final testing of configuration files as superuser to ensure that your testing is compatible with sendmail's normal operating mode.

INDEX

For information specific to either Caldera OpenLinux, Debian, or Red Hat Linux, please see their individual listings.

Symbols

C

D

E

F

G

H

J

K

L

M

N

O

P

Q

R

S

T

V

W

Y

Z

Other Related Titles

Sams Teach Yourself GIMP in 24 Hours
Joshua Pruitt and Ramona Pruitt
0-672-31509-2
$24.99 US / $37.95 CAN

Sams Teach Yourself C in 21 Days, Fourth Edition
Peter Aitken and Bradley L. Jones
0-672-31069-4
$29.99 US / $44.95 CAN

Sams Teach Yourself StarOffice 5 for Linux in 24 Hours
Nicholas Wells
0-672-31412-6
$19.99 US / $29.95 CAN

Sams Teach Yourself C++ in 21 Days, Third Edition
Jesse Liberty
0-672-31515-7
$29.99 US / $42.95 CAN

Sams Teach Yourself TCP/IP Network Administration in 21 Days
Brian Komar
0-672-31250-6
$29.99 US / $44.95 CAN

Bob Lewis's IS Survival Guide
Bob Lewis
0-672-31437-1
$24.99 US / $37.95 CAN

Maximum Security, Second Edition
Anonymous
0-672-31341-3
$49.99 US / $74.95 CAN

Sams Teach Yourself Java 2 Platform in 21 Days, Professional Reference Edition
Rogers Cadenhead
0-672-31438-X
$49.99 US / $74.95 CAN

SAMS
www.samspublishing.com

Maximum RPM
Edward Bailey
0-672-31105-4
$39.99 US / $59.95 CAN

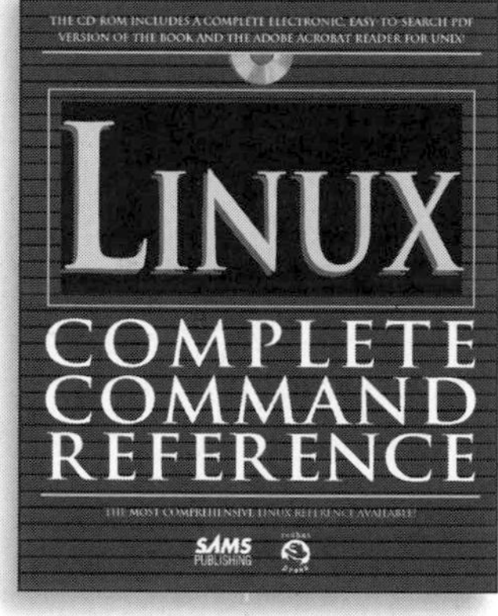

Linux Complete Command Reference
Red Hat
0-672-31104-6
$49.99 US / $74.95 CAN

Sams Teach Yourself Samba in 24 Hours
Gerald Carter
0-672-31609-9
$24.99 US / $37.95 CAN

All prices are subject to change.